Modern Management

Adding Digital Focus

NINTH EDITION

Samuel C. Certo

Steinmetz Professor of Management
Roy E. Crummer Graduate School of Business
Rollins College

Prentice Hall

Upper Saddle River, New Jersey 07458

Library of Congress Cataloging-in-Publication Data

Certo, Samuel C.
    Modern management : adding digital focus / Samuel C. Certo—9th ed.
        p. cm.
    Includes bibliographical references and index.
    ISBN 0-13-067089-8
        1. Management. 2. Industrial management. 3. Social responsibility of business.
    4. Technological innovations. I. Title.

    HD31 .C4125 2003
    658—dc21

Executive Editor: David Shafer
Editor-in-Chief: Jeff Shelstad
Senior Managing Editor (Editorial): Jennifer Glennon
Assistant Editor: Melanie Olsen
Editorial Assistant: Kevin Glynn
Media Project Manager: Michele Faranda
Senior Marketing Manager: Shannon Moore
Marketing Assistant: Christine Genneken
Managing Editor (Production): Judy Leale
Production Editor: Cindy Spreder
Production Assistant: Dianne Falcone
Permissions Supervisor: Suzanne Grappi
Associate Director, Manufacturing: Vincent Scelta
Production Manager: Arnold Vila
Manufacturing Buyer: Diane Peirano
Design Manager: Patricia Smythe
Designer: Steve Frim
Interior Design: Jill Little
Cover Design: Steve Frim
Cover Illustration/Photo: Wendy Chan/Image Bank
Illustrator (Interior): Electra Graphics
Associate Director, Multimedia: Karen Goldsmith
Manager, Print Production: Christy Mahon
Page Formatter: Ashley Scattergood
Composition: Rainbow Graphics
Full-Service Project Management: Rainbow Graphics
Printer/Binder: Courier Kendallville

Credits and acknowledgments borrowed from other sources and reproduced,
with permission, in this textbook appear on pages 542–571.

Pearson Education LTD.
Pearson Education Australia PTY, Limited
Pearson Education Singapore, Pte. Ltd
Pearson Education North Asia Ltd
Pearson Education, Canada, Ltd
Pearson Educación de Mexico, S.A. de C.V.
Pearson Education—Japan
Pearson Education Malaysia, Pte. Ltd

10 9 8 7 6 5
ISBN 0-13-067089-8

To Matthew

A Cherished son with wisdom well beyond his years. I am very proud of his spiritual fiber that inspires all who truly know him!

Contents in Brief

Contents

Modern management is exciting indeed! Never in the past have managers had the wealth of reported research and experiences of practicing managers to provide insights for building organizational success. The arrival of the Internet and related digital applications provide managers with the most revolutionary and powerful tools since Henry Ford and the development of the assembly line. Your career as a manager will be extremely interesting and your rewards for competence will be very significant.

As it was in the previous eight editions of *Modern Management*, the purpose of this text is to prepare students to be managers. Coverage includes a wealth of conventional wisdom related to traditional management tasks. Contemporary management challenges related to such issues as people, diversity, quality, ethics, and the global environment are prominently featured and integrated. Examples of many different types of organizations are also presented throughout the text to give students background regarding various industries. New to this edition is an emphasis on management's digital dimension. A new chapter is dedicated to this topic and a new highlight called "Digital Focus" is integrated throughout the text.

This book is carefully crafted to present traditional management concepts, important contemporary management issues, and insights regarding ways that students should use both to ensure organizational success.

The ninth edition of the *Modern Management* **Learning Package,** the text plus its ancillaries, continues a recognized and distinctive tradition in management education that has extended well over 20 years. This tradition emphasizes clear, concise, current, and thorough coverage based on an understanding of and a determination to enhance the student learning process. Only instructional support materials that contribute to the design and conduct of the highest quality principles of management course are included in the package.

As in the past, revisions to this *Modern Management* **Learning Package** have been focused on a single objective—improve student learning. All revisions reflect responsiveness to instructor and student feedback regarding ways to refashion the package in order to further enhance student learning. Starting with the text, the following sections explain each major component of this revision.

TEXT: THEORY OVERVIEW

Decisions about which concepts to include in this revision were indeed difficult. Such decisions were heavily influenced by information from accrediting agencies such as the American Assembly of Collegiate Schools of Business (AACSB), organizations established by professional managers such as the American Management Association (AMA), and organizations established by management scholars such as the Academy of Management. Overall, management theory in this edition is divided into the following seven main sections as opposed to the six of last edition:

- Introduction to Management
- Modern Management Challenges
- Planning
- Organizing
- Influencing
- Controlling
- Topics for Special Emphasis

For this edition, extensive updates of theory and examples have been made throughout the text. Highlights of content and other revisions follow.

Part One: Introduction to Management

This section lays the groundwork necessary for studying management.

> **Chapter 1, "Modern Management: *A Digital Focus,*"** is a heavily revised chapter for this edition. The chapter exposes students to what management is and gives them insights about how to build their careers. This chapter discusses the arrival of the Internet and how digital tools should be integrated within the management process. A new "Introductory Case" in this chapter covers how Lands' End's management team is learning how to use the Web. The chapter also has a new concluding case on eBay.

> **Chapter 2, "Managing: *History and Current Thinking,*"** presents several fundamental, but different ways, in which managers can perceive their jobs. The work of management pioneers like Frederick W. Taylor, Frank and Lilian Gilbreth, and Henry L. Gantt is highlighted. Students are given insights into how to combine the work of management pioneers into a more comprehensive view of management. A new concluding case for this chapter focuses on Albertson's excitement about a new CEO. The revision also includes new coverage of the Baldrige Award.

Part Two: Modern Management Challenges

This section helps students focus on understanding major challenges that modern managers face. Special highlights or boxed features based on these challenges are integrated throughout the text.

> **Chapter 3, "Corporate Social Responsibility and Business Ethics,"** discusses the responsibilities that managers have to society and how business ethics applies to modern management. Valuable discussion focuses on determining if social responsibility exists in a particular situation. A new "Introductory Case" illustrates how IBM uses its Web site to help manage social responsibility activities. A new concluding case focuses on controversy surrounding Ford's Explorer situation. New examples focus on global social responsibility issues at Maxwell company and how the Endangered Species Chocolate Company lives up to its social obligations in the food processing industry.

> **Chapter 4, "Management and Diversity,"** is presented earlier in this edition to allow students to reflect on diversity as a management challenge throughout the text. The chapter defines *diversity*, explains the advantages of promoting diversity in organizations, and outlines ways in which managers can promote it. This chapter also discusses some key challenges and dilemmas that managers face in attempting to build a diverse workforce.

> **Chapter 5, "Managing in the Global Arena,"** focuses on domestic versus international, multinational, and transnational organizations. The chapter also emphasizes expatriates, repatriation, and international market agreements like the European Union (EU) and the North American Free Trade Agreement (NAFTA). Discussion also extends to the evolving international market agreement among countries in the Pacific Rim. This chapter appears early in the text to better enable students to reflect on global management issues through-

out the course. The chapter has a new "Introductory Case" depicting Wal-Mart reaching out to the Japanese market and a concluding case emphasizing McDonald's experience in India. Special focus has been added on how IBM manages women abroad and how Nissan handles global management issues in the automobile manufacturing industry.

Part Three: Planning

This section elaborates on planning as a primary management function.

➤ **Chapter 6, "Principles of Planning,"** is heavily revised in this edition. This chapter discusses fundamentals of planning and features organizational objectives as a critical component of organizational planning. The new "Introductory Case" features planning for Internet use at American Airlines and new examples on planning for social responsibility.

➤ **Chapter 7, "Making Decisions,"** discusses the decision process as a component of the planning process. Coverage focuses on group decision processes like brainstorming, the nominal group technique, and the Delphi technique. Coverage also focuses on advantages and disadvantages of having groups make decisions and problems in evaluating the group decision process. New coverage of Ben & Jerry's decision process for choosing foreign markets is highlighted as well as Nestlé's decisions about creating appropriate digital activities. A new concluding case for this chapter focuses on decision making within Speednames, Inc., a domain name registrar.

➤ **Chapter 8, "Strategic Planning,"** highlights Porter's model for industry analysis, the BCG Growth-Share Matrix, the GE Portfolio Matrix, strategy implementation, and strategic control. New illustrations include a concluding case on strategic planning at JetBlue, a fledgling airline. New coverage highlights McMurray Publishing's strategic values code emphasizing social responsibility, Goodall Rubber Company including a quality focus in its strategic planning, and S. C. Johnson & Son of the consumer products industry using diversity as an organizational strategy.

➤ **Chapter 9, "Plans and Planning Tools,"** discusses various planning tools, such as forecasting and scheduling, that are available to help formulate plans. A new "Introductory Case" for this chapter discusses planning to improve production and new focus emphasizes how Shell plans for its global customer service sites. A new concluding case focuses on planning tool issues like finding appropriate plant locations for White Wave, a company providing innovative soy products.

Part Four: Organizing

This section discusses organizing activities as a major management function.

➤ **Chapter 10, "Fundamentals of Organizing,"** presents the basic principles of organizing. Concepts featured are organization structure, division of labor, span of management, and scalar relationships. A new concluding case for this chapter features organizational issues at Southwest Airlines. Special new focus highlights McDonald's organizing activities.

➤ **Chapter 11, "Responsibility, Authority, and Delegation,"** focuses on ways to organize worker activities. Emphasis is on holding organization members accountable for carrying out their obligations. A new "Introductory Case" features how Procter & Gamble has organized for its Internet push and a new concluding case highlights authority and decentralization issues at Gateway. New highlights show how Security One Systems used incentives to enhance the success of organization structure.

➤ **Chapter 12, "Managing Human Resources,"** discusses hiring and developing people who will make desirable contributions to the attainment of organizational objectives. Recruitment, selection, performance appraisal, and training are all major topics. Human resources issues at Intel are emphasized in a new concluding case. New coverage shows how Coca-Cola is holding managers accountable for reaching diversity goals and how The Container Store focuses on people issues to enhance its success.

➤ **Chapter 13, "Organizational Change and Stress,"** emphasizes ways in which managers change organizations and the stress-related issues that can accompany such action. Coverage also emphasizes increasing virtuality in organizations by establishing virtual

offices, building alternative work situations, and communicating successfully in virtual offices. A new concluding case shows how Merrily Orsini is striving to create a stress-free work zone at My Virtual Corporation. New coverage also illustrates how social responsibility impacts production changes at Mazda and how companies like GoTraining provide virtual training for client organizations.

Part Five: Influencing

This section discusses ways in which managers should deal with people. Reflecting the spirit of AACSB guidelines encouraging thorough coverage of human factors in the business curriculum, the influencing section is comprehensive.

➤ **Chapter 14, "Fundamentals of Influencing and Communication,"** introduces the topic of managing people, defines interpersonal communication, and presents organizational communication as the primary vehicle that managers use to interact with people. A new concluding case explores communication at Gucci and an interesting new highlight explores how Joe Torre, manager of the New York Yankees, influences his players.

➤ **Chapter 15, "Leadership,"** highlights more traditional concepts, such as the Vroom-Yetton-Jago leadership model, the path-goal theory of leadership, and the life cycle theory of leadership. Coverage also includes more recently developed concepts, like transformational leadership, coaching, super-leadership, and entrepreneurial leadership. A new concluding case explores a leadership issue at Cerner Corporation. Interesting new coverage also focuses on training leaders in social responsibility and how Cisco Systems trains its leaders online.

➤ **Chapter 16, "Motivation,"** defines *motivation*, describes the motivation process, and provides useful strategies that managers can use in attempting to motivate organization members. A new "Introductory Case" focuses on Bristol-Meyers Squibb and a new concluding case emphasizes events at Axis Communications. Additional new content focuses on reinforcing diversity at Raffa and Associates and reinforcing sales at Xerox.

➤ **Chapter 17, "Groups, Teams, and Corporate Culture,"** emphasizes managing clusters of people as a means of accomplishing organizational goals. This chapter covers the management of teams. Discussion focuses on groups versus teams, virtual teams, problem solving, self-managed and cross-functional teams, states of team development, empowerment, and factors contributing to team effectiveness. A new "Introductory Case" highlights building teamwork at Xerox and a new concluding case emphasizes a team culture at Alberto-Culver. New coverage on diversity and teams at Continental as well as Weyerhaeuser quality teams is included. An update of teams at Harley-Davidson is also provided.

➤ **Chapter 18, "Understanding People: Attitudes, Perception, and Learning,"** focuses on important characteristics of people that managers must understand. First, the relationship among attitudes, values, and beliefs is described. Then, the role of attitudes in influencing behavior is discussed. The chapter then turns to perception and the perceptual process, including detailed analyses of attribution theory and perceptions of procedural justice. Finally, the concept of learning is studied. New chapter-related illustrations focus on Webvan and the Indian company Hindustan Lever Ltd.

Part Six: Controlling

This section presents control as a major management function. Major topics include fundamentals of control, controlling production, information, and the Internet as a management tool.

➤ **Chapter 19, "Principles of Controlling,"** discusses the basics of control. Power and control as well as types of control are important topics. A new "Introductory Case" discusses how DaimlerChrysler controls through its Web-based *FastCar* and a new concluding case illustrates how control is key to success at Knight Transportation. New illustrations cover how Best Western uses feedback control to manage company diversity and how management takes corrective action at Luby's cafeterias.

➤ **Chapter 20, "Production Management and Control,"** focuses on the creation of goods and services, paying special attention on automation and production strategies, systems, and processes available to managers. A new concluding case discusses how Pirelli has revolutionized tire manufacturing. Interesting discussion has also been added concerning production issues at Firestone.

➤ **Chapter 21, "Information and the Internet,"** in keeping with the spirit of AACSB guidelines, has significant coverage of current information technology via Internet-related discussion. The chapter emphasizes recent technology developments ranging from e-mail, electronic data interchange, and videoconferencing to the Internet and the World Wide Web. Emphasis on intranets and firewalls complete this section. Discussion focuses on becoming a better manager by using technological tools, *not* by understanding the intricacies of technology. A new concluding case discusses Loudcloud, a company run by Marc Andreessen, the 29-year-old cofounder of Netscape.

Part Seven: Topics for Special Emphasis

This last section of *Modern Management* discusses additional issues important to managers operating in an organization in today's challenging, global environment. Quality, competitiveness, innovation, and management's digital dimension are all major topics. Digital coverage in this section is new to this edition.

➤ **Chapter 22, "Competitiveness: Quality and Innovation,"** emphasizes building competitiveness through quality and innovation. Discussion focuses on defining quality, achieving quality through strategic planning, and describing the management skills necessary to build quality throughout an organization. The ideas of such internationally known quality experts as Philip B. Crosby, W. Edwards Deming, and Joseph M. Juran are highlighted. Discussion highlights the role of innovation in being organizationally competitive. Topics discussed include innovation and creativity, creativity in individuals, and encouraging creativity in organizations. A new case focuses on Lear Corporation, a manufacturer of welded and stamped steel assemblies for the automotive and aircraft industries. A new focus on innovation is emphasized by explaining how Siemens uses ShareNet.

➤ **Chapter 23, "Management's Digital Dimension,"** is new to this edition and provides students with timely information on how managers should integrate traditional planning, organizing, influencing, and controlling activities with new digital dimensioning activities. The chapter defines digital dimensioning as the process of designing and implementing those digital activities that will best help a specific organization to reach its goals. The chapter emphasizes how managers use Internet activities or business activities to enhance organizational success. The "Introductory Case" focuses on digital excellence at Office Depot and the concluding case focuses on digital dimensioning for a small business school.

TEXT STUDENT LEARNING AIDS

Several features of this text were designed to make the study of management more efficient, effective, and enjoyable. New learning aids have been added to further improve the student learning process. The following is a list of these features and an explanation of each.

Learning Objectives

The opening pages of each chapter contain a set of learning objectives that are intended as guidelines for focusing study within the chapter.

Chapter Outlines

The opening pages of each chapter also contain a chapter outline that reviews the textual material, and helps the reader keep the information in perspective while it is being read.

Chapter Highlights

Chapter highlights are an exciting feature of this text. Highlights are extended examples or boxes emphasizing the wide range of contemporary issues in real companies that modern managers face. Each chapter has three highlights. The highlights have been significantly revised in this edition and include the following elements in each chapter:

> **Spotlights**   Spotlights focus on the following major management themes: diversity, quality, ethics, people, and the global environment. Two Spotlights appear in each chapter, with all topics receiving equivalent emphasis throughout the book. In Chapter 5, for instance, a "Diversity Spotlight" focuses on how IBM is tackling the challenge of managing women in global work situations. In the same chapter, a "People Spotlight" reports on helping expatriates to adjust.

➤ **Across Industries** "*Across Industries*" is a highlight that illustrates how chapter content relates to a specific industry. "*Across Industries*" are spread throughout the text and appear in about half of the chapters. The purpose of this feature is to ensure that students get a full, rich understanding of how management can be applied to many different situations. Situations presented in "*Across Industries*" emphasize companies and industries such as Nissan Motor Company in automobile manufacturing, Endangered Chocolates in the food processing industry, Harley-Davidson in the motorcycle manufacturing industry, and CMS in the electric utilities industry.

➤ **Digital Focus** New to this edition, "*Digital Focus*" is a highlight that emphasizes the Internet as a new, evolving, and practical management tool. "*Digital Focus*" highlights are spread throughout the text and appear in about half of the chapters. Given the unprecedented growth of the Internet, today's management students must acquire a useful, applied knowledge of the Internet. Organizations and issues discussed in this feature include the Equal Employment Opportunity Commission (EEOC) using the Internet to inform managers about the specifics of sexual harassment, Sega considering the Internet in how it develops organizational objectives, Nestlé USA employing the Internet to speed up worldwide decision making, and GoTrain offering online training programs to help other companies reap the advantages of virtual training.

"Introductory Cases" with "Back-to-the-Case" Sections

The opening of each chapter contains a case study that introduces readers to management problems related to chapter content. Detailed "Back-to-the-Case" sections appear throughout each chapter, applying specific areas of management theory discussed in the chapter to the "Introductory Case." All cases involve real companies ranging from AT&T and Gateway 2000 to US Air, Heinz, and Gillette. Over half the cases in this edition are new or updated. New cases in this edition include focus on companies like IBM, Wal-Mart, American Airlines, and Procter & Gamble.

End-of-Chapter Pedagogy

New for this edition, end-of-chapter pedagogy has been completely revamped and presented as a comprehensive "Management Skills Module." "Management Skills Modules" are built on the premise that sound management skills are based on an understanding of management concepts and the ability to apply those concepts in management situations. Each "Management Skills Module" is divided into the following two sections to heighten student understanding of management concepts as well as applying those concepts in various management situations.

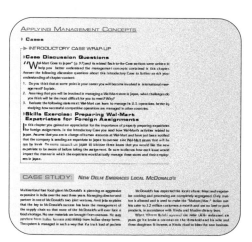

Section One: Understanding Management Concepts This first section of the "Management Skills Module" contains an "Action Summary," an "Action Summary Answer Key," and "Issues for Review and Discussion." An "Action Summary" is an action-oriented chapter summary that allows students to respond to several objective questions that are clearly linked to the learning objectives stated at the beginning of the chapter. Students can refer to the "Action Summary Answer Key" to check their answers. This key also lists the pages in the chapter that the students can reference for a full explanation of the answers. "Issues for Review and Discussion" contains a set of discussion questions that test the understanding of chapter material and can serve as a vehicle for independent study or class discussion.

Section Two: Applying Management Concepts This second section of the "Management Skills Module" focuses on helping students to acquire ability to use management concepts to solve management problems. This section contains cases, video exercises, and Internet activities aimed at helping students to develop this ability.

➤ **Skills Module Cases** This section contains both an "Introductory Case" Wrap-Up and a Concluding Case. The "Introductory Case" Wrap-Up includes learning materials to further illustrate the application of chapter content to the "Introductory Case." The Wrap-Up section has two distinct parts. Part one is a set of *case discussion questions* intended to extend discussion of the application of chapter content to the case. Part two is a *skills exercise* that focuses on building the management abilities of students via the case. Sample exercises are "Designing an MBO Program," "Building Useful Organization Charts," "Using Reinforcement Strategies," "Determining Symptoms and Problems," "Applying Total Quality Management," and "Evaluating a Web Site."

Each Management Skills Module also contains a completely new concluding case for students to analyze. These new cases include: "CEO Ted Waitt Comes Back to Save Gateway," "At Gucci De Sole Reigns Supreme," "Hindustan Lever Ltd. Reaches India's Poorest Villages," and "eBay Races Ahead Despite Slow Economy." Each new case is followed by a set of questions intended to guide student thought and discussion.

> **New Skills Live! Video Cases, Discussion Questions, and Experiential Exercises can be found in appropriate chapters.** All of the skills video cases now have a new feature called ". . . and You." This exercise gives students the chance to apply management concepts in their own lives. These exciting videos are scenario-based and feature actors demonstrating important management skills. They are based on two different companies: a television production company (Quicktakes) and a dot-com merging with a more traditional magazine publisher (Conmedia). They include questions at the end of each segment that relate to the material in the previous section of the book. Dr. Certo appears throughout the video to comment on how the text material relates to the case.

New to This Edition

Mastering Management   Packaged with every copy of *Modern Management, Mastering Management* uses video and interactive exercises to help students learn core concepts. This powerful learning tool focuses on CanGo, a fictional e-commerce company that sells a variety of entertainment products and services. The CD contains 12 case studies or episodes that show students how all of the functional areas of business work together to ensure the growth of the company as well as how to apply business theories to CanGo's daily operations. These can be found at the end of appropriate chapters.

Additional Text Features

> **Marginal Notes**   Each chapter contains marginal notes that can be helpful both in initial reading and for review. These notes highlight key terms in each chapter while providing brief definitions for student review.

> **Glossary**   Major terms and their definitions are gathered at the end of the text. Terms appear in boldface type and include references to the text pages on which the discussion of the term appears.

> **Illustrations**   Figures, tables, and photographs depicting various management situations are used throughout the text to help bridge the gap between management theory and real-world facts and figures.

Additional Teaching Materials

> **Instructor's Resource Manual**   Designed to guide the educator through the text, each chapter in the Instructor's Manual contains a brief summary, brief chapter outline, detailed lecture outline, suggested answers and solutions to questions in the text, a comprehensive video guide with discussion questions based on the Skills Video, *Mastering Management*, and Internet support.

> **Test Item File**   Each chapter contains true-false, multiple choice, and essay questions. Together the questions cover the content of each chapter in a variety of ways, providing flexibility in testing the student's knowledge of the text.

> **PowerPoint Electronic Transparencies**   A comprehensive package allowing access to the figures from the text, these PowerPoint transparencies are designed to aid the educator and supplement in-class lectures and can be found on the Instructor's Resource CD-ROM.

> **Color Transparencies**   Designed to aid the educator and enhance classroom lectures, 100 of the most critical PowerPoint electronic transparencies have been chosen for inclusion in this package as full-color acetates and are provided on high-quality mylar.

> **Instructor's Resource CD-ROM**   The Instructor's Resource CD-ROM includes the electronic Instructor's Manual, PowerPoint Electronic Transparencies, and the Windows/Prentice Hall Test Manager. The Test Manager contains all of the questions in the printed Test Item File. Test Manager is a comprehensive suite of tools for testing and assessment. Test Manager allows educators to easily create and distribute tests for their courses, either by printing and distributing through traditional methods or by online delivery via a Local Area Network (LAN) server.

> **Study Guide**   Designed to aid student comprehension of the concepts presented in the text, a Study Guide is available containing chapter objectives, detailed chapter outlines, review, discussion, and study questions.

> **Companion Web Site** is a fully customizable environment that ties students and faculty to text-specific resources. This powerful Prentice Hall Web site offers chapter-specific current events, internet exercises, online study guide, and downloadable supplements.

Special Features:

> **Individual homepages for students and faculty.** These pages provide easy, one-click navigation to our vast, dynamic database of online teaching and learning resources. Faculty and students can organize the online resources for all of their classes on this single, customizable homepage.

> **A powerful new point-and-click syllabus creation tool** that faculty can use for each course and section they teach. Additionally, faculty can annotate and link each resource on the Web site to their syllabi.

> **Faculty can even upload their own personal resources to our site** and have these resources available to their students via their personalized syllabus.

> Check it out: *www.prenhall.com/certo*

ACKNOWLEDGMENTS

I feel very blessed that the positive feedback regarding the Modern Management Learning Package has now continued for over 20 years. This package has become known as a standard for high-quality learning materials in colleges and universities, as well as in professional management-training programs throughout the world. Well over half a million students have now used this book. These materials have been translated into foreign languages, the most recent Spanish translation being published in 2001.

Although I have received much professional recognition for the success of this text, considerable recognition for this success rightfully belongs to valuable contributions made by many of my respected colleagues. I am pleased to recognize the contributions of these individuals and extend to them my warmest personal gratitude for their professional insights, as well as for their personal support and encouragement throughout the life of this project.

Professor Lee A. Graf, Illinois State University, has been a special supporter throughout the life of this project. Over the years, Dr. Graf's countless significant contributions in many areas have helped to keep this text a market leader since its first edition in 1980. His overall professionalism has been a constant encouragement. More importantly, I consider him a close friend.

Many other colleagues have also made important contributions to the Modern Management Learning Package over the years. I would like to thank these individuals for their dedication and professionalism in making this project all that it can be. The following professionals have made special contributions to the shaping of this project: Robert E. Kemper (Northern Arizona University), Toni Carol Kind (Binghamton University), Maurice Manner (Marymount College), Richard Ratliff, Shari Tarnutzer, and their colleagues (Utah State University), Larry Waldorf (Boise State University), and Michael Carrell (Morehead State University).

Every author appreciates the valuable contribution reviewers make to the development of a text project. Reviewers offer the different viewpoint that requires an author to constructively question his or her work. I again had an excellent team of reviewers. Thoughtful comments, concern for student learning, and insights regarding instructional implications of the written work characterized the high-quality feedback I received. I am pleased to be able to recognize members of the review team for this edition and their valuable contributions to the development of this text: Jacqueline Marks, Lon Doty (San Jose State University), Steven E. Huntley (Florida Community College at Jacksonville), Dan Baugher (Pace University), Randi L. Sims (Nova Southern University), Joe Simon (Casper College), Charles I. Stubbart (Southern Illinois University Carbondale), James I. Phillips (Northeastern State University), and Gloria Walker (Florida Commmunity College at Jacksonville.)

Members of my Prentice Hall family deserve personal and sincere recognition. The staff at Prentice Hall has provided outstanding wisdom and understanding throughout this project. David Shafer, my executive editor, constantly amazes me with his insights regarding what Modern Management should become. David is a market expert and his constancy in seeking text excellence is a true inspiration. Best of all, I consider David a friend. Jennifer Glennon, my senior managing editor, has a remarkable sense of text design and learning impact. Having graduated from Rollins College during my tenure at Rollins, Jennifer is an excellent example of why professors should be nice to their students! Other Prentice Hall professionals who have assisted greatly in this book are the following: Melanie Olsen, assistant editor; Kim Marsden, editorial assistant; Judy Leale, managing editor; Cindy Spreder, production editor; Diane Peirano, manufacturing buyer; and Steve Frim, designer. I thank them.

Orlando businessman, Charles Steinmetz, a longtime leader in the pest control industry, and his wife, Lynn, recently established the Steinmetz Chair in Management to recruit or retain a nationally recognized scholar for the management program in the Roy E. Crummer Graduate School of Business at Rollins College. I am extremely honored and personally excited to be the first recipient of the Steinmetz Chair of Management. I feel very fortunate to have been selected for this honor and can only hope to relate to students the keen business acumen and high moral and ethical standards that have made Charles Steinmetz a world-class entrepreneur and manager. I would like to thank Dr. Rita Bornstein, Rollins College President, and Dr. Craig McAllaster, Crummer Dean, for creating an educational climate in which professionalism can grow and flourish and for supporting me as the first recipient of the Steinmetz Chair in Management.

On a personal note, my family is very special to me and has been a source of energy and dedication throughout this project. Very special thanks go to my wife, Mimi, for her love and support throughout all aspects of my life. She constantly helps me to maintain the needed spiritual, family, and professional dimensions of my life. Our children Brian, Sarah, Matthew, and Trevis continually support me through their unconditional love. They have a profound impact on who I am and what I do. I'm especially thankful for Sarah's professional input in helping me sift through the lastest management research to be included in this book. In giving us Samuel Skylar Certo, the beginning of our family's next generation, our son Trevis and his wife Melissa help me to understand how important it is to focus on the future through projects of this nature. Lastly, my parents, Sam and Annette, have instilled within me a discipline necessary to complete long-run projects of this nature. Their devotion to building my life has not gone unnoticed.

chapter
1 Modern Management:
A Digital Focus

Objectives

From studying this chapter, I will attempt to acquire

- An understanding of the importance of management to society and individuals
- An understanding of the role of management
- An ability to define *management* in several different ways
- An ability to list and define the basic functions of management
- Working definitions of managerial effectiveness and managerial efficiency
- An understanding of basic management skills and their relative importance to managers
- An understanding of the universality of management
- Insights concerning what management careers are and how they evolve
- An understanding of management's digital focus

CHAPTER OUTLINE

Introductory Case: *Lands' End Management Learning How to Use the Web*

The Importance of Management
The Management Task
The Role of Management
Defining Management
The Management Process: Management Functions
Management Process and Goal Attainment
Management and Organizational Resources

The Universality of Management
The Theory of Characteristics

Management Careers
A Definition of Career
Career Stages, Life Stages, and Performance
Promoting Your Own Career
Special Career Issues

Modern Management's Digital Focus
Defining Digital Dimension
Digital Dimensioning and Traditional Management Functions

Special Features for the Remaining Chapters
Spotlights
Across Industries
Digital Focus

Lands' End Management Learning
How to Use the Web

REMINDER: THE INTRODUCTORY CASE WRAP-UP (P. 21) CONTAINS DISCUSSION QUESTIONS AND A SKILLS EXERCISE TO FURTHER ILLUSTRATE THE APPLICATION OF CHAPTER CONCEPTS TO THIS VIGNETTE.

The need to harness Internet technology in new and competitive ways challenges many managers today. Lands' End managers have successfully translated the company's well-known, mail-order selling strategies to its popular Web site.

Gary C. Comer originally founded Lands' End in 1963 in Chicago, to sell sailboat hardware and equipment via direct mail catalogs. In the early 1970s, catalog offerings were expanded to include a sampling of outerwear and casual clothing. In 1977, because the demand for casual clothing appeared to be strong and growing, the management decided to shift the company's primary focus to selling clothing and soft luggage. By 1979, Lands' End had moved to Dodgeville, Wisconsin, increased the selections of clothing in its catalog, and begun to recruit personnel experienced in the areas of fabrics and clothing manufacturing.

Today, Lands' End sells traditionally styled, casual clothing for men, women, and children, and has broadened its catalog to include accessories, domestics, shoes, and soft luggage. Lands' End works directly with mills and manufacturers in order to eliminate the middlemen, and the savings generated allow Lands' End to offer customers the best possible price. The company sells merchandise through direct mail catalogs as well as through the Internet and retail outlet stores. It ships directly to customers anywhere in the world. Overall, this way of doing business allows the shopper to avoid driving to a mall, running from store to store to find just the right product, or waiting in lines.

Recently, the Lands' End traditional commitment to quality and innovation has prompted its management to apply new Internet-related technology, for the purpose of providing new and better customer service. The first groundbreaking step was putting "Your Personal Model" on its Web site. Designed to facilitate online sales of women's apparel, Your Personal Model invited customers to input their measurements. From this information, the company Web site created a virtual model that allowed buyers to "try on" clothes and view a picture of exactly how the garments would fit.

Lands' End then relaunched the model and renamed it "My Virtual Model." Now, for both men and women, My Virtual Model attempts to more accurately reflect customers' measurements, through the use of a body scanner. The scanner was introduced during a U.S. promotional bus tour that allowed people to visit the Lands' End "My Virtual Model Tour" trailer to be "scanned" for 12 seconds

(continued)

by a laser that measures 200,000 points on the body. The scanner technology will soon be available to consumers in mall kiosks throughout the country. Lands' End has received much attention and praise for the project.

The Lands' End name has become well-known both nationally and internationally. Over the years, the management has molded the organization into a highly successful contender. Continuing to apply new Internet technologies to the traditional business practices should enable Lands' End to become a formidable competitor in the years to come.

What's Ahead

As discussed in the Introductory Case, Lands' End has recently gone online with "My Virtual Model." Although the building of this segment of the Lands' End Web site is a significant accomplishment in itself, the future success or failure of My Virtual Model rests in the hands of management. Assume that you are the president of Lands' End and that all company operations including the Web site are your responsibility. The information in this chapter is designed to help you understand the basics of your management job. Management is defined through:

1) A discussion of its importance both to society and to individuals

2) A description of the management task

3) A discussion of its universality

4) Insights about management careers

5) Coverage of modern management's digital dimension

THE IMPORTANCE OF MANAGEMENT

Managers influence all phases of modern organizations. Plant managers run manufacturing operations that produce the clothes we wear, the food we eat, and the automobiles we drive. Sales managers maintain a sales force that markets goods. Personnel managers provide organizations with a competent and productive workforce. The "jobs available" section in the classified advertisements of any major newspaper describes many different types of management activities and confirms the importance of management (see Figure 1.1).

THE MANAGEMENT TASK

Besides understanding the significance of managerial work to themselves and society and its related benefits, prospective managers need to know what the management task entails. The sections that follow introduce the basics of the management task through discussions of the role and definition of management, the management process as it pertains to management functions and organizational goal attainment, and the need to manage organizational resources effectively and efficiently.

Our society could neither exist as we know it today nor improve without a steady stream of managers to guide its organizations. Peter Drucker emphasized this point when he stated that effective management is probably the main resource of developed countries and the most needed resource of developing ones.[1] In short, all societies desperately need good managers.

Besides its importance to society as a whole, management is vital to many individuals who earn their livings as managers. Government statistics show that management positions have increased approximately from 10 percent to 18 percent of all jobs since 1950. Managers

SR. MANAGEMENT DEVELOPMENT SPECIALIST

We are a major metropolitan service employer of over 5,000 employees seeking a person to join our management development staff. Prospective candidates will be degreed with 5 to 8 years experience in the design, implementation, and evaluation of developmental programs for first-line and mid-level management personnel. Additionally, candidates must demonstrate exceptional oral and written communications ability and be skilled in performance analysis, programmed instruction, and the design and implementation of reinforcement systems.

If you meet these qualifications, please send your résumé, including salary history and requirements to:

Box RS-653
An Equal Opportunity Employer

BRANCH MGR

$30,500. Perceptive pro with track record in administration and lending has high visibility with respected firm.

Box PH-185

HUMAN RESOURCE MANAGER

Publicly owned, national manufacturer with 12 plants, 700 employees, seeks first corporate personnel director. We want someone to administer programs in:

- Position and rate evaluation
- Employee safety engineering
- Employee training
- Employee communications
- Employee benefits
- Federal compliance

Qualifications: Minimum of 3–5 years personnel experience in mfg. company, ability to tactfully deal with employees at all levels from all walks of life, free to travel. Position reports to Vice President, Operations. Full range of company benefits, salary $32,000–$40,000. Reply in complete confidence to:

Box JK-236

AVIATION FBO MANAGER NEEDED

Southeast Florida operation catering to corporate aviation. No maintenance or aircraft sales—just fuel and the best service. Must be experienced. Salary plus benefits commensurate with qualifications. Submit complete résumé to:

Box LJ0688

DIVISION CREDIT MANAGER

Major mfg. corporation seeks an experienced credit manager to handle the credit and collection function of its Midwest division (Chicago area). Interpersonal skills are important, as is the ability to communicate effectively with senior management. Send résumé with current compensation to:

Box NM-43

ACCOUNTING MANAGER

Growth opportunity. Michigan Ave. location. Acctg. degree, capable of supervision. Responsibilities include G/L, financial statements, inventory control, knowledge of systems design for computer applications. Send résumé, incl. salary history to:

Box RJM-999
An Equal Opportunity Employer

FINANCIAL MANAGER

CPA/MBA (U of C) with record of success in management positions. Employed, now seeking greater opportunity. High degree of professionalism, exp. in dealing w/financial inst., strong communication & analytical skills, stability under stress, high energy level, results oriented. Age 34, 11 yrs. exper. incl. major public acctng., currently 5 years as Financial VP of field leader. Impressive references.

Box LML-666

MARKET MANAGER

Major lighting manufacturer seeks market manager for decorative outdoor lighting. Position entails establishing and implementing marketing, sales, and new product development programs including coordination of technical publications and related R&D projects. Must locate at Denver headquarters. Send résumé to

Box WM-214
No agencies please

GENERAL MANAGER

Small industrial service company, privately owned, located in Springfield, Missouri, needs aggressive, skilled person to make company grow in profits and sales. Minimum B.S. in Business, experienced in all facets of small business operations. Must understand profit. Excellent opportunity and rewards. Salary and fringes commensurate with experience and performance.

Box LEM-116

FOUNDRY SALES MANAGER

Aggressive gray iron foundry located in the Midwest, specializing in 13,000 tons of complex castings yearly with a weight range of 2 to 400 pounds, is seeking experienced dynamic sales manager with sound sales background in our industry. Salary commensurate with experience.

Box MO-948

The variety of management positions available

Figure 1.1

come from varying backgrounds and have diverse educational specialties. Many people who originally trained to be accountants, teachers, financiers, or even writers eventually make their livelihoods as managers. Although in the short term, the demand for managers varies somewhat, in the long term, managerial positions can yield high salaries, status, interesting work, personal growth, and intense feelings of accomplishment.

In fact, there is some concern that certain managers are paid *too* much. For example, consider the notable criticism regarding the high salaries paid to managers at the Walt Disney Company. Disapproval of the excessive compensation paid to Disney's top management has recently surfaced in the popular press as well as in statements by stockholders. An article in *The Economist*, for example, questions whether Michael Eisner, head of Walt Disney, is worth the amount he receives.[2] In the end, Eisner's compensation should be determined by how much value he adds to the company.[3] The more value he adds, the more compensation he deserves. The overall compensation for Eisner and three other top managers for the fiscal year ending September 2000 appears in Table 1.1.

> ►‾ Back to the Case
>
> The information just presented furnishes you, as CEO of Lands' End, with insights concerning the significance of your role as manager. That role is important not only to society as a whole but to you as an individual. As a manager you make some contribution to creating the standard of living that we all enjoy, and you earn corresponding rewards. Lands' End is making societal contributions aimed at providing clothing to people throughout the world. As its president, you would be helping Lands' End in this endeavor. If you exert significant impact, the company's contribution to society, and your personal returns, will be heightened considerably.

The Role of Management

Essentially, the role of managers is to guide organizations toward goal accomplishment. All organizations exist for certain purposes or goals, and managers are responsible for combining and using organizational resources to ensure that their organizations achieve their purposes. Management moves an organization toward its purposes or goals by assigning activities that organization members perform. If the activities are designed effectively, the production of each individual worker will contribute to the attainment of organizational goals. Management strives to encourage individual activity that will lead to reaching organizational goals and to discourage individual activity that will hinder the accomplishment of those goals. "There is no idea more important to managing than goals. Management has no meaning apart from its goals."[4] Managers must, therefore, keep organizational goals in mind at all times.

Defining Management

Students of management should be aware that the term *management* can be, and often is, used in different ways. For instance, it can refer simply to the process that managers follow in order to accomplish organizational goals. It can also refer to a body of knowledge; in this context, management is a cumulative body of information that furnishes insights on how to manage. The term *management* can also refer to the individuals who guide and direct organizations or to a career devoted to the task of guiding and directing organizations. An understanding of the various uses and related definitions of the term will help you avoid miscommunication during management-related discussions.

Table 1.1	Overall Compensation for Four Disney Top Managers: Fiscal Year 2000[a]				
Name and Title	Salary	Bonus	Total Annual Compensation	Options/Other	Fiscal Year Total
Michael D. Eisner Chairman of Board, Chief Executive Officer	$ 813,462	$8,500,000	$9,313,462	$3,004,020	$12,317,482
Robert A. Iger President, Chief Operating Officer, Director	1,084,615	5,000,000	6,084,615	3,135,128	9,219,743
Thomas O. Staggs Senior Executive Vice President, President, Chief Financial Officer	700,000	1,500,000	2,200,000	4,020	2,202,020
Peter E. Murphy Senior Executive Vice President, Chief Strategic Officer	700,000	1,500,000	2,200,000	4,020	2,204,020

[a]Figures based on company records

As used most commonly in this text, **management** is the process of reaching organizational goals by working with and through people and other organizational resources. A comparison of this definition with the definitions offered by several contemporary management thinkers shows that there is broad agreement that management has the following three main characteristics:

1. It is a process or series of continuing and related activities
2. It involves and concentrates on reaching organizational goals
3. It reaches these goals by working with and through people and other organizational resources

A discussion of each of these characteristics follows.

Management is the process of reaching organizational goals by working with and through people and other organizational resources.

The Management Process: Management Functions

The four basic **management functions**—activities that make up the management process—are described in the following sections.

Management functions are activities that make up the management process. The four basic management activities are planning, organizing, influencing, and controlling.

Planning   Planning involves choosing tasks that must be performed to attain organizational goals, outlining how the tasks must be performed, and indicating when they should be performed. Planning activity focuses on attaining goals. Through their plans, managers outline exactly what organizations must do to be successful. Planning is concerned with organizational success in the near future (short term) as well as in the more distant future (long term).[5]

Organizing   Organizing can be thought of as assigning the tasks developed under the planning function to various individuals or groups within the organization. Organizing, then, creates a mechanism to put plans into action. People within the organization are given work assignments that contribute to the company's goals. Tasks are organized so that the output of individuals contributes to the success of departments, which, in turn, contributes to the success of divisions, which ultimately contributes to the success of the organization.

Influencing   Influencing is another of the basic functions within the management process. This function—also commonly referred to as *motivating*, *leading*, *directing*, or *actuating*—is concerned primarily with people within organizations.* Influencing can be defined as guiding the activities of organization members in appropriate directions. An appropriate direction is any direction that helps the organization move toward goal attainment. The ultimate purpose of influencing is to increase productivity. Human-oriented work situations usually generate higher levels of production over the long term than do task-oriented work situations, because people find the latter type distasteful.

▶ Jeff Taylor, CEO of Monster.com, is proud of having created a friendly and informal workplace. Among the other managerial challenges he faces are over 35,000 competing online recruitment Web sites, a slowing economy that will reduce hiring, and customer demands for increased online services. Right now, Monster.com has 34 percent of the market for online recruiting and, unlike most of its competitors, has posted a profit for 12 straight quarters.

Controlling   Controlling is the management function for which managers:

1. Gather information that measures recent performance within the organization
2. Compare present performance to preestablished performance standards
3. From this comparison, determine if the organization should be modified to meet preestablished standards

Controlling is an ongoing process. Managers continually gather information, make their comparisons, and then try to find new ways of improving production through organizational modification.

Management Process and Goal Attainment

Although we have discussed the four functions of management individually, planning, organizing, influencing, and controlling are integrally related and therefore cannot be separated in practice. Figure 1.2 illustrates this interrelationship and also indicates that managers use these activi-

---

*In early management literature, the term *motivating* was more commonly used to signify this people-oriented management function. The term *influencing* is used consistently throughout this text because it is broader and permits more flexibility in discussing people-oriented issues. Later in the text, motivating is discussed as a major part of influencing.

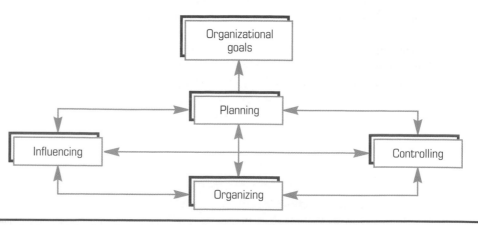

Figure 1.2 *Interrelations of the four functions of management to attain organizational goals*

ties solely for reaching organizational goals. Basically, these functions are interrelated because the performance of one depends on the performance of the others. For example, organizing is based on well-thought-out plans developed during the planning process, and influencing systems must be tailored to reflect both these plans and the organizational design used to implement them. The fourth function, controlling, involves possible modifications to existing plans, organizational structure, or the motivation system used to develop a more successful effort.

To be effective, a manager must understand how the four management functions are practiced, not simply how they are defined and related. Thomas J. Peters and Robert H. Waterman, Jr., studied numerous organizations—including Frito-Lay and Maytag—for several years to determine what management characteristics best describe excellently run companies. In their book *In Search of Excellence,* Peters and Waterman suggest that planning, organizing, influencing, and controlling should be characterized by a bias for action; a closeness to the customer; autonomy and entrepreneurship; productivity through people; a hands-on, value-driven orientation; "sticking to the knitting"; a simple organizational form with a lean staff; and simultaneous loose-tight properties.

The information in this section has given you but a brief introduction to the four management functions. Later sections are devoted to developing these functions in much more detail.

Management and Organizational Resources

Management must always be aware of the status and use of **organizational resources.** These resources, composed of all assets available for activation during the production process, are of four basic types:

Organizational resources are all assets available for activation during normal operations; they include human resources, monetary resources, raw materials resources, and capital resources.

▶ Among the many management decisions made by Lynn and Alan Kuwahara since 1996 were the choice to switch their company, Hawaiian Greenhouse of Pahoa, Hawaii, from a wholesaler to a mail order retailer, to automate their shipping and ordering processes, to increase the scope of their small but growing international business, and to open a retail Web site at *www.hawaiiangreenhouse.com.* The Kuwaharas also face the need to control costs as they compete against companies from Costa Rica, the Philippines, and Thailand in a global marketplace.

1. Human
2. Monetary
3. Raw materials
4. Capital

As Figure 1.3 shows, organizational resources are combined, used, and transformed into finished products during the production process.

Human resources are the people who work for an organization. The skills they possess and their knowledge of the work system are invaluable to managers. Monetary resources are amounts of money that managers use to purchase goods and services for the organization. Raw materials are ingredients used directly in the manufacturing of products. For example, rubber is a raw material that Goodyear would purchase with its monetary resources and use directly in manufacturing tires. Capital resources are machines used during the manufacturing process. Modern machines, or equipment, can be a major factor in maintaining desired production levels. Worn-out or antiquated machinery can make it impossible for an organization to keep pace with competitors.

Managerial Effectiveness   As managers use their resources, they must strive to be both effective and efficient. **Managerial effectiveness** refers to management's use of organizational resources in meeting organizational goals. If organizations are using their resources to attain their goals, the managers are said to be effective. In reality, however, there are degrees of managerial effectiveness. The closer an organization comes to achieving its goals, the more effective its managers are considered to be. Managerial effectiveness, then, exists on a continuum ranging from *ineffective* to *effective.*

> **Managerial effectiveness** refers to management's use of organizational resources in meeting organizational goals.

Managerial Efficiency   **Managerial efficiency** is the proportion of total organizational resources that contribute to productivity during the manufacturing process.[6] The higher this proportion, the more efficient the manager. The more resources wasted or unused during the production process, the more inefficient the manager. In this situation, *organizational resources* refers not only to raw materials that are used in manufacturing goods or services but also to related human effort.[7] Like management effectiveness, management efficiency is best described as being on a continuum ranging from inefficient to efficient. *Inefficient* means that a very small proportion of total resources contributes to productivity during the manufacturing process; *efficient* means that a very large proportion contributes.

> **Managerial efficiency** is the degree to which organizational resources contribute to productivity. It is measured by the proportion of total organizational resources used during the production process.

As Figure 1.4 shows, the concepts of managerial effectiveness and efficiency are obviously related. A manager could be relatively ineffective—with the consequence that the organization is making very little progress toward goal attainment—primarily because of major inefficiencies or poor utilization of resources during the production process. In contrast, a manager could be somewhat effective despite being inefficient if demand for the finished goods is so high that the manager can get an extremely high price per unit sold and thus absorb inefficiency costs.

For example, oil companies in Saudi Arabia can probably absorb many managerial inefficiencies when oil is selling at a high price. Management in this situation has a chance to be somewhat effective despite its inefficiency. Thus a manager can be effective without being efficient and vice versa. To maximize organizational success, however, both effectiveness and efficiency are essential.

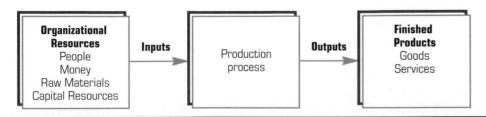

Transformation of organizational resources into finished products through the production process

Figure 1.3

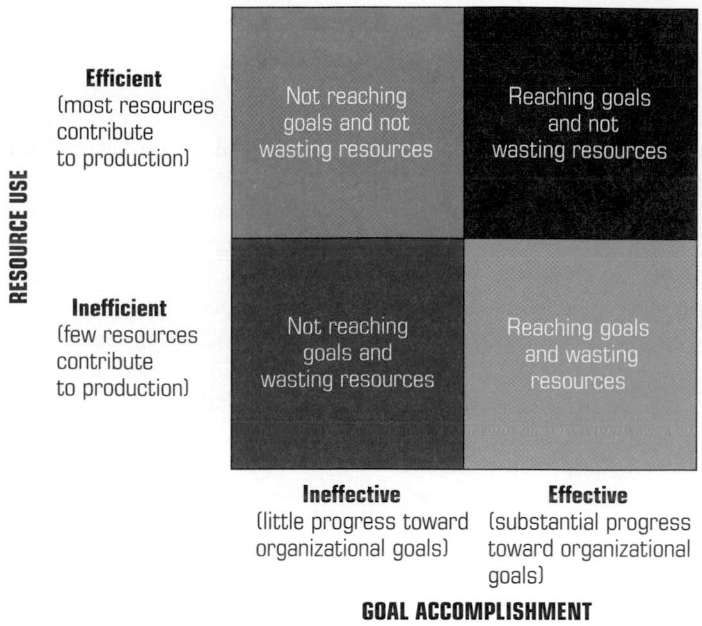

	Ineffective (little progress toward organizational goals)	**Effective** (substantial progress toward organizational goals)
Efficient (most resources contribute to production)	Not reaching goals and not wasting resources	Reaching goals and not wasting resources
Inefficient (few resources contribute to production)	Not reaching goals and wasting resources	Reaching goals and wasting resources

RESOURCE USE

GOAL ACCOMPLISHMENT

Figure 1.4 *Various combinations of managerial effectiveness and managerial efficiency*

▶ Back to the Case

The previous discussion contains more specific explanations of what management is and what managers do. According to this information, as CEO at Lands' End, you must have a clear understanding of the company's objectives, and you must guide its operations in a way that helps the company reach those objectives. This guidance will involve your working directly with people like sales managers, other upper managers like the vice president of global operations, and the delivery system personnel.

You must be sure that planning, organizing, influencing, and controlling are being carried out appropriately. You must outline how jobs are to be performed to reach objectives, assign these jobs to appropriate workers, encourage the workers to perform their jobs, and make any changes necessary to ensure the achievement of company objectives. As you perform these four functions, remember that the activities themselves are interrelated and must blend together appropriately.

Your wise use of Lands' End's organizational resources is critical. Strive to make sure that Lands' End is both effective and efficient, reaching company objectives without wasting company resources.

Management Skills   No discussion of organizational resources would be complete without the mention of management skills, perhaps the primary determinant of how effective and efficient managers will be.

According to a classic article by Robert L. Katz, managerial success depends primarily on performance rather than personality traits.[8] Katz also states that managers' ability to perform is a result of their managerial skills. A manager with the necessary management skills will probably perform well and be relatively successful. One without the necessary skills will probably perform poorly and be relatively unsuccessful.

Katz indicates that three types of skills are important for successful management performance: technical, human, and conceptual skills.

> **Technical skills** involve using specialized knowledge and expertise in executing work-related techniques and procedures. Examples of these skills are engineering, computer programming, and accounting. Technical skills are mostly related to working with "things"—processes or physical objects.

Technical skills are skills involving the ability to apply specialized knowledge and expertise to work-related techniques and procedures.

➤ **Human skills** are skills that build cooperation within the team being led. They involve working with attitudes and communication, individual and group interests—in short, working with people.

➤ **Conceptual skills** involve the ability to see the organization as a whole. A manager with conceptual skills is able to understand how various functions of the organization complement one another, how the organization relates to its environment, and how changes in one part of the organization affect the rest of the organization.

As one moves from lower-level management to upper-level management, conceptual skills become more important and technical skills less important (see Figure 1.5). The supportive rationale is that as managers advance in an organization, they become less involved with the actual production activity or technical areas and more involved with guiding the organization as a whole. Human skills, however, are extremely important to managers at top, middle, and lower (or supervisory) levels.[9] The common denominator of all management levels, after all, is people.

Human skills are skills involving the ability to build cooperation within the team being led.

Conceptual skills are skills involving the ability to see the organization as a whole.

THE UNIVERSALITY OF MANAGEMENT

Management principles are **universal:** That is, they apply to all types of organizations (businesses, churches, sororities, athletic teams, hospitals, and so on) and organizational levels. Naturally, managers' jobs vary somewhat from one type of organization to another because each organizational type requires the use of specialized knowledge, exists in a unique working and political environment, and uses different technology. However, there are job similarities across organizations because the basic management activities—planning, organizing, influencing, and controlling—are common to all organizations.

Universality of management means that the principles of management are applicable to all types of organizations and organizational levels.

The Theory of Characteristics

Henri Fayol, one of the earliest management writers, stated that all managers should possess certain characteristics, such as positive physical and mental qualities and special knowledge related to the specific operation.[10] B. C. Forbes has emphasized the importance of certain more personal qualities, inferring that enthusiasm, earnestness of purpose, confidence, and faith in their own worthwhileness are primary characteristics of successful managers. Forbes has described Henry Ford as follows:

> *At the base and birth of every great business organization was an enthusiast, a man consumed with earnestness of purpose, with confidence in his powers, with faith in the worthwhileness of his endeavors. The original Henry Ford was the quintessence of enthusiasm. In the days of his difficulties, disappointments, and discouragements, when he was wrestling with his bulky motor engine—and wrestling likewise with poverty—only his inexhaustible enthusiasm saved him from defeat.[11]*

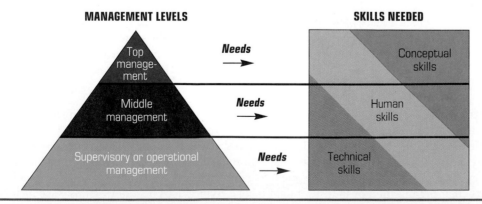

MANAGEMENT LEVELS

- Top management
- Middle management
- Supervisory or operational management

SKILLS NEEDED

- Needs → Conceptual skills
- Needs → Human skills
- Needs → Technical skills

As a manager moves from the supervisory to the top-management level, conceptual skills become more important than technical skills, but human skills remain equally important

Figure 1.5

Fayol and Forbes can describe desirable characteristics of successful managers only because of the universality concept: The basic ingredients of successful management are applicable to all organizations.

▶ Back to the Case

You will be a successful manager at Lands' End only if you possess technical skills, human skills, and conceptual skills. In order to succeed, a relatively low-level manager at Lands' End would need, in order of importance, human skills, technical skills, and conceptual skills.

As top manager at Lands' End, you would normally need, again in order of importance, human skills, conceptual skills, and technical skills. As lower-level managers at Lands' End take over middle and upper-level management positions, the ranking of skills importance changes by adding more importance to conceptual skills and less importance to technical skills.

As you gain experience at Lands' End, you will no doubt find that your cumulative management experience is valuable in similar management positions in other companies, or even in some other type of business. You are also likely to discover that as your enthusiasm, earnestness, confidence, and faith in your own worthwhileness become more pronounced, you will become a more successful manager.

Management Careers

Thus far, this chapter has focused on outlining the importance of management to society, presenting a definition of management and the management process, and explaining the universality of management. Individuals commonly study such topics because they are interested in pursuing a management career. This section presents information that will help you preview your own management career. It also describes some of the issues you may face in attempting to manage the careers of others within an organization. The specific focus is on career definition, career and life stages and performance, and career promotion.

A Definition of Career

A **career** is a sequence of work-related positions occupied by a person over the course of a lifetime.

A **career** is a sequence of work-related positions occupied by a person over the course of a lifetime.[12] As the definition implies, a career is cumulative in nature: As people accumulate successful experiences in one position, they generally develop abilities and attitudes that qualify them to hold more advanced positions. In general, management positions at one level tend to be stepping-stones to management positions at the next higher level.

Career Stages, Life Stages, and Performance

Careers are generally viewed as evolving through a series of stages.[13] These evolutionary stages—exploration, establishment, maintenance, and decline—are shown in Figure 1.6, which highlights the performance levels and age ranges commonly associated with each stage. Note that the levels and ranges in the figure indicate what has been more traditional at each stage, not what is inevitable. According to the Bureau of the Census, the proportion of men in the U.S. population age 65 and older that will participate in the labor force in 2008 will reach 17.8 percent. This is the highest participation rate since 1985. The same proportion for women will be 9.1 percent the highest since 1975.[14] As more workers beyond age 65 exist in the workforce, more careers will be maintained beyond the traditional benchmark age of 65 depicted in Figure 1.6.

The **exploration stage** is the first stage in career evolution; it occurs at the beginning of a career, when the individual is typically 15 to 25 years of age, and it is characterized by self-analysis and the exploration of different types of available jobs.

Exploration Stage   The first stage in career evolution is the **exploration stage,** which occurs at the beginning of a career and is characterized by self-analysis and the exploration of different types of available jobs. Individuals at this stage are generally about 15 to 25 years old and are involved in some type of formal training, such as college or vocational education. They often pursue part-time employment to gain a richer understanding of what a career in a particular organization or industry might be like. Typical jobs held during this stage include cooking at Burger King, stocking at a Federated Department Store, and working as an office assistant at a Nationwide Insurance office.

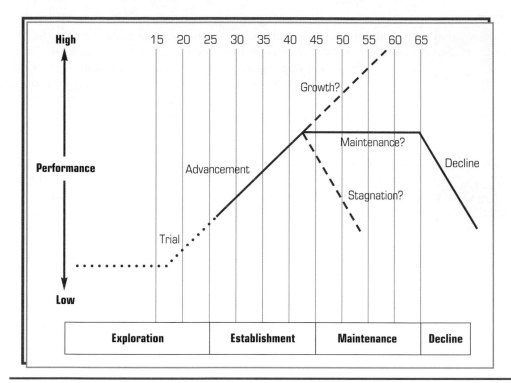

The relationships among career stages, life stages, and performance

Figure 1.6

Establishment Stage   The second stage in career evolution is the **establishment stage,** during which individuals about 25 to 45 years old start to become more productive, or higher performers (as Figure 1.6 indicates by the upturn in the dotted line and its continuance as a solid line). Employment sought during this stage is guided by what was learned during the exploration stage. In addition, the jobs sought are usually full-time. Individuals at this stage commonly move to different jobs within the same company, to different companies, or even to different industries.

Maintenance Stage   The third stage in career evolution is the **maintenance stage.** In this stage, individuals who are about 45 to 65 years old show either increased performance (career growth), stabilized performance (career maintenance), or decreased performance (career stagnation).

From the organization's viewpoint, it is better for managers to experience career growth than maintenance or stagnation. That is why some companies, such as IBM, Monsanto, and Brooklyn Union Gas, have attempted to eliminate **career plateauing**—defined as a period of little or no apparent progress in the growth of a career.[15]

Decline Stage   The last stage in career evolution is the **decline stage,** which involves people about 65 years old whose productivity is declining. These individuals are either close to retirement, semiretired, or fully retired. People in the decline stage may find it difficult to maintain prior performance levels, perhaps because they have lost interest in their careers or have failed to keep their job skills up-to-date.

As Americans live longer and stay healthier into late middle age, many of them choose to become part-time workers in businesses such as Publix supermarkets and McDonald's or in volunteer groups such as the March of Dimes and the American Heart Association. Some retired executives put their career experience to good social use by working with the government-sponsored organization Service Corps of Retired Executives (SCORE) to offer management advice and consultation to small businesses trying to gain a foothold in their market.

Promoting Your Own Career

Both practicing managers and management scholars agree that careful formulation and implementation of appropriate tactics can enhance the success of a management career.[16] Planning your

The **establishment stage** is the second stage in career evolution; individuals of about 25 to 45 years of age typically start to become more productive, or higher performers.

The **maintenance stage** is the third stage in career evolution; individuals of about 45 to 65 years of age either become more productive, stabilize, or become less productive.

Career plateauing is a period of little or no apparent progress in the growth of a career.

The **decline stage** is the fourth and last stage in career evolution; it occurs near retirement age, when individuals of about 65 years of age show declining productivity.

▶ Patricia F. Russo, executive vice president for strategy and administration, is Lucent Technologies' highest-ranking woman. Although they now make up nearly half the workforce, women, and particularly minority women, still find it difficult to achieve positions such as Russo's. Savings institutions and financial firms tend to have the highest percentage of women officers, while trucking, semiconductor, and waste management industries have the lowest.

career path—the sequence of jobs that you will fill in the course of your working life—is the first step you need to take in promoting your career. For some people, a career path entails ascending the hierarchy of a particular organization. Others plan a career path within a particular profession or series of professions. Everyone, however, needs to recognize that career planning is an ongoing process, beginning with the career's early phases and continuing throughout the career.

In promoting your own career, you must be proactive and see yourself as a business that you are responsible for developing. You should not view your plan as limiting your options. First consider both your strengths and your liabilities and assess what you need from a career. Then explore all the avenues of opportunity open to you, both inside and outside the organization. Set your career goals, continually revise and update these goals as your career progresses, and take the steps necessary to accomplish these goals.

Another important tactic in promoting your own career is to work for managers who carry out realistic and constructive roles in the career development of their employees.[17] Table 1.2 outlines what career development responsibility, information, planning, and follow-through generally include. It also outlines the complementary career development role for a professional employee.

To enhance your career success, you must learn to be *proactive* rather than *reactive*.[18] That is, you must take specific actions to demonstrate your abilities and accomplishments. You must also have a clear idea of the next several positions you should seek, the skills you need to acquire to function appropriately in those positions, and plans for acquiring those skills. Finally, you need to think about the ultimate position you want and the sequence of positions you must hold in order to gain the skills and attitudes necessary to qualify for that position.

Special Career Issues

In the business world of today, there are countless special issues that significantly affect how careers actually develop. Three issues that have had a significant impact on career development in recent years are:

1. Women managers
2. Dual-career couples
3. Modern management's digital focus

The following sections discuss each of these factors.

Women Managers   Women in their roles as managers must meet the same challenges in their work environments that men do. However, since they have only recently joined the ranks of management in large numbers, women often lack the social contacts that are so important in the development of a management career. Another problem for women is that, traditionally, they have been expected to manage families and households while simultaneously handling the pressures and competition of paid employment. Finally, women are more likely than men to encounter sexual harassment in the workplace.

 Table 1.2   Manager and Employee Roles in Enhancing Employee Career Development

Dimension	Professional Employee	Manager
Responsibility	Assumes responsibility for individual career development	Assumes responsibility for employee development
Information	Obtains career information through self-evaluation and data collection: What do I enjoy doing? Where do I want to go?	Provides information by holding up a mirror of reality: How manager views the employee How others view the employee How "things work around here"
Planning	Develops an individual plan to reach objectives	Helps employee assess plan
Follow-through	Invites management support through high performance on the current job by understanding the scope of the job and taking appropriate initiative	Provides coaching and relevant information on opportunities

Interestingly, Tom Peters, author of the aforementioned classic management book *In Search of Excellence,* believes that women may have an enormous advantage over men in future management situations.[19] He predicts that networks of relationships will replace rigid organizational structures and star workers will be replaced by teams made up of workers at all levels who are empowered to make decisions. Detailed rules and procedures will be replaced by a flexible system that calls for judgments based on key values and a constant search for new ways to get the job done. Strengths often attributed to women—emphasizing interrelationships, listening, and motivating others—will be the dominant virtues in the corporation of the future.

▶ DaimlerChrysler's workforce reflects diversity at all levels of the corporation, as evidenced by this group of senior executives. When support for diversity comes from the top of the organization, it is more successful at attracting and keeping a diverse workforce.

Dual-Career Couples Because of the growing number of women at work, many organizations have been compelled to consider how dual-career couples affect the workforce.[20] The traditional scenario in which a woman takes a supporting role in the development of her spouse's career is being replaced by one of equal work and shared responsibilities for spouses. This requires a certain amount of flexibility on the part of the couple as well as the organizations for which they work. Today such burning issues as whose career takes precedence if a spouse is offered a transfer to another city and who takes the ultimate responsibility for family concerns point to the fact that dual-career relationships involve trade-offs and that it is very difficult to "have it all."

How Dual-Career Couples Cope Studies of dual-career couples reveal that many cope with their career difficulties in one of the following ways.[21] The couple might develop a commitment to both spouses' careers so that when a decision is made, the right of each spouse to pursue a career is taken into consideration. Both husband and wife are flexible about handling home- and job-oriented issues. They work out coping mechanisms, such as negotiating child care or scheduling shared activities in advance, to better manage their work and their family responsibilities. Often, dual-career couples find that they must limit their social lives and their volunteer responsibilities in order to slow their lives to a manageable pace. Finally, many couples find that they must take steps to consciously facilitate their mutual career advancement. An organization that wants to retain an employee may find that it needs to assist that employee's spouse in his or her career development as well.

MODERN MANAGEMENT'S DIGITAL FOCUS

Thus far, this chapter has defined modern management as the process of working with and through people and other organizational resources to accomplish organizational goals. Related discussion has focused on management wisdom accumulated over the last century by practicing managers as well as management scholars. Overall, this wisdom indicates that managers reach organizational goals by performing four primary functions: planning, organizing, influencing, and controlling.

Recent significant developments support the notion that modern management should include a digital dimension to complement, support, and enhance planning, organizing, influencing, and controlling. The following sections define this "digital dimension" and outline a useful relationship between it and the traditional management functions.

Defining Digital Dimension

In this book, the term **digital** refers to the Internet as well as all Internet-supporting technologies such as voice recognition technology or wireless technology. **Digital dimension,** therefore, refers to that segment of modern management that focuses on meeting management challenges through the application of the Internet and related enhancing technologies. In creating a digital dimension, which is called **"digital dimensioning,"** managers apply the specific combination of Internet and supportive electronic technologies that best help management meet unique organizational challenges and thereby enhance organizational goal attainment.[22] Fundamentally, the focus of management's digital dimension is on employing the Internet and related technologies to maximize organizational goal attainment. Chapter 23, "Management's Digital Dimension," discusses digital dimensioning in detail.

Digital pertains to components related to the Internet and Internet-supporting technologies like voice recognition or wireless technologies.

A **digital dimension** is that segment of management that focuses on meeting management challenges through the application of the Internet and Internet-supportive technologies.

Digital dimensioning is the process of determining and using a unique combination of Internet and Internet-supportive tools that best helps management meet organizational challenges and thereby enhance organizational goal attainment.

As an example of how digital dimensioning works, consider that a manager presently uses a desktop computer to perform organizational activities like making travel arrangements, accessing performance data, or accessing e-mail. The purpose of these activities is to help the manager reach organizational goals; however, this manager recently discovered a new device, a cellular phone with Internet access capability.[23]

For this manager, digital dimensioning would include evaluating this new cell phone in areas like speed of accessing the Internet, ease of use, and cost, to determine if using the phone would increase organizational efficiency and effectiveness. The manager could then determine whether its use would enhance planning, organizing, influencing, controlling, and as a result, organizational goal attainment.

Digital Dimensioning and Traditional Management Functions

Overall, digital dimensioning can impact the way a manager plans, organizes, influences, and controls, and, if appropriate for a specific organization, can lead to improvement in all these areas.

Planning is the process of establishing organizational goals, choosing tasks that must be performed in order to reach those goals, outlining how the tasks should be performed, and determining when the tasks should be performed. Digital dimensioning can have a significant impact on planning. For example, many managers use the Internet to allow employees throughout the world to have input on what organizational plans should be. Such input not only helps managers to develop more appropriate plans, it also helps to build employee commitment to carrying out plans once they are formulated.

Organizing is the process of establishing orderly uses for all resources within an organization. Resources include the organization's people, raw materials, equipment, and financial assets. Digital dimensioning can seriously impact organizing. For example, many managers decide to coordinate activities with different company divisions located throughout the world by communicating with them via Internet videoconferencing. Caterpillar is an example of a company that has been a strong proponent of such videoconferencing for more than a decade.[24] Caterpillar manufactures products like construction and mining equipment, diesel and natural gas engines, and industrial gas turbines. Although it is headquartered in Peoria, Illinois, the company also has operations in countries like Indonesia, Italy, Japan, Mexico, Northern Ireland, and Poland. In this company, videoconferencing plays an important role in coordinating projects that span Caterpillar's global facilities. With continuing technology development making videoconferencing more effective, efficient, and Internet-compatible, such communication at companies like Caterpillar will become much more common in the future.

Influencing is the process of guiding the activities of people in appropriate directions. Appropriate directions are those that lead to the attainment of organizational goals. Digital dimensioning can impact the success of management's influencing efforts. For example, as a means of motivating organization members, many managers choose to award gift certificates to people who do outstanding work. For some companies, it might make sense to award gift certificates and have employees redeem them at nearby stores. For other organizations, it might make sense to enlist the services of an organization specializing in the design and administration of such programs. Some programs, like those at GiftCertificates.com, are Internet-based.[25] GiftCertificates.com offers a special gift certificate, called the Super-Certificate, which stresses maximum flexibility. Employees can use their SuperCertificates to personally choose their gifts, or redeem them for original gift certificates at over 500 popular stores, restaurants, travel merchants, Internet retailers, spas, and movie theaters. SuperCertificates can be exchanged for gift certificates from well-known retailers like J. Crew, Macy's, Barnes and Noble, Sam Goody, and Bloomingdale's. Such rewards for doing good work are designed to motivate employees to continue doing good work.

Controlling is the process of making sure that events occur as planned. As with planning, organizing, and influencing, digital dimensioning can also impact controlling. Consider recently reported events at T.G.I. Friday's.[26] T.G.I. Friday's is a chain of full-service, casual dining restaurants featuring a wide selection of freshly prepared, popular foods and beverages served in relaxed settings. Friday's Web site was purposefully designed to include features for providing management with a continuing stream of evaluative digital information such as the number of people visiting the company Web site, times of the day and days of the week when the Web site was most often visited, and the length of time each visitor stayed after logging on to the Web site. In essence, digital activities at Friday's were designed to generate information that could help management control company efforts by improving its Web site.

SPECIAL FEATURES FOR THE REMAINING CHAPTERS

The **law of the situation,** based on the classic work of Mary Parker Follett, indicates that managers must continually analyze the unique circumstances within their organizations and apply management concepts to fit those circumstances.[27] Managers can understand planning, organizing, influencing, and controlling, but unless they are able to apply these concepts in dealing with specific organizational circumstances, their knowledge will be of little value.

> The **law of the situation** indicates that managers must continually analyze the unique circumstances within their organizations and apply management concepts to fit those circumstances.

Spotlights, Across Industries, and *Digital Focus* are special features in the remaining chapters that provide a wealth of examples on how chapter concepts can be applied to managing organizations. These features have been purposely designed to convey a practical understanding of chapter content by emphasizing the application of management principles by real managers in real organizations. Overall, they offer a rich assortment of applications in top-level to lower-level managerial positions in service, manufacturing, nonprofit, for-profit, and other types of organizations. Additionally, smaller and midsize companies like Opryland, Roadhouse Grill, Luby's, and Endangered Species Chocolate Company are highlighted, as well as larger, better-known companies like IBM, Cisco, Xerox, Weyerheauser, and Coca-Cola.

Spotlights

Spotlights appear throughout the text to focus attention on important contemporary management themes: global management, business or corporate ethics, diversity in organizations, quality in organizations, and people in organizations. Each chapter contains at least two *Spotlight* features, with all themes being equally developed throughout the book. Each type of *Spotlight* is discussed in the following paragraphs.

Global Spotlight
Modern managers are faced with many challenges involving global business. Some of these challenges involve building organizations in developing countries, fighting foreign competition, developing joint ventures with foreign companies, and building a productive workforce across several foreign countries. This feature illustrates the application of management concepts to meeting international challenges.

Ethics Spotlight
Modern managers face the challenge of developing and maintaining social responsibility and ethical practices that are appropriate for their particular organizations. Some challenges involve such issues as settling on who within an organization should perform socially responsible activities, determining the role of ethics in an organization, encouraging ethical behavior throughout the organization, and determining internal funding for socially responsible activities.[28] This feature illustrates the application of management concepts to meeting a firm's social responsibility and ethical challenges.

Diversity Spotlight
Modern managers constantly face the challenge of handling situations involving diversity in organizations. *Diversity* is defined as differences in people such as age, gender, ethnicity, nationality, and ability. In essence, today's managers must continually deal with significant variability in the people who interface with the organization. Thus organization members as well as customers may be a mix of African Americans, Hispanics, Asians, and Native Americans.[29] Or the mix may involve people who are older, women, and the handicapped. This management feature presents practical insights for appropriately building organizational diversity into a resource so that the organization can understand and respond to diversity in its broader environment (e.g., among customers) and thereby enhance its success. In addition, diversity is discussed in Chapter 4, "Management and Diversity."

Quality Spotlight
Contemporary managers, perhaps more than any other generation of managers, face the challenge of developing and maintaining high quality in the goods and services they offer.[30] High-quality products are defined as goods or services that customers rate as

excellent. Most management theorists and practicing managers agree that if an organization is to be successful in today's national and international markets, it must offer high-quality goods and services to its customers.

Virtually every activity a manager performs can have some impact on the quality of goods or services that that manager's organization produces. Developing organizational objectives, training organization members, practicing strategic management, and designing organization structures—all affect the quality of a company's output. This management feature illustrates how various management activities affect product quality. In addition, quality is discussed in detail in Chapter 22, "Competitiveness: Quality and Innovation."

You will find it valuable to study all of these management spotlights carefully, as they will help you build realistic expectations about your career as a manager. The cases detailed in the spotlights illustrate that as managers show the ability to solve various organizational problems, they become more valuable to organizations and are more likely to receive the organizational rewards of promotion and significant pay increases.

People Spotlight   This *Spotlight* concentrates on human issues in organizations. This feature emphasizes how crucial managing people is and illustrates that no management topic exists independently of people issues. In addition, the Influencing section of this text provides an in-depth theoretical look at many people-oriented topics, such as communication, managing teams, and motivation. The *People Spotlight* complements this theoretical focus by integrating human topics and their application into the entire book.

Across Industries

Managers apply management principles daily in many different industries across the world. A rich understanding of management includes insights about how managers react to the varied situations that confront them. Studying how management principles are applied in different industries can provide managers with invaluable insights about facing the challenges of their industries. *Across Industries* is a proven feature of this book that illustrates how management concepts are applied in different industries. An *Across Industries* highlight appears in half of the chapters. Industries highlighted in this text are varied and include mail-order retailing, food processing, automobile tire manufacturing, and government.

Digital Focus

Earlier in this chapter we discussed modern management's digital focus, an emphasis on using the Internet and Internet-enhancing technologies like voice recognition technology and wireless technology to improve planning, organizing, influencing, controlling, and ultimately, organizational goal attainment. *Digital Focus*, a new feature for this text edition, aims at providing students with insights about how modern management's digital dimension can enhance organizational success. *Digital Focus* highlights appear in half of the chapters and illustrate how managers are using digital tools to meet management challenges. Examples of topics in this feature include organizational learning via the Web, using the Web to survey employee attitudes, and using digital tools to enhance organizational efficiency.

▶ Back to the Case

As is the case with managers of any company, the managers at Lands' End are at various stages of career development. As an example of how those stages might relate to managers at Land's End, let us focus on one particular manager, Martin Plane. Assume that Martin Plane is a manager overseeing product delivery. He is 45 years old and is considered a member of middle management.

Plane began his career (exploration stage) in college by considering various areas of study and by working at a number of different types of part-time positions. He delivered pizzas for Domino's Pizza and worked for Scott's, a lawn care company. He began college at age 18 and graduated when he was 22.

Plane then moved into the establishment stage of his career. For a few years immediately after graduation, he held full-time trial positions in the retail industry as well as in the delivery industry. What he had learned during the career exploration stage helped him choose the types of full-time trial positions to pursue.

At the age of 26, he accepted a trial position as an assistant delivery manager at Lands' End in Dodgeville, Wisconsin. Through this position he discovered that he wanted to remain in the delivery end of retailing in general and more specifically with Lands' End. From age 27 to age 45, he held a number of supervisory and management positions at Lands' End.

Now Plane is moving into an extremely critical part of his career, the maintenance stage. He could probably remain in his present position and maintain his productivity for several more years. However, he wants to advance his career. Therefore, he must emphasize a proactive attitude by formulating and implementing tactics aimed at enhancing his career success, such as seeking training to develop critical skills, or moving to a position that is a prerequisite for other, more advanced positions at Lands' End.

In the future, as Plane approaches the decline stage of his career, it is probable that his productivity will decrease somewhat. From a career viewpoint, he may want to go from full-time employment to semiretirement. Perhaps he could work for Lands' End or another retail-based company on a part-time advisory basis or even pursue part-time work in another industry. For example, he might be able to teach a management course at a nearby community college.

It is not too late for Plane to focus on adding a digital dimension to his management activities. In essence, he should use the Internet and related enhancing technologies to help Land's End reach its goals and meet organizational challenges. Overall, such tools can help Plane to better plan, organize, influence, and control.

Management Skills Module

This section is specially designed to help you develop management skills. An individual's management skill is based on an understanding of management concepts and the ability to apply those concepts in management situations. As a result, the following activities are designed both to heighten your understanding of management concepts and to help you gain facility in applying those concepts in various management situations.

UNDERSTANDING MANAGEMENT CONCEPTS

▶ Action Summary

Reread the learning objectives below. Each objective is followed by questions. Answering these questions accurately will help you retain the most important concepts discussed in this chapter. After answering each question, check your answer against the answer key at the end of this chapter. (*Hint:* If you have any doubts regarding the correct response, consult the page number that follows the answer.)

Circle:

From studying this chapter, I will attempt to acquire

1. An understanding of the importance of management to society and individuals.
   - T F   **a.** Managers constitute less than 1 percent of the U.S. workforce.
   - T F   **b.** Management is important to society.
2. An understanding of the role of management.
   - a b c d e   **a.** The role of a manager is to: (a) make workers happy (b) satisfy only the manager's needs (c) make the most profit (d) survive in a highly competitive society (e) achieve organizational goals.
   - T F   **b.** Apart from its goals, management has no meaning.
3. An ability to define *management* in several different ways.
   - a b c d e   **a.** Management is: (a) a process (b) reaching organizational goals (c) utilizing people and other resources (d) all of the above (e) a and b.
   - T F   **b.** Management is the process of working with people and through people.
4. An ability to list and define the basic functions of management.
   - a b c d e   **a.** Which of the following is not a function of management: (a) influencing (b) planning (c) organizing (d) directing (e) controlling.
   - a b c d e   **b.** The process of gathering information and comparing this information to preestablished standards is part of: (a) planning (b) influencing (c) motivating (d) controlling (e) commanding.
5. Working definitions of managerial effectiveness and managerial efficiency.
   - T F   **a.** If an organization is using its resources to attain its goals, the organization's managers are efficient.
   - T F   **b.** A manager who is reaching goals but wasting resources is efficient but ineffective.
6. An understanding of basic management skills and their relative importance to managers.
   - a b c d e   **a.** Conceptual skills require that management view the organization as: (a) a profit center (b) a decision-making unit (c) a problem-solving group (d) a whole (e) individual contributions.
   - T F   **b.** Managers require fewer and fewer human skills as they move from lower to higher management levels.
7. An understanding of the universality of management.
   - T F   **a.** The statement that management principles are universal means that they apply to all types of organizations and organizational levels.
   - T F   **b.** The universality of management means that management principles are taught the same way in all schools.
8. Insights concerning what management careers are and how they evolve.
   - T F   **a.** In general, as careers evolve, individuals tend to further develop job skills but show very little or no change in attitude about various job circumstances.
   - T F   **b.** Individuals tend to show the first significant increase in performance during the establishment career stage.
9. An understanding of management's digital focus
   - T F   **a.** "Digital" refers exclusively to Internet technology.
   - T F   **b.** Digital dimensioning should focus on enhancing controlling, but not planning.

▶ Action Summary Answer Key

1. a. F, p. 4	4. a. d, p. 7	6. a. d, p. 11	8. a. F, pp. 12–13
b. T, p. 4	b. d, p. 7	b. F, p. 11	b. T, p. 13
2. a. e, p. 6	5. a. F, p. 9	7. a. T, p. 11	9. a. F, p. 15
b. T, p. 6	b. F, pp. 9–10	b. F, p. 11	b. F, p. 16
3. a. d, pp. 7–9			
b. F, p. 7			

▶ Issues for Review and Discussion

1. What is the main point illustrated in the introductory case on Lands' End?
2. How important is the management function to society?
3. How important is the management function to individuals?
4. What is the basic role of the manager?
5. How is *management* defined in this text? What main themes are contained in this definition?
6. List and define each of the four functions of management.
7. Outline the relationship among the four management functions.
8. List and describe five of Peters and Waterman's characteristics of excellent companies, and explain how each of these characteristics could affect planning, organizing, influencing, and controlling.
9. List and define the basic organizational resources managers have at their disposal.
10. What is the relationship between organizational resources and production?
11. Draw and explain the continuum of managerial effectiveness.
12. Draw and explain the continuum of managerial efficiency.
13. Are managerial effectiveness and managerial efficiency related concepts? If so, how are they related?
14. According to Katz, what are the three primary types of skills important to management success? Define each of these types of skills.
15. Describe the relative importance of each of these three types of skills to lower-level, middle-level, and upper-level managers.
16. What is meant by "the universality of management"?
17. What is a career?
18. Discuss the significance of the maintenance career stage.
19. What tips contained in this chapter for promoting the success of a career do you find most valuable? Explain.
20. What does the law of the situation tell you about the success of your management career?
21. What is meant by "digital dimensioning" and how can it help a manager like the president of Coca-Cola Company?

APPLYING MANAGEMENT CONCEPTS

▶ Cases

➡ INTRODUCTORY CASE WRAP-UP

▶ Case Discussion Questions

"Lands' End Management Learning How to Use the Web" (pp. 2–3) and Its related Back-to-the-Case sections were written to help you better understand the management concepts contained in this chapter. Answer the following discussion questions about this introductory case to further enrich your understanding of the chapter content:

1. Do you think that it will be difficult for you to become a successful manager? Explain.
2. What do you think you would like most about being a manager? What would you like least?
3. As part of this case, you were asked to assume that you are the CEO of Lands' End. As such, list and describe five activities that you think you will have to perform as part of this job.

▶ Skills Exercise: Interviewing for a Lands' End Management Position

Despite your lack of managerial experience, you have made it through the initial stages for executive employment at Lands' End and are getting ready to interview for the position called "Delivery Manager, Southeast Region." Review the discussion of management functions in the text and prepare for your interview using the following heads: (1) Planning, (2) Influencing, (3) Controlling, and (4) Organizing. Under each head, list experiences that you have had that meet the definition of that managerial function, however broadly, and that you think would appeal to executive recruiters at Lands' End. Review your lists and select the *one* experience that you will discuss in your interview. Write a short description of the experience, highlighting those aspects that you plan to emphasize when you actually interview.

eBay's primary colors invite you to play, but logging on to eBay is no game. Millions of people conduct serious business on the site each day—buying and selling with a passion. Founded in 1995, eBay is the world's largest online trading community, selling over 8,000 categories of merchandise from a nineteenth-century pair of Levi's jeans valued at over $25,000.00 to art work to automobile parts to AC/DC albums. It facilitates auctions for individuals across the United States, Canada, and much of Europe, Japan, South Korea, Australia, and New Zealand.

CEO Meg Whitman predicts eBay will handle $30 billion in sales and be established in 25 foreign countries by 2005. This represents an annual growth rate of about 50 percent. Unlike rival Amazon.com, which has invested millions in warehouses to store the goods it sells, and ships to buyers, eBay has few infrastructure costs. At eBay it is the seller's responsibility to package and ship the goods to the buyer once an auction is completed.

Whitman believes that revenues should exceed expenses and runs her new-economy company according to old-economy rules. Under her tenure, eBay has survived aggressive competition from Yahoo!, Lycos, and Amazon.com; a string of power outages; some phony auctions featuring human organs; and the appearance of Nazi swastikas on the site.

Whitman has polished eBay's image by having it take out an insurance policy to protect buyers and sellers from fraud. She has lobbied Washington for a bill that could help fend off "auction aggregators," who collect listings and post them in one location. At one point the site was down for 22 hours and she worked 100 hours a week for a month to fix the outages. "We put in cots, and I was just there. I lived it," she said in an interview with Computerworld.

Whitman travels the globe to bring eBay to an ever-growing population. She even scheduled a stop at a women's college on her recent trip to Seoul, South Korea, where she spoke to students about the future of the Internet industry.

Meg Whitman was born in Long Island, New York, in 1957. She is the youngest child of a businessman and a headstrong homemaker. When Meg was 6 years old her mother took her and her older brother and sister on a drive up the Alaskan highway in a Ford Econoline van for the summer. "We camped for three months. No hotels," said Meg. In 1977, Whitman graduated from Princeton University with a B.A. in economics and earned her M.B.A. from Harvard Business School in 1979. "Go figure out what you want to do, and do it," Meg's mother told her. She landed a job as a brand assistant with Proctor & Gamble and worked her way up to brand manager.

In 1981, Whitman moved to San Francisco when her husband, a neurosurgeon, began a residency at the University of California. Whitman then found work as a consultant for Bain & Company, where she stayed for the next eight years. Moving to the Walt Disney Company in 1989 as a senior vice president of marketing, Whitman opened Disney's first stores in Japan. After her husband

took a new position in Boston, she accepted a job as president of Stride Rite shoes, putting "Keds" back in the public eye. In 1995 she left Stride Rite for the challenge of revamping the floundering Florists' Transworld Delivery (FTD). She fought the corporate higher-ups and transformed it into a privately held company. In 1997, Whitman changed jobs again to go to Hasbro, Inc., where she was general manager of the Playskool division handling Mr. Potato Head and the Teletubbies.

Then, in November 1997, Whitman was contacted by a headhunter who told her about a job with an Internet start-up called "Auction Web" (later renamed eBay). Reluctant to uproot her husband and two sons, she turned it down. The headhunter persisted, and when she saw the offices in San Jose, she changed her mind, accepting the job in February 1998. In a recent *Fast Company* interview, Whitman said, when eBay's founder Pierre Omidyar told her that people had met their best friends on eBay, she "just knew this was huge," and she wanted to be a part of it. Whitman came in as CEO, found out what was going right, and nurtured it. "I think sometimes when a new senior executive comes into a company the instinctive thing to do is to find out what's wrong and fix it. That doesn't actually work very well. People are very proud of what they've created and it just feels like you are second guessing them all the time," Whitman said.

As one of *Worth*'s top 50 CEOs for 2001, Meg Whitman is said to have the "foresight, judgement and competitive juice to make her investors happy"; but it is not only on shareholders that Whitman focuses. Her priorities for the twenty-first century are training and mentoring in order to develop middle managers and senior leaders who will be able to build a strong global trading platform for eBay. Whitman believes in hiring people who are able to work in a team. All executives are held up to collective scrutiny and ego is frowned upon. Her approach is upbeat. When asked by *Fast Company* how she felt about having a cubicle like everyone else instead of an executive office, Meg Whitman had this to say: "(laughing) I don't actually miss the trappings of the offices I used to have. I love being in a smaller environment, feeling like I'm in a bit of a PT boat, as opposed to a battleship." Not only is eBay thriving, but Meg Whitman has become one of the Internet's wealthiest CEOs, worth more than $1 billion on paper.

QUESTIONS

1. As CEO at eBay, is Meg Whitman a manager? Explain fully using facts from the case.
2. Which stage of her management career is Meg Whitman in now? What do you believe her next career stage will be? Why?
3. List three ways that Whitman could use the Internet to make eBay a better-managed company. Could your suggestions make a significant difference in how eBay is managed? Explain fully.

CONMEDIA SEGMENT ONE

A Digital Focus

Viewing this five-video sequence will allow you to observe how employees and managers from a traditional corporate background merge with those who are used to a more casual entrepreneurial work environment. You will get a glimpse of just how complicated it can be to put management theory into practice in our ever-changing world. Take note of the particular group or character you most closely identify with in each segment, and you will learn something about your own potential as a manager in the process.

In the opening video on Conmedia you meet Sam, Ruth, and Ashley, three generations of employees at *Modern Lady,* a women's magazine that has been on the market for 75 years. Sam has taken Ruth, the magazine's editor of 13 years, and Ashley, the fledgling managing editor of 6 months, out to lunch. Think about what his reasons may be for taking them to a restaurant to tell them that their parent company, Conmedia, has just acquired the webzine, Allaboutself.com. You will notice that Sam doesn't tell them the two entities will be merged until after they have finished eating. Be aware of Ruth's reaction as she hears Sam's news. You may want to take note of the difference in Ashley's response. At this point, begin to clarify exactly which career stage Ashley, Ruth, and Sam are in. This should help you see how their relationships to one another and to the company as a whole have evolved and are continuing to evolve as the scene unfolds.

Pay attention to Ruth so that you will be able to gage the range of her professional experience and what she will need to understand about the real effects digital dimensioning could have on her job as a manager. Sam clearly wants little to do with the day-to-day decision making of the merger. (His comments seem to be motivated by organizational objectives rather than by personal beliefs. This may or may not turn out to be the best way to achieve change.) Ashley, on the other hand, is keen on being in on every step of the merger. She may feel as vulnerable being a newcomer as Ruth does being a veteran of the old order. Notice how Ashley feels when she learns that Ruth will be meeting Mia Cipriano, founder of the webzine, alone.

The meeting between Ruth and Mia starts out with each woman defending her own turf. When Mia picks up on Ruth's insecurity, she lets her guard down by volunteering that Allaboutself.com has had difficulty in finding advertisers. The dialogue between them will give you an understanding of the differences between print media and an online site. As they open up to one another, they find common ground and a spark of excitement that starts them off on the planning stage. Their success or failure will now depend heavily on their managerial skills. As this first segment closes, consider how digital dimensioning might enhance controlling at Conmedia.

QUESTIONS

1. How effective is Sam as a senior manager? Based on his behavior in this segment, how would you rate him in terms of technical, human, and conceptual skills?

2. Would you consider Ashley *proactive* or *reactive* regarding her position at *Modern Lady*?

3. What career stage is Ruth in? What career stage is Mia in? Support your answer using both the text and the video.

4. Which qualities often attributed to women managers are demonstrated in the last scene between Mia and Ruth?

5. How do you see the new digital focus at Conmedia being used as a tool to enhance management's ability to make a profit?

THE DIGITAL DIMENSION AND *YOU*

It is snowing out, and it is the first night of winter break. You are stuck in your empty dorm watching a rerun of *The Simpsons.* Your grandparents are probably at the airport in Los Angles right now waiting for you. You booked your midnight bargain flight on the Web and when you arrived at the airport it had been canceled. The Web site was never updated and you cannot reach your grandparents because they do not have a cell phone. It looks like there are no flights available for the next two days. What are you going to do now?

1. What does this experience teach you about technology as a tool to be used in planning your activities? How will this be useful to you in the future when you might be faced with business plans that are impacted by a "glitch" in technology?

www.prenhall.com/certo

This book is accompanied by a rich assortment of online activities aimed at developing your management skills. Reviewing news headlines, Internet exercises, an online study guide, and other research and Internet resources can help personalize management skills development for individual students or an entire class.

2 Managing: *History and Current Thinking*

Objectives

From studying this chapter, I will attempt to acquire

- An understanding of the classical approach to management

- An appreciation for the work of Frederick W. Taylor, Frank and Lillian Gilbreth, Henry L. Gantt, and Henri Fayol

- An understanding of the behavioral approach to management

- An understanding of the studies at the Hawthorne Works and the human relations movement

- An understanding of the management science approach to management

- An understanding of how the management science approach has evolved

- An understanding of the system approach to management

- Knowledge about the learning organization approach to management

- An understanding of how triangular management and the contingency approach to management are related

A Problem at McDonald's

REMINDER: THE INTRODUCTORY CASE WRAP-UP (P. 43) CONTAINS DISCUSSION QUESTIONS AND A SKILLS EXERCISE TO FURTHER ILLUSTRATE THE APPLICATION OF CHAPTER CONCEPTS TO THIS VIGNETTE.

McDonald's is banking on its new "one order at a time" method of preparing its traditional burger and fries menu to help recover its dominant market share in the fast-food industry. Reduced waste, lower cost, and higher customer satisfaction are the goals.

McDonald's Corporation, perhaps the premier hamburger retailer in the world for decades, now faces significant problems. Within the last 10 years, McDonald's share of fast-food sales in the United States has slipped almost two percentage points. The drop has come despite the company's increasing its number of restaurants by 50 percent, thereby leading the industry.

How is McDonald's trying to regain its lost sales? The primary solution involves reengineering the company's system for making hamburgers. In the past, McDonald's used a *standard* method for making hamburgers. The customer could get a *custom* hamburger, but it would take much longer. In essence, it was a choice between a preferred hamburger and speed of service.

The new food preparation method requires McDonald's to prepare orders one at a time as opposed to its traditional method of preparing it in batches. Besides being more customer oriented, this "one order at a time" method should help McDonald's compete more effectively with Burger King and Wendy's, two of its primary competitors.

The new system has many advantages. First of all, it is very quick and accurate since its operation is computerized. Indeed, the system had to be designed to be quick because customers want food promptly and sandwiches are not made until customers actually order them. As another advantage, the new system will lower food costs. Company officials believe that the old system's batch-related cost of having to discard prepared food held too long in the warmer will be eliminated. Finally, since food is no longer held in a warmer, the quality should be raised even further.

Michael Quinlan, CEO at McDonald's, is very excited about the new system being introduced in his restaurants. He believes the speedier system will enable restaurants to serve more people at peak hours and offer more and different products. Quinlan, however, is an astute manager, and he knows that many problems will arise before the system contributes all that it can to the success of the organization.

There are several different ways to approach management situations and to solve related organizational problems. Managers like Michael Quinlan, the CEO of McDonald's mentioned in the Introductory Case, as well as all other managers at McDonald's, must understand these approaches if they are to build successful organizations. This chapter explains six such approaches:

1) The classical approach
2) The behavioral approach
3) The management science approach
4) The contingency approach
5) The system approach
6) The learning organization approach

Chapter 1 focused primarily on defining *management*. This chapter presents various approaches to analyzing and reacting to the management situation, each characterized by a basically different method of analysis and a different type of recommended action.

There has been much disagreement on how many different approaches to management there are and what each approach entails. In an attempt to simplify the discussion of the field of management without sacrificing significant information, Donnelly, Gibson, and Ivancevich combined the ideas of Koontz, O'Donnell, and Weihrich with those of Haynes and Massie, and concluded that there were three basic approaches to management:[1]

1. Classical approach
2. Behavioral approach
3. Management science approach

The following sections build on the work of Donnelly, Gibson, and Ivancevich in presenting the classical, behavioral, and management science approaches to analyzing the management task. The contingency approach is discussed as a fourth primary approach, while the system approach is presented as a recent trend in management thinking. The learning organization is continually evolving and is discussed as the newest form for analyzing management.

THE CLASSICAL APPROACH

The **classical approach to management** is a management approach that emphasizes organizational efficiency to increase organizational success.

The **classical approach to management** was the product of the first concentrated effort to develop a body of management thought. In fact, the management writers who participated in this effort are considered the pioneers of management study. The classical approach recommends that managers continually strive to increase organizational efficiency in order to increase production. Although the fundamentals of this approach were developed some time ago, contemporary managers are just as concerned with finding the "one best way" to get the job done as their predecessors were. To illustrate this concern, notable management theorists see striking similarities between the concepts of scientific management developed many years ago and the more current management philosophy of building quality into all aspects of organizational operations.[2]

For discussion purposes, the classical approach to management can be broken down into two distinct areas. The first, lower-level management analysis, consists primarily of the work of Frederick W. Taylor, Frank and Lillian Gilbreth, and Henry L. Gantt. These individuals studied mainly the jobs of workers at lower levels of the organization. The second area, comprehensive analysis of management, concerns the management function as a whole. The primary contributor to this category was Henri Fayol. Figure 2.1 illustrates the two areas in the classical approach.

Lower-Level Management Analysis

Lower-level management analysis concentrates on the "one best way" to perform a task; that is, it investigates how a task situation can be structured to get the highest production from workers. The process of finding this "one best way" has become known as the *scientific method of management,* or simply, **scientific management.** Although the techniques of scientific managers could conceivably be applied to management at all levels, the research, research applications, and illustrations relate mostly to lower-level managers. The work of Frederick W. Taylor, Frank and Lillian Gilbreth, and Henry L. Gantt is summarized in the sections that follow.

Frederick W. Taylor (1856–1915) Because of the significance of his contributions, Frederick W. Taylor is commonly called the "father of scientific management." His primary goal was to increase worker efficiency by scientifically designing jobs. His basic premise was that there was one best way to do a job and that this way should be discovered and put into operation.

Work at Bethlehem Steel Co. Perhaps the best way to illustrate Taylor's scientific method and his management philosophy is to describe how he modified the job of employees whose sole responsibility was shoveling materials at Bethlehem Steel Company.[3] During the modification process, Taylor made the assumption that any worker's job could be reduced to a science. To construct the "science of shoveling," he obtained answers—through observation and experimentation—to the following questions:

1. Will a first-class worker do more work per day with a shovelful of 5, 10, 15, 20, 30, or 40 pounds?
2. What kinds of shovels work best with which materials?
3. How quickly can a shovel be pushed into a pile of materials and pulled out properly loaded?
4. How much time is required to swing a shovel backward and throw the load a given horizontal distance at a given height?

As Taylor formulated answers to these types of questions, he developed insights on how to increase the total amount of materials shoveled per day. He raised worker efficiency by matching shovel size with such factors as the size of the worker, the weight of the materials, and the

Scientific management emphasizes the "one best way" to perform a task.

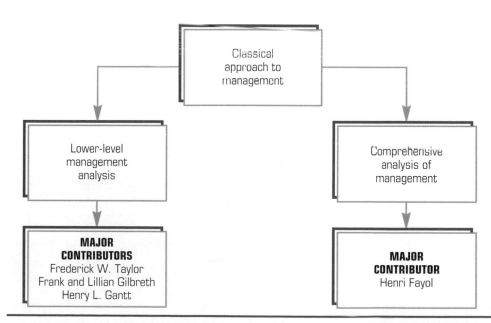

Division of classical approach to management into two areas and the major contributors to each area

Figure 2.1

height and distance the materials were to be thrown. By the end of the third year after Taylor's shoveling efficiency plan was implemented, records at Bethlehem Steel showed that the total number of shovelers needed had been reduced from about 600 to 140, the average number of tons shoveled per worker per day had risen from 16 to 59, the average earnings per worker per day had increased from $1.15 to $1.88, and the average cost of handling a long ton (2,240 pounds) had dropped from $0.072 to $0.033—all in all, an impressive demonstration of the applicability of scientific management to the task of shoveling.[4]

Frank Gilbreth (1868–1924) and Lillian Gilbreth (1878–1972)

The Gilbreths were also significant contributors to the scientific method. As a point of interest, the Gilbreths focused on handicapped as well as normal workers.[5] Like other contributors to the scientific method, they subscribed to the idea of finding and using the one best way to perform a job. The primary investigative tool in the Gilbreths' research was **motion study,** which consists of reducing each job to the most basic movements possible. Motion analysis is used today primarily to establish job performance standards. Each movement, or motion, that is used to do a job is studied to determine how much time the movement takes and how necessary it is to performing the job. Inefficient or unnecessary motions are pinpointed and eliminated.[6]

Frank Gilbreth's experience as an apprentice bricklayer led him to do motion studies of bricklaying. He found that bricklayers could increase their output significantly by concentrating on performing some motions and eliminating others. Table 2.1 shows a simplified portion of the results of one of Gilbreth's bricklaying motion studies. For each bricklaying operation, Gilbreth indicated whether it should be omitted for the sake of efficiency and why. He reduced the five motions per brick listed under "The Wrong Way" to the one motion per brick listed under "The Right Way." Overall, Gilbreth's bricklaying motion studies resulted in the reducing of the number of motions necessary to lay a brick by approximately 70 percent and the consequently tripling bricklaying production.

Lillian Gilbreth, who began as her husband's collaborator, continued to research and write on motion studies after his death. She is noted especially for her application of the scientific method to the role of the homemaker and to the handicapped.

Henry L. Gantt (1861–1919)

The third major contributor to the scientific management approach was Henry L. Gantt. He, too, was interested in increasing worker efficiency. Gantt attributed unsatisfactory or ineffective tasks and piece rates (incentive pay for each product piece an individual produces) primarily to the fact that these tasks and rates were set

A **motion study** finds the best way to accomplish a task by analyzing the movements necessary to perform that task.

▶ Unlike the women working in this World War I munitions factory, who had to contend with isolating and repetitive work in noisy surroundings, today's employee teams have the freedom to devise their own solutions to problems and put them into effect. Even factory workers in many firms are members of such teams.

▶ The members of this consulting team have just completed a project for Macy's, an elaborate computer model that will help the store determine how many salespeople are needed in each department, based on how shoppers behave.

Operation No.	The Wrong Way	The Right Way	Pick and Dip Method: The Exterior 4 Inches (Laying to the Line)
1	Step for mortar	Omit	On the scaffold, the inside edge of the mortar box should be plumb with the inside edge of the stock platform. On the floor, the inside edge of the mortar box should be 21 inches from the wall. Mortar boxes should never be over 4 feet apart.
2	Reach for mortar	Reach for mortar	Do not bend any more than absolutely necessary to reach mortar with a straight arm.
3	Work up mortar	Omit	Provide mortar of the right consistency. Examine sand screen and keep it in repair so that no pebbles can get through. Keep tender on scaffold to temper up and keep mortar worked up right.
4	Step for brick	Omit	If tubs are kept 4 feet apart, no stepping for brick will be necessary on scaffold. On the floor, keep brick in a pile not nearer than 1 foot or more than 4 feet 6 inches from wall.
5	Reach for brick	Included in 2	Brick must be reached for at the same time that the mortar is reached for, and picked up at exactly the same time the mortar is picked up. If it is not picked up at the same time, allowance must be made for operation.

according to what had been done by workers in the past or on somebody's *opinion* of what workers could do. According to Gantt, *exact scientific knowledge* of what could be done by a worker should be substituted for opinion. He considered this the role of scientific management.

Gantt's management philosophy is encapsulated in his statement that "the essential differences between the best system of today and those of the past are the manner in which tasks are 'scheduled' and the manner in which their performance is rewarded."[7] Using this rationale, he sought to improve systems or organizations through task-scheduling innovation and the rewarding of innovation.

Scheduling Innovation   The Gantt chart, the primary scheduling device that Gantt developed, is still the scheduling tool most commonly used by modern managers.[8] Basically, this chart provides managers with an easily understood summary of what work was scheduled for specific time periods, how much of this work has been completed, and by whom it was done.

Special computer software like MacSchedule has been developed to help managers more efficiently and effectively apply the concept of the Gantt chart today.[9] MacSchedule allows managers to easily monitor complicated and detailed scheduling issues like the number of units planned for production during a specified period, when work is to begin and to be completed, and the percentage of work that was actually completed during a period. (The Gantt chart is covered in much more detail in Chapter 8.)

Rewarding Innovation   Gantt was more aware of the human side of production than either Taylor or the Gilbreths. He wrote that "the taskmaster (manager) of the past was practically a slave driver, whose principal function was to force workmen to do that which they had no desire to do, or interest in doing. The task setter of today under any reputable system of management is not a driver. When he asks the workmen to perform tasks, he makes it to their interest to accomplish them, and is careful not to ask what is impossible or unreasonable."[10]

In contrast to Taylor, who pioneered a piece-rate system under which workers were paid according to the amount they produced and who advocated the use of wage-incentive plans, Gantt developed a system wherein workers could earn a bonus in addition to the piece rate if they exceeded their daily production quota. Gantt, then, believed in worker compensation that corresponded not only to production (through the piece-rate system) but also to overproduction (through the bonus system).

▶ Utz Quality Foods, Inc., the number three U.S. maker of salty snacks, now uses sophisticated software and the Internet to create daily sales reports that match promotions against results. Marketing manager Dylan Lissette (right, with CEO Michael W. Rice) can track every product by store, so if store shelves should empty, they can be filled within a day. Such state-of-the-art operations techniques build on the work of early management theorists like the Gilbreths and Henry Gantt.

► Back to the Case

Michael Quinlan, the CEO of McDonald's mentioned in the Introductory Case, could attempt to use a classical approach to management to stress organizational efficiency—the "one best way" to perform jobs at McDonald's restaurants—and thereby increase productivity. To take a simplified example, McDonald's managers might want to check whether the dispenser used to apply mustard and catsup is of the appropriate size to require only one squirt or whether more than one squirt is necessary to adequately cover a hamburger.

To complement his new "made-to-order cooking system," Quinlan could use motion studies to eliminate unnecessary or wasted motions by his employees. For example, are Big Macs, french fries, and drinks located for easy insertion into customer bags, or must an employee walk unnecessary steps during the sales process? Also, would certain McDonald's employees be more efficient over an entire working day if they sat, rather than stood, while working?

The classical approach to management might also guide Quinlan to stress efficient scheduling. By ensuring that an appropriate number of people with the appropriate skills are scheduled to work during peak hours and that fewer such individuals are scheduled to work during slower hours, McDonald's would maximize the return on their labor costs.

Quinlan and other McDonald's managers also might want to consider offering their employees some sort of bonus if they reach certain work goals. Management should make sure, however, that the goals it sets are realistic, because unreasonable or impossible goals tend to make workers resentful and unproductive. For example, management might ask that certain employees reduce errors in filling orders by 50 percent during the next month. If and when these employees reached the goal, McDonald's could give them a free lunch as a bonus.

Comprehensive analysis of management involves studying the management function as a whole.

Comprehensive Analysis of Management

Whereas scientific managers emphasize job design approaching the study of management, managers who embrace the comprehensive view—the second area of the classical approach—are concerned with the entire range of managerial performance.

Among the well-known contributors to the comprehensive view are Chester Barnard,[11] Alvin Brown, Henry Dennison, Luther Gulick and Lyndall Urwick, J. D. Mooney and A. C. Reiley, and Oliver Sheldon.[12] Perhaps the most notable contributor, however, was Henri Fayol. His book *General and Industrial Management* presents a management philosophy that still guides many modern managers.[13]

Henri Fayol (1841–1925)   Because of his writings on the elements and general principles of management, Henri Fayol is usually regarded as the pioneer of administrative theory. The elements of management he outlined—planning, organizing, commanding, coordinating, and control—are still considered worthwhile divisions under which to study, analyze, and effect the management process.[14] (Note the close correspondence between Fayol's elements of management and the management functions outlined in Chapter 1—planning, organizing, influencing, controlling.)

The general principles of management suggested by Fayol are still considered useful in contemporary management practice. Here are the principles in the order developed by Fayol, accompanied by corresponding definitional themes:[15]

1. *Division of work*—Work should be divided among individuals and groups to ensure that effort and attention are focused on special portions of the task. Fayol presented work specialization as the best way to use the human resources of the organization.
2. *Authority*—The concepts of authority and responsibility are closely related. *Authority* was defined by Fayol as the right to give orders and the power to exact obedience. *Responsibility* involves being accountable, and is therefore naturally associated with authority. Whoever assumes authority also assumes responsibility.
3. *Discipline*—A successful organization requires the common effort of workers. Penalties should be applied judiciously to encourage this common effort.
4. *Unity of command*—Workers should receive orders from only one manager.

5. *Unity of direction*—The entire organization should be moving toward a common objective, in a common direction.
6. *Subordination of individual interests to the general interests*—The interests of one person should not take priority over the interests of the organization as a whole.
7. *Remuneration*—Many variables, such as cost of living, supply of qualified personnel, general business conditions, and success of the business, should be considered in determining a worker's rate of pay.
8. *Centralization*—Fayol defined *centralization* as lowering the importance of the subordinate role. *Decentralization* is increasing the importance. The degree to which centralization or decentralization should be adopted depends on the specific organization in which the manager is working.
9. *Scalar chain*—Managers in hierarchies are part of a chainlike authority scale. Each manager, from the first-line supervisor to the president, possesses certain amounts of authority. The president possesses the most authority; the first-line supervisor, the least. Lower-level managers should always keep upper-level managers informed of their work activities. The existence of a scalar chain and adherence to it are necessary if the organization is to be successful.
10. *Order*—For the sake of efficiency and coordination, all materials and people related to a specific kind of work should be assigned to the same general location in the organization.
11. *Equity*—All employees should be treated as equally as possible.
12. *Stability of tenure of personnel*—Retaining productive employees should always be a high priority of management. Recruitment and selection costs, as well as increased product-reject rates, are usually associated with hiring new workers.
13. *Initiative*—Management should take steps to encourage worker initiative, which is defined as new or additional work activity undertaken through self-direction.
14. *Esprit de corps*—Management should encourage harmony and general good feelings among employees.[16]

Fayol's general principles of management cover a broad range of topics, but organizational efficiency, the handling of people, and appropriate management action are the three general themes he stresses. With the writings of Fayol, the study of management as a broad, comprehensive activity began to receive the attention it deserved.

Limitations of the Classical Approach

Contributors to the classical approach felt encouraged to write about their managerial experiences largely because of the success they enjoyed. Structuring work to be more efficient and defining the manager's role more precisely yielded significant improvements in productivity, which individuals such as Taylor and Fayol were quick to document.

The classical approach, however, does not adequately emphasize human variables. People today do not seem to be as influenced by bonuses as they were in the nineteenth century. It is generally agreed that critical interpersonal areas, such as conflict, communication, leadership, and motivation, were shortchanged in the classical approach.

THE BEHAVIORAL APPROACH

The **behavioral approach to management** emphasizes increasing production through an understanding of people. According to proponents of this approach, if managers understand their people and adapt their organizations to them, organizational success will usually follow.

> The **behavioral approach to management** is a management approach that emphasizes increasing organizational success by focusing on human variables within the organization.

The Hawthorne Studies

The behavioral approach is usually described as beginning with a series of studies conducted between 1924 and 1932, which investigated the behavior and attitudes of workers at the Hawthorne (Chicago) Works of the Western Electric Company.[17] Accounts of the Hawthorne Studies are usually divided into two phases: the relay assembly test room experiments and the bank wiring observation room experiment. The following sections discuss each of these phases.

Bobbe White is a business development officer at State Street Bank and Trust Company in Quincy, Illinois, and she is also a certified laughter leader who runs weekly laughter exercises for fellow employees. The idea behind these sessions is to reduce stress by engaging in communal mirth, the full-blown, belly-laughing kind. White begins with warm-ups and proceeds to such exercises as one in which employees imitate a lion roaring with laughter. The laughter group is strictly voluntary, and not everyone participates, but those who have tried it say the experience is invigorating and improves their attitudes and behavior for the rest of the workday.

The Relay Assembly Test Room Experiments   The relay assembly test room experiments originally had a scientific management orientation. The experimenters believed that if they studied productivity long enough under different working conditions (including variations in weather conditions, temperature, rest periods, work hours, and humidity), they would discover the working conditions that maximized production. The immediate purpose of the relay assembly test room experiments was to determine the relationship between intensity of lighting and worker efficiency, as measured by worker output. Two groups of female employees were used as subjects. The light intensity for one group was varied, while the light intensity for the other group was held constant.

The results of the experiments surprised the researchers: No matter what conditions employees were exposed to, production increased. There seemed to be no consistent relationship between productivity and lighting intensity. An extensive interviewing campaign was undertaken to determine why the subjects continued to increase production under all lighting conditions. The following are the main reasons, as formulated from the interviews:

1. The subjects found working in the test room enjoyable
2. The new supervisory relationship during the experiment allowed the subjects to work freely, without fear
3. The subjects realized that they were taking part in an important and interesting study
4. The subjects seemed to become friendly as a group

The experimenters concluded that human factors within organizations could significantly influence production. More research was needed, however, to evaluate the potential impact of this human component in organizations.

The Bank Wiring Observation Room Experiment   The purpose of the bank wiring observation room experiment was to analyze the social relationships in a work group. Specifically, the study focused on the effect of group piecework incentives on a group of men who assembled terminal banks for use in telephone exchanges. The group piecework incentive system dictated that the harder a group worked as a whole, the more pay each member of that group would receive.

The experimenters believed that the study would show that members of the work group pressured one another to work harder so that each group member would receive more pay. To their surprise, they found the opposite: The work group pressured the faster workers to slow down their work rate. The men whose work rate would have increased individual salaries were being pressured by the group, rather than the men whose work rate would have decreased individual salaries. Evidently, the men were more interested in preserving work group solidarity than in making more money. The researchers concluded that social groups in organizations could effectively exert pressure to influence individuals to disregard monetary incentives.[18]

Recognizing the Human Variable

Taken together, the series of studies conducted at the Hawthorne plant gave management thinkers a new direction for research. Obviously, the human variable in the organization needed much more analysis, since it could either increase or decrease production drastically. Managers began to realize that they needed to understand this influence so they could maximize its positive effects and minimize its negative effects. This attempt to understand people is still a major force in today's organizational research.[19] The cartoon below humorously illustrates how a manager's lack of understanding of an employee results in employee discontent and may eventually produce a less productive employee. More current behavioral findings and their implications for management are presented in greater detail later in this text.

The Human Relations Movement

The Hawthorne Studies sparked the **human relations movement,** a people-oriented approach to management in which the interaction of people in organizations is studied to judge its impact on organizational success. The ultimate objective of this approach is to enhance organizational success by building appropriate relationships with people. To put it simply, when management stimulates high productivity and worker commitment to the organization and its goals, human relations are said to be effective; and when management precipitates low productivity and uncommitted workers, human relations are said to be ineffective. **Human relations skill** is defined as the ability to work with people in a way that enhances organizational success.

The **human relations movement** is a people-oriented approach to management in which the interaction of people in organizations is studied to judge its impact on organizational success.

Human relations skill is the ability to work with people in a way that enhances organizational success.

The human relations movement has made some important contributions to the study and practice of management. Advocates of this approach to management have continually stressed the need to use humane methods in managing people. Abraham Maslow, perhaps the best-known contributor to the human relations movement, believed that managers must understand the physiological, safety, social, esteem, and self-actualization needs of organization members. Douglas McGregor, another important contributor to the movement, emphasized a management philosophy built upon the views that people can be self-directed, accept responsibility, and consider work to be as natural as play. The ideas of both Maslow and McGregor are discussed thoroughly in Chapter 16. As a result of the tireless efforts of theorists like Maslow and McGregor, modern managers better understand the human component in organizations and how to appropriately work with it to enhance organizational success.

▶ Back to the Case

The comprehensive analysis of organizations implies that Michael Quinlan might be able to further improve success at McDonald's by evaluating the entire range of managerial performance—especially organizational efficiency, the handling of people, and appropriate management action. For example, Quinlan should make sure that McDonald's employees receive orders

(continued)

cathy®   **by Cathy Guisewite**

Cathy Copyright © 1990, Cathy Guisewite. Reprinted with permission of Universal Press Syndicate.

from only one source (be sure that one manager does not instruct an employee to serve french fries moments before another manager directs the same employee to prepare milk shakes). Along the same lines, Quinlan might want to make sure that all McDonald's employees are treated equally—that fry cooks, for example, do not get longer breaks than order takers.

The behavioral approach to management suggests that Quinlan strongly encourages McDonald's managers to consider the people working for them and evaluate the impact of their employees' feelings and relationships on restaurants' productivity. A McDonald's manager, for example, should try to make the work more enjoyable, perhaps by allowing employees to work at different stations (grill, beverage, or cash register) each day. A McDonald's manager might also consider creating opportunities for employees to become more friendly with one another, perhaps through a McDonald's employee picnic. In essence, the behavioral approach to management stresses that McDonald's managers should recognize the human variable in their restaurants and strive to maximize its positive effects.

THE MANAGEMENT SCIENCE APPROACH

The **management science approach** is a management approach that emphasizes the use of the scientific method and quantitative techniques to increase organizational success.

Churchman, Ackoff, and Arnoff define the management science, or operations research (OR), approach as (1) an application of the scientific method to problems arising in the operation of a system and (2) the solution of these problems by solving mathematical equations representing the system.[20] The **management science approach** suggests that managers can best improve their organizations by using the scientific method and mathematical techniques to solve operational problems.

The Beginning of the Management Science Approach

The management science, or operations research, approach can be traced to World War II, an era in which leading scientists were asked to help solve complex operational problems in the military.[21] The scientists were organized into teams that eventually became known as operations research (OR) groups. One OR group, for example, was asked to determine which gun sights would best stop German attacks on the British mainland.

These early OR groups typically included physicists and other "hard" scientists, who used the problem-solving method with which they had the most experience: the scientific method. The scientific method dictates that scientists:

1. Systematically *observe* the system whose behavior must be explained to solve the problem
2. Use these specific observations to *construct* a generalized framework (a model) that is consistent with the specific observations and from which consequences of changing the system can be predicted
3. Use the model to *deduce* how the system will behave under conditions that have not been observed but could be observed if the changes were made
4. Finally, *test* the model by performing an experiment on the actual system to see if the effects of changes predicted using the model actually occur when the changes are made[22]

The OR groups proved very successful at using the scientific method to solve the military's operational problems.

Management Science Today

After World War II, America again became interested in manufacturing and selling products. The success of the OR groups in the military had been so obvious that managers were eager to try management science techniques in an industrial environment. After all, managers also had to deal with complicated operational problems.

By 1955, the management science approach to solving industrial problems had proved very effective. Many people saw great promise in refining its techniques and analytical tools. Managers and universities alike pursued these refinements.

By 1965, the management science approach was being used in many companies and being applied to many diverse management problems, such as production scheduling, plant location, and product packaging.

In the 1980s, surveys indicated that management science techniques were used extensively in very large, complex organizations. Smaller organizations, however, had not yet fully realized the benefits of using these techniques. Finding ways to apply management science techniques to smaller organizations is undoubtedly a worthwhile challenge for managers in the twenty-first century.[23]

Baldrige Award: Evaluating a Company's Quality

Since it was established in 1987, the Malcolm Baldrige National Quality Award has become the sought-after award for quality standards among U.S. businesses. In fact, it is to corporate America what the Oscars are to the motion picture industry and the Grammys to the music industry.

The Baldrige Award's evaluation of a company's quality includes an examination of both efficiency and effectiveness. The guidelines for award application provide a detailed plan for improving quality in all areas of a company's business.

Six prizes are offered each year, two each for manufacturing and service companies and two for small businesses with fewer than 500 employees. Winners of the Baldrige Award for 2000 are Dana Corporation's Spicer Driveshaft Division in the area of manufacturing, KARLEE Company also in manufacturing, Operations Management International in the area of service, and Los Alamos National Bank in the area of small business. Some past winners are Motorola, Globe

Metallurgical, IBM Rochester, Federal Express, Wallace Company, the Ritz-Carlton Hotel Company, AT&T Universal Card Services, Texas Instruments Defense Systems & Electronics Group, and Granite Rock Company.

The Baldrige Award is administered by the National Institute of Standards and Technology. To apply, a large company must pay a fee of about $4,000 and submit responses to a comprehensive, 75-page questionnaire. A small company pays approximately $1,200 and answers a somewhat less comprehensive questionnaire.

Applications are scored by volunteer examiners, largely from industry. Companies that survive the initial screening enter the second phase of the competition, which includes an on-site visit by four to six examiners who verify information presented in the application.

Finally, application scores and examiners' reports are given to a panel of nine judges who submit their choices to the U.S. Secretary of Commerce. ■

Characteristics of Management Science Applications

Four primary characteristics are usually present in situations in which management science techniques are applied.[24] First, the management problems studied are so complicated that managers need help in analyzing a large number of variables. Management science techniques increase the effectiveness of the managers' decision making in such a situation. Second, a management science application generally uses economic implications as guidelines for making a particular decision. Perhaps this is because management science techniques are best suited for analyzing quantifiable factors such as sales, expenses, and units of production.

Third, the use of mathematical models to investigate the decision situation is typical in management science applications. Models constructed to represent reality are used to determine how the real-world situation might be improved. The fourth characteristic of a management science application is the use of computers. The great complexity of managerial problems and the sophisticated mathematical analysis of problem-related information required are two factors that make computers very valuable to the management science analyst.

Today managers use such management science tools as inventory control models, network models, and probability models to aid them in the decision-making process. Later parts of this text will outline some of these models in more detail and illustrate their applications to management decision making. Because management science thought is still evolving, more and more sophisticated analytical techniques can be expected in the future.

THE CONTINGENCY APPROACH

In simple terms, the **contingency approach to management** emphasizes that what managers do in practice depends on, or is contingent upon, a given set of circumstances—a situation.[25] In essence, this approach emphasizes "if–then" relationships: "If" this situational variable exists, "then" this is the action a manager probably would take. For example, if a manager has a group of inexperienced subordinates, then the contingency approach would recommend that he or she lead in a different fashion than if the subordinates were experienced.

The **contingency approach to management** is a management approach emphasizing that what managers do in practice depends on a given set of circumstances—a situation.

In general, the contingency approach attempts to outline the conditions or situations in which various management methods have the best chance of success.[26] This approach is based on the premise that, although there is probably no one best way to solve a management problem in all organizations, there probably is one best way to solve any given management problem in any one organization. Perhaps the main challenges of using the contingency approach are the following:

1. Perceiving organizational situations as they actually exist
2. Choosing the management tactics best suited to those situations
3. Competently implementing those tactics

The notion of a contingency approach to management is not novel. It has become a popular discussion topic for contemporary management thinkers. The general consensus of their writings is that if managers are to apply management concepts, principles, and techniques successfully, they must consider the realities of the specific organizational circumstances they face.[27]

DIGITAL FOCUS

▶ easyEverything Internet Café Opens in New York

Following the tenets of the contingency approach to management, *if* people surf the Internet in groups and in social settings, *then,* at least based on this one issue, it seems reasonable that management could take action to establish a cyber café. A cyber café is a place that sells computer access, along with light food and refreshments.

easyEverything has just opened the world's largest Internet café in New York City. It has 800 PCs in 18,300 square feet. Internet access is only $1 and related services such as Internet phones and Webcams are also available. The café offers competitive prices for in-store Internet access, services and refreshments, state-of-the-art high-speed computers, and access 24 hours a day, 7 days a week, 365 days a year.

easyEverything Internet cafés started 18 months ago in London and quickly expanded into Italy, Spain, and France. It is estimated that in one month, 1.25 million people in Europe will stop by an easyEverything cyber café. There is some question about whether easyEverything cafés, popular in Europe where fewer people have Internet access, will be a success in the U.S. market, where many more people have Internet access. In the United States, technology and Internet access are less expensive than in Europe. For example, many European offices still have only one or two computers available for use by several people.

A contingency that easyEverything management may have to address sometime in the near future is: If new U.S. cafés do not become popular, *then . . .*

THE SYSTEM APPROACH

The **system approach to management** is a management approach based on general system theory—the theory that to understand fully the operation of an entity, the entity must be viewed as a system. This requires understanding the interdependence of its parts.

A **system** is a number of interdependent parts functioning as a whole for some purpose.

A **closed system** is one that is not influenced by, and does not interact with, its environment.

An **open system** is one that is influenced by, and is continually interacting with, its environment.

The **system approach to management** is based on general system theory. Ludwig von Bertalanffy, a scientist who worked mainly in physics and biology, is recognized as the founder of general system theory.[28] The main premise of the theory is that to understand fully the operation of an entity, the entity must be viewed as a system. A **system** is a number of interdependent parts functioning as a whole for some purpose. For example, according to general system theory, to fully understand the operations of the human body, one must understand the workings of its interdependent parts (ears, eyes, and brain). General system theory integrates the knowledge of various specialized fields so that the system as a whole can be better understood.

Types of Systems

According to von Bertalanffy, there are two basic types of systems: closed and open. **Closed systems** are not influenced by, and do not interact with, their environments. They are mostly mechanical and have predetermined motions or activities that must be performed regardless of the environment. A clock is an example of a closed system. Regardless of its environment, a clock's wheels, gears, and so forth must function in a predetermined way if the clock as a whole is to exist and serve its purpose. The second type of system, the **open system,** is continually interacting with its environment. A plant is an example of an open system. Constant interaction with the environment influences the plant's state of existence and its future. In fact, the environment determines whether or not the plant will live.

Systems and "Wholeness"

The concept "wholeness" is very important in general system analysis. The system must be viewed as a whole and modified only through changes in its parts. Before modifications of the parts can be made for the overall benefit of the system, a thorough knowledge of how each part functions and the interrelationships among the parts must be present. L. Thomas Hopkins suggested the following six guidelines for anyone doing system analysis:[29]

1. The whole should be the main focus of analysis, with the parts receiving secondary attention
2. Integration is the key variable in wholeness analysis. It is defined as the interrelatedness of the many parts within the whole
3. Possible modifications in each part should be weighed in relation to possible effects on every other part
4. Each part has some role to perform so that the whole can accomplish its purpose
5. The nature of the part and its function is determined by its position in the whole
6. All analysis starts with the existence of the whole. The parts and their interrelationships should then evolve to best suit the purpose of the whole

Because the system approach to management is based on general system theory, analysis of the management situation as a system is stressed. The following sections present the parts of the management system and recommend information that can be used to analyze the system.

The Management System

As with all systems, the **management system** is composed of a number of parts that function interdependently to achieve a purpose. The main parts of the management system are organizational input, organizational process, and organizational output. As discussed in Chapter 1, these parts consist of organizational resources, the production process, and finished goods, respectively. The parts represent a combination that exists to achieve organizational objectives, whatever they may be.

The management system is an open system—that is, one that interacts with its environment (see Figure 2.2). Environmental factors with which the management system interacts include the government, suppliers, customers, and competitors. Each of these factors represents a potential environmental influence that could significantly change the future of the management system.

Environmental impact on management cannot be overemphasized. As an example, the federal government, through its Occupational Safety and Health Act (OSHA) of 1970, encourages management to take costly steps to safeguard workers. Many managers believe that these mandated safeguards are not only too expensive but also unnecessary.

The critical importance of managers knowing and understanding various components of their organizations' environments is perhaps best illustrated by the constant struggle of super-

The **management system** is an open system whose major parts are organizational input, organizational process, and organizational output.

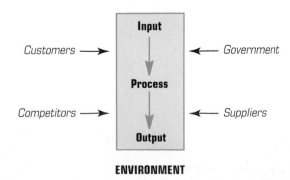

Customers → **Input** ← Government

Process

Competitors → ← Suppliers

Output

ENVIRONMENT

The open management system

Figure 2.2

market managers to know and understand their customers. Supermarket managers fight for the business of a national population that is growing by less than one percent per year. Survival requires that they know their customers better than the competition does. That is why many food retailers conduct market research to uncover customer attitudes about different kinds of foods and stores. Armed with a thorough understanding of their customers, gained from this kind of research, they hope to win business from competitors who are not benefiting from the insights made possible by such research.[30]

Information for Management System Analysis

As noted earlier, general system theory supports the use of information from many specialized disciplines to better understand a system. This certainly holds true for the management system. Information from any discipline that can increase the understanding of management system operations enhances the success of the system. This is a sweeping statement. Where do managers go to get this broad information? The concise answer: To the first three approaches to management outlined in this chapter.

Thus the information used to discuss the management system in the remainder of this text comes from three primary sources:

1. Classical approach to management
2. Behavioral approach to management
3. Management science approach to management

The use of these three sources of information to analyze the management system is referred to as **triangular management.** Figure 2.3 presents the triangular management model. The three sources of information depicted in the model are not meant to represent all the information that can be used to analyze the management system. Rather, these are the three bodies of management-related information that probably would be most useful in analysis.

A synthesis of classically based information, behaviorally based information, and management science–based information is critical to effective use of the management system. This information is integrated and presented in the five remaining parts of this book. These parts discuss, respectively, management systems and planning (Chapters 6–9), organizing (Chapters 10–13), influencing (Chapters 14–18), controlling (Chapters 19–21), and topics for special emphasis (Chapters 22–23). In addition, some information in these parts of the text is pre-

Triangular management is a management approach that emphasizes using information from the classical, behavioral, and management science schools of thought to manage the open management system.

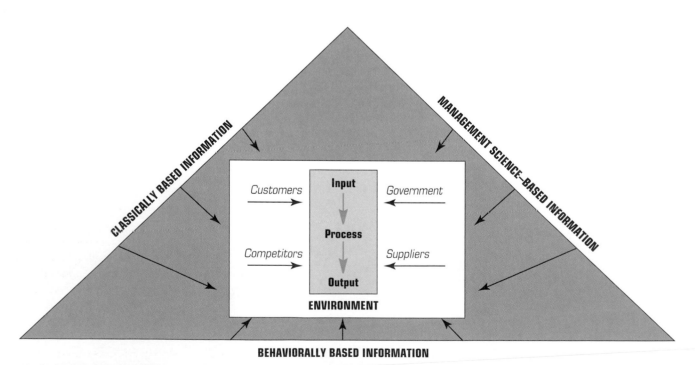

Figure 2.3   *Triangular management model*

sented from a contingency viewpoint to emphasize the practical application of management principles.

Learning Organization: A New Approach?

The preceding material in this chapter provides a history of management by discussing a number of different approaches to management that have evolved over time. Each approach developed over a number of years and focused on the particular needs of organizations at the time.

In more recent times, managers seem to be searching for new approaches to management.[31] Fueling this search is a range of new issues that modern managers face but that their historical counterparts did not. These issues include a concern about the competitive decline of Western firms, the accelerating pace of technological change, the sophistication of customers, and an increasing emphasis on globalization.

A new approach to management that is evolving to handle this new range of issues can be called the *learning organization approach*. A **learning organization** is an organization that does well in creating, acquiring, and transferring knowledge, and in modifying behavior to reflect new knowledge.[32] Learning organizations emphasize systematic problem solving, experimenting with new ideas, learning from experience and past history, learning from the experiences of others, and transferring knowledge rapidly throughout the organization. Managers attempting to build a learning organization must create an environment conducive to learning and encourage the exchange of information among all organization members. Honda, Corning, and General Electric are successful learning organizations.

> A **learning organization** is an organization that does well in creating, acquiring, and transferring knowledge, and in modifying behavior to reflect new knowledge.

The learning organization represents a specific, new *management paradigm,* or fundamental way of viewing and contemplating management. Peter Senge started serious discussion of learning organizations in 1990 with his book *The Fifth Discipline: The Art & Practice of the Learning Organization.*[33] Since then, Senge, his colleagues at MIT, and many others have made significant progress in developing the learning organization concept. According to Senge, building a learning organization entails building five features within an organization:

1. *Systems Thinking*—Every organization member understands his or her own job and how the jobs fit together to provide final products to the customer.
2. *Shared Vision*—All organization members have a common view of the purpose of the organization and a sincere commitment to accomplish the purpose.
3. *Challenging of Mental Models*—Organization members routinely challenge the way business is done and the thought processes people use to solve organizational problems.
4. *Team Learning*—Organization members work together, develop solutions to new problems together, and apply the solutions together. Working as teams rather than individuals will help organizations gather collective force to achieve organizational goals.
5. *Personal Mastery*—All organization members are committed to gaining a deep and rich understanding of their work. Such an understanding will help organizations to reach important challenges that confront them.

The learning organization concept is being applied in many different sizes and types of organizations. The following People Spotlight discusses how Signicast Corporation took specific steps to help its employees become competent members of a learning organization.

People for a New Learning Organization at Signicast

Signicast Corporation, a castings manufacturer based in Milwaukee, makes products like kickstands for Harley-Davidson motorcycles and various parts for John Deere tractors. When Signicast's executives decided to build a new $12 million automated plant, they knew they would need more than new technology—they would need new, learning focused employees. Management decided to use the building of the new plant as a tool to transform employees into competent members of a learning organization.

In participating in the building of the new plant, employees were taught to become responsible and immersed in organizational issues, and to face and solve new and unique organizational problems. Every Signicast employee had an opportunity to contribute to how the new facility would finally appear. A core group of five executives would develop an idea, send it to employees, and ask for evaluation, soliciting both positive and negative reactions. Employees would meet with management to explain why plans would or would not work, how

(continued)

equipment would fit into the planned facility, and how expenses related to the new plant could be controlled. Employees even had the final word, through a formal vote, on whether the plant should be built. Employees saw that there were certain by-products of the process: It was necessary to work 12-hour shifts, learn many different jobs, and be part of a team if the new plant was to be successful. Overall, management at Signicast initiated a learning culture by putting management and employees on the same team in planning for a new plant and by giving employees the power to function as real members of that team. ∎

▶ Back to the Case

This chapter suggests that Michael Quinlan could enhance the success of McDonald's by encouraging managers to use the management science approach to solve operational problems. According to the scientific method, a McDonald's manager would first spend some time observing. Next, the manager would use these observations to outline exactly how the restaurant operates as a whole. Third, the manager would apply this understanding of McDonald's operations by predicting how various changes might help or hinder the restaurant as a whole. Before implementing possible changes, the manager would test them on a small scale to see if they actually affected the restaurant as desired.

If McDonald's managers were to follow the contingency approach to management, their actions as managers would depend on the situation. For example, *if* some customers had not been served within a reasonable period because the equipment needed to make chocolate sundaes had broken down, *then* management probably would not hold employees responsible. But *if* management knew that the equipment had broken down because of employee mistreatment or neglect, *then* reaction to the situation would likely be very different.

A McDonald's manager could also apply the system approach and view a restaurant as a system, or a number of interdependent parts that function as a whole, to reach restaurant objectives. A McDonald's restaurant would be viewed as an open system—one that exists in and is influenced by its environment. Major factors within the environment of a McDonald's restaurant would be its customers, suppliers, competitors, and the government. For example, if a McDonald's competitor lowered its price for hamburgers well below McDonald's price, McDonald's management might be forced to consider modifying different parts of its restaurant system in order to meet or beat that price.

Lastly, a McDonald's manager could apply the learning organization approach. Using this approach, a restaurant manager, for example, would see the restaurant as an organizational unit that needs to be good at creating, acquiring, and transferring knowledge, and at modifying behavior to reflect new knowledge. For example, all McDonald's employees at a restaurant would be involved in gathering new thoughts and ideas about running the restaurant and would be on a team with management, possessing a significant voice in establishing how the restaurant exists and operates.

Management Skills Module

This section is specially designed to help you develop management skills. An individual's management skill is based on an understanding of management concepts and the ability to apply those concepts in management situations. As a result, the following activities are designed both to heighten your understanding of management concepts and to help you gain facility in applying those concepts in various management situations.

UNDERSTANDING MANAGEMENT CONCEPTS

▶ Action Summary

Reread the learning objectives below. Each objective is followed by questions. Answering these questions accurately will help you retain the most important concepts discussed in this chapter. After answering each question, check your answer against the answer key at the end of this chapter. (*Hint:* If you have any doubts regarding the correct response, consult the page number that follows the answer.)

Circle:

From studying this chapter, I will attempt to acquire

1. An understanding of the classical approach to management.
   - T F   **a.** The classical management approach established what it considered the "one best way" to manage.
   - a b c d e   **b.** The process of finding the "one best way" to perform a task is called: (a) comprehensive analysis of management (b) the concept of wholeness (c) the Hawthorne Studies (d) the management science approach (e) scientific management.

2. An appreciation for the work of Frederick W. Taylor, Frank and Lillian Gilbreth, Henry L. Gantt, and Henri Fayol.
   - a b c d e   **a.** Fayol defines 14 principles of management. Which of the following is *not* one of those principles: (a) scalar chain of authority (b) esprit de corps (c) centralization (d) unity of command (e) directedness of command.
   - a b c d e   **b.** Which of the following theorists assumed that any worker's job could be reduced to a science: (a) Gilbreth (b) Gantt (c) Mayo (d) Fayol (e) Taylor.
   - T F   **c.** Gantt increased worker efficiency by setting standards according to top management's opinion of what maximum performance should be.

3. An understanding of the behavioral approach to management.
   - T F   **a.** The behavioral approach to management emphasizes striving to increase production through an understanding of the organization itself.
   - a b c d e   **b.** The behavioral approach began with: (a) the Hawthorne Studies (b) the mental revolution (c) the industrial revolution (d) motion studies (e) the Bethlehem Steel Studies.

4. An understanding of the studies at the Hawthorne Works and the human relations movement.
   - T F   **a.** The Hawthorne Studies showed a direct relationship between lighting and efficiency.
   - T F   **b.** The Hawthorne experimenters found that people were more concerned with preserving the work group than with maximizing their pay.
   - T F   **c.** The human relations movement deemphasized the importance of people in organizations.

5. An understanding of the management science approach to management.
   - a b c d e   **a.** Which of the following is *not* one of the philosophies of the management science approach: (a) managers can improve the organization by using scientific methods (b) mathematical techniques can solve organizational problems (c) models should be used to represent the system (d) individual work is better than teamwork (e) observation of the system must take place.
   - T F   **b.** In the management science theory, models are used to represent reality and then to determine how the real-world situation might be improved.

6. An understanding of how the management science approach has evolved.
   - a b c d e   **a.** The management science approach emerged after: (a) World War I (b) the Civil War (c) the Korean War (d) World War II (e) the 1930s Depression.
   - T F   **b.** Although management science was first applied to military problems, it is now applied by companies to diverse management problems.

7. An understanding of the system approach to management.

a b c d e   **a.** An organization that interacts with external forces is: (a) a closed system (b) a model (c) an independent entity (d) an open system (e) a contingency.

a b c d e   **b.** Which of the following is *not* one of the guidelines proposed by Hopkins for doing system analysis according to the concept of wholeness: (a) the whole should be the main focus of analysis (b) all analysis starts with the existence of the whole (c) the nature of the part is determined by its position in the whole (d) each part has some role to perform so that the whole can accomplish its purpose (e) modifications should be made as problems occur.

8. Knowledge about the learning organization approach to management.

T F   **a.** The learning organization approach to management reflects an old management paradigm.

a b c d e   **b.** A learning organization is typically least characterized by: (a) systems thinking (b) shared vision (c) rigid job procedures (d) team learning (e) challenging mental models.

9. An understanding of how triangular management and the contingency approach to management are related.

a b c d e   **a.** The contingency approach emphasizes the viewpoint that what managers do in practice depends overall on: (a) the worker (b) the situation (c) the task (d) the environment (e) the manager's personality.

a b c d e   **b.** The three sources of information in triangular management are: (a) input, process, and output (b) management science, the classical approach to management, and the behavioral approach to management (c) mathematics, psychology, and sociology (d) managers, directors, and stockholders (e) executives, administrators, and supervisors.

▶ Action Summary Answer Key

1. a. T, p. 26
   b. e, p. 27
2. a. e, pp. 30–31
   b. e, p. 27
   c. F, pp. 28–29
3. a. F, p. 31
   b. a, pp. 31–32

4. a. F, p. 32
   b. T, p. 32
   c. F, p. 33
5. a. d, pp. 34–35
   b. T, p. 35

6. a. d, p. 34
   b. T, p. 34
7. a. d, p. 36
   b. e, p. 37

8. a. P, p. 39
   b. c, p. 39
9. a. b, p. 35
   b. b, p. 38

▶ Issues for Review and Discussion

1. List the five approaches to managing.
2. Define the classical approach to management.
3. Compare and contrast the contributions to the classical approach made by Frederick W. Taylor, Frank and Lillian Gilbreth, and Henry L. Gantt.
4. How does Henri Fayol's contribution to the classical approach differ from the contributions of Taylor, the Gilbreths, and Gantt?
5. What is scientific management?
6. Describe motion study as used by the Gilbreths.
7. Describe Gantt's innovation in the area of worker bonuses.
8. List and define Fayol's general principles of management.
9. What is the primary limitation to the classical approach to management?
10. Define the behavioral approach to management.
11. What is the significance of the studies carried out at the Hawthorne Works of the Western Electric Company?
12. Describe the human relations movement.
13. What is the management science approach to management?
14. What are the steps in the scientific method of problem solving?
15. List and explain three characteristics of situations in which management science applications usually are made.
16. Define the contingency approach to management.
17. What is a system?
18. What is the difference between a closed system and an open system?
19. Explain the relationship between system analysis and "wholeness."
20. What are the parts of the management system?
21. Explain in your own words what is meant by a learning organization.

APPLYING MANAGEMENT CONCEPTS

❱ Cases

❱➤ INTRODUCTORY CASE WRAP-UP

❱Case Discussion Questions

"A Problem at McDonald's" (p. 25) and its related Back-to-the-Case sections were written to help you better understand the management concepts contained in this chapter. Answer the following discussion questions about this Introductory Case to further enrich your understanding of the chapter content:

1. Based on information in the introductory case, list three problems that you think future McDonald's managers will have to solve.
2. What action(s) do you think the managers will have to take to solve these problems?
3. From what you know about fast-food restaurants, how easy would it be to manage a McDonald's restaurant? Why?

❱Skills Exercise: Applying a Comprehensive View of Management

In this chapter you studied a comprehensive view of management as outlined by 14 principles developed by Henri Fayol. Reflecting on the overall situation depicted in the Introductory Case about McDonald's, discuss how you, as a manager of a McDonald's restaurant, would apply each of these principles to help ensure organizational success.

CASE STUDY: ALBERTSON'S PINS ITS HOPES ON NEW CEO

Albertson's has been doing business the old-fashioned way since 1939 when Joe Albertson opened his first grocery store in Boise, Idaho. He called it "Idaho's largest and finest food store." His philosophy was to "give the customer the merchandise they want at a price they can afford, complete with lots of tender loving care." He was the first to introduce unheard-of extras like a scratch bakery, magazine racks, homemade ice cream, popcorn, and an automatic donut machine. Today, Albertson's is the second largest supermarket chain in the United States, and it operates about 2,500 stores in 37 states, some of which are under the names Acme, Jewel, Super Saver, and Max Foods. Albertson's continues to follow Joe's vision by merging with food and drug companies that offer high-quality goods and friendly service.

For the past few years, Albertson's sales have been low. Convenience and warehouse stores have threatened the company's survival. Also, Albertson's has not been successful in integrating the newly acquired American Stores Co. Since the acquisition, the company has strengthened its marketing and merchandising operations by doing away with a regional structure and reorganizing to better serve its customers neighborhood by neighborhood.

Albertson's is now facing tough competition from local stores, restaurants, coffee bars, and bagel shops that offer convenience items such as roasted chicken and pre-cut, mixed salad. People are looking to save time in every aspect of their lives.

In an effort to better serve its customers, Albertson's has offered online service in Seattle since 1999, where orders are filled from five designated supermarkets. It is presently testing "self-checkout," enabling shoppers to load their own groceries onto the belt, run them over the scanner, bag the goods, and pay by cash or charge at the end of the transaction.

As it moves into the technological age, Albertson's still runs a Pillsbury Kids' Bake-Off at the Los Angeles Zoo as a way of maintaining its traditional image as a community store. The company was honored by the food industry for its commitment to fighting hunger in the United States through the donation of money, food, and nonfood items to hunger-relief efforts across the country. However, the supermarket giant needs to stretch even further to remain the number one choice among shoppers.

Albertson's has high hopes that its newly appointed CEO, Lawrence R. Johnston, can come up with a plan to bring American stores into line and save Albertson's place in the food and drug industry. Johnston, a former General Electric appliance executive, has no experience in the retail grocery business. He began his career at GE in 1972 as a sales trainee. He told a *Wall Street Journal* reporter that he left because he has burning desire to run his own company.

Johnston spent a lot of time at GE working with consumer focus groups, and he knows what it takes to deliver what customers want. He believes that Albertson's needs to cut costs to become more competitive. The board of directors is counting on Johnston, as an outsider, to bring a new perspective to its operations.

In an interview that aired on CNBC, Johnston said he felt there were a lot of untapped opportunities left in the integration between Albertson's and American Stores. "I think one of the things I bring to this party is that I don't have any baggage. I haven't been in the industry . . . so I'm going to be looking very hard at every corner of the company," he said. As CEO of Medical Systems Europe for General Electric, Johnston did about 26 mergers, acquisitions, and joint ventures in 30 months. The board of directors of Albertson's believes this experience will give him the insight to boost the company's profits. Paul Corddry, an Albertson's board member who led the CEO search, explained that Johnston was chosen because he "embodied the best strategic planning skills and the ability to be a change agent. It's the right time to have a change agent at this company."

Johnston is a "results-oriented executive" who is unafraid of change and eager to lead Albertson's into the twenty-first century.

QUESTIONS

1. Could understanding the management science approach to management help Johnston to make better decisions at Albertson's? Explain.
2. What does the human relations movement tell Johnston about how to best integrate American Stores with established Albertson's operations?
3. What does the system approach to management tell Johnston about best integrating the two companies?

▶ Video

QUICKTAKES SEGMENT ONE
Introduction to Modern Management

A video has been created for your textbook. It looks at specific areas which have been covered in detail in the individual chapters. The idea is not to isolate a point and focus on it exclusively. Instead, scenarios are developed that resemble situations you might experience in the real world. As a result, concepts are mixed together, experiences are not sequential (as they often are in a chapter in a textbook), and you may have to think about what you see to get the point. In fact, you will probably see things differently than some of your classmates. Each of you will see these scenes with the influence of what you have learned from the book, with influences from life's experiences, and from things that are important to you.

In the opening video, you are introduced to some of the main characters that appear throughout the series. John is a young guy who is trying to land a job as a production manager with a company that produces educational and news-type programs. He has experience in the field as a cameraman. This job, if he gets it, may begin to steer his career in a different direction. We get the feeling that he wants it to. You also meet Hal and Karen. They are partners who own the company, Quicktakes, with which John is trying to get a job.

A lot is going on in this opening segment. There are a few things for which you may want to be on the lookout. First, pay attention to John as he prepares at home for the upcoming interview. He and his wife do not necessarily agree about the opportunity that exists at Quicktakes. Think about what the job really entails as you listen to the discussion John has with Hal and Karen, and pay attention to the way Hal and Karen interact. As partners, they both probably have a lot at stake in planning for the success and growth of this company. It is interesting to notice the way each sees the specific job John is applying for and also the way each views the overall objectives and plans for the company.

From a more general perspective, you may wish to consider how this company fits with some of the management concepts you have learned about; how well this company is suited for doing business in other countries, under other social norms and standard business practices; and how well this company might do at adjusting to changes in its operating environment or to other changes in its internal environment as it grows.

QUESTIONS

1. John and his wife seem to have different ideas about the job description of the position John is applying for and different ideas about how qualified John is for the opening. What factors do you think influence an individual's perception, and why do you think they come up with different perspectives?

2. Hal and Karen are partners, but they seem to have their own ideas about the company and the way it runs. Do you think it is good for partners to have their own, and sometimes differing, opinions, or should they agree more? What do you think is good for the success of a company?

3. John was asked about how he would handle two particular issues in the company. One dealt with staffing multiple projects and one dealt with his use of company equipment to film a wedding for a friend. If you were Hal and Karen, what other hypothetical situations might you want to ask John about?

MODERN MANAGEMENT AND *YOU*

It is your senior year and you have your sights set on becoming head of the activities committee. You role play for hours in preparation for the interview before the faculty advisory board. Your friends grill you on leadership models, ways to motivate your peers, and life experiences that would make you perfect for the job. Standing in front of the board members, you are confident, and able to clearly articulate your vision for this year's event. When the interview ends, you leave feeling that things could not have gone better. The next day you are told that someone else has been given the position. You know that this person is a real "brown noser." You have been appointed to a secretarial position on the committee instead.

1. How do you react? How can you turn your anger or disappointment into a valuable experience? What have you learned already about working in an organization? How might this help you later on when you find yourself caught in the politics of the workplace? How might this make you a better manager someday?

www.prenhall.com/certo

This book is accompanied by a rich assortment of online activities aimed at developing your management skills. Reviewing news headlines, Internet exercises, an online study guide, and other research and Internet resources can help personalize management skills development for individual students or an entire class.

chapter

chapterchapterchapterchapterchapterchapter

3 Corporate Social Responsibility and Business Ethics

Objectives

From studying this chapter, I will attempt to acquire

- An understanding of the term *corporate social responsibility*

- An appreciation of the arguments both for and against the assumption of social responsibilities by business

- Useful strategies for increasing the social responsiveness of an organization

- Insights into the planning, organizing, influencing, and controlling of social responsibility activities

- A practical plan for how society can help business meet its social obligations

- An understanding of the relationship between ethics and management

CHAPTER OUTLINE

Introductory Case: *IBM Uses Web Site to Promote Social Responsibility Goals*

Fundamentals of Social Responsibility
The Davis Model of Corporate Social Responsibility
Areas of Corporate Social Responsibility

Across Industries ▶ Food Processing—Endangered Species Chocolate Company Protects Threatened Animals
Varying Opinions on Social Responsibility
Conclusions About the Performance of Social Responsibility Activities by Business

Global Spotlight ▶ Maxell Sensitive to the Global Environment

Social Responsiveness
Determining if a Social Responsibility Exists
Social Responsiveness and Decision Making
Approaches to Meeting Social Responsibilities

Diversity Spotlight ▶ Social Responsiveness and the Equal Opportunity Act at Opryland

Social Responsibility Activities and Management Functions
Planning Social Responsibility Activities
Organizing Social Responsibility Activities
Influencing Individuals Performing Social Responsibility Activities
Controlling Social Responsibility Activities

How Society Can Help Business Meet Social Obligations
Business Ethics
A Definition of Ethics
Why Ethics Is a Vital Part of Management Practices
A Code of Ethics
Creating an Ethical Workplace

IBM Uses Web Site to Promote Social Responsibility Goals

REMINDER: THE INTRODUCTORY CASE WRAP-UP (PP. 69–70) CONTAINS DISCUSSION QUESTIONS AND A SKILLS EXERCISE TO FURTHER ILLUSTRATE THE APPLICATION OF CHAPTER CONCEPTS TO THIS VIGNETTE.

International Business Machines Corporation (IBM) provides business solutions to customers through the use of advanced information technology such as computers, software, and management information systems. IBM uses its company Web site to inform stakeholders about company activities in the area of social responsibility and to promote stakeholder participation in these activities, and because of this, information about IBM's social responsibility activities is both focused and well organized.

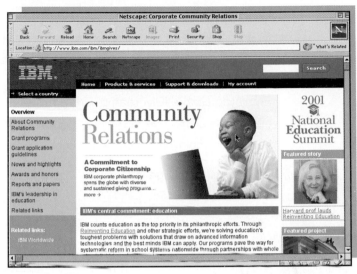

IBM is a long-standing corporate supporter of nonprofit and educational institutions around the world. Its Web site demonstrates that it puts its cutting edge technology at the service of many of the communities to which it belongs.

For the last 10 years, IBM has been one of the largest corporate contributors of cash, equipment, and people to nonprofit organizations and educational institutions across the United States and around the world. The company's central focus is on helping people use information technology to improve the quality of life for themselves and others.

IBM believes that the same information technology innovations that are revolutionizing businesses can provide important breakthroughs for public and nonprofit organizations. These technologies have the potential to help organizations deliver better services, manage costs, maximize effectiveness, and implement exciting new programs.

Company commitment to solutions-oriented innovation for these organizations involves both monetary contributions and working hand-in-hand with the organizations themselves to design technology solutions that address specific problems. This commitment focuses on several priority areas:

> *Education.* IBM realizes the worldwide power and importance of education. Through major initiatives such as Reinventing Education, KidSmart, and Project FIRST, the company hopes to promote knowledge and skills that will ensure that communities thrive around the globe.

> *Adult Training and Workforce Development.* IBM invests in helping others to use technology as a powerful tool in education and job training programs for adults. There is a special focus on using technology to broaden opportunities and strengthen programs available to adults in need of new skills and employment.

(continued)

> *Arts and Culture.* IBM's support of the arts stems from its strong commitment to bettering its communities. By joining with libraries, museums, and other cultural institutions in exciting partnerships that leverage IBM expertise, the company demonstrates the critical role technology plays in enhancing the arts.

> *Helping Communities in Need.* Wherever IBM does business around the globe, it forms connections to communities and supports a range of civic and nonprofit activities that help those in need. All of IBM's efforts demonstrate how technology can enrich and expand access to services and assistance.

> *Environment.* IBM supports preservation of the environment by promoting the optimal use of leading-edge technology to conduct environmental research for new knowledge and enhanced understanding of important issues.

> *Employee Giving.* IBM teams with employees to support organizations and causes in the communities where they live and work. Community-level grant making and extensive volunteer programs help IBM employees become personally involved in community projects.

The overall message is clear: IBM strives to be a socially responsible member of the communities in which it does business.

What's Ahead

The Introductory Case describes several IBM initiatives in the area of social responsibility. IBM gives back to the communities in which it does business in areas like education, environmental care, and culture. This chapter presents material that management in a company like IBM should use in deliberating how, or even if, to "give back" to a community. Specifically, the chapter discusses

1) Fundamentals of social responsibility
2) Social responsiveness
3) Social responsibility activities and management functions
4) How society can help business meet social obligations
5) Ethics

FUNDAMENTALS OF SOCIAL RESPONSIBILITY

Corporate social responsibility is the managerial obligation to take action that protects and improves both the welfare of society as a whole and the interests of the organization.

The term *social responsibility* means different things to different people. For purposes of this chapter, however, **corporate social responsibility** is the managerial obligation to take action that protects and improves both the welfare of society as a whole and the interests of the organization. According to the concept of corporate social responsibility, a manager must strive to achieve societal as well as organizational goals.[1]

The amount of attention given to the area of social responsibility by both management and society has increased in recent years and probably will continue to increase.[2] The following sections present the fundamentals of social responsibility of businesses by discussing these topics:

1. The Davis model of corporate social responsibility
2. Areas of corporate social responsibility
3. Varying opinions on social responsibility
4. Conclusions about the performance of social responsibility activities by business

The Davis Model of Corporate Social Responsibility

A generally accepted model of corporate social responsibility was developed by Keith Davis.[3] Stated simply, Davis's model is a list of five propositions that describe why and how business should adhere to the obligation to take action that protects and improves the welfare of society as well as of the organization:

Proposition 1: Social responsibility arises from social power—This proposition is derived from the premise that business has a significant amount of influence on, or power over, such critical social issues as minority employment and environmental pollution. In essence, the collective action of all businesses in the country primarily determines the proportion of minorities employed and the prevailing condition of the environment in which all citizens must live.

Davis reasons that since business has this power over society, society can and must hold business responsible for social conditions that result from the exercise of this power. Davis explains that society's legal system does not expect more of business than it does of each individual citizen exercising personal power.

Proposition 2: Business shall operate as a two-way open system, with open receipt of inputs from society and open disclosure of its operations to the public—According to this proposition, business must be willing to listen to what must be done to sustain or improve societal welfare. In turn, society must be willing to listen to business reports on what it is doing to meet its social responsibilities. Davis suggests that there must be ongoing, honest, and open communications between business and society's representatives if the overall welfare of society is to be maintained or improved.

Proposition 3: The social costs and benefits of an activity, product, or service shall be thoroughly calculated and considered in deciding whether to proceed with it—This proposition stresses that technical feasibility and economic profitability are not the only factors that should influence business decision making. Business should also consider both the long- and short-term societal consequences of all business activities before undertaking them.

Proposition 4: The social costs related to each activity, product, or service shall be passed on to the consumer—This proposition states that business cannot be expected to completely finance activities that may be socially advantageous but economically disadvantageous. The cost of maintaining socially desirable activities within business should be passed on to consumers through higher prices for the goods or services related to these activities.

Proposition 5: Business institutions, as citizens, have the responsibility to become involved in certain social problems that are outside their normal areas of operation—This last proposition points out that if a business possesses the expertise to solve a social problem with which it may not be directly associated, it should be held responsible for helping society solve that problem. Davis reasons that because business eventually will reap an increased profit from a generally improved society, business should share in the responsibility of all citizenry to generally improve society.

▶ Gethal Amazonas recently became the first tropical plywood maker in the world to be fully certified by the nonprofit Forest Stewardship Council. The certified lumber, marked with yellow paint, is guaranteed to come from a well-managed forest, and the Council hopes to eventually squeeze out competitors whose harvesting practices are harmful to the rainforest. Other members of the Council include Friends of the Earth, Greenpeace, Home Depot, IKEA, and lumber companies in the Americas, Europe, and Asia.

▶ Back to the Case

Social responsibility is the obligation of management to take action that protects and improves the welfare of society in conjunction with the interests of the organization. Based on the Introductory Case, IBM protects and improves its communities through the use of information technology to improve the quality of life. IBM presently makes substantial contributions in employing technology in many different areas of community life and concern. According to Keith Davis's social responsibility model, making such investments in the welfare of society is essential to being a good business citizen. Corporations, however, must also take steps to protect their own interests while making social investments. For example, donating IBM equip-

(continued)

ment for use in educational programs could benefit the company by turning students into future IBM customers.

Following Davis's model of social responsibility further, IBM should commit to benefiting society because of the vast power the company possesses in creating such benefit. It should be remembered, however, that the costs of social responsibility activities can be passed to consumers, and action should be taken only if it is financially feasible. For IBM to invest in social responsibility activities to its own financial detriment would be socially irresponsible given the company's commitment to employees and stockholders.

Areas of Corporate Social Responsibility

The areas in which business can act to protect and improve the welfare of society are numerous and diverse. Perhaps the most publicized of these areas are urban affairs, consumer affairs, environmental affairs, and employment practices affairs. The following Across Industries feature explains how one company protects its environment by helping to protect endangered animals.

▶ Food Processing—Endangered Species Chocolate Company Protects Threatened Animals

The Web site of the Endangered Species Chocolate Company boldly announces its company mission:

Our Mission at the Endangered Species Chocolate Company is to use the universal appeal of chocolate to spread a positive environmental message as far as possible. The company accomplishes this mission by creating the highest quality, all-natural chocolate products possible, wrapped into appealing packaging that highlights the importance of animals and their habitats to educate and inspire those who purchase our chocolate. We add to the impact of each bar by donating a percentage of our profits to a variety of nonprofit environmental groups who are working to help endangered species and preserve their habitat. We also place an utmost importance in maintaining absolute consistency and integrity in the quality of our products and service.

Jon Stocking founded the Endangered Species Chocolate Company in 1993, in Talent, Oregon. At that time, Stocking's background included having worked as a cook on a commercial fishing boat. In that role, he had personally witnessed the deaths of many dolphins and would often climb into nets to free drowning dolphins.

As a result of this experience with dolphins and many other endangered animals, Stocking decided to help protect the environment by attempting to make it a better place for animals.

The primary purpose of the Endangered Species Chocolate Company is to make a fair return for its stakeholders while living up to its commitment and social responsibility to help endangered animals.

Varying Opinions on Social Responsibility

Although numerous businesses are already involved in social responsibility activities, there is much controversy about whether such involvement is necessary or even appropriate. The following two sections present some arguments for and against businesses performing social responsibility activities.[4]

Arguments *for* Business Performing Social Responsibility Activities The best-known argument for the performance of social responsibility activities by business was alluded to earlier in this chapter. This argument begins with the premise that business as a whole is a subset of society, one that exerts a significant impact on the way society exists. Since business is such an influential member of society, the argument continues, it has the responsibility to help maintain and improve the overall welfare of society. Since society puts this responsibility on its individual members, why should its corporate members be exempt?

In addition, some people argue that business should perform social responsibility activities because profitability and growth go hand in hand with responsible treatment of employees, customers, and the community. This argument says, essentially, that performing social responsibility activities is a means of earning greater organizational profit.[5]

However, empirical studies have not demonstrated any clear relationship between corporate social responsibility and profitability. In fact, several companies that were acknowledged leaders in social commitment during the 1960s and 1970s—including Control Data Corporation, Atlantic Richfield, Dayton-Hudson, Levi Strauss, and Polaroid—experienced serious financial difficulties during the 1980s.[6] (No relationship between corporate social responsibility activities and these financial difficulties was shown, however.)

Arguments *Against* Business Performing Social Responsibility Activities

The best-known argument against business performing social responsibility activities has been advanced by Milton Friedman, one of America's most distinguished economists. Friedman argues that making business managers simultaneously responsible to business owners for reaching profit objectives and to society for enhancing societal welfare sets up a conflict of interest that could potentially cause the demise of business as it is known today. According to Friedman, this demise will almost certainly occur if business is continually forced to perform socially responsible actions that directly conflict with private organizational objectives.[7]

Friedman also argues that to require business managers to pursue socially responsible objectives may, in fact, be unethical, because it compels managers to spend money on some individuals that rightfully belongs to other individuals.[8]

> In a free enterprise, private property system, a corporate executive is an employee of the owners of the business. He has direct responsibility to his employers. That responsibility is to conduct the business in accordance with their desires, which generally will be to make as much money as possible while conforming to the basic rules of society, both those embodied in law and those embodied in ethical custom. . . . Insofar as his actions reduce returns to stockholders, he is spending their money. Insofar as his actions raise the price to customers, he is spending the customers' money.

An example that Friedman could use to illustrate his argument is the Control Data Corporation. Former chairman William Norris involved Control Data in many socially responsible programs that cost the company millions of dollars—from building plants in the inner city and employing a minority workforce to researching farming on the Alaskan tundra. When Control Data began to incur net losses of millions of dollars in the mid-1980s, critics blamed Norris's "do-gooder" mentality. Eventually, a new chairman was installed to restructure the company and return it to profitability.[9]

▶ Back to the Case

There are many different areas of social responsibility in which IBM could become involved. The company's present activities are clearly in education, arts and culture, community needs, the environment, and employee giving; other possibilities include women's rights, health, and racial equality. No matter how much IBM does in pursuing social responsibility goals, however, it will no doubt be criticized by someone for not doing enough. At this point, IBM's activities in the area of social responsibility appear to be highly significant.

Anything IBM does within the sphere of social responsibility could result in a short-run profit decrease simply because of the costs. Although, at first glance, such action might seem unbusinesslike, performing social responsibility activities could significantly improve IBM's public image of and could be instrumental in generating increased sales.

Conclusions About the Performance of Social Responsibility Activities by Business

The preceding section presented several major arguments for and against businesses performing social responsibility activities. Regardless of which argument or combination of arguments particular managers embrace, they generally should make a concerted effort to do the following:

1. Perform all legally required social responsibility activities
2. Consider voluntarily performing social responsibility activities beyond those legally required

3. Inform all relevant individuals of the extent to which their organization will become involved in performing social responsibility activities

Performing Required Social Responsibility Activities   Federal legislation requires that businesses perform certain social responsibility activities. In fact, several government agencies have been established expressly to enforce such business-related legislation (see Table 3.1). The Environmental Protection Agency, for instance, has the authority to require businesses to adhere to certain socially responsible environmental standards. Examples of specific legislation requiring the performance of corporate social responsibility activities are the Equal Pay Act of 1963, the Equal Employment Opportunity Act of 1972, the Highway Safety Act of 1978, and the Clean Air Act Amendments of 1990.[10]

Voluntarily Performing Social Responsibility Activities   Adherence to legislated social responsibilities is the minimum standard of social responsibility performance that business managers must achieve. Managers must ask themselves, however, how far beyond the minimum they should go.

Determining how far to go is a simple process to describe, yet it is difficult and complicated to implement. It entails assessing the positive and negative outcomes of performing social responsibility activities over both the short and the long terms, and then performing only those activities that maximize management system success while making a desirable contribution to the welfare of society.

Events at the Sara Lee Bakery plant in New Hampton, Iowa, illustrate how company management can voluntarily take action to protect employees' health. Many employees at the plant began to develop carpal tunnel syndrome, a debilitating wrist disorder caused by repeated hand motions. Instead of simply having its employees go through physical therapy—and, as the principal employer in the town, watching the morale of the town drop—Sara Lee thoroughly investigated the problem. Managers took suggestions from factory workers and had their engineers design tools to alleviate the problem. The result was a virtual elimination of carpal tunnel syndrome at the plant within a very short time.[11]

Sandra Holmes asked top executives in 560 major firms, in such areas as commercial banking, life insurance, transportation, and utilities, to state the possible negative and positive outcomes their firms could expect from performing social responsibility activities.[12] Table 3.2 lists these outcomes and indicates the percentage of executives questioned who expected them. Although this information furnishes managers with insights into how involved their organizations should become in social responsibility activities, it does not give them a clear-cut indication of what to do. Managers can determine the appropriate level of social responsi-

Table 3.1

Primary Functions of Several Federal Agencies That Enforce Social Responsibility Legislation

Federal Agency	Primary Agency Functions
Equal Employment Opportunity Commission	Investigates and conciliates employment discrimination complaints that are based on race, sex, or creed
Office of Federal Contract Compliance Programs	Ensures that employers holding federal contracts grant equal employment opportunity to people regardless of their race or sex
Environmental Protection Agency	Formulates and enforces environmental standards in such areas as water, air, and noise pollution
Consumer Product Safety Commission	Strives to reduce consumer misunderstanding of manufacturers' product design, labeling, and so on, by promoting clarity of these messages
Occupational Safety and Health Administration	Regulates safety and health conditions in nongovernment workplaces
National Highway Traffic Safety Administration	Attempts to reduce traffic accidents through the regulation of transportation-related manufacturers and products
Mining Enforcement and Safety Administration	Attempts to improve safety conditions for mine workers by enforcing all mine safety and equipment standards

Outcomes of Social Responsibility Involvement Expected by Executives and the Percent Who Expected Them

Table 3.2

Expected Outcomes	Percent of Executives Expecting Them
Positive Outcomes	
Enhanced corporate reputation and goodwill	97.4
Strengthening of the social system in which the corporation functions	89.0
Strengthening of the economic system in which the corporation functions	74.3
Greater job satisfaction among all employees	72.3
Avoidance of government regulation	63.7
Greater job satisfaction among executives	62.8
Increased chances for survival of the firm	60.7
Ability to attract better managerial talent	55.5
Increased long-term profitability	52.9
Strengthening of the pluralistic nature of American society	40.3
Maintaining or gaining customers	38.2
Investor preference for socially responsible firms	36.6
Increased short-term profitability	15.2
Negative Outcomes	
Decreased short-term profitability	59.7
Conflict of economic or financial and social goals	53.9
Increased prices for consumers	41.4
Conflict in criteria for assessing managerial performance	27.2
Disaffection of stockholders	24.1
Decreased productivity	18.8
Decreased long-term profitability	13.1
Increased government regulation	11.0
Weakening of the economic system in which the corporation functions	7.9
Weakening of the social system in which the corporation functions	3.7

Maxell Sensitive to the Global Environment

SPOTLIGHT global

Maxell was established in 1961. Since then, it has developed and introduced products in the fields of data, energy, sound, and vision, including audiocassettes, headphones, camcorder tapes, and floppy diskettes. The company's many years of experience in research and product development have built the utmost customer trust and confidence in the Maxell brand name. To its credit, management at Maxell has created a global network to meet the special demands of each market it serves around the world.

One area in which Maxell is clearly committed to the communities it serves is protecting the global environment. Norio Akai, president of Hitachi Maxell, believes that preservation of the global environment is an issue which requires solutions that ignore national boundaries.

According to Akai, a company that does not take fast and effective action to help remedy global environmental problems will not survive; hence this is a serious concern at Maxell. As a reflection of that concern, the waiting room for visitors to Maxell's Works Center in the United Kingdom contains a site plan showing the measures taken, in building the site, to protect local "green" features such as the fishing ponds and lakes.

Maxell has become a model for how global companies can help to protect the global environment. Its achievements in this area have undoubtedly contributed not only to company success, but to a higher-quality environment in the communities it serves throughout the world. ■

▶ Volunteers for Habitat for Humanity put up low-income housing in Washington, DC. Many firms encourage employee contributions to such socially responsible programs by allowing them time off to participate.

bility involvement for a specific organization only by examining and reacting to specific factors related to that organization.

Communicating the Degree of Social Responsibility Involvement Determining the extent to which a business should perform social responsibility activities beyond legal requirements is a subjective process. Despite this subjectivity, however, managers should have a well-defined position in this vital area and should inform all organization members of that position.[13] Taking these steps will ensure that managers and organization members behave consistently to support the position and that societal expectations of what a particular organization can achieve in this area are realistic.

Nike, the world famous athletic-gear manufacturer, recently felt so strongly that its corporate philosophy on social responsibility issues should be clearly formulated and communicated that the company created a new position, vice president of corporate and social responsibility. Maria Eitelto, a former public-relations executive at Microsoft, was hired to fill that position and is now responsible for clearly communicating Nike's thoughts on social responsibility both inside and outside the organization.[14]

▶ **Back to the Case**

Some social responsibility activities are legislated and therefore *must* be performed by businesses. Most of the legislated activities, however, are aimed at larger companies like IBM. Such legislation has to do with required levels of product safety and employee safety. Legislated support for community arts probably doesn't exist.

Since IBM is not required by law to support things like adult education or community arts, whatever it might contribute to such areas would be strictly voluntary. In making a decision about how to support society, IBM management should assess the positive and negative outcomes of such support over both the long and short terms, and then establish whatever support, if any, would maximize its success and offer some desirable contribution to society. IBM should communicate to all organization members, as well as society, those areas it will support, and why. The use of its Web site greatly facilitates this communication.

SOCIAL RESPONSIVENESS

The previous section discussed social responsibility, a business's obligation to take action that protects and improves the welfare of society along with the business's own interests. This section defines and discusses **social responsiveness,** the degree of effectiveness and efficiency an organization displays in pursuing its social responsibilities.[15] The greater the degree of effectiveness and efficiency, the more socially responsive the organization is said to be. The next three sections take up the following issues:

1. Determining if a social responsibility exists
2. Social responsiveness and decision making
3. Approaches to meeting social responsibilities

Social responsiveness is the degree of effectiveness and efficiency an organization displays in pursuing its social responsibilities.

Determining if a Social Responsibility Exists

One challenge facing managers who are attempting to be socially responsive is to determine which specific social obligations are implied by their business situation. Managers in the tobacco industry, for example, are probably socially obligated to contribute to public health by pushing for the development of innovative tobacco products that do less harm to people's health than present products do, but they are not socially obligated to help reclaim shorelines contaminated by oil spills.

Clearly, management has an obligation to be socially responsible toward its stakeholders. **Stakeholders** are all those individuals and groups that are directly or indirectly affected by an organization's decisions.[16] Managers of successful organizations typically have many different stakeholders to consider: stockholders, or owners of the organization; suppliers; lenders; government agencies; employees and unions; consumers; competitors; and local communities as well as society at large. Table 3.3 lists these stakeholders and gives a corresponding example of how a manager is socially obligated to each of them.

Stakeholders are all individuals and groups that are directly or indirectly affected by an organization's decisions.

Social Responsiveness and Decision Making

The socially responsive organization that is both effective and efficient meets its social responsibilities without wasting organizational resources in the process. Determining exactly which social responsibilities an organization should pursue and then deciding how to pursue them are the two most critical decisions for maintaining a high level of social responsiveness within an organization.

Figure 3.1 is a flowchart that managers can use as a general guideline for making social responsibility decisions that enhance the social responsiveness of their organization. This figure implies that for managers to achieve and maintain a high level of social responsiveness within an organization, they must pursue only those responsibilities their organization possesses and has a right to undertake. Furthermore, once managers decide to meet a specific social responsibility, they must determine the best way to undertake activities related to meeting this obligation. That is, managers must decide whether their organization should undertake the activities on its own or acquire the help of outsiders with more expertise in the area.

As an example of how the guidelines in Figure 3.1 can be used profitably, consider a recent decision made by Radisson Hotels International. Radisson's management determined that the

Stakeholders of a Typical Modern Organization and Examples of Social Obligations Managers Owe to Them

 Table 3.3

Stakeholder	Social Obligations Owed
Stockholders/owners of the organization	To increase the value of the organization
Suppliers of materials	To deal with them fairly
Banks and other lenders	To repay debts
Government agencies	To abide by laws
Employees and unions	To provide safe working environment and to negotiate fairly with union representatives
Consumers	To provide safe products
Competitors	To compete fairly and to refrain from restraints of trade
Local communities and society at large	To avoid business practices that harm the environment

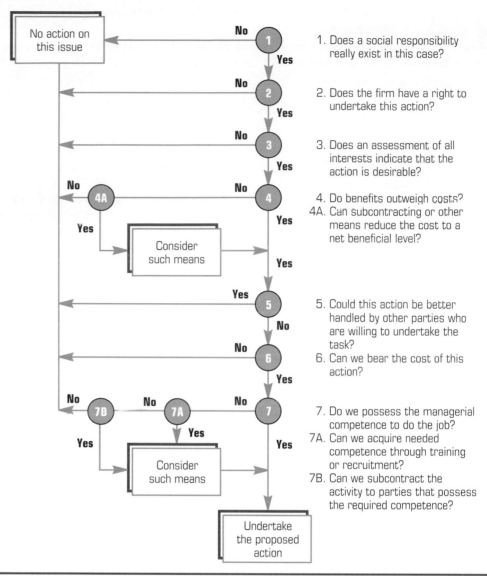

No action on this issue

No ① Yes
1. Does a social responsibility really exist in this case?

No ② Yes
2. Does the firm have a right to undertake this action?

No ③ Yes
3. Does an assessment of all interests indicate that the action is desirable?

No ④A No ④ Yes
Yes

Consider such means
Yes

4. Do benefits outweigh costs?
4A. Can subcontracting or other means reduce the cost to a net beneficial level?

Yes ⑤ No
5. Could this action be better handled by other parties who are willing to undertake the task?

No ⑥ Yes
6. Can we bear the cost of this action?

No ⑦B No ⑦A No ⑦ Yes
Yes
Yes

Consider such means

7. Do we possess the managerial competence to do the job?
7A. Can we acquire needed competence through training or recruitment?
7B. Can we subcontract the activity to parties that possess the required competence?

Undertake the proposed action

Figure 3.1 🖑 *Flowchart of social responsibility decision making that generally will enhance the social responsiveness of an organization*

---

company had an obligation to help preserve the environment. To proactively meet this obligation, management initiated a new concept called Green Suites. Along with the normally expected suite appointments, Green Suites feature recycled paper goods because Radisson managers believe that by offering its customers recycled paper products, the company can discourage the unnecessary cutting of trees. In order for this decision to be considered truly socially responsible, however, it must actually help to preserve the environment by saving trees and attract customer dollars that will help Radisson Hotels International reach such organizational objectives as making a profit.[17]

Approaches to Meeting Social Responsibilities

Various managerial approaches to meeting social obligations are another determinant of an organization's level of social responsiveness. According to Lipson, a desirable and socially responsive approach to meeting social obligations does the following:[18]

1. Incorporates social goals into the annual planning process
2. Seeks comparative industry norms for social programs
3. Presents reports to organization members, the board of directors, and stockholders on social responsibility progress

4. Experiments with different approaches for measuring social performance
5. Attempts to measure the cost of social programs as well as the return on social program investments

S. Prakash Sethi presents three management approaches to meeting social obligations:[19]

1. Social obligation approach
2. Social responsibility approach
3. Social responsiveness approach

Each of these approaches entails behavior that reflects a somewhat different attitude toward performance of social responsibility activities by business. The **social obligation approach,** for example, considers business as having primarily economic purposes and confines social responsibility activity mainly to existing legislation. The **social responsibility approach** sees business as having both economic and societal goals. The **social responsiveness approach** considers business as having both societal and economic goals as well as the obligation to anticipate potential social problems and work actively toward preventing their occurrence.

Organizations characterized by attitudes and behaviors consistent with the social responsiveness approach are generally more socially responsive than organizations characterized by attitudes and behaviors consistent with either the social responsibility or the social obligation approach. And organizations that take the social responsibility approach usually achieve higher levels of social responsiveness than organizations that take the social obligation approach. In other words, as one moves along the continuum from social obligation to social responsiveness, one generally finds management becoming more proactive. Proactive managers do what is prudent from a business viewpoint to reduce liabilities regardless of whether such action is required by law.

> The **social obligation approach** is an approach to meeting social obligations that considers business to have primarily economic purposes and confines social responsibility activity largely to conformance to existing legislation.
>
> The **social responsibility approach** is an approach to meeting social obligations that considers business as having both societal and economic goals.
>
> The **social responsiveness approach** is an approach to meeting social obligations that considers business to have societal and economic goals as well as the obligation to anticipate potential social problems and to work actively toward preventing them from occurring.

Social Responsiveness and the Equal Opportunity Act at Opryland

The Equal Opportunity Act was passed in 1972 to eliminate employment discrimination based on race, sex, or color. Management's attitude toward performing Equal Opportunity Act social responsibility activities at Opryland illustrates the social responsiveness approach.

The inevitability of having a future workforce characterized by cultural diversity is driving many hotels to aggressively recruit minorities for management-level positions. Such hotels see the careful building of a diverse workforce as a means not only of enhancing worker productivity but also of attracting a more diverse customer base since minorities are a growing segment of their market.

Because the pool of minority candidates for hotel manager positions is relatively small, many hotels and hotel chains are aggressively recruiting. At the Opryland Hotel, for example, the human resource department supports a wide range of special minority recruitment programs. One such program, called INROADS, gives minority college students the financial means to experience four years of hotel-management training. Upon completion of such a college program, students are qualified for entry-level management positions in a hotel such as Opryland. Although participating in INROADS will not solve Opryland Hotel's minority recruitment problems in the short run, it will certainly increase the supply of minority candidates to fill the company's management positions in the longer run. ■

▶ Back to the Case

IBM should strive to maintain a relatively high level of social responsiveness in pursuing its social responsibility activities. To do this, management should make decisions focusing on IBM's established social responsibility areas and approach meeting those responsibilities in appropriate ways.

In terms of supporting adult education, for example, management must first decide if IBM has a social responsibility to become involved, through the design and application of its products, in society's adult education problem. Assuming it was decided that IBM *has* such a responsibility, it must then determine how to accomplish the activities necessary to meet it. For example, IBM might employ its expertise to develop new, computer-based educational methods and content aimed specifically at adult learning needs. Making appropriate decisions will help IBM meet social obligations effectively and efficiently.

In terms of implementing an approach to meeting social responsibilities that will increase IBM's social responsiveness, management should try to view the company as having both societal and economic goals. In addition, management should attempt to anticipate social problems and actively work to prevent them.

This section considers social responsibility as a major organizational activity subject to the same management techniques used in other major organizational activities, such as production, personnel, finance, and marketing. Managers have known for some time that to achieve desirable results in these areas, they must be effective in planning, organizing, influencing, and controlling. Achieving social responsibility results is no different. The following sections discuss planning, organizing, influencing, and controlling social responsibility activities.

Planning Social Responsibility Activities

Planning was defined in Chapter 1 as the process of determining how the organization will achieve its objectives, or get where it wants to go. Planning social responsibility activities, then, involves determining how the organization will achieve its social responsibility objectives, or get where it wants to go in the area of social responsibility. The following sections discuss how the planning of social responsibility activities is related to the organization's overall planning process and how its social responsibility policy can be converted into action.

The Overall Planning Process   The model presented in Figure 3.2 illustrates how social responsibility activities can be handled as part of the overall planning process of the organization. As shown in this figure, social trends forecasts should be performed within the organizational environment along with the more typically performed economic, political, and technological trends forecasts. Examples of social trends are prevailing and future societal attitudes toward water pollution, safe working conditions, and the national education system.[20] Each of the forecasts would influence the development of the organization's long-run plans, or plans for the more distant future, and short-run plans, or plans for the relatively near future.

Converting Organizational Policies on Social Responsibility into Action   A *policy* is a management tool that furnishes broad guidelines for channeling management thinking in specific directions. Managers should establish organizational policies in the social responsibility area just as they do in some of the more generally accepted areas, such as hiring, promotion, and absenteeism.

To be effective, social responsibility policies must be converted into appropriate action. As shown in Figure 3.3, this conversion involves three distinct and generally sequential phases.

➤ *Phase 1* consists of the recognition by top management that the organization has some social obligation. Top management then must formulate and communicate some policy about the acceptance of this obligation to all organization members.

➤ *Phase 2* involves staff personnel as well as top management. In this phase, top management gathers information related to meeting the social obligation accepted in phase 1. Staff personnel are generally involved at this point to give advice on technical matters related to meeting the accepted social obligation.

➤ *Phase 3* involves division management in addition to the organization personnel already involved from the first two phases. During this phase, top management strives to obtain

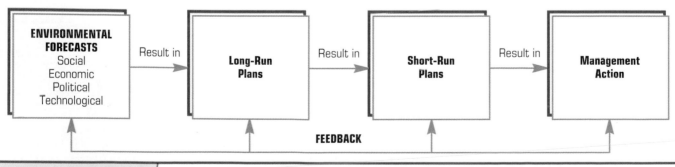

Figure 3.2   *Integration of social responsibility activities and planning activities*

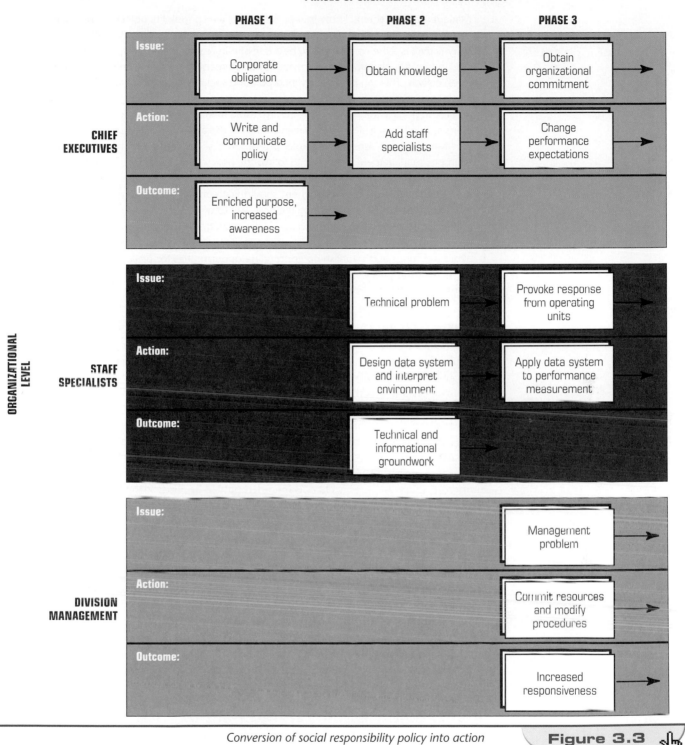

PHASES OF ORGANIZATIONAL INVOLVEMENT

	PHASE 1	PHASE 2	PHASE 3
CHIEF EXECUTIVES — Issue:	Corporate obligation	Obtain knowledge	Obtain organizational commitment
Action:	Write and communicate policy	Add staff specialists	Change performance expectations
Outcome:	Enriched purpose, increased awareness		
STAFF SPECIALISTS — Issue:		Technical problem	Provoke response from operating units
Action:		Design data system and interpret environment	Apply data system to performance measurement
Outcome:		Technical and informational groundwork	
DIVISION MANAGEMENT — Issue:			Management problem
Action:			Commit resources and modify procedures
Outcome:			Increased responsiveness

ORGANIZATIONAL LEVEL

Conversion of social responsibility policy into action

Figure 3.3

the commitment of organization members to live up to the accepted social obligation and attempts to create realistic expectations about the effects of such a commitment on organizational productivity. Staff specialists encourage the responses within the organization necessary to meet the accepted social obligation properly; and division management commits resources and modifies existing procedures so that appropriate socially oriented activities can and will be performed within the organization.

Managers at IBM should know that pursuing social responsibility objectives is a major management activity. Therefore, they must plan, organize, influence, and control IBM's social responsibility activities if the company is to be successful in reaching social responsibility objectives.

In terms of planning these activities, management should determine how IBM will achieve its objectives. This can be done by incorporating social responsibility planning into IBM's overall planning process; that is, social trends forecasts can be made along with economic, political, and technological trends forecasts. In turn, these forecasts would influence the development of plans and, ultimately, the action taken by IBM in the area of social responsibility.

Management also must be able to turn IBM's social responsibility policy into action. For example, management may want to follow the policy of making IBM's laptop computers more affordable to customers, thereby facilitating the company's role in promoting education. To convert this into action, management should first communicate the policy to all organization members. Next, it must determine the best way to generate lower product costs that can ultimately be passed on to the customers. Finally, management should make sure everyone at IBM is committed to meeting this social responsibility objective and that lower-level managers are allocating funds and establishing appropriate opportunities for organization members to help implement this policy.

Organizing Social Responsibility Activities

Organizing was discussed in Chapter 1 as the process of establishing orderly uses for all the organization's resources. These uses emphasize the attainment of management system objectives and flow naturally from management system plans. Correspondingly, organizing for social responsibility activities entails establishing for all organizational resources logical uses that emphasize the attainment of the organization's social objectives and that are consistent with its social responsibility plans.

Figure 3.4 shows how Standard Oil Company of Indiana decided to organize for the performance of its social responsibility activities. The vice president for law and public affairs has primary responsibility in the area of societal affairs and oversees the related activities of numerous individuals. This chart is intended only as an illustration of how a company might include its social responsibility area on its organization chart. Specific organizing in this area should always be tailored to the unique needs of a company.

Influencing Individuals Performing Social Responsibility Activities

Influencing was defined in Chapter 1 as the management process of guiding the activities of organization members to help attain organizational objectives. As applied to the social responsibility area, then, influencing is the process of guiding the activities of organization members to help attain the organization's social responsibility objectives. More specifically, to influence appropriately in this area, managers must lead, communicate, motivate, and work with groups in ways that result in the attainment of the organization's social responsibility objectives.

Controlling Social Responsibility Activities

Controlling, as discussed in Chapter 1, is making things happen as they were planned to happen. To control, managers assess or measure what is occurring in the organization and, if necessary, change these occurrences in some way to make them conform to plans. Controlling in the area of social responsibility entails the same two major tasks. The following sections discuss various areas in which social responsibility measurement takes place and examine the social audit, a tool for determining and reporting progress in the attainment of social responsibility objectives.

Areas of Measurement   Measurements to gauge organizational progress in reaching social responsibility objectives can be taken in any number of areas. The specific areas in which individual companies decide to take such measurements will vary according to the spe-

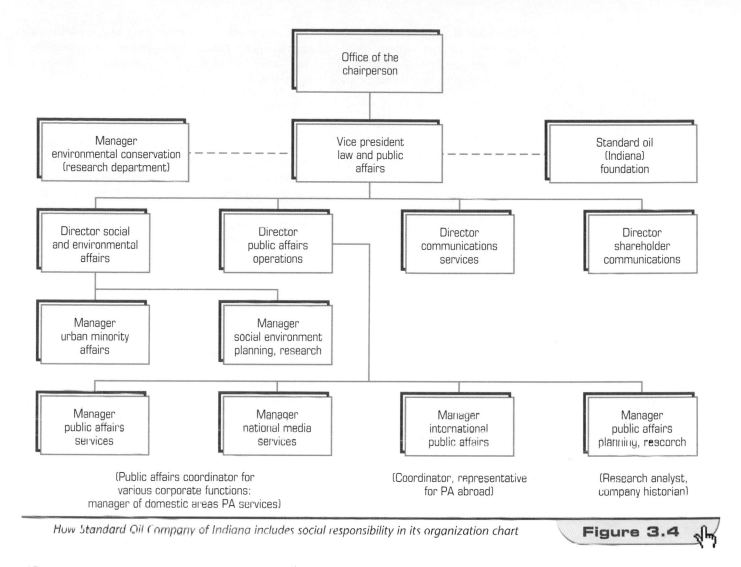

How Standard Oil Company of Indiana includes social responsibility in its organization chart

Figure 3.4

cific social responsibility objectives to be met. All companies, however, should take social responsibility measurements in at least the following four major areas:[21]

1. *The economic function area*   A measurement should be made of whether the organization is performing such activities as producing goods and services that people need, creating jobs for society, paying fair wages, and ensuring worker safety. This measurement gives some indication of the economic contribution the organization is making to society.

2. *The quality-of-life area*—The measurement of quality of life should focus on whether the organization is improving or degrading the general quality of life in society. Producing high-quality goods, dealing fairly with employees and customers, and making an effort to preserve the natural environment are all indicators that the organization is upholding or improving the general quality of life. As an example of degrading the quality of life, some people believe that cigarette companies, because they produce goods that can harm the health of society overall, are socially irresponsible.[22]

3. *The social investment area*—The measurement of social investment deals with the degree to which the organization is investing both money and human resources to solve community social problems. Here, the organization could be involved in assisting community organizations dedicated to education, charities, and the arts.

4. *The problem-solving area*—The measurement of problem solving should focus on the degree to which the organization deals with social problems, such as participating in long-range community planning and conducting studies to pinpoint social problems.

The Social Audit: A Progress Report   A **social audit** is the process of measuring the present social responsibility activities of an organization to assess its performance in this area.

A **social audit** is the process of measuring the present social responsibility activities of an organization. It monitors, measures, and appraises all aspects of an organization's social responsibility performance.

The basic steps in conducting a social audit are monitoring, measuring, and appraising all aspects of an organization's social responsibility performance. Although some companies that pioneered concepts of social reporting, like General Electric, are still continuing their efforts, few companies, unfortunately, are joining their ranks.[23]

▶ Back to the Case

In addition to planning social responsibility activities at IBM, management must organize, influence, and control them. To organize these activities, orderly use of all resources at IBM must be established to carry out the company's social responsibility plans. Developing an organization chart that shows the social responsibility area with corresponding job descriptions, responsibilities, and specifications for the positions would be an appropriate step for management to take.

To influence social responsibility activities, organization members should be guided in directions that will enhance the attainment of IBM's social responsibility objectives. Management must lead, communicate, motivate, and work with groups in ways that are appropriate for meeting those objectives.

To control, management must make sure that social responsibility activities occur as planned. If they do not, changes should be made to ensure that activities will be handled properly in the near future. One tool that can be used to check IBM's progress in meeting social responsibilities is the social audit. The audit will enable management to check and assess system performance in such areas as economic functions, quality of life, social investment, and problem solving.

HOW SOCIETY CAN HELP BUSINESS MEET SOCIAL OBLIGATIONS

Although the point was made early in this chapter that there must be an open and honest involvement of both business and society for business to meet desirable social obligations, the bulk of the chapter has focused on what business should do in the area of social responsibility. This section emphasizes actions that society should take to help business accomplish its social responsibility objectives.

Jerry McAfee, chairman of the board and CEO of Gulf Oil Corporation, says that although business has some responsibilities to society, society also has the following responsibilities to business:[24]

1. *Set rules that are clear and consistent*—This is one of the fundamental things that society, through government, ought to do. Although it may come as a surprise to some, I believe that industry actually needs an appropriate measure of regulation. By this I mean that the people of the nation, through their government, should set the bounds within which they want industry to operate.

    But the rules have got to be clear. Society must spell out clearly what it is it wants the corporations to do. The rules can't be vague and imprecise. Making the rules straight and understandable is what government is all about. One of my colleagues described his confusion when he read a section of a regulation that a federal regulatory representative had cited as the reason for a certain decision that had been made. "You're right," the official responded, "that's what the regulation says, but that's not what it means."

2. *Keep the rules technically feasible*—Business cannot be expected to do the impossible. Yet the plain truth is that many of today's regulations are unworkable. Environmental standards have on occasion exceeded those of Mother Nature. For example, the Rio Blanco shale-oil development in Colorado was delayed because air-quality standards, as originally proposed, required a higher quality of air than existed in the natural setting.

3. *Make sure the rules are economically feasible*—Society cannot impose a rule that society is not prepared to pay for because, ultimately, it is the people

▶ New York Life Insurance surveyed its employees to find out what kind of community services and volunteer programs they would like to be involved with, and it now has a three-year-old Volunteers for LIFE program, which experiments with different volunteer partnerships to find out where the firm's social responsibility efforts can have the greatest impact. The program focuses on children from kindergarten through grade 12 and relies on mentoring and after-school programs run with five different organizations. Employee Julia Warren works with the Big Brothers Big Sisters program.

who must pay, either through higher prices or higher taxes, or both. Furthermore, the costs involved include not only those funds constructively spent to solve problems, but also the increasingly substantial expenditures needed to comply with red-tape requirements. Although the total cost of government regulation of business is difficult to compute, it is enormous. To cite an example, the Commission on Federal Paperwork estimated the energy industry's annual cost of complying with federal energy-reporting requirements at possibly $335 million per year.

4. *Make the rules prospective, not retroactive*—Nowadays, there is an alarming, distressing trend toward retroactivity, toward trying to force retribution for the past. Certain patterns of taxation and some of the regulations and applications of the law are indications of this trend.

   As a case in point, the U.S. government recently filed a multimillion-dollar lawsuit against Borden Chemicals & Plastics, a company operating in Louisiana and Illinois that produces various chemical products for construction, industrial, and agricultural markets.[25] The suit alleges that Borden released significant amounts of cancer-causing and other hazardous contaminants into the groundwater at its Louisiana complex. Borden maintains that recent changes to hazardous waste regulations are being applied retroactively to force the company to pay penalties for actions it took before the law existed. Borden charges that this type of action by the government violates the basic concepts of fairness and due process.

   It is counterproductive to make today's rules apply retroactively to yesterday's ball game.

5. *Make the rules goal-setting, not procedure-prescribing*—The proper way for the people of the nation, through their government, to tell their industries how to operate is to set the goals, set the fences, set the criteria, set the atmosphere, but don't tell us how to do it. Tell us what you want made, but don't tell us how to make it. Tell us the destination we're seeking, but don't tell us how to get there. Leave it to the ingenuity of American industry to devise the best, the most economical, the most efficient way to get there, for industry's track record in this regard has been good.

BUSINESS ETHICS

The study of ethics in management can be approached from many different directions. Perhaps the most practical approach is to view ethics as catalyzing managers to take socially responsible actions. The movement to include the study of ethics as a critical part of management education began in the 1970s, grew significantly in the 1980s, and is expected to continue growing into the twenty-first century. John Shad, chairman of the Securities and Exchange Commission during the 1980s when Wall Street was shaken by a number of insider trading scandals, recently pledged a $20 million trust fund to the Harvard Business School to create a curriculum in business ethics for M.B.A. students. Television producer Norman Lear gave $1 million to underwrite the Business Enterprise Trust, which will give national awards to companies and "whistle blowers . . . who demonstrate courage, creativity, and social vision in the business world."[26]

The following sections define ethics, explain why ethical considerations are a vital part of management practices, discuss a workable code of business ethics, and present some suggestions for creating an ethical workplace.

A Definition of Ethics

The famous missionary physician and humanitarian Albert Schweitzer defined ethics as "our concern for good behavior. We feel an obligation to consider not only our own personal well-being, but also that of other human beings." This is similar to the precept of the Golden Rule: Do unto others as you would have them do unto you.[27]

In business, **ethics** can be defined as the capacity to reflect on values in the corporate decision-making process, to determine how these values and decisions affect various stakeholder groups, and to establish how managers can use these observations in day-to-day company management. Ethical managers strive for success within the confines of sound management practices which are characterized by fairness and justice.[28] Interestingly, using ethics as a major

Ethics is our concern for good behavior; our obligation to consider not only our own personal well-being but also that of other human beings.

Business ethics involves the capacity to reflect on values in the corporate decision-making process, to determine how these values and decisions affect various stakeholder groups, and to establish how managers can use these observations in day-to-day company management.

guide in making and evaluating business decisions is not only popular in the United States but also in the very different societies of India and Russia.[29]

Why Ethics Is a Vital Part of Management Practices

John F. Akers, former chairman of the board of IBM, recently said that it makes good business sense for managers to be ethical. Unless they are ethical, he believes, companies cannot be competitive in either national or international markets. According to Akers:[30]

Ethics and competitiveness are inseparable. We compete as a society. No society anywhere will compete very long or successfully with people stabbing each other in the back; with people trying to steal from one another; with everything requiring notarized confirmation because you can't trust the other person; with every little squabble ending in litigation; and with government writing reams of regulatory legislation, trying business hand and foot to keep it honest.

Although ethical management practices may not be linked to specific indicators of financial profitability, there is no inevitable conflict between ethical practices and making a profit. As Akers' statement suggests, our system of competition presumes underlying values of truthfulness and fair dealing. The employment of ethical business practices can enhance overall corporate health in three important areas: productivity, stakeholder relations, and government regulation.

Productivity The employees of a corporation constitute one major stakeholder group that is affected by management practices. When management is resolved to act ethically toward stakeholders, then employees will be positively affected. For example, a corporation may decide that business ethics requires it to make a special effort to ensure the health and welfare of its employees. To this end, many corporations have established Employee Advisory Programs (EAPs) to help employees with family, work, financial, or legal problems, or with mental illness or chemical dependency. These programs have even enhanced productivity in some corporations. For instance, Control Data Corporation found that its EAP reduced health costs and sick-leave usage significantly.[31]

Stakeholder Relations The second area in which ethical management practices can enhance corporate health is by positively affecting "outside" stakeholders such as suppliers and customers. A positive public image can attract customers who view such an image as desirable. For example, Johnson & Johnson, the world's largest maker of health-care products, is guided by a "Credo" addressed over 50 years ago by General Robert Wood Johnson to the company's employees and stockholders and members of its community (see Figure 3.5).

Government Regulation The third area in which ethical management practices can enhance corporate health is in minimizing government regulation. Where companies are believed to be acting unethically, the public is more likely to put pressure on legislators and other government officials to regulate those businesses or to enforce existing regulations. For example, in 1995, Texas state legislators held public hearings on the operations of the psychiatric hospital industry. These hearings arose, at least partly, out of the perception that private psychiatric hospitals were not following ethical pricing practices.[32]

A Code of Ethics

A **code of ethics** is a formal statement that acts as a guide for the ethics of how people within a particular organization should act and make decisions. Ninety percent of *Fortune* 500 firms, and almost half of all other firms, have ethical codes. Moreover, many organizations that do not already have an ethical code are giving serious consideration to developing one.[33]

Codes of ethics commonly address such issues as conflict of interest, competitors, privacy of information, gift giving, and giving and receiving political contributions or business. A code of ethics recently developed by Nissan of Japan, for example, barred all Nissan employees from accepting almost all gifts or entertainment from, or offering them to, business partners and government officials. The new code was drafted by Nissan President Yoshikazu Hanawa and sent to 300 major suppliers.[34]

A **code of ethics** is a formal statement that acts as a guide for making decisions and acting within an organization.

We believe our first responsibility is to the doctors, nurses, and patients, to mothers
    and all others who use our products and services.
In meeting their needs everything we do must be of high quality.
We must constantly strive to reduce our costs in order to maintain reasonable prices.
Customers' orders must be serviced promptly and accurately.
Our suppliers and distributors must have an opportunity to make a fair profit.
We are responsible to our employees, the men and women who work with us
    throughout the world.
Everyone must be considered as an individual.
We must respect their dignity and recognize their merit.
They must have a sense of security in their jobs.
Compensation must be fair and adequate, and working conditions clean, orderly, and
    safe.
Employees must feel free to make suggestions and complaints.
There must be equal opportunity for employment, development, and advancement for
    those qualified.
We must provide competent management, and their actions must be just and ethical.
We are responsible to the communities in which we live and work and to the world
    community as well.
We must be good citizens—support good works and charities and bear our fair share
    of taxes.
We must encourage civic improvements and better health and education.
We must maintain in good order the property we are privileged to use, protecting the
    environment and natural resources.
Our final responsibility is to our stockholders.
Business must make a sound profit.
We must experiment with new ideas.
Research must be carried on, innovative programs developed, and mistakes paid for.
New equipment must be purchased, new facilities provided, and new products
    launched.
Reserves must be created to provide for adverse times.
When we operate according to these principles, the stockholders should realize a fair
    return.

The Johnson & Johnson Credo　　　　　**Figure 3.5**

According to a recent survey, the development and distribution of a code of ethics is perceived as an effective and efficient means of encouraging ethical practices within organizations.[35] The code of ethics that Johnson & Johnson drew up to guide company business practices (Figure 3.5) is distributed in its annual report, as well as to employees.

Managers cannot assume that merely because they have developed and distributed a code
of ethics, organization members have all the guidelines they need to determine what is ethical
and to act accordingly. It is impossible to cover all ethical and unethical conduct within an
organization in one code. Managers should view codes of ethics as tools that must be evaluated and refined periodically so that they will be comprehensive and usable guidelines for
making ethical business decisions efficiently and effectively.

Creating an Ethical Workplace

Managers commonly strive to encourage ethical practices, not only to be morally correct, but
also to gain whatever business advantage lies in projecting an ethical image to consumers and
employees.[36] Creating, distributing, and continually improving a company's code of ethics is
one common step managers can take to establish an ethical workplace.

Another step managers can take to create an ethical workplace is to set up a special office
or department responsible for ensuring that the organization's practices are ethical. For example, management at Martin Marietta, a major supplier of missile systems and aircraft components, has established a corporate ethics office as a tangible sign to all employees that management is serious about encouraging ethical practices within the company (see Figure 3.6).

Another way to promote ethics in the workplace is to furnish organization members with
appropriate training. General Dynamics, McDonnell Douglas, Chemical Bank, and American

To ensure continuing attention to matters of ethics and standards on the part of all Martin Marietta employees, the Corporation has established the Corporate Ethics Office. The Director of Corporate Ethics is charged with responsibility for monitoring performance under this Code of Ethics and for resolving concerns presented to the Ethics Office.

Martin Marietta calls on every employee to report any violation or apparent violation of the Code. The Corporation strongly encourages employees to work with their supervisors in making such reports, and in addition, provides to employees the right to report violations directly to the Corporate Ethics Office. Prompt reporting of violations is considered to be in the best interest of all.

Employee reports will be handled in absolute confidence. No employee will suffer indignity or retaliation because of a report he or she makes to the Ethics Office. . . .

The Chairman of the Corporate Ethics Committee will be the President of the Corporation. The Committee will consist of five other employees of the Corporation, including representatives of the Corporation's operating elements, each of whom will be appointed by the Chairman of the Committee subject to the approval of the Audit and Ethics Committee of the Corporation's Board of Directors.

The Chairman of the Corporate Ethics Committee reports to the Audit and Ethics Committee of the Martin Marietta Corporation Board of Directors.

Figure 3.6 *Martin Marietta's corporate ethics statement*

Can Company are examples of corporations that conduct training programs aimed at encouraging ethical practices within their organizations.[37] Such programs do not attempt to teach managers what is moral or ethical, but rather to give them criteria they can use to help determine how ethical a certain action might be. Managers can feel confident that a potential action will be considered ethical by the general public if it is consistent with one or more of the following standards:[38]

1. *The golden rule*—Act in a way you would expect others to act toward you.
2. *The utilitarian principle*—Act in a way that results in the greatest good for the greatest number of people.
3. *Kant's categorical imperative*—Act in such a way that the action taken under the circumstances could be a universal law, or rule, of behavior.

▶ Some firms have established formal programs to monitor ethics and social responsibility efforts. Gale C. Andrews is Vice President for Ethics and Business Conduct at Boeing Company, where employees at every level are required to take at least one hour of ethical training a year and managers five hours.

4. *The professional ethic*—Take actions that would be viewed as proper by a disinterested panel of professional peers.
5. *The TV test*—Managers should always ask, "Would I feel comfortable explaining to a national TV audience why I took this action?"
6. *The legal test*—Is the proposed action or decision legal? Established laws are generally considered minimum standards for ethics.
7. *The four-way test*—Managers can feel confident that a decision is ethical if they can answer "yes" to the following questions: Is the decision truthful? Is it fair to all concerned? Will it build goodwill and better friendships? Will it be beneficial to all concerned?

Finally, managers can take responsibility for creating and sustaining conditions in which people are likely to behave ethically and for minimizing conditions in which people might be tempted to behave unethically. Two practices that commonly inspire unethical behavior in organizations are to give unusually high rewards for good performance and unusually severe punishments for poor performance. By eliminating such factors, managers can reduce any pressure on employees to perform unethically in organizations.[39]

▶ Back to the Case

As indicated earlier, there is no legislation that requires IBM to support societal areas such as education or community arts. If such legislation were being developed, however, there are certain steps legislators could take to help management meet social responsibilities in these areas. For example, laws should be clear, consistent, and technically feasible, which would ensure that management knows what action is expected and that the means actually exist to take this action.

Laws should also be economically feasible, emphasize the future, and allow flexibility. IBM should be able to follow them without going bankrupt and should not be penalized for past practices. It also should be given the flexibility to follow these laws to the best advantage of the company; IBM should not be told to conform to laws by following specific steps.

Assuming that management at IBM is ethical, its decisions would focus on enhancing the well-being of all company stakeholders. In essence, management should follow the Golden Rule by acting in a way that it would expect others to act toward it. Decisions at IBM will always be ethical if they are truthful and fair to all concerned, if they build goodwill and better friendships, and if they are beneficial to all concerned.

Management Skills Module

This section is specially designed to help you develop management skills. An individual's management skill is based on an understanding of management concepts and the ability to apply those concepts in management situations. As a result, the following activities are designed both to heighten your understanding of management concepts and to help you gain facility in applying those concepts in various management situations.

UNDERSTANDING MANAGEMENT CONCEPTS

▌ Action Summary

Reread the learning objectives below. Each objective is followed by questions. Answering these questions accurately will help you retain the most important concepts discussed in this chapter. After answering each question, check your answer against the answer key at the end of this chapter. (*Hint:* If you have any doubts regarding the correct response, consult the page number that follows the answer.)

Circle:

From studying this chapter, I will attempt to acquire

1. An understanding of the term *corporate social responsibility*.

   T F　　**a.** According to Davis, since business has certain power over society, society can and must hold business responsible for social conditions that result from the exercise of this power.

   a b c d e　　**b.** Major social responsibility areas in which business can become involved include all of the following except: (a) urban affairs (b) consumer affairs (c) pollution control (d) natural resource conservation (e) all of the above are areas of potential involvement.

2. An appreciation of the arguments both for and against the assumption of social responsibilities by business.

   T F　　**a.** Some argue that since business is an influential component of society, it has the responsibility to help maintain and improve the overall welfare of society.

   a b c d e　　**b.** Milton Friedman argues that business cannot be held responsible for performing social responsibility activities. He does *not* argue that: (a) doing so has the potential to cause the demise of American business as we know it today (b) doing so is in direct conflict with the organizational objectives of business firms (c) doing so would cause the nation to creep toward socialism, which is inconsistent with American business philosophy (d) doing so is unethical because it requires business managers to spend money that rightfully belongs to the firm's investors (e) doing so ultimately would either reduce returns to the firm's investors or raise prices charged to consumers.

3. Useful strategies for increasing the social responsiveness of an organization.

   a b c d e　　**a.** When using the flowchart approach in social responsibility decision making, which one of the following questions is out of sequential order: (a) Can we afford this action? (b) Does a social responsibility actually exist? (c) Does the firm have a right to undertake this action? (d) Does an assessment of all interests indicate that the act is desirable? (e) Do benefits outweigh costs?

   T F　　**b.** The social obligation approach to performing social responsibility activities is concerned primarily with complying with existing legislation on the topic.

4. Insights into the planning, organizing, influencing, and controlling of social responsibility activities.

   T F　　**a.** Organizational policies should be established for social responsibility matters in the same manner as, for example, for personnel relations problems.

   a b c d e　　**b.** Companies should take social responsibility measurements in all of the following areas except: (a) economic utility area (b) economic function area (c) quality-of-life area (d) social investment area (e) problem-solving area.

5. A practical plan for how society can help business meet its social obligations.

   T F　　**a.** Ultimately, it is the citizens in a society who must finance the social responsibility activities of business by paying higher prices for goods and services or higher taxes or both.

   a b c d e　　**b.** The following is *not* one of the responsibilities that society has toward business, as listed by Jerry McAfee: (a) setting rules that are clear and concise (b) making rules prospective, not retroactive (c) making rules goal-setting, not procedure-prescribing (d) making rules subjective, not objective (e) making sure rules are economically feasible.

Circle: **6.** An understanding of the relationship between ethics and management.

T F   **a.** The utilitarian principle suggests that managers should act in such a way that an action taken under specific circumstances could be a universal law, or rule, of behavior.

a b c d e   **b.** Management might strive to encourage ethical behavior in organizations in order to: (a) be morally correct (b) gain a business advantage by having employees perceive their company as ethical (c) gain a business advantage by having customers perceive the company as ethical (d) avoid possible costly legal fees (e) all of the above.

T F   **c.** Once developed, a company's code of ethics generally does not have to be monitored or revised for at least two years.

T F   **d.** Some managers create a special "office of ethics" to show employees the critical importance of ethics.

▶ Action Summary Answer Key

1. a. T, p. 49   **3. a.** a, p. 56   **5. a.** T, pp. 62–63   **6. a.** F, p. 66
   b. e, p. 50   **b.** T, p. 57   **b.** d, pp. 62–63   **b.** e, p. 65
2. a. T, p. 50   **4. a.** T, p. 58   **c.** F, p. 65
   b. c, p. 51   **b.** a, p. 61   **d.** T, p. 65

▶ Issues for Review and Discussion

1. Define *corporate social responsibility.*

2. Explain three of the major propositions in the Davis model of corporate social responsibility.

3. Summarize three arguments that support the pursuit of social responsibility objectives by business.

4. Summarize Milton Friedman's arguments against the pursuit of social responsibility objectives by business.

5. What is meant by the phrase *performing required social responsibility activities?*

6. What is meant by the phrase *voluntarily performing social responsibility activities?*

7. List five positive and five negative outcomes a business might experience as a result of performing social responsibility activities.

8. What is the difference between social responsibility and social responsiveness?

9. Discuss the decision-making process that can help managers increase the social responsiveness of their organizations.

10. In your own words, explain the main differences among Sethi's three approaches to meeting social responsibilities.

11. Which of Sethi's approaches has the most potential for increasing the social responsiveness of a management system? Explain.

12. What is the overall relationship between the four main management functions and the performance of social responsibility activities by business?

13. What suggestions does this chapter make concerning planning social responsibility activities?

14. Describe the process of turning social responsibility policy into action.

15. How do organizing and influencing social responsibility activities relate to planning social responsibility activities?

16. List and define four main areas in which any management system can take measurements to control social responsibility activities.

17. What is a social audit? How should the results of a social audit be used by management?

18. How can society help business meet its social responsibilities?

19. What is the relationship between ethics and social responsibility?

20. Explain how managers can try to judge if a particular action is ethical.

21. What steps can managers take to make their organizations more ethical workplaces?

APPLYING MANAGEMENT CONCEPTS

▶ Cases

▶ INTRODUCTORY CASE WRAP-UP

▶ Case Discussion Questions

"IBM Uses Web Site to Promote Social Responsibility Goals" (p.47) and its related Back-to-the-Case sections were written to help you better understand the management concepts con-

(continued)

tained in this chapter. Answer the following discussion questions about this Introductory Case to further enrich your understanding of chapter content:

1. Do you think that IBM has a responsibility to support adult education in the communities in which it does business? Explain.
2. Assuming that IBM has such a responsibility, in what instances would it be relatively easy for the company to be committed to living up to it?
3. Assuming that IBM has such a responsibility, in what instances would it be relatively difficult for the company to be committed to living up to it?

▶Skills Exercise: Setting Social Responsibility Goals at IBM

In this chapter you studied several different areas in which management can take measurements to conduct a social audit for a company: economic function area, quality-of-life area, social investment area, and problem-solving area. Based only on the information in the Introductory Case, perform a social responsibility audit for IBM in each of these areas. Based on the results of your audit, develop suggestions for IBM management about how to focus its future social responsibility efforts.

CASE STUDY: FORD MOTOR CO. GOES GREEN

William Clay Ford Jr., chairman and CEO of Ford, great-grandson of founder Henry Ford, has been a Ford employee since 1979. Still in his early forties, he is sincere, optimistic, open, and an enthusiastic environmentalist. When interviewed by Jeffrey Garten, the author of *The Mind of the C.E.O.*, this is what he had to say about his vision for the future: "When it comes to fuel sources, we hope to lead a clean revolution. The company has certified all its plants around the world under the toughest environmental standards . . . and we have committed to have cars on the road for sale in 2004 running on fuel cells. It means that the only thing that comes out the tailpipe is water vapor."

"I've staked much of my personal reputation on the environment. I wake up sometimes wondering whether I'm the only one who feels this way," says Ford. He worries that he is steering his company on a course that may not pay off in the end. "We are trying to build up a lot of trust," he said, "trust that our product is good, trust that we will stand for something that our customers and employees can be proud of."

In 1997, an Environmental and Public Policy Committee of the Board of Directors was established at Ford and chaired by Bill Ford as part of his Corporate Citizenship Strategy. He wanted to set up a globally responsible foundation for Ford's actions and decisions, and he wanted to inspire his employees while keeping an open dialogue with stakeholders. Ford Motor Company agreed on three priorities to be pursued: improving human rights in the developing nations where Ford does business; persuading the financial markets to place greater value on corporate social efforts, including the environment; and addressing the problem of global warming. In an effort to be more "transparent," Ford voluntarily submitted to outside audits, which was unheard of corporate behavior just a few years ago.

However, in late 1998, all Ford's good intentions were called into question when the public learned of problems with Firestone tires suddenly failing on Ford sport utility vehicles in Venezuela. By August 2000, after extensive investigations by highway safety regu-

lators, the tire problems were blamed for hundreds of accidents, 174 deaths, and 700 injuries in the United States alone. By May 2001, Ford and Firestone were blaming each other for the debacle and parted ways, breaking a 100-year-old business relationship. At a cost of $3 billion, Ford replaced 13 million Firestone tires as a precautionary measure. Ford is planning to recall 47,000 year-2002 SUVs to replace tires damaged during assembly.

For former Ford CEO Jacques Nasser, damage control was the new number one job of his corporate career. In his address on Corporate Citizenship, Nasser said that at one time, businesses believed that "what was good for them was good for the world." He thought that this trend may be reversed and that corporate decisions needed to take into account a consideration for others and their fundamental needs.

Nasser hoped to achieve unprecedented profitability and success by connecting directly with customers. For example, more than 25,000 Ford employees spent a day last year meeting individually with car and truck owners to listen to them talk about their vehicles. In this way the company learned to view both products and services from a customer's perspective. Nasser's "Let's Chat" e-mails to Ford employees received an enthusiastic response, especially in the area of environmental issues. People wanted to feel proud of the company they worked for and wanted to build a better future for their children.

Nasser acknowledged how difficult the tire recall was for everyone, and Ford is now covering tires under the vehicle warranty program. It is also working to create an "early warning system," linked to a computer database of tire information. Ford also introduced a number of shareholder value initiatives in an effort to keep everyone happy.

Ford is now promoting its redesigned 2002 Explorer without any mention of safety—an attempt to steer consumers' thoughts to the good times they'll enjoy as Explorer owners.

Meanwhile, the company continues to try to establish an environmentally friendly image in an effort to sell more cars. It said that it would increase the average fuel economy of its SUVs by 25 percent by 2005, and plans to sell a gasoline-electric hybrid version of the SUV by 2003.

Ford has not explained how it plans to reduce its vehicles' carbon dioxide emissions. The company continues to lobby with other automakers against the environmentalists' CAFE regulation, which would require vehicles to go farther on a gallon of gasoline. Bill Ford admitted in May 2001, "we don't have a game plan yet."

QUESTIONS

1. Which phase of converting organizational policies on social responsibility into action would you say Ford Motor Company is in? Explain.
2. Do you feel that a company like Ford should perform social responsibility activities? Why? Is there any doubt in your mind?
3. What do you think William Clay Ford Jr., should do about the Ford Explorer situation?

▶ **Video**

MASTERING MANAGEMENT: EPISODE 1 — ETHICAL ISSUES

Mastering Management is a series of innovative, interactive learning activities specially designed to help you develop management skills emphasized in various text chapters. Ethics is the major focus of this chapter. Episode 1 of *Mastering Management* focuses on doing the right thing and covers several different areas related to the general topic of ethical behavior in organizations. In this episode, Andrew is faced with a dilemma about whether or not to breach a confidence. How he handles the situation could affect his job, the jobs of others, and the future of CanGo. Review Episode 1 on your *Mastering Management* CD and then answer the following questions.

QUESTIONS

1. Is this ethical issue facing Andrew important to a manager? Why? Why not?

2. Write a Code of Ethics for CanGo that, among other issues, relates to the breach of confidence facing Andrew.

3. If you were Andrew, which one or more of the ethical standards would you use to judge the appropriateness of your behavior in this situation? Why?

www.prenhall.com/certo

This book is accompanied by a rich assortment of online activities aimed at developing your management skills. Reviewing news headlines, Internet exercises, an online study guide, and other research and Internet resources can help personalize management skills development for individual students or an entire class.

chapter

4 Management and Diversity

Advantica Making Great Strides in Building a Diverse Company

REMINDER: THE INTRODUCTORY CASE WRAP-UP (P. 92) CONTAINS DISCUSSION QUESTIONS AND A SKILLS EXERCISE TO FURTHER ILLUSTRATE THE APPLICATION OF CHAPTER CONCEPTS TO THIS VIGNETTE.

Advantica Restaurant Group is working hard to achieve diversity among its employees and (despite some problems) to reflect an appreciation of customers' diversity in the service it provides in its restaurants. The firm recently moved to the number-one spot on Fortune *magazine's "Best Companies for Minorities" list.*

Advantica Restaurant Group, Inc. is one of the largest U.S. restaurant companies including more than 1,800 Denny's restaurants, 480 Coco's, and over 120 Carrows restaurants. Denny's is one of the largest national family restaurant chains in market share and sales volume. Denny's restaurants recently reached the benchmark of operating in all 50 states and 5 foreign countries. Advantica has 22 percent of its Denny's restaurants in California, 11 percent in Florida, and 9 percent in Texas.

Through its Denny's chain, Advantica has suffered some negative publicity regarding alleged racist employees. A black family is suing the Denny's restaurant chain for $10 million claiming that their group of 25 people was refused service. The suit alleges that the family waited for nearly two hours and was ultimately refused service based solely on their race. Rachelle Hood-Phillips, chief diversity officer for Advantica Restaurant Group Inc., apologized for the poor service but asked that people not confuse a delay of service with discrimination. In 1994, Denny's settled a similar suit for $46 million that claimed black customers were denied service or forced to pay in advance.

Advantica has had much to gleam about regarding its diversity efforts. Because the Denny's chain has been making great strides in diversity, Advantica recently gained the number-one position on *Fortune's* "Best Companies for Minorities" list. The following factors helped the company achieve this acclaim: (1) the board of directors consists of 11 directors of which 36 percent are women and people of color, (2) the senior management committee consists of 33 percent women and people of color, and (3) all of Denny's employees, management and nonmanagement, have completed diversity training.

In addition, Advantica's workforce is highly diverse. Of Advantica's more than 46,221 company employees, 48 percent are minorities. Of the minorities, 11 percent are African Americans and 31 percent are Hispanic American. Minorities hold 32 percent of Advantica's restaurant and supervisory positions. Also, minority employees represent 32 percent of Advantica's management team with African Americans, Hispanic Americans, and Asian Pacific Americans accounting for 12 percent, 14 percent, and 6 percent, respectively.

Advantica's management is focusing on building a diverse workplace. Unlike some companies, Advantica is achieving real success in building company diversity. Such success should be a major contributor to long run company viability.

The Introductory Case discusses Advantica Restaurant Group's number-one position on *Fortune's* "Best Companies for Minorities" list. This chapter provides insights on why managers like those at Advantica might set the goal of building a more diversified company and discusses diversity issues and concepts that could impact obtaining that goal. More specifically, the chapter discusses:

1) The definition and social implications of diversity
2) Advantages of diversity in organizations
3) Challenges confronting managers who work with diverse populations
4) Managerial strategies for promoting organizational diversity
5) The role of managers in promoting effective workforce diversity

DEFINING DIVERSITY

Diversity is the degree of basic human differences among a given population. Major areas of diversity are gender, race, ethnicity, religion, social class, physical ability, sexual orientation, and age.

Diversity refers to characteristics of individuals that shape their identities and the experiences they have in society. This chapter provides information about workforce diversity and discusses the strengths and problems of a diverse workforce. Understanding diversity is essential for managers today because managing diversity will undoubtedly constitute a large portion of the management agenda well into the twenty-first century.[1]

This chapter describes some strategies for promoting social diversity in organizations. It also explains how diversity is related to the four management functions. Given the nature of this topic, you will probably find yourself reflecting on diversity as you study future chapters. For example, you will reflect on diversity as you study the legal foundation for developing an inclusive workforce—affirmative action and Equal Employment Opportunity (EEO), discussed in Chapter 12, and ideas about organizational change, discussed in Chapter 13.

The Social Implications of Diversity

Workforce diversity is not a new issue in the United States. People from various other regions and cultures have been immigrating to these shores since colonial times, so the American population has always been a heterogeneous mix of races, ethnicities, religions, social classes, physical abilities, and sexual orientations.[2] These differences—along with the basic human differences of age and gender—comprise diversity. The purpose of exploring diversity issues in a management textbook is to suggest how managers might include diverse employees equally, accepting their differences and utilizing their talents.

Majority group refers to that group of people in the organization who hold most of the positions that command decision-making power, control of resources and information, and access to system rewards.

Minority group refers to that group of people in the organization who are smaller in number or who possess fewer granted rights and lower status than the majority groups.

Majority and Minority Groups   Managers must understand the relationship between two groups in organizations: majority groups and minority groups. **Majority group** refers to that group of people in the organization who hold most of the positions that command decision-making power, control of resources and information, and access to system rewards. Note that the majority is not *always* the group with a numerical majority. **Minority group** refers to that group of people in the organization who are smaller in number or who lack critical power, resources, acceptance, and social status. Together, the minority and majority group members form the entire social system of the organization.

Note that the minority group is not *always* lesser in number than the majority group. For example, women are seen as a minority group in most organizations because they do not have the critical power to shape organizational decisions and to control resources. Moreover, they have yet to achieve full acceptance and social status in most workplaces. In most health care organizations, for instance, women outnumber men. Although men are numerical minorities, however, they are seldom denied social status because white males hold most positions of power in the health care system hierarchy, such as physician and health care administrator.

Managers are becoming more dedicated to seeking a wide range of talents from every group in American culture because they now realize that there are distinct advantages to doing so.[3] For one thing, as you will see in Chapter 17, group decisions often improve the quality of decision making. For another, work groups or teams that can draw on the contributions of a multicultural membership gain the advantage of a larger pool of information and a richer array of approaches to work problems.

Ann Morrison carried out a comprehensive study of 16 private and public organizations in the United States. In the resulting book, *The New Leaders: Guidelines on Leadership Diversity in America,* she outlines the several other advantages of diversity, each of which is discussed here.[4]

There are many ways to define diversity, including age, gender, race, color, religious belief, sexual orientation, and physical ability. Despite the passage of the Americans with Disabilities Act in 1990, only about 25 percent of the 15 million disabled people of working age are employed. Freddy Laboy, who works at a midtown Manhattan Gap store, is one of those. Of the remaining 75 percent, polls indicate that two thirds would like to work.

Gaining and Keeping Market Share

Today managers must understand increasingly diverse markets. Failure to discern customers' preferences can cost a company business in the United States and abroad. Some people argue that one of the best ways to ensure that the organization is able to penetrate diverse markets is to include diverse managers among the organization's decision makers.[5]

Diversity in the managerial ranks has the further advantage of enhancing company credibility with customers. Employing a manager who is of the same gender or ethnic background as customers may imply to those customers that their day-to-day experiences will be understood. One African American female manager found that her knowledge of customers paid off when she convinced her company to change the name of a product it intended to sell at Wal-Mart. "I knew that I had shopped for household goods at Wal-Mart, whereas the CEO of this company, a white, upper-middle class male, had not. He listened to me and we changed the name of the product."

Morrison cites a case in which one company lost an important opportunity for new business in a southwestern city's predominantly Hispanic community. The lucrative business ultimately went to a competitor that had put a Hispanic manager in charge of the project who solicited input from the Hispanic community.

Cost Savings

Companies incur high costs in recruiting, training, relocating, and replacing employees and in providing competitive compensation packages. According to Morrison, Corning Corporation's high turnover among women and people of color was costing the company an estimated $2 million to $4 million a year. Many managers that were questioned for her study felt that the personnel expenses associated with turnover—often totaling as much as two-thirds of an organization's budget—could be cut by instituting diversity practices that would give nontraditional managers more incentive to stay. When nontraditional managers remain with the organization, nontraditional employees at lower levels feel more committed to the company.

In addition to the personnel costs, executives are distressed by the high legal fees and staggering settlements resulting from lawsuits brought by employees who feel they have been discriminated against. For example, $17.7 million in damages was awarded to a woman employed by Texaco who claimed she had been passed over for a management promotion because of her gender. Executives are learning that such sums would be better spent on promoting diversity.

Increased Productivity and Innovation

Many executives quoted in Morrison's study believe productivity is higher in organizations that focus on diversity. These managers have found that employees who feel valued, competent, and at ease in their work setting enjoy coming to work and perform at a high level.

Morrison also cites a study by Donna Thompson and Nancy DiTomaso, which concluded that a multicultural approach has a positive effect on employees' perception of equity. This, in turn, positively affects employees' morale, goal setting, effort, and performance. The managers in Morrison's study also saw innovation as a strength of a diverse workforce.

Better-Quality Management

Morrison also found that including nontraditional employees in fair competition for advancement usually improves the quality of management by providing a wider pool of talent. According to the research she cites, exposure to diverse colleagues helps managers develop breadth and openness.

The quality of management can also be improved by building more effective personnel policies and practices that, once developed, will benefit all employees in the organization, not just minorities. According to Morrison's study, many of the programs initially developed for nontraditional managers resulted in improvements that were later successfully applied throughout the organization. Ideas such as adding training for mentors, upgrading techniques for developing managers, and improving processes for evaluating employees for promotion—all concepts originally intended to help nontraditional managers—were later adopted for wider use. (See Table 4.1 for more information on the advantages of a diverse workforce.)

► Back to the Case

An organization like Advantica that uses the diverse talents of a multicultural workforce can reap many rewards. Some experts believe that one of the best ways for a company like Advantica to capture a diverse customer base is to make sure that its decision makers are a diverse group. For example, Advantica's family restaurants could use menu offerings, internal décor, and employees that reflect the wants and desires of a diverse customer population. Promoting a diverse group of decision makers will ensure a sensitivity to such issues, giving a company like Advantica a better chance of establishing restaurants characterized by such diversity.

The progress of a company like Advantica in its diversity program will enhance the productivity of its diverse workforce. An organization's diversity programs will help a diverse workforce to feel valued and at ease in their work setting thereby performing better than workers who feel that their organization has little respect for them as people. As a result of its required diversity training, Advantica can retain employees, thereby lowering personnel costs related to recruiting and training.

Table 4.1 Advantages of a Diverse Workforce

- ➤ Improved ability to gain and keep market share
- ➤ Cost savings
- ➤ Increased productivity
- ➤ A more innovative workforce
- ➤ Minority and women employees who are more motivated
- ➤ Better quality of managers
- ➤ Employees who have internalized the message that "different" does not mean "less than"
- ➤ Employees who are accustomed to making use of differing worldviews, learning styles, and approaches in the decision-making process and in the cultivation of new ideas
- ➤ Employees who have developed multicultural competencies, such as learning to recognize, surface, discuss, and work through work-related issues pertaining to global, cultural, or intergroup differences
- ➤ A workforce that is more resilient when faced with change

General Electric Values Global Sensitivity

General Electric Aircraft Company has promoted specific values to indicate what management views as effective leadership. According to these guidelines, effective leaders should "have the capacity to develop global brains and global sensitivity." In keeping with this appreciation of global diversity, the company has developed diversity training sessions for all employees.

One especially innovative approach developed by General Electric Aircraft is a program titled "Leveraging Differences (Cultural Diversity)." This program, which uses an Interactive Video Disk (IVD), consists of the following five components:

1. An introduction explains how a company evolves from "homogeneous, to assimilative, to heterogeneous, and finally to multicultural"
2. "Walk a Mile in My Shoes" focuses on problems women face in the workplace

3. "Something I've Always Wanted to Ask You People" gives trainees a chance to express their curiosity about members of other groups, specifically Asians, African Americans, Hispanics, and women
4. "You Decide" presents the trainee with a variety of problem-solving situations that have implications for diversity
5. A summary concludes the video with closing remarks by John Rittenhouse, General Electric's senior vice president

The strengths of this program on IVD are that the components are easily understandable by a wide range of employees, available for use on company time, and require responses from employees. "Leveraging Differences (Cultural Diversity)" reflects management's leadership values statement, which includes the following goals: selecting "the most talented team members available"; fully utilizing people "regardless of race, gender, ethnic origin, culture, or age"; and learning to see "the priority of all aspects of diversity to business success." ∎

CHALLENGES THAT MANAGERS FACE IN WORKING WITH DIVERSE POPULATIONS

As you have seen, there are compelling reasons for an organization to encourage diversity in its workforce. For managers to fully appreciate the implications of promoting diversity, however, they must understand some of the challenges they face in managing a diverse workforce. Changing demographics and several issues arising out of these changes are discussed in the following sections.

Changing Demographics

Demographics are statistical characteristics of a population. Demographics are an important tool that managers can use to study workforce diversity, and they are discussed further in Chapter 8. According to a report done for the U.S. Department of Labor by the Hudson Institute, the workforce and jobs of the twenty-first century will parallel changes in society and in the economy. This report indicates that five demographic issues will be very important to managers in the twenty-first century:[6]

Demographics are statistical characteristics of a population.

▶ Many firms are reaping the advantages of a highly diverse workforce. At Query Object Systems Corporation, a software manufacturer in Roslyn Heights, New York, about a third of the company's 60 highly skilled employees, like those shown here, come from foreign countries including Poland, Kashmir, China, Russia, India, and Ukraine. The chairman and CEO, Robert Thompson, is from Canada, where he was always called Mr. Thompson. At Query Object, he is known as Bob. "It takes a bit of getting used to for those of us who come here from other cultures," he says.

1. The population and the workforce will grow more slowly than at any time since the 1930s
2. The average age of the population and the workforce will rise, and the pool of young workers entering the labor market will shrink
3. More women will enter the workforce
4. Minorities will make up a larger share of new entrants into the labor force
5. Immigrants will represent the largest share of the increase in both the general population and the workforce

The changing demographics of a population over 16 years can give managers insight regarding future diversity management challenges. For example, Figure 4.1 provides four snapshots of selected U.S. population minorities at 10-year intervals over the 1978–2008 period. Four events have had significant impact on these changes: (1) the scarcity of births in the 1920s and 1930s, (2) the baby boom of the 1940s through the 1960s, (3) a modest increase in births from the 1970s through the 1990s, and (4) increased migration to the United States. The effect of migration on the demographic composition of the population is reflected in the rapid growth rate of the Asian and Hispanic percentages. Although growth of these groups is expected to slow from 1998–2008, the projected growth rates for these groups are nevertheless much faster than for other U.S. population groups. Such demographic statistics trends seem to indicate that the ability to handle diversity challenges will be valuable to managers in the future.

Ethnocentrism and Other Negative Dynamics

The changing demographics described in the Hudson Institute's report set in motion certain social dynamics that can interfere with workforce productivity. If an organization is to be successful in diversifying, it must neutralize these dynamics.

Ethnocentrism and Stereotyping   Our natural tendency is to judge other groups less favorably than our own. This tendency is the source of **ethnocentrism,** the belief that one's own group, culture, country, or customs are superior to others'. Two related dynamics are prejudices and stereotypes. A **prejudice** is a preconceived judgment, opinion, or assumption about an issue, behavior, or group of people.[7] **Stereotype** is a positive or negative assessment of members of a group or their perceived attributes. It is important for managers to know

Ethnocentrism is the belief that one's own group, culture, country, or customs are superior to others'.

A **prejudice** is a preconceived judgment, opinion, or assumption about an issue, behavior, individual, or group of people.

A **stereotype** is a positive or negative assessment of members of a group or their perceived attributes.

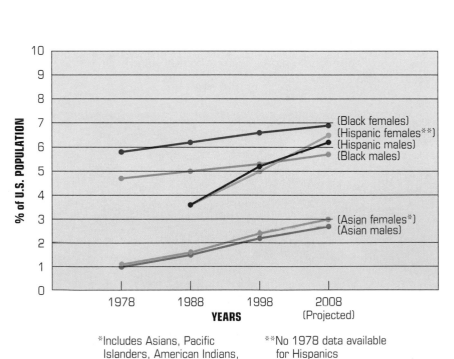

*Includes Asians, Pacific Islanders, American Indians, and Alaska Natives

**No 1978 data available for Hispanics

Figure 4.1   *Percentages of U.S. population over the age of 16 for selected minorities*

AT&T Connects the World

AT&T offers five consumer services to travelers and consumers living outside the United States: AT&T USADirect, AT&T World Connect, AT&T USADirect Service In-Language, AT&T Calling Card, and AT&T TeleTicket Service. The oldest service, USADirect, introduced in 1985, allows users to save on cost when calling the United States from 113 different countries. The newest service, USADirect Service In-Language, is offered to residents in 16 countries. Consumers using this service can make calls to the United States through operators who speak their languages. Both services are drawing more customers—and, consequently, increasing AT&T's need to hire diverse employees. Only 15 months after instituting USADirect Service In-Language, the company had to add 250 Spanish-speaking operators. Similar hiring increases occurred when the service was expanded to appeal to Polish and Hungarian speakers.

African consumers are a large market for the more established USADirect Service. According to Yaw Osei-Amoako, market development manager for Africa in Morristown, New Jersey, more than 50,000 USADirect calls are made per week from Ghana—mostly by Ghanaians calling their U.S. relatives.

With respect to global diversity, Osei-Amoako, himself a Ghanaian, says, "Patience is the key virtue here. The Europeans understand this better than the Americans because of their colonial experience. Americans want to come in, make a deal, go home. The Africans want to get to know you personally, know all about your family, what you like, what you don't like, where you come from."

In Africa, USADirect Service In-Language was initially offered only in Liberia. Now it is available in 10 African countries. Africa is an emerging market that is also being pursued by Sprint and MCI. Its skills in global diversity may give AT&T a competitive edge in this market. ■

---

about these negative dynamics so they can monitor their own perceptions and help their employees view diverse coworkers more accurately.

Discrimination   When verbalized or acted upon, these negative dynamics can cause discomfort and stress for the judged individual. In some cases, there is outright discrimination. **Discrimination** is the act of treating an issue, person, or behavior unjustly or inequitably on the basis of stereotypes and prejudices. Consider the disabled person who is turned down for promotion because the boss feels this employee is incapable of handling the regular travel required for this particular job. The boss's prejudgment of this employee's capabilities on the basis of "difference," and implementation of the prejudgment through differential treatment, constitutes discrimination.

> **Discrimination** is the act of treating an issue, person, or behavior unjustly or inequitably on the basis of stereotypes or prejudices.

Tokenism and Other Challenges   Discrimination occurs when stereotypes are acted upon in ways that affect hiring, pay, or promotion practices—for example, where older employees are steered into less visible job assignments that are unlikely to provide opportunities for advancement. Other challenges facing minorities and women include the pressure to conform to the organization's culture, high penalties for mistakes, and tokenism. **Tokenism** refers to being one of very few members of your group in the organization.[8] "Token" employees are given either very high or very low visibility in the organization. One African American male indicated that he was "discouraged" by his white female manager from joining voluntary committees and task forces within the company—but at the same time criticized in his performance appraisal by her for being "aloof" and taking a "low-profile approach."

> **Tokenism** refers to being one of very few members of a group in an organization.

In other cases, minorities are seen as representatives or "spokespeople" for all members of their group. As such, they are subject to high expectations and scrutiny from members of their own group. One Latino male employee described how other Latinos in the company "looked up to him" for his achievements in the organization. In general, ethnocentrism, prejudices, and stereotypes inhibit our ability to accurately process information.

Negative Dynamics and Specific Groups

The following sections more fully discuss these negative dynamics as they pertain to women, minorities, older workers, and workers with disabilities.

Women   Rosabeth Kanter has researched the pressures women managers face. In her classic study of gender dynamics in organizations, she emphasized the high expectations women have of other women as one of those pressures.[9]

Gender Roles   Women in organizations confront **gender-role stereotypes,** or perceptions about people based on what our society believes are appropriate behaviors for men and

> **Gender-role stereotypes** are perceptions about the sexes based on what society believes are appropriate behaviors for men and women.

▶ Some firms have helped pave the way for women to rise through the management ranks. Though women in positions of power are still rare in the financial world and class-action sexual-discrimination suits have been filed against some prominent firms, at Fiduciary Trust International, a global asset-management firm based in Manhattan, 51 percent of the 700 employees are women, and women hold 30 percent of the senior management positions. Anne M. Tatlock, center front with some of those managers, advises other women, "If you're at a firm that's not interested in creating a culture where you can grow, cut out of there fast."

women. Both sexes find their self-expression constrained by gender-role stereotyping. For example, women in organizations are often assumed to be good listeners. This attribution is based on our societal view that women are nurturing. Although this is a positive assessment, it is not true of all women or of any woman all the time—hence the negative side of this stereotypical expectation for women in the workplace.

Women professionals, for instance, often remark that they are frequently sought out by colleagues who want to discuss non–work-related problems. Women managers also describe the subtle sanctions they experience from both men and women when they do not fulfill expectations that they will be nurturing managers.

The *Glass Ceiling* and Sexual Harassment   A serious form of discrimination affecting women in organizations has been dubbed the *glass ceiling*.[10] The glass ceiling refers to an invisible "ceiling," or barrier to advancement. This term, originally coined to describe the limits confronting women, is also used to describe the experiences of other minorities in organizations. Although both women and men struggle to balance work and family concerns, it is still more common for women to assume primary responsibility for household management as well as their careers, and sometimes they are denied opportunities for advancement because of this stereotype.

Sexual harassment is another form of discrimination that disproportionately affects female employees. *Sexual harassment* is defined as any unwanted sexual language, behavior, or imagery negatively affecting an employee.[11]

Minorities   Racial, ethnic, and cultural minorities also confront inhibiting stereotypes about their group. Like women, they must deal with misunderstandings and expectations based on their ethnic or cultural origins.

Many members of ethnic or racial minority groups have been socialized to be members of two cultural groups—the dominant culture and their particular racial or ethnic culture. Ella Bell, professor of organizational behavior at MIT, refers to this dual membership as *biculturalism*. In her study of African American women, she identifies the stress of coping with membership in two cultures simultaneously as **bicultural stress**.[12] She also indicates that **role conflict**—having to fill competing roles because of membership in two cultures—and **role overload**—having too many expectations to comfortably fulfill—are common characteristics of bicultural stress. Although these are problems for many minority groups, they are particularly intense for women of color. This is because this group experiences negative dynamics affecting *both* minorities and women.

Socialization in one's culture of origin can lead to misunderstandings in the workplace. This is particularly true when a manager relies solely on the cultural norms of the majority group. According to the norms of American culture, for example, it is acceptable—even positive—to publicly praise an individual for a job well done. However, in cultures that place pri-

Bicultural stress is stress resulting from having to cope with membership in two cultures simultaneously.

Role conflict is the conflict that results when a person has to fill competing roles because of membership in two cultures.

Role overload refers to having too many expectations to comfortably fulfill.

mary value on group harmony and collective achievement, this way of rewarding an employee causes emotional discomfort because employees fear that, if praised publicly, they will "lose face" in their group.

Older Workers   Older workers are a significant and valuable component of today's labor force.[13] The "baby boomers" born in the late 1940s and 1950s are now middle aged, while the previous generation of workers is approaching retirement. Organizations need to learn how to tap the rich knowledge and experience of these workers and how to help older workers avoid the occupational stagnation of later careers. These are especially important concerns given the *Workforce 2000* predictions that the supply of younger workers is dwindling and that huge numbers of baby boomers will reach the preretirement phase of their careers simultaneously, creating fierce competition for scarce jobs.

Stereotypes and Prejudices   Older workers present some specific challenges for managers. Stereotypes and prejudices link age with senility, incompetence, and lack of worth in the labor market. Jeffrey Sonnenfeld, an expert on senior executives and older workers, compiled research findings from several studies of older employees. He found that managers view older workers as "deadwood," and seek to "weed them out" through pension incentives, biased performance appraisals, and other methods.[14]

Actually, Sonnenfeld's compilation of research indicates that while older managers are more cautious, less likely to take risks, and less open to change than younger managers, many are high performers. Studies that tracked individuals' careers over the long term conclude that there is a peak in performance around age 45 to 50, and a second peak around 55 to 60. Performance in some fields (e.g., sales) either improves with age or does not significantly decline.

It is the manager's responsibility to value older workers for their contributions to the organization and to see to it that they are treated fairly. This requires an understanding of and sensitivity to the physiological and psychological changes that older workers are experiencing. Supporting older workers also requires paying attention to how performance appraisal processes, retirement incentives, training programs, blocked career paths, union insurance pensions, and affirmative action goals affect this segment of the workforce.

Workers with Disabilities   People with disabilities are subject to the same negative dynamics that plague women, minorities, and older workers. For example, one manager confessed that before he attended diversity training sessions offered through a nearby university, he felt "uncomfortable" around disabled people. One disabled professional reported that she was always received warmly by phone and told that her background was exactly what companies were looking for, but when she showed up for job interviews, she was often rebuffed and informed that her credentials were insufficient.

The stereotyping, prejudice, and discrimination women and minorities often suffer in organizations are summarized in Figure 4.2. Managers who learn to recognize and deal with these negative dynamics will be better prepared to manage a diverse workforce.

STRATEGIES FOR PROMOTING DIVERSITY IN ORGANIZATIONS

This section looks at several approaches to diversity and strategies that managers can consider as they plan for promoting cultural diversity in their organizations. First, the six strategies for modern management offered by the Hudson Institute report focusing on the twenty-first century workforce are explored. Then the requirements of the Equal Employment Opportunity Commission, which is legally empowered to regulate organizations to ensure that management practices enhance diversity, are discussed, along with affirmative action. Finally, the wisdom of moving beyond these legal requirements and striving for pluralism is considered, and five approaches to pluralism are described.

Hudson Institute's Recommended Strategies
According to the Hudson Institute, six major issues demand the full attention of U.S. business leaders of the twenty-first century and require them to take the following actions:[15]

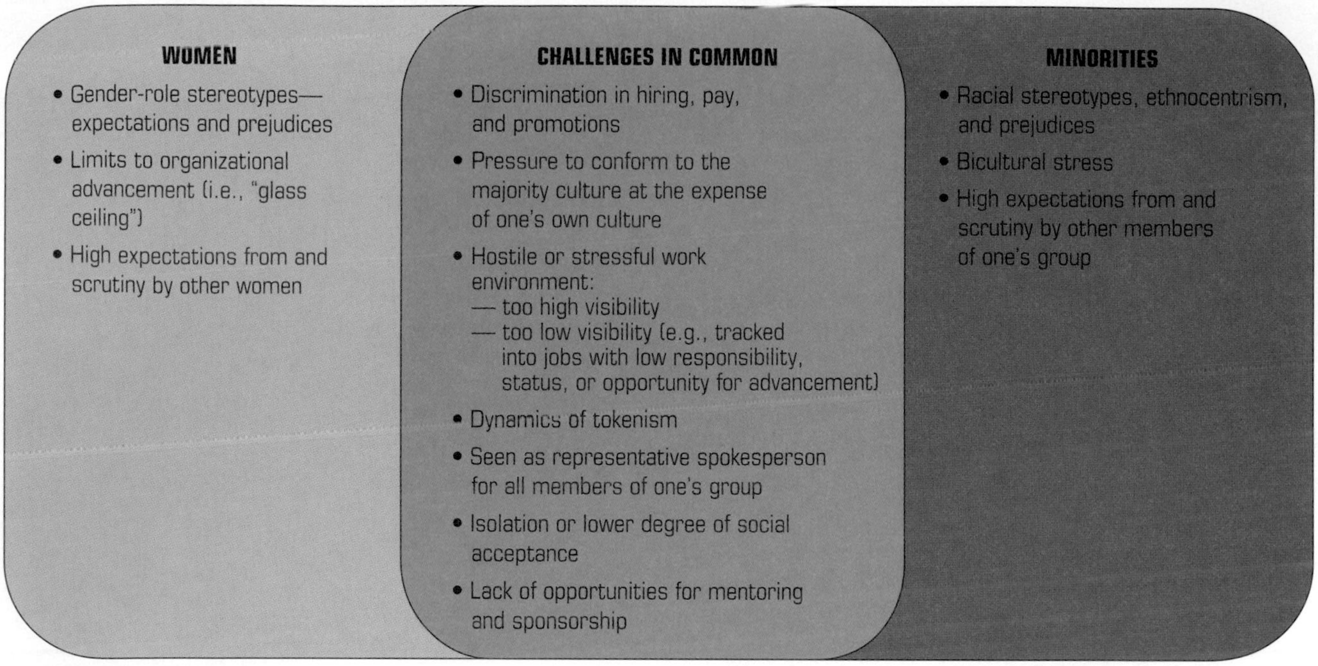

WOMEN	CHALLENGES IN COMMON	MINORITIES
• Gender-role stereotypes—expectations and prejudices • Limits to organizational advancement (i.e., "glass ceiling") • High expectations from and scrutiny by other women	• Discrimination in hiring, pay, and promotions • Pressure to conform to the majority culture at the expense of one's own culture • Hostile or stressful work environment: — too high visibility — too low visibility (e.g., tracked into jobs with low responsibility, status, or opportunity for advancement) • Dynamics of tokenism • Seen as representative spokesperson for all members of one's group • Isolation or lower degree of social acceptance • Lack of opportunities for mentoring and sponsorship	• Racial stereotypes, ethnocentrism, and prejudices • Bicultural stress • High expectations from and scrutiny by other members of one's group

Figure 4.2 *Negative dynamics confronting women and minorities in organizations*

1. *Stimulate balanced world growth*—The United States must pay less attention to its share of world trade and more to the growth of the economies of other nations of the world, including those nations in Europe, Latin America, and Asia with which the United States competes.

2. *Accelerate productivity increases in service industries*—Prosperity will depend much more on how fast output per worker increases in health care, education, retailing, government, and other services than on gains in manufacturing.

3. *Maintain the dynamism of an aging workforce*—As the age of the average American worker climbs toward 40, the nation must make sure that its workforce does not lose its adaptability and willingness to learn.

4. *Reconcile the conflicting needs of women, work, and families*—There has been a huge influx of women into the workforce in the last two decades, but organizational policies covering pay, fringe benefits, time away from work, pensions, welfare, and many other issues do not yet reflect this new reality.

5. *Fully integrate African American and Hispanic workers into the economy*—The decline in the number of "traditional" white male workers among the young, the rapid pace of industrial change, and the rising skill requirements of the emerging economy make the full utilization of minority workers a particularly urgent challenge between now and 2000.

6. *Improve the education and skills of all workers*—Human capital (knowledge, skills, organization, and leadership) is the key to economic growth and competitiveness.

As these key strategies for modern management suggest, many of the most significant managerial challenges that lie ahead derive from dramatic demographic shifts and other complex societal issues. Organizations—and, ultimately, their leaders and managers—will need to clarify their own social values as they confront these dynamics. *Social values,* discussed further in Chapter 8, refer to the relative worth society places on different ways of existence and functions.

The six strategies outlined in the report strongly imply that organizations need to become more inclusive—that is, to welcome a broader mix of employees and to develop an organizational culture that maximizes the value and potential of each worker. As with any major initiative, commitment to developing an inclusive organization begins at the top of the organizational hierarchy. However, on a day-to-day operational basis, each manager's level of commitment is a critical determinant of how well or how poorly the organization's strategies and approaches will be implemented.

Equal Employment and Affirmative Action

The Equal Employment Opportunity Commission (EEOC) is the federal agency that enforces the laws regulating recruiting and other management practices. Chapter 12 contains a more extended discussion of the EEOC. Affirmative action programs are designed to eliminate barriers against and increase opportunities for underutilized or disadvantaged individuals. These programs are positive steps toward promoting diversity and have created career opportunities for both women and minority groups.

Still, organizations can do much more. For example, some employees are hostile toward affirmative action programs because they feel these programs have been misused to create **reverse discrimination**—that is, they discriminate against members of the majority group in order to help groups that are underrepresented in the organization. When management implements appropriate legal approaches but stops short of developing a truly multicultural organization, intergroup conflicts are highly likely.

Reverse discrimination is the term used to describe inequities affecting members of the majority group as an outcome of programs designed to help underrepresented groups.

DIGITAL FOCUS

▶ EEOC Uses Web Site to Inform Managers About Sexual Harassment

As you have learned in this chapter, the EEOC is a federal agency that enforces laws regarding fairness in recruiting and other management practices. The following information about sexual harassment is from the EEOC Web site and appears as an example of how managers can stay informed about EEOC issues by reviewing its Web site.

Facts About Sexual Harassment

Sexual harassment is a form of sex discrimination that violates Title VII of the Civil Rights Act of 1964. Unwelcome sexual advances, requests for sexual favors, and other verbal or physical conduct of a sexual nature constitute sexual harassment when submission to or rejection of this conduct explicitly or implicitly affects an individual's employment, unreasonably interferes with an individual's work performance, or creates an intimidating, hostile, or offensive work environment.

Sexual harassment can occur in a variety of circumstances, including but not limited to the following:

➤ The victim as well as the harasser may be a woman or a man. The victim does not have to be of the opposite sex.
➤ The harasser can be the victim's supervisor, an agent of the employer, a supervisor in another area, a coworker, or a nonemployee.

➤ The victim does not have to be the person harassed but could be anyone affected by the offensive conduct.
➤ Unlawful sexual harassment may occur without economic injury to or discharge of the victim.
➤ The harasser's conduct must be unwelcome.

It is helpful for the victim to directly inform the harasser that the conduct is unwelcome and must stop. The victim should use any employer complaint mechanism or grievance system available.

When investigating allegations of sexual harassment, EEOC looks at the whole record: the circumstances, such as the nature of the sexual advances, and the context in which the alleged incidents occurred. A determination on the allegations is made from the facts on a case-by-case basis.

Prevention is the best tool to eliminate sexual harassment in the workplace. Employers are encouraged to take the steps necessary to prevent sexual harassment from occurring. They should clearly communicate to employees that sexual harassment will not be tolerated. They can do so by establishing an effective complaint or grievance process and taking immediate and appropriate action when an employee complains.

▶ Back to the Case

Legislation and government involvement cannot provide complete direction for building diversity in organizations. Advantica's management understands that organizations should not wait for laws and government to provide guidelines for building a diverse organization. Instead, management of a company like Advantica should recreate the company to reflect the environment in which it operates. For example, given demographics reflecting environmental population trends, Advantica will probably be recruiting and hiring a greater proportion of Asian and Hispanic employees.

(continued)

If an organization like Advantica increases the proportion of Asian and Hispanic employees, company diversity training programs should be modified to include a sensitivity toward factors relevant to the Asian and Hispanic cultures. Factors like religion, values, and behavioral norms specific to these two groups should be emphasized. Such modification of diversity training at Advantica would be aimed at eliminating ethnocentrism within the company relating to these two demographic groups.

Organizational Commitment to Diversity

Figure 4.3 shows the range of organizational commitment to multiculturalism. At the bottom of the continuum are organizations that have committed resources, planning, and time to the ongoing shaping and sustaining of a multicultural organization. At the top of the continuum are organizations that make no efforts whatever to achieve diversity in their workforces. Most organizations fall somewhere between the extremes depicted in the figure.

Ignoring Differences Some organizations make no effort to promote diversity and do not even bother to comply with affirmative action and EEOC standards. They are sending a

---

No diversity efforts:
- Noncompliance with affirmative action and EEOC

Diversity efforts based on:
- Compliance with affirmative action and EEOC policies
- Inconsistent enforcement and implementation (those who breach policies may not be sanctioned unless noncompliance results in legal action)
- Support of policies is not rewarded; organization relies on individual managers' interest or commitment

Diversity efforts based on:
- Compliance with and enforcement of affirmative action and EEOC policies
- No organizational supports with respect to education, training
- Inconsistent or poor managerial commitment

Diversity efforts based on:
- Narrowly defined affirmative action and EEOC policies combined with one-shot education and/or training programs
- Inconsistent managerial commitment; rewards not tied to effective implementation of diversity programs and goal achievement
- No attention directed toward organizational climate

Diversity efforts based on:
- Effective implementation of affirmative action and EEOC policies
- Ongoing education and training programs
- Managerial commitment tied to organizational rewards
- Minimal attention directed toward cultivating an inclusive and supportive organizational climate

Broad-based diversity efforts based on:
- Effective implementation of affirmative action and EEOC policies
- Organization-wide assessment and management's top-down commitment to diversity
- Managerial commitment tied to organizational rewards
- Ongoing processes of organization assessment and programs for the purpose of creating an organizational climate that is inclusive and supportive of diverse groups

Figure 4.3 *Organizational diversity continuum*

strong message to their employees that the dynamics of difference are unimportant. By ignoring EEOC policies, they are sending an even more detrimental message to their managers: that it is permissible to maintain exclusionary practices.

Complying with External Policies   Some organizations base their diversity strategy solely on compliance with affirmative action and EEOC policies. They make no attempt to provide education and training for employees, nor do they use the organization's reward system to reinforce managerial commitment to diversity. Managers in some companies in this category breach company affirmative action and EEOC policies with impunity. When top management does not punish them, the likelihood of costly legal action against the organization rises.

Enforcing External Policies   Some organizations go so far as to enforce affirmative action and EEOC policies, but provide no organizational supports for education or training for diversity. Managerial commitment to a diverse workforce is either weak or inconsistent.

Responding Inadequately   Other organizations fully comply with affirmative action and EEOC policies, but define these policies quite narrowly. Organizational systems and structures are inadequate to support real organizational change. Education and training in diversity are sporadic, and managerial rewards for implementing diversity programs are inconsistent or nonexistent. Although these organizations may design some useful programs, they are unlikely to result in any long-term organizational change, so the organizational climate never becomes truly receptive to diverse groups.

Implementing Adequate Programs   Some organizations effectively implement affirmative action and EEOC policies, provide ongoing education and training programs pertaining to diversity, and tie managerial rewards to success in meeting diversity goals and addressing diversity issues. However, such companies make only a minimal attempt to cultivate the kind of inclusive and supportive organizational climate diverse populations of employees will feel comfortable in.

Taking Effective Action   The most effective diversity efforts are based on managerial implementation of affirmative action and EEOC policies that are developed in conjunction with an organization-wide assessment of the company's systems and structures. Such an assessment is necessary to determine how these systems and structures support or hinder diversity goals.

Generally, for such a comprehensive assessment to take place, top management must "buy" the idea that diversity is important to the company. Actually, support from the top is critical to all successful diversity efforts and underlies tying organizational rewards to managers' commitment to diversity. Ongoing assessment and continuing programs are also necessary to create an organizational climate that is inclusive and supportive of diverse groups.

▶ Back to the Case

In an organization like Advantica, management's commitment to diversity is a significant contributor to the company's diversity success. Certainly, Advantica had to face very difficult diversity-related issues as minority groups began to sue the company alleging discriminatory practices against customers. Such allegations implied that one of Advantica's major restaurant chains, Denny's, was made up of employees who discriminated against blacks. The continued commitment of Advantica's management to diversity programs ultimately assisted the company in receiving the *Fortune* "Best Companies for Minorities" ranking.

In terms of the organizational diversity continuum, Advantica's commitment to diversity seems very broad based. This broad-based commitment is reflected in company-wide practices related to recruiting, hiring, and training a diverse workforce. The broad-based commitment is also evident through Advantica's building of minority representation within influential company groups like the board of directors and the senior management advisory board.

Pluralism

Pluralism is an environment in which cultural, group, and individual differences are acknowledged, accepted, and viewed as significant contributors to the entirety.

Pluralism refers to an environment in which differences are acknowledged, accepted, and seen as significant contributors to the entirety. A diverse workforce is most effective when managers are capable of guiding the organization toward achieving pluralism. Approaches, or strategies, to achieve effective workforce diversity have been classified into five major categories by Jean Kim of Stanford University:[16]

1. "Golden Rule" approach
2. Assimilation approach
3. "Righting-the-wrongs" approach
4. Culture-specific approach
5. Multicultural approach

Each approach is described briefly in the following sections.

"Golden Rule" Approach The "Golden Rule" approach to diversity relies on the biblical dictate, "Do unto others as you would have them do unto you."[17] The major strength of this approach is that it emphasizes individual morality. Its major flaw is that individuals apply the Golden Rule from their own particular frame of reference without knowing the cultural expectations, traditions, and preferences of the other person.

One African American male manager recalled a situation in which he was having difficulty scheduling a work-related event. In exasperation, he volunteered to schedule the event on Saturday. He was reminded by another employee that many of the company's Jewish employees went to religious services on Saturday. He was initially surprised—then somewhat embarrassed—that he had simply assumed that "all people" attended "church" on Sunday.

Assimilation Approach The assimilation approach advocates shaping organization members to fit the existing culture of the organization. This approach pressures employees who do not belong to the dominant culture to conform—at the expense of renouncing their own cultures and worldviews. The end result is the creation of a homogeneous culture that suppresses the creativity and diversity of views that could benefit the organization.

One African American woman in middle management said, "I always felt uncomfortable in very formal meetings. I tend to be very animated when I talk, and this is not the norm for the company. Until I became more comfortable with myself and my style, I felt inhibited. I was tempted to try to change my style to fit in."

"Righting-the-Wrongs" Approach "Righting-the-wrongs" is an approach that addresses past injustices experienced by a particular group. When a group's history places its members at a disadvantage for achieving career success and mobility, policies are developed to create a more equitable set of conditions. For example, the original migration of African Americans to the United States was forced on them as slaves. Righting-the-wrongs approaches are designed to compensate for the damages African Americans have suffered because of historical inequalities.

This approach most closely parallels the affirmative action policies to be discussed in Chapter 12. It goes beyond affirmative action, however, in that it emphasizes tapping the unique talents of each group in the service of organizational productivity.

Culture-Specific Approach The culture-specific approach teaches employees the norms and practices of another culture to prepare them to interact with people from that culture effectively. This approach is often used to help employees prepare for international assignments. The problem with it is that it usually fails to give employees a genuine appreciation for the culture they are about to encounter.

Stewart Black and Hal Gregerson, in their study of managers on assignment in foreign countries, found that some identify much more with their parent firm than with the local operation.[18] One male manager, for instance, after spending two years opening retail outlets throughout Europe, viewed Europeans as "lazy and slow to respond to directives." Obviously, his training and preparation had failed to help him adjust to European host countries or to appreciate their peoples and cultures.

Multicultural Approach The multicultural approach gives employees the opportunity to develop an appreciation for both differences of culture and variations in personal characteristics. This approach focuses on how interpersonal skills and attitudinal changes relate to organizational performance. One of its strengths is that it assumes the organization itself—as well as individuals working within it—will be required to change in order to accommodate the diversity of the organization's workforce.

The multicultural approach is probably the most effective approach to pluralism because it advocates change on the part of management, employees, and organization systems and structures. It has the added advantage of stressing the idea that equity demands making some efforts to "right the wrongs" so that underrepresented groups will be fairly included throughout the organization.

THE ROLE OF THE MANAGER

Managers play an essential role in tapping the potential capacities of each person within their departments. To do this requires competencies that are anchored in the four basic management functions of planning, organizing, influencing, and controlling. In this context, planning refers to the manager's role in developing programs to promote diversity, while organizing, influencing, and controlling take place in the implementation phases of those programs.

Planning

Recall from Chapter 1 that planning is a specific action proposed to help the organization achieve its objectives. It is an ongoing process that includes troubleshooting and continually defining areas where improvements can be made. Planning for diversity may involve selecting diversity training programs for the organization or setting diversity goals for employees within the department.

Setting recruitment goals for members of underrepresented groups is a key component of diversity planning. If top management has identified Hispanics as an underrepresented group within the company, every manager throughout the company will need to collaborate with the human resources department to achieve the organizational goal of higher Hispanic representation. For example, a manager might establish goals and objectives for the increased representation of this group within five years. To achieve this five-year vision, the manager will need to set benchmark goals for each year.

Organizing

According to Chapter 1, organizing is the process of establishing orderly uses for all resources within the management system. To achieve a diverse workplace, managers have to work with human resource professionals in the areas of recruitment, hiring, and retention so that the best match is made between the company and the employees it hires. Managerial responsibilities in this area may include establishing task forces or committees to explore issues and provide ideas, carefully choosing work assignments to support the career development of all employees, and evaluating the extent to which diversity goals are being achieved.

After managers have begun hiring from a diverse pool of employees, they will need to focus on retaining them. This means paying attention to the many concerns of a diverse workforce. In the case of working women and men with families, skillfully using the organization's resources to support their need for day care for dependents, allowing flexible work arrangements in keeping with company policy, and assigning and reassigning work responsibilities equitably to accommodate family leave usage are all examples of managers applying the organizing function.

Influencing

According to Chapter 1, influencing is the process of guiding the activities of organization members in appropriate directions. Integral to this management function are an effective leadership style, good communication skills, knowledge about how to motivate others, and an understanding of the organization's culture and group dynamics. In the area of diversity, influencing organization members means that managers must not only encourage and support employees to participate constructively in a diverse work environment, but must themselves engage in the career development and training processes that will give them the skills to facilitate the smooth operation of a diverse work community.

Managers are accountable as well for informing their employees of breaches of organizational policy and etiquette. Let us assume that the diversity strategy selected by top management includes educating employees about organizational policies concerning diversity (e.g., making sure that employees understand what constitutes sexual harassment) as well as providing workshops for employees on specific cultural diversity issues. The manager's role in this case would be to hold employees accountable for learning about company diversity policies and complying with them. This could be accomplished by consulting with staff and holding regular group meetings and one-on-one meetings when necessary. To encourage participation in diversity workshops, the manager may need to communicate to employees the importance the organization places on this knowledge base. Alternatively, the manager might choose to tie organizational rewards to the development of diversity competencies. Examples of such rewards are giving employees public praise or recognition and providing workers with opportunities to use their diversity skills on desirable work assignments.

Controlling

Overseeing compliance with the legal stipulations of EEOC and affirmative action is one aspect of the controlling function in the area of diversity. According to Chapter 1, controlling is the set of activities that make something happen as planned. Hence the evaluation activities necessary to assess diversity efforts are part of the controlling role that managers play in shaping a multicultural workforce.

Managers may find this function the most difficult one of the four to execute. It is hard to evaluate planned-change approaches in general, and it is particularly hard to do so in the area of diversity. Many times the most successful diversity approaches reveal more problems as employees begin to speak openly about their concerns. Moreover, subtle attitudinal changes in one group's perception of another group are very difficult to measure. What *can* be accurately measured are the outcome variables of turnover; representation of women, minorities, and other underrepresented groups at all levels of the company; and legal problems stemming from inappropriate or illegal behaviors (e.g., discrimination and sexual harassment).

Managers engaged in the controlling function in the area of diversity need to continually monitor their units' progress with respect to diversity goals and standards. They must decide what control measures to use (e.g., indicators of productivity, turnover, absenteeism, or promotion) and how to interpret the information these measures yield in light of diversity goals and standards.

For example, a manager may need to assess whether the low rate of promotions for African American men in her department is due to subtle biases toward this group or group members' poor performance compared to others in the department. She may find she needs to explore current organizational dynamics, as well as create effective supports for this group. Such supports might include fostering greater social acceptance of African American men among other employees, learning more about the African American male's bicultural experience in the company, making mentoring or other opportunities available to members of this group, and providing them with some specific job-related training.

▶ Every manager can have an impact on the way his or her company handles employee diversity. At Coca-Cola Company, as part of a discrimination lawsuit settlement, a seven-member panel has been created to make binding recommendations about how the company hires, promotes, and evaluates employees who are women or minorities. Alexis M. Herman, the former labor secretary, will head the panel.

Management Development and Diversity Training

Given the complex set of managerial skills needed to promote diversity, it is obvious that managers themselves will need organizational support if the company is to achieve its diversity goals. One important component of the diversity strategy of a large number of companies is diversity training. **Diversity training** is a learning process designed to raise managers' awareness and develop their competencies to deal with the issues endemic to managing a diverse workforce.

Diversity training is a learning process designed to raise managers' awareness and develop their competencies to deal with the issues endemic to managing a diverse workforce.

Basic Themes of Diversity Training **Training** is the process of developing qualities in human resources that will make them more productive and better able to contribute to organizational goal attainment. Some companies develop intensive programs for management and less intensive, more generalized programs for other employees. Such programs are discussed further in Chapter 12 and generally focus on the following five components or themes:

Training is the process of developing qualities in human resources.

1. Behavioral awareness
2. Acknowledgment of biases and stereotypes
3. Focus on job performance
4. Avoidance of assumptions
5. Modification of policy and procedure manuals

Stages in Managing a Diverse Workforce Donaldson and Scannell, authors of *Human Resource Development: The New Trainer's Guide*, have developed a four-stage model to describe how managers progress in managing a diverse workforce.[19] In the first stage, known as "unconscious incompetence," managers are unaware of behaviors they engage in that are problematic for members of other groups. In the second stage, "conscious incompetence," managers go through a learning process in which they become conscious of behaviors that make them incompetent in their interactions with members of diverse groups.

The third stage is one of becoming "consciously competent": Managers learn how to interact with diverse groups and cultures by deliberately thinking about how to behave. In the last stage, "unconscious competence," managers have internalized these new behaviors and feel so comfortable relating to others different from themselves that they need to devote little conscious effort to doing so:

> *Managers who have progressed to the "unconscious competence" stage will be the most effective with respect to interacting in a diverse workforce. Effective interaction is key to carrying out the four management functions previously discussed.*

Table 4.2 summarizes our discussion of the challenges facing those who manage a diverse workforce. Managers, who are generally responsible for controlling organizational goals and outcomes, are accountable for understanding these diversity challenges and recognizing the dynamics described here. In addition to treating employees fairly, they must influence other employees to cooperate with the company's diversity goals.

Organizational Challenges and Supports Related to Managing a Diverse Workforce — Table 4.2

Organizational Challenges	Organizational Supports
Employee's Difficulties in Coping with Cultural Diversity	**Educational Programs and Training to Assist Employees in Working Through Difficulties**
➤ Resistance to change	**Top-Down Management Support for Diversity**
➤ Enthnocentrism	➤ Managers who have diversity skills and competence
➤ Lack of information and misinformation	➤ Education and training
➤ Prejudices, biases, and stereotypes	➤ Awareness raising
Reasons Employees Are Unmotivated to Understand Cultural Differences	➤ Peer support
➤ Lack of time and energy and unwillingness to assume the emotional risk necessary to explore issues of diversity	➤ Organizational climate that support diversity
➤ Absence of social or concrete rewards for investing in diversity work (e.g., lack of peer support and monetary rewards, unclear linkage between multicultural competence and career mobility)	➤ Open communication with manager about diversity issues
➤ Interpersonal and intergroup conflicts arising when diversity issues are either ignored or mismanaged	➤ Recognition for employee development of diversity skills and competencies
Work Group Problems	➤ Recognition for employee contributions to diversity goals
➤ Lack of cohesiveness	➤ Organizational rewards for managers' implementation of organizational diversity goals and objectives
➤ Communication problems	
➤ Employee stress	

Understanding and Influencing Employee Responses Managers cannot rise to the challenge of managing a diverse workforce unless they recognize that many employees have difficulties in coping with diversity. Among these difficulties are natural resistance to change, ethnocentrism, and lack of information and outright misinformation about other groups, as well as prejudices, biases, and stereotypes. Some employees lack the motivation to understand and cope with cultural differences—which requires time, energy, and a willingness to take some emotional risks.

Another problem is that employees often receive no social rewards (e.g., peer support and approval) or concrete rewards (e.g., financial compensation or career opportunities) for cooperating with the organization's diversity policies.

For all these difficulties, managers cannot afford to ignore or mismanage diversity issues because the cost of doing so is interpersonal and intergroup conflicts. These conflicts very often affect the functioning of the work group by destroying cohesiveness and causing communications problems and employee stress.

Managers who are determined to deal effectively with their diverse workforce can usually obtain organizational support. One primary support is education and training programs designed to help employees work through their difficulties in coping with diversity. Besides recommending such programs to their employees, managers may find it helpful to enroll in available programs themselves.

Getting Top-Down Support Another very important source of support for managers dealing with diversity issues is top management. Organizations that provide top-down support are more likely to boast the following features:

1. Managers skilled at working with a diverse workforce
2. Effective education and diversity training programs
3. An organizational climate that promotes diversity and fosters peer support for exploring diversity issues
4. Open communication between employees and managers about diversity issues
5. Recognition for employees' development of diversity skills and competencies
6. Recognition for employee contributions to diversity goals
7. Organizational rewards for managers' implementation of organizational diversity goals and objectives

▶ Back to the Case

Consistent with diversity initiatives in most organizations, Advantica managers are given extensive diversity training. Managers in a company like Advantica who know how to interact with people of different cultures will be the most successful in building productive multi-cultural teams in organizations. Overall, diversity training for managers in a company like Advantica is aimed to help managers become more sensitive to other cultures and thereby more capable of using planning, organizing, influencing, and controlling skills to help organizations meet diversity goals.

In addition to managers, non-managers within organizations can be a focus of specially designed diversity training. Mentioned earlier, Denny's restaurant chain has faced allegations of discriminatory practices against customers of color. Perhaps partially in attempting to make the chain more sensitive to customers of color as well as other minority groups, all of Denny's non-management employees were required to complete a specially designed diversity training program.

Focusing on workforce composition can help a restaurant chain like Denny's to minimize discrimination against minority groups. Building a workforce more reflective of minority groups in the environment should help management of any organization to lessen discrimination against customers who are members of those groups. For example, building a workforce with notable proportions of African Americans, Hispanic Americans, and Asian Pacific Americans should help to lower the probability of customers from these groups being discriminated against.

Management Skills Module

This section is specially designed to help you develop management skills. An individual's management skill is based on an understanding of management concepts and the ability to apply those concepts in management situations. As a result, the following activities are designed both to heighten your understanding of management concepts and to help you gain facility in applying those concepts in various management situations.

UNDERSTANDING MANAGEMENT CONCEPTS

▶ Action Summary

Reread the learning objectives below. Each objective is followed by questions. Answering these questions accurately will help you retain the most important concepts discussed in this chapter. After answering each question, check your answer against the answer key at the end of this chapter. (*Hint:* If you have any doubts regarding the correct response, consult the page number that follows the answer.)

Circle:

From studying this chapter, I will attempt to acquire

1. A definition of diversity and an understanding of its importance in the corporate structure.

T F   **a.** Diversity refers to characteristics that shape people's identities and the experiences they have in society.

a b c d e   **b.** The following is *not* true of workforce diversity: (a) it is a new issue (b) it stems from workforce demographics (c) it involves developing an inclusive organization (d) it includes age and physical ability (e) it is a strength that can be built on.

2. An understanding of the advantages of having a diverse workforce.

a b c d e   **a.** All of the following are advantages of a diverse workforce *except:* (a) employees who develop multicultural competencies (b) cost savings (c) similarity in thinking and approaches (d) increased productivity (e) improved ability to gain and keep market share.

T F   **b.** A diverse workforce results in a "better quality of management" because managers are recruited from a wider pool of talent.

3. An awareness of the challenges facing managers within a diverse workforce.

a b c d e   **a.** Challenges facing American corporations include all of the following *except:* (a) the need to look beyond traditional sources of personnel (b) the need to assess the opportunities suggested by demographic projections (c) the need to adapt to changes in the structure of the workforce (d) the need to prepare for a huge influx of younger workers (e) the need to improve the educational preparation of all workers.

a b c d e   **b.** The following is a potential challenge facing American business leaders: (a) reconciling the conflicting needs of women, work, and families (b) fully assimilating into the economy African American and Hispanic workers (c) maintaining the dynamism of an aging workforce (d) accelerating productivity increases in service industries (e) all of the above.

a b c d e   **c.** The dynamics of coping with diverse populations include: (a) "the glass ceiling" (b) tokenism (c) bicultural stress (d) ethnocentrism (e) all of the above.

4. An understanding of the strategies for promoting diversity in organizations.

T F   **a.** Following the appropriate affirmative action and EEOC guidelines will resolve intergroup conflicts and result in an effectively diverse organization.

a b c d e   **b.** The following is true regarding strategies for promoting diversity in organizations: (a) organizations vary widely with respect to the strategies they employ (b) all organizations comply with affirmative action and EEOC guidelines (c) exclusionary practices have no effect on an organization (d) diversity programs always result in comprehensive culture change (e) all of the above.

5. Insights into the role of the manager in promoting diversity in the organization.

a b c d e   **a.** A manager engaged in the four functions of management with respect to diversity might take all of the following actions *except:* (a) establishing hiring goals for specific, underrepresented groups (b) granting family leave time (c) communicating the importance of diversity training (d) letting employees know they are not accountable for knowing diversity-related policies (e) assessing progress toward diversity goals.

T F   **b.** In a diverse organization, the highest level of diversity competence is described as "conscious competence."

❯ Action Summary Answer Key

1. a. T, p. 74	**3. a.** d, pp. 77–80
b. a, p. 74	**b.** e, pp. 77–80
2. a. c, pp. 75–76	**c.** e, pp. 77–80
b. T, p. 76	

4. a. F, p. 83	**5. a.** d, pp. 87–88
b. a, pp. 84–85	**b.** F, p. 89

❯ Issues for Review and Discussion

1. What is diversity?
2. Why is diversity an important contemporary management issue?
3. List the six challenges facing American businesses according to the Hudson Institute study.
4. Define *pluralism*.
5. Describe the five major approaches organizations can employ in responding to diversity.
6. List the advantages of a diverse workforce.
7. List the managerial challenges presented by a diverse workforce.

8. Give a detailed description of the dynamics encountered by diverse populations in the workplace.
9. Outline the organizational supports available to help managers address the challenges of a diverse workforce.
10. Describe the range of strategies organizations employ to implement workforce diversity.
11. Explain the concept of reverse discrimination.
12. What is the relationship between the four management functions and the implementation of diversity goals?
13. Why should managers undergo diversity training?
14. What is the meaning of "unconscious competence" and why is it desirable for managers?

APPLYING MANAGEMENT CONCEPTS

❯ Cases

➤ INTRODUCTORY CASE WRAP-UP

❯Case Discussion Questions

"Advantica Making Great Strides in Building a Diverse Company" (p. 73) and its related Back-to-the Case sections were written to help you better understand the management concepts contained in this chapter. Answer the following discussion questions about this Introductory Case to enrich your understanding of the chapter content:

1. How important is having a diverse workforce to Advantica? Discuss fully.
2. How would you control diversity activities at Advantica if you were top management?
3. As Advantica's top management, what steps would you take to build commitment for diversity throughout the organization? Be as specific as possible.

❯Skills Exercise: Defending Advantages of a Diverse Workforce

The Introductory Case on Advantica emphasizes management's success in building a diverse organization. Using Table 4.1 as a guide, present an argument outlining how a diverse workforce at Advantica would contribute to organizational success. In your argument, list the items in the table that you believe will contribute to the success and explain why. Also list items in the table that you think will not contribute to the success and explain why.

On February 3, 2000, president and CEO of CBS Leslie Moonves signed a pact with Kweisi Mfume, president and CEO of the National Association for the Advancement of Colored People (NAACP), who had joined forces with the Hispanic Media Coalition, the Asian Pacific American Media Coalition, and the American Indians in Film and Television to request that CBS help to increase ethnic presence in the television industry. The agreement stipulated that CBS would increase minority participation both on- and off-screen by June 30, 2000.

In April 2000, CBS announced the appointment of Josie Thomas to the newly created position of Senior Vice President of Diversity at CBS Television. Her job was to improve outreach and recruitment, hiring, promotion, and mentoring practices in all divisions of CBS. That fall Moonves announced that 16 of the 21 CBS shows, including news magazines, would prominently feature minorities. "We think we are a leader in this area," Moonves said. "We think we are ahead of the curve."

Despite Moonves's statement that as "broadcasters, we believe strongly that it is our duty to reflect the public that makes up our viewing audience," there were many who did not feel the company was sincere in its efforts to improve hiring practices. The National Hispanic Foundation for the Arts criticized CBS for not scheduling "American Family," a pilot drama about a middle class Hispanic family. Moonves said "American Family" simply did not fit in CBS's schedule, since there were already too many strong dramas planned. He said he took the unusual step of allowing the show's producers to pitch the CBS-developed networks but no one picked it up. Meanwhile, the June 30 deadline had come and gone without much outward sign of change at CBS Television.

Josie Thomas is committed to CBS's new mandate for multicultural diversity. Twelve of CBS's prime-time series will have minorities in permanent roles and other series will have a minority in a recurring role. Four of the network's shows—*C.S.I., The District, The Fugitive,* and *Welcome to New York* have minorities in leading roles.

Since signing the agreement, CBS has established a strong working relationship with the National Minority Supplier Council in order to help minority and women's businesses. The company has bolstered its internship program to include paid internships on the West Coast, pairing up interns with their areas of interest, such as finance or entertainment. There are 10 minority interns in the program. Moreover, CBS has now made diversity a factor in employee job performance evaluation. "Each area of the network has developed a detailed plan for diversity," said Thomas. "Managers will be reviewed with respect to their diversity efforts and that will be a factor in compensation decisions." Ms. Thomas noted that Ghen Maynard, an Asian American Pacific Islander, had just been promoted from director to vice president of alternative programming for the entertainment division.

"We all believe there is a long way to go," Thomas said. "What I have found is there are some things that already exist that are positive, such as newsmagazines having minority anchors. We think *City of Angels'* renewal was an important step. The ratings were mediocre to low, and we did feel the program was a risk. It says a lot about our commitment."

In June 2001, the coalition gave the Big 4 Broadcast Networks (all of whom had signed an agreement) a report card for their efforts to diversify shows on-air and behind the scenes. CBS got a D-plus.

Mr. Nogales, of the National Hispanic Media Coalition, said he was disappointed. "We expect progress; we signed for progress." "The numbers in comparison to last year actually look better," Nogales says. "There have been gains for people of color. There was movement. But it has to be movement across the board, not just for one group." He is referring to the fact that most of the gains have been made by black actors, writers, and producers. Black actors appear as regulars in at least 19 of the six major networks' 30 new prime-time series. Hispanics show up in only eight, Asians in five, and Native Americans in one.

The pressure being put on the networks—including threats of "boycott" and "legal action"—is having results. At CBS the number of minority writers and producers has more than tripled, from four to fourteen, including six executive or coexecutive producers. However, obstacles to a fully integrated future remain serious—particularly because of misconceptions about the nature of the television audience and about the way pop culture works. Network executives worry that "ghetto shows" might promote stereotypes. They wonder if shows like *The Cosby Show* are "black" enough. Then again, they think that casting too many minorities may drive white viewers away. Some network executives are afraid to cast minority actors in "negative" roles because they may be criticized for it. Minority writers, who have been getting more work lately, wonder if they are not just "tokens"; and despite some progress it is still almost impossible for Hispanic actors to get non-Hispanic roles.

Both the NAACP and the Coalition have been battling discrimination for years. CBS is just finding out that a profound change toward pluralism can take place only with true insight on the part of management. CBS spokesperson Chris Ender says, "We have made tremendous strides to increase diversity on screen, behind the camera and in the executive suites. However, we certainly recognize that more can be done and more will be done."

As far as Nogales is concerned, "It's still a white guy's world," and the June 2001 statistics for network television prove he is right.

QUESTIONS

1. What advantages would accrue to CBS if it became a more diverse workplace?
2. Where would you have placed CBS on the organizational diversity continuum (Figure 4.3) in 1999, and where would you place CBS now? Why?
3. Which approach(es) to pluralism best sums up the diversity policy that is being developed at CBS? Explain.
4. How do the attitudes of management at CBS as depicted in your case study affect the company's progress toward forming a more diverse workforce? Explain.

CONMEDIA SEGMENT 2
Management and Diversity

Segment two in the Conmedia company videos opens at the Allaboutself.com office just as six members of the staff are gathering for a meeting. Everyone is guessing that their boss, Mia Cipriano, has bad news for them. In segment one you learned that their dot-com has just been sold to a conglomerate that owns a variety of publications. It seems they have been through some ups and downs together before. On the whole, the group feels valued and respected by Mia and is open with her. You will notice that unlike the employees we met at Conmedia, these people are not all white. Their opening comments will make it possible for you to understand each individual's response to this potentially threatening change. Keep in mind that diversity is still an emotionally charged issue for many of us.

Notice how Mia puts a positive spin on the merger and easily quiets Brian's fears that he will no longer be needed. When Joan raises the issue a lack of diversity at Conmedia, Mia is genuinely concerned. The next scene finds Mia in an important meeting she has requested with Sam, Ruth, and Ashley.

Notice Sam's initial reaction to Mia's questions about Conmedia's policy on diversity as well as to his later comments about his own role in the merger. Sam's attitude will help you assess management's commitment to diversity. As Ruth reveals the various problems that Conmedia has had in fostering *pluralism* such as the absence of training programs and internships, consider some possible solutions. The dynamic between Mia, Ruth, and Ashley will provide you with information about the future development of a multicultural workforce at Conmedia.

QUESTIONS

1. Using the organizational diversity continuum as a guide, would you say Conmedia has responded to affirmative action and EEOC policies adequately or inadequately? Explain your answers based on the dialogue between Mia, Ruth, Sam, and Ashley in this segment. Include Mia's allusion to the glass ceiling in your answer.

2. Which approach or combination of approaches to pluralism do you think would work best when Conmedia and Allabout.com merge?

3. How important is getting top-down support for managers like Ruth and Mia who want to create an environment of acceptance and growth? Do you think they will get it at Conmedia?

4. How do you think Joan, Brian, and Kim will feel working for Conmedia?

DIVERSITY AND *YOU*

You are a white middle-class student attending a state college. It is spring semester of your junior year and you are working part-time for a limousine service to help pay tuition. You get a call to pick up a visiting CEO who is staying at the most expensive hotel in town. You are asked to drive this senior executive to a country club to address a large business association. When you arrive at the hotel there is a Hispanic looking man on the corner dressed in a white linen jacket and tan pants with a leather travel bag over his shoulder. You don't see anyone who looks like a CEO, so you radio your boss that your fare is a "no show." Then the man motions to you. He *is* the CEO.

1. Did you judge him because he was casually dressed or because he was Hispanic? Why? Did you have a preconception of what a CEO should look like? Do you think of yourself as being prejudiced? Do you think of yourself as being ethnocentric? How might your mistake help you to be more sensitive to a diverse workforce in your future career as a manager?

www.prenhall.com/certo

This book is accompanied by a rich assortment of online activities aimed at developing your management skills. Reviewing news headlines, Internet exercises, an online study guide, and other research and Internet resources can help personalize management skills development for individual students or an entire class.

5 Managing in the Global Arena

Wal-Mart Goes to Japan

REMINDER: THE INTRODUCTORY CASE WRAP-UP (P. 119) CONTAINS DISCUSSION QUESTIONS AND A SKILLS EXERCISE TO FURTHER ILLUSTRATE THE APPLICATION OF CHAPTER CONCEPTS TO THIS VIGNETTE.

Wal-Mart looks abroad to continue the rapid expansion it achieved under the leadership of its late founder and CEO, Sam Walton. With stores in nine foreign countries to date, the retail chain now looks to Japan.

When Sam Walton opened the first Wal-Mart store in 1962, it was the beginning of an American success story that has become famous throughout the world. As evidence of the success of Wal-Mart, the company recently appeared on *Fortune* magazine's list of "The World's Most Admired Companies," a list compiled by surveying industry executives as well as Wall Street analysts. Today, Wal-Mart has about 3,800 stores scattered throughout the 50 states and nine foreign countries. The company is the nation's largest private employer, with a staggering 1.1 million associates.

Walton had had experience in operating variety stores in small towns in Arkansas and Missouri, and based on this experience, he was convinced that consumers would be drawn to a discount store offering a wide variety of merchandise that was accompanied by friendly service. Walton was absolutely correct.

In a few decades, Wal-Mart has become the world's number-one retailer. Company growth has come not only from the success of the original Wal-Mart concept, but also from diversified concepts such as the availability of grocery products to customers in Wal-Mart Supercenters and general merchandise being offered in countries like Brazil, Argentina, and China. Also, SAM'S Clubs (a subsidiary of Wal-Mart), membership warehouse clubs, have undoubtedly aided company growth.

Upon Sam Walton's death in 1992, many company analysts were concerned that Wal-Mart was coming upon hard times. Analysts believed that Sam Walton was the personification of Wal-Mart's positive corporate culture and that without him it would erode. Time has shown, however, that the culture does not seem to have eroded, and indeed appears as strong or even stronger now than ever. Store openings are still conducted with high enthusiasm and operating stores look better than ever. The company cheer is still done regularly at store openings and meetings—the only difference is that now the cheer is done in many different countries and in many different languages.

John Menzer is president and CEO of Wal-Mart's international division and is responsible for executing Wal-Mart's international strategies. Menzer did not have direct responsibility for international operations prior to his appointment, but did serve as the company's CFO for three years. Menzer's challenges include overseeing the opening of 100 to 110 new units in existing foreign markets, while planning an entry into the Japanese marketplace. Anonymous sources claim that Wal-Mart has begun recruiting employees and scouting store locations in Japan. Japan's status as the world's second largest economy makes this new marketplace very promising for Wal-Mart. However, the recent opening of Japanese stores by competitor Costco indicates that success in Japan may not be as easy for Wal-Mart as the company would like.

The Introductory Case illustrates several steps that Wal-Mart has taken to maintain its growth. Perhaps the boldest of these steps is opening stores in foreign countries. Such a move toward expanding its international presence, however, seems consistent with the trend among many managers throughout the world. The material in this chapter provides insights into the challenges that a manager like John Menzer, CEO of Wal-Mart's international division, faces in this expansion, and provides an overview of the international management area. Major topics covered include the need to manage internationally, the multinational corporation and its workforce, management functions and multinational corporations, transnational organizations, and special issues in international management.

MANAGING ACROSS THE GLOBE: WHY?

Most U.S. companies see great opportunities in the international marketplace today.[1] Although the U.S. population is growing slowly, but steadily the population in many other countries is exploding. For example, it has been estimated that in 1990, China, India, and Indonesia together had more than 2 billion people, or 40 percent of the world's population.[2] Obviously, such countries offer a strong profit potential for aggressive businesspeople throughout the world.

This potential does not come without serious risk, however. Managers who attempt to manage in a global context face formidable challenges. Some of these challenges are the cultural differences among workers from different countries, different technology levels from country to country, and laws and political systems that can vary immensely from one nation to the next.

The remaining sections of this chapter deal with the intricacies of managing in a global context by emphasizing the following:

1. Fundamentals of international management
2. Categories of organizations by international involvement
3. Comparative management (with an emphasis on Japanese management)

FUNDAMENTALS OF INTERNATIONAL MANAGEMENT

International management is the performance of management activities across national borders.

International management is simply the performance of management activities across national borders. It entails reaching organizational objectives by extending management activities to include an emphasis on organizations in foreign countries. The trend toward increased international management, or *globalization,* is now widely recognized. The primary question for most firms is not *whether* to globalize, but *how* and *how fast* to do so and how to measure global progress over time.[3]

International management can take several different forms, from simply analyzing and fighting competition in foreign markets to establishing a formal partnership with a foreign company. AMP, Inc., for example, has been vigorously fighting competition in a foreign market. This company, a manufacturer of electrical parts, headquartered in Harrisburg, Pennsylvania, has achieved outstanding success by gaining significant control over a portion of its multinational market. The company built factories in 17 countries because experience showed management that competitors could best be beaten in foreign markets if AMP actually produced products within those markets. A message recently sent to AMP stockholders by company president William J. Hudson indicates that the company is continuing to make good progress in the international arena. Hudson has promised to persist in his efforts to develop AMP into a "globe-able" organization.[4]

An example of a formal international partnership involves Toshiba Corporation and Time Warner. Toshiba Corporation, a Japanese computer manufacturer, and Time Warner, a communications conglomerate that owns a major Hollywood film studio, formed a partnership to develop a new technology for presenting movies to consumers. This technology, now available in the marketplace, called digital video disc (DVD). In a natural division of labor, Toshiba focused on making the hardware needed to deliver the new technology, and Time Warner provided the movies to be presented on DVD. Both companies hoped the partnership would give them an edge over formidable competitors like Sony.[5]

The notable trend that already exists in the United States and other countries toward developing business relationships in and with foreign countries is expected to accelerate even more in the future. As Figure 5.1 illustrates, U.S. investment in foreign countries and investment by foreign countries in the United States has grown since 1982 and is expected to continue growing, with only slight slowdowns or setbacks in recessionary periods. As an interesting side note, in the 1990s the growth rate of foreign investment in developing countries like India and China has increased, while the growth rate of foreign investment in the United States, Japan, and the European Community has slowed somewhat.[6] Information of this nature has spurred both management educators and practicing managers to insist that a knowledge of international management is necessary for a thorough understanding of the contemporary fundamentals of management.[7]

▶ Back to the Case

As the Introductory Case shows, Wal-Mart is an organization involved in international management. The company now operates in countries like China and Brazil, and has recently decided to expand into Japan. Manager John Menzer will be performing international management activities in a number of countries, and given today's trend toward greater foreign investment, Wal-Mart is likely to continue to emphasize global expansion. In addition, it is likely that foreign companies will attempt to compete with Wal-Mart in the United States.

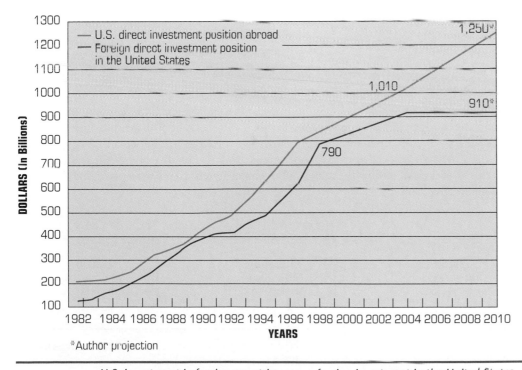

*Author projection

U.S. investment in foreign countries versus foreign investment in the United States

Figure 5.1

A number of different categories have evolved to describe the extent to which organizations are involved in the international arena. These categories are domestic organizations, international organizations, multinational organizations, and transnational or global organizations. As Figure 5.2 suggests, this categorization format actually describes a continuum of international involvement, with domestic organizations representing the least and transnational organizations the most international involvement. Although the format may not be perfect, it is very useful for explaining primary ways in which companies operate in the international realm.[8] The following sections describe these categories in more detail.

Domestic Organizations

A **domestic organization** is a company that essentially operates within a single country.

Domestic organizations are organizations that essentially operate within a single country. These organizations normally not only acquire necessary resources within a single country but also sell their goods or services within that same country. Although domestic organizations may occasionally make an international sale or acquire some needed resource from a foreign supplier, the overwhelming bulk of their business activity takes place within the country where they are based.

Although this category is not determined by size, most domestic organizations today are quite small. Even smaller business organizations, however, are following the trend and becoming increasingly involved in the international arena.

International Organizations

An **international organization** is a company primarily based within a single country but having continuing, meaningful transactions in other countries.

International organizations are organizations that are primarily based within a single country but have continuing, meaningful international transactions—such as making sales and/or purchases of materials—in other countries. Nu Horizons is an example of a small company that can be classified as an international organization. This distributor of electronic goods made mainly by some 40 U.S. manufacturers has about 5,000 customers and is the fastest-growing company in Melville, New York. Nu Horizons is an international organization because an important part of its business is to act as the primary North American distributor of electronic components made by Japan's NIC Components Corp.[9]

In summary, international organizations are more extensively involved in the international arena than are domestic organizations, but less so than either multinational or transnational organizations.

Multinational Organizations: The Multinational Corporation

The *multinational organization,* commonly called the *multinational corporation* (MNC), represents the third level of international involvement. This section of the text defines the multinational corporation, discusses the complexities involved in managing such a corporation, describes the risks associated with its operations, explores the diversity of the multinational workforce, and explains how the major management functions relate to managing the multinational corporation.

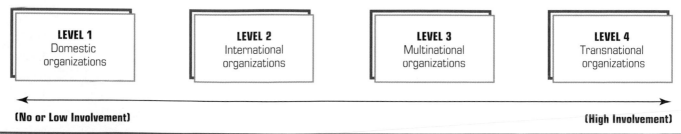

| LEVEL 1 Domestic organizations | LEVEL 2 International organizations | LEVEL 3 Multinational organizations | LEVEL 4 Transnational organizations |

(No or Low Involvement) ⟶ (High Involvement)

Figure 5.2   *Continuum of international involvement*

Defining the Multinational Corporation

The term *multinational corporation* first appeared in American dictionaries around 1970, and has since been defined in various ways in business publications and textbooks. For the purposes of this text, a **multinational corporation** is a company that has significant operations in more than one country. Essentially, a multinational corporation is an organization that is involved in doing business at the international level. It carries out its activities on an international scale that disregards national boundaries, and it is guided by a common strategy from a corporation center.[10]

A **multinational corporation** (MNC) is a company that has significant operations in more than one country.

Several companies listed on the *Forbes* Global 500 are presented in Table 5.1. These multinationals are some of America's most powerful and appear on this list as a result of combined tabulation of company sales, profits, market value, and total assets. Foreign sales as a percent of total sales indicates how very important global operations are to managers in these companies.

A list of the 12 largest foreign investments in the United States (see Table 5.2) includes an investment in Shell Oil by Royal Dutch/Shell Oil, an investment in BP America by British Petroleum, and an investment in MCI Communications by British Telecommunications. Other significant investments on the list include those in popular companies like Burger King, Pillsbury, Sony Electronics, Tyco, Siemens, and Verizon Wireless. Foreign investment in the United States has reached a record high in recent years and will almost certainly continue to grow significantly in the future.

Neil H. Jacoby explains that companies go through six stages to reach the highest degree of multinationalization. As Table 5.3 indicates, multinational corporations can range from slightly multinationalized organizations that simply export products to a foreign country to highly multinationalized organizations that have some of their owners in other countries. According to Alfred M. Zeien, CEO of Gillette Company, it can take up to 25 years to build a management team with the requisite skills, experience, and abilities to mold an organization into a highly developed multinational company.[11]

In general, the larger the organization, the greater the likelihood it participates in international operations of some sort. Companies such as General Electric, Lockheed, and DuPont, which have annually accumulated over $1 billion from export sales, support this generalization. There are exceptions, however, BRK Electronics, for example, a small firm in Aurora, Illinois, has won a substantial share of world sales of smoke detectors. By setting up local distributors in Italy, France, and England, BRK caused its export sales to climb from $124,000 in one year to $4 million five years later.[12] As noted earlier, an increasing number of smaller organizations are undertaking international operations.

Complexities of Managing the Multinational Corporation

From the discussion so far, it should be clear that international management and domestic management are quite different. Classic management thought indicates that international management differs from domestic management because it involves operating:[13]

Selected Multinational Companies Appearing on the 2001 *Forbes* Global 500

 **Table 5.1**

Company	Sales ($mil)	Foreign Sales as % of Total	Net Profits ($mil)	Assets ($mil)	Market Value ($mil)	Enterprise Value ($mil)
General Electric	129,853	33	12,735	437,006	406,525	613,268
Exxon Mobil	206,083	69	15,990	149,000	286,348	312,381
Verizon Communications	64,707	3	10,810	164,735	126,724	219,504
IBM	88,396	58	8,093	88,349	167,206	194,097
Wal-Mart Stores	191,329	17	6,295	77,895	210,827	228,897
Philip Morris	63,276	51	8,510	79,067	105,977	140,827
Ford Motor	170,064	30	5,410	284,421	52,907	214,815
General Motors	184,632	26	4,452	303,100	48,643	187,907
Intel	33,726	59	10,535	47,945	195,245	194,620
Procter & Gamble	39,595	50	3,618	36,825	86,572	99,846

Table 5.2   The 12 Largest Foreign Investments in the United States

2001 Rank	Foreign Investor	Country	US Investment	% Owned	Industry	Revenue ($mil)	Net Income[1] ($mil)	Assets ($mil)
1	DaimlerChrysler AG*	Germany	DaimlerChrysler Corp	100	automotive	73,144	NA	82,722
			Freightliner	100	commercial vehicles	10,469	NA	3,601
			Mercedes-Benz US Intl	100	automotive	2,458	NA	901
						86,071		
2	BP Amoco Plc*	UK	BP Amoco	100	energy	38,786	3,001	27,348
			Atlantic Richfield	100	energy	13,055	2,509	26,272
						51,841		
3	Royal Ahold*	Netherlands	Ahold USA	100	supermarkets	19,344	954	7,226
			US Foodservice	100	food service distribution	6,198	212	2,013
						25,542		
4	Sony*	Japan	Sony Music Entertainment	100	music			
			Sony Pictures Entertainment	100	film	21,117	918	NA
			Sony Electronics	100	consumer electronics			
5	Royal Dutch/ Shell Group*	Netherlands/ UK	Shell Oil	100	energy, chemicals	18,438	2,486	26,111
6	Toyota Motor*	Japan	Toyota Motor Mfg	100	automotive	10,800 E	NA	NA
			New United Motor Mfg	50	automotive	4,700 E	NA	NA
	Denso	Japan	Denso International America	100	automotive systems	2,583	NA	1,888
						17,863 E		
7	Diageo*	UK	Burger King	100	fast food	10,900	NA	NA
			Pillsbury	100	food processing	5,936	NA	NA
			Utd Distillers & Vintners (US)	100	wines and spirits	703	NA	NA
						17,539		
8	ING Group*	Netherlands	ING North America Insurance	100	insurance	14,197	442	NA
			ING Barings (US)	100	financial services	800	−75	NA
						14,997		
9	Deutsche Bank AG*	Germany	Deutsche Bank Americas	100	financial services		NA	270,000
			DB Alex Brown	100	financial services	**14,500 E**		
10	Tyco International*	Bermuda	Tyco International (US)	100	diversified mfg & services	**14,409**	NA	21,434
11	Siemens AG*	Germany	Siemens US	100	electronics	**14,350**	NA	NA
12	Vodafone AirTouch*	UK	Verizon Wireless	45	telecommunications	**14,000 E**	NA	NA

Note: Some foreign investors on the list own U.S. companies indirectly through companies in italics. *Publicly traded in the U.S. in shares or ADRs [1]Earnings before interest and taxes. E: Estimate NA: Not available.

1. Within different national sovereignties
2. Under widely disparate economic conditions
3. Among people living within different value systems and institutions
4. In places experiencing the industrial revolution at different times
5. Often over greater geographical distance
6. In national markets varying greatly in population and area

Figure 5.3 shows some of the more important management implications of these six variables and some of the relationships among them. Consider, for example, the first variable.

Table 5.3

Stage 1	Stage 2	Stage 3	Stage 4	Stage 5	Stage 6
Exports its products to foreign countries	Establishes sales organizations abroad	Licenses use of its patterns and know-how to foreign firms that make and sell its products	Establishes foreign manufacturing facilities	Multinationalizes management from top to bottom	Multinationalizes ownership of corporate stock

Different national sovereignties generate different legal systems. In turn, each legal system implies a unique set of rights and obligations involving property, taxation, antitrust (control of monopoly) law, corporate law, and contract law. In turn, these rights and obligations require the firm to acquire the skills necessary to assess the international legal considerations. Such skills are very different from those required in a purely domestic setting.

IBM Attacks Complexity of Managing Women Abroad

International Business Machines Corporation (IBM) uses cutting-edge technology to provide customers with solutions to business problems. IBM offers a broad array of products and services such as personal computers, servers, and Web hosting. The following quote at the company Web site, by Louis V. Gerstner Jr., chairman and CEO of IBM, describes his worldwide vision for the company:

At IBM, we strive to lead in the creation, development and manufacture of the industry's most advanced information technologies, including computer systems, software, networking systems, storage devices and microelectronics.
And our worldwide network of IBM solutions and services professionals translates these advanced technologies into business value for our customers.

To support Gerstner's worldwide vision, the company recently organized its first Global Women Leaders Conference. At the confer-ence, IBM brought together 81 women executives from 19 different countries. Its purpose was to identify and eliminate common barriers to the advancement of IBM women managers worldwide. Women executives indicated that major cultural barriers limiting their success at IBM worldwide included:

1. IBM's culture was too male dominated
2. Women had difficulty balancing personal and work responsibilities
3. Women had too few mentors
4. The IBM culture does not allow enough risk-taking with women

Certainly, success in eliminating these barriers will aid in maintaining the company's needed worldwide sexual diversity and accomplishing Gerstner's worldwide view. ∎

▶ The idea of an international bakery might seem unlikely, but Lionel Poilâne's Paris bakery, which sells 15,000 loaves of rich and chewy bread every day, has a shop in London as well as two in Paris and also sends bread by FedEx to devoted customers in 20 countries around the world. FedEx's nearby hub at Roissy-Charles-de-Gaulle airport ships Poilâne's bread early in the morning and is on dinner tables as far away as the United States by the next night. Global sales are growing, partly fueled by the Internet. In 2000, exports were up 30 percent.

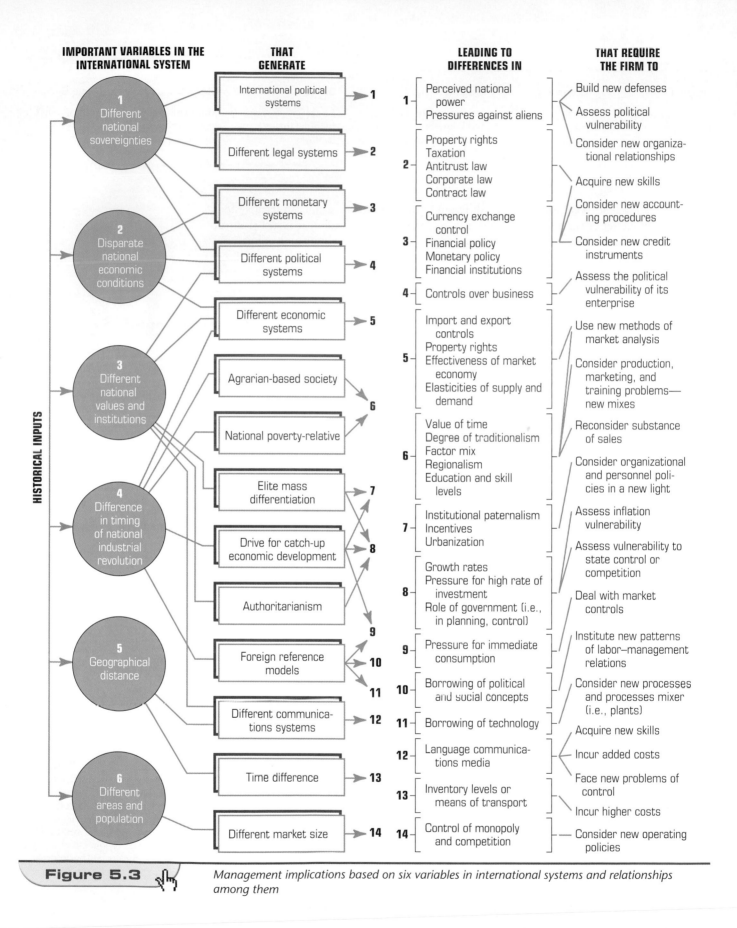

Figure 5.3 Management implications based on six variables in international systems and relationships among them

▶ Since 1987, Japan's Matsushita Electrical Industrial Co. has opened 13 new subsidiaries in the nation of Malaysia. The company has shown its sensitivity to the large Muslim segment of its workforce by providing special prayer rooms in each plant and permitting two prayer sessions during each shift.

Risk and the Multinational Corporation

Developing a multinational corporation obviously requires a substantial investment in foreign operations. Normally, managers who make foreign investments expect that such investments will accomplish the following:[14]

1. Reduce or eliminate high transportation costs
2. Allow participation in the rapid expansion of a market abroad
3. Provide foreign technical, design, and marketing skills
4. Earn higher profits

Unfortunately, many managers decide to internationalize their companies without having an accurate understanding of the risks involved in making such a decision.[15] For example, political complications involving the **parent company** (the company investing in the international operations) and various factions within the **host country** (the country in which the investment is made) could prevent the parent company from realizing the desirable outcomes just listed. Some companies attempt to minimize this kind of risk by adding standard clauses to their contracts stipulating that in the event a business controversy cannot be resolved by the parties involved, they will agree to mediation by a mutually selected mediator.[16]

The likelihood of achieving desirable outcomes related to foreign investments will probably be somewhat uncertain and will certainly vary from country to country. Nevertheless, managers faced with making a foreign investment must assess this likelihood as accurately as possible. Obviously, a poor decision to invest in another country can cause serious financial problems for the organization.

The **parent company** is the company investing in international operations.

The **host country** is the country in which an investment is made by a foreign company.

The Workforce of Multinational Corporations

As organizations become more global, their organization members tend to become more diverse. Managers of multinational corporations face the continual challenge of building a competitive business team made up of people of different races who speak different languages and come from different parts of the world. The following sections perform two functions that should help managers build such teams:

1. They furnish details and related insights about the various types of organization members generally found in multinational corporations
2. They describe the adjustments members of multinational organizations normally must make in order to become efficient and effective contributors to organization goal attainment, and they suggest how managers can facilitate these adjustments

Types of Organization Members Found in Multinational Corporations

Workers in multinational organizations can be divided into three basic types:

➤ *Expatriates*—Organization members who live and work in a country where they do not have citizenship
➤ *Host-Country Nationals*—Organization members who are citizens of the country in which the facility of a foreign-based organization is located
➤ *Third-Country Nationals*—Organization members who are citizens of one country and who work in another country for an organization headquartered in still another country

Organizations that operate in the global businessplace often employ all three types of worker. The use of host-country nationals, however, is increasing because they are normally the least expensive to employ. Such employees, for example, do not need to be relocated or undergo training in the culture, language, or tax laws of the country where the organization is doing business. Both expatriates and third-country nationals, on the other hand, would have to be relocated and normally undergo such training.

Workforce Adjustments   Working in a multinational corporation requires more difficult adjustments than working in an organization that focuses primarily on domestic activities. Probably the two most difficult challenges, which pertain to expatriates and third-country nationals rather than to host-country nationals, are adjusting to a new culture and repatriation.

Adjusting to a New Culture   Upon arrival in a foreign country, many people experience confusion, anxiety, and stress related to the need to make cultural adjustments in their organizational and personal lives. From a personal viewpoint, food, weather, and language may all be dramatically different, and driving may be done on the "wrong" side of the road. As an example of personal anxiety that can be caused by adjusting to a new culture, a U.S. expatriate recently working in Sao Paulo, Brazil, drove out of a parking lot by nudging his way into a terrible traffic jam. When a Brazilian woman allowed him to cut in front of her, the expatriate gave her the "ok" signal. To his personal dismay, he was told that in the Brazilian culture, forming a circle with one's first finger and thumb is considered vulgar.[17]

From an organizational viewpoint, there may be different attitudes toward work and different perceptions of time in the workplace. To illustrate, the Japanese are renowned for their hard-driving work ethic, but Americans take a slightly more relaxed attitude toward work. On the other hand, in many U.S. companies, working past quitting time is seen as exemplary, but in Germany, someone who works late is commonly criticized.

Members of multinational corporations normally have the formidable task of adjusting to a drastically new organizational situation. Managers must help these people adjust quickly and painlessly so they can begin contributing to organizational goal attainment as soon as possible.

Repatriation   **Repatriation** is the process of bringing individuals who have been working abroad back to their home country and reintegrating them into the organization's home-country operations.[18] Repatriation has its own set of adjustment problems, especially with people who have lived abroad for a long time. Some individuals become so accustomed to the advantages of an overseas lifestyle that they greatly miss it when they return home. Others idealize their homeland so much while they are abroad that they become disappointed when it fails to live up to their expectations upon their return. Still others acquire foreign-based habits that are undesirable from the organization's viewpoint and that are hard to break.

Managers must be patient and understanding with repatriates. Some organizations provide repatriates with counseling so that they will be better prepared to handle readjustment problems. Others have found that providing employees, before they leave for foreign duty, with a written agreement specifying what their new duties and career path will be when they return home reduces friction and facilitates the repatriate's adjustment.

Repatriation is the process of bringing individuals who have been working abroad back to their home country and reintegrating them into the organization's home-country operations.

▶ Back to the Case

As Wal-Mart continues its international expansion it will become more of a multinational corporation—an organization with significant operations in more than one country. In any company, management under international circumstances is a complex matter. As Wal-Mart continues to grow internationally, the complexity is related to the necessity for managing within different foreign countries that are separated by significant distances and that are characterized by different economic conditions, people, levels of technology, market sizes, and laws. Wal-Mart's success with foreign expansion illustrates the potential rewards to managers who can handle the complexity of doing business in other countries.

Management at Wal-Mart is attempting to minimize risk in its decisions to make foreign investments. However, few managers would see expansion into a country like Japan as too risky. This country is considered to be economically stable and very safe for foreign investors, whereas expansion into a country characterized by civil upheaval and military action would certainly be risky.

The United States has normal trading relationships with Japan, and Wal-Mart may have much to gain by being successful merchandisers in Japan. Management must be aware, however, that the political situation between the United States and other countries can change very rapidly. As a result, the company should constantly monitor the political relationship between the United States and the countries in which it does business, in order to enable a quick response to any changes.

Wal-Mart management has apparently decided that foreign investment in Japan represents a tolerable amount of risk when weighed against the prospect of increased return from operations in Japan. Only actual operation in Japan will furnish feedback indicating whether or not this decision was sound.

Perhaps the most important variable in making the Japanese Wal-Marts successful will be the people it employs. The company must decide on the best combination of people to run the stores—expatriates, host-country nationals, or third-country nationals. Whatever blend of human resources is decided on, management must be sensitive in helping individuals adjust both personally and organizationally to an international situation. In addition, if expatriates are involved in running the stores, the company should be sensitive to helping them adjust when they are repatriated.

MANAGEMENT FUNCTIONS AND MULTINATIONAL CORPORATIONS

The sections that follow discuss the four major management functions—planning, organizing, influencing, and controlling—as they occur in multinational corporations.

Planning in Multinational Corporations

Planning was defined in Chapter 1 as determining how an organization will achieve its objectives. This definition is applicable to the management of both domestic and multinational organizations, but with some differences.

The primary difference between planning in multinational and domestic organizations is in the plans' components. Plans for the multinational organization include components that focus on the international arena, whereas plans for the domestic organization do not. For example, plans for multinational organizations could include the following:

1. Establishing a new sales force in a foreign country
2. Developing new manufacturing plants in other countries through purchase or construction
3. Financing international expansion
4. Determining which countries represent the most suitable candidates for international expansion

Components of International Plans   Although planning for multinational corporations varies from organization to organization, the following four components are commonly included in international plans:

➤ Imports/Exports
➤ License agreements
➤ Direct investing
➤ Joint ventures

This section discusses these four components as well as the responses of multinational corporations to international market agreements.

Imports/Exports   Imports/Exports planning components emphasize reaching organizational objectives by **importing** (buying goods or services from another country) or **exporting** (selling goods or services to another country).

Organizations of all sizes import and export. On the one hand, there are companies like Auburn Farms, Inc., a relatively small producer of all-natural, fat-free snack foods that imports products to be resold. Auburn Farms is the exclusive U.S. importer of Beacon Sweets & Chocolates of South Africa. Auburn sees its importing activities as a way of expanding and diversifying.[19] On the other hand, there are extremely large and complex organizations, such as Eastman Kodak, which export photographic products to a number of foreign countries.[20]

License Agreements   A **license agreement** is a right granted by one company to another to use its brand name, technology, product specifications, and so on, in the manufacture or sale of goods and services. The company to which the license is extended pays some fee for the privilege. International planning components in this area involve reaching organizational objectives through either the purchase or the sale of licenses at the international level.

For example, the Tosoh Corporation recently purchased a license agreement from Mobil Research and Development Corporation to commercialize Mobil's newly developed process for extracting mercury from natural gas. Tosoh, a Japanese firm, will use its subsidiaries in the United States, Japan, the Netherlands, Greece, Canada, and the United Kingdom as bases of operations from which to profit from Mobil's new process.[21]

Direct Investing   **Direct investing** is using the assets of one company to purchase the operating assets (for example, factories) of another company. International planning in this area emphasizes reaching organizational objectives through the purchase of the operating assets of another company in a foreign country.

A number of Japanese firms have recently been making direct investments in the United States. In fact, many people believe that a new wave of direct Japanese investment in the United States is building. Several large Japanese companies have announced plans to expand their U.S. production facilities. These planned direct investments are focused on building competitive clout for Japanese companies in such core industries as automobiles, semiconductors, electronics, and office products. Lower manufacturing wages and lower land costs in the United States are key attractions for the Japanese firms. For example, because the cost of building a factory was 30 percent cheaper in the United States than in Japan, Ricoh Company decided to spend $30 million to start making thermal paper products near Atlanta, Georgia. One of the largest Japanese direct investments in the United States was Toyota Motor Company's $900 million expansion of its Georgetown, Kentucky, plant. The lower costs associated with expanding and operating the Georgetown plant were the key reason Toyota decided to make this investment.[22]

Joint Ventures   An **international joint venture** is a partnership formed by a company in one country with a company in another country for the purpose of pursuing some mutually desirable business undertaking. International planning components that include joint ventures emphasize the attainment of organizational objectives through partnerships with foreign companies.

Joint ventures between car manufacturers are becoming more and more common as companies strive for greater economies of scale and higher standards in product quality and delivery.

General Motors and Suzuki Motor Company recently formed CAMI Automotive as a joint venture to manufacture the Geo Metro, touted as Chevrolet's most affordable car model. General Motors is based in the United States and is known throughout the world for its prowess as an automobile manufacturer. Suzuki is a leading minicar and motorcycle manufacturer based in Japan. General Motors' substantial size and marketing muscle make the joint venture desirable from Suzuki's viewpoint, and Suzuki's international presence through its subsidiaries in Spain, Canada, Australia, New Zealand, Germany, France, Italy, Belgium, the

---

Importing is buying goods or services from another country.

Exporting is selling goods or services to another country.

A **license agreement** is a right granted by one company to another to use its brand name, technology, product specifications, and so on in the manufacture or sale of goods and services.

Direct investing is using the assets of one company to purchase the operating assets of another company.

An **international joint venture** is a partnership formed by a company in one country with a company in another country for the purpose of pursuing some mutually desirable business undertaking.

Philippines, Pakistan, and Colombia makes the partnership desirable from General Motors' viewpoint.[23]

Planning and International Market Agreements   In order to plan properly, managers of a multinational corporation, or any other organization participating in the international arena, must understand numerous complex and interrelated factors present within the organization's international environment. Managers should have a practical grasp of such international environmental factors as the economic and cultural conditions, the laws and political circumstances, of foreign countries within which their companies operate.

One international environmental factor impacting strategic planning that has lately received significant attention is the international market agreement. An **international market agreement** is an arrangement among a cluster of countries that facilitates a high level of trade among these countries. In planning, managers must consider existing international market agreements as they relate to countries in which their organizations operate. If an organization is from a country that is party to an international market agreement, the organization's plan should include steps for taking maximum advantage of that agreement. On the other hand, if an organization is from a country that is *not* party to an international market agreement, the organization's plan must include steps for competing with organizations from nations that are parties to such an agreement. The most notable international market agreements are discussed here.

An **international market agreement** is an arrangement among a cluster of countries that facilitates a high level of trade among these countries.

The European Community (EC)   The European Community (EC) is an international market agreement first formed in 1958 and dedicated to facilitating trade among member nations. To that end, the nations in the EC have agreed to eliminate tariffs among themselves and work toward meaningful deregulation in such areas as banking, insurance, telecommunications, and airlines. Longer-term members of the EC are Denmark, the United Kingdom, Portugal, the Netherlands, Belgium, Spain, Ireland, Luxembourg, France, Germany, Italy, and Greece. More recent members include Austria, Finland, and Sweden. Swedish businesses are particularly excited about their country's entrance into the EC because they are sure that membership will ultimately boost exports and encourage foreign investment from other member nations. The significance of the EC as an international environmental factor can only increase, since the number of member countries is expected to grow to over 25 by 2010.[24]

North American Free Trade Agreement (NAFTA)   The North American Free Trade Agreement is an international market agreement aimed at facilitating trade among member nations. Current NAFTA members are the United States, Canada, and Mexico. To facilitate trade among themselves, these countries have agreed to such actions as the phasing out of tariffs on U.S. farm exports to Mexico, the opening up of Mexico to American trucking, and the safeguarding of North American pharmaceutical patents in Mexico.

NAFTA has had significant impact since its implementation in January 1994. Recent figures show that since the agreement went into effect, there has been a 30 percent increase in U.S. exports to Mexico and a 15 percent increase in Mexican exports to the United States. Trade between the United States and Canada has exploded since NAFTA took effect. As with the EC, the significance of NAFTA as an international environmental factor can only grow in the future as other countries in the Caribbean and South America apply for membership.[25]

▶ Sometimes the best-sounding plans for international marketing can go wrong. Microsoft's Venus, a product that was to allow Chinese customers Internet access via their televisions, failed. Observers say that Microsoft misjudged how willing the Chinese would be to buy such a product when PCs now sell for as little as $600, and at least one local television maker never got behind the Venus because it felt Microsoft was not fully committed to the concept. Said Microsoft's General Manager in China, Jack Gao, "We have a lot of things to improve."

The Evolving Pacific Rim   Countries in the Pacific Rim area are commonly believed to be interested in developing an international market agreement among themselves that is as effective as the EC has proved to be in Europe. The countries categorized as belonging to the Pacific Rim are Japan, China, Malaysia, Singapore, Indonesia, South Korea, Thailand, Taiwan, Hong Kong, the Philippines, New Zealand, Pakistan, Sri Lanka, and Australia. One country on this list, Japan, is presently a world economic power, while others, like Taiwan and South Korea, are making good progress toward that status. The Pacific Rim countries as a group are anxious to develop an international trade agreement that can best serve their particular economic needs.[26]

To sum up, numerous countries throughout the world are already signatories to international market agreements. Moreover, the number of countries that are parties to such agreements should grow significantly in the future.

Organizing Multinational Corporations

Organizing was generally defined in Chapter 1 as the process of establishing orderly uses for all resources within the organization. This definition applies equally to the management of domestic and multinational organizations. Two organizing topics as they specifically relate to multinational corporations, however, bear further discussion. These topics are organization structure and the selection of managers.[27]

Organization Structure

Basically, *organization structure* is the sum of all established relationships among resources within the organization, and the *organization chart* is the graphic illustration of organization structure.

Figure 5.4 illustrates several ways in which organization charts can be designed for multinational corporations. Briefly, multinational organization charts can be set up according to major business functions the organization performs, such as production or marketing; major products the organization sells, such as brakes or electrical parts; geographic areas within which the organization does business, such as North America or Europe; customers the organization serves, such as the Japanese or Swiss; or the way in which the organization manufactures and assembles its products. The topic of organization structure is discussed in much more detail in Chapter 10.

As with domestic organizations, there is no one best way to organize a multinational corporation. Instead, managers must analyze the multinational circumstances that confront them and develop an organization structure that best suits those circumstances.

Selection of Managers

For multinational organizations to thrive, they must have competent managers. One characteristic believed to be a primary determinant of how competently managers can guide multinational organizations is their attitude toward how such organizations should operate.

Managerial Attitudes Toward Foreign Operations   Over the years, management theorists have identified three basic managerial attitudes toward the operation of multinational corporations: ethnocentric, polycentric, and geocentric. The **ethnocentric attitude** reflects the belief that multinational corporations should regard home-country management practices as superior to foreign-country management practices. Managers with an ethnocentric attitude are prone to stereotype home-country management practices as sound and reasonable and foreign management practices as faulty and unreasonable. The **polycentric attitude** reflects the belief that because foreign managers are closer to foreign organizational units, they probably understand them better, and therefore foreign management practices should generally be viewed as more insightful than home-country management practices. Managers with a **geocentric attitude** believe that the overall quality of management recommendations, rather than the location of managers, should determine the acceptability of management practices used to guide multinational corporations.[28]

Advantages and Disadvantages of Each Management Attitude   It is extremely important to understand the potential advantages and disadvantages of these three attitudes within multinational corporations. The ethnocentric attitude has the advantage of keeping the organization simple, but it generally causes organizational problems because it prevents the organization from receiving feedback from its foreign operations. In some cases, the ethnocentric attitude even causes resentment toward the home country within the foreign society. The polycentric attitude permits the tailoring of foreign organizational segments to their cultures, which can be an advantage. Unfortunately, this attitude can lead to the substantial disadvantage of creating numerous foreign organizational segments that are individually run and rather unique, which makes them difficult to control.

The **ethnocentric attitude** reflects the belief that multinational corporations should regard home-country management practices as superior to foreign-country management practices.

The **polycentric attitude** reflects the belief that because foreign managers are closer to foreign organizational units, they probably understand them better, and therefore foreign management practices should generally be viewed as more insightful than home-country management practices.

The **geocentric attitude** reflects the belief that the overall quality of management recommendations, rather than the location of managers, should determine the acceptability of management practices used to guide multinational corporations. The geocentric attitude is considered most appropriate for long-term organizational success.

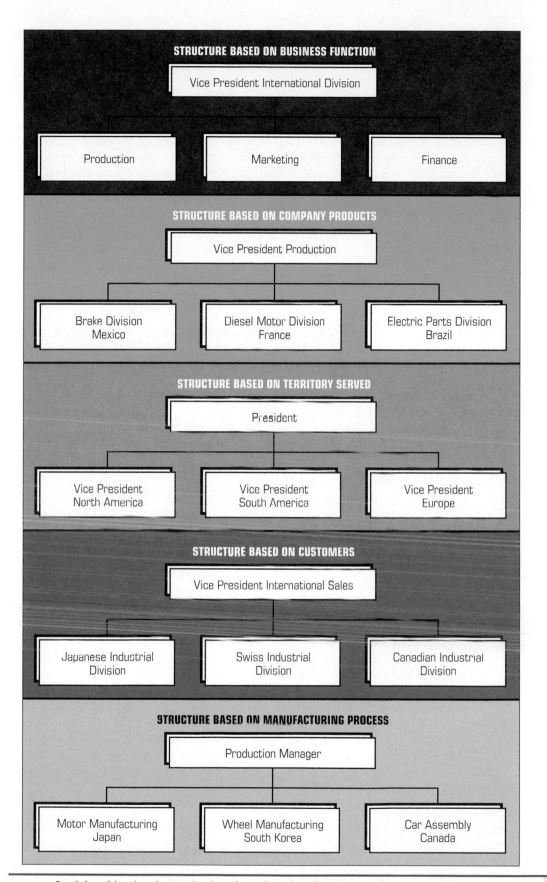

STRUCTURE BASED ON BUSINESS FUNCTION

Vice President International Division

- Production
- Marketing
- Finance

STRUCTURE BASED ON COMPANY PRODUCTS

Vice President Production

- Brake Division Mexico
- Diesel Motor Division France
- Electric Parts Division Brazil

STRUCTURE BASED ON TERRITORY SERVED

President

- Vice President North America
- Vice President South America
- Vice President Europe

STRUCTURE BASED ON CUSTOMERS

Vice President International Sales

- Japanese Industrial Division
- Swiss Industrial Division
- Canadian Industrial Division

STRUCTURE BASED ON MANUFACTURING PROCESS

Production Manager

- Motor Manufacturing Japan
- Wheel Manufacturing South Korea
- Car Assembly Canada

Partial multinational organization charts based on function, product, territory, customers, and manufacturing process

Figure 5.4

The geocentric attitude is generally thought to be the most appropriate for managers in multinational corporations. This attitude promotes collaboration between foreign and home-country management and encourages the development of managerial skills regardless of the organizational segment or country in which managers operate. An organization characterized by the geocentric attitude generally incurs high travel and training expenses, and many decisions are made by consensus. Although the risks from such a wide distribution of power are real, the potential payoffs—better-quality products, worldwide utilization of the best human resources, increased managerial commitment to worldwide organizational objectives, and increased profit—generally outweigh the potential harm. Overall, managers with a geocentric attitude contribute more to the long-term success of the multinational corporation than managers with an ethnocentric or polycentric attitude.

Influencing People in Multinational Corporations

Influencing was generally defined in Chapter 1 as guiding the activities of organization members in appropriate directions through communicating, leading, motivating, and managing groups. Influencing people in a multinational corporation, however, is more complex and challenging than in a domestic organization.

A **culture** is the set of characteristics of a given group of people and their environment.

Culture   The factor that probably contributes most to this increased complexity and challenge is culture. **Culture** is the set of characteristics of a given group of people and their environment. The components of a culture that are generally designated as important are customs, beliefs, attitudes, habits, skills, state of technology, level of education, and religion. As a manager moves from a domestic corporation involving basically one culture to a multinational corporation involving several, the task of influencing usually becomes more difficult.

To successfully influence employees, managers in multinational corporations should:

1. *Acquire a working knowledge of the languages used in countries that house foreign operations*—Multinational managers attempting to operate without such knowledge are prone to making costly mistakes.
2. *Understand the attitudes of people in countries that house foreign operations*—An understanding of these attitudes can help managers design business practices that are suitable for unique foreign situations. For example, Americans generally accept competition as a tool to encourage people to work harder. As a result, U.S. business practices that include some competitive aspects seldom create significant disruption within organizations. Such practices could cause disruption, however, if introduced into either Japan or the typical European country.
3. *Understand the needs that motivate people in countries housing foreign operations*—For managers in multinational corporations to be successful at motivating employees in different countries, they must present these individuals with the opportunity to satisfy personal needs while being productive within the organization. In designing motivation strategies, multinational managers must understand that employees in different countries often have quite different personal needs. For example, the Swiss, Austrians, Japanese, and Argentineans tend to have high security needs; whereas Danes, Swedes, and Norwegians tend to have high social needs. People in Great Britain, the United States, Canada, New Zealand, and Australia tend to have high self-actualization needs.[29] Thus, to be successful at influencing, multinational managers must understand their employees' needs and mold such organizational components as incentive systems, job design, and leadership style to correspond to these needs.

Controlling Multinational Corporations

Controlling was generally defined in Chapter 1 as making something happen the way it was planned to happen. As with domestic corporations, control in multinational corporations requires that standards be set, performance be measured and compared to standards, and corrective action be taken if necessary. In addition, control in such areas as labor costs, product quality, and inventory is important to organizational success regardless of whether the organization is domestic or international.

▶ **Automobile Manufacturing—Controlling at Multinational Nissan Motor Company**

The Nissan Motor Company is one of the world's premier automobile manufacturing companies. Headquartered in Japan, popular company brand names include Centra, Maxima, Xterra, and Altima. Throughout its history, Nissan Motor Company has often been cited for outstanding success.

In recent times, however, the company's severe financial difficulties have been the main topic of discussion. In an attempt to control the situation at Nissan, Carlos Ghosn, Nissan's new CEO from Brazil, has ordered a number of severe company cutbacks. Ghosn's plan calls for the elimination of 30 percent of Nissan's production capacity by closing three assembly lines and two powertrain plants in Japan. Thousands of jobs will also be eliminated in Japan. Ghosn's plan does not call for cutting any overseas production-related jobs,

but to help stop the acceleration of expenses, Nissan will also close its offices in New York and Washington, DC.

Ghosn's plan also takes aim at Nissan's long-standing *keiretsu*. *Keiretsu* is a Japanese term describing a loose conglomeration of firms that coordinate effort, without owning equity in one another, to enhance the success of partner companies. Ghosn's plan calls for breaking up Nissan's present *keiretsu*, because in Ghosn's opinion, this system of relationships isn't working for the company.

Recent events at Nissan illustrate that, as with purely domestic organizations, management must control company operations to enhance success. With multinational corporations, however, controlling focuses on ensuring that "events occur as planned" across national borders.

Special Difficulties Control of a multinational corporation involves certain complexities. First, there is the problem of different currencies. Management must decide how to compare profits generated by organizational units located in different countries and therefore expressed in terms of different currencies.

Another complication is that organizational units in multinational corporations are generally more geographically separated. This increased distance normally makes it difficult for multinational managers to keep a close watch on operations in foreign countries.

Improving Communication One action successful managers take to help overcome the difficulty of monitoring geographically separated foreign units is carefully designing the communication network or information system that links them. A significant part of this design requires all company units to acquire and install similar computer equipment in all offices, both foreign and domestic, to ensure the likelihood of network hookups when communication becomes necessary. Such standardization of computer equipment also facilitates communication among all foreign locations and makes equipment repair and maintenance easier and therefore less expensive.[30]

▶ Working across five different time zones created some communications difficulties for Andy Pada Jr., vice president and chief operating officer of 1st 2nd Mortgage Co. of N.J. Inc. His Honolulu branch manager had trouble reaching the home office in New Jersey before it closed for the day, and if she waited for it to reopen, it would be after midnight in Hawaii. Pada solved the problem by ordering a unified messaging service to consolidate his own messages and gave each of his 75 employees (scattered across 10 states) an e-mail account that provides e-mail, fax, and voice messaging at a single toll-free phone number or e-mail address. Calls can be forwarded too, and the system has voice-to-speech capabilities.

Transnational Organizations

Transnational organizations, also called *global organizations,* take the entire world as their business arena. Doing business wherever it makes sense is primary; national borders are considered inconsequential. The transnational organization transcends any single home country, with ownership, control, and management being from many different countries. Transnational organizations represent the fourth, and maximum, level of international activity as depicted on the continuum of international involvement presented earlier in this chapter. Seeing great opportunities in the global marketplace, some MNCs have transformed themselves from home-based companies with worldwide interests into worldwide companies pursuing business activities across the globe and claiming no singular loyalty to any one country.

Perhaps the most commonly cited example of a transnational organization is Nestlé.[31] Although Nestlé is headquartered in Veney, Switzerland, its arena of daily business activity is truly the world. Nestlé has a very diversified list of products, including instant coffee, cereals, pharmaceuticals, coffee creamers, dietetic foods, ice cream, chocolates, and a wide array of snack foods. Its recent acquisition of the French company Perrier catapulted Nestlé into mar-

Transnational organizations also called *global organizations,* take the entire world as their business arena.

ket leadership in the mineral water industry. Nestlé has over 210,000 employees and operates 494 factories in 71 countries worldwide, including the United States, Germany, Portugal, Brazil, France, New Zealand, Australia, Chile, and Venezuela. Of Nestlé's sales and profits, about 45 percent come from Europe, 35 percent from North and South America, and 25 percent from other countries.

▶ Back to the Case

Planning is equally valuable to both domestic and international companies. The primary difference between planning for Wal-Mart as a domestic company and as an international company would be reflected in components of company plans. As an international corporation, Wal-Mart would have planning components that focus on the international sector, whereas a totally domestic organization would not. Such components could include establishing a partnership with a Japanese construction company to build Wal-Mart stores throughout Japan; building nearby training facilities that could provide well-trained employees for Japanese stores and stores in nearby countries; choosing additional store locations in other countries; and selling the rights to a foreign company to use the Wal-Mart name in mass merchandising.

Regarding organizing a company such as Wal-Mart along international lines, organization structure generally should be based on one or more of the variables of function, product, territory, customers, or manufacturing process. Wal-Mart managers must consider all of the variables within the situations that confront them and then design the organization structure that is most appropriate for those situations. In fact, Wal-Mart is organized internationally on a geographic basis; for example, it has a CEO for its European division.

Over the long term, management at Wal-Mart should try to select for international positions the managers who possess geocentric attitudes, as opposed to polycentric or ethnocentric attitudes. Such managers would tend to build operating units in other countries, would use the best human resources available, and would be highly committed to the attainment of organizational objectives.

As Wal-Mart becomes more multinational, influencing people within the company will become more complicated. The cultures of people in countries like Japan and other countries in which Wal-Mart does international business must be thoroughly understood. Managers of foreign operations who may be U.S. citizens must have a working knowledge of the languages spoken in the host country and an understanding of the attitudes and personal needs that motivate individuals within the foreign workforce. If motivation strategy is to be successful for Wal-Mart as a whole, rewards used to motivate Japanese workers may need to be much different from the rewards used to motivate U.S. workers.

The control process at Wal-Mart should involve standards, measurements, and needed corrective action, just as it should within a purely domestic company. The different currencies used in countries like Japan, however, tend to make control more complicated for an international organization than for a domestic one. The significant distance of countries like Japan from the United States would also tend to complicate the issue of control at Wal-Mart.

INTERNATIONAL MANAGEMENT: SPECIAL ISSUES

The preceding section of this chapter discussed planning, organizing, influencing, and controlling multinational corporations. This section focuses on two special issues that can help to ensure management success in the international arena: maintaining ethics in international management, and preparing expatriates for foreign assignments.[32]

Maintaining Ethics in International Management

As discussed in Chapter 3, *ethics* is a concern for "good" behavior and reflects an obligation that forces managers to consider not only their own personal well-being, but that of other human beings as they lead organizations. Having a manager define what is ethical behavior can indeed be challenging. Defining what behavior is ethical becomes increasingly challenging as managers consider the international implications of management action. What seems ethical in a manager's home country can be unethical in a different country.

The following guidelines can help managers ensure that management action taken across national borders is indeed ethical. According to these guidelines, managers can ensure that such action is ethical by the following:

Respecting Core Human Rights   This guideline underscores the notion that all people deserve an opportunity to achieve economic advancement and an improved standard of living. In addition, all people have the right to be treated with respect. Much effort has been made recently by major sporting goods companies, including Nike and Reebok, to ensure that this guideline is followed in business operations they are conducting in other countries.[33] These companies have joined forces to crack down on child labor, establish minimum wages comparable to existing individual country standards, establish a maximum 60-hour workweek with at least one day off, and support the establishment of a mechanism for inspecting apparel factories worldwide. These companies have also committed themselves to the elimination of forced labor, harassment, abuse, and discrimination in the workplace.

Respecting Local Traditions   This guideline suggests that managers hold the customs of foreign countries in which they conduct business in high regard. In Japan, for example, people have a long-standing tradition that those individuals who do business together exchange gifts. Sometimes, these gifts can be very expensive. When U.S. managers started doing business in Japan, accepting a gift felt like accepting a bribe. As a result, many of these managers thought that the practice of gift giving might be wrong. As U.S. managers have come to know and respect this Japanese tradition, most have come to tolerate, and even encourage, the practice as ethical behavior in Japan. Some managers even set different limits on gift giving in Japan than they do elsewhere.

Determining Right from Wrong by Examining Context   This guideline suggests that managers should evaluate the specifics of the international situation confronting them in determining if a particular management activity is ethical. Although some activities are wrong no matter where they take place, some that are unethical in one setting may be acceptable in another. For instance, the chemical EDB, a soil fungicide, is banned from use in the United States. In hot climates, however, it quickly becomes harmless through exposure to intense solar radiation and high soil temperatures. As long as the chemical is monitored, companies may be able to use EDB ethically in certain parts of the world.

Most managers and management scholars agree that implementing ethical management practices across national borders enhances organizational success. Although following the above guidelines does not guarantee that management action taken across national borders will be ethical, it should increase the probability.

Preparing Expatriates for Foreign Assignments

The trend of U.S. companies forming joint ventures and other strategic alliances that emphasize foreign operations is increasing. As a result, the number of expatriates being sent from the United States to other countries is also rising.[34]

The somewhat casual approach of the past toward preparing expatriates for foreign duty is being replaced by the attitude that these managers need special tools to be able to succeed in difficult foreign assignments.[35] To help expatriates adjust, home companies are helping them find homes and high quality health care in host countries. Companies are also responding to expatriate feelings that they need more help from home companies on career planning related to foreign assignments, career planning for spouses forced to go to the foreign assignment country to look for work, and better counseling for the personal challenges they will face during their foreign assignment.

Many companies prepare their expatriates for foreign assignments by using special training programs. Specific features of these programs vary from company to company, depending on the situation. Most of these programs, however, usually contain the following core elements:

> ➤ *Culture profiles*—Here, expatriates learn about the new culture in which they will be working.

> *Cultural adaptation*—Here, expatriates learn how to survive the difficulties of adjusting to a new culture.

> *Logistical information*—Here, expatriates learn basic information, such as personal safety, who to call in an emergency, and how to write a check.

> *Application*—Here, expatriates learn about specific organizational roles they will perform.

Expatriates generally play a critical role in determining the success of an organization's foreign operations. The tremendous personal and professional adjustments that expatriates must make, however, can delay their effectiveness and efficiency in foreign settings. Sound training programs can lower the amount of time expatriates need to adjust and can thereby help them become productive more quickly. The following People Spotlight discusses more detail on helping expatriates adjust.

Helping Expatriates to Adjust

As more companies initiate or expand overseas operations, the need to send employees on international assignments will increase. Because many companies use overseas assignments as a means of assessing which employees should be promoted to top-level positions, success in such positions is critical to both the individual and the organization.

Unfortunately, the success rate in foreign assignments is unimpressive. Up to 40 percent of expatriate employees leave their posts early. The reasons vary, but early termination is generally accompanied by negatives for both the organization and the employee. Each failure to complete a foreign assignment costs companies between $50,000 and $150,000 and usually derails the employee's career.

The primary reason for early termination is that the employee was not properly prepared for the foreign assignment. Poorly prepared expatriates find it very difficult to make the personal and organizational adjustments necessary for success in positions abroad.

Management can take certain steps to better prepare organization members for expatriate positions. For example, organization members who are eligible for expatriate positions should be involved in discussions concerning the challenges of working in another country before they are actually given an international assignment.

Employees chosen for an assignment should be given an early start on learning the language and etiquette of the host country where they will work, as well as the culture and value system of that country.

Finally, management should develop and refine the stress management skills of future expatriates. These employees will undoubtedly encounter high levels of stress related to their new foreign jobs, and they must know how to manage such stress if they are to be successful organization members. ■

Back to the Case

Based on the above information, managers at Wal-Mart should be concerned with promoting ethical behavior in the company's foreign operations. This can be done by taking action that respects the core human rights of foreign citizens, respects foreign local traditions, and reflects what is "right" in the particular foreign context. Examples of ethical behavior could be forbidding foreign children to be hired as employees, paying a fair wage that reflects foreign national wage levels, and eliminating abuse and discrimination in Wal-Mart stores.

In addition, Wal-Mart must properly prepare expatriates who are going to work in other countries, such as Japan, if these individuals are to be as productive as possible as quickly as possible. The company should take steps to help the expatriates find appropriate housing and health care, to explain how the assignment impacts the expatriates' long-term career at Wal-Mart, and to provide counseling for personal problems that the expatriates could face simply by living in Japan or elsewhere. Formal training of expatriates going to Japan should probably include a description of the Japanese culture; steps that expatriates can take to adapt to that culture; basic information about logistics of life in Japan, such as who to call in case of emergency; and specifics about the job they will be performing.

Management Skills Module

This section is specially designed to help you develop management skills. An individual's management skill is based on an understanding of management concepts and the ability to apply those concepts in management situations. As a result, the following activities are designed both to heighten your understanding of management concepts and to help you gain facility in applying those concepts in various management situations.

UNDERSTANDING MANAGEMENT CONCEPTS

▶ Action Summary

Reread the learning objectives below. Each objective is followed by questions. Answering these questions accurately will help you retain the most important concepts discussed in this chapter. After answering each question, check your answer against the answer key at the end of this chapter. (*Hint:* If you have any doubts regarding the correct response, consult the page number that follows the answer.)

Circle:

From studying this chapter, I will attempt to acquire

1. An understanding of international management and its importance to modern managers.

   T F   **a.** To reach organizational objectives, management may extend its activities to include an emphasis on organizations in foreign countries.

   a b c d e   **b.** The U.S. multinational corporation with the highest foreign revenue as a percent of total revenue in 2001 was: (a) BP Amoco (b) DaimlerChrysler (c) Royal Ahold (d) Sony (e) Deutsch Bank.

2. An understanding of what constitutes a multinational corporation.

   a b c d e   **a.** According to Jacoby, the first stage in a corporation's multinationalization is when the corporation: (a) multinationalizes ownership of corporate stock (b) multinationalizes management from top to bottom (c) establishes foreign manufacturing facilities (d) establishes sales organizations abroad (e) exports its products.

   T F   **b.** In general, the smaller the organization, the greater the likelihood that it participates in international operations of some sort.

3. Insights concerning the risk involved in investing in international operations.

   a b c d e   **a.** Managers who make foreign investments believe that such investments: (a) reduce or eliminate high transportation costs (b) allow participation in the rapid expansion of a market abroad (c) provide foreign technical, design, and marketing skills (d) earn higher profits (e) a, b, c, and d.

   T F   **b.** A manager's failure to understand different national sovereignties, national conditions, and national values and institutions can lead to poor investment decisions.

4. Insights about those who work in multinational corporations.

   a b c d e   **a.** People who work in multinational corporations are generally categorized as: (a) expatriates (b) third-country nationals (c) host-country nationals (d) all of the above (e) a and b only.

   T F   **b.** Personal adjustments that employees of multinational corporations must make can influence how productively they work.

   T F   **c.** Repatriation is the process of sending an individual out of his or her home country to work for a multinational corporation.

5. Knowledge about managing multinational corporations.

   T F   **a.** The primary difference between planning in multinational versus domestic organizations probably involves operational planning.

   a b c d e   **b.** The attitude that regards home-country management practices as superior to foreign-country
   T F   practices is known as a(n): (a) egocentric attitude (b) ethnocentric attitude (c) polycentric attitude (d) geocentric attitude (e) isocentric attitude.

6. Knowledge about managing multinational organizations versus transnational organizations.

   T F   **a.** Generally speaking, a transnational organization transcends any home country, whereas a multinational organization does not.

   T F   **b.** A multinational organization is basically the same as a transnational organization.

Circle:

7. An understanding of how ethics and the preparation of expatriates relate to managing internationally.

T F   **a.** Examining context can help a manager determine if action taken in a foreign country or countries is ethical.

a b c d e   **b.** Which of the following is NOT commonly discussed in training programs aimed at preparing expatriates for foreign assignments: (a) culture profiles (b) cultural adaption (c) application (d) logistical information (e) all of the above are commonly discussed.

▶ Action Summary Answer Key

1. **a.** T, p. 98
   b. b, p. 102
2. **a.** e, p. 101
   b. F, p. 101
3. **a.** e, p. 105
   b. T, p. 104

4. **a.** d, p. 106
   b. T, p. 106
   c. F, p. 106

5. **a.** F, p. 107
   b. b, p. 110
6. **a.** T, p. 113
   b. F, p. 113

7. **a.** T, p. 115
   b. e, pp. 115–116

▶ Issues for Review and Discussion

1. More and more organizations are initiating business ventures in foreign countries. Explain why in detail.
2. Define *international management.*
3. How significant is the topic of international management to the modern manager? Explain fully.
4. What is meant by the term *multinational corporation?*
5. List and explain four factors that contribute to the complexity of managing multinational corporations.
6. Choose an organization and describe how it has become multinational by progressing through two or more stages of Jacoby's six stages of multinationalization.
7. List and define three types of organization members generally found in multinational corporations.
8. Describe personal and professional adjustments that members of multinational corporations generally must make. How should managers respond to employees making such adjustments? Why?
9. What is the difference between direct investing and joint ventures at the international level?
10. What is an international market agreement? Explain how these agreements can impact organization plans.

11. Draw segments of organization charts that organize a multinational corporation on the basis of product, function, and customers.
12. Is there one best way to organize all multinational corporations? Explain your answer fully.
13. What are the differences between ethnocentric, polycentric, and geocentric attitudes? Describe advantages and disadvantages of each.
14. How does culture affect the international management process?
15. Discuss three suggestions that would be helpful to a manager attempting to influence organization members in different countries.
16. What is a transnational organization? How does it differ from a multinational organization?
17. How can comparative management help managers of today?
18. Discuss three guidelines that managers can use to ensure that action taken across national borders is ethical.

APPLYING MANAGEMENT CONCEPTS

❯ Cases

➤ INTRODUCTORY CASE WRAP-UP

❯Case Discussion Questions

"Wal-Mart Goes to Japan" (p. 97) and its related Back-to-the-Case sections were written to help you better understand the management concepts contained in this chapter. Answer the following discussion questions about this Introductory Case to further enrich your understanding of chapter content:

1. Do you think that at some point in your career you will become involved in international management? Explain.
2. Assuming that you will be involved in managing a Wal-Mart store in Japan, what challenges do you think will be the most difficult for you to meet? Why?
3. Evaluate the following statement: Wal-Mart can learn to manage its U.S. operations better by studying how successful competitive operations are managed in other countries.

❯Skills Exercise: Preparing Wal-Mart Expatriates for Foreign Assignments

In this chapter you gained an appreciation for the importance of properly preparing expatriates for foreign assignments. In the Introductory Case you read how Wal-Mart's activities related to Japan. Assume that you are in charge of human resources at Wal-Mart and have just been notified that the company is sending an expatriate to Japan to oversee nine Wal-Mart stores that will be run by locals. Do some research on Japan to uncover three issues that you would like the new expatriate to be aware of before taking the assignment. Be sure to discuss how each issue would impact the manner in which the expatriate would actually manage these stores and their employees in Japan.

Multinational fast-food giant McDonald's is planning an aggressive expansion in India over the next three years. Managing director and partner in one of McDonald's two joint ventures, Amit Jatia, explains that the key to McDonald's success has been the management of the supply chain so that none of the McDonald's will ever face a food shortage. No raw materials are brought from oversees. He uses produce from Indian farmers and sheep from Indian sheep farms. The system is managed in such a way that if a truck load of packets goes from one McDonald's to another the truck doesn't come back empty, ensuring that customers will always be served instantly. Workers' wages are low in the Indian branches to offset low prices and high costs of hygienic quality control.

Mr. Vikram Bakshi, North India franchise holder for McDonald's and owner of the New Delhi restaurants, helped adapt McDonald's to prices and tastes suited to the Indian palate. Under his direction, a full-time "menu-vision" team was hired to reinvent the McDonald's selection to appeal to native taste buds. The team toiled for years to come up with an Indian version of the company's special sauce that is an egg-less mayonnaise laced with mint for its vegetarian products. Then they invented a "McAloo Tikki burger," based on a mix of potatoes, green peas, carrots, coriander, and cumin. Every summer, when India's delicious Alfonso mangoes are ripe, they make a mango topping for their 6-rupee (20-cent) ice cream cones.

McDonald's has respected the local culture: Meat and vegetarian cooking and processing are completely segregated. Only mutton is allowed and is used to make the "Maharaj Mac." Indian outlets cater to 3.2 million customers a month and use no beef or pork products, in accordance with Hindu and Muslim dietary laws.

When Vikram Bakshi opened the New Delhi restaurant six years go he broke a coconut on the threshold and his wife and three daughters lit incense, a Hindu ritual to bless the new business.

Bakshi and Jatia and their suppliers plan to invest $75 million to increase outlets from 26 to 80 by the year 2003. Bakshi said McDonald's India, whose emblem is a peacock's wings spread behind the familiar golden arches, is 50 percent owned by Indian investors and cannot be called "foreign." Right-wing fundamentalist leader Jai Bhagwan Goel does not agree and recently threatened to close down McDonald's India. He accused McDonald's of being a foreign firm that has made a habit of "dumping things here without any regard to feelings of people."

After newspapers reported a lawsuit filed in Seattle on behalf of Hindus and vegetarians against McDonald's, charging the company with using beef fat to flavor its French fries, Goel led protests out-side the corporate office. McDonald's said the French fries sold in the United States were never marketed as vegetarian. The switch to vegetable oil in 1990 was "all about healthy hearts eliminating cholesterol," according to Walt Riker, spokesman for McDonald's. He explained that in the United States McDonald's added beef flavoring to the fries before they were flash frozen in compliance with FDA regulations; only vegetable oil is used in India.

On May 4, 2001, a group of over 500 Hindu fundamentalists vandalized the McDonald's restaurant in a Bombay suburb. They asked customers to leave before smashing furniture, lights, and equipment. They then smeared signs in the outlets with cow dung.

The violence did not seem to deter middle-class Indians from frequenting their local McDonald's eateries. For those who have cash to spend in this poor country, there is snob appeal that draws people to foreign food. As the health authorities in India prepared to test McDonald's French fries at the insistence of the fundamentalist party Shiv Sena, a reporter for the American-based radio show "Marketplace Morning Report" (820 AM in New York) recorded the sounds inside Bakshi's franchise.

On May 9, 2001, the outlet, located in New Delhi's plush Ansel Plaza Shopping Complex, was teeming with college students, mothers and children, and business executives. Here are some quotes from the live broadcast: "whenever you want to go somewhere, go to Macki. Forget about everything. It feels very good." "One rice burger with cheese combo"; "it's cheap. We've got very good crowd here, air conditioning, and music. And we like that stuff. It's not what you regularly find in other Indian restaurants."

According to Mr. Bakshi, after five years of labor, "People think of us as their own McDonald's—not some place which is multinational. I think we've been accepted more as a good, local chain."

QUESTIONS

1. Kentucky Fried Chicken recently closed its outlets in India, unable to compete with local restaurants. How has McDonald's corporate motto "thinking global, acting local" saved it from the fate of its competitor?

2. Define *joint venture.* In what way(s) does a joint venture benefit McDonald's? In what way(s) does it benefit Mr. Jatia and Mr. Bakshi?

3. What are some of the problems that McDonald's might still have to face as it continues its expansion plans into this vast country?

www.prenhall.com/certo

This book is accompanied by a rich assortment of online activities aimed at developing your management skills. Reviewing news headlines, Internet exercises, an online study guide, and other research and Internet resources can help personalize management skills development for individual students or an entire class.

chapter
chapterchapterchapterchapterchapterchapter

6 Principles of Planning

objectivesobjectivesobjectives

 Objectives

From studying this chapter, I will attempt to acquire

- A definition of planning and an understanding of the purposes of planning

- Insights into how the major steps of the planning process are related

- An understanding of the relationship between planning and organizational objectives

- A knowledge of the areas in which managers should set organizational objectives

- An appreciation for the potential of a management-by-objectives (MBO) program

- A knowledge of how the chief executive relates to the planning process

- An understanding of the qualifications and duties of planners and how planners can be evaluated

CHAPTER OUTLINE

Introductory Case: *American Airlines Planning to Make the Internet Work*

General Characteristics of Planning
Defining Planning
Purposes of Planning
Planning: Advantages and Potential Disadvantages
Primacy of Planning

Ethics Spotlight ▶ Wal-Mart Plans Social Responsibility Activity Very Carefully

Steps in the Planning Process
The Planning Subsystem
Organizational Objectives: Planning's Foundation
Definition of Organizational Objectives

Areas for Organizational Objectives

Digital Focus ▶ Internet Trend Causes Sega to Alter Objectives: A Classic Example

Working with Organizational Objectives
Guidelines for Establishing Quality Objectives

Management by Objectives (MBO)
Factors Necessary for a Successful MBO Program
MBO Programs: Advantages and Disadvantages

Planning and the Chief Executive
Final Responsibility
Planning Assistance

Quality Spotlight ▶ Including the Right People in Planning Enhances Quality at Sun Microsystems

The Planner
Qualifications of Planners
Evaluation of Planners

American Airlines Planning to Make the Internet Work

REMINDER: THE INTRODUCTORY CASE WRAP-UP (P. 140) CONTAINS DISCUSSION QUESTIONS AND A SKILLS EXERCISE TO FURTHER ILLUSTRATE THE APPLICATION OF CHAPTER CONCEPTS TO THIS VIGNETTE.

To build its new digital strategy, American Airlines' managers devoted a great deal of time to detailed planning. Information from department heads, those closest to day-to-day operations, provided the basis for the plans.

American Airlines is one of the largest passenger airlines in the world, providing scheduled jet service to more than 169 destinations throughout North America, the Caribbean, Latin America, Europe, and the Pacific. In addition, it is one of the world's largest providers of air freight and mail services.

American Airlines has recently established a new digital strategy that employs the Internet in many different ways. To develop that strategy, American relied heavily on advice from its department heads. It was believed that since the department heads were closely and continually involved in running their departments on a day-to-day basis, they were in the best position to advise management on how to use the Internet to the best advantage of the company.

American's new digital strategy supports the company's wide array of operating activities, including the company call center, sales management, and employee scheduling. In terms of the call center, digital activities provide support by allowing customers to purchase tickets through the company Web site, in addition to the telephone. In terms of sales management, the company's online presence allows dead inventory or empty seats to be sold at discounted prices. This activity is very valuable in that it adds incremental dollars to company sales efforts. In terms of employee scheduling, the company's online presence allows employees to access work schedules quickly and easily from anywhere in the world.

American Airlines was one of the first to formulate and implement a digital strategy, although some of its U.S. competitors, such as Delta Air Lines and United Air Lines, are also making important strides in that area. American appears to hold a significant competitive advantage over some of its foreign competitors, such as Malaysia Airlines and Thai Airways International, who are in the preliminary phases of establishing a competitive digital presence. Malaysia Airlines' Web site is mostly limited to providing customers with flight schedules, while Thai Airways requires customers who book tickets through its Web site to physically go to a Thai Airways office to pay for tickets rather than paying online.

American's domestic and foreign competitors are emphasizing the development of digital thrust in order to generate competitive advantage. Therefore, if it is to continue to maintain a position of strength in the industry, American Airlines must have a sound plan for making the Internet work to its advantage.

The Introductory Case focuses on a new Internet strategy at American Airlines, which consists of many different Internet applications aimed at making the company more competitive. The case ends with the implication that this new Internet strategy will only be successful if it is based on sound planning principles. The material in this chapter will help managers to understand why planning is so important, not only for ensuring the success of a new Internet strategy but also for carrying out virtually any other organizational activity. The fundamentals of planning are described, and specifically, this chapter:

1) Outlines the general characteristics of planning

2) Discusses steps in the planning process

3) Describes the planning subsystem

4) Elaborates on the relationship between organizational objectives and planning

5) Discusses the relationship between planning and the chief executive

6) Summarizes the qualifications of planners and explains how planners can be evaluated

GENERAL CHARACTERISTICS OF PLANNING

The first part of this chapter is a general introduction to planning. The sections in this part discuss the following topics:

1. Definition of planning
2. Purposes of planning
3. Advantages and potential disadvantages of planning
4. Primacy of planning

Defining Planning

Planning is the process of determining how the management system will achieve its objectives; it determines how the organization can get where it wants to go.

Planning is the process of determining how the organization can get where it wants to go, and what will do to accomplish its objectives. In more formal terms, planning is "the systematic development of action programs aimed at reaching agreed business objectives by the process of analyzing, evaluating, and selecting among the opportunities which are foreseen."[1]

Planning is a critical management activity regardless of the type of organization being managed. Modern managers face the challenge of sound planning in small and relatively simple organizations as well as in large, more complex ones, and in nonprofit organizations such as libraries as well as in for-profit organizations such as General Motors.[2]

Purposes of Planning

Over the years, management writers have presented several different purposes of planning. For example, a classic article by C. W. Roney indicates that organizational planning has two purposes: protective and affirmative. The protective purpose of planning is to minimize risk by reducing the uncertainties surrounding business conditions and clarifying the consequences of related management actions. The affirmative purpose is to increase the degree of organizational success.[3] For an example of this affirmative purpose, consider Whole Foods Market, a health food chain in Texas. This company uses planning to ensure success as measured by the systematic opening of new stores. Company head John Mackey believes that increased company success is not an accident, but a direct result of careful planning.[4] Still another purpose of planning is to establish a coordinated effort within the organization. Where planning is absent, so, usually, are coordination and organizational efficiency.

The fundamental purpose of planning, however, is to help the organization reach its objectives. As Koontz and O'Donnell put it, the primary purpose of planning is "to facilitate the accomplishment of enterprise and objectives."[5] All other purposes of planning are spin-offs of this fundamental purpose.

Planning: Advantages and Potential Disadvantages

A vigorous planning program produces many benefits. First, it helps managers to be future-oriented. They are forced to look beyond their normal everyday problems to project what situations may confront them in the future.[6] Second, a sound planning program enhances decision coordination. No decision should be made today without some idea of how it will affect a decision that might have to be made tomorrow. The planning function pushes managers to coordinate their decisions. Third, planning emphasizes organizational objectives. Because organizational objectives are the starting points for planning, managers are continually reminded of exactly what their organization is trying to accomplish.

Overall, planning is very advantageous to an organization. According to an often-cited survey, as many as 65 percent of all newly started businesses are not around to celebrate a fifth anniversary. This high failure rate seems primarily a consequence of inadequate planning. Successful businesses have an established plan, a formal statement that outlines the objectives the organization is attempting to achieve. Planning does not eliminate risk, of course, but it does help managers identify and deal with organizational problems before they cause havoc in a business.[7]

The downside is that if the planning function is not well executed, planning can have several disadvantages for the organization. For example, an overemphasized planning program can take up too much managerial time. Managers must strike an appropriate balance between time spent on planning and time spent on organizing, influencing, and controlling. If they don't, some activities that are extremely important to the success of the organization may be neglected.

Overall, the advantages of planning definitely outweigh the disadvantages. Usually, the disadvantages of planning result from the planning function's being used incorrectly.

Primacy of Planning

Planning is the primary management function—the one that precedes and is the basis for the organizing, influencing, and controlling functions of managers. Only after managers have developed their plans can they determine how they want to structure their organization, place their people, and establish organizational controls. As discussed in Chapter 1, planning, organizing, influencing, and controlling are interrelated. Planning is the foundation function and the first one to be performed. Organizing, influencing, and controlling are all based on the results of planning. Figure 6.1 shows this interrelationship.

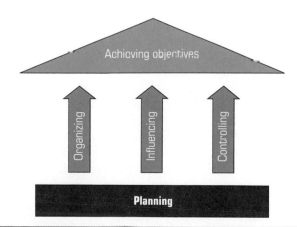

Planning as the foundation for organizing, influencing, and controlling

Figure 6.1

SPOTLIGHT *ethics*

Wal-Mart is mainly engaged in the operation of mass-merchandising stores. The company has three primary operating segments: (1) the Wal-Mart Stores segment includes the company's discount stores and Supercenters in the United States; (2) the SAM'S Club segment includes the warehouse membership clubs in the United States; (3) the international segment includes operations in nine different countries, including Argentina, Brazil, China, Germany, Korea, and the United Kingdom. Founded by Sam Walton, the company presently operates over 1,700 discount stores, 800 Supercenters, and 450 SAM's Clubs.

Wal-Mart management believes that each of its units should operate not only for the welfare of its stockholders, but should also contribute to the well-being of the local communities in which the units are located. Wal-Mart's more than 3,000 sites distribute approximately $128 million annually to support social causes in their communities. Because it touches millions of lives, Wal-Mart was recently recognized as a leading business in the area of social responsibility.

The Company's management plans its social responsibility activities very carefully. First, the Wal-Mart Foundation was created as its unit for carrying out community support efforts. Through the Foundation, Wal-Mart focuses its efforts on education, environment, children, the economy, and neighbors. Although certain programs affect organizations on a national scale, most programs are local. Activities such as company-sponsored Teacher of the Year Awards, free vision checks for underprivileged children at company vision centers, and company scholarships to minority students highlight Wal-Mart's social responsibility efforts. ∎

▶ Back to the Case

It seems apparent from facts in the Introductory Case that American Airlines' managers must focus heavily on planning if its Internet strategy is to be successful. Such a process should help to determine issues such as what equipment must be purchased and when, to actually implement the strategy; who will maintain the equipment once purchased; and how to build an Internet focus into the fabric of the organization's culture.

Because of the many benefits of planning, the company's managers should make certain that the planning process is thorough and comprehensive. One particularly notable benefit of this thoroughness and completeness is the probability of increased profits. However, the planning function must be well executed and not overemphasized, in order to gain positive results.

Since planning is the primary management function, managers should not begin to organize, influence, or control while introducing Internet activities, until planning for the Internet is complete. All other management functions should be based on planning.

STEPS IN THE PLANNING PROCESS

The planning process consists of the following six steps:

1. *State organizational objectives*—Since planning focuses on how the management system will reach organizational objectives, a clear statement of those objectives is necessary before planning can begin. In essence, objectives stipulate those areas in which organizational planning must occur.[8]

2. *List alternative ways of reaching objectives*—Once organizational objectives have been clearly stated, a manager should list as many available alternatives as possible for reaching those objectives.

3. *Develop premises on which to base each alternative*—To a large extent, the feasibility of using any one alternative to reach organizational objectives is determined by the **premises,** or assumptions, on which the alternative is based. For example, two alternatives a manager could generate to reach the organizational objective of increasing profit might be: (a) increase the sale of products presently being produced or (b) produce and sell a completely new product. Alternative (a) is based on the premise that the organization can gain a larger share of the existing market. Alternative (b) is based on the premise that a new product would capture a significant portion of a new market. A manager should list all of the premises for each alternative.

4. *Choose the best alternative for reaching objectives*—An evaluation of alternatives must include an evaluation of the premises on which the alternatives are based. A manager usually finds that some premises are unreasonable and can therefore be excluded from fur-

Premises are the assumptions on which an alternative to reaching an organizational objective is based.

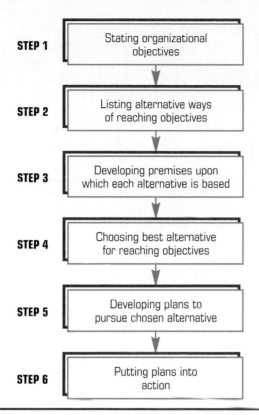

STEP 1	Stating organizational objectives
STEP 2	Listing alternative ways of reaching objectives
STEP 3	Developing premises upon which each alternative is based
STEP 4	Choosing best alternative for reaching objectives
STEP 5	Developing plans to pursue chosen alternative
STEP 6	Putting plans into action

Elements of the planning process   **Figure 6.2**

ther consideration. This elimination process helps the manager determine which alternative would best accomplish organizational objectives. The decision making required for this step is discussed more fully in Chapter 7.

5. *Develop plans to pursue the chosen alternative*—After an alternative has been chosen, a manager begins to develop strategic (long-range) and tactical (short-range) plans.[9] More information about strategic and tactical planning is presented in Chapters 8 and 9.

6. *Put the plans into action*—Once plans that furnish the organization with both long-range and short-range direction have been developed, they must be implemented. Obviously, the organization cannot directly benefit from the planning process until this step is performed.

Figure 6. 2 shows the sequencing of the six steps of the planning process.

THE PLANNING SUBSYSTEM

Once managers thoroughly understand the basics of planning, they can take steps to implement the planning process in their organization. Implementation is the key to a successful planning process. Even though managers might be experts on facts related to planning and the planning process, if they cannot transform this understanding into appropriate action, they will not be able to generate useful organizational plans.

One way to approach implementation is to view planning activities as an organizational subsystem. A **subsystem** is a system created as part of the overall management system. Figure 6.3 illustrates the relationship between the overall management system and a subsystem. Subsystems help managers organize the overall system and enhance its success.

Figure 6.4 presents the elements of the planning subsystem. The purpose of this subsystem is to increase the effectiveness of the overall management system by helping managers identify, guide, and direct planning activities within the overall system.[10]

A **subsystem** is a system created as part of the process of the overall management system. A planning subsystem increases the effectiveness of the overall management system.

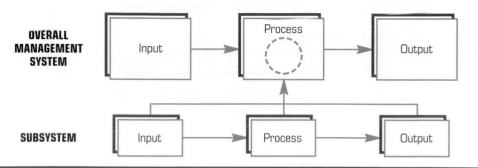

Figure 6.3

Relationship between overall management system and subsystem

Obviously, only a portion of organizational resources can be used as input in the planning subsystem. This input is allocated to the planning subsystem and transformed into output through the steps of the planning process.

▶ Back to the Case

Managers like those at American Airlines who are initiating Internet activities should use their planning process to produce a practical plan for the activities. The process of developing this plan should consist of six steps, beginning with a statement of an organizational objective to successfully design the plan and ending with guidelines for putting Internet plans into action.

To implement a planning process, planning should be viewed as a subsystem that is part of the process of the overall management system, and a portion of all the organizational resources available should be used, for the purpose of Internet-related planning. Following our new Internet strategy example, the output of this subsystem would be the actual plans used to introduce and use the strategy. Areas like integrating Internet systems throughout departments and establishing online relationships with traveling customers should be emphasized. A comprehensive planning effort at American Airlines would also focus on many other organizational areas, such as obtaining needed funds and establishing new flight schedules.

ORGANIZATIONAL OBJECTIVES: PLANNING'S FOUNDATION

The previous section made the point that managers start planning by stating or formulating organizational objectives. Only after they have a clear view of organizational objectives can they appropriately carry out subsequent steps of the planning process. Organizational objectives serve as the foundation upon which all subsequent planning efforts are built. The follow-

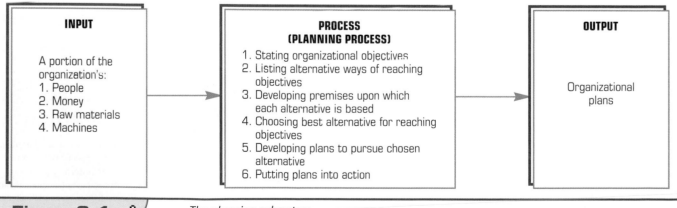

INPUT	PROCESS (PLANNING PROCESS)	OUTPUT
A portion of the organization's: 1. People 2. Money 3. Raw materials 4. Machines	1. Stating organizational objectives 2. Listing alternative ways of reaching objectives 3. Developing premises upon which each alternative is based 4. Choosing best alternative for reaching objectives 5. Developing plans to pursue chosen alternative 6. Putting plans into action	Organizational plans

Figure 6.4

The planning subsystem

CEO Gordon M. Bethune has stated quite clearly his objectives for Continental Airlines: He intends to reduce jobs, costs, and cut-rate fares while simultaneously improving service. The two prongs of the attack may seem contradictory, but Bethune is operating on a specific premise: Continental management, he maintains, can achieve both goals if it becomes more market-savvy and customer-oriented and less willing to let strictly financial considerations dictate marketing decisions.

ing sections focus on organizational objectives, a critical component of the planning process, by:

1. Defining organizational objectives
2. Pinpointing areas in which organizational objectives should be established
3. Illustrating how managers work with organizational objectives
4. Discussing management by objectives, an approach to management based mainly on organizational objectives

Definition of Organizational Objectives

Organizational objectives are the targets toward which the open management system is directed. Organizational input, process, and output—topics discussed in Chapter 2—all exist to reach organizational objectives (see Figure 6.5). Properly developed organizational objectives reflect the purpose of the organization—that is, they flow naturally from the organization's mission. The **organizational purpose** is what the organization exists to do, given a particular group of customers and customer needs. Table 6.1 contains several statements of organizational purpose, or mission, as developed by actual companies. If an organization is accomplishing its objectives, it is accomplishing its purpose and thereby justifying its reason for existence.

Organizational objectives are the targets toward which the open management system is directed. They flow from the organization's purpose or mission.

The **organizational purpose** is what the organization exists to do, given a particular group of customers and customer needs.

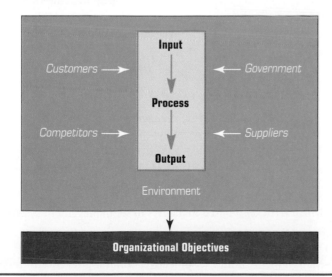

How an open management system operates to reach organizational objectives

Figure 6.5

Table 6.1   Examples of Statements of Organizational Purpose

DuPont	DuPont is a multinational, high-technology company that manufactures and markets chemically related products. It services a diversified group of markets in which proprietary technology provides the competing edge.
Polaroid	Polaroid manufactures and sells photographic products based on its inventions in the field of one-step instant photography and light-polarizing products. Utilizing its inventions in the field of polarized light, the company considers itself to be engaged in one line of business.
Central Soya	The basic mission of Central Soya is to be a leading producer and merchandiser of products for the worldwide agribusiness and food industry.
General Portland Cement	It has long been a business philosophy of Central Portland that "we manufacture and sell cement, but we market concrete." The company sees its job as manufacturing top-quality cement and working with customers to develop new applications for concrete while expanding current uses.

Organizations exist for various purposes and thus have various types of objectives. A hospital, for example, may have the primary purpose of providing high-quality medical services to the community. Therefore, its objectives are aimed at furnishing this assistance. The primary purpose of a business organization, in contrast, is usually to make a profit. The objectives of the business organization, therefore, concentrate on ensuring that a profit is made. Some companies, however, assume that if they focus on such organizational objectives as producing a quality product at a competitive price, profits will be inevitable. For example, although the Lincoln Electric Company is profit oriented, management has stated organizational objectives in these terms.[11]

The goal of the organization must be this—to make a better and better product to be sold at a lower and lower price. Profit cannot be the goal. Profit must be a by-product. This is a state of mind and a philosophy. Actually, an organization doing this job as it can be done will make large profits which must be properly divided between user, worker, and stockholder. This takes ability and character.

In a 1956 article that has become a classic, John F. Mee suggested that organizational objectives for businesses can be summarized in three points.[12]

1. Profit is the motivating force for managers
2. Service to customers by the provision of desired economic values (goods and services) justifies the existence of the business
3. Managers have social responsibilities in accordance with the ethical and moral codes of the society in which the business operates

Deciding on the objectives for an organization, then, is one of the most important actions managers take. Unrealistically high objectives are frustrating for employees, while objectives that are set too low do not push employees to maximize their potential. Managers should establish performance objectives that they know from experience are within reach for employees, but not within *easy* reach.[13]

AREAS FOR ORGANIZATIONAL OBJECTIVES

Peter F. Drucker, one of the most influential management writers of modern times, believed that the very survival of a management system was endangered when managers emphasized only the profit objective because this single-objective emphasis encourages managers to take action that will make money today with little regard for how a profit will be made tomorrow.[14]

Managers should strive to develop and attain a variety of objectives in all areas where activity is critical to the operation and success of the management system. Following are the eight key areas in which Drucker advised managers to set management system objectives:

1. *Market standing*—Management should set objectives indicating where it would like to be in relation to its competitors
2. *Innovation*—Management should set objectives outlining its commitment to the development of new methods of operation
3. *Productivity*—Management should set objectives outlining the target levels of production

4. *Physical and financial resources*—Management should set objectives regarding the use, acquisition, and maintenance of capital and monetary resources
5. *Profitability*—Management should set objectives that specify the profit the company would like to generate
6. *Managerial performance and development*—Management should set objectives that specify rates and levels of managerial productivity and growth
7. *Worker performance and attitude*—Management should set objectives that specify rates of worker productivity as well as desirable attitudes for workers to possess
8. *Public responsibility*—Management should set objectives that indicate the company's responsibilities to its customers and society and the extent to which the company intends to live up to those responsibilities

According to Drucker, since the first five goal areas relate to tangible, impersonal characteristics of organizational operation, most managers would not dispute their designation as key areas. Designating the last three as key areas, however, could arouse some managerial opposition because these areas are more personal and subjective. Regardless of this potential opposition, an organization should have objectives in all eight areas to maximize its probability of success.

The information in this section pertains to all the different areas in which managers can establish organizational objectives. One relatively new area in which managers are setting objectives involves Internet usage. The following Digital Focus discusses how one company recently altered its organizational objectives because of an increasing trend toward more Internet usage.

DIGITAL FOCUS

▶ Internet Trend Causes Sega to Alter Objectives: A Classic Example

Sega Enterprises, Inc., develops and markets video games and video game consoles. In 1997, the video game industry enjoyed record revenues of $5.5 billion, but Sega's once formidable grip on the industry virtually disappeared. In fact, Sega captured only 4 percent of the console market in 1997 while its main competitors, Sony and Nintendo, captured most of the remaining market. In the past, Sega's executives worried only about maintaining its huge market share, but two dynamics have forced the company to change its objectives: intense industry competition and the evolution of the Internet.

Due to intense industry competition, Sega changed its market share objective. More specifically, Sega's executives hope that sales of its new Dreamcast video game console, due to launch in the fall of 1999, match those of Sony's Playstation launch in 1995. In other words, Sega's objective changed from leading the market to simply keeping up with the market leader. Sega is concerned, however, that some consumers might skip its Dreamcast launch and wait until Sony introduces its new Playstation the following year.

Although intense competition obviously altered Sega's objectives, the company's executives might be even more concerned with the evolution of the Internet. Lower prices have made computers more affordable, and this increased computer ownership has provided more people with access to the Internet. This trend concerns Sega's executives because the Internet has spawned new games that enable users to play against thousands of strangers in real time on the Internet. As a result, Sega's new Dreamcast machine will include a first: a modem that allows users to connect to the Internet. With the modem, Sega executives hope to establish a presence in the Internet video game market. Obviously, these changes in the marketplace caused Sega to alter its objectives quite dramatically.

WORKING WITH ORGANIZATIONAL OBJECTIVES

Appropriate objectives are fundamental to the success of any organization. Theodore Levitt noted that some leading U.S. industries could be facing the same financial disaster as the railroads faced years earlier because their objectives were inappropriate for their organizations.[15]

Managers should approach the development, use, and modification of organizational objectives with the utmost seriousness. In general, an organization should set three types of objectives:

1. **Short-term objectives**—targets to be achieved in one year or less
2. **Intermediate-term objectives**—targets to be achieved in one to five years
3. **Long-term objectives**—targets to be achieved in five to seven years

Short-term objectives are targets to be achieved in one year or less.

Intermediate-term objectives are targets to be achieved within one to five years.

Long-term objectives are targets to be achieved within five to seven years.

The **principle of the objective** is a management guideline that recommends that before managers initiate any action, they should clearly determine, understand, and state organizational objectives.

The necessity of predetermining appropriate organizational objectives has led to the development of a management guideline called the **principle of the objective.** This principle holds that before managers initiate any action, they should clearly determine, understand, and state organizational objectives.

Developing a Hierarchy of Objectives In practice, an organizational objective must be broken down into subobjectives so that individuals at different levels and sections of the organization know what they must do to help reach the overall organizational objective.[16] An organizational objective is attained only after the subobjectives have been reached.

A **hierarchy of objectives** is the overall organizational objectives and the subobjectives assigned to the various people or units of the organization.

Suboptimization is a condition wherein organizational subobjectives are conflicting or not directly aimed at accomplishing the overall organizational objectives.

The overall organizational objective and the subobjectives assigned to the various people or units of the organization are referred to as a **hierarchy of objectives.** Figure 6.6 presents a sample hierarchy of objectives for a medium-sized company.

Suboptimization is a condition wherein subobjectives are conflicting or not directly aimed at accomplishing the overall organizational objective. Suboptimization is possible within the company whose hierarchy of objectives is depicted in Figure 6.6 if the first subobjective for the finance and accounting department clashes with the second subobjective for the supervisors. This conflict would occur if supervisors needed new equipment to maintain production and the finance and accounting department couldn't approve the loan without the company's borrowing surpassing 50 percent of company assets. In such a situation, in which established subobjectives are aimed in different directions, a manager would have to choose which subobjective would better contribute to obtaining overall objectives and should therefore take precedence.

Controlling suboptimization in organizations is part of a manager's job. Managers can minimize suboptimization by developing a thorough understanding of how various parts of

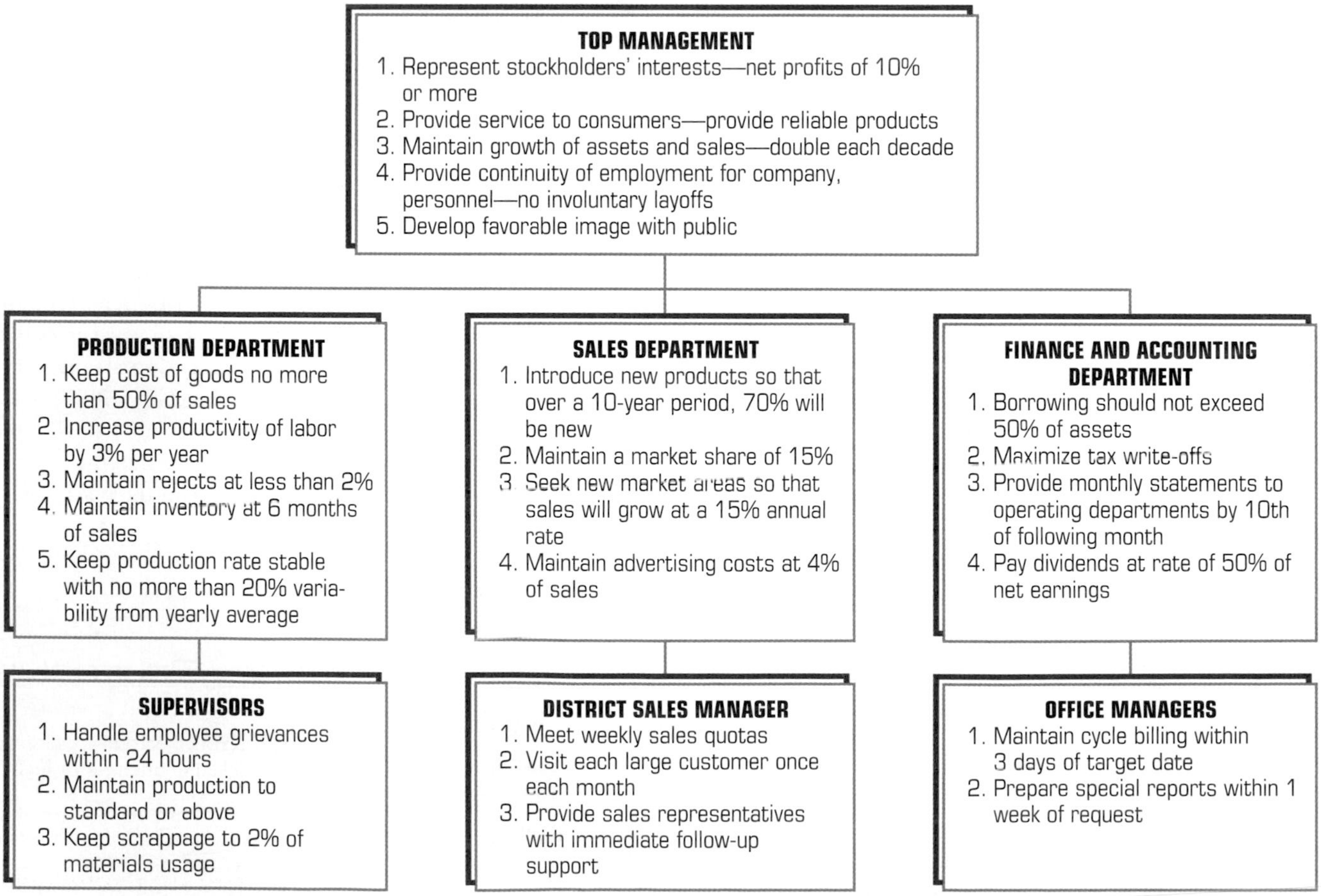
TOP MANAGEMENT
1. Represent stockholders' interests—net profits of 10% or more
2. Provide service to consumers—provide reliable products
3. Maintain growth of assets and sales—double each decade
4. Provide continuity of employment for company, personnel—no involuntary layoffs
5. Develop favorable image with public
PRODUCTION DEPARTMENT
1. Keep cost of goods no more than 50% of sales
2. Increase productivity of labor by 3% per year
3. Maintain rejects at less than 2%
4. Maintain inventory at 6 months of sales
5. Keep production rate stable with no more than 20% variability from yearly average
SALES DEPARTMENT
1. Introduce new products so that over a 10-year period, 70% will be new
2. Maintain a market share of 15%
3. Seek new market areas so that sales will grow at a 15% annual rate
4. Maintain advertising costs at 4% of sales
FINANCE AND ACCOUNTING DEPARTMENT
1. Borrowing should not exceed 50% of assets
2. Maximize tax write-offs
3. Provide monthly statements to operating departments by 10th of following month
4. Pay dividends at rate of 50% of net earnings
SUPERVISORS
1. Handle employee grievances within 24 hours
2. Maintain production to standard or above
3. Keep scrappage to 2% of materials usage
DISTRICT SALES MANAGER
1. Meet weekly sales quotas
2. Visit each large customer once each month
3. Provide sales representatives with immediate follow-up support
OFFICE MANAGERS
1. Maintain cycle billing within 3 days of target date
2. Prepare special reports within 1 week of request

Figure 6.6 *Hierarchy of objectives for a medium-sized organization*

the organization relate to one another and by ensuring that subobjectives properly reflect these relations.

▶ Back to the Case

Planning at American Airlines, as at any other company, begins with a statement of organizational objectives; these should reflect the purpose and goals of the company, which for American Airlines include profit targets, customer service targets, and social responsibility targets. Other organizational objectives for most companies would focus on market standing, innovation, productivity, and worker performance and attitude.

Overall objectives for a company like American Airlines should be of three basic types: short-term objectives that are to be achieved in a year or less; intermediate objectives, to be achieved in one to five years; and long-term objectives, to be achieved in five to seven years. Additionally, a company such as American Airlines would develop a hierarchy of objectives so that individuals at different levels of the organization know what they must do to help reach organizational targets.

Planning for Internet activities should emphasize implementation of those activities to help reach various organizational targets. American's planning for the Internet should focus on enhancing the accomplishment of its short-term, intermediate-term, and long-term objectives as they exist throughout the company's hierarchy of objectives.

Guidelines for Establishing Quality Objectives

The quality of goal statements, like that of all humanly developed commodities, can vary drastically. Here are some general guidelines that managers can use to increase the quality of their objectives:[17]

1. *Let the people responsible for attaining the objectives have a voice in setting them*—Often the people responsible for attaining the objectives know their job situation better than the managers do and can therefore help to make the objectives more realistic. They will also be better motivated to achieve objectives they have had a say in establishing. Work-related problems that these people face should be thoroughly considered when objectives are being developed.
2. *State objectives as specifically as possible*—Precise statements minimize confusion and ensure that employees have explicit directions for what they should do. Research shows that when objectives are not specific, the productivity of individuals attempting to reach those objectives tends to fluctuate significantly over time.
3. *Relate objectives to specific actions whenever necessary*—In this way, employees do not have to infer what they should do to accomplish their goals.
4. *Pinpoint expected results*—Employees should know exactly how managers will determine whether or not an objective has been reached.
5. *Set goals high enough that employees will have to strive to meet them, but not so high that employees give up trying to meet them*—Managers want employees to work hard but not to become frustrated.
6. *Specify when goals are expected to be achieved*—Employees must have a time frame for accomplishing their objectives. They then can pace themselves accordingly.
7. *Set objectives only in relation to other organizational objectives*—In this way, suboptimization can be kept to a minimum.
8. *State objectives clearly and simply*—The written or spoken word should not impede communicating a goal to organization members.

Management by Objectives (MBO)

Some managers find organizational objectives such an important and fundamental part of management that they use a management approach based exclusively on them. This approach, called **management by objectives** (MBO), was popularized mainly through the writings of Peter Drucker. Although mostly discussed in the context of profit-oriented companies, MBO

Management by objectives (MBO) is a management approach that uses organizational objectives as the primary means of managing organizations.

is also a valuable management tool for nonprofit organizations like libraries and community clubs. The MBO strategy has three basic parts:[18]

1. All individuals within an organization are assigned a specialized set of objectives that they try to reach during a normal operating period. These objectives are mutually set and agreed upon by individuals and their managers
2. Performance reviews are conducted periodically to determine how close individuals are to attaining their objectives
3. Rewards are given to individuals on the basis of how close they come to reaching their goals

The MBO process consists of five steps (see Figure 6.7):

1. *Review organizational objectives*—The manager gains a clear understanding of the organization's overall objectives
2. *Set worker objectives*—The manager and worker meet to agree on worker objectives to be reached by the end of the normal operating period
3. *Monitor progress*—At intervals during the normal operating period, the manager and worker check to see if the objectives are being reached
4. *Evaluate performance*—At the end of the normal operating period, the worker's performance is judged by the extent to which the worker reached the objectives
5. *Give rewards*—Rewards given to the worker are based on the extent to which the objectives were reached

Factors Necessary for a Successful MBO Program

Certain key factors are essential to the success of an MBO program. First, top management must be committed to the MBO process and set appropriate objectives for the organization. Since all individual MBO goals will be based on these overall objectives, if the overall objectives are inappropriate, individual MBO objectives will also be inappropriate and related individual work activity will be nonproductive. Second, managers and subordinates together must develop and agree on each individual's goals. Both managers and subordinates must feel that the individual objectives are just and appropriate if each party is to seriously regard them as a guide for action. Third, employee performance should be conscientiously evaluated against established objectives. This evaluation helps determine whether the objectives are fair and if appropriate means are being used to attain them. Fourth, management must follow through on employee performance evaluations by rewarding employees accordingly.

If employees are to continue striving to reach their MBO program objectives, managers must reward those who do reach, or surpass, their objectives more than those whose performance falls short of their objectives. It goes without saying that such rewards must be given

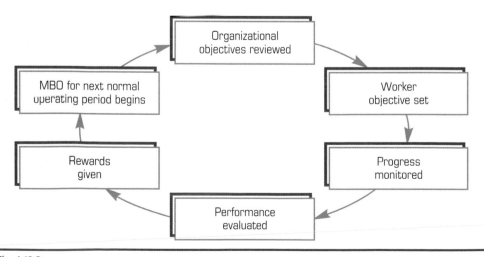

Figure 6.7 The MBO process

out fairly and honestly. Managers must be careful, though, not to automatically conclude that employees have produced at an acceptable level simply because they have reached their objectives. The objectives may have been set too low in the first place, and managers may have failed to recognize it at the time.[19]

MBO Programs: Advantages and Disadvantages

Experienced MBO managers say that there are two advantages to the MBO approach. First, MBO programs continually emphasize what should be done in an organization to achieve organizational goals. Second, the MBO process secures employee commitment to attaining organizational goals. Because managers and subordinates have developed objectives together, both parties are sincerely interested in reaching those goals.

MBO managers also admit that MBO has certain disadvantages. One is that the development of objectives can be time consuming, leaving both managers and employees less time in which to do their actual work. Another is that the elaborate written goals, careful communication of goals, and detailed performance evaluations required in an MBO program increase the volume of paperwork in an organization.

On balance, however, most managers believe that MBO's advantages outweigh its disadvantages. Therefore, they find MBO programs beneficial.

▶ Back to the Case

The higher the quality of the organizational objectives at a company like American Airlines the more valuable the planning activities. To increase the quality of objectives, managers can take steps such as allowing people responsible for attaining objectives to have a voice in setting them, stating objectives as clearly and simply as possible, and pinpointing expected results when objectives are achieved.

Managers at American Airlines might be so committed to managing via organizational targets that MBO becomes the primary management approach. Such an approach would involve monitoring the progress that workers are making in reaching established objectives and using rewards and punishments to hold workers accountable for reaching the objectives. An MBO program could be very advantageous to American Airlines because it would continually emphasize what needs to be accomplished to reach organizational targets. On the other hand, an MBO program could be extremely time consuming, and benefits might not outweigh the costs.

PLANNING AND THE CHIEF EXECUTIVE

More than two decades ago, Henry Mintzberg pointed out that the top managers—the chief executives—of organizations have many different roles to perform.[20] As organizational figureheads, they must represent their organizations in a variety of social, legal, and ceremonial situations. As leaders, they must ensure that organization members are properly guided toward achieving organizational goals. As liaisons, they must establish themselves as links between their organizations and factors outside their organizations. As monitors, they must assess organizational progress. As disturbance handlers, they must settle disputes between organization members. And as resource allocators, they must determine where resources should be placed to benefit their organizations best.

Final Responsibility

In addition to these many varied roles, chief executives have the final responsibility for organizational planning. As the scope of planning broadens to include a larger portion of the management system, it becomes increasingly important for chief executives to get involved in the planning process.

As planners, chief executives seek answers to the following broad questions:[21]

1. In what direction should the organization be going?
2. In what direction is the organization going now?

▶ Richard Branson, CEO and founder of the innovative Virgin Atlantic Airways, has continued to strike out in new business directions with Virgin Records. While some planners have their hands full managing one type of business, Branson has managed to achieve success in two widely different business ventures due to his superb planning skills.

3. Should something be done to change this direction?
4. Is the organization continuing in an appropriate direction?

Keeping informed about social, political, and scientific trends is of utmost importance in helping chief executives to answer these questions.

Planning Assistance

Given the necessity to participate in organizational planning while performing other time-consuming roles, more and more top managers have established the position of organization planner to obtain the planning assistance they require. Just as managers can ask others for help and advice in making decisions, so can they involve others in formulating organizational plans.[22]

The chief executive of a substantial organization almost certainly needs planning assistance.[23] The remainder of this chapter assumes that the organization planner is an individual who is not the chief executive of the organization, but rather a manager inside the organization who is responsible for assisting the chief executive on organizational planning issues.[24] Where the planner and the chief executive are the same person, however, the following discussion of the planner can, with slight modifications, be applied to the chief executive.

Including the Right People in Planning Enhances Quality at Sun Microsystems

Sun Microsystems, Inc., is an integrated portfolio of businesses that supply computing technologies, products, and services. Its computing solutions include networked workstations and multiprocessing servers, operating system software, silicon designs, and other value-added technologies.

Management at Sun Microsystems has developed a team approach to planning. The planning team, known within the company as the business team, consists of representatives from design engineering, manufacturing, customer service, finance, and marketing. It is used primarily during the introduction of a new product.

The business team follows a very specific process. First, it creates a formal plan for the new-product introduction and submits it to an executive-level committee within the corporation. This plan, known as the Product Initiation Form (PIF), is essentially a business plan for a single new product. Once the executive committee approves a PIF, implementation proceeds by establishing an implementation team, which also consists of a number of individuals representing several different operational areas.

Through this cross-functional deployment of individuals in both business and implementation teams, Sun Microsystems has achieved more effective planning. This improved planning, in turn, has enhanced overall product quality by contributing to more on-time delivery of products, better product designs, and a higher proportion of manufactured products meeting established quality standards. ∎

The planner is probably the most important input in the planning subsystem. This individual combines all other inputs and influences the subsystem process so that its output is effective organizational plans. The planner is responsible not only for developing plans but also for advising management on what actions should be taken to implement those plans. Regardless of who actually does the planning or what organization the planning is being done in, the qualifications, duties, and evaluations of the planner are all very important considerations for an effective planning subsystem.

Qualifications of Planners

Planners should have four primary qualifications:

- First, they should have considerable practical experience within their organization. Preferably, they should have been executives in one or more of the organization's major departments. This experience will help them develop plans that are both practical and tailor-made for the organization.
- Second, planners should be capable of replacing any narrow view of the organization they may have acquired while holding other organizational positions with an understanding of the organization as a whole. They must know how all parts of the organization function and interrelate. In other words, they must possess an abundance of the conceptual skills mentioned in Chapter 1.
- Third, planners should have some knowledge of and interest in the social, political, technical, and economic trends that could affect the future of the organization. They must be skillful in defining those trends and possess the expertise to determine how the organization should react to the trends to maximize its success. This qualification cannot be overemphasized.
- The fourth and last qualification for planners is that they be able to work well with others. Their position will inevitably require them to work closely with several key members of the organization, so its is essential that they possess the personal characteristics necessary to collaborate and advise effectively. The ability to communicate clearly, both orally and in writing, is one of the most important of these characteristics.[23]

▶ Liz Cobb founded Incentive Systems Inc., a sales-management software maker, with a large supply of venture capital and plenty of sales and marketing savvy. The firm took off and began to grow, especially with the rise of e-commerce, and Cobb soon realized the firm was in need of a strong management team. Being product champion, Web visionary, and chief executive was too much for one person. Cobb planned the appointment of Mike Byers carefully, hiring him as chief financial officer, promoting him to chief operating officer, and finally announcing his new role as CEO. Cobb continues as president of the firm, which thanks to her planning has made a smooth transition under Byers and looks forward to its IPO.

Evaluation of Planners

Planners, like all other organization members, should be evaluated according to the contribution they make toward helping the organization achieve its objectives.[26] The quality and appropriateness of the planning system and the plans that the planner develops for the organization are the primary considerations in this evaluation. Because the organizing, influencing, and controlling functions of managers all vitally depend on the fundamental planning function, an accurate evaluation of the planner is critically important to the organization.

Objective Indicators   Although the assessment of planners is necessarily somewhat subjective, there are several objective indicators. The use of appropriate techniques is one objective indicator. A planner who uses appropriate techniques is probably doing an acceptable job. The degree of objectivity displayed by the planner is another indicator. The planner's advice should be largely based on a rational analysis of appropriate information.[27] This is not to say that planners should abandon subjective judgment altogether; only that their opinions should be based chiefly on specific and appropriate information.

Malik suggests that a planner is doing a reputable job if the following objective criteria are met:[28]

1. Organizational plan is in writing
2. Plan is the result of all elements of the management team working together
3. Plan defines present and possible future business of the organization
4. Plan specifically mentions organizational objectives

5. Plan identifies future opportunities and suggests how to take advantage of them
6. Plan emphasizes both internal and external environments
7. Plan describes the attainment of objectives in operational terms whenever possible
8. Plan includes both long- and short-term recommendations

These eight criteria furnish objective guidelines for evaluating the performance of planners. However, management's evaluation of planners should never be completely objective. Important subjective considerations include how well planners get along with key members of the organization, the amount of organizational loyalty they display, and their perceived potential.

▶ Back to the Case

Technically, the CEO at American Airlines is responsible for planning for the organization as a whole, and for performing such related, time-consuming functions as keeping abreast of internal and external trends that could affect the future of the company. Because planning requires so much time, and because most CEOs have many other responsibilities within the company, they might want to consider appointing a director of planning.

The director of planning at American Airlines would need certain qualities, such as having had some experience at American Airlines; being able to see the company as an entire organization; having some ability to gauge and react to major trends that probably will affect the company's future, and being able to work well with others. The planner must oversee the planning process, evaluate developed plans, and solve planning problems. An evaluation of an American Airlines organization planner would be based on both objective and subjective appraisals of that planner's performance. Perhaps the first issue a company planner would want to address is the introduction of the new Internet strategy.

Management Skills Module

This section is specially designed to help you develop management skills. An individual's management skill is based on an understanding of management concepts and the ability to apply those concepts in management situations. As a result, the following activities are designed both to heighten your understanding of management concepts and to help you gain facility in applying those concepts in various management situations.

UNDERSTANDING MANAGEMENT CONCEPTS

▶ Action Summary

Reread the learning objectives below. Each objective is followed by questions. Answering these questions accurately will help you retain the most important concepts discussed in this chapter. After answering each question, check your answer against the answer key at the end of this chapter. (*Hint:* If you have any doubts regarding the correct response, consult the page number that follows the answer.)

Circle:

From studying this chapter, I will attempt to acquire

1. A definition of planning and an understanding of the purposes of planning.

    T F   **a.** The affirmative purpose of planning is to increase the degree of organizational success.

a b c d e   **b.** The following is *not* one of the purposes of planning: (a) systematic (b) protective (c) affirmative (d) coordination (e) fundamental.

2. Insights on how the major steps of the planning process are related.

a b c d e   **a.** The first major step in the planning process is: (a) developing premises (b) listing alternative ways of reaching organizational objectives (c) stating organizational objectives (d) developing plans to pursue chosen alternatives (e) putting plans into action.

a b c d e   **b.** The assumptions on which alternatives are based are usually referred to as: (a) objectives (b) premises (c) tactics (d) strategies (e) probabilities.

3. An understanding of the relationship between planning and organizational objectives.

    T F   **a.** Organizational objectives should reflect the organization's purpose.

a b c d e   **b.** The targets toward which an open management system is directed are referred to as: (a) functional objectives (b) organizational objectives (c) operational objectives (d) courses of action (e) individual objectives.

4. A knowledge of the areas in which managers should set organizational objectives.

a b c d e   **a.** The eight key areas in which Peter F. Drucker advises managers to set objectives include all of the following except: (a) market standing (b) productivity (c) public responsibility (d) inventory control (e) manager performance and development.

    T F   **b.** Long-term objectives are defined as targets to be achieved in one to five years.

5. An appreciation for the potential of a management-by-objectives (MBO) program.

    T F   **a.** Both performance evaluations and employee rewards should be tied to objectives assigned to individuals when the firm is using MBO.

a b c d e   **b.** A method under which a manager is given specific objectives to achieve and is evaluated according to the accomplishment of these objectives is: (a) means–ends analysis (b) operational objectives (c) individual objectives (d) management by objectives (e) management by exception.

6. A knowledge of how the chief executive relates to the planning process.

    T F   **a.** The responsibility for organizational planning rests with middle management.

a b c d e   **b.** The final responsibility for organizational planning rests with: (a) the planning department (b) the chief executive (c) departmental supervisors (d) the organizational planner (e) the entire organization.

7. An understanding of the qualifications and duties of planners and how planners can be evaluated.

    T F   **a.** The performance of planners should be evaluated with respect to the contribution they make toward helping the organization achieve its objectives.

a b c d e   **b.** The organizational planner's full responsibilities are: (a) developing plans only (b) advising about action that should be taken relative to the plans that the chief executive developed (c) advising about action that should be taken relative to the plans of the board of directors (d) selecting the person who will oversee the planning process (e) none of the above.

Action Summary Key

Issues for Review and Discussion

1. What is planning?
2. What is the main purpose of planning?
3. List and explain the advantages of planning.
4. Why are the disadvantages of planning called *potential* disadvantages?
5. Explain the phrase *primacy of planning*.
6. List the six steps in the planning process.
7. Outline the relationships among the six steps in the planning process.
8. What is an organizational subsystem?
9. List the elements of the planning subsystem.
10. What are organizational objectives and how do they relate to organizational purpose?
11. Explain why objectives are important to an organization.
12. List four areas in which organizational objectives can act as important guidelines for performance.
13. List and define eight key areas in which organizational objectives should be set.
14. What is a hierarchy of objectives?
15. Explain the purpose of a hierarchy of objectives.
16. How does suboptimization relate to a hierarchy of objectives?
17. List eight guidelines a manager should follow to establish quality organizational objectives.
18. Define MBO and describe its main characteristics.
19. List and describe the factors necessary for an MBO program to be successful.
20. Discuss the advantages and disadvantages of MBO.
21. How do the many roles of a chief executive relate to his or her role as organization planner?
22. Explain the basic qualifications of an organization planner.
23. How would you evaluate the performance of an organization planner?

APPLYING MANAGEMENT CONCEPTS

Cases

INTRODUCTORY CASE WRAP-UP

Case Discussion Questions

"American Airlines Planning to Make the Internet Work" (p. 123) and its related Back-to-the-Case sections were written to help you better understand the management concepts contained in this chapter. Answer the following discussion questions about this Introductory Case to further enrich your understanding of chapter content:

1. What special challenges will American Airlines face in planning for its new Internet thrust? What steps would you take to meet these challenges?
2. Would you have the American Airlines CEO or an appointed planning executive do the planning for the new Internet activities? Why?
3. List three criteria you would use to evaluate the planning for Internet activities done for American Airlines. Explain why you chose each criterion.

Skills Exercise: Designing a Management by Objectives (MBO) Program

In the Introductory Case, it is clear that one of American Airlines' objectives is to provide better customer service. To reach this objective, design an MBO program that relates the objectives of selected employees with the organizational objective of providing better customer service. First, identify the most important aspects of customer service and determine how to measure them. Second, establish what levels of performance result in employee awards. Last, determine the appropriate employee awards that would allow both employees and an organization member like the American Airlines manager of customer service to realize the successes of improved customer service. Focus your MBO program on American Airlines' improving customer service via the Internet.

CASE STUDY: *CAN ACCUSHIP OUTRUN FEDEX?*

Not so long ago, when a package needed to be mailed it went via the U.S. Postal Service or UPS. Then in 1971, Fred Smith founded Federal Express (known as FedEx)—introducing the concept of overnight delivery. Now businesses cannot do without it. Twenty-five years ago Smith hired a young man named Mason C. Kauffman to work for him at FedEx.

Kauffman was one of the University of Memphis M.B.A. students who were sitting in the audience when Fred Smith said, "If you want to create a business, go to a party and listen. You'll hear people complain." After working at FedEx for 16 years in sales, operations, engineering, and information management, Kauffman remembered Smith's advice. At age 40 he started listening to the frustrations of the company managers he was dealing with. They seemed overwhelmed by the ever-changing process of shipping and needed help figuring out how to find faster, cheaper, and easier ways to ship and keep track of their goods.

In 1994, Kauffman left FedEx and his $100,000-a-year salary to start a consulting business. His vision was to "offer one global solution" for transport and logistics services. Seven years later, his brainchild, Accuship, is a successful dot-com enterprise whose clients include Reebok International Ltd. and Verizon Communications. He wants to change how the average company finds and books its international freight services by offering his customers a neutral network in which to decide what is most cost effective for their particular needs. Right now he is working on a system based on "Sabre Systems," the principal means by which air passenger tickets are booked.

"We want to be everywhere in the world," Kauffman says. His plan is to target corporate giants first and then work down to smaller companies. Accuship is already responsible for shipping over 100,000 purchases made each day on the Home Shopping Network to people's homes in record time. Last year Accuship saved Coca-Cola $500,000 in shipping costs with a 99 percent reduction in paper invoices requiring manual processing.

Accuship's Web site integrates easily with organizations' in-house applications such as customer databases and accounting systems. Customers have the ability to choose and implement all the steps of the shipping process with a click of the mouse. Accuship currently turns over more than 500,000 transactions per day. Kauffman says this translates into a savings of $160 million overall to clients. Accuship even tracks packages en route and alerts the sender of any problems via e-mail.

How does Kauffman's virtual company with no planes, trucks, or warehouses do it? Kauffman operates in the Web-world but he sticks to land-based principles. He started Accuship with his own savings and did not receive any outside funding until the business was six years old. He took no salary the first year and worked alone using his attic as an office. Then he slowly built his staff, hiring people only after he already had new accounts. Now the Germantown, Tennessee–based dot-com has 100 employees on its payroll.

What is most striking about Accuship's leadership team is their collective traditional corporate background. Together these renegades from such powerhouses as Goldman Sachs, IBM, and Xerox are growing a successful dot-com. Last year the company received help from outside investors for the first time. Kauffman says it is part of his plan to make Accuship number one in the online shipping logistics field. He continues to expand to new countries and to add new services such as same-day delivery to any city in North America.

Right now, Accuship has a solid satisfied customer base, a real revenue stream, and a plan for growth. Kauffman says, "Timing is everything. . . . So I'm reminding everyone that we can't be in every country tomorrow and we can't be in every company tomorrow . . . Growth can kill companies."

Look out FedEx! If Kauffman takes his own advice and doesn't move too quickly, he might just win the race.

QUESTIONS

1. Would you recommend that a manager like Mason Kauffman develop a detailed plan for a business before starting it? Why?
2. If you were Kauffman, in which areas would you develop objectives for Accuship? Why?
3. Would you use MBO at Accuship? Explain.

QUICKTAKES SEGMENT 2
Planning

Remember John from the first part-ending video case? In this episode, we find out that John got the production manager job at Quicktakes. We meet up with John on his first day on the job; we join him at his first meeting at Quicktakes and are reintroduced to Hal and Karen, the owners of the company. We also meet Alexandra, the company's general manager. It seems that the purpose of this meeting is to give John an idea of how the company is organized, what its goals are, and how things run.

What can you learn from this meeting that relates to what you have learned about planning? Before considering this question, we might want to make some assumptions about the management of the company. Given that this meeting is set up to introduce John to the company, we assume that the people invited are those that the owners believe are important in setting the direction and focus of the company, or are those who are most responsible for keeping it running. This may not be a correct assumption, but it is logical that John might get this idea. He will only know for sure after he has been at Quicktakes for a while.

This meeting is John's first real chance to learn about who is really running Quicktakes and about how the people interact. In this meeting he gets some idea about how Hal and Karen operate and interact on the job. It is likely that someday, maybe soon, you will be in a meeting like this and you will be in John's shoes. Think about the kinds of information you would hope to get, the expectations you might have of new employers, and the kinds of things you would hope your new employer thinks are important. With these things in mind, you might now consider how you think John feels after this meeting.

There are a couple of important areas covered in this orientation meeting. First, we get some idea about the culture at Quicktakes. This comes across in the comments Hal makes to John about a dress code and the degree of formality that you observe in the meeting. You also get some hints about what Hal and Karen, and to some degree Alexandra, think Quicktakes' main product focus is. They tell John about things they think make them different from their competitors and things that they seem to think are important.

It is interesting that John asks about plans and goals, more than once. This gives us an idea about what is important to John. He does not necessarily get the answer he is looking for and seems to think that there might be more to planning than what is currently considered at Quicktakes.

QUESTIONS

1. Hal and Karen talk about their ideas for the company. Do you think they are both moving in the same direction and aiming for the same target? If not, how do you think this affects the ongoing operation of the company?

2. It was explained to John that it is difficult to plan because of changes in economic conditions and areas of public interest. What areas of Quicktakes' operation might economic and market factors affect the most? Do you think that these issues make it impossible to develop a general plan and goal for the company? What areas might be important to consider anyway?

3. There was some discussion of things that Quicktakes does other than video production. Why do you think they do these other things? To what degree should a small company like Quicktakes spread itself across multiple products?

PLANNING AND *YOU*

You are a popular junior at a mid-size college on the East Coast. You can't wait to start your new job as alumni liaison. The first big task is to organize homecoming weekend. First you call the alumni representatives from each class year to notify them of the date. It seems easy enough until everyone starts asking for the same location for his or her group. No one is willing to be in the outdoor tent. Finally after many phone calls, you explain to the younger attendees that they will just have to take the space available, since the older alumni should have the more comfortable rooms. All that is left now is to recruit your friends and classmates to help prepare banners, mail invitations, set up refreshment tables, and prepare the rooms for each party. Many of the friends whose help you thought you could count on let you down. You call meetings to clarify and delegate the various tasks, but your classmates don't show up. It seems everyone has an excuse. Either they have to make a practice or study for an exam.

1. You can't do this job alone. How do you recruit people to help you? Do you think the school should pay them to work? Might the Internet provide you with some shortcuts? Do you think you could devise a system of rewards or benefits so that your fellow students will join you in your efforts to make Homecoming weekend a success? What do you think the difficulties you face in dealing with both alumni and your own classmates might teach you about the principles of management and planning?

7 Making Decisions

Objectives

From studying this chapter, i will attempt to acquire

● A fundamental understanding of the term *decision*

● An understanding of each element of the decision situation

● An ability to use the decision-making process

● An appreciation for the various situations in which decisions are made

● An understanding of probability theory and decision trees as decision-making tools

● Insights into groups as decision makers

Gateway Chief Makes Daring Decisions

REMINDER: THE INTRODUCTORY CASE WRAP-UP (P. 163) CONTAINS DISCUSSION QUESTIONS AND A SKILLS EXERCISE TO FURTHER ILLUSTRATE THE APPLICATION OF CHAPTER CONCEPTS TO THIS VIGNETTE.

Ted Waitt and partner Mike Hammond founded Gateway as a telephone sales operation using a $10,000 CD from Ted's grandmother as collateral for a loan. On the way to earning $7.5 billion in 1998, Waitt has learned to be comfortable making risky decisions.

Although many are familiar with the histories of Bill Gates and Michael Dell, few know the story of Ted Waitt. Like Gates and Dell, Waitt left college to form Gateway, a multibillion-dollar company in the computer industry.

Gateway was started in an Iowa farmhouse by Waitt and Mike Hammond, who is now senior vice president of manufacturing for the company. Waitt's grandmother helped the two entrepreneurs secure a loan by offering a $10,000 CD from her nest egg as collateral. Waitt and Hammond started out by selling hardware peripherals and software to owners of Texas Instruments PCs. They then began designing and assembling their own fully configured PC-compatible systems for direct sale.

As the company grew, Waitt refused to abandon his Midwestern roots. In fact, he used these roots to differentiate the North Sioux City, South Dakota–based company from its competitors. More specifically, Gateway's use of cow spots helped it to establish a brand image, which is very difficult in the standardized computer industry. Waitt used Holstein cow–like themes in every way he could imagine. For example, Gateway shipped its computers to consumers in white boxes with cow-like black spots, and the company served cow-shaped cookies at its annual shareholder meetings. This brand image helped the company build a loyal customer base, and in 1998, Gateway reported revenues of $7.5 billion and a net income of $346 million.

However, in order to sustain the company's phenomenal growth, Waitt felt that he needed to make some changes. In April 1998, Gateway announced a major decision: Waitt, top executives, and assistants were relocating to an administrative headquarters in San Diego. The expansion move was designed to help attract executive-level talent and place the company closer to partners and suppliers. Waitt also decided that the company needed to reduce its reliance on the cow motif to improve Gateway's position in the profitable business market. Some business executives may not clearly see the connection between high-quality computers and cows.

Although Waitt views these decisions as necessary to increase the company's growth, some think the decisions are too risky. Waitt believes that these decisions will benefit the company, and he is well aware of the risks.

This case contributed by S. Trevis Certo, Texas A & M University

The Introductory Case discusses two decisions that Gateway's management recently made—to move the company's top management team to San Diego and to discontinue the use of its trademark cow logo in marketing campaigns. The information in this chapter discusses specifics surrounding a decision-making situation and provides insights about the steps that management at Gateway might have taken in making the decisions. This chapter discusses the following:

1) The fundamentals of decisions
2) The elements of the decision situation
3) The decision-making process
4) Various decision-making conditions
5) Decision-making tools

These topics are critical to managers and other individuals who make decisions.

FUNDAMENTALS OF DECISIONS

Definition of a Decision

A **decision** is a choice made between two or more available alternatives.

A **decision** is a choice made between two or more available alternatives. *Decision making* is the process of choosing the best alternative for reaching objectives. Decision making is covered in the planning section of this text, but since managers must also make decisions when performing the other three managerial functions—organizing, influencing, and controlling—the subject requires a separate chapter.

We all face decision situations every day. A decision situation may involve simply choosing whether to spend the day studying, swimming, or golfing. It does not matter which alternative is chosen, only that a choice is made.[1]

Managers make decisions affecting the organization daily and communicate those decisions to other organization members.[2] Not all managerial decisions are of equal significance to the organization. Some affect a large number of organization members, cost a great deal of money to carry out, or have a long-term effect on the organization. Such significant decisions can have a major impact, not only on the management system itself, but also on the career of the manager who makes them. Other decisions are fairly insignificant, affecting only a small number of organization members, costing little to carry out, and producing only a short-term effect on the organization.

Types of Decisions

Decisions can be categorized according to how much time a manager must spend in making them, what proportion of the organization must be involved in making them, and the organizational functions on which they focus. Probably the most generally accepted method of categorizing decisions, however, is based on computer language; it divides all decisions into two basic types: programmed and nonprogrammed.[3]

Programmed decisions are decisions that are routine and repetitive and that typically require specific handling methods.

Programmed decisions are routine and repetitive, and the organization typically develops specific ways to handle them. A programmed decision might involve determining how products will be arranged on the shelves of a supermarket. For this kind of routine, repetitive problem, standard-arrangement decisions are typically made according to established management guidelines.

Nonprogrammed decisions are typically one-shot decisions that are usually less structured than programmed decisions.

Nonprogrammed decisions, in contrast, are typically one-shot decisions that are usually less structured than programmed decisions. An example of the type of nonprogrammed decision that more and more managers are having to make is whether to expand operations into the "forgotten continent" of Africa.[4] Another example is deciding whether a supermarket should carry an additional type of bread. The manager making this decision must consider whether the new bread will merely stabilize bread sales by competing with existing bread carried in the store or actually increase bread sales by offering a desired brand of bread to customers who have never before bought bread in the store. These types of issues must be dealt with before the manager can finally decide whether to offer the new bread. Table 7.1 shows traditional and modern ways of handling programmed and nonprogrammed decisions.

Programmed and nonprogrammed decisions should be thought of as being at opposite ends of the decision programming continuum, as illustrated in Figure 7.1. As the figure indicates, however, some decisions are neither programmed nor nonprogrammed, falling somewhere between the two.

DIGITAL FOCUS

▶ Nestlé USA, Inc. Uses Internet to Speed Up Decisions

Nestlé is headquartered in Vevey, Switzerland. With a total workforce of over 224,000 people worldwide, it is Switzerland's largest industrial company, and with about 480 factories worldwide, Nestlé is also the world's largest food company. Its product line is extensive and diverse, and includes Taster's Choice coffee, Powerbar energy food, Baby Ruth and Butterfinger candy bars, and Alpo and Mighty Dog pet foods. Nestlé products are available in nearly every country in the world.

Nestlé USA, the U.S. operating arm of the company, is headquartered in Glendale, California. Joe Weller, CEO and chairman of the operation, is on a campaign to make Nestlé USA more efficient and faster moving. According to Weller, people in his company are wasting too much time in meetings, and he is urging managers to focus on making decisions more quickly, and in some cases, more independently.

Weller's primary tool for speeding up decisions and operations at Nestlé is the Internet. He is relying on it to help overhaul much of what the company does in areas ranging from buying raw materials to processing purchase orders to marketing its nearly 2,000 products and 200 brands. Speeding up planning decisions and activities in these major operational areas should be a significant factor in making Nestlé more competitive. Weller wants Nestlé to do business the e-business way, and he is convinced the Internet is the solution.

The Responsibility for Making Organizational Decisions

Many different kinds of decisions must be made within an organization—such as how to manufacture a product, how to maintain machines, how to ensure product quality, and how to establish advantageous relationships with customers. Since organizational decisions are so

Traditional and Modern Ways of Handling Programmed and Nonprogrammed Decisions

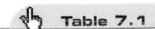 Table 7.1

Types of Decisions	Decision-Making Techniques	
	Traditional	Modern
Programmed:		
Routine, repetitive decisions	1. Habit	1. Operations research: Mathematical analysis models Computer simulation
Organization develops specific processes for handling them	2. Clerical routine: Standard operating procedures	2. Electronic data processing
	3. Organization structure: Common expectations A system of subgoals Well-defined information channels	
Nonprogrammed:		
One-shot, ill-structured, novel policy decisions	1. Judgment, intuition, and creativity	1. Heuristic problem-solving techniques applied to: Training human decision makers Constructing heuristic computer programs
Handled by general problem-solving processes	2. Rules of thumb	
	3. Selection and training of executives	

Figure 7.1   *Decision programming continuum*

varied, some type of rationale must be developed to stipulate who within the organization has the responsibility for making which decisions.

One such rationale is based primarily on two factors: the scope of the decision to be made and the levels of management. The **scope of the decision** is the proportion of the total management system that the decision will affect. The greater this proportion, the broader the scope of the decision is said to be. *Levels of management* are simply lower-level management, middle-level management, and upper-level management. The rationale for designating who makes which decisions is this: the broader the scope of a decision, the higher the level of the manager responsible for making that decision. Figure 7.2 illustrates this rationale.

One example of this decision-making rationale is the manner in which E. I. DuPont de Nemours and Company handles decisions related to the research and development function.[5] As Figure 7.3 shows, this organization makes both narrow-scope research and development decisions, such as "which markets to test" (decided by lower-level managers), and broad-scope research and development decisions, such as "authorize full-scale plant construction" (decided by upper-level managers).

The manager who is responsible for making a particular decision can ask the advice of other managers or subordinates before settling on an alternative. In fact, some managers prefer to use groups to make certain decisions.

Consensus is one method a manager can use in getting a group to arrive at a particular decision. **Consensus** is an agreement on a decision by all the individuals involved in making

The **scope of the decision** is the proportion of the total management system that a particular decision will affect. The broader the scope of a decision, the higher the level of the manager responsible for making that decision.

Consensus is an agreement on a decision by all individuals involved in making that decision.

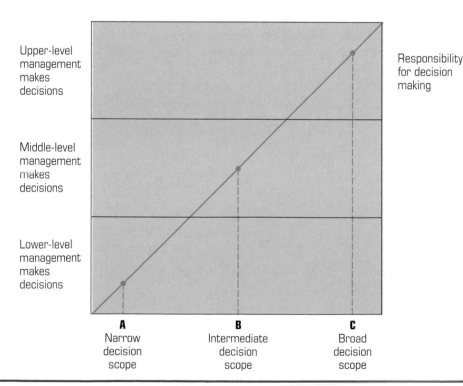

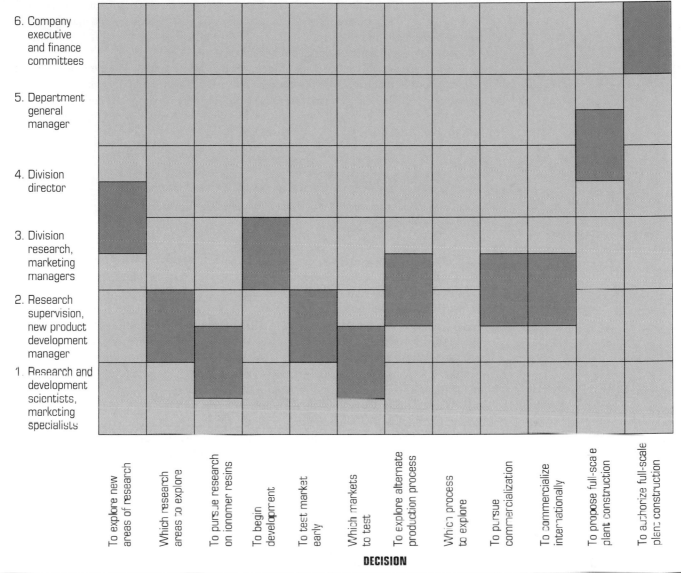

How scope of decision affects management level making decision at DuPont

Figure 7.3

that decision. It usually occurs after lengthy deliberation and discussion by members of the decision group, who may be either all managers or a mixture of managers and subordinates.[6]

The manager who asks a group to produce a consensus decision must bear in mind that groups will sometimes be unable to arrive at a decision. Lack of technical skills or poor interpersonal relations may prove insurmountable barriers to arriving at a consensus. When a group is stalemated, a manager needs to offer assistance in making the decision or simply make it herself.

Decisions arrived at through consensus have both advantages and disadvantages. One advantage of this method is that it focuses "several heads" on the decision. Another is that employees are more likely to be committed to implementing a decision if they helped make it. The main disadvantage of this method is that it often involves time-consuming discussions relating to the decision, which can be costly to the organization.

▶ Back to the Case

Evaluating whether to move the location of its corporate headquarters to San Diego is definitely a formal decision situation; that is, one that requires management at Gateway to choose

(continued)

between a number of alternatives. Gateway's management must scrutinize this decision carefully because of the significance to the organization and to the careers of the managers themselves. Technically, this decision is nonprogrammed in nature and therefore is characterized more by judgment than by simple, quantitative data.

Ted Waitt, the CEO at Gateway, would probably have the ultimate responsibility, with the approval of the board of directors, for making such a broad-scope decision. This does not mean, however, that Waitt would have to make the decision by himself. He could ask for advice from other Gateway employees and perhaps even appoint a group of managers and employees to arrive at a consensus on which alternative the company should implement.

Elements of the Decision Situation

Wilson and Alexis isolate several basic elements in the decision situation.[7] Five of these elements are defined and discussed in this section.

The Decision Makers   Decision makers, the first element of the decision situation, are the individuals or groups that actually make the choice among alternatives. According to Ernest Dale, weak decision makers usually have one of four orientations: receptive, exploitative, hoarding, and marketing.[8]

Decision makers who have a *receptive* orientation believe that the source of all good is outside themselves, and therefore they rely heavily on suggestions from other organization members. Basically, they want others to make their decisions for them.

Decision makers with an *exploitative* orientation also believe that the source of all good is outside themselves, and they are willing to steal ideas as necessary in order to make good decisions. They build their organizations on others' ideas and typically hog all the credit themselves, extending little or none to the originators of the ideas.

The *hoarding* orientation is characterized by the desire to preserve the status quo as much as possible. Decision makers with this orientation accept little outside help, isolate themselves from others, and are extremely self-reliant. They are obsessed with maintaining their present position and status.

Marketing-oriented decision makers look upon themselves as commodities that are only as valuable as the decisions they make. Thus they try to make decisions that will enhance their value and are highly conscious of what others think of their decisions.

The ideal decision-making orientation emphasizes the realization of the organization's potential as well as that of the decision maker. Ideal decision makers try to use all of their talents when making a decision and are characterized by reason and sound judgment. They are

In retail stores like this Folsom, California Wal-Mart, lower-level managers oversee the stocking of inventory and numerous other functions on the selling floor. Sometimes called first-line managers, they also spend a good deal of their time working with and supervising the employees who report directly to them. They also interact with suppliers and middle-level managers at the home office.

Decision Makers at Ben & Jerry's Make Decisions About Entering Foreign Markets

Ben & Jerry's Homemade, Inc. is a Vermont-based manufacturer of ice cream, frozen yogurt, and sorbet. Childhood friends Ben Cohen and Jerry Greenfield founded the company in 1978 in a renovated gas station in Burlington, Vermont. The pair started the company with a $12,000 investment, $4,000 of which was borrowed. The company soon became popular for its innovative flavors made from fresh Vermont milk and cream. Its products are currently distributed nationwide as well as in selected foreign countries.

The foreign countries to which Ben & Jerry's distributes product include the United Kingdom, France, The Netherlands, and Japan. The decision to enter a particular foreign market is very complicated and somewhat dependent on the country being considered. To decide to enter a country like Japan, for example, management must con-

sider issues such as the culture of Japan, existing channels for product distribution within Japan, and the overall trustworthiness of the Japanese government and its citizenry.

An interesting variable that Ben & Jerry's management considers when making the decision to distribute product within a country is the opportunity the company will have to perform socially responsible activities in that country. Ben & Jerry's mission focuses on operating in a way that actively recognizes the central role that business plays in the structure of society by initiating innovative ways to improve the quality of life of local, national, and international communities. A country must be sensitive to social responsibility issues and be able to afford the company avenues for social responsibility activities before Ben & Jerry decide to participate in its marketplace. ■

---

largely free of the qualities of the four undesirable decision-making orientations just described.

Goals to Be Served The goals that decision makers seek to attain are another element of the decision situation. In the case of managers, these goals should most often be organizational objectives. (Chapter 6 discusses the specifics of organizational objectives.)

Relevant Alternatives The decision situation is usually composed of at least two relevant alternatives. A **relevant alternative** is one that is considered feasible for solving an existing problem and for implementation. Alternatives that will not solve an existing problem *or* cannot be implemented are irrelevant and should be excluded from the decision-making situation.

Relevant alternatives are alternatives that are considered feasible for solving an existing problem and for implementation.

Ordering of Alternatives The decision situation requires a process or mechanism for ranking alternatives from most desirable to least desirable. This process can be subjective, objective, or some combination of the two. Past experience of the decision maker is an example of a subjective process, and the rate of output per machine is an example of an objective process.

Choice of Alternatives The last element of the decision situation is the actual choice between available alternatives. This choice establishes the decision. Typically, managers choose the alternative that maximizes long-term return for the organization.

▶ Back to the Case

As Gateway's management evaluates its decision about whether or not to abandon the company's popular cow-based marketing campaign, it must be aware of all the elements in the decision situation. Both the internal and external environments of Gateway would be one focus of the analysis. For example, internally, is there a sense of employee morale associated with the company's image? Externally, do customers in the highly profitable business market negatively perceive the company's products because of its cow-based marketing campaign? Management needs reason and sound judgment in making this decision. Also, management would have to keep Gateway's organizational objectives in mind and list relevant alternatives for additional marketing campaigns. For example, the company may decide to segment the market by keeping its current marketing campaign for consumers purchasing personal computers for home use while creating a new marketing campaign designed specifically for the business market. In addition, management would need to list such relevant alternatives in some order of desirability before choosing an alternative to implement.

THE DECISION-MAKING PROCESS

The **decision-making process** comprises the steps the decision maker takes to make a decision.

A decision is a choice of one alternative from a set of available alternatives. The **decision-making process** comprises the steps the decision maker takes to arrive at this choice. The process a manager uses to make decisions has a significant impact on the quality of those decisions. If managers use an organized and systematic process, the probability that their decisions will be sound is higher than if they use a disorganized and unsystematic process.[9]

A model of the decision-making process that is recommended for managerial use is presented in Figure 7.4. In order, the decision-making steps this model depicts are as follows:

1. Identify an existing problem
2. List possible alternatives for solving the problem
3. Select the most beneficial of these alternatives
4. Implement the selected alternative
5. Gather feedback to find out if the implemented alternative is solving the identified problem

The paragraphs that follow elaborate on each of these steps and explain their interrelationships.[10]

This model of the decision-making process is based on three primary assumptions.[11] First, the model assumes that humans are economic beings with the objective of maximizing satisfaction or return. Second, it assumes that within the decision-making situation all alternatives and their possible consequences are known. Its last assumption is that decision makers have some priority system to guide them in ranking the desirability of each alternative. If each of these assumptions is met, the decision made will probably be the best possible one for the organization. In real life, unfortunately, one or more of these assumptions is often not met, and therefore the decision made is less than optimal for the organization.

Identifying an Existing Problem

Decision making is essentially a problem-solving process that involves eliminating barriers to organizational goal attainment. The first step in this elimination process is identifying exactly what the problems or barriers are, for only after the barriers have been adequately identified can management take steps to eliminate them. Several years ago, Molson, a Canadian manufacturer of beer as well as of cleaning and sanitizing products, faced a barrier to success: a free-trade agreement that threatened to open Canadian borders to U.S. beer. Although the borders were not due to open for another five years, Molson decided to deal with the problem of increased beer competition from the United States immediately by increasing production and sales of its specialty chemical products. Within four years, Molson's chemical sales exceeded its beer sales. Essentially, the company identified its problem—the threat of increased U.S. competition for beer sales—and dealt with it by emphasizing sales in a different division.[12]

Chester Barnard has stated that organizational problems are brought to the attention of managers mainly by the following means:[13]

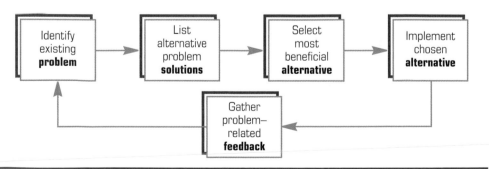

Figure 7.4 🖑 *Model of the decision-making process*

1. Orders issued by managers' supervisors
2. Situations relayed to managers by their subordinates
3. The normal activity of the managers themselves

Listing Alternative Solutions

Once a problem has been identified, managers should list the various possible solutions. Very few organizational problems are solvable in only one way. Managers must search out the numerous available alternative solutions to most organizational problems.

Before searching for solutions, however, managers should be aware of five limitations on the number of problem-solving alternatives available:[14]

1. Authority factors (for example, a manager's superior may have told the manager that a certain alternative is not feasible)
2. Biological or human factors (for example, human factors within the organization may be inappropriate for implementing certain alternatives)
3. Physical factors (for example, the physical facilities of the organization may be inappropriate for certain alternatives)
4. Technological factors (for example, the level of organizational technology may be inadequate for certain alternatives)
5. Economic factors (for example, certain alternatives may be too costly for the organization)

Figure 7.5 presents additional factors that can limit a manager's decision alternatives. This diagram uses the term *discretionary area* to depict all the feasible alternatives available to managers. Factors that limit or rule out alternatives outside this area are legal restrictions, moral and ethical norms, formal policies and rules, and unofficial social norms.[15]

Selecting the Most Beneficial Alternative

Decision makers can select the most beneficial solution only after they have evaluated each alternative very carefully. This evaluation should consist of three steps. First, decision makers should list, as accurately as possible, the potential effects of each alternative as if the alternative had already been chosen and implemented. Second, they should assign a probability factor to each of the potential effects; that is, indicate how probable the occurrence of the effect would be if the alternative were implemented. Third, keeping organizational goals in mind, decision makers should compare each alternative's expected effects and the respective probabilities of those effects.[16] After these steps have been completed, managers will know which alternative seems most advantageous to the organization.

Beth Crandall is vice president of research operations at Klein Associates, Inc. Her study of decision making among intensive-care nurses in a Dayton, Ohio, hospital showed that nurses relied on specific criteria in diagnosing dangerously fast-acting infections in newborns. Although the nurses said they "just knew" when to take emergency action to save a baby's life, Crandall showed that in reality their identification of the problem relied on their matching a set of subtle visual cues, such as skin color and behavior, to criteria they had learned to associate with danger. After learning that half the cues did not appear in the medical literature, Crandall developed a set of training materials for the nurses.

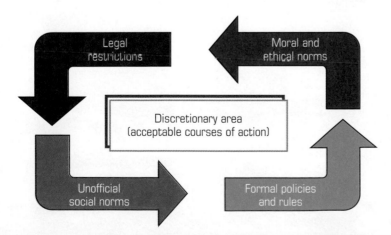

Additional factors that limit a manager's number of acceptable alternatives

Figure 7.5

Implementing the Chosen Alternative

The next step is to put the chosen alternative into action. Decisions must be supported by appropriate action if they are to have a chance of success.

Gathering Problem-Related Feedback

After the chosen alternative has been implemented, decision makers must gather feedback to determine the effect of the implemented alternative on the identified problem. If the identified problem is not being solved, managers need to search out and implement some other alternative.

The text presents the decision-making process essentially as a problem-solving process. The following People Spotlight feature illustrates how top management at John Deere and Company decided to solve significant problems by getting employees more involved in the company.

▶ Back to the Case

To illustrate the above material, assume that Gateway's management is facing a decision to introduce a new line of computers. Management would first need to identify the problem. For example, management could find out that business customers are purchasing computers from other companies because they perceive Gateway's computers as inferior. Once the problem is identified, management would have to list all possible problem solutions—for example: Can the quality of computer parts be improved? Would a new line of computers capture more consumers? Would a new marketing campaign improve customer perception of Gateway's products?

After eliminating infeasible solutions, Gateway's management would have to evaluate all remaining solutions, select one, and implement it. If either improving the quality of parts or designing a brand new line of computers required too much capital, the best alternative might be to create a new marketing campaign for Gateway's products. Management would then have to initiate appropriate action to formulate and implement a new campaign. Problem-related feedback would be extremely important once the new campaign was formulated. For example, the marketing department could conduct a survey to evaluate the effectiveness of the new campaign. Management could then find out if the new campaign did, in fact, positively influence consumers' perceptions of product quality. If the campaign failed, management would need to decide what other actions should be taken to improve customer perception of Gateway's computers.

▶ Choosing the best location for e-commerce warehouses is a matter of finding low-cost real estate and a plentiful labor force. E-Toys found such a location in Ontario, California, about 40 miles east of Los Angeles, where Alarick Palencia stocks toys. According to the firm's senior vice president for logistics, Ted Augustine, location, price, and freeway and rail access to Los Angeles and Long Beach were key considerations. "This is the nonglamorous stuff," he says, "but . . . it's increasingly seen as critical for success."

Decision at Deere & Company: Eliminate Problems by Building Employee Involvement

Hans W. Becherer, chief executive of Deere & Company, a firm that manufactures and sells farm equipment, recently faced two significant company problems: (1) the long-term demand for company products was weakening, and (2) competition from other companies was intensifying.

Becherer decided that the best way to deal with these problems was to get employees more involved in the company. For example, assembly-line workers were trained and then traveled across North America to explain Deere's new products to dealers and farmers. Becherer believed that this action would help the company fight its competition by impressing customers and dealers with the quality of Deere employees and hence its products. Becherer was also convinced that making production workers marketing emissaries for

Deere's products would strengthen their commitment to manufacturing only the best products because they would feel more responsible for output once they had developed personal relationships with customers and dealers.

Another move Becherer has taken is to encourage employee involvement in maintaining customer relationships and monitoring product-quality feedback.

As Becherer expands the responsibilities of his employees, he has been careful to step up their training so they will be well prepared for their new roles. Preliminary reports indicate that Becherer's implementation of his decision to involve employees has indeed helped him solve Deere's problems of weakening product demand and increased product competition. ∎

DECISION-MAKING CONDITIONS

In most instances, it is impossible for decision makers to know exactly what the future consequences of an implemented alternative will be. The word *future* is the key in discussing decision-making conditions. Because organizations and their environments are constantly changing, future consequences of implemented decisions are not perfectly predictable.

In general, there are three different conditions under which decisions are made. Each of these conditions is based on the degree to which the future outcome of a decision alternative is predictable. The conditions are as follows:[17]

1. Complete certainty
2. Complete uncertainty
3. Risk

Complete Certainty Condition

The **complete certainty condition** exists when decision makers know exactly what the results of an implemented alternative will be. Under this condition, managers have complete knowledge about a decision, so all they have to do is list outcomes for alternatives and then choose the outcome with the highest payoff for the organization. For example, the outcome of an investment in government bonds is, for all practical purposes, completely predictable because of established government interest rates. Deciding to implement this alternative, then, would be making a decision in a complete certainty situation. Unfortunately, most organizational decisions are made outside the complete certainty situation.

> The **complete certainty condition** is the decision-making situation in which the decision maker knows exactly what the results of an implemented alternative will be.

Complete Uncertainty Condition

The **complete uncertainty condition** exists when decision makers have absolutely no idea what the results of an implemented alternative will be. The complete uncertainty condition would exist, for example, if there were no historical data on which to base a decision. Not knowing what happened in the past makes it difficult to predict what will happen in the future. In this situation, decision makers usually find that sound decisions are mostly a matter of chance. An example of a decision made in a complete uncertainty situation is choosing to pull the candy machine lever labeled "Surprise of the Day" rather than the lever that would deliver a familiar candy bar. Fortunately, few organizational decisions need to be made in the complete uncertainty condition.

> The **complete uncertainty condition** is the decision-making situation in which the decision maker has absolutely no idea what the results of an implemented alternative will be.

Risk Condition

The primary characteristic of the **risk condition** is that decision makers have only enough information about the outcome of each alternative to estimate how probable an outcome will

> The **risk condition** is the decision-making situation in which the decision maker has only enough information to estimate how probable the outcome of implemented alternatives will be.

be.[18] Obviously, the risk condition lies somewhere between complete certainty and complete uncertainty. The manager who hires two extra salespeople in order to increase annual organizational sales is deciding in a risk situation. He may believe that the probability is high that these two new salespeople will raise total sales, but it is impossible for him to know that for sure. Therefore, some risk is associated with this decision.

The risk condition is a broad one in which *degrees* of risk can be associated with decisions. The lower the quality of information about the outcome of an alternative, the closer the situation is to complete uncertainty and the higher is the risk in choosing that alternative. Most decisions made in organizations have some amount of risk associated with them.

▶ Back to the Case

If Gateway's management decides to alter its marketing campaign, it must also face a decision regarding how to handle competition from other computer manufacturers like Dell and IBM. The decision-making condition for such a situation is somewhere between complete certainty and complete uncertainty about the outcome of the proposed alternatives. Gateway's management could decide, for example, to either lower prices or increase advertising to fight off the competition, but management has no guarantee that such measures would produce the desired results. Management does know, however, how its competitors have responded to price cuts in the past, and thus is not dealing with a complete unknown. Therefore, any decision that Gateway's management would make about handling increased competition would be made under the risk condition. In other words, management would have to determine the outcome probability for each proposed alternative and choose the alternative that looked most advantageous.

DECISION-MAKING TOOLS

Most managers develop an intuition about what decisions to make—a largely subjective feeling, based on years of experience in a particular organization or industry, that gives them insights into decision making for that industry or organization.[19] Although intuition is often an important factor in making a decision, managers generally emphasize more objective decision-making tools. The two most widely used such tools are probability theory and decision trees.[20]

Probability Theory

Probability theory is a decision-making tool used in risk situations—situations in which decision makers are not completely sure of the outcome of an implemented alternative. *Probability* refers to the likelihood that an event or outcome will actually occur. It is estimated by calculating an expected value for each alternative considered. Specifically, the **expected value (EV)** for an alternative is the income (I) that alternative would produce multiplied by its probability of producing that income (P). In formula form, $EV = I \times P$. Decision makers generally choose and implement the alternative with the highest expected value.[21]

An example will clarify the relationship of probability, income, and expected value. A manager is trying to decide where to open a store that specializes in renting surfboards. She is considering three possible locations (A, B, and C), all of which seem feasible. For the first year of operation, the manager has projected that, under ideal conditions, her company would earn $90,000 in Location A, $75,000 in Location B, and $60,000 in Location C. After studying historical weather patterns, however, she has determined that there is only a 20 percent chance—or a .2 probability—of ideal conditions occurring during the first year of operation in Location A. Locations B and C have a .4 and a .8 probability, respectively, for ideal conditions during the first year of operations. Expected values for each of these locations are as follows: Location A—$18,000; Location B—$30,000; Location C—$48,000. Figure 7.6 shows the situation this decision maker faces. According to her probability analysis, she should open a store in Location C, the alternative with the highest expected value.

Decision Trees

In the previous section, probability theory was applied to a relatively simple decision situation. Some decisions, however, are more complicated and involve a series of steps. These steps are

Probability theory is a decision-making tool used in risk situations—situations in which the decision maker is not completely sure of the outcome of an implemented alternative.

Expected value (EV) is the measurement of the anticipated value of some event, determined by multiplying the income an event would produce by its probability of producing that income ($EV = I \times P$).

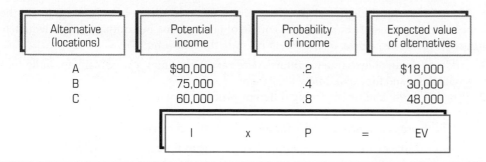

Alternative (locations)	Potential income	Probability of income	Expected value of alternatives
A	$90,000	.2	$18,000
B	75,000	.4	30,000
C	60,000	.8	48,000
	I	x	P	=	EV

Expected values from locating surfboard rental store in each of three possible locations

Figure 7.6

interdependent; that is, each step is influenced by the step that precedes it. A **decision tree** is a graphic decision-making tool typically used to evaluate decisions involving a series of steps.[22]

John F. Magee has developed a classic illustration that outlines how decision trees can be applied to a production decision.[23] In his illustration (see Figure 7.7), the Stygian Chemical Company must decide whether to build a small or a large plant to manufacture a new product with an expected life of 10 years (Decision Point 1 in Figure 7.7). If the choice is to build a large plant, the company could face high or low average product demand, or high initial and then low demand. If, however, the choice is to build a small plant, the company could face either initially high or initially low product demand. If the small plant is built and there is high product demand during an initial two-year period, management could then choose whether to expand the plant (Decision Point 2). Whether the decision is made to expand or not to expand, management could then face either high or low product demand.

A **decision tree** is a graphic decision-making tool typically used to evaluate decisions involving a series of steps.

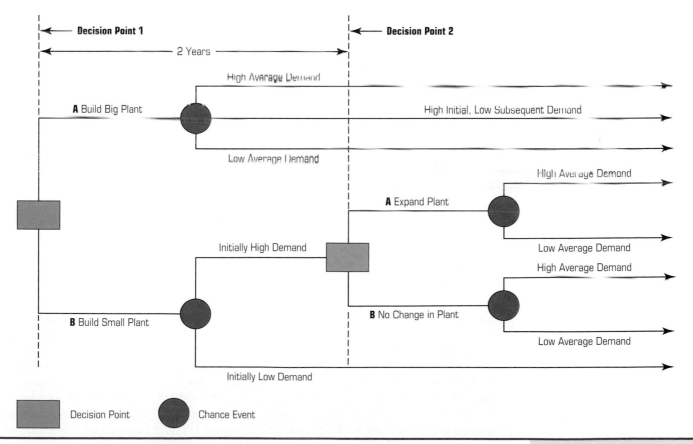

A basic decision tree illustrating the decision facing Stygian management

Figure 7.7

Now that various possible alternatives related to this decision have been outlined, the financial consequence of each different course of action must be compared. To adequately compare these consequences, management must do the following:

1. Study estimates of investment amounts necessary for building a large plant, for building a small plant, and for expanding a small plant
2. Weigh the probabilities of facing different product demand levels for various decision alternatives
3. Consider projected income yields for each decision alternative

Analysis of the expected values and net expected gain for each decision alternative helps management to decide on an appropriate choice.[24] *Net expected gain* is defined in this situation as the expected value of an alternative minus the investment cost. For example, if building a large plant yields the highest net expected gain, Stygian management should decide to build the large plant.

▶ Back to the Case

According to the previous information, managers at Gateway have two tools that they can use to make better decisions. First, they can use probability theory to obtain an expected value for various decision alternatives and then implement the alternative with the highest expected value. For example, in determining a tactic for handling Dell and IBM competition, Gateway's management may need to decide either to devote more of the company's resources to making higher quality computers or to initiate more effective advertising for its existing products. This decision would depend on the projected value of each alternative once implemented.

Second, with decisions that involve a series of steps related to each of several alternatives, Gateway's management could use a decision tree to assist in picturing and evaluating each alternative. For example, to handle the competition, Gateway's management could choose to design an entirely new line of high-powered computers or to devote more resources to the improvement of its existing lines. Each of these alternatives would lead to different decision-making steps.

Gateway's management must remember, however, that business judgment is an essential adjunct to the effective use of any decision-making tool. The purpose of the tool is to improve the quality of the judgment, not to replace it. In other words, Gateway's management must not only choose alternatives based on probability theory and decision trees, but must also use good judgment in deciding what is best for the company.

GROUP DECISION MAKING

Earlier in this chapter, decision makers were defined as individuals or groups that actually make a decision—that is, choose a decision alternative from those available. This section focuses on groups as decision makers. The two key topics discussed here are the advantages and disadvantages of using groups to make decisions, and the best processes for making group decisions.

Advantages and Disadvantages of Using Groups to Make Decisions

Groups commonly make decisions in organizations.[25] For example, groups are often asked to decide what new product should be offered to customers, how policies for promotion should be improved, and how the organization should reach higher production goals. Groups are so often asked to make organizational decisions because there are certain advantages to having a group of people rather than an individual manager make a decision. One is that a group can generally come up with more and better decision alternatives than an individual can. The reason for this is that a group can draw on collective, diverse organizational experiences as the foundation for decision making, while the individual manager has only the limited experiences of one person to draw on.[26] Another advantage is that when a group makes a decision, the members of that group tend to support the implementation of the decision more fervently

Employee-involvement groups entrusted with decision making are becoming increasingly common in the workplace. The Bic Corporation, for instance, relies on group decision making in its employee-involvement program, which uses employee suggestions to boost morale and productivity. Charlie Tichy, bottom right in the photo, leads a meeting where recent suggestions are discussed and tabulated. Last year 2,999 suggestions were submitted, and almost 2,400 were carried out on the recommendation of the group.

than they would if the decision had been made by an individual. This can be of significant help to a manager in successfully implementing a decision. A third advantage of using a group rather than an individual to make a decision is that group members tend to perceive the decision as their own, and this ownership perception makes it more likely that they will strive to implement the decision successfully rather than prematurely giving in to failure.

There are also several disadvantages to having groups rather than individual managers make organizational decisions. Perhaps the one most often discussed is that it takes longer to make a group decision because groups must take the time to present and discuss all the members' views. Another disadvantage is that group decisions cost the organization more than individual decisions do simply because they take up the time of more people in the organization. Finally, group decisions can be of lower quality than individual decisions if they become contaminated by the group members' efforts to maintain friendly relationships among themselves. This phenomenon of compromising the quality of a decision to maintain relationships within a group is referred to as *groupthink* and is discussed more fully in Chapter 17, "Groups, Teams, and Corporate Culture."

Managers must weigh all these advantages and disadvantages of group decision making carefully, factoring in unique organizational situations and give a group authority to make a decision only when the advantages of doing so clearly outweigh the disadvantages.

Processes for Making Group Decisions

Making a sound group decision regarding complex organizational circumstances is a formidable challenge. Fortunately, several useful processes have been developed to assist groups in meeting this challenge. The following sections discuss three such processes: brainstorming, nominal group technique, and Delphi technique.

Brainstorming   **Brainstorming** is a group decision-making process in which negative feedback on any suggested alternative by any group member is forbidden until all members have presented alternatives that they perceive as valuable.[27] Figure 7.8 shows this process. Brainstorming is carefully designed to encourage all group members to contribute as many viable decision alternatives as they can think of. Its premise is that if the evaluation of alternatives starts before all possible alternatives have been offered, valuable alternatives may be overlooked. During brainstorming, group members are encouraged to state their ideas, no matter how wild they may seem, while an appointed group member records all ideas for discussion.

Armstrong International's David Armstrong discovered an intriguing method for discouraging the premature evaluation of ideas during a brainstorming session. He allows only one negative comment per group member. Before discussion begins, he hands every member one piece of M&M's candy. Once a member makes a negative comment, he or she must eat the piece of candy. Because a group member is required to have an uneaten piece of candy in order

Brainstorming is a group decision-making process in which negative feedback on any suggested alternative to any group member is forbidden until all group members have presented alternatives that they perceive as valuable.

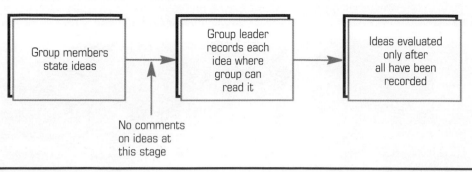

Figure 7.8   *The brainstorming process*

to make a negative comment, members use their sole opportunity to be negative very carefully.[28] Once everyone's ideas have been presented, the group evaluates them and chooses the one that holds the most promise.

Nominal group technique is a group decision-making process in which every group member is assured of equal participation in making the group decision. After each member writes down individual ideas and presents them orally to the group, the entire group discusses all the ideas and then votes for the best idea in a secret ballot.

Nominal Group Technique   The **nominal group technique** is another useful process for helping groups make decisions. This process is designed to ensure that each group member has equal participation in making the group decision.[29] It involves the following steps:

➤ *Step 1*—Each group member writes down individual ideas on the decision or problem being discussed.
➤ *Step 2*—Each member presents individual ideas orally. The ideas are usually written on a board for all other members to see and refer to.
➤ *Step 3*—After all members present their ideas, the entire group discusses these ideas simultaneously. Discussion tends to be unstructured and spontaneous.
➤ *Step 4*—When discussion is completed, a secret ballot is taken to allow members to support their favorite ideas without fear. The idea receiving the most votes is adopted and implemented.

Delphi technique is a group decision-making process that involves circulating questionnaires on a specific problem among group members, sharing the questionnaire results with them, and then continuing to recirculate and refine individual responses until a consensus regarding the problem is reached.

Delphi Technique   The **Delphi technique** is a third useful process for helping groups make decisions. The Delphi technique involves circulating questionnaires on a specific problem among group members, sharing the questionnaire results with them, and then continuing to recirculate and refine individual responses until a consensus regarding the problem is reached.[30] In contrast to the nominal group technique or brainstorming, the Delphi technique does not have group members meet face to face. The formal steps followed in the Delphi technique are:

➤ *Step 1*—A problem is identified.
➤ *Step 2*—Group members are asked to offer solutions to the problem by providing anonymous responses to a carefully designed questionnaire.
➤ *Step 3*—Responses of all group members are compiled and sent out to all group members.
➤ *Step 4*—Individual group members are asked to generate a new individual solution to the problem after they have studied the individual responses of all other group members compiled in Step 3.
➤ *Step 5*—Steps 3 and 4 are repeated until a consensus problem solution is reached.

Evaluating Group Decision-Making Processes   All three of the processes presented here for assisting groups in reaching decisions have both advantages and disadvantages. Brainstorming offers the advantage of encouraging the expression of as many useful ideas as possible, but the disadvantage of wasting the group's time on ideas that are wildly impractical. The nominal group technique, with its secret ballot, offers a structure in which individuals can support or reject an idea without fear of recrimination. Its disadvantage is that there is no way of knowing why individuals voted the way they did. The advantage of the Delphi technique is that ideas can be gathered from group members who are too geographically separated or busy to meet face to face. Its disadvantage is that members are unable to ask questions of one another.

As with any other management tool, managers must carefully weigh the advantages and disadvantages of these three group decision-making tools and adopt the one—or some combination of the three—that best suits their unique organizational circumstances.

▶ Back to the Case

The material in this section of the text offers insights about how a group at Gateway could be entrusted with the decision of whether to replace its marketing campaign. First, a decision of this magnitude and importance should probably be made by a group of top managers drawn from many different organizational areas. A group decision would almost certainly be better than an individual decision in this case because a group would have a broader view of Gateway and the market than any one person in the company would. Therefore, the group would be more likely to make an appropriate decision.

Perhaps the group decision-making process used in this case should be a combination of the three processes discussed in the text. Brainstorming sessions would ensure that all thoughts and ideas related to this crucial decision surface, while the nominal group technique would focus group members on the urgency of making the decision by requiring them to vote on whether or not to make the change. The Delphi technique could be used to obtain important input on the decision from experts around the country by asking them to present their written views through a specially designed questionnaire.

Unquestionably, using a group to make this decision would be time consuming and expensive. Once the decision is made, however, group members will be committed to it, perceive it as their own, and do all in their power to ensure that they are successful—even if the decision is *not* to change the marketing campaign.

Management Skills Module

This section is specially designed to help you develop management skills. An individual's management skill is based on an understanding of management concepts and the ability to apply those concepts in management situations. As a result, the following activities are designed both to heighten your understanding of management concepts and to help you gain facility in applying those concepts in various management situations.

UNDERSTANDING MANAGEMENT CONCEPTS

▶ Action Summary

Reread the learning objectives below. Each objective is followed by questions. Answering these questions accurately will help you retain the most important concepts discussed in this chapter. After answering each question, check your answer against the answer key at the end of this chapter. (*Hint:* If you have any doubt regarding the correct response, consult the page number that follows the answer.)

Circle:

From studying this chapter, I will attempt to acquire

1. A fundamental understanding of the term *decision.*

   T F   **a.** A decision is a choice made between two or more alternatives.

   a b c d e   **b.** Decision making is involved in the following function: (a) planning (b) organizing (c) controlling (d) influencing (e) all of the above.

2. An understanding of each element of the decision situation.

   a b c d e   **a.** The following type of decision-making orientation involves the belief that the source of all good is outside oneself and that, therefore, one must rely heavily on suggestions from other organizational members: (a) exploitation (b) hoarding (c) marketing (d) natural (e) receptive.

   a b c d e   **b.** According to Wilson and Alexis, all of the following are elements of the decision situation except: (a) the ordering of alternatives (b) the decision makers (c) the goals to be served (d) the timeliness of the decision (e) the relevant alternatives.

3. An ability to use the decision-making process.

   a b c d e   **a.** After identifying an existing problem, the next major step in the decision-making process is: (a) defining the terminology in the problem statement (b) listing possible alternatives to solve the problem (c) investigating possible alternatives to determine their effect on the problem (d) determining what parties will participate in the problem-solving process (e) identifying sources of alternatives to solve the problem.

   a b c d e   **b.** After going through the decision-making process, if the identified problem is not being solved as a result of the implemented alternative, the manager should: (a) attempt to redefine the problem (b) turn attention to another problem (c) search out and implement some other alternative (d) attempt to implement the alternative until the problem is solved (e) accept the fact that the problem cannot be solved.

4. An appreciation for the various situations in which decisions are made.

   T F   **a.** The risk condition exists when decision makers have absolutely no idea of what the results of an implemented alternative will be.

   T F   **b.** When operating under the complete uncertainty condition, decision makers usually find that sound decisions are a matter of chance.

5. An understanding of probability theory and decision trees as decision-making tools.

   a b c d e   **a.** Expected value is determined by using the formula: (a) $EV = I \times P$ (b) $EV = I/P$ (c) $EV = I + P$ (d) $EV = P - I$ (e) $EV = 2P \times I$.

   a b c d e   **b.** In the case of the Stygian Chemical Company, the problem was solved through the use of: (a) executive experience (b) decision tree technique (c) queuing theory (d) linear programming (e) demand probability.

6. Insights about groups as decision makers.

   T F   **a.** One disadvantage of using a group to make a decision is that members of the group will feel ownership of the decision.

   a b c d e   **b.** The process for group decision making that involves the use of questionnaires is: (a) brainstorming (b) nominal group technique (c) Delphi technique (d) a and b (e) all of the above.

Action Summary Answer Key

1. **a.** T, p. 146
   b. e, p. 146
2. **a.** e, p. 150
   b. d, pp. 150–151

3. **a.** b, p. 152
   b. c, p. 153
4. **a.** F, pp. 155–156
   b. T, p. 155

5. **a.** a, p. 156
   b. b, p. 157

6. **a.** F, pp. 158–159
   b. c, p. 160

Issues for Review and Discussion

1. What is a decision?
2. Describe the difference between a significant decision and an insignificant decision. Which would you rather make? Why?
3. List three programmed and three nonprogrammed decisions that the manager of a nightclub would probably have to make.
4. Explain the rationale for determining which managers in the organization are responsible for making which decisions.
5. What is the consensus method of making decisions? When would you use it?
6. List and define five basic elements of the decision-making situation.
7. How does the receptive orientation for decision making differ from the ideal orientation for decision making?
8. List as many undesirable traits of a decision maker as possible. (They are implied within the explanations of the receptive, exploitative, hoarding, and marketing orientations to decision making.)

9. What is a relevant alternative? An irrelevant alternative?
10. Draw and describe in words the decision-making process presented in this chapter.
11. What is meant by the term *discretionary area*?
12. List the three assumptions on which the decision-making process presented in this chapter is based.
13. Explain the difference between the complete certainty and complete uncertainty decision-making situations.
14. What is the risk decision-making situation?
15. Are there degrees of risk associated with various decisions? Why?
16. How do decision makers use probability theory? Be sure to discuss expected value in your answer.
17. What is a decision tree?
18. Under what conditions are decision trees usually used as decision-making tools?
19. Discuss the advantages and disadvantages of using a group to make an organizational decision.
20. In what ways are brainstorming, nominal group technique, and the Delphi technique similar? How do they differ?

APPLYING MANAGEMENT CONCEPTS

Cases

▶ INTRODUCTORY CASE WRAP-UP

Case Discussion Questions

"Gateway Chief Makes Daring Decisions" (p. 145) and its related Back-to-the-Case sections were written to help you better understand the management concepts contained in this chapter. Answer the following discussion questions about this Introductory Case to further enrich your understanding of the chapter content:

1. List three alternatives for handling competition that Gateway's management might consider *before* making a decision to abandon its popular marketing campaign.
2. What information would management need in order to evaluate these three alternatives?
3. Do you think that you would enjoy making this decision of whether to abandon the advertising campaign at Gateway? Explain.

Skills Exercise: Using Brainstorming to Make a Decision

Working in a group of four or five people, brainstorm as many alternatives as possible to Gateway's decision of how to improve market share in a highly profitable business market (use the brainstorming process as outlined in Figure 7.8). As a group, examine each suggested alternative and choose the one you think is best. Now, list three disadvantages and three advantages of using brainstorming to solve such a problem. Will you use brainstorming when you become a manager? Explain.

CASE STUDY: SPEEDNAMES, INC.: YOUNG AND SWIFT

Speednames was created in 1999 and launched in Europe and Asia Pacific. In just two years the company has become the world's largest international digital domain-name registrar. Customers can search for, register, and protect their domain names in English and over 10 European languages, including German, French, Spanish, Italian, Dutch, Swedish, Danish, and Norwegian.

The creative power behind Speednames is 25-year-old Nikolaj Nyholm. He was only 23 when he and his friend Clausen started their "i-technology company" in their native Denmark. Last year Nyholm gave up the position of CEO of his own company and named someone with more experience to the post. As heads of a successful start-up enterprise, Nyholm and Clausen soon found themselves growing too fast with too little capital. Nyholm knew they needed management help. He went to Internet Ventures Scandia (IVS), which supplied funding and assigned Morgens Nielsen as director. "Had we not made that decision, Speednames would not be alive today," says Nyholm.

Nielsen brought to the company the leadership and decision-making skills he acquired in his career as Vice President of business development for a leading Danish CRM software vendor, and founder and CEO of a leading international vendor of e-business software in Denmark.

In an interview with Flemming Fflyvholm, editor of Denmark's oldest and most prestigious newspaper *Berlingske Tidende,* Nyholm spoke openly about the short, happy life of his company. The interview was published in *Wireless,* and is the source for the following excerpts.

According to Nyholm, drive and confidence are typical of his generation. "We don't really see any barriers," he says. "We just go after what we want. . . . When you have an idea, you have to give it shape and form and an existence in the real world."

Nyholm believes in applied education rather than education for its own sake. He holds a degree in economics from Tufts University in Boston, Massachusetts. As a student at Tufts, he took a summer job with NetNames, and his work there eventually gave him the idea for Speednames. The atmosphere on the Tufts campus was "very intense" and "very inspirational," according to Nyholm. After returning to Denmark, he studied economics at the University of Copenhagen, where he felt frustrated. "I just couldn't grasp economics the way they were teaching it to us," he explains. "Their whole approach was to elevate economics to a high science on a par with physics or mathematics. Whereas I had always viewed economics as a tool." Nyholm also studied economics at the Universidad Naçional in San Jose, Costa Rica, and at the University of Roskilde in Denmark; but his fascination with pure economics began to lessen and he became more and more interested in business.

Nyholm now hires newly graduated university students to hold jobs at Speednames. When he interviews prospective candidates he is more concerned with their character than with their degree. "A pioneer spirit is the most important thing that any start-up needs," he says. "At Speednames that's what we seek to hang on to." He emulates Microsoft Corporation's dedication to its goals. "Our staff live and breathe their work. It's the only way we can make any forward progress overall. The entire team, quite simply, has to have the hots for the project."

He does not shy away from hiring people without business experience because he feels "they are very malleable, so as a company we can shape them to a large extent—they are so keen to get going that they are happy to work within the initial parameters we set them." He recognizes that as new graduates, "they've usually only had to work with projects involving themselves," and they need to be given guidelines set by top-level management at Speednames. Part of the challenge of being an employer is to hire a staff that can eventually work as a strong, productive team.

Nyholm talks openly about the financial problems Speednames had last year. "We had a business that in the first quarter of 2000 boomed incredibly. We had $2 million in the bank, but we still hadn't sufficient cash reserves to keep up with the bills." He and cofounder Clausen went to Internet Ventures Scandinavia (IVS) and were matched with a partner who had the expertise to remedy the situation.

The chief executive position was given to businessman Morgens Nielsen, a move that Nyholm didn't see as a defeat in any way. On the contrary, "It was something we requested of IVS," he says. "Speednames clearly needed a new CEO." Not only did Nielsen take over Nyholm's position, but he also brought in a whole management team with a new marketing director and a new financial director. They were all exceptionally talented and Nyholm says he experienced a huge sense of relief at being replaced as the head of Speednames. "You have to be able to let go of mere power and identify your core competency," he explains. "For me, that's the product design. It's what I like best, and I believe I'm pretty good at it. I like above all technology that can be turned into a product and beyond that into an entire business. Product development is where technology and the marketplace interface, and it's a minefield."

He is now, fittingly, Vice President of Product Development at Speednames and the young company has come through its first crisis with flying colors. In the coming months its services will become available to customers in Asian languages. Speednames continues to grow, combining the know how of experienced business executives with the ideas and energy of a young staff.

QUESTIONS

1. In a start-up company like Speednames, are decision-making conditions more often likely to be in the complete certainty category, the complete uncertainty category, or the risk category? Explain.

2. List the advantages and disadvantages of using groups to make decisions at a small company such as Speednames.

3. According to the description of decision makers in your text, what type of decision maker is 25-year-old Nikolaj Nyholm? Explain.

MASTERING MANAGEMENT: EPISODE 2—DECISION MAKING

Mastering Management is a series of innovative, interactive learning activities specially designed to help you develop management skills emphasized in various text chapters. Making decisions is the major focus of this chapter. Episode 2 of *Mastering Management* focuses on the decision-making process in organizations. In the introductory video, Andrew is faced with the decision of whether or not to leave CanGo in order to pursue a career elsewhere. Andrew finds this decision difficult to make and laden with stress. Review Episode 2 on your *Mastering Management* CD and then answer the following questions.

QUESTIONS

1. Is the decision facing Andrew of whether or not to leave CanGo a programmed or a nonprogrammed decision? Explain.

2. Would the model of the decision-making process presented in the chapter be useful to Andrew in making this decision? Why?

3. Under what decision-making conditions would Andrew be making this decision? Explain.

---

www.prenhall.com/certo

This book is accompanied by a rich assortment of online activities aimed at developing your management skills. Reviewing news headlines, Internet exercises, an online study guide, and other research and Internet resources can help personalize management skills development for individual students or an entire class.

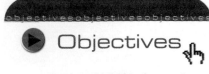

chapter
chapterchapterchapterchapterchapterchapter

8 Strategic Planning

Gillette's New Strategy: Women

REMINDER: THE INTRODUCTORY CASE WRAP-UP (P. 187) CONTAINS DISCUSSION QUESTIONS AND A SKILLS EXERCISE TO FURTHER ILLUSTRATE THE APPLICATION OF CHAPTER CONCEPTS TO THIS VIGNETTE.

G illette has been producing technologically advanced safety razors since 1903. Although Gillette has long been concerned with men's faces, the company now has a new strategy: women's legs. Gillette executives hope that the market for women's razors will provide the company with growth well into the next century.

Gillette virtually ignored the women's market until 1975, when it unveiled the Daisy razor. However, the Daisy represented little more than a pink version of the Good News disposable men's razor that it was already selling. Gillette's executives were afraid to invest too heavily in this market because they thought that it was too small, and their hesitation translated into poor unit sales. According to Mary Ann Pesce, vice presi-

Strategic planning is what brings a business like Gillette's line of shaving products for women from zero in 1975 to nearly $400 million in 1998.

dent of female shaving for Gillette's North Atlantic group, women were not buying the new Daisy—literally.

In 1992, the introduction of the Sensor for Women, designed by a female industrial engineer, showed that management had taken a different view toward the women's market. Today, Gillette has turned its shaving line for women into a global business worth nearly $400 million. In the United States, women's blades represent 20 percent of Gillette's sales, compared to just 3 percent in 1991.

Gillette recognizes the opportunity that the women's market provides, and so do its competitors. For example, Warner Lambert, the producer of Schick razors, has introduced its Silk Effects line for women. For Warner Lambert, shaving products for women represent 35 percent of its total U.S. blade sales, compared with 20 percent for Gillette.

Although the women's line represents a larger portion of Warner Lambert's sales, Gillette is still the clear market leader. More specifically, Gillette's women's shaving products boast nearly a 13 percent share of the $1.3 billion U.S. market, which represents a substantial portion of Gillette's overall 67 percent share. At the same time, Warner Lambert has a 16.5 percent share for both men's and women's products.

Gillette hopes to build on its women's market share by offering women their own version of the Mach3, Gillette's new three-bladed shaving system for men, and through its new "Gillette Women: Are

(continued)

You Ready?" advertising campaign. This campaign evolved from Gillette's market research showing that women regarded shaving as a chore separate from primping with makeup or clothing, and it attempts to establish a link between smooth-shaven legs and sex appeal.

Gillette's management shows a clear history of investing in its strategy of developing and selling its women's product line. In 1998, the company planed to spend $41 million to promote its women's line in the United States and Western Europe. For 2001–2002, the company is preparing to spend $150 million for the global advertising of its Venus shaving system for women. According to management, this campaign represents its largest marketing expenditure for a woman's product.

This case contributed by S. Trevis Certo, Texas A & M University

What's Ahead

The Introductory Case highlights the new competitive course taken by Gillette. Developing a new course of this sort is actually part of Gillette's strategic planning process. The material in this chapter explains how developing a competitive strategy fits into strategic planning and discusses the strategic planning process as a whole. Major topics included in this chapter are as follows:

1) Strategic planning
2) Tactical planning
3) Comparing and coordinating strategic and tactical planning
4) Planning and levels of management

STRATEGIC PLANNING

If managers are to be successful strategic planners, they must understand the fundamentals of strategic planning and how to formulate strategic plans.

Fundamentals of Strategic Planning

This section presents the basic principles of strategic planning. In doing so, it discusses definitions of both *strategic planning* and *strategy* in detail.

Strategic planning is long-range planning that focuses on the organization as a whole.

Defining Strategic Planning   **Strategic planning** is long-range planning that focuses on the organization as a whole. In doing strategic planning, managers consider the organization as a total unit and ask themselves what must be done in the long term to attain organizational goals. *Long range* is usually defined as a period of time extending about three to five years into the future. Hence, in strategic planning, managers try to determine what their organization should do to be successful three to five years from now. The most successful managers tend to be those who are capable of encouraging innovative strategic thinking within their organization.[1]

The **commitment principle** is a management guideline that advises managers to commit funds for planning only if they can anticipate, in the foreseeable future, a return on planning expenses as a result of the long-range planning analysis.

Managers may have a problem trying to decide exactly how far into the future they should extend their strategic planning. As a general rule, they should follow the **commitment principle,** which states that managers should commit funds for planning only if they can anticipate, in the foreseeable future, a return on planning expenses as a result of long-range planning analysis. Realistically, planning costs are an investment and therefore should not be incurred unless a reasonable return on that investment is anticipated.

Strategy is a broad and general plan developed to reach long-term organizational objectives; it is the end result of strategic planning.

Defining Strategy   **Strategy** is defined as a broad and general plan developed to reach long-term objectives. Organizational strategy can, and generally does, focus on many different

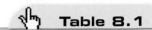
Company	Type of Business	Sample Organizational Objectives	Strategy to Accomplish Objectives
Ford Motor Company	Automobile manufacturing	1. Regain market share recently lost to General Motors 2. Regain quality reputation that was damaged because of Pinto gas tank explosions	1. Resize and downsize present models 2. Continue to produce subintermediate, standard, and luxury cars 3. Emphasize use of programmed combustion engines instead of diesel engines
Burger King	Fast food	1. Increase productivity	1. Increase people efficiency 2. Increase machine efficiency
CP Railroad	Transportation	1. Continue company growth 2. Continue company profits	1. Modernize 2. Develop valuable real estate holdings 3. Complete an appropriate railroad merger

organizational areas, such as marketing, finance, production, research and development, and public relations. It gives broad direction to the organization.[2]

Strategy is actually the end result of strategic planning. Although larger organizations tend to be more precise in developing organizational strategy than smaller organizations are, every organization should have a strategy of some sort.[3] For a strategy to be worthwhile, though, it must be consistent with organizational objectives, which, in turn, must be consistent with organizational purpose. Table 8.1 illustrates this relationship between organizational objectives and strategy by presenting sample organizational objectives and strategies for three well-known business organizations.

Strategy Management

Strategy management is the process of ensuring that an organization possesses and benefits from the use of an appropriate organizational strategy. In this definition, an appropriate strategy is one best suited to the needs of an organization at a particular time.

The strategy management process is generally thought to consist of five sequential and continuing steps:[4]

1. Environmental analysis
2. Establishment of an organizational direction
3. Strategy formulation
4. Strategy implementation
5. Strategic control

The relationships among these steps are illustrated in Figure 8.1.

Strategy management is the process of ensuring that an organization possesses and benefits from the use of an appropriate organizational strategy.

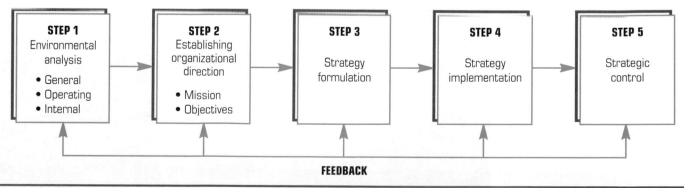

| STEP 1
Environmental analysis

• General
• Operating
• Internal | STEP 2
Establishing organizational direction

• Mission
• Objectives | STEP 3

Strategy formulation | STEP 4

Strategy implementation | STEP 5

Strategic control |

FEEDBACK

Steps of the strategy management process **Figure 8.1**

In developing a plan to vie with its competitors, management at Gillette would begin by thinking strategically. That is, management should try to determine what can be done to ensure that Gillette will be successful with its women's shaving line three to five years in the future. Developing a women's shaving line that best suits the marketplace is part of this thinking. Gillette's management must be careful, however, to spend funds on strategic planning only if they can anticipate a return on these expenses in the foreseeable future.

The end result of Gillette's overall strategic planning will be a strategy—a broad plan that outlines what must be done to reach long-range objectives and carry out the organizational purpose of the company. This strategy will focus on many organizational areas, one of which will be competing with other companies that develop similar shaving products. Once the strategy has been formulated using the results of an environmental analysis, Gillette's management must conscientiously carry out the remaining steps of the strategy management process: strategy implementation and strategic control.

Environmental analysis is the study of the organizational environment to pinpoint environmental factors that can significantly influence organizational operations.

Environmental Analysis   The first step of the strategy management process is environmental analysis. Chapter 2 presented organizations as open management systems that are continually interacting with their environments. In essence, an organization can be successful only if it is appropriately matched to its environment. **Environmental analysis** is the study of the organizational environment to pinpoint environmental factors that can significantly influence organizational operations. Managers commonly perform environmental analyses to help them understand what is happening both inside and outside their organizations and to increase the probability that the organizational strategies they develop will appropriately reflect the organizational environment.

In order to perform an environmental analysis efficiently and effectively, a manager must thoroughly understand how organizational environments are structured. For purposes of environmental analysis, the environment of an organization is generally divided into three distinct levels: general environment, operating environment, and internal environment.[5] Figure 8.2 illustrates the positions of these levels relative to one another and to the organization; it also shows the important components of each level. Managers must be well aware of these three environmental levels, understand how each level affects organizational performance, and then formulate organizational strategies in response to this understanding.

The General Environment   The level of an organization's external environment that contains components having broad long-term implications for managing the organization is

▶ Factors that firms consider in formulating strategic plans to do business overseas, such as shipping these U.S.-grown apples to Yokohama, Japan, include aspects of the general environment such as possible legal considerations (tariffs, quotas, and so on); the operating environment, such as consumer tastes and preferences; and the internal environment, such as the firm's ability to transport perishable merchandise without loss.

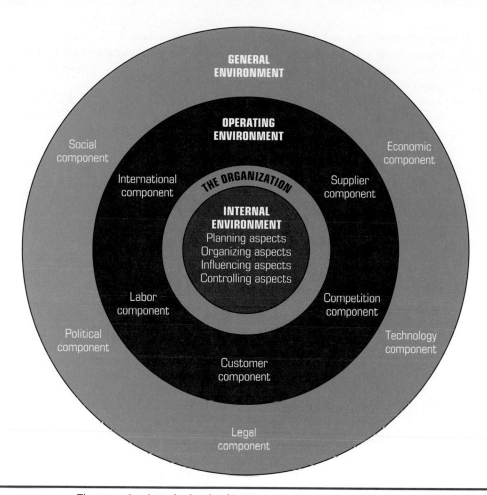

The organization, the levels of its environment, and the components of those levels

Figure 8.2

the **general environment.** The components normally considered part of the general environment are economic, social, political, legal, and technological.

The Economic Component. The economic component is that part of the general environment that indicates how resources are being distributed and used within the environment. This component is based on **economics,** the science that focuses on understanding how people of a particular community or nation produce, distribute, and use various goods and services. Important issues to be considered in an economic analysis of an environment are generally the wages paid to labor, inflation, the taxes paid by labor and businesses, the cost of materials used in the production process, and the prices at which produced goods and services are sold to customers.

Economic issues like these can significantly influence the environment in which a company operates, and the ease or difficulty the organization experiences in attempting to reach its objectives. For example, it should be somewhat easier for an organization to sell its products at higher prices if potential consumers in the environment are earning relatively high wages and paying relatively low taxes than if these same potential customers are earning relatively low wages and have significantly fewer after-tax dollars to spend.

Organizational strategy should reflect the economic issues in the organization's environment. To build on the preceding example, if the total amount of after-tax income that potential customers earn has significantly declined, an appropriate organizational strategy might be to lower the price of goods or services to make them more affordable. Such a strategy should be evaluated carefully, however, because it could have a serious impact on organizational profits.

The Social Component. The social component is part of the general environment that describes the characteristics of the society in which the organization exists. Two important features of a society commonly studied during environmental analysis are demographics and social values.[6]

The **general environment** is the level of an organization's external environment that contains components normally having broad long-term implications for managing the organization; its components are economic, social, political, legal, and technological.

Economics is the science that focuses on understanding how people of a particular community or nation produce, distribute, and use various goods and services.

Demographics are the statistical characteristics of a population. Organizational strategy should reflect demographics.

Demographics are the statistical characteristics of a population. These characteristics include changes in numbers of people and income distribution among various population segments. Such changes can influence the reception of goods and services within the organization's environment and thus should be reflected in organizational strategy.

For example, the demand for retirement housing would probably increase dramatically if both the number and the income of retirees in a particular market area doubled.[7] Effective organizational strategy would include a mechanism for dealing with such a probable increase in demand within the organization's environment.

An understanding of demographics is also helpful for developing a strategy aimed at recruiting new employees to fill certain positions within an organization. Knowing that only a small number of people have a certain type of educational background, for example, would tell an organization that it should compete more intensely to attract these people. To formulate a recruitment strategy, managers need a clear understanding of the demographics of the groups from which employees eventually will be hired.

Social values are the relative degrees of worth society places on the manner in which it exists and functions.

Social values are the relative degrees of worth that society places on the ways in which it exists and functions. Over time, social values can change dramatically, causing significant changes in how people live. These changes alter the organizational environment and, as a result, have an impact on organizational strategy. It is important for managers to remember that although changes in the values of a particular society may come either slowly or quickly, they are inevitable.

The Political Component. The political component is that part of the general environment related to government affairs. Examples include the type of government in existence, government's attitude toward various industries, lobbying efforts by interest groups, progress on the passage of laws, and political party platforms and candidates. The reunification of Germany and the shift from a Marxist-Socialist government in the Soviet Union in the 1980s illustrate how the political component of an organization's general environment can change at the international level.

The Legal Component. The legal component is that part of the general environment that contains passed legislation. This component comprises the rules or laws that society's members must follow. Some examples of legislation specifically aimed at the operation of organizations are the Clean Air Act, which focuses on minimizing air pollution; the Occupational Safety and Health Act, which aims at ensuring a safe workplace; the Comprehensive Environmental Response, Compensation, and Liability Act, which emphasizes controlling hazardous waste sites; and the Consumer Products Safety Act, which upholds the notion that businesses must provide safe products for consumers. Over time, new laws are passed and some old ones are amended or eliminated.

▶ Since former President Bill Clinton lifted the embargo against trade with Vietnam in February 1994, the communist country in Southeast Asia has ordered an annual average of 300,000 fiber-optic phone lines (plus advanced digital switches)—despite a per capita income of $220. Political factors, it seems, have been overridden by economic factors: Like most of their Third World counterparts, Vietnam's leaders realize that economic progress is dependent on a modern telecommunications infrastructure.

The Technology Component.   The technology component is that part of the general environment that includes new approaches to producing goods and services. These approaches can be new procedures as well as new equipment. The trend toward exploiting robots to improve productivity is an example of the technology component. The increasing use of robots in the next decade should vastly improve the efficiency of U.S. industry.

The Operating Environment   The level of an organization's external environment that contains components normally having relatively specific and immediate implications for managing the organization is the **operating environment**. As Figure 8.2 shows, major components of this environmental level are customers, competition, labor, suppliers, and international issues.

> The **operating environment** is the level of the organization's external environment that contains components normally having relatively specific and immediate implications for managing the organization.

The Customer Component.   The customer component is the operating environment segment that is composed of factors relating to those who buy goods and services provided by the organization. Businesses commonly create profiles, or detailed descriptions, of those who buy their products. Developing such profiles helps management generate ideas for improving customer acceptance of organizational goods and services.

The Competition Component.   The competition component is the operating environment segment that is composed of those with whom an organization must battle in order to obtain resources. Organizational strategy requires searching for a plan of action that will give the organization an advantage over its competitors. Because understanding competitors is a key factor in developing effective strategy, understanding the competitive environment is a fundamental challenge to management. Basically, the purpose of competitive analysis is to help management comprehend the strengths, weaknesses, capabilities, and likely strategies of existing and potential competitors.[8]

The Labor Component.   The labor component is the operating environment segment that is composed of factors influencing the supply of workers available to perform needed organizational tasks. Issues such as skill levels, trainability, desired wage rates, and average age of potential workers are important to the operation of the organization. Another important, but often overlooked, issue is potential employees' desire to work for particular organizations.

The Supplier Component.   The supplier component is the operating environment segment that comprises all variables related to the individuals or agencies that provide organizations with the resources they need to produce goods or services. These individuals or agencies are called **suppliers**. Issues such as how many suppliers offer specified resources for sale, the relative quality of the materials offered by different suppliers, the reliability of supplier deliveries, and the credit terms provided by suppliers are all important to managing an organization effectively and efficiently.

> **Suppliers** are individuals or agencies that provide organizations with the resources they need to produce goods and services.

The International Component.   The international component is the operating environment segment that is composed of all the factors relating to the international implications of organizational operations. Although not all organizations must deal with international issues, the number that have to do so is increasing dramatically and continually in the early twenty-first century. Significant factors in the international component include other countries' laws, culture, economics, and politics.[9] Important variables within each of these four categories are presented in Table 8.2.

The Internal Environment   The level of an organization's environment that exists inside the organization and normally has immediate and specific implications for managing the organization is the **internal environment**. In broad terms, the internal environment includes marketing, finance, and accounting. From a more specific management viewpoint, it includes planning, organizing, influencing, and controlling within the organization.

> The **internal environment** is the level of an organization's environment that exists inside the organization and normally has immediate and specific implications for managing the organization.

▶ Back to the Case

As part of the strategy development process, Gillette's management should spend time analyzing the organization's environment. They should focus on Gillette's general, operating, and internal environments. Environmental factors that would be important for them to consider as they pursue strategic planning include the number of companies with which Gillette competes

(continued)

and knowing if this number will be increasing or decreasing, strengths and weakness of their products when compared to competitive companies, the reasons why people pay to use high-quality shaving products, and the methods competitors like Warner Lambert are using to promote their products to customers. Obtaining information about environmental issues such as these will increase the probability that any strategy developed for Gillette will be appropriate for its environment, and that the company will be successful in the long term.

Establishing Organizational Direction   The second step of the strategy management process is establishing organizational direction. Through an interpretation of information gathered during environmental analysis, managers can determine the direction in which an organization should move. Two important ingredients of organizational direction are organizational mission and organizational objectives.

Determining Organizational Mission   The most common initial act in establishing organizational direction is determining an organizational mission. **Organizational mission** is the purpose for which—the reason why—an organization exists. In general, the firm's organizational mission reflects such information as what types of products or services it produces, who its customers tend to be, and what important values it holds. Organizational mission is a very broad statement of organizational direction and is based on a thorough analysis of information generated through environmental analysis.[10]

The **organizational mission** is the purpose for which, or the reason why, an organization exists.

Developing a Mission Statement   A **mission statement** is a written document developed by management, normally based on input by managers as well as nonmanagers, that describes and explains what the mission of an organization actually is. The mission is expressed in writing to ensure that all organization members will have easy access to it and thoroughly understand exactly what the organization is trying to accomplish. Here, for example, is the mission statement of FedEx:

A **mission statement** is a written document developed by management, normally based on input by managers as well as nonmanagers, that describes and explains the organization's mission.

> *FedEx is committed to our People-Service-Profit philosophy. We will produce outstanding financial returns by providing totally reliable, competitively superior, global air-ground transportation of high-priority goods and documents that require rapid, time-certain deliv-*

Table 8.2   Important Aspects of the International Component of the Organization's Operating Environment

Legal Environment

Legal tradition
Effectiveness of legal system
Treaties with foreign nations
Patent and trademark laws
Laws affecting business firms

Economic Environment

Level of economic development
Population
Gross national product
Per capita income
Literacy level
Social infrastructure
Natural resources
Climate
Membership in regional economic blocs
(EEC, LAFTA, etc.)
Monetary and fiscal policies
Nature of competition
Currency convertibility
Inflation
Taxation system
Interest rates
Wage and salary levels

Cultural Environment

Customs, norms, values, beliefs
Language
Attitudes
Motivations
Social institutions
Status symbols
Religious beliefs

Political System

Form of government
Political ideology
Stability of government
Strength of opposition parties and groups
Social unrest
Political strife and insurgency
Government attitude toward foreign firms
Foreign policy

McMurry Publishing Values Code Includes Social Responsibility

McMurry Publishing is one of the largest custom publishers in the United States. Based in Phoenix, Arizona, it also has offices in New York City. The company publishes and distributes custom magazines and other periodicals for over 300 corporate clients.

In little more than 10 years, McMurry Publishing has grown from a company of four people publishing a single custom magazine to over 80 employees publishing 18 magazines for 78 million readers in 23 countries. The management of such growth is extremely challenging, and critical to its success is a documented values code that gives employees broad, general direction regarding how they are to act and make decisions within the company. Employees are asked to sign the code to declare commitment to it.

McMurry's value code is designed to enable the company to fulfill its organizational mission. Overall, the code reflects how employees build and maintain relationships with company staff, vendors, and

clients. The values code focuses on social responsibility as well as other critical areas, and entails the following:

1. Do the right thing
2. Help one another
3. Deliver outstanding customer service
4. Produce quality always
5. Exceed expectations
6. Embrace change
7. Accept social responsibility
8. Earn a reasonable profit

Many at McMurry believe that the values code has been instrumental in building company success. According to Preston McMurry, chairman and president, the company has never borrowed money and has been profitable in 48 of the last 49 quarters. ■

---

ery. Equally important, positive control of each package will be maintained utilizing real time electronic tracking and tracing systems. A complete record of each shipment and delivery will be presented with our request for payment. We will be helpful, courteous, and professional to each other and the public. We will strive to have a completely satisfied customer at the end of each transaction.

The Importance of Organizational Mission An organizational mission is very important to an organization because it helps management increase the probability that the organization will be successful. There are several reasons why it does this. First, the existence of an organizational mission helps management focus human effort in a common direction. The mission makes explicit the major targets the organization is trying to reach and helps managers keep these targets in mind as they make decisions. Second, an organizational mission serves as a sound rationale for allocating resources. A properly developed mission statement gives managers general, but useful, guidelines about how resources should be used to best accomplish organizational purpose. Third, a mission statement helps management define broad but important job areas within an organization and therefore critical jobs that must be accomplished.[11]

▶ Organizational direction is set at the highest level of the firm. When she was appointed CEO of Hewlett-Packard in 1999, Carly Fiorina wanted to return the company to the peak of success and effective management it had maintained for most of its 60-year existence. In her view, that required the biggest reorganization in the company's history. Many observers say her decision to redirect the firm by introducing sweeping changes at every level may work—and it may not.

SPOTLIGHT *quality*

Goodall Rubber Company was established by Howard W. Goodall in 1905. In the early years Goodall was primarily a distributor, but when it acquired Whitehead Bros. Rubber Company in 1925 the company began manufacturing and distributing its own products. This strategy was successful until the early 1980s when economic conditions forced Goodall to examine its business more closely. Things became more difficult and in 1985 the Swedish industrial group Trelleborg AB bought Goodall and operated it as a subsidiary.

Goodall Rubber now faced the issue of whether to be a manufacturer, a distributor, or both. Management decided to do what it did best and focus on being a distributor. It established a new direction for

Goodall, called "Total Quality Distribution," and designed and launched a marketing campaign for the purpose of helping Goodall employees and customers understand the firm's new direction. Part of management's efforts to establish the new direction entailed developing a new mission statement outlining Goodall's commitment to high-quality distribution, and a new slogan was developed to maintain the new direction: "Goodall, The Total Quality Distributor."

The history of Goodall Rubber illustrates management flexibility in changing the direction of a company. It also illustrates how a mission statement can be used to reinforce an established new direction like "total quality." The change of direction has had a positive effect, and today Goodall Rubber is one of the largest hose and accessories distributorships in the United States. ■

The Relationship Between Mission and Objectives Organizational objectives were defined in Chapter 6 as the targets toward which the open management system is directed. Sound organizational objectives reflect and flow naturally from the purpose of the organization. The organization's purpose is expressed in its mission statement. As a result, useful organizational objectives must reflect and flow naturally from an organizational mission that, in turn, was designed to reflect and flow naturally from the results of an environmental analysis.

Strategy Formulation: Tools After managers involved in the strategic management process have analyzed the environment and determined organizational direction through the development of a mission statement and organizational objectives, they are ready to formulate strategy. **Strategy formulation** is the process of determining appropriate courses of action for achieving organizational objectives and thereby accomplishing organizational purpose.

> **Strategy formulation** is the process of determining appropriate courses of action for achieving organizational objectives and thereby accomplishing organizational purpose. Strategy development tools include critical question analysis, SWOT analysis, business portfolio analysis, and Porter's Model for Industry Analysis.

Managers formulate strategies that reflect environmental analysis, lead to fulfillment of organizational mission, and result in reaching organizational objectives. Special tools they can use to assist them in formulating strategies include the following:

1. Critical question analysis
2. SWOT analysis
3. Business portfolio analysis
4. Porter's Model for Industry Analysis

These four strategy development tools are related but distinct. Managers should use the tool or combination of tools that seems most appropriate for them and their organizations.

Critical Question Analysis A synthesis of the ideas of several contemporary management writers suggests that formulating appropriate organizational strategy is a process of **critical question analysis**—answering the following four basic questions:[12]

> **Critical question analysis** is a strategy development tool that consists of answering basic questions about the present purposes and objectives of the organization, its present direction and environment, and actions that can be taken to achieve organizational objectives in the future.

> ➤ *What are the purposes and objectives of the organization?* The answer to this question will tell management where the organization should be going. As indicated earlier, appropriate strategy reflects both organizational purpose and objectives. By answering this question during the strategy formulation process, managers are likely to remember this important point and thereby minimize inconsistencies among the organization's purposes, objectives, and strategies.

> ➤ *Where is the organization presently going?* The answer to this question can tell managers if the organization is achieving its goals, and if it is, whether the level of progress is satisfactory. Whereas the first question focuses on where the organization should be going, this one focuses on where the organization is actually going.

> ➤ *In what kind of environment does the organization now exist?* Both internal and external environments—factors inside and outside the organization—are covered in this question. For example, assume that a poorly trained middle-management team and a sudden influx

of competitors in a market are factors in, respectively, the internal and external environments of an organization. Any strategy formulated, if it is to be appropriate, must deal with these factors.

➤ *What can be done to better achieve organizational objectives in the future?* It is the answer to this question that results in the strategy of the organization. The question should be answered, however, only *after* managers have had an adequate opportunity to reflect on the answers to the previous three questions. Managers cannot develop an appropriate organizational strategy unless they have a clear understanding of where the organization wants to go, where it is going, and in what environment it exists.

SWOT Analysis   **SWOT analysis** is a strategic development tool that matches internal organizational strengths and weaknesses with external opportunities and threats. (SWOT is an acronym for a firm's **S**trengths and **W**eaknesses and its environmental **O**pportunities and **T**hreats.) SWOT analysis is based on the assumption that if managers carefully review such strengths, weaknesses, opportunities, and threats, a useful strategy for ensuring organizational success will become evident to them.[13]

SWOT analysis is a strategy development tool that matches internal organizational strengths and weaknesses with external opportunities and threats.

Business Portfolio Analysis   Business portfolio analysis is another strategy development tool that has gained wide acceptance. **Business portfolio analysis** is an organizational strategy formulation technique that is based on the philosophy that organizations should develop strategy much as they handle investment portfolios. Just as sound financial investments should be supported and unsound ones discarded, sound organizational activities should be emphasized and unsound ones deemphasized. Two business portfolio tools are the BCG Growth-Share Matrix and the GE Multifactor Portfolio Matrix.

Business portfolio analysis is the development of business-related strategy based primarily on the market share of businesses and the growth of markets in which businesses exist.

The BCG Growth-Share Matrix.   The Boston Consulting Group (BCG), a leading manufacturing consulting firm, developed and popularized a portfolio analysis tool that helps managers develop organizational strategy based on market share of businesses and the growth of markets in which businesses exist.

The first step in using the BCG Growth-Share Matrix is identifying the organization's strategic business units (SBUs). A **strategic business unit** is a significant organization segment that is analyzed to develop organizational strategy aimed at generating future business or revenue. Exactly what constitutes an SBU varies from organization to organization. In larger organizations, an SBU could be a company division, a single product, or a complete product line. In smaller organizations, it might be the entire company. Although SBUs vary drastically in form, each has the following four characteristics:[14]

A **strategic business unit** (SBU) is, in business portfolio analysis, a significant organizational segment that is analyzed to develop organizational strategy aimed at generating future business or revenue. SBUs vary in form, but all are a single business (or collection of businesses), have their own competitors and a manager accountable for operations, and can be independently planned for.

1. It is a single business or collection of related businesses
2. It has its own competitors
3. It has a manager who is accountable for its operation
4. It is an area that can be independently planned for within the organization

After SBUs have been identified for a particular organization, the next step in using the BCG Matrix is to categorize each SBU within one of the following four matrix quadrants (see Figure 8.3):

➤ *Stars*—SBUs that are "stars" have a high share of a high-growth market and typically need large amounts of cash to support their rapid and significant growth. Stars also generate large amounts of cash for the organization and are usually segments in which management can make additional investments and earn attractive returns.

➤ *Cash Cows*—SBUs that are cash cows have a large share of a market that is growing only slightly. Naturally, these SBUs provide the organization with large amounts of cash, but since their market is not growing significantly, the cash is generally used to meet the financial demands of the organization in other areas, such as the expansion of a star SBU.

➤ *Question Marks*—SBUs that are question marks have a small share of a high-growth market. They are dubbed "question marks" because it is uncertain whether management should invest more cash in them to gain a larger share of the market or deemphasize or eliminate them. Management will choose the first option when it believes it can turn the question mark into a star, and the second when it thinks further investment would be fruitless.

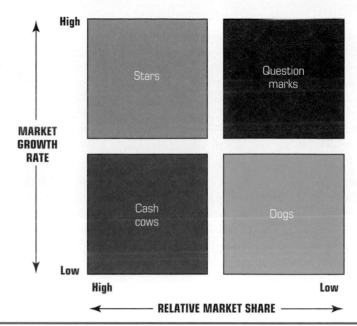

Figure 8.3 👆   *The BCG Growth-Share Matrix*

> *Dogs*—SBUs that are dogs have a relatively small share of a low-growth market. They may barely support themselves; in some cases, they actually drain off cash resources generated by other SBUs. Examples of dogs are SBUs that produce typewriters or cash registers.

Companies such as Westinghouse and Shell Oil have successfully used the BCG Matrix in their strategy management processes. This technique, however, has some potential pitfalls. For one thing, the matrix does not consider such factors as (1) various types of risk associated with product development, (2) threats that inflation and other economic conditions can create in the future, and (3) social, political, and ecological pressures. These pitfalls may be the reason for recent research results indicating that the BCG Matrix does not always help managers make better strategic decisions.[15] Managers must remember to weigh such factors carefully when designing organizational strategy based on the BCG Matrix.

The GE Multifactor Portfolio Matrix.   With the help of McKinsey and Company, a leading consulting firm, the General Electric Company (GE) has developed another popular portfolio analysis tool. Called the GE Multifactor Portfolio Matrix, this tool helps managers develop organizational strategy that is based primarily on market attractiveness and business strengths. The GE Multifactor Portfolio Matrix was deliberately designed to be more complete than the BCG Growth-Share Matrix.

Its basic use is illustrated in Figure 8.4. Each of the organization's businesses or SBUs is plotted on a matrix in two dimensions: industry attractiveness and business strength. Each of these two dimensions is actually a composite of a variety of factors that each firm must determine for itself, given its own unique situation. As examples, industry attractiveness might be determined by such factors as the number of competitors in an industry, the rate of industry growth, and the weakness of competitors within an industry; while business strengths might be determined by such factors as a company's financially solid position, its good bargaining position over suppliers, and its high level of technology use.

Several circles appear on Figure 8.4, each representing a company line of business or SBU. Circle size indicates the relative market size for each line of business. The shaded portion of a circle represents the proportion of the total SBU market that a company has captured.

Specific strategies for a company are implied by where their businesses (represented by circles) fall on the matrix. Businesses falling in the cells that form a diagonal from lower left to upper right are medium-strength businesses that should be invested in only selectively. Businesses above and to the left of this diagonal are the strongest and the ones that the company should invest in and help to grow. Businesses in the cells below and to the right of the diagonal are low in overall strength and are serious candidates for divestiture.

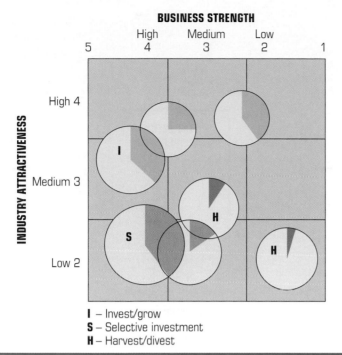

BUSINESS STRENGTH

I – Invest/grow
S – Selective investment
H – Harvest/divest

GE's Multifactor Portfolio Matrix

Figure 8.4

Portfolio models are graphic frameworks for analyzing relationships among the businesses of an organization, and they can provide useful strategy recommendations. However, no such model yet devised gives managers a universally accepted approach for dealing with these issues. Portfolio models, then, should never be applied in a mechanistic fashion, and any conclusions they suggest must be carefully considered in light of sound managerial judgment and experience.

Porter's Model for Industry Analysis   Perhaps the best-known tool for formulating strategy is a model developed by Michael E. Porter, an internationally acclaimed strategic management expert.[16] Essentially, Porter's model outlines the primary forces that determine competitiveness within an industry and illustrates how those forces are related. The model suggests that in order to develop effective organizational strategies, managers must understand and react to those forces within an industry that determine an organization's level of competitiveness within that industry.

Porter's model is presented in Figure 8.5. According to the model, competitiveness within an industry is determined by the following: new entrants or new companies within the industry; products that might act as a substitute for goods or services that companies within the industry produce; the ability of suppliers to control issues like costs of materials that industry companies use to manufacture their products; the bargaining power that buyers possess within the industry; and the general level of rivalry or competition among firms within the industry. According to the model, then, buyers, product substitutes, suppliers, and potential new companies within an industry all contribute to the level of rivalry among industry firms.

Strategy Formulation: Types   Understanding the forces that determine competitiveness within an industry should help managers develop strategies that will make their companies more competitive within the industry. Porter has developed three generic strategies to illustrate the kind of strategies managers might develop to make their organizations more competitive.

Differentiation   **Differentiation,** the first of Porter's strategies, focuses on making an organization more competitive by developing a product or products that customers perceive as being different from products offered by competitors. Differentiation includes uniqueness

Differentiation is a strategy that focuses on making an organization more competitive by developing a product or products that customers perceive as being different from products offered by competitors.

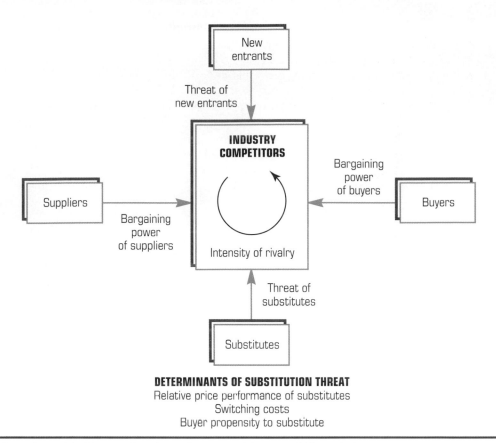

DETERMINANTS OF SUBSTITUTION THREAT
Relative price performance of substitutes
Switching costs
Buyer propensity to substitute

Figure 8.5   *Porter's model of factors that determine competitiveness within an industry*

in such areas as product quality, design, and level of after-sale service. Examples of products that customers commonly purchase because they perceive them as being different are Nike's Air Jordan shoes (because of their high-technology "air" construction) and Honda automobiles (because of their high reliability).

Cost leadership is a strategy that focuses on making an organization more competitive by producing products more cheaply than competitors can.

Cost Leadership   **Cost leadership** is a strategy that focuses on making an organization more competitive by producing products more cheaply than competitors can. According to the logic behind this strategy, by producing products more cheaply than its competitors do, an organization will be able to offer products to customers at lower prices than competitors can, and thereby increase its market share. Examples of tactics managers might use to gain cost leadership are obtaining lower prices for product parts purchased from suppliers and using technology like robots to increase organizational productivity.

Focus is a strategy that emphasizes making an organization more competitive by targeting a particular customer.

Focus   **Focus** is a strategy that emphasizes making an organization more competitive by targeting a particular customer. Magazine publishers commonly use a focus strategy in offering their products to specific customers. *Working Woman* and *Ebony* are examples of magazines that are aimed, respectively, at the target markets of employed women and African Americans.

Sample Organizational Strategies   Analyzing the organizational environment and applying one or more of the strategy tools—critical question analysis, SWOT analysis, business portfolio analysis, and Porter's model—will give managers a foundation on which to formulate an organizational strategy. The four common organizational strategies that evolve this way are growth, stability, retrenchment, and divestiture. The following discussion of these organizational strategies features business portfolio analysis as the tool used to arrive at the strategy, although the same strategies could result from critical question analysis, SWOT analysis, or Porter's model.

Growth   **Growth** is a strategy adopted by management to increase the amount of business that an SBU is currently generating. The growth strategy is generally applied to star SBUs or question mark SBUs that have the potential to become stars. Management generally invests substantial amounts of money to implement this strategy and may even sacrifice short-term profit to build long-term gain.[17]

Managers can also pursue a growth strategy by purchasing an SBU from another organization. For example, Black & Decker, not satisfied with being an international power in power tools, purchased General Electric's small-appliance business. Through this purchase, Black & Decker hoped that the amount of business it did would grow significantly over the long term. Similarly, President Enterprises, the largest food company in Taiwan, recently bought the American Famous Amos brand of chocolate chip cookies. Despite a downturn in the U.S. cookie market, management at President saw the purchase as important for company growth because it gave the company a nationally recognized product line in the United States.[18]

Stability   **Stability** is a strategy adopted by management to maintain or slightly improve the amount of business that an SBU is generating. This strategy is generally applied to cash cows, since these SBUs are already in an advantageous position. Management must be careful, however, that in its pursuit of stability it does not turn cash cows into dogs.

Retrenchment   In this section, *retrench* is used in the military sense: to defend or fortify. Through **retrenchment** strategy, management attempts to strengthen or protect the amount of business an SBU is generating. This strategy is generally applied to cash cows or stars that are beginning to lose market share.

Douglas D. Danforth, the chief executive of Westinghouse, is convinced that retrenchment is an important strategy for his company. According to Danforth, bigger profits at Westinghouse depend not only on fast-growing new products but also on the revitalization of Westinghouse's traditional businesses of manufacturing motors and gears.[19]

Divestiture   **Divestiture** is a strategy adopted to eliminate an SBU that is not generating a satisfactory amount of business and that has little hope of doing so in the near future. In essence, the organization sells or closes down the SBU in question. This strategy is usually applied to SBUs that are dogs or question marks that have failed to increase market share but still require significant amounts of cash.

> **Growth** is a strategy adopted by management to increase the amount of business that a strategic business unit is currently generating.

> **Stability** is a strategy adopted by management to maintain or slightly improve the amount of business a strategic business unit is generating.

> **Retrenchment** is a strategy adopted by management to strengthen or protect the amount of business a strategic business unit is currently generating.

> **Divestiture** is a strategy adopted to eliminate a strategic business unit that is not generating a satisfactory amount of business and has little hope of doing so in the future.

▶ Consumer Products—Diversity as a Strategy at S. C. Johnson and Son

S. C. Johnson and Son started in 1886 as a parquet flooring company, and soon earned a reputation for quality and innovation through one of its earliest products, Johnson's Paste Wax. The wax was a product specially designed to help customers care for parquet flooring after installation. Today the company produces numerous products that have become household names, including Shout, Windex, Ziploc, Glade, Vanish, Raid, and OFF!, and it now employs more than 9,500 people in nearly 60 countries.

Notably, S. C. Johnson and Son has appeared on *Fortune* magazine's list of America's 50 Best Companies for Minorities for the last two years. The company got high marks for minority presence in the areas of new hires, present executives, and even members of the board of directors.

Knowing that having a diverse workforce is a prerequisite for long-term company success, S. C. Johnson and Son has a strategy for establishing workforce diversity. This includes sending out recruiting teams to historically black colleges and creating fellowships for minority M.B.A. candidates. These fellowships are accompanied by a flexible company policy that allows minority executives to commute from headquarters in Racine, Wisconsin, to Chicago or Milwaukee to attend M.B.A. classes.

S. C. Johnson and Son understands that diversity today should be a business strategy and not just something achieved because of established laws. The company not only has such a strategy, but takes appropriate steps to make sure that it is implemented successfully.

Strategy implementation, the fourth step of the strategy management process, is putting formulated strategy into action.

Strategy Implementation

Strategy implementation, the fourth step of the strategy management process, is putting formulated strategies into action. Without successive implementation, valuable strategies developed by managers are virtually worthless.[20]

The successful implementation of strategy requires four basic skills:[21]

1. *Interacting skill* is the ability to manage people during implementation. Managers who are able to understand the fears and frustrations others feel during the implementation of a new strategy tend to be the best implementers. These managers empathize with organization members and bargain for the best way to put a strategy into action.
2. *Allocating skill* is the ability to provide the organizational resources necessary to implement a strategy. Successful implementers are talented at scheduling jobs, budgeting time and money, and allocating other resources that are critical for implementation.
3. *Monitoring skill* is the ability to use information to determine whether a problem has arisen that is blocking implementation. Good strategy implementers set up feedback systems that continually tell them about the status of strategy implementation.
4. *Organizing skill* is the ability to create throughout the organization a network of people who can help solve implementation problems as they occur. Good implementers customize this network to include individuals who can handle the special types of problems anticipated in the implementation of a particular strategy.

Overall, then, the successful implementation of a strategy requires handling people appropriately, allocating resources necessary for implementation, monitoring implementation progress, and solving implementation problems as they occur. Perhaps the most important requirements are knowing which people can solve specific implementation problems and being able to involve them when those problems arise.

Strategic control, the last step of the strategy management process, consists of monitoring and evaluating the strategy management process as a whole to ensure that it is operating properly.

Strategic Control

Strategic control, the last step of the strategy management process, consists of monitoring and evaluating the strategy management process as a whole to ensure that it is operating properly. Strategic control focuses on the activities involved in environmental analysis, organizational direction, strategy formulation, strategy implementation, and strategic control itself—checking that all steps of the strategy management process are appropriate, compatible, and functioning properly.[22] Strategic control is a special type of organizational control, a topic that is featured in Chapters 19, 20, and 21.

▶ Back to the Case

Based on the previous information, after Gillette has performed its environmental analysis, it must determine the direction in which it will move regarding its competitive position. Issues like adding shaving products for women will naturally surface. Developing a mission statement with related objectives would be clear signals to all Gillette's employees about the role of new shaving products for women in the organization's future. Gillette's management has several tools available to assist them in formulating strategy. If they are to be effective in this area, how-

▶ Ted Fang (left) and David Black (right) are among some daily newspaper publishers who are testing a new strategy—reviving dying papers in cities that would otherwise have only one daily left. Ted Fang purchased the *San Francisco Examiner* from Hearst Corp., and Black bought the *Honolulu Star-Bulletin* for only $10,000. How well their strategy works will depend in part on whether advertising revenues go up or down.

ever, they must use the tools in conjunction with environmental analysis. One of the tools, critical question analysis, would require management to analyze Gillette's purpose, direction, environment, and goals.

SWOT analysis, another strategy development tool, would require management to generate information regarding the internal strengths and weaknesses of Gillette as well as the opportunities and threats that exist within Gillette's environment. Management probably would classify the products of competitors like Warner Lambert's Schick division as threats and significant factors to be considered in their strategy development process.

One approach to business portfolio analysis would suggest that Gillette's management classify each major product line (SBU) within the company as a star, cash cow, question mark, or dog, depending on the growth rate of the market interested and the market share the Gillette product line possesses. Management could decide, for example, to consider the new Mach3 and each of its other major product lines as a unit for SBU analysis and categorize them according to the four classifications. As a result of this categorization process, they could develop, perhaps for each different product line that they offer, growth, stability, retrenchment, or divestiture strategies. Gillette's management should use whichever strategy development tools they think would be most useful. Their objective in this case is to develop an appropriate strategy for the development of Gillette's product lines.

To be successful at using the strategy it develops, Gillette's management must apply its interacting, allocating, monitoring, and organizing skills. In addition, management must be able to improve the strategy management process when necessary.

TACTICAL PLANNING

Tactical planning is short-range planning that emphasizes the current operations of various parts of the organization. *Short range* is defined as a period of time extending about one year or less into the future. Managers use tactical planning to outline what the various parts of the organization must do for the organization to be successful at some point one year or less into the future.[23] Tactical plans are usually developed in the areas of production, marketing, personnel, finance, and plant facilities.

Tactical planning is short-range planning that emphasizes the current operations of various parts of the organization.

Comparing and Coordinating Strategic and Tactical Planning

In striving to implement successful planning systems within organizations, managers must remember several basic differences between strategic planning and tactical planning:

1. Because upper-level managers generally have a better understanding of the organization as a whole than lower-level managers do, and because lower-level managers generally have a better understanding of the day-to-day organizational operations than upper-level managers do, strategic plans are usually developed by upper-level management and tactical plans by lower-level management.

2. Because strategic planning emphasizes analyzing the future and tactical planning emphasizes analyzing the everyday functioning of the organization, facts on which to base strategic plans are usually more difficult to gather than are facts on which to base tactical plans.

3. Because strategic plans are based primarily on a prediction of the future and tactical plans on known circumstances that exist within the organization, strategic plans are generally less detailed than tactical plans.

4. Because strategic planning focuses on the long term and tactical planning on the short term, strategic plans cover a relatively long period of time whereas tactical plans cover a relatively short period of time.

All of these major differences between strategic and tactical planning are summarized in Table 8.3.

Despite their differences, tactical and strategic planning are integrally related. As Russell L. Ackoff states, "We can look at them separately, even discuss them separately, but we cannot

Table 8.3   Major Differences Between Strategic and Tactical Planning

Area of Difference	Strategic Planning	Tactical Planning
Individuals involved	Developed mainly by upper-level management	Developed mainly by lower-level management
Facts on which to base planning	Facts are relatively difficult to gather	Facts are relatively easy to gather
Amount of detail in plans	Plans contain relatively little detail	Plans contain substantial amounts of detail
Length of time plans cover	Plans cover long periods of time	Plans cover short periods of time

separate them in fact."[24] In other words, managers need both tactical and strategic planning programs, and these programs must be closely related to be successful. Tactical planning should focus on what to do in the short term to help the organization achieve the long-term objectives determined by strategic planning.

PLANNING AND LEVELS OF MANAGEMENT

An organization's top management is primarily responsible for seeing that the planning function is carried out. Although all management levels are involved in the typical planning process, upper-level managers usually spend more time planning than lower-level managers do. Lower-level managers are highly involved in the everyday operations of the organization and therefore normally have less time to contribute to planning than top managers do. Middle-level managers usually spend more time planning than lower-level managers, but less time than upper-level managers. Figure 8.6 shows how planning time increases as a manager moves from lower-level to upper-level management. In small as well as large organizations, determining the amount and nature of the work that each manager should personally handle is extremely important.

The type of planning done also changes as a manager moves up in the organization. Typically, lower-level managers plan for the short term, middle-level managers for the somewhat longer term, and upper-level managers for the even longer term. The expertise of lower-level managers in everyday operations makes them the best planners for what can be done in the short term to reach organizational objectives—in other words, they are best equipped to do tactical planning. Upper-level managers usually have the best understanding of the whole organizational situation and are therefore better equipped to plan for the long term—or to develop strategic plans.[25]

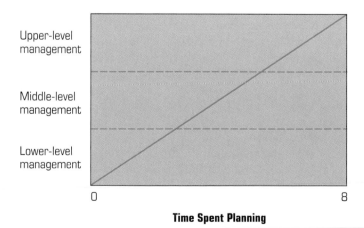

Time Spent Planning

Figure 8.6   *Increase in planning time as manager moves from lower-level to upper-level management*

In addition to developing strategic plans for its organization, Gillette's management should consider tactical, or short-range, plans that would complement its strategic plans. Tactical plans for Gillette should emphasize what can be done within approximately the next year to reach the organization's three- to five-year objectives and to steal competition from its competitors. For example, Gillette could devote more resources to aggressive, short-range advertising campaigns or increase sales by aggressively reducing the introductory prices of new products.

In addition, Gillette's management must closely coordinate strategic and tactical planning within the company. It must keep in mind that strategic planning and tactical planning are different types of activities that may involve different people within the organization and result in plans with different degrees of detail. Yet it must also remember that these two types of plans are interrelated. While lower-level managers would be mostly responsible for developing tactical plans, upper-level managers would mainly spend time on long-range planning and developing strategic plans that reflect company goals.

Management Skills Module

This section is specially designed to help you develop management skills. An individual's management skill is based on an understanding of management concepts and the ability to apply those concepts in management situations. As a result, the following activities are designed both to heighten your understanding of management concepts and to help you gain facility in applying those concepts in various management situations.

UNDERSTANDING MANAGEMENT CONCEPTS

▶ Action Summary

Reread the learning objectives below. Each objective is followed by questions. Answering these questions accurately will help you retain the most important concepts discussed in this chapter. After answering each question, check your answer against the answer key at the end of this chapter. (*Hint:* If you have any doubts regarding the correct response, consult the page number that follows the answer.)

Circle:

From studying this chapter, I will attempt to acquire

1. Definitions of both strategic planning and strategy.

    T F
    a. Strategic planning is long-range planning that focuses on the organization as a whole.

    a b c d e
    b. Strategy: (a) is a specific, narrow plan designed to achieve tactical planning (b) is designed to be the end result of tactical planning (c) is a plan designed to reach long-range objectives (d) is timeless, so the same strategy can meet organizational needs anytime (e) is independent of organizational objectives and therefore need not be consistent with them.

2. An understanding of the strategy management process.

    a b c d e
    a. Which of the following is *not* one of the steps in strategy management: (a) strategy formulation (b) strategy implementation (c) strategy control (d) environmental analysis (e) all of the above are steps.

    T F
    b. The steps of the strategy management process are sequential but usually not continuing.

3. A knowledge of the impact of environmental analysis on strategy formulation.

    T F
    a. Environmental analysis is the strategy used to change an organization's environment to satisfy the needs of the organization.

    a b c d e
    b. All of the following are factors to be considered in environmental analysis except: (a) suppliers (b) economic issues (c) demographics (d) social values (e) none of the above.

4. Insights about how to use critical question analysis and SWOT analysis to formulate strategy.

    a b c d e
    a. The following is *not* one of the four basic questions used in critical question analysis: (a) Where has the organization been? (b) Where is the organization presently going? (c) What are the purposes and objectives of the organization? (d) In what kind of environment does the organization now exist? (e) What can be done to better achieve organizational objectives in the future?

    T F
    b. SWOT is an acronym for "Strengths and Weaknesses, Objectives and Tactics."

5. An understanding of how to use business portfolio analysis and industry analysis to formulate strategy.

    a b c d e
    a. Using the BCG Matrix requires considering the following factors: (a) types of risk associated with product development (b) threats that economic conditions can create in the future (c) social factors (d) market shares and growth of markets in which products are selling (e) political pressures.

    a b c d e
    b. To users of the BCG Matrix, products that capture a high share of a rapidly growing market are known as: (a) cash cows (b) milk products (c) sweepstakes products (d) stars (e) dog products.

    T F
    c. Use of the GE Multifactor Portfolio Matrix requires considering total market size for an SBU but usually not the amount of the market that the SBU has won.

6. Insights into what tactical planning is and how strategic and tactical planning should be coordinated.

    T F
    a. Tactical plans generally are developed for one year or less and usually contain fewer details than strategic plans.

    a b c d e
    b. The following best describes strategic planning: (a) facts are difficult to gather, and plans cover short periods of time (b) facts are difficult to gather, and plans cover long periods of time (c) facts are difficult to gather, and plans are developed mainly by lower-level managers (d) facts are easy to gather, and plans are developed mainly by upper-level managers (e) facts are easy to gather, and plans are developed mainly by lower-level managers.

Action Summary Answer Key

1. a.	T, p. 168	**3. a.**	F, p. 170	**5. a.**	d, pp. 177–178	**6. a.**	F, p. 183	
b.	c, pp. 168–169	**b.**	e, pp. 170–172	**b.**	d, p. 177	**b.**	b, p. 184	
2. a.	e, p. 169	**4. a.**	a, pp. 176–177	**c.**	F, p. 178			
b.	F, p. 169	**b.**	F, p. 177					

Issues for Review and Discussion

1. What is strategic planning?
2. How does the commitment principle relate to strategic planning?
3. Define *strategy* and discuss its relationship to organizational objectives.
4. What are the major steps in the strategy management process? Discuss each step fully.
5. Why is environmental analysis an important part of strategy formulation?
6. List one major factor from each environmental level that could have a significant impact on specific strategies developed for an organization. How could the specific strategies be affected by each factor?
7. Discuss the significance of the questions answered during critical question analysis.
8. Explain in detail how SWOT analysis can be used to formulate strategy.
9. What is business portfolio analysis?
10. Discuss the philosophy on which business portfolio analysis is based.
11. What is an SBU?
12. Draw and explain the BCG Growth-Share Matrix.
13. What potential pitfalls must managers avoid in using this matrix?
14. Explain three major differences in using the GE Multifactor Portfolio Matrix to develop organizational strategy as opposed to the BCG Matrix.
15. Draw and explain Porter's model of factors that determines competitiveness within an industry. What is the significance of this model for developing an organizational strategy?
16. List and define four sample strategies that can be developed for organizations.
17. What is tactical planning?
18. How do strategic and tactical planning differ?
19. What is the relationship between strategic and tactical planning?
20. How do time spent planning and scope of planning vary according to management levels?

APPLYING MANAGEMENT CONCEPTS

Cases

▶ INTRODUCTORY CASE WRAP-UP

Case Discussion Questions

"Gillette's New Strategy: Women" (p. 167) and its related Back-to-the-Case sections were written to help you better understand the management concepts contained in this chapter. Answer the following discussion questions about this Introductory Case to further enrich your understanding of chapter content:

1. For Gillette's management, is improving its women's line of shaving products a strategic management issue? Explain.
2. Give three factors in Gillette's internal environment that management should be assessing in determining the company's organizational direction. Why are these factors important?
3. Using the business portfolio matrix, categorize the new women's line of shaving products as a dog, question mark, star, or cash cow. From a strategic planning viewpoint, what do you recommend that Gillette management do as a result of this categorization? Why?

Skills Exercise: Performing an Environmental Analysis

In this chapter you learned how managers study the environment to form a strategic plan. The Introductory Case details the new strategy at Gillette and how the company has increased its focus on women's shaving products. Describe two factors from each of Gillette's environments—general, operating, and internal—and discuss how each factor could increase the probability that the new women-oriented strategy will be successful. Discuss how each factor could decrease the probability that the new strategy will be unsuccessful.

CASE STUDY: JetBlue at Your Service

If you log on to fledgling airline JetBlue's Web page, you will see the words "redefining and rethinking"—and that's just what CEO and founder David Neeleman has done with his latest business venture. JetBlue Airways was launched in February 2000, and became profitable six months later. Neeleman refers to his company not as an airline but as a services company.

Neeleman believes in rolling up his sleeves and helping out—even vacuuming planes and hauling luggage. He and JetBlue staff have made 3:00 A.M. phone calls to notify passengers that their 6:00 A.M. flight had been delayed and they should not bother going to the airport early. Neeleman's devotion to service is contagious. Passengers who had been grounded on a flight were surprised when the pilot came into the cabin to offer them use of his cell phone. "We don't want jaded people working here. If you don't like people or can't deal with rude customers you'll be fired," says Neeleman.

Raised in Utah, the 41-year-old CEO is a devout Mormon and a college dropout who wears jeans to his office. In his spare time he likes to hang out with his nine children or read history books. "He's a genius entrepreneur," says Kevin Murphy, a friend, and airline analyst at Morgan Stanley.

As JetBlue's founder and CEO, Neeleman worked with top New York politicians to get their backing of his use of John F. Kennedy airport. He worked with the Port Authority of New York to make access to the airport easier for passengers, and held long discussions with the Federal Aviation Administration and air traffic control officials to learn which flight paths are overused so he could avoid them. Despite the conventional wisdom that JFK is too expensive and too far from Manhattan when compared with LaGuardia airport, Neeleman based JetBlue at JFK.

He then hired a top-notch management team with plenty of experience in the air carrier industry. Together they decided to buy brand-new planes, figuring they would save in maintenance. All the money saved in repairs would more than pay for the difference between a new plane and an old one. Then they opted for luxurious leather seats that cost twice as much as the cloth ones but last twice as long.

In order to really set his airline apart, Neeleman invested in live TV and saved the difference in food. JetBlue serves only snacks and passengers can have as much as they like of the blue chips, animal crackers, chocolate chip cookies, and sodas available. (Neeleman is working on a deal for blue M&M's.) There are no carts clogging the aisles and passengers love being able to get up and move around.

Next, Neeleman attracted big investors based on the strength of the executive staff and their plans for future operations and expansion. Chase Capital and billionaire George Soros together invested $160 million in JetBlue.

By starting from scratch, JetBlue could "do more with fewer employees," Neeleman says. For example, crews do most of the cleaning between flights, which cuts down on turnaround time and expense. More than 30 percent of its tickets are booked through the Internet and it employs no unionized workers. Neeleman planned for JetBlue to be an ultra-efficient corporation. All 300 full-time reservationists work from home, and all of its new planes were purchased from Airbus Industries rather than the more popular but costly Boeing. The Airbus plane seats 162 as compared with 132 in the Boeing plane, and the A320 by Airbus is also cheaper to maintain and more fuel-efficient—a plus in the face of a 53 percent jump in fuel prices.

Even the location of JetBlue's corporate office is well chosen. It is near the airport, in case Neeleman has to dash to the terminal. He flies JetBlue about twice a week and spends the flight time talking to customers or crew and passing out snacks. Neeleman is constantly coming up with new ideas such as making one of the back bathrooms "for women only" and checking people in at the curb using hand-held devices.

JetBlue's management plans to add 11 new A320s by the end of 2001. The airline's goal is to produce an operating profit of 10 percent. Within six years, JetBlue plans to have 82 planes flying as many as 480 daily flights—up from 64 in 2000. As its next step, JetBlue will launch a frequent-flyer program, giving passengers retroactive credit for past flights. Passengers will earn a free ticket after 10 round-trip flights.

Neeleman knows that JetBlue's profit-sharing plan motivates employees to work harder, and everyone has a stake in the company's future. "We have a culture," says Neeleman. "When the plane lands, every employee on the plane, be it the CEO or someone from sales, pitches in and helps get the airplane ready. The pilots even come back and do it."

"I love to work. I love my job," Neeleman says. So far, people who fly seem to love JetBlue as well.

QUESTIONS

1. Based on facts in the case, write a mission statement for JetBlue. Was it easy to write this statement? Why?
2. List three strategies that Neeleman has taken to make JetBlue successful. What will determine whether these strategies will be successful in the future?
3. How would you advise Neeleman to strategically control JetBlue?

9 Plans and Planning Tools

CHAPTER OUTLINE

Introductory Case: *Ford Plans to Improve the Explorer*

Plans: A Definition

Ethics Spotlight ▶ Toyota Uses Philanthropy Plan to Take Aim at General Motors

Dimensions of Plans
Types of Plans

Digital Focus ▶ Salomon Smith Barney Establishes Rules to Deal with Internet

Why Plans Fail
Planning Areas: Input Planning

Global Spotlight ▶ Shell Picks Global Customer Center Sites

Planning Tools
Forecasting

Ford Plans to Improve the Explorer

REMINDER: THE INTRODUCTORY CASE WRAP-UP (P. 209) CONTAINS DISCUSSION QUESTIONS AND A SKILLS EXERCISE TO FURTHER ILLUSTRATE THE APPLICATION OF CHAPTER CONCEPTS TO THIS VIGNETTE.

In addition to producing cars and trucks, Ford Motor Company and its subsidiaries conduct business in other areas such as manufacturing automotive components, financing vehicle purchases for customers, and renting vehicles. The company's vehicle brand names include Ford, Mercury, Lincoln, Volvo, and Jaguar.

Recently, one of Ford's vehicles, the Explorer, created a monumental problem for the company, and although it involves many customers and many Explorers, the problem is probably best illustrated through the experiences of Donna Bailey.

Plans to improve the Ford Explorer's safety performance may rely on forecasting tools that can predict, for instance, what would cause the vehicle to roll over in an accident. Engineers use such information to redesign for greater safety and stability.

She and two friends were driving a Ford Explorer toward Enchanted Rock, a favorite climbing spot north of Austin, Texas. Suddenly, the Explorer took a vicious swerve; the tire simply started separating and the driver lost control of the vehicle. The pavement was dry, but the Explorer skidded and rolled anyway. Although Bailey's friends were fine, Donna, a 43-year-old mother of two, was left paralyzed from the neck down as a result of the accident. Bailey became a ventilator-dependent quadriplegic, and she had to learn how to navigate a wheelchair via a breathing tube.

Donna Bailey wanted justice. Her lawyers sued Ford as well as its tire supplier, Bridgestone/Firestone. Bailey's lawyers claimed that a defective tire—and more important, a defective car—took her livelihood. Bailey's attorney, Tab Turner, claimed that a bad tire on a bad car caused his client's accident.

Donna Bailey's megamillion-dollar lawsuit never got to court because Ford settled. In addition, Ford settled over 20 other tire-related injury and death claims involving other people who experienced similar circumstances. Ford's case was undoubtedly damaged when the National Highway Traffic and Safety Administration released "rollover" ratings to help consumers figure out which cars and trucks are more or less prone to rollovers. Most cars received top marks earning, four or five out of a possible five stars. However, SUVs were lucky to get three stars, and most, like the Explorer, received only two stars. Two stars means that there is a 30 percent to 40 percent risk that a particular vehicle will flip during a crisis on the road.

The record shows that Ford management had been making and implementing plans to improve the Ford Explorer even before the Donna Bailey incident. Only the future will tell if the improvement plans were appropriate and implemented properly.

The Introductory Case ends with the notion that management at Ford Motor Company has been planning to improve its Ford Explorer. This chapter emphasizes several fundamental issues about plans that should be useful to managers like those at Ford who are involved in such planning. This chapter describes what plans are and discusses several valuable tools that can be used in actually developing plans.

PLANS: A DEFINITION

A **plan** is a specific action proposed to help the organization achieve its objectives.

A **plan** is a specific action proposed to help the organization achieve its objectives. A critical part of the management of any organization is developing logical plans and then taking the steps necessary to put the plans into action.[1] Regardless of how important experience-related intuition may be to managers, successful management actions and strategies typically are based on reason. Rational managers are crucial to the development of an organizational plan.

Toyota Uses Philanthropy Plan to Take Aim at General Motors

The Toyota Motor Company, a Japanese firm, is one of the largest automobile manufacturers in the world. Toyota's top management has created a philanthropy plan to help the company to better compete with General Motors.

Toyota has designed a comprehensive plan for the organization that has both domestic and overseas components. It outlines an enormous undertaking that calls for annual automobile production and sales equaling more than 6 million units within three to five years. Toyota's president, Shoichiro Toyoda, believing that the world automobile market has plenty of room to grow, is determined to overtake General Motors as the world's largest automaker.

Although GM's output and sales have declined in recent years while Toyota's output and sales have increased, some industry analysts doubt Toyota has the ability to develop a marketing effort that will enable the company to surpass GM. Toyota's management team, however, insists that the company's aspirations to overtake GM are realistic. One reason for Toyota's optimism is the company's philanthropy plan, which channels corporate profits into local communities, enhancing Toyota's public image and thus boosting sales. Over the last few years, Toyota has channeled about 1.5 percent of its profits into philanthropic programs. In the near future, the company's level of philanthropy will probably remain about the same or even increase. ■

Dimensions of Plans

Kast and Rosenzweig identify a plan's four major dimensions as follows:[2]

1. Repetitiveness
2. Time
3. Scope
4. Level

Each dimension is an independent characteristic of a plan and should be considered during plan development.

The **repetitiveness dimension** of a plan is the extent to which the plan is to be used over and over again.

Repetitiveness The **repetitiveness dimension** of a plan is the extent to which the plan is used over and over again. Some plans are specially designed for one situation that is relatively short term in nature. Plans of this sort are essentially nonrepetitive. Other plans, however, are designed to be used time after time for long-term recurring situations. These plans are basically repetitive in nature.

The **time dimension** of a plan is the length of time the plan covers.

Time The **time dimension** of a plan is the length of time the plan covers. In Chapter 8, strategic planning was defined as long term in nature, while tactical planning was defined as short term. It follows, then, that strategic plans cover relatively long periods of time and tactical plans cover relatively short periods of time.

The **scope dimension** of a plan is the portion of the total management system at which the plan is aimed.

Scope The **scope dimension** of a plan is the portion of the total management system at which the plan is aimed. Some plans are designed to cover the entire open management sys-

▶ Engineer Ron Shriver and his Japan-based counterpart Hiroyuki Itoh (second and third from the left, respectively) are celebrating the successful completion of a project to reduce the costs of building the Civic at Honda Motor Co.'s plant in East Liberty, Ohio. The project was a model of both team-based problem solving and creating plans across management levels. Originally, for instance, Shriver and Itoh had formed separate teams, but once they had begun pooling their resources, they were able to gather money-saving suggestions from suppliers and factory workers in both the United States and Japan.

tem: the organizational environment, inputs, process, and outputs. Such a plan is often referred to as a *master plan*. Other plans are developed to cover only a portion of the management system. An example of the latter would be a plan that covers the recruitment of new workers—a portion of the organizational input segment of the management system. The greater the portion of the management system that a plan covers, the broader the plan's scope is said to be.

Level   The **level dimension** of a plan is the level of the organization at which the plan is aimed. Top-level plans are those designed for the organization's top management, whereas middle- and lower-level plans are designed for middle and lower management, respectively. Because all parts of the management system are interdependent, however, plans designed for any level of the organization have some effect on all other levels.

The **level dimension** of a plan is the level of the organization at which the plan is aimed.

Figure 9.1 illustrates the four dimensions of an organizational plan. This figure indicates that when managers develop a plan, they should consider the degree to which it will be used over and over again, the period of time it will cover, the parts of the management system on which it focuses, and the organizational level at which it is aimed.

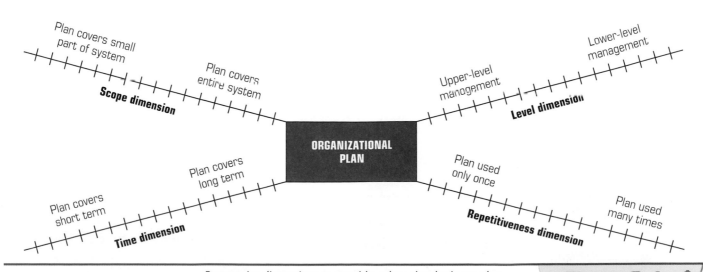

Four major dimensions to consider when developing a plan

Figure 9.1

In developing plans in a company like Ford, management is actually developing recommendations for future actions. As such, plans should be action oriented; they should state precisely what management is going to do in order to achieve its goals.

In developing the plans, managers like those at Ford should consider how often the plans will be used and the length of time they will cover. Will a plan be implemented only once or be used on a long-term basis to handle an ongoing issue like maintaining product quality? A plan like Ford's to improve product quality might not be used very often by most companies and would be designed to cover a specific amount of time.

In addition, managers like those at Ford should consider what part of the organization the plans they develop will be aimed at and on what level the plans will focus. For instance, a plan to cut costs may encompass all Ford operations, whereas a plan to improve product quality may affect only one part of the production process, such as the part involving the Explorer. Similarly, a plan to cut costs may be aimed at top-level management, whereas a product-quality plan may be aimed toward lower-level management and the auto assemblers themselves. Managers like those at Ford must realize that since management systems are interdependent, any plans they implement will affect the system as a whole.

Types of Plans

Standing plans are plans that are used over and over because they focus on organizational situations that occur repeatedly.

Single-use plans are plans that are used only once—or, at most, several times—because they focus on unique or rare situations within the organization.

A **policy** is a standing plan that furnishes broad guidelines for channeling management toward taking action consistent with reaching organizational objectives.

With the repetitiveness dimension as a guide, organizational plans are usually divided into two types: standing and single-use. **Standing plans** are used over and over again because they focus on organizational situations that occur repeatedly. **Single-use plans** are used only once—or, at most, several times—because they focus on unique or rare situations within the organization. As Figure 9.2 illustrates, standing plans can be subdivided into policies, procedures, and rules and single-use plans into programs and budgets.

Standing Plans: Policies, Procedures, and Rules A **policy** is a standing plan that furnishes broad guidelines for taking action consistent with reaching organizational objectives. For example, an organizational policy relating to personnel might be worded as follows: "Our organization will strive to recruit only the most talented employees." This policy statement is very broad, giving managers only a general idea of what to do in the area of recruitment. The policy is intended to emphasize the extreme importance management attaches to hiring competent employees and to guide managers' actions accordingly.

As another example of an organizational policy, consider companies' responses to studies showing that one out of every four workers in the United States was attacked, threatened, or harassed on the job during a recent 12-month operating period. To deal with this problem, many managers are developing weapons policies. A sample policy could be: "Management strongly discourages any employee from bringing a weapon to work." This policy would encourage managers to deal forcefully and punitively with employees who bring weapons into the workplace.[3]

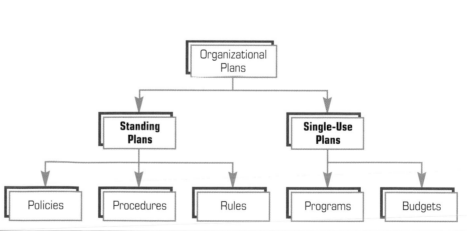

Figure 9.2   *Standing plans and single-use plans*

A **procedure** is a standing plan that outlines a series of related actions that must be taken to accomplish a particular task. In general, procedures outline more specific actions than policies do. Organizations usually have many different sets of procedures covering the various tasks to be accomplished. Managers must be careful to apply the appropriate organizational procedures for the situations they face and to apply them properly.[4]

A **rule** is a standing plan that designates specific required action. In essence, a rule indicates what an organization member should or should not do and allows no room for interpretation. An example of a rule that many companies are now establishing is No Smoking. The concept of rules may become clearer if one thinks about the purpose and nature of rules in such games as Scrabble and Monopoly.

Although policies, procedures, and rules are all standing plans, they are different from one another and have different purposes within the organization. As Figure 9.3 illustrates, however, for the standing plans of an organization to be effective, policies, procedures, and rules must be consistent and mutually supportive.

A **procedure** is a standing plan that outlines a series of related actions that must be taken to accomplish a particular task.

A **rule** is a standing plan that designates specific required action.

DIGITAL FOCUS

▶ Salomon Smith Barney Establishes Rules to Deal with Internet

For many companies, the Internet has created opportunities that were once unimaginable. This technology has allowed some companies to reach markets that were once impossible, and it has helped other companies to literally start new businesses that did not exist previously. Although these benefits would seemingly result in a no-lose situation for all companies, some are struggling with the problems resulting from increased Internet use. Some of these problems include employees using company computers to access sports-related and pornographic Web sites and to send inappropriate e-mail messages.

To deal with these problems, some companies have created new rules, procedures, and policies. Surprisingly, however, there are many companies that still have not addressed these issues. According to a recent survey conducted by the Society for Human Resource Management, 70 percent of the organizations polled had no written Internet rules or policies. In addition, only half of the same organiza-

tions had written rules or procedures regarding the proper use of e-mail.

Salomon Smith Barney is one company that created new rules to protect it from the problems resulting from the Internet. Recently, the company fired two high-level executives for sending pornography over the company's message system. After the firing, the company sent a loud message to the remaining employees regarding proper use of the company's Internet and e-mail resources. This loud message came in the form of an e-mail message, and the company told employees that anyone engaging in similar activities could assume that he or she would be terminated immediately. The company hopes that this message will make employees think long and hard before behaving similarly. With clearly stated rules and policies such as this one, companies can increase the likelihood that employees will use their resources strictly for productive purposes.

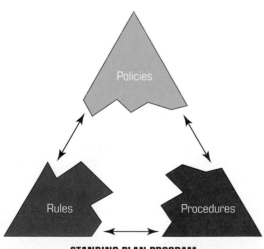

STANDING PLAN PROGRAM

A successful standing plan program with mutually supportive policies, procedures, and rules

Figure 9.3

A **program** is a single-use plan designed to carry out a special project in an organization that, if accomplished, will contribute to the organization's long-term success.

A **budget** is a control tool that outlines how funds in a given period will be spent, as well as how they will be obtained.

Single-Use Plans: Programs and Budgets

A **program** is a single-use plan designed to carry out a special project within an organization. The project itself is not intended to remain in existence over the entire life of the organization. Rather, it exists to achieve some purpose that, if accomplished, will contribute to the organization's long-term success.

A common example is the management development program found in many organizations. This program exists to raise the skill levels of managers in one or more of the areas mentioned in Chapter 1: technical, conceptual, or human relations skills. Increasing managerial skills, however, is not an end in itself. The end or purpose of the program is to produce competent managers who are equipped to help the organization be successful over the long term. In fact, once managerial skills have been raised to a desired level, the management development program can be deemphasized. Activities on which modern management development programs commonly focus include understanding and using the computer as a management tool, handling international competition, and planning for a major labor shortage.[5]

A **budget** is a single-use financial plan that covers a specified length of time. It details how funds will be spent on labor, raw materials, capital goods, information systems, marketing, and so on, as well as how the funds will be obtained.[6] Although budgets are planning devices, they are also strategies for organizational control. They are discussed in more detail in Chapter 20.

Why Plans Fail

If managers know why plans fail, they can take steps to eliminate the factors that cause failure and thereby increase the probability that their plans will be successful. A study by K. A. Ringbakk determined that plans fail when:[7]

1. Corporate planning is not integrated into the total management system
2. There is a lack of understanding of the different steps of the planning process
3. Management at different levels in the organization has not properly engaged in or contributed to planning activities
4. Responsibility for planning is wrongly vested solely in the planning department
5. Management expects that plans developed will be realized with little effort
6. In starting formal planning, too much is attempted at once
7. Management fails to operate by the plan
8. Financial projections are confused with planning
9. Inadequate inputs are used in planning
10. Management fails to grasp the overall planning process

Planning Areas: Input Planning

As discussed earlier, organizational inputs, process, outputs, and environment are major factors in determining how successful a management system will be. Naturally, a comprehensive organizational plan should focus on each of these factors. The following two sections cover planning in two areas normally associated with the input factor: plant facilities planning and human resource planning. Planning in areas such as these is called **input planning**—the development of proposed action that will furnish sufficient and appropriate organizational resources for reaching established organizational objectives.

Input planning is the development of proposed action that will furnish sufficient and appropriate organizational resources for reaching established organizational objectives.

Plant facilities planning is input planning that involves developing the type of work facility an organization will need to reach its objectives.

Site selection involves determining where a plant facility should be located. It may use a weighting process to compare site differences.

Plant Facilities Planning

Plant facilities planning involves determining the type of buildings and equipment an organization needs to reach its objectives. A major part of this determination is called **site selection**—deciding where a plant facility should be located. Table 9.1 lays out several major areas to be considered in plant site selection and gives sample questions that can be asked as these areas are being explored. The specifics of site selection will vary from organization to organization.[8]

One factor that significantly influences site selection is foreign location. Management in a foreign country planning to select a site must deal with such issues as differences among foreign governments in time taken to approve site purchases and political pressures that may slow down or prevent the purchase of a site. For example, Japanese investors who locate businesses in the United States tend to select those states that have low unionization rates, low employment rates, relatively impoverished populations, and the highest possible educational

Major Areas of Consideration in Site Selection	Sample Questions to Be Asked
Profit	
Market Location	Where are our customers in relation to the site?
Competition	What competitive situation exists at the site?
Operating costs	
Suppliers	Are materials available near the site at reasonable cost?
Utilities	What are utility rates at the site? Are utilities available in sufficient amounts?
Wages	What wage rates are paid by comparable organizations near the site?
Taxes	What are tax rates on income, sales, property, and so on for the site?
Investment costs	
Land/development	How expensive are land and construction at the site?
Others	
Transportation	Are airlines, railroads, highways, and so on accessible from the site?
Laws	What laws related to zoning, pollution, and so on will influence operations if the site is chosen?
Labor	Does an adequate labor supply exist around the site?
Unionization	What is the degree of unionization in the site area?
Living conditions	Are housing, schools, and so on around the site appropriate?
Community relations	Does the community support the organization's moving into the area?

levels under those conditions. Japanese managers believe that these factors enhance the chances of success of Japanese business in the United States.[9]

Many organizations use a weighting process to compare site differences among foreign countries. Basically, this process involves the following steps:

1. Deciding on a set of variables critical to obtaining an appropriate site
2. Assigning each of these variables a weight reflecting its relative importance
3. Ranking alternative sites according to how they reflect these different variables

Table 9.2 shows the results of such a weighting process for seven site variables in six countries. In this table, "living conditions" are worth 100 points and are the most important vari-

Shell Picks Global Customer Center Sites

Shell Chemicals is a worldwide conglomerate engaged in the chemicals business. The company was formed through a 1907 alliance between Royal Dutch Petroleum Company in the Netherlands and The "Shell" Transport and Trading Company of the United Kingdom.

Today, Shell Chemicals has several prominent core businesses: chemicals, exploration and production, oil products, and gas and power generation; and it operates in more than 130 countries. Shell products impact almost everyone's life, and are used by other companies to produce countless finished goods relating to homes, shops, workplaces, schools, clubs, cars, boats, and planes.

Shell is radically altering the way it views customer needs by changing the way it sells and delivers products to customers. The company recognizes that different customers have different needs and it is attempting to build facilities to meet those needs. To best serve its clientele, Shell is building an array of international service centers at which customers can have a "one-stop-shopping" experience. At the service centers patrons will be able to place orders, have technical questions answered, and settle accounts, which will help to complete day-to-day transactions more quickly, more easily, and more efficiently.

However, Shell must be careful to choose sites that are convenient and extensive enough to allow comprehensive customer service. Present and planned locations include the United Kingdom, Germany, France, and the Netherlands. ■

▶ Planning for plant facilities increasingly means planning to expand them overseas. At the Mexico factory of the South Korean electronics firm Daewoo, Lorena Lopez performs a quality control check on a computer monitor. Human resource planning is also needed to ensure that enough employees with the right skills are hired to run the plant, and quality planning must be done to provide guidelines for jobs such as Lopez's.

able; "effect on company reputation" is worth 35 points and is the least important variable. The six countries are given a number of points for each variable, depending on the importance of the variable and how well it is reflected within the country. The table shows that, using this particular set of weighted criteria, Japan, Mexico, and France are more desirable sites than Chile, Jamaica, and Australia.

Human Resource Planning   Human resources are another area of concern to input planners. Organizational objectives cannot be attained without appropriate personnel. Future needs for human resources are influenced mainly by employee turnover, the nature of the present workforce, and the rate of growth of the organization.[10]

The following are representative of the kinds of questions personnel planners should try to answer:

1. What types of people does the organization need to reach its objectives?
2. How many of each type are needed?
3. What steps should the organization take to recruit and select such people?
4. Can present employees be further trained to fill future needed positions?
5. At what rate are employees being lost to other organizations?

Figure 9.4 shows the human resource planning process developed by Bruce Coleman. According to his model, **human resource planning** involves reflecting on organizational objectives to determine overall human resource needs; comparing these needs to the existing

Human resource planning is input planning that involves obtaining the human resources necessary for the organization to achieve its objectives.

☜ **Table 9.2**	Results of Weighting Seven Site Variables for Six Countries						
	Maximum Value Assigned	**Sites**					
Criteria		**Japan**	**Chile**	**Jamaica**	**Australia**	**Mexico**	**France**
Living conditions	100	70	40	45	50	60	60
Accessibility	75	55	35	20	60	70	70
Industrialization	60	40	50	55	35	35	30
Labor availability	35	30	10	10	30	35	35
Economics	35	15	15	15	15	25	25
Community capability and attitude	30	25	20	10	15	25	15
Effect on company reputation	35	25	20	10	15	25	15
Total	370	260	190	165	220	275	250

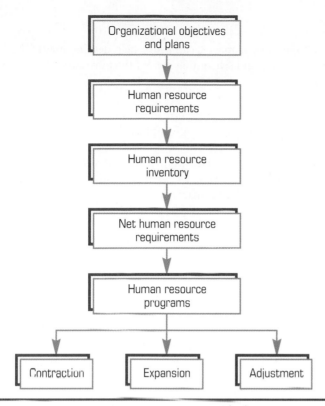

The human resource planning process

Figure 9.4

human resource inventory to determine net human resource needs; and, finally, seeking appropriate organization members to meet the net human resource needs.

► Back to the Case

Managers like those at Ford would normally use both standing plans and single-use plans in a company. Standing plans include policies, procedures, and rules and should be developed for situations that occur repeatedly. For example, one policy Ford management could develop might focus on the level of product quality they want to emphasize with employees.

Single-use plans include programs and budgets and should be developed to help manage less repetitive situations. For example, the Introductory Case implies that Ford management has worked on a budget that allows it to improve its Explorer. In developing such plans, managers should thoroughly understand the reasons that plans fail and take steps to avoid those pitfalls.

Plant facilities planning and human resource planning are two types of planning that managers commonly pursue. In the case of Ford, plant facilities planning would entail developing the types of factories the company needs to reach its objectives. Automotive companies like Ford often focus on plant facilities planning. Such planning emphasizes questions like where a new plant should be located, how to expand and remodel an existing factory, and how to lay out a plant to best facilitate the effective and efficient production of vehicles.

Human resource planning involves obtaining or developing the personnel an organization needs to reach its objectives. In this area, for example, Ford management might discuss the types of engineers needed to improve existing products or design new products that meet specified safety requirements. Discussion would inevitably focus on issues like how many new employees, if any, Ford will need as economic conditions vary; in what areas they will be needed; when such employees would be needed; how they will be obtained; and how they will be trained appropriately.

Planning tools are techniques managers can use to help develop plans.

Forecasting is a planning tool used to predict future environmental happenings that will influence the operation of the organization.

Planning tools are techniques managers can use to help develop plans. The remainder of this chapter discusses forecasting and scheduling, two of the most important of these tools.

Forecasting

Forecasting is the process of predicting future environmental happenings that will influence the operation of the organization. Although sophisticated forecasting techniques have been developed only rather recently, the concept of forecasting can be traced at least as far back in the management literature as Fayol. The importance of forecasting lies in its ability to help managers understand the future makeup of the organizational environment, which, in turn, helps them formulate more effective plans.[11]

How Forecasting Works

William C. House, in describing the Insect Control Services Company, has developed an excellent illustration of how forecasting works. In general, Insect Control Services forecasts by attempting to do the following:[12]

1. Establish relationships between industry sales and national economic and social indicators
2. Determine the impact government restrictions on the use of chemical pesticides will have on the growth of chemical, biological, and electro-magnetic energy pest-control markets
3. Evaluate sales growth potential, profitability, resources required, and risks involved in each of its market areas (commercial, industrial, institutional, governmental, and residential)
4. Evaluate the potential for expansion of marketing efforts in geographical areas of the United States as well as in foreign countries
5. Determine the likelihood of technological breakthroughs that would make existing product lines obsolete

Types of Forecasts

In addition to the general type of organizational forecasting done by Insect Control Services, there are specialized types of forecasting, such as economic, technological, social trends, and sales forecasting. Although a complete organizational forecasting process should, and usually does, include all these types of forecasting, sales forecasting is considered the key organizational forecast. A *sales forecast* is a prediction of how high or low sales of the organization's products and/or services will be over the period of time under consideration. It is the key forecast for organizations because it serves as the fundamental guideline for planning. Only after the sales forecast has been completed can managers decide, for example, if more salespeople should be hired, if more money for plant expansion must be borrowed, or if layoffs and cutbacks in certain areas are necessary. Managers must continually monitor forecasting methods to improve them and to reformulate plans based on inaccurate forecasts.[13]

▶ The Internet is proving to be a versatile tool for planning of various kinds. Nestlé, for instance, has over 70 people around the world who need to buy hazelnuts for various chocolate products made by the 135-year-old firm. Each of them used to visit processing plants in Italy and Turkey, trying to hedge the wild swings in price and quality to which hazelnuts are prone. But when Pietro Senna, a buyer for Nestlé Switzerland, posted his report on Turkish hazelnut plants on the Internet, the other Nestlé buyers around the world had read it within a week and were saved the effort of repeating the trip.

Methods of Sales Forecasting

Modern managers have several different methods available for forecasting sales. Popular methods are the jury of executive opinion method, the salesforce estimation method, and the time series analysis method. Each of these methods is discussed in this section.

The **jury of executive opinion method** is a method of predicting future sales levels primarily by asking appropriate managers to give their opinions on what will happen to sales in the future.

Jury of Executive Opinion Method The **jury of executive opinion method** of sales forecasting is straightforward. Appropriate managers within the organization assemble to discuss their opinions on what will happen to sales in the future. Since these discussion sessions usually revolve around hunches or experienced guesses, the resulting forecast is a blend of informed opinions.

A similar, more recently developed forecasting method, called the *Delphi method,* also gathers, evaluates, and summarizes expert opinions as the basis for a forecast, but the procedure is more formal than that for the jury of executive opinion method.[14] The basic Delphi method employs the following steps:

- *Step 1*—Various experts are asked to answer, independently and in writing, a series of questions about the future of sales or whatever other area is being forecasted.
- *Step 2*—A summary of all the answers is then prepared. No expert knows how any other expert answered the questions.
- *Step 3*—Copies of the summary are given to the individual experts with the request that they modify their original answers if they think it necessary.
- *Step 4*—Another summary is made of these modifications, and copies again are distributed to the experts. This time, however, expert opinions that deviate significantly from the norm must be justified in writing.
- *Step 5*—A third summary is made of the opinions and justifications, and copies are once again distributed to the experts. Justification in writing for *all* answers is now required.
- *Step 6*—The forecast is generated from all of the opinions and justifications that arise from step 5.

Salesforce Estimation Method   The **salesforce estimation method** is a sales forecasting technique that predicts future sales by analyzing the opinions of salespeople as a group. Salespeople continually interact with customers, and from this interaction they usually develop a knack for predicting future sales. As with the jury of executive opinion method, the resulting forecast normally is a blend of the informed views of the group.

The salesforce estimation method is considered to be a very valuable management tool and is commonly used in business and industry throughout the world. Although the accuracy of this method is generally good, managers have found that it can be improved by taking such simple steps as providing salespeople with sufficient time to forecast and offering incentives for accurate forecasts. Some companies help their salespeople to become better forecasters by training them to better interpret their interactions with customers.[15]

Time Series Analysis Method   The **time series analysis method** predicts future sales by analyzing the historical relationship between sales and time. Information showing the relationship between sales and time typically is presented on a graph, as in Figure 9.5. This presentation clearly displays past trends, which can be used to predict future sales.

Although the actual number of years included in a time series analysis will vary from company to company, as a general rule, managers should include as many years as necessary to

> The **salesforce estimation method** predicts future sales levels primarily by asking appropriate salespeople for their opinions of what will happen to sales in the future.

> The **time series analysis method** is a method of predicting future sales levels by analyzing the historical relationship in an organization between sales and time.

Time series analysis method

Figure 9.5

Chapter 9 ▶ Plans and Planning Tools   201

ensure that important sales trends do not go undetected. At the Coca-Cola Company, for example, management believes that in order to validly predict the annual sales of any one year, it must chart annual sales in each of the 10 previous years.[16]

The time series analysis in Figure 9.5 indicates steadily increasing sales for B. J.'s Men's Clothing over time. However, since in the long term products generally go through what is called a product life cycle, the predicted increase based on the last decade of sales should probably be considered overly optimistic. A **product life cycle** is the five stages through which most products and services pass. These stages are introduction, growth, maturity, saturation, and decline.

Product Stages.   Figure 9.6 shows how the five stages of the product life cycle are related to sales volume for seven products over a period of time. In the introduction stage, when a product is brand new, sales are just beginning to build (Web-capable cell phones). In the growth stage, the product has been in the marketplace for some time and is becoming more accepted, so product sales continue to climb (e.g., cellular phones and compact disc players). During the maturity stage, competitors enter the market, and although sales are still climbing, they are climbing at a slower rate than they did in the growth stage (e.g., personal computers). After the maturity stage comes the saturation stage, when nearly everyone who wanted the product has it (e.g., refrigerators and freezers). Sales during the saturation stage typically are due to the need to replace a worn-out product or to population growth. The last product life cycle stage—decline—finds the product being replaced by a competing product (e.g., black-and-white televisions).

Managers may be able to prevent some products from entering the decline stage by improving product quality or by adding innovations. Other products, such as scissors, may never reach this last stage of the product life cycle because there are no competing products to replace them.

Evaluating Sales Forecasting Methods   The sales forecasting methods just described are not the only ones available to managers. Other, more complex methods include the statistical correlation method and the computer simulation method.[17] The methods just discussed, however, do provide a basic foundation for understanding sales forecasting.

In practice, managers find that each sales forecasting method has distinct advantages and disadvantages. Before deciding to use a particular sales forecasting method, a manager must carefully weigh these advantages and disadvantages as they relate to the manager's organization. The best decision may be to use a combination of methods to forecast sales rather than just one. Whatever method or methods are finally adopted, the manager should be certain the framework is logical, fits the needs of the organization, and can be adapted to changes in the environment.

A **product life cycle** is the five stages through which most products and services pass: introduction, growth, maturity, saturation, and decline.

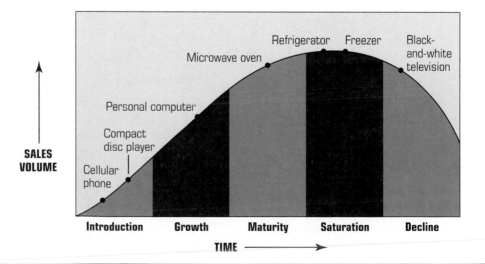

Figure 9.6   *Stages of the product life cycle*

One of the planning tools available to Ford management is forecasting, which involves predicting future environmental events that could influence the operation of the company. Although various specific types of forecasting—such as economic, technological, and social trends forecasting—are available to them, Ford management would probably use sales forecasting as its key, since it will predict how high or low their sales will be during the time period they are considering. Although the sales history of the Explorer has been impressive, such events as the Donna Bailey situation do significantly decrease forecasted future sales.

In order to forecast sales, managers should follow the jury of executive opinion method by having Ford executives discuss their opinions of future sales. This method would be quick and easy to use and, assuming that Ford executives have a good feel for product demand, might be as valid as any other method the company might use.

Ford management could also ask their auto retailers (salesforce) for opinions on predicted sales. Although the opinions of such car dealers may not be completely reliable, these people are closest to the market and must ultimately make the sales.

Finally, Ford management could use the time series analysis method by analyzing the relationship between sales and time. Although this method takes into account the cyclical patterns and past history of sales, it also assumes the continuation of these patterns in the future without considering outside influences such as economic downturns, which could cause the patterns to change.

Since each sales forecasting method has advantages and disadvantages, managers like those at Ford should carefully analyze them before deciding which method or combination of methods should be used.

Scheduling   **Scheduling** is the process of formulating a detailed listing of activities that must be accomplished to attain an objective, allocating the resources necessary to attain the objective, and setting up and following timetables for completing the objective. Scheduling is an integral part of every organizational plan. Two popular scheduling techniques are Gantt charts and the program evaluation and review technique (PERT).

Gantt Charts   The **Gantt chart**, a scheduling device developed by Henry L. Gantt, is essentially a bar graph with time on the horizontal axis and the resource to be scheduled on the vertical axis. It is used for scheduling resources, including management system inputs such as human resources and machines.

Scheduling is the process of formulating a detailed listing of activities that must be accomplished to attain an objective, allocating the resources necessary to attain the objective, and setting up and following timetables for completing the objective.

The **Gantt chart** is a scheduling tool composed of a bar chart with time on the horizontal axis and the resource to be scheduled on the vertical axis. It is used for scheduling resources.

▶ Computers and the Internet are becoming common tools for scheduling in the trucking industry. Bill Ensell is a Houston-based driver, shown here at a Denver rest stop where computer workstations allow access to "load boards," Web sites where truckers can find out about loads in need of transport. Says Scott Barnes, another driver, "You had better not be scared of computers any more if you drive a truck for a living. It's how you communicate, how you find your next load, how you do your accounts, how other people find you."

Figure 9.7 shows a completed Gantt chart for a work period entitled "Workweek 28." The resources scheduled over the five workdays on this chart were the human resources Wendy Reese and Peter Thomas. During this workweek, both Reese and Thomas were supposed to produce 10 units a day. Note, however, that actual production deviated from planned production. There were days when each of the two workers produced more than 10 units, as well as days when each produced fewer than 10 units. Cumulative actual production for workweek 28 shows that Reese produced 40 units and Thomas 45 units over the five days.

Features   Although simple in concept and appearance, the Gantt chart has many valuable managerial uses. First, managers can use it as a summary overview of how organizational resources are being employed. From this summary, they can detect such facts as which resources are consistently contributing to productivity and which are hindering it. Second, managers can use the Gantt chart to help coordinate organizational resources. The chart can show which resources are not being used during specific periods, thereby allowing managers to schedule those resources for work on other production efforts. Third, the chart can be used to establish realistic worker output standards. For example, if scheduled work is being completed too quickly, output standards should be raised so that workers are scheduled for more work per time period.

Program Evaluation and Review Technique (PERT)   The main weakness of the Gantt chart is that it does not contain any information about the interrelationship of tasks to be performed. Although all tasks to be performed are listed on the chart, there is no way of telling if one task must be performed before another can be started. The **program evaluation and review technique (PERT)**, a technique that evolved partly from the Gantt chart, is a scheduling tool that does emphasize the interrelationship of tasks.

Defining PERT   PERT is a network of project activities showing both the estimates of time necessary to complete each activity and the sequence of activities that must be followed to complete the project. This scheduling tool was developed in 1958 for designing and building the Polaris submarine weapon system. The people who were managing this project found Gantt charts and other existing scheduling tools of little use because of the complicated nature of the Polaris project and the interdependence of the tasks to be performed.[18]

The PERT network contains two primary elements: activities and events. **Activities** are specified sets of behavior within a project, and **events** are the completions of major project tasks. Within the PERT network, each event is assigned corresponding activities that must be performed before the event can materialize.[19]

The **program evaluation and review technique (PERT)** is a scheduling tool that is essentially a network of project activities showing estimates of time necessary to complete each activity and the sequence of activities that must be followed to complete the project.

Activities and events are the primary elements of a PERT network. **Activities** are specified sets of behavior within a project. **Events** are the completions of major project tasks.

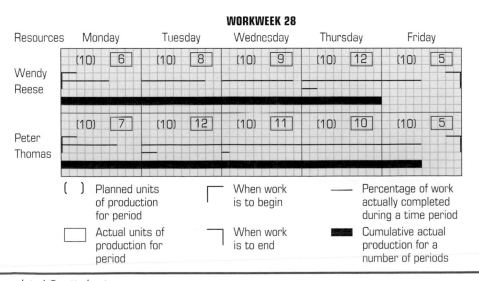

WORKWEEK 28

Completed Gantt chart

Figure 9.7

204   Part Three ▶ Planning

Features A sample PERT network designed for building a house is presented in Figure 9.8. Events are symbolized by circles and activities by arrows. To illustrate, the figure indicates that after the event "Foundation Complete" (represented by a circle) has materialized, certain activities (represented by an arrow) must be performed before the event "Frame Complete" (represented by another circle) can materialize.

Two other features of the network shown in Figure 9.8 should be emphasized. First, the left-to-right presentation of events shows how the events interrelate or the sequence in which they should be performed. Second, the numbers in parentheses above each arrow indicate the units of time necessary to complete each activity. These two features help managers ensure that only necessary work is being done on a project and that no project activities are taking too long.

Critical Path Managers need to pay close attention to the **critical path** of a PERT network—the sequence of events and activities requiring the longest period of time to complete. This path is called *critical* because a delay in completing this sequence results in a delay in completing the entire project. The critical path in Figure 9.8 is indicated by thick arrows; all other paths are indicated by thin arrows. Managers try to control a project by keeping it within the time designated by the critical path. The critical path helps them predict which features of a schedule are becoming unrealistic and provides insights into how those features might be eliminated or modified.[20]

> A **critical path** is the sequence of events and activities within a program evaluation and review technique (PERT) network that requires the longest period of time to complete.

Steps in Designing a PERT Network When designing a PERT network, managers should follow four primary steps:[21]

> ➤ *Step 1*—List all the activities/events that must be accomplished for the project and the sequence in which these activities/events should be performed
> ➤ *Step 2*—Determine how much time will be needed to complete each activity/event
> ➤ *Step 3*—Design a PERT network that reflects all of the information contained in steps 1 and 2
> ➤ *Step 4*—Identify the critical path

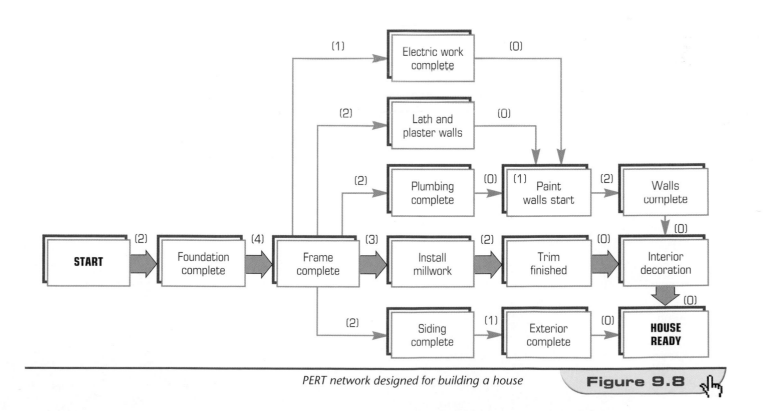

PERT network designed for building a house

Figure 9.8

Scheduling is another planning tool available to Ford management. It involves the detailed listing of activities that must be accomplished to reach an objective. For example, if Ford's goal is to have all of its employees working proficiently on updated equipment within two years, management needs to schedule activities such as installing the equipment, training the employees, and establishing new output standards.

Two scheduling techniques available to Ford management are Gantt charts and PERT. To schedule employee production output, the managers might want to use Gantt charts—bar graphs with time on the horizontal axis and the resource to be scheduled on the vertical axis. They might also find these charts helpful for evaluating worker performance and setting new production standards.

If managers like those at Ford want to see the relationships among tasks, they could use PERT to develop a flowchart showing activities, events, and the amount of time necessary to complete each task. For example, a PERT network would be helpful in scheduling the installation of new machines, since this type of schedule would allow management to see which equipment needed to be installed first, the amount of time each installation would require, and how other activities in renovating an existing factory would be affected before the installation was completed.

PERT would also help the managers to discern the critical path they must follow for successful installation. This path represents the sequence of activities and events requiring the longest amount of time to complete, and it indicates the total time it will take to finish the project. If, for example, new welding machinery takes longer to install than other types of equipment, management should target the completion of the entire equipment installation on the basis of this equipment's installation time.

Management Skills Module

This section is specially designed to help you develop management skills. An individual's management skill is based on an understanding of management concepts and the ability to apply those concepts in management situations. As a result, the following activities are designed both to heighten your understanding of management concepts and to help you gain facility in applying those concepts in various management situations.

UNDERSTANDING MANAGEMENT CONCEPTS

▶ Action Summary

Reread the learning objectives below. Each objective is followed by questions. Answering these questions accurately will help you retain the most important concepts discussed in this chapter. After answering each question, check your answer against the answer key at the end of this chapter. (*Hint:* If you have any doubts regarding the correct response, consult the page number that follows the answer.)

Circle:

From studying this chapter, I will attempt to acquire

1. A complete definition of a plan.

a b c d e **a.** A plan is: (a) the company's buildings and fixtures (b) a specific action proposed to help the company achieve its objectives (c) a policy meeting (d) a projection of future sales (e) an experiment to determine the optimal distribution system.

a b c d e **b.** The following is generally *not* an important component of a plan: (a) the evaluation of relevant information (b) the assessment of probable future developments (c) a statement of a recommended course of action (d) a statement of manager intuition (e) strategy based on reason or rationality.

2. Insights regarding various dimensions of plans.

T F **a.** Most plans affect top management only.

a b c d e **b.** The following is one of the four major dimensions of a plan: (a) repetitiveness (b) organization (c) time (d) a and c (e) b and c.

3. An understanding of various types of plans.

a b c d e **a.** Standing plans that furnish broad guidelines for channeling management thinking in specified directions are called: (a) procedures (b) programs (c) single-use plans (d) policies (e) rules.

a b c d e **b.** Programs and budgets are examples of: (a) single-use plans (b) standing rules (c) procedures (d) Gantt chart components (e) critical paths.

4. Insights into why plans fail.

a b c d e **a.** The following is a reason that plans fail: (a) adequate inputs are used in planning (b) corporate planning is integrated into the total management system (c) management expects that plans developed will be realized with little effort (d) management operates by the plan (e) responsibility for planning is vested in more than just the planning department.

T F **b.** The confusion of planning with financial projections will have no effect on the success of plans.

5. A knowledge of various planning areas within an organization.

T F **a.** Input planning includes only site selection planning.

a b c d e **b.** Personnel planners who reflect on organizational objectives to determine overall human resource needs and compare needs to existing human resource inventory are engaging in a type of planning called: (a) process layout (b) plant facilities (c) input (d) life cycle (e) Delphi.

6. A definition of forecasting.

T F **a.** Forecasting is the process of setting objectives and scheduling activities.

a b c d e **b.** According to the text, the following product is in the growth stage of the product life cycle: (a) microwave oven (b) cellular phone (c) black-and-white television (d) personal computer (e) refrigerator.

7. An ability to see the advantages and disadvantages of various methods of sales forecasting.

a b c d e **a.** The sales forecasting technique that utilizes specialized knowledge based on interaction with customers is: (a) jury of executive opinion (b) sales force estimation (c) time series analysis (d) a and b (e) b and c.

T F   **b.** One of the advantages of the jury of executive opinion method is that it may be the only feasible means of forecasting sales, especially in the absence of adequate data.

  8. A definition of scheduling.

a b c d e   **a.** Scheduling can best be described as: (a) the evaluation of alternative courses of action (b) the process of formulating goals and objectives (c) the process of formulating a detailed listing of activities (d) the calculation of the break-even point (e) the process of defining policies.

T F   **b.** Scheduling is the process of predicting future environmental happenings that will influence the operations of the organization.

  9. An understanding of Gantt charts and PERT.

a b c d e   **a.** The following is *not* an acceptable use of a Gantt chart: (a) as a summary overview of how organizational resources are being used (b) to help coordinate organizational resources (c) to establish realistic worker output standards (d) to determine which resources are consistently contributing to productivity (e) none of the above (all are acceptable uses of Gantt charts).

a b c d e   **b.** In a PERT network, the sequence of events and activities requiring the longest period of time to complete is: (a) called the network (b) indicated by thin arrows (c) the path that managers avoid (d) the critical path (e) eliminated from the rest of the project so the project will not take too long.

▶ Action Summary Answer Key

1. a. b, p. 192
  b. d, p. 192
2. a. F, pp. 192–193
  b. d, pp. 192–193
3. a. d, p. 194
  b. a, p. 196

4. a. c, p. 196
  b. F, p. 196
5. a. F, p. 196
  b. c, pp. 198–199

6. a. F, p. 200
  b. d, p. 202
7. a. b, p. 201
  b. T, pp. 200–201

8. a. c, p. 203
  b. F, p. 203
9. a. e, pp. 203–204
  b. d, p. 205

▶ Issues for Review and Discussion

1. What is a plan?
2. List and describe the basic dimensions of a plan.
3. What is the difference between standing plans and single-use plans?
4. Compare and contrast policies, procedures, and rules.
5. What are the two main types of single-use plans?
6. Why do organizations have programs?
7. Of what use is a budget to managers?
8. Summarize the 10 factors that cause plans to fail.
9. What is input planning?
10. Evaluate the importance of plant facilities planning to the organization.
11. What major factors should be involved in site selection?
12. Describe the human resource planning process.
13. What is a planning tool?
14. Describe the measurements usually employed in forecasting. Why are they taken?
15. Draw and explain the product life cycle.
16. Discuss the advantages and disadvantages of three methods of sales forecasting.
17. Elaborate on the statement that all managers should spend some time scheduling.
18. What is a Gantt chart? Draw a simple chart to assist you in your explanation.
19. How can information related to the Gantt chart be used by managers?
20. How is PERT a scheduling tool?
21. How is the critical path related to PERT?
22. List the steps necessary to design a PERT network.

Applying Management Concepts

▸ Cases

➡ INTRODUCTORY CASE WRAP-UP

▸ Case Discussion Questions

"Ford Plans to Improve the Explorer" (p. 191) and its related Back-to-the-Case sections were written to help you better understand the management concepts contained in this chapter. Answer the following discussion questions about this Introductory Case to further enrich your understanding of chapter content:

1. Should Ford's plan to improve the Explorer be related to its human resource planning? Explain.
2. Explain this statement: "The quality of Ford's decision about how to improve the Explorer is largely determined by product improvement planning."
3. Do you think that Ford management should use forecasted Explorer sales as a component of product improvement planning? Explain.

▸ Skills Exercise: Writing Plans for Improving Ford's Explorer

In the Introductory Case, Ford's management was planning to improve the quality of the Explorer before Donna Bailey's tragic accident. Assume that you are presently a manager at Ford in charge of this planning. Write a policy, a procedure, and a rule that should help to upgrade the Explorer. Explain why each of these standing plans that you write will enhance the quality.

CASE STUDY: *White Wave Wins with Soy*

Colorado-based White Wave's CEO Steve Demos, refers to himself as an entrepreneurial "soy mogul." His favorite beverages are strong coffee and Silk soymilk smoothies. For 23 years his mission has been the "creative integration of soy into the average American diet." Finally, his perseverance is paying off with his innovative Silk soymilk. Silk is the first nationally distributed, refrigerated soy beverage, and the top seller in the United States. White Wave also produces the Silk brands of soy creamer and dairy-free yogurt, as well as the White Wave brands of tofu and tempeh. The company's products are sold through natural food and grocery stores across the United States and Canada, as well as on military bases in Asia and Europe.

A self-proclaimed hippie, Demos grew up in a meat-eating family, in Philadelphia. He was inspired to found White Wave after spending a few years meditating and living inside a cave in India. Now a 52-year-old vegetarian, he still wears his hair long, practices yoga each day, and lives in a handcrafted wood cabin 8,500 feet up in the Colorado Rockies. Demos has waited a long time for success. He hopes that Silk will turn White Wave, a private company with 120 employees, into a big player in the food industry.

Pat Calhoun, senior vice president and CFO of White Wave, is Demos's friend from college days. She said White Wave's business practices are based on the "right livelihood philosophy." It is derived from a meditation practice they both learned in India, consisting of ethical decision making based on nonviolent products.

White Wave has been through some tough times, having reached a low point in the 1980s when a *Los Angeles Times* poll named tofu the second most hated food in the nation, right behind liver. Demos continued to work in his kitchen, refusing to give up

trying to make soy pleasing to the American consumer. "At one time Steve had 200 products out there," recalls Peter Globitz, an industry consultant and longtime friend. "He'd just throw products at the wall and see what stuck."

Finally, in 1996, Demos hit on a way to make soymilk more appealing. He added sugar and vanilla to disguise the beany flavor and packaged it in a classic milk carton to be stocked in the dairy case right next to regular milk. He put instructions on the carton like "Shake well and buy often"; he spent $10 million on an ad campaign that featured slogans like "Have a nice life span," and gave away more than 3 million half-pints of Silk in 5,000 stores. (Demos believes in-store tastings to be too aggressive.)

Calhoun credits the 1999 Food and Drug Administration's recommendation that consuming 25 grams of soy protein per day lowers cholesterol levels with boosting sales of Silk soymilk over the top. Silk chocolate soymilk actually beat Hershey's chocolate milk in a taste test conducted by *Good Housekeeping* magazine in 2000!

With the growth spurt of Silk, Demos found himself in uncharted territory. He got help by doing some strategic partnering with Dean Foods, the second largest dairy in the United States. In exchange for a minority stake in White Wave, Dean Foods gives Demos access to its operations and distribution network, crucial to delivering more Silk to mainstream supermarkets. Demos's dedication is paying off. Silk sales have more than doubled every year since it was launched. The changing demographics in the nation are also working in his favor. A high percentage of African Americans and Hispanics are lactose-intolerant, which means more people could switch to nondairy milk.

Demos's executive staff has grown with Silk's success. He has hired Sheryl Lambs, former Peace Corps volunteer and natural foods guru, to head sales and marketing. He also hired another old college friend, James Terman, to create packaging, after James sent him a postcard with a picture of an unemployed man that said, "Will work for tofu." "I didn't pick M.B.A.s, I picked cultural connects," says Demos.

According to observations by Peter Globitz, soymilk sales in the United States are slated to hit $1 billion by 2005, up from $420 million in 2001. In anticipation, White Wave is building two processing plants, one in Utah and one in New Jersey. "If you don't plan for success, what are you going to do when you get there?" Demos asks. (While breaking ground in Utah, the company spent $4,000 to relocate 26 prairie dogs that lived on the property.)

Demos also has ideas for new products like breakfast cereal topping and soy snacks. Meanwhile, larger companies like The Hain Celestial, Suiza Foods, Tofutti Brands, and Kellogg are trying to cash in on the demand for soy products. When asked whether he feared competition from these giants, he said, "We're going to be outspent, so we have to outthink. I'm racing, they're chasing."

Steve Demos's passion and persistence will surely be put to the test as he tries to guide White Wave to new heights.

QUESTIONS

1. List three factors that White Wave should consider in choosing the locations of its two new processing plants. Why is each factor important?

2. How might use of the Internet aid Demos's planning in the future?

3. Which of the three methods of sales forecasting described in your text would be most helpful for Demos at this critical time in his company's growth? Why?

▶ Video

MASTERING MANAGEMENT: EPISODE 3—PLANNING

Mastering Management is a series of innovative, interactive learning activities specially designed to help you develop management skills emphasized in various text chapters. Plans and planning tools are major focuses of this chapter. Episode 3 of *Mastering Management* focuses on how to plan and focuses on two CanGo projects that require careful planning. In this episode, one of CanGo's best technical people has difficulty developing a worthwhile plan. Review Episode 3 on your *Mastering Management* CD and then answer the following questions.

QUESTIONS

1. Do you believe that plans will fail at CanGo? Why?

2. How might CanGo use PERT as a planning tool?

3. Is CanGo using human resource planning appropriately? Explain.

www.prenhall.com/certo

This book is accompanied by a rich assortment of online activities aimed at developing your management skills. Reviewing news headlines, Internet exercises, an online study guide, and other research and Internet resources can help personalize management skills development for individual students or an entire class.

chapter

chapterchapterchapterchapterchapterchapter

10 Fundamentals of Organizing

objectivesobjectivesobjectives

▶ Objectives

From studying this chapter, I will attempt to acquire

● An understanding of the organizing function

● An appreciation for the complexities of determining appropriate organizational structure

● Insights into the advantages and disadvantages of division of labor

● A working knowledge of the relationship between division of labor and coordination

● An understanding of span of management and the factors that influence its appropriateness

● An understanding of scalar relationships

CHAPTER OUTLINE

Introductory Case: *Lucent Technologies Organizes to Be More Competitive*

A Definition of Organizing
Fayol's Guidelines
The Importance of Organizing
The Organizing Process
The Organizing Subsystem

Classical Organizing Theory
Weber's Bureaucratic Model
Structure

Global Spotlight ▶ McDonald's Organizes by Global Territory

Division of Labor

Quality Spotlight ▶ DaimlerChrysler Improves Coordination to Improve Product Quality

Span of Management
Scalar Relationships

Across Industries ▶ Health Care—Circular Organization Chart at Our Lady of the Way Hospital

Lucent Technologies Organizes to Be More Competitive

REMINDER: THE INTRODUCTORY CASE WRAP-UP (P. 230) CONTAINS DISCUSSION QUESTIONS AND A SKILLS EXERCISE TO FURTHER ILLUSTRATE THE APPLICATION OF CHAPTER CONCEPTS TO THIS VIGNETTE.

Lucent Technologies, headquartered in Murray Hill, New Jersey, designs, builds, and delivers a wide range of public and private networks, communications systems and software, wired and wireless business telephone systems, and microelectronics components. For businesses it produces and sells call center systems, Internet systems, and mobile phone systems.

Two years ago Lucent was spun off from AT&T and established as a stand-alone company. Major competitors of the newly formed company are Motorola, Tellabs, Harris Corporation, and Applied Signal. Even given such formidable competition, Lucent has shown amazing success. The company reached annual revenues of more than $26 billion with a 20 percent annual growth rate. Lucent's outstanding performance has gained both national and international attention and respect.

Lucent Technologies' organizational structure speeds up the product development process by giving individual groups greater autonomy and the ability to respond quickly to the marketplace.

A large part of the credit for this success goes to Lucent's organization structure. The company built a structure that facilitates internal autonomy to speed up the product development process and get products to market sooner. Managers can make decisions about what must be done and when it can be done without having to get constant approval from managers higher up.

Lucent's organization structure also gives groups within the company the ability to respond quickly to an ever-changing marketplace. The company was divided into 11 groups, with each group focusing on a major product or service being offered. According to Karyn Mashima, a vice president of the area called Enterprise Networks and Data Networks Systems, such groupings will help Lucent to get focused and be efficient in some very competitive business areas.

The new, group-oriented structure allows groups autonomy but also encourages them to work together. For example, the Global Service Provider group was formed to support sales and service of several other groups. Groups are accountable for their individual missions, which at times include independence from other groups and at other times cooperation with other groups.

There are some questions as to whether Lucent can continue its rate of growth and success. According to Richard A. McGinn, Lucent CEO, the company's organization structure is one factor that assures this continuance.

What's Ahead

The Introductory Case describes, in general, how Lucent is being organized in order to be more competitive. Information in this chapter would be useful to a manager like Richard A. McGinn, Lucent's CEO, in contemplating organizing issues. This chapter emphasizes both a definition of organizing and principles of classical organizing theory that can be useful in organizing a company.

A DEFINITION OF ORGANIZING

Organizing is the process of establishing orderly uses for all the organization's resources.

Organizing is the process of establishing orderly uses for all resources within the management system. Orderly uses emphasize the attainment of management system objectives and assist managers not only in making objectives apparent but also in clarifying which resources will be used to attain them. A primary focus of organizing is determining both what individual employees will do in an organization and how their individual efforts should best be combined to advance the attainment of organizational objectives.[1] *Organization* refers to the result of the organizing process.

Fayol's Guidelines

In essence, each organizational resource represents an investment from which the management system must get a return. Appropriate organization of these resources increases the efficiency and effectiveness of their use. Henri Fayol developed 16 general guidelines for organizing resources:[2]

1. Judiciously prepare and execute the operating plan
2. Organize the human and material facets so that they are consistent with objectives, resources, and requirements of the concern
3. Establish a single competent, energetic guiding authority (formal management structure)
4. Coordinate all activities and efforts
5. Formulate clear, distinct, and precise decisions
6. Arrange for efficient selection so that each department is headed by a competent, energetic manager and all employees are placed where they can render the greatest service
7. Define duties
8. Encourage initiative and responsibility
9. Offer fair and suitable rewards for services rendered
10. Make use of sanctions against faults and errors
11. Maintain discipline
12. Ensure that individual interests are consistent with the general interests of the organization
13. Recognize the unity of command
14. Promote both material and human coordination
15. Institute and effect controls
16. Avoid regulations, red tape, and paperwork

The Importance of Organizing

The organizing function is extremely important to the management system because it is the primary mechanism managers use to activate plans. Organizing creates and maintains relationships between all organizational resources by indicating which resources are to be used for specified activities and when, where, and how they are to be used. A thorough organizing effort helps managers minimize costly weaknesses, such as duplication of effort and idle organizational resources.

Some management theorists consider the organizing function so important that they advocate the creation of an organizing department within the

▶ If a bumper crop is the objective, the organizing process can be divided into major tasks, such as tilling, planting, fertilization, watering, and so on; then allocating resources like equipment and labor to accomplish subtasks like sorting the harvest; and finally evaluating the result for quality and quantity produced.

management system. Typical responsibilities of this department would include developing the following:[3]

1. Reorganization plans that make the management system more effective and efficient
2. Plans to improve managerial skills to fit current management system needs
3. An advantageous organizational climate within the management system

The Organizing Process

The five main steps of the organizing process are presented in Figure 10.1:[4]

1. Reflect on plans and objectives
2. Establish major tasks
3. Divide major tasks into subtasks
4. Allocate resources and directives for subtasks
5. Evaluate the results of implemented organizing strategy

As the figure implies, managers should continually repeat these steps. Through repetition, they obtain feedback that will help them improve the existing organization.

The management of a restaurant can serve as an illustration of how the organizing process works. The first step the restaurant manager would take to initiate the organizing process would be to reflect on the restaurant's plans and objectives. Because planning involves determining how the restaurant will attain its objectives, and organizing involves determining how the restaurant's resources will be used to activate plans, the restaurant manager must start to organize by understanding planning.

The second and third steps of the organizing process focus on tasks to be performed within the management system. The manager must designate major tasks or jobs to be done within the restaurant. Two such tasks are serving customers and cooking food. Then the tasks must be divided into subtasks. For example, the manager might decide that serving customers includes the subtasks of taking orders and clearing tables.

The fourth organizing step is determining who will take orders, who will clear the tables, and what the details of the relationship between these individuals will be. The size of tables and how they are to be set are other factors to be considered at this point.

In the fifth step, evaluating the results of the implemented organizing strategy, the manager gathers feedback on how well the strategy is working. This feedback should furnish information that can be used to improve the existing organization. For example, the manager may find that a particular type of table is not large enough and that larger ones must be purchased if the restaurant is to attain its goals.

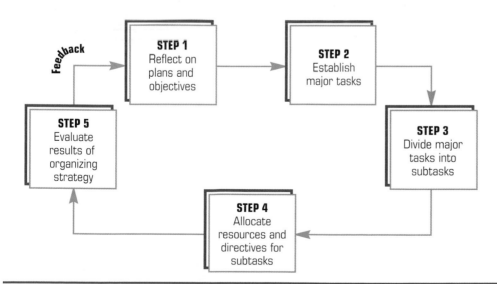

The five main steps of the organizing process

Figure 10.1

The Organizing Subsystem

The organizing function, like the planning function, can be visualized as a subsystem of the overall management system (see Figure 10.2). The primary purpose of the organizing subsystem is to enhance the goal attainment of the general management system by providing a rational approach for using organizational resources. Figure 10.3 presents the specific ingredients of the organizing subsystem. The input is a portion of the total resources of the organization, the process is the steps involved in the organizing function, and the output is organization.

► Back to the Case

In contemplating how Lucent should be organized, a manager like Richard A. McGinn can focus on answering several important questions. These questions should be aimed at establishing an orderly use of Lucent's organizational resources. Because these resources represent an investment on which he must get a return, McGinn's questions should be geared toward gaining information that will be used to maximize this return. Overall, such questions should focus on determining what use of Lucent's resources will best accomplish its goals.

Some preliminary questions could be as follows:

1. What organizational objectives exist at Lucent? For example, does Lucent want to focus on international markets as well as domestic markets? Does Lucent want to grow or maintain its present size?
2. What plans does Lucent have to accomplish these objectives? Is Lucent going to open more offices abroad? Are additional training programs being added to enable employees to effectively work abroad?
3. What are the major tasks Lucent must accomplish to offer message and voice products? For example, how many steps are involved in developing a new wireless telephone and making it available to appropriate customers?
4. What resources does Lucent have to run its operations? Answers to this question focus on issues such as the number of employees, financial resources available, and equipment being used.

McGinn should also begin thinking of some mechanism for evaluating the organizing strategy he develops. Once the strategy is implemented, McGinn must be able to get feedback

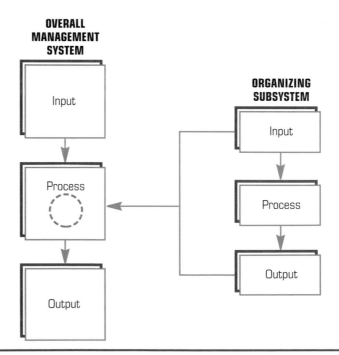

Figure 10.2    *Relationships between overall management system and organizing subsystem*

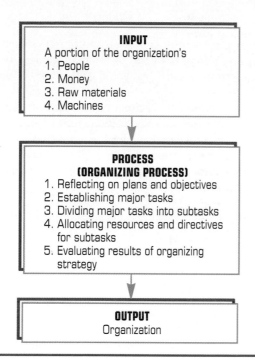

INPUT
A portion of the organization's
1. People
2. Money
3. Raw materials
4. Machines

PROCESS
(ORGANIZING PROCESS)
1. Reflecting on plans and objectives
2. Establishing major tasks
3. Dividing major tasks into subtasks
4. Allocating resources and directives for subtasks
5. Evaluating results of organizing strategy

OUTPUT
Organization

Organizing subsystem   **Figure 10.3**

on how all of Lucent's resources are functioning so he can improve his organizing efforts. For example, he may find that in order for Lucent to become more competitive he needs more Internet systems capability in one country than another and more employees in the consumer products area as opposed to the commercial area. With appropriate feedback, McGinn can continually improve Lucent's existing organizational system.

CLASSICAL ORGANIZING THEORY

Classical organizing theory comprises the cumulative insights of early management writers on how organizational resources can best be used to enhance goal attainment. The writer who probably had the most profound influence on classical organizing theory was Max Weber.[5] According to Weber, the main components of an organizing effort are detailed procedures and rules, a clearly outlined organizational hierarchy, and impersonal relationships among organization members.

Classical organizing theory comprises the cumulative insights of early management writers on how organizational resources can best be used to enhance goal attainment.

Weber's Bureaucratic Model

Weber used the term **bureaucracy** to label the management system that contains these components. Although he firmly believed in the bureaucratic approach to organizing, he was concerned that managers were inclined to overemphasize the merits of a bureaucracy. He cautioned that a bureaucracy is not an end in itself, but rather a means to the end of management system goal attainment. The main criticism of Weber's bureaucracy model, as well as the concepts of other classical organizing theorists, is that they give short shrift to the human variable within organizations. In fact, it is recognized today that the bureaucratic approach without an appropriate emphasis on the human variable is almost certainly a formula for organizational failure.[6]

The rest of this chapter summarizes four main considerations of classical organizing theory that all modern managers should incorporate into their organizing efforts:

1. Structure
2. Division of labor
3. Span of management
4. Scalar relationships

Bureaucracy is the term Max Weber used to describe a management system characterized by detailed procedures and rules, a clearly outlined organizational hierarchy, and impersonal relationships among organization members.

Structure

Structure refers to the designated relationships among resources of the management system.

In any organizing effort, managers must choose an appropriate structure. **Structure** refers to the designated relationships among resources of the management system. Its purpose is to facilitate the use of each resource, individually and collectively, as the management system attempts to attain its objectives.[7]

An **organization chart** is a graphic representation of organizational structure.

Organization structure is represented primarily by means of a graphic illustration called an **organization chart.** Traditionally, an organization chart is constructed in pyramid form, with individuals toward the top of the pyramid having more authority and responsibility than those toward the bottom.[8] The relative positioning of individuals within boxes on the chart indicates broad working relationships, and lines between boxes designate formal lines of communication between individuals.

Authority and Responsibility Figure 10.4 is an example of an organization chart. The dotted line is not part of the organization chart but has been added to emphasize the chart's pyramid shape. The position of restaurant manager is at the point of the pyramid, and those positions close to the restaurant manager's involve more authority and responsibility, while those positions farther away involve less authority and responsibility. The locations of positions also indicate broad working relationships. For example, the positioning of the head chef over the three other chefs indicates that the head chef has authority over them and is responsible for their productivity. The lines between the individual chefs and the restaurant manager indicate that formal communication from chef 1 to the restaurant manager must go through the head chef.

Structure and Gender Pyramidal organization structures are probably modeled on the hierarchical structure of military command. In the Western world, the structure of organized religion has also been hierarchical, with authority derived from the top. Some researchers have found that women are not comfortable with this type of structure. As more and more women enter the management field, therefore, a new type of structural model may be needed. In *The Female Advantage: Women's Ways of Leadership,* Sally Helgesen postulates that women create networks or "webs" of authority and that women's leadership styles are relational rather than hierarchical and authoritarian. Management writer Tom Peters suggests that these styles are inherently better suited to the new kinds of organizational structures, featuring teamwork and participative management, required for the competitive global environment of the twenty-first century.[9]

Formal structure is defined as the relationships among organizational resources as outlined by management.

Formal and Informal Structure There are two basic types of structure within management systems: formal and informal. **Formal structure** is defined as the relationships

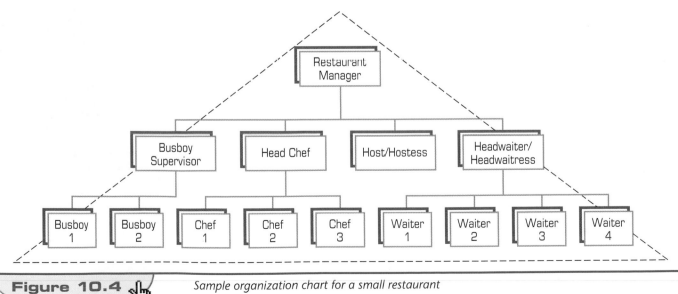

Figure 10.4   *Sample organization chart for a small restaurant*

among organizational resources as outlined by management. It is represented primarily by the organization chart.

Informal structure is defined as the patterns of relationships that develop because of the informal activities of organization members. It evolves naturally and tends to be molded by individual norms and values and social relationships. Essentially, an organization's informal structure is the system or network of interpersonal relationships that exists within, but is not usually identical to, the organization's formal structure.[10] This chapter focuses on formal structure. Details on informal structure are presented in Chapter 17.

Departmentalization and Formal Structure: A Contingency Viewpoint The most common method of instituting formal relationships among resources is to establish departments. Basically, a **department** is a unique group of resources established by management to perform some organizational task. The process of establishing departments within the management system is called **departmentalization.** Typically, these departments are based on, or contingent upon, such situational factors as the work functions being performed, the product being assembled, the territory being covered, the customer being targeted, and the process designed for manufacturing the product. (For a quick review of the contingency approach to management, see Chapter 2.)

Functional Departmentalization Perhaps the most widely used basis for establishing departments within the formal structure is the type of *work functions* (activities) being performed within the management system.[11] Functions are typically divided into the major categories of marketing, production, and finance. Figure 10.5 is an organization chart showing structure based primarily on function for a hypothetical organization, Greene Furniture Company.

Product Departmentalization Organization structure based primarily on *product* departmentalizes resources according to the products being manufactured. As more and more products are manufactured by a company, it becomes increasingly difficult for management to coordinate activities across the organization. Organizing according to product permits the logical grouping of resources necessary to produce each product. Figure 10.6 is an organization chart for Greene Furniture Company showing structure based primarily on product.

Geographic Departmentalization Structure based primarily on *territory* departmentalizes according to the places where the work is being done or the geographic markets on which the management system is focusing. The physical distances can range from quite short (between two points in the same city) to quite long (between two points in the same state, in

Informal structure is defined as the patterns of relationships that develop because of the informal activities of organization members.

A **department** is a unique group of resources established by management to perform some organizational task.

Departmentalization is the process of establishing departments within the management system.

▶ Formal organizational structure defines the hierarchy within the firm and establishes departments, like this one at the Social Security center in Baltimore, Maryland. As a service operation, the Social Security office is more likely to operate under functional departmentalization.

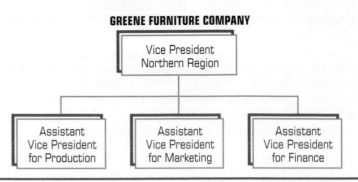

Organization structure based primarily on function

Figure 10.5

different states, or even in different countries).[12] As market areas and work locations expand, the physical distances between places can make the management task extremely cumbersome. To minimize this problem, resources can be departmentalized according to territory. Figure 10.7 is an organization chart for Greene Furniture Company based primarily on territory.

McDonald's Organizes by Global Territory

McDonald's Corporation operates fast-food restaurants under the brand name McDonald's. The popular restaurants serve varied, yet limited, value-priced meals in 120 countries throughout the world.

Reacting to its recent poor financial performance, McDonald's decided to reorganize its global senior management team. This involved creating two geographic areas of responsibility: One of the new positions focuses on managing operations in the Americas while the other focuses on managing operations in Europe, Asia, and the Pacific.

According to Jack Greenberg, McDonald's chairman and CEO, the new organization hierarchy evolved over many months as a vehicle for creating clearer lines of responsibility over the two territories as well as more focus on and accountability for the company's financial performance within the territories. The new structure was also aimed at helping the company to make business decisions more quickly. Greenberg believes that the reorganization should improve McDonald's capability for making necessary change, innovating, and being more consistent in its management across the globe. ■

Customer Departmentalization Structure based primarily on the *customer* establishes departments in response to the organization's major customers. This structure, of course, assumes that major customers can be identified and divided into logical categories. Figure 10.8 is an organization chart for Greene Furniture Company based primarily on customers. Greene Furniture obviously can clearly identify its customers and divide them into logical categories.

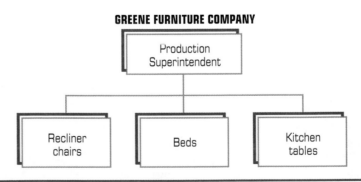

Organization structure based primarily on product

Figure 10.6

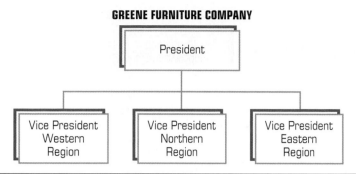

GREENE FURNITURE COMPANY

President

Vice President Western Region

Vice President Northern Region

Vice President Eastern Region

Organization structure based primarily on territory

Figure 10.7

Manufacturing Process Departmentalization Structure based primarily on *manufacturing process* departmentalizes according to the major phases of the process used to manufacture products. In the case of Greene Furniture Company, the major phases are wood-cutting, sanding, gluing, and painting. Figure 10.9 is the organization chart that reflects these phases.

If the situation warrants it, individual organization charts can be combined to show all five of these factors. Figure 10.10 shows how all the factors are included on the same organization chart for Greene Furniture Company.

Forces Influencing Formal Structure According to Shetty and Carlisle, the formal structure of a management system is continually evolving. Four primary forces influence this evolution:[13]

1. Forces in the manager
2. Forces in the task
3. Forces in the environment
4. Forces in the subordinates

The evolution of a particular organization is actually the result of a complex and dynamic interaction among these forces.

Forces in the manager are the unique way in which a manager perceives organizational problems.[14] Naturally, background, knowledge, experience, and values influence the manager's perception of what the organization's formal structure should be or how it should be changed.

Forces in the task include the degree of technology involved in performing the task and the task's complexity. As task activities change, a force is created to change the existing organization. Forces in the environment include the customers and suppliers of the management system, along with existing political and social structures. Forces in the subordinates include the needs and skill levels of subordinates. Obviously, as the environment and subordinates change, forces are created simultaneously to change the organization.

GREENE FURNITURE COMPANY

Sales Manager

Sales Representatives for Educational Sales

Sales Representatives for Residential Sales

Sales Representatives for Commercial Sales

Organization structure based primarily on customers

Figure 10.8

GREENE FURNITURE COMPANY

Production
Superintendent

| Woodcutting Department | Sanding Department | Gluing Department | Painting Department |

Figure 10.9 🖑   *Organization structure based primarily on manufacturing process*

▶ Back to the Case

In order to develop a sound organizing effort, a manager like McGinn should take classical organizing theory into consideration. Of the four major elements of classical organizing theory, the first to be considered here is structure. McGinn's considerations regarding the structure of Lucent would be aimed at creating working relationships among all Lucent employees. In order to develop an effective organizational structure, McGinn must analyze situational factors in the company, such as functions, products, geographic locations, customers, and processes involved in offering its products to customers.

Within the case there is information indicating that McGinn's organization structure for Lucent is based primarily on products or services offered. For example, 2 of the 11 main areas at

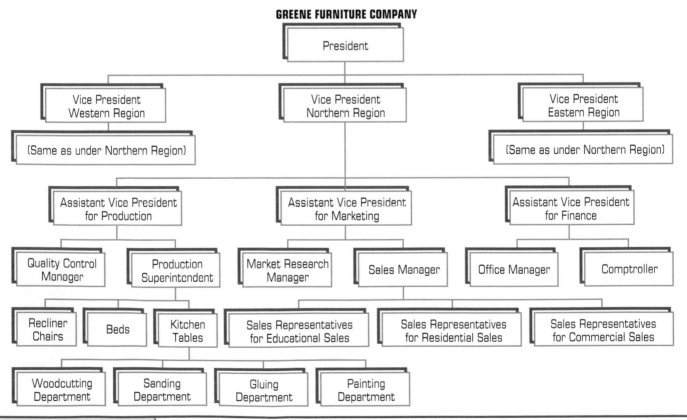

Figure 10.10 🖑   *Combined organization chart for Greene Furniture Company*

Lucent are Global Service Provider and Enterprise Networks and Data Networks Systems. In essence, Lucent is arranging its resources to focus on its 11 main product/service areas.

A manager like McGinn typically uses an organization chart to represent organization structure. Such a chart would allow McGinn not only to see the lines of authority and responsibility at Lucent, but also to understand the broad working relationships among its employees.

Division of Labor

The second main consideration of any organizing effort is how to divide labor. **Division of labor** is the assignment of various portions of a particular task among a number of organization members.[15] Rather than one individual doing the entire job, several individuals perform different parts of it. Production is divided into a number of steps, with the responsibility for completing various steps assigned to specific individuals. The essence of division of labor is that individuals specialize in doing part of a task rather than the entire task.

A commonly used illustration of division of labor is the automobile production line. Rather than one person assembling an entire car, specific portions of the car are assembled by various workers. The following sections discuss the advantages and disadvantages of division of labor and the relationship between division of labor and coordination.

Division of labor is the assignment of various portions of a particular task among a number of organization members. Division of labor calls for specialization.

Advantages and Disadvantages of Division of Labor

Even the peerless physicist Albert Einstein, famous for his independent theorizing, believed that division of labor could be very advantageous in many undertakings.[16] Several explanations have been offered for the usefulness of division of labor. First, when workers specialize in a particular task, their skill at performing that task tends to increase. Second, workers who have one job and one place in which to do it do not lose valuable time changing tools or locations. Third, when workers concentrate on performing only one job, they naturally try to make the job easier and more efficient. Lastly, division of labor creates a situation in which workers need only to know how to perform their part of the work task rather than the entire process for producing the end product. The task of understanding their work, therefore, does not become too burdensome.

Arguments have also been presented against the use of an extreme division of labor.[17] Essentially, these arguments contend that division of labor focuses solely on efficiency and economic benefit and overlooks the human variable in organizations. Work that is extremely specialized tends to be boring and therefore will eventually cause production rates to go down as workers become resentful of being treated like machines. Clearly, managers need to find a reasonable balance between specialization and human motivation. How to arrive at this balance is discussed in Chapter 16.

Division of Labor and Coordination

In a division-of-labor situation, the importance of effective coordination of the different individuals doing portions of the task is obvious. Mooney has defined **coordination** as "the orderly arrangement of group effort to provide unity of action in the pursuit of a common purpose." In essence, coordination is a means for achieving any and all organizational objectives.[18] It involves encouraging the completion of individual portions of a task in a synchronized order that is appropriate for the overall task. Groups cannot maintain their productivity without coordination.[19] Part of the synchronized order of assembling an automobile, for example, is that seats are installed only after the floor has been installed; adhering to this order of installation is an example of coordination.

Coordination is the orderly arrangement of group effort to provide unity of action in the pursuit of a common purpose. It involves encouraging the completion of individual portions of a task in an appropriate, synchronized order.

Establishing and maintaining coordination may require close supervision of employees, though managers should try to break away from the idea that coordination can only be achieved this way.[20] They can, instead, establish and maintain coordination through bargaining, formulating a common purpose for the group, or improving on specific problem solutions so the group will know what to do when it encounters those problems. Each of these efforts is considered a specific management tool.

Follett's Guidelines on Coordination

Mary Parker Follett provided valuable advice on how managers can establish and maintain coordination within the organization. First, Follett said that coordination can be attained with the least difficulty through direct horizontal relationships and personal communications. In other words, when a coordination problem arises, peer discussion may be the best way to resolve it. Second, Follett suggested that coordination be a discussion topic throughout the planning process. In essence, managers should plan for coordination. Third, maintaining coordination is a continuing process and should be treated as such. Managers cannot assume that because their management system shows coordination today it will show coordination tomorrow.

Follett also noted that coordination can be achieved only through purposeful management action—it cannot be left to chance. Finally, she stressed the importance of the human element and advised that the communication process is an essential consideration in any attempt to encourage coordination. Employee skill levels and motivation levels are also primary considerations, as is the effectiveness of the human communication process used during coordination activities.[21]

DaimlerChrysler Improves Coordination to Improve Product Quality

Improving coordination can improve the effectiveness and efficiency of the workforce in virtually any organization. DaimlerChrysler executives focus on improving coordination to improve product quality.

Although they acknowledge that new competitors such as Lexus and Infinity have made an impact in the upscale automobile market, DaimlerChrysler executives are neither discouraged nor digressing from decades-old organizational objectives. The company remains dedicated to the needs and wants of the upscale-but-unpretentious buyer who is looking for a vehicle that balances style and performance with form and function.

As in the past, the company will compete by remaining firmly committed to improving the overall quality of its products. KlausDieter Vohringer, a member of the DaimlerChrysler top management team, says the company will demonstrate this commitment to product quality through a plan that focuses on improving coordination among three different manufacturing and assembly plants. This major restructuring of the manufacturing process at DaimlerChrysler is expected to result not only in better product quality but also in more productive uses of existing facilities, quicker responses to changing customers' needs and competitive products, and lowered product costs. According to Vohringer, DaimlerChrysler has developed a sophisticated understanding of its customers over the years. In order to maintain a high level of customer satisfaction, management knows that it must constantly be on the alert for new methods of improving product quality, and is convinced that better coordination in the manufacturing process will help DaimlerChrysler achieve its quality goals. ■

▶ Back to the Case

In developing the most appropriate way to organize Lucent employees, a manager like McGinn can reflect on the second major element in classical organizing theory, division of labor. He could decide, for example, that instead of having one person do all the work involved in servicing a business customer, the labor could be divided so that for each business customer one person would make the initial contact, another would assess the communication needs of the organization, and a third would explore the alternative ways that Lucent could offer to meet those needs. In this way, employees could work more quickly and specialize in one area of business customer relations, such as business needs assessment or meeting business customer needs.

In considering the appropriateness of division of labor at Lucent, a manager like McGinn could also consider creating a mechanism for enhancing coordination. In order to develop such a mechanism, McGinn must have a thorough understanding of how various Lucent business processes occur so he can divide various tasks and maintain coordination within the various Lucent divisions. In addition, a manager like McGinn must stress communication as a prerequisite for coordination. Without Lucent employees continually communicating with one another, coordination will be virtually impossible. In taking action aimed at enhancing organizational coordination, McGinn must also continually plan for and take action toward maintaining such coordination.

Span of Management

The **span of management** is the number of individuals a manager supervises.

The third main consideration of any organizing effort is **span of management**—the number of individuals a manager supervises. The more individuals a manager supervises, the greater the span of management. Conversely, the fewer individuals a manager supervises, the smaller the span of management. The span of management has a significant effect on how well managers carry out their responsibilities. Span of management is also called *span of control, span of authority, span of supervision,* and *span of responsibility.*[22]

The central concern of span of management is to determine how many individuals a manager can supervise effectively. To use the organization's human resources effectively, managers should supervise as many individuals as they can best guide toward production quotas. If they are supervising too few people, they are wasting a portion of their productive capacity. If they are supervising too many, they are losing part of their effectiveness.

Designing Span of Management: A Contingency Viewpoint   As reported by Harold Koontz, several important situational factors influence the appropriateness of the size of an individual's span of management:[23]

> *Similarity of functions*—the degree to which activities performed by supervised individuals are similar or dissimilar. As the similarity of subordinates' activities increases, the span of management appropriate for the situation widens. The converse is also generally true.

> *Geographic continuity*—the degree to which subordinates are physically separated. In general, the closer subordinates are physically, the more of them managers can supervise effectively.

> *Complexity of functions*—the degree to which workers' activities are difficult and involved. The more difficult and involved the activities are, the more difficult it is to manage a large number of individuals effectively.

> *Coordination*—the amount of time managers must spend synchronizing the activities of their subordinates with the activities of other workers. The greater the amount of time that must be spent on such coordination, the smaller the span of management should be.

> *Planning*—the amount of time managers must spend developing management system objectives and plans and integrating them with the activities of their subordinates. The more time managers must spend on planning activities, the fewer individuals they can manage effectively.

Table 10.1 summarizes the factors that tend to increase and decrease the span of management.

When Bolt, Inc., began to grow, it grew by leaps and bounds. The New York–based teen-communications platform went from 15 people to about 175, and management had to find additional space in the building the firm occupied, often on different floors. Jane Mount, Executive Vice President for Empowerment, wanted to retain the feeling of closeness that employees and managers had enjoyed when the span of management was much smaller. Her solution was to house sales reps, programmers, Web producers, accountants, and the company's founders together in "hives," rather than to seat everyone by department. "Because everyone is intermingled," says Mount, "they've adopted a common, overarching goal. And this isn't the goal of Bolt sales or Bolt marketing: It's the goal of Bolt, Inc."

Graicunas and Span of Management   Perhaps the best-known contribution to span-of-management literature was made by the management consultant V. A. Graicunas.[24] He developed a formula for determining the number of *possible* relationships between a manager and subordinates when the number of subordinates is known. **Graicunas' formula** is as follows:

$$C = n\left(\frac{2^n}{2} + n - 1\right)$$

C is the total number of possible relationships between manager and subordinates, and *n* is the known number of subordinates. As the number of subordinates increases arithmetically,

Graicunas' formula is a formula that makes the span-of-management point that as the number of a manager's subordinates increases arithmetically, the number of possible relationships between the manager and the subordinates increases geometrically.

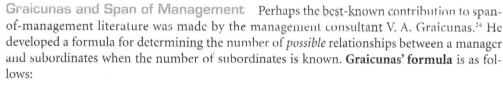

Major Factors That Influence the Span of Management   Table 10.1

Factor	Factor Has Tendency to Increase Span of Management When—	Factor Has Tendency to Decrease Span of Management When—
1. Similarity of functions	1. Subordinates have similar functions	1. Subordinates have different functions
2. Geographic contiguity	2. Subordinates are physically close	2. Subordinates are physically distant
3. Complexity of functions	3. Subordinates have simple tasks	3. Subordinates have complex tasks
4. Coordination	4. Work of subordinates needs little coordination	4. Work of subordinates needs much coordination
5. Planning	5. Manager spends little time planning	5. Manager spends much time planning

the number of possible relationships between the manager and those subordinates increases geometrically.

A number of criticisms have been leveled at Graicunas' work. Some have argued that he failed to take into account a manager's relationships outside the organization and that he considered only *potential* relationships rather than *actual* relationships. These criticisms have some validity, but the real significance of Graicunas' work lies outside them. His main contribution, in fact, was to point out that span of management is an important consideration that can have a far-reaching impact on the organization.[25]

Height of Organization Chart There is a definite relationship between span of management and the height of an organization chart. Normally, the greater the height of the organization chart, the smaller the span of management, and the lower the height of the chart, the greater the span of management.[26] Organization charts with little height are usually referred to as **flat,** while those with much height are usually referred to as **tall.**

Figure 10.11 is a simple example of the relationship between organization chart height and span of management. Organization chart A has a span of management of six, and organization chart B has a span of management of two. As a result, chart A is flatter than chart B. Note that both charts have the same number of individuals at the lowest level. The larger span of management in A is reduced in B merely by adding a level to B's organization chart.

An organization's structure should be built from top to bottom to ensure that appropriate spans of management are achieved at all levels. Increasing spans of management merely to eliminate certain management positions and thereby reduce salary expenses may prove to be a very shortsighted move. Increasing spans of management to achieve such objectives as speeding up organizational decision making and building a more flexible organization is more likely to help the organization achieve success in the long run.[27] A survey of organization charts of the 1990s reveals that top managers were creating flatter organizational structures than top managers used in the 1980s.

Scalar Relationships

The fourth main consideration of any organizing effort is **scalar relationships**—the chain of command. Every organization is built on the premise that the individual at the top possesses the most authority and that other individuals' authority is scaled downward according to their relative position on the organization chart. The lower a person's position on the organization chart, then, the less authority that person possesses.[28]

The scalar relationship, or chain of command, is related to the unity of command. **Unity of command** is the management principle that recommends that an individual have only one boss. If too many bosses give orders, the result will probably be confusion, contradiction, and frustration—a sure recipe for ineffectiveness and inefficiency in an organization. Although the unity-of-command principle made its first appearance in management literature well over 75 years ago, it is still discussed today as a critical ingredient of successful organizations.[29]

A **flat organization chart** is an organization chart characterized by few levels and a relatively broad span of management.

A **tall organization chart** is an organization chart characterized by many levels and a relatively narrow span of management.

Scalar relationships refer to the chain-of-command positioning of individuals on an organization chart.

Unity of command is the management principle that recommends that an individual have only one boss.

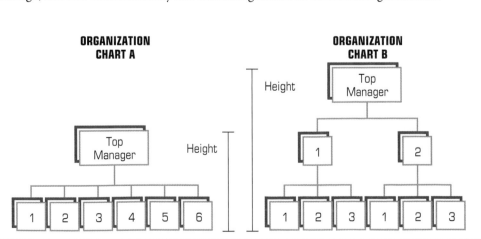

ORGANIZATION CHART A

ORGANIZATION CHART B

Figure 10.11 *Relationship between organization chart height and span of management*

▶ **Health Care—Circular Organization Chart at Our Lady of the Way Hospital**

Reflecting traditional organization theory, this chapter is filled with examples and discussions of organization charts built linearly and vertically. Given such organization chart construction, issues like height are relevant and important. However, in more recent times, some managers use circular organization charts.

Our Lady of the Way Hospital is a small, 39-bed hospital located in Martin, Kentucky. Like most hospitals, Our Lady of the Way historically had an organization chart built on straight lines and boxes that reflected a typical bureaucratic organization. The CEO of Our Lady of the Way Hospital had direct management responsibility for several functional departments.

Recently, however, management replaced the traditional, hierarchical organization chart with a circular structure. According to management, the new structure was built to emphasize an increased need for reliance on team processes throughout the hospital. The circular organization chart is represented by a series of diagrams in which the circle, a geometric form with no beginning or end points, symbolizes the ongoing nature of the team process. The circle also implies that decisions are reached by consensus, that no expertise within the organization is more important than any other, and that each person on the team is equally responsible for advancing its work.

Fayol's Guidelines on Chain of Command Fayol has indicated that strict adherence to the chain of command is not always advisable.[30] Figure 10.12 explains his rationale. If individual F needs information from individual G and follows the concept of chain of command, F has to go through individuals D, B, A, C, and E before reaching G. The information would get back to F only by going from G through E, C, A, B, and D. Obviously, this long, involved process can be very time consuming and therefore expensive for the organization.

To avoid this long, involved, expensive process, Fayol has recommended that in some situations a bridge, or **gangplank,** be used to allow F to go directly to G for information. This bridge is represented in Figure 10.12 by the dotted line connecting F and G. Managers should be very careful in allowing the use of these organizational bridges, however, because although F might get the information from G more quickly and cheaply that way, individuals D, B, A, C, and E would be excluded from the communication channel, and their ignorance might prove

A **gangplank** is a communication channel extending from one organizational division to another but not shown in the lines of communication outlined on an organization chart. Use of Fayol's gangplank may be quicker, but could prove costly in the long run.

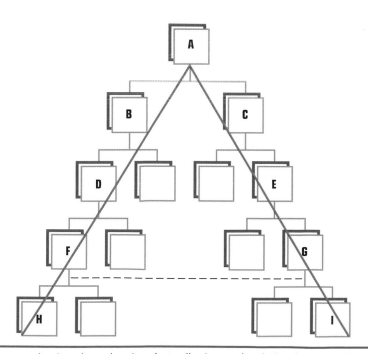

Sample organization chart showing that adhering to the chain of command is not advisable

Figure 10.12

more costly to the organization in the long run than would following the established chain of command. When managers allow the use of an organizational bridge, they must be extremely careful to inform all other appropriate individuals within the organization of any information received that way.

▶ Back to the Case

The last two major elements in classical organizing theory that a manager like McGinn could reflect on are span of management and scalar relationships. Span of management focuses on the number of subordinates that managers in various roles at Lucent can successfully supervise. In thinking about span of management McGinn might explore several important situational factors, such as similarities among various Lucent activities, the extent to which Lucent workers being managed are physically separated and the complexity of various Lucent work activities.

For example, McGinn should consider that selling cordless phones to consumer outlets can be fairly simple and that installing a special equipment network within a company can be much more involved and complicated. Therefore, the span of management for workers doing the former job should generally be larger than the span of management for workers doing the latter job. Other important factors McGinn should consider in determining spans of management for various Lucent managers are the amount of time managers must spend coordinating workers' activities and the amount of time managers spend planning. With all of this information, a manager like McGinn should be quite capable of determining appropriate spans of management for their managers.

Management Skills Module

This section is specially designed to help you develop management skills. An individual's management skill is based on an understanding of management concepts and the ability to apply those concepts in management situations. As a result, the following activities are designed both to heighten your understanding of management concepts and to help you gain facility in applying those concepts in various management situations.

UNDERSTANDING MANAGEMENT CONCEPTS

▶ Action Summary

Reread the learning objectives below. Each objective is followed by questions. Answering these questions accurately will help you retain the most important concepts discussed in this chapter. After answering each question, check your answer against the answer key at the end of this chapter. (*Hint:* If you have any doubts regarding the correct response, consult the page number that follows the answer.)

Circle:

From studying this chapter, I will attempt to acquire

1. An understanding of the organizing function.

a b c d e   **a.** Of the five steps in the organizing process, the following is grossly out of order: (a) reflect on plans and objectives (b) establish major tasks (c) allocate resources and directives for subtasks (d) divide major tasks into subtasks (e) evaluate results of the implemented organizational strategy.

T F   **b.** Proper execution of the organizing function normally results in minimal duplication of effort.

2. An appreciation for the complexities of determining appropriate organizational structure.

a b c d e   **a.** The XYZ Corporation is organized as follows: it has (1) a president, (2) a vice president in charge of finance, (3) a vice president in charge of marketing, and (4) a vice president in charge of human resources management. This firm is organized on the: (a) functional basis (b) manufacturing process basis (c) customer basis (d) territorial basis (e) production basis.

a b c d e   **b.** All of the following forces are influences on the evolution of formal structure except: (a) forces in the manager (b) forces in subordinates (c) forces in the environment (d) forces in the division of labor (e) forces in the task.

3. Insights into the advantages and disadvantages of division of labor.

a b c d e   **a.** Extreme division of labor tends to result in: (a) human motivation (b) boring jobs (c) nonspecialized work (d) decreased work skill (e) all of the above.

a b c d e   **b.** The following is *not* a generally accepted advantage of division of labor within an organization: (a) workers' skills in performing their jobs tend to increase (b) workers need to know only how to perform their specific work tasks (c) workers do not waste time in moving from one task to another (d) workers naturally tend to try to make their individual tasks easier and more efficient (e) none of the above (all are advantages of the division of labor).

4. A working knowledge of the relationship between division of labor and coordination.

T F   **a.** Effective coordination is best achieved through close employee supervision.

T F   **b.** Mary Parker Follett contended that managers should plan for coordination.

5. An understanding of span of management and the factors that influence its appropriateness.

a b c d e   **a.** Of the factors listed, the following would have a tendency to increase (expand) the span of management: (a) subordinates are physically distant (b) subordinates have similar functions (c) subordinates have complex tasks (d) subordinates' work needs close coordination (e) manager spends much time in planning.

a b c d e   **b.** The concept of span of management concerns: (a) seeing that managers at the same level have equal numbers of subordinates (b) employee skill and motivation levels (c) supervision of one less than the known number of subordinates (d) a determination of the number of individuals a manager can effectively supervise (e) a and d.

6. An understanding of scalar relationships.

a b c d e   **a.** The management concept that recommends that employees should have one and only one boss is termed: (a) departmentalization (b) function (c) unity of command (d) scalar relationship (e) none of the above.

T F   **b.** According to Fayol, under no circumstances should a gangplank be used in organizations.

Action Summary Answer Key

1. a. c, p. 215	**3. a.** b, p. 223	**5. a.** b, p. 225	**6. a.** c, p. 226
b. T, p. 214	**b.** e, p. 223	**b.** d, p. 225	**b.** F, p. 227
2. a. a, p. 219	**4. a.** F, pp. 223–224		
b. d, p. 221	**b.** T, pp. 223–224		

Issues for Review and Discussion

1. What is organizing?
2. Explain the significance of organizing to the management system.
3. List the steps in the organizing process. Why should managers continually repeat these steps?
4. Can the organizing function be thought of as a subsystem? Explain.
5. Fully describe what Max Weber meant by the term *bureaucracy.*
6. Compare and contrast formal structure with informal structure.
7. List and explain three factors that management structure is based on, or contingent upon. Draw three sample portions of organization charts that illustrate the factors you listed.
8. Describe the forces that influence formal structure. How do these forces collectively influence structure?
9. What is division of labor?
10. What are the advantages and disadvantages of employing division of labor within a management system?
11. Define *coordination.*
12. Does division of labor increase the need for coordination? Explain.
13. Summarize Mary Parker Follett's thoughts on how to establish and maintain coordination.
14. Is span of management an important management concept? Explain.
15. Do you think that similarity of functions, geographic contiguity, complexity of functions, coordination, and planning influence appropriate span of control in all management systems? Explain.
16. Summarize and evaluate Graicunas' contribution to span-of-management literature.
17. What is the relationship between span of management and *flat* and *tall* organizations?
18. What are scalar relationships?
19. Explain the rationale behind Fayol's position that always adhering to the chain of command is not necessarily advisable.
20. What caution should managers exercise when they use the gangplank Fayol described?

APPLYING MANAGEMENT CONCEPTS

Cases

➤ INTRODUCTORY CASE WRAP-UP

Case Discussion Questions

"Lucent Technologies Organizes to Be More Competitive" (p. 213) and its related Back-to-the-Case sections were written to help you better understand the management concepts contained in this chapter. Answer the following discussion questions about this Introductory Case to further enrich your understanding of the chapter content:

1. Does it seem reasonable that McGinn is attempting to better organize Lucent in order to remain more competitive? Explain.
2. List five questions that McGinn should ask himself in exploring how to best organize Lucent.
3. Explain why it would be important for McGinn to ask each of the questions you listed.

Skills Exercise: Building a Useful Organization Chart

In this chapter you studied several topics that apply to building organization charts. The Introductory Case discusses organizational structure at Lucent Technologies and how its CEO, Richard A. McGinn, has divided the organization into 11 operational units. Draw a partial organization chart for Lucent showing 11 vice presidents reporting to him (you do not need to name each area). Now, draw another chart showing 2 executive vice presidents between McGinn and the 11 vice presidents. Construct an argument for using this second chart at Lucent as opposed to the first chart.

CASE STUDY: BUSINESS LOOKS TO THE INSECT WORLD FOR SOLUTIONS

Sometimes the competitive environment in the new economy can be fierce. In order to survive without being bought out by a larger corporation, CEOs need to get creative. When the heads of Southwest Airlines in Texas, Pina Petroli in Switzerland, and Capital One in Virginia, found themselves losing revenue they turned to scientific researchers for help.

Southwest Airlines' cargo routing and handling system was experiencing difficulties. Even though the company was only using 7 percent of its cargo space, at some airports there wasn't enough room for the loads of freight Southwest had scheduled. This inefficiency created bottlenecks, making it harder and harder to meet delivery times. Airline personnel worked around the clock just to keep up with cargo that needed to be moved from one plane to another. Often, loads had to be transferred in the middle of the night in order for Southwest to keep its customers satisfied. The system at the time was to load freight on the first plane going in the right direction.

Scientists studied Southwest's problems and devised a plan to remedy them based on the behavior of ants. They looked at the way ants forage for food and discovered that it can be more efficient to leave cargo on a plane headed in the wrong direction. Let us say a package needed to go from Chicago to Boston. It might be faster and cheaper to leave it on a plane headed for Atlanta and then back to Boston than to take it off and put it on the next flight to Boston.

Scientific findings helped Southwest to cut freight transfer rates by 80 percent at the busiest airports, decreased the workload for employees by 20 percent, and greatly reduced the number of overnight transfers. Its new system made it possible for Southwest to cut back on the number of storage warehouses it needs. Now that there are fewer overnight transfers, the company doesn't have to worry about paying so many wages, and because fewer planes are flying full, there is more room for new business. These scientific advancements are also helping Southwest's bottom line—Southwest reported an annual gain of $10 million.

Over the past 20 years, Eric Bonabeau, Christopher Meyer, and other researchers have developed mathematical models based on the behavior of social insects such as ants, bees, and termites. *Swarm Intelligence* is the phrase scientists use to define the "collective behavior that emerges from a group of social insects." Social insects work without supervision, functioning as a team and organizing themselves. Together, their actions result in efficient solutions to difficult problems (such as finding the shortest route to a food source).

The scientists believe that the survival of social insects everywhere in the ecosystem is related to three characteristics:

1. *Flexibility:* the group can adapt to a changing environment
2. *Robustness:* even when one or more workers fail the group can still perform its task
3. *Self-organization:* the group needs relatively little supervision or control

Furthermore, scientists agree that robustness and flexibility are largely the result of self-organization

In order to make Southwest's cargo operations more effective, scientists observed a species of ant that uses "swarm intelligence" to find the shortest path to a food source. By laying and following their own secretions of pheromones they are able to get from their nest to the food and back in the fastest way. The ant that gets to the food first comes back first so the next insect will pick up its scent and emit its own pheromones following the same path back—making the scent of the shortest path stronger than that of any other path that may have been used by other ants, and so on. In this way the shortest path will be followed by the most ants and the group will get the work done in the most efficient way. By observing how the ants forage for food, researchers were able to fine-tune mathematical formulas to create backup routes.

This allowed Southwest Airlines to adjust quickly to last-minute changes due to weather conditions or cargo volume. The same scientific thinking enabled Pina Petroli heating oil company to improve its business in Switzerland. Pina Petroli was having trouble meeting its delivery schedule to residential customers. First the company had to take into account the different truck sizes and hose lengths, and street accessibility. Most of the customers could be home for delivery only at certain times and there were always emergency calls for service. There were also the unknown variables of traffic and weather—especially during the winter months when delivery was most crucial. Using an ant-behavior–based plan, scientists were able to help Pina Petroli to make all its deliveries with fewer trucks than ever before with less hours spent on the road.

Studies of "swarm intelligence" have shown that *complex* collective behavior can emerge from individuals following *simple* rules. Insects have had millions of years of evolution to perfect those rules; but researchers believe that managers can develop similar rules to shape the behavior of employees and replace command-control structures.

The CIO of Capital One was fascinated by this and tried it out, with great success. In 1994 he had a staff of 150 people based in one location. The company was expanding fast and by 1999 he found himself in charge of 1,800 employees in 10 different cities, 3 of which were outside the United States. The command-control structure that worked in his small office wasn't working anymore.

Based on "swarm intelligence," he came up with four simple rules to get everyone focused on a common goal:

> Always put the goals of the company first.
> Spend the money like it is yours.
> Be flexible.
> Have empathy for others.

Then he gave out 10,000 gaming chips to his departmental managers. If a staffer followed the guidelines he or she got a chip. If he or she followed all four guidelines at once a special chip was received from the CIO himself. After a year, the rules became second nature. Not only did they unify the entire group of 1,800 people but they empowered the staff to make decisions on their own with little supervision from top-down management.

Meanwhile, scientists go on decoding the secrets of the insect world and how insects survive in large and small colonies in both hostile and friendly environments. Who can say how their findings will be used in the future?

1. In your opinion, do Fayol's organizational guidelines include the basic concept of "swarm intelligence"? Explain.
2. Discuss how following the five steps of the organizing process might help Southwest's management eliminate the company's cargo handling difficulties.

3. Could inappropriate "span of management" or "division of labor" be contributing to Southwest's cargo-handling problems? If so, how? If not, why not?

▶ Video

QUICKTAKES SEGMENT 3
Organizing

In this segment, our new production manager is being tested by a Quicktakes producer. We are not given an organizational chart to look at, but it comes across as if Susan does not report directly to John, but that she is at a lower level in the organization's overall scheme. Given John's broader role and responsibility, it seems appropriate that the decisions that need to be made in this video segment are John's shots to call. As a result, we get our first idea of how John handles conflict and whether or not he accepts the responsibility that comes along with the job he has taken. In segment one, we heard John tell his wife that he wanted to be a manager; in this segment, he gets his chance to be just that.

It is not uncommon for new employees to be tested by people who have been working at a company for a long time. This is especially true when someone inside the company thinks that they were more qualified for the job than the newcomer. Pressure like John is getting from Susan is pretty common. We learn a lot about John, Susan, and Hal from watching how all three of them deal with the task of getting a couple shoots set up. We also learn about how this company is organized by watching who takes, or gets stuck with, certain parts of the task.

A final thought might be to consider why Susan got upset about the way the shoots were planned. It could have been her basic frustration with John. On the other hand, maybe something else is going on. Hal talks about Susan as if she has been with Quicktakes for a long time. Perhaps Susan is showing some of her feelings toward the way the company is changing. Very few successful companies stand still. Sometimes people who work at a company roll with the changes and progress with the company, and sometimes people are overwhelmed and wish it was the "same old company" it used to be. We do not know exactly what Susan's concerns are but there are certainly many ideas to think about.

QUESTIONS

1. John and Susan get into a debate about resource allocation. John seems to be understanding but stern in his approach. He addressed Susan's concerns by stating that he knows the crew she is worried about, but he does not back down. Do you think he handles this situation properly? How else might he have handled it?

2. After he deals with staffing assignments and Susan's disagreement, John talks with Hal. Why do you think he does this? What might John be hoping to get from Hal? Do you think he gets it?

3. In the end, Susan runs into trouble and John's plan seems to have paid off. He and Susan have a phone discussion and come up with a solution to their dilemma. What do you think about the way Susan and John dealt with the issue? Think about other ways each might have dealt with the problem. What do you think would be some of the advantages and disadvantages to your solution?

ORGANIZING AND *YOU*

You are responsible for organizing your college's job fair. Since there are many engineering majors at your school, you were able to attract recruiters from large companies like GE. You stayed in your dorm on many Friday nights, searching databases, and contacting appropriate corporate representatives to come to your campus. Students are working on their résumés and setting up interviews. There is a real buzz surrounding your event. One week before the big day, the dean notifies you that the job fair has to be rescheduled.

1. What do you do first? Remember that you will need to communicate as quickly and effectively as possible in order to try to hold the corporate recruiters to their commitments. You will also have to arrange for use of the meeting room again. Will you have to start reorganizing from scratch? Can you use e-mail? How much of the organizing material have you stored in your computer? Might this help you now? How might this setback prepare you for managerial challenges in a corporate structure?

chapter

11 Responsibility, Authority, and Delegation

Organizing P&G's New Internet Push

REMINDER: THE INTRODUCTORY CASE WRAP-UP (P. 252) CONTAINS DISCUSSION QUESTIONS AND A SKILLS EXERCISE TO FURTHER ILLUSTRATE THE APPLICATION OF CHAPTER CONCEPTS TO THIS VIGNETTE.

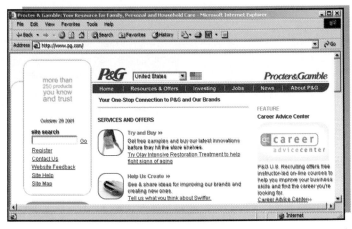

The Procter & Gamble Company (P&G), headquartered in Cincinnati, Ohio, is a world-renowned manufacturer and marketer of consumer products. The wide array of products offered by the company includes household names like Tide laundry detergent, Folger's coffee, Secret anti-perspirant, Downy fabric softener, Crest toothpaste, and Ivory soap.

Procter & Gamble's effort to increase sales includes $1 billion worth of technology improvements that include business-to-business e-commerce systems and Web-based relationships with its suppliers. Delegation is required to properly organize all the tasks in this kind of complex undertaking.

Since William Procter and James Gamble started P&G in 1837, the company has been very proactive and focused on the goal of doubling sales every decade. Although historically the company has been largely successful in reaching this sales-doubling goal, recently the target has been in jeopardy. Annual sales growth has been slowing over the last few years, from about a 5 percent increase in 1996 to about a 2.5 percent increase more recently.

A. G. Lafley was recently appointed as P&G's new CEO with the apparent mandate of again reaching the sales-doubling goal. To carry out this mandate, Lafley will likely support the "spirit" of a program that he inherited, called "Organization 2005." This new program focuses on revitalizing P&G's recent stagnant sales growth through innovation and product improvement. Overall, Organization 2005 aims at changing P&G's corporate culture from a conservative, slow-moving bureaucracy to a modern, fast-moving, Internet-savvy organization. The company needs to make faster and better decisions, cut red tape, and stimulate innovation.

The catalyst for overhauling the P&G culture is technology. The company is spending $1 billion annually on new technology initiatives such as establishing online collaborative technology to facilitate planning and marketing, business-to-consumer e-commerce systems, Web-based relationships with P&G's supply chain, and decision systems that deliver timely data to P&G desktops worldwide.

P&G is obviously building an Internet thrust that could be very advantageous to future success. The way in which Mr. Lafley manages the company's Internet efforts is critical, because they can only be effective if they are properly organized.

The Introductory Case describes P&G's new focus on the Internet. This includes activities like building online relationships with suppliers as well as providing managers with better information on which to make decisions. A. G. Lafley, P&G's new top manager, has much to gain by building a successful Internet thrust in the organization. To be successful, Internet activities must be properly organized. Lafley must answer questions like: Who is responsible for building and maintaining Internet activities? Who will actually use the Internet at P&G? Who has authority over the new Internet thrust? Information in this chapter should be of great value to managers, since organizing the job activities of individuals within a company is the principal topic of this chapter. Three major elements of organizing are presented:

1) Responsibility
2) Authority
3) Delegation

Chapter 10 dealt with applying the principles of organizational structure, division of labor, span of management, and scalar relationships to establish an orderly use of resources within the management system. Productivity in any management system, however, results from specific activities performed by individuals within that organization. An effective organizing effort, therefore, includes not only a rationale for the orderly use of management system resources but also three other elements of organizing that specifically channel the activities of organizational members: responsibility, authority, and delegation.

RESPONSIBILITY

Responsibility is the obligation to perform assigned activities.

Perhaps the most fundamental method of channeling the activity of individuals within an organization, **responsibility** is the obligation to perform assigned activities. It is the self-assumed commitment to handle a job to the best of one's ability. The source of responsibility lies within the individual. A person who accepts a job agrees to carry out a series of duties or activities or to see that someone else carries them out.[1] The act of accepting the job means that the person is obligated to a superior to see that job activities are successfully completed. Because responsibility is an obligation that a person *accepts*, there is no way it can be delegated or passed on to a subordinate.

The Job Description

A **job description** is a list of specific activities that must be performed to accomplish some task or job.

An individual's job activities within an organization are usually summarized in a formal statement called a **job description**—a list of specific activities that must be performed by whoever holds the position. Unclear job descriptions can confuse employees and may cause them to lose interest in their jobs. On the other hand, a clear job description can help employees to become successful by focusing their efforts on the issues that are important for their position. When properly designed, job descriptions communicate job content to employees, establish performance levels that employees must maintain, and act as a guide that employees should follow to help the organization reach its objectives.[2]

Job activities are delegated by management to enhance the accomplishment of management system objectives. Management analyzes its objectives and assigns specific duties that will lead to reaching those objectives. A sound organizing strategy delineates specific job activities for every individual in the organization. Note, however, that as objectives and other conditions within the management system change, so will individual job activities.

Information Systems Job Descriptions Focus More on Internet

The growth and popularity of the Internet have undeniably changed the way many managers are creating job descriptions for people working in Information Systems (IS) departments. In the past, IS job descriptions have focused mainly on programming. Programs were mostly written to facilitate handling and analyzing data related to various organizational functions. IS personnel were mainly attentive to designing their programs to best help "end users," people inside the organization who normally used the programs and data created by them.

With the growth of the Internet, management is seeing many new and exciting ways for IS personnel to assist in reaching organizational goals. As a result, many new job descriptions are being written to emphasize Internet usage, or existing ones are being changed, reducing the programming focus and emphasizing an Internet focus. This new Internet focus emphasizes not only communicating more closely with customers, but also having employees communicate more efficiently and effectively via Internet e-mail.

Managers are realizing more and more that a high-quality Internet presence is a prerequisite for organizational success. Success is encouraged as IS personnel make organizational information directly available to customers. Products are explained, press releases are posted, and management's views and philosophy are communicated. Success is also encouraged as management reaps the potential rewards of Internet commerce. Conducting business via Internet payments is becoming more commonplace every day. Organizations that fail to capitalize on Internet possibilities are not only missing an opportunity today, but may be risking their future success if Internet business transactions become a dominant method of transacting business.

The following three areas are related to responsibility:

1. Dividing job activities
2. Clarifying job activities of managers
3. Being responsible

Each of these topics is discussed in the sections that follow.

Dividing Job Activities

Obviously, one person cannot be responsible for performing all of the activities that take place within an organization. Because so many people work in a given management system, organizing necessarily involves dividing job activities among a number of individuals. Some method of distributing these job activities is essential.

The Functional Similarity Method   The **functional similarity method** is, according to many management theorists, the most basic method of dividing job activities. Simply stated, the method suggests that management should take four basic interrelated steps to divide job activities in the following sequence:

The **functional similarity method** is a method for dividing job activities in the organization.

1. Examine management system objectives
2. Designate appropriate activities that must be performed to reach those objectives
3. Design specific jobs by grouping similar activities
4. Make specific individuals responsible for performing those jobs

Figure 11.1 illustrates this sequence of activities.

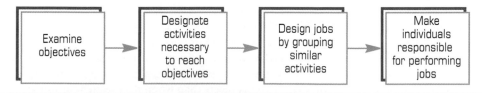

Sequence of activities for the functional similarity method of dividing job activities

Figure 11.1

At least three additional guides can be used to supplement the functional similarity method.[3] The first of these supplemental guides suggests that overlapping responsibility should be avoided when making job activity divisions. **Overlapping responsibility** refers to a situation in which more than one individual is responsible for the same activity. Generally speaking, only one person should be responsible for completing any one activity. When two or more employees are unclear about who should do a job because of overlapping responsibility, it usually leads to conflict and poor working relationships.[4] Often the job does not get done because each employee assumes the other will do it.

The second supplemental guide suggests that responsibility gaps should be avoided. A **responsibility gap** exists when certain tasks are not included in the responsibility area of any individual organization member. This results in a situation in which nobody within the organization is obligated to perform certain necessary activities.

The third supplemental guide suggests that management should avoid creating job activities for accomplishing tasks that do not enhance goal attainment. Organization members should be obligated to perform *only* those activities that lead to goal attainment.

The absence of clear, goal-related, nonoverlapping responsibilities undermines organizational efficiency and effectiveness.[5]

When job responsibilities are distributed inappropriately, the organization will have both responsibility gaps and overlapping responsibilities.

The effects of responsibility gaps on product quality are obvious, but overlapping responsibilities also impair product quality. When two (or more) employees are uncertain as to who is responsible for a task, four outcomes are possible:

1. One of the two may perform the job. The other may either forget to or choose not to do the job—and neither of these is a desirable outcome for product quality control.
2. Both employees may perform the job. At the least, this results in duplicated effort, which dampens employee morale. At worst, one employee may diminish the value of the other employee's work, resulting in a decrement in product quality.
3. Neither employee may perform the job because each assumed the other would do it.
4. The employees may spend valuable time negotiating each aspect and phase of the job to carefully mesh their job responsibilities, thus minimizing both duplication of effort and responsibility gaps. Though time consuming, this is actually the most desirable option in terms of product quality.

Note that each of these outcomes negatively affects both product quality and overall productivity.

▶ Back to the Case

Lafley, the manager in the Introductory Case, is faced with the challenge of organizing the Internet activities of various individuals within P&G. This activity should help to ensure the success of the new Internet program if the activities directly reflect company objectives. Lafley's specific steps to organize these should include the analysis of company objectives, the outlining of specific Internet-related activities that must be performed to reach those objectives, the designing of Internet-related jobs by the grouping of similar activities, and the assigning of these jobs to company personnel. To supplement these steps, Lafley must be careful not to create overlapping responsibilities, responsibility gaps, or responsibilities for Internet activities that do not lead directly to the attainment of P&G's goals.

Clarifying Job Activities of Managers

Clarifying the job activities of managers is even more important than dividing the job activities of nonmanagers because managers affect greater portions of resources within the management system. Responsibility gaps, for instance, usually have a more significant impact on the management system when they relate to managers than when they relate to nonmanagers.

One process used to clarify management job activities "enables each manager to actively participate with his or her superiors, peers, and subordinates in systematically describing the

Overlapping responsibility refers to a situation in which more than one individual is responsible for the same activity.

A **responsibility gap** exists when certain organizational tasks are not included in the responsibility area of any individual organization member.

managerial job to be done and then clarifying the role each manager plays in relationship to his or her work group and to the organization."[6] The purpose of this interaction is to ensure that there are no overlaps or gaps in perceived management responsibilities and that managers are performing only those activities that lead to the attainment of management system objectives. Although this process is typically used to clarify the responsibilities of managers, it can also be effective in clarifying the responsibilities of nonmanagers.

Management Responsibility Guide A specific tool developed to implement this interaction process is the **management responsibility guide,** some version of which is used in most organizations. This guide helps management to describe the various responsibility relationships that exist in the organization and to summarize how the responsibilities of various managers relate to one another.

> A **management responsibility guide** is a tool that is used to clarify the responsibilities of various managers in the organization.

The seven main organizational responsibility relationships covered by the management responsibility guide are listed in Table 11.1. Once it is decided which of these relationships exist within the organization, the relationships between these responsibilities can be defined.

Responsible Managers Managers can be described as responsible if they perform the activities they are obligated to perform.[7] Because managers have more impact on an organization than nonmanagers, responsible managers are a prerequisite for management system success. Several studies have shown that responsible management behavior is highly valued by top executives because the responsible manager guides many other individuals within the organization in performing their duties appropriately.

The degree of responsibility that a manager possesses can be determined by appraising the manager on the following four dimensions:

1. Attitude toward and conduct with subordinates
2. Behavior with upper management
3. Behavior with other groups
4. Personal attitudes and values

Table 11.2 summarizes what each of these dimensions entails.

▶ **Back to the Case**

In organizing the Internet activities of employees, Lafley must recognize, for example, that a department manager's Internet activities within the company, as well as those of his or her subordinates, are a major factor in company success. Because Internet activity of department managers can impact all personnel within that department, the activities of the department manager must be well-defined. From the viewpoint of company divisions, one department manager's Internet activities should be coordinated with those of other departments. Lafley

(continued)

Seven Responsibility Relationships Among Managers, as Used in the Management Responsibility Guide  **Table 11.1**

1. *General Responsibility*—The individual who guides and directs the execution of the function through the person accepting operating responsibility.

2. *Operating Responsibility*—The individual who is directly responsible for the execution of the function.

3. *Specific Responsibility*—The individual who is responsible for executing a specific or limited portion of the function.

4. *Must Be Consulted*—The individual whose area is affected by a decision who must be called on to render advice or relate information before any decision is made or approval is granted. This individual does not, however, make the decision or grant approval.

5. *May Be Consulted*—The individual who may be called on to relate information, render advice, or make recommendations before the action is taken.

6. *Must Be Notified*—The individual who must be notified of any action that has been taken.

7. *Must Approve*—The individual (other than persons holding general and operating responsibility) who must approve or disapprove the decision.

Behavior with Subordinates	Behavior with Upper Management	Behavior with Other Groups	Personal Attitudes and Values
Responsible managers—	Responsible managers—	Responsible managers—	Responsible managers—
1. Take complete charge of their work groups	1. Accept critism for mistakes and buffer their groups from excessive criticism	1. Make sure that any gaps between their areas and those of other managers are securely filled.	1. Identify with the group
2. Pass praise and credit along to subordinates	2. Ensure that their groups meet management expectations and objectives		2. Put organizational goals ahead of personal desires or activities
3. Stay close to problems and activities			3. Perform tasks for which there is no immediate reward but that help subordinates, the company, or both
4. Take actions to maintain productivity and are willing to terminate poor performers if necessary			4. Conserve corporate resources as if the resources were their own

could use the management responsibility guide process to achieve this coordination of Internet responsibilities.

Overall, for managers at P&G to be responsible, they must perform the Internet activities they are obligated to perform. They must also employ the Internet to build relationships with their subordinates, their superiors in the company, and their peer managers.

AUTHORITY

Authority is the right to perform or command.

Individuals are assigned job activities to channel their behavior within the organization appropriately. Once they have been given specific assignments, they must be given a commensurate amount of authority to perform those assignments satisfactorily.

Authority is the right to perform or command. It allows its holder to act in certain designated ways and to directly influence the actions of others through orders. It also allows its holder to allocate the organization's resources to achieve organizational objectives.[8]

Authority on the Job

The following example illustrates the relationship between job activities and authority. Two primary tasks for which a particular service station manager is responsible are pumping gasoline and repairing automobiles. The manager has the authority necessary to perform both of these tasks, or he or she may choose to delegate automobile repair to the assistant manager. Along with the activity of repairing, the assistant should also be delegated the authority to order parts, to command certain attendants to help, and to do anything else necessary to perform repair jobs. Without this authority, the assistant manager may find it impossible to complete the delegated job activities.

Practically speaking, authority merely increases the probability that a specific command will be obeyed.[9] The following excerpt emphasizes that authority does not always exact obedience:[10]

> *People who have never exercised power have all kinds of curious ideas about it. The popular notion of top leadership is a fantasy of capricious power: the top man [or woman] presses a button and something remarkable happens; he [or she] gives an order as the whim strikes him [or her], and it is obeyed. Actually, the capricious use of power is relatively rare except in some large dictatorships and some small family firms. Most leaders are hedged around by constraints—tradition, constitutional limitations, the realities of the external situation, rights and privileges of followers, the requirements of teamwork, and most of all, the inexorable demands of large-scale organization, which does not operate on capriciousness. In short, most power is wielded circumspectly.*

Acceptance of Authority

As Chapter 10 showed, the positioning of individuals on an organization chart indicates their relative amount of authority. Those positioned toward the top of the chart possess more authority than those positioned toward the bottom. Chester Barnard writes, however, that the exercise of authority is determined less by formal organizational decree than by acceptance among those under the authority. According to Barnard, authority exacts obedience only when it is accepted.

In line with this rationale, Barnard defines *authority* as the character of communication by which an order is accepted by an individual as governing the actions that individual takes within the system. Barnard maintains that authority will be accepted only under the following conditions:

1. The individual can understand the order being communicated
2. The individual believes the order is consistent with the purpose of the organization
3. The individual sees the order as compatible with his or her personal interests
4. The individual is mentally and physically able to comply with the order

The fewer of these four conditions that are present, the lower the probability that authority will be accepted and obedience be exacted.

Barnard offers some guidance on what managers can do to raise the odds that their commands will be accepted and obeyed. He maintains that more and more of a manager's commands will be accepted over the long term if:[11]

1. The manager uses formal channels of communication and these are familiar to all organization members
2. Each organization member has an assigned formal communication channel through which orders are received
3. The line of communication between manager and subordinate is as direct as possible
4. The complete chain of command is used to issue orders
5. The manager possesses adequate communication skills
6. The manager uses formal communication lines only for organizational business
7. A command is authenticated as coming from a manager

▶ Back to the Case

Lafley must be sure that any individuals within P&G who are delegated job activities, including Internet-related activities, also are delegated a commensurate amount of authority to give orders and carry out those activities. Managers throughout P&G must recognize, however, that authority must be accepted if obedience is to be exacted. To increase the probability of acceptance, care should be taken to ensure that individuals understand internal orders and see orders as being consistent with the objectives of both the department they work in and the company. Employees should perceive the orders they receive as being compatible with their individual interest, and they should see themselves as being mentally and physically able to follow those orders. Lafley must be very careful to delegate Internet-related jobs only to those organization members who are mentally and physically able to carry them out.

Types of Authority

Three main types of authority can exist within an organization:

1. Line authority
2. Staff authority
3. Functional authority

Each type exists only to enable individuals to carry out the different types of responsibilities with which they have been charged.

Line and Staff Authority **Line authority,** the most fundamental authority within an organization, reflects existing superior–subordinate relationships. It consists of the right to make decisions and to give orders concerning the production-, sales-, or finance-related

Line authority consists of the right to make decisions and to give orders concerning the production-, sales-, or finance-related behavior of subordinates.

behavior of subordinates. In general, line authority pertains to matters directly involving management system production, sales, and finance and, as a result, the attainment of objectives. People directly responsible for these areas within the organization are delegated line authority to assist them in performing their obligatory activities.[12]

Whereas line authority involves giving orders concerning production activities, **staff authority** consists of the right to advise or assist those who possess line authority as well as other staff personnel. Staff authority enables those responsible for improving the effectiveness of line personnel to perform their required tasks. Examples of organization members with staff authority are people working in the accounting and human resource departments. Obviously, line and staff personnel must work together closely to maintain the efficiency and effectiveness of the organization. To ensure that line and staff personnel do work together productively, management must make sure both groups understand the organizational mission, have specific objectives, and realize that they are partners in helping the organization reach its objectives.[13]

Size is perhaps the most significant factor in determining whether or not an organization will have staff personnel. Generally speaking, the larger the organization, the greater the need and ability to employ staff personnel. As an organization expands, it usually needs employees with expertise in diversified areas. Although small organizations may also require this kind of diverse expertise, they often find it more practical to hire part-time consultants to provide it as needed than to hire full-time staff personnel, who may not always be kept busy.

Line–Staff Relationships Figure 11.2 shows how line-staff relationships can be presented on an organization chart. The plant manager on this chart has line authority over each immediate subordinate—the human resource manager, the production manager, and the sales manager. However, the human resource manager has staff authority in relation to the plant manager, meaning the human resource manager possesses the right to advise the plant manager on human resource matters. Still, final decisions concerning human resource matters are in the hands of the plant manager, the person holding line authority. Similar relationships exist between the sales manager and the sales research specialist, as well as between the production manager and the quality control manager.

Roles of Staff Personnel Harold Stieglitz has pinpointed three roles that staff personnel typically perform to assist line personnel:[14]

1. *The advisory or counseling role*—In this role, staff personnel use their professional expertise to solve organizational problems. The staff personnel are, in effect, internal consultants whose relationship with line personnel is similar to that of a professional and a client. For example, the staff quality control manager might advise the line production

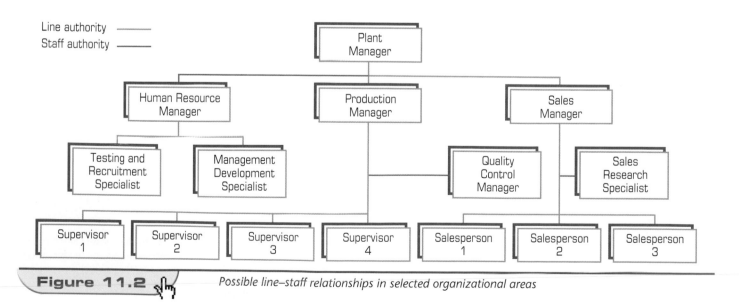

Figure 11.2 *Possible line–staff relationships in selected organizational areas*

manager on possible technical modifications to the production process that will enhance the quality of the organization's products.

2. *The service role*—Staff personnel in this role provide services that can more efficiently and effectively be provided by a single centralized staff group than by many individuals scattered throughout the organization. This role can probably best be understood if staff personnel are viewed as suppliers and line personnel as customers. For example, members of a human resource department recruit, employ, and train workers for all organizational departments. In essence, they are the suppliers of workers, and the various organizational departments needing workers are their customers.

3. *The control role*—In this role, staff personnel help establish a mechanism for evaluating the effectiveness of organizational plans. Staff personnel exercising this role are representatives, or agents, of top management.

These three are not the only roles performed by staff personnel, but they are the major ones. In the final analysis, the roles of staff personnel in any organization should be specially designed to best meet the needs of that organization. In some organizations, the same staff people must perform all three major roles.

General Electric Staff Organizes Renovation

At General Electric, a social responsibility project was organized and managed by one of GE's staff personnel, Bob Hess, a marketing specialist. As part of a sales meeting, GE salespeople renovated San Diego's Vincent de Paul–Joan Kroc urban center for the homeless. This project was part of a company program in which tired buildings used by worthy nonprofit organizations are selected to be renovated by GE employees. At the beginning of the renovation day at San Diego, GE workers formed teams, each with a captain, a safety expert, and a task expert. In about eight hours, the work teams completed 95 percent of the job, renovating space for 400 beds and preparing space for 200 additional beds.

The renovation program at General Electric reflects a very progressive management attitude. Through staff activities, the company has been able to demonstrate its desire and ability to make a worthwhile contribution to society. ■

Conflict in Line–Staff Relationships   Most management practitioners readily admit that a noticeable amount of organizational conflict centers around line–staff relationships.[15] From the viewpoint of line personnel, conflict is created because staff personnel tend to assume line authority, do not give sound advice, steal credit for success, fail to keep line personnel informed of their activities, and do not see the whole picture. From the viewpoint of staff personnel, conflict is created because line personnel do not make proper use of staff personnel, resist new ideas, and refuse to give staff personnel enough authority to do their jobs.

Staff personnel can often avert line–staff conflicts if they strive to emphasize the objectives of the organization as a whole, encourage and educate line personnel in the appropriate use of staff personnel, obtain any necessary skills they do not already possess, and deal intelligently with resistance to change rather than view it as an immovable barrier. Line personnel can do their part to minimize line–staff conflict by using staff personnel wherever possible, making proper use of the staff abilities, and keeping staff personnel appropriately informed.[16]

▶ Back to the Case

Assuming that a main objective of P&G is to produce and sell the highest quality of household products possible, company personnel who are directly responsible for achieving this objective should possess line authority to perform their responsibilities. For example, individuals responsible for manufacturing laundry detergents must be given the right to do everything necessary to produce the highest quality laundry detergent possible.

As with most organizations of substantial size, P&G needs individuals who are charged with the responsibility of assisting the line through a staff position. A new, Internet-oriented market research position in the company might be a good example of such a staff position. For example, a market researcher within P&G might be given the responsibility of designing online market research applications focusing mainly on customer satisfaction surveys. Results of such

(continued)

online surveys could be used for advising P&G management on issues such as how to raise the perceived quality of P&G laundry detergents in the eyes of the customers. Any individuals responsible for advising the line should be delegated appropriate staff authority.

As in all organizations, the potential for conflict between P&G line and staff personnel could be significant. Lafley should be aware of this potential and encourage both line and staff personnel to minimize it.

Functional authority consists of the right to give orders within a segment of the management system in which the right is normally nonexistent.

▶ Accountability is high in jobs that require dealing with nonroutine situations. Susan Barters is a customer service representative for Unum Provident, a leading insurance firm in New York. She handles up to 100 customer calls a day that can range from simple claims or billing questions to the occasional attempted fraud, and she is responsible for helping customers while following the company's established procedures.

Accountability refers to the management philosophy whereby individuals are held liable, or accountable, for how well they use their authority or live up to their responsibility of performing predetermined activities.

Functional Authority   **Functional authority** consists of the right to give orders within a segment of the organization in which this right is normally nonexistent. This authority is usually assigned to individuals to complement the line or staff authority they already possess. Functional authority generally covers only specific task areas and is operational only for designated amounts of time. Typically, it is given to individuals who, in order to meet responsibilities in their own areas, must be able to exercise some control over organization members in other areas.

The vice president for finance in an organization is an example of someone with functional authority. Among his or her basic responsibilities is the obligation to monitor the financial situation of the whole management system. To do so requires having appropriate financial information continually flowing in from various segments of the organization. The vice president for finance, therefore, is usually delegated the functional authority to order various departments to furnish the kinds and amounts of information he or she needs to perform an analysis. In effect, this functional authority allows the vice president for finance to give orders to personnel within departments in which he or she normally cannot give orders.

From this discussion of line authority, staff authority, and functional authority, it is logical to conclude that although authority can exist within an organization in various forms, these forms should be used in a combination that will best enable individuals to carry out their assigned responsibilities and thereby best help the management system accomplish its objectives. When trying to decide on an optimal authority combination for a particular organization, managers should be aware that each type of authority has both advantages and disadvantages. The organization chart illustrated in Figure 11.3 shows how the three types of authority could be combined for the overall benefit of a hospital management system.

Accountability

Accountability refers to the management philosophy whereby individuals are held liable, or accountable, for how well they use their authority and live up to their responsibility of performing predetermined activities.[17] The concept of accountability implies that if an individual does not perform predetermined activities, some type of penalty, or punishment, is justifiable. The punishment theme of accountability has been summed up by one company executive: "Individuals who do not perform well simply will not be around too long."[18] The accountability concept also implies that some kind of reward will follow if predetermined activities are performed well.

▶ Back to the Case

Functional authority and accountability are two additional factors that Lafley must consider when organizing employee activities within P&G. Some Internet-focused employees may have to be delegated functional authority to supplement the line or staff authority they already have. An Internet applications designer (staff person), for example, who may advise management on using the Internet to build consumer relationships online may need to gather information regarding various products throughout the company. Functional authority would enable staff individuals to command that this information be channeled to them.

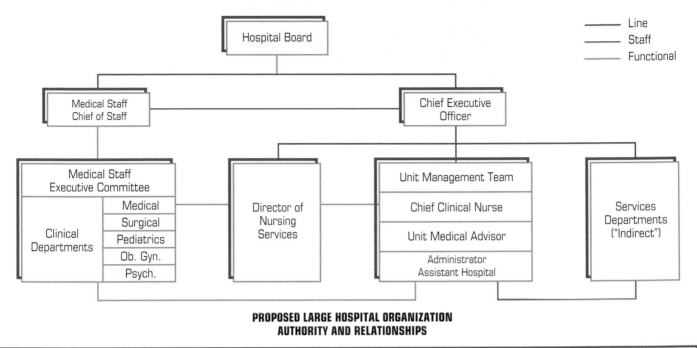

**PROPOSED LARGE HOSPITAL ORGANIZATION
AUTHORITY AND RELATIONSHIPS**

Proposed design for incorporating three types of authority in a hospital

Figure 11.3

In organizing Internet as well as all other employee activity, Lafley should also stress the concept of accountability—that living up to assigned responsibilities brings rewards and not living up to them brings negative consequences.

So far in this chapter we have discussed responsibility and authority as complementary factors that channel activity within the organization. **Delegation** is the actual process of assigning job activities and corresponding authority to specific individuals within the organization. This section focuses on the following topics:

1. Steps in the delegation process
2. Obstacles to the delegation process
3. Elimination of obstacles to the delegation process
4. Centralization and decentralization

Delegation is the process of assigning job activities and related authority to specific individuals in the organization.

Steps in the Delegation Process

According to Newman and Warren, the delegation process consists of three steps, all of which may be either observable or implied.[19] The first step is assigning specific duties to the individual. In all cases, the manager must be sure that the subordinate assigned to specific duties has a clear understanding of what these duties entail. Whenever possible, the activities should be stated in operational terms so the subordinate knows exactly what action must be taken to perform the assigned duties. The second step of the delegation process involves granting appropriate authority to the subordinate—that is, the subordinate must be given the right and power within the organization to accomplish the duties assigned. The last step involves creating the obligation for the subordinate to perform the duties assigned. The subordinate must be aware of the responsibility to complete the duties assigned and must accept that responsibility. Table 11.3 offers several guidelines that managers can follow to ensure the success of the delegation process.

Table 11.3   Guidelines for Making Delegation Effective

➤ Give employees freedom to pursue tasks in their own way

➤ Establish mutually agreed-upon results and performance standards for delegated tasks

➤ Encourage employees to take an active role in defining, implementing, and communicating progress on tasks

➤ Entrust employees with completion of whole projects or tasks whenever possible

➤ Explain the relevance of delegated tasks to larger projects or to department or organization goals

➤ Give employees the authority necessary to accomplish tasks

➤ Allow employees access to all information, people, and departments necessary to perform delegated tasks

➤ Provide training and guidance necessary for employees to complete delegated tasks satisfactorily

➤ When possible, delegate tasks on the basis of employee interests

Obstacles to the Delegation Process

Obstacles that can make delegation within an organization difficult or even impossible can be classified into three general categories:

1. Obstacles related to the supervisor
2. Obstacles related to subordinates
3. Obstacles related to organizations

An example of the first category is the supervisor who resists delegating his authority to subordinates because he cannot bear to part with any authority. Two other supervisor-related obstacles are the fear that subordinates will not do a job well and the suspicion that surrendering some authority may be seen as a sign of weakness. Moreover, if supervisors are insecure in their jobs or believe certain activities are extremely important to their personal success, they may find it hard to put the performance of these activities into the hands of others.

Supervisors who do wish to delegate to subordinates may encounter several subordinate-related roadblocks. First, subordinates may be reluctant to accept delegated authority because they are afraid of failing, lack self-confidence, or feel the supervisor doesn't have confidence in them.[20] These obstacles will be especially apparent in subordinates who have never before used delegated authority. Other subordinate-related obstacles are the fear that the supervisor will be unavailable for guidance when needed and the reluctance to exercise authority that may complicate comfortable working relationships.

Characteristics of the organization itself may also make delegation difficult. For example, a very small organization may present the supervisor with only a minimal number of activities to be delegated. In organizations where few job activities and little authority have been delegated in the past, an attempt to initiate the delegation process may make employees reluctant and apprehensive, for the supervisor would be introducing a significant change in procedure and change is often strongly resisted.

Eliminating Obstacles to the Delegation Process

Since delegation has significant advantages for the organization, eliminating obstacles to the delegation process is important to managers. Among the advantages of delegation are enhanced employee confidence, improved subordinate involvement and interest, more free time for the supervisor to accomplish tasks, and, as the organization gets larger, assistance from subordinates in completing tasks the manager simply wouldn't have time for otherwise. True, there are potential disadvantages to delegation—such as the possibility that the manager will lose track of the progress of a delegated task—but the potential advantages of some degree of delegation generally outweigh the potential disadvantages.[21]

What can managers do to eliminate obstacles to the delegation process? First of all, they must continually strive to uncover any obstacles to delegation. Then they should approach taking action to eliminate these obstacles with the understanding that they may be deeply ingrained and therefore require much time and effort to overcome. Among the most effective managerial actions that can be taken to eliminate obstacles to delegation are building subordinate confidence in the use of delegated authority, minimizing the impact of delegated authority on established working relationships, and helping delegatees cope with problems whenever necessary.[22]

Koontz, O'Donnell, and Weihrich believe that overcoming the obstacles to delegation requires certain critical characteristics in managers. These characteristics include the willingness to consider the ideas of others seriously, the insight to allow subordinates the free rein necessary to carry out their responsibilities, trust in the abilities of subordinates, and the wisdom to allow people to learn from their mistakes without suffering unreasonable penalties for making them.[23]

▶ Back to the Case

To delegate Internet as well as all other activities effectively within P&G, Lafley must assign specific duties to individuals, grant corresponding authority to these individuals, and make sure these individuals are aware that they are obligated to perform these activities.

In encouraging the use of delegation within P&G, Lafley must be aware that obstacles to delegation may exist on the part of company managers, their subordinates, or the departments in which they work. He must be sure that managers can meet the delegation challenge by discovering which obstacles exist in their work environments and taking steps to eliminate them. If Lafley is to be a successful delegator, he also must be willing to consider the ideas of his subordinates, allow them the free rein necessary to perform their assigned tasks, trust them, and help them learn from their mistakes without suffering unreasonable penalties.

Centralization and Decentralization

There are noticeable differences from organization to organization in the relative number of job activities and the relative amount of authority delegated to subordinates. This difference is seldom a case of delegation existing in one organization and not existing in another. Rather, the difference is degree of delegation.

The terms **centralization** and **decentralization** describe the general degree to which delegation exists within an organization. They can be visualized as opposite ends of the delegation continuum depicted in Figure 11.4. It is apparent from this figure that centralization implies that a minimal number of job activities and a minimal amount of authority have been delegated to subordinates by management, whereas decentralization implies the opposite.

The issues practicing managers usually face are determining whether to further decentralize an organization and, if that course of action is advisable, deciding how to decentralize.[24] The section that follows presents practical suggestions on both issues.

Centralization refers to the situation in which a minimal number of job activities and a minimal amount of authority are delegated to subordinates.

Decentralization refers to the situation in which a significant number of job activities and a maximum amount of authority are delegated to subordinates.

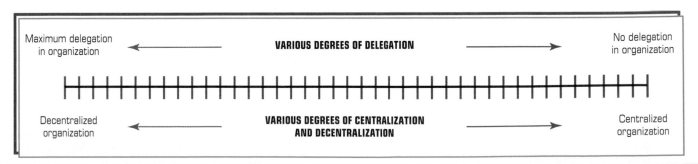

Centralized and decentralized organizations on delegation continuum

Figure 11.4

Security One Systems Uses Bonus to Support Decentralization

Security One Systems is based in Fort Lauderdale, Florida. In operation since 1990, the company provides professional security managers with customized security solutions. Its products include burglar alarm systems, fire alarm tests and inspections, employee identification badge systems, and video surveillance systems.

Much of the company's success in acquiring thousands of statewide clients is attributed to its providing customers with same-day service, and it is one of very few security contractors who are committed to offering high quality as well as same-day security service.

Cofounders and partners Bob Newman, president, and Jim Pasquarello, vice president of operations, decided that they had to decentralize operations if the company was to continue to grow. Although the "same-day service" motto was successful in gaining cus-

tomers, providing them with that service from one location was becoming very difficult, if not impossible. Initially, Security One Systems established three separate offices in Florida. Shortly thereafter, two more Florida offices were added.

According to Newman, decentralizing to five branches strategically placed throughout Florida definitely increased the company's capability to deliver same-day service. Newman admits, however, that such decentralization also created challenges in managing people. For example, Newman found that, away from his watchful eye, employee technicians were only averaging four customer visits per day. Rather than punish the technicians, Newman decided to offer a bonus to those who made an extra visit or two daily. Overall, Newman's bonus has resulted in technicians making more customer visits within the same time frame, which is an increase in employee productivity. ∎

Decentralizing an Organization: A Contingency Viewpoint The appropriate degree of decentralization for an organization depends on the unique situation of that organization. Some specific questions managers can use to determine the amount of decentralization appropriate for a situation are as follows:

▶ At its unconventional jet-engine assembly plant in Durham, NC, General Electric employs a highly decentralized structure in which all 170 employees report to the same person, plant manager Paula Sims. On a day-to-day basis, that means that the factory's work teams essentially run themselves, enjoying wide latitude in choosing the means by which they reach their goals—loading completed engines on outbound trucks on the scheduled day. The teams have responsibility for deciding on training, vacations, overtime, process improvements, and other internal matters. "More and more of what I do involves listening to people, to teams, to councils, to ideas, trying to find common themes," says Sims.

1. *What is the present size of the organization?* As noted earlier, the larger the organization, the greater the likelihood that decentralization will be advantageous. As an organization increases in size, managers have to assume more and more responsibility and different types of tasks. Delegation is typically an effective means of helping them manage this increased workload.

   In some cases, however, top management will conclude that the organization is actually too large and decentralized. One signal that an organization is too large is labor costs that are very high relative to other organizational expenses. In this instance, increased centralization of certain organizational activities could reduce the need for some workers and thereby lower labor costs to a more acceptable level.[25]

2. *Where are the organization's customers located?* As a general rule, the more physically separated the organization's customers are, the more viable a significant amount of decentralization is. Decentralization places appropriate management resources close to customers and thereby makes quick customer service possible. JCPenney, for example, decentralized its purchasing activities to give its managers the ability to buy merchandise best suited to the customers of its individual stores.[26]

3. *How homogeneous is the organization's product line?* Generally, as the product line becomes more heterogeneous, or diversified, the appropriateness of decentralization increases. Different kinds of decisions, talents, and resources are needed to manufacture different products. Decentralization usually minimizes the confusion that can result from diversification by separating organizational resources by product and keeping pertinent decision making close to the manufacturing process.

4. *Where are organizational suppliers?* The location of raw materials needed to manufacture the organization's products is another important consideration. Time loss and high transportation costs associated with shipping raw materials over great distances from supplier to manufacturer could signal the need to decentralize certain functions.

For example, the wood necessary to manufacture a certain type of bedroom set may be available only from tree growers in certain northern states. If the bedroom set in question is an important product line for a furniture company and if the costs of transporting the lumber are substantial, a decision to decentralize may be a sound one. The effect of this decision would probably be building a plant that produces only bedroom sets in a northern state close to where the necessary wood is readily available. The advantages of such a costly decision, of course, would accrue to the organization only over the long term.

5. *Is there a need for quick decisions in the organization?* If speedy decision making is essential, a considerable amount of decentralization is probably in order. Decentralization cuts red tape and allows the subordinate to whom authority has been delegated to make on-the-spot decisions when necessary. It goes without saying that this delegation is advisable only if the potential delegatees have the ability to make sound decisions. If they don't, faster decision making results in no advantage for the organization. Quite the contrary, the organization may find itself saddled with the effects of unsound decisions.

6. *Is creativity a desirable feature of the organization?* If creativity is desirable, then some decentralization is advisable, for decentralization allows delegatees the freedom to find better ways of doing things. The mere existence of this freedom encourages the incorporation of new and more creative techniques within the task process.[27]

Decentralization at Massey-Ferguson: A Classic Example   Positive decentralization is decentralization that is advantageous for the organization in which it is being implemented; negative decentralization is disadvantageous for the organization. To see how an organization should be decentralized, it is worthwhile to study a classic example of an organization that achieved positive decentralization: Massey-Ferguson.[28]

Guidelines for Decentralization   Massey-Ferguson is a worldwide farm equipment manufacturer that has enjoyed noticeable success with decentralization over the past several years. The company has three guidelines for determining the degree of decentralization of decision making that is appropriate for a situation:

1. The competence to make decisions must be possessed by the person to whom authority is delegated. A derivative of this principle is that the superior must have confidence in the subordinate to whom authority is delegated.

2. Adequate and reliable information pertinent to the decision is required by the person making the decision. Decision-making authority therefore cannot be pushed below the point at which all information bearing on the decision is available.

3. If a decision affects more than one unit of the enterprise, the authority to make the decision must rest with the manager accountable for the most units affected by the decision.

Delegation as a Frame of Mind   Massey-Ferguson also encourages a definite attitude toward decentralization in its managers. The company's organization manual indicates that delegation is not delegation in name only but a frame of mind that includes both what a supervisor says to subordinates and the way the supervisor acts toward them. Managers at Massey-Ferguson are prodded to allow subordinates to make a reasonable number of mistakes and to help them learn from these mistakes.

Complementing Centralization   Another feature of the positive decentralization at Massey-Ferguson is that decentralization is complemented by centralization:

The organization plan that best serves our total requirements is a blend of centralized and decentralized elements. Marketing and manufacturing responsibilities, together with supporting service functions, are located as close as possible to local markets. Activities that determine the long-range character of the company, such as the planning and control of the product line, the planning and control of facilities and money; and the planning of the strategy to react to changes in the patterns of international trade, are highly centralized.

Thus, Massey-Ferguson management recognizes that decentralization is not necessarily an either/or decision and uses the strengths of both centralization and decentralization to its advantage.

Management Responsibilities   Not all activities at Massey-Ferguson are eligible for decentralization. Only management is allowed to follow through on the following responsibilities:

1. Responsibility for determining the overall objectives of the enterprise
2. Responsibility for formulating the policies that guide the enterprise
3. Final responsibility for control of the business within the total range of the objectives and policies, including control over any changes in the nature of the business
4. Responsibility for product design where a product decision affects more than one area of accountability
5. Responsibility for planning for achievement of overall objectives and for measuring actual performance against those plans
6. Final approval of corporate plans or budgets
7. Decisions pertaining to availability and application of general company funds
8. Responsibility for capital investment plans

▶ Back to the Case

Centralization implies that few job activities and little authority have been delegated to subordinates; decentralization implies that many job activities and much authority have been delegated. Lafley will have to determine the best degree of delegation for his subordinates regarding Internet-related as well as all other job activities. For guidelines, Lafley and all other P&G managers can rely on certain rules of thumb to determine that greater degrees of delegation will be appropriate for the company: (1) as departments becomes larger, (2) as manufacturing facilities become more geographically dispersed and diversified, and (3) as the needs for quick decision making and creativity increase.

The Massey-Ferguson decentralization situation could provide Lafley and all other P&G managers with many valuable insights on what characteristics the decentralization process within the company should assume. First, managers should use definite guidelines to decide whether their situation warrants added decentralization. In general, additional delegation probably is warranted within the company as the competence of subordinates increases, as managers' confidence in their subordinates increases, and as more adequate and reliable decision-making information within the company becomes available to subordinates. For delegation to be advantageous for P&G, company managers must help subordinates learn from their mistakes. Depending on their situations, individual P&G managers may want to consider supplementing decentralization with centralization.

Management Skills Module

This section is specially designed to help you develop management skills. An individual's management skill is based on an understanding of management concepts and the ability to apply those concepts in management situations. As a result, the following activities are designed both to heighten your understanding of management concepts and to help you gain facility in applying those concepts in various management situations.

UNDERSTANDING MANAGEMENT CONCEPTS

▌ Action Summary

Reread the learning objectives below. Each objective is followed by questions. Answering these questions accurately will help you retain the most important concepts discussed in this chapter. After answering each question, check your answer against the answer key at the end of this chapter. (*Hint:* If you have any doubts regarding the correct response, consult the page number that follows the answer.)

Circle:

From studying this chapter, I will attempt to acquire

1. An understanding of the relationship of responsibility, authority, and delegation.
   - T F **a.** Responsibility is a person's self-assumed commitment to handle a job to the best of his or her ability.
   - a b c d e **b.** The following element is *not* an integral part of an effective organizing effort: (a) rationale for the orderly use of management system resources (b) responsibility (c) authority (d) delegation (e) none of the above (they are all important).
2. Information on how to divide and clarify the job activities of individuals working within an organization.
   - a b c d e **a.** The following is *not* one of the four basic steps for dividing responsibility by the functional similarity method: (a) designing specific jobs by grouping similar activities (b) examining management system objectives (c) formulating management system objectives (d) designating appropriate activities that must be performed to reach objectives (e) making specific individuals responsible for performing activities.
   - a b c d e **b.** A management responsibility guide can assist organization members in the following way: (a) by describing the various responsibility relationships that exist in their organization (b) by summarizing how the responsibilities of various managers within the organization relate to one another (c) by identifying manager work experience (d) a and b (e) none of the above.
3. Knowledge of the differences among line authority, staff authority, and functional authority.
   - a b c d e **a.** The production manager has mainly: (a) functional authority (b) staff authority (c) line authority (d) a and c (e) all of the above.
   - T F **b.** An example of functional authority is the vice president of finance being delegated the authority to order various departments to furnish him or her with the kinds and amounts of information needed to perform an analysis.
4. An appreciation for the issues that can cause conflict in line and staff relationships.
   - a b c d e **a.** From the viewpoint of staff personnel, a major reason for line–staff conflict is that line personnel: (a) do not make proper use of staff personnel (b) resist new ideas (c) do not give staff personnel enough authority (d) a and c (e) all of the above.
   - a b c d e **b.** From the viewpoint of line personnel, a major reason for line–staff conflict is that staff personnel: (a) assume line authority (b) do not offer sound advice (c) steal credit for success (d) fail to keep line personnel informed (e) all of the above.
5. Insights into the value of accountability to the organization.
   - T F **a.** Accountability refers to how well individuals live up to their responsibility for performing predetermined activities.
   - a b c d e **b.** Rewarding employees for good performance is most closely related to: (a) simplicity (b) a clear division of authority (c) centralization (d) decentralization (e) accountability.
6. An understanding of how to delegate.
   - T F **a.** The correct ordering of steps in the delegation process is: assignment of duties, creation of responsibility, and granting of authority.
   - a b c d e **b.** The following are obstacles to the delegation process: (a) obstacles related to supervisors (b) obstacles related to subordinates (c) obstacles related to the organization (d) all of the above (e) none of the above.

Action Summary Answer Key

1. a. T, p. 236
   b. e, p. 236
2. a. c, p. 237
   b. d, p. 239

3. a. c, pp. 241–244
   b. T, p. 244
4. a. e, p. 243
   b. e, p. 243

5. a. F, p. 244
   b. e, p. 244

6. a. F, p. 245
   b. d, p. 246

Issues for Review and Discussion

1. What is responsibility, and why it is so important in organizations?
2. Explain the process a manager would go through to divide responsibility within an organization.
3. What is a management responsibility guide, and how is it used?
4. List and summarize the four main dimensions of responsible management behavior.
5. What is authority, and why is it so important in organizations?
6. Describe the relationship between responsibility and authority.
7. Explain Barnard's notion of authority and acceptance.
8. What steps can managers take to increase the probability that subordinates will accept their authority? Be sure to explain how each of these steps increases that probability.
9. Summarize the relationship that exists between line and staff personnel in most organizations.
10. Explain three roles that staff personnel can perform in organizations.

11. List five possible causes of conflict in line–staff relationships and suggest appropriate action to minimize the effect of these causes.
12. What is functional authority?
13. Give an example of how functional authority actually works in an organization.
14. Compare the relative advantages and disadvantages of line, staff, and functional authority.
15. What is accountability?
16. Define *delegation* and list the steps of the delegation process.
17. List three obstacles to the delegation process and suggest actions for eliminating them.
18. What is the relationship between delegation and decentralization?
19. What is the difference between decentralization and centralization?

APPLYING MANAGEMENT CONCEPTS

Cases

INTRODUCTORY CASE WRAP-UP

Case Discussion Questions

"Organizing P&G's New Internet Push" (p. 235) and its related Back-to-the-Case sections were written to help you better understand the management concepts contained in this chapter. Answer the following discussion questions about this Introductory Case to further enrich your understanding of the chapter content:

1. What first step would you recommend that Lafley take in organizing the Internet activities of individuals within the company? Why?
2. Discuss the roles of responsibility, authority, and accountability in organizing the Internet activities of individuals at P&G.
3. At this time, do you think that P&G's Internet activities should be more centralized or more decentralized? Why?

Skills Exercise: Managing P&G's Line and Staff Personnel

The Introductory Case emphasizes that the new head of P&G is focusing on changing the company from a slow-moving bureaucracy to a modern, fast-moving, Internet-savvy organization. List two *line* positions and two *staff* positions that you think should exist as this "new" company is established. Describe the responsibility(ies) and authority that you think would characterize each position. What steps would you take to minimize conflict between the line and staff personnel?

Known for his humor, his patched jeans, and his cowboy boots, Ted Waitt wears his hair tied back in a pony tail. He loves Gateway, the company he cofounded in 1985 when he was 22 years old. At the time he was working for a computer retailer in Des Moines, Iowa. He talked coworker Mike Hammond (now vice president operations) into setting up a business with him selling personal computer peripherals and add-ons.

For capital his grandmother guaranteed him a $10,000 loan. His father, a cattle trader, let him use an old barn on the family's cattle farm in North Sioux City, South Dakota. The business expanded into computer sales when Waitt figured out that he could build them for one-half the price his supplier was charging. Selling by phone and over the Internet, Waitt and Hammond eventually turned Gateway into a company of 20,000 employees, 15 call centers, and 5 manufacturing plants worldwide.

In the mid-1990s they invested a huge amount of time and money into building a corporate salesforce only to find that the company was still not strong enough to compete with industry rivals like Dell. Waitt reasoned that by hiring a seasoned corporate executive to head a strong management team, he could keep Gateway profitable. He hired Jeffrey Weitzen, executive vice president of AT&T's Business Markets division, to steer Gateway in the right direction.

Waitt had always maintained the company's "country" roots—with an easygoing work environment. Rock music was always playing in the manufacturing plant; the shipping boxes had a cow-spot design; Waitt made frequent visits to the assembly line and sales floor; Gateway employees were crazy about their CEO. A Gateway shipping operator describes him this way: "He's a normal dude, an everyday guy you'd go out and have a pizza with."

Weitzen was more strategy oriented. He improved Gateway's financial system, requiring every department to draft a budget. He introduced the concept of "Beyond the Box" and offered customers financing and Internet training with the purchase of a PC. It seemed that by opening Gateway Country retail stores Weitzen had really turned things around.

The two men got along well and sales grew. By the end of 1999, sales were up again and Gateway was flying high. In January 2000, Waitt went into semiretirement so that he could spend more time with his wife and children. He gave the job of CEO to Weitzen, retaining the title of chairman. Waitt spent his days at a family foundation that provides scholarships and technology to the disadvantaged. However, at Gateway there were already signs of friction among lower management. Weitzen recruited new high-level mangers from big corporations like GE and PepsiCo. Gateway veterans felt that the company was becoming a bureaucracy. They weren't used to formal memos and meetings. Conversely, the new management team viewed them as unpolished country boys, lacking college credentials.

By the end of 2000, Weitzen's plans weren't working anymore and Dell computers was taking away Gateway's customers with its Internet sales. Waitt had stayed in touch with managers at Gateway. When he learned that Weitzen had demoted many of the original managerial staff, that some had chosen to leave, and that his stock was going down, he was worried.

Weitzen had made no effort to establish a rapport with Gateway workers. He set up policies and procedures for everything—from when employees ate lunch to what was allowed in their cubicles. He instituted two-hour daily conference calls for all sales managers. He put a time limit on customer service calls—which put pressure on sales reps to do less rather than more for their buyers, and eventually damaged sales. Weitzen spent a lot of the company's money opening new stores, and soon Gateway could not afford to match competitor's prices.

By Thanksgiving 2001, morale had hit bottom at Gateway, and it looked as though the company might go out of business. As chairman, Waitt had given Weitzen free reign to make changes that would help Gateway to recover and to grow, but once he became aware that there were serious problems. Waitt started showing up and asking questions.

A year after he had left, Waitt decided to come back. Weitzen didn't want to be subordinate to Waitt, so he quit. Waitt sent out a corporate e-mail that read, "Hi. That's right. It's me. I'm back." He immediately fired six of Weitzen's eight managers and rehired his old management crew. He revoked 21 initiatives and 14 "stupid policies" Weitzen had put in place. He replaced Weitzen's "Beyond the Box" with "Back to Basics." "We have to be successful in the box if we're going to go beyond the box," Waitt said. Within three months after Waitt's return, Gateway cut costs by offering fewer products, handling its own advertising, pulling out of some foreign markets, and abandoning plans for any new stores.

Gateway is now guaranteeing its customers that it will match the price of its competitors in order to take back business. The company is using software to track its rivals' price offers and will use the program to verify its competitors' print and online prices. To get the low-cost message across to senior managers Waitt has tied bonuses to reducing marketing expenses and supplying superior customer service.

With more than one-half of U.S. households already owning a PC, buyers are harder to find than ever. Waitt says he doesn't expect to return to growth and profitability for another year. He has a lot of work ahead of him, but he is prepared to do whatever it takes to bring Gateway back. The company's new advertising slogan is "You've got a friend in the business." "We feel that line really, truly captures what Gateway is all about," says returned CEO Ted Waitt.

QUESTIONS

1. Do you think that line–staff relationships at Gateway changed when Weitzen took over? If so, how? If not, why?
2. Do you think that Gateway employees accepted the authority of the new executives that Weitzen recruited? Explain.
3. Assuming that you are the CEO at Gateway, should you make your organization more centralized or more decentralized? Why?

CONMEDIA SEGMENT 3
Responsibility, Authority, and Delegation

In this segment you will see the organizing function at work. Conmedia management is activating its operating plan so that each department will be able to incorporate the ex-dot-coms employees from the former Allaboutself.com. This means that new staffers will be working to make the merged print/web magazine as efficient as possible right from the start. Although Mike may not realize it, the list of activities Mia has requested from him is very important. It will be used to write a formal job description that will clarify Mike's responsibilities, so that he knows what is expected of him. From a management perspective, you might want to ask yourself the importance of ensuring that there is no overlap between his job and someone who is already working at Conmedia. Observe closely how Mia uses her managerial influence to show both Mike and Joan the positive side of this merger and how it may give both of them a career boost. As you listen to Joan's question, consider whether she has a good grasp of line authority, staff authority, and functional authority. Imagine what your own responses to an employee like Joan might be.

You already know from the first segment that Mike, the Web guru, is more easily placated than Joan, the writer, is. Like Mike, Joan is upset by the new definition of line–staff relationships between her coworkers and herself and especially between Mia and herself. Once again, Mia is able to present Joan with both the negatives and the positives of what will essentially be a growth opportunity for her. Note that Mike and Joan's fears are well founded since big changes often cause conflict. In this scene, think carefully about the key issues of responsibility and authority.

While Mia is astute at managing her original staff, there is no guarantee that her management style will work at Conmedia. As senior vice president for new development, Mia will be accountable to the CEO and the board. You might want to think about what this will mean for Mia in terms of her responsibilities as an executive.

As we leave these three, they are all dreaming of making a successful, financially lucrative future for themselves. But first they will have to negotiate the realities of being absorbed by a bigger company. Most importantly they will have to demonstrate that their combined talent and Internet know-how can turn a hybrid like *New Century Woman* into a profitable venture. Remember that increased digital dimensioning at Conmedia will impact not just the two merged magazines, but the entire organizational structure, affecting almost every aspect of internal communication as well as the larger issue of centralization versus decentralization.

QUESTIONS

1. What conflict in line–staff relationships do you see ahead for Mike and Joan?

2. Using the four key dimensions of responsible management behavior in Table 11.2, rate Mia as a manager.

3. Based on his conversation with Mia, do you think Mike will be a good manager?

4. In her future capacity as an editor, do you think Joan will be able to understand how to delegate? Is she motivated to adjust to a more corporate culture?

5. Do you think that it would be better for management at Conmedia to use centralization or decentralization in their reorganization?

RESPONSIBILITY, AUTHORITY, DELEGATION, AND *YOU*

You are in your sophomore year at a small, conservative, private college. As a new Resident Assistant, you don't pay for housing and you don't have a roommate. You are responsible for making sure the 20 students on your floor follow all the rules of your college. Weekly meetings with other RAs have been really helpful; since it is easier to get advice from your peers than from the dean you report to. So far, you've had to report someone for having alcohol on campus twice, and charge a few people who lost their room keys. No big deal.

1. Yesterday, you walked into your friend's room to get the notes from accounting class and found that your friend was logged on to a porn site. According to college rules, no one is allowed on a porn site. As an RA, you have the authority and the responsibility to report any student violating this rule. But this person is your friend. What do you do? Do you handle this yourself? Do you react immediately? Do you seek advice? Is there a way to delegate this, so you do not have to tell your friend directly? REMEMBER, YOU ARE ENJOYING THE PRIVILEGES THAT COME WITH BEING AN RA AND YOU TAKE YOUR JOB AND THE REPUTATION OF YOUR COLLEGE VERY SERIOUSLY.

chapter

chapterchapterchapterchapterchapterchapter

12 Managing Human Resources

Objectives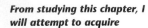

objectivesobjectivesobjectives

From studying this chapter, I will attempt to acquire

● An overall understanding of how appropriate human resources can be provided for the organization

● An appreciation for the relationship among recruitment efforts, an open position, sources of human resources, and the law

● Insights into the use of tests and assessment centers in employee selection

● An understanding of how the training process operates

● A concept of what performance appraisals are and how they can best be conducted

CHAPTER OUTLINE

Introductory Case: *Northwestern Mutual Life Focuses on Recruitment*

Defining Appropriate Human Resources

Steps in Providing Human Resources
Recruitment
Selection
Training

People Spotlight ▶ Training at The Container Store Stresses Employees Caring for Each Other

Across Industries ▶ Furniture Manufacturing—Training Is Critical at Keller Manufacturing

Performance Appraisal

Diversity Spotlight ▶ Coca-Cola Uses Performance Appraisal to Tie Pay to Diversity

Northwestern Mutual Life Focuses on Recruitment

REMINDER: THE INTRODUCTORY CASE WRAP-UP (P. 275) CONTAINS DISCUSSION QUESTIONS AND A SKILLS EXERCISE TO FURTHER ILLUSTRATE THE APPLICATION OF CHAPTER CONCEPTS TO THIS VIGNETTE.

Northwestern Mutual Life is a Milwaukee-based insurance company. It specializes in life and disability insurance and is the nation's sixth largest insurer with over $63 billion in assets. The company's major competitors include John Hancock Mutual Life, Aetna, and Prudential Insurance of America.

Since 1983, *Fortune* magazine has annually surveyed senior executives, outside directors, and securities analysts of the nation's largest companies to determine the most admired company in their industry based on eight key attributes of reputation. They are innovativeness, quality of man-

Northwestern Mutual recently focused on tackling the challenge of recruiting outstanding employees and agents. One of its initiatives revolves around an Internet-based qualifying exam. Those who pass are interviewed by the Northwestern recruiter closest to their home, and the results are e-mailed to the home office.

agement, employee talent, quality of products/services, long-term investment value, financial soundness, social responsibility, and use of corporate assets. Each year, Northwestern Mutual has been rated first in the life insurance industry.

Despite Northwestern Mutual's outstanding reputation, recruiting good employees is a major challenge and concern. The company is finding it very difficult to attract new, good people. This difficulty, however, is being experienced throughout the insurance industry. John Sheaffer, assistant director of career recruitment at Northwestern Mutual, believes that it takes as many as 20 to 40 referrals to lead to one new prospect.

Sheaffer recently decided to concentrate on solving this recruitment problem. He established a committee for recruitment improvement and included Michael Van Grinsven, a commercial life underwriter and assistant director of campus recruitment; Blaise Beaulier, manager of systems development; and Laura Schmidt, project manager. The initial focus of the group was to automate the recruitment process. To start, the company's recruitment data was stored on a mainframe computer and was retrievable. Each area of the company, however, maintained its own manual recruitment tracking system, and people were reluctant to use the centralized mainframe system. Overall, the results of the mainframe-based recruiting were somewhat disappointing.

Next, the company began developing an Internet-based recruiting process. Following this process, any prospective recruits who enter Northwestern Mutual's recruitment Web site must register and

(continued)

take a qualifying exam. Registrant demographic information and test scores are then automatically and electronically forwarded to the Northwestern Mutual home office. Information on the acceptable registrants is then e-mailed from the home office to company recruiters located in areas closest to the candidates. Recruiters interview candidates and then communicate interview results back to the home office via e-mail from their laptop computers. Depending on the results of the field interview, the recruitment process of a candidate is either continued or terminated.

Northwestern Mutual's management is excited about the potential of the company's new Internet-based recruitment process. As the process is used, improvements will undoubtedly be made to increase efficiency and effectiveness.

What's Ahead

The Introductory Case discusses an intense effort by John Sheaffer and others at Northwestern Mutual to recruit good new people. The task of recruiting and hiring not just any people, but the *right* people is part of managing human resources in an organization. This chapter outlines that process of managing human resources within an organization and illustrates how recruiting and ultimately hiring the right people fit within this process.

The emphasis in Chapter 11 was on organizing the activity of individuals within the management system. To this end, responsibility, authority, and delegation were discussed in detail. This chapter continues to explore the relationship between individuals and organizing by discussing how appropriate human resources can be provided for the organization.[1]

DEFINING APPROPRIATE HUMAN RESOURCES

Appropriate human resources are the individuals in the organization who make a valuable contribution to management system goal attainment.

The phrase **appropriate human resources** refers to the individuals within the organization who make a valuable contribution to management system goal attainment. This contribution results from their productivity in the positions they hold. The phrase *inappropriate human resources* refers to organization members who do not make a valuable contribution to the attainment of management system objectives. For one reason or another, these individuals are ineffective in their jobs.

Productivity in all organizations is determined by how human resources interact and combine to use all other management system resources. Such factors as background, age, job-related experience, and level of formal education all play a role in determining how appropriate the individual is for the organization. Although the process of providing appropriate human resources for the organization is involved and somewhat subjective, the following section offers insights on how to increase the success of this process.

STEPS IN PROVIDING HUMAN RESOURCES

To provide appropriate human resources to fill both managerial and nonmanagerial openings, managers follow four sequential steps.[2]

1. Recruitment
2. Selection
3. Training
4. Performance appraisal

Figure 12.1 illustrates these steps.

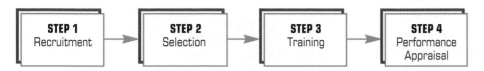

STEP 1	STEP 2	STEP 3	STEP 4
Recruitment	Selection	Training	Performance Appraisal

Four sequential steps to provide appropriate human resources for an organization

Figure 12.1

Recruitment

Recruitment is the initial attraction and screening of the supply of prospective human resources available to fill a position. Its purpose is to narrow a large field of prospective employees to a relatively small group of individuals from which someone eventually will be hired. To be effective, recruiters must know the following:

1. The job they are trying to fill
2. Where potential human resources can be located
3. How the law influences recruiting efforts

Knowing the Job Recruitment activities must begin with a thorough understanding of the position to be filled so the broad range of potential employees can be narrowed down intelligently. The technique commonly used to gain that understanding is known as **job analysis.** Basically, job analysis is aimed at determining a **job description** (the activities a job entails) and a **job specification** (the characteristics of the individual who should be hired for the job). Figure 12.2 shows the relationship of job analysis to job description and job specification.[3]

The U.S. Civil Service Commission has developed a procedure for performing a job analysis. As with all job analysis procedures, the Civil Service procedure uses information gathering as the primary means of determining what workers do and how and why they do it. Naturally, the quality of the job analysis depends on the accuracy of information gathered. This information is used to develop both a job description and a job specification.[4]

> **Recruitment** is the initial attraction and screening of the supply of prospective human resources available to fill a position.

> **Job analysis** is a technique commonly used to gain an understanding of what a task entails and the type of individual who should be hired to perform that task.

> A **job description** is a list of specific activities that must be performed to accomplish some task or job.

> A **job specification** is a list of the characteristics of the individual who should be hired to perform a specific task or job.

▶ Back to the Case

In hiring new employees for an organization like Northwestern Mutual, management must be careful to emphasize not just hiring workers, but hiring the right workers. For Northwestern Mutual, appropriate human resources are those people who will make a valuable contribution to the attainment of the company's organizational objectives. In hiring sales agents, for example, management should consider hiring only those people who will best help the organization become successful. In finding appropriate human resources, management at Northwestern Mutual has to follow four basic steps: (1) recruitment, (2) selection, (3) training, and (4) performance appraisal.

Basically, recruitment would entail the initial screening of individuals available to fill open positions at Northwestern Mutual. For recruitment efforts to be successful at a company like Northwestern Mutual, recruiters have to know the jobs they are trying to fill, where potential human resources can be located, and how the law influences recruiting efforts.

Recruiters could acquire an understanding of open positions at a company like Northwestern Mutual by performing a job analysis. The job analysis would force them to determine the job description of the position—the activities of a salesperson, for example—and the job specification of the position, including the type of individual who should be hired to fill that position.

▶ Mike Abrashoff is the founder of a leadership-consulting firm called Grassroots Leadership LLC. He believes that recruitment is an ongoing process: "Recruit your people every day, even though your crew is already on board. You have to grow your people to grow your business . . . growing my people is a cold, hard business decision to compete in today's rapid-fire economy."

Knowing Sources of Human Resources Besides a thorough knowledge of the position the organization is trying to fill, recruiters must be able to pinpoint sources of human resources. Since the supply of individuals from

```
                    ┌─────────────────────────┐
                    │      JOB ANALYSIS       │
                    │   A process for obtaining│
                    │    all pertinent job facts│
                    └─────────────────────────┘
              ┌──────────────────┴──────────────────┐
┌───────────────────────────────┐   ┌───────────────────────────────┐
│      JOB DESCRIPTION          │   │      JOB SPECIFICATION         │
│  A statement containing items │   │  A statement of the human      │
│  such as:                     │   │  qualifications necessary to do │
│      Job title                │   │  the job. Usually contains such │
│      Location                 │   │  items as:                     │
│      Job summary              │   │      Education                 │
│      Duties                   │   │      Experience                │
│      Machines, tools, equipment│  │      Training                  │
│      Materials and forms used │   │      Judgment                  │
│      Supervision given or received│ │    Initiative                │
│      Working conditions       │   │      Physical effort           │
│      Hazards                  │   │      Physical skills           │
│                               │   │      Responsibilities          │
│                               │   │      Communication skills       │
│                               │   │      Emotional characteristics  │
│                               │   │      Unusual sensory demands,   │
│                               │   │         such as sight, smell, hearing│
└───────────────────────────────┘   └───────────────────────────────┘
```

Figure 12.2   *Relationship of job analysis, job description, and job specification*

which to recruit is continually changing, there will be times when finding appropriate human resources will be much harder than at other times. Human resources specialists in organizations continually monitor the labor market so they will know where to recruit suitable people and what kind of strategies and tactics to use to attract job applicants in a competitive marketplace.[5]

Sources of human resources available to fill a position can be generally categorized in two ways:

1. Sources inside the organization
2. Sources outside the organization

Sources Inside the Organization   The pool of employees within the organization is one source of human resources. Some individuals who already work for the organization may be well qualified for an open position. Although existing personnel are sometimes moved laterally within an organization, most internal movements are promotions. Promotion from within has the advantages of building employee morale, encouraging employees to work harder in hopes of being promoted, and enticing employees to stay with the organization because of the possibility of future promotions. Companies such as Exxon and General Electric find it very rewarding to train their managers for advancement within the organization.[6]

Human Resource Inventory.   A **human resource inventory** consists of information about the characteristics of organization members. The focus is on past performance and future potential, and the objective is to keep management up to date about the possibilities for filling a position from within. This inventory should indicate which individuals in the organization would be appropriate for filling a position if it became available. In a classic article, Walter S. Wikstrom proposed that organizations keep three types of records that can be combined to maintain a useful human resource inventory.[7] Although Wikstrom focused on filling managerial positions, slight modifications to his inventory forms would make his records equally useful for filling nonmanagerial positions. Many organizations computerize records like the ones Wikstrom suggests to make their human resource inventory system more efficient and effective.

A **human resource inventory** is an accumulation of information about the characteristics of organization members; this information focuses on members' past performance as well as on how they might be trained and best used in the future.

➤ The first of Wikstrom's three record-keeping forms for a human resource inventory is the **management inventory card.** The management inventory card in Figure 12.3 has been completed for a fictional manager named Mel Murray. It indicates Murray's age, year of employment, present position and the length of time he has held it, performance ratings, strengths and weaknesses, the positions to which he might move, when he would be ready to assume these positions, and additional training he would need to fill the positions. In short, this card contains both an organizational history of Murray and an indication of how he might be used in the future.

➤ Figure 12.4 shows Wikstrom's second human resource inventory form—the **position replacement form.** This form focuses on position-centered information rather than the people-centered information maintained on the management inventory card. Note that the form in Figure 12.4 indicates little about Murray, but much about two individuals who could replace him. The position replacement form is helpful in determining what would happen to Murray's present position if Murray were selected to be moved within the organization or if he decided to leave the organization.

➤ Wikstrom's third human resource inventory form is the **management manpower replacement chart** (see Figure 12.5). This chart presents a composite view of the individuals management considers significant for human resource planning. Note on Figure 12.5 how Murray's performance rating and promotion potential can easily be compared with those of other employees when the company is trying to determine which individual would most appropriately fill a particular position.

The management inventory card, the position replacement form, and the management manpower replacement chart are three separate record-keeping devices for a human resource

The **management inventory card** is a form used in compiling a human resource inventory. It contains the organizational history of an individual and indicates how that individual might be used in the organization in the future.

The **position replacement form** is used in compiling a human resource inventory. It summarizes information about organization members who could fill a position should it open up.

The **management manpower replacement chart** is a form used in compiling a human resource inventory. It is people oriented and presents a composite view of individuals management considers significant to human resource planning.

NAME Murray, Mel	AGE 47	EMPLOYED 1985
PRESENT POSITION Manager, Sales (House Fans Division)		**ON JOB** 6 years
PRESENT PERFORMANCE Outstanding—exceeded sales goal in spite of stiffer competition.		
STRENGTHS Good planner—motivates subordinates very well—excellent communication.		
WEAKNESSES Still does not always delegate as much as situation requires. Sometimes does not understand production problems.		
EFFORTS TO IMPROVE Has greatly improved in delegating in last two years; also has organized more effectively after taking a management course on own time and initiative.		
COULD MOVE TO Vice President, Marketing		**WHEN** 2003
TRAINING NEEDED More exposure to problems of other divisions (attend top staff conference?). Perhaps university program stressing staff role of corporate marketing versus line sales.		
COULD MOVE TO Manager, House or Industrial Fans Division		**WHEN** 2004 2005
TRAINING NEEDED Course in production management; some project working with production people; perhaps a good business game somewhere.		

Management inventory card

Figure 12.3

POSITION	Manager, Sales (House Fans Division)		
PERFORMANCE Outstanding	**INCUMBENT** Mel Murray	**SALARY** $44,500	**MAY MOVE** 1 Year
REPLACEMENT 1 Earl Renfrew		**SALARY** $39,500	**AGE** 39
PRESENT POSITION Field Sales Manager, House Fans		**EMPLOYED:** Present Job 3 years	Company 10 years
TRAINING NEEDED Special assignment to study market potential for air conditioners to provide forecasting experience.			**WHEN READY** Now
REPLACEMENT 2 Bernard Storey		**SALARY** $38,500	**AGE** 36
PRESENT POSITION Promotion Manager, House Fans		**EMPLOYED:** Present Job 4 years	Company 7 years
TRAINING NEEDED Rotation to field sales. Marketing conference in fall.			**WHEN READY** 2 years

Figure 12.4

Position replacement form

inventory. Each form furnishes different data on which to base a hiring-from-within decision. These forms help management to answer the following questions:

1. What is the organizational history of an individual, and what potential does that person possess (management inventory card)?
2. If a position becomes vacant, who might be eligible to fill it (position replacement form)?
3. What are the merits of one individual being considered for a position compared to those of another individual under consideration (management manpower replacement chart)?

Considering the answers to these three questions collectively should help management make successful hiring-from-within decisions. Computer software is available to aid managers in keeping track of the organization's complex human resource inventories and in making better decisions about how employees can best be deployed and developed.[8]

Sources Outside the Organization If a position cannot be filled by someone presently employed by the organization, management has available numerous sources of human resources outside the organization. These sources include the following:

1. *Competitors*—One often-tapped external source of human resources is competing organizations. Since there are several advantages to luring human resources away from competitors, this type of piracy has become a common practice. Among the advantages are the following:

   ➤ The individual knows the business.
   ➤ The competitor will have paid for the individual's training up to the time of hire.
   ➤ The competing organization will probably be weakened somewhat by the loss of the individual.
   ➤ Once hired, the individual will be a valuable source of information about how to best compete with the other organization.

2. *Employment agencies*—Employment agencies help people find jobs and help organizations find job applicants. Such agencies can be either public or private. Public employment agencies do not charge fees, whereas private ones collect a fee from either the person hired or the organization doing the hiring, once the hire has been finalized.

3. *Readers of certain publications*—Perhaps the most widely used external source of human resources is the readership of certain publications. To tap this source, recruiters simply place an advertisement in a suitable publication. The advertisement describes the open

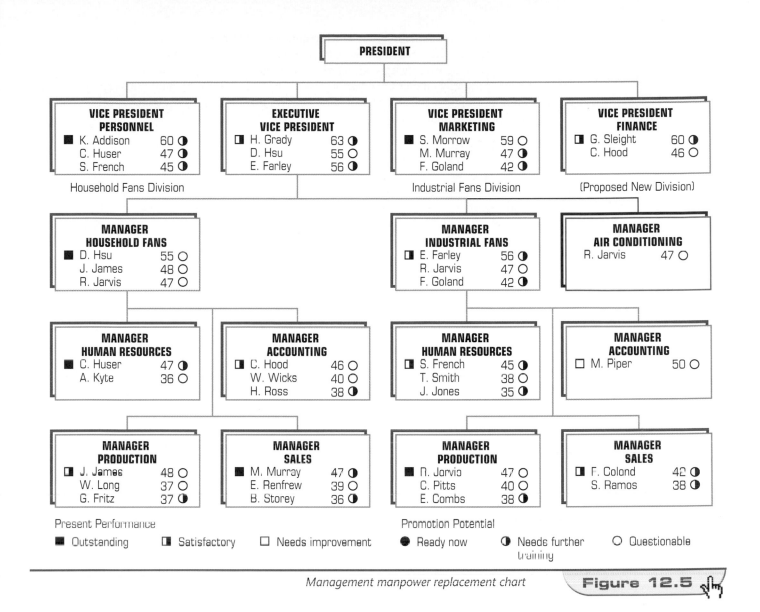

PRESIDENT

VICE PRESIDENT PERSONNEL
- ■ K. Addison 60 ◑
- C. Huser 47 ◑
- S. French 45 ◑

Household Fans Division

EXECUTIVE VICE PRESIDENT
- ◧ H. Grady 63 ◑
- D. Hsu 55 ○
- E. Farley 56 ◑

VICE PRESIDENT MARKETING
- ■ S. Morrow 59 ○
- M. Murray 47 ◑
- F. Goland 42 ◑

Industrial Fans Division

VICE PRESIDENT FINANCE
- ◧ G. Sleight 60 ◑
- C. Hood 46 ○

(Proposed New Division)

MANAGER HOUSEHOLD FANS
- ■ D. Hsu 55 ○
- J. James 48 ○
- R. Jarvis 47 ○

MANAGER INDUSTRIAL FANS
- ◧ E. Farley 56 ◑
- R. Jarvis 47 ○
- F. Goland 42 ◑

MANAGER AIR CONDITIONING
- R. Jarvis 47 ○

MANAGER HUMAN RESOURCES
- ■ C. Huser 47 ◑
- A. Kyte 36 ○

MANAGER ACCOUNTING
- ◧ C. Hood 46 ○
- W. Wicks 40 ○
- H. Ross 38 ◑

MANAGER HUMAN RESOURCES
- ◧ S. French 45 ◑
- T. Smith 38 ○
- J. Jones 35 ◑

MANAGER ACCOUNTING
- □ M. Piper 50 ○

MANAGER PRODUCTION
- ◧ J. James 48 ○
- W. Long 37 ○
- G. Fritz 37 ◑

MANAGER SALES
- ■ M. Murray 47 ◑
- E. Renfrew 39 ○
- B. Storey 36 ◑

MANAGER PRODUCTION
- ■ R. Jarvis 47 ○
- C. Pitts 40 ○
- E. Combs 38 ◑

MANAGER SALES
- ◧ F. Goland 42 ◑
- S. Ramos 38 ◑

Present Performance
- ■ Outstanding
- ◧ Satisfactory
- □ Needs improvement

Promotion Potential
- ● Ready now
- ◑ Needs further training
- ○ Questionable

Management manpower replacement chart   **Figure 12.5**

position in detail and announces that the organization is accepting applications from qualified individuals. The type of position to be filled determines the type of publication in which the advertisement is placed. The objective is to advertise in a publication whose readers are likely to be interested in filling the position. An opening for a top-level executive might be advertised in the *Wall Street Journal,* a training director opening might be advertised in the *Journal of Training and Development,* and an educational opening might be advertised in the *Chronicle of Higher Education.*

4. *Educational institutions*—Many recruiters go directly to schools to interview students close to graduation time. Liberal arts schools, business schools, engineering schools, junior colleges, and community colleges all have somewhat different human resources to offer. Recruiting efforts should focus on the schools with the highest probability of providing human resources appropriate for the open position.

Knowing the Law   Legislation has had a major impact on modern organizational recruitment practices. Managers need to be aware of the laws that govern recruitment efforts. The Civil Rights Act passed in 1964 and amended in 1972 created the **Equal Employment Opportunity Commission (EEOC)** to enforce federal laws prohibiting discrimination on the basis of race, color, religion, sex, and national origin in recruitment, hiring, firing, layoffs, and all other employment practices. The EEOC report was amended in 1978 to include the

The Equal Employment Opportunity Commission (EEOC) is an agency established to enforce federal laws regulating recruiting and other employment practices.

Pregnancy Discrimination Act, which requires employers to treat pregnancy, insofar as leave and insurance are concerned, like any other form of medical disability.

Equal opportunity legislation protects the right of a citizen to work and obtain a fair wage based primarily on merit and performance. The EEOC seeks to uphold this right by overseeing the employment practices of labor unions, private employers, educational institutions, and government bodies.

Affirmative Action   In response to equal opportunity legislation, many organizations have established **affirmative action programs.** Translated literally, *affirmative action* means positive movement: "In the area of equal employment opportunity, the basic purpose of positive movement or affirmative action is to eliminate barriers and increase opportunities for the purpose of increasing the utilization of underutilized and/or disadvantaged individuals."[9] An organization can judge how much progress it is making toward eliminating such barriers by taking the following steps:

1. Determining how many minority and disadvantaged individuals it presently employs
2. Determining how many minority and disadvantaged individuals it should be employing according to EEOC guidelines
3. Comparing the numbers obtained in steps 1 and 2

If the two numbers obtained in step 3 are nearly the same, the organization's employment practices probably should be maintained; if they are not nearly the same, the organization should modify its employment practices accordingly.

Modern management writers recommend that managers follow the guidelines of affirmative action, not merely because they are mandated by law, but also because of the characteristics of today's labor supply.[10] According to these writers, more than half of the U.S. workforce now consists of minorities, immigrants, and women. Since the overall workforce is so diverse, it follows that employees in today's organizations will also be more diverse than in the past. Thus today's managers face the challenge of forging a productive workforce out of an increasingly diverse labor pool, and this task is more formidable than simply complying with affirmative action laws.

> ## ▶ Back to the Case
>
> A successful recruitment effort at Northwestern Mutual would require recruiters to know where to locate the available human resources to fill open positions. These sources may be both within Northwestern and outside of it. In this case, employees at Aetna, John Hancock Mutual Life, and Prudential Insurance of America would probably be good candidates.
>
> In supporting plans for the future, Northwestern Mutual's management must devise ways to obtain needed appropriate human resources along with other resources like equipment and buildings. To do this, management can keep current on the possibilities of filling positions from within by maintaining some type of human resource inventory. This inventory can help management organize information about (1) the organizational histories and potentials of various Northwestern employees, (2) the employees in other Northwestern positions who might be eligible to fill various roles in the future, and (3) the relative abilities of various Northwestern employees to fill openings. Some of the sources of potential human resources outside of Northwestern that a manager like John Sheaffer could be aware of are competitors, public and private employment agencies, the readers of industry-related publications, users of the Internet, and various types of educational institutions.
>
> Northwestern's management must also be aware of how the law influences its recruitment efforts. Basically, the law says that Northwestern's recruitment practices cannot discriminate on the basis of race, color, religion, sex, or national origin. If recruitment practices at Northwestern are found to be discriminatory, the company is subject to prosecution by the Equal Employment Opportunity Commission.

Selection

The second major step involved in providing human resources for the organization is **selection**—choosing an individual to hire from all those who have been recruited.[11] Selection, obviously, is dependent on the first step, recruitment.

Affirmative action programs are organizational programs whose basic purpose is to eliminate barriers against and increase employment opportunities for underutilized or disadvantaged individuals.

Selection is choosing an individual to hire from all those who have been recruited.

Selection is represented as a series of stages through which job applicants must pass in order to be hired.[12] Each stage reduces the total group of prospective employees until, finally, one individual is hired. Figure 12.6 lists the specific stages of the selection process, indicates reasons for eliminating applicants at each stage, and illustrates how the group of potential employees is narrowed down to the individual who ultimately is hired. Two tools often used in the selection process are testing and assessment centers.

Testing   **Testing** is examining human resources for qualities relevant to performing available jobs. Although many different kinds of tests are available for organizational use, they generally can be divided into the following four categories.[13]

1. *Aptitude tests*—Tests of aptitude measure the potential of an individual to perform a task. Some aptitude tests measure general intelligence, while others measure special abilities, such as mechanical, clerical, or visual skills.[14]
2. *Achievement tests*—Tests that measure the level of skill or knowledge an individual possesses in a certain area are called achievement tests. This skill or knowledge may have been acquired through various training activities or through experience in the area. Examples of skill tests are typing and keyboarding tests.
3. *Vocational interest tests*—Tests of vocational interest attempt to measure an individual's interest in performing various kinds of jobs. They are administered on the assumption that certain people perform jobs well because they find the job activities stimulating. The basic purpose of this type of test is to select for an open position the individual who finds most aspects of that position interesting.
4. *Personality tests*—Personality tests attempt to describe an individual's personality dimensions in such areas as emotional maturity, subjectivity, honesty, and objectivity. These tests can be used advantageously if the personality characteristics needed to do well in a particular job are well defined and if individuals possessing those characteristics can be identified and selected. Managers must be careful, however, not to expose themselves to legal prosecution by basing employment decisions on personality tests that are invalid and unreliable. Test validity and reliability are discussed under "Testing Guidelines."[15]

Testing Guidelines   Several guidelines should be observed when tests are used as part of the selection process. First, care must be taken to ensure that the test being used is both valid and reliable. A test is *valid* if it measures what it is designed to measure and *reliable* if it measures similarly time after time.[16] Second, test results should not be used as the sole determinant

Testing is examining human resources for qualities relevant to performing available jobs.

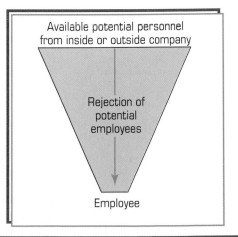

STAGES OF THE SELECTION PROCESS	REASONS FOR ELIMINATION
Preliminary screening from records, data sheets, etc.	Lack of adequate educational and performance record
Preliminary interview	Obvious misfit from outward appearance and conduct
Intelligence tests	Failure to meet minimum standards
Aptitude tests	Failure to have minimum necessary aptitude
Personality tests	Negative aspects of personality
Performance references	Unfavorable or negative reports on past performance
Diagnostic interview	Lack of necessary innate ability, ambition, or other qualities
Physical examination	Physically unfit for job
Personal judgment	Remaining candidate placed in available position

Summary of major factors in the selection process

Figure 12.6

▶ Some jobs, such as firefighting, the military, and law enforcement, require testing for color blindness, which many people are unaware they have. Glen Holmes of Los Angeles failed a color-vision test at the Union Pacific railroad, where he had worked for three years after passing the field test. Turned down for a job as a city firefighter because of his color deficiency, he appealed the decision and advanced to the next stage of the hiring process. New tests are being developed that might identify color problems in childhood and help people learn to cope with them. Blinking lights and signals that rely on design rather than color differences can also be used in industry to help the color-blind compensate.

of a hiring decision. People change over time, and someone who doesn't score well on a particular test might still develop into a productive employee. Such factors as potential and desire to obtain a position should be assessed subjectively and used along with test scores in the final selection decision. Third, care should be taken to ensure that tests are nondiscriminatory; many tests contain language or cultural biases that may discriminate against minorities, and the EEOC has the authority to prosecute organizations that use discriminatory testing practices.

Assessment Centers Another tool often used in employee selection is the assessment center. Although the assessment center concept is discussed in this chapter primarily as an aid to selection, it is also used in such areas as human resource training and organization development. The first industrial use of the assessment center is usually credited to AT&T. Since AT&T's initial efforts, the assessment center concept has expanded greatly, and today it is used not only as a means for identifying individuals to be hired from outside an organization, but also for identifying individuals from inside the organization who should be promoted. Corporations that have used assessment centers extensively include JCPenney, Standard Oil of Ohio, and IBM.[17]

An **assessment center** is a program (not a place) in which participants engage in a number of individual and group exercises constructed to stimulate important activities at the organizational levels to which they aspire.[18] These exercises can include such activities as participating in leaderless discussions, giving oral presentations, and leading a group in solving some assigned problem. The individuals performing the activities are observed by managers or trained observers who evaluate both their ability and their potential. In general, participants are assessed according to the following criteria:[19]

An **assessment center** is a program in which participants engage in, and are evaluated on, a number of individual and group exercises constructed to simulate important activities at the organizational levels to which they aspire.

1. Leadership
2. Organizing and planning ability
3. Decision making
4. Oral and written communication skills
5. Initiative
6. Energy
7. Analytical ability
8. Resistance to stress
9. Use of delegation
10. Behavior flexibility

11. Human relations competence
12. Originality
13. Controlling
14. Self-direction
15. Overall potential

▶ Back to the Case

After the initial screening of potential human resources, Northwestern Mutual will be faced with the task of selecting the individuals to be hired from those who have been screened. Two tools that Northwestern could suggest to help in this selection process are testing and assessment centers.

For example, after screening potential employees for positions at Northwestern, management could use aptitude tests, achievement tests, vocational interest tests, or personality tests to see if any of the individuals screened had the qualities to work a specific job. In using these tests, however, management must make sure that the tests are both valid and reliable, that they were not the sole basis for its selection decision, and that they are nondiscriminatory.

Northwestern can also use assessment centers to simulate the tasks necessary to perform jobs that workers will be performing. Individuals who performed well on these tasks would probably be more appropriate for the positions than would those who did poorly. The use of assessment centers might be particularly appropriate in evaluating applications for the position of sales agent. Simulating this job would probably give management an excellent idea of how prospective sales agents would actually interact with customers during sales presentations.

Training

After recruitment and selection, the next step in providing appropriate human resources for the organization is training. **Training** is the process of developing qualities in human resources that will enable them to be more productive and thus to contribute more to organizational goal attainment. The purpose of training is to increase the productivity of employees by influencing their behavior. Table 12.1 provides an overview of the types and popularity of training being offered by organizations today.

The training of individuals is essentially a four-step process:

1. Determining training needs
2. Designing the training program
3. Administering the training program
4. Evaluating the training program

These steps are presented in Figure 12.7 and are described in the sections that follow.

Training is the process of developing qualities in human resources that will enable them to be more productive.

Management Training Topics for Police Within the Alabama Department of Public Safety

▶ Table 12.1

- Organization Theory	- Effective Communication
- Leadership	- Hiring Practices
- Organizational Goals	- Training Process
- Media Relations	- Measuring Productivity
- Problem Solving	- Employee Evaluations
- Decision Making	- Discipline
- Time Management	- Legal Aspects of Discipline and Termination
- Stress Management	- Motivation
- Ethics and Integrity	- Contingency Planning

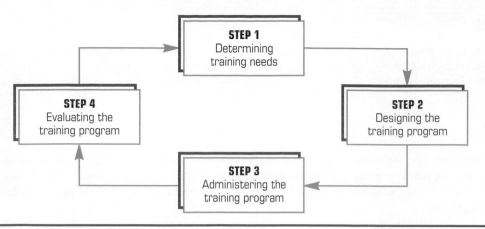

Figure 12.7 🖑

Steps of the training process

Training needs are the information or skill areas of an individual or group that require further development to increase the productivity of that individual or group.

Determining Training Needs   The first step of the training process is determining the organization's training needs.[20] **Training needs** are the information or skill areas of an individual or group that require further development to increase the productivity of that individual or group. Only if training focuses on these needs can it be productive for the organization.

The training of organization members is typically a continuing activity. Even employees who have been with the organization for some time and who have undergone initial orientation and skills training need continued training to improve their skills.

Determining Needed Skills   There are several methods of determining which skills to focus on with established human resources. One method calls for evaluating the production process within the organization. Such factors as excessive rejected products, unmet deadlines, and high labor costs are clues to deficiencies in production-related expertise. Another method for determining training needs calls for getting direct feedback from employees on what they believe are the organization's training needs. Organization members are often able to verbalize clearly and accurately exactly what types of training they require to do a better job. A third way of determining training needs involves looking into the future. If the manufacture of new products or the use of newly purchased equipment is foreseen, some type of corresponding training almost certainly will be needed.

Designing the Training Program   Once training needs have been determined, a training program aimed at meeting those needs must be designed. Basically, designing a program entails assembling various types of facts and activities that will meet the established training needs. Obviously, as training needs vary, so will the facts and activities designed to meet those needs.

Training at The Container Store Stresses Employees Caring for Each Other

In 1978, Kip Tindell and Garrett Boone cofounded The Container Store. The company was established to offer storage and organization products. Today, Tindell is the CEO and president of the company while Boone is the chairman.

The Container Store retail outlets are spread across the United States, varying in size from 22,000 to 25,000 square feet. The stores give customers unparalleled service, fresh ideas, and an interactive shopping experience. The Container Store products such as shelving relate to using kitchen, home office, garage, and closet space more efficiently. In addition, The Container Store products such as luggage, beltpacks, and backpacks help travelers use their space more efficiently.

The success of The Container Store chain is undeniable, and it commonly receives awards such as the Optimas Award, recently given to the company by *Workforce* magazine for overall excellence. According to management, much of this success is attributable to the special people emphasis that the company puts on training employees; it trains them to care about one another. Rather than simply lecturing about this point in the training program, The Container Store typically stresses care for one another by using a barrage of interactive techniques. Trainees focus on what it means philosophically to "care for one another" as opposed to simply memorizing what the phrase means. Management believes that such training methods provide its employees with a deeper sense for working together, which in turn significantly contributes to company success. ■

After hiring new employees, Northwestern Mutual must train them to be productive organization members. To train effectively, Northwestern must determine training needs, design a corresponding training program, and administer and evaluate the program.

Designing a training program requires that Northwestern assemble facts and activities that address specific company training needs. These needs are simply information or skill areas that must be further developed in Northwestern's employees in order to make them more productive. Over the long term, training at Northwestern should focus on more established employees as well as newly hired employees.

For a company like Northwestern, future plans probably include continued expansion. In this situation, management should probably try to learn as much as possible from training programs that the company operated to support past expansion. Knowing strengths and weaknesses of training programs aimed at past expansion would undoubtedly help management at Northwestern in designing efficient and effective training programs for its newest expansion plans.

Administering the Training Program   The next step in the training process is administering the training program—that is, actually training the individuals selected to participate in the program. Various techniques exist for both transmitting necessary information and developing needed skills in training programs, and several of these techniques are discussed in the sections that follow.

Techniques for Transmitting Information   Two techniques for transmitting information in training programs are lectures and programmed learning. Although it could be argued that these techniques develop some skills in individuals as well as transmit information to them, they are primarily devices for the dissemination of information.

1. *Lectures*—Perhaps the most widely used technique for transmitting information in training programs is the lecture. The **lecture** is primarily a one-way communication situation in which an instructor orally presents information to a group of listeners. The instructor typically does most of the talking, and trainees participate primarily through listening and note taking.

   An advantage of the lecture is that it allows the instructor to expose trainees to a maximum amount of information within a given time period. The lecture, however, has some serious disadvantages:[21]

   > *The lecture generally consists of a one-way communication: the instructor presents information to the group of passive listeners. Thus, little or no opportunity exists to clarify meanings, to check on whether trainees really understand the lecture material, or to handle the wide diversity of ability, attitude, and interest that may prevail among the trainees. Also, there is little or no opportunity for practice, reinforcement, knowledge of results, or overlearning. . . . Ideally, the competent lecturer should make the material meaningful and intrinsically motivating to his or her listeners. However, whether most lectures achieve this goal is a moot question. . . . These limitations, in turn, impose further limitations on the lecture's actual content. A skillful lecturer may be fairly successful in transmitting conceptual knowledge to a group of trainees who are ready to receive it; however, all the evidence available indicates that the nature of the lecture situation makes it of minimal value in promoting attitudinal or behavioral change.*

2. *Programmed learning*—Another commonly used technique for transmitting information in training programs is called programmed learning. **Programmed learning** is a technique for instructing without the presence or intervention of a human instructor.[22] Small parts of information that require related responses are presented to individual trainees. The trainees can determine from checking their responses against provided answers whether their understanding of the information is accurate. The types of responses

A **lecture** is primarily a one-way communication situation in which an instructor trains an individual or group by orally presenting information.

Programmed learning is a technique for instructing without the presence or intervention of a human instructor. Small pieces of information requiring responses are presented to individual trainees, and the trainees determine from checking their responses against provided answers whether their understanding of the information is accurate.

required of trainees vary from situation to situation but usually are multiple-choice, true-false, or fill-in-the-blank.

Like the lecture method, programmed learning has both advantages and disadvantages. Among the advantages are that it can be computerized and students can learn at their own pace, know immediately if they are right or wrong, and participate actively in the learning process. The primary disadvantage of this method is that no one is present to answer a confused learner's questions.

Techniques for Developing Skills   Techniques for developing skills in training programs can be divided into two broad categories: on-the-job and classroom. Techniques for developing skills on the job, referred to as **on-the-job training,** reflect a blend of job-related knowledge and experience. They include coaching, position rotation, and special project committees. *Coaching* is direct critiquing of how well an individual is performing a job.[23] *Position rotation* involves moving an individual from job to job to enable the person to gain an understanding of the organization as a whole. *Special project committees* are vehicles for assigning a particular task to an individual to furnish him or her with experience in a designated area.[24]

Classroom techniques for developing skills also reflect a blend of job-related knowledge and experience. The skills addressed through these techniques can range from technical, such as computer programming skills, to interpersonal, such as leadership skills. Specific classroom techniques aimed at developing skills include various types of management games and role-playing activities. The most common format for *management games* requires small groups of trainees to make and then evaluate various management decisions. The *role-playing format* typically involves acting out and then reflecting on some people-oriented problem that must be solved in the organization.

In contrast to the typical one-way communication of the lecturer, the skills instructor in the classroom encourages high levels of discussion and interaction among trainees, develops a climate in which trainees learn new behavior from carrying out various activities, clarifies related information, and facilitates learning by eliciting trainees' job-related knowledge and experience in applying that knowledge. The difference between the instructional role in information dissemination and the instructional role in skill development is dramatic.[25]

Evaluating the Training Program   After the training program has been completed, management should evaluate its effectiveness.[26] Because training programs represent an investment—costs include materials, trainer time, and production loss while employees are being trained rather than doing their jobs—a reasonable return is essential.

Basically, management should evaluate the training program to determine if it meets the needs for which it was designed. Answers to questions like the following help determine training program effectiveness:

1. Has the excessive reject rate of products declined?
2. Are deadlines being met more regularly?
3. Are labor costs per unit produced decreasing?

If the answer to such questions is yes, the training program can be judged as at least somewhat successful, though perhaps its effectiveness could be enhanced through certain selective changes. If the answer is no, significant modification to the training program is warranted.

In a noteworthy survey of businesspeople, 50 percent of respondents thought that their sales per year would be unaffected if training programs for experienced salespeople were halted.[27] This is the kind of feedback management should seek and scrutinize to see if present training programs should be discontinued, slightly modified, or drastically altered to make them more valuable to the organization. The results of the survey just mentioned indicate a need to make significant changes in sales training programs at the companies covered by the survey.

On-the-job training is a training technique that blends job-related knowledge with experience in using that knowledge on the job.

▶ New hires at Capital One Financial Corp. are plentiful—the workforce recently tripled to 15,000 employees. Once on board, new employees are quickly exposed to the company's enterprising culture with a week of classroom and outdoor sessions that are designed to foster teamwork and spur creative thinking. The firm recently planned to invest over $9,000 in training each of its top 570 managers.

▶ Furniture Manufacturing—Training Is Critical at Keller Manufacturing

The Keller Manufacturing Company, located in Corydon, Indiana, manufactures high-quality solid wood furniture for both dining rooms and bedrooms. Recently, management introduced a new, very complex, computer-assisted manufacturing system for better serving the customer through quicker and more reliable delivery of finished products. The process involved using more than 6,000 different components and more than 100 different procedures.

Training employees in how to use the new system was key to implementing it successfully, according to Marvin Miller, vice president of information services and the manager in charge of implementing the new process. The training program first focused on employees on the shop floor. A training room was set up to introduce

10 people at a time to the new system. Training began with 18 hours of keyboard work, learning how to operate the new system via the computer. Extensive on-the-job training in which employees actually operated the new system and gained insights followed keyboard training.

Miller evaluates the worth of this training by seeing how many employees opt to take voluntary, more advanced training. Results from one plant indicated that 93 percent of the employees volunteered for the extra training. Miller sees such feedback as indicating that employees value the training and feel that it is instrumental in doing good work.

▶ Back to the Case

After training needs at Northwestern Mutual have been determined and programs have been designed to meet those needs, the programs must be administered. Administering training programs at Northwestern might involve the lecture technique as well as the programmed learning technique for transmitting information to trainees. For actually developing skills in trainees, Northwestern could use on the job training methods, such as coaching, position rotation, or special project committees. For developing skills in a classroom setting, Northwestern could use instructional techniques, such as role-playing activities. For example, flight attendants could be asked to handle passengers with various kinds of attitudes and different family sizes. These situations then could be analyzed from the viewpoint of how to improve attendant–passenger relationships.

Once a Northwestern training program has been completed, it must be evaluated to determine if it met the training need for which it was designed. Training programs aimed at specific, tangible skills such as word processing or building electronic spreadsheets would be much easier to evaluate than would training programs aimed at interpersonal skills such as effective interpersonal communication or motivating employees. The evaluation of any training program at Northwestern, of course, should emphasize how to improve the program the next time it is implemented.

Performance Appraisal

Even after individuals have been recruited, selected, and trained, the task of making them maximally productive within the organization is not finished. The fourth step in the process of providing appropriate human resources for the organization is **performance appraisal**—the process of reviewing individuals' past productive activity to evaluate the contribution they have made toward attaining management system objectives. Like training, performance appraisal—which is also called *performance review* and *performance evaluation*—is a continuing activity that focuses on both established human resources within the organization and newcomers. Its main purpose is to furnish feedback to organization members about how they can become more productive and useful to the organization in its quest for quality.[28] Table 12.2 describes several methods of performance appraisal.

Performance appraisal is the process of reviewing past productive activity to evaluate the contribution individuals have made toward attaining management system objectives.

Why Use Performance Appraisals?

Most U.S. firms engage in some type of performance appraisal. Douglas McGregor has suggested the following three reasons for using performance appraisals:[29]

 **Table 12.2** Descriptions of Several Methods of Performance Appraisal

Appraisal Method	Description
Rating scale	Individuals appraising performance use a form containing several employee qualities and characteristics to be evaluated (e.g., dependability, initiative, leadership). Each evaluated factor is rated on a continuum or scale ranging, for example, from 1 to 7.
Employee comparisons	Appraisers rank employees according to such factors as job performance and value to organization. Only one employee can occupy a particular ranking.
Free-form essay	Appraisers simply write down their impressions of employees in paragraph form.
Critical-form essay	Appraisers write down particularly good or bad events involving employees as these events occur. Records of all documented events for any one employee are used to evaluate that persons performance.

1. They provide systematic judgments to support salary increases, promotions, transfers, and sometimes demotions or terminations.
2. They are a means of telling subordinates how they are doing and of suggesting needed changes in behavior, attitudes, skills, or job knowledge; they let subordinates know where they stand with the boss.
3. They furnish a useful basis for the coaching and counseling of individuals by superiors.

Coca-Cola Uses Performance Appraisal to Tie Pay to Diversity

The Coca-Cola Company is the world's largest manufacturer, distributor, and marketer of soft drink concentrates and syrups. Overall, the company's beverage products are sold in nearly 200 countries throughout the world. In most of these countries, Coke products are leading sellers in the marketplace, and they include popular names like Coca-Cola, Coca-Cola Classic, Diet Coke, Fanta, Sprite, and Minute Maid.

In April 1999, Coca-Cola employees filed suit against the company, accusing it of having a corporate hierarchy in which African Americans floundered at the bottom of the pay scale. As a result of this suit, Coca-Cola has made the highest-ever company settlement involving racial discrimination suits, with a whopping payment of $192.5 million. This settlement, heralded as the largest financial settlement of its kind, signals a major breakthrough in the Coca-Cola workplace. Company supporters believe that Coca-Cola has assumed both social and business leadership roles throughout its history. With this settlement, supporters believe that Coca-Cola has positioned itself as an example of how business should positively respond to diversity issues in a big-business situation.

To ensure that the company continues to support diversity in the future, Doug Daft, Coca-Cola's new chief executive, has indicated that he will link executive pay, including his own, to meeting diversity goals. Daft believes that what gets measured in organizations gets accomplished. As a result, he is committed to holding executives accountable for making progress in reaching company diversity goals. To further ensure progress in this area, Daft is establishing a new position called Vice President and Director of Diversity Strategies, which will report directly to Daft. ■

Handling Performance Appraisals If performance appraisals are not handled well, their benefits to the organization will be minimal. Several guidelines can assist management in increasing the appropriateness with which appraisals are conducted. The first guideline is that performance appraisals should stress both performance in the position the individual holds and the success with which the individual is attaining organizational objectives. Although conceptually separate, performance and objectives should be inseparable topics of discussion during performance appraisals. The second guideline is that appraisals should emphasize how well the individual is doing the job, not the evaluator's impression of the individual's work habits. In other words, the goal is an objective analysis of performance rather than a subjective evaluation of habits.

The third guideline is that the appraisal should be acceptable to both the evaluator and the subject—that is, both should agree that it has benefit for the organization and the worker. The fourth, and last, guideline is that performance appraisals should provide a base for improving individuals' productivity within the organization by making them better equipped to produce.[30]

Potential Weaknesses of Performance Appraisals   To maximize the payoff of performance appraisals to the organization, managers must avoid several potential weaknesses of the appraisal process, including the following pitfalls:[31]

1. Performance appraisals focus employees on short-term rewards rather than on issues that are important to the long-run success of the organization.
2. Individuals involved in performance appraisals view them as a reward–punishment situation.
3. The emphasis of performance appraisal is on completing paperwork rather than on critiquing individual performance.
4. Individuals being evaluated view the process as unfair or biased.
5. Subordinates react negatively when evaluators offer unfavorable comments.

To avoid these potential weaknesses, supervisors and employees should look on the performance appraisal process as an opportunity to increase the worth of the employee through constructive feedback, not as a means of rewarding or punishing the employee through positive or negative comments. Paperwork should be viewed only as an aid in providing this feedback, not as an end in itself. Also, care should be taken to make appraisal feedback as tactful and objective as possible to minimize negative reactions.

▶ Back to the Case

The last step in providing appropriate human resources at Northwestern Mutual is performance appraisal. This means that the contributions that Northwestern's employees make toward attaining management system objectives must be evaluated. Naturally, the performance appraisal process should focus on more recently hired employees as well as more established Northwestern employees.

It would be difficult to visualize a Northwestern employee who could not benefit from a properly conducted performance appraisal. Such an appraisal would stress activities on the job and effectiveness in accomplishing job objectives. An objective appraisal would provide Northwestern's employees with tactful, constructive criticism that should help to increase their productivity. Handled properly, Northwestern's appraisals would not be a reward or a punishment in themselves, but rather an opportunity to increase their value to the company. Such objective, productive analysis of performance should help Northwestern's employees to become more productive over time rather than to be without guidance and perhaps moving toward the inevitable outcome of being fired.

Management Skills Module

This section is specially designed to help you develop management skills. An individual's management skill is based on an understanding of management concepts and the ability to apply those concepts in management situations. As a result, the following activities are designed both to heighten your understanding of management concepts and to help you gain facility in applying those concepts in various management situations.

UNDERSTANDING MANAGEMENT CONCEPTS

▶ Action Summary

Reread the learning objectives below. Each objective is followed by questions. Answering these questions accurately will help you retain the most important concepts discussed in this chapter. After answering each question, check your answer against the answer key at the end of this chapter. (*Hint:* If you have any doubts regarding the correct response, consult the page number that follows the answer.)

Circle:

From studying this chapter, I will attempt to acquire

1. An overall understanding of how appropriate human resources can be provided for the organization.

T F   **a.** An appropriate human resource is an individual whose qualifications are matched to job specifications.

a b c d e   **b.** The term *appropriate human resources* refers to: (a) finding the right number of people to fill positions (b) individuals being satisfied with their jobs (c) individuals who help the organization achieve management system objectives (d) individuals who are ineffective (e) none of the above.

2. An appreciation for the relationship among recruitment efforts, an open position, sources of human resources, and the law.

a b c d e   **a.** The process of narrowing a large number of candidates to a smaller field is called: (a) rushing (b) recruitment (c) selection (d) enlistment (e) enrollment.

a b c d e   **b.** The characteristics of the individual who should be hired for the job are indicated by the: (a) job analysis (b) job specification (c) job description (d) job review (e) job identification.

3. Insights on the use of tests and assessment centers in employee selection.

a b c d e   **a.** The level of skill or knowledge an individual possesses in a particular area is measured by: (a) aptitude tests (b) achievement tests (c) acuity tests (d) assessment tests (e) vocational interest tests.

a b c d e   **b.** The following guideline does *not* apply when tests are used in selecting potential employees: (a) the tests should be both valid and reliable (b) the tests should be nondiscriminatory in nature (c) the tests should not be the sole source of information for determining whether someone is to be hired (d) such factors as potential and desire to obtain a position should not be assessed subjectively (e) none of the above—all are important guidelines.

4. An understanding of how the training process operates.

a b c d e   **a.** Four steps involved in training individuals are: (1) designing the training program (2) evaluating the training program (3) determining training needs (4) administering the training program. The correct sequence for these steps is:
   (a) 1, 3, 2, 4
   (b) 3, 4, 1, 2
   (c) 2, 1, 3, 4
   (d) 3, 1, 4, 2
   (e) none of the above

T F   **b.** The lecture offers learners an excellent opportunity to clarify meanings and ask questions, since communication is two-way.

5. A concept of what performance appraisals are and how they can best be conducted.

a b c d e   **a.** Performance appraisals are important in an organization because they: (a) provide systematic judgments to support promotions (b) provide a basis for coaching (c) provide a basis for counseling (d) let subordinates know where they stand with the boss (e) all of the above.

a b c d e   **b.** To achieve the maximum benefit from performance evaluations, a manager should: (a) focus only on the negative aspects of performance (b) punish the worker with negative feedback (c) be as subjective as possible (d) focus only on the positive aspects of performance (e) use only constructive feedback.

▶ Action Summary Answer Key

1. **a.** F, p. 258
   b. c, p. 258
2. **a.** b, p. 259
   b. b, p. 259

3. **a.** b, p. 265
   b. d, pp. 265–266

4. **a.** d, p. 267
   b. F, p. 269

5. **a.** e, pp. 271–272
   b. e, p. 273

▶ Issues for Review and Discussion

1. What is the difference between appropriate and inappropriate human resources?
2. List and define the four major steps in providing appropriate human resources for the organization.
3. What is the purpose of recruitment?
4. How are job analysis, job description, and job specification related?
5. List the advantages of promotion from within.
6. Compare and contrast the management inventory card, the position replacement form, and the management manpower replacement chart.
7. List three sources of human resources outside the organization. How can these sources be tapped?
8. Does the law influence organizational recruitment practices? If so, how?
9. Describe the role of the Equal Employment Opportunity Commission.
10. Can affirmative action programs be useful in recruitment? Explain.
11. Define *selection.*
12. What is the difference between aptitude tests and achievement tests?
13. Discuss three guidelines for using tests in the selection process.
14. What are assessment centers?
15. List and define the four main steps of the training process.
16. Explain two possible ways of determining organizational training needs.
17. What are the differences between the lecture and programmed learning as alternative methods of transmitting information in the training program?
18. On-the-job training methods include coaching, position rotation, and special project committees. Explain how each of these methods works.
19. What are performance appraisals, and why should they be used?
20. If someone asked your advice on how to conduct performance appraisals, describe in detail what you would say.

APPLYING MANAGEMENT CONCEPTS

▶ Cases

➤ INTRODUCTORY CASE WRAP-UP

▶ Case Discussion Questions

"Northwestern Mutual Life Focuses on Recruitment" (pp. 257–258) and its related Back-to-the-Case sections were written to help you better understand the management concepts contained in this chapter. Answer the following discussion questions about this Introductory Case to further enrich your understanding of the chapter content:

1. How important is the training of employees to an organization such as Northwestern? Explain.
2. What actions besides training must an organization such as Northwestern take to make employees as productive as possible?
3. Based on information in the case, what do you think will be the biggest challenge for Northwestern's management in successfully providing appropriate human resources for the future? Explain.

▶ Skills Exercise: Performing a Job Analysis

In this chapter, you learned that performing a job analysis entails determining a job description and a job specification. Assume that you are John Sheaffer (as discussed in the Introductory Case) and are doing a job analysis of the "Insurance Sales Agent" position at Northwestern Mutual. Recognizing that you are not an insurance expert, write a job description and a job specification for this position.

CASE STUDY: *EVEN IN ECONOMIC DOWNTURN INTEL STRIVES TO MAINTAIN STUDENT INTEREST*

Not long ago, high-technology companies were wooing college graduates with promises of signing bonuses and luxury perks, to entice them to accept jobs. Now, companies like chipmaker Intel are cutting costs and going through the painful process of laying off workers at every level.

Craig Barnett, CEO of Intel, believes 100 percent in the importance of his workforce. He considers the people who work for Intel "a vital asset." "After all," he recently told *Fast Company* magazine, "a company's most valuable knowledge often resides not in a database but in someone's head." Intel recruits heavily from both community colleges and M.B.A. programs. They need skilled technicians to run their plants and innovative minds to design and create new models of information technology.

For college students thinking of applying to Intel, there is a special site on its home page dedicated specifically to answering any questions they might have about available jobs and corporate environment.

Intel respects the ideas of new hires. It even includes a segment on "constructive confrontation" in its recruitment-training program. According to Michael Fors, a co-manager, and instructor for Intel University, "we have this common way to disagree. We don't spend time being defensive or taking things personally." Intel tries to be responsive to everyone's ideas and cognizant of people's needs. For instance, if there is a merger, the day the deal is finalized, all new employees can access their new benefits information and start contributing to and learning about Intel via the company's own intranet. The Intel staff is welcome to go online to file expenses or select benefit options, to order supplies, and to perform a lot of small things to make their day go more smoothly on a personal level. Fundamentally, it allows everyone who works for Intel to use the Web easily and to identify with customers who want to be able to use it just as easily.

Normally, Intel recruits 2,000 seniors to work for it after graduation. In March, Intel announced it would be cutting 5,000 jobs. In order to soften the blow, Intel spokesperson Chuck Malloy says the company has instituted a "reverse signing bonus" of two months' salary for the college recruit to walk away. This also gives the manager one less job to eliminate.

Additionally, Intel is offering incentives for current employees to leave. In some cases, the company will eliminate the job but send the worker to be redeployed, meaning he or she would have to find another job within the company. "This is where the signing bonus comes in," explains Malloy. "Let's say Intel has an engineer-ing opening that's been offered to a college student but a manager also has a ten-year veteran engineer whose job has just been eliminated. . . . He could then take the Intel engineer, put him in the job and offer the signing bonus to the prospective employee. The prospective employee could reject the offer and opt to join Intel anyway with the understanding that they won't get the job they interviewed for. They'll get a different job."

Despite the hiring freeze, it was reported by the *Wall Street Journal* that Intel spent more than $10,000 to send 5 Intel employees and 12 community college presidents and deans on a three-day junket in New Mexico and Texas. They were treated to a tour of Intel's chip-making plant in Albuquerque and visits to four community colleges that Intel considers models. Intel's goal is to make sure that five years from today it will have enough highly qualified workers to run its new plants in Colorado and Massachusetts. It is easier to raise capital for new equipment than it is to find smart, skilled employees.

"Intel will resume hiring someday," says Intel workforce development manager Pat Foy. "Training programs can't be turned on and off like a spigot." Intel needs to know that graduating students will be there when the need arises, and it works hard to attract them. That is why sponsoring scholarships, hiring interns, and donating equipment to schools are not enough to set Intel apart from competing high-tech companies.

Even entry-level jobs at Intel require at least a two-year college degree with courses in math, physics, and chemistry. First-rung jobs at Intel pay nearly $40,000 a year. Intel plans to go on courting potential hires, certain that its good public relations will pay off in the long run when the tech sector picks up again. Everyone hopes it will be soon.

QUESTIONS

1. What steps has the Human Resources Management of Intel taken to try to maintain a positive image in the eyes of potential employees?

2. In what ways can Intel's intranet system be used to make recruitment, selection, training, and performance appraisals more efficient?

3. Should Intel be looking inside its company as a source of human resources? Why? If you think that "looking inside" would be good for Intel, suggest some broad steps for a process that could be used in such a search.

MASTERING MANAGEMENT: EPISODE 4—PERFORMANCE APPRAISAL

Mastering Management is a series of innovative, interactive learning activities specially designed to help you develop management skills emphasized in various text chapters. Evaluating employee performance is the major focus of this chapter. Episode 4 of *Mastering Management* focuses on appraising employee performance and highlights how CanGo, a cutting edge company, evaluates its people. In the introductory video, Warren is faced with the challenge of appraising the performance of a poorly performing subordinate. Review Episode 4, "Performance Appraisal," on your *Mastering Management* CD and then answer the following questions.

QUESTIONS

1. Explain why the situation facing Warren about customer complaints could be a performance appraisal problem. What steps would you take to solve this problem?

2. Explain why the situation facing Warren about customer complaints could be a training problem. What steps would you take to solve this problem?

3. Explain why the situation facing Warren about customer complaints could be a selection problem. What steps would you take to solve this problem?

www.prenhall.com/certo

This book is accompanied by a rich assortment of online activities aimed at developing your management skills. Reviewing news headlines, Internet exercises, an online study guide, and other research and Internet resources can help personalize management skills development for individual students or an entire class.

chapter

chapterchapterchapterchapterchapterchapter

13 Organizational Change and Stress

Objectives

From studying this chapter, I will attempt to acquire

- A working definition of *changing an organization*

- An understanding of the relative importance of change and stability to an organization

- Some ability to recognize what kinds of changes should be made within an organization

- An appreciation for why the people affected by a change should be considered when the change is being made

- Some facility at evaluating change

- An understanding of how organizational change and stress are related

- Knowledge about virtuality as a vehicle for organizational change

CHAPTER OUTLINE

AT&T Changes Where
and How People Work

REMINDER: THE INTRODUCTORY CASE WRAP-UP (P. 300) CONTAINS DISCUSSION QUESTIONS AND A SKILLS EXERCISE TO FURTHER ILLUSTRATE THE APPLICATION OF CHAPTER CONCEPTS TO THIS VIGNETTE.

About 12 percent of AT&T's workforce has a formal telecommuting arrangement with management, works from a virtual office, or works from a remote location.

AT&T is one of the world's premier communications and information services companies, serving more than 90 million consumer, business, and government customers. The company has annual revenues of more than $52 billion and employs more than 130,000 workers. It runs the world's largest, most sophisticated communications network and is the leading provider of long distance and wireless services. AT&T operates in more than 200 countries and territories around the world. The company also offers online services and access to home entertainment, and has begun to deliver local telephone service. AT&T's mission statement is as follows:

> We aspire to be the most admired and valuable company in the world. Our goal is to enrich our customers' personal lives and to make their businesses more successful by bringing to market exciting and useful communications services, building shareowner value in the process.

In late 1994, AT&T formed an eight-member Alternative Work Arrangements (AWA) team. The purpose of this team was to assess and propose various new company options for alternative work arrangements—new and different work situations that could be instituted within the company. In essence, AWA was to develop a comprehensive plan for implementing new, desirable work situations. The plan was to include conclusions that were based on surveying employee ideas and assessing company work needs. In addition, the plan was to include proposed guidelines for implementing recommended new work situations along with new training packages necessary to acclimate people to these new situations. Last, the plan was to include recommended purchases of equipment, if any, necessary to make the new work situations functional.

Although AWA studied several options like continuously changing work schedules and a compressed workweek, the team finally settled on endorsing only the initiation of telecommuting, employees essentially working from home via e-mail, videoconferencing, and other information technology advances. One area of concern about instituting a new telecommuting work situation came from supervisors at AT&T. They were concerned about how to measure the productivity of telecommuting employees. In order to address this issue, AWA actually devised a new feedback form focusing on

(continued)

telecommuter productivity. This form gave supervisors a new, useful tool for evaluating the performance of telecommuting workers.

Based on the recommendation of AWA, AT&T instituted a new telecommuting program. By the beginning of 1995, almost 28 percent of AT&T managers had become telecommuters. Although not without its problems, the general consensus today at AT&T is that the telecommuting program continues to be successful. The company benefits in areas like reduced office expenses because employees work from home and increased productivity because workers are generally not interrupted as much at home as in traditional offices. Perhaps most important to employees, the new program gives them a better balance between their work and family lives.

What's Ahead

In essence, the Alternative Work Arrangements (AWA) team discussed in the Introductory Case is faced with making a recommendation about what changes to make within AT&T and how to make them. The changes AWA must recommend focus on implementing new and better ways to do work. Members of teams like AWA as well as individual managers who face making similar organizational changes would find the major topics in this chapter very useful and practical. These topics are the following: fundamentals of changing an organization, factors to consider when changing the organization, organizational change and stress, and virtuality.

FUNDAMENTALS OF CHANGING AN ORGANIZATION

Thus far, discussion in this "Organizing" section of the text has centered on the fundamentals of organizing, furnishing appropriate human resources for the organization, authority, delegation, and responsibility. This chapter focuses on changing the organization.

Defining Changing an Organization

Changing an organization is the process of modifying an existing organization to increase organizational effectiveness.

Changing an organization is the process of modifying an existing organization to increase organizational effectiveness—that is, the extent to which an organization accomplishes its objectives. These modifications can involve virtually any organizational segment, but typically affect the lines of organizational authority, the levels of responsibility held by various organization members, and the established lines of organizational communication. Driven by new technology, expanding global opportunities, and the trend toward organizational streamlining, almost all modern organizations are changing in some way.[1]

The Importance of Change Most managers agree that if an organization is to thrive, it must change continually in response to significant developments in the environment, such as changing customer needs, technological breakthroughs, and new government regulations. The study of organizational change is extremely important because all managers at all organizational levels are faced throughout their careers with the task of changing their organization. Managers who can determine appropriate changes and then implement such changes successfully enable their organizations to be more flexible and innovative. Because change is such a fundamental part of organizational existence, such managers are very valuable to organizations of all kinds.[2]

Many managers consider change to be so critical to organizational success that they encourage employees to continually search for areas in which beneficial changes can be made.

To take a classic example, General Motors provides employees with a "think list" to encourage them to develop ideas for organizational change and to remind them that change is vital to the continued success of GM. The think list contains the following questions:[3]

1. Can a machine be used to do a better or faster job?
2. Can the fixture now in use be improved?
3. Can handling of materials for the machine be improved?
4. Can a special tool be used to combine the operations?
5. Can the quality of the part being produced be improved by changing the sequence of the operation?
6. Can the material used be cut or trimmed differently for greater economy or efficiency?
7. Can the operation be made safer?
8. Can paperwork regarding this job be eliminated?
9. Can established procedures be simplified?

Change Versus Stability

In addition to organizational change, some degree of stability is a prerequisite for long-term organizational success. Figure 13.1 presents a model developed by Hellriegel and Slocum that shows the relative importance of change and stability to organizational survival. Although these authors use the word *adaptation* in their model rather than *change*, the two terms are essentially synonymous.

The model stresses that organizational survival and growth are most probable when both stability and adaptation are high within the organization (number 3 on the model depicted in Figure 13.1). The organization without enough stability to complement change is at a definite disadvantage. When stability is low, the probability of organizational survival and growth declines. Change after change without regard for the essential role of stability typically results in confusion and employee stress.[1]

▶ Back to the Case

The above information furnishes several insights about how AWA should make decisions, such as whether or not to recommend a particular type of change in AT&T's work arrangements. AWA should evaluate whether a change would better enable AT&T to accomplish its objectives. It should also understand that making such change is extremely important. If AT&T is to have continued success over the long run, change will probably have to be made a number of times. In fact, appropriate change is so important to a company like AT&T that AWA might want to

(continued)

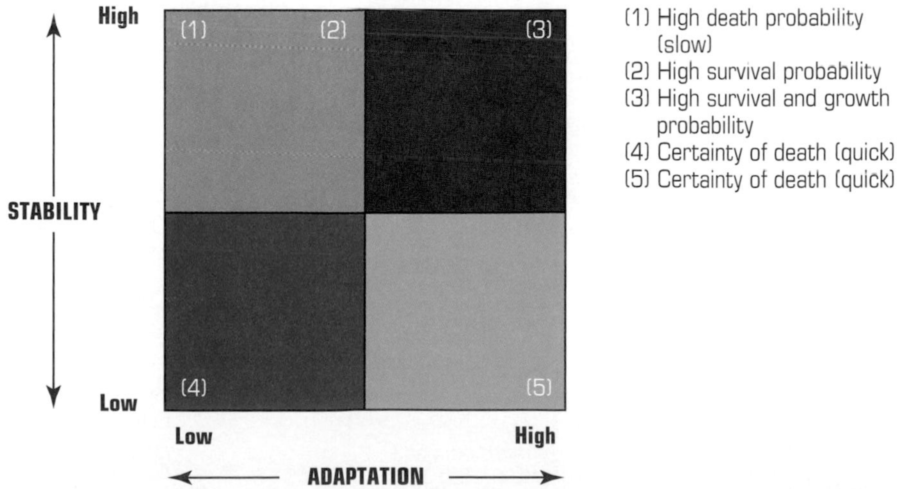

(1) High death probability (slow)
(2) High survival probability
(3) High survival and growth probability
(4) Certainty of death (quick)
(5) Certainty of death (quick)

Adaptation, stability, and organizational survival

Figure 13.1

consider initiating some type of program that would encourage employees to submit their ideas continually on new alternative work ideas that could increase company effectiveness. When considering possible changes, however, AWA will have to keep in mind that some level of work arrangements stability is also necessary to survival and growth.

FACTORS TO CONSIDER WHEN CHANGING AN ORGANIZATION

How managers deal with the major factors that need to be considered when an organizational change is being made will largely determine how successful that change will be. The following factors should be considered whenever change is being contemplated:

1. The change agent
2. Determining what should be changed
3. The kind of change to make
4. Individuals affected by the change
5. Evaluation of the change

Although the following sections discuss each of these factors individually, Figure 13.2 makes the point that it is a collective influence that ultimately determines the success of a change.

The Change Agent

Perhaps the most important factor managers need to consider when changing an organization is who will be the **change agent**—the individual inside or outside the organization who tries to modify the existing organizational situation. The change agent might be a self-designated manager within the organization, or an outside consultant hired because of a special expertise in a particular area. This individual might be responsible for making very broad changes, like altering the culture of the whole organization; or more narrow ones, like designing and implementing a new safety program or a new quality program.[5] Although in some circumstances the change agent will not be a manager, the term *manager* and *change agent* are used synonymously throughout this chapter.

Special skills are necessary for success as a change agent. Among them are the ability to determine how a change should be made, the skill to solve change-related problems, and facility in using behavioral science tools to influence people appropriately during the change process. Perhaps the most overlooked skill of successful change agents, however, is the ability to determine how much change employees can withstand.[6]

A **change agent** is an individual inside or outside the organization who tries to modify an existing organizational situation.

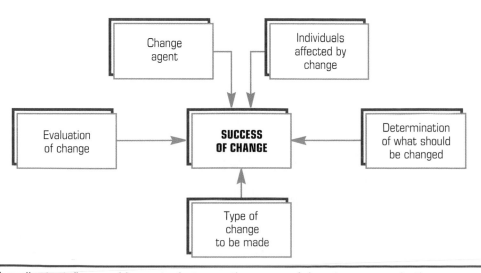

Overall, managers should choose change agents who have the most expertise in all these areas. A potentially beneficial change might not result in any advantages for the organization if a person without expertise in these areas is designated as change agent.

► Scott Cook, cofounder of software maker Intuit Inc. in Mountain View, California, operates in a business where almost every employee can function as a change agent. "We've been able to change by identifying our most passionate people and by letting them set our course," says Cook. "And then we have acted as cheerleaders for them, protecting them, encouraging them, and empowering them with every resource that they need to succeed."

►Back to the Case

An appointed manager at AT&T would undoubtedly have the main role in deciding what structural changes to make or which new alternative work arrangements to implement. Therefore, this manager would be the change agent, who should be carefully selected giving special consideration to individuals with abilities to determine if and how particular changes recommended by AWA should be made. The individual best suited for this change agent role is probably the individual best suited in the company to evaluate the advantages and disadvantages of having one type of structure or work situation as opposed to another.

The change agent must have the ability to use behavioral science tools to influence organization members during the implementation of planned change. As examples, the change agent must determine how much structural or new work situation change AT&T employees can withstand and be able to influence employees so that they learn to work together in their new roles. He or she must then implement this change, perhaps gradually, so employees will not be overwhelmed. Overall, the ability to use behavioral science tools will help the change agent to be successful in implementing needed work situation changes at AT&T.

Determining What Should Be Changed

Another major factor managers need to consider is exactly what should be changed within the organization. In general, managers should make only those changes that will increase organizational effectiveness.

It has been generally accepted for many years that organizational effectiveness depends primarily on activities centering around three classes of factors:

1. People
2. Structure
3. Technology

People factors are attitudes, leadership skills, communication skills, and all other characteristics of the human resources within the organization. **Structural factors** are organizational controls, such as policies and procedures; and **technological factors** are any types of equipment or processes that assist organization members in the performance of their jobs.

For an organization to maximize its effectiveness, appropriate people must be matched with appropriate technology and appropriate structure. Thus, people factors, technological factors, and structural factors are not independent determinants of organizational effectiveness. Instead, as Figure 13.3 shows, organizational effectiveness is determined by the relationship of these three factors.

People factors are attitudes, leadership skills, communication skills, and all other characteristics of the organization's employees.

Structural factors are organizational controls, such as policies and procedures.

Technological factors are any types of equipment or processes that assist organization members in the performance of their jobs.

Social Responsibility Slowing Mazda's Production Change

SPOTLIGHT ethics

Mazda Motor Corporation is based in Hiroshima, Japan. Mazda manufactures both passenger cars and commercial vehicles and is one of western Japan's largest companies, employing about 24,000 people. In one year, Mazda manufactures as many as 800,000 cars and trucks at its two production sites in Japan, Hiroshima and Hofu. It also operates joint venture plants in the state of Michigan and in Thailand, and Mazda cars and trucks are assembled in 16 countries.

Mark Fields, the new president of Mazda, presently faces a formidable change-related challenge. More than 80 percent of the cars Mazda sells are made in Japan, where labor and production costs are very high. As result, Fields is considering shifting some production

(continued)

from its flagship plant in Hiroshima to foreign plants, in order to reduce these costs.

Predictably, many longtime organization members are resisting the pressure to shift production to other locations. Mazda has an overwhelming presence in the Hiroshima community. Estimates are that in addition to the 24,000 people that Mazda employs in Hiroshima, another 200,000 people in the area have jobs related to its business. Hiroshima prospers when Mazda vehicles roll out of its factory.

After having been president for several months, analysts and investors are wondering why Fields has not aggressively shifted production from the Hiroshima plant to other locations. The reason seems simple: It will take time for him to determine and implement a solution to the high production costs while meeting Mazda's social responsibility obligation to the Hiroshima community. ■

The Kind of Change to Make

The kind of change to make is the third major factor that managers need to consider when they set out to change an organization. Most changes can be categorized as one of three kinds:

1. Technological
2. Structural
3. People

Note that these three kinds of change correspond to the three main determinants of organizational effectiveness—each change is named for the determinant it emphasizes.

For example, **technological change** emphasizes modifying the level of technology in the management system. Because this kind of change so often involves outside experts and highly technical language, it is more profitable to discuss structural change and people change in detail in this text.

Structural Change Structural change emphasizes increasing organizational effectiveness by changing controls that influence organization members during the performance of their jobs. The following sections further describe this approach and discuss matrix organizations (organizations modified to complete a special project) as an example of structural change.

Describing Structural Change **Structural change** is change aimed at increasing organizational effectiveness through modifications to the existing organizational structure. These modifications can take several forms:

1. Clarifying and defining jobs
2. Modifying organizational structure to fit the communication needs of the organization

Technological change is a type of organizational change that emphasizes modifying the level of technology in the management system.

Structural change is a type of organizational change that emphasizes modifying an existing organizational structure.

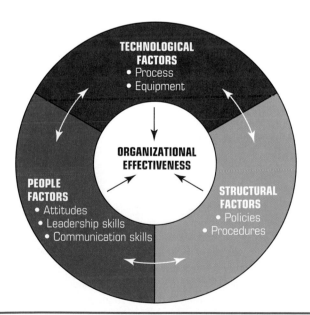

Figure 13.3

Determination of organizational effectiveness by the relationship of people, technological, and structural factors

3. Decentralizing the organization to reduce the cost of coordination, increase the controllability of subunits, increase motivation, and gain greater flexibility

Although structural change must take account of people and technology to be successful, its primary focus is obviously on changing organizational structure. In general, managers choose to make structural changes within an organization if information they have gathered indicates that the present structure is the main cause of organizational ineffectiveness. The precise structural changes they choose to make will vary from situation to situation, of course. After changes to organizational structure have been made, management should conduct periodic reviews to make sure the changes are accomplishing their intended purposes.[7]

Matrix Organizations   Matrix organizations provide a good illustration of structural change. According to C. J. Middleton, a **matrix organization** is a traditional organization that is modified primarily for the purpose of completing some kind of special project. Essentially, a matrix organization is one in which individuals from various functional departments are assigned to a project manager responsible for accomplishing some specific task.[8] For this reason, matrix organizations are also called *project organizations*. The project itself may be either long term or short term, and the employees needed to complete it are borrowed from various organizational segments.

> A **matrix organization** is a traditional organizational structure that is modified primarily for the purpose of completing some kind of special project.

John F. Mee has developed a classic example showing how a traditional organization can be changed into a matrix organization.[9] Figure 13.4 presents a portion of a traditional organizational structure based primarily on product line. Although this design is generally useful, management might learn, for example, that it makes it impossible for organization members to give adequate attention to three government projects of extreme importance to long-term organizational success.

Making the Change to Matrix: An Example.   Figure 13.5 illustrates one way management could change this traditional organizational structure into a matrix organization to facilitate completion of the three government projects. A manager would be appointed for each of the three projects and allocated personnel with appropriate skills to complete the project. The three project managers would have authority over the employees assigned to them and be accountable for the performance of those people. Each of the three project managers would be placed on the chart in Figure 13.5 in one of the three boxes labeled Venus Project, Mars Project, and Saturn Project, and the work flow related to each project would go from right to left on the chart. After the projects were completed, the organization chart would revert to its original design—assuming that design is more advantageous under most circumstances.

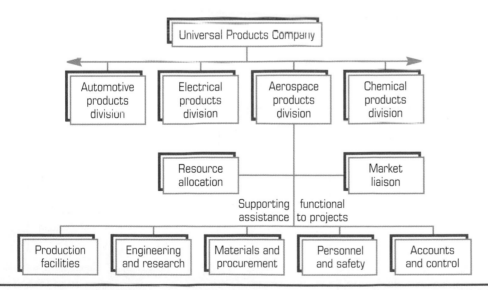

Portion of a traditional organizational structure based primarily on product line

Figure 13.4

Intel Corporation, which holds a near-monopoly over the microprocessor chip, still strives to make technological change a key factor in its market leadership. In particular, Intel uses its resources to push technological advancements faster than its competitors, and one of the company's formal goals is to render its own products obsolete before other chipmakers do it.

There are several advantages and disadvantages to making structural changes such as those reflected by the matrix organization. The major advantages are that such structural changes generally result in better control of a project, better customer relations, shorter project development time, and lower project costs. In addition, matrix organizations are flexible enough to allow managers to shift resources to special projects as needed. The downside is that

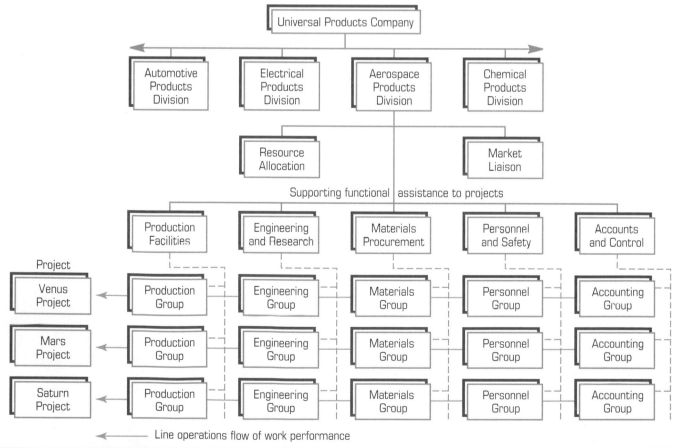

Figure 13.5   *Traditional organization chart transformed into matrix organization chart*

such structural changes generally create more complex internal operations, which commonly cause conflict, encourage inconsistency in the application of company policy, and result in a more difficult situation to manage.

The advantages and disadvantages of changing a traditional organization into a matrix organization will have different weights according to the situation. One point is clear, however: For a matrix organization to be effective and efficient, organization members must be willing to learn and execute somewhat different organizational roles than they are used to.[10]

▶ Back to the Case

The AT&T change agent chosen to put AWA recommendations into action must make different types of changes. The preceding information discussed how a change agent can change technological factors, people factors, and structural factors in order to increase organizational effectiveness. AWA's recommendation will likely include change in all these factors. New work arrangements would be categorized as changing structural factors. In addition, however, such new work arrangements would include technological change centering on features like using new computers and the Internet. Last, the new work situation changes must focus on people—changing the way people actually do their work at AT&T will be facilitated through actions such as the change agent communicating with off-site workers, molding off-site workers into a team with a distinctive culture, and motivating off-site workers.

People change is a type of organizational change that emphasizes modifying certain aspects of organization members to increase organizational effectiveness.

Organization development (OD) is the process that emphasizes changing an organization by changing organization members and bases these changes on an overview of structure, technology, and all other organizational ingredients.

Grid organization development (grid OD) is a commonly used organization development technique based on a theoretical model called the *managerial grid*.

People Change   Although successfully changing people factors necessarily involves some consideration of structure and technology, the primary emphasis is on people. The following sections discuss people change and examine grid organization development, one commonly used means of changing organization members.

Describing People Change: Organization Development (OD)   People change emphasizes increasing organizational effectiveness by changing certain aspects of organization members. The focus of this kind of change is on such factors as employee's attitudes and leadership skills. In general, managers should attempt to make this kind of change when human resources are shown to be the main cause of organizational ineffectiveness.

McDonald's Corporation Is Changing the Way Employees Think About Disabled Workers

In 1990, President George Bush signed into law the Americans with Disabilities Act (ADA), which bans discrimination against disabled workers. Although some employers may be concerned about hiring the disabled, companies like DuPont and Target Stores have found that employing the disabled is a sound business practice. Their history in this area shows that many disabled workers are loyal, enthusiastic employees and make valuable contributions toward attaining organizational goals.

To effectively integrate disabled workers into the organization, however, some managers have discovered that they must change the way other employees think of their disabled coworkers. These managers have developed specific programs to prepare employees for appropriate interaction with disabled workers. For example, McDon-ald's Corporation sponsors awareness training in which employees role-play disabled workers to experience how these workers feel and how they may react to other employees' statements or attitudes concerning them. The experience of companies with a successful history of employing and integrating the disabled into the workforce indicates that awareness training should avoid prejudging disabled people's limitations. Employees who have not had direct experience with disabled workers often overestimate their limitations and consequently buffer them from challenges they can actually handle quite well.

Hiring the disabled can provide significant benefits to an organization. One is that the disabled usually are loyal and productive workers and managers. Another is that consumers commonly develop a deep sense of respect for companies that hire the disabled. ■

The process of people change can be referred to as **organization development (OD).** Although OD focuses mainly on changing certain aspects of people, these changes are based on an overview of structure, technology, and all other organizational ingredients.

Grid OD   One commonly used OD technique for changing people in organizations is called **grid organization development,** or **grid OD.**[11] The **managerial grid,** a basic model

A **managerial grid** is a theoretical model based on the premise that concern for people and concern for production are the two primary attitudes that influence management style.

describing various managerial styles, is used as the foundation for grid OD. The managerial grid is based on the premise that various managerial styles can be described by means of two primary attitudes of the manager: concern for people and concern for production. Within this model, each attitude is placed on an axis, which is scaled 1 through 9 and is used to generate five managerial styles. Figure 13.6 shows the managerial grid, its five managerial styles, and the factors that characterize each of these styles.

The Ideal Style.　The central theme of this managerial grid is that 9,9 management (as shown on the grid in Figure 13.6) is the ideal managerial style. Managers using this style have a high concern for both people and production. Managers using any other style have lesser degrees of concern for people or production, and are thought to reduce organizational success accordingly. The purpose of grid OD is to change organization managers so they will use the 9,9 management style.

Main Training Phases.　How is a grid OD program conducted? The program has six main training phases that are used with all managers within the organization. The first two phases focus on acquainting managers with the managerial grid concept and assisting them in determining which managerial style they most commonly use. The last four phases of the grid OD program concentrate on encouraging managers to adopt the 9,9 management style and showing them how to use this style within their specific job situation. Emphasis throughout the program is on developing teamwork within the organization.

Some evidence suggests that grid OD is effective in enhancing profit, positively changing managerial behavior, and positively influencing managerial attitudes and values.[12] Grid OD will have to undergo more rigorous testing for an extended period of time, however, before conclusive statements about it can be made.

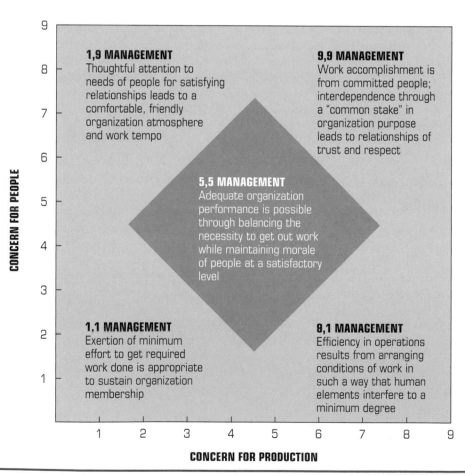

Figure 13.6　*The managerial grid*

The Status of Organization Development   If the entire OD area is taken into consideration, changes that emphasize both people and the organization as a whole seem to have inherent strength. There are, however, several commonly voiced weaknesses in OD efforts. These weaknesses are as follows:[13]

1. The effectiveness of an OD program is difficult to evaluate
2. OD programs are generally too time consuming
3. OD objectives are commonly too vague
4. The total costs of an OD program are difficult to gauge at the time the program starts
5. OD programs are generally too expensive

These weaknesses, however, should not eliminate OD from consideration, but rather should indicate areas to perfect within it. Managers can improve the quality of OD efforts by doing the following:[14]

1. Systematically tailoring OD programs to meet the specific needs of the organization
2. Continually demonstrating exactly how people should change their behavior
3. Conscientiously changing organizational reward systems so organization members who change their behavior in ways suggested by the OD program are rewarded

Managers have been employing OD techniques for several decades, and broad and useful applications of these techniques continue to be documented in the more recent management literature. OD techniques are currently being applied not only to business organizations, but also to many other types of organizations, such as religious organizations. Moreover, OD applications are being documented throughout the world, with increasing use being reported in countries like Hungary, Poland, and the United Kingdom.[15]

▶ Back to the Case

Technically, changing work situations at AT&T would not be classified as people change. Although the people involved in the change must be considered to some extent, the main emphasis of this change is on structural factors.

If, however, a change agent at AT&T believed that problems with human resources are the main cause of organizational ineffectiveness and *not* the work situation, he or she would probably plan and initiate an organization development program rather than a work situation improvement focus. On the other hand, the change agent may find it necessary to use grid OD in order to modify management styles and produce more cooperative team effort once established work changes are in place and a "new" kind of worker is operating.

Individuals Affected by the Change

A fourth major factor to be considered by managers when changing an organization is the people who will be affected by the change. A good assessment of what to change and how to make the change will be wasted if organization members do not support the change. To increase the chances of employee support, managers should be aware of the following factors:

1. The usual employee resistance to change
2. How this resistance can be reduced

Resistance to Change   Resistance to change within an organization is as common as the need for change. After managers decide to make some organizational change, they typically meet with employee resistance aimed at preventing that change from occurring.[16] Behind this resistance by organization members lies the fear of some personal loss, such as a reduction in personal prestige, a disturbance of established social and working relationships, and personal failure because of inability to carry out new job responsibilities.

Reducing Resistance to Change   To ensure the success of needed modifications, managers must be able to reduce the effects of the resistance that typically accompanies proposed change. Resistance can usually be lowered by following these guidelines:[17]

1. *Avoid surprises*—People need time to evaluate a proposed change before management implements it. Unless they are given time to evaluate and absorb how the change will affect them, employees are likely to be automatically opposed to it. Whenever possible, therefore, individuals who will be affected by a change should be informed of the kind of change being considered and the probability that it will be adopted.

2. *Promote real understanding*—When fear of personal loss related to a proposed change is reduced, opposition to the change is also reduced. Most managers find that ensuring that organization members thoroughly understand a proposed change is a major step in reducing this fear. Understanding may even generate enthusiastic support for the change if it focuses employees on individual gains that could materialize as a result of it. People should be given information that will help them answer the following change-related questions they invariably will have:

   ➤ Will I lose my job?
   ➤ Will my old skills become obsolete?
   ➤ Am I capable of producing effectively under the new system?
   ➤ Will my power and prestige decline?
   ➤ Will I be given more responsibility than I care to assume?
   ➤ Will I have to work longer hours?
   ➤ Will it force me to betray or desert my good friends?

3. *Set the stage for change*—Perhaps the most powerful tool for reducing resistance to change is management's positive attitude toward the change. This attitude should be displayed openly by top and middle management as well as by lower management. In essence, management should convey that change is one of the basic prerequisites for a successful organization. Management should also strive to encourage change for increasing organizational effectiveness, rather than for the sake of trying something new. To reinforce this positive attitude toward change, some portion of organizational rewards should be earmarked for those organization members who are most instrumental in implementing constructive change.

4. *Make tentative change*—Resistance to change can also be reduced if the changes are made on a tentative basis. This approach establishes a trial period during which organization members spend some time working under a proposed change before voicing support or nonsupport of it. Tentative change is based on the assumption that a trial period during which organization members live under a change is the best way of reducing feared personal loss. Judson has summarized the benefits of using the tentative approach:

   ➤ Employees affected by the change are able to test their reactions to the new situation before committing themselves irrevocably to it.
   ➤ Those who will live under the change are able to acquire more facts on which to base their attitudes and behavior toward the change.
   ➤ Those who had strong preconceptions about the change are in a better position to assess it with objectivity. Consequently, they may review and modify some of their preconceptions.
   ➤ Those involved are less likely to regard the change as a threat.
   ➤ Management is better able to evaluate the method of change and make any necessary modifications before carrying it out more fully.

Evaluation of the Change

As with all other managerial actions, managers should spend some time evaluating the changes they make. The purpose of this evaluation is not only to gain insights into how the change itself might be modified to further increase its organizational effectiveness, but also to determine whether the steps taken to make the change should be modified to increase organizational effectiveness the next time they are used.

According to Margulies and Wallace, making this evaluation may be difficult because the data from individual change programs may be unreliable.[18] Nevertheless, managers must do their best to evaluate change in order to increase the organizational benefits from the change.

Evaluation of change often involves watching for symptoms that indicate that further change is necessary. For example, if organization members continue to be oriented more to the past than the future, if they recognize the obligations of rituals more readily than they do the challenges of current problems, or if they pay greater allegiance to departmental goals than to overall company objectives, the probability is high that further change is necessary.

A word of caution is needed at this point. Although symptoms such as those listed in the preceding paragraph generally indicate that further change is warranted, this is not always the case. The decision to make additional changes should not be made solely on the basis of symptoms. More objective information should be considered. In general, additional change is justified if it will accomplish any of the following goals:[19]

1. Further improve the means for satisfying someone's economic wants
2. Increase profitability
3. Promote human work for human beings
4. Contribute to individual satisfaction and social well-being

> ## Back to the Case

The change agent at AT&T must realize that even though he or she may formulate a structural change that would be beneficial to the company, any attempt to implement this change could prove unsuccessful if it does not appropriately consider the people affected by the change. For example, if a new work arrangement is implemented requiring certain employees to work from home, employees may fear that this change will diminish their opportunities for promotion within the company. As a result, they may subtly resist the change.

To overcome such resistance, the change agent could use strategies like giving employees enough time to fully evaluate and understand the change, presenting a positive attitude about the change, and, if resistance is very strong, making the proposed change tentative until it is fully evaluated.

All work situation changes at AT&T need to be evaluated after implementation to discover if further organizational change is necessary and if the change process used might be improved for future use. For example, concerning the change of establishing a new work situation requiring certain workers to work only from home, the evaluation process could indicate that managers needed more personal contact with workers and that workers should work only half-time at home and half-time in the office.

CHANGE AND STRESS

Whenever managers implement changes, they should be concerned about the stress they may be creating. If the stress is significant enough, it may well cancel out the improvement that was anticipated from the change. In fact, stress could result in the organization being *less* effective than it was before the change was attempted. This section defines stress and discusses the importance of studying and managing it.

Defining Stress

The bodily strain that an individual experiences as a result of coping with some environmental factor is **stress**. Hans Selye, an early authority on this subject, said that stress constitutes the factors affecting wear and tear on the body. In organizations, this wear and tear is caused primarily by the body's unconscious mobilization of energy when an individual is confronted with organizational or work demands.[20]

Stress is the bodily strain that an individual experiences as a result of coping with some environmental factor.

The Importance of Studying Stress

There are several sound reasons for studying stress:[21]

> Stress can have damaging psychological and physiological effects on employees' health and on their contributions to organizational effectiveness. It can cause heart disease, and it can prevent employees from concentrating or making decisions.
> Stress is a major cause of employee absenteeism and turnover. Certainly, such factors severely limit the potential success of an organization.
> A stressed employee can affect the safety of other workers or even the public.

➤ Stress represents a very significant cost to organizations. Some estimates put the cost of stress-related problems in the U.S. economy at $150 billion a year. As examples of these costs, many modern organizations spend a great deal of money treating stress-related employee problems through medical programs, and they must absorb expensive legal fees when handling stress-related lawsuits.

Managing Stress in Organizations

Because stress is felt by virtually all employees in all organizations, insights about managing stress are valuable to all managers. This section is built on the assumption that in order to appropriately manage stress in organizations, managers must do the following:

1. Understand how stress influences worker performance
2. Identify where unhealthy stress exists in organizations
3. Help employees handle stress

Understanding How Stress Influences Worker Performance To deal with stress among employees, managers must understand the relationship between the amount of stress felt by a worker and the worker's performance. This relationship is shown in Figure 13.7. Note that extremely high and extremely low levels of stress tend to have negative effects on production. Additionally, while increasing stress tends to bolster performance up to some point (Point A in the figure), when the level of stress increases beyond this point, performance will begin to deteriorate.

In sum, a certain amount of stress among employees is generally considered to be advantageous for the organization because it tends to increase production. However, when employees experience too much or too little stress, it is generally disadvantageous for the organization because it tends to decrease production. The cartoon on the next page lightheartedly illustrates the profoundly negative effect that too much stress can have on job performance.

Identifying Unhealthy Stress in Organizations Once managers understand the impact of stress on performance, they must identify where stress exists within the organization.[22] After areas of stress have been pinpointed, managers must then determine whether the stress is at an appropriate level or is too high or too low. Because most stress-related organizational problems involve too much stress rather than too little, the remainder of this section focuses on how to relieve undesirably high levels of stress.

Managers often find it difficult to identify the people in the organization who are experiencing detrimentally high levels of stress. Part of this difficulty is that people respond to high stress in different ways, and part is that physiological reactions to stress are hard, if not impossible, for managers to observe and monitor. Such reactions include high blood pressure, pounding heart, and gastrointestinal disorders.

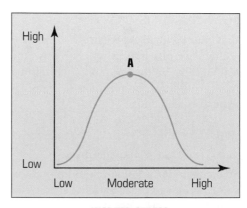

Figure 13.7    *The relationship between worker stress and the level of worker performance*

Harvard Business Review (July/August 1987), 64. © Lee Lorenz 1989.

Keller is a good man but totally lacking in stress-management skills.

Nevertheless, there are several observable symptoms of undesirably high stress levels that managers can learn to recognize. These symptoms are as follows:[23]

➤ Constant fatigue
➤ Low energy
➤ Moodiness
➤ Increased aggression
➤ Excessive use of alcohol
➤ Temper outbursts
➤ Compulsive eating
➤ High levels of anxiety
➤ Chronic worrying

A manager who observes one or more of these symptoms in employees should investigate to determine if those exhibiting the symptoms are indeed under too much stress. If so, the manager should try to help those employees handle their stress and/or should attempt to reduce stressors in the organization.

> A **stressor** is an environmental demand that causes people to feel stress.

Helping Employees Handle Stress   A **stressor** is an environmental demand that causes people to feel stress. Stressors are common in situations where individuals are confronted by circumstances for which their usual behaviors are inappropriate or insufficient and where negative consequences are associated with failure to deal properly with the situation. Organizational change characterized by continual layoffs or firings is an obvious stressor, but many other factors related to organizational policies, structure, physical conditions, and processes can also act as stressors.[24]

Reducing Stressors in the Organization   Stress is seldom significantly reduced until the stressors causing it have been coped with satisfactorily or withdrawn from the environment. For example, if too much organizational change is causing undesirably high levels of stress, management may be able to reduce that stress by improving organizational training that is aimed at preparing workers to deal with job demands resulting from the change. Management might also choose to reduce such stress by refraining from making further organizational changes for a while.[25]

Management can also adopt several strategies to help prevent the initial development of unwanted stressors in organizations. Three such strategies follow:[26]

1. *Create an organizational climate that is supportive of individuals*—Organizations commonly evolve into large bureaucracies with formal, inflexible, impersonal climates. This setup leads to considerable job stress. Making the organizational environment less formal and more supportive

▶ Karen Borgnes runs the aircraft repair firm Pacific Aerotech in Seattle on a 30-hour workweek. She has reduced stress in her own life by making use of her consummate organizing skills and putting in place a strong management team with whom she keeps in close touch. Her 18 employees enjoy stress relief options at work as well—11 of 12 workers in the window department have chosen a compressed workweek of four 10-hour days, and other workers have part-time schedules or take earlier shifts so they can attend school in the afternoon. Everyone gets a paid week off at Christmas, and sunny June days, rare in Seattle, have been the occasion for sending the entire staff home early.

of employee needs will help prevent the development of unwanted organizational stressors.

2. *Make jobs interesting*—Routine jobs that do not allow employees some degree of freedom often result in undesirable employee stress. If management focuses on making jobs as interesting as possible, this should help prevent the development of stressors related to routine, boring jobs.

3. *Design and operate career counseling programs*—Employees often experience considerable stress when they do not know what their next career step might be or when they might take it. If management can show employees that next step and when it can realistically be achieved, it will discourage unwanted organizational stressors in this area.

IBM is an example of a company that for many years has focused on career planning for its employees as a vehicle for reducing employee stress.[27] IBM has a corporationwide program to encourage supervisors to annually conduct voluntary career planning sessions with employees that result in one-page career action plans. Thus, IBM employees have a clear idea of where their careers are headed.

▶ Back to the Case

The change agent should be careful not to create too much stress on other organization members as a result of planned change. Such stress could be significant enough to eliminate any expected improvement at AT&T and could eventually result in such stress-related effects on employees as physical symptoms and the inability to make sound decisions.

Although some additional stress on organization members as a result of a change agent's newly implemented work situations could enhance productivity, too much stress could have a negative impact on production. The change agent could look for such signs as constant fatigue, increased aggression, temper outbursts, and chronic worrying.

If the change agent determines that undesirably high levels of stress have resulted from new work situation changes, he or she should try to reduce the stress. The change agent may be able to do so through training programs aimed at better equipping organization members to execute new job demands resulting from the change, or he or she may want to simply slow the rate of planned change.

It would probably be wise for the change agent to take action that would prevent unwanted stressors from developing as a result of work situation change. In this regard, the change agent could ensure that the organizational climate at AT&T is supportive of individual needs and that jobs resulting from the planned change are as interesting as possible.

VIRTUALITY

One specific, commonplace type of organizational change being made in modern organizations throughout the world is the trend toward "virtuality." Since this trend is indeed significant and expected to grow even more in the future, this section emphasizes it by defining a virtual organization, discussing degrees of virtuality in organizations, and describing the virtual office.[28]

Defining a Virtual Organization

Virtual organization is an organization having the essence of a traditional organization, but without some aspect(s) of traditional boundaries and structure.

Overall, a **virtual organization** has the essence of a traditional organization, but without some aspect of traditional boundaries and structure.[29] Virtual organizations are also referred to as *network organizations* or *modular corporations*.[30] In essence, managers go beyond traditional boundaries and structure for the good of the organization by using recent developments in information technology. Perhaps the most prominent of these developments are the Internet, the World Wide Web, and hardware and software tools enabling managers to use these two more easily.[31] Both large and small organizations can have virtual aspects.[32]

Degrees of Virtuality

Virtual corporation is an organization that goes significantly beyond the boundaries and structure of a traditional organization.

Organizations can vary drastically in terms of their degree of virtuality. Perhaps the company exhibiting the most extensive degree is known as the **virtual corporation,** an organization that goes significantly beyond the boundaries and structure of a traditional organization by comprehensively "tying together" a company's stakeholders like employees, suppliers, and customers via an elaborate system of e-mail, the World Wide Web, and other Internet-related vehicles like videoconferencing. This tying together allows all stakeholders to communicate and participate in helping the organization to become more successful.

On the other hand, some organizations have much lesser degrees of virtuality. For example, some organizations limit their virtuality to **virtual teams,** groups of employees formed by managers that go beyond the boundaries and structure of traditional teams by having members in geographically dispersed locations meeting via real-time messaging on an intranet or the Internet to discuss special or unanticipated organizational problems.[33] As another example, organizations may limit their virtuality to **virtual training,** a training process that goes beyond the boundaries and structure of traditional training. Such training can go beyond traditional training limits by, for example, instructing employees via Internet-assisted learning materials.[34] The following sections discuss virtual offices, a popular type of virtuality being introduced into many organizations.

Virtual teams are groups of employees formed by managers that go beyond the boundaries and structure of traditional teams.

Virtual training is a training process that goes beyond the boundaries and structure of traditional training.

DIGITAL FOCUS

▶ GoTrain Provides Virtual Training for Organizations

GoTrain.net provides virtual learning systems to other companies. Its products are envisioned as training experiences that improve the performance of those who use them while providing substantial training-cost savings to client companies. GoTrain has reformed the old classroom delivery system by providing innovative learning experiences through Internet applications. It provides courses in human resources that focus on areas like a drug-free workplace, sexual harassment, and stress management, and the more technical courses focus on fundamentals in areas like chemistry, electronics, and refrigeration.

GoTrain classes use the Internet to deliver computer based instruction. Companies like Circuit City and Radio Shack are experimenting with using instruction via the Internet because of the advantages it seems to provide. Internet-based training allows trainees to study from various locations at various times, and also integrates video, graphics, and sound to maximize trainee engagement in the learning experience. Also, Internet-based learning allows trainees to learn at their own pace and incorporates frequent feedback exercises and testing to apprise trainees of their learning progress.

Some managers are skeptical of virtual training for employees because they see the absence of social interaction among trainees and the unavailability of an instructor to answer questions and clarify concepts being taught as significant disadvantages. Overall, managers must carefully weigh the specifics of their organizational situations and use virtual training only if and when appropriate.

The Virtual Office

This section discusses an exciting component of organization virtuality, the virtual office.[35] The following sections discuss the definition of the term, various reasons for establishing a virtual office, and challenges to managing a virtual office.

Defining a Virtual Office   A **virtual office** is a work arrangement that extends beyond the structure and boundaries of the traditional office arrangement. Specifics of the arrangements vary from organization to organization but can be conceptualized using the alternative work arrangements continuum shown in Figure 13.8. This continuum is based on the degree of worker mobility reflected within a particular virtual office, moving from "occasional telecommuting" to "fully mobile." The definitions of the alternative work arrangements shown on the continuum follow.

A **virtual office** is a work arrangement that extends beyond the structure and boundaries of the traditional office arrangement.

Occasional Telecommuting   Workers have fixed, traditional offices and work schedules but occasionally work at home. In this situation, most are traditional workers in traditional office situations.

Hoteling   Workers come into the traditional office frequently, but because they are not always physically present, they are not allocated permanent office space. Instead, workers can

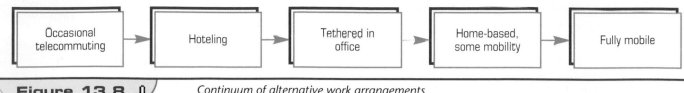

| Occasional telecommuting | → | Hoteling | → | Tethered in office | → | Home-based, some mobility | → | Fully mobile |

Figure 13.8 *Continuum of alternative work arrangements*

reserve a room or cubicle in advance of their arrival, sometimes called a "hotel room," where they can receive and return telephone calls and link into a computer network.

Tethered in Office "Tethered" workers have some mobility but are expected to report to the office on a regular basis. As an example, some tethered workers are expected to appear at the office in the morning to receive a cellular phone and portable computer. The equipment is returned to the office in the afternoon, sometimes accompanied by a meeting or progress report for the workday.

Home-Based, Some Mobility A home-based worker has no traditional office. The workspace of this type of worker could be a kitchen table or a bedroom desk. A home-based worker may visit customers or go outside the home occasionally, but his or her work is mainly done via the telephone or computer inside the home. Some companies support home-based workers through activities like leasing office furniture, providing computers, and procuring high-speed phone lines.

Fully Mobile A worker who is fully mobile works out of a car. In essence, the car is an office containing equipment like a cellular phone, portable computer, and fax machine. This type of worker is expected to be on the road or at work areas like customer locations during the entire workday, and they are typically field sales representatives or customer service specialists.

Reasons for Establishing a Virtual Office Managers design and implement virtual offices for many different reasons. Cost reduction is the most commonly cited reason, and real estate or rental costs are the most commonly cited costs to be reduced. Traditional office space needed for an organization can be reduced by over 50 percent by using virtual offices. Managers also use virtual offices to increase productivity. History in some organizations shows that people work faster and are interrupted less when working at home. Third, firms also establish virtual offices as part of redesigning jobs to make employees more effective and efficient. For example, some organizations need to decrease the amount of time necessary for eliminating customer problems. Some managers meet this need by establishing fully mobile customer service employees. According to the rationale, fully mobile customer service employees have a better chance of arriving at customer locations quickly than customer service employees in traditional offices, and thereby have a better chance of solving problems quickly.

Challenges to Managing a Virtual Office Undoubtedly, managers face many new and different challenges when using the virtual office concept. For example, virtual offices make it more difficult to build desired corporate culture. For employees, traditional offices represent a place to become familiar with fellow workers and socialize into a purposefully designed corporate culture. Due simply to their lack of proximity, employees working in virtual offices are more physically distant from other employees and more difficult for managers to build into the fabric of organizational culture. Another management challenge to using virtual offices is that such offices make it more difficult for managers to control workers. An individual's presence in a traditional office can give a manager constant feedback throughout the day concerning worker commitment and performance, whereas in a virtual office situation, it is not as easy. Last, virtual offices make communication more difficult. Planned or unplanned face-to-face communication that takes place in a traditional office is essentially nonexistent in a virtual office. As a result, management has a difficult time gathering information relevant to employee attitudes and work concerns.

►Back to the Case

This last chapter section contains material that illustrates the type of content the AWA team's report could feature. First, the AWA report could recommend establishing a virtual organization at AT&T. This type of recommendation would focus on keeping the essence of traditional organization, but without some aspects of traditional boundaries and structure. The team's recommendation probably would not propose drastic measures like establishing AT&T as a virtual corporation, but rather some degree of virtuality like establishing virtual teams.

As the Introductory Case indicates, the AWA team's actual recommendation focused on establishing a type of virtual office that had workers telecommute. Other options available for establishing a virtual office at AT&T could have included workers hoteling, tethered in the office, home-based with some mobility, or fully mobile. The AWA team's rationale for establishing this type of virtual office at AT&T probably included cost reductions due to rent savings and enhanced worker productivity.

The AWA team's report probably also included challenges that must be met in order for a newly established virtual office at AT&T to be successful. Perhaps the most significant of these challenges is appropriately integrating virtual workers into the AT&T corporate culture. The report probably reasoned that building good communication among AT&T's managers and virtual workers is an important step for integrating these workers into the culture and maintaining their continued presence. To build this communication, AT&T's managers could take steps like establishing regular communication times with virtual workers, publishing an online newsletter aimed at helping virtual workers deal with their unique problems, and having regular social events where virtual workers can meet and interact with other virtual workers as well as with AT&T's employees in traditional work settings.

Management Skills Module

This section is specially designed to help you develop management skills. An individual's management skill is based on an understanding of management concepts and the ability to apply those concepts in management situations. As a result, the following activities are designed both to heighten your understanding of management concepts and to help you gain facility in applying those concepts in various management situations.

UNDERSTANDING MANAGEMENT CONCEPTS

▶ Action Summary

Reread the learning objectives below. Each objective is followed by questions. Answering these questions accurately will help you retain the most important concepts discussed in this chapter. After answering each question, check your answer against the answer key at the end of this chapter. (*Hint:* If you have any doubts regarding the correct response, consult the page number that follows the answer.)

Circle:

From studying this chapter, I will attempt to acquire

1. A working definition of *changing an organization.*

   T F
   a. The purpose of organizational modifications is to increase the extent to which an organization accomplishes its objectives.

   a b c d e
   b. Organizational modifications typically include changing: (a) overall goals and objectives (b) established lines of organizational authority (c) levels of responsibility held by various organization members (d) b and c (e) all of the above.

2. An understanding of the relative importance of change and stability to an organization.

   a b c d e
   a. According to the Hellriegel and Slocum model, the following is the most likely outcome when both adaptation and stability are high: (a) high probability of slow death (b) high probability of survival (c) high probability of survival and growth (d) certainty of quick death (e) probability of slow death.

   T F
   b. According to Hellriegel and Slocum, repeated changes in an organization without concern for stability typically result in employees with a high degree of adaptability.

3. Some ability to recognize what kind of changes should be made within an organization.

   T F
   a. Although managers can choose to change an organization in many ways, most changes can be categorized as one of three kinds: (1) people change (2) goal or objective change and (3) technological change.

   a b c d e
   b. Decentralizing an organization is a structural change aimed at: (a) reducing the cost of coordination (b) increasing the controllability of subunits (c) increasing motivation (d) all of the above (e) a and b.

4. An appreciation for why the people affected by a change should be considered when the change is being made.

   a b c d e
   a. The following is *not* an example of personal loss that organization members fear as a result of change: (a) possibility of a reduction in personal prestige (b) disturbance of established social relationships (c) reduction in overall organizational productivity (d) personal failure because of an inability to carry out new job responsibilities (e) disturbance of established working relationships.

   T F
   b. Support for a proposed change may be altered by focusing attention on possible individual gains that could materialize as a result of the change.

5. Some facility at evaluating change.

   a b c d e
   a. Symptoms indicating that further change is necessary are that organization members: (a) are oriented more to the future than to the past (b) recognize the challenge of current problems more than the obligations of rituals (c) pay more allegiance to overall company goals than to departmental goals (d) none of the above (e) a and b.

   T F
   b. Additional organizational change is justified nowadays if the change results in greater profitability.

6. An understanding of how organizational change and stress are related.

T F   **a.** Stress is simply the rate of wear and tear on the body.

T F   **b.** From a managerial viewpoint, stress on employees can be either too high or too low.

T F   **c.** Stressors are the factors within an organization that reduce employee stress.

7. Knowledge about virtuality as a vehicle for organizational change.

a b c d e   **a.** The continuum of alternative work arrangements contains a work circumstance called: (a) work surfing (b) fully tethered (c) fully mobile (d) occasional hoteling (e) none of the above.

T F   **b.** Lowering expenses is the reason managers least cite for establishing a virtual office.

T F   **c.** Workers in virtual office work situations are harder for managers to control.

❱ Action Summary Answer Key

1. a. T, p. 280   **4. a.** c, p. 290   **6. a.** T, p. 291   **7. a.** c, pp. 295–296
    b. d, p. 280   **b.** T, p. 290   **6.** T, p. 292   **b.** F, p. 296
2. a. c, p. 281   **5. a.** d, pp. 290–291   **c.** F, p. 293   **c.** T, p. 296
    b. F, p. 281   **b.** T, p. 291
3. a. F, p. 283
    b. d, p. 285

❱ Issues for Review and Discussion

1. What is meant in this chapter by the phrase *changing an organization*?
2. Why do organizations typically undergo various changes?
3. Does an organization need both change and stability? Explain.
4. What major factors should a manager consider when changing an organization?
5. Define *change agent* and list the skills necessary to be a successful change agent.
6. Explain the term *organizational effectiveness* and describe the major factors that determine how effective an organization will be.
7. Describe the relationship between "determining what should be changed within an organization" and "choosing a kind of change for the organization."
8. What is the difference between structural change and people change?
9. Is matrix organization an example of a structural change? Explain.
10. Draw and explain the managerial grid.
11. Is grid OD an example of a technique used to make structural change? Explain.
12. What causes resistance to change?
13. List and explain the steps managers can take to minimize employee resistance to change.
14. How and why should managers evaluate the changes they make?
15. Define *stress* and explain how it influences performance.
16. List three stressors that could exist within an organization. For each stressor, discuss a specific management action that could be taken to reduce or eliminate it.
17. What effect can career counseling have on employee stress? Explain.
18. Define *virtual organization* and explain how different organizations can have different degrees of virtuality.
19. Discuss three challenges that you might face in managing a virtual organization. Be sure to explain why the issues you raise are indeed challenges.
20. Discuss three suggestions that you would make for maintaining good communication between a manager and workers in a virtual office situation.

APPLYING MANAGEMENT CONCEPTS

▶ Cases

➡ INTRODUCTORY CASE WRAP-UP

▶Case Discusssion Questions

"AT&T Changes Where and How People Work" (p. 279) and its related Back-to-the-Case sections were written to help you better understand the management concepts contained in this chapter. Answer the following discussion questions about this Introductory Case to further enrich your understanding of chapter content:

1. How complicated would it be for a change agent at AT&T to implement the change of establishing new work situations in the company? Explain.
2. Do you think that certain AT&T employees would subtly resist this change? Why or why not?
3. What elements of this change could cause organization members to experience stress, and what might the change agent do to help alleviate this stress? Be specific.

▶Skills Exercise: Building a Matrix Organization

The Introductory Case discusses AT&T's efforts to change where and how people work. Assume that you have been appointed a project manager at AT&T who is responsible for implementing needed changes in these areas. Draw a matrix organization chart that you would use to implement these needed changes. Explain in as much detail as possible how your matrix organization would function. The name your project has been given is "Alternative Work Project."

CASE STUDY: MY VIRTUAL CORP. PIONEERS EXTREME OUTSOURCING

Conflict experts say stress in the workplace is not only manageable, but also useful. Stress can help a company grow by pinpointing exactly what needs changing.

Entrepreneur Merrily Orsini has gone to great lengths to completely avoid corporate stress. As founder and CEO of an eldercare company, she managed 250 employees. "I felt like their mother. I didn't want to feel like that anymore," she says; so after 15 years, she sold her company.

At My Virtual Corp., her latest challenge is aiming for a stress-free, employee-free work zone. Merrily outsources work that has been outsourced to her by companies looking to cut cost; that way she no longer deals with employee conflict. These companies farm out work that isn't at the core of their business, like creating marketing brochures, logo designs, or employee benefit packages. They are looking for professionals with expertise in these areas whom they will not have to hire or train. Their only investment will be the payment for services of My Virtual Corp., which takes care of these things and presents the client with completed work at the agreed-upon date. There are no meetings, no wasted time, and no conflict. When things go well, the virtual experience minimizes stress and maximizes productivity for everyone.

Orsini has a five-member management team and 135 associates working on dozens of projects at one time. She has never even met most of them; they are her virtual employees. Orsini has only one full-time employee who oversees all work in progress and directs "team leaders" who then manage associates on a project deadline.

The 54-year-old Orsini vigilantly screens each job candidate who applies to My Virtual Corp. via a series of targeted questions on her Web site. She looks only for applicants who have at least five years of corporate experience in a niche market. "We don't look for people good at everything, because usually they're not good at anything," she explains. If they pass that stage, she hires them to work on a sample project for her. She makes sure they do high-quality work, that they know how to deal with a virtual environment, and they are able to meet deadlines. She truly believes that she is hiring the top 5 percent of America's workforce. "I'm amazed at the quality of people we get who want to work this way—it's like a gold mine," she says. Some people work for My Virtual Corp. because it allows them to focus on what they do best. Jen Cosgrove, a freelance advertising copywriter, does not like negotiating with clients. My Virtual Corp. does that for her, and she can concentrate on writing copy.

Orsini pays workers only after she has lined up a job, so she has "virtually" no overhead expenses. Her own office is in the basement of her home on a wooded property in the suburbs of Louisville. Her only full-time employee, Tammy Brown, works from her own house, and the 135 associates under her watchful eye are scattered across the United States and Canada.

According to a Dun & Bradstreet's survey, outsourcing is up 15 percent in large corporations since 1999 and up 25 percent in small businesses. Right now businesses need to compete in a global economy where information technology is making it possible to produce more in a shorter time with fewer employees. Orsini's virtual teams might just be the wave of the future.

Dress code, office hours, traffic jams, cultural differences, personal habits, friendships, and prejudices don't affect the work flow of Orsini's employees on-screen. My Virtual Corp.'s raw material is information, and its most valuable human resource is the professional team, skilled in obtaining quickly and effectively the precise information the client needs. Staff members are not monitored (though they easily could be) but are held accountable for a specific list of outcomes and expectations. Orsini believes in a system of mutual trust, empowering her workers to make their own decisions. She knows that the better her teams become at making judgments, the better it is for her clients and the goals of My Virtual Corp.

Because people can become overwhelmed by the workload, associates work *only on* projects they think they can complete without being overstressed. On a personal level, the virtual organization gives members enough time for outside activities and encourages them to belong to networking and business groups. This gives people an opportunity to exchange ideas with others.

Right now, Orsini's biggest challenge is marketing the company's services. My Virtual Corp.'s former vice president of sales and marketing Kelly Kitchen says many big corporations are afraid to give their work to a company whose employees have never even met one another. At first, all projects were delivered without any actual physical interaction between people, but when clients began asking for face-to-face meetings, Merrily complied and now routinely offers meetings as an option to her customers.

In the two years since My Virtual Corp. has been in business, Orsini has spent about $500,000 and expects to put in another $100,000 before the company's Web site and intranet are running smoothly. Revenues are expected to top $600,000 by the end of 2001. Plans for expansion into South Africa are currently under way—impressive growth for a start-up with a full-time staff of one.

QUESTIONS

1. Evaluate Orsini's goal to make My Virtual Corp. a stress-free work zone.
2. List three stressors that might exist in a virtual office setting. How would you ensure that these stressors do not negatively influence worker productivity?
3. What four tips to ensure good communication in a virtual office would you give Merrily Orsini? Why is each tip important?

▶ Video

MASTERING MANAGEMENT: EPISODE 5—ORGANIZATIONAL CHANGE

Mastering Management is a series of innovative, interactive learning activities specially designed to help you develop management skills emphasized in various text chapters. Organizational change is the major focus of this chapter. Episode 5 of *Mastering Management* focuses on changing an organization and illustrates how even a small, progressive company like CanGo can have difficulties in changing the way it operates. In the introductory video, Liz, CanGo's CEO, begins the process of changing her company. Review Episode 5, "Organizational Change" on your *Mastering Management* CD and then answer the following questions.

QUESTIONS

1. What should Liz know about adaptation, stability, and organizational survival as she thinks about changes at CanGo?

2. Does the concept of grid OD apply to even a small company like CanGo? Explain.

3. If you were making changes at CanGo, do you think that you would encounter resistance to the changes from employees? If so, how would you reduce the resistance?

www.prenhall.com/certo

This book is accompanied by a rich assortment of online activities aimed at developing your management skills. Reviewing news headlines, Internet exercises, an online study guide, and other research and Internet resources can help personalize management skills development for individual students or an entire class.

14 Fundamentals of Influencing and Communication

Eaton Managers Concentrate
on Influencing People

REMINDER: THE INTRODUCTORY CASE WRAP-UP (P. 321) CONTAINS DISCUSSION QUESTIONS AND A SKILLS EXERCISE TO FURTHER ILLUSTRATE THE APPLICATION OF CHAPTER CONCEPTS TO THIS VIGNETTE.

It is 7:30 A.M., time for the morning quiz at Eaton Corporation's factory. Ten union workers, each representing work teams, sit around a boardroom table. "What were our sales yesterday?" asks a supervisor at the head of the table. A worker, glancing at a computer printout, replies that they were $625,275. "And in the month?" From another worker comes the response: $6,172,666.

Eaton may not be a household name, and its products—including gears, engine valves, truck axles, and, at Lincoln, Nebraska, circuit breakers—aren't glamorous, but its success in raising

These team workers at Eaton Corporation are planning and evaluating their own work. The company provides them with the financial information and other data they need to make their own decisions.

productivity and cutting costs throws plenty of doubt on recent hand-wringing about unmotivated American workers and flaccid American corporations.

Getting people to think for themselves—and work in teams—is important to Eaton. The company starts by hiring managers who are not autocratic and training them to accept encroachments on their authority. Not everyone can hack it: When engineers at Lincoln were evicted from their office enclave and the department was moved out onto the shop floor, the department chief and a colleague quit in protest.

Managers who adjust, however, tend to stay at one plant a long time. The same person has been plant manager at Lincoln since 1980. The Kearney manager, Nebraskan Robert Dyer, is an area native who was hired as a machine operator in 1969, when the plant opened. That, too, is not unusual: 23 of Lincoln's salaried staff of 57 came up through the rank and file.

Management shares extensive data with employees. At Eaton's plant in Kearney, Nebraska, a TV monitor in the cafeteria indicates how specific shifts and departments did the previous day against their cost and performance goals. Lincoln gets the message out via computer printouts. "It gives you a sense of direction," says Ricky Rigg, a metal fabricator, "and makes you appreciate what you do more."

At Kearney, where workers labor amid the noise and heat of hot forged metal, bonuses are based on the entire plant's performance compared with the prior year. In one quarter, for instance, Kearney

(continued)

topped the year-earlier profit and cost criteria by 7 percent—and workers got a quarterly bonus of 7 percent, or about $500 each. Kearney employees have regularly earned a quarterly bonus since the system was introduced.

There's noncash recognition as well. As a celebration, the Kearney plant recently held a lunchtime barbecue to mark the first shift's 365th consecutive day without any injuries. The plant manager and his staff prepared the meal—hamburgers, hot dogs, potato salad, and baked beans—while the first shift chowed down.

Eaton's management is pleased with the performance of its Kearney plant. As an indication of this performance, Ford Motor Company has given quality awards to Eaton for the high-quality automobile components that it supplies.

Due to its success at the Kearney plant, Eaton recently opened another plant in nearby Hastings, Nebraska. Management wants to hire the same type of people in Hastings as they have in Kearney. A company spokesman said that the people hired in Hastings are living up to the reputation established by Eaton's 800 associates in the company's top component plant in Kearney. If people are managed in the Hastings plant similarly to the way they are managed in the Kearney plant, the Hastings plant can be as successful as the Kearney plant.

What's Ahead

In the Introductory Case, Eaton Corporation's success in enhancing company productivity and efficiency is credited largely to how its managers manage people. According to the case, Eaton managers encourage employees to think for themselves, to make decisions about who is hired at Eaton, and to make changes in the organization that will result in improvements. The information in this chapter emphasizes the value of such managers and offers insights into what additional steps managers might take to guide organization members' activities in directions that lead to the attainment of management system objectives. The chapter is divided into two main parts:

1) Fundamentals of influencing
2) Communication

FUNDAMENTALS OF INFLUENCING

The four basic managerial functions—planning, organizing, influencing, and controlling—where introduced in Chapter 1. *Planning* and *organizing* have already been discussed; *influencing* is the third of these basic functions covered in this text. A definition of *influencing* and a discussion of the influencing subsystem follow.

Defining Influencing

Influencing is the process of guiding the activities of organization members in appropriate directions. *Appropriate directions*, of course, are those that lead to the attainment of management system objectives. Influencing involves focusing on organization members as people and dealing with such issues as morale, arbitration of conflicts, and the development of good working relationships. It is a critical part of a manager's job. In fact, the ability to influence others is a primary determinant of how successful a manager will be.[1]

> **Influencing** is the process of guiding the activities of organization members in appropriate directions. It involves the performance of four management activities: (1) leading, (2) motivating, (3) considering groups, and (4) communicating.

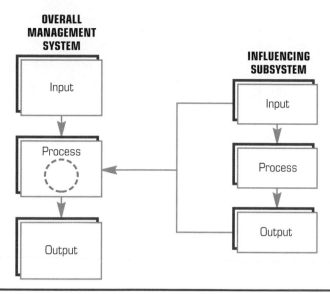

Relationship between overall management system and influencing subsystem

Figure 14.1

The Influencing Subsystem

Like the planning and organizing functions, the influencing function can be viewed as a subsystem within the overall management system (see Figure 14.1). The primary purpose of the influencing subsystem, as stated above, is to enhance the attainment of management system objectives by guiding the activities of organization members in appropriate directions.

Figure 14.2 shows the constituents of the influencing subsystem. The input of this subsystem is composed of a portion of the total resources of the overall management system, and its output is appropriate organization member behavior. The process of the influencing subsystem involves the performance of four primary management activities:

1. Leading
2. Motivating
3. Considering groups
4. Communicating

Managers transform a portion of organizational resources into appropriate organization member behavior mainly by performing these four activities.

As Figure 14.2 shows, leading, motivating, and considering groups are interrelated. Managers accomplish each of these influencing activities, to some extent, by communicating with organization members. For example, managers can only decide what kind of leader they need to be after they analyze the characteristics of the various groups with which they will interact and determine how those groups can best be motivated. Then, regardless of the leadership strategy they adopt, their leading, motivating, and working with groups will be accomplished—at least party—through communication with other organization members.

In fact, all management activities are accomplished at least partly through communication or communication-related endeavors. Because communication is used repeatedly by managers, ability to communicate is often referred to as the fundamental management skill.

A recent survey of chief executives supports this notion that communication is the fundamental management skill. The results, which appear in Table 14.1 on page 307, show that CEOs ranked oral and written communication skills first (along with interpersonal skills) among the skills that should be taught to management students.

▶ Back to the Case

One of the primary functions of Eaton's management is influencing—guiding the activities of Eaton's employees to enhance the accomplishment of organizational objectives. Illustrations in

(continued)

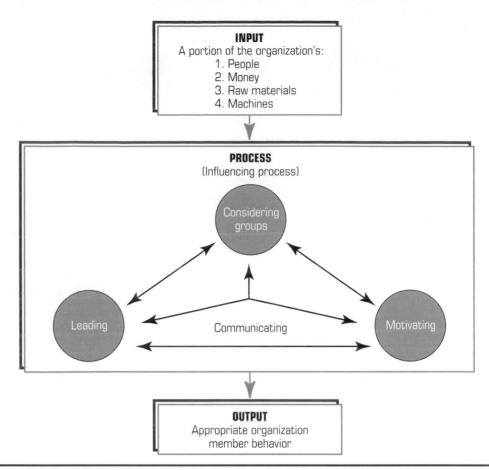

INPUT
A portion of the organization's:
1. People
2. Money
3. Raw materials
4. Machines

PROCESS
(Influencing process)

Considering groups

Leading

Communicating

Motivating

OUTPUT
Appropriate organization member behavior

Figure 14.2

The influencing subsystem

the case give clear examples of how the company influences people through leadership (hiring managers who aren't autocratic), motivation (granting cash and noncash rewards for jobs done well), managing groups (operating work teams to enhance company success), and communicating (giving workers feedback on exactly how well they are doing).

Of all of these influencing activities, communication is the most important. In subsequent Back-to-the-Case sections, discussion will focus on communication as it relates to Robert Dyer, Eaton's plant manager in Lincoln, Nebraska. As mentioned in the Introductory Case, Dyer communicates to employees how well the plant is performing, what problems and challenges it faces, and how those problems and challenges will be addressed. Communication, in fact, is the main tool through which he accomplishes his duties as plant manager. Almost any work that Dyer does at Eaton (planning, organizing, or controlling) requires him to communicate with other Eaton employees. In essence, Dyer must be a good communicator if he is to be a successful plant manager.

Communication is discussed further in the rest of this chapter. Leading, motivating, and considering groups are discussed in Chapters 15, 16, and 17, respectively.

COMMUNICATION

Communication is the process of sharing information with other individuals. Information, as used here, is any thought or idea that managers desire to share with other individuals. In general, communication involves one person projecting a message to one or more other people that results in everyone's arriving at a common understanding of the message. Because communication is a commonly used management skill and ability and is often cited as the skill

Joe Torre, manager of the New York Yankees, heads a major league baseball team steeped in tradition. Recent accomplishments of the team reflect this history; for example, in 1998, the Yankees swept the San Diego Padres in the World Series. In 1999, the Yankees completed a four-game sweep of the Atlanta Braves to capture their 25th World Championship. In 2000, the Yankees won their 26th World Championship by defeating the New York Mets in five games, the first "Subway Series" since 1956.

Most would agree that Joe Torre gets the most out of his workers, the players. Many in the Yankees organization see him as a type of organizational psychologist. Overall, Torre seems to have an uncanny ability to look inside another person and see what motivates

him. His management style primarily involves personal talks with players rather than impersonal team meetings. Roger Clemens, one of Torre's pitchers, believes that Torre has been a success because he knows how to build a player's confidence. Paul O'Neill, one of Torre's famous outfielders, believes that players like to perform well for Torre because he doesn't put undue pressure on them when they're not performing well. Overall, Torre seems to be a master at influencing his players appropriately, encouraging them to do their best to contribute to Yankees wins.

Torre doesn't run a *Fortune* 500 company, and perhaps couldn't. How he influences the players to create success, however, is important for all managers to understand. ■

most responsible for a manager's success, prospective managers must learn how to communicate. To help managers become better interpersonal communicators, new training techniques are constantly being developed and evaluated.[2]

The communication activities of managers generally involve interpersonal communication—sharing information with other organization members. The following sections feature both the general topic of interpersonal communication and the more specific topic of interpersonal communication in organizations.

Interpersonal Communication

To be a successful interpersonal communicator, a manager must understand the following:

1. How interpersonal communication works
2. The relationship between feedback and interpersonal communication
3. The importance of verbal versus nonverbal interpersonal communication

	Chief Executives, Ranking of Skills They Believe Should Be Taught to Management Students	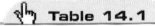 Table 14.1

Rank[a]	Key Learning Area	Frequency Indicated
1	Oral and written communication skills	25
1	Interpersonal skills	25
3	Financial/managerial accounting skills	22
4	Ability to think, be analytical, and make decisions	20
5	Strategic planning and goal setting—concern for long-term performance	13
6	Motivation and commitment to the firm—giving 110%	12
7	Understanding of economics	11
8	Management information systems and computer applications	9
8	Thorough knowledge of your business, culture, and overall environment	9
8	Marketing concept (the customer is king) and skills	9
11	Integrity	7
11	Knowledge of yourself: setting long- and short-term career objectives	7
13	Leadership skills	6
13	Understanding of the functional areas of the business	6
13	Time management: setting priorities—how to work smart, not long or hard	1

[a]1 is most important.

How Interpersonal Communication Works   Interpersonal communication is the process of transmitting information to others.[3] To be complete, the process must have the following three basic elements:

1. *The source/encoder*—The **source/encoder** is the person in the interpersonal communication situation who originates and encodes information to be shared with others. Encoding is putting information into a form that can be received and understood by another individual. Putting one's thoughts into a letter is an example of encoding. Until information is encoded, it cannot be shared with others. (From here on, the *source/encoder* will be referred to simply as the *source.*)
2. *The signal*—Encoded information that the source intends to share constitutes a **message.** A message that has been transmitted from one person to another is called a **signal.**
3. *The decoder/destination*—The **decoder/destination** is the person or persons with whom the source is attempting to share information. This person receives the signal and decodes, or interprets, the message to determine its meaning. Decoding is the process of converting messages back into information. In all interpersonal communication situations, message meaning is a result of decoding. (From here on, the *decoder/destination* will be referred to simply as the *destination.*)

The classic work of Wilbur Schramm clarifies the role played by each of the three elements of the interpersonal communication process. As implied in Figure 14.3, the source determines what information to share, encodes this information in the form of a message, and then transmits the message as a signal to the destination. The destination decodes the transmitted message to determine its meaning and then responds accordingly.

A manager who desires to assign the performance of a certain task to a subordinate would use the communication process in the following way: First, the manager would determine exactly what task he or she wanted the subordinate to perform. Then the manager would encode and transmit a message to the subordinate that would accurately reflect this assignment. The message transmission itself could be as simple as the manager's telling the subordinate what the new responsibilities include. Next, the subordinate would decode the message transmitted by the manager to ascertain its meaning and then respond to it appropriately.

Successful and Unsuccessful Interpersonal Communication **Successful communication** refers to an interpersonal communication situation in which the information the source intends to share with the destination and the meaning the destination derives from the transmitted message are the same. Conversely, **unsuccessful communication** is an interpersonal communication situation in which the information the source intends to share with the destination and the meaning the destination derives from the transmitted message are different.

To increase the probability that communication will be successful, the message must be encoded so that the source's experience of the way a signal should be decoded is equivalent to the destination's experience of the way it should be decoded. If this is done, the probability is high that the destination will interpret the signal as intended by the source. Figure 14.4 illustrates these overlapping fields of experience that ensure successful communication.

On sunny days, Mike Bouissey takes his notebook computer and heads for the roof of Philadelphia's Center City, where his employer, WebLinc, is located. A project manager for the firm, Bouissey relies on technology to keep him constantly in touch with clients and coworkers. He forwards calls to his cell phone and uses radio waves to access the company's LAN on his notebook computer, through which he also sends and receives e-mail, builds Web pages, and tracks the progress of his WebLinc team. Says Bouissey of today's communications technology, "You can get away and still be connected."

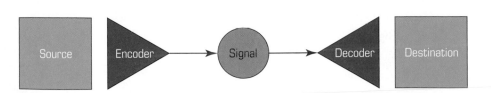

Figure 14.3   *Role of the source, signal, and destination in the communication process*

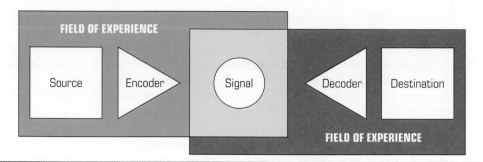

FIELD OF EXPERIENCE

Source → Encoder → Signal ← Decoder ← Destination

FIELD OF EXPERIENCE

Overlapping fields of experience that ensure successful communication

Figure 14.4

Barriers to Successful Interpersonal Communication   Factors that decrease the probability that communication will be successful are called *communication barriers*. A clear understanding of these barriers will help managers maximize their communication success. The following sections discuss both communication macrobarriers and communication microbarriers.

Macrobarriers.   **Communication macrobarriers** are factors that hinder successful communication in a general communication situation.[4] These factors relate primarily to the communication environment and the larger world in which communication takes place. Some common macrobarriers are the following:[5]

1. *The increasing need for information*—Because society is changing constantly and rapidly, individuals have a greater and greater need for information. This growing need tends to overload communication networks, thereby distorting communication. To minimize the effects of this barrier, managers should take steps to ensure that organization members are not overloaded with information. Only information critical to the performance of their jobs should be transmitted to them.

2. *The need for increasingly complex information*—Because of today's rapid technological advances, most people are confronted with complex communication situations in their everyday lives. If managers take steps to emphasize simplicity in communication, the effects of this barrier can be lessened. Furnishing organization members with adequate training to deal with more technical areas is another strategy for overcoming this barrier.

3. *The reality that people in the United States are increasingly coming into contact with people who use languages other than English*—As U.S. business becomes more international in scope and as organization members travel more frequently, the need to know languages other than English increases. The potential communication barrier of this multilanguage situation is obvious. Moreover, people who deal with foreigners need to be familiar not only with their languages, but also with their cultures. Formal knowledge of a foreign language is of little value unless the individual knows which words, phrases, and actions are culturally acceptable.

4. *The constant need to learn new concepts cuts down on the time available for communication*—Many managers feel pressured to learn new and important concepts that they did not have to know in the past. Learning about the intricacies of international business or computer usage, for example, takes up significant amounts of managerial time. Many managers also find that the increased demands that training employees makes on their time leaves them with less time for communicating with other organization members.

Microbarriers.   **Communication microbarriers** are factors that hinder successful communication in a specific communication situation.[6] These factors relate directly to such variables as the communication message, the source, and the destination. Among the microbarriers are the following:[7]

1. *The source's view of the destination*—The source in any communication situation has a tendency to view the destination in a specific way, and this view influences the messages sent. For example, individuals usually speak differently to people they think are informed about a subject than to those they believe are uninformed. The destination can sense the

Unsuccessful communication refers to an interpersonal communication situation in which the information the source intends to share with the destination and the meaning the destination derives from the transmitted message are different.

Communication macrobarriers are factors hindering successful communication that relate primarily to the communication environment and the larger world in which communication takes place.

Communication microbarriers are factors hindering successful communication that relate primarily to such variables as the communication message, the source, and the destination.

source's attitudes, which often block successful communication. Managers should keep an open mind about the people with whom they communicate and be careful not to imply any negative attitudes through their communication behaviors.

2. *Message interference*—Stimuli that compete with the communication message for the attention of the destination are called **message interference,** or noise. An instance of message interference is a manager talking to an office worker while the worker is trying to input data into a word processor. The inputting of data is message interference here because it is competing with the manager's communication message. Managers should attempt to communicate only when they have the total attention of the individuals with whom they wish to share information. An amusing example of message interference is depicted in the cartoon below.

3. *The destination's view of the source*—Certain attitudes of the destination toward the source can also hinder successful communication. If, for example, a destination believes that the source has little credibility in the area about which the source is communicating, the destination may filter out much of the source's message and pay only slight attention to that part of the message actually received. Managers should attempt to consider the worth of messages transmitted to them independently of their personal attitudes toward the source. Many valuable ideas will escape them if they allow their personal feelings toward others to influence which messages they attend to.

4. *Perception*—**Perception** is an individual's interpretation of a message. Different individuals may perceive the same message in very different ways. The two primary factors that influence how a stimulus is perceived are the destination's education level and the destination's amount of experience. To minimize the negative effects of this perceptual factor on interpersonal communication, managers should try to send messages with precise meanings. Ambiguous words generally tend to magnify negative perceptions.

5. *Multimeaning words*—Because many words in the English language have several meanings, a destination may have difficulty deciding which meaning should be attached to the words of a message. A manager should not assume that a word means the same thing to all the people who use it.

A classic study by Lydia Strong substantiates this point. Strong concluded that for the 500 most common words in our language, there are 4,070 different dictionary definitions. On the average, each of these words has over 18 usages. The word *run* is an example:[8]

> *Babe Ruth scored a* run.
> *Did you ever see Jesse Owens* run?
> *I have a* run *in my stocking.*
> *There is a fine* run *of salmon this year.*
> *Are you going to* run *this company or am I?*
> *You have the* run *of the place.*
> *What headline do you want to* run?
> *There was a* run *on the bank today.*
> *Did he* run *the ship aground?*
> *I have to* run *(drive the car) downtown.*

BEETLE BAILEY ®   **By Mort Walker**

Who will run *for president this year?*
Joe flies the New York–Chicago run *twice a week.*
You know the kind of people they run *around with.*
The apples run *large this year.*
Please run *my bathwater.*

When encoding information, managers should be careful to define the terms they are using whenever possible, never use obscure meanings for words when designing messages, and strive to use words in the same way their destination uses them.

► Back to the Case

In discussing Robert Dyer's ability to communicate, we are really discussing his ability to share ideas with other Eaton employees. For Dyer to be a successful communicator, he must concentrate on the three essential elements of the communication process. The first element is the source—the individual who wishes to share information with another. In this case, the source is Dyer. The second element is the signal—the message transmitted by Dyer. The third element is the destination—the Eaton employee with whom Dyer wishes to share information. Dyer should communicate with Eaton's employees by first determining exactly what information he wants to share, encoding the information, and only then transmitting the message. Communication is complete when his subordinates interpret the message and respond accordingly. Dyer's communication would be termed successful if his subordinates interpreted his messages as he intended.

If Dyer is to be a successful communicator, he must also learn to minimize the impact of numerous communication barriers. These barriers include the following:

1. Eaton's employees need to have more information and more complex information to do their jobs
2. Message interference
3. Dyer's view of the destination as well as the destination's view of Dyer
4. The perceptual processes of the people involved in the communication attempt
5. Multimeaning words

Feedback and Interpersonal Communication   **Feedback** is the destination's reaction to a message. Feedback can be used by the source to ensure successful communication. For example, if the destination's message reaction is inappropriate, the source can conclude that communication was unsuccessful and that another message should be transmitted. If the destination's message reaction is appropriate, the source can conclude that communication was successful (assuming, of course, that the appropriate reaction did not happen merely by chance). Because of its potentially high value, managers should encourage feedback whenever possible and evaluate it carefully.[9]

Feedback is, in the interpersonal communication situation, the destination's reaction to a message.

Gathering and Using Feedback   Feedback can be either verbal or nonverbal.[10] To gather verbal feedback, the source can simply ask the destination pertinent message-related questions; the destination's answers should indicate whether the message was perceived as intended. To gather nonverbal feedback, the source can observe the destination's nonverbal response to a message. Say a manager has transmitted a message to a subordinate specifying new steps that must be taken in the normal performance of the subordinate's job. Assuming there are no other problems, if the subordinate does not follow the steps accurately, this constitutes nonverbal feedback telling the manager that the initial message needs to be clarified.

If managers discover that their communication effectiveness is relatively low over an extended period of time, they should assess the situation to determine how to improve their communication skills. It may be that their vocabulary is confusing to their destinations. For example, a study conducted by Group Attitudes Corporation found that when managers used certain words repeatedly in communicating with steelworkers, the steelworkers usually became confused.[11] Among the words causing confusion were *accrue, contemplate, designate, detriment, magnitude,* and *subsequently.*

Achieving Communication Effectiveness　In general, managers can sharpen their communication skills by adhering to the following "ten commandments of good communication" as closely as possible:[12]

1. *Seek to clarify your ideas before communicating*—The more systematically you analyze the problem or idea to be communicated, the clearer it becomes. This is the first step toward effective communication. Many communications fail because of inadequate planning. Good planning must consider the goals and attitudes of those who will receive the communication and those who will be affected by it.

2. *Examine the true purpose of each communication*—Before you communicate, ask yourself what you really want to accomplish with your message—obtain information, initiate action, change another person's attitude? Identify your most important goal and then adapt your language, tone, and total approach to serve that specific objective. Don't try to accomplish too much with each communication. The sharper the focus of your message, the greater its chances of success.

3. *Consider the total physical and human setting whenever you communicate*—Meaning and intent are conveyed by more than words alone. Many other factors influence the overall impact of a communication, and managers must be sensitive to the total setting in which they communicate. Consider, for example, your sense of timing—that is, the circumstances under which you make an announcement or render a decision; the physical setting—whether you communicate in private or otherwise, for example, the social climate that pervades work relationships within your company or department and sets the tone of its communications; and custom and practice—the degree to which your communication conforms to, or departs from, the expectations of your audience. Be constantly aware of the total setting in which you communicate. Like all living things, communication must be capable of adapting to its environment.

4. *Consult with others, when appropriate, in planning communications*—Frequently, it is desirable or necessary to seek the participation of others in planning a communication or in developing the facts on which to base the communication. Such consultation often lends additional insight and objectivity to your message. Moreover, those who have helped you plan your communication will give it their active support.

5. *Be mindful of the overtones while you communicate rather than merely the basic content of your message*—Your tone of voice, your expression, your apparent receptiveness to the responses of others—all have a significant effect on those you wish to reach. Frequently overlooked, these subtleties of communication often affect a listener's reaction to a message even more than its basic content. Similarly, your choice of language—particularly your awareness of the fine shades of meaning and emotion in the words you use—predetermines in large part the reactions of your listeners.

6. *Take the opportunity, when it arises, to convey something of help or value to the receiver*—Consideration of the other person's interests and needs—trying to look at things from the other person's point of view—frequently points out opportunities to convey something of immediate benefit or long-range value to the other person. Subordinates are most responsive to managers whose messages take the subordinates' interests into account.

7. *Follow up your communication*—Your best efforts at communication may be wasted, and you may never know whether you have succeeded in expressing your true meaning and intent, if you do not follow up to see how well you have put your message across. You can do this by asking questions, by encouraging the receiver to express his or her reactions, by following up on contacts, and by subsequently reviewing performance. Make certain that you get feedback for every important communication so that complete understanding and appropriate action result.

8. *Communicate for tomorrow as well as today*—Even though communications may be aimed primarily at meeting the demands of an immediate situation, they must be planned with the past in mind if they are to be viewed as consistent by the receiver. Most importantly, however, communications must be consistent with long-range interests and goals. For example, it is not easy to communicate frankly on such matters as poor performance or the shortcomings of a loyal subordinate, but postponing disagreeable communications makes these matters more difficult in the long run and is actually unfair to your subordinates and your company.

9. *Be sure your actions support your communications*—In the final analysis, the most persuasive kind of communication is not what you say, but what you do. When your actions or attitudes contradict your words, others tend to discount what you have said. For every manager, this means that good supervisory practices—such as clear assignment of responsibility and authority, fair rewards for effort, and sound policy enforcement—communicate more than all the gifts of oratory.

10. *Last, but by no means least: Seek not only to be understood, but also to understand—be a good listener*—When you start talking, you often cease to listen, or at least to be attuned to the other person's unspoken reactions and attitudes. Even more serious is the occasional inattentiveness you may be guilty of when others are attempting to communicate with you. Listening is one of the most important, most difficult, and most neglected skills in communication. It demands that you concentrate, not only on the explicit meanings another person is expressing, but also on the implicit meanings, unspoken words, and undertones that may be far more significant.

Verbal and Nonverbal Interpersonal Communication

Interpersonal communication is generally divided into two types: verbal and nonverbal. Up to this point, the chapter has emphasized **verbal communication**—communication that uses either spoken or written words to share information with others.

Nonverbal communication is the sharing of information without using words to encode thoughts. Factors commonly used to encode thoughts in nonverbal communication are gestures, vocal tones, and facial expressions.[13] In most interpersonal communication, verbal and nonverbal communications are not mutually exclusive. Instead, the destination's interpretation of a message is generally based both on the words contained in the message and on such nonverbal factors as the source's gestures and facial expressions.

Verbal communication is the sharing of information through words, either written or spoken.

Nonverbal communication is the sharing of information without using words.

The Importance of Nonverbal Communication

In an interpersonal communication situation in which both verbal and nonverbal factors are present, nonverbal factors may have more influence on the total effect of the message. Over two decades ago, Albert Mehrabian developed the following formula to show the relative contributions of verbal and nonverbal factors to the total effect of a message: Total message impact = .07 words + .38 vocal tones + .55 facial expressions. Other nonverbal factors besides vocal tones that can influence the effect of a verbal message are facial expressions, gestures, gender, and dress. Managers who are aware of this great potential influence of nonverbal factors on the effect of their communications will use nonverbal message ingredients to complement their verbal message ingredients whenever possible.[14]

Nonverbal messages can also be used to add content to verbal messages. For instance, a head might be nodded or a voice toned to show either agreement or disagreement.

▶ Nonverbal communication uses symbols, gestures, and facial expressions to convey meaning without words. These brokers on the Chicago Mercantile Exchange are reacting to a drop in stock prices that followed an announcement by the Federal Reserve late in 2000.

Managers must be especially careful when they are communicating that verbal and nonverbal factors do not present contradictory messages. For example, if the words of a message express approval while the nonverbal factors express disapproval, the result will be message ambiguity that leaves the destination frustrated.

Managers who are able to communicate successfully through a blend of verbal and nonverbal communication are critical to the success of virtually every organization. In fact, a recent survey of corporate recruiters across the United States, commissioned by the Darden Graduate School of Business at the University of Virginia, revealed that the skill organizations most seek in prospective employees is facility at verbal and nonverbal communication.

▶ Back to the Case

Employee's reactions to Dyer's messages can provide him with perhaps his most useful tool for honing his communication skills—feedback. He must be alert to both verbal and nonverbal feedback. When feedback seems inappropriate, Dyer should transmit another message to clarify the meaning of his first one. Over time, if feedback indicates that he is a relatively unsuccessful communicator, he should analyze his situation carefully to improve his communication effectiveness. He might find, for instance, that he is using a vocabulary that is generally inappropriate for certain employees or that he is not following one or more of the 10 commandments of good communication.

In addition, Dyer must remember that he communicates to others without using words. His facial expressions, gestures, even the tone of his voice say things to his employees. In most communication situations, in fact, Dyer is sending both verbal and nonverbal messages to Eaton's employees. Because a message's impact is often most dependent on its nonverbal components, Dyer must make certain that his nonverbal messages complement his verbal messages.

Interpersonal Communication in Organizations

To be effective communicators, managers must understand not only general interpersonal communication concepts, but also the characteristics of interpersonal communication within organizations, or **organizational communication.** Organizational communication directly relates to the goals, functions, and structure of human organizations.[15] To a major extent, organizational success is determined by the effectiveness of organizational communication.

Although organizational communication was frequently referred to by early management writers, the topic did not receive systematic study and attention until after World War II. From World War II through the 1950s, the discipline of organizational communication made significant advances in such areas as mathematical communication theory and behavioral communication theory, and the emphasis on organizational communication has grown stronger in colleges of business throughout the nation since the 1970s.[16] The following sections focus on three fundamental organizational communication topics:

1. Formal organizational communication
2. Informal organizational communication
3. The encouragement of formal organizational communication

Formal Organizational Communication In general, organizational communication that follows the lines of the organization chart is called **formal organizational communication.**[17] As discussed in Chapter 10, the organization chart depicts relationships of people and jobs and shows the formal channels of communication among them.

Types of Formal Organizational Communication There are three basic types of formal organizational communication:

1. Downward
2. Upward
3. Lateral

Downward organizational communication is communication that flows from any point on an organization chart downward to another point on the organization chart. This type of

Organizational communication is interpersonal communication within organizations.

Formal organizational communication is organizational communication that follows the lines of the organization chart.

Downward organizational communication is communication that flows from any point on an organization chart downward to another point on the organization chart.

formal organizational communication relates primarily to the direction and control of employees. Job-related information that focuses on what activities are required, when they should be performed, and how they should be coordinated with other activities within the organization must be transmitted to employees. This downward communication typically includes a statement of organizational philosophy, management system objectives, position descriptions, and other written information relating to the importance, rationale, and interrelationships of various departments.

Upward organizational communication is communication that flows from any point on an organization chart upward to another point on the organization chart.[18] This type of organizational communication contains primarily the information managers need to evaluate the organizational area for which they are responsible and to determine if something is going wrong within it. Techniques that managers commonly use to encourage upward organizational communication are informal discussions with employees, attitude surveys, the development and use of grievance procedures, suggestion systems, and an "open door" policy that invites employees to come in whenever they would like to talk to management.[19] Organizational modifications based on the feedback provided by upward organizational communication will enable a company to be more successful in the future.

Lateral organizational communication is communication that flows from any point on an organization chart horizontally to another point on the organization chart. Communication that flows across the organization usually focuses on coordinating the activities of various departments and developing new plans for future operating periods. Within the organization, all departments are related to all other departments. Only through lateral communication can these departmental relationships be coordinated well enough to enhance the attainment of management system objectives.

▶ Open, inviting office spaces in bright and cheerful colors are a trend in organizational decor in some industries. Some people feel they encourage formal organizational communication in all directions, although employees may need to adjust to the relative lack of privacy that comes with extremely open spaces. Jay Chiat, of the advertising agency TBWA Chiat/Day, is shown here enjoying his own "virtual office."

ACROSS INDUSTRIES

Local Government—How David Bell Communicates with City Employees

The previous information discusses organizational communication and describes various directions in which it can occur. David Bell, a city administrator in Columbus, Nebraska, understands that sound organizational communication is important in building successful city government. Bell believes that public administrators should encourage employee participation and feedback on such issues as working conditions, employee benefits, and personnel policies. To encourage this feedback, Bell constantly strives to maintain good relationships with diverse employee groups like police officers, firefighters, and street maintenance workers.

According to Bell, public administrators must make a serious effort to improve the quality of communication in their organizations. Local government employees want to know more about their organizations, and a lack of information flowing from administrators to employees forces employees to rely on the local newspaper and the rumor mill as their two primary sources of information. Unless employees are kept informed of a local government's activities, they seek out information elsewhere—and that information may be drastically incorrect. Also, administrators should strive to improve organizational communication because such improvement generally leads to improved employee relations and, resultantly, better city government.

Bell has his own style in staff meetings. These meetings with department heads occur directly after the city council meets. Bell presents issues and official actions of the council in a written summary. Department heads then post the meeting summary on all employee bulletin boards on the same day to ensure that employees have quick access to the information.

According to Bell's philosophy, communicating with employees is also the key to updating and improving personnel policies. City government personnel policies should be updated annually to reflect both changes in employment law and organizational and employee needs. Bell encourages all departments to review and suggest changes in personnel policies. City employees are aware of problems in the day-to-day administration of these policies and generally have excellent ideas for improvement. In addition, employee participation in improving such policies leads to greater employee acceptance of the policies and greater ease for Bell in implementing the policies.

Modern managers in city governments face the serious and formidable challenge of building successful organizations. Building sound organizational communication within city government seems to be an important key to meeting this challenge.

Upward organizational communication is communication that flows from any point on an organization chart upward to another point on the organization chart.

Lateral organizational communication is communication that flows from any point on an organization chart horizontally to another point on the organization chart.

A **serial transmission** involves the passing of information from one individual to another in a series.

Patterns of Formal Organizational Communication   By its very nature, organizational communication creates patterns of communication among organization members. These patterns evolve from the repeated occurrence of various serial transmissions of information. According to Haney, a **serial transmission** involves passing information from one individual to another in a series. It occurs under the following circumstances:[20]

> A *communicates a message to* B; B *then communicates A's message (or rather his or her interpretation of A's message) to* C; C *then communicates his or her interpretation of B's interpretation of A's message to* D; *and so on. The originator and the ultimate recipient of the message are separated by middle people.*

One obvious weakness of a serial transmission is that messages tend to become distorted as the length of the series increases. Research has shown that message details may be omitted, altered, or added in a serial transmission.

The potential inaccuracy of transmitted messages is not the only weakness of serial transmissions. A classic article by Alex Bavelas and Dermot Barrett[21] makes the case that serial transmissions can also influence morale, the emergence of a leader, the degree to which individuals involved in the transmissions are organized, and their efficiency. Three basic organizational communication patterns and the corresponding effects on the variables just mentioned are shown in Figure 14.5.

▶ Back to the Case

As a plant manager at Eaton, Robert Dyer must strive to understand the intricacies of organizational communication—that is, interpersonal communication as it takes place within the organization—since this is such an important factor in determining the company's level of success. Dyer can communicate with his people in two basic ways: formally and informally.

In general, Dyer's formal communication should follow the lines on the organization chart. He can communicate downward to, for example, a department head, or he can communicate upward to, for example, George Dettloff, Eaton's engine components division general manager and Dyer's boss, as mentioned in the Introductory Case. Dyer's downward communication will commonly focus on the activities his subordinates are performing. His upward communication will usually concentrate on how the company is performing. Dyer can get

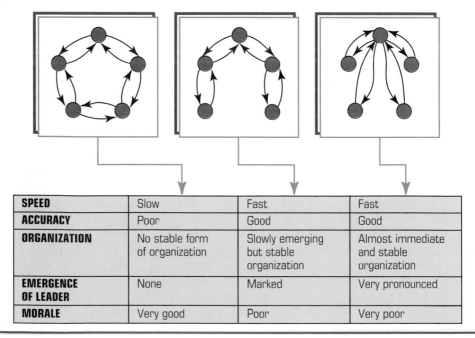

SPEED	Slow	Fast	Fast
ACCURACY	Poor	Good	Good
ORGANIZATION	No stable form of organization	Slowly emerging but stable organization	Almost immediate and stable organization
EMERGENCE OF LEADER	None	Marked	Very pronounced
MORALE	Very good	Poor	Very poor

Figure 14.5    *Comparison of three patterns of organizational communication on the variables of speed, accuracy, organization, emergence of leader, and morale*

advice on problems and improve coordination by communicating laterally with other plant managers, like the manager of Eaton's Lincoln, Nebraska, plant. He should take steps to ensure that lateral communication also occurs at other organizational levels to enhance planning and coordination within his plant.

Enhanced Formal Communication Contributes to Improving Quality at Holiday Inn

Improving the flow of communication dictated by the organization chart can be of immense benefit to an organization. Holiday Inn discovered that improving the flow of such communication enhanced the quality of customer service throughout the organization.

Marketing and product quality were the themes at a recent Holiday Inn Worldwide Franchise Conference. Individual Holiday Inn operators expressed more confidence in the company after it announced it had a new plan to improve customer service as well as customer attitudes toward Holiday Inn by improving Holiday Inn's for-

mal communication system. The company stated it would extend its satellite communication system into Europe to allow for more efficient communication of hotel room rate information between North American and European operations.

Mike Leven, president of the Holiday Inn franchise division, said that franchisees have always depended on Holiday Inn's commitment to maintaining quality service. Company Chairman Bryan Langton believes that this focus on quality has helped Holiday Inn outperform others in the industry in occupancy rates in recent years. ■

Informal Organizational Communication   **Informal organizational communication** is organizational communication that does not follow the lines of the organization chart.[22] Instead, this type of communication typically follows the pattern of personal relationships among organization members: One friend communicates with another friend, regardless of their relative positions on the organization chart. Informal organizational communication networks generally exist because organization members have a desire for information that is not furnished through formal organizational communication.

> **Informal organizational communication** is organizational communication that does not follow the lines of the organization chart.

Patterns of Informal Organizational Communication   The informal organizational communication network, or **grapevine,** has three main characteristics:

1. It springs up and is used irregularly within the organization.
2. It is not controlled by top executives, who may not even be able to influence it.
3. It exists largely to serve the self-interests of the people within it.

> The **grapevine** is the network of informal organizational communication.

Understanding the grapevine is a prerequisite for a complete understanding of organizational communication. It has been estimated that 70 percent of all communication in organizations flows along the organizational grapevine. Not only do grapevines carry great amounts of communication, but they carry it at very rapid speeds. Employees commonly cite the company grapevine as the most reliable and credible source of information about company events.[23]

Like formal organizational communication, informal organizational communication uses serial transmissions. The difference is that it is more difficult for managers to identify organization members involved in these transmissions than members of the formal communication network. A classic article by Keith Davis that appeared in the *Harvard Business Review* has been a significant help to managers in understanding how organizational grapevines spring up and operate. Figure 14.6 sketches the four most common grapevine patterns as outlined by Davis. They are as follows:[24]

1. *The single-strand grapevine*—A tells B, who tells C, who tells D, and so on. This type of grapevine tends to distort messages more than any other.
2. *The gossip grapevine*—A informs everyone else on the grapevine.
3. *The probability grapevine*—A communicates randomly—for example, to F and D. F and D then continue to inform other grapevine members in the same way.
4. *The cluster grapevine*—A selects and tells C, D, and F. F selects and tells I and B, and B selects and tells J. Information in this grapevine travels only to selected individuals.

Dealing with Grapevines.   Clearly, grapevines are a factor managers must deal with because they can, and often do, generate rumors that are detrimental to organizational success. Exactly how individual managers should deal with the grapevine, of course, depends on the

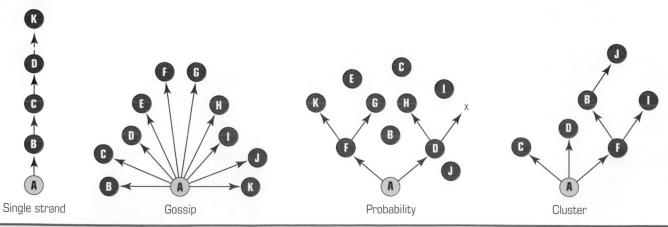

Single strand   Gossip   Probability   Cluster

Figure 14.6   *Four types of organizational grapevines*

specific organizational situation in which they find themselves. Managers can use grapevines advantageously to maximize information flow to employees. When employees have what they view as sufficient organizational information, it seems to build their sense of belonging to the organization and their level of productivity. Some writers even argue that managers should encourage the development of grapevines and strive to become grapevine members in order to gain feedback that could be very valuable in improving the organization.[25]

Encouraging Formal Organizational Communication   Since the organization acts only in the way that its organizational communication directs it to act, organizational communication is often called the nervous system of the organization. Formal organizational communication is generally the more important type of communication within an organization, so managers should encourage its free flow.

One strategy for doing this is to listen attentively to messages that come through formal channels. Listening shows organization members that the manager is interested in what subordinates have to say and encourages them to use formal communication channels in subsequent situations. Table 14.2 presents some general guidelines for listening well.

Some other strategies to encourage the flow of formal organizational communication are as follows:

> ➤ Support the flow of clear and concise statements through formal communication channels. Receiving an ambiguous message through a formal organizational communication channel can discourage employees from using that channel again.

▶ Formal organizational communication is taking place more and more frequently on intranets, or internal Internets for in-house communication. Ford Motor Company, the financial brokerage house Charles Schwab, and building materials manufacturer Certain Teed are among the growing number of corporate intranet users. Another is IBM, whose Ronda Rattray is able to volunteer at her son's high school a few afternoons a month and log back on to the company intranet in the evening to continue working from her Atlanta home. The system holds information about current projects and travel-planning material that allows Rattray to work on her own schedule.

1. *Stop talking!*
   You cannot listen if you are talking.
   Polonius (*Hamlet*): "Give every man thine ear, but few thy voice."

2. *Put the talker at ease.*
   Help the talker feel free to talk.
   This is often called establishing a permissive environment.

3. *Show the talker that you want to listen.*
   Look and act interested. Do not read your mail while he or she talks.
   Listen to understand rather than to oppose.

4. *Remove distractions.*
   Do not doodle, top, or shuffle papers.
   Will it be quieter if you shut the door?

5. *Empathize with the talker.*
   Try to put yourself in the talker's place so that you can see his or her point of view.

6. *Be patient.*
   Allow plenty of time. Do not interrupt the talker.
   Do not start for the door to walk away.

7. *Hold your temper.*
   An angry person gets the wrong meaning from words.

8. *Go easy on argument and criticism.*
   This puts the talker on the defensive. He or she may "clam up" or get angry.
   Do not argue: even if you win, you *lose*.

9. *Ask questions.*
   This encourages the talker and shows you are listening.
   It helps to develop points further.

10. *Stop talking!*
    This is the first and last commandment, because all other commandments depend on it. You just can't do a good listening job while you are talking. Nature gave us two ears but only one tongue, which is a gentle hint that we should listen more than we talk.

➤ Take care to ensure that all organization members have free access to formal communication channels. Obviously, organization members cannot communicate formally within the organization if they don't have access to the formal communication network.

➤ Assign specific communication responsibilities to staff personnel who could be of enormous help to line personnel in spreading important information throughout the organization.

▶ Back to the Case

It is virtually certain that there is an extensive grapevine in Dyer's plant—there is one in nearly every organization. Although Dyer must deal with this grapevine, he may not be able to influence it significantly. Eaton employees at his plant, like employees everywhere else, will latch on to a grapevine out of self-interest or because the formal organization has not furnished them with the information they believe they need.

By developing certain social relationships, Dyer could conceivably become part of the grapevine and obtain valuable feedback from it. Also, because grapevines generate rumors that could have a detrimental effect on the success of Dyer's plant, he should make sure that all personnel at his plant receive all the information they need to do their jobs well through formal organizational communication channels, thereby reducing their reliance on the grapevine.

Because formal organizational communication is vitally important to Dyer's plant, he should strive to encourage it by listening intently to messages that come to him over formal channels, supporting the flow of clear messages through formal channels, and making sure that all employees at his plant have access to these formal channels.

Management Skills Module

This section is specially designed to help you develop management skills. An individual's management skill is based on an understanding of management concepts and the ability to apply those concepts in management situations. As a result, the following activities are designed both to heighten your understanding of management concepts and to help you gain facility in applying those concepts in various management situations.

UNDERSTANDING MANAGEMENT CONCEPTS

▶ Action Summary

Reread the learning objectives below. Each objective is followed by questions. Answering these questions accurately will help you retain the most important concepts discussed in this chapter. After answering each question, check your answer against the answer key at the end of this chapter. (*Hint:* If you have any doubts regarding the correct response, consult the page number that follows the answer.)

Circle:

From studying this chapter, I will attempt to acquire

1. An understanding of influencing.
   T F
   a. The influencing function can be viewed as forcing the activities of organization members in appropriate directions.
   a b c d e
   b. The following activity is *not* a major component of the influencing process: (a) motivating (b) leading (c) communicating (d) correcting (e) considering groups.

2. An understanding of interpersonal communication.
   a b c d e
   a. Communication is best described as the process of: (a) sharing emotion (b) sharing information (c) sending messages (d) feedback formulation (e) forwarding information.
   a b c d e
   b. The basic elements of interpersonal communication are: (a) source/encoder, signal, decoder/destination (b) sender/message, encoder, receiver/decoder (c) signal, source/sender, decoder/destination (d) signal, source/decoder, encoder/destination (e) source/sender, signal, receiver/destination.

3. A knowledge of how to use feedback.
   T F
   a. Feedback is solely verbal.
   a b c d e
   b. Feedback can be used: (a) as a microbarrier (b) as a way for sources to evaluate their communication effectiveness (c) to ensure that instructions will be carried out (d) to evaluate the decoder (e) all of the above.

4. An appreciation for the importance of nonverbal communication.
   T F
   a. In interpersonal communication, nonverbal factors often play a more influential role than verbal factors.
   T F
   b. Nonverbal messages can contradict verbal messages, creating frustration in the destination.

5. Insights into formal organizational communication.
   a b c d e
   a. The following is *not* upward communication: (a) cost accounting reports (b) purchase order summary (c) production reports (d) corporate policy statement (e) sales reports.
   a b c d e
   b. The primary purpose served by lateral organizational communication is: (a) coordinating (b) organizing (c) direction (d) evaluation (e) control.

6. An appreciation for the importance of the grapevine.
   a b c d e
   a. The following statement concerning the grapevine is *not* correct: (a) grapevines generally are irregularly used in organizations (b) a grapevine can and often does generate harmful rumors (c) the grapevine is used largely to serve the self-interests of the people within it (d) some managers use grapevines to their advantage (e) in time, and with proper pressure, the grapevine can be eliminated.
   T F
   b. The grapevine is much slower than formal communication channels.

7. Some hints on how to encourage organizational communication.
   a b c d e
   a. To encourage formal organizational communication, managers should: (a) support the flow of clear and concise statements through formal channels (b) ensure free access to formal channels for all organization members (c) assign specific communication responsibilities to staff personnel (d) a and b (e) all of the above.
   T F
   b. Since formal organizational communication is the most important type of communication within an organization, managers must restrict its flow if the organization is to be successful.

▶ Action Summary Answer Key

1. **a.** F, p. 304	3. **a.** F, p. 311	5. **a.** d, p. 315	7. **a.** e, pp. 318–319
b. d, p. 305	**b.** b, p. 311	**b.** a, p. 315	**b.** F, p. 318
2. **a.** b, p. 306	4. **a.** T, p. 313	6. **a.** e, p. 317	
b. a, p. 308	**b.** T, p. 314	**b.** F, p. 317	

▶ Issues for Review and Discussion

1. What is influencing?
2. Describe the relationship between the overall management system and the influencing subsystem.
3. What factors make up the input, process, and output of the influencing subsystem?
4. Explain the relationship between the factors that compose the process section of the influencing subsystem.
5. What is communication?
6. How important is communication to managers?
7. Draw the communication model presented in this chapter and explain how it works.
8. How does successful communication differ from unsuccessful communication?
9. Summarize the significance of field of experience to communication.
10. List and describe three communication macrobarriers and three communication microbarriers.
11. What is feedback, and how should managers use it when communicating?

12. How is the communication effectiveness index calculated, and what is its significance?
13. Name the 10 commandments of good communication.
14. What is nonverbal communication? Explain its significance.
15. How should managers use nonverbal communication?
16. What is organizational communication?
17. How do formal and informal organizational communication differ?
18. Describe three types of formal organizational communication, and explain the general purpose of each type.
19. Can serial transmissions and other formal communication patterns influence communication effectiveness and the individuals using the patterns? If so, how?
20. Draw and describe the four main types of grapevines that exist in organizations.
21. How can managers encourage the flow of formal organizational communication?

APPLYING MANAGEMENT CONCEPTS

▶ Cases

➤ INTRODUCTORY CASE WRAP-UP

▶ Case Discussion Questions

"Eaton Managers Concentrate on Influencing People" (p. 303) and its related Back-to-the-Case sections were written to help you better understand the management concepts contained in this chapter. Answer the following discussion questions about this Introductory Case to enrich your understanding of the chapter content.

1. List three problems that could be caused at Eaton's Kearney plant if Robert Dyer were a poor communicator.
2. Explain *how* the problems you listed in number 1 could be caused by Dyer's inability to communicate.
3. Assuming that Dyer is a good communicator, discuss three ways that he is having a positive impact on Eaton's Kearney plant as a result of his communication expertise.

▶ Skills Exercise: Encouraging Formal Organizational Communication

In this chapter, you studied about encouraging formal interpersonal communication in organizations. The Introductory Case explains how Eaton Corporation focuses on building work teams. Assume that you supervise a work team at Eaton. List five actions you would take to encourage upward formal organizational communication from the team to you. Be sure to explain why you would take each action.

In 1881, Guccio Gucci was born to the owners of a straw hat–making business in Florence, Italy. The business failed and the couple was forced to declare bankruptcy. As a teenager, Guccio hopped a freighter and worked his way to England, where he got a job at London's Savoy Hotel. Four years later, at the age of 21, he returned to Florence, married his sweetheart, and went to work for a local leather crafts company. In 1938, with his savings and a loan from an acquaintance, Guccio Gucci opened the first Gucci leather goods shop in an elegant Florentine neighborhood, hoping to attract the class of travelers he had seen at the Savoy. By the time he was in his seventies, the Gucci name had become a symbol of luxury. At the birth of each grandchild, Guccio would say, "Let him smell a piece of leather, for it is the smell of his future."

Eventually, Gucci's son Aldo became the driving force in the business and opened the first American store in New York in 1953. Guccio's youngest son Roberto took charge, but Aldo visited the store often, much as his father had before him, treating employees like members of the family and even giving them personal loans. Guccio kept his sons on stipends and did not trust them to make decisions on their own. It was Aldo who built the Gucci name from a $6,000 corporation and a small shop in the Savoy Plaza into an empire reaching as far as Tokyo and Hong Kong.

At the age of 70, ill with cancer, Rodolfo saw that Aldo was trying to control the company and he was afraid his own young son Maurizio would get cheated out of his share of the business. He hired Domenico De Sole, a Harvard Law School graduate from Calabria, Italy, to advise him. Aldo looked down on De Sole for his bad taste in clothes and his lower-class background, but Rodolfo admired him and retained his services. After Rodolfo died, De Sole became Maurizio's attorney.

Aldo still called all the shots at Gucci until September 1983, when the Internal Revenue Service investigated him and the U.S. Attorney's office found him guilty of tax evasion.

Meanwhile, De Sole had discovered that in addition to illegally transferring millions of dollars out of Gucci America into his own offshore companies, Aldo had personally cashed a stack of checks made out to the company that were worth hundreds of thousands of dollars.

De Sole helped Maurizio to take over the board and create a new Gucci while Aldo was in prison. In 1984, Maurizio asked De Sole to become president of Gucci's U.S. business. De Sole only agreed to work for the Guccis part time. He preferred to keep his lucrative law firm position in Washington, DC. He hired Art Leshin as Gucci's CFO, thinking he would be able to sort out the finances. "When we got there we freaked out!" De Sole recalled. "It was a disaster, total chaos. There were no inventories, no accounting procedures. It took us months to make head or tail of what was going on. Aldo ran the business with intuition—and his marketing genius was so great, he had gotten away with it!"

In January 1988, the Gucci company went into debt to pay the IRS $21 million in back taxes and fines. In 1987, with 18 cases pending against the Gucci family in various courts around the world, Maurizio sought help from Morgan Stanley and Investcorp.

"You have taken a thoroughbred racehorse and reduced it to a carriage horse!" Aldo wrote to De Sole from jail.

In 1993, Gucci was sold to Investcorp. For the first time since Guccio Gucci had opened his Florentine shop in 1938, Gucci was not in the hands of a family member. In 1995, on the way to his private office on a tree-lined street in Milan, Maurizio Gucci was killed by a pistol shot. He was 47 years old.

Domenico De Sole is now CEO. Over the past 16 years, De Sole has put together a group of talented senior executives who lately have become his war team against cutthroat competitors LVMH (the fashion powerhouse that includes Louis Vuitton, Givenchy, and Fendi) and Prada.

CEO of LVMH Bernard Arnault came close to taking Gucci over in 1999, but in a brilliant last-minute maneuver, De Sole bought Yves Saint Laurent Rive Gauche for $1 billion and blocked Arnault's move. He also stole designer Alexander McQueen away from LVMH's Givenchy division. According to Sara Gay Forden, author of "The House of Gucci," his critics say he is ruthless, mercenary, and self-serving. "But friends say in business negotiations he is 'natural, straightforward and talkative.' "

Most recently, De Sole has closed 5 of Japan's 10 Yves Saint Laurent stores. He believes that for a brand to be exclusive, it must have limited distribution. "The stores were just horrible," the 57-year-old De Sole told Forbes. In Parisian perfume shops, he is pulling the Yves Saint Laurent perfume "Opium" from all but the top stores and relaunching it without the trademark tassel on the box. The tassel added one minute to the production time and made it more expensive to manufacture. Yves Saint Laurent Beauté has closed 1,300 of its 20,000 outlets during what have come to be called "terminator tours."

Last year, Gucci won a restraining order against a French Web site that was selling Yves Saint Laurent perfumes without permission. Gucci constantly scans the Web for unauthorized, independent sellers of Gucci products. Yves Saint Laurent cut jobs in 2000 from 963 to 341. "You have to execute quickly," says De Sole. "The most dangerous thing in business is not making decisions. I learned that from Maurizio Gucci—he couldn't decide anything." More than anything, De Sole wants to ensure that Gucci remains a great luxury brand. "Great brands all have one thing in common," says De Sole. "They have a great uniformity of style." De Sole himself chooses the location of every single store for Gucci and for Yves Saint Laurent. For Gucci to continue growing, it will have to sell an ever-wider array of luxury goods through fewer outlets.

One of De Sole's first acts as CEO of Gucci was to eliminate 6 of Gucci's 50 leather manufacturers. To the others, he offered financial and technical support in electronic leather-cutting and inventory systems—bringing in new technology to increase production.

It remains to be seen whether De Sole's strategies can keep LVMH and Prada at bay. His tactics are corporate and his priority is to be accountable to stakeholders. Unlike the Guccis who charmed both clients and employees, De Sole's focus is on keeping Gucci lean and profitable.

QUESTIONS

1. According to the definition in your text, do you think De Sole will be a successful communicator who will be able to lead Gucci to greater heights? Why?

2. Do you think the channels of communication in a family-run business are different than in a nonfamily business? Explain.

3. Are different communication and influencing skills needed in a "luxury goods" business than in a "nonluxury goods" business? Explain.

▶ Video

MASTERING MANAGEMENT: EPISODE 6—COMMUNICATION

Mastering Management is a series of innovative, interactive learning activities specially designed to help you develop management skills emphasized in various text chapters. Communication in organizations is the major focus of this chapter. Episode 6 of *Mastering Management* focuses on organizational communication and illustrates that even a small company like CanGo that has mostly face-to-face communication does indeed have communication challenges. The introductory video portrays a rather amusing miscommunication between Andrew and a new employee. Review Episode 6, "Communication," on your *Mastering Management* CD and then answer the following questions.

QUESTIONS

1. Is communication skill as important to managers in a small company like CanGo as in a large company? Explain.

2. Describe the most significant communication problem that you see at CanGo. How should management solve this problem?

3. Is the problem described in this segment a formal organizational communication problem? Explain.

www.prenhall.com/certo

This book is accompanied by a rich assortment of online activities aimed at developing your management skills. Reviewing news headlines, Internet exercises, an online study guide, and other research and Internet resources can help personalize management skills development for individual students or an entire class.

chapter

chapterchapterchapterchapterchapterchapter

15 Leadership

Objectives

From studying this chapter, I will attempt to acquire

- A working definition of leadership

- An understanding of the relationship between leading and managing

- An appreciation for the trait and situational approaches to leadership

- Insights into using leadership theories that emphasize decision-making situations

- Insights into using leadership theories that emphasize more general organizational situations

- An understanding of alternatives to leader flexibility

- An appreciation of emerging leadership styles and leadership issues of today

CHAPTER OUTLINE

Introductory Case: *The President of H. J. Heinz Company Sends a Letter*

Defining Leadership
Leader Versus Manager

Ethics Spotlight ▶ Ford Motor Company Trains Leaders in Social Responsibility

The Trait Approach to Leadership
The Situational Approach to Leadership: A Focus on Leader Behavior
Leadership Situations and Decisions

Digital Focus ▶ Cisco Uses Online Learning to Influence "Forces in Managers"

Leadership Behaviors

Leadership Today
Transformational Leadership
Coaching
Superleadership
Entrepreneurial Leadership

Current Topics in Leadership
Substitutes for Leadership
Women as Leaders
Ways Women Lead

Diversity Spotlight ▶ For James G. Kaiser of Corning, Being Employee-Centered Includes a Focus on Diversity

The President of H.J. Heinz Company Sends a Letter

REMINDER: THE INTRODUCTORY CASE WRAP-UP (P. 349) CONTAINS DISCUSSION QUESTIONS AND A SKILLS EXERCISE TO FURTHER ILLUSTRATE THE APPLICATION OF CHAPTER CONCEPTS TO THIS VIGNETTE.

H einz Company manufactures and markets an extensive line of processed food products throughout the world, including ketchup and sauces, condiments, pet food, baby food, frozen potato products, and low-calorie products. The following is a recent letter sent to Heinz stockholders by its president.

This is a selection of Heinz Company's extensive product offerings around the world. Raw ingredients are gathered worldwide as well, including cereals from Russia and infant formula from the Czech Republic.

Dear Fellow Shareholders:

I feel deeply privileged to have been selected as the new chief executive officer of H.J. Heinz Company and to lead one of the world's enduring corporations into a new century of growth.

Your management team has rededicated itself to the future through a formula we have dubbed "V5V" or "V × 5 = Victory." Through Vision, Voracity, Value, Volume, and Velocity, we can achieve Victory.

Victory. Victory for Heinz means delivering superior shareholder value. It means realizing ambitious, but realistic, performance goals that we have set for the coming years, including consistent 10 to 12 percent annual earnings growth; 4 to 5 percent real unit growth; gross profit margins of more than 40 percent; a return on invested capital of more than 30 percent; and world-class "value chain" status from procurement to manufacturing to distribution.

Vision. To accomplish this requires *Vision*—the vision of a truly global Heinz, turning from reliance on affiliate strategies and manufacturing to global leverage of our eight core categories of food service: infant feeding; ketchup, sauces and condiments; pet food; tuna; weight control; frozen food; and convenience meals.

Voracity. We will propel our global vision with a new culture of *Voracity.* We are stimulating our management team's voracious appetite to succeed through "centralized decentralization." By this we mean our strategy will be global, directed by ambitious centralized goals. There will be decentralized local accountability, motivated by a creative, entrepreneurial zeal.

(continued)

Value. Our global team is intently focused on delivering sustainable growth in shareholder *Value.* We anticipate continued progress in such key investment concerns as: increased sales and market shares, higher margins, and greater capital efficiency.

Volume. A primary factor in our company's valuation is top-line performance, fueled by greater *Volume* around the world. A mix of global expansion, improved marketing, and new products will achieve this—all supported by increased margins and continued cost reduction. Opportunities abound in trends, such as meal solutions, nutraceuticals, the growing global popularity of pets, and the increasing world appetite for eating out.

Velocity. We are particularly impatient about pursuing change. Hence, the stress on *Velocity.* The transformation of Heinz will not be glacial; it will be lightning quick. We begin Fiscal 1999 with new senior management appointments to help drive our new philosophy forward immediately.

To summarize the "V5V" equation: Heinz will achieve victory through a vision based on global category management and growth; a voracious appetite for success; an unyielding focus on enhancing shareholder value; a dedication to volume growth fueled by cost containment; and a high-velocity commitment to change. This formula is the key to greater shareholder return and a dynamic future for Heinz as the most dependable growth and performance company in the global food industry.

William R. Johnson
President, Chief Executive Officer, and Chairman

What's Ahead

William R. Johnson is the new president and CEO of Heinz Company. With this new job, Johnson is facing a whole set of new professional challenges in leading Heinz into a new century of growth. The case, Johnson's letter, ends by noting that Heinz will achieve victory through the 5 Vs. The information in this chapter would be helpful to an individual such as Johnson as the basis for developing a useful leadership strategy to achieve such success. This chapter discusses the following:

1) How to define leadership
2) The difference between a leader and a manager
3) The trait approach to leadership
4) The situational approach to leadership
5) Leadership today
6) Current topics in leadership

DEFINING LEADERSHIP

Leadership is the process of directing the behavior of others toward the accomplishment of objectives.

Leadership is the process of directing the behavior of others toward the accomplishment of some objective. Directing, in this sense, means causing individuals to act in a certain way or to follow a particular course. Ideally, this course is perfectly consistent with such factors as established organizational policies, procedures, and job descriptions. The central theme of leadership is getting things accomplished through people.[1]

As indicated in Chapter 14, leadership is one of the four main interdependent activities of the influencing subsystem and is accomplished, at least to some extent, by communicating with others. It is extremely important that managers have a thorough understanding of what leadership entails. Leadership has always been considered a prerequisite for organizational success. Today, given the increased capability afforded by enhanced communication technology and the rise of international business, leadership is more important than ever before.[2]

Leader Versus Manager

Leading is not the same as managing. Many executives fail to grasp the difference between the two and therefore labor under a misapprehension about how to carry out their organizational duties. Although some managers are leaders and some leaders are managers, leading and managing are not identical activities.[3] According to Theodore Levitt, management consists of[4]

> the rational assessment of a situation and the systematic selection of goals and purposes (what is to be done); the systematic development of strategies to achieve these goals; the marshalling of the required resources; the rational design, organization, direction, and control of the activities required to attain the selected purposes; and, finally, the motivating and rewarding of people to do the work.

Leadership, as one of the four primary activities of the influencing function, is a subset of management. Managing is much broader in scope than leading and focuses on nonbehavioral as well as behavioral issues. Leading emphasizes mainly behavioral issues. Figure 15.1 makes the point that although not all managers are leaders, the most effective managers over the long term are leaders.

Merely possessing management skills is no longer sufficient for success as an executive in the business world. Modern executives need to understand the difference between managing and leading and know how to combine the two roles to achieve organizational success. A manager makes sure that a job gets done, and a leader cares about and focuses on the people who do the job. To combine management and leadership, therefore, requires demonstrating a calculated and logical focus on organizational processes (management) along with a genuine concern for workers as people (leadership).[5]

Ford Motor Company Trains Leaders in Social Responsibility

Ford Motor Company produces and sells automotive vehicles under the brand names Ford, Mercury, Lincoln, Volvo, and Jaguar. Ford also owns 33.4 percent of Mazda Motor Corporation and engages in other businesses such as car rental, through its Hertz Corporation subsidiary.

Ford is very serious about training new leaders who will help the company to prepare for a new business era and reach its goal of making a difference in the world. Ford provides training for its leaders in the Ford Leadership Center, where the focus is on building leaders, both men and women, who know how to get things done through the talents of their people. These leaders also learn to think "outside of the box" by abandoning their comfort zones in everything from selecting a work project to working with new people.

Leadership training at the Center also focuses on social responsibility. Training activities reflect the ideas of William Clay Ford Jr., company chairman, which Ford published in its 2000 Corporate Citizenship Report. The report stresses that the company sees no conflict between business goals and social and environmental needs. According to Ford, the distinction between a good company and a great one is that a good company delivers excellent products and services while a great company delivers excellent products and services and strives to improve the world. Overall, Ford believes that the company needs leaders who can make informed business decisions and who can help the company better meet customer needs, increase shareholder value, and honor responsibilities to society. ■

The most effective managers over the long term are also leaders

Figure 15.1

THE TRAIT APPROACH TO LEADERSHIP

The **trait approach to leadership** is an outdated view of leadership that sees the personal characteristics of an individual as the main determinants of how successful that individual could be as a leader.

The **trait approach to leadership** is based on early leadership research that seemed to assume that a good leader is born, not made. The mainstream of this research attempted to describe successful leaders as precisely as possible. The reasoning was that if a complete profile of the traits of a successful leader could be drawn, it would be fairly easy to identify the individuals who should and should not be placed in leadership positions.

Many of the early studies that attempted to summarize the traits of successful leaders were documented. One of these summaries concludes that successful leaders tend to possess the following characteristics:[6]

1. Intelligence, including judgment and verbal ability
2. Past achievement in scholarship and athletics
3. Emotional maturity and stability
4. Dependability, persistence, and a drive for continuing achievement
5. The skill to participate socially and adapt to various groups
6. A desire for status and socioeconomic position

Evaluations of these trait studies, however, have concluded that their findings are inconsistent. One researcher says that 50 years of study have failed to produce one personality trait or set of qualities that can be used consistently to differentiate leaders from nonleaders.[7] It follows, then, that no trait or combination of traits guarantees that someone will be a successful leader. Leadership is apparently a much more complex issue.

Contemporary management writers and practitioners generally agree that leadership ability cannot be explained by an individual's traits or inherited characteristics. They believe, rather, that individuals can be trained to be good leaders. In other words, leaders are made, not born. That is why thousands of employees each year are sent through leadership training programs.[8]

▶ Back to the Case

From the preceding material, a manager like William Johnson, the president of H.J. Heinz Company, should understand that his leadership activities relating to achieving "victory" are those activities that involve directing the behavior of organization members so that the company will achieve its success. A manager like Johnson also should understand that leading and managing are not the same thing. When managing, Johnson is involved with planning, organizing, influencing, and controlling. When leading, he is performing an activity that is part of the influencing function of management. To maximize his long-term success, Johnson should strive to be both a manager and a leader.

In assessing his leadership at Heinz, Johnson should not fall into the trap of trying to increase his leadership success by changing his personal traits or attitudes to mirror those of successful leaders that he might know. Studies based on the trait approach to leadership should indicate to Johnson that merely changing his characteristics will not guarantee his success as a leader.

THE SITUATIONAL APPROACH TO LEADERSHIP: A FOCUS ON LEADER BEHAVIOR

The **situational approach to leadership** is a relatively modern view of leadership that suggests that successful leadership requires a unique combination of leaders, followers, and leadership situations.

Leadership studies have shifted emphasis from the trait approach to the situational approach, which suggests that leadership style must be appropriately matched to the situation the leader faces. The more modern **situational approach to leadership** is based on the assumption that each instance of leadership is different and therefore requires a unique combination of leaders, followers, and leadership situations.

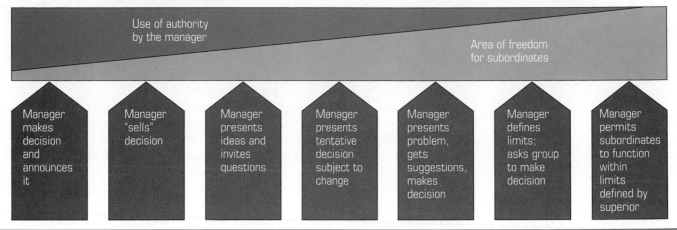

Use of authority
by the manager

Area of freedom
for subordinates

| Manager makes decision and announces it | Manager "sells" decision | Manager presents ideas and invites questions | Manager presents tentative decision subject to change | Manager presents problem, gets suggestions, makes decision | Manager defines limits; asks group to make decision | Manager permits subordinates to function within limits defined by superior |

Continuum of leadership behavior that emphasizes decision making

Figure 15.2

This interaction is commonly expressed in formula form: $SL = f(L,F,S)$, where SL is *successful leadership;* f stands for *function of;* and L, F, and S are, respectively, the *leader,* the *follower,* and the *situation.*[9] Translated, this formula says that successful leadership is a function of a leader, follower, and situation that are appropriate for one another.

Leadership Situations and Decisions

The Tannenbaum and Schmidt Leadership Continuum Since one of the most important tasks of a leader is making sound decisions, all practical and legitimate leadership thinking emphasizes decision making. Tannenbaum and Schmidt, who wrote one of the first and perhaps most often quoted articles on the situational approach to leadership, stress situations in which a leader makes decisions.[10] Figure 15.2 presents their model of leadership behavior.

This model is actually a continuum, or range, of leadership behavior available to managers when they are making decisions. Note that each type of decision-making behavior depicted in the figure has both a corresponding degree of authority used by the manager and a related amount of freedom available to subordinates. Management behavior, at the extreme left of the model, characterizes the leader who makes decisions by maintaining high control and allowing subordinates little freedom. Behavior at the extreme right characterizes the leader who makes decisions by exercising little control and allowing subordinates much freedom and self-direction. Behavior in between the extremes reflects graduations in leadership from autocratic to democratic.

Managers displaying leadership behavior toward the right of the model are more democratic, and are called *subordinate-centered* leaders. Those displaying leadership behavior toward the left of the model are more autocratic, and are called *boss-centered* leaders.

Each type of leadership behavior in this model is explained in more detail in the following list:

1. *The manager makes the decision and announces it*—This behavior is characterized by the manager (a) identifying a problem, (b) analyzing various alternatives available to solve it, (c) choosing the alternative that will be used to solve it, and (d) requiring followers to implement the chosen alternative. The manager may or may not use coercion, but the followers have no opportunity to participate directly in the decision-making process.

2. *The manager "sells" the decision*—As above, the manager identifies the problem and independently arrives at a decision. Rather than announce the decision to subordinates for implementation, however, the manager tries to persuade subordinates to accept the decision.

3. *The manager presents ideas and invites questions*—Here, the manager makes the decision and attempts to gain acceptance through persuasion. One additional step is taken, however: Subordinates are invited to ask questions about the decision.

4. *The manager presents a tentative decision that is subject to change*—The manager allows subordinates to have some part in the decision-making process but retains the responsibility for identifying and diagnosing the problem. The manager then arrives at a tentative decision that is subject to change on the basis of subordinate input. The final decision is made by the manager.

5. *The manager presents the problem, gets suggestions, and then makes the decision*—This is the first leadership activity described thus far that allows subordinates the opportunity to offer problem solutions before the manager does. The manager, however, is still the one who identifies the problem.

6. *The manager defines the limits and asks the group to make a decision*—In this type of leadership behavior, the manager first defines the problem and sets the boundaries within which a decision must be made. The manager then enters into partnership with subordinates to arrive at an appropriate decision. The danger here is that if the group of subordinates does not perceive that the manager genuinely desires a serious group decision-making effort, it will tend to arrive at conclusions that reflect what it thinks the manager wants rather than what the group actually wants and believes is feasible.

7. *The manager permits the group to make decisions within prescribed limits*—Here the manager becomes an equal member of a problem-solving group. The entire group identifies and assesses the problem, develops possible solutions, and chooses an alternative to be implemented. Everyone within the group understands that the group's decision will be implemented.

Determining How to Make Decisions as a Leader   The true value of the model developed by Tannenbaum and Schmidt lies in its use in making practical and desirable decisions. According to these authors, the three primary factors, or forces, that influence a manager's determination of which leadership behavior to use in making decisions are as follows:

1. *Forces in the Manager*—Managers should be aware of four forces within themselves that influence their determination of how to make decisions as a leader. The first force is the manager's values, such as the relative importance to the manager of organizational efficiency, personal growth, the growth of subordinates, and company profits. For example, a manager who values subordinate growth highly will probably want to give group members the valuable experience of making a decision, even though he or she could make the decision much more quickly and efficiently alone.

    The second influencing force is level of confidence in subordinates. In general, the more confidence a manager has in his or her subordinates, the more likely it is that the manager's decision-making style will be democratic, or subordinate-centered. The reverse is also true: The less confidence a manager has in subordinates, the more likely it is that the manager's decision-making style will be autocratic, or boss-centered.

    The third influencing force within the manager is personal leadership strengths. Some managers are more effective in issuing orders than in leading group discussions, and vice versa. Managers must be able to recognize their own leadership strengths and capitalize on them.

    The fourth influencing force within the manager is tolerance for ambiguity. The move from a boss-centered style to a subordinate-centered style means some loss of certainty about how problems should be solved. A manager who is disturbed by this loss of certainty will find it extremely difficult to be successful as a subordinate-centered leader.

▶ Cisco Uses Online Learning to Influence "Forces in Managers"

As has been discussed, a manager's level of personal development can impact the way in which he or she makes decisions. Companies commonly use various types of training to influence this level of personal development and positively influence managerial decision making. Cisco Systems is one such company. Headquartered in San Jose, California, it provides networking for the Internet, including hardware, software, and various services to assist clients throughout the world in gaining seamless Internet access to information. Overall, this Internet access is aimed at helping Cisco's clients to achieve a significant competitive advantage, and many of them point to advantages like greater information efficiency and closer relationships with customers, suppliers, and employees that are a result of using Cisco's products.

John Chambers, Cisco's CEO, has taken a strong position on how he would like to impact the personal development of managers and thereby impact managerial decision making. Chambers has declared strong support for training his managers online, because it is fast and results-oriented and because it can help to develop managers any time and any place. Overall, online training at Cisco focuses on information, communication, education, and training, and it is currently developing over 10,000 systems engineers and account managers. To carry out his ambitious online learning plans, Chambers has established the Internet Learning Solutions Group, a centralized training organization with about 165 staff members. The mission of this group is to implement Chambers's vision for online training across the entire company.

▶ Back to the Case

The situational approach to leadership affords more insights into how William Johnson can help Heinz achieve success than does the trait approach. The situational approach would suggest that successful leadership for Johnson is determined by the appropriateness of a combination of three factors: (1) William Johnson as a leader, (2) Heinz's employees as followers, and (3) the situation(s) within the company that Johnson faces. Each of these factors plays a significant role in determining whether or not Johnson is successful as a leader.

One of the most important activities that a manager like Johnson performs as a leader is making decisions. He can make decisions in any number of ways, ranging from authoritarian to democratic. For example, Johnson could make the decision to sell Weight Watchers, an extensive line of low-fat, weight-control products owned by Heinz. The Weight Watchers line includes products like frozen chicken dinners and low-fat ice cream. On the other hand, Johnson could generally define the type of food lines he sees in the future of Heinz, discuss the situation with appropriate Heinz personnel, and allow personnel to come up with and implement its own conclusions about which food lines to keep and which to sell. Of course, Johnson could also be less extreme in his decision making, in that his leadership behavior could fall in the middle of the continuum. For example, he could suggest to appropriate Heinz personnel the type of company Heinz is to be, ask them to develop ideas for the type of food lines needed, and then make the decision on the basis of his own ideas and those of the staff.

2. *Forces in Subordinates*—A manager also should be aware of forces within subordinates that influence the manager's determination of how to make decisions as a leader.[11] To lead successfully, the manager needs to keep in mind that subordinates are both somewhat different and somewhat alike and that any cookbook approach to leading all subordinates is therefore impossible. Generally speaking, however, managers can increase their leadership success by allowing subordinates more freedom in making decisions when:

   ➤ The subordinates have a relatively high need for independence (people differ greatly in the amount of direction they desire)
   ➤ They have a readiness to assume responsibility for decision making (some see additional responsibility as a tribute to their ability; others see it as someone above them "passing the buck")
   ➤ They have a relatively high tolerance for ambiguity (some employees prefer to be given clear-cut directives; others crave a greater degree of freedom)
   ➤ They are interested in the problem and believe it is important to solve it

▶ Michael S. Funk is credited with turning around a desperate situation at United Natural Foods when he took over as CEO at the end of 1999. With the company losing $1 million a week, Funk made a quick decision to gather a "SWAT team" of operations experts from its West Coast offices and take them to Dayville, Connecticut headquarters, where he dismissed 12 employees, hired information technology consultants to fix the firm's computer problems, and rehired the former chief financial officer, who had resigned to protest the former CEO's decisions in running the troubled eastern division. "It looks like we're out of the woods," says Funk.

> They understand and identify with the organization's goals
> They have the necessary knowledge and experience to deal with the problem
> They have learned to expect to share in decision making (people who have come to expect strong leadership and then are suddenly told to participate more fully in decision making are often upset by this new experience; conversely, people who have enjoyed a considerable amount of freedom usually resent the boss who assumes full decision-making powers)

If subordinates do not have these characteristics, the manager should probably assume a more autocratic, or boss-centered approach to making decisions.

3. *Forces in the Situation*—The last group of forces that influence a manager's determination of how to make decisions as a leader are forces in the leadership situation. The first such situational force is the type of organization in which the leader works. Organizational factors like the size of working groups and their geographic distribution are especially important influences on leadership style. Extremely large work groups or wide geographic separations of work groups, for example, could make a subordinate-centered leadership style impractical.

The second situational force is the effectiveness of a group. To gauge this force, managers should evaluate such issues as the experience of group members in working together and the degree of confidence they have in their ability to solve problems as a group. As a general rule, managers should assign decision-making responsibilities only to effective work groups.

The third situational force is the problem to be solved. Before deciding to act as a subordinate-centered leader, a manager should be sure that the group has the expertise necessary to make a decision about the problem in question. If it does not, the manager should move toward more boss-centered leadership.

The fourth situational force is the time available to make a decision. As a general guideline, the less time available, the more impractical it is to assign decision making to a group because a group typically takes more time than an individual to reach a decision.

As the situational approach to leadership implies, managers will be successful decision makers only if the method they use to make decisions appropriately reflects the leader, the followers, and the situation.

Determining How to Make Decisions as a Leader: An Update   Tannenbaum and Schmidt's 1957 article on leadership decision making was so widely accepted that the two authors were invited by the *Harvard Business Review* to update their original work in the 1970s.[12] In this update, they warned that in modern organizations, the relationship among forces within the manager, subordinates, and situation had become more complex and more interrelated since the 1950s and that this obviously made it harder for managers to determine how to lead.

The update also pointed out that new organizational environments had to be considered in determining how to lead. For example, such factors as affirmative action and pollution control—which hardly figured in the decision making of managers in the 1950s—have become significant influences on the decision making of leaders since the 1970s.

The Vroom-Yetton-Jago Model   Another major decision-focused theory of leadership that has gained widespread attention was first developed in 1973 and refined and expanded in 1988.[13] This theory, which we will call the **Vroom–Yetton–Jago (VYJ) Model of leadership** after its three major contributors, focuses on how much participation to allow subordinates in the decision-making process. The VYJ Model is built on two important premises:

1. Organizational decisions should be of high quality (should have a beneficial impact on performance)
2. Subordinates should accept and be committed to organizational decisions that are made

The **Vroom–Yetton–Jago (VYJ) Model of leadership** is a modern view of leadership that suggests that successful leadership requires determining, through a decision tree, what style of leadership will produce decisions that are beneficial to the organization and will be accepted and committed to by subordinates.

Decision Styles   The VYJ Model suggests that there are five different decision styles or ways that leaders can make decisions. These styles range from autocratic (the leader makes the

DECISION STYLE	DEFINITION
AI	Manager makes the decision alone.
AII	Manager asks for information from subordinates but makes the decision alone. Subordinates may or may not be informed about what the situation is.
CI	Manager shares the situation with individual subordinates and asks for information and evaluation. Subordinates do not meet as a group, and the manager alone makes the decision.
CII	Manager and subordinates meet as a group to discuss the situation, but the manager makes the decision.
GII	Manager and subordinates meet as a group to discuss the situation, and the group makes the decision.
A = autocratic; C = consultative; G = group	

The five decision styles available to a leader according to the Vroom–Yetton–Jago Model

Figure 15.3

decision) to consultative (the leader makes the decision after interacting with the followers) to group-focused (the manager meets with the group, and the group makes the decision). All five decision styles within the VYJ Model are described in Figure 15.3.

Using the Model The VYJ Model, presented in Figure 15.4, is a method for determining when a leader should use which decision style. As you can see, the model is a type of decision tree. To determine which decision style to use in a particular situation, the leader starts at the left of the decision tree by stating the organizational problem being addressed. Then the leader asks a series of questions about the problem as determined by the structure of the decision tree until he or she arrives at a decision style appropriate for the situation at the far right side of the model.

Consider, for example, the very bottom path of the decision tree. After stating an organizational problem, the leader determines that a decision related to that problem has a low quality requirement, that it is important that subordinates be committed to the decision, and it is very uncertain whether a decision made solely by the leader will be committed to by subordinates. In this situation, the model suggests that the leader use the GII decision—that is, the leader should meet with the group to discuss the situation, and then allow the group to make the decision.

The VYJ Model seems promising. Research on an earlier version of this model has yielded some evidence that managerial decisions consistent with the model are more successful than are managerial decisions inconsistent with the model.[14] The model is rather complex, however, and therefore difficult for practicing managers to apply.

▶ Back to the Case

Based on the previous information, in trying to decide exactly how to make his decisions as Heinz's leader, William Johnson should consider forces in himself as manager, forces in his subordinates, and forces in the specific organizational situation he faces. Forces within William Johnson include his own ideas about how to lead and his level of confidence in the Heinz employees that he is leading. If Johnson believes he is more knowledgeable about achieving *victory*, for example, than his staff is, he will be likely to make boss-centered decisions about what steps to take to create *victory* at Heinz. Forces within his subordinates, such as the need for independence, the readiness to assume responsibility, and the knowledge of and interest in the issues to be decided, also affect Johnson's decisions as a leader. If his staff is relatively independent and responsible and its members feel strongly about what *victory* means and how it should be achieved, then Johnson should be inclined to allow his employees more freedom in deciding how to achieve that *victory*.

(continued)

Forces within the company include the number of people making decisions and the problem to be solved. For example, if Johnson's staff is small, he will be more likely to use a democratic decision-making style, allowing his employees to become involved in such decisions as how to best achieve *victory*. He will also be likely to use a subordinate-centered leadership style if his staff is knowledgeable about what makes a company like Heinz victorious. The VYJ Model suggests that William Johnson should try to make decisions in such a fashion that the quality of decisions is enhanced and followers are committed to the decisions. Johnson can try to ensure that such decisions are made by matching his decision style (autocratic, consultative, or group) to the particular situation he faces.

Leadership Behaviors

The failure to identify predictive leadership traits led researchers in this area to turn to other variables to explain leadership success. Rather than looking at traits leaders should possess, the

QR	Quality Requirement:	*How important is the technical quality of this decision?*
CR	Commitment Requirement:	*How important is subordinate commitment to the decision?*
LI	Leader's Information:	*Do you have sufficient information to make a high-quality decision?*
ST	Problem Structure:	*Is the problem well structured?*
CP	Commitment Probability:	*If you were to make the decision by yourself, is it reasonably certain that your subordinate(s) would be committed to the decision?*
GC	Goal Congruence:	*Do subordinates share the organizational goals to be attained in solving this problem?*
CO	Subordinate Conflict:	*Is conflict among subordinates over preferred solution likely?*
SI	Subordinate Information:	*Do subordinates have sufficient information to make a high-quality decision?*

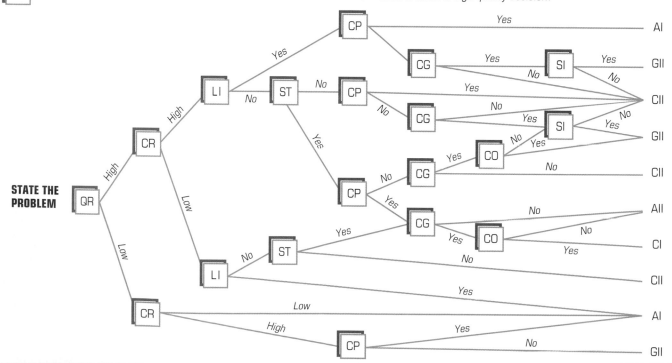

Figure 15.4 *The Vroom–Yetton–Jago Model*

behavioral approach looked at what good leaders do. Are they concerned with getting a task done, for instance, or do they concentrate on keeping their followers happy and maintaining high morale?

Two major studies series were conducted to identify leadership behavior, one by the Bureau of Business Research at Ohio State University (referred to as the OSU studies), and another by the University of Michigan (referred to as the Michigan studies).

The OSU Studies

The OSU studies concluded that leaders exhibit two main types of behavior:

➤ **Structure behavior** is any leadership activity that delineates the relationship between the leader and the leader's followers or establishes well-defined procedures that followers should adhere to in performing their jobs. Overall, structure behavior limits the self-guidance of followers in the performance of their tasks, but while it can be relatively firm, it is never rude or malicious.

Structure behavior can be useful to leaders as a means of minimizing follower activity that does not significantly contribute to organizational goal attainment. Leaders must be careful, however, not to go overboard and discourage follower activity that *will* contribute to organizational goal attainment.

➤ **Consideration behavior** is leadership behavior that reflects friendship, mutual trust, respect, and warmth in the relationship between leader and followers. This type of behavior generally aims to develop and maintain a good human relationship between the leader and the followers.

Leadership Style The OSU studies resulted in a model that depicts four fundamental leadership styles. A **leadership style** is the behavior a leader exhibits while guiding organization members in appropriate directions. Each of the four leadership styles depicted in Figure 15.5 is a different combination of structure behavior and consideration behavior. For example, the high structure/low consideration leadership style emphasizes structure behavior and deemphasizes consideration behavior.

The OSU studies made a significant contribution to our understanding of leadership, and the central ideas generated by these studies still serve as the basis for modern leadership thought and research.[15]

The Michigan Studies

Around the same time the OSU leadership studies were being carried out, researchers at the University of Michigan, led by Rensis Likert, were also conduct-

---

Structure behavior is leadership activity that (1) delineates the relationship between the leader and the leader's followers or (2) establishes well-defined procedures that the followers should adhere to in performing their jobs.

Consideration behavior is leadership behavior that reflects friendship, mutual trust, respect, and warmth in the relationship between leader and followers.

Leadership style is the behavioral pattern a leader establishes while guiding organization members in appropriate directions.

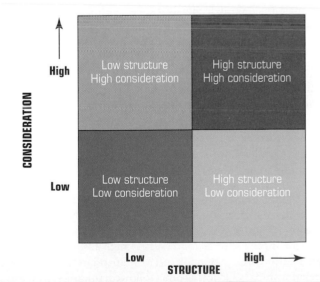

Four fundamental leadership styles based on structure behavior and consideration behavior

Figure 15.5

ing a series of historically significant leadership studies.[16] After analyzing information based on interviews with both leaders and followers (managers and subordinates), the Michigan studies pinpointed two basic types of leader behavior: job-centered behavior and employee-centered behavior.

Job-centered behavior is leader behavior that focuses primarily on the work a subordinate is doing.

Employee-centered behavior is leader behavior that focuses primarily on subordinates as people.

Job-Centered Behavior   **Job-centered behavior** is leader behavior that focuses primarily on the work a subordinate is doing. The job-centered leader is very interested in the job the subordinate is doing and in how well the subordinate is performing at that job.

Employee-Centered Behavior   **Employee-centered behavior** is leader behavior that focuses primarily on subordinates as people. The employee-centered leader is very attentive to the personal needs of subordinates and is interested in building cooperative work teams that are satisfying to subordinates and advantageous for the organization.

The results of the OSU studies and the Michigan studies are very similar. Both research efforts indicated two primary dimensions of leader behavior: a work dimension (structure behavior/job-centered behavior) and a people dimension (consideration behavior/employee-centered behavior). The following section focuses on determining which of these two primary dimensions of leader behavior is more advisable for a manager to adopt.

Effectiveness of Various Leadership Styles   An early investigation of high school superintendents concluded that desirable leadership behavior is associated with high leader emphasis on both structure and consideration and that undesirable leadership behavior is associated with low leader emphasis on both dimensions. Similarly, the managerial grid described in Chapter 13 implies that the most effective leadership style is characterized by high consideration and high structure. Results of a more recent study indicate that high consideration is always preferred by subordinates.[17]

Comparing Styles   One should be cautious, however, about concluding that any single leadership style is more effective than any other. Leadership situations are so varied that pronouncing one leadership style as the most effective is an oversimplification. In fact, a successful leadership style for managers in one situation may prove ineffective in another situation. Recognizing the need to link leadership styles to appropriate situations, A. K. Korman notes, in a classic article, that a worthwhile contribution to leadership literature would be a rationale for systematically linking appropriate styles with various situations so as to ensure effective leadership.[18] The life cycle theory of leadership, which is covered in the next section, provides such a rationale.

The **life cycle theory of leadership** is a leadership concept that hypothesizes that leadership styles should reflect primarily the maturity level of the followers.

The Hersey–Blanchard Life Cycle Theory of Leadership   The **life cycle theory of leadership** is a rationale for linking leadership styles with various situations so as to ensure effective leadership. This theory posits essentially the same two types of leadership behavior as the OSU leadership studies, but it calls them "task" and "relationships" rather than "structure" and "consideration."

Maturity   The life cycle theory is based on the relationship among follower maturity, leader task behavior, and leader relationship behavior. In general terms, according to this theory, leadership style should reflect the maturity level of the followers. Maturity is defined as the ability of followers to perform their job independently, to assume additional responsibility, and to desire to achieve success. The more of each of these characteristics that followers possess, the more mature they are said to be. (Maturity here is not necessarily linked to chronological age.)

The Life Cycle Model   Figure 15.6 illustrates the life cycle theory of leadership model. The curved line indicates the maturity level of the followers: Maturity level increases as the maturity curve runs from right to left. In more specific terms, the theory indicates that effective leadership behavior should shift as follows:[19] (1) high-task/low-relationships behavior to (2) high-task/high-relationships behavior to (3) high-relationships/low-task behavior to (4) low-task/low-relationships behavior, as one's followers progress from immaturity to maturity. In sum, a manager's leadership style will be effective only if it is appropriate for the maturity level of the followers.

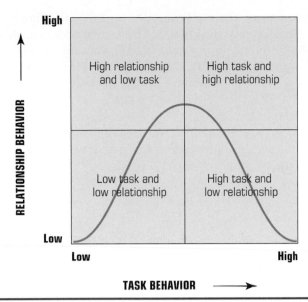

The life cycle theory of leadership model

Figure 15.6

Exceptions to the Model There are some exceptions to the general philosophy of the life cycle theory. For example, if there is a short-term deadline to meet, a leader may find it necessary to accelerate production through a high-task/low-relationships style rather than use a low-task/low-relationships style, even if the followers are mature. A high-task/low-relationships leadership style carried out over the long term with such followers, though, would typically result in a poor working relationship between leader and subordinates.

Applying Life Cycle Theory Following is an example of how the life cycle theory applies to a leadership situation:

➤ A man has just been hired as a salesperson in a men's clothing store. At first, this individual is extremely immature—that is, unable to solve task-related problems independently. According to the life cycle theory, the appropriate style for leading this salesperson at his level of maturity is high-task/low-relationships—that is, the leader should tell the salesperson exactly what should be done and how to do it. The salesperson should be shown how to make cash and charge sales and how to handle merchandise returns. The leader should also begin laying the groundwork for developing a personal relationship with the salesperson. Too much relationship behavior at this point, however, should be avoided, since it can easily be misinterpreted as permissiveness.

➤ As time passes and the salesperson gains somewhat in job-related maturity, the appropriate style for leading him would be high-task/high-relationships. Although the salesperson's maturity has increased somewhat, the leader still needs to watch him closely because he requires guidance and direction at times. The main difference between this leadership style and the first one is the amount of relationship behavior displayed by the leader. Building on the groundwork laid during the period of the first leadership style, the leader can now start to encourage an atmosphere of mutual trust, respect, and friendliness between herself and the salesperson.

➤ As more time passes and the salesperson's maturity level increases still further, the appropriate style for leading this individual will become high-relationships/low-task. The leader can now deemphasize task behavior because the salesperson is of above-average maturity in his job and is capable of solving most job-related problems independently. The leader would continue to develop a human relationship with her follower.

➤ Once the salesperson's maturity level reaches its maximum, the appropriate style for leading him is low-task/low-relationships. Again, the leader deemphasizes task behavior because the follower is thoroughly familiar with the job. Now, however, the leader can also deemphasize relationship behavior because she has fully established a good working relationship with the follower. At this point, task behavior is seldom needed, and relationship behavior is used primarily to nurture the good working rapport that has developed between the leader and the follower. The salesperson, then, is left to do his job without close supervision, knowing that he has a positive working relationship with a leader who can be approached for guidance whenever necessary.

The life cycle approach more than likely owes its acceptance to its intuitive appeal. Although at first glance it appears to be a useful leadership concept, managers should bear in mind that there is little scientific investigation verifying its worth, and therefore it should be applied very carefully.[20]

> ### ▶ Back to the Case
>
> The OSU leadership studies should furnish a manager like William Johnson with insights into leadership behavior in general situations. According to these studies, Johnson can exhibit two general types of leadership behavior: structure and consideration. He will be using structure behavior if he tells Heinz's personnel what to do—for example, exactly how to design new, plastic containers for 9-Lives Cat Food. He will be using consideration behavior if he attempts to develop a more human rapport with his employees by discussing their concerns and developing friendships with them.
>
> Of course, depending on how Johnson emphasizes these two behaviors, his leadership style can reflect a combination of structure and consideration ranging from high structure/low consideration to low structure/high consideration. For example, if Johnson stresses giving orders to employees and deemphasizes developing relationships, he will be exhibiting high structure/low consideration. If he emphasizes a good rapport with his staff and allows its members to function mostly independently of him, his leadership style will be termed low structure/high consideration.
>
> Although no single leadership style is more effective than any other in all situations, the life cycle theory of leadership furnishes William Johnson with a strategy for using various styles in various situations. According to this theory, Johnson should make his style consistent primarily with the maturity level of the Heinz organization members that he is leading. As Johnson's followers progress from immaturity to maturity, his leadership style should shift systematically from (1) high-task/low-relationships behavior to (2) high-task/high-relationships behavior to (3) high-relationships/low-task behavior to (4) low-task/low-relationships behavior.

Leader flexibility is the ability to change leadership style.

The **contingency theory of leadership** is a leadership concept that hypothesizes that, in any given leadership situation, success is determined primarily by (1) the degree to which the task being performed by the followers is structured, (2) the degree of position power possessed by the leader, and (3) the type of relationship that exists between the leader and the followers.

Fiedler's Contingency Theory   Situational theories of leadership like the life cycle theory are based on the concept of **leader flexibility**—the idea that successful leaders must change their leadership styles as they encounter different situations. Can any leader be so flexible as to span all major leadership styles? The answer to this question is that some leaders can be that flexible, and some cannot. Unfortunately, there are numerous obstacles to leader flexibility. One is that a leadership style is sometimes so ingrained in a leader that it takes years to even approach flexibility. Another is that some leaders have experienced such success in a basically static situation that they believe developing a flexible style is unnecessary.

Changing the Organization to Fit the Leader   One strategy, proposed by Fred Fiedler, for overcoming these obstacles is changing the organizational situation to fit the leader's style, rather than changing the leader's style to fit the organizational situation.[21] Applying this idea to the life cycle theory of leadership, an organization may find it easier to shift leaders to situations appropriate for their leadership styles than to expect those leaders to change styles as situations change. After all, it would probably take three to five years to train a manager to use a concept like life cycle theory effectively, while changing the situation that the leader faces can be done very quickly simply by exercising organizational authority.

According to Fiedler's **contingency theory of leadership**, leader–member relations, task structure, and the position power of the leader are the three primary factors that should be considered when moving leaders into situations appropriate for their leadership styles:

> *Leader–member relations* is the degree to which the leader feels accepted by the followers.
> *Task structure* is the degree to which the goals—the work to be done—and other situational factors are outlined clearly.
> *Position power* is determined by the extent to which the leader has control over the rewards and punishments followers receive.

How these three factors can be arranged in eight different combinations, called *octants,* is presented in Table 15.1.

Figure 15.7 shows how effective leadership varies among the eight octants. From an organizational viewpoint, this figure implies that management should attempt to match permissive, passive, and considerate leaders with situations reflecting the middle of the continuum containing the octants. It also implies that management should try to match controlling, active, and structuring leaders with the extremes of this continuum.

Fiedler suggests some actions that can be taken to modify the leadership situation. They are as follows:[22]

1. In some organizations, we can change the individual's task assignment. We may assign to one leader very structured tasks that have implicit or explicit instructions telling him what to do and how to do it, and we may assign to another the tasks that are nebulous and vague. The former are the typical production tasks; the latter are exemplified by committee work, by the development of policy, and by tasks that require creativity.

2. We can change the leader's position power. We not only can give him a higher rank and corresponding recognition, we also can modify his position power by giving him subordinates who are equal to him in rank and prestige or subordinates who are two or three ranks below him. We can give him subordinates who are experts in their specialties or subordinates who depend on the leader for guidance and instruction. We can give the leader the final say in all decisions affecting his group, or we can require that he make decisions in consultation with his subordinates, or even that he obtain their concurrence. We can channel all directives, communications, and information about organizational plans through the leader alone, giving him expert power, or we can provide these communications concurrently to all his subordinates.

3. We can change the leader–member relations in this group. We can have the leader work with groups whose members are very similar to him in attitude, opinion, technical background, race, and cultural background, or we can assign him subordinates with whom he differs in any one or several of these important aspects. Finally, we can assign the leader to a group in which the members have a tradition of getting along well with their supervisors or to a group that has a history and tradition of conflict.

Fiedler's work certainly helps destroy the myths that there is one best leadership style and that leaders are born, not made. Further, his work supports the theory that almost every manager in an organization can be a successful leader if placed in a situation appropriate to that person's leadership style. This, of course, assumes that someone in the organization has the

Eight Combinations, or Octants, of Three Factors: Leader–Member Relations, Task Structure, and Leader Position Power

Table 15.1

Octant	Leader–Member Relations	Task Structure	Leader Position Power
I	Good	High	Strong
II	Good	High	Weak
III	Good	Weak	Strong
IV	Good	Weak	Weak
V	Moderately poor	High	Strong
VI	Moderately poor	High	Weak
VII	Moderately poor	Weak	Strong
VIII	Moderately poor	Weak	Weak

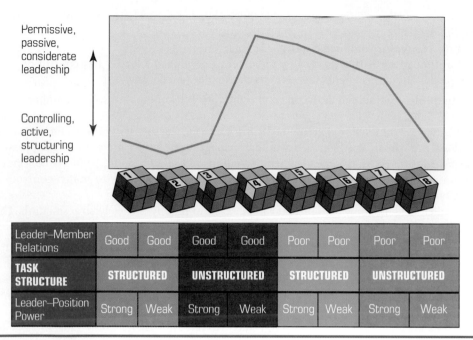

Leader–Member Relations	Good	Good	Good	Good	Poor	Poor	Poor	Poor
TASK STRUCTURE	STRUCTURED		UNSTRUCTURED		STRUCTURED		UNSTRUCTURED	
Leader–Position Power	Strong	Weak	Strong	Weak	Strong	Weak	Strong	Weak

Figure 15.7   *How effective leadership style varies with Fiedler's eight octants*

ability to assess the characteristics of the organization's leaders and of other important organizational variables and then to match the two accordingly.

Fiedler's model, like all theoretical models, has its limitations, but although it may not provide concrete answers, it does emphasize the importance of situational variables in determining leadership effectiveness. As said earlier, it may actually be easier to change the leadership situation or move the leader to a more favorable situation than to try to change a leader's style.[23]

The Path–Goal Theory of Leadership   The **path–goal theory of leadership** suggests that the primary activities of a leader are to make desirable and achievable rewards available to organization members who attain organizational goals and to clarify the kinds of behavior that must be performed to earn those rewards.[24] The leader outlines the goals that followers should aim for and clarifies the path that followers should take to achieve those goals and earn the rewards contingent on doing so. Overall, the path–goal theory maintains that managers can facilitate job performance by showing employees how their performance directly affects their reception of desired rewards.

Leadership Behavior   According to the path–goal theory of leadership, leaders exhibit four primary types of behavior:

1. *Directive behavior*—Directive behavior is aimed at telling followers what to do and how to do it. The leader indicates what performance goals exist and precisely what must be done to achieve them.
2. *Supportive behavior*—Supportive behavior is aimed at being friendly with followers and showing interest in them as human beings. Through supportive behavior, the leader demonstrates sensitivity to the personal needs of followers.
3. *Participative behavior*—Participative behavior is aimed at seeking suggestions from followers regarding business operations to the extent that followers are involved in making important organizational decisions. Followers often help to determine the rewards that will be available to them in organizations and what they must do to earn those rewards.
4. *Achievement behavior*—Achievement behavior is aimed at setting challenging goals for followers to reach and expressing and demonstrating confidence that they will measure up to the challenge. This leader behavior focuses on making goals difficult enough that employees will find achieving them challenging, but not so difficult that they will view them as impossible and give up trying to achieve them.

Path–goal theory of leadership is a theory of leadership that suggests that the primary activities of a leader are to make desirable and achievable rewards available to organization members who attain organizational goals and to clarify the kinds of behavior that must be performed to earn those rewards.

Adapting Behavior to Situations   As with other situational theories of leadership, the path–goal theory proposes that leaders will be successful if they appropriately match these four types of behavior to situations that they face. For example, if inexperienced followers do not have a thorough understanding of a job, a manager may appropriately use more directive behavior to develop this understanding and to ensure that serious job-related problems are avoided. For more experienced followers, who have a more complete understanding of a job, directive behavior would probably be inappropriate and might create interpersonal problems between leader and followers.

If jobs are very structured, with little room for employee interpretation of how the work should be done, directive behavior is less appropriate than if there is much room for employees to determine how the work gets done. When followers are deriving much personal satisfaction and encouragement from work and enjoy the support of other members of their work group, supportive behavior by the leader is not as important as when followers are gaining little or no satisfaction from their work or from personal relationships in the work group.

The primary focus of the path–goal theory of leadership is on how leaders can increase employee effort and productivity by clarifying performance goals and the path to be taken to achieve those goals. This theory of leadership has gained increasing acceptance in recent years. In fact, research suggests that the path–goal theory is highly promising for enhancing employee commitment to achieving organizational goals and thereby increasing the probability that organizations will be successful. It should be pointed out, however, that the research done on this model has been conducted mostly on its parts rather than on the complete model.[25]

▶ Back to the Case

The life cycle theory suggests that William Johnson should be flexible enough to behave as required by situations at Heinz. If Johnson finds it extremely difficult to be flexible, however, he should attempt to structure his situation so as to make it appropriate for his style. As suggested by Fiedler, if Johnson's leadership style is high-task in nature, he generally will be a more successful leader in situations best described by octants 1, 2, 3, and 8 in Table 15.1 and Figure 15.7. If, however, Johnson's leadership style is more relationship-oriented, he will probably be a more successful leader in situations representative of octants 4, 5, 6, and 7. Overall, Fiedler's work provides Johnson with insights into how to engineer situations at Heinz so they will be appropriate for his leadership style.

The path–goal theory of leadership suggests that in leading Heinz, Johnson should emphasize clarifying what rewards are available to followers in the organization, how those rewards can be earned, and eliminating barriers that could prohibit followers from earning the rewards. Johnson can use directive behavior, supportive behavior, participative behavior, and achievement behavior in implementing the path–goal theory.

LEADERSHIP TODAY

Leaders in modern organizations have been confronting many situations rarely encountered by organizational leaders of the past.[26] Today's leaders are often called upon to make massive personnel cuts in order to eliminate unnecessary levels of organizations and thereby lower labor expenses, to introduce work teams in order to enhance organizational decision making and work flow, to reengineer work so that organization members will be more efficient and effective, and to initiate programs designed to improve the overall quality of organizational functioning.

In reaction to these new situations, organizations are emphasizing leadership styles that concentrate on getting employees involved in the organization and giving them the freedom to use their abilities as they think best. This is a dramatically different type of leadership from that known in organizations of the past, which largely concentrated on controlling people and work processes. Figure 15.8 contrasts the "soul" of the new leader with the "mind" of the manager.

LEADER	MANAGER
SOUL	**MIND**
Visionary	Rational
Passionate	Consultative
Creative	Persistent
Flexible	Problem-solving
Inspirational	Tough-minded
Innovative	Analytical
Courageous	Structured
Imaginative	Deliberate
Experimental	Authoritative
Independent	Stabilizing

Figure 15.8 *Characteristics of the emerging leader versus characteristics of the manager*

Transformational leadership is leadership that inspires organizational success by profoundly affecting followers' beliefs in what an organization should be, as well as their values, such as justice and integrity.

The information in this section of the text points out the trend among today's leaders to get employees involved in their organizations and to give them the freedom to make and carry out decisions.

Four leadership styles have emerged in recent years to suit these new situations: transformational leadership, coaching, "superleadership," and entrepreneurial leadership.[27] Each of these new styles is discussed in the following sections.

Transformational Leadership

Transformational leadership is leadership that inspires organizational success by profoundly affecting followers' beliefs in what an organization should be, as well as their values, such as justice and integrity.[28] This style of leadership creates a sense of duty within an organization, encourages new ways of handling problems, and promotes learning for all organization members. Transformational leadership is closely related to concepts like charismatic leadership and inspirational leadership.

Perhaps transformational leadership is receiving more attention nowadays because of the dramatic changes that many organizations are going through and the critical importance of transformational leadership in "transforming" or changing organizations successfully. Lee Iacocca is often cited as an exemplar of transformational leadership because of his success in transforming Chrysler Corporation from a company on the verge of going under into a successful company.[29]

▶ Joe Weller, chairman and CEO of Nestlé USA, has worked to bring about organizational changes that support his vision of the firm as one in which, among other things, Friday afternoons are reserved for strategizing and setting priorities for the coming week. Most Fridays, he prowls the company's 21-story headquarters in Glendale, California, breaking up meetings that are still running after 10 A.M. Ted Manion, a member of the advertising and marketing team, was holding such a meeting when Weller interrupted. "I hate to admit this," says Manion, "but I didn't think he'd come back," and the group continued to work after Weller had walked away. A few minutes later, Weller reappeared in the doorway. "I am sincere," he said.

The Tasks of Transformational Leaders Transformational leaders perform several important tasks. First, they raise followers' awareness of organizational issues and their consequences. Organization members must understand an organization's high-priority issues and what will happen if these issues are not successfully resolved. Second, transformational leaders create a vision of what the organization should be, build commitment to that vision throughout the organization, and facilitate organizational changes that support the vision. In sum, transformational leadership is consistent with strategy developed through an organization's strategic management process.[30]

Managers of the future will continue to face the challenge of significantly changing their organizations, primarily because of the accelerating trend to position organizations to be more competitive in a global business environment. Therefore, transformational leadership will probably get increasing attention in the leadership literature. Although there is much practical appeal and interest in this style of leadership, more research is needed to develop insights into how managers can become successful transformational leaders.

Coaching

Coaching is leadership that instructs followers on how to meet the special organizational challenges they face.[31] Operating like an athletic coach, the coaching leader identifies inappropriate behavior in followers and suggests how they might correct that behavior. The increasing use of teams has elevated the importance of coaching in today's organizations. Characteristics of an effective coach are presented in Table 15.2.

Coaching is a leadership that instructs followers on how to meet the special organizational challenges they face.

Coaching Behavior   A successful coaching leader is characterized by many different kinds of behavior. Among these behaviors are the following:

➤ *Listens closely*—The coaching leader tries to gather both the facts in what is said and the feelings and emotions behind what is said. Such a leader is careful to really listen and not fall into the trap of immediately rebutting statements made by followers.

➤ *Gives emotional support*—The coaching leader gives followers personal encouragement.[32] Such encouragement should constantly be aimed at motivating them to do their best to meet the high demands of successful organizations.

➤ *Shows by example what constitutes appropriate behavior*—The coaching leader shows followers, for instance, how to handle an employee problem or a production glitch. By demonstrating expertise, the coaching leader builds the trust and respect of followers.

Superleadership

Superleadership is leading by showing others how to lead themselves. If superleaders are successful, they develop followers who are productive, work independently, and need only minimal attention from the superleader.

Superleadership is leadership that inspires organizational success by showing followers how to lead themselves.

Characteristics of an Effective Coach  Table 15.2

Trait, Attitude, or Behavior	Action Plan for Improvement
1. Empathy (putting self in other person's shoes)	*Sample:* Will listen and understand person's point of view. *Your own:*
2. Listening skill	*Sample:* Will concentrate extra-hard on listening. *Your own:*
3. Insight into people (ability to size them up)	*Sample:* Will jot down observations about people on first meeting, then verify in the future. *Your own:*
4. Diplomacy and tact	*Sample:* Will study book of etiquette. *Your own:*
5. Patience toward people	*Sample:* Will practice staying calm when someone makes a mistake. *Your own:*
6. Concern for welfare of people	*Sample:* When interacting with another person, will ask myself, "How can this person's interests best be served?" *Your own:*
7. Minimum hostility toward people	*Sample:* Will often ask myself, "Why am I angry at this person?" *Your own:*
8. Self-confidence and emotional stability	*Sample:* Will attempt to have at least one personal success each week. *Your own:*
9. Noncompetitiveness with team members	*Sample:* Will keep reminding myself that all boats rise with the same tide. *Your own:*
10. Enthusiasm for people	*Sample:* Will search for the good in each person. *Your own:*

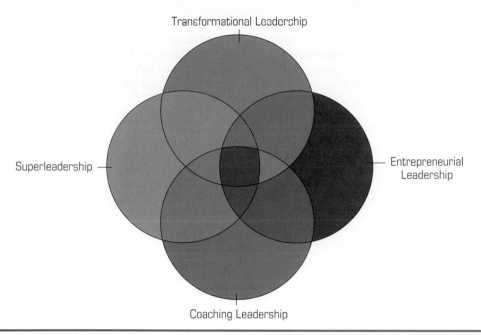

Transformational Leadership

Superleadership

Entrepreneurial Leadership

Coaching Leadership

Figure 15.9 *Various combinations of transformational, coaching, superleader, and entrepreneurial leadership styles*

In essence, superleaders teach followers how to think on their own and act constructively and independently.[33] They encourage people to eliminate negative thoughts and beliefs about the company and coworkers and to replace them with more positive and constructive beliefs. An important aspect of superleadership is building the self-confidence of followers by convincing them that they are competent, have a significant reservoir of potential, and are capable of meeting the difficult challenges of the work situation.

The objective of superleaders is to develop followers who require very little leadership. This is an important objective in the typical organization of today, whose structure is flatter than that of organizations of the past and which therefore has fewer leader–managers. Organizations cannot be successful in such a situation unless their members become proficient at leading themselves.

Entrepreneurial Leadership

Entrepreneurial leadership is leadership that is based on the attitude that the leader is self-employed. Leaders of this type act as if they are playing a critical role in the organization rather than a mostly unimportant one. In addition, they behave as if they are taking the risk of losing money but will receive the profit if one is made. They approach each mistake as if it were a significant error rather than a smaller error that will be neutralized by the normal functioning of the organization.[34]

Each of these four contemporary leadership styles has received notable attention in recent management literature. Managers should realize that these four styles are not mutually exclusive; they can be combined in various ways to generate a unique style. For example, a leader can assume both a coaching and an entrepreneurial role. Figure 15.9 shows the various combinations of these four leadership styles that a leader can adopt. The shaded portion of the figure represents a leader whose style comprises all four.

CURRENT TOPICS IN LEADERSHIP

Two currently popular leadership topics are leadership substitutes and women leaders. Both are discussed in the following sections under the heads "Substitutes for Leadership," "Women as Leaders," and "Ways Women Lead."

Marginal note: **Entrepreneurial leadership** is leadership that is based on the attitude that the leader is self-employed.

Substitutes for Leadership

There are times when leaders do not have to lead or, for one reason or another, cannot lead. In these circumstances, situational substitutes can have as much influence on employees as any leader.

You have probably heard or observed situations in which the nominal leader—for a number of reasons, including factors beyond the leader's control—had little or no impact on the outcome of a situation. Because so many factors can affect a situation, some people argue that leadership is really irrelevant to many organization outcomes. Under various conditions—for instance, strong subordinates, knowledge of the task, organizational constraints—subordinates may not need or even want leadership.

Substitute leadership theory attempts to identify those situations in which the input of leader behavior is partly or wholly canceled out by characteristics of the subordinate or the organization. Here are some examples: A subordinate may have such high levels of ability, experience, education, and internal motivation that little or no leadership is required or desired; task characteristics may be so routine that the subordinate does not require much, if any, leadership; organizational characteristics such as group cohesion and a high degree of formalization may reduce the need for leadership. Recall, also, from our earlier discussion of life cycle theory the situation in which the leader delegates tasks to highly mature followers in a low-task/low-relationship situation.[35]

Throughout this chapter, we have concentrated on a number of factors affecting leadership effectiveness. Much of this attention has centered on leadership characteristics, situations, and leader behavior. Substitute theory tends to downplay the importance of these dimensions. Why? Meindl and Ehrlich suggest one possible answer: Throughout history, human beings have had a tendency to romanticize leadership, treating it as more important than it actually is.[36] Substitute theory reminds us that—at least in some situations with some people in some organizations—things just seem to get done regardless of the quality of leadership.

▶ Orpheus, the renowned leaderless chamber orchestra, relies on several substitutes for a conductor's traditional leadership. Body language allows all the musicians to begin together, and they watch one another closely while playing in order to come in on cue at the slightest gesture. A core group of musicians from the orchestra meets to decide how to play each new piece, and the first violinist, also known as the concertmaster, typically leads rehearsals. The group relies on consensus-building to resolve disputes; when that fails, they take a vote. The orchestra has become a management model for many flat-hierarchy firms.

Women as Leaders

One can read Stogdill's *Handbook of Leadership* (1974) and find barely any reference to women leaders, except as a subject deserving further research. This is probably because in 1970 only 15 percent of all managers were women. By 1989, this figure had risen to more than 40 percent. By 1995, women made up about 63 percent of the total workforce. Just how many women will become leaders in their companies or industries remains to be seen. Currently, only 3 of every 100 top jobs in the largest U.S. companies are held by women—about the same number as a decade ago. A Labor Department study of the early 1990s concluded that the so-called glass ceiling was keeping women from moving into leadership positions. The glass ceiling is the subtle barrier of negative attitudes and prejudices that prevents women from reaching seemingly attainable top-management positions.[37]

Ways Women Lead

Women who have broken through the glass ceiling have found that there is no one mold for effective leadership. In the past, women leaders modeled their leadership styles after successful male managers. Today's women managers, however, often describe their leadership styles as transformational—getting workers to transform or subordinate their individual self-interests into group consensus directed toward a broader goal. This leadership style attributes power to such personal characteristics as charisma, personal contacts, and interpersonal skills rather than to the organizational structure.

Men, on the other hand, are more likely to characterize their leadership as transactional. They see their jobs as involving a series of transactions between themselves and their subordinates. This leadership style involves exchanging rewards for service or dispensing punishment for inadequate performance.[38]

For James G. Kaiser of Corning, Being Employee-Centered Includes a Focus on Diversity

James G. Kaiser is a senior vice president at Corning, Inc. Kaiser is responsible for keeping the Technical Products Division competitive in the global marketplace and for masterminding the strategic planning for his division's operations. In addition, he oversees research and development for new products and is responsible for seeking business partners with whom the company can pursue joint ventures. Last, Kaiser is in charge of a series of export and sales offices in several locations.

Kaiser considers himself to be a people-oriented leader. He is an African American manager who sees his race as an asset in managing people from different cultures because it gives him a broader perspective on the differences among various types of employees. He focuses formally on cultural diversity at Corning largely through the

Executive Leadership Council, a group whose mission is to offer guidance and leadership to other up-and-coming African American executives. As president of Corning's Executive Leadership Council, Kaiser provides minority executives with a network and a discussion forum that help them to understand what the achievement of excellence means within and for the African American community and how they can personally excel.

Because Kaiser is an African American leader, it could be argued that he has special insights for advising and helping minority employees to be successful leaders. For their own long-run success, however, leaders like Kaiser must be careful not to become "specialists" who deal with only one culture, but rather "generalists" who develop the skills to successfully manage people from many different cultures. ∎

▶ Back to the Case

Based on the preceding information, during his tenure at Heinz, William Johnson could focus on being a transformational leader, a leader who inspires followers to seriously focus on achieving organizational objectives. As a transformational leader, he would strive to encourage new ideas, create a sense of duty, and encourage employees to learn and grow. As Heinz experiences more and more significant change, the importance of Johnson being a transformational leader increases.

Three other popular leadership styles also offer a manager like Johnson insights about how to lead at Heinz. As a coaching leader, Johnson can focus on instructing Heinz's followers to meet special challenges they face, such as expansion through global acquisition. In the role of a coaching leader, he would listen closely, give emotional support, and show by example what should be done. As a superleader, Johnson would teach followers how to think on their own and act constructively and independently. As an entrepreneurial leader, Johnson would act much like a self-employed owner of Heinz. He would act, for example, like an individual personally incurring the risk of developing a new "hot" ketchup sauce, but also benefiting from the profit if it is made.

Overall, a manager like Johnson must keep in mind that these leadership styles are aimed at getting people involved in an organization and giving them the freedom to use their abilities as they think best. Such leaders must always keep in mind that regardless of the type of leader they may be, they must earn and maintain the trust of their followers if they are to be successful in the long run.

Management Skills Module

This section is specially designed to help you develop management skills. An individual's management skill is based on an understanding of management concepts and the ability to apply those concepts in management situations. As a result, the following activities are designed both to heighten your understanding of management concepts and to help you gain facility in applying those concepts in various management situations.

UNDERSTANDING MANAGEMENT CONCEPTS

▶ Action Summary

Reread the learning objectives below. Each objective is followed by questions. Answering these questions accurately will help you retain the most important concepts discussed in this chapter. After answering each question, check your answer against the answer key at the end of the chapter. (*Hint*: If you have any doubts regarding the correct response, consult the page number that follows the answer.)

Circle:

From studying this chapter, I will attempt to acquire

1. A working definition of leadership.

a b c d e   **a.** The process of directing others toward the accomplishment of some objective is: (a) communication (b) controlling (c) leadership (d) managing (e) none of the above.

a b c d e   **b.** Directing must be consistent with: (a) organizational policies (b) procedures (c) job descriptions (d) none of the above (e) all of the above.

2. An understanding of the relationship between leading and managing.

T F   **a.** Leading and managing are the same process.

a b c d e   **b.** In the relationship between managers and leaders, one could say that: (a) all managers are leaders (b) all leaders are managers (c) some leaders are not managers (d) managers cannot be leaders (e) management is a subset of leadership.

3. An appreciation for the trait and situational approaches to leadership.

a b c d e   **a.** The following is true about the conclusions drawn from the trait approach to leadership: (a) the trait approach identifies traits that consistently separate leaders from nonleaders (b) there are certain traits that guarantee that a leader will be successful (c) the trait approach is based on early research that assumes that a good leader is born, not made (d) leadership is a simple issue of describing the traits of successful leaders (e) none of the above.

a b c d e   **b.** The situational approach to leadership takes into account: (a) the leader (b) the follower (c) the situation (d) a and b (e) a, b, and c.

4. Insights into using leadership theories that emphasizes decision-making situations.

a b c d e   **a.** Forces within the manager that determine leadership behavior include: (a) the manager's values (b) the manager's confidence in subordinates (c) the manager's strengths (d) the manager's tolerance for ambiguity (e) all of the above.

a b c d e   **b.** Limiting the self-guidance of the follower and specifically defining procedures for the follower's task performance are called: (a) initiating behavior (b) structure behavior (c) maturity behavior (d) consideration behavior (e) relationship behavior.

T F   **c.** The VYJ Model suggests that a leader should match one of five decision-making styles to the particular situation the leader faces.

5. Insights into using leadership theories that emphasize more general organizational situations.

a b c d e   **a.** The ability of followers to perform their jobs independently and to assume additional responsibilities in their desire to achieve success is called: (a) maturity (b) authority (c) aggressiveness (d) assertiveness (e) consideration.

a b c d e   **b.** Usually, on entrance into an organization, an individual is unable to solve task-related problems independently. According to the life cycle theory, the appropriate style of leadership for this person is: (a) high-task/low-relationships (b) high-task/high-relationships (c) high-relationships/low-task (d) low-task/low-relationships (e) none of the above.

T F   **c.** According to the path-goal theory of leadership, a leader should carefully inform followers of the rewards that are available to them in the organization and then allow them to pick their own methods of earning the rewards.

6. An understanding of alternatives to leader flexibility.

a b c d e   **a.** According to Fiedler, the three primary factors that should be used as a basis for moving leaders into more appropriate situations are: (a) task behavior, consideration behavior, maturity (b) maturity, job knowledge, responsibility (c) the worker, the leader, the situation (d) leader–member relations, task structure, position power (e) task structure, leadership style, maturity.

T F   **b.** Fiedler's studies have proven true the myths that leaders are born, not made, and that there is one best leadership style.

7. An appreciation of emerging leadership styles and leadership issues of today.

T F   **a.** Transformational leaders modify organizations by precisely carrying out strategic plans and emphasizing only slightly the values that followers may have.

a b c d e   **b.** The coaching leader: (a) listens closely (b) gives emotional support (c) shows by example (d) a and c (e) all of the above.

T F   **c.** The superleader and entrepreneurial leadership styles are basically the same.

T F   **d.** Even though there are situations in which a leader has little or no impact on the outcome, the leader is nevertheless an important part of management.

▌ Action Summary Answer Key

1. a. c, p. 326   **4. a.** e, p. 330   **6. a.** d, p. 339   **7. a.** F, p. 342
   b. e, p. 326   **b.** b, p. 335   **b.** F, p. 339   **b.** e, p. 343
2. a. F, p. 327   **c.** T, p. 332   **c.** F, p. 343
   b. c, p. 327   **5. a.** a, p. 336   **d.** F, p. 345
3. a. c, p. 327   **b.** a, pp. 336–337
   b. e, p. 329   **c.** F, p. 340

▌ Issues for Review and Discussion

1. What is leadership?
2. How does leadership differ from management?
3. Explain the trait approach to leadership.
4. What relationship exists between successful leadership and leadership traits?
5. Explain the situational approach to leadership.
6. Draw and explain Tannenbaum and Schmidt's leadership model.
7. List the forces within the manager, the subordinates, and the situation that ultimately determine how a manager should make decisions as a leader.
8. How is the VYJ Model similar to Tannenbaum and Schmidt's model? How is it different?
9. What contribution did the OSU studies make to leadership theory?
10. Can any one of the major leadership styles resulting from the OSU studies be called more effective than the others? Explain.
11. Compare the results of the OSU studies with the results of the Michigan studies.
12. What is meant by *maturity* as it is used in the life cycle theory of leadership?
13. Draw and explain the life cycle theory of leadership model.
14. What is meant by *leadership flexibility*?
15. Describe some obstacles to leader flexibility.
16. In general, how might obstacles to leader flexibility be overcome?
17. In specific terms, how does Fiedler suggest that obstacles to leader flexibility be overcome?
18. Based on the path-goal theory of leadership, how would you advise a friend to lead?
19. Describe three challenges that a transformational leader must face.
20. Compare and contrast the coaching leader and the entrepreneurial leader.
21. Describe the leadership style indicated by the shaded portion of Figure 15.9.

APPLYING MANAGEMENT CONCEPTS

▶ Cases

▶ INTRODUCTORY CASE WRAP-UP

▶Case Discussion Questions

"The President of H.J. Heinz Company Sends a Letter" (p. 325) and its related Back-to-the-Case sections were written to help you better understand the management concepts contained in this chapter. Answer the following discussion questions about this Introductory Case to further enrich your understanding of chapter content:

1. List and define five activities that William Johnson might perform as a manager moving his company toward *victory* as defined in the Introductory Case.
2. Do you feel that Johnson should use more of a boss-centered or subordinate-centered leadership style in making decisions about achieving this *victory?* Why?
3. If you were Johnson, would understanding the transformational and the entrepreneurial leadership styles be valuable to you in leading Heinz employees to this *victory?* Explain fully.

▶Skills Exercise: Applying the VYJ Leadership Model

The Introductory Case discussed some of William R. Johnson's plans as the new president of H.J. Heinz Company. Assume that you are Mr. Johnson and you want to decide whether or not to create a new line of instant fruit juices for infants. Use Figure 15.4 to help you decide which style you would use to make this decision. Be sure to explain the rationale you use to choose each branch of the VYJ decision tree.

CASE STUDY: *THREATENING E-MAIL FROM CERNER CEO HEARD ROUND THE WORLD*

On January 8, 2001, *Fortune* published its list of the 100 Best Companies to Work For. The Kansas City, Missouri–based health software developer Cerner Corporation ranked number 56, heralded by its employees as "being a place that knows how to treat workers right." A few weeks later, CEO Neal Patterson hit the "send" button on an e-mail to his top management team, unleashing a "firestorm" that ultimately caused the company's stock to drop 28 percent in three days.

Patterson's message, later posted on Yahoo! by angry staff members, included the following: "We are getting less than 40 hours of work from a large number of our K.C.-based EMPLOYEES. The parking lot is sparsely used at 8 A.M.; likewise at 5 P.M. As managers, you either do not know what your EMPLOYEES are doing, or you do not CARE. NEVER in my career have I allowed a team that worked for me to think they had a 40-hour job. I have allowed YOU to create a culture, which is permitting this. NO LONGER."

Six potential punishments were listed, including laying off 5 percent of the staff in Kansas City, where about 2,000 of Cerner's 3,100 employees work. "Hell will freeze over before this CEO implements ANOTHER EMPLOYEE benefit in this Culture," Patterson declared, going on to recommend that managers start scheduling 7 A.M., 6 P.M., and Saturday team meetings. He said the company parking lot would be a key measure of success. "It should be substantially full at 7:30 A.M. and 6:30 P.M. The pizza man should show up at 7:30 P.M. to feed the starving teams working late. The lot

should be half full on Saturday mornings.   You have two weeks. Tick, tock."

The day after the memo was posted on the World Wide Web, trading in Cerner's shares, which typically runs to about 650,000, in one day shot up to 1.2 million shares. The following day, volume surged to 4 million. In three days, the stock price fell to $34 from almost $44.

Patterson, who holds an M.B.A. from Oklahoma State, grew up on his family's 4,000-acre wheat farm. He attributes his management style to the long days he spent riding a tractor through the fields alone with his thoughts. He came to the conclusion then, he said, that life was about building things in your head, then going out and acting on them. He worked as a consultant at Arthur Andersen before forming Cerner with two partners in 1979. As chairman and CEO of Cerner, he has devoted the last 20 years to creating an open, trusting corporate culture focused on transforming the health care industry.

Cerner has "clients," not "customers." Staff members are "associates" who share Cerner's sense of mission and values, not "employees" who punch a clock. Patterson meets with all new associates during their first month at Cerner to share the company's vision with them. He uses "Town Hall" meetings and informal "Neal Notes" to communicate with the Cerner "associate community." People who know the 51-year-old CEO describe him variously as "arrogant," "candid," and "passionate." Neal Patterson sees himself as both a visionary and an entrepreneur. "Leaders lead," he says. "Look behind you. If people are following you, congratulations, you are a leader." He sees a leader as someone able to *energize* others to achieve goals that may not seem possible, someone capable of making unpopular decisions when it is necessary, and, above all, someone who shoulders full responsibility for making those decisions.

Cerner has grown over the last two decades, literally doubling in size every two to four years. In 1999, the workforce was faced with the enormous task of completing a rewrite of all its software to overcome the Y2K challenge. Because Cerner associates had to work harder than ever (and in acknowledgment of the extra effort), Patterson felt that during early 2000, Cerner should take a short "breather." However, he was troubled that part of the organization—particularly in Kansas City—had lost its focus and never really clicked back into gear. The impetus for his e-mail was to regain the momentum to push the company over the next hill.

When Patterson realized his corporate memo had been leaked, he took immediate action, sending out a "Neal Note" of apology to anyone who might have been offended by the original "Management Directive." "Unfortunately, I used an intense coach's half-time speech with our team, some of whom have never been in the locker room with me. . . . As with many things in life, looking back, I would clearly approach it differently. But once you hit the 'send' button, it is difficult to change it. However, I stand behind my message." Just three weeks after the original memo was sent, Cerner reported record results for the first quarter of 2001. This marked the fifth consecutive quarter in which the company exceeded consensus estimates.

Contemplating the trouble his e-mail caused, Patterson had this to say: "We've all got more to learn about managing in this environment. There's the temptation to not be as open and candid as I've been in the past." As the use of e-mail becomes a primary mode of communication within corporations, Patterson may have to learn to adjust his leadership style.

QUESTIONS

1. As one of Cerner's front-line managers, what would your response be to Patterson's e-mail?
2. Using Figure 15.9 as an example, draw a diagram showing the ideal combination of transformational, super, coaching, and entrepreneurial leadership that Patterson might use to modify his own leadership style in the future.
3. Is Patterson a CEO you would feel comfortable with as a member of the company's board of directors? Why?

▶ Video

CONMEDIA SEGMENT 4
Leadership

In this segment, the focus shifts from the editorial and IT departments to Conmedia's art department, headed by Ted Baker. You will learn that Ted, who's been with the company for over 10 years, is still considered a star by the "old boy network." Listen for Ted's reactions as he struggles to find a way to accept the introduction of the Internet into his graphic design operation. There does not seem to be any corporate vision for the future of this merger, allowing Ted's own fears to bring out the worst in him. Remember that Sam, the publisher, has remained aloof. Your own understanding of the relationship between leading and management should help you to assess the strengths and weaknesses of each person in this episode.

As the first scene unfolds, Ruth tries to boost Ted's confidence by telling him that "good design is good design," on or off the Web. You will learn quickly that Ruth and Ted have very different leadership styles. Keep this in mind as you watch how Ted handles the interchange with his two new Web designers from Allaboutself.com, Jack and Sarah. He fails to address their concerns or to appreciate the valuable insight into the Web that they want to share with him. As a result, he leaves them both dissatisfied. Think about the reasons for Jack and Sarah's sense of isolation.

The final scene takes place two months later in Ruth's office. She has called Sam and Mia in to discuss the problem in Ted's department. Ruth has obviously assessed the situation thoroughly before calling this meeting. When Ruth starts talking, it is Mia who is caught off guard. At this moment, Ruth is very much the team player she promised Sam she would be in the opening video of this series. You might want to keep in mind the emerging leadership issues of today and how very different they are from what they were when Ruth started out at *Modern Lady*.

As the scene comes to a close, you might want to think about why Mia is now out of touch with her staff. From her facial expressions and her comments, try to ascertain whether Mia's dot-com leadership skills are effective in this more impersonal setting. Listen closely as Ruth and Mia seem to join together in response to Sam.

QUESTIONS

1. Which of the four leadership styles—transformational, coaching, superleadership, or entrepreneurial—apply to Ruth? Which of the four leadership styles applies to Mia?

2. Take a guess at Ruth's motives for wanting to replace Ted. Do you think she has organizational goals in mind, or do you think she might have her own objective in mind? Do you think Jack and

Sarah will decide to stay if the assistant art director, who is more of a consensus builder, replaces Ted?

3. How might Fiedler's contingency theory of leadership be useful to Conmedia as the company tries to move from a traditional structure to a more modern structure incorporating the use of the Internet? When answering, keep in mind *leader–member relations, task structure,* and *position power.*

LEADERSHIP AND *YOU*

You have been voted captain of the intercollegiate swim team at your school. Everyone did well at the first interscholastic meet of the season. The coach calls you in for a meeting and tells you to make sure morale stays up because your next meet will be against an undefeated team. You are working hard to improve your own time and to keep your teammates' minds on victory in the next competition. You are respected among your teammates as a leader. You abide by all the rules

pertaining to athletes at your college and expect your fellow swimmers to do the same. One night, as you and the best butterfly racer the team has are leaving the pool, a container of protein vitamins falls out of his/her bag. Everyone in your league signed a contract at the beginning of the semester stipulating that protein vitamins are not allowed.

1. Which of your leadership skills are you going to use? (Remember leadership involves influencing others.) Will you try to convince your teammate to stop using the vitamins by letting him/her know you care about their well-being? Will you try to motivate them to stop by pointing out how unfair they are being to the rest of the swimmers? Will you try to inspire them with your own dedication to the sport, the team, and the school? Will you threaten to tell the coach and have them kicked off the team? Will you say nothing and then hold a meeting with the rest of the team and try to exert peer pressure? Can you think of a better way to lead in this situation? Do you think being a team captain may help you develop leadership skills you will use as a manager in business?

MASTERING MANAGEMENT: EPISODE 7—LEADERSHIP

Mastering Management is a series of innovative, interactive learning activities specially designed to help you develop management skills emphasized in various text chapters. Leadership is the major focus of this chapter. Episode 7 of *Mastering Management* focuses on leading individuals as well as groups and covers behavioral and contingency theories of leadership. In this episode, we will take a look at how the CanGo president, Liz, handles her role as leader in two different employee groups. Review Episode 7, "Leadership," on your *Mastering Management* CD and then answer the following questions.

QUESTIONS

1. Do you see evidence that managers at CanGo are also leaders? Explain.

2. Do you believe that the Hersey-Blanchard Life Cycle Theory of Leadership can be applied to improve leadership at CanGo? Explain.

3. Reflecting on leadership concepts in this chapter, if you were president of CanGo, what leadership style would you adopt for yourself? Why?

www.prenhall.com/certo

This book is accompanied by a rich assortment of online activities aimed at developing your management skills. Reviewing news headlines, Internet exercises, an online study guide, and other research and Internet resources can help personalize management skills development for individual students or an entire class.

16 Motivation

Bristol-Myers Squibb Stresses Motivation in Internet Implementation

REMINDER: THE INTRODUCTORY CASE WRAP-UP (P. 371) CONTAINS DISCUSSION QUESTIONS AND A SKILLS EXERCISE TO FURTHER ILLUSTRATE THE APPLICATION OF CHAPTER CONCEPTS TO THIS VIGNETTE.

Bristol-Myers Squibb is a world-renowned manufacturer of personal care products and over-the-counter pharmaceuticals, which produces and markets popular household brands like Bufferin, Excedrin, and Nuprin. The company's annual sales exceed $18 billion. With its international infrastructure, ever-changing marketplace, and competitive industry, Bristol-Myers has a lot to consider in formulating and refining its Internet strategy.

Change is difficult. When a firm adopts a new strategy, such as Bristol Myers Squibb's Internet strategy, managers can help to motivate employees to accept the accompanying changes.

Formulating the strategy is only the beginning. After the strategy is formulated, it must be implemented. Jack Cooper, a top Bristol-Myers manager, champions many of the company's activities aimed at implementing Internet strategy. Cooper coordinates implementation activities with a firm grasp of the organization's business priorities. According to Cooper, implementing Internet strategy can be very tricky. Implementing Internet strategy is challenging because it requires implementing multiple project phases concurrently. To be successful in implementing Internet strategy, managers need to know how to commit resources, set deadlines, and control implementation costs.

In addition to the technical issues involved in implementing Internet strategy, there are also people issues involved. Managers implementing Internet strategy in organizations must be sound leaders. Motivating people involved in implementing Internet strategy is key. According to Cooper, it is easy for people to see reasons why Internet strategy implementation will not work. Managers must help people see beyond those reasons if Internet strategy implementation is to be successful. Managers must emphasize the desire to win and to create solutions in the face of adversity.

The lesson seems clear. Even if management at Bristol-Myers Squibb develops the very best plan to implement Internet strategy, it is of little value if people are not motivated to carry out the plan.

Jack Cooper, a member of top management at Bristol-Myers Squibb in the Introductory Case, focuses on implementing Internet strategy within the company. According to the case, in implementing Internet strategy, Cooper focuses on more technical issues like properly committing resources, setting deadlines, and controlling related costs. Cooper knows that if he is to be successful in implementing Internet strategy, however, he must focus on related people issues in addition to such technical issues. The material in this chapter discusses insights into why managers such as Cooper should focus on motivating workers in such situations and how this might be accomplished. Major topics in this chapter are:

1) The motivation process
2) Motivating organization members

THE MOTIVATION PROCESS

To be successful in working with subordinates, managers need to acquire a thorough understanding of the motivation process. To this end, the definition of motivation, various motivation models, and theories of people's needs are the main discussion topics in this section of the chapter.

Defining Motivation

Motivation is the inner state that causes an individual to behave in a way that ensures the accomplishment of some goal.[1] In other words, motivation explains why people act as they do. The better a manager understands organization members' behavior, the more able that manager will be to influence subordinates' behavior to make it more consistent with the accomplishment of organizational objectives. Because productivity is a result of the behavior of organization members, motivating organization members is the key to reaching organizational goals.[2]

Several motivation theories have been proposed over the years. Most of these theories can be categorized into two basic types: process theories and content theories. **Process theories of motivation** are explanations of motivation that emphasize how individuals are motivated. They focus, essentially, on the steps that occur when an individual is motivated. **Content theories of motivation** are explanations of motivation that emphasize people's internal characteristics. They focus on the need to understand what needs people have and how these needs can be satisfied. The following sections discuss important process and content theories of motivation and establish a relationship between them that should prove useful to managers in motivating organization members.

Process Theories of Motivation

There are four important theories that describe how motivation occurs:

1. Needs-goal theory
2. Vroom expectancy theory
3. Equity theory
4. Porter–Lawler theory

These theories build on one another to furnish a description of the motivation process that begins at a relatively simple and easily understood level and culminates at a somewhat more intricate and realistic level.

The Needs-Goal Theory of Motivation   The **needs-goal theory** of motivation, diagrammed in Figure 16.1, is the most fundamental of the motivation theories discussed in this chapter. As the figure indicates, motivation begins with an individual feeling a need. This need is then transformed into behavior directed at supporting, or allowing, the performance of goal behavior to reduce the felt need. Theoretically, goal-supportive behavior and goal behavior itself continue until the felt need has been significantly reduced.

Motivation is the inner state that causes an individual to behave in a way that ensures the accomplishment of some goal.

Process theories of motivation are explanations of motivation that emphasize how individuals are motivated.

Content theories of motivation are explanations of motivation that emphasize people's internal characteristics.

The **needs-goal theory** is a motivation model that hypothesizes that felt needs cause human behavior.

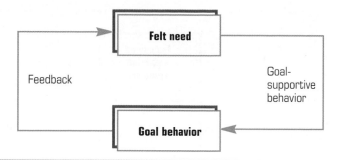

The needs-goal theory of motivation

Figure 16.1

When an individual feels hunger, for example, this need is typically transformed first into behavior directed at supporting the performance of the goal behavior of eating. This supportive behavior could include such activities as buying, cooking, and serving the food to be eaten. The goal-supportive behaviors and the goal behavior itself—eating—generally continue until the individual's hunger substantially subsides. When the individual experiences hunger again, however, the entire cycle is repeated.

The Role of Individual Needs   If managers are to have any success in motivating employees, they must understand the personal needs of those employees. When managers offer rewards that are not relevant to employees' personal needs, the employees will not be motivated. For example, if a top executive is already extremely well paid, more money is not likely to be an effective motivator. What is required is a more meaningful incentive—perhaps a higher-level title or an offer of partnership in the firm. Managers must be familiar with needs their employees have and offer them rewards that can satisfy these needs.[3]

The Vroom Expectancy Theory of Motivation   In reality, the motivation process is more complex than supposed by the needs-goal theory. The **Vroom expectancy theory** of motivation encompasses some of these complexities.[4] Like the needs-goal theory, the Vroom expectancy theory is based on the premise that felt needs cause human behavior. However, the Vroom theory also addresses the issue of **motivation strength**—an individual's degree of desire to perform a behavior. As this desire increases or decreases, motivation strength fluctuates correspondingly.

Motivation and Perceptions   Vroom's expectancy theory is shown in equation form in Figure 16.2. According to this theory, motivation strength is determined by the perceived value of the result of performing a behavior and the perceived probability that the behavior performed will cause the result to materialize. As both of these factors increase, so does motivation strength, or the desire to perform the behavior. People tend to perform the behaviors that maximize their personal rewards over the long term.

To see how Vroom's theory applies to human behavior, suppose that a college student has been offered a summer job painting three houses at the rate of $200 a house. Assuming that the student needs money, her motivation strength, or desire, to paint the houses will be determined by two major factors: her perception of the value of $600 and her perception of the

The **Vroom expectancy theory** is a motivation theory that hypothesizes that felt needs cause human behavior and that motivation strength depends on an individual's degree of desire to perform a behavior.

Motivation strength is an individual's degree of desire to perform a behavior.

$$\text{Motivation strength} = \text{Perceived value of result of performing behavior} \times \text{Perceived probability that result will materialize}$$

Vroom's expectancy theory of motivation in equation form

Figure 16.2

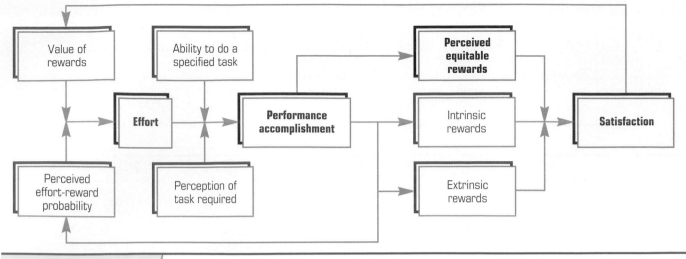

Figure 16.3 👆 *The Porter–Lawler theory of motivation*

probability that she can actually paint the houses satisfactorily and receive the $600. As the student's perceived value of the $600 reward and perceived probability that she can paint the houses increase, the student's motivation strength to paint the houses will also increase.

Equity theory is an explanation of motivation that emphasizes the individual's perceived fairness of an employment situation and how perceived inequities can cause certain behaviors.

Equity Theory of Motivation   **Equity theory,** the work of J. Stacy Adams, looks at an individual's perceived fairness of an employment situation and finds that perceived inequities can lead to changes in behavior. Adams found that when individuals believe they have been treated unfairly in comparison with their coworkers, they will react in one of the following ways to try to right the inequity:[5]

1. Some will change their work inputs to better match the rewards they are receiving. If they believe they are being paid too little, they will decrease their work outputs; if they believe they are being paid more than their coworkers, they will increase their work outputs to match their rewards.
2. Some will try to change the compensation they receive for their work by asking for a raise or by taking legal action.
3. If attempts to change the actual inequality are unsuccessful, some will try to change their own perception of the inequality. They may do this by distorting the status of their jobs or by rationalizing away the inequity.
4. Some will leave the situation rather than try to change it. People who feel they are being treated unfairly on the job may decide to quit that job rather than endure the inequity.

Perceptions of inequities can arise in any number of management situations—among them, work assignments, promotions, ratings reports, and office assignments—but they occur most often in the area of pay. All of these issues are emotionally charged, however, because they pertain to people's feelings of self-worth. What is a minor inequity in the mind of a manager can loom as extremely important in the mind of an employee. Effective managers strive to deal with equity issues because the steps that workers are prone to take to balance the scales are often far from good for the organization.

The Porter–Lawler theory is a motivation theory that hypothesizes that felt needs cause human behavior and that motivation strength is determined primarily by the perceived value of the result of performing the behavior and the perceived probability that the behavior performed will cause the result to materialize.

The Porter–Lawler Theory of Motivation   Porter and Lawler developed a motivation theory that provides a more complete description of the motivation process than either the needs-goal theory or the Vroom expectancy theory.[6] Still, the **Porter–Lawler theory** of motivation (see Figure 16.3) is consistent with those two theories in that it accepts the premises that felt needs cause human behavior and that effort expended to accomplish a task is determined by the perceived value of rewards that will result from finishing the task and the probability that those rewards will materialize.

The Motivation Process   In addition, the Porter–Lawler motivation theory stresses three other characteristics of the motivation process:

1. The perceived value of a reward is determined by both intrinsic and extrinsic rewards that result in need satisfaction when a task is accomplished. **Intrinsic rewards** come directly from performing the task, while **extrinsic rewards** are extraneous to the task. For example, when a manager counsels a subordinate about a personal problem, the manager may get some intrinsic reward in the form of personal satisfaction at helping another individual. In addition to this intrinsic reward, however, the manager also receives an extrinsic reward in the form of the overall salary the manager is paid.

> **Intrinsic rewards** are rewards that come directly from performing a task.
>
> **Extrinsic rewards** are rewards that are extraneous to the task accomplished.

Xerox Makes Extrinsic Commission Reward Harder for Salespeople to Earn

Xerox Corporation is a leader in the global documents market as a result of productivity-oriented document solutions that it provides customers. Xerox develops, manufactures, markets, and services a complete range of document-processing products including printers, copiers, scanners, and fax machines. The company primarily distributes its products throughout the Western Hemisphere as well as Europe, Africa, the Middle East, and parts of Asia.

A company like Xerox needs a well qualified, highly motivated sales force to maintain its success. Richard Thoman was recently fired as Xerox's CEO partially because the steps he took to make salespeople more productive ultimately ended in salespeople becoming frustrated and less productive. For years, Xerox copier salespeople sold machines to individual customers within assigned geographic

regions. Thoman decided to ask the sales force to focus on industries rather than geographic territories. Rather than selling photocopiers in Ohio, for example, salespeople were asked to focus on customers in a specific industry, like the auto industry, regardless of the territories in which they existed.

Salespeople who once received desirable commissions, focusing on customers within certain territories, seemed hampered by trying to focus on customers within a certain industry when these customers were outside of the territories they knew and understood.

When Thoman's plan became operational, the sales force became frustrated. Commissions became harder to get because of the new territories, and salespeople began to leave Xerox at twice the regular rate. ■

2. The extent to which an individual effectively accomplishes a task is determined primarily by two variables: the individual's perception of what is required to perform the task and the individual's ability to perform the task. Effectiveness at accomplishing a task increases as the perception of what is required to perform the task becomes more accurate and the ability to perform the task increases.

3. The perceived fairness of rewards influences the amount of satisfaction produced by those rewards. The more equitable an individual perceives the rewards to be, the greater the satisfaction that individual will experience as a result of receiving them.

▶ Back to the Case

Motivation is an inner state that causes individuals to act in certain ways that ensure the accomplishment of some goal. Jack Cooper in the Introductory Case seems to have an accurate understanding of the motivation process. He is focusing on influencing the behavior of his employees to enhance the success of his digital strategy program at Bristol-Myers Squibb. Cooper encourages employees within the company to be creative and efficient in implementing digital strategy. Cooper's focus on motivation should be a valuable tool in making his Internet strategy implementation efforts effective.

To motivate employees at Bristol-Myers Squibb, Cooper must keep five specific principles of human motivation clearly in mind: (1) felt needs cause behavior aimed at reducing those needs, (2) the degree of desire to perform a particular behavior is determined by an individual's perceived value of the result of performing the behavior and the perceived probability that the behavior will cause the result to materialize, (3) the perceived value of a reward for a particular behavior is determined by both intrinsic and extrinsic rewards that result in need satisfaction when the behavior is accomplished, (4) individuals can effectively accomplish a task only if they understand what the task requires and have the ability to perform the task, and (5) the perceived fairness of a reward influences the degree of satisfaction generated when the reward is received.

Content Theories of Motivation: Human Needs

The motivation theories discussed thus far imply that an understanding of motivation is based on an understanding of human needs. There is some evidence that most people have strong needs for self-respect, respect from others, promotion, and psychological growth.[7] Although identifying all human needs is impossible, several theories have been developed to help managers better understand these needs:

1. Maslow's hierarchy of needs
2. Alderfer's ERG theory
3. Argyris's maturity-immaturity continuum
4. McClelland's acquired needs theory

Maslow's Hierarchy of Needs   Perhaps the most widely accepted description of human needs is the hierarchy of needs concept developed by Abraham Maslow.[8] Maslow states that human beings possess the five basic needs described below and theorizes that these five basic needs can be arranged in a hierarchy of importance—the order in which individuals generally strive to satisfy them. The needs and their relative positions in the hierarchy of importance are shown in Figure 16.4

Physiological needs are Maslow's first set of human needs—for the normal functioning of the body, including the desires for water, food, rest, sex, and air.

Security, or **safety, needs** are Maslow's second set of human needs—reflecting the human desire to keep free from physical harm.

Social needs are Maslow's third set of human needs—reflecting the human desire to belong, including longings for friendship, companionship, and love.

Esteem needs are Maslow's fourth set of human needs—including the desires for self-respect and respect from others.

> **Physiological needs** relate to the normal functioning of the body. They include the needs for water, food, rest, sex, and air. Until these needs are met, a significant portion of an individual's behavior will be aimed at satisfying them. Once the needs are satisfied, however, behavior is aimed at satisfying the needs on the next level of Maslow's hierarchy.

> **Security,** or **safety, needs** relate to the individual's desire to be free from harm, including both bodily and economic disaster.
>   Traditionally, management has best helped employees satisfy their physiological and security needs through adequate wages or salaries, which employees use to purchase such things as food and housing.

> **Social needs** include the desire for love, companionship, and friendship. These needs reflect a person's desire to be accepted by others. As they are satisfied, behavior shifts to satisfying esteem needs.

> **Esteem needs** are concerned with the desire for respect. They are generally divided into two categories: self-respect and respect from others. Once esteem needs are satisfied, the individual moves to the pinnacle of the hierarchy and emphasizes satisfying self-actualization needs.

▶ When General Motors workers struck at the Flint, Michigan, plant in the summer of 1998, their concerns focused on subcontracting and other competitive issues. They were responding to what they perceived as a security need, in this case, a buffer against a serious economic challenge to the operation.

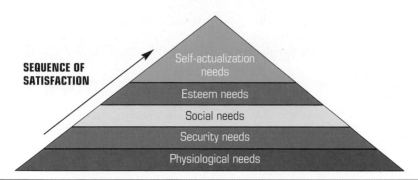

SEQUENCE OF
SATISFACTION

Self-actualization
needs

Esteem needs

Social needs

Security needs

Physiological needs

Maslow's hierarchy of needs

Figure 16.4

> **Self-actualization needs** refer to the desire to maximize whatever potential an individual possesses. For example, in the nonprofit public setting of a high school, a principal who seeks to satisfy self-actualization needs would strive to become the best principal possible. Self-actualization needs occupy the highest level of Maslow's hierarchy.[9]

Self-actualization needs are Maslow's fifth, and final, set of human needs—reflecting the human desire to maximize personal potential.

The traditional concerns about Maslow's hierarchy are that it has no research base, that it may not accurately pinpoint basic human needs, and that it is questionable whether human needs can be neatly arranged in such a hierarchy. Nevertheless, Maslow's hierarchy is probably the most popular conceptualization of human needs to date, and it continues to be positively discussed in management literature.[10] Still, the concerns expressed about it should remind managers to look upon Maslow's hierarchy more as a subjective statement than an objective description of human needs.

Alderfer's ERG Theory   Clayton Alderfer responded to some of the criticisms of Maslow's work by conducting his own study of human needs.[11] He identified three basic categories of needs:

1. Existence needs—the need for physical well-being
2. Relatedness needs—the need for satisfying interpersonal relationships
3. Growth needs—the need for continuing personal growth and development

The first letters of these needs form the acronym ERG, by which the theory is now known.

Alderfer's ERG theory is similar to Maslow's theory except in three major respects. First, Alderfer identified only three orders of human needs, compared to Maslow's five orders. Second, in contrast to Maslow, Alderfer found that people sometimes activate their higher-level needs before they have completely satisfied all of their lower-level needs. Third, Alderfer concluded that movement in his hierarchy of human needs is not always upward. For instance—and this is reflected in his frustration-regression principle—he found that a worker frustrated by his failure to satisfy an upper-level need might regress by trying to fulfill an already satisfied lower-level need.

Alderfer's ERG theory is an explanation of human needs that divides them into three basic types: existence needs, relatedness needs, and growth needs.

Alderfer's work, in conjunction with Maslow's, has implications for management. Employees frustrated by work that fails to provide opportunities for growth or development on the job might concentrate their energy on trying to make more money, thus regressing to a lower level of needs. To counteract such regression, management might use job enrichment strategies designed to help people meet their higher-order needs.

Argyris's Maturity-Immaturity Continuum   **Argyris's maturity-immaturity continuum** also furnishes insights into human needs.[12] This continuum concept focuses on the personal and natural development of people to explain human needs. According to Argyris, as people naturally progress from immaturity to maturity, they move:

1. From a state of passivity as an infant to a state of increasing activity as an adult
2. From a state of dependence on others as an infant to a state of relative independence as an adult
3. From being capable of behaving only in a few ways as an infant to being capable of behaving in many different ways as an adult

Argyris's maturity-immaturity continuum is a concept that furnishes insights into human needs by focusing on an individual's natural progress from immaturity to maturity.

4. From having erratic, casual, shallow, and quickly dropped interests as an infant to having deeper, more lasting interests as an adult
5. From having a short time perspective as an infant to having a much longer time perspective as an adult
6. From being in a subordinate position as an infant to aspiring to occupy an equal or superordinate position as an adult
7. From a lack of self-awareness as an infant to awareness and control over self as an adult

According to Argyris's continuum, then, as individuals mature, they have increasing needs for more activity, enjoy a state of relative independence, behave in many different ways, have deeper and more lasting interests, are capable of considering a relatively long time perspective, occupy an equal position vis-à-vis other mature individuals, and have more awareness of themselves and control over their own destiny. Note that, unlike Maslow's needs, Argyris's needs are not arranged in a hierarchy. Like Maslow's hierarchy, however, Argyris's continuum is a primarily subjective explanation of human needs.

McClelland's Acquired Needs Theory   Another theory about human needs, called **McClelland's acquired needs theory,** focuses on the needs that people acquire through their life experiences. This theory, formulated by David C. McClelland in the 1960s, emphasizes three of the many needs human beings develop in their lifetimes:

1. *Need for achievement (nAch)*—the desire to do something better or more efficiently than it has ever been done before
2. *Need for power (nPower)*—the desire to control, influence, or be responsible for others
3. *Need for affiliation (nAff)*—the desire to maintain close, friendly, personal relationships

The individual's early life experiences determine which of these needs will be highly developed and therefore dominate the personality.

McClelland's studies of these three acquired human needs have significant implications for management.

Need for Achievement   McClelland claims that in some businesspeople, the need to achieve is so strong that it is more motivating than the quest for profits. To maximize their satisfaction, individuals with high achievement needs set goals for themselves that are challenging, yet achievable. Although such people are willing to assume risk, they assess it very carefully because they do not want to fail. Therefore, they will avoid tasks that involve too much risk. People with a low need for achievement, on the other hand, generally avoid challenges, responsibilities, and risk.

Need for Power   People with a high need for power are greatly motivated to influence others and to assume responsibility for subordinates' behavior. They are likely to seek advancement and to take on increasingly responsible work activities to earn that advancement. Power-oriented managers are comfortable in competitive situations and enjoy their decision-making role.

Need for Affiliation   Managers with a high need for affiliation have a cooperative, team-centered managerial style. They prefer to influence subordinates to complete tasks through team efforts. The danger is that managers with a high need for affiliation can lose their effectiveness if their need for social approval and friendship interferes with their willingness to make managerial decisions.[13]

> ► Back to the Case

Jack Cooper undoubtedly understands the basic motivation principle that felt needs cause behavior. Before managers like Cooper can have maximum impact on motivating their organization members, they must meet the more complex challenge of being thoroughly familiar with various individual human needs of their employees.

According to Maslow, people generally possess physiological needs, security needs, social needs, esteem needs, and self-actualization needs arranged in a hierarchy of importance. Argyris suggests that as people mature, they have increasing needs for activity, independence, flexibility, deeper interests, analyses of longer time perspectives, a position of equality with other mature individuals, and control over personal destiny. McClelland believes that the need for achievement—the desire to do something better or more efficiently than it has ever been done before—is a strong human need.

By guaranteeing every worker a position with no pay cuts as part of the Internet strategy implementation program, Cooper could focus on satisfying employee physiological and safety needs. Other possible features of Cooper's implementation program to further motivate employees could be "Best Implementer of the Month" or "Best Implementation Idea of the Week" to focus on other needs that employees might have.

MOTIVATING ORGANIZATION MEMBERS

People are motivated to perform behavior that satisfies their personal needs. Therefore, from a managerial viewpoint, motivation is the process of furnishing organization members with the opportunity to satisfy their needs by performing productive behavior within the organization. In reality, managers do not motivate people. Rather, they create environments in which organization members motivate themselves.[14]

As discussed in Chapter 14, motivation is one of the four primary interrelated activities of the influencing function performed by managers to guide the behavior of organization members toward the attainment of organizational objectives. The following sections discuss the importance of motivating organization members and present some strategies for doing so.

The Importance of Motivating Organization Members

Figure 16.5 makes the point that unsatisfied needs can lead organization members to perform either appropriate or inappropriate behavior. Successful managers minimize inappropriate behavior and maximize appropriate behavior among subordinates, thus raising the probability that productivity will increase and lowering the probability that it will decrease.

Strategies for Motivating Organization Members

Managers have various strategies at their disposal for motivating organization members. Each strategy is aimed at satisfying subordinates' needs (consistent with the descriptions of human needs in Maslow's hierarchy, Alderfer's ERG theory, Argyris's maturity-immaturity continuum, and McClelland's acquired needs theory) through appropriate organizational behavior. These managerial motivation strategies are as follows:

▶ Motivating highly creative employees like Aaron Schatz, 26, who is the author of a daily Internet trend-spotting report called the *Lycos 50*, calls for an equally creative approach to work and the workplace that allows free spirits to thrive. Shown in his office, Schatz has what his friends call wide interests and a highly retentive memory.

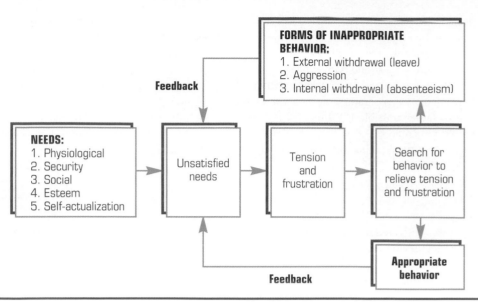

FORMS OF INAPPROPRIATE BEHAVIOR:
1. External withdrawal (leave)
2. Aggression
3. Internal withdrawal (absenteeism)

NEEDS:
1. Physiological
2. Security
3. Social
4. Esteem
5. Self-actualization

Unsatisfied needs

Tension and frustration

Search for behavior to relieve tension and frustration

Appropriate behavior

Feedback

Feedback

Figure 16.5 *Unsatisfied needs of organization members resulting in either appropriate or inappropriate behavior*

1. Managerial communication
2. Theory X–Theory Y
3. Job design
4. Behavior modification
5. Likert's management systems
6. Monetary incentives
7. Nonmonetary incentives

The strategies are discussed in the sections that follow.

Throughout the discussion, it is important to remember that no single strategy will always be more effective for a manager than any other. Most managers find that some combination of these strategies is most effective in the organization setting.

Managerial Communication   Perhaps the most basic motivation strategy for managers is to communicate well with organization members. Effective manager–subordinate communication can satisfy such basic human needs as recognition, a sense of belonging, and security. For example, such a simple managerial action as attempting to become better acquainted with subordinates can contribute substantially to the satisfaction of each of these three needs. For another example, a message praising a subordinate for a job well done can help satisfy the subordinate's recognition and security needs.

As a general rule, managers should strive to communicate often with other organization members, not only because communication is the primary means of conducting organizational activities, but also because it is a basic tool for satisfying the human needs of organization members.

Theory X–Theory Y   Another motivation strategy involves managers' assumptions about human nature. Douglas McGregor identified two sets of assumptions: **Theory X** involves negative assumptions about people that McGregor believes managers often use as the basis for dealing with their subordinates (e.g., the average person has an inherent dislike of work and will avoid it whenever he or she can). **Theory Y** represents positive assumptions about people that McGregor believes managers should strive to use (e.g., people will exercise self-direction and self-control in meeting their objectives).[15]

McGregor implies that managers who use Theory X assumptions are "bad" and that those who use Theory Y assumptions are "good." Reddin, how-

▶ This wall of gloves at the New York offices of OXO International, an award-winning maker of household products, is actually a message from the company's managers. "When I moved to New York," says president Alex Lee, "I started noticing all the gloves on the sidewalk. . . . I told everyone to keep collecting gloves" to build a sense of community. Now new staffers look forward to contributing to the wall, and it has taken on a new meaning. Says Lee, "These gloves represent all the kinds of hands that our products must fit."

ever, argues that production might be increased by using *either* Theory X or Theory Y assumptions, depending on the situation the manager faces: "Is there not a strong argument for the position that any theory may have desirable outcomes if appropriately used?" The difficulty is that McGregor considered only the ineffective application of Theory X and the effective application of Theory Y. Reddin proposes a **Theory Z**—an effectiveness dimension that implies that managers who use either Theory X or Theory Y assumptions when dealing with people can be successful, depending on their situation.

The basic rationale for using Theory Y rather than Theory X in most situations is that managerial activities that reflect Theory Y assumptions generally are more successful in satisfying the human needs of most organization members than are managerial activities that reflect Theory X assumptions. Therefore, activities based on Theory Y assumptions are more apt to motivate organization members than are activities based on Theory X assumptions.

▶ Back to the Case

Once a manager like Jack Cooper understands that felt needs cause behavior and is aware of people's different types of needs, he is ready to apply this information to motivating his workforce. From Cooper's viewpoint, motivating employees means furnishing them with the opportunity to satisfy their human needs by performing their jobs. This is a very important notion because successful motivation tends to increase employee productivity. If Cooper does not furnish his employees with an opportunity to satisfy their human needs while working, low morale within the company will eventually develop. Signs of this low morale might be only a few employees initiating new ideas, people avoiding the confrontation of tough situations, and employees resisting innovation.

What does the above information recommend that Cooper actually do to motivate employees involved in his digital strategy implementation efforts? One strategy he might follow is taking time to communicate with his employees. Manager–employee communication can help satisfy employee needs for recognition, belonging, and security. Another of Cooper's strategies might be based on McGregor's Theory X–Theory Y concept. In following this concept when dealing with employees, Cooper should assume that work is as natural as play; that employees can be self-directed in goal accomplishment; that the granting of rewards encourages the achievement of implementation objectives; that employees seek and accept responsibility; and that most employees are creative, ingenious, and imaginative. The adoption of such assumptions by Cooper can lead to satisfying many of the needs defined by Maslow, Argyris, and McClelland.

Job Design A third strategy managers can use to motivate organization members involves designing jobs that organization members perform. The following two sections discuss earlier and more recent job design strategies.

Earlier Job Design Strategies A movement has long existed in American business to make jobs simpler and more specialized in order to increase worker productivity. The idea behind this movement is to make workers more productive by enabling them to be more efficient. Perhaps the best example of a job design inspired by this movement is the automobile assembly line. The negative result of work simplification and specialization, however, is job boredom. As jobs become simpler and more specialized, they typically become more boring and less satisfying to workers, and, consequently, productivity suffers.

Job Rotation. The first major attempt to overcome job boredom was **job rotation**—moving workers from job to job rather than requiring them to perform only one simple and specialized job over the long term. For example, a gardener would do more than just mow lawns; he might also trim bushes, rake grass, and sweep sidewalks.

Although job rotation programs have been known to increase organizational profitability, most of them are ineffective as motivation strategies because, over time, people become bored with all the jobs they are rotated into.[16] Job rotation programs, however, are often effective for achieving other organizational objectives, such as training, because they give individuals an overview of how the various units of the organization function.

Theory X is a set of essentially negative assumptions about human nature.

Theory Y is a set of essentially positive assumptions about human nature.

Theory Z is the effectiveness dimension that implies that managers who use either Theory X or Theory Y assumptions when dealing with people can be successful, depending on their situation.

Job rotation is the process of moving workers from one job to another rather than requiring them to perform only one simple and specialized job over the long term.

▶ Pharmaceuticals: Eli Lilly and Company Benefits from Job Rotation

Management research suggests that job rotation programs can provide organizations with many different types of significant benefits. A recent study of a job rotation program at Eli Lilly and Company, a major pharmaceutical manufacturer, found support for the validity of this suggestion.

Lilly has used job rotation longer and more often than most other large organizations. Although job rotation is not a formal program at Lilly, rotating employees from job to job has been viewed for many years as an integral part of the company's plan for professional development. One of Lilly's strongest recruiting tools in recent years has been its reputation for successfully implementing its job rotation program. Although management sees job rotation as an important training and development tool, moving around the organization is not required of every employee. In general, providing employees with different, attractive job options has increased overall employee job satisfaction as well as satisfaction with Lilly as a company.

At Lilly, job rotation has proven to be a valuable training and development tool. History shows that job rotation at Lilly enhances employees' technical skills like accounting, finance, and operating procedures. In addition, Lilly's job rotation also enhances employees' financial, planning, communication, interpersonal, leadership, and computer skills. Although much valuable training is accomplished through job rotation at Lilly, the program does not focus on the development of *all* employee skills. For example, employees generally do not use job rotation at Lilly to improve their knowledge of the external business environment and how to develop other people.

The advantages of Lilly's job rotation program must be compared to its disadvantages. First, job rotation at Lilly sometimes results in increased workload and decreased productivity for the rotating employee as well as for the new work group to whom the employee is being rotated. This decreased productivity is normally due to the learning curve that can occur on new jobs, like time spent learning the new job, training costs related to the newly rotated employee, costly errors that employees often make while learning a new job, and integration of a new member into an established work group.

Job enlargement is the process of increasing the number of operations an individual performs in a job.

Job Enlargement. Another strategy developed to overcome the boredom of doing very simple and specialized jobs is **job enlargement,** or increasing the number of operations an individual performs in order to enhance the individual's satisfaction in work. According to the job enlargement concept, the gardener's job would become more satisfying as such activities as trimming bushes, raking grass, and sweeping sidewalks were added to his initial activity of mowing grass. Some research supports the contention that job enlargement does make jobs more satisfying, and some does not.[17] Still, job enlargement programs are more successful at increasing job satisfaction than job rotation programs.

A number of other job design strategies have evolved since the development of job rotation and job enlargement programs. Two of these more recent strategies are job enrichment and flextime.

Hygiene, or **maintenance, factors** are items that influence the degree of job dissatisfaction.

Motivating factors, or **motivators,** are items that influence the degree of job satisfaction.

Job Enrichment Frederick Herzberg has concluded from his research that the degrees of satisfaction and dissatisfaction organization members feel as a result of performing a job are two different variables determined by two different sets of items.[18] The items that influence the degree of job dissatisfaction are called **hygiene,** or **maintenance, factors,** while those that influence the degree of job satisfaction are called **motivating factors,** or **motivators.** Hygiene factors relate to the work environment, and motivating factors to the work itself. The items that make up Herzberg's hygiene and motivating factors are presented in Table 16.1.

Herzberg believes that when the hygiene factors of a particular job situation are undesirable, organization members will become dissatisfied. Making these factors more desirable—for example, by increasing salary—will rarely motivate people to do a better job, but it will keep them from becoming dissatisfied. In contrast, when the motivating factors of a particular job situation are high, employees usually are motivated to do a better job. People tend to be more motivated and productive as more motivators are built into their job situation.

Job enrichment is the process of incorporating motivators into a job situation.

The process of incorporating motivators into a job situation is called **job enrichment.** Early reports indicated that companies such as Texas Instruments and Volvo had notable success in motivating organization members through job enrichment programs. More recent reports, though they continue to support the value of job enrichment, indicate that for a job enrichment program to be successful, it must be carefully designed and administered.[19]

Dissatisfaction: Hygiene or Maintenance Factors	Satisfaction: Motivating Factors
1. Company policy and administration	1. Opportunity for achievement
2. Supervision	2. Opportunity for recognition
3. Relationship with supervisor	3. Work itself
4. Relationship with peers	4. Responsibility
5. Working conditions	5. Advancement
6. Salary	6. Personal growth
7. Relationship with subordinates	

Job Enrichment and Productivity.   Herzberg's overall conclusions are that the most productive organization members are those involved in work situations that have both desirable hygiene and motivating factors. The needs in Maslow's hierarchy that desirable hygiene factors and motivating factors generally satisfy are shown in Figure 16.6. Esteem needs can be satisfied by both types of factors. An example of esteem needs satisfied by a hygiene factor is a private parking space—a status symbol and a working condition evidencing the employee's importance to the organization. An example of esteem needs satisfied by a motivating factor is an award given for outstanding performance—a public recognition of a job well done that displays the employee's value to the organization.

Flextime   Another more recent job design strategy for motivating organization members is based on a concept called *flextime*. Perhaps the most common traditional characteristic of work in the United States is that jobs are performed within a fixed eight-hour workday. This tradition has been challenged. Faced with motivation problems and excessive absenteeism, many managers have turned to scheduling innovations as a possible solution.[20]

The main purpose of these scheduling innovations is not to reduce the total number of work hours, but rather to give workers greater flexibility in scheduling their work hours. The main thrust of **flextime,** or flexible working hours programs, is that it allows workers to complete their jobs within a workweek of a normal number of hours that they arrange themselves.[21] The choices of starting and finishing times can be as flexible as the organizational situation allows. To ensure that flexibility does not become counterproductive within the organization, however, many flextime programs stipulate a core period during which all employees must be on the job.

Advantages of Flextime.   Various kinds of organizational studies have indicated that flextime programs have some positive organizational effects. Douglas Fleuter, for example, has reported that flextime contributes to greater job satisfaction, which typically results in greater

Flextime is a program that allows workers to complete their jobs within a workweek of a normal number of hours that they schedule themselves.

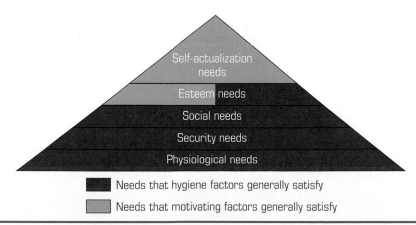

Needs that hygiene factors generally satisfy

Needs that motivating factors generally satisfy

Needs in Maslow's hierarchy of needs that desirable hygiene and motivating factors generally satisfy

Figure 16.6

productivity. Other researchers have concluded that flextime programs can result in higher motivation levels of workers. Because organization members generally consider flextime programs desirable, organizations that have such programs can usually better compete with other organizations in recruiting qualified new employees. (A listing of the advantages and disadvantages of flextime programs appears in Table 16.2.) Although many well-known companies, such as Scott Paper, Sun Oil, and Samsonite, have adopted flextime programs,[22] more research is needed before flextime's true worth can be conclusively assessed.

> ### ▶ Back to the Case
>
> Jack Cooper could use two major job design strategies to motivate his employees at Bristol-Myers Squibb. With job enrichment, Cooper can incorporate into employee jobs such motivating factors as opportunities for achievement, recognition, and personal growth. Cooper's allowing workers to transfer back and forth among work teams and not work on just one product can be viewed as a type of job enrichment allowing workers opportunities for personal growth. However, for maximum success, hygiene factors at Bristol-Myers Squibb—company policy and administration, supervision, salary, and working conditions, for example—also should be perceived as desirable by employees.
>
> The second major job design strategy that Cooper can use to motivate his employees is flextime. With flextime, his employees could have some freedom in scheduling the beginning and ending of workdays. This freedom could be somewhat limited by organizational factors such as the urgency of Internet strategy implementation or the availability of skilled employees to perform implementation jobs.

Behavior Modification   A fourth strategy that managers can use to motivate organization members is based on a concept known as behavior modification. As stated by B. F. Skinner, the Harvard psychologist considered by many to be the father of behavioral psychology, **behavior modification** focuses on encouraging appropriate behavior by controlling the consequences of that behavior.[23] According to the law of effect, behavior that is rewarded tends to be repeated, while that which is punished tends to be eliminated.

Although behavior modification programs typically involve the administration of both rewards and punishments, it is rewards that are generally emphasized because they are more effective than punishments in influencing behavior. Obviously, the main theme of behavior modification is not new.

Behavior modification is a program that focuses on managing human activity by controlling the consequences of performing that activity.

Reinforcement   Behavior modification theory asserts that if managers want to modify subordinates' behavior, they must ensure that appropriate consequences occur as a result of

---

🖰 Table 16.2   Advantages and Disadvantages of Using Flextime Programs

Advantages	Disadvantages
Improved employee attitude and morale	Lack of supervision during some hours of work
Accommodation of working parents	Key people unavailable at certain times
Decreased tardiness	Understaffing at times
Fewer commuting problems—workers can avoid congested streets and highways	Problem of accommodating employees whose output is the input for other employees
Accommodation of those who wish to arrive at work before normal workday interruptions begin	Employee abuse of flextime program
Increased production	Difficulty in planning work schedules
Facilitation of employees scheduling of medical, dental, and other types of appointments	Problem of keeping track of hours worked or accumulated
Accommodation of leisure-time activities of employees	Inability to schedule meetings at convenient times
Decreased absenteeism	Inability to coordinate projects
Decreased turnover	

that behavior. **Positive reinforcement** is a reward that consists of a desirable consequence of behavior, and **negative reinforcement** is a reward that consists of the elimination of an undesirable consequence of behavior.[24]

If arriving at work on time is positively reinforced, or rewarded, the probability increases that a worker will arrive on time more often. If arriving late for work causes a worker to experience some undesirable outcome, such as a verbal reprimand, that worker will be negatively reinforced when this outcome is eliminated by on-time arrival. According to behavior modification theory, positive reinforcement and negative reinforcement are both rewards that increase the likelihood that a behavior will continue.

Positive reinforcement is a reward that consists of a desirable consequence of behavior.

Negative reinforcement is a reward that consists of the elimination of an undesirable consequence of behavior.

Positive Reinforcement Impacts Diversity at Raffa and Associates

Raffa and Associates is an accounting, tax, and consulting practice that specializes in the non-profit sector. Established in 1984, the company is presently one of the largest independent accounting firms in Washington, D.C. The firm has doubled its size in the last two years to around 70 employees, and a significant portion of the staff are black, Hispanic, or Asian. The Southern Christian Leadership Conference recently honored Raffa and Associates for its support of national civil rights and humanitarianism through its hiring and employment.

For Raffa and Associates, diversity reflects its client base and enables the company to communicate better and establish relationships with clients. Clients in the nonprofit sector tend to have a diverse employee base and lean toward aligning themselves with firms that share their commitment to diversity. Raffa and Associates tends to have clients that are not only diverse, but also international.

Tom Raffa, managing partner of Raffa and Associates, maintains diversity in his company. Since Raffa sees diversity as an important reason why his company has been successful, he is essentially being rewarded for building a diverse company. As a result, the probability is high that Raffa will continue to maintain employee diversity at Raffa and Associates. ■

Punishment **Punishment** is the presentation of an undesirable behavior consequence or the removal of a desirable behavior consequence that decreases the likelihood that the behavior will continue. To use our earlier example, a manager could punish employees for arriving late for work by exposing them to some undesirable consequence, such as verbal reprimand, or by removing a desirable consequence, such as their wages for the amount of time they are late.[25] Although punishment would probably quickly convince most workers to come to work on time, it might have undesirable side effects, such as high absenteeism and turnover, if it is emphasized over the long term.

Punishment is the presentation of an undesirable behavior consequence or the removal of a desirable one that decreases the likelihood that the behavior will continue.

Applying Behavior Modification Behavior modification programs have been applied both successfully and unsuccessfully in a number of organizations. Management at Emery Worldwide, for example, found that an effective feedback system is crucial to making a behavior modification program successful.[26] This feedback system should be aimed at keeping employees informed of the relationship between various behaviors and their consequences.

Other ingredients of successful behavior modification programs are the following:[27]

1. Giving different levels of rewards to different workers according to the quality of their performances
2. Telling workers what they are doing wrong
3. Punishing workers privately in order not to embarrass them in front of others
4. Always giving out rewards and punishments that are earned to emphasize that management is serious about its behavior modification efforts

The behavior modification concept is also being applied to cost control in organizations, with the objective of encouraging employees to be more cost conscious. Under this type of behavior modification program, employees are compensated in a manner that rewards cost control and cost reduction and penalizes cost acceleration.[28]

Likert's Management Systems Another strategy that managers can use to motivate organization members is based on the work of Rensis Likert, a noted management scholar.[29]

After studying several types and sizes of organizations, Likert concluded that management styles in organizations can be categorized into the following systems:

➤ *System 1*—This style of management is characterized by a lack of confidence or trust in subordinates. Subordinates do not feel free to discuss their jobs with superiors and are motivated by fear, threats, punishments, and occasional rewards. Information flow in the organization is directed primarily downward; upward communication is viewed with great suspicion. The bulk of all decision making is done at the top of the organization.

➤ *System 2*—This style of management is characterized by a condescending master-to-servant–style confidence and trust in subordinates. Subordinates do not feel very free to discuss their jobs with superiors and are motivated by rewards and actual or potential punishments. Information flows mostly downward; upward communication may or may not be viewed with suspicion. Although policies are made primarily at the top of the organization, decisions within a prescribed framework are made at lower levels.

➤ *System 3*—This style of management is characterized by substantial, though not complete, confidence in subordinates. Subordinates feel fairly free to discuss their jobs with superiors and are motivated by rewards, occasional punishments, and some involvement. Information flows both upward and downward in the organization. Upward communication is often accepted, though at times, it may be viewed with suspicion. Although broad policies and general decisions are made at the top of the organization, more specific decisions are made at lower levels.

➤ *System 4*—This style of management is characterized by complete trust and confidence in subordinates. Subordinates feel completely free to discuss their jobs with superiors and are motivated by such factors as economic rewards based on a compensation system developed through employee participation and involvement in goal setting. Information flows upward, downward, and horizontally. Upward communication is generally accepted—but even where it is not, employees' questions are answered candidly. Decision making is spread widely throughout the organization and is well coordinated.

Styles, Systems, and Productivity   Likert has suggested that as management style moves from system 1 to system 4, the human needs of individuals within the organization tend to be more effectively satisfied over the long term. Thus, an organization that moves toward system 4 tends to become more productive over the long term.

Figure 16.7 illustrates the comparative long- and short-term effects of both system 1 and system 4 on organizational production. Managers may increase production in the short term by using a system 1 management style, because motivation by fear, threat, and punishment is generally effective in the short run. Over the long run, however, this style usually causes production to decrease, primarily because of the long-term nonsatisfaction of organization members' needs and the poor working relationships between managers and subordinates.

Conversely, managers who initiate a system 4 management style will probably face some decline in production initially but will see an increase in production over the long term. The short-term decline occurs because organization members must adapt to the new system management is implementing. The production increase over the long term materializes as a result of organization members' adjustment to the new system, greater satisfaction of their needs, and good working relationships that develop between managers and subordinates.

This long-term production increase under system 4 can also be related to decision-making differences in the two management systems. Because decisions reached in system 4 are more likely to be thoroughly understood by organization members than decisions reached in system 1, decision implementation is more likely to be efficient and effective in system 4 than in system 1.

Monetary Incentives   A number of firms make a wide range of money-based compensation programs available to their employees as a form of motivation. For instance, employee stock ownership plans (ESOPs) motivate employees to boost production by offering them shares of company stock as a benefit. Managers are commonly given stock bonuses as an incentive to think more like an owner and ultimately do a better job of building a successful organization. Other incentive plans include lump-sum bonuses—one-time cash payments— and gain-sharing, a plan under which members of a team receive a bonus when their team

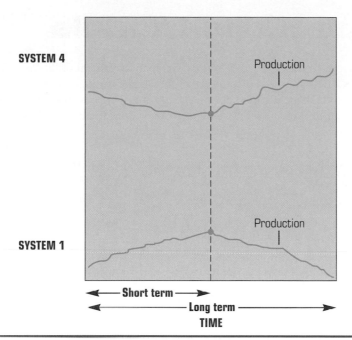

SYSTEM 4

Production

SYSTEM 1

Production

◄—— **Short term** ——►
◄—————— **Long term** ——————►
TIME

Comparative long-term and short-term effects of system I and system 4 on organizational production

Figure 16.7

exceeds a goal. All of these plans link pay closely to performance. Many organizations have found that by putting more of their employees' pay at risk, they can peg more of their total wage costs to sales, which makes expenses more controllable in a downturn.[30]

Nonmonetary Incentives   A firm can also keep its employees committed and motivated by nonmonetary means. For instance, some companies have a policy of promoting from within. They go through an elaborate process of advertising jobs internally before going outside to fill vacancies. Another nonmonetary incentive emphasizes quality, on the theory that most workers are unhappy when they know their work goes to producing a shoddy product.[31]

▶ Back to the Case

Jack Cooper can apply behavior modification to his situation at Bristol-Myers Squibb by rewarding appropriate employee behavior and punishing inappropriate employee behavior. Punishment has to be used very carefully, however. If used continually, the working relationship between Cooper and his employees can be destroyed. For the behavior modification program to be successful, Cooper has to furnish employees with feedback on which behaviors are appropriate and inappropriate, to give workers different rewards depending on the quality of their performance, to tell workers what they were doing wrong, to punish workers privately, and to consistently give rewards and punishments when earned.

To use Likert's system 4 management style to motivate employees over the long term, Cooper has to demonstrate complete confidence in his workers and to encourage workers to feel completely free to discuss problems with him. In addition, communication among those involved in digital strategy implementation at Bristol-Myers Squibb has to flow freely in all directions within the organization structure, with upward communication discussed candidly. Cooper's decision-making process under system 4 has to involve many employees. Cooper can use the principle of supportive relationships as the basis for his system 4 management style. No single strategy mentioned in this chapter for motivating organization members would necessarily be more valuable to managers such as Cooper than any of the other strategies. In reality, Cooper will probably find that some combination of all of these strategies is most useful in motivating Internet strategy implementation workers at Bristol-Myers Squibb.

Management Skills Module

This section is specially designed to help you develop management skills. An individual's management skill is based on an understanding of management concepts and the ability to apply those concepts in management situations. As a result, the following activities are designed both to heighten your understanding of management concepts and to help you gain facility in applying those concepts in various management situations.

UNDERSTANDING MANAGEMENT CONCEPTS

▶ Action Summary

Reread the learning objectives below. Each objective is followed by questions. Answering these questions accurately will help you retain the most important concepts discussed in this chapter. After answering each question, check your answer against the answer key at the end of this chapter. (*Hint:* If you have any doubts regarding the correct response, consult the page number that follows the answer.)

Circle:

From studying this chapter, I will attempt to acquire

1. A basic understanding of human motivation.

a b c d e   **a.** An individual's inner state that causes him or her to behave in such a way as to ensure accomplishment of a goal is: (a) ambition (b) drive (c) motivation (d) need (e) leadership.

T F   **b.** According to the needs-goal theory of motivation, a fulfilled need is a motivator.

a b c d e   **c.** The following most comprehensively describes how motivation takes place: (a) the Vroom expectancy theory (b) the needs-goal theory (c) the Porter–Lawler theory (d) all of the above (e) none of the above.

2. Insights into various human needs.

a b c d e   **a.** The following is a rank-ordered listing of Maslow's hierarchy of needs from lowest to highest: (a) self-actualization, social, security, physiological, esteem (b) social, security, physiological, self-actualization (c) esteem, self-actualization, security, social, physiological (d) physiological, security, social, esteem, self-actualization (e) physiological, social, esteem, security, self-actualization.

a b c d e   **b.** According to Argyris, as individuals mature, they have an increasing need for: (a) greater dependence (b) a shorter-term perspective (c) more inactivity (d) deeper interests (e) youth.

a b c d e   **c.** The desire to do something better or more efficiently than it has ever been done before is known as the need for: (a) acceleration (b) achievement (c) acclamation (d) actualization (e) none of the above.

3. An appreciation for the importance of motivating organization members.

T F   **a.** From a managerial viewpoint, motivation is the process of furnishing organization members with the opportunity to satisfy their needs by performing productive behaviors within the organization.

T F   **b.** The concepts of motivation and appropriate behavior are closely related.

4. An understanding of various motivation strategies.

a b c d e   **a.** The following is a Theory Y assumption: (a) the average person prefers to be directed (b) most people must be threatened and coerced before they will put forth adequate effort (c) commitment to objectives is a function of the rewards associated with achievement (d) the average person seeks no responsibility (e) all of the above.

a b c d e   **b.** The process of incorporating motivators into the job situation is called: (a) job enlargement (b) flextime (c) satisfying (d) job enrichment (e) Theory X.

a b c d e   **c.** People will exercise self direction in meeting their objectives by: (a) giving rewards and punishments when earned (b) giving rewards according to performance quality (c) telling workers what they are doing wrong (d) punishing workers privately (e) all of the above.

Action Summary Answer Key

1. **a.** c, p. 354
   b. F, p. 354
   c. c, p. 356

2. **a.** d, pp. 358–359
   b. d, p. 360
   c. b, p. 360

3. **a.** T, p. 361
   b. T, p. 361

4. **a.** c, p. 362
   b. d, p. 364
   c. e, pp. 366–367

Issues for Review and Discussion

1. Define *motivation* and explain why managers must understand it.
2. Describe the difference between process and content theories of motivation.
3. Draw and explain a model that illustrates the needs-goal theory of motivation.
4. Explain Vroom's expectancy theory of motivation.
5. List and explain three characteristics of the motivation process described in the Porter–Lawler motivation theory that are not contained in either the needs-goal theory of motivation or Vroom's expectancy theories.
6. What is the main theme of the equity theory of motivation?
7. What does Maslow's hierarchy of needs tell us about the relationship between personal needs and workplace needs?
8. What concerns have been expressed about Maslow's hierarchy of needs?
9. What are the similarities and differences between Maslow's hierarchy of needs and Alderfer's ERG theory?
10. Explain Argyris's maturity-immaturity continuum.
11. What is the need for achievement?
12. Summarize the characteristics of individuals who have a high need for achievement.
13. Explain "motivating organization members."
14. Is the process of motivating organization members important to managers? Explain.
15. How can managerial communication be used to motivate organization members?
16. Describe Theory X, Theory Y, and Theory Z. What does each of these theories tell us about motivating organization members?
17. What is the difference between job enlargement and job rotation?
18. Describe the relationship of hygiene factors, motivating factors, and job enrichment.
19. Define *flextime* and *behavior modification*.
20. What basic ingredients are necessary to make a behavior modification program successful?
21. In your own words, summarize Likert's four management systems.
22. What effect do Likert's systems 1 and 4 generally have on organizational production in both the short and the long term? Why do these effects occur?
23. List three nonmonetary incentives that you personally would find desirable as an employee. Why would these incentives be desirable to you?

APPLYING MANAGEMENT CONCEPTS

Cases

▶ INTRODUCTORY CASE WRAP-UP

Case Discussion Questions

"Bristol-Myers Squibb Stresses Motivation in Internet Implementation" (p. 353) and its related Back-to-the-Case sections were written to help you better understand the management concepts contained in this chapter. Answer the following discussion questions about this Introductory Case to further enrich your understanding of chapter content:

1. Do you think it would be unusual for a manager like Jack Cooper to spend a significant portion of his time motivating his workforce? Explain.
2. Which of the needs on Maslow's hierarchy of needs could implementing Internet strategy at Bristol-Myers Squibb help satisfy? Why? If you have omitted one or more of the needs, explain why the implementation would not satisfy those needs.
3. Is it possible for Cooper's efforts to be successful in motivating workers yet detrimental to organizational success? Explain.

Skills Exercise: Analyzing Worker Needs at Bristol-Myers Squibb

The Introductory Case discussed how motivating employees is a key to successfully implementing Internet strategy at Bristol-Myers Squibb. Describe three jobs that would probably be involved in implementing such a strategy in this company. After describing these jobs, list the human needs that workers performing the jobs would have the opportunity to satisfy? Be sure to explain how the jobs actually provide these opportunities. Use Maslow's hierarchy of needs to guide your analysis and related discussion.

Mikael Karlsson, chairman of Axis Communications, offers his customers printer servers, CD/DVD servers, Network Document servers, Network cameras, and video servers all from one source. This makes it possible for the businesses using Axis Communications's wireless products to enable their entire workgroup to communicate and share information for a cheaper price than the present Internet technology.

According to industry analysts IDC, the market for this type of wireless equipment will be about $5.5 billion by 2004. Axis is the first company to offer Bluetooth Access Point. Bluetooth is a technology designed to enable short-range wireless communication for cheap portable devices. It uses radio to transmit and receive data.[a] It is estimated that 20 million access points will be installed by 2005.[b] Karlsson's vision is to dominate the global market with Bluetooth Access Point.

Founded in 1984 by Karlsson and his high school friend Martin Gren, Axis is now a $75 million enterprise employing over 500 people worldwide. Its products are sold in over 60 countries. Axis is headquartered in Lund, Sweden, and has 28 offices throughout North America, Asia, and Europe.

When Karlsson and Gren started out, their basic philosophy was to develop a product before anyone else, produce it, sell it, and get paid. This is still their basic concept. "What we know is that Axis is the first communication company in the world that can present the new Bluetooth technology with functioning access points, that is available now," says Karlsson.

"The capital market gives companies time to develop products," he says. "This can result in innovative companies getting into complex systems, which take much longer to develop. We could never spend three years finding the perfect solution. I believe this vision is basic to everyone at Axis: we must be innovative and fast."

It is this shared corporate vision that motivates employees at all levels to work together to achieve company goals. Working without vast capital resources can be an advantage according to Karlsson. Being the underdog makes people work harder; so do Axis Core Values.

The Axis Core Values were established in 1985, and today, every single member of the company internalizes them. "All employees know them," says Karlsson. "I see this sometimes in e-mails. For example, someone will write: I don't think we are sticking to point 6 on Split vision."

Karlsson calls the following core values The Stone Tablets:

1. Axis increases the value of the network
2. Growth in volume niches
3. Always open
4. Make it happen!
5. Never satisfied
6. Split vision

[a]For a description, refer to www.bluetooth.com/developer/specification/specification.asp.

[b]Cahners industry forecast.

Karlsson's favorite core value is number 4. Each core value contains four or five subvalues. For example, number 4's expanded definition is:

Take initiative and responsibility. Stand up for what you believe in. And dare to say no. Mistakes are accepted if you learn from them. "Why" is more important than "who." Don't just talk. Dig in when needed. No self-importance. Give credit to those who "make it happen."

Karlsson has succeeded in creating a culture that makes each employee personally responsible to contribute to the corporation's success. Axis even has a customer advisory board, which can be accessed via e-mail. This enables customers to influence the development of existing and future products. The board includes Axis employees as well as other information technology professionals.

Two years ago, Axis started developments in wireless Internet. This year, a separate division was created—the Mobile Internet Division. Karlsson believes that all you need is a mobile phone or a computer at a little micro base station and an access point in a broadband wall outlet to connect to the wireless Internet.

Karlsson shares his plans with his staff and they in turn supply him with support and fresh ideas. Right now he sees two ways to expand. One is via large telecom operators and their partners, and the other is through smaller operators like offices, hotels, and airports where local mobile networks can offer employees or customers wireless data and phone services right at the location. In order to do this, operators need access points like Bluetooth.

Axis Communications views itself as a leader in network connectivity for the 21st century. By offering the people who work there a role in product development and empowering them to test their ideas in the workplace, Axis provides an ongoing challenge. In this way, the entire corporation is connected not only via the Internet, but via a shared vision.

QUESTIONS

1. Do employees at Axis receive both intrinsic and extrinsic rewards from their work? Using the Porter–Lawler theory of motivation, explain the probable impact of such rewards on motivation within the company.
2. Use Maslow's hierarchy of needs to identify employee needs focused on by Karlsson's management style. Can Karlsson improve this focus? Explain.
3. Would you say that a significant proportion of employees at Axis have enriched jobs? Why?
4. Would you say that Karlsson's management style comes closest to Likert's system 1, 2, 3, or 4? Given this system, what productivity would you expect within the company?

MASTERING MANAGEMENT: EPISODE 8—WORK MOTIVATION

Mastering Management is a series of innovative, interactive learning activities specially designed to help you develop management skills emphasized in various text chapters. Motivation is the major focus of this chapter. Episode 8 of *Mastering Management* focuses on motivating people in organizations and gives special attention to the expectancy theory of motivation. In this episode, we will take a look at how members of CanGo's work team focusing on the development of online gaming attempt to motivate one another. Review Episode 8, "Work Motivation," on your *Mastering Management* CD and then answer the following questions.

QUESTIONS

1. Do you believe that employees at CanGo are motivated to perform well? Explain.

2. Use the Porter–Lawler theory of motivation to provide more detail to your answer above.

3. Do unsatisfied needs of employees at CanGo result in appropriate or inappropriate behavior? Explain.

MASTERING MANAGEMENT: EPISODE 9 —WORK DESIGN

Mastering Management is a series of innovative, interactive learning activities specially designed to help you develop management skills emphasized in various text chapters. Job design is a major focus of this chapter. Episode 9 of *Mastering Management* focuses on how to design work and gives special attention to job rotation, job enlargement, and job enrichment. In this episode, Nick is dissatisfied with his current job. Review Episode 9, "Work Design," on your *Mastering Management* CD and then answer the following questions.

QUESTIONS

1. Can job enlargement and job rotation have a positive impact on success at CanGo? Why?

2. Would you consider using a job enrichment program at CanGo to improve company success? Discuss.

3. How might managers at CanGo use behavior modification to improve employee performance? Be as specific as you can.

---

www.prenhall.com/certo

This book is accompanied by a rich assortment of online activities aimed at developing your management skills. Reviewing news headlines, Internet exercises, an online study guide, and other research and Internet resources can help personalize management skills development for individual students or an entire class.

chapter
chapterchapterchapterchapterchapterchapter

17 Groups, Teams, and Corporate Culture

Objectives

From studying this chapter, I will attempt to acquire

- A definition of the term *group* as used in the context of management

- A thorough understanding of the difference between formal and informal groups

- Knowledge of the types of formal groups that exist in organizations

- An understanding of how managers can determine which groups exist in an organization

- An appreciation for what teams are and how to manage them

- Insights into managing corporate culture to enhance organizational success

CHAPTER OUTLINE

Introductory Case: *Teamwork Builds Success at Xerox*

Groups
Kinds of Groups in Organizations
Formal Groups
Informal Groups

Managing Work Groups
Determining Group Existence
Understanding the Evolution of Informal Groups

Teams
Groups Versus Teams
Types of Teams in Organizations

Quality Spotlight ▶ Problem-Solving Teams Focus on Improving Quality at Weyerhaeuser Insurance Department

Across Industries ▶ Motorcycle Manufacturing—Cross-Functional Teams Design New Products at Harley-Davidson

Diversity Spotlight ▶ Building Diverse Flight Teams Benefits Continental Airlines

Stages of Team Development
Team Effectiveness
Trust and Effective Teams

Corporate Culture
Status Symbols
Traditions and History
Physical Environment
The Significance of Corporate Culture

Teamwork Builds Success at Xerox

REMINDER: THE INTRODUCTORY CASE WRAP-UP (P. 395) CONTAINS DISCUSSION QUESTIONS AND A SKILLS EXERCISE TO FURTHER ILLUSTRATE THE APPLICATION OF CHAPTER CONCEPTS TO THIS VIGNETTE.

Xerox Corporation is a global leader in providing document solutions that enhance business productivity, and its focus is on developing, manufacturing, marketing, servicing, and financing a complete range of document-processing products designed to make organizations around the world more productive. The company's digital output includes color copiers and printers with production speeds ranging from 20 to 65 pages per minute. Xerox also offers a wide range of other document-processing merchandise including equipment for reproducing large engineering

Many of Xerox's most successful initiatives in asset management depend on the work of teams. Team members work closely together to coordinate the specifications and conduct the user training and maintenance that keep customers' document-processing products working productively.

and architectural drawings, facsimile products, and scanners. Among other worldwide locations, its products are distributed in Europe, Africa, and parts of Asia including Hong Kong, India, and China.

Xerox manages an extremely complex logistics system focusing on asset management, which entails tracking and coordinating thousands of pieces of equipment at hundreds of customer work locations. The company must keep track of the specific equipment requirements involving issues like space, electricity, cooling, network connectivity, supplies, and maintenance. Solutions also have to be developed for helping customer organizations coordinate equipment service, related training, and ordering of supplies from almost anywhere in the world.

Asset management at Xerox also involves the proper billing of customers. This means that customers must be billed for every single piece of equipment based on its specific usage, and they need invoices that clearly delineate equipment usage costs but don't overwhelm with too much information.

Another component of Xerox's asset management includes providing outstanding service and support to customers, who can call a toll-free number with questions, problems, and requests related to thousands of equipment assets. At Xerox, after equipment is sold or leased, the formidable challenge of technical support begins.

According to company officials, asset management at Xerox is a very challenging and labor-intensive job. Alan Asher, one of the managers, believes that successful asset management requires a tremendous amount of coordination and is exceedingly difficult to pull off, because you must have processes in place that are really detailed and really tight, or things can fall through the cracks.

(continued)

The Houston office has had some success because of a small, tightly knit work team, but it has had to confront a serious problem in operations: managing fleets of office equipment at multiple sites from a remote location. Evelyn Grubb, the customer account manager in Houston, explains: "We've got a group of people here that truly works together. It's really a family. Everyone works together. If we didn't have that spirit here, none of this would have happened."

What's Ahead

The Introductory Case highlights the important role that work groups play in the success of operations at Xerox. The material in this chapter should help managers like those at Xerox to gain insights into work group management. This chapter:

1) Defines groups
2) Discusses the kinds of groups that exist in organizations
3) Explains what steps managers should take to manage groups appropriately.

The previous chapters in Part 5 dealt with three primary activities of the influencing function: communication, leadership, and motivation. This chapter focuses on managing groups, the last major influencing activity to be discussed in this text. As with the other three activities, managing work groups requires guiding the behavior of organization members in ways that increase the probability of reaching organizational objectives.

GROUPS

A **group** is any number of people who (1) interact with one another, (2) are psychologically aware of one another, and (3) perceive themselves to be a group.

To deal with groups appropriately, managers must have a thorough understanding of the nature of groups in organizations.[1] As used in management-related discussions, a **group** is not simply a gathering of people. Rather, it is "any number of people who (1) interact with one another, (2) are psychologically aware of one another, and (3) perceive themselves to be a group."[2] Groups are characterized by frequent communication among members over time and a size small enough to permit each member to communicate with all other members on a face-to-face basis. As a result of this communication, each group member influences and is influenced by all other group members.

The study of groups is important to managers because the most common ingredient of all organizations is people and the most common technique for accomplishing work through these people is dividing them into work groups. In a classic article, Cartwright and Lippitt list four additional reasons why managers should study groups:[3]

1. Groups exist in all kinds of organizations
2. Groups inevitably form in all facets of organizational existence
3. Groups can cause either desirable or undesirable consequences within the organization
4. An understanding of groups can help managers raise the probability that the groups with which they work will cause desirable consequences within the organization[4]

KINDS OF GROUPS IN ORGANIZATIONS

A **formal group** is a group that exists within an organization by virtue of management decree to perform tasks that enhance the attainment of organizational objectives.

Organizational groups are typically divided into two basic types: formal and informal.

Formal Groups

A **formal group** is a group that exists within an organization by virtue of management decree to perform tasks that enhance the attainment of organizational objectives.[5] Figure 17.1 is an

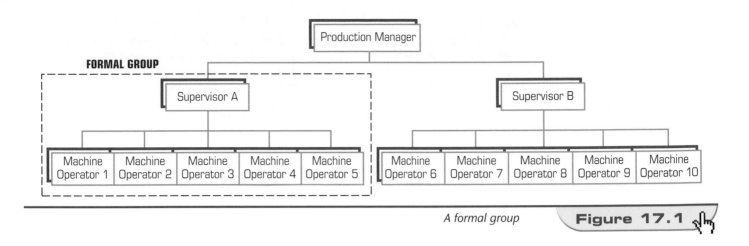

FORMAL GROUP

Production Manager

Supervisor A | Supervisor B

Machine Operator 1 | Machine Operator 2 | Machine Operator 3 | Machine Operator 4 | Machine Operator 5 | Machine Operator 6 | Machine Operator 7 | Machine Operator 8 | Machine Operator 9 | Machine Operator 10

A formal group

Figure 17.1

organization chart showing a formal group. The placements of organization members in such areas as marketing departments, personnel departments, and production departments are examples of establishing formal groups.

Actually, organizations are made up of a number of formal groups that exist at various organizational levels. The coordination of and communication among these groups is the responsibility of managers, or supervisors, commonly called "linking pins."

Formal groups are clearly defined and structured. The next sections discuss the following topics:

1. The basic kinds of formal groups
2. Examples of formal groups as they exist in organizations
3. The four stages of formal group development

Kinds of Formal Groups   Formal groups are commonly divided into command groups and task groups. **Command groups** are formal groups that are outlined in the chain of command on an organization chart. They typically handle routine organizational activities.

Task groups are formal groups of organization members who interact with one another to accomplish most of the organization's nonroutine tasks. Although task groups are usually made up of members on the same organizational level, they can consist of people from different levels in the organizational hierarchy. For example, a manager might establish a task group to consider the feasibility of manufacturing some new product and include representatives from various levels of such organizational areas as production, market research, and sales.[6]

A **command group** is a formal group that is outlined in the chain of command on an organization chart. Command groups handle routine activities.

A **task group** is a formal group of organization members who interact with one another to accomplish nonroutine organizational tasks. Members of any one task group can and often do come from various levels and segments of an organization.

▶ Back to the Case

In order for managers to be able to manage work they need to understand the definition of the term *group*, and they need to understand that there are several types of groups that exist in organizations. A group at Xerox or any other organization is any number of people who interact, who are psychologically aware of each other, and who perceive themselves as a group. A company like Xerox is made up of formal groups, the groups that appear on the company's organization charts, such as the marketing department. Managers of groups act as the "linking pins" among departments. The ability of Xerox managers to coordinate and communicate with these groups and their success in dealing with their own departments are certainly important factors in the future success of the company as a whole.

At times, managers at Xerox can form new groups to handle some of the more nonroutine challenges. For example, management could form a task group by choosing two people from each of several different departments and getting them together on developing a new and more efficient system for improving company asset management procedures. Then, as with any other organization, Xerox also has informal groups (those that do not appear on the organization chart) to consider. More discussion on informal groups will follow in later Back-to-the-Case sections.

Examples of Formal Groups Two formal groups that are often established in organizations are committees and work teams. Committees are the more traditional formal group; work teams have only recently gained acceptance and support in U.S. organizations. The part of this text dealing with the managerial function of organizing emphasized command groups; however, the examples here emphasize task groups.

A **committee** is a task group that is charged with performing some type of specific activity.

Committees A **committee** is a group of individuals charged with performing some type of specific activity and is usually classified as a task group. From a managerial viewpoint, there are four major reasons for establishing committees:[7]

1. To allow organization members to exchange ideas
2. To generate suggestions and recommendations that can be offered to other organizational units
3. To develop new ideas for solving existing organizational problems
4. To assist in the development of organizational policies

Committees exist in virtually all organizations and at all organizational levels. As Figure 17.2 suggests, however, the larger the organization, the greater the probability that it will use committees on a regular basis. The following two sections discuss why managers should use committees and what makes a committee successful.

Why Managers Should Use Committees. Managers generally agree that committees have several uses in organizations.

➤ Committees can improve the quality of decision making. As more people become involved in making a decision, the strengths and weaknesses of various alternatives tend to be discussed in greater detail and the chances of reaching a higher-quality decision increase.

➤ Committees encourage the expression of honest opinions. Committee members feel protected enough to say what they really think because the group output of a committee cannot be associated with any one member of that group.

➤ Committees also tend to increase organization members' participation in decision-making and thereby enhance the chances of widespread support of decisions. Another result of this increased participation is that committee members satisfy their social or self-esteem needs through committee work.

➤ Finally, committees ensure the representation of important groups in the decision-making process. Managers must choose committee members wisely, however, to achieve appropriate representation, for if a committee does not adequately represent various interest groups, any decision it comes to may well be counter to the interests of some important organizational group.

Although executives vary somewhat in their enthusiasm about using committees in organizations, a study reported by McLeod and Jones concludes that most executives favor using

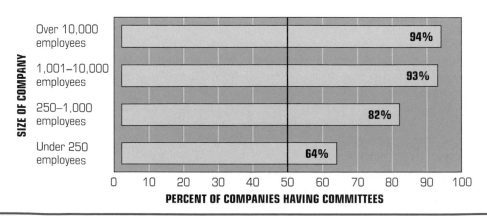

Figure 17.2 Percent of companies that have committees, by size of company

committees. The executives who took part in this study said they got significantly more information from organizational sources other than committees, but found the information from committees more valuable than the information from any other source. Nevertheless, some top executives express only qualified support for using committees as work groups, and others had negative feelings toward committees. Still, the executives who feel positive about committees or who display qualified acceptance of them in general outnumber those who look upon committees negatively.

What Makes Committees Successful. Although committees have become an accepted management tool, managerial action taken to establish and run them is a major variable in determining their degree of success.

Procedural Steps. Several procedural steps can be taken to increase the probability that a committee will be successful:[8]

➢ The committee's goals should be clearly defined, preferably in writing. This will focus the committee's activities and reduce the time members devote to discussing just what it is the committee is supposed to be doing.

➢ The committee's authority should be specified. Is it merely to investigate, advise, and recommend, or is it authorized to implement decisions?

➢ The optimum size of the committee should be determined. With fewer than 5 members, the advantages of group work may be diminished. With more than 10 or 15 members, the committee may become unwieldy. Although optimal size varies with the circumstances, the ideal number of committee members for most tasks seems to be from 5 to 10.

➢ A chairperson should be selected on the basis of ability to run an efficient meeting—that is, the ability to keep committee members from getting bogged down in irrelevancies and to see to it that the necessary paperwork gets done.

➢ Appointing a permanent secretary to handle communications is often useful.

➢ The agenda and all supporting material for the meeting should be distributed before the meeting takes place. When members have a chance to study each item beforehand, they are likely to stick to the point and be prepared to make informed contributions.

➢ Meetings should start on time, and their ending time should be announced at the outset.

People-Oriented Guidelines. In addition to these procedural steps, managers can follow a number of more people-oriented guidelines to increase the probability that a committee will succeed. In particular, a manager can raise the quality of committee discussions by doing the following:[9]

➢ *Rephrasing ideas already expressed*—This rephrasing ensures that the manager as well as other people on the committee clearly understand what has been said.

➢ *Bringing all members into active participation*—Every committee member is a potential source of useful information, so the manager should serve as a catalyst to spark individual participation whenever appropriate.

➢ *Stimulating further thought by members*—The manager should encourage committee members to think ideas through carefully and thoroughly, for only this type of analysis will generate high-quality committee output.

Groupthink. Managers should also help the committee avoid a phenomenon called "groupthink." **Groupthink** is the mode of thinking that group members engage in when the desire for agreement so dominates the group that it overrides the need to realistically appraise alternative problem solutions. Groups tend to slip into groupthink when their members become overly concerned about being too harsh in judging one another's ideas and lose their objectivity. Such groups tend to seek complete support on every issue to avoid conflicts that might endanger the "we-feeling" atmosphere.[10]

Work Teams **Work teams** are another example of task groups used in organizations. Contemporary work teams in the United States evolved out of the problem-solving teams—based on Japanese-style quality circles—that were widely adopted in the 1970s. Problem-

▶ This team of engineers traveled a year-long path to the creation of the Smartphone, which combines a Palm OS digital assistant with a high-end mobile phone. The challenges that brought them together included the need to match design and function; the sale of their unit to another firm in mid-project; budgeting crises; and finally, a lack of support within the firm that led team leader Gary Koerper (far right) to outsource the final product test. Sprint PCS and Verizon are now eagerly marketing the phone nationwide. Other members of the vindicated team include (l. to r.) Kyle Halkola, Brett Kayzar, and Mike Barnwell.

Groupthink is the mode of thinking that group members engage in when the desire for agreement so dominates the group that it overrides the need to realistically appraise alternative problem solutions.

A **work team** is a task group used in organizations to achieve greater organizational flexibility or to cope with rapid growth.

solving teams consist of 5 to 12 volunteer members from different areas of the department who meet weekly to discuss ways to improve quality and efficiency.

Special-Purpose and Self-Managed Teams.   Special-purpose teams evolved in the early to middle 1980s out of problem-solving teams. The typical special-purpose team consists of workers and union representatives meeting together to collaborate on operational decisions at all levels. The aim is to create an atmosphere conducive to quality and productivity improvements.

Special-purpose teams laid the foundation for the self-managed work teams that arose in the 1990s, and it is these teams that appear to be the wave of the future. Self-managed teams consist of 5 to 15 employees who work together to produce an entire product. Members learn all the tasks required to produce the product and rotate from job to job. Self-managed teams even take over such managerial duties as scheduling work and vacations and ordering materials. Because these work teams give employees so much control over their jobs, they represent a fundamental change in how work is organized. (Self-managed teams will be discussed in some detail later in this chapter.)

Employing work teams allows a firm to draw on the talent and creativity of all its employees, not just a few maverick inventors or top executives, to make important decisions. As product quality becomes more and more important in the business world, companies will need to rely more and more on the team approach in order to stay competitive. Consider a recent situation at Yellow Freight Systems, a shipping company, whose management was intent on giving its customers excellent service. To address this concern, management established a work team made up of employees from many different parts of the company, including marketing, sales, operations, and human resources. The overall task of the work team was to run an excellence-in-service campaign that management had initiated.[11]

▶ Back to the Case

Xerox management could decide to form a committee to achieve some specific goal. For example, a committee might be formed on how to enhance the quality of copiers offered by Xerox, which could allow various Xerox departments to exchange quality improvement ideas and generate related suggestions to management. Such a committee could improve Xerox decision making in general by encouraging honest feedback from employees about quality issues in the organization. It could also be used to get fresh ideas about enhancing product quality, and to encourage Xerox employees to more seriously participate in actually improving the quality of equipment offered by the company. This approach would help to ensure that all appropriate departments are represented in important quality decisions, so when Xerox takes action to improve the quality of its copiers, for example, every important angle would be considered, including design, production, marketing, sales, and so on.

In managing such a quality committee at Xerox, management should encourage the members to take certain steps that can help the committee to be successful, since a poorly run committee wastes a lot of time. For example, the committee should develop a clear definition of its goals and the limits of its authority: Is it just going to come up with quality improvement ideas, or should it also take the initial steps toward implementing its ideas?

In addition, the quality committee should not have too few or too many members. Issues such as appointing a secretary to handle communications and appointing a chairperson who is people-oriented must be addressed. Such a quality committee needs someone who can rephrase ideas clearly to ensure that everyone understands; and someone who can get members to participate and think about the issues while avoiding "groupthink": Original ideas should be generated by the committee, not by a unanimous opinion because everyone is trying to avoid conflict.

Stages of Formal Group Development   Another requirement for successfully managing formal groups is understanding the stages of formal group development. In a classic book, Bernard Bass suggested that group development is a four-stage process that unfolds as the group learns how to use its resources.[12] Although these stages may not occur sequentially, for the purpose of clarity, the discussion that follows will assume that they do.

The Acceptance Stage   It is common for members of a new group to mistrust one another somewhat initially. The acceptance stage occurs only after this initial mistrust melts and the group has been transformed into one characterized by mutual trust and acceptance.

The Communication and Decision-Making Stage   Once they have passed through the acceptance stage, group members are better able to communicate frankly with one another. This frank communication provides the basis for establishing and using an effective group decision-making mechanism.

The Group Solidarity Stage   Group solidarity comes naturally as the mutual acceptance of group members increases and communication and decision making continue within the group. At this stage, members become more involved in group activities and cooperate, rather than compete, with one another. Members find belonging to the group extremely satisfying and are committed to enhancing the group's overall success.

The Group Control Stage   A natural result of group solidarity is group control. In this stage, group members attempt to maximize the group's success by matching individual abilities with group activities and by assisting one another. Flexibility and informality usually characterize this stage.

As a group passes through each of these four stages, it generally becomes more mature and effective—and therefore more productive. The group that reaches maximum maturity and effectiveness is characterized by the following traits in its members:

- *Members function as a unit*—The group works as a team. Members do not disturb one another to the point of interfering with their collaboration.
- *Members participate effectively in group effort*—Members work hard when there is something to do. They seldom loaf, even if they have the opportunity to do so.
- *Members are oriented toward a single goal*—Group members work for the common purpose; they do not waste group resources by moving in different directions.
- *Members have the equipment, tools, and skills necessary to attain the group's goals*—Members are taught the various parts of their jobs by experts and strive to acquire whatever resources they need to attain group objectives.
- *Members ask and receive suggestions, opinions, and information from one another*—A member who is uncertain about something stops working and asks another member for information. Group members generally talk to one another openly and frequently.

▶ Back to the Case

Managers in companies like Xerox must be patient and understand that it will take some time for a new group to develop into a productive working unit. The members in any new work group must start by trusting and accepting one another and then begin communicating and exchanging ideas. Once this acceptance and communication increases, group solidarity and control come naturally. The group members get involved, cooperate, and try to maximize the group's success.

With the quality committee that is being used as an example, Xerox management must be patient and let it mature before maximum effectiveness and productivity can be expected. If given time to grow, the group will function as a unit, members will participate willingly and effectively, and the group will reach valuable decisions about what needs to be done to improve the quality of equipment that Xerox offers.

Informal Groups

An **informal group** is a collection of individuals whose common work experiences result in the development of a system of interpersonal relations that extend beyond those established by management.

Informal groups, the second major kind of group that can exist within an organization, are groups that develop naturally as people interact. An **informal group** is defined as a collection of individuals whose common work experiences result in the development of a system of interpersonal relations that extend beyond those established by management.[13]

As Figure 17.3 shows, informal group structures can deviate significantly from formal group structures. As is true of Supervisor A in the figure, an organization member can belong to more than one informal group at the same time. In contrast to formal groups, informal groups are not highly structured in procedure and are not formally recognized by management.

The next sections discuss the following subjects:

1. Various kinds of informal groups that exist in organizations
2. The benefits people usually reap from belonging to informal groups

An **interest group** is an informal group that gains and maintains membership primarily because of a common concern members have about a specific issue.

A **friendship group** is an informal group that forms in organizations because of the personal affiliation members have with one another.

Kinds of Informal Groups Informal groups are divided into two general types: interest groups and friendship groups. **Interest groups** are informal groups that gain and maintain membership primarily because of a common concern members have about a specific issue. An example is a group of workers pressing management for better pay or working conditions. Once the interest or concern that instigated the formation of the informal group has been eliminated, the group will probably disband.

As its name implies, **friendship groups** are informal groups that form in organizations because of the personal affiliation members have with one another. Such personal factors as

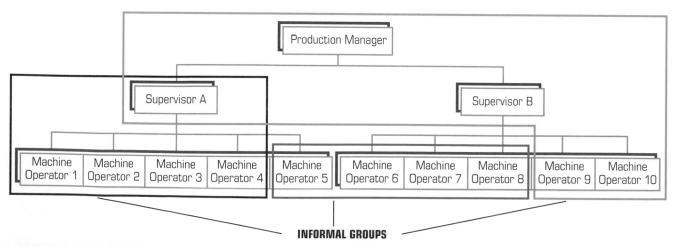

Figure 17.3 🖑   *Three informal groups that deviate significantly from formal groups within the organization*

recreational interests, race, gender, and religion serve as foundations for friendship groups. As with interest groups, the membership of friendship groups tends to change over time. Here, however, membership changes as friendships dissolve or new friendships are made.

Benefits of Informal Group Membership   Informal groups tend to develop in organizations because of various benefits that group members obtain:[14]

1. Perpetuation of social and cultural values that group members consider important
2. Status and social satisfaction that people might not enjoy without group membership
3. Increased ease of communication among group members
4. Increased desirability of the overall work environment

These benefits may be one reason that employees who are on fixed shifts or who continually work with the same groups tend to be more satisfied with their work than employees whose shifts are continually changing.

Back to the Case

There are also issues regarding informal groups that could impact the success of work groups at Xerox. Employee groups get together at times because of certain issues. For example, certain minority employees could get together as a group to increase the opportunities for their professional growth at Xerox; and employees from friendship groups, which ease communication and provide feelings of satisfaction in a company. In general, such informal groups can improve the work environment for everyone involved, so it can be advantageous for management to encourage their development.

Perhaps Xerox management could accelerate the development of a quality committee into a productive unit by including individuals who already know and trust one another through membership in one or more informal groups at Xerox. For example, some members of the newly formed quality committee might know and trust one another immediately as a result of membership on a company bowling or softball team. Under such circumstances, a trust developed among employees through past informal group affiliations could help the formal quality committee to develop into a productive group more quickly.

MANAGING WORK GROUPS

To manage work groups effectively, managers must simultaneously consider the effects of both formal and informal group factors on organizational productivity. This consideration requires two steps:

1. Determining group existence
2. Understanding the evolution of informal groups

Determining Group Existence

The most important step that managers need to take in managing work groups is to determine what informal groups exist within the organization and who their members are. **Sociometry** is an analytical tool managers can use to do this. They can also use sociometry to get information on the internal workings of an informal group, including the identity of the group leader, the relative status of group members, and the group's communication networks.[15] This information on informal groups, combined with an understanding of the established formal groups shown on the organization chart, will give managers a complete picture of the organization's group structure.

Sociometry is an analytical tool that can be used to determine what informal groups exist in an organization and who the members of those groups are.

Sociometric Analysis   The procedure for performing a sociometric analysis in an organization is quite basic. Various organization members simply are asked, through either an interview or a questionnaire, to name several other organization members with whom they would like to spend free time. A sociogram is then constructed to summarize the informal relationships among group members. **Sociograms** are diagrams that visually link individuals within

A **sociogram** is a sociometric diagram that summarizes the personal feelings of organization members about the people in the organization with whom they would like to spend free time.

the population queried according to the number of times they were chosen and whether the choice was reciprocated.

Applying the Sociogram Model   Figure 17.4 shows two sample sociograms based on a classic study of two groups of boys in a summer camp—the Bulldogs and the Red Devils. An analysis of these sociograms leads to several interesting conclusions. First, more boys within the Bulldogs than within the Red Devils were chosen as being desirable to spend time with. This probably implies that the Bulldogs are a closer-knit informal group than the Red Devils. Second, the greater the number of times an individual was chosen, the more likely it was that the individual would be the group leader. Thus, individuals C and E in Figure 17.4 are probably Bulldog leaders, while L and S are probably Red Devil leaders. Third, communication between L and most other Red Devils members is likely to occur directly, whereas communication between C and other bulldogs is likely to pass through other group members.

Sociometric analysis can give managers many useful insights concerning the informal groups within their organization. Managers who do not want to perform a formal sociometric analysis can at least casually gather information on what form a sociogram might take in a particular situation. They can pick up this information through normal conversations with other organization members as well as through observations of how various organization members relate to one another.

Understanding the Evolution of Informal Groups

As we have seen, the first prerequisite for managing groups effectively is knowing what groups exist within an organization and what characterizes the membership of those groups. The second prerequisite is understanding how informal groups evolve. This understanding will give managers some insights on how to encourage the development of appropriate informal groups, that is, groups that support the attainment of organizational objectives and whose members maintain good relationships with formal work groups.

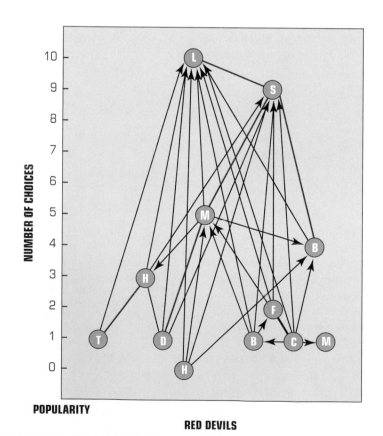

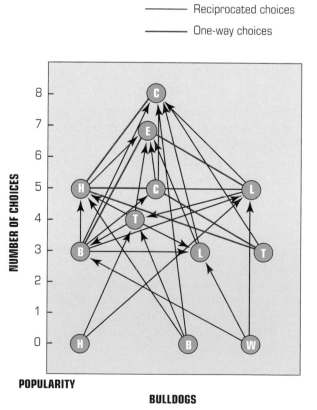

Figure 17.4   *Sample sociograms*

Homans' Model   Perhaps the most widely accepted framework for explaining the evolution of informal groups was developed by George Homans.[16] Figure 17.5 broadly summarizes his theory. According to Homans, the informal group is established to provide satisfaction and growth for its members. At the same time, the sentiments, interactions, and activities that emerge within an informal group result from the sentiments, interactions, and activities that already exist within a formal group. Given these two premises, it follows that feedback on the functioning of the informal group can give managers ideas about how to modify the formal group so as to increase the probability that informal group members will achieve the satisfaction and growth they desire. The ultimate consequence will be to reinforce the solidarity and productiveness of the formal group—to the advantage of the organization.

Applying the Homans Model   To see what Homans' concept involves, suppose that 12 factory workers are members of a formal work group that manufactures toasters. According to Homans, as these workers interact to assemble toasters, they might discover common personal interests that encourage the evolution of one or more informal groups that would maximize the satisfaction and growth of their members. Once established, these informal groups will probably resist changes in the formal work group that threaten the satisfaction and growth of the informal group's members. On the other hand, modifications in the formal work group that enhance the satisfaction and growth of the informal group's members will tend to be welcomed.

Back to the Case

In order for a company like Xerox to be successful, managers must be able to consider how both formal and informal groups affect organizational productivity, and they need to determine what informal groups exist, know who the group members are, and understand how these groups form. Armed with this information, Xerox management can strive to make their work groups more effective.

One way management can get information about the groups at Xerox is to use sociometry. A questionnaire can be designed asking their employees with whom they spend time and a sociogram can be constructed to summarize this information. Managers could also do a more casual analysis by just talking to their employees and observing how they interact with one another.

Managers in a company like Xerox should try to understand how informal groups evolve and should be aware that an organization's formal structure influences how the informal groups develop within it. For example, assume that in one department at Xerox there are 30 people who work on copier design. Many of them are interested in sports, have become friends because of this common interest, and work well together as a result. If a manager needed to make some changes in such a department, he or she should try to accommodate such informal friendship groups to keep employees satisfied. Only with very good reason should a manager of such a department damage the existence of the productive friendship group by transferring any informal group members out of the design department.

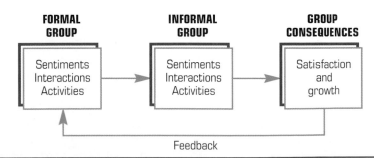

FORMAL GROUP	INFORMAL GROUP	GROUP CONSEQUENCES
Sentiments Interactions Activities	Sentiments Interactions Activities	Satisfaction and growth

Feedback

Homans' ideas on how informal groups develop

Figure 17.5

The preceding sections of this chapter discussed groups—what they are, what kinds exist in organizations, and how such groups should be managed. This section focuses on a special type of group: teams. It covers the following topics:

1. Difference between groups and teams
2. Types of teams that exist in organizations
3. Stages of development that teams go through
4. What constitutes an effective team
5. Relationship between trust and team effectiveness

Groups Versus Teams

A **team** is a group whose members influence one another toward the accomplishment of (an) organizational objective(s).

The terms *group* and *team* are not synonymous. As we have seen, a group consists of any number of people who interact with one another, are psychologically aware of one another, and think of themselves as a group. A **team** is a group whose members influence one another toward the accomplishment of an organizational objective(s).

Not all groups in organizations are teams, but all teams are groups. A group qualifies as a team only if its members focus on helping one another to accomplish organizational objectives. In today's quickly changing business environment, teams have emerged as a requirement for success.[17] Therefore, good managers constantly try to help groups become teams. This part of the chapter provides insights on how managers can facilitate the evolution of groups into teams.

Types of Teams in Organizations

Organizational teams take many different forms. The following sections discuss three types of teams commonly found in today's organizations: problem-solving teams, self-managed teams, and cross-functional teams.

Problem-Solving Teams

Management confronts many different organizational problems daily. Examples are production systems that are not manufacturing products at the desired levels of quality; workers who appear to be listless and uninvolved; and managers who are basing their decisions on inaccurate information.

A **problem-solving team** is an organizational team set up to help eliminate a specified problem within the organization.

For assistance in solving such formidable problems, management commonly establishes special teams. A team set up to help eliminate a specified problem within the organization is called a **problem-solving team.** The typical problem-solving team has 5 to 12 members and is formed to discuss ways to improve quality in all phases of the organization, to make organizational processes more efficient, or to improve the overall work environment.[18]

After the problem-solving team reaches a consensus, it makes recommendations to management about how to deal with the specified problem. Management may respond to the team's recommendations by implementing them in their entirety, by modifying and then implementing

Problem-Solving Teams Focus on Improving Quality at Weyerhaeuser Insurance Department

Weyerhaeuser is engaged in the growing and harvesting of timber for the manufacture and sale of lumber and other forest products needed in real estate development and related construction activities. The company was founded in 1900 and employs approximately 47,000 people. Although Weyerhaeuser operates in 17 countries, its primary presence is in the United States and Canada, and its annual sales average about $16 billion.

Weyerhaeuser is a world-class company. It is one of North America's largest producers of forest products and the world's largest producer of softwood lumber. In addition, Weyerhaeuser is a leading recycler of office wastepaper, a top forest-products exporter in the United States, and one of the largest producers of container packaging.

The company has many different departments due to the diversity of its products. One such department has recently received acclaim for its successful focus on a particular problem—improving the quality of operations. Weyerhaeuser's insurance department is focusing on doing things right the first time by creating teams to apply total quality management principles to confront many challenges. Basically, the department's approach to quality management involves encouraging continual improvement. Teams are formed based on members' expertise and members meet to determine ways to improve department operations. Brainstorming to encourage the department's continual improvement has included improving customer service and motivating vendors to improve their services to Weyerhaeuser. ■

them, or by requesting further information to assess them. Once the problem that management asked the problem-solving team to address has been solved, the team is generally disbanded.

Self-Managed Teams The **self-managed team,** sometimes called a *self-managed work group* or *self-directed team,* is a team that plans, organizes, influences, and controls its own work situation with only minimal intervention and direction from management. This creative team design involves a highly integrated group of several skilled individuals who are cross-trained and have the responsibility and authority to perform some specified activity.

Activities typically carried out by management in a traditional work setting—creating work schedules, establishing work pace and breaks, developing vacation schedules, evaluating performance, determining the level of salary increases and rewards received by individual workers, and ordering materials to be used in the production process—are instead carried out by members of the self-managed team. Generally responsible for whole tasks as opposed to "parts" of a job,[19] the self-managed team is an important new way of structuring, managing, and rewarding work. Since these teams require only minimum management attention, they free managers to pursue other management activities like strategic planning.

Reports of successful self-managed work teams are plentiful.[20] These teams are growing in popularity because today's business environment seems to require such work teams to solve complex problems independently, because American workers have come to expect more freedom in the workplace, and because the speed of technological change demands that employees be able to adapt quickly. Not all self-managed teams are successful. To ensure the success of a self-managed team, the manager should carefully select and properly train its members.[21]

Cross-functional teams operate in all kinds of situations. The members of this pit crew team must depend on one another to get the job done, with each one contributing his or her expertise in a particular task.

Cross-Functional Teams A **cross-functional team** is a work team composed of people from different functional areas of the organization—marketing, finance, human resources, and operations, for example—who are all focused on a specified objective. Cross-functional teams may or may not be self-managed, though self-managed teams are generally cross-functional. Because cross-functional team members are from different departments within the organization, the team possesses the expertise to coordinate all the department activities within the organization that impact its own work.

> A **self-managed team** is an organizational team established to plan, organize, influence, and control its own work situation with only minimal direction from management.

> A **cross-functional team** is an organizational team composed of people from different functional areas of the organization who are all focused on a specified objective.

ACROSS INDUSTRIES

▶ Motorcycle Manufacturing—Cross-Functional Teams Design New Products at Harley-Davidson

Harley-Davidson, Inc. designs, manufactures, and markets heavyweight motorcycles, motorcycle parts and accessories, and motorcycle collectibles and riding apparel. The company offers four popular motorcycle platforms: Sportster, Dyna, Softail, and Touring. In recent years, Harley-Davidson's products have gained much popularity, notoriety, and applause.

In addition, management at Harley-Davidson has been recognized worldwide for its successful use of progressive, cutting-edge management techniques. One specific area in which Harley-Davidson's management has received acclaim is its use of cross-functional teams to design new products. To some extent, cross-functional advice has always been considered within the new product design process at Harley-Davidson. Representatives from engineering, purchasing, manufacturing, and marketing have always had some influence on the future direction of new products.

More recently, management has underscored its commitment to cross-functional teams for designing new products by opening a new Product Development Center (PDC) near its plant in Wauwatosa, Wisconsin. For years the motorcycle maker has been consistently moving toward more emphasis on using cross-functional teams for new product development. The PDC accelerated this move by locating design engineers, purchasers, manufacturing personnel, and other crucial players in a single building. These team members work together daily and are totally dedicated to the new product development process on a full-time basis.

At Harley-Davidson, management's commitment to new product design via cross-functional teams is clear. In addition, management is implementing self-managed work teams to help meet the challenges of manufacturing its products in a timely fashion. Harley-Davidson's self-managed work teams are on the way to becoming the standard for the industry.

Some examples of cross-functional teams are teams established to choose and implement new technologies throughout the organization; teams formed to improve marketing effectiveness within the organization; and teams established to control product costs.[22]

This section discussed three types of teams that exist in organizations: problem-solving, self-directed, and cross-functional. It should be noted here that managers can establish various combinations of these three types of teams. Figure 17.6 illustrates some possible combinations that managers could create. For example, *a* in the figure represents a team that is problem-solving, self-directed, and cross-functional, while *b* represents one that is problem-solving, but neither cross-functional nor self-directed. Before establishing a team, managers should carefully study their own unique organizational situation and set up the type of team that best suits that situation.

Building Diverse Flight Teams Benefits Continental Airlines

Continental Airlines is a major U.S. air carrier that transports passengers, cargo, and mail. Continental and its subsidiaries, Continental Express and Continental Micronesia, serve about 230 airports. Continental flies to over 125 domestic cities, and 90 international destinations including flights to Europe, South America, Japan, and Central America.

The Continental Airlines Web site proudly proclaims news, in *Aviation Week & Space Technology*, that the company has received its highest rating for outstanding management among U.S.-based global carriers. For the second straight year, the publication gave Continental the highest rating of any major U.S. airline for management of company assets to achieve goals.

Many airline executives believe one reason the company is enjoying such notable success is its aggressive attitude in hiring, training,

and retaining minority employees. Continental's diverse workforce is an important competitive advantage for serving an increasingly diverse customer base. For example, it has recruited a number of bilingual employees (speaking Spanish and English) to serve areas with concentrated Hispanic customer bases. As a result of such efforts, Continental recently became the official airline of the U.S. Hispanic Chamber of Commerce. Servicing customers in their native language with diversified flight teams, and with their native cuisine, is one of Continental's diversity-based strategies that keeps customers coming back to Continental. The recognition that Continental continues to receive, such as repeat appearances on the Hispanic business list of best places for Latinos to work, should help the company to maintain its diversified flight teams well into the future. ■

Stages of Team Development

More and more modern managers are using work teams to accomplish organizational tasks. Simply establishing such a team, however, does not guarantee it will be productive. In fact, managers should be patient when an established work team is not initially productive, for teams generally need to pass through several developmental stages before they become productive. Managers must understand this developmental process so they can facilitate it. The following sections discuss the various stages a team usually must pass through before it becomes fully productive.[23]

▶ Cross-functional teams operate in all kinds of situations. The members of this pit crew team must depend on one another to get the job done, with each one contributing his or her expertise in a particular task.

Forming   **Forming** is the first stage of the team development process. During this stage, members of the newly formed team become oriented to the team and acquainted with one another. This period is characterized by exploring issues related to the members' new job situation, such as what is expected of them, who has what kind of authority within the team, what kind of people are team members, and what skills team members possess.

The forming stage of team development is usually characterized by uncertainty and stress. Recognizing that team members are struggling to adjust to their new work situations and to one another, managers should be tolerant of lengthy, informal discussions exploring team specifics and not regard them as time wasters. The newly formed team must be allowed an exploratory period if it is to become truly productive.

Storming   After a team has formed, it begins to storm. **Storming,** the second stage of the team development process, is characterized by conflict and disagreement as team members become more assertive in clarifying their indi-

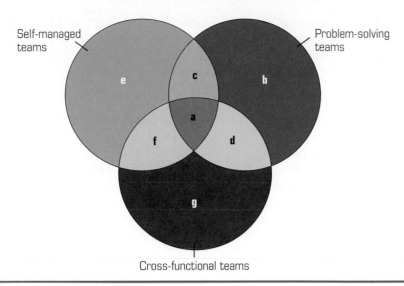

Self-managed teams

Problem-solving teams

Cross-functional teams

Possible team types based on various combinations of self-directed, problem-solving, and cross-functional teams

Figure 17.6

vidual roles. During this stage, the team seems to lack unity because members are continually challenging the way the team functions.

To help the team progress beyond storming, managers should encourage team members to feel free to disagree with any team issues and to discuss their own views fully and honestly. Most of all, managers should urge team members to arrive at agreements that will help the team reach its objective(s).

Norming   When the storming stage ends, norming begins. **Norming,** the third stage of the team development process, is characterized by agreement among team members on roles, rules, and acceptable behavior while working on the team. Conflicts generated during the storming stage are resolved in this stage.

Managers should encourage teams that have entered the norming stage to progress toward developing team norms and values that will be instrumental in building a successful organization. The process of determining what behavior is and is not acceptable within the team is critical to the work team's future productivity.

Performing   The fourth stage of the team development process is **performing.** At this stage, the team fully focuses on solving organizational problems and on meeting assigned challenges. The team is now productive: after successfully passing through the earlier stages of team development, it knows itself and has settled on team roles, expectations, and norms.

During this stage, managers should recognize the team's accomplishments regularly, for productive team behavior must be reinforced to enhance the probability that it will continue in the future.

Adjourning   The fifth, and last, stage of the team development process is known as **adjourning.** Now the team is finishing its job and preparing to disband. This stage normally occurs only in teams established for some special purpose to be accomplished in a limited time period. Special committees and task groups are examples of such teams. During the adjourning stage, team members generally feel disappointment that their team is being broken up because disbandment means the loss of personally satisfying relationships or an enjoyable work situation.

During this phase of team development, managers should recognize team members' disappointment and sense of loss as normal and assure them that other challenging and exciting organizational opportunities await them. It is important that management then do everything necessary to integrate these people into new teams or other areas of the organization.

Although some work teams do not pass through every one of the development stages just described, understanding the stages of forming, storming, norming, performing, and

Forming is the first stage of the team development process, during which members of the newly formed team become oriented to the team and acquainted with one another as they explore issues related to their new job situation.

Storming, the second stage of the team development process, is characterized by conflict and disagreement as team members try to clarify their individual roles and challenge the way the team functions.

Norming, the third stage of the team development process, is characterized by agreement among team members on roles, rules, and acceptable behavior while working on the team.

Performing, the fourth stage of the team development process, is characterized by a focus on solving organizational problems and meeting assigned challenges.

Adjourning, the fifth and last stage of the team development process, is the stage in which the team finishes its job and prepares to disband.

adjourning will give managers many useful insights on how to build productive work teams. Above all, managers must realize that new teams are different from mature teams and that their challenge is to build whatever team they are in charge of into a mature, productive work team.

Team Effectiveness

Earlier in this chapter, teams were defined as groups of people who influence one another to reach organizational targets. It is easy to see why effective teams are critical to organizational success. Effective teams are those that come up with innovative ideas, accomplish their goals, and adapt to change when necessary. Their individual members are highly committed to both the team and organizational goals. Such teams are highly valued by upper management and recognized and rewarded for their accomplishments.[24]

Figure 17.7 sketches the characteristics of an effective team. Note the figure's implications for the steps managers need to take to build effective work teams in organizations. *People-related steps* include the following:[25]

1. Trying to make the team's work satisfying
2. Developing mutual trust among team members and between the team and management
3. Building good communication—from management to the team as well as within the team
4. Minimizing unresolved conflicts and power struggles within the team
5. Dealing effectively with threats toward and within the team
6. Building the perception that the jobs of team members are secure

Organization-related steps managers can take to build effective work teams include:

1. Building a stable overall organization or company structure that team members view as secure
2. Becoming involved in team events and demonstrating interest in team progress and functioning
3. Properly rewarding and recognizing teams for their accomplishments
4. Setting stable goals and priorities for the team

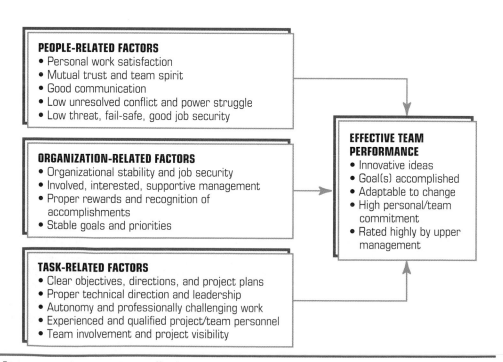

Finally, Figure 17.7 implies that managers can build effective work teams by taking six *task-related steps*:

1. Developing clear objectives, directions, and project plans for the team
2. Providing proper technical direction and leadership for the team
3. Establishing autonomy for the team and challenging work within the team
4. Appointing experienced and qualified team personnel
5. Encouraging team involvement
6. Building visibility within the organization for the team's work

Trust and Effective Teams

Probably the most fundamental ingredient of effective teams is trust. Trust is belief in the reliance, ability, and integrity of another. Unless team members trust one another, the team leader, and management, managers may well find that building an effective work team is impossible.[26]

Today there is significant concern that management is not inspiring the kind of trust that is essential to team effectiveness. In fact, subordinates' trust in their managers is critically low, and employee opinion polls indicate that it may well decline even further in the future.

Management urgently needs to focus on reversing this trend. There are many strategies managers can use to build trust within groups.[27]

- *Communicate often to team members*—This is a fundamental strategy. Keeping team members informed of organizational news, explaining why certain decisions have been made, and sharing information about organizational operations are examples of how managers should communicate to team members.
- *Show respect for team members*—Managers need to show team members that they are highly valued. They can demonstrate their respect for team members by delegating tasks to them, listening intently to feedback from the group, and acting on it appropriately.
- *Be fair to team members*—Team members must receive the rewards they have earned. Managers must therefore conduct fair performance appraisals and objectively allocate and distribute rewards. It should go without saying that showing favoritism in this area sows mistrust and resentment.
- *Be predictable*—Managers must be consistent in their actions. Team members should usually be able to forecast what decisions management will make before those decisions are made. Moreover, managers must live up to commitments made to team members. Managers who make inconsistent decisions and fail to live up to commitments will not be trusted by teams.
- *Demonstrate competence*—To build team trust, managers must show team members that they are able to diagnose organizational problems and have the skill to implement solutions to those problems. Team members tend to trust managers they perceive as competent and distrust those they perceive as incompetent.

CORPORATE CULTURE

So far, this chapter has focused on managing smaller work groups. This section, in contrast, discusses corporate culture as an important ingredient for managing organization members as a total group.

Corporate culture is a set of shared value and beliefs that organization members have regarding the functioning and existence of their organization. What type of corporate culture is present in any organization can be discovered by studying that organization's special combination of status symbols, traditions, history, and physical environment. A management that understands the significance of all these factors can use them to develop a corporate culture that is beneficial to the firm.

Corporate culture is a set of shared values and beliefs that organization members have regarding the functioning and existence of their organization.

Status Symbols

Looking at the status symbols of an organization—the visible, external signs of social position that are associated with the various positions in the firm—gives an observer a feeling for the organization's social hierarchy. The size and location of an organization member's office, as well as the member's access to executive clubs and reserved parking, indicates the status level of that member's job.

Traditions and History

A firm's history and traditions can determine how workers in that particular firm act on a daily basis. Typically, traditions developed over time let workers know exactly what is expected of them. By developing traditions, therefore, managers can steer the everyday behaviors that go on in an organization.

Physical Environment

The firm's physical environment makes a statement about its corporate culture. For instance, closed offices and few common areas where organization members can meet indicate a closed form of culture. On the other hand, a building with open offices and extensive common areas where employees can interact indicates a more open culture. Management that wants an open culture, then, will see to it that office doors are usually open; management that wants a more formal type of corporate culture will encourage closed office doors.

The Significance of Corporate Culture

The significance of corporate culture for management is that it influences the behavior of everyone within an organization and, if carefully crafted, can have a significant positive effect on organizational success.[28] If not properly managed, however, corporate culture can help doom an organization. Typically, top management and other present or past organizational leaders are the key agents influencing corporate culture.

The current management literature is full of advice about the way managers should handle corporate culture issues. One especially practical and helpful book suggests that there are five primary mechanisms for developing and reinforcing the desired corporate culture.[29]

> *What leaders pay attention to, measure, and control*—Leaders can communicate very effectively what their vision of the organization is and what they want done by consistently emphasizing the same issues in meetings, in casual remarks and questions, and in strategy discussions. For example, if product quality is the dominant value to be inculcated in employees, leaders may consistently inquire about the effect of any proposed changes on product quality.

> *Leaders' reactions to critical incidents and organizational crises*—The manner in which leaders deal with crises can create new beliefs and values and reveal underlying organiza-

▶ The corporate culture at Interval Research in Palo Alto, California, is less a reflection of what the company does (conducting "pure research" on consumer goods and services for the information highway) than of how it goes about it. To build this futuristic kitchen, for example, researchers "collected" samples of people's everyday behavior in the real world. Then they brought it back to the office, where the workday consisted of freewheeling "informances"—informative performances in which staffers "play act" the imagined lives of imaginary consumers.

tional assumptions. For example, when a firm faces a financial crisis but does not lay off any employees, the message is that the organization sees itself as a "family" that looks out for its members.

➤ *Deliberate role modeling, teaching, and coaching*—The behaviors of leaders in both formal and informal settings have an important effect on employee beliefs, values, and behaviors. For example, if the CEO regularly works very long hours and on weekends, other managers will probably respond by spending more time at work also.

➤ *Criteria for allocation of rewards and status*—Leaders can firmly communicate their priorities and values by consistently linking rewards and punishments to the behaviors that concern them. For example, if a weekly bonus is given for exceeding production or sales quotas, employees will recognize the value placed on these activities and focus their efforts on them.

➤ *Criteria for recruitment, selection, promotion, and retirement of employees*—The kinds of people who are hired and who succeed in an organization are those who accept the organization's values and behave accordingly. For example, if managers who are action oriented and who implement strategies effectively consistently move up the organizational ladder, the organization's priorities will come through loud and clear to other managers.

To influence the type of culture that exists within an organization, a manager must first determine what culture would be appropriate for the organization, and then take calculated and overt steps to encourage the establishment, growth, and maintenance of that culture. Merely allowing a corporate culture to develop without planned management influence can result in an inappropriate culture that limits the organization's success.

▶ Back to the Case

Managers in a company like Xerox should consider the four major factors that influence work group effectiveness. First, the size of the work group can be important to its productivity. A 20-person quality committee would probably be somewhat large and would hamper the group's effectiveness. Remember also, however, that managers should consider informal groups before making changes in group size. The quality committee could end up being less productive without one or more of its respected members than it would be if it were slightly too large.

Another important factor that influences work group effectiveness is group cohesiveness, since a more cohesive group will tend to be more effective. The Introductory Case mentions that the cohesiveness of the asset management work group at Xerox's Houston office was very instrumental in its success. Evelyn Grubb increased the cohesiveness of her formal asset management group by doing such things as allowing members to take breaks together or rewarding informal group members for a job well done.

Group norms, or appropriate behaviors required within the informal group, are a third factor that affects the productivity of formal group behavior at a company like Xerox. Since these norms affect profitability, managers must be aware of them and understand how to influence them within the formal group structure. For example, assume that a smaller informal group of workers within Xerox's asset management department normally maintains the quality of asset management by focusing mainly on tracking the durability of Xerox equipment. Unfortunately, because of this quality norm, the informal group members are taking too much time tracking durability and too little time servicing customer requests via e-mail feedback. Management could try to improve this situation by giving bonuses to group members who best service e-mail requests while tracking equipment durability. This reward would probably increase the formal group productivity while encouraging a positive norm within the informal group.

Status within the informal groups also impacts work group productivity. For example, if Xerox managers want to increase productivity for a group, management should try to encourage the informal group's leaders, as well as the group's formal supervisor. Chances are that a targeted group will become more productive if its informal, high-status members support that objective.

Overall, if a company like Xerox wants to maximize work group effectiveness, management must remember both the formal and informal dimensions of its work groups while considering the four main factors that influence work group productivity.

Management Skills Module

This section is specially designed to help you develop management skills. An individual's management skill is based on an understanding of management concepts and the ability to apply those concepts in management situations. As a result, the following activities are designed both to heighten your understanding of management concepts and to help you gain facility in applying those concepts in various management situations.

UNDERSTANDING MANAGEMENT CONCEPTS

▶ Action Summary

Reread the learning objectives below. Each objective is followed by questions. Answering these questions accurately will help you retain the most important concepts discussed in this chapter. After answering each question, check your answer against the answer key at the end of this chapter. (*Hint*: If you have any doubts regarding the correct response, consult the page number that follows the answer.)

Circle:

From studying this chapter, I will attempt to acquire

1. A definition of the term *group* as used in the context of management.

T F   **a.** A group is made up of people who interact with one another, perceive themselves to be a group, and are primarily physically aware of one another.

a b c d e   **b.** According to Cartwright and Lippitt, it is *not* true to say that: (a) groups exist in all kinds of organizations (b) groups inevitably form in all facets of organizational existence (c) groups cause undesirable consequences within the organization, so their continued existence should be discouraged (d) understanding groups can assist managers in increasing the probability that the groups with which they work will cause desirable consequences within the organization (e) all of the above are true.

2. A thorough understanding of the difference between formal and informal groups.

T F   **a.** An informal group is one that exists within an organization by virtue of management decree.

T F   **b.** A formal group is one that exists within an organization by virtue of interaction among organization members who work in proximity to one another.

3. Knowledge of the types of formal groups that exist in organizations.

a b c d e   **a.** The type of group that generally handles more routine organizational activities is the: (a) informal task group (b) informal command group (c) formal task group (d) formal command group (e) none of the above.

a b c d e   **b.** Managers should be encouraged to take the following steps to increase the success of a committee: (a) clearly define the goals of the committee (b) rephrase ideas that have already been expressed (c) select a chairperson on the basis of ability to run an efficient meeting (d) a and b (e) a, b, and c.

4. An understanding of how managers can determine which groups exist in an organization.

T F   **a.** The technique of sociometry involves asking people whom they would like to manage.

a b c d e   **b.** A sociogram is defined in the text as: (a) a letter encouraging group participation (b) a diagram that visually illustrates the number of times that the individuals were chosen within the group and whether the choice was reciprocal (c) a composite of demographic data useful in determining informal group choices (d) a computer printout designed to profile psychological and sociological characteristics of the informal group (e) none of the above.

5. An appreciation for what teams are and how to manage them.

T F   **a.** A cross-functional team can also be a problem-solving team, but it cannot be a self-managed team.

a b c d e   **b.** Which of the following is *not* a stage of team development: (a) storming (b) alarming (c) forming (d) performing (e) norming.

T F   **c.** Trust is probably the most fundamental ingredient of effective teams.

6. Insights into managing corporate culture to enhance organizational success.

T F   **a.** The concept of corporate culture usually does not include the set of beliefs that organization members have about their organization and its functioning.

a b c d e   **b.** Mechanisms that managers can use to influence corporate culture include: (a) what leaders pay attention to (b) criteria that leaders use to make organizational awards (c) criteria leaders use to select new employees (d) all of the above (e) none of the above.

Action Summary Answer Key

Issues for Review and Discussion

1. How is the term *group* defined in this chapter?
2. Why is the study of groups important to managers?
3. What is a formal group?
4. Explain the significance of linking pins to formal groups in organizations.
5. List and define two types of formal groups that can exist in organizations.
6. Why should managers use committees in organizations?
7. What steps can managers take to ensure that a committee will be successful?
8. Explain how work teams can be valuable to an organization.
9. Describe the stages a group typically goes through as it matures.
10. What is an informal group?
11. List and define two types of informal groups in organizations.
12. What benefits generally accrue to members of informal groups?
13. What is the relationship between work teams and informal groups?
14. Are formal groups more important to managers than informal groups? Explain.
15. Describe the sociometric procedure used to study the informal group membership. What can the results of a sociometric analysis tell managers about members of an informal group?
16. Explain Homans' concept of how informal groups develop.
17. What is the difference between a group and a team? Is this an important difference for a manager to understand? Why?
18. Discuss how managers can develop effective teams in organizations.
19. What steps can managers take to develop trust in work teams? Is developing this trust important? Why?
20. Define corporate culture. Can managers actually build corporate culture? Explain.

APPLYING MANAGEMENT CONCEPTS

Cases

➤ INTRODUCTORY CASE WRAP-UP

Case Discussion Questions

"Teamwork Builds Success at Xerox" (pp. 375–376) and its related Back-to-the-Case sections were written to help you better understand the management concepts contained in this chapter. Answer the following discussion questions about this Introductory Case to further enrich your understanding of chapter content:

1. Describe the characteristics of an effective work team at Xerox.
2. As a manager at Xerox, what steps would you take to turn a work group into an effective team? Explain the importance of each step.

Skills Exercise: Building a Work Team at Xerox

The Introductory Case explains how Xerox's Houston office has been successful in large part because of a small, tightly knit work team. Assume that you are the manager of Xerox's Houston office giving advice to a manager opening a new, similar office in San Francisco. What advice would you give this manager about how to develop an effective work team in the San Francisco office? Use Figure 17.7 as the basis for your advice.

In 1955, Carol Lavin Bernick's father and mother started Alberto-Culver North America with a single product: Alberto VO5 Hairdressing. It earned $100,000 in sales the first year. By sponsoring the television programs of the day like *What's My Line?*, Alberto VO5 became a household name, enabling the small company to hold its own against giants like Proctor & Gamble and Gillette. Since then, the Alberto-Culver Company has grown into a $2.25 billion manufacturer and marketer of personal care, specialty grocery, and household products, with 13,000 employees worldwide.

However, in 1994, when Bernick's parents turned the company over to her and her husband, Alberto-Culver was facing flattened sales, slipping margins, and a high rate of attrition among its employees. As newly appointed president of Alberto-Culver, Bernick wanted to turn members of her North American group into committed team players with a "hunger for innovation." She cared deeply about the company and wanted to make it more fun to work there. She blamed the existing corporate culture for the employee's dissatisfaction, and she realized that the company policy had always been to shield staff from the day-to-day operations of the business. People worked hard but they were just taking orders and had no real input into business decisions. Many of them wound up leaving for other companies where their ideas could have more of an impact.

Together with her husband and her top executives, she tackled the question: "Do we make people happy and then business gets better, or do we fix the business, which will make people happier?" They couldn't find the definitive answer, so they decided to focus on both.

The first step was to call a meeting at which Bernick delivered a "state of the company address." In reality this was a forum for teaching the company's members about the behind-the-scenes problems at Alberto-Culver. It was also an invitation for staff to participate in the challenge of overcoming those problems. In order to further empower its employees, Alberto-Culver assigned each person an IEV or "individual economic value." The IEV is a short description of how each person contributes to the company's profitability; for instance, the IEV of a woman who works in the consumer relations department is "I turn every customer I talk to into a company fan."

"If there is one move I credit more than anything else for the success of our cultural makeover, it's our decision to create a role called the 'growth development leader' (GDL)," says Bernick. Each GDL mentors about a dozen people, and their job is to assist people in making their IEVs, help with performance reviews, and explain all benefits and human resource policies, including a fund for personal financial difficulties and a scholarship program for children. What the GDL does is to build team spirit at the small group level by helping people to balance their personal and work lives.

It is considered an honor to be a GDL, and anyone from any level of the company can become one. Bernick says they have all been "handpicked for qualities like empathy, communication skills, positive attitude, and even the ability to let one's hair down and

have fun." A GDL must also excel at his or her job. To get promoted at Alberto-Culver, it is not enough to be a "superstar;" you must also be a good team player. GDLs meet with Bernick every six weeks and bring a group member as a guest. Sales and earnings, new programs, workplace rumors, new products, stock ratings, and whatever else is on their minds is discussed. Then the GDL reports back to the group.

Each year there is a meeting dedicated to "macros and irritations." GDLs and their guests are split into four subgroups and given 15 minutes to brainstorm on the four greatest business challenges the company faces and the four most annoying aspects of daily life on the job. Then Bernick says, "Okay, you're the CEO. You have only so many resources, and you can't do it all. Which four deserve our focus?" After the vote is in, different group members are assigned to work on possible solutions. Each person working at Alberto-Culver really does have the power to make changes and to be rewarded for his or her efforts. Stock rewards go to GDLs who make a real difference. Business Builders Awards are given to individuals and to teams who have contributed to corporate growth and profitability. Someone who worked in Mexico for a month updating information systems was rewarded with a BBA.

Bernick believes in letting everyone know about the company's triumphs. She had a bonfire in the parking lot to celebrate cutting paperwork by 30 percent and a surprise thank-you party with entertainment and 700 pounds of popcorn to celebrate a great fiscal year. Everyone at Alberto-Culver North America receives a special gift for work anniversaries and personal milestones. GDLs and coworkers often reward a team member's extra effort with an appropriate present. Sales for 2000 were up 18.2 percent for Alberto-Culver North America and corporate net earnings were up 12.6 percent; employee turnover has been cut in half, and once again the company is attracting top talent.

Alberto-Culver is a much happier place to work in today than it was in 1994, thanks to its finely tuned corporate culture. Today it is a company in which every individual truly feels valued and motivated to work hard to achieve corporate goals. According to Bernick, "companies don't succeed—people do."

QUESTIONS

1. In what ways is it advantageous for an employee to be a member of a group in which a GDL is assigned to him or her? In what ways is it disadvantageous? Be specific in your answers.
2. How should Bernick use informal groups in her company? Is there any evidence in the case indicating that she understands informal groups and how they contribute to productivity in organizations?
3. Using the stages of group development as described in your text, what advice would you give Lavin Bernick about building groups at Alberto-Culver North America?

MASTERING MANAGEMENT: EPISODE 10—ORGANIZATIONAL CULTURE

Mastering Management is a series of innovative, interactive learning activities specially designed to help you develop management skills emphasized in various text chapters. Groups, teams, and corporate culture are the major focuses of this chapter. Episode 10 of *Mastering Management* focuses on organizational culture and gives special attention to maintaining a culture that spawns creative ideas. In this episode, Liz realizes that CanGo's culture may have changed to the point where the company is losing its creative edge. Review Episode 10, "Organizational Culture," on your *Mastering Management* CD and then answer the following questions.

QUESTIONS

1. Do you believe that "employees being creative" should be part of the CanGo culture? Discuss.

2. Can you think of ways to use status symbols, traditions, and history to build a culture at CanGo that fosters employee creativity? Discuss.

3. How might managers at CanGo use the physical environment to build a culture that fosters employee creativity? Be as specific as you can.

MASTERING MANAGEMENT: EPISODE 11—WORKING IN GROUPS AND TEAMS

Mastering Management is a series of innovative, interactive learning activities specially designed to help you develop management skills emphasized in various text chapters. Groups, teams, and corporate culture are the major focuses of this chapter. Episode 11 of *Mastering Management* focuses on groups and teams and gives special attention to forming effective work teams. In this episode, a team is formed at CanGo whose assignment is to develop a *dog and pony* show for presentation to CanGo's potential investors. Review Episode 11, "Groups and Teams," on your *Mastering Management* CD and then answer the following questions.

QUESTIONS

1. Is the CanGo group formed to develop a "dog and pony show" also a team? Why?

2. In what stage of team development does this group appear to be? Discuss.

3. What advice would you give CanGo's management for building trust within this team? How could management help to build this trust?

---

www.prenhall.com/certo

This book is accompanied by a rich assortment of online activities aimed at developing your management skills. Reviewing news headlines, Internet exercises, an online study guide, and other research and Internet resources can help personalize management skills development for individual students or an entire class.

chapter

chapterchapterchapterchapterchapterchapter

18 Understanding People: Attitudes, Perception, and Learning

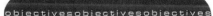

▶ Objectives 🖐

From studying this chapter, I will attempt to acquire

- An understanding of employee workplace attitudes

- Insights into how to change employee attitudes

- An appreciation of the impact of employee perceptions on employee behaviors

- Knowledge of employee perceptions of procedural justice

- An understanding that adult learners are different from younger students

CHAPTER OUTLINE

Introductory Case: *Where Was the People Focus at Webvan?*

What Are Attitudes?
How Beliefs and Values Create Attitudes
Attitude Surveys

Digital Focus ❱ H.T.E. Uses the Internet to Study Employee Attitudes

Quality Spotlight ❱ Nucor Steel

Perception
Perception and the Perceptual Process
Attribution Theory: Interpreting the Behavior of Others
Perceptual Distortions

Global Spotlight ❱ The Wide, Wide World of Cultural Perceptions

Perceptions of Procedural Justice

Learning
Operant Learning
Cognitive Learning
Learning Strategies

Where Was the People Focus
at Webvan?

REMINDER: THE INTRODUCTORY CASE WRAP-UP (P. 416) CONTAINS DISCUSSION QUESTIONS AND A SKILLS EXERCISE TO FURTHER ILLUSTRATE THE APPLICATION OF CHAPTER CONCEPTS TO THIS VIGNETTE.

Webvan, an online grocer, was a recent casualty of the downturn in online-business growth. Could its managers have failed to understand how its customers' attitudes and perceptions about the Internet were shaped?

A few years ago, the Internet was gobbling up venture capital, and one start-up company that was much heralded and attracted more than $120 million from investors was Webvan, an online grocer. Perhaps the reason Webvan drew so much investment money was because it was launched by Louis Borders, former chairman and founder of Borders Books. Webvan's goal was to sell $300 million in groceries annually from one warehouse located in Oakland, California, and it already had plans to locate additional warehouses in Atlanta and other key cities around the country. The Webvan warehouse concept was to include automated systems that would yield a 10 percent advantage in profit margin over traditional supermarket warehouses.

In addition, groceries were only part of the plan at Webvan. Logistics were developed so that Webvan could deliver perishables such as kiwi fruit and live lobsters within a specified 30-minute period. According to company officials, once the delivery system was in place, the sky would be the limit. Along with groceries, Webvan could deliver dry cleaning, newly processed photos, and almost anything else to homes. Potential rewards for the company seemed huge. In fact, the prospects for Webvan seemed so promising that respected managers from other industries were leaving established companies to share in the Webvan dream. For example, George Shaheen, who had been CEO for Andersen Consulting for 10 years, left his company to become CEO at Webvan. Many people were buying into Webvan's future.

News about Webvan, however, turned sour. Its stock began trading for as low as 34 cents per share, far below its 52-week high of $14.88. Louis Borders resigned from the company's board to end his last official connection with the Internet grocer; Webvan struggled and doubts grew that it could make a profit delivering groceries to consumers.

Borders was focused on long-term, visionary planning, but other board members were more interested in executing the company's near-term business plan, because they felt that without a focus on the near term, there would be no future. Mr. Borders had hoped to overcome some of the cost problems with motorized carousels and other warehouse equipment that would make filling orders more

(continued)

efficient. The building of this equipment, however, saddled Webvan with enormous start-up costs stemming from its network of high-tech, automated warehouses and the fleet of trucks needed to deliver orders.

Most of the plans at Webvan seem to have focused on understanding the technology component of the company's business model. Curiously, very little evidence can be found to indicate that management understood how the people component fits into the Webvan business model.

What's Ahead

In the Introductory Case, Louis Borders resigned from the board of Webvan, an Internet grocery company. As implied by the case, management at Webvan seems to have a thorough understanding of the technology component of its business model but may be somewhat lacking in its understanding of the people component. The information in this chapter provides insights on concepts concerning people for managers like those at Webvan. More precisely, this chapter studies people by discussing the following topics:

1) Attitudes
2) Perception
3) Learning

The previous chapters in this section discussed people issues important to managing like influencing and communication, leadership, motivation, and groups and teamwork. This chapter continues the study of people issues important to managing by elaborating upon characteristics of individuals in organizations. Characteristics discussed in the following sections are attitudes, perception, and learning.

WHAT ARE ATTITUDES?

An **attitude** is a predisposition to react to a situation, person, or concept with a particular response.

An **attitude** is a predisposition to react to a situation, person or concept with a particular response. This response can be either positive or negative. It is a learned reaction—one that results from an individual's past observations, direct experiences, or exposure to others' attitudes. For example, someone may say, "I love baseball," thus communicating to others a general attitude about the sport. Some baseball fans developed their love for the sport while playing it in childhood; direct experience shaped their attitude. Others never played the game but developed a love for the sport by watching games at the ballpark or on television. Still others had friends or family members who influenced their attitudes by communicating their love for the game.

Attitudes are internal and may be largely kept to oneself, or they may be made known to others through overt behaviors. Generally, attitudes have three primary components:[1]

1. *Cognitive*—information and beliefs about a particular person or object
2. *Affective*—a positive or negative feeling about a particular person or object
3. *Behavioral*—an intent or desire to behave in a certain way toward a particular person or object

Again, a conversation among coworkers may help illustrate these differences:

Maria: *Did you hear about the training program that starts next week?*
Lex: *Yes, I've read several reviews on that software. It may make my job much easier and help me to produce better newsletters and reports.*
David: *I hate going to training programs and having to learn new software. Just when you really get comfortable with one, they change to a new one.*
Maria: *Well, I intend to pick it up as quickly as possible so I can expand my skills and possibly bid for a higher-grade job.*

In this brief exchange, Lex communicates one attitude about the specific training program. The information that he has learned about it has given him an attitude of awareness (a cognitive component), but no positive or negative feelings toward the program. David, however, expresses both awareness and a negative attitude (an affective component) toward the training program, probably based on his own past experiences or those of others. Maria not only has knowledge of the program (cognitive) and a positive feeling toward it (affective), but also has decided how she will approach it (a behavioral component).

How Beliefs and Values Create Attitudes

Overall, an individual's attitudes are a result of the beliefs and values held by the individual. **Beliefs** are accepted facts or truths about an object or person that have been gained from either direct experience or a secondary source. For example, what people believe about McDonald's restaurants or the Publisher's Clearinghouse Sweepstakes tends to form their attitudes about each and influences the way they react to each.

Values are levels of worth placed by an individual on various factors in the environment. Values tend to be broad views of life and are influenced by parents, peer groups, and associates. Values tend to guide one's actions and judgments across a variety of situations. Thus, a person's workplace values may be defined as those concepts, principles, people, objects, or activities that he or she considers important. Values are those things for which a person may make sacrifices and work hard. In the workplace, such factors as compensation, recognition, and status are often regarded as common values.[2]

One way in which the relationship among attitudes, values, and beliefs can affect people's behavior in the workplace is illustrated in Figure 18.1.[3] For example, direct past experiences or observations of others may have led our hypothetical manager to believe that software vendors usually exaggerate the virtues of their products. In fact, this person has developed a rule of thumb: New office software programs cost twice as much as their initial price (because of add-on charges, upgrades, training expenses, and so forth) and deliver only half the level of promised service. This general belief has led the manager to develop an attitude of distrust toward any new software. When the manager's skepticism is applied to a specific new product, this attitude influences his behavior—he denies the request for the software. We can see that the manager's decision-making process was not objective. Instead, the process was negatively biased because of an attitude—an attitude resulting from general beliefs and values formed by past experiences and observations.

▶ People bring different attitudes to work with them. Terry Murray, who roller-skates to his job as an engineering manager in Cambridge, Massachusetts, says the trip, which he makes in stretch pants, fluorescent top, and helmet with blinking red lights on top, is a highlight of his day. His feelings about it changed last year when he started skating the 10-mile route through woods, lakes, and streams. "I feel like a warrior on my way to work," he says. "Every commute is like a day of skiing."

Beliefs are accepted facts or truths about an object or person that have been gained from either direct experience or a secondary source.

Values are the global beliefs that guide one's actions and judgments across a variety of situations.

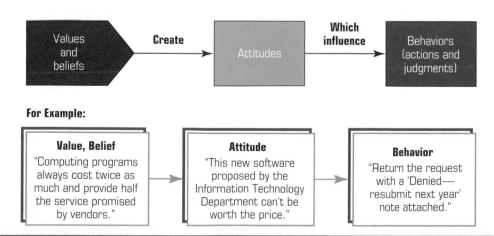

For Example:

Value, Belief		Attitude		Behavior
"Computing programs always cost twice as much and provide half the service promised by vendors."	→	"This new software proposed by the Information Technology Department can't be worth the price."	→	"Return the request with a 'Denied—resubmit next year' note attached."

Situation: Based on personal attitudes, beliefs, and values, a manager decides to deny a request for new software

Figure 18.1

Attitude Surveys

In election years, political candidates spend millions of dollars on public opinion surveys. In addition, the media publish their own polls on candidates and issues. Why are such surveys done? In the case of the candidate, survey information can be used to plan future campaign strategy. The most important reason for such surveys, however, is that a professionally conducted poll will almost invariably predict the outcome of an election. Polls tend to be accurate because the people surveyed express *attitudes* on which they are likely to base *behavior*.

Managers also use attitude surveys.[4] Faced with such employee problems as excessive turnover and absenteeism, low productivity, and poor-quality work, they may use surveys to predict employee behavior or determine the sources of existing problems. In the workplace, surveys are sometimes called "polling-attitude surveys" or simply "job-satisfaction surveys." In recent years, attitude surveys have gained in popularity because they often determine the sources of employee dissatisfaction. If an employer addresses problem areas identified in attitude surveys, organizational problems like low productivity and poor-quality products can often be reduced, employee morale improved, and productivity increased.

DIGITAL FOCUS

▶ H.T.E. Uses the Internet to Study Employee Attitudes

Attitude surveys can be extremely useful in helping managers pinpoint existing organizational problems. Dennis Harward, founder and president of H.T.E. Enterprises, recently used an attitude survey to gauge employee attitudes toward organizational communication. H.T.E. develops, markets, implements, and supports software applications designed for public sector organizations, like police and fire departments. Harward has had outstanding success recently. For the six months ended June 1998, revenues rose 45 percent to $43.8 million. Net income during the same period rose 43 percent to $2.5 million.

Faced with the challenge of assessing and improving organizational communication within his company, Harward assembled an employee group along with an outside consultant to plan and implement a communication survey. The employee group represented major segments within the company and included representatives from areas like accounting, human resources, sales and marketing, operations, and strategic planning. Representing various organizational levels, employees within the group possessed titles like president, vice president, director, salesperson, and project manager. The consultant was a professor of management at a local graduate school of business.

As group meetings passed, the group made excellent progress. The group eventually settled on a survey that asked H.T.E. employees to rate several different organizational communication factors. These factors included receiving information from others, sending information to others, following up on information sent, sources of information, and channels of communication. Although survey responses were completely anonymous, employees were also asked to identify themselves as a manager or nonmanager. Through this partial identity, the committee planned to see if managers saw communication at H.T.E. differently than nonmanagers.

The group decided to use the Internet to actually administer the survey. A Web services company, Websolvers Incorporated, was hired to design a Web site that would house or host the survey. According to plan, employees would access the survey on the Internet, answer it online, and then e-mail answers to Websolvers. Part of Websolvers' job was to e-mail all employee answers to the survey analyst. Basically, Websolvers was hired to eliminate any possibility that employees would think someone could identify their answers within H.T.E.

The implementation of the survey plan was virtually flawless. The real value of the survey rests on its role in helping Harward to improve organizational communication at H.T.E. This survey experience, however, does support the notion that the Internet can play a useful and major role in conducting attitude surveys in organizations.

Theory of Reasoned Action   Research indicates that the attitudes employees hold toward their jobs and employers are quite stable over time: People with both generally positive and generally negative attitudes tend to retain them over time.[5] This finding is important to managers because it means they can feel reasonably confident that measuring attitudes is likely to produce useful information.

At the same time, however, changing employees' attitudes toward specific aspects of their jobs is usually a challenging task for management. Researchers generally agree that while attitudes "influence" employee behaviors in the workplace, they are not perfect predictors of behaviors. Thus, behavioralists Martin Fishbein and others have developed a model designed to provide a more complete examination of the attitude–behavior relationship. This model, called the **theory of reasoned action**, is summarized in Figure 18.2. According to the model, when a behavior is a matter of *choice*, the best predictor of the behavior is the person's *intention* to perform it. Intention is best predicted from two factors:

1. Person's attitude toward performing the behavior
2. Person's subjective norm—the perception that he or she is expected by peers or others to perform a certain behavior

According to this view, then, attitude is a person's positive or negative feeling toward performing a behavior.

The *reasoned action* model further suggests that a person's attitude can be predicted by his or her belief that a certain behavior will lead to certain outcomes. Also important is the value that the person places on those outcomes. Similarly, a person's subjective norm can sometimes be predicted from his or her belief that other individuals (supervisors, coworkers, friends) think that the person should (or should not) perform a behavior. Not surprisingly, when people have strong beliefs and attitudes about a certain behavior and perceive that it is expected of them, they are more likely to perform it. The reverse, of course, is also true.[6]

The **theory of reasoned action** states that when a behavior is a matter of *choice*, the best predictor of the behavior is the person's *intention* to perform it.

Employee Attitudes   Many managers find employee attitudes complex and difficult to understand—and even more difficult to change. What job factors are important determinants of employee attitudes? Academic research and the hands-on experience of managers have produced at least three theories concerning the primary determinations of employee attitudes (see Figure 18.3).

The first approach focuses on the *design of the job* and stresses such factors as task design, work autonomy, and level of challenge. The second approach stresses *social influence*, assuming that employees' attitudes toward their jobs are affected by the attitudes or beliefs of their peers.

The third theory, called the *dispositional approach,* stresses personal characteristics that are fairly stable over time. This theory holds that people are *generally predisposed* to like or dislike both the overall quality of their jobs and such specific job characteristics as the work itself, supervision, compensation, and work rules. The dispositional approach does not deny potentially positive or negative situational influences—say, changes in supervision, work assignment, job design—but it holds that individuals enter the workplace with predisposed job attitudes formed from past experiences and personal beliefs. Changes such as pay increases, job redesign, and flexible hours can improve job attitudes, at least temporarily, but in the long run, the best predictor of employees' current job attitudes is their prior work attitudes.[7]

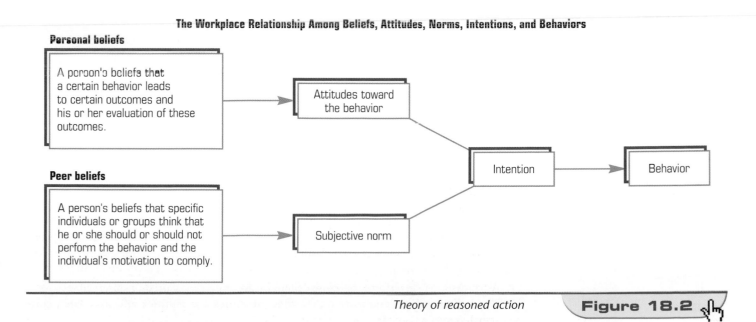

The Workplace Relationship Among Beliefs, Attitudes, Norms, Intentions, and Behaviors

Personal beliefs

A person's beliefs that a certain behavior leads to certain outcomes and his or her evaluation of these outcomes.

→ Attitudes toward the behavior

Peer beliefs

A person's beliefs that specific individuals or groups think that he or she should or should not perform the behavior and the individual's motivation to comply.

→ Subjective norm

Intention → Behavior

Theory of reasoned action   **Figure 18.2**

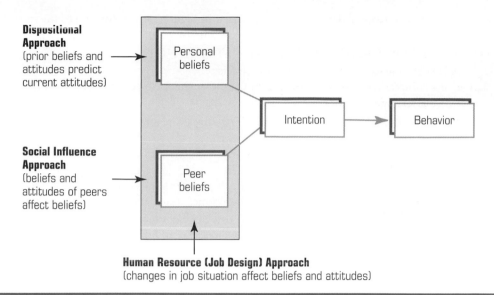

Dispositional Approach
(prior beliefs and attitudes predict current attitudes)

Personal beliefs

Social Influence Approach
(beliefs and attitudes of peers affect beliefs)

Peer beliefs

Intention

Behavior

Human Resource (Job Design) Approach
(changes in job situation affect beliefs and attitudes)

Figure 18.3

Three theories of job attitudes applied to the theory of reasoned action

Attitude Theory and Reasoned Action All three of these attitude theories can be adapted to the theory of reasoned action. Thus, a change in job design may alter the general workplace situation to the extent that a worker's beliefs are changed. Social influence theory would say that the beliefs that predict a person's subjective norm will change when the beliefs and attitudes of the person's peers are changed. Finally, the dispositional approach would argue that a person's own prior beliefs and attitudes are the strongest predictor of job attitudes—and thus of intentions and behaviors while performing a newly designed job.

Changing Attitudes   Behaviors and attitudes can best be predicted by knowing two factors:

1. A person's beliefs
2. The social norms that influence a person's intentions

Managers may strive to change attitudes, intentions, and behaviors by changing workplace situations—that is, by changing such work factors as compensation, job design, and work hours. However, they must realize that employee attitudes are both fairly stable over time and slow to change. Thus, selecting employees who come to their positions with positive job attitudes might be the most effective way to build a workforce with a positive attitude.

Human Resource Approach Research has also supported a related managerial philosophy often called the *human resource approach* to job satisfaction. Consistently providing personnel activities that are highly valued by employees will in the long run improve attitudes, intentions, and behaviors. This approach typically works because employees' attitudes are favorably affected by their belief that the organization is committed to providing a positive work environment. Studies have shown that employees who believe that their employer cares about them will reciprocate with more positive attitudes, reduced absenteeism, increased quality and productivity, and greater creative input.[8] Thus, the basic principles of the human resource approach, which are listed in Table 18.1, can favorably influence employee attitudes when consistently applied by managers.

As a practical matter, what does the manager do with the employee who has a "bad attitude"? Unfortunately, managerial experience and research both indicate that changing attitudes is very difficult. Fortunately, a "bad attitude" is often not the problem. Rather, the problem is usually unacceptable *behavior*. Attitude, of course, influences behaviors, as we have seen, but there are two good reasons why managers should not focus too sharply on attitudes:

1. Attitudes are *internal* and therefore cannot be accurately measured or observed
2. The beliefs, values, and norms that affect attitudes are complex and have been constructed over a lifetime

Nucor Steel

F. Kenneth Iverson is the chief executive officer of Nucor Corporation. Nucor is America's seventh-largest steel company and the only one to consistently make a profit over the past 20 years. Nucor has increased its dividend annually and operated profitably in each quarter since 1968—this is quite an accomplishment in an industry that has lost money overall in more than half of those years. In addition, while the U.S. steel industry has laid off over 300,000 workers and shut down numerous plants in the past two decades, Nucor has not laid off a single worker. According to former U.S. Secretary of Labor Ann McLaughlin, "Every manager who wonders what it will take to compete in the twenty-first century needs to know the Nucor story."

Why has Nucor succeeded while the other U.S. steel firms have struggled? Ken Iverson proudly but without hesitation cites four practices that are directly related to the company's human resources policies:

1. *Employee Teams*—All tasks in Nucor's mills are performed by employee teams. Each team is in charge of complete tasks and receives a production bonus every week in which work standards are exceeded. This program is an excellent example of applied behavior modification with continuous reinforcement.

2. *Levels of Management*—Iverson believes that those closest to the work should make the decisions concerning that work whenever possible. Thus, the greater the autonomy given to teams, the fewer levels of management that are necessary.

3. *Limited Staff*—Iverson also believes that staff tend to obstruct effective work teams. Nucor, therefore, operates 6 steel mills, 6 joist plants, and 2 products divisions with only 22 staff members. All staff are located at the corporate headquarters in Charlotte, North Carolina.

4. *No-Layoffs Policy*—For well over 20 years, Nucor has maintained a no-layoffs policy in an industry that has laid off over 350,000 U.S. workers. During lean times, Nucor prefers a "share the pain" policy. This plan reduces the number of days per week that a team works. In addition, management, including Iverson, also takes a pay reduction.

These principles have helped Nucor build an environment in which autonomous teams of employees strive for maximum productivity—a goal that, if achieved, maximizes bonuses and minimizes interference from management or staff. In addition, the teams have a great deal of job security because of the no-layoffs policy. As a result, Nucor employees have consistently maintained higher levels of productivity and far more positive work attitudes than their counterparts elsewhere in the steel industry. ■

Behaviors, on the other hand, are not only observable, but can also be documented and measured. Most importantly, managers can deal successfully with unacceptable performance.

Not surprisingly, then, the correct identification, analysis, and resolution of behavioral problems are an important task for managers. Of course, poor attitude or motivation is only one potential cause of unsatisfactory behavior or performance. Determining exactly *why* an employee is performing at an unsatisfactory level is critical because problems cannot be corrected unless their causes are known. Effective managers not only look for performance problems, but also recognize that they stem from a variety of causes. Human resource specialists have identified at least four major causes of behavior problems:[9]

1. *Lack of Skills*—Organizations often place employees in jobs without giving them sufficient training. Once identified, the skills-deficiency problem can be remedied in one of

---

Basic Principles of the Human Resource Approach    **Table 18.1**

Providing employee training

Communicating about human resource programs and policies

Helping new employees learn about their job and the company

Providing advancement opportunities within the company

Providing job security

Hiring qualified employees

Having enough people to get the job done

Asking my opinions about how one can improve one's own job

Asking my opinion about making the company successful

Asking for employee suggestions

Acting on employee suggestions

three ways: (a) train the employee to remove the skill deficiency, (b) transfer the employee to a job that better uses his or her current skills, (c) terminate the employee.

2. *Lack of Positive Attitude*—Although there are numerous approaches to attitude and motivation problems, most strategies rest on one seemingly simple axiom: *Determine what the employee needs and offer it as a reward for good performance.* (Yet, as most managers know, determining the needs of an employee and providing a corresponding change in job design or work environment is a challenging task.)

3. *Rule Breaking*—Rule breakers are employees who are occasionally absent or late to work without good reason, who violate dress codes, or who refuse to follow safety procedures. They have the necessary skills and normally do good work, but they disregard the organization's policies and regulations. The most effective approach to this form of behavior is to apply positive discipline. This means providing a written policy of expected behaviors and a written program detailing progressive disciplinary steps (e.g., first offense—oral warning; second offense—written warning; third offense—suspension; fourth offense—termination).

4. *Personal Problems*—A final type of unsatisfactory behavior is associated with the *troubled employee*—one whose personal problems are so significant that they prevent the employee from performing satisfactorily at work. The troubled employee may suffer from a variety of problems, including emotional illness, financial crisis, alcohol or drug dependency, chronic physical problems, and family unrest.

▶ Back to the Case

At Webvan, as within any other company, each employee developed job-related attitudes. In turn, these attitudes impacted the way employees acted in the organization. The attitudes are shaped by the employee's values and beliefs, as well as by the norms confirmed by the employee's peers and other organization members. Assume that a Webvan employee had a negative attitude about the company. Perhaps the employee had lackluster feelings about the quality of his or her supervisor. In turn, this negative attitude would limit the contribution that the employee made to attaining Webvan goals. Overall, the more negative the attitude, the less the employee will contribute to organizational goal attainment.

Once a negative attitude was developed at Webvan, management should have understood that it could not be changed quickly or easily. Management could not change an attitude from negative to positive simply by changing situational (external) factors such as a difficult boss, a frustrating coworker, or unchallenging work; employees' attitudes change as their values and beliefs about the organization change. So by helping employees to change their values and beliefs about Webvan, management could have influenced employee attitudes and ultimately improved morale and productivity.

PERCEPTION

Perception is the psychological process of selecting stimuli, organizing the data into recognizable patterns, and interpreting the resulting information.

The **perceptual process** is the series of actions that individuals follow in order to select, organize, and interpret stimuli from the environment.

The above material focused on individuals by discussing attitudes. This major chapter section continues the discussion of individuals by emphasizing perception. Topics discussed below are as follows:

1. Defining perception and the perceptual process
2. Attribution theory
3. Perceptual distortions

Perception and the Perceptual Process

Perception is the psychological process of selecting stimuli, organizing the data into recognizable patterns, and interpreting the resulting information. The **perceptual process** is the series of actions that individuals follow in order to select, organize, and interpret stimuli from the environment. Every second of every day individuals are bombarded by countless stimuli through the human senses of sight, hearing, touch, smell, and taste. We attend to only a small portion of these stimuli.

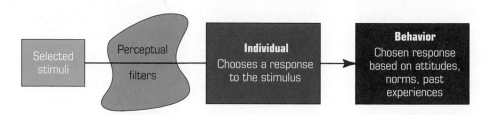

Process of perception

Figure 18.4

Thus, as you can see in Figure 18.4, the perceptual process links the individual with his or her environment. Since we can only select and process a limited number of the stimuli, we are never aware of everything that occurs around us. Moreover, the limited stimuli that we do perceive are subjected to perceptual filters that are largely determined by our past experiences, attitudes, and beliefs. Just as importantly, stimuli that are inconsistent with our predispositions are often ignored or distorted. Thus, we can become "closed-minded" without realizing it.

Attribution Theory: Interpreting the Behavior of Others

Attribution is the process by which people *interpret* the behavior of others by assigning to it motives or causes. For example, if an employee is routinely late to work, a manager might try to determine the cause of the behavior. Is it lack of motivation or lack of ability? Is it some personal factor or a situational factor such as the way the job is structured or scheduled? The manager may believe that poor attitude is the cause of the behavior and try to motivate the employee to arrive on time. As a rule, managers do *not* consider situational factors. Why? Much of the conflict that occurs between managers and subordinates stems from the tendency of managers to act on their own perception and interpretation of a given situation, which may be quite different from those of subordinates; they may not even coincide with the facts of the situation. Managers can avoid inappropriate attributions in three ways:[10]

> **Attribution** is the process by which people *interpret* the behavior of others by assigning to it motives or causes.

1. By making a greater effort to see situations as they are perceived by others
2. By guarding against perceptual distortions
3. By paying more attention to individual differences among subordinates

The underlying assumption of attribution theory is that managers are typically motivated to understand the *causes* of employee behavior. They tend to question whether the behavior is the result of internal or external causes. *Internal* causes include attitude or motivation, ability, and lack of knowledge of the desired (correct) behavior. *External* causes include the difficulty of tasks and the actions of others, both of which may exert influence beyond the control of the individual. Research indicates that people generally focus on three factors when making attributions:[11]

1. *Consensus*—The extent to which they believe that the person being observed is behaving in a manner consistent with the behavior of his or her peers. High consensus exists when the person's actions reflect, or are similar to, the actions of the groups; low consensus exists when the person's actions do not.
2. *Consistency*—The extent to which they believe that the person being observed behaves consistently—in a similar fashion—when confronted on other occasions with the same or similar situations. High consistency exists when the person repeatedly acts in the same way when faced with similar stimuli.
3. *Distinctiveness*—The extent to which they believe that the person being observed would behave consistently when faced with different situations. Low distinctiveness exists when the person acts in a similar manner in response to different stimuli. High distinctiveness exists when the person varies his or her response in different situations.

Thus, a manager would be more likely to attribute an employee's behavior to external causes under at least three circumstances:

1. If other employees behave the same way
2. If the employee has behaved the same way in similar situations in the past
3. If this behavior is highly unusual or distinctive

Internal causes might be attributed if other employees do not behave in the same manner or if the employee usually behaves in the same manner under most circumstances.

Perceptual Distortions

Managers, like everyone else, make judgments and decisions based on their perceptions. To help ensure that these judgments and decisions are worthwhile, managers must strive to avoid common perceptual distortions, including stereotypes, halo effects, projection, self-serving bias, attribution error, selective perception, and recency. Each of these distortions is discussed below.

A stereotype is a fixed, distorted generalization about members of a group.

Stereotypes A **stereotype** is a fixed, distorted generalization about members of a group.[12] Stereotyping—which often stems from such aspects of diversity as race, gender, age, physical abilities/qualities, social background, and occupation—attributes incomplete, exaggerated, or distorted qualities to individual members of groups. Stereotyping results from the nature of our information-processing tendencies. As human beings, we process information through learned knowledge gained by means of past experience, observation, or contact with other individuals who influence us, such as our family, friends, and coworkers. Stereotyping, therefore, is not generalization. A stereotype is usually *learned* through outside sources rather than through direct individual experiences.

The halo effect results from allowing one particular aspect of someone's behavior to influence one's evaluation of all other aspects of that person's behavior.

Halo Effect When a manager allows one particular aspect of an employee's behavior to influence his or her evaluation of all other aspects of that employee's behavior, the so-called **halo effect** has occurred. For example, the manager who knows that a particular employee always arrives at work early and helps to open the business may let the "halo" of the employee's dependability influence his or her perceptions of the employee in other areas—say, customer relations or products knowledge. Thus, even if the employee is only mediocre in these areas, the manager perceives overall strength.

Of course, a negative halo—"devil's horns"—may also affect perceptions. If an accountant performs poorly only when working directly with plant managers on annual budget projects, a supervisor may allow this one negative behavior to cloud his or her judgment of the employee's other behaviors.

The halo problem can be minimized by supervisory training that focuses on the fact that it is not unusual for employees to perform well in some areas and less effectively in others.

Projection is the unconscious tendency to assign one's own traits, motives, beliefs, and attitudes to others.

Projection The unconscious tendency to assign (project) our own traits, motives, beliefs, and attitudes to others is called **projection.** Consider, for example, a manager who enjoys

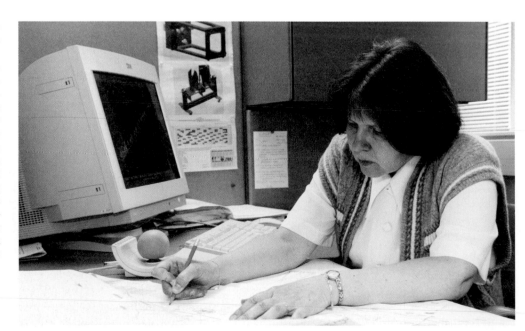

▶ Its search for highly qualified engineers led Boeing to Moscow, where it operates an engineering design center. Here Nadezhda Frolenova and other Russian engineers work on creating improved designs for overhead storage bins and in-flight bunks for Boeing's aircraft. Aleksandr Amelin, a design manager for Boeing in Russia, recalls a Russian and an American engineer confounding each other's stereotypes when they solved a design problem together using drawings, since neither spoke the other's language. "The thing that surprised me most," Amelin said, "is how similar we are. Engineers think the same whether at Boeing or in a Russian company."

working as part of a quality-improvement team. This manager may strongly encourage subordinates to join similar teams, and then be disappointed in those who refuse to do so. This classic form of perceptual distortion assumes that others have the same needs and desires as oneself. Not surprisingly, this assumption is rarely accurate.

Self-Serving Bias and Attribution Error　　In practice, when asked to identify the causes of an employee's poor performance, managers will usually choose internal causes, such as motivation, ability, or effort, rather than external causes, such as lack of support from others or circumstances beyond the employee's control. This tendency to overestimate internal causes of behavior and underestimate external ones is called **attribution error.** Interestingly, many of the same managers, when asked to identify the causes of their own performance, refer to external causes. This form of perceptual distortion is called **self-serving bias:** the tendency to attribute personal success to internal causes and personal failures to external causes.

Selective Perception　　When bombarded with too many external stimuli, people may resort to perceptual filters in order to reduce their awareness of the stimuli. In particular, we tend to attend to stimuli that are consistent with our own motives, beliefs, and attitudes. Thus, we are prone to collect information that not only supports our perceptions, but also minimizes the emotional distress caused by unfamiliar or troublesome stimuli. This form of perceptual distortion is called **selective perception.**

Recency　　For example, let us say that a manager notices a few unusually negative comments in the weekly stack of customer comment cards. However, because the majority of the cards contain positive comments about the service that the manager believes accurately reflect the work of her staff, she ignores the negative messages. A few weeks later, she notices a substantial number of negative comments. An investigation reveals that one newly hired employee is the cause of the negative comments—but this discovery comes too late to prevent negative impressions of the service among a good many customers. What went wrong here? The manager allowed her own perceptions to filter out early information that did not conform to her beliefs. Only later did she seek reliable data to check the accuracy of her perceptions.

> **Attribution error** is the tendency to overestimate internal causes of behavior and underestimate external ones when judging other people's behavior.
>
> The **self-serving bias** is the tendency to overestimate external causes of behavior and underestimate internal ones when judging one's own behavior.
>
> **Selective perception** is the tendency to collect information that not only supports one's own motives, beliefs, and attitudes, but also minimizes the emotional distress caused by unfamiliar or troublesome stimuli.

The Wide, Wide World of Cultural Perceptions

On a sea voyage, you are traveling with your spouse, your child, and your mother. The ship develops problems and starts to sink. Of your family, you are the only one who can swim, and you can save only one other individual. Who will you save?

This question was posed to a group of men in Asia and the United States. In the United States, more than 60 percent of respondents said they would save the child, 40 percent the spouse, and none the mother. In the Asian countries, 100 percent of respondents said they would save the mother. Their rationale? You can always remarry and have more children, but you can never have another mother.

When doing business overseas, Americans cannot rely only on uniquely American perceptions and behavior patterns. What seems good in one place ("Father is getting to the age where he would probably be happier in the senior citizen home in Arizona") is scandalous in another ("Look at how Americans treat older people—it's awful").

Cross-cultural mistakes can be expensive. For example, many companies spend a minimum of $125,000 per year to employ one U.S. manager in an overseas position. Another less obvious factor is the human cost accrued when someone does poorly or returns early from an overseas assignment. Premature return of an employee and family may cost the company between $50,000 and $200,000 when replacement expenses are included. Mistakes of corporate representatives because of language or intercultural incompetence can jeopardize millions of dollars in negotiations and purchases, sales, and contracts, as well as undermine customer relations. No doubt, managers' cultural ineptitude damages organizational productivity and profitability.

The price of providing employees with education and training for intercultural effectiveness is miniscule compared to the financial losses that can occur because of personnel "faux pas" in cross-cultural business relations. The benefits from developing human resources can be enormous. ■

Perceptions of Procedural Justice

Perhaps the most important workplace perception formed by employees, however, is of **procedural justice:** the perceived fairness of the process used for deciding outcomes such as merit increases and promotions. The most important of these processes are performance appraisals, job applicant interviewing systems, pay systems, grievance or dispute-resolution

> **Procedural justice** is the perceived fairness of the process used for deciding workplace outcomes such as merit increases and promotions.

systems, and participative decision making. Most employees continually evaluate for themselves not only the fairness of these systems, but also their consequences.

Procedures and Outcomes   Employees actually form separate perceptions about the organization's process for deciding outcomes on the one hand and the consequences on the other hand. *Procedural justice* examines the fairness of the process itself: Are decisions made according to clear standards? Is the process used consistently for everyone? Can I appeal the decision? Will I be able to have input? *Distributive justice*, on the other hand, examines only the outcome of a decision or policy: Did I receive the promotion? Did I get the raise? Research indicates that employees often view these two types of workplace justice quite differently.[13]

Obviously, then, employees expect managers to be fair in making selection and promotion decisions, in assigning tasks and scheduling work, in choosing people for training and promotion opportunities, in conducting performance appraisals, and in making pay decisions. Of all these processes, the one most likely to affect attitudes and morale is performance appraisal. Probably because of the highly personal nature of the process, employees are especially sensitive to perceived unfairness in this area. Consequently, they base a large portion of their overall perceptions about procedural justice on their perceptions of performance appraisals.

A history of perceived fairness, therefore, can be a major asset to a manager in shaping employee perceptions of fairness, positive job attitudes, and productive behaviors. The manager with such a history is also often seen as honest, ethical, and trustworthy. Such a manager may, moreover, be judged less harshly when he or she is perceived as having made an unfavorable decision.[14]

Dispute Resolution   Another critical factor in employees' evaluations of fairness is how managers resolve disputes. Experienced managers are likely to use *mediation* techniques— they listen to the points of view of the parties involved, offer resources to help resolve the dispute, and encourage the parties to seek inventive solutions. Managers who resort to formal authority and simply impose their own settlements are less likely to be perceived as fair, regardless of the quality of their decisions.[15]

Employee Responses   How do employees respond to perceptions of unfairness? Those with seniority usually decide that they have invested too many years in the organization either to leave or to cause a disturbance. Instead, they may respond by performing marginally until retirement. Newer employees are more likely to leave for (perceived) better opportunities elsewhere. The costs of unfair employee treatment are difficult to compute. Research has determined that employees' perceptions of unfair treatment are very strong predictors of job absence and turnover—two costly employee behaviors. Other consequences of unfair treatment include lower production quantity and quality, less initiative, diminished morale, lack of cooperation, spread of dissatisfaction to coworkers, fewer suggestions, and less self-confidence. Each result has a substantial organizational cost, whether direct or indirect.[16]

Measuring Employee Attitudes   Considering the effects on the organization of employee responses to perceived unfairness, it is not surprising that managers often try to measure employees' perceptions of their treatment. However, measuring employee feelings is a complex and difficult process. Getting honest answers in interviews and group discussions is hardly assured; the most practical alternative is to use anonymous survey techniques. One advantage of using written questionnaires is that they make it easier to identify the dimensions of perceived unfairness. For example, results of a written survey can be compared across departments, jobs, and supervisors. A survey taken for Lens Lab, Inc., a national chain of eyeglass stores, found, overall, a high level of perceived fairness. However, in two of eight stores, the levels reported were significantly lower on two dimensions—work pace and pay administration. An investigation led to changes in policy and supervision at those stores, which resulted in higher levels of perceived fairness, and higher store profitability, the following year.

Management at Webvan should have understood that employee perceptions are what generated their views of the company. Employees' views of the company are not objective; they are interpretations of reality influenced by many different filters. Employee perception can be distorted through stereotyping (making of generalizations about various groups of people), the halo effect (allowing one aspect of an employee to influence feelings about all other aspects of the employee), or projection (assigning their own traits, beliefs, and motives as traits of others). Webvan management should also have been aware of their own perceptual challenges. Overall, it is important to try to minimize the possible negative impact of the human perceptual process on the achievement of Webvan's goals.

In addition, Webvan managers should have been aware that procedural justice and fairness within the company could have significantly impacted employees' perceptions. Much depends on how Webvan management settled disputes. Employees might have responded to a feeling that Webvan was an unfair company by leaving the company, performing marginally, or even sabotaging company efforts. Even the best technology components purchased by Webvan management could have been rendered useless if employees perceived the organization to be unjust.

LEARNING

Learning can be defined as a relatively permanent change in behavior resulting from practice, experience, education, or training. Behavioral change includes the acquisition of skills, knowledge, and ability. In organizations, people learn specific job-related skills, knowledge, and abilities. They also learn about organizational norms—what is expected from them and how things are accomplished. Both of these learning situations affect employee beliefs, attitudes, intentions, and behaviors. This section will focus on two of the traditional approaches to learning that are of particular value in the workplace: operant and cognitive learning.

> **Learning** is a more or less permanent change in behavior resulting from practice, experience, education, or training.

Operant Learning

Operant learning, also called operant conditioning, is based on the belief that behavior is a function of its consequences.[17] If a person perceives that a behavior will lead to a positive consequence, that person will be more likely to repeat the behavior. For example, a salesperson who has taken a client to lunch at a favorite restaurant and has always subsequently received a large order from that client is likely to arrange a similar lunch meeting on the client's next visit. Conversely, if a person perceives that a behavior will likely lead to a negative conse-

> **Operant learning** is an approach that holds the behavior leading to positive consequences is more likely to be repeated.

▶ Technology has had a tremendous impact on the way in which we learn. With more and more employees already comfortable with the Internet, firms like Circuit City can rely on online training classes that can be completed in short modules and fit into flexible schedules for people like Adan Berishaj, a sales associate. Berishaj (center, on the computer) took an online course that helped him develop customer relations skills he recently tested with customer Derek Blasberg (right). Circuit City chose the online program because it was less expensive and more efficient than sending its many sales representatives to an off-site training program.

quence, that person will be more likely to avoid the behavior. An employee who receives a written disciplinary warning after submitting a report 24 hours late is more likely to submit the report on time next month.

Cognitive Learning

Cognitive learning is an approach theory that focuses on thought processes and assumes that human beings have a high capacity to act in a purposeful manner, and so to choose behaviors that will enable them to achieve long-run goals.

The approach theory that focuses on thought processes is known as **cognitive learning**. This theory assumes that human beings have a high capacity to act in a purposeful manner, and so to choose behaviors that will enable them to achieve long-run goals. Thus, employees will evaluate the work environment and choose behaviors that will enable them to achieve such goals as pay bonuses, promotions, and recognition.

Goal-Setting Strategies

Cognitive learning theory is the basis for "goal-setting" strategies and has therefore become the most widely applied learning theory in the business world. Goal setting is the basis for individual incentive plans like commissions or piecework, group-incentive plans, and organizationwide incentive plans like profit sharing and gainsharing. The widespread use of goal setting in organizations is attributed to several advantages these strategies offer:[18]

1. *Directed Behavior*—Goals help people focus their daily decisions and behaviors in specific ways.
2. *Challenges*—Individuals are more motivated, and thus achieve higher levels of performance, when given specific objectives instead of such nondirective responses as "keep up the good work."
3. *Resource Allocation*—Critical decisions involving resources (people, time, equipment, money) are more consistent with organizational goals when goal-setting strategies are used.
4. *Structure*—The formal and informal organizational structure can be shaped to set communication patterns and provide each position with a degree of authority and responsibility that supports employee and organizational goals.

Basically, goal-setting strategies involve a systematic process wherein managers and subordinates discuss and agree on a set of specific, jointly determined goals. If the process is functioning effectively, the final result will be a set of goals in keeping with the overall goals of the organization. Moreover, managers will have exact, measurable objectives by which to gauge each subordinate's performance. In this process, feedback on progress is periodically supplied, enabling workers to recognize and make necessary corrections in their work performance. Above all, the link among performance and evaluation and organizational rewards (goals) is made explicitly clear to the subordinate, with emphasis on *what* was achieved and *how*.

Goal Setting and Problem Solving

Managers use goal setting to correct problems as well as achieve new objectives. For example, if the manager of a video store is told in her annual review that she should "cut down on the total number of employee hours," how will she react? This vague reference to a perceived problem may cause the manager to do any one of a number of things, ranging from laying off several employees (and negatively affecting service) to simply worrying about the suggestion for a few days until it's forgotten. The problem: Her supervisor did not give her a specific measurable goal, require a plan of action, and provide a framework for feedback to see if the plan is working.

Moreover, the manager cannot be sure how achieving the goal (or failure to do so) will directly affect *her*—a necessary link in cognitive learning. Management by objectives (MBO), as discussed in detail in Chapter 6, is perhaps the most common application of goal setting. In an MBO process, the supervisor and store manager would jointly discuss and agree on a goal such as: "20 percent reduction of total employee hours per month to be achieved by reducing the number of 10:00 A.M.–5:00 P.M. personnel by 33 percent under a flextime program. The program is to be developed by the store manager, approved before implementation, and reported on monthly. This goal is one of three that will determine midyear bonuses."

▶ Working with different types of people presents new challenges in goal setting, as women who break through to nontraditional occupations often discover. What kinds of goals might women in the construction industries have?

Learning Strategies

Many strategies have evolved that managers can use to enhance the learning of organization members. These strategies are positive strategy, avoidance strategy, escape strategy, and punishment and are discussed further in the following sections.

Reinforcement Strategy Managers often use the principle of *reinforcement* when attempting to shape employee behavior. Reinforcement is based on operant conditioning theory: It is assumed that employees will repeat behavior that is reinforced or rewarded. Forms of reinforcement may include positive recognition by a supervisor, a "pass" on a checklist training item, or even simple praise ("You've mastered that, so let's move on to something new"). Of course, formal awards and monetary compensation also work. To shape or strengthen employee behavior, the manager can select from any combination of the following four reinforcement strategies:[19]

1. *Positive Reinforcement*—Any stimulus that causes a behavior to be repeated is a positive reinforcer. Common examples of positive reinforcement are praise, recognition, pay, and support. It is essential that the reinforcer directly follow the desired behavior. For example, if a manager witnesses an employee superbly handling an irate customer, immediate praise (or praise offered no later than the end of the day) is much more effective than a comment three months later during a performance appraisal.

2. *Avoidance Strategy*—Behavior that can prevent the onset of an undesired consequence often results from *avoidance learning*. In recent years, for example, many employers have adopted strict policies regarding the use of illegal drugs by employees. Research indicates that such strict "avoidance" policies have contributed to the overall decline in casual drug use, both in organizations and within the larger society. Indeed, one major pharmaceutical firm reported a drop in the number of job applicants testing positive for drug use from 7 percent in 1985 to less than 1 percent 10 years later.[20]

3. *Escape Strategy*—When a manager provides an arrangement in which a desired response will terminate an undesired consequence, that manager is using the *escape strategy*. For example, a manager may first set employees the least desired task, such as cleaning and setting up equipment, and inform them that once the equipment has passed inspection, they can move on to a more desirable task.

4. *Punishment Strategy*—When an *undesired* behavior by an employee is followed by an undesired response by management, a punishment strategy is being used. Organizations commonly select such punishment strategies—usually, they are called "disciplinary actions"—as oral and written warnings, demotion, suspension, and termination. The primary objective of a disciplinary program is to warn employees that certain undesired

behaviors are considered serious enough to invoke discipline. The purpose, of course, is to motivate employees to comply with work rules and performance standards. A second objective is to establish and maintain a climate of respect and mutual trust between employees and managers.

▶ Back to the Case

Over time, Webvan employees had to learn to change their behavior as a result of practice, education, experience, or training. In helping employees to learn, Webvan management might have focused on cognitive strategy, influencing employee thought processes to help them choose those behaviors that will be most productive. For example, educating employees about various methods for efficiently loading a truck with groceries could have helped them to decide which technique to employ in order to be most productive.

As another strategy to help employees learn, Webvan management could have employed learning concepts. Operant learning purports that employees can learn new behaviors by trying new behaviors and witnessing the outcomes of those behaviors. If, for example, employees at Webvan could earn bonuses by using a new technique for loading groceries, employees would have learned to use that technique continually. On the other hand, the employees would have learned to use some other loading techniques if using the new ones resulted in some type of verbal admonishment or punishment from management. Management must learn to use positive reinforcement as well as punishment and other reinforcement strategies in shaping employee behavior.

As learning situations change, Webvan management should have used cognitive learning strategy, operant learning strategy, or some combination of the two. Overall, as learning circumstances vary, Webvan management should have emphasized intellectual understanding as well as reinforcement strategies in helping employees learn.

Management Skills Module

This section is specially designed to help you develop management skills. An individual's management skill is based on an understanding of management concepts and the ability to apply those concepts in management situations. As a result, the following activities are designed both to heighten your understanding of management concepts and to help you gain facility in applying those concepts in various management situations.

UNDERSTANDING MANAGEMENT CONCEPTS

▶ Action Summary

Read the learning objectives below. Each objective is followed by questions. Answering these questions accurately will help you retain the most important concepts discussed in this chapter. After answering each question, check your answer against the answer key at the end of this chapter. (*Hint*: If you have any doubts regarding the correct response, consult the page number that follows the answer.)

Circle:

From studying this chapter, I will attempt to acquire

1. An understanding of employee workplace attitudes.
   - T F   **a.** Attitudes are largely shaped by personal beliefs and values.
   - a b c d e   **b.** Primary attitude components are: (a) cognitive (b) affective (c) behavioral (d) all of the above (e) none of the above.

2. Insights into how to change employee attitudes.
   - T F   **a.** Employee workplace attitudes are fairly stable over time and slow to change.
   - a b c d e   **b.** Managers should keep in mind that of the following employee characteristics, only one is *external* and thus should be subject to potential disciplinary action: (a) bad attitude (b) negative intention (c) poor behavior (d) inappropriate values (e) false beliefs.

3. An appreciation of the impact of employee perceptions on employee behaviors.
   - T F   **a.** Managers can usually correctly attribute poor employee behavior to lack of motivation.
   - a b c d e   **b.** When a manager evaluates an employee highly on all aspects of his or her job performance even though, in reality, the employee excels at only one aspect, the manager is guilty of (a) the halo effect (b) stereotyping (c) attribution error (d) selective perception (e) recency.

4. Knowledge of employee perceptions of procedural justice.
   - T F   **a.** Employee perceptions of the fairness of the processes used in reaching organizational decisions are often as important as the fairness of the decisions themselves.
   - a b c d e   **b.** Managers are most likely to be perceived as fair in their dispute-resolution strategy if they: (a) impose their own ideas for a settlement (b) stay out of all disputes (c) use mediation techniques (d) side with one party quickly (e) refer disputes to the human resource department.

5. An understanding that adult learners are different from younger students.
   - T F   **a.** Adult learners seek skills and knowledge that they can apply to their work or use to further their careers.
   - a b c d e   **b.** At Nucor Steel, employees have very positive work attitudes and production records owing to: (a) the use of employee teams (b) a "no-layoffs" policy (c) weekly production bonuses (d) limited levels of staff (e) all of the above.

▶ Action Summary Answer Key

1. **a.** T, p. 401	3. **a.** F, p. 407	4. **a.** T, pp. 409–410	5. **a.** T, p. 411
b. c, p. 400	**b.** a, p. 408	**b.** c, p. 410	**b.** e, p. 405
2. **a.** T, p. 402			
b. c, pp. 404–405			

Issues for Review and Discussion

1. Define *attitude*.
2. Explain how people's own values and beliefs affect their job behaviors.
3. How do employees communicate their job attitudes to their coworkers?
4. In your own words, explain the theory of reasoned action.
5. Why are people with positive job attitudes often the best-liked employees?
6. How would you rate your current ability to maintain a positive attitude when you have a task to perform? Are you satisfied with your ability? How could you improve it?
7. What strategies should managers use in striving to improve employee attitudes?
8. What are the most common sources of unsatisfactory employee performance?
9. Do you really believe that hiring employees who have a positive attitude can be critical to the success of a company? Explain.
10. Do employees form mental sets about their managers that are at odds with reality?
11. Why do people "filter out" stimuli that do not match their perceptions?
12. Describe the differences between perceptions of objects and perceptions of people.
13. To provide for more effective communication, what seating arrangement should a manager utilize (around a desk or table) when discussing a behavioral problem with an employee?
14. How common is "attribution error" among managers when they are evaluating employees' behavioral problems?
15. List several employee stereotypes you have heard from coworkers.
16. How can a manager guard against selective perception?
17. Why do employees often form more negative perceptions of the organizations they work for after their first year on the job?
18. Which of the two traditional approaches to learning is more often used in organizations?
19. Describe several effective forms of managerial positive reinforcement.

APPLYING MANAGEMENT CONCEPTS

Cases

INTRODUCTORY CASE WRAP-UP

Case Discussion Questions

"Where Was the People Focus at Webvan?" (pp. 399–400) and its related Back-to-the-Case sections were written to help you better understand the management concepts contained in this chapter. Answer the following discussion questions about this Introductory Case to enrich your understanding of the chapter content:

1. Do you agree that management in a company like Webvan needed to understand people as well as technology in designing and implementing a business model? Explain.
2. What advice would you have given Webvan management about how to manage employee attitudes?
3. Describe a situation where procedural justice might have built negative employee attitudes at Webvan. Once this situation has occurred, what steps would you have taken as the Webvan CEO to minimize its impact?

Skills Exercise: Using Reinforcement Strategies at Webvan

The Introductory Case focuses on a company that delivered groceries to customers. Assume that you managed the van drivers who delivered the groceries for Webvan. One of your drivers seldom showed up for work on time and was commonly 15 to 20 minutes late. How would you have used the four reinforcement strategies discussed in this chapter to encourage the driver to arrive at work on time?

India is a country of contradictions. It is recognized as a high-tech superpower with a strong information technology industry, yet only half of the 1 billion people living there have access to television or know how to read, and only 37 percent have running water. Some people use mud for soap and twigs for dental care.

The Anglo-Dutch Hindustan Lever Ltd. is considered by many to be the best-run company in India. For two decades, it has been painstakingly building a distribution system to sell soap and detergent to all of India. It is now expanding to reach even the very poorest population. "Everybody wants brands," claims Keki Dadiseth, a company veteran of 25 years, who began his business career as an accountant.

Today, Dadiseth is chairman of India's $2.9 billion Hindustan Lever Ltd. He is still constantly in and out of stores along India's poorest rural roads keeping track of how briskly his bars of Lux soap are moving. "You learn a lot about your own products—and the competition's," he says. According to Dadiseth, "To be a global business and to have a global market share you have to participate in all segments." He understands his products from the perspective of his poorest customers. If you have only 2 rupees (4 cents) to spare, you want quality products for your children, not the inferior knock offs usually offered to those who are not rich or middle class. All people want "the real thing."

Lever's strengths come from constant cost cutting, tight control on inventories, a thorough grasp of local markets, and sensitivity to cultural values of remote villagers. "While most of Lever's executives come from India's top schools," says the CIO of Birla Capital Asset Management: "they aren't suited, booted, out-of-touch urban sophisticates."

For Lever managers, the real world consists mainly of villages where 70 percent of the nation's population resides. Clearly, creativity is encouraged and rewarded at Lever. Aside from marketing at public watering holes, managers and staff have plastered promotional tiles for shampoo and soap at village wells, and even hung tin plates with ads in trees over bathing ponds. In many rural villages, walking around with a bar of Lux is a status symbol and "a clear sign you've moved up in life," says Arun Aadhikari, executive director for personal products.

In 2000, when Lever's share of the market dropped from 62 percent to 60 percent, the staff decided to stick 4-gram gold coins (worth $30 apiece) into a number of randomly selected bars of Lux soap. The word spread and millions of people bought Lux hoping to be the lucky winner. Lux sales promptly rose 9 percent as a result.

Hindustan Lever's executives believe that marketing well-made products to the poor isn't just a business opportunity: It is a sign of commercial respect for people whose needs are usually overlooked. Unilever, with current annual revenues of $43 billion, predicts that by 2010, half of its sales will come from the developing world. India's rural villagers comprise 12 percent of the world's population, which represents a huge untapped market. In order to reach that market, Unilever must understand the attitudes and perceptions of its prospective customers.

That is why every Lever management trainee begins his or her career by spending six to eight weeks in a rural village, eating, sleeping, and talking with the locals. Each trainee is required to participate in community projects. Marketing executives like M. Venkatesh, a regional sales manager, make frequent two-day trips to low-income areas, visiting stores and markets. If Lever products are hidden behind those of a competitor, he rearranges the display. He smells soap to make sure it is still fresh. He uses an IBM Thinkpad to keep track of the demographics for every village on his route. He knows by looking at the digital spreadsheet the number of bank deposits above a certain amount and the literacy rates. He knows his customers and they respond to him. "You build brands by offering choices and benefits. It lets consumers know that you're investing in them," he says.

In villages of the more rural states of northeastern India, people wash infrequently. Executives at Lever realized that people didn't wash their hands after washing clothes in the river or feeding cows. They didn't see dirt, so they assumed their hands were clean. In order to educate the villagers, Hindustan Lever staff members joined 70 million pilgrims in a religious festival at one of India's sacred rivers. They brought along an ultraviolet-light wand to wave over people's hands to show them the presence of dirt and germs, teaching them about the role of soap in avoidance of disease.

In India, women keep long hair throughout their lives. Many poor women cannot afford fancy jewelry or saris, and taking care of their hair may be their only luxury. This insight led to the two-in-one soap, allowing women to enjoy the luxury of caring for themselves while at the same time keeping the habit of using only one product for hair and body.

Executives at Lever are extremely responsive to the ideas of their product developers and sales management teams. They realize that in order to become more profitable in this new market, they must allocate a substantial sum of money to research and development. Dr. V. M. Naik, deputy of Hindustan Lever's Research Laboratory in Bangalore, spends about 70 percent of his time in the lab working on new products like low-cost two-in-one soap to be used for both hair and body. "New products require new principles," he says.

Through perseverance and a willingness to invest in new strategies, Hindustan Lever Ltd. has become a part of the changing face of twenty-first-century India.

QUESTIONS

1. Does Hindustan Lever Ltd.'s training program for new recruits address the organization member challenges of attitudes, perceptions, and learning? Explain.
2. Define halo effect, selective perception, and recency, and discuss how each might limit Hindustan Lever Ltd.'s success.
3. In what way is success and profitability dependent on breaking through stereotypes at Hindustan Lever Ltd.?
4. Do you think the information available to M. Venkatesh via his IBM Thinkpad influences his perception of his customers? Explain.

QUICKTAKES SEGMENT 4

Influencing

This segment consists of a pretty serious discussion between Susan and Hal. We get the idea that Susan and John have not sorted out their differences. Actually, it is not clear whether John sees that there is really anything to worry about. Perhaps, as far as he is concerned, he is doing the job he was hired to do, and over time, things will smooth out between him and Susan.

Susan, on other hand, sees "nothing but trouble" with John in the production manager slot. As she talks with Hal, we see at least two issues that Susan has: one directly related to John and his style of management, and the other related to the fact that Hal is less involved in the day-to-day operations at Quicktakes. Maybe Susan would be unhappy with anybody who was in the job—it just happens to be John. It would be helpful for us to know if these are Susan's feelings alone or if others in the company feel the same way. It is important for managers to understand when issues are individual in nature and when they affect a group of employees.

This segment shifts gears somewhat when Hal asks Susan to be part of a group he is assembling to identify issues in the company and provide suggestions to him for improvement. There are at least two lessons we get from Hal's attempt to change the direction of the discussion. First, we get an idea of how he decided to handle Susan's concerns. Second, we are introduced to a plan he has for getting feedback about the operations at Quicktakes. We do not know much, but it looks like he wants this advisory group to be made up of people who are not in his top management team. Think about how the group will interact. Also, consider whether it would be different if higher managers in the organization participated.

QUESTIONS

1. Susan came to Hal with what she believed is a problem at Quicktakes. By the end of the conversation, do you think Susan saw things the same way or differently from when she began talking with Hal?

2. After his discussion with Susan about John, Hal asks her to be part of a team he is establishing to identify issues and provide recommendations to him about the operations at Quicktakes. Why do you think Hal asked Susan to be on the team? Do you think asking her to be on the team was a good idea?

3. It seems like Hal dealt with Susan in a professional manner. He reacted to and expressed his interest in her concern. There are other ways Hal might have handled Susan's concerns. How else might he have dealt with this situation? What do you think are the strengths and weaknesses of your ideas?

4. Hal is setting up a team to identify issues and provide some possible solutions for problems that they identify at Quicktakes. This is basically a good idea but not one that is without risk. If you were advising Hal, what advice might you give him about setting up the team and in presenting them with his expectations of their work?

INFLUENCING AND *YOU*

The manager of a local steakhouse has hired you and five of your dorm mates as valet parking attendants on Saturday nights. Usually, there is a huge crowd and a good chance of earning some big tips. All of you have agreed to pool the money and split it evenly. That way everyone will do his/her fair share of the work. You notice that one of your friends is pocketing the large bills and handing in only the singles. This person is making a profit and cheating the rest of you. Right now you all get along with one another, and you would like to keep it that way.

1. How might you be able to influence him/her to stop without creating an awkward situation? Do you think trying to right this wrong will be a useful experience in your future role as a manager?

Mastering Management is a series of innovative, interactive learning activities specially designed to help you develop management skills emphasized in various text chapters. Attitudes, perception, and learning are the major focuses of this chapter. Episode 12 of *Mastering Management* focuses on what causes individual behavior and gives special attention to attribution and the halo effect. In this episode, Warren's task is to determine who will be CanGo's next order fulfillment manager. Review Episode 12, "Individual Behavior," on your *Mastering Management* CD and then answer the following questions.

QUESTIONS

1. Should Warren consider employee attitudes in determining who will be the next order fulfillment manager? Why?

2. What advice would you give Warren about minimizing the influence of the "halo effect" in making his decision?

3. What advice would you give Warren about minimizing the influence of "attribution" in making his decision?

---

www.prenhall.com/certo

This book is accompanied by a rich assortment of online activities aimed at developing your management skills. Reviewing news headlines, Internet exercises, an online study guide, and other research and Internet resources can help personalize management skills development for individual students or an entire class.

---

chapter

chapterchapterchapterchapterchapterchapter

19 Principles of Controlling

Objectives

From studying this chapter, I will attempt to acquire

● A definition of *control*

● A thorough understanding of the controlling subsystem

● An appreciation for various kinds of control and for how each kind can be used advantageously by managers

● Insights into the relationship between power and control

● Knowledge of the various potential barriers that must be overcome to implement successful control

● An understanding of steps that can be taken to increase the quality of a controlling subsystem

CHAPTER OUTLINE

DaimlerChrysler Controls by Initiating Web-Based *FastCar*

REMINDER: THE INTRODUCTORY CASE WRAP-UP (P. 437) CONTAINS DISCUSSION QUESTIONS AND A SKILLS EXERCISE TO FURTHER ILLUSTRATE THE APPLICATION OF CHAPTER CONCEPTS TO THIS VIGNETTE.

One of DaimlerChrysler's newest products, FastCar, is not a car at all but a Web-based initiative to deliver built-to-order cars on a mass scale while controlling production time and cost.

DaimlerChrysler recently unveiled a new Web-based initiative aimed at enhancing its overall competitive advantage. The company manufactures a wide array of products including passenger cars, trucks, and commercial and military aircraft. The company's most well-known passenger car brands are Mercedes-Benz, Chrysler, Dodge, and Jeep.

The new initiative, called FastCar, will focus on deploying Web linkages that will provide tighter communication among design, engineering, manufacturing, quality, finance, procurement, and sales and marketing units in the Chrysler division. Overall, FastCar is designed to deliver built-to-order cars on a mass scale while trimming costs.

Prior to FastCar, months would elapse before suppliers knew what new DaimlerChrysler car models would include, but now, approved product design changes will be communicated instantly to other departments within the company as well as to external suppliers that are involved in equipping a new car. Such changes in communication alone could cut vehicle production costs by as much as 20 percent and trim production cycles by three months, a step the company has been looking for as profits have slowed in its Chrysler unit.

One real benefit of FastCar will be to help project managers in various parts of the company to better plan for ordering products and find optimal parts to be included in the production process, and the new Web-based infrastructure will allow 4,100 internal employees and 5,000 external users to communicate and access design changes and production requirements.

Competitive pressures in the e-business arena are creating a necessity for the company to initiate FastCar as quickly as possible. One of DaimlerChrysler's most formidable competitors, General Motors (GM), recently announced the development of a comprehensive, Web-based initiative similar to FastCar. GM created a new operating unit to coordinate and manage the global proliferation of its new Web thrust, and its purpose is to use the Internet to connect with car buyers in a new, exciting fashion that will lead to better relationships with customers. The scope of GM's Internet activities, while certainly including customer emphasis, will also be broad enough to reap the benefits of Internet-related relationships with many other GM stakeholders such as suppliers, the communities in which GM operates, and employees.

Both companies are headed in the same direction, and these improvements illustrate a recently established dimension in which managers must now compete.

According to the Introductory Case, issues at Daimler-Chrysler such as production costs, internal communication, communication with suppliers, and customer relations need to be improved. The management function called *control* can help managers like those at DaimlerChrysler improve such issues, and the material in this chapter explains why this would be considered controlling. The following material also elaborates on the control function as a whole. Major topics in this chapter are:

1) Fundamentals of controlling
2) The controller and control
3) Power and control
4) Performing the control function

THE FUNDAMENTALS OF CONTROLLING

As the scale and complexity of modern organizations grow, so does the problem of control in organizations. Prospective managers, therefore, need a working knowledge of the essentials of the controlling function.[1] To this end, the following sections provide a definition of control, a definition of the process of controlling, and a discussion of the various types of control that can be used in organizations.

Defining Control

Control is making something happen the way it was planned to happen.

Stated simply, **control** is making something happen the way it was planned to happen. As implied by this definition, planning and control are virtually inseparable functions.[2] In fact, these two functions have been called the Siamese twins of management. According to Robert L. Dewelt:[3]

The importance of the planning process is quite obvious. Unless we have a soundly charted course of action, we will never quite know what actions are necessary to meet our objectives. We need a map to identify the timing and scope of all intended actions. This map is provided through the planning process.

But simply making a map is not enough. If we don't follow it or if we make a wrong turn along the way, chances are we will never achieve the desired results. A plan is only as good as our ability to make it happen. We must develop methods of measurement and control to signal when deviations from the plan are occurring so that corrective action can be taken.

Murphy's Law is a lighthearted adage making the serious point that managers should continually control—that is, check to see that organizational activities and processes are going as planned. According to Murphy's Law, anything that can go wrong will go wrong.[4] This law reminds managers to remain alert for possible problems, because even if a management system appears to be operating well, it might be eroding under the surface. Managers must always seek feedback on how the system is performing and make corrective changes whenever warranted.

Defining Controlling

Controlling is the process managers go through to control. It is a systematic effort to compare performance to predetermined standards, plans, or objectives to determine whether performance is in line with those standards or needs to be corrected.

Controlling is the process managers go through to control. According to Roberto Mockler, controlling is[5]

a systematic effort by business management to compare performance to predetermined standards, plans, or objectives to determine whether performance is in line with these standards and presumably to take any remedial action required to see that human and other corporate resources are being used in the most effective and efficient way possible in achieving corporate objectives.

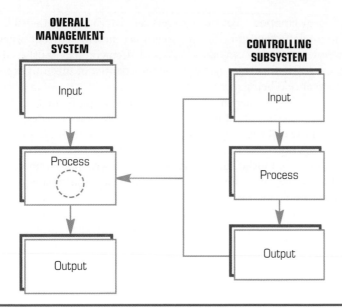

Relationship between overall management system and controlling subsystem

Figure 19.1

For example, production workers generally have daily production goals. At the end of each working day, the number of units produced by each worker is recorded so weekly production levels can be determined. If these weekly totals are significantly below weekly goals, the supervisor must take corrective action to ensure that actual production levels equal planned ones. If, on the other hand, production goals are being met, the supervisor should allow work to continue as it has in the past.[6]

The following sections discuss the controlling subsystem and provide more details about the control process itself.

Back to the Case

The above information supports the notion that high production costs (as well as the other issues mentioned in the Introductory Case) at DaimlerChrysler actually should be categorized as a control problem. Control is making things happen at DaimlerChrysler in a way they were planned to happen. In this case, because profits were obviously not reaching planned levels, management decided to initiate FastCar to help in reducing production costs. FastCar should help to ensure that profit levels achieved in the future are more in line with expected returns. DaimlerChrysler's control must be closely linked to its planning activities.

Going one step further, the process of controlling is the action that management takes in order to control. Ideally, this process at DaimlerChrysler, as within any company, would include a determination of company plans, standards, and objectives for manufacturing products like the PT Cruiser, so steps can be taken to eliminate company characteristics that caused deviation from these factors.

The Controlling Subsystem   As with the planning, organizing, and influencing functions described in earlier chapters, controlling can be viewed as a subsystem of the overall management system. The purpose of this subsystem is to help managers enhance the success of the overall management system through effective controlling. Figure 19.1 shows the specific components of the controlling subsystem.

The Controlling Process   As Figure 19.2 illustrates, there are three main steps in the controlling process:

1. Measuring performance
2. Comparing measured performance to standards
3. Taking corrective action

Measuring Performance   Before managers can determine what must be done to make an organization more effective and efficient, they must measure current organizational performance.[7] However, before they can take such a measurement, they must establish some unit of measure that gauges performance and observe the quantity of this unit as generated by the item whose performance is being measured.

How to Measure.   A manager who wants to measure the performance of five janitors, for example, first must establish units of measure that represent janitorial performance—such as the number of floors swept, the number of windows washed, or the number of light bulbs changed. After designating these units of measure, the manager has to determine the number of each of these units accomplished by each janitor. The process of determining both the units of measure and the number of units associated with each janitor furnishes the manager with a measure of janitorial performance.

What to Measure.   Managers must always keep in mind that there is a wide range of organizational activities that can be measured as part of the control process. For example, the amounts and types of inventory on hand are commonly measured to control inventory, while the quality of goods and services being produced is commonly measured to control product quality. Performance measurements can relate as well to various effects of production, such as the degree to which a particular manufacturing process pollutes the atmosphere.

The degree of difficulty in measuring various types of organizational performance, of course, is determined primarily by the activity being measured. For example, it is far more dif-

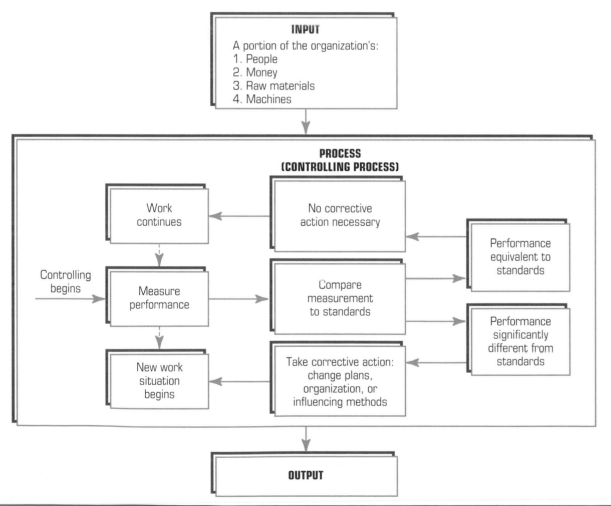

Figure 19.2   *The controlling subsystem*

ficult to measure the performance of a highway maintenance worker than to measure the performance of a student enrolled in a college-level management course.

Comparing Measured Performance to Standards Once managers have taken a measure of organizational performance, their next step in controlling is to compare this measure against some standard. A **standard** is the level of activity established to serve as a model for evaluating organizational performance. The performance evaluated can be for the organization as a whole or for some individuals working within the organization.[8] In essence, standards are the yardsticks that determine whether organizational performance is adequate or inadequate.[9]

A **standard** is the level of activity established to serve as a model for evaluating organizational performance.

▶ Hotels—Marriott Hotels Set Performance Standards Through the First Ten Program

This section emphasizes that in order to control, managers must compare measured performance to standards. Based on this comparison, managers take corrective action, if necessary, to make what is taking place in organizations more consistent with achieving organizational goals. This chapter feature discusses action taken by Marriott Hotels to set and enforce customer service standards.

Marriott International owns Marriott Hotels and is the world's leading hospitality company. Marriott Hotels has more than 4,700 units and serves more than 4 million customers a day. Marriott International operates the broadest portfolio of brands of any lodging company in the world through its company-owned chains. In addition to Marriott Hotels, these chains include the Ritz Carlton, Marriott Executive Residences, Courtyard by Marriott, Ramada International, and Fairfield Suites by Marriott. Through all of its chains, Marriott International offers more than 229,000 rooms worldwide.

Recent financial results at Marriott International indicate that its focus on high-quality customer service is paying off. For the first half of 1998, total revenues rose 15 percent to $4.73 billion. For this same period, net income rose 24 percent to $190 million. Increased revenues reflect higher room revenues due to higher average room rates and the addition of properties. Overall, Marriott International's reputation is very positive among its customers.

One example of customer service focus at Marriott Hotels is the newly implemented First Ten program. Essentially, the First Ten program set a standard within the company for hassle-free check-in. The concept behind the program's name is simple: Guests ideally should be in their hotel rooms within the first 10 minutes of their arrival. In measuring actual performance and comparing it to the First Ten standard, management has discovered many ways to improve operational efficiency related to getting customers to their rooms. Improvements in areas like check-in procedure and luggage handling help employees to meet the First Ten standard. Overall, management believes that the First Ten program has increased customer satisfaction.

Studying operations at General Electric (GE) will give us some insights into the different kinds of standards managers can establish. GE has established the following standards:

1. *Profitability standards*—In general, these standards indicate how much money GE would like to make as profit over a given time period—that is, its return on investment. More and more, GE is using computerized preventive maintenance on its equipment to help maintain profitability standards. Such maintenance programs have reduced labor costs and equipment downtime and thereby have helped raise company profits.

2. *Market position standards*—These standards indicate the share of total sales in a particular market that GE would like to have relative to its competitors. GE market position standards were set by company chairman John F. Welch Jr., in 1988, when he announced that henceforth any product his company offers must achieve the highest or second-highest market share compared to similar products offered by competitors or it would be eliminated or sold to another firm.

3. *Productivity standards*—How much various segments of the organization should produce is the focus of these standards. Management at GE has found that one of the best ways to convince organization members to commit themselves to increasing company productivity is simply to treat them with dignity and make them feel they are part of the GE team.

4. *Product leadership standards*—GE intends to assume a leading position in product innovation in its field. Product leadership standards indicate what must be done to attain such a position. Reflecting this interest in innovation, GE has pioneered the development of synthetic diamonds for industrial use. In fact, GE is considered the leader in this area, having recently discovered a method for making synthetic diamonds at a purity of 99.9 percent. In all probability, such diamonds will eventually be used as a component of super-high-speed computers.

5. *Personnel development standards*—Standards in this area indicate the type of training programs GE personnel should undergo to develop properly. GE's commitment to sophisticated training technology is an indication of the seriousness with which the company takes personnel development standards. Company training sessions are commonly supported by sophisticated technology like large-screen projection systems, computer-generated visual aids, combined video and computer presentations, and laser videos.

6. *Employee attitudes standards*—These standards indicate what types of attitudes GE managers should strive to inculcate in GE employees. Like many other companies today, GE is trying to build positive attitudes toward product quality in its employees.

7. *Social responsibility standards*—GE recognizes its responsibility to make a contribution to society. Standards in this area outline the level and types of contributions management believes GE should make. One recent activity that reflects social responsibility standards at GE is the renovation of San Diego's Vincent de Paul Joan Kroc center for the homeless, accomplished by work teams made up of GE employees. These teams painted, cleaned, and remodeled a building to create a better facility for some of San Diego's disadvantaged citizens.

8. *Standards reflecting the relative balance between short- and long-range goals*—These standards express the relative emphasis that should be placed on attaining various short and long-range goals. GE recognizes that short-range goals exist to enhance the probability that long-range goals will be attained.

Successful managers pinpoint all important areas of organizational performance and establish corresponding standards in each area.[10] For instance, American Airlines has set two very specific standards for appropriate performance of its airport ticket offices: (1) at least 95 percent of the flight arrival times posted should be accurate, meaning that actual arrival times do not deviate more than 15 minutes from posted times, and (2) at least 85 percent of customers coming to the airport ticket counter should not have to wait more than 5 minutes to be serviced.

► Back to the Case

In theory, DaimlerChrysler's management should view controlling activities within the company as a subsystem of the organization's overall management system. For management to achieve organizational control, the controlling subsystem requires a portion of the people, money, raw materials, and machines available within the company.

The process portion of the controlling subsystem at DaimlerChrysler involves three steps:

1. Measuring the performance levels of various productive units
2. Comparing these performance levels to predetermined performance standards for these units
3. Taking any corrective action necessary to make sure that planned performance levels are consistent with actual performance levels

Based on information in the Introductory Case, one area in which management should emphasize standards is in the arena of desired profitability. According to the case, high production costs are a primary reason that the company is not as profitable as management would like it to be. Because it is not presently earning a desirable level of profits, management is initiating FastCar, an Internet-based program aimed at reducing production costs, among other targets.

Taking Corrective Action After actual performance has been measured and compared with established performance standards, the next step in the controlling process is to take corrective action if necessary. **Corrective action** is managerial activity aimed at bringing organizational performance up to the level of performance standards.[11] In other words, corrective action focuses on correcting organizational mistakes that are hindering organizational performance. Before taking any corrective action, however, managers should make sure that the standards they are using were properly established and that their measurements of organizational performance are valid and reliable.

Recognizing Problems. At first glance, it seems a fairly simple proposition that managers should take corrective action to eliminate **problems**—factors within an organization that are barriers to organizational goal attainment.[12] In practice, however, it often proves difficult to pinpoint the problem causing some undesirable organizational effect. Let us suppose that a performance measurement indicates a certain worker is not adequately passing on critical information to fellow workers. If the manager is satisfied that the communication standards are appropriate and that the performance measurement information is both valid and reliable, the manager should take corrective action to eliminate the problem causing this substandard performance.

Recognizing Symptoms. What exactly is the problem causing substandard communication in this situation? Is it that the worker is not communicating adequately simply because he or she doesn't want to communicate? Is it that the job makes communication difficult? Is it that the worker does not have the necessary training to communicate in an appropriate manner? Before attempting to take corrective action, the manager must determine whether the worker's failure to communicate is a problem in itself or a **symptom**—a sign that a problem exists.[13] For example, the worker's failure to communicate adequately could be a symptom of inappropriate job design or a cumbersome organizational structure.

Once the problem has been properly identified, corrective action can focus on one or more of the three primary management functions of planning, organizing, and influencing. That is, corrective action can include such activities as modifying past plans to make them more suitable for future organizational endeavors, making an existing organizational structure more suitable for existing plans and objectives, or restructuring an incentive program to ensure that high producers are rewarded more than low producers. Note that because planning, organizing, and influencing are closely related, there is a good chance that corrective action taken in one area will necessitate some corresponding action in one or both of the other two areas.

Corrective action is managerial activity aimed at bringing organizational performance up to the level of performance standards.

Problems are factors within an organization that are barriers to organizational goal attainment.

A **symptom** is a sign that a problem exists.

▶ Back to the Case

In determining that corrective action is necessary at DaimlerChrysler, management must be certain that the action is aimed at organizational problems rather than at symptoms of problems. For example, if production costs are too high because workers are not trained well

(continued)

enough to operate their equipment properly, the symptom will disappear as a result of improved training of production workers.

Inevitably, corrective action at DaimlerChrysler, such as improved worker training, must focus on further planning, organizing, or influencing efforts. As examples: How must DaimlerChrysler's scheduling of workers change if production workers are being more carefully trained? Does the company still need the same number of production supervisors if workers become more competent as a result of improved training?

Lubys Takes Corrective Action by Providing Incentives

Lubys, Inc. operates 219 cafeteria-style restaurants in many states including Florida, Arizona, Missouri, and Oklahoma. Each restaurant offers a broad and diverse menu, typically serving about 12 entrees, 12 vegetable dishes, 15 salads, and 18 desserts. Food is prepared in small quantities several times a day and checked frequently to ensure that quality is maintained. The Lubys cafeterias are usually located close to retail centers, business parks, and neighborhoods. Customers are primarily shoppers and business personnel for lunch and families for dinner. Lubys restaurants are open seven days a week, and take-out orders are available.

Recent financial news at Lubys has been discouraging. For the first time in its history, because of declining sales for the restaurant chain as a whole, the company suspended the payment of dividends to stockholders. The poor sales results were followed by a flurry of resignations including the president and CEO, the chief financial officer, and the vice president of human resources.

David Daviss, interim president and CEO, has taken a number of steps to try to control this situation, the most notable of which is providing new pay incentives for restaurant managers. A source of frustration at Lubys has been its pay plan. The new incentive system provides that managers will get a percentage of profits on a monthly basis and an extra bonus for increased sales or earnings. As a result of this program, some managers who left Lubys are applying to rejoin the company. ■

Types of Control

Three types of management control are possible:

1. Precontrol
2. Concurrent control
3. Feedback control

What type is used is determined primarily by the work phase in which the control is needed.

Precontrol is control that takes place before some unit of work is actually performed.

Precontrol   Control that takes place before work is performed is called **precontrol,** or *feedforward control.*[14] Managers using this type of control create policies, procedures, and rules aimed at eliminating behavior that will cause undesirable work results. For example, the manager of a small record shop may find that a major factor in attracting return customers is having salespeople discuss records with customers. This manager might use precontrol by establishing a rule that salespeople cannot talk to one another while a customer is in the store. This rule is a precontrol measure because it is aimed at eliminating an anticipated problem: salespeople who are so engrossed in conversations with one another that they neglect to chat with customers about records. In sum, precontrol focuses on eliminating predicted problems.

Concurrent control is control that takes place as some unit of work is being performed.

Concurrent Control   Control that takes place as work is being performed is called **concurrent control.** It relates not only to employee performance, but also to such nonhuman areas as equipment performance and department appearance. For example, most supermarkets have rigid rules about the amount of stock that should be placed on the selling floor. The general idea is to display generous amounts of all products on the shelves, with no empty spaces. A concurrent control aimed at ensuring that shelves are stocked as planned could consist of a stock manager's making periodic visual checks throughout a work period to evaluate the status of the sales shelves and, correspondingly, the performance of the stock crew.[15]

Feedback control is control that takes place after some unit of work has been performed.

Feedback Control   Control that concentrates on past organizational performance is called **feedback control.**[16] Managers exercising this type of control are attempting to take corrective action by looking at organizational history over a specified time period. This history may involve only one factor, such as inventory levels, or it may involve the relationships among many factors, such as net income before taxes, sales volume, and marketing costs.

> ## Back to the Case
>
> In controlling at DaimlerChrysler, management should use an appropriate combination of pre-control, concurrent control, and feedback control. Precontrol would emphasize the elimination of the factors that could cause poor annual profitability before the year actually begins. Through concurrent control, management would be able to assess the profitability of Daimler Chrysler during a particular operating period. Last, feedback control would enable management to control at the end of some operating period. With feedback control, management would improve future performance by analyzing a segment of history of DaimlerChrysler.
>
> Some use of each of these types of control could increase the probability of DaimlerChrysler eliminating problems of profitability before they become too overwhelming. Management must not make the common mistake of emphasizing feedback control to the exclusion of concurrent control and precontrol.

Best Western Uses Feedback Control for Diversity

Best Western International is known as the world's largest hotel chain, with over 4,000 independently owned and operated hotels throughout regions like Australia, Asia, South Africa, Canada, and the United States. Best Western International has been in operation for over 50 years and focuses on providing customers with high quality, superior service, and outstanding value.

Despite the success of Best Western, many of its executives believe that in the past several years, the company has not kept pace with the demands of the digital marketplace. In addition, some insiders believe that Best Western has lagged in diversity efforts. To illustrate that point, in 1997, the NAACP ranked Best Western last among hotels in diversity efforts.

Based on this feedback, the Best Western board charged James P. Evans, the company president and CEO, with changing the company's culture from one based mostly on the good-old-boy network to one more reflective of a diverse world population. To promote company diversity, Evans hired Vicki A. Winston as the director of human resources. Winston was Best Western's first female executive. To enhance diversity, Winston is taking action by increasing the number of Best Western minority vendors, increasing the number of African American owners of Best Western facilities, developing a marketing plan aimed at minority groups, and educating employees about diversity issues and how they can impact the company. ■

THE CONTROLLER AND CONTROL

Organization charts developed for medium- and large-sized companies typically contain a position called *controller*. The sections that follow explain the job of the controller and discuss its relationship to the control function and how much control is needed within an organization.

The Job of the Controller

The **controller** (also sometimes called the *comptroller*) is the staff person who gathers information that helps managers control. From the preceding discussion, it is clear that managers are responsible for comparing planned and actual performance and for taking corrective action when necessary. In smaller organizations, managers may also be completely responsible for gathering information about various aspects of the organization and developing necessary reports based on this information. In medium- or large-sized companies, however, the controller handles much of this work. The controller's basic responsibility is to assist line managers with the controlling function by gathering appropriate information and generating reports that reflect this information.[17] The controller usually works with information about the following financial dimensions of the organization:[18]

1. Profits
2. Revenues

The **controller** is the staff person whose basic responsibility is to assist line managers with the controlling function by gathering appropriate information and generating necessary reports that reflect this information.

3. Costs
4. Investments
5. Discretionary expenses

The sample job description of a controller in Table 19.1 shows that the controller is responsible for generating information managers rely on when exercising the control function. Because the controller is seldom directly responsible for taking corrective action within the organization but instead advises managers on what sort of action to take, the controller position is considered a staff position.

How Much Control Is Needed?

As with all organizational endeavors, control activities should be pursued if the expected benefits of performing such activities are greater than the costs of performing them. The process of comparing the cost of any organizational activity with the expected benefit of performing the activity is called **cost–benefit analysis**.[19] In general, managers and controllers should collaborate to determine exactly how much controlling is justified in a given situation.

Figure 19.3 graphs controlling activity at a certain company over an extended period of time. Note how controlling costs increase steadily as more and more controlling activities are performed. Also note that because the controlling function requires start-up costs, controlling costs are usually greater than the income generated from increased controlling at first. As controlling starts to correct major organizational errors, however, the income from increased controlling eventually equals controlling costs (point X_1 on Figure 19.3) and ultimately surpasses them by a large margin.

As more and more controlling activity is added beyond X_1, however, controlling costs and the income from increased controlling eventually become equal again (point X_2 on Figure

 Managers must decide how much control is enough, based on cost–benefit analysis. Dick Hunter is Dell Computer Corporation's vice president who oversees supply chain management, and in Dell's "lean manufacturing" environment, he sees the efficiency of the supply chain as an "absolutely critical" component of cost control. "Materials costs account for about 74 percent of our revenues. We spent around $21 million on materials last year. Shaving 0.1 percent off can have a bigger impact than, say, improving manufacturing productivity by 10 percent," he says.

✋ Table 19.1   **Sample Job Description for a Controller in a Large Company**

Objectives

The controller (or comptroller) is responsible for all accounting activities within the organization.

Functions

1. *General accounting*—Maintain the company's accounting books, accounting records, and forms. This includes:
   a. Preparing balance sheets, income statements, and other statements and reports
   b. Giving the president interim reports on operations for the recent quarter and fiscal year to date
   c. Supervising the preparation and filing of reports to the SEC

2. *Budgeting*—Prepare a budget outlining the company's future operations and cash requirements.

3. *Cost accounting*—Determine the cost to manufacture a product and prepare internal reports for management of the processing divisions. This includes:
   a. Developing standard costs
   b. Accumulating actual cost data
   c. Preparing reports that compare standard costs to actual costs and highlight unfavorable differences

4. *Performance reporting*—Identify individuals in the organization who control activities and prepare reports to show how well or how poorly they perform.

5. *Data processing*—Assist in the analysis and design of a computer-based information system. Frequently, the data-processing department is under the controller, and the controller is involved in management of that department as well as other communications equipment.

6. *Other duties*—Other duties may be assigned to the controller by the president or by corporate bylaws. Some of these include:
   a. Tax planning and reporting
   b. Service departments such as mailing, telephone, janitors, and filing
   c. Forecasting
   d. Corporate social relations and obligations

Relationship

The controller reports to the vice president of finance.

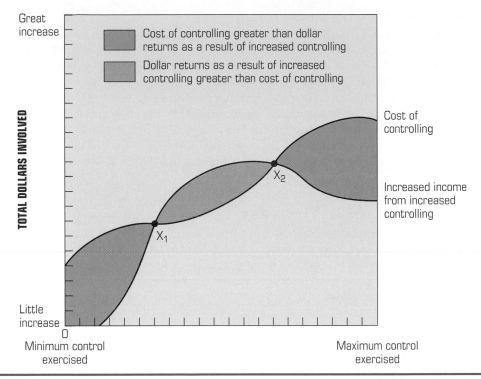

Great
increase

▢ Cost of controlling greater than dollar
returns as a result of increased controlling

▢ Dollar returns as a result of increased
controlling greater than cost of controlling

TOTAL DOLLARS INVOLVED

Cost of
controlling

X₂

Increased income
from increased
controlling

X₁

Little
increase

0

Minimum control
exercised

Maximum control
exercised

Value of additional controlling

Figure 19.3

19.3). As more controlling activity is added beyond X₂, controlling costs again surpass the income from increased controlling. The main reason for this last development is that major organizational problems probably were detected much earlier, so most corrective measures at this point are aimed at smaller and less costly problems.

Cost–benefit analysis is the process of comparing the cost of some activity with the benefit or revenue that results from the activity to determine the activity's total worth to the organization.

▶ Back to the Case

The job of a controller at DaimlerChrysler would be to gather information for reports that management could use to take corrective action. The controller him or herself would not take any corrective action, but would simply advise management as to what should be done.

To operate properly, management must determine, with the advice of the controller, exactly how much control is necessary: in this case, which production costs seem the most detrimental and how these are to be reduced. Management should continue to increase controlling as long as the benefits from the control activities (enhanced profitability) exceed their cost. DaimlerChrysler management should keep in mind that too much control can cause too much paperwork and slow decision making to an undesirable level.

POWER AND CONTROL

To control successfully, managers must understand not only the control process, but also how organization members relate to it. Up to this point, the chapter has emphasized the nonhuman variables of controlling. This section focuses on power, perhaps the most important human-related variable in the control process. The following sections discuss power by:

1. Presenting its definition
2. Elaborating on the total power of managers
3. Listing the steps managers can take to increase their power over other organization members

A Definition of Power

Power is the extent to which an individual is able to influence others so that they respond to orders.

Perhaps the two most often confused terms in management are *power* and *authority*. Authority was defined in Chapter 11 as the right to command or give orders. The extent to which an individual is able to influence others so that they respond to orders is called **power**.[20] The greater this ability, the more power an individual is said to have.

Obviously, power and control are closely related. To illustrate, after comparing actual performance with planned performance and determining that corrective action is necessary, a manager usually gives orders to implement this action. Although the orders are issued by virtue of the manager's organizational authority, they may or may not be followed precisely, depending on how much power the manager has over the individuals to whom the orders are addressed.

Total Power of a Manager

Total power is the entire amount of power an individual in an organization possesses. It is made up of position power and personal power.

Position power is power derived from the organizational position a manager holds.

Personal power is the power derived from a manager's relationships with others.

The **total power** a manager possesses is made up of two different kinds of power: position power and personal power. **Position power** is power derived from the organizational position a manager holds. In general, a manager moving from lower-level management to upper-level management accrues more position power. **Personal power** is power derived from a manager's relationships with others.[21]

Steps for Increasing Total Power

Managers can increase their total power by enhancing either their position power or their personal power or both. Position power is generally enhanced by a move to a higher organizational position, but most managers have little personal control over when they will move up in an organization. Managers do, however, have substantial control over the amount of personal power they hold over other organization members. John P. Kotter stresses the importance of developing personal power:[22]

> *To be able to plan, organize, budget, staff, control, and evaluate, managers need some control over the many people on whom they are dependent. Trying to control others solely by directing them and on the basis of the power associated with one's position simply will not work—first, because managers are always dependent on some people over whom they have no formal authority, and second, because virtually no one in modern organizations will passively accept and completely obey a constant stream of orders from someone just because he or she is the "boss."*

To increase personal power, a manager should attempt to develop the following attitudes and beliefs in other organization members:[23]

1. *A sense of obligation toward the manager*—If a manager succeeds in developing this sense of obligation, other organization members will allow the manager to influence them within certain limits. The basic strategy suggested for creating this sense of obligation is to do personal favors for people.

2. *A belief that the manager possesses a high level of expertise within the organization*—In general, a manager's personal power increases as organization members perceive that the manager's level of expertise is increasing. To raise perceptions of their expertise, managers must quietly make their significant achievements visible to others and build up a successful track record and a solid professional reputation.

3. *A sense of identification with the manager*—The manager can strive to develop this identification by behaving in ways that other organization members respect and by espousing goals, values, and ideals commonly held by them. The following description illustrates how a certain sales manager took steps to increase the degree to which his subordinates identified with him:[24]

> *One vice-president of sales in a moderate-sized manufacturing company was reputed to be so much in control of his sales force that he could get them to respond to new and different marketing programs in a third of the time taken by the company's best competitors. His power over his employees was based primarily on their strong identification with him and what he stood for. Emigrating to the United States at age seventeen, this person worked his way up "from nothing." When made a sales manager in 1965, he*

began recruiting other young immigrants and sons of immigrants from his former country. When made vice-president of sales in 1970, he continued to do so. In 1975, 85 percent of his sales force was made up of people whom he hired directly or who were hired by others he brought.

4. *The perception that they are dependent on the manager*—The main strategy here is to clearly convey the amount of authority the manager has over organizational resources— not only those necessary for organization members to do their jobs, but also those organization members personally receive in such forms as salaries and bonuses. This strategy is aptly reflected in the managerial version of the Golden Rule: "He who has the gold makes the rules."

> ### ▶ Back to the Case
>
> For DaimlerChrysler's management to be successful in controlling, they have to be aware not only of the intricacies of the control process itself, but also of how to deal with people as they relate to the control process. With regard to people and control, managers must consider the amount of power they hold over organization members—that is, their ability to encourage workers to follow orders. Based on the Introductory Case, many of these orders would probably be related to implementing new and better production methods as well as improved communication with stakeholders like suppliers and customers.
>
> The total amount of power that DaimlerChrysler management possesses comes from the positions they hold and from their personal relationships with other organization members. For example, the top managers already have more position power than any other managers in the organization. Therefore, to increase their total power, they would have to develop their personal power. Top management might attempt to do this by developing
>
> 1. A sense of obligation in other organization members toward top managers
> 2. The belief in other organization members that top management has a high level of task-related expertise
> 3. A sense of identification that other organization members have with top management
> 4. The perception in organization members that they are dependent on top management

Performing the Control Function

Controlling can be a detailed and intricate function, especially as the size of an organization increases. The following two sections furnish valuable guidelines for successfully executing this complicated function. They discuss potential barriers to successful controlling and how to make controlling successful.

Potential Barriers to Successful Controlling

To avoid potential barriers to successful controlling, managers should take action in the following areas.[25]

Long-Term Versus Short-Term Production   A manager, in striving to meet planned weekly production quotas, might be tempted to "push" machines in a particular area so hard they cannot be serviced properly. This kind of management behavior would ensure that planned performance and actual performance are equivalent in the short term, but it might well cause the machines to deteriorate to the point where it is impossible to meet long-term production quotas.

Employee Frustration and Morale   Worker morale tends to be low when management exerts too much control. Employees become frustrated when they perceive management is too rigid in its thinking and will not allow them the freedom they need in order to do a good job. Overcontrol may also make employees suspect that control activities are merely a tactic to pressure them to work harder and harder to increase production.

Filing of Reports   Employees may perceive that management is basing corrective action solely on department records with no regard for extenuating circumstances. If this is the case, they may feel pressured to falsify reports so that corrective action pertaining to their organizational unit will not be too drastic. For example, employees may overstate actual production figures to make their unit look good to management, or they may understate the numbers to create the impression that planned production is too high, thereby tricking management into thinking that a lighter workload is justified.

A well-publicized instance of falsifying control reports involved the Federal Aviation Administration (FAA) and Eastern Airlines.[26] The FAA is a government organization charged with controlling airlines' safety. As part of the FAA's controlling process, airline companies must fill out service reports and return them to the FAA for monitoring and evaluation. Before Eastern went out of business, the company and its senior maintenance executives were charged by a federal grand jury with conspiring to falsify aircraft maintenance records and returning improperly maintained aircraft to passenger service. The indictment charged that on 52 different occasions, company managers signed off on, or coerced aircraft mechanics and mechanics supervisors to sign off on, maintenance that had not been completed. Management seems to have regarded the falsification of maintenance reports as a way of reducing maintenance costs and thereby boosting Eastern's poor profit performance. The pressure of poor profits at Eastern Airlines caused certain company managers to falsify service reports, making it impossible for the FAA to properly control the airline company.

Perspective of Organization Members   Although controls can be designed to focus on relatively narrow aspects of an organization, managers must remember to consider any prospective corrective action not only in relation to the specific activity being controlled, but also in relation to all other organizational units.

For example, a manager may determine that actual and planned production are not equivalent in a specific organizational unit because during various periods, a low inventory of needed parts causes some production workers to pursue other work activities instead of producing a product. The appropriate corrective action in this situation would seem to be simply raising the level of inventory, but this would be taking a narrow perspective of the problem. The manager should take a broader perspective by asking the following questions before initiating any corrective action: Is there enough money on hand to raise current inventory levels? Are there sufficient personnel presently in the purchasing department to effect the necessary increase? Who will do the work the production workers are now doing when they run out of parts?

Mean Versus Ends   Control activities are not the goals of the control process; they are merely the means to eliminating problems. Managers must keep in mind throughout the control process that the information gathering and report generating done to facilitate taking corrective action are activities that can be justified only if they yield some organizational benefit that exceeds the cost of performing them.

Making Controlling Successful

In addition to avoiding the potential barriers to successful controlling mentioned in the previous section, managers can perform certain activities to make the control process more effective. To increase the quality of the controlling subsystem, managers should make sure that controlling activities take all of the following factors into account.

Specific Organizational Activities Being Focused On   Managers should make sure the various facets of the control process are appropriate to the control activity under consideration. For example, standards and measurements concerning a line worker's productivity are much different from standards and measurements concerning a vice president's productivity. Controlling ingredients related to the productivity of these individuals, therefore, must be different if the control process is to be applied successfully.

▶ A budget is among the most basic control devices managers have at their disposal. One of the ways in which Dr. Regina S. Peruggi will be able to judge the success of her leadership of New York's Central Park Conservancy, the private nonprofit organization that manages and raises money for Central Park, will be whether she can further the organization's goals of restoration and conservation within its $20 million budget.

Different Kinds of Organizational Goals   According to Jerome, control can be used for such different purposes as standardizing performance, protecting organizational assets from theft and waste, and standardizing product quality.[27] Managers should remember that the control process can be applied to many different facets of organizational life and that, if the organization is to receive maximum benefit from controlling, each of these facets must be emphasized.

Timely Corrective Action   Some time will necessarily elapse as managers gather control-related information, develop necessary reports based on this information, and decide what corrective action should be taken to eliminate a problem. However, managers should take the corrective action as promptly as possible to ensure that the situation depicted by the information gathered has not changed. Unless corrective actions are timely, the organizational advantage of taking them may not materialize.

Communication of the Mechanics of the Control Process   Managers should take steps to ensure that people know exactly what information is required for a particular control process, how that information is to be gathered and used to compile various reports, what the purposes of the various reports actually are, and what corrective actions are appropriate given those reports. The lesson here is simple: For control to be successful, all individuals involved in controlling must have a working knowledge of how the control process operates.[28]

▶ Back to the Case

In addition to understanding the intricacies of control and how people fit into the control process, DaimlerChrysler management must be aware of the potential barriers to successful controlling and the action they could take to increase the probability that controlling activities would be successful, that is, to increase the probability that factors such as new and improved production techniques will be performed efficiently, effectively, and without resistance.

To overcome the potential control-related barriers at DaimlerChrysler, management must balance its emphasis on short-term versus long-term objectives, minimize the negative influence controlling can have on the morale of organization members, eliminate forces that can lead to the falsification of control-related reports, implement a control perspective that has appropriately combined narrow and broad organizational focuses, and stress controlling as a means rather than an end.

With regard to the action that can be taken to increase the probability of effective controlling activities, DaimlerChrysler management must be sure that various facets of its controlling subsystem are appropriate for company activities, that components of the controlling subsystem are flexible and suited to many purposes, that corrective action is based on timely information, and that the controlling subsystem is understood by all organization members involved in its operation.

chapter

20 Production Management and Control

USAir Focuses on Turnaround to Build Productivity

REMINDER: THE INTRODUCTORY CASE WRAP-UP (P. 466) CONTAINS DISCUSSION QUESTIONS AND A SKILLS EXERCISE TO FURTHER ILLUSTRATE THE APPLICATION OF CHAPTER CONCEPTS TO THIS VIGNETTE.

E d Vilchis is in a hurry. So is his employer, USAir.

A ramp-agent supervisor at the company's Baltimore–Washington airport terminal, Vilchis used to have 45 minutes to see that bags moved off and on planes between flights. These days, he and his crews have about half that (see below). "Once that plane rolls in, you basically attack it," says Vilchis, a 17-year USAir veteran. "You load it, fuel it, cater it, push it back, and it's gone."

What's the rush? It's all part of the "quick-turn" strategy being implemented by some U.S. airlines. To improve productivity and lower operating costs, these carriers are trying to cut the time that planes on nonconnecting flights stay on the ground. After all, planes earn money flying passengers, not sitting on the tarmac.

The strategy offers flyers one big advantage. Because of delays in boarding, "people were telling

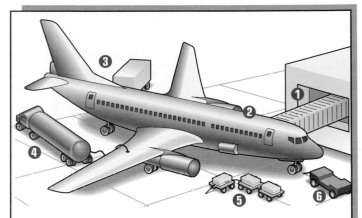

USAir is attempting to cut the turnaround time on some commercial flights from the current 45 minutes to 20 minutes for Boeing 737s. Below is a list of procedures that must be completed before the flight can depart:
1. Ticket agent takes flight plan to pilot, who loads information into aircraft computer. About 130 passengers disembark from the plane.
2. Workers clean trash cans, seat pockets, lavatories, etc.
3. Catering personnel board plane and replenish supply of drinks and ice.
4. A fuel truck loads up to 5,300 gallons of fuel into aircraft's wings.
5. Baggage crews unload up to 4,000 pounds of luggage and 2,000 pounds of freight. "Runners" rush the luggage to baggage claim area in terminal.
6. Ramp agents, who help park aircraft upon arrival, "push" plane back away from gate.

The quick turn at USAir.

us they weren't getting their business done in one day," says a USAir spokeswoman. Stripping away amenities such as meals, pillows, and blankets means caterers and cleaners can turn the flights around more quickly and passengers can get where they going faster, she maintains.

However, flyers do lose some amenities, and there are other pitfalls. Some customers don't like the stricter boarding procedures. USAir, for example, has a "10-minute rule," which requires boarding 10 minutes or more before departure time. It also insists that all carry-on luggage fit into a "sizer box" at the gate, which is roughly the size of an overhead compartment. The box is intended to keep passengers from bringing on huge bags and holding up seating.

Some workers grumble about having to move faster. "They're not used to working this hard," says Tim Goodrich, a USAir ground-crew worker in Baltimore. "In the old days, you'd come to work and have 30 or 40 minutes before you did anything. Now, they've got to pick up the pace or get out."

USAir's competitors also use turnaround as a critical productivity measure. To ensure that service is at acceptable levels, JetBlue insists on a 35-minute turnaround for its planes. Southwest maintains a 40-minute turnaround as first or second in terms of domestic passenger volume. To remain competitive, USAir must continue to focus on turnarounds to build and maintain company productivity.

The Introductory Case describes one airline company's attempt to raise productivity. It explains how USAir is shortening the amount of time that its planes stay on the ground between flights by speeding up procedures for preparing a plane for takeoff. This chapter is designed to help managers in a company like USAir increase employee productivity.

This chapter emphasizes the fundamentals of **production control**—ensuring that an organization produces goods and services as planned. The primary discussion topics in the chapter are as follows:

1) Production
2) Operations management
3) Operations control
4) Selected operations control tools

Production control ensures that an organization produces goods and services as planned.

PRODUCTION

To reach organizational goals, all managers must plan, organize, influence, and control to produce some type of goods or services. Naturally, these goods and services vary significantly from organization to organization. This section of the chapter defines production and productivity and discusses the relationship between quality and productivity and automation.

Defining Production

Production is the transformation of organizational resources into products.[1] In this definition, *organizational resources* are all assets available to a manager to generate products, *transformation* is the set of steps necessary to change these resources into products, and *products* are various goods or services aimed at meeting human needs. Inputs at a manufacturing firm, for example, would include raw materials, purchased parts, production workers, and even schedules. The transformation process would encompass the preparation of customer orders, the design of various products, the procurement of raw materials, and the production, assembly, and (perhaps) warehousing of products. Outputs, of course, would consist of products fit for customer use.

"Production" occurs at service organizations as well. Inputs at a hospital, for instance, would include ambulances, rooms, employees (doctors, nurses, administrators, receptionists), supplies (medicines, bandages, food), and (as at a manufacturer) funds, schedules, and records. The transformation process might begin with transporting patients to the facility and end with discharging them. In between, the hospital would attend to patients' needs (nursing and feeding them, administering their medication, recording their progress). The output here is health care.

Production is the transformation of organizational resources into products.

Productivity

Productivity is an important consideration in designing, evaluating, and improving modern production systems. We can define **productivity** as the relationship between the total amount of goods or services being produced (output) and the organizational resources needed to produce them (input). This relationship is usually expressed by the following equation:[2]

$$\text{productivity} = \frac{\text{outputs}}{\text{inputs}}$$

Productivity is the relationship between the total amount of goods or services being produced (output) and the organizational resources needed to produce them (input).

The higher the value of the ratio of outputs to inputs, the higher the productivity of the operation.

Managers should continually strive to make their production processes as productive as possible. It is no secret that over the last 20 years, the rate of productivity growth related to production management and innovation in U.S. manufacturing has lagged significantly behind that of countries such as Japan, West Germany, and France.[3] Some of the more traditional strategies for increasing productivity are as follows:[4]

1. Improving the effectiveness of the organizational workforce through training
2. Improving the production process through automation
3. Improving product design to make products easier to assemble
4. Improving the production facility by purchasing more modern equipment
5. Improving the quality of workers hired to fill open positions

DIGITAL FOCUS

▶ Sallie Mae Uses the Internet to Improve Productivity

Productivity is discussed in this chapter as the total amount of goods or services produced given the resources needed to produce them. This section describes recent action taken at the Student Loan Marketing Association (Sallie Mae) to try to improve productivity. In this case, management attempted to improve productivity by using the Internet to improve customer service while reducing the time customer representatives spent on customers.

Sallie Mae is a lending institution committed to making college education more affordable for students and their families. Borrowing from a Sallie Mae lender enables students to participate in money-saving programs and flexible repayment plans. Sallie Mae is one of the nation's largest financial services companies, providing funds for education loans and servicing accounts to borrowers.

Recently, Sallie Mae went live with a new Web site that lets users directly access individual loan information that is stored on main-frame computers from any browser-equipped client. A variety of options on Sallie Mae's Internet self-service menu lets users quickly get information on loan balances and details on any other services or options available. Previously, students and other users had to call Sallie Mae service representatives to get the information.

Israel Gotay, vice president of information technology at Sallie Mae, believes that the new Internet application has created an easier way for the organization to offer services to its customers while increasing customer representative productivity. According to Gotay, Sallie Mae initiated its Web site to contain costs. Like any institution that provides call-center service, there is some advantage to having information on the Web instead of having customers call an operator.

Quality and Productivity

Quality can be defined as how well a product does what it is intended to do—how closely it satisfies the specifications to which it was built. In a broad sense, quality is the degree of excellence on which products or services can be ranked on the basis of selected features or characteristics. It is customers who determine this ranking, and customers define quality in terms of appearance, performance, availability, flexibility, and reliability. Product quality determines an organization's reputation.

During the last decade or so, managerial thinking about the relationship between quality and productivity has changed drastically. Many earlier managers chose to achieve higher levels of productivity simply by producing a greater number of products given some fixed level of available resources. They saw no relationship between improving quality and increasing productivity. Quite the contrary: They viewed quality improvement as a controlling activity that took place toward the end of the production process and largely consisted of rejecting a number of finished products that were too obviously flawed to be offered to customers. Under this approach, quality improvement efforts were generally believed to *lower* productivity.

Focus on Continual Improvement Management theorists have more recently discovered that concentrating on improving product quality throughout all phases of a production process actually improves the productivity of the manufacturing system.[5] U.S. companies were far behind the Japanese in making this discovery. As early as 1948, Japanese companies observed that continual improvements in product quality throughout the production process normally resulted in improved productivity. How does this happen? According to Dr. W. Edwards Deming, a world-renowned quality expert, a serious and consistent quality focus normally reduces nonproductive variables such as the reworking of products, production mistakes, delays and production snags, and inefficient use of time and materials.

Quality is the extent to which a product reliably does what it is intended to do.

Quality inspectors check out a new Mustang at Ford Motor Company's Rouge Center, a 1917 factory in Dearborn, Michigan, that was long in decline and that the company now plans to rebuild and rehabilitate with production techniques that minimize long-term environmental damage. With numerous new skylights, overhead walkways to protect workers from machinery, conference rooms, cafeterias, redesigned and ergonomic work stations, and a "living roof" of plants intended to reduce harmful runoff and insulate the building, employees should experience a much improved workplace. Says United Auto Workers' Jerry Sullivan, president of Local 600, "If you feel good while you're working, I think quality and productivity will increase, and Ford thinks that, too, otherwise they wouldn't do this."

Deming believed that for continual improvement to become a way of life in an organization, managers need to understand their company and its operations. Most managers feel they do know their company and its operations, but when they begin drawing flowcharts, they discover that their understanding of strategy, systems, and processes is far from complete. Deming recommended that managers question every aspect of an operation and involve workers in discussion before they take action to improve operations. He maintained that a manager who seriously focuses on improving product quality throughout all phases of a production process will initiate a set of chain reactions that benefits not only the organization, but also the society in which the organization exists.

Bridgestone/Firestone and Ford: Product Quality Triggers Social Responsibility Debate

In 1990, Bridgestone U.S.A. merged with the Firestone Tire & Rubber Company to form Bridgestone/Firestone, Inc. The merger resulted in the establishment of a powerful international tire manufacturer with 38 production facilities throughout the Americas.

Bridgestone/Firestone prides itself on being a leader in tire technology. The company has research and development centers in Tokyo, Akron, and Rome, and to test its products, it has world-class proving grounds in Ft. Stockton, Texas; Sao Pedro, Brazil; and Acuna, Mexico.

Despite all of this focus on research, significant controversy has recently arisen concerning the quality of the company's products. Firestone has admitted that design and manufacturing problems contributed to tire failures resulting in 148 U.S. traffic deaths. For example, Lori Erickson, 25 years old, and her husband Scott Erickson, 28,

died when the tread came off a Firestone tire on her Ford Explorer, a very popular sport utility vehicle.

Following a growing number of such incidents involving the combination of Bridgestone/Firestone tires and Ford Explorers, no one seems any closer to finding the root cause of this safety crisis. Ford now charges that it has found new damning evidence indicating that the quality of Firestone tires is the cause of the problem. Bridgestone/Firestone has countered by claiming that its evidence clearly shows that the design quality of the Ford Explorer is at fault. Given this controversy, the federal government's Department of Transportation may have to get involved to delineate where the social responsibilities exist in this situation and how they should be met. ■

Focus on Quality and Integrated Operations   Deming's flow diagram for improving product quality (see Figure 20.1) contains a complete set of organizational variables. It introduces the customer into the operations process and introduces the idea of continually refining knowledge, design, and inputs into the process in order to constantly increase customer satisfaction. The diagram shows the operations process as an integrated whole, from the first input to actual use of the finished product; a problem at the beginning of the process will impact the

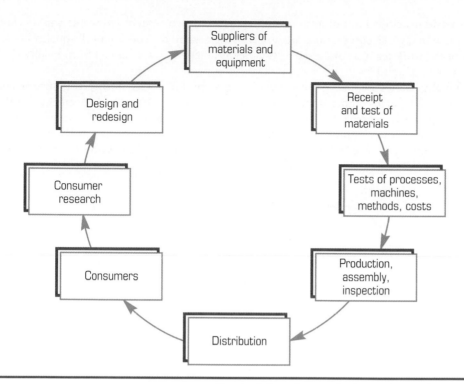

Deming's flow diagram for improving product quality

Figure 20.1

whole process and the end product. In Deming's scheme, there are no barriers between the company and the customer, between the customer and suppliers, or between the company and its employees. Since the process is unified, the greater the harmony among all its components, the better the results will be.

An organization's interpretation of quality is expressed in its strategies. The following sections elaborate on the relationship between quality and production by discussing quality assurance and quality circles as part of organizational strategy.

Quality Assurance   **Quality assurance** is an operations process involving a broad group of activities aimed at achieving the organization's quality objectives.[6] Quality assurance is a continuum of activities that starts when quality standards are set and ends when quality goods and services are delivered to the customer. Although the precise activities involved in quality assurance vary from organization to organization, activities like determining the safest system for delivering goods to customers and maintaining the quality of parts or materials purchased from suppliers are part of most quality assurance efforts.

Statistical Quality Control   Statistical quality control is a much narrower concept than quality assurance. **Statistical quality control** is the process used to determine how many products should be inspected to calculate a probability that the total number of products will meet organizational quality standards. An effective quality assurance strategy reduces the need for quality control and subsequent corrective actions.

"No Rejects" Philosophy   Quality assurance works best when management adopts a "no rejects" philosophy. Unfortunately, such a philosophy is not economically feasible for most mass-produced products. What is possible is training employees to approach production with a "do not make the same mistake once" mind set. Mistakes are costly. Detecting defective products in the final quality control inspection is very expensive. Emphasizing quality in the early stages—during product and process design—will reduce rejects and production costs.

Quality Circles   The recent trend in U.S. organizations is to involve all company employees in quality control by soliciting their ideas for judging and maintaining product quality.

Quality assurance is an operations process involving a broad group of activities that are aimed at achieving the organization's quality objectives.

Statistical quality control is the process used to determine how many products should be inspected to calculate a probability that the total number of products will meet organizational quality standards.

This trend developed out of a successful Japanese control system known as *quality circles*. Although many U.S. corporations are now moving beyond the concept of the quality circle to that of the work team, as discussed in Chapter 17, many ideas generated from quality circles continue to be valid.[7]

Quality circles are small groups of workers that meet to discuss quality assurance of a particular project and to communicate their solutions to these problems to management directly at a formal presentation session. Figure 20.2 shows the quality circle problem-solving process.

Most quality circles operate in a similar manner. The circle usually has fewer than eight members, and the circle leader is not necessarily the members' supervisor. Members may be

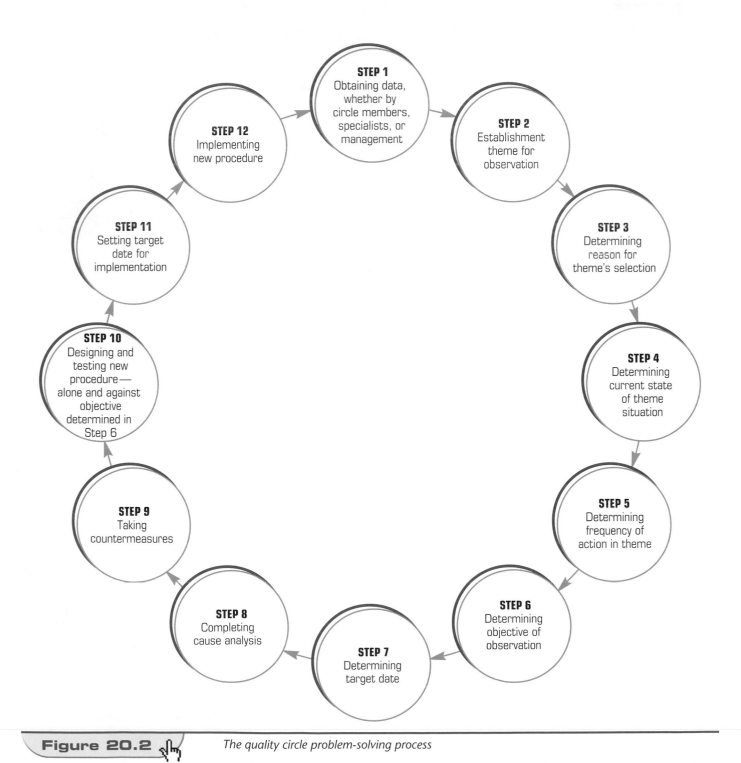

Figure 20.2   *The quality circle problem-solving process*

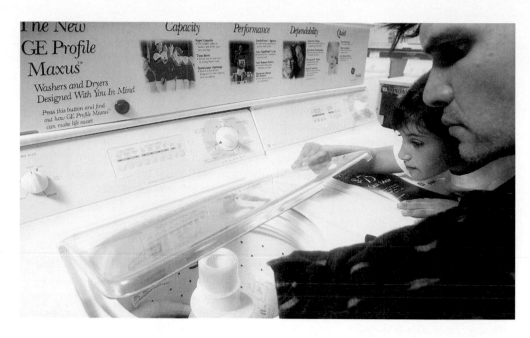

The bad news is that productivity is a little sluggish: General Electric cannot make quite enough Maxus washing machines to keep up with demand. The good news: With 40 percent fewer parts, a larger tub, and a new suspension that reduces both noise and vibration, the Maxus is a high-quality product. GE collected data from both market research studies and service technicians in order to design its first really new washing machine in over 40 years, and managers attribute productivity snags to predictable but temporary start-up problems.

workers on the project and/or outsiders. The focus is on operational problems rather than interpersonal ones. The problems discussed in the quality circle may be ones assigned by management or ones uncovered by the group itself.

Focusing on Quality at Adidas USA

Adidas USA, Inc., an athletic apparel company, is best known for its athletic footwear. Events at Adidas illustrate that, without proper control aimed at enhancing profit, an organization may not last long enough to have the opportunity to focus on enhancing product quality.

Although Adidas USA lost significant amounts of money in the late 1980s, the company seemed to turn the corner in the early 1990s. It went from a $63 million loss in 1989 to a $2 million profit in 1990. This profit, although small, was highly significant because it was achieved despite an 11 percent drop in revenues, to $249 million. Staff reductions and an emphasis on collecting overdue receivables were important control measures that helped to produce the turnaround in earnings. The company also exercised control by analyzing product lines weekly to assess and increase the contributions to profit that each line was making.

Adidas's chief financial officer, Andrew P. Hines, conceded that these and other cost controls instituted by the company were primarily one-time measures. According to Hines, after the company was once again profitable, its challenge was to build lasting quality in both its staff and its products. Adidas USA dominated the U.S. market for athletic footwear in the 1970s, but strong competition and internal problems in the 1980s caused its market share to dwindle from more than 60 percent to 4 percent. Hines believed that such measures as creating a pay-for-performance plan, clarifying and documenting job responsibilities, and instituting critical training programs allowed Adidas to build more quality into its staff and its products.

In 1992, Adidas was acquired by Britain's Pentland Group, which plans to invigorate the Adidas brand name by upgrading products, improving distribution, and signing up more big-name endorsers. ■

Automation

The preceding section discussed the relationship between quality and productivity organizations. This section introduces the topic of automation, which shows signs of increasing organizational productivity in a revolutionary way.[8]

Automation is defined as the replacement of human effort by electromechanical devices in such operations as welding, materials handling, design, drafting, and decision making. It includes robots—mechanical devices built to perform repetitive tasks efficiently—and **robotics**—the study of the development and use of robots.

Over the past 20 years, a host of advanced manufacturing systems have been developed and implemented to support operations. Most of these are automated systems that combine hardware-industrial robots and computers—and software. The goals of new automation

Robotics is the study of the development and use of robots.

include reduced inventories, higher productivity, and faster billing and product distribution cycles. So far, the industrialized Asian countries appear to be doing the best job of making optimal use of company resources through automation.

Strategies, Systems, and Processes

According to Kemper and Yehudai, an effective and efficient operations manager is skilled not only in management, production, and productivity, but also in strategies, systems, and processes. A *strategy* is a plan of action. A *system* is a particular linking of organizational components that facilitates carrying out a process. A *process* is a flow of interrelated events toward a goal, purpose, or end. Strategies create interlocking systems and processes when they are comprehensive, functional, and dynamic—when they designate responsibility and provide criteria for measuring output.[9]

► Back to the Case

Increasing productivity at USAir, as described in the Introductory Case, is mainly a matter of integrating resources such as people, equipment, and materials to provide better customer service.

Although productivity at USAir was far from disastrous, management seems to have decided that it was necessary to lower operating costs through improved productivity in order to stay competitive in the increasingly combative airline carrier business. USAir's first move to increase productivity has been the "quick-turn" strategy described in the Introductory Case—taking less time to ready a plane for takeoff after it has landed so customers will have shorter waits for flights. To improve productivity even further, USAir might consider implementing more effective training programs for employees and instituting more selective hiring procedures. In addition, company managers could evaluate the possibility of using robots to further shorten airport turnaround time. This strategy has the added advantage that robots would make fewer errors than humans.

To maintain and improve the quality of customer services like shorter turnaround time, USAir management could establish a quality assurance program that continually monitors services to ensure that they are at acceptable levels. Quality circles could be established to involve employees in the effort to improve customer service in both the specific area of turnaround time and in more general terms.

OPERATIONS MANAGEMENT

Operations management deals with managing the production of goods and services in organizations. The sections that follow define *operations management* and discuss various strategies that managers can use to make production activities more effective and efficient.

Defining Operations Management

Operations management is performance of managerial activities entailed in selecting, designing, operating, controlling, and updating production systems.

According to Chase and Aquilano, **operations management** is performance of managerial activities entailed in selecting, designing, operating, controlling, and updating production systems.[10] Figure 20.3 describes these activities and categorizes them as either periodic or continual. The distinction between periodic and continual activities is one of relative frequency of performance: Periodic activities are performed from time to time, while continual activities are performed essentially without interruption.

Operations Management Considerations

Overall, *operations management* is the systematic direction and control of operations processes that transform resources into finished goods and services.[11] The concept conveys three key notions:

➤ Operations management involves managers—people who get things done by working with or through other people
➤ Operations management takes place within the context of objectives and policies that drive the organization's strategic plans

```
                    ┌─────────────────────────┐
                    │ OPERATIONS MANAGEMENT   │
                    │        ACTIVITIES       │
                    └─────────────────────────┘
                ┌──────────────┴──────────────┐
          ┌──────────┐                   ┌──────────┐
          │ Periodic │                   │ Continual│
          └──────────┘                   └──────────┘
```

SELECTING	DESIGNING	UPDATING	OPERATING, CONTROLLING
Selecting products, processes, equipment, and workforce	Designing products, processes, equipment, jobs, methods, wage payments, and operating and control systems	Revising the production system in light of new products and processes, technological breakthroughs, shifts in demand, new managerial techniques, research findings, and failures in existing products, processes, or operating and control systems	Setting production levels and scheduling production and workforce, managing inventory, and overseeing quality assurance programs

Major activities performed to manage production

Figure 20.3

➤ The criteria for judging the actions taken as a result of operations management are standards for effectiveness and efficiency

Effectiveness is the degree to which managers attain organizational objectives: "doing the right things." **Efficiency** is the degree to which organizational resources contribute to productivity: "doing things right." A review of organizational performance based on these standards is essential to enhancing the success of any organization.

Operations strategies—capacity, location, product, process, layout, and human resources—are specific plans of action designed to ensure that resources are obtained and used effectively and efficiently. An operational strategy is implemented by people who get things done with and through people. It is achieved in the context of objectives and policies derived from the organization's strategic plan.

Capacity Strategy   **Capacity strategy** is a plan of action aimed at providing the organization with the right facilities to produce the needed output at the right time. The output capacity of the organization determines its ability to meet future demands for goods and services. *Insufficient capacity* results in loss of sales that, in turn, affects profits. *Excess capacity* results in higher production costs. A strategy that aims for *optimal capacity,* where quantity and timing are in balance, provides an excellent basis for minimizing operating costs and maximizing profits.

Capacity flexibility enables the company to deliver its goods and services to its customers in a shorter time than its competitors. This component of capacity strategy involves having flexible plants and processes, broadly trained employees, and easy and economical access to external capacity, such as suppliers.

Managers use capacity strategy to balance the costs of overcapacity and undercapacity. The difficulty of accurately forecasting long-term demand makes this balancing task risky. Modifying long-range capacity decisions while in production is both hard and costly. In a highly competitive environment, construction of a new high-tech facility might take longer than the life cycle of the product. Correcting overcapacity by closing a plant saddles management with high economic costs and even higher social costs—such as lost jobs that devastate both employees and the community in which the plant operates—that will have a long-term adverse effect on the firm.

Effectiveness is the degree to which managers attain organizational objectives; it is doing the right things.

Efficiency is the degree to which organizational resources contribute to production; it is doing things right.

Capacity strategy is an operational plan of action aimed at providing the organization with the right facilities to produce the needed output at the right time.

The traditional concept of economies of scale led management to construct large plants that tried to do everything. The more modern concept of the focused facility has led management to conclude that better performance can be achieved in more specialized plants that concentrate on fewer tasks and are therefore smaller.

Five Steps in Capacity Decisions   Managers are more likely to make sound strategic capacity decisions if they adhere to the following five-step process:

1. Measure the capacity of currently available facilities
2. Estimate future capacity needs on the basis of demand forecasts
3. Compare future capacity needs and available capacity to determine whether capacity must be increased or decreased
4. Identify ways to accommodate long-range capacity changes (expansion or reduction)
5. Select the best alternative based on a quantitative and qualitative evaluation

Location Strategy
Location strategy is a plan of action that provides the organization with a competitive location for its headquarters, manufacturing, services, and distribution activities. A competitive location results in lower transportation and communication costs among the various facilities. These costs—which run as high as 20 to 30 percent of a product's selling price—greatly affect the volume of sales and amount of profit generated by a particular product. Many other quantitative and qualitative factors are important when formulating location strategy.

Factors in a Good Location   A successful location strategy requires a company to consider the following major factors in its location study:

➤ Nearness to market and distribution centers
➤ Nearness to vendors and resources
➤ Requirements of federal, state, and local governments
➤ The character of direct competition
➤ The degree of interaction with the rest of the corporation
➤ The quality and quantity of labor pools
➤ The environmental attractiveness of the area
➤ Taxes and financing requirements
➤ Existing and potential transportation
➤ The quality of utilities and services

The dynamic nature of these factors could make what is a competitive location today an undesirable location in five years.

Product Strategy
Product strategy is an operational plan of action outlining which goods and services an organization will produce and market.[12] Product strategy is a main component of an organization's operations strategy—in fact, it is the link between the operations strategy and the other functional strategies, especially marketing and research and development. In essence, product, marketing, and research and development strategies must fit together if management is to be able to build an effective overall operations strategy. A business's product and operations strategies should take into account the strengths and weaknesses of operations, which are primarily internal, as well as those of other functional areas concerned more with external opportunities and threats.

Cooperation and coordination among its marketing, operations, and research and development departments from the inception of a new product are strongly beneficial to a company. At the very least, it ensures a smooth transition from research and development to production, since operations people will be able to contribute to the quality of the total product, rather than merely attempt to improve the quality of the components. Even the most sophisticated product can be designed so that it is relatively simple to produce, thus reducing the number of units that must be scrapped or reworked during production, as well as the need for

▶ Procter & Gamble's efforts to prevent assembly line breakdowns in the manufacture of its paper towel products have saved billions of dollars in wasted materials since 1990. The technical and statistical innovations the firm developed in the process have proven so successful in increasing efficiency that P&G is now preparing to market its toolbox of "reliability engineering" methods to other firms.

Location strategy is an operational plan of action that provides the organization with a competitive location for its headquarters, manufacturing, services, and distribution activities.

Product strategy is an operational plan of action outlining which goods and services an organization will produce and market.

highly trained and highly paid employees. All of these strategies lower production costs and hence increase the product's price competitiveness or profits or both.

Process Strategy

Process strategy is a plan of action outlining the means and methods the organization will use to transform resources into goods and services. Materials, labor, information, equipment, and managerial skills are resources that must be transformed. A competitive process strategy will ensure the most efficient and effective use of these organizational resources.

Process strategy is an operational plan of action outlining the means and methods the organization will use to transform resources into goods and services.

Types of Processes

All manufacturing processes may be grouped into three different types. The first is the *continuous process*, a product-oriented, high-volume, low-variety process used, for example, in producing chemicals, beer, and petroleum products. The second is the *repetitive process*, a product-oriented production process that uses modules to produce items in large lots. This mass-production or assembly-line process is characteristic of the auto and appliance industries.

The third type of manufacturing process is used to produce small lots of custom-designed products such as furniture. This high-variety, low-volume system, commonly known as the *job-shop process*, includes the production of one-of-a-kind items as well as unit production. Spaceship and weapons systems production are considered job-shop activities.

Organizations commonly employ more than one type of manufacturing process at the same time and in the same facility.

Process strategy is directly linked to product strategy. The decision to select a particular process strategy is often the result of external market opportunities or threats. When this is true, the corporation decides what it wants to produce, then selects a process strategy to produce it. The product takes center stage and the process becomes a function of the product.

The function of process strategy is to determine what equipment will be used, what maintenance will be necessary, and what level of automation will be most effective and efficient. The type of employees and the level of employee skills needed are dependent on the process strategy chosen.

Layout Strategy

Layout strategy is a plan of action that outlines the location and flow of all organizational resources around, into, and within production and service facilities. A cost-effective and cost-efficient layout strategy is one that minimizes the expenses of processing, transporting, and storing materials throughout the production and service cycle.

Layout strategy is an operational plan that determines the location and flow of organizational resources around, into, and within production and service facilities.

Layout strategy—which is usually the last part of operations strategy to be formulated—is closely linked, either directly or indirectly, with all other components of operations strategy: capacity, location, product, process, and human resources. It must target capacity and process requirements. It must satisfy the organization's product design, quality, and quantity requirements. It must target facility and location requirements. Finally, to be effective, the layout strategy must be compatible with the organization's established quality of work life.

A **layout** is the overall arrangement of equipment, work areas, service areas, and storage areas within a facility that produces goods or provides services.[13] There are three basic types of layouts for manufacturing facilities:

A **layout** is the overall arrangement of equipment, work areas, service areas, and storage areas within a facility that produces goods or provides services.

1. A **product layout** is designed to accommodate high production volumes, highly specialized equipment, and narrow employee skills. It is appropriate for organizations that produce and service a limited number of different products. It is not appropriate for an organization that experiences constant or frequent changes of products.

A **product layout** is a layout designed to accommodate a limited number of different products that require high volumes, highly specialized equipment, and narrow employee skills.

2. A **process (functional) layout** is a layout pattern that groups together similar types of equipment. It is appropriate for organizations involved in a large number of different tasks. It best serves companies whose production volumes are low, whose equipment is multipurpose, and whose employees' skills are broad.

A **process (functional) layout** is a layout pattern based primarily on grouping together similar types of equipment.

3. The **fixed-position layout** is one in which the product is stationary while resources flow. It is appropriate for organizations involved in a large number of different tasks that require low volumes, multipurpose equipment, and broad employee skills. A *group technology layout* is a product layout cell within a larger process layout. It benefits organizations that require both types of layout.

A **fixed-position layout** is a layout plan appropriate for organizations involved in a large number of different tasks that require low volumes, multipurpose equipment, and broad employee skills.

Figure 20.4 illustrates the three basic layout patterns. Actually, most manufacturing facilities are a combination of two or more different types of layouts. Various techniques are avail-

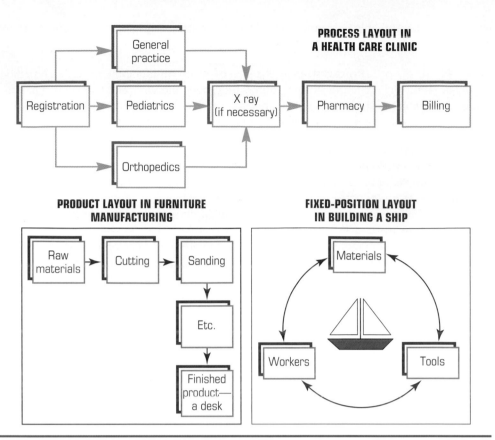

PROCESS LAYOUT IN A HEALTH CARE CLINIC

General practice

Registration

Pediatrics

X ray (if necessary)

Pharmacy

Billing

Orthopedics

PRODUCT LAYOUT IN FURNITURE MANUFACTURING

Raw materials → Cutting → Sanding

Etc.

Finished product— a desk

FIXED-POSITION LAYOUT IN BUILDING A SHIP

Materials

Workers

Tools

Figure 20.4

The three basic layout patterns

able to assist management in designing an efficient and effective layout that meets the required specifications.

Human Resources Strategy *Human resources* is the term used for individuals engaged in any of the organization's activities. There are two human resource imperatives:

1. It is essential to optimize individual, group, and organizational effectiveness
2. It is essential to enhance the quality of organizational life

A **human resources strategy** is an operational plan to use the organization's human resources effectively and efficiently while maintaining or improving the quality of work life.[14]

As discussed in Chapter 12, human resource management is about employees—who are the best means of enhancing organizational effectiveness. Whereas financial management attempts to increase organizational effectiveness through the allocation and conservation of financial resources, human resource management (personnel management) attempts to increase organizational effectiveness through such factors as the establishment of personnel policies, education and training, and procedures.

Operational Tools in Human Resources Strategy Operations management attempts to increase organizational effectiveness by employing the methods used in the manufacturing and service processes. Human resources, one very important factor of operations, must be compatible with operations tasks.

Manpower planning is the primary focus of the operations human resources strategy. It is an operational plan for hiring the right employees for a job and training them to be productive. This is a lengthy and costly process. A human resources strategy must be founded on fair treatment and trust. The employee, not operations, must take center stage.

Job design is an operational plan that determines who will do a specific job and how and where the job will be done. The goal of job design is to facilitate productivity. Successful job

A **human resources strategy** is an operational plan to use the organization's human resources effectively and efficiently while maintaining or improving the quality of work life.

Manpower planning is an operational plan that focuses on hiring the right employees for a job and training them to be productive.

Job design is an operational plan that determines who will do a specific job and how and where the job will be done.

design takes efficiency and behavior into account. It also guarantees that working conditions are safe and that the health of employees will not be jeopardized in the short or the long run.

Work methods analysis is an operational tool used to improve productivity and ensure the safety of workers. It can be performed for new or existing jobs. **Motion-study techniques** are another set of operational tools used to improve productivity.

Work measurement methods are operational tools used to establish labor standards. These standards are useful for planning, control, productivity improvements, costing and pricing, bidding, compensation, motivation, and financial incentives.

> ## ► Back to the Case
>
> In attempting to speed up plane turnaround, USAir's management is involved in operations management. Most of the issues mentioned in the Introductory Case pertain to the "periodic updating" segment of operations management activities—revising systems to provide better customer service. USAir's periodic updating should focus on the appropriate use of company resources like ticket agents, caterers, fuel trucks, and ramp agents. Once established, the new operations procedure must be continually monitored by USAir's management for both effectiveness—"doing the right things"—and efficiency—"doing things right."
>
> Factors USAir's management must consider in making operations decisions are: *capacity strategy*, making sure that the airline has appropriate resources to perform needed functions at appropriate times; *location strategy*, making sure that airline resources are appropriately postured for work when the work must be performed; *product strategy*, making sure that appropriate customer services are targeted and provided; *process strategy*, making sure that USAir is employing appropriate steps in providing various customer services; *layout strategy*, making sure that the flow of USAir's resources in the process of providing customer services is desirable; and *human resources strategy*, making sure that USAir has appropriate people providing services to customers.

Work methods analysis is an operational tool used to improve productivity and ensure the safety of workers.

Motion-study techniques are operational tools that are used to improve productivity.

Work measurement methods are operational tools that are used to establish labor standards.

OPERATIONS CONTROL

Once a decision has been made to design an operational plan of action, resource allocations are considered. After management has decided on a functional operations strategy, using marketing and financial plans of action, it determines what specific tasks are necessary to accomplish functional objectives. This is known as *operations control*.

Operations control is defined as making sure that operations activities are carried out as planned. The major components of operations control are *just-in-time inventory control*, *maintenance control*, *cost control*, *budgetary control*, *ratio analysis*, and *materials control*. Each of these components is discussed in detail in the following sections.

Just-in-Time Inventory Control

Just-in-time (JIT) inventory control is a technique for reducing inventories to a minimum by arranging for production components to be delivered to the production facility "just in time" to be used.[15] The concept, developed primarily by the Toyota Motor Company of Japan, is also called "zero inventory" or *kanban*—the latter a Japanese term referring to purchasing raw materials by using a special ordering form.[16]

JIT is based on the management philosophy that products should be manufactured only when customers need them and only in the quantities customers require in order to minimize the amounts of raw materials and finished goods inventories manufacturers keep on hand. It emphasizes maintaining organizational operations by using only the resources that are absolutely necessary to meet customer demand.

Best Conditions for JIT JIT works best in companies that manufacture relatively standardized products for which there is consistent demand. Such companies can comfortably order materials from suppliers and assemble products in small, continuous batches. The result is a smooth, consistent flow of purchased materials and assembled products, with little inven-

Operations control is an operational plan that specifies the operational activities of an organization.

Just-in-time (JIT) inventory control is a technique for reducing inventories to a minimum by arranging for production components to be delivered to the production facility "just in time" to be used.

tory buildup. Companies that manufacture nonstandardized products for which there is sporadic or seasonal demand, however, generally face more irregular purchases of raw materials from suppliers, more uneven production cycles, and greater accumulations of inventory.

Advantages of JIT   When successfully implemented, JIT enhances organizational performance in several important ways. First, it reduces the unnecessary labor expenses generated by manufacturing products that are not sold. Second, it minimizes the tying up of monetary resources in purchases of production-related materials that do not result in timely sales. Third, it helps management hold down inventory expenses—particularly storage and handling costs. Better inventory management and control of labor costs, in fact, are the two most commonly cited benefits of JIT.

Characteristics of JIT   Experience indicates that successful JIT programs have certain common characteristics:[17]

1. *Closeness of suppliers*—Manufacturers using JIT find it beneficial to use raw materials suppliers who are based only a short distance from them. When a company is ordering smaller quantities of raw materials at a time, suppliers must sometimes be asked to make one or more deliveries per day. Short distances make multiple deliveries per day feasible.
2. *High quality of materials purchased from suppliers*—Manufacturers using JIT find it especially difficult to overcome problems caused by defective materials. Since they keep their materials inventory small, defective materials purchased from a supplier may force them to discontinue the production process until another delivery from the supplier can be arranged. Such production slowdowns can be disadvantageous, causing late delivery to customers or lost sales.
3. *Well-organized receiving and handling of materials purchased from suppliers*—Companies using JIT must be able to receive and handle raw materials effectively and efficiently. Materials must be available for the production process where and when they are needed, because if they are not, extra costs will be built into the production process.
4. *Strong management commitment*—Management must be strongly committed to the concept of JIT. The system takes time and effort to plan, install, and improve—and is therefore expensive to implement. Management must be willing to commit funds to initiate the JIT system and to support it once it is functioning.

Maintenance Control

Maintenance control is aimed at keeping the organization's facility and equipment functioning at predetermined work levels. In the planning stage, managers must select a strategy that will direct personnel to fix equipment either before it malfunctions or after it malfunctions. The first strategy is referred to as a **pure-preventive maintenance policy**—machine adjustments, lubrication, cleaning, parts replacement, painting, and needed repairs and overhauls are done regularly, before facilities or machines malfunction. At the other end of the maintenance control continuum is the **pure-breakdown (repair) policy,** which decrees that facilities and equipment be fixed only after they malfunction.

Most organizations implement a maintenance strategy somewhere in the middle of the maintenance continuum. Management usually tries to select a level and a frequency of maintenance that minimize the cost of both preventive maintenance and breakdowns (repair). Since no level of preventive maintenance can eliminate breakdowns altogether, repair will always be an important activity.

Whether management decides on a pure-preventive or pure-breakdown policy, or on something in between, the prerequisite for a successful maintenance program is the availability of maintenance parts and supplies or replacement (standby) equipment. Some organizations choose to keep standby machines to protect themselves against the consequences of breakdowns. Plants that use special-purpose equipment are more likely to invest in standby equipment than those that use general-purpose equipment.

Cost Control

Cost control is broad control aimed at keeping organizational costs at planned levels.[18] Since cost control relates to all organizational costs, it emphasizes activities in all organizational

Pure-preventive maintenance policy is a maintenance control policy that tries to ensure that machine adjustments, lubrication, cleaning, parts replacement, painting, and needed repairs and overhauls will be performed before facilities or machines malfunction.

Pure-breakdown (repair) policy is a maintenance control policy that decrees that machine adjustments, lubrication, cleaning, parts replacement, painting, and needed repairs and overhaul will be performed only after facilities or machines malfunction.

According to auto industry analysts, "Toyota wants nothing less than to be the world's lowest-cost producer of the highest-quality automobiles." A major part of achieving that goal is cost-cutting, and Toyota plans to cut $1.5 billion from its procurements costs. But will it be enough? With sales less than half its rival's, Nissan expects to cut a full 10 percent from its parts costs, a savings of at least $2.25 billion, by more tightly managing its suppliers. Thus, operational controls loom large in the profit strategies of both firms.

areas, such as research and development, operations, marketing, and finance. If an organization is to be successful, costs in all organizational areas must be controlled. Cost control is therefore an important responsibility of all managers in an organization.

Operations activities are very cost-intensive—perhaps the most cost-intensive of all organizational activities—so when significant cost savings are realized in organizations, they are generally realized at the operations level.

Operations managers are responsible for the overall control of the cost of goods or services sold. Since producing goods and services at or below planned cost levels is their principal objective, operations managers are commonly evaluated primarily on their cost control activities. When operations costs are consistently above planned levels, the organization may need to change its operations management.

Stages in Cost Control The general cost control process has four stages:

1. Establishing standard or planned cost amounts
2. Measuring actual costs incurred
3. Comparing planned costs to incurred costs
4. Making changes to reduce actual costs to planned costs when necessary

Following these stages for specific operations cost control, the operations manager must first establish planned costs or cost standards for operations activities like labor, materials, and overhead. Next, the operations manager must actually measure or calculate the costs incurred for these activities. Third, the operations manager must compare actual operations costs to planned operations costs, and fourth, take steps to reduce actual operations costs to planned levels if necessary.

Budgetary Control

As described in Chapter 9, a budget is a single-use financial plan that covers a specified length of time. An organization's **budget** is its financial plan outlining how funds in a given period will be obtained and spent.

In addition to being a financial plan, however, a budget can be the basis for *budgetary control*—that is, for ensuring that income and expenses occur as planned. As managers gather information on actual receipts and expenditures within an operating period, they may uncover significant deviations from budgeted amounts. If that be the case, they should develop and implement a control strategy aimed at bringing actual performance into line with planned performance. This, of course, assumes that the plan contained in the budget is appropriate for the organization. The following sections discuss some potential pitfalls of budgets and human relations considerations that may make a budget inappropriate.

A **budget** is a control tool that outlines how funds will be obtained and spent in a given period.

Potential Pitfalls of Budgets To maximize the benefits of using budgets, managers must avoid several potential pitfalls. Among these pitfalls are the following:

1. *Placing too much emphasis on relatively insignificant organizational expenses*—In preparing and implementing a budget, managers should allocate more time for dealing with significant organizational expenses and less time for relatively insignificant organizational expenses. For example, the amount of time managers spend on developing and implementing a budget for labor costs typically should be much more than the amount of time they spend on developing and implementing a budget for office supplies.

2. *Increasing budgeted expenses year after year without adequate information*—It does not necessarily follow that items contained in last year's budget should be increased this year. Perhaps the best-known method for overcoming this potential pitfall is zero-base budgeting.[19] **Zero-base budgeting** is a planning and budgeting process that requires mangers to justify their entire budget request in detail rather than simply referring to budget amounts established in previous years.

    Some management theorists believe that zero-base budgeting is a better management tool than traditional budgeting—which simply starts with the budget amount established in the prior year—because it emphasizes focused identification and control of each budget item. It is unlikely, however, that this tool will be implemented successfully unless management adequately explains what zero-base budgeting is and how it is to be used in the organization. One of the earliest and most commonly cited successes in implementing a zero-base budgeting program took place in the Department of Agriculture's Office of Budget and Finance.

3. *Ignoring the fact that budgets must be changed periodically*—Managers should recognize that such factors as costs of materials, newly developed technology, and product demand change constantly and that budgets must be reviewed and modified periodically in response to these changes.

A special type of budget called a *variable budget* is sometimes used to determine automatically when such changes in budgets are needed. A **variable budget**, also known as a *flexible budget,* outlines the levels of resources to be allocated for each organizational activity according to the level of production within the organization. It follows, then, that a variable budget automatically indicates an increase in the amount of resources allocated for various organizational activities when production levels go up and a decrease when production goes down.

Human Relations Considerations in Using Budgets   Many managers believe that although budgets are valuable planning and control tools, they can result in major human relations problems in an organization. A classic article by Chris Argyris, for example, shows how budgets can build pressures that unite workers against management, cause harmful conflict between management and factory workers, and create tensions that result in worker inefficiency and worker aggression against management.[20] If such problems are severe enough, a budget may result in more harm to the organization than good.

Reducing Human Relations Problems   Several strategies have been suggested to minimize the human relations problems caused by budgets. The most often recommended strategy is to design and implement appropriate human relations training programs for finance personnel, accounting personnel, production supervisors, and all other key people involved in the formulation and use of budgets. These training programs should emphasize both the advantages and disadvantages of applying pressure on people through budgets and the possible results of using budgets to imply that an organization member is a success or a failure at his or her job.

Ratio Analysis

Another type of control uses ratio analysis.[21] A *ratio* is a relationship between two numbers that is calculated by dividing one number into the other. **Ratio analysis** is the process of generating information that summarizes the financial position of an organization through the calculation of ratios based on various financial measures that appear on the organization's balance sheet and income statements.

The ratios available to managers for controlling organizations, shown in Table 20.1, can be divided into four categories:

1. Liquidity ratios
2. Leverage ratios

Zero-base budgeting requires managers to justify their entire budget request in detail rather than simply referring to budget amounts established in previous years.

A variable budget (also known as a *flexible budget*) is one that outlines the levels of resources to be allocated for each organizational activity according to the level of production within the organization.

Ratio analysis is a control tool that summarizes the financial position of an organization by calculating ratios based on various financial measures.

Type	Example	Calculation	Interpretation
Profitability	Return on investment (ROI)	$\dfrac{\text{Profit after taxes}}{\text{Total assets}}$	Productivity of assets
Liquidity	Current ratio	$\dfrac{\text{Current assets}}{\text{Current liabilities}}$	Short-term solvency
Activity	Inventory turnover	$\dfrac{\text{Sales}}{\text{Inventory}}$	Efficiency of inventory management
Leverage	Debt ratio	$\dfrac{\text{Total debt}}{\text{Total assets}}$	How a company finances itself

3. Activity ratios

4. Profitability ratios

Using Ratios to Control Organizations   Managers should use ratio analysis in three ways to control an organization:[22]

➤ Managers should evaluate all ratios simultaneously. This strategy ensures that they will develop and implement a control strategy appropriate for the organization as a whole rather than one that suits only one phase or segment of the organization.

➤ Managers should compare computed values for ratios in a specific organization with the values of industry averages for those ratios. (The values of industry averages for the ratios can be obtained from Dun & Bradstreet; Robert Morris Associates, a national association of bank loan officers; the Federal Trade Commission; and the Securities and Exchange Commission.) Managers increase the probability of formulating and implementing appropriate control strategies when they compare their financial situation to that of competitors in this way.

➤ Managers' use of ratios should incorporate trend analysis. Managers must remember that any set of ratio values is actually only a determination of relationships that existed in a specified time period (often a year). To employ ratio analysis to maximum advantage, they need to accumulate ratio values for several successive time periods to uncover specific organizational trends. Once these trends are revealed, managers can formulate and implement appropriate strategies for dealing with them.

Materials Control

Materials control is an operations control activity that determines the flow of materials from vendors through an operations system to customers. The achievement of desired levels of product cost, quality, availability, dependability, and flexibility heavily depends on the effective and efficient flow of materials. Materials management activities can be broadly organized into six groups or functions: purchasing, receiving, inventorying, floor controlling, trafficking, and shipping and distributing.

Procurement of Materials   Over 50 percent of the expenditures of a typical manufacturing company are for the procurement of materials, including raw materials, parts, subassemblies, and supplies. This procurement is the responsibility of the purchasing department. Actually, purchases of production materials are largely automated and linked to a resources requirement planning system. Purchases of all other materials, however, are based on requisitions from users. The purchasing department's job does not end with the placement of an order; order follow-up is just as crucial.

Materials control is an operational activity that determines the flow of materials from vendors through an operations system to customers.

▶ One of the innovative ways in which building-products manufacturer USG Corporation controls the materials used in its East Chicago, Indiana, wallboard plant also happens to be good for the environment. The company gets all the gypsum it uses for fueling the plant from chemical sludge produced by scrubbing pollutants from smokestack gases to prevent acid rain. It also uses waste heat from its gas-fired kilns in Texas and New York to generate electricity, and it saves 35 million gallons of water a day by recycling at least 90 percent of the waste water at its seven paper mills.

Receiving, Shipping, and Trafficking   Receiving activities include unloading, identifying, inspecting, reporting, and storing inbound shipments. Shipping and distribution activities are similar. These may include preparing documents, packaging, labeling, loading, and directing outbound shipments to customers and to distribution centers. Shipping and receiving are sometimes organized as one unit.

A traffic manager's main responsibilities are selection of the transportation mode, coordination of the arrival and departure of shipments, and auditing freight bills.

Inventory and Shop-Floor Control   Inventory control activities ensure the continuous availability of purchased materials. Work-in-process and finished-goods inventory are inventory control subsystems. Inventory control specifies what, when, and how much to buy. Held inventories buffer the organization against a variety of uncertainties that can disrupt supply, but since holding inventory is costly, an optimal inventory control policy provides a predetermined level of certainty of supply at the lowest possible cost.

Shop-floor control activities include input/output control, scheduling, sequencing, routing, dispatching, and expediting.

While many materials management activities can be programmed, the human factor is the key to a competitive performance. Skilled and motivated employees are therefore crucial to successful materials control.

> ### ▶ Back to the Case
>
> Operations control activities help USAir's management make certain that customer services are carried out as planned. *Just-in-time inventory control,* for example, would ensure that pillows, blankets, ticketing materials, and packing materials are available just when customers need them. Putting money into large surpluses of these items would needlessly tie up company resources and reduce company profitability. *Maintenance control* would ensure that equipment (e.g., baggage conveyors) needed to provide customer services is operating at a desirable level. *Cost control* would ensure that USAir is not providing services to customers too expensively. *Budgetary control* would focus on acquiring company resources and using them to provide customer services as stipulated by USAir's financial plan.
>
> Operations control at USAir can also include ratio analysis, or determining relationships between various factors on USAir's income statement and balance sheet to arrive at a good indication of the company's financial position. Through ratio analysis, USAir's management could monitor issues like customer services to determine their overall impact on company profitability, liquidity, and leverage. To assess the impact of providing various customer services on the financial condition of USAir, management would track ratios over time to discern trends.
>
> Finally, operations control at USAir would need to include materials control to ensure that materials purchased from suppliers are flowing appropriately from vendors to customers in the form of customer services. For example, the goal of monitoring the drinks, snacks, and meals that caterers are providing to USAir's passengers would be to improve the quality of such items in terms of temperature, freshness, and nutritional value.

SELECTED OPERATIONS CONTROL TOOLS

A **control tool** is a specific procedure or technique that presents pertinent organizational information in a way that helps managers to develop and implement an appropriate control strategy.

In addition to understanding production, operations management, and operations control, managers also need to be aware of various operations control tools that are useful in an operations facility. A **control tool** is a specific procedure or technique that presents pertinent organizational information in a way that helps managers and workers develop and implement an appropriate control strategy. That is, a control tool aids managers and workers in pinpointing the organizational strengths and weaknesses on which a useful control strategy must focus. This section discusses specific control tools for day-to-day operations as well as for longer-run operations.

Using Control Tools to Control Organizations

Continual improvement of operations is a practical, not a theoretical, managerial concern. It is, essentially, the development and use of better methods. Different types of organizations have different goals and strategies, but all organizations struggle daily to find better ways of doing things. This goal of continual improvement applies not just to money-making enterprises, but to those with other missions as well. Since organizational leaders are continually changing systems and personal styles of management, everyone within the organization is continually learning to live with change.

Inspection

Traditionally, managers believed that if you wanted good quality, you hired many inspectors to make sure an operation was producing at the desired quality level. These inspectors examined and graded finished products or components, parts, or services at any stage of operation by measuring, tasting, touching, weighing, disassembling, destroying, and testing. The goal of inspection was to detect unacceptable quality levels before a bad product or service reached a customer. Whenever a lot of defects were found, management blamed the workers and hired more inspectors.

To Inspect or Not to Inspect   Today, managers know that inspection cannot catch problems built into the system. The traditional inspection process does not result in improvement and does not guarantee quality. In fact, according to Deming, inspection is a limited, grossly overused, and often misused tool. He recommended that management stop relying on mass inspection to achieve quality, and advocated instead either 100 percent inspection in those cases where defect-free work is impossible or no inspection at all where the level of defects is acceptably small.

Management by Exception

Management by exception is a control technique that allows only significant deviations between planned and actual performance to be brought to a manager's attention. Management by exception is based on the *exception principle*, a management principle that appears in early management literature.[23] This principle recommends that subordinates handle all routine organizational matters, leaving managers free to deal with nonroutine, or exceptional, organizational issues.

Establishing Rules   Some organizations rely on subordinates or managers themselves to detect the significant deviations between standards and performance that signal exceptional issues. Other organizations establish rules to ensure that exceptional issues surface as a matter of normal operating procedure. Settings rules must be done very carefully to ensure that all true deviations are brought to the manager's attention.

Two examples of rules based on the exception principle are the following:[24]

1. A department manager must immediately inform the plant manager if actual weekly labor costs exceed estimated weekly labor costs by more than 15 percent
2. A department manager must immediately inform the plant manager if actual dollars spent plus estimated dollars to be spent on a special project exceed the funds approved for the project by more than 10 percent

Although these two rules happen to focus on production-related expenditures, detecting and reporting significant rules deviations can be established in virtually any organizational area.

If appropriately administered, the management-by-exception control technique ensures the best use of managers' time. Because only significant issues are brought to managers' attention, the possibility that managers will spend their valuable time working on relatively insignificant issues is automatically eliminated.

Of course, the significant issues brought to managers' attention could be organizational strengths as well as organizational weaknesses. Obviously, managers should try to reinforce the first and eliminate the second.

Management by Objectives

In management by objectives, which was discussed in Chapter 5, the manager assigns a specialized set of objectives and action plans to workers and then rewards those workers on the basis of how close they come to reaching their goals. This control technique has been imple-

Management by exception is a control tool that allows only significant deviations between planned and actual performance to be brought to a manager's attention.

mented in corporations intent on using an employee-participative means to improve productivity.

Break-Even Analysis

Another production-related control tool commonly used by managers is break-even analysis. **Break-even analysis** is the process of generating information that summarizes various levels of profit or loss associated with various levels of production. The next sections discuss three facets of this control tool:

1. Basic ingredients of break-even analysis
2. Types of break-even analysis available to managers
3. Relationship between break-even analysis and controlling

Break-even analysis is a control tool that summarizes the various levels of profit or loss associated with various levels of production.

Basic Ingredients of Break-Even Analysis
Break-even analysis typically involves reflection, discussion, reasoning, and decision making relative to the following seven major aspects of production:

1. *Fixed costs*—**Fixed costs** are expenses incurred by the organization regardless of the number of products produced. Some examples are real estate taxes, upkeep to the exterior of a business building, and interest expenses on money borrowed to finance the purchase of equipment.
2. *Variable costs*—Expenses that fluctuate with the number of products produced are called **variable costs.** Examples are costs of packaging a product, costs of materials needed to make the product, and costs associated with packing products to prepare them for shipping.
3. *Total costs*—**Total costs** are simply the sum of the fixed and variable costs associated with production.
4. *Total revenue*—**Total revenue** is all sales dollars accumulated from selling manufactured products or services. Naturally, total revenue increases as more products are sold.
5. *Profits*—**Profits** are defined as the amount of total revenue that exceeds the total costs of producing the products sold.
6. *Loss*—**Loss** is the amount of the total costs of producing a product that exceeds the total revenue gained from selling the product.
7. *Break-even point*—The **break-even point** is that level of production where the total revenue of an organization equals its total costs—that is, the point at which the organization is generating only enough revenue to cover its costs. The company is neither gaining a profit nor incurring a loss.

Fixed costs are expenses incurred by the organization regardless of the number of products produced.

Variable costs are expenses that fluctuate with the number of the products produced.

Total costs are the sum of fixed costs and variable costs.

Total revenue is all sales dollars accumulated from selling the goods or services produced by the organization.

Profits are the amount of total revenue that exceeds total costs.

Loss is the amount of the total costs of producing a product that exceeds the total revenue gained from selling the product.

The **break-even point** is that level of production where the total revenue of an organization equals its total costs.

Types of Break-Even Analysis
There are two somewhat different procedures for determining the same break-even point for an organization: algebraic break-even analysis and graphic break-even analysis.

Algebraic Break-Even Analysis   The following simple formula is commonly used to determine the level of production at which an organization breaks even:

$$BE = \frac{FC}{P - VC}$$

where

      BE = the level of production at which the firm breaks even
      FC = total fixed costs of production
      P   = price at which each individual unit is sold to customers
      VC = variable costs associated with each product manufactured and sold

In using this formula to calculate a break-even point, two sequential steps must be followed. First, the variable costs associated with producing each unit must be subtracted from the price at which each unit will sell. The purpose of this calculation is to determine how much of the selling price of each unit sold can go toward covering total fixed costs incurred from producing all products. Second, the remainder calculated in the first step must be divided into total fixed costs. The purpose of this calculation is to determine how many units

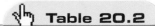
Fixed Costs (Yearly Basis)		Variable Costs per Book Sold	
1. Real estate taxes on property	$1,000	1. Printing	$2.00
2. Interest on loan to purchase equipment	5,000	2. Artwork	1.00
3. Building maintenance	2,000	3. Sales commission	.50
4. Insurance	800	4. Author royalties	1.50
5. Salaried labor	80,000	5. Binding	1.00
Total fixed costs	$88,800	Total variable costs per book	$6.00

must be produced and sold to cover fixed costs. This number of units is the break-even point for the organization.

Say a book publisher faces the fixed and variable costs per paperback book presented in Table 20.2. If the publisher wants to sell each book for $12, the break-even point could be calculated as follows:

$$BE = \frac{\$88,800}{\$12 - \$6}$$

$$BE = \frac{\$88,800}{\$6}$$

$$BE = 14,800 \text{ copies}$$

This calculation indicates that if expenses and selling price remain stable, the book publisher will incur a loss if book sales are fewer than 14,800 copies, will break even if book sales equal 14,800 copies, and will make a profit if book sales exceed 14,800 copies.

Graphic Break-Even Analysis   Graphic break-even analysis entails the construction of a graph showing all the critical elements in a break-even analysis. Figure 20.5 is such a graph for the book publisher. Note that in a break-even graph, the total revenue line starts at zero

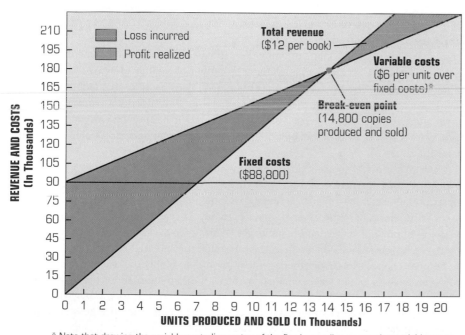

* Note that drawing the variable costs line on top of the fixed costs line means that variable costs have been added to fixed costs. Therefore, the variable costs line also represents total costs.

Break-even analysis for a book publisher   **Figure 20.5**

Advantages of Using the Algebraic and Graphic Break-Even Methods   Both the algebraic and the graphic methods of break-even analysis for the book publisher result in the same break-even point—14,800 books produced and sold—but the processes used to arrive at this point are quite different.

Which break-even method managers should use is usually determined by the situation they face. For a manager who desires a quick yet accurate determination of a break-even point, the algebraic method generally suffices. For a manager who wants a more complete picture of the cumulative relationships between the break-even point, fixed costs, and escalating variable costs, the graphic break-even method is more useful. For example, the book publisher could quickly and easily see from Figure 20.5 the cumulative relationships of fixed costs, escalating variable costs, and potential profit and loss associated with various levels of production.

Control and Break-Even Analysis   Break-even analysis is a useful control tool because it helps managers understand the relationships between fixed costs, variable costs, total costs, and profit and loss within an organization. Once these relationships are understood, managers can take steps to modify one or more of the variables to reduce deviation between planned and actual profit levels.[25]

Increasing costs or decreasing selling prices has the overall effect of increasing the number of units an organization must produce and sell to break even. Conversely, the managerial strategy for decreasing the number of products an organization must produce and sell to break even entails lowering or stabilizing fixed and variables costs or increasing the selling price of each unit. The exact break-even control strategy a particular manager should develop and implement is dictated primarily by that manager's unique organizational situation.

► Back to the Case

There are several useful production control tools that USAir's management can use to ensure that various services are provided to customers as planned. First, management can have customer services inspected to determine which, if any, services should be improved and how to improve them. Second, USAir can use management by exception to control customer services. In this case, USAir's workers would handle all routine customer service issues and bring only exceptional matters to management's attention. To successfully use management by exception at USAir, it would be necessary to implement a number of carefully designed rules. One such rule might be that when 5 percent or more of luggage bags handled on a flight are damaged, a baggage handler must report this fact to a supervisor. The supervisor would then carefully inspect the baggage-handling process to see why this is happening—perhaps because of improper procedures or malfunctioning equipment—and management would take steps to correct the situation.

USAir might prefer to use management by objectives to control customer service issues. For example, management could set such customer service objectives as answering a ticket counter phone within five rings, ticketing a passenger within 5 minutes, and making sure that passengers do not wait longer than 30 minutes to buy a ticket at the airport. If such objectives are deemed both worthwhile and realistic, yet USAir's employees are not reaching them consistently, management would take steps to ensure that they are met.

Another control tool USAir's management might find highly useful is break-even analysis. Break-even analysis would furnish management with information about the various levels of profit or loss associated with various levels of revenue. To use this tool, USAir would have to determine the total fixed costs necessary to operate the airline, the price at which flights are sold, and the variable costs associated with various flights.

For example, if management wanted to determine how many tickets had to be sold before the company would break even on a particular flight, it could arrive at this break-even point algebraically by following three steps. First, all fixed costs attributable to operating the flight—for example, airport facility rent—would be totaled. Second, all the variable costs of furnishing a flight to a passenger would be totaled, and from this total, management would subtract the revenue that a ticket will generate. Variable costs include such expenses as meal costs, fuel costs, and labor needed to furnish the flight. Finally, the answer calculated in step 2 would be divided into the answer derived in step 1, and this figure would tell management how many tickets must be sold at the projected revenue level to break even.

USAir's management also could choose to determine the break-even point by constructing a graph showing fixed costs, variable costs, and revenue per flight. Such a graph would probably give managers a more useful picture for formulating profit-oriented flight plans.

Other Broad Operations Control Tools

Some of the best-known and most commonly used operations control tools are discussed in the following sections. The primary purpose of these tools is to control the production of organizational goods and services.[26]

Decision Tree Analysis

Decision tree analysis, as you recall from Chapter 7, is a statistical and graphical multiphased decision-making technique containing a series of steps showing the sequence and interdependence of decisions. Decision trees allow a decision maker to deal with uncertain events by determining the relative expected value of each alternative course of action. The probabilities of different possible events are known, as are the monetary payoffs that result from a particular alternative and a particular event. Decision trees are best suited to situations in which capacity decisions involve several capacity expansion alternatives and the selection of the alternative with the highest expected profit or the lowest expected cost is necessary.

> **Decision tree analysis** is a statistical and graphical multiphased decision-making technique that shows the sequence and interdependence of decisions.

Process Control

Statistical process control, known as **process control,** is a technique that assists in monitoring production processes. Production processes must be monitored continually to ensure that the quality of their output is acceptable. The earlier the detection of a faulty production process, the better. If detection occurs late in the production process, the company may find parts that do not meet quality standards, and scrapping or reworking these is a costly proposition. If a production process results in unstable performance or is downright out of control, corrective action must be taken. Process control can be implemented with the aid of graphical charts known as control charts.

> **Process control** is a technique that assists in monitoring production processes.

Value Analysis

Value analysis is a cost control and cost reduction technique that aids managers controlling operations by focusing primarily on material costs. The goal of this analysis, which is performed by examining all the parts and materials and their functions, is to reduce costs by using cheaper components and materials in such a way that product quality or appeal is not affected. Simplification of parts—which lowers production costs—is also a goal of value analysis. Value analysis can result not only in cost savings, but also in an improved product.

Value analysis requires a team effort. The team, if not companywide, should at least include personnel from operations, purchasing, engineering, and marketing.

> **Value analysis** is a cost control and cost reduction technique that examines all the parts, materials, and functions of an operation.

Computer-Aided Design

Computer-aided design (CAD) systems include several automated design technologies. *Computer graphics* is used to design geometric specifications for parts, while *computer-aided engineering (CAE)* is employed to evaluate and perform engineering analyses on a part. CAD also includes technologies used in process design. CAD functions to ensure the quality of a product by guaranteeing not only the quality of parts in the product, but also the appropriateness of the product's design.

> **Computer-aided design (CAD)** is a computerized technique for designing new products or modifying existing ones.

Computer-Aided Manufacturing

Computer-aided manufacturing (CAM) employs computers to plan and program equipment used in the production and inspection of manufactured items. Linking CAM and CAD processes through a computer is very beneficial when production processes must be altered, because when CAD and CAM systems can share information easily, design changes can be implemented in a very short period of time.

> **Computer-aided manufacturing (CAM)** is a technique that employs computers to plan and program equipment used in the production and inspection of manufactured items.

Decision tree analysis, process control, value analysis, computer-aided design, and computer-aided manufacturing were presented in the text as broader operations tools that are highly useful to managers exercising the control function. Of all these tools, value analysis would have the most application to USAir's service-oriented operation. USAir's management could use this cost control and cost reduction technique to examine the cost and worth of every component of customer service. To gain a complete picture of customer service components and their usefulness, USAir might establish a team comprising members from different customer service areas.

For instance, a team composed of a ticket agent, a flight attendant, a maintenance supervisor, and a baggage handler might explore different options for establishing comfortable cabin temperature while a plane is being loaded but before it taxis to the runway to await takeoff. If this team concludes, for example, that expediting the baggage-handling process would expose passengers to uncomfortable temperatures for shorter periods of time, management could take steps to speed up the process. Implementation of more efficient ways of handling baggage would result not only in better customer service, but also in lower airline operating costs.

Management Skills Module

This section is specially designed to help you develop management skills. An individual's management skill is based on an understanding of management concepts and the ability to apply those concepts in management situations. As a result, the following activities are designed both to heighten your understanding of management concepts and to help you gain facility in applying those concepts in various management situations.

UNDERSTANDING MANAGEMENT CONCEPTS

▶ Action Summary

Reread the learning objectives below. Each objective is followed by questions. Answering these questions accurately will help you retain the most important concepts discussed in this chapter. After answering each question, check your answer against the answer key at the end of this chapter. (*Hint*: If you have any doubts regarding the correct response, consult the page number that follows the answer.)

Circle:

From studying this chapter, I will attempt to acquire

1. Definitions of production, productivity, and quality.

a b c d e   **a.** *Production* is the transformation of organizational resources into: (a) profits (b) plans (c) forecasts (d) processes (e) products.

a b c d e   **b.** *Productivity* is the relationship between the amount of goods or services produced and: (a) profits (b) the organizational resources needed to produce them (c) quality (d) operations management activities (e) advanced manufacturing support.

T F   **c.** Quality is the extent to which a product reliably does what it is intended to do.

2. An understanding of the importance of operations and production strategies, systems, and processes.

a b c d   **a.** The flow of interrelated events moving toward a goal, purpose, or end is known as a: (a) system (b) process (c) strategy (d) plan.

a b c d   **b.** A particular linkage of mission, goals, strategies, policies, rules, human resources, and raw materials that facilitates carrying out a process is a: (a) system (b) process (c) strategy (d) plan.

3. Insights into the role of operations management concepts in the workplace.

T F   **a.** The criteria relevant for judging the actions taken as a result of operations management are effectiveness and efficiency.

a b c d   **b.** An operations strategy is achieved in a context of objectives and policies derived from the organization's: (a) capacity strategy (b) product strategy (c) strategic plan (d) human resources strategy.

a b c d   **c.** The reputation of an organization is determined by its: (a) size (b) style of management (c) profits (d) product quality.

4. An understanding of how operations control procedures can be used to control production.

T F   **a.** Just-in-time inventory control is an inventory control technique based on the management philosophy that products should be manufactured when customers need them.

a b c d e   **b.** Potential pitfalls of using budgets as control tools include: (a) placing too much emphasis on relatively insignificant organizational expenses (b) changing budgets periodically (c) increasing budgeted expenses year after year without adequate information (d) a and c (e) a and b.

a b c d   **c.** Managers can use ratio analysis in the following way to control an organization:
        a. Evaluate all ratios simultaneously to get a picture of the organization as a whole.
        b. Compare computer values for ratios with values of industry averages.
        c. Accumulate values for ratios for successive time periods to uncover specific organizational trends.
        d. a, b, and c.

5. Insights into operations control tools and how they evolve into a continual improvement approach to production management and control.

T F   **a.** By using inspection, managers can expect to catch any problems that are built into the system.

T F   **b.** Management by exception is a control technique that allows only significant deviations between planned and actual performance to be brought to the manager's attention.

a b c d e   **c.** The overall effect on the break-even point of increasing costs or decreasing selling prices is that: (a) the number of products an organization must sell to break even increases (b) the amount of profit a firm will receive at a fixed number of units sold increases (c) the number of products an organization must sell to break even decreases (d) a and b (e) there is no effect on the break-even point.

chapter

chapterchapterchapterchapterchapterchapter

21 Information Technology and the Internet

Making Changes Without the Right Information at Sunbeam?

REMINDER: THE INTRODUCTORY CASE WRAP-UP (P. 495) CONTAINS DISCUSSION QUESTIONS AND A SKILLS EXERCISE TO FURTHER ILLUSTRATE THE APPLICATION OF CHAPTER CONCEPTS TO THIS VIGNETTE.

S unbeam Corporation develops, manufactures, and markets consumer products in the areas of home appliances, home health care, and outdoor cooking. The company offers a very diverse product line ranging from electric blankets to gas grills.

Sunbeam Corporation recently announced the firing of Albert J. Dunlap as chairman and chief executive officer. Contrary to earlier projections, the company appeared headed for an operating loss. The ouster of Mr. Dunlap, whose aggressive layoffs and other cost-cutting tactics have made

Sunbeam Corporation has long maintained its profile as a progressive firm driven by new-product evolution.

him one of corporate America's premier downsizers, was decided in an emergency meeting of Sunbeam's independent directors in New York. It marked the culmination of a week during which the board's support for him collapsed as its worries about his leadership and the company's deteriorating performance increased.

Mr. Dunlap, 60 years old, earned the nickname "Chain Saw Al" by obliterating thousands of jobs and firing managers who failed to deliver at several companies he ran over the past 15 years. Now Sunbeam's board decided that Mr. Dunlap was failing to turn around the Delray Beach, Florida, company.

Mr. Dunlap succeeded in slashing costs at Sunbeam, eliminating about half the company's 12,000 jobs. But he wasn't able to deliver on his promise to transform the company into a high-growth profit machine.

A series of disclosures about Sunbeam's worsening financial performance sapped investors' confidence. Despite thumping assurances from Mr. Dunlap that his turnaround plan was working, the stock price sank steadily.

Given Mr. Dunlap's outstanding record of success in turning around other organizations, one can only wonder why he was unsuccessful at Sunbeam. Perhaps the information on which he was basing his decisions was of low quality.

The Introductory Case discusses how Albert J. Dunlap had a successful career as one of America's premier downsizers until he failed at Sunbeam. The case ends with the possibility that Dunlap failed because he based downsizing decisions on faulty information. This chapter presents material that should be useful to a manager like Dunlap who should scrutinize the overall worth of information before making important decisions based upon it. Major topics in this chapter are the following:

1) Essentials of information

2) The management information system (MIS)

3) Information technology

4) The management decision support system (MDSS)

5) Computer networks including both local area networks and the Internet

Controlling is the process of making things happen as planned. Of course, managers cannot make things happen as planned if they lack information on the manner in which various events in the organization occur. This chapter discusses the fundamental principles of handling information in an organization by first presenting the essentials of information and then examining both the management information system (MIS) and information technology.

ESSENTIALS OF INFORMATION

Data are facts or statistics.

Information is the set of conclusions derived from data analysis.

The process of developing information begins with gathering some type of facts or statistics, called **data.** Once gathered, data typically are analyzed in some manner. In general terms, **information** is the set of conclusions derived from data analysis. In management terms, information is the set of conclusions derived from the analysis of data that relate to the operation of an organization. As examples to illustrate the relationship between data and information, managers gather data regarding pay rates that individuals are receiving within industries in order to collect information about how to develop competitive pay rates, data regarding hazardous-materials accidents in order to gain information about how to improve worker safety, and data regarding customer demographics in order to gain information about product demand in the future.[1]

The information that managers receive heavily influences managerial decision making, which, in turn, determines the activities that will be performed within the organization, which, in turn, dictate the eventual success or failure of the organization. Some management writers consider information to be of such fundamental importance to the management process that they define *management* as the process of converting information into action through decision making.[2] The next sections discuss the following aspects of information and decision making:

1. Factors that influence the value of information
2. How to evaluate information
3. Computer assistance in using information

Factors Influencing the Value of Information

Some information is more valuable than other information.[3] The value of information is defined in terms of the benefit that can accrue to the organization through its use. The greater this benefit, the more valuable the information.

Four primary factors determine the value of information:

1. Information appropriateness
2. Information quality
3. Information timeliness
4. Information quantity

In general, management should encourage generation, distribution, and use of organizational information that is appropriate, of high quality, timely, and of sufficient quantity. Following this guideline will not necessarily guarantee sound decisions, but it will ensure that important resources necessary to make such decisions are available.[4] Each of the factors that determines information value is discussed in more detail in the paragraphs that follow.

Information Appropriateness

Information appropriateness is defined in terms of how relevant the information is to the decision-making situation the manager faces. If the information is quite relevant, then it is said to be appropriate. Generally, as the appropriateness of information increases, so does the value of that information.

Figure 21.1 shows the characteristics of information appropriate for the following common decision-making situations:[5]

1. Operational control
2. Management control
3. Strategic planning

Operational Control, Management Control, and Strategic Planning Decisions

Operational control decisions relate to ensuring that specific organizational tasks are carried out effectively and efficiently. *Management control decisions* relate to obtaining and effectively and efficiently using the organizational resources necessary to reach organizational objectives. *Strategic planning decisions* relate to determining organizational objectives and designating the corresponding action necessary to reach them.

As Figure 21.1 shows, characteristics of appropriate information change as managers shift from making operational control decisions to making management control decisions to making strategic planning decisions. Strategic planning decision makers need information that focuses on the relationship of the organization to its external environment, emphasizes the future, is wide in scope, and presents a broad view. Appropriate information for this type of decision is generally not completely current, but more historical in nature. In addition, this information does not need to be completely accurate because strategic decisions tend to be characterized by some subjectivity and focus on areas, like customer satisfaction, that are difficult to measure.

Information appropriate for making operational control decisions has dramatically different characteristics from information appropriate for making strategic planning decisions. Operational control decision makers need information that focuses for the most part on the internal organizational environment, emphasizes the performance history of the organization, and is well-defined, narrow in scope, and detailed. In addition, appropriate information for this type of decision is both highly current and highly accurate.

Information appropriate for making management control decisions generally has characteristics that fall somewhere between the extreme of appropriate operational control information and appropriate strategic planning information.

> **Information appropriateness** is the degree to which information is relevant to the decision-making situation the manager faces.

CHARACTERISTICS OF INFORMATION	OPERATIONAL CONTROL	MANAGEMENT CONTROL	STRATEGIC PLANNING
Source	Largely internal	⟶	External
Scope	Well defined, narrow	⟶	Very wide
Level of aggregation	Detailed	⟶	Aggregate
Time horizon	Historical	⟶	Future
Currency	Highly current	⟶	Quite old/historical
Required accuracy	High	⟶	Low
Frequency of use	Very frequent	⟶	Infrequent

Characteristics of information appropriate for decisions related to operational control, management control, and strategic planning

Figure 21.1

Information Quality

Information quality is the degree to which information represents reality.

The second primary factor that determines the value of information is **information quality**—the degree to which information represents reality. The more closely information represents reality, the higher the quality and the greater the value of that information. In general, the higher the quality of information available to managers, the better equipped managers are to make appropriate decisions and the greater the probability that the organization will be successful over the long term.

Perhaps the most significant factor in producing poor-quality information is *data contamination*. Inaccurate data gathering can result in information that is of very low quality—a poor representation of reality.[6]

Information Timeliness

Information timeliness is the extent to which the receipt of information allows decisions to be made and action to be taken so the organization can gain some benefit from possessing the information.

Information timeliness, the third primary factor that determines the value of information, is the extent to which the receipt of information allows decisions to be made and action to be taken so the organization can gain some benefit from possessing the information. Information received by managers at a point when it can be used to the organization's advantage is said to be timely.

For example, a product may be selling poorly because its established market price is significantly higher than the price of competitive products. If this information is received by management after the product has been discontinued, the information will be untimely. If, however, it is received soon enough to adjust the selling price of the product and thereby significantly increase sales, it will be timely.

Information Quantity

Information quantity is the amount of decision-related information a manager possesses.

The fourth and final determinant of the value of information is **information quantity**—the amount of decision-related information managers possess. Before making a decision, managers should assess the quantity of information they possess that relates to the decision being made. If this quantity is judged to be insufficient, more information should be gathered before the decision is made. If the amount of information is judged to be as complete as necessary, managers can feel justified in making the decision.

There is such a thing as *too* much information. According to Rick Feldcamp of Century Life of America, information overload—too much information to consider properly—can make managers afraid to make decisions and result in important decisions going unmade. Information overload is generally considered to be the major cause of indecision in organizations—commonly referred to as "paralysis by analysis."[7]

Evaluating Information

Evaluating information is the process of determining whether the acquisition of specified information is justified. As with all evaluations of this kind, the primary concern of management is to weigh the dollar value of benefit gained from using some quantity of information against the cost of generating that information.

▶ Boeing Corp. supplies its customers with literally tons of information needed to keep their fleets in top flying condition. Each year the Seattle firm has spent millions of dollars to print and mail technical manuals, parts lists, and other maintenance documents that would make a stack of paper 130,000 feet in height. However, thanks to Barbara Claitman, director of e-business for the firm's commercial aviation division, Boeing recently transferred all that technical information, plus links to news stories and maintenance chats, to a Web site called myboeingfleet.com. Better and more up-to-date information in a two-way flow should be the result.

Identifying and Evaluating Data

According to the flowchart in Figure 21.2, the first major step in evaluating organizational information is to ascertain the value of that information by pinpointing the data to be analyzed, and then determine the expected value or return to be received from obtaining perfect information based on these data. Then this expected value is reduced by the amount of benefit that will not be realized because of deficiencies and inaccuracies expected to appear in the information.

Evaluating the Cost of Data

Next, the expected value of organizational information is compared with the expected cost of obtaining that information. If the expected cost does not exceed the expected value, the information should be gathered. If it does exceed the expected value, managers either must increase the information's expected value or decrease its expected cost before the information gathering can be justified. If neither of these objectives is possible, management cannot justify gathering the information.

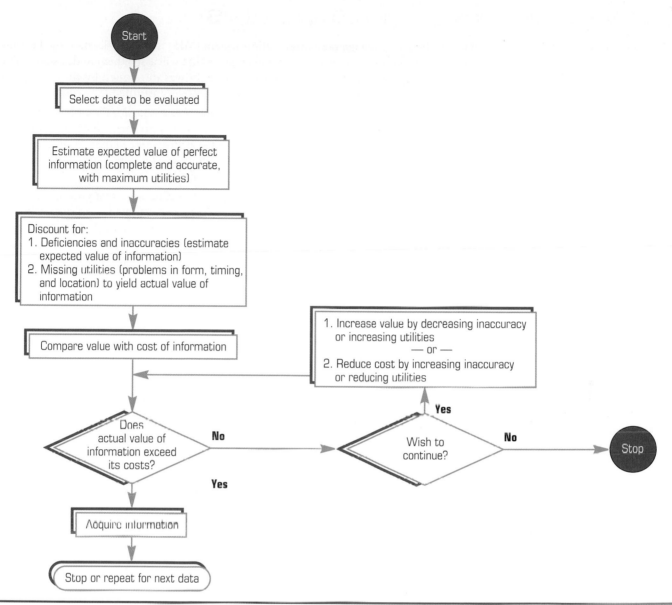

Flowchart of main activities in evaluating information

Figure 21.2

Back to the Case

According to the preceding material, information at Sunbeam Corporation can be defined as conclusions derived from the analysis of data relating to the way in which the company operates. The case implies that managers at Sunbeam will be better able to make sound decisions, including better control decisions, because of the successful data handling achieved by its information system. One important factor in evaluating the overall worth of Sunbeam Corporation's information handling system would be the overall impact of the system on the value of information that company managers would receive. A manager like Dunlap must see that investing in computers, satellites, and other data-handling devices at a reasonable cost can enhance the value of information that he receives and improve the appropriateness of downsizing decisions. That is, investments in improving information system components can enhance the appropriateness, quality, timeliness, and quantity of information that Dunlap can use to make downsizing decisions. Dunlap must believe and act on the notion that the benefits of making investments in computers and information systems will outweigh the costs of the equipment by significantly improving his downsizing decisions.

THE MANAGEMENT INFORMATION SYSTEM (MIS)

A **management information system (MIS)** is a network established within an organization to provide managers with information that will assist them in decision making. An MIS gets information to where it is needed.

In simple terms, a **management information system (MIS)** is a network established within an organization to provide managers with information that will assist them in decision making.[8] The following, more complete definition of an MIS was developed by the Management Information System Committee of the Financial Executives Institute.[9]

> An MIS is a system designed to provide selected decision-oriented information needed by management to plan, control, and evaluate the activities of the corporation. It is designed within a framework that emphasizes profit planning, performance planning, and control at all levels. It contemplates the ultimate integration of required business information subsystems, both financial and nonfinancial, within the company.

The typical MIS is a formally established organizational network that gives managers continual access to vital information. For example, the MIS normally provides managers with ongoing reports relevant to significant organizational activities like sales, worker productivity, and labor turnover. As this example implies, the purview of an MIS is usually limited to internal organizational events. Based on information they gain via an MIS, managers make decisions that are aimed at improving organizational performance. Because the typical MIS is characterized by computer usage, managers can use an MIS to gain online access to company records and condensed information in the form of summaries and reports. Overall, the MIS is a planned, systematic mechanism for providing managers with relevant information in a systematic fashion.[10]

The title of the specific organization member responsible for developing and maintaining an MIS varies from organization to organization. In smaller organizations, a president or vice president may have this responsibility. In larger organizations, an individual with a title such as "director of information systems" may be solely responsible for appropriately managing an entire MIS department. The term *MIS manager* is used in the sections that follow to indicate the person within the organization who has the primary responsibility for managing the MIS. The term *MIS personnel* is used to designate the nonmanagement individuals within the organization who possess the primary responsibility for actually operating the MIS. Examples of nonmanagement individuals are computer operators and computer programmers. The sections that follow describe an MIS more fully and outline the steps managers take to establish an MIS.

Pohang Iron & Steel Company Needs a Complex MIS

A management information system is used in managing activities at virtually all levels of an organization. Thus, although a given MIS may be relatively simple, managers at some organizations have to develop and use a very complex MIS, especially if their organizations are of significant size.

Management at the Pohang Iron & Steel Company in Korea faced a challenge of developing a complex MIS to manage Pohang's organizational activities efficiently and effectively. A complex MIS was needed primarily because of the large size of the company and the complexity of the activities involved in manufacturing steel. Pohang established an MIS that permits managers to monitor any phase of the steel production process. In addition, the system continually monitors about 60,000 items that are critical in controlling production costs and, at specified intervals, automatically updates the status of these items. To best interpret and react to information that flows on its MIS, management uses regularly scheduled video conferences with organization members in different locations. Pohang is the only Korean company to use regularly scheduled video conferences in this fashion. Pohang was founded in 1973 by the government of the Republic of Korea and is now the second largest and most competitive steel maker in the world. The company's success is largely credited to its development and use of its sophisticated MIS. ■

Describing the MIS

The MIS is perhaps best described by a summary of the steps necessary to properly operate it,[11] and by a discussion of the different kinds of information various managers need to make job-related decisions.

Operating the MIS MIS personnel generally need to perform six sequential steps to properly operate an MIS.[12] Figure 21.3 summarizes the steps and indicates the order in which they are performed. The first step is to determine what information is needed within the organization, when it will be needed, and in what form it will be needed. Because the basic purpose

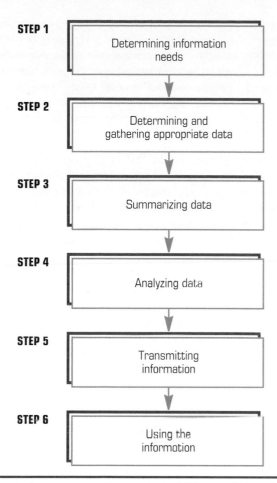

STEP 1 — Determining information needs

STEP 2 — Determining and gathering appropriate data

STEP 3 — Summarizing data

STEP 4 — Analyzing data

STEP 5 — Transmitting information

STEP 6 — Using the information

The six steps necessary to operate an MIS properly in order of their performance

Figure 21.3

of the MIS is to assist management in making decisions, one way to begin determining management information needs is to analyze the following:

1. Decision areas in which management makes decisions
2. Specific decisions within these decision areas that management must actually make
3. Alternatives that must be evaluated to make these specific decisions

For example, insights regarding what information management needs in a particular organization can be gleaned by understanding that management makes decisions in the area of plant and equipment, that a specific decision related to this area involves acquiring new equipment, and that two alternatives that must be evaluated relating to this decision are buying newly developed, high-technology equipment versus buying more standard equipment that has been around for some time in the industry.

Target's MIS Focuses on Hispanic Workers

According to Target's vice president of public and consumer affairs, George Hite, and its president, Warren Feldberg, Target Stores is implementing aggressive expansion plans. Target, a consumer products retailer, has gained its success primarily by designing merchandise programs that reflect lifestyle trends. Company success has been significant enough to yield plans to add about 300 new stores over the next three years. Target managers are being prepared for expansion through comprehensive planning and a strong emphasis on management development.

Several MIS challenges face a company as substantial as Target. For example, management must have certain information: how competitive the company must be in order to hire an adequate number of workers; current trends in technology that might help Target become more efficient; financial results that the company is generating; the

(continued)

kind of continuing education necessary to build a productive workforce; international factors, such as the desirability of purchasing cheaper products abroad; and the level of workforce diversity that the company possesses and should aspire to.

The MIS at Target has provided management with a foundation of information upon which to make diversity-related decisions. For example, in southern California, the company is monitoring changing demographics of the population surrounding Target stores and attempting to build a workforce that reflects the diversity of that population. As a result, in southern California, Target is hiring a greater proportion of Hispanic workers. In order to help these workers become more productive, Target is offering them free English classes. ■

The second major step in operating the MIS is pinpointing and collecting data that will yield needed organizational information. This step is just as important as determining information needs of the organization. If collected data do not relate properly to information needs, it will be impossible to generate needed information.

After information needs of the organization have been determined and appropriate data have been pinpointed and gathered, summarizing the data and analyzing the data are, respectively, the third and fourth steps MIS personnel generally should take to properly operate an MIS. It is in the performance of these steps that MIS personnel find computer assistance of great benefit.

The fifth and sixth steps are transmitting the information generated by data analysis to appropriate managers and getting the managers to actually use the information. The performance of these last two steps results in managerial decision making. Although each of the six steps is necessary if an MIS is to run properly, the time spent on performing each step will naturally vary from organization to organization.

Different Managers Need Different Kinds of Information For maximum benefit, an MIS must collect relevant data, transform that data into appropriate information, and transmit that information to the appropriate managers. Appropriate information for one manager within an organization, however, may not be appropriate information for another. Robert G. Murdick suggests that the degree of appropriateness of MIS information for a manager depends on the activities for which the manager will use the information, the organizational objectives assigned to the manager, and the level of management at which the manager functions.[13] All of these factors are closely related.

Murdick's thoughts on this matter are best summarized in Figure 21.4. As you can see from this figure, because the overall job situations of top managers, middle managers, and first-line managers are significantly different, the kinds of information these managers need to satisfactorily perform their jobs are also significantly different.

▶ L. L. Bean retail operations have grown from its original catalog business, which still accounts for the bulk of its sales, to include a Web site and a few retail stores like this one in McLean, Virginia. Another 12 to 15 more stores are scheduled to open in the next few years. Managers of each of L. L. Bean's retail arms require different kinds of information. Consider, for instance, how data about shoppers' access to technology and their privacy concerns is important to the company's Web site manager, while the demographics of the local labor supply are likely to be important for peak hiring periods faced by managers of the company's telephone centers and retail stores.

Organizational Level	Type of Management	Manager's Organizational Objectives	Appropriate Information from MIS	How MIS Information Is Used
1. Top management	CEO, president, vice president	Survival of the firm, profit growth, accumulation and efficient use of resources	Environmental data and trends, summary reports of operations, exception reports of problems, forecasts	Corporate objectives, policies, constraints, decisions on strategic plans, decisions on control of the total company
2. Middle management	Middle managers in such areas as marketing, production, and finance	Allocation of resources to assigned tasks, establishment of plans to meet operating objectives, control of operations	Summaries and exception reports of operating results, corporate objectives, policies, constraints, decisions on strategic plans, relevant actions and decisions of other middle managers	Operating plans and policies, exception reports, operating summaries, control procedures, decisions on resource allocations, actions and decisions related to other middle managers
3. First-line management	First-line managers whose work is closely related	Production of goods to meet marketing needs, supplying budgets, estimates of resource requirements, movement and storage of materials	Summary reports of transactions, detailed reports of problems, operating plans and policies, control procedures, actions and decisions of related first-line managers	Exception reports, progress reports, resource requests, dispatch orders, cross-functional reports

Appropriate MIS Information under various sets of organizational circumstances

Figure 21.4

Back to the Case

In order for a company like Sunbeam Corporation to get maximum benefit from its computer assistance, management must appropriately build each main ingredient of its MIS. The MIS at a company like Sunbeam is the organizational network established to provide managers with information that helps them make job-related decisions. Such a system would normally necessitate the use of several MIS personnel who would help determine information needs at the company, help determine and collect appropriate Sunbeam data, summarize and analyze these data, transmit analyzed data to appropriate Sunbeam managers, and generally help managers in interpreting received MIS information.

To make sure that managers get appropriate information, Sunbeam's MIS personnel must appreciate how different managers need different kinds of information. As an example, a top manager like Albert Dunlap would normally need information that summarizes trends like consumer tastes, competitor moves, and perhaps most importantly for a downsizer, summary reports for productivity and costs related to various organizational units. Middle managers would need information that focuses more on specific operating divisions or units within the company, such as all specifics regarding home appliance production. More lower-level managers, perhaps production supervisors, would normally need information about daily production rates, regular versus overtime labor costs, and the status of meeting production goals.

Establishing an MIS

The process of establishing an MIS involves four stages:

1. Planning for the MIS
2. Designing the MIS
3. Implementing the MIS
4. Improving the MIS

Planning for the MIS The planning stage is perhaps the most important stage of the process. Commonly cited factors that make planning for the establishment of an MIS an absolute necessity are the typically long periods of time needed to acquire MIS-related data-processing equipment and to integrate it into the operations of the organization, the difficulty of hiring competent equipment operators, and the major amounts of financial and managerial resources typically needed to operate an MIS.[14]

The specific types of plans for an MIS vary from organization to organization. However, a sample plan for the establishment of an MIS at a large consumer-products company is shown in Figure 21.5. This hypothetical plan, of course, is abbreviated; much more detailed outlines of each of the areas in this plan would be needed before it could be implemented. Notice that this plan includes a point (about a third of the way down the figure) at which management must decide if there is enough potential benefit to be gained from an MIS to continue the process of establishing such a system. This particular plan specifies that if management decides there is insufficient potential benefit to be gained from an MIS, given its total costs, the project should be terminated.

Designing the MIS Although data-processing equipment is normally an important component of management information systems, the designing of an MIS should not begin with a comparative analysis of the types of such equipment available. Many MIS managers mistakenly think that data-processing equipment and an MIS are synonymous.

Analyzing Managers' Decisions Stoller and Van Horn indicate that because the purpose of an MIS is to provide information that will assist managers in making better decisions, the designing of an MIS should begin with an analysis of the kinds of decisions the managers actually make in a particular organization.[15] These authors suggest that designing an MIS should consist of the following four steps:

1. Defining various decisions that must be made to run an organization
2. Determining the types of existing management policies that may influence the ways in which these decisions should be made
3. Pinpointing the types of data needed to make these decisions
4. Establishing a mechanism for gathering and appropriately processing the data to obtain needed information

Implementing the MIS The third stage in the process of establishing an MIS within an organization is implementation—that is, putting the planned-for and designed MIS into operation. In this stage, the equipment is acquired and integrated into the organization. Designated data are gathered, analyzed as planned, and distributed to appropriate managers within the organization. Line managers make decisions based on the information they receive from the MIS.

Making sure that the MIS is as simple as possible and serves the information needs of management is critical to a successful implementation of an MIS. If the MIS is overly complicated or does not meet management's information needs, the implementation of the system will encounter much resistance and will probably have only limited success.

Enlisting Management Support Management of the implementation process of the MIS can determine the ultimate success or failure of the system.[16] To help ensure that this process will be successful, management can attempt to find an executive sponsor—a high-level manager who understands and supports the MIS implementation process. The support of such a sponsor will be a sign to all organization members that the MIS implementation is important to the organization and that all organization members should cooperate in making the implementation process successful.

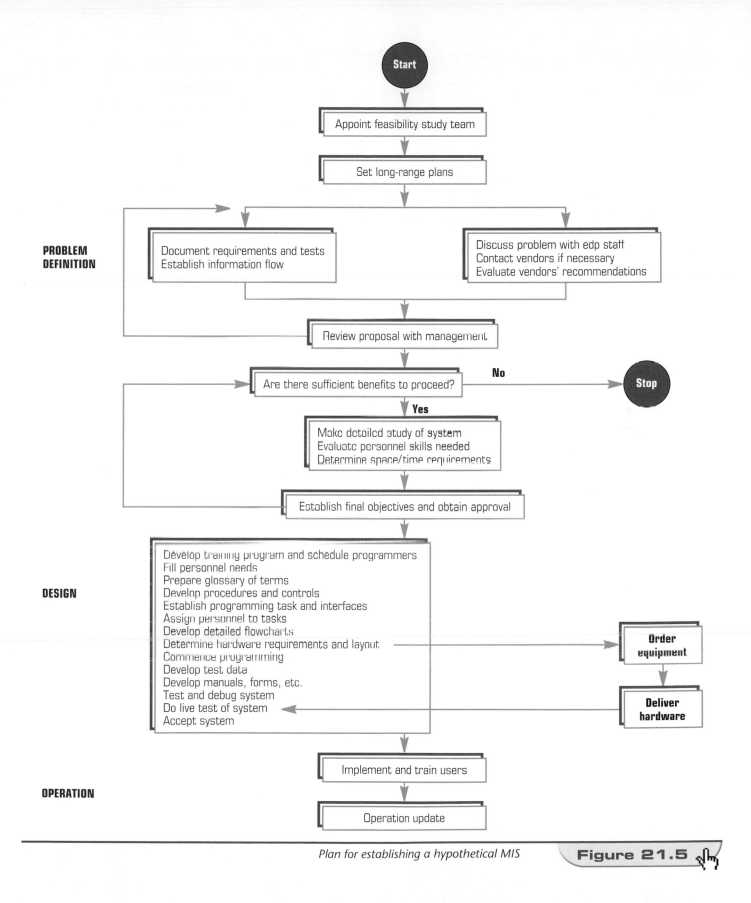

Plan for establishing a hypothetical MIS

Figure 21.5

Table 21.1   Symptoms of an Inadequate MIS

Operational	Psychological	Report Content
Large physical inventory adjustments	Surprise at financial results	Excessive use of tabulations of figures
Capital expenditure overruns	Poor attitude of executives about usefulness of information	Multiple preparation and distribution of identical data
Inability of executives to explain changes from year to year in operating results	Lack of understanding of financial information on part of nonfinancial executives	Disagreeing information from different sources
Uncertain direction of company growth	Lack of concern for environmental changes	Lack of periodic comparative information and trends
Cost variances unexplainable	Executive homework reviewing reports considered excessive	Lateness of information
No order backlog awareness		Too little or excess detail
No internal discussion of reported data		Inaccurate information
Insufficient knowledge about competition		Lack of standards for comparison
Purchasing parts from outside vendors when internal capability and capacity to make are available		Failure to identify variances by cause and responsibility
Record of some "sour" investments in facilities, or in programs such as R&D and advertising		Inadequate externally generated information

Improving the MIS   Once the MIS is operating, MIS managers should continually strive to maximize its value. The two sections that follow provide insights on how MIS improvements might be made.

Symptoms of an Inadequate MIS   To improve an MIS, MIS managers must first find symptoms or signs that the existing MIS is inadequate. A list of such symptoms, developed by Bertram A. Colbert, a principal of Price Waterhouse & Company, is presented in Table 21.1.[17]

Colbert divides the symptoms into three types:

1. Operational
2. Psychological
3. Report content

Operational symptoms and psychological symptoms relate, respectively, to the operation of the organization and the functioning of organization members. Report content symptoms relate to the actual makeup of the information generated by the MIS.

Although the symptoms listed in the table are clues that an MIS is inadequate, the symptoms, by themselves, may not actually pinpoint MIS weaknesses. Therefore, after such symptoms are detected, MIS managers usually must gather additional information to determine what MIS weaknesses exist. Answering questions such as the following helps MIS managers to determine these weaknesses:[18]

1. Where and how do managers get information?
2. Can managers make better use of their contacts to get information?
3. In what areas is managers' knowledge weakest, and how can managers be given information to minimize these weaknesses?
4. Do managers tend to act before receiving information?
5. Do managers wait so long for information that opportunities pass them by and the organization becomes bottlenecked?

Typical Improvements to an MIS   MIS inadequacies vary from situation to situation, depending on such factors as the quality of an MIS plan, the appropriateness of an MIS design, and the kinds of individuals operating an MIS. However, several activities have the potential of improving the MIS of most organizations:[19]

1. *Building cooperation among MIS personnel and line managers*—Cooperation of this sort encourages line managers to give MIS personnel honest opinions of the quality of infor-

mation being received. Through this type of interaction, MIS designers and operators should be able to improve the effectiveness of an MIS.

2. *Constantly stressing that MIS personnel should strive to accomplish the purpose of the MIS— providing managers with decision-related information*—In this regard, it probably would be of great benefit to hold line managers responsible for continually educating MIS personnel on the types of decisions organization members make and the corresponding steps taken to make these decisions. The better MIS personnel understand the decision situations that face operating managers, the higher the probability that MIS information will be appropriate for decisions these managers must make.

3. *Holding, wherever possible, both line managers and MIS personnel accountable for MIS activities on a cost–benefit basis*—This accountability reminds line managers and MIS personnel that the benefits the organization receives from MIS functions must exceed the costs. In effect, this accountability emphasis helps increase the cost consciousness of both line managers and MIS personnel.

4. *Operating an MIS in a "people-conscious" manner*—An MIS, like the formal pyramidal organization, is based on the assumption that organizational affairs can and should be handled in a completely logical manner. Logic, of course, is important to the design and implementation of an MIS. However, MIS activities should also take human considerations into account. After all, even when MIS activities are well-thought-out and completely logical, an MIS can be ineffective simply because people do not use it as intended.

▶ Back to the Case

Assume that Dunlap has just decided to establish an MIS within his company. Sunbeam Corporation, like any other company, would probably gain significantly by carefully planning the way in which its MIS would be established. For example, perhaps the answers to the following questions during the planning stage of Sunbeam Corporation's MIS would be useful. Is an appropriate computer-based system being acquired and integrated? Does the company need new MIS personnel or will present personnel require further training in order to operate the new MIS? Will managers need additional training in order to operate the new MIS?

About the design and implementation stages of Sunbeam's new MIS, Dunlap should seek answers to such questions as: How do we design the new MIS based upon managerial decision making? How can we ensure that the new MIS as designed and implemented will actually exist and be functional?

Dunlap as well as MIS personnel should continually try to improve the new MIS. All users of MIS should be aware of the symptoms of an inadequate MIS and should be constantly attempting to pinpoint and eliminate corresponding weaknesses. Suggestions for improving the new MIS could include (1) building additional cooperation between MIS managers, MIS personnel, and line managers; (2) stressing that the purpose of the MIS is to provide managers with decision-related information; (3) using cost–benefit analysis to evaluate MIS activities; and (4) ensuring that the MIS operates in a people-conscious manner.

INFORMATION TECHNOLOGY

Technology consists of any type of equipment or process that organization members use in the performance of their work. This definition includes tools as old as a blacksmith's anvil and tools as new and innovative as virtual reality. This section discusses one segment of technology, **information technology,** or technology that focuses on the use of information in the performance of work. Some recent information technology introductions are covered in more detail through the following topics: computer assistance in using information, the management decision support system (MDSS), and computer networks.

Technology consists of any type of equipment or process that organization members use in the performance of their work.

Information technology is technology that focuses on the use of information in the performance of work.

Computer Assistance in Using Information

Managers have an overwhelming amount of data to gather, analyze, and transform into information before making numerous decisions. In fact, many managers in the United States as well as in the United Kingdom and other foreign countries are currently complaining that they are overloaded with information.[20] A computer is a tool managers can use to assist in the complicated and time-consuming task of generating this information.

A **computer** is an electronic tool capable of accepting data, interpreting data, performing ordered operations on data, and reporting on the outcome of these operations. Computers give managers the ability to store vast amounts of financial, inventory, and other data so that the data will be readily accessible for making day-to-day decisions. These decisions can be quite diverse and focus on issues like billing customers more efficiently, keeping track of receivables that are past due, ordering materials in appropriate quantities, paying vendors on a timely basis, and making sure that planned projects are on schedule.

The sections that follow discuss the main functions of computers and possible pitfalls in using computers.

Main Functions of Computers   A computer function is a computer activity that must be performed to generate organizational information. Computers perform five main functions:

1. Input
2. Storage
3. Control
4. Processing
5. Output

The relationships among these functions are shown in Figure 21.6.

Input   The **input function** consists of computer activities through which the computer enters the data to be analyzed and the instructions to be followed to analyze the data appropriately. As Figure 21.6 shows, the purpose of the input function is to provide data and instructions to be used in the performance of the storage, processing, control, and output functions.

A **computer** is an electronic tool capable of accepting data, interpreting data, performing ordered operations on data, and reporting on the outcome of these operations. Computers are extremely helpful in generating information from raw data.

The five main functions of computers are:

1. The **input function**—computer activities through which the computer enters the data to be analyzed and the instructions to be followed to analyze the data appropriately.

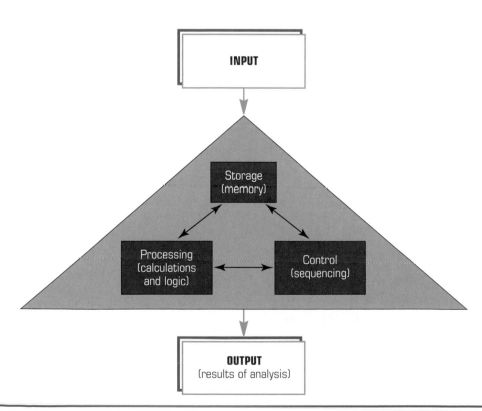

Figure 21.6   *Relationships among the five main functions of a computer*

INPUT

Storage
(memory)

Processing
(calculations
and logic)

Control
(sequencing)

OUTPUT
(results of analysis)

Storage   The **storage function** consists of computer activities involved with retaining the material entered into the computer during the performance of the input function. The storage unit, or memory, of a computer is similar to the human memory in that various facts can be stored until they are needed for processing. In addition, facts can be stored, used in processing, and then restored as many times as necessary. As Figure 21.6 demonstrates, the storage, processing, and control activities are dependent on one another and ultimately yield computer output.

Processing   The **processing function** consists of the computer activities involved with performing both logic and calculation steps necessary to analyze data appropriately. Calculation activities include virtually any numeric analysis. Logic activities include such analysis as comparing one number to another to determine which is larger. Data, as well as directions for processing the data, are furnished by input and storage activities.

Control   Computer activities that dictate the order in which other computer functions are performed compose the **control function.** Control activities indicate the following:

1. When data should be retrieved after storage
2. When and how the data should be analyzed
3. If and when the data should be restored after analysis
4. If and when additional data should be retrieved
5. When output activities (described in the next paragraph) should begin and end

Output   The **output function** comprises the activities that take the results of the input, storage, processing, and control functions and transmit them outside the computer. These results can appear in such diverse forms as data on magnetic tape or characters typed on paper. Obviously, the form in which output appears is determined primarily by how the output is to be used. Output that appears on magnetic tape, for example, can be used as input for another computer analysis but is of little value for analysis by human beings.

Possible Pitfalls in Using Computers   The computer is a sophisticated management tool with the potential to make a significant contribution to organizational success. For this potential to materialize, however, the following possible pitfalls should be avoided:[21]

1. *Thinking that a computer is capable of independently performing creative activities*   A computer does not lessen the organization's need for a manager's personal creative ability and professional judgment. A computer is capable only of following precise and detailed instructions provided by the computer user. The individual using the computer must tell

2. The **storage function**—computer activities involved with retaining the material entered into the computer during the performance of the input function.

3. The **processing function**—computer activities involved with performing the logic and calculation steps necessary to analyze data appropriately.

4. The **control function**—computer activities that dictate the order in which other computer functions are performed.

5. The **output function**—computer activities that take the results of input, storage, processing, and control functions and transmit them outside the computer.

Orlando Sentinel (May 1, 1989).

Sorry, but according to our brand-new $40,000 computer, we don't have any paintbrushes — and if we did, it wouldn't know how much to charge for one.

the computer exactly what to do, how to do it, and when to do it. Computers are simply pieces of equipment that must be directed very precisely by computer users to perform some function.

2. *Spending too much money on computer assistance*—In general, computers can be of great assistance to managers. The initial cost of purchasing a computer and the costs of updating it when necessary, however, can be high. Managers need to keep comparing the benefits obtained from computer assistance with the costs of obtaining it. In essence, an investment in a computer should be expected to help the organization generate enough added revenue not only to finance the computer but also to contribute an acceptable level of net profit.

3. *Overestimating the value of computer output*—Some managers fall into the trap of assuming that they have "the answer" once they have received information generated by computer analysis. The preceding cartoon illustrates the kind of problems that can arise when organization members think that computers generate "the answer." Managers must recognize that computer output is only as good as the quality of data and directions for analyzing the data that human beings have put into the computer. Inaccurate data or inappropriate computer instructions yield useless computer output. A commonly used phrase to describe such an occurrence is "garbage in, garbage out."

▶ Back to the Case

The computer would certainly be a valuable tool for Dunlap in making downsizing decisions as well as other decisions at Sunbeam. The computer can accept data within the company such as daily production levels of various products, perform operations on the data like percentage increases of various products shipped to customers daily or weekly, and quickly distribute the results of this analysis to managers. To be able to distribute such results to management, data must be put into Sunbeam's computers, and it must be stored as well as appropriately controlled and processed.

In addition to providing such valuable decision-related information as the production and shipping reports, computers at a company like Sunbeam can perform many other functions. As examples, computers can generate and track bills to Sunbeam's customers, generate payroll checks to employees, and write orders for materials as they are needed from suppliers. Despite the great value of computers, Dunlap must keep in mind that they, like any other management tool, have limitations. As an example, Dunlap must keep in mind that computer assistance at Sunbeam Corporation, as within any company, is only as good as the people running the computers, and that managers should not expect computers to independently perform creative activities.

The Management Decision Support System (MDSS)

Traditionally, the MIS that uses electronic assistance in gathering data and providing related information to managers has been invaluable. This MIS assistance has been especially useful in areas where programmed decisions (see Chapter 7) are necessary, because the computer continually generates the information that helps managers make these decisions. An example is using the computer to track cumulative labor costs by department. The computer can automatically gather and update the cumulative labor costs per department, compare these costs to corresponding annual budgets, and calculate the percentage of the budget that each department has reached to date. Such information is normally very useful in controlling department labor costs.

A **management decision support system (MDSS)** is an interdependent set of computer-oriented decision aids that help managers make nonprogrammed decisions. The following characteristics are typical of an MDSS.

Closely related to the MIS is the **management decision support system (MDSS)**—an interdependent set of decision aids that help managers make nonprogrammed decisions (see Chapter 7).[22] Figure 21.7 illustrates possible components of the MDSS and describes what they do. The MDSS is typically characterized by the following.[23]

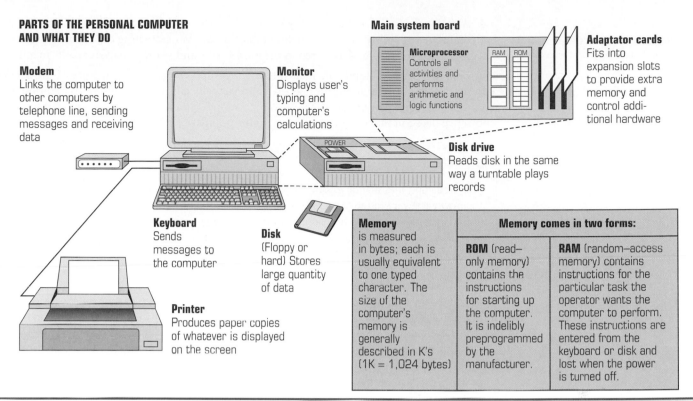

PARTS OF THE PERSONAL COMPUTER AND WHAT THEY DO

Modem
Links the computer to other computers by telephone line, sending messages and receiving data

Monitor
Displays user's typing and computer's calculations

Main system board

Microprocessor
Controls all activities and performs arithmetic and logic functions

RAM ROM

Adaptator cards
Fits into expansion slots to provide extra memory and control additional hardware

Disk drive
Reads disk in the same way a turntable plays records

Keyboard
Sends messages to the computer

Disk
(Floppy or hard) Stores large quantity of data

Printer
Produces paper copies of whatever is displayed on the screen

Memory is measured in bytes; each is usually equivalent to one typed character. The size of the computer's memory is generally described in K's (1K = 1,024 bytes)	**Memory comes in two forms:**	
	ROM (read–only memory) contains the instructions for starting up the computer. It is indelibly preprogrammed by the manufacturer.	**RAM** (random–access memory) contains instructions for the particular task the operator wants the computer to perform. These instructions are entered from the keyboard or disk and lost when the power is turned off.

Possible components of a management decision support system (MDSS)

Figure 21.7

1. *One or more corporate databases*—A **database** is a reservoir of corporate facts consistently organized to fit the information needs of a variety of organization members. These data bases (also termed *corporate databases*) tend to contain facts about all of the important facets of company operations, including both financial and nonfinancial information. These facts are used to explore issues important to the corporation. For example, a manager might find facts from the corporate databases useful for forecasting profits for each of the next three years.

2. *One or more user databases*—In addition to the corporate database, an MDSS usually contains several user databases. A **user database** is a database developed by an individual manager or other user. Such databases may be derived from, but are not necessarily limited to, the corporate database. They tend to address specific issues peculiar to the individual user. For example, a production manager might be interested in exploring the specific issue of lowering production costs. To do so, the manager might build a simple user database that includes departmental facts about reject rates of materials purchased from various suppliers. The manager might be able to lower production costs by eliminating the purchase of materials from suppliers with the highest reject rates.

3. *A set of quantitative tools stored in a model base*—A **model base** is a collection of quantitative computer programs that can assist MDSS users in analyzing data within databases. For example, the production manager discussed in item 2 might use a correlation analysis program stored in a model base to accurately determine if there is any relationship between reject rates and the materials from various suppliers.

   One desirable feature of a model base is its ability to allow the user to perform **"what if" analysis**—the simulation of a business situation over and over again, using somewhat different data for selected decision areas. For example, a manager might first determine the profitability of a company under present conditions. The manager might then ask *what* would happen *if* materials costs increased by 5 percent. Or *if* products were sold at a different price. Popular programs such as Lotus 1-2-3 and the Interactive Financial Planning System (IFPS)[24] allow managers to ask as many "what if" questions as they want to and save their answers without changing their original data.

A **database** is a reservoir of corporate facts consistently organized to fit the information needs of a variety of organization members.

A **user database** is a database developed by an individual manager or other user

A **model base** is a collection of quantitative computer programs that can assist MDSS users in analyzing data within databases.

"What if" analysis is the simulation of a business situation over and over again, using somewhat different data for selected decision areas.

4. *A dialogue capability*—The ability of an MDSS user to interact with an MDSS is called **dialogue capability.** Such interaction typically involves extracting data from a database, calling up various models stored in the model base, and storing analysis results in a file.

Technological developments related to microcomputers have made the use of the MDSS concept feasible and its application available to virtually all managers today. In addition, the continual development of extensive software to support information analysis related to more subjective decision making is contributing to the popularity of these systems.

A **dialogue capability** is the ability of an MDSS user to interact with an MDSS.

► Back to the Case

The preceding information about MDSS implies that Dunlap and other managers could use their own software to tap into corporate databases relevant to making decisions like downsizing. In order for Sunbeam to gain maximum advantage from an MIS, its managers should be able to use an MDSS efficiently and effectively. If Sunbeam's managers are not familiar with the MDSS concept, they can undergo training and could thus use the MDSS to help them make both programmed and nonprogrammed decisions.

In building and using the most advantageous MIS possible, management at a company like Sunbeam should ensure that MIS users within the company have adequate equipment to operate an MDSS, have adequate access to a corporate database, are properly employing user databases, have appropriate model bases available, and have adequate dialogue capability within the company's MDSS. If management is successful in ensuring that these issues reflect MDSS use within the company, then the probability is high that the company MDSS is being properly used. If, on the other hand, management is not successful in ensuring these issues reflect MDSS use within the company, management would probably be able to improve operations by encouraging organization members to appropriately use an MDSS.

COMPUTER NETWORKS

A **computer network** is a system of two or more connected computers that allows computer users to communicate, cooperate, and share resources.

A **computer network** is a system of two or more connected computers that allows computer users to communicate, cooperate, and share resources. When working properly, a computer network is an information technology tool that encourages employees to maximize their potential and their productivity. The next sections discuss the two computer networks that have received the most attention recently from modern managers: local area networks and the Internet.

The Local Area Network

A **local area network (LAN)** is a computer network characterized by software that manages how information travels through cables to arrive at a number of connected single-user computer workstations.

One type of computer network commonly used in modern organizations is called a **local area network (LAN).** An LAN is a computer network characterized by software that manages how information travels through cables to arrive at a number of connected single-user computer workstations. One rule of thumb recommends that when an organization reaches the use of five independent computer workstations, the computers should probably be connected as an LAN.[25] At this number of computers, the cost of networking should be outweighed by the gain of important organizational advantages—for example, allowing computer users to communicate more efficiently and effectively with one another and enabling workers to share the use of expensive software.

Figure 21.8 indicates the growth of management interest in usage of LANs by illustrating the continuing upward trend of sales of equipment used to build LANs. Although this growing enthusiasm for LANs has prompted many computer support companies to expand the array of LAN products they offer to organizations, managers should be cautious and refrain from investing in LAN products that do not satisfy a rigorous cost–benefit analysis.[26]

The Internet

The **Internet** is a large interconnected network of computer networks linking people and computers all over the world via phone lines, satellites, and other telecommunications systems.

The **Internet,** an information technology tool, is a large, interconnected network of computer networks linking people and computers all over the world via phone lines, satellites, and other telecommunications systems. Simply stated, the Internet is an expansive computer network

An LAN, or local area network, is a network for managing the flow of information to individual but connected workstations. Here a Microsoft employee monitors Microsoft's LAN.

linking about 1 million smaller networks worldwide.[27] The following quote contains a worthwhile description of the Internet.[28]

> Probably the best model or analogy is that of a giant highway system that connects computers. The Internet connects all kinds of computers, no matter who made them, what programs run on them, or who they belong to—computers as large as the biggest supercomputers in the world or as small as a laptop PC. By connecting these computers, the Internet connects the people who use the computers. It's called the Internet because it connects not only the computers, but all the different kinds of regional and local networks that hook up

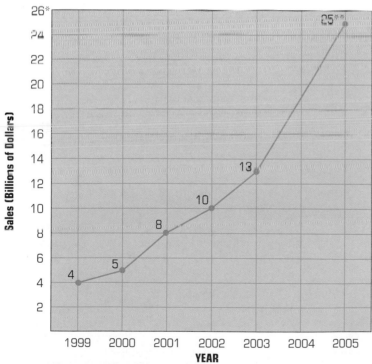

*Sales stated in billions of dollars
**Author estimate based on historical trends

Total dollar sales of equipment used to build LANs in organizations

Figure 21.8

these computers as well. Like the highway system, the Internet consists of interstates and state highways, and little roads. The number of computers and people linked by the Internet is now in the tens of millions and growing at an ever-faster rate.

The Internet as we know it today evolved out of a project conceived and initiated by the U.S. Department of Defense in the early 1970s to allow scientists and researchers to better communicate and exchange data. Today, the Internet is extremely popular and is characterized by a growing number of users throughout the general world population. According to the 2001 *Neilsen/Net Ratings Survey*, the number of Internet users is growing exponentially as it has in past years.[29] According to the survey, the number of people with Internet access in the United States has risen to about 56 percent of the population. The United States now has about 100 million Internet users.

Growth in the use of the Internet, however, is not limited to the United States. According to a study by the Gartner Group, there will be huge growth for Internet use in Asia. Internet subscribers in the Asia–Pacific region, for example, will climb from 41.8 million at the end of 1999 to a forecasted 188 million at the end of 2004, a near five fold increase. This region includes Japan, which is expected to surpass 72 million Internet users by 2004. Of the predicted 188 million Internet subscribers in this region for 2004, 51 million are expected in China and 10.1 million in India. China and India are expected to experience average annual compound growth in Internet subscribers through 2004 to 36.6 percent and 47 percent respectively.

Managers are using the Internet in many different ways. Some use it to continually monitor and gather late-breaking news that can impact their organization in the short run. For example, news regarding fluctuations in interest rates and the latest moves of competitors is readily available on the Internet. Other managers use the Internet to monitor and track government trends that can impact an organization's long-run viability. For example, issues like the evolving trade relationship between the United States and China or the latest turn in affirmative action legislation are easily monitored on the Internet. The following Management and the Internet feature describes how Dell Computer Corporation uses the Internet to reach customer service as well as company image objectives.

The following sections elaborate on the Internet by discussing the World Wide Web, e-mail, and intranets, illustrating how these factors help managers achieve organizational goals. Some managers even use the Internet to find new employees (see Figure 21.9).

The World Wide Web   Perhaps the fastest-growing segment of the Internet is the World Wide Web.[30] The **World Wide Web** is a system that allows managers to have an information location called a **Web site** that is available 24 hours a day, 7 days a week, to anyone who is using the Internet. Each Web site has a beginning page called a **home page,** and each home page generally has several supporting pages called **branch pages** that expand on the thoughts and ideas

The **World Wide Web** is a segment of the Internet that allows managers to have an information location called a **Web site** available continually to Internet users. Each Web site has a beginning page called a **home page,** and each home page generally has several supporting pages called **branch pages** that expand on the thoughts and ideas contained in the home page.

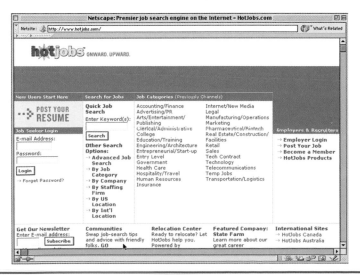

 **Figure 21.9**   *Hotjobs is an Internet site where managers can list open positions and prospective applicants can review them*

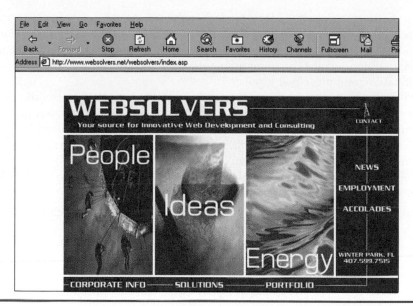

The World Wide Web home page of WebSolvers

Figure 21.10

contained in the home page. Special programming features allow Web site visitors to quickly visit branch pages and quickly return to a home page.

For example, Figure 21.10 is the actual home page of WebSolvers, a company that provides professional Web site services to managers across the world. With the click of a computer mouse on any words at the bottom of the home page, the site visitor quickly shifts to a branch page that provides more information regarding the highlighted topic. A similar click on the branch page quickly returns the visitor to the home page. For example, clicking on "Portfolio" on the WebSolvers home page will give the site visitor more information on a branch page about the company's customers and accomplishments. Another click on the branch page will quickly return the visitor to the WebSolvers home page.

The number of managers establishing Web sites has been growing exponentially, and it is predicted that the number will continue to increase rapidly in the foreseeable future. Managers are using Web sites to perform a wide array of activities ranging from soliciting venture capital to making business travel arrangements.[31]

Managers should not rush into establishing Web sites, but rather should take great care to design and implement a Web site that is consistent with organizational goals. Recall that the fundamental job of the manager is to reach organizational goals through the use of organizational resources. A properly designed and used Web site is an organizational resource that can help managers reach organizational goals like the following:

➤ *Marketing products more effectively*—Marketing is a very popular use of a Web site. Organizations already offer thousands of diverse products, including T-shirts, computers, books, financial services, travel advice and arrangements, and candy, on Web sites. An appropriately organized Web site can help managers promote products through an electronic brochure that is cost-efficient, easily updated, and instantaneously distributed across the world.

➤ *Enhancing the quality of recruits to the organization*—A properly designed Web site enables management to recruit highly qualified people to the organization. Managers using Web sites appropriately can project the image of a progressive organization that keeps abreast of meaningful business trends and that uses any and all innovative tools available to ensure its success. This image should be useful in attracting the finest human resources.

➤ *Enhancing product quality*—An important part of establishing a high-quality product is the ability to offer high-quality service and to maintain communication with customers after the product is purchased. A Web site gives managers an effective and efficient vehicle for communicating with customers *after* an organization's product is purchased.

> ➤ *Communicating globally*—Many modern managers need to communicate across the globe. A Web site enables them to reach out quickly and easily to almost anywhere in the world—and communicating globally via a Web site is generally less costly than using the more traditional global communication vehicles. In addition, a Web site can bring international communities closer together.

> ➤ *Encouraging creativity in organization members*—Every successful organization maintains its success by devising creative solutions to problems. If appropriately designed and administered, a Web site can be a creative solution to myriad organizational problems. Perhaps more importantly, by establishing a Web site, management is sending a clear signal to all organization members that it is willing to provide technological tools for creatively solving problems, and also that it expects members to strive to develop their own creative solutions to their job problems.

Establishing a corporate Web site to help management reach such goals can be an extremely complicated matter. Many modern managers are finding that their organizations do not contain the skills necessary to build and maintain an appropriate Web site. In such cases, managers typically engage the services of an Internet consultant to establish a desirable Web site. WebSolvers, the company mentioned above, is an example of such a consultant. Figure 21.11 shows the results of a survey of 167 Web design consultants outlining fee levels being charged to *Fortune* 500 companies for a typical Web project.

E-Mail   **E-mail**[32] or **electronic mail** is a computerized information system that allows individuals the electronic capability to create, edit, and send messages to one another. Messages are sent to a recipient's "mailbox" where they can be read, saved, answered, forwarded, downloaded, or discarded. This section focuses on e-mail via the Internet, the fastest growing area of such messaging.

Evidence of the growing use of Internet e-mail abounds. For example, a recent report indicated that the U.S. Postal Service delivers 330 million first-class letters a day to the 270 mil-

E-mail is a computerized information system that allows individuals the electronic capability to create, edit, and send messages to one another.

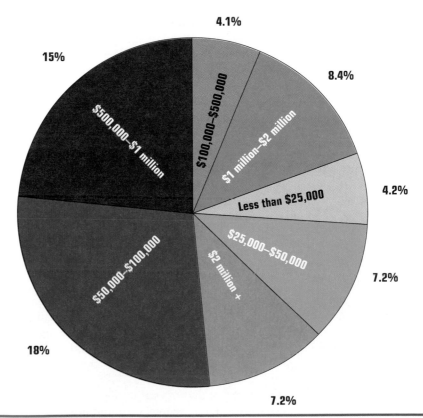

Figure 21.11

Fees for typical Web project charged to Fortune *500 clients and percent of Web consulting firms surveyed charging those fees*

lion people living in the United States. On the other hand, America Online, a worldwide Internet service provider, delivers 225 million "instant" e-mail messages daily to its 12.5 million subscribers.[33] The country's largest Internet provider appears to be rapidly catching up to the volume of daily mail sent via the traditional U.S. mail system. E-mail enthusiasts commonly refer to mail sent via the traditional system as "snail mail."

Using e-mail in organizations provides a means of communicating with unprecedented speed and convenience. Messages can literally be sent and received across the world within seconds from almost any location as long as a connection to the Internet can be procured. Overall, most agree that e-mail significantly enhances the efficiency and effectiveness of communication in organizations. As the following Across Industries feature illustrates, however, technical glitches can render e-mail and its accompanying advantages worthless.

▶ Accounting—Technical Glitch at Arthur Andersen Renders E-Mail Useless

Andersen Consulting, a big purveyor of computer networks to corporate America, recently got a firsthand lesson in just how vulnerable computer networks can be: An Andersen employee made an inadvertent computer error that spread to hundreds of other computers, and suddenly thousands of Andersen employees could not get electronic mail.

The first sign of trouble came for managing partner Lyle Ginsburg late one Friday after he had sent a series of e-mail memos via modem from his hotel. Dialing up Andersen's computer network to check on the messages, he found his mailbox full of a repeated error message: "user . . . not found in name and address file."

That unsettling error message was showing up in mailboxes around the world because an employee—Andersen would not say who or where—unwittingly installed a new directory in the local "server" computer that stores, sends, and receives e-mail. The new directory replaced the existing one, which contained 24,000 user names and addresses. Then, the wayward computer   doing precisely what it was programmed to do—automatically contacted the other 300 or so servers around the world and had them replace their directories with the new one. Without the user names, the network did not know where anyone was.

Using e-mail in organizations can be very challenging. Because e-mail lacks the context of the body language, facial expression, and tone and pitch of voice that face-to-face or even telephone communication provides, electronic messages can be misread or misinterpreted if the words in messages aren't well chosen and to the point. Although some e-mail programs offer a kind of voice mail, they still are not perfect replications of the speaker's natural intonations. Keystroke versions of "happy faces" abound, for instance, :) for happy, and :(for sad, and so on, but they have little application in business writing. Also, because sending a message is as easy as clicking a button, the temptation is to fire off a message without stopping to give it a second reading, either for proofreading or for reconsidering your choice of words. Finally, because messages are so easy to send, the e-mail system in an organization, by its very nature, can increase the number of messages sent resulting in information overload. Table 21.2 contains a number of suggestions for how to e-mail appropriately.

Intranets   **Intranets** are internal corporate communications networks that use the structure and standards of the Internet to allow employees of a single firm to communicate and share information with each other electronically. Figure 21.12 is the home page for an actual intranet at HTE, Inc., a software company in Lake Mary, Florida. Although software to enable firms to set up their own intranets with relative ease is becoming more affordable, the high value of involving professional consultants in designing and building intranets is undeniable. Some of these new programs are Intranetics 97, Involv Intranet, e:Folders, and HotOffice. However, the task is not cheap. The primary costs are training employees how to use the intranet and identifying someone to manage it.[34]

To give access to selected business partners, vendors, or clients, firms can expand their intranets with an **extranet** program that allows outsiders to place orders and check the status

Intranet is an internal corporate communication network that uses the structure and standards of the Internet to allow employees of a single firm to communicate and share information with each other electronically.

Extranet is a program that expands an Intranet to allow organizational outsiders to perform such activities such as placing orders and checking on the status of their orders.

 **Table 21.2**   Hints on How to E-Mail

1. Consider e-mail as you would a hard-copy letter. Proofread all your messages carefully before sending. If your program includes a spell-checker, learn how to use it.

2. Research and follow your company's policies about sending copies to the appropriate colleagues.

3. Remember that e-mail can be monitored in some firms, and that it has been retrieved from hard drives and used as evidence in court cases. Do not use e-mail to start or circulate rumors, repeat damaging information, or spread misinformation.

4. Be sure your message is clear and unambiguous. It should indicate whether or not you require a reply.

5. Do not reply to e-mails that are just confirmations or acknowledgments. Your e-mail will multiply unnecessarily if you do.

6. Write a letter when angry if you must, but do not send or save it.

7. Use a simple filing system for e-mails you need to save.

8. Do not send or reply to chain letters. They clog the system and have been known to shut down entire networks.

9. Be conservative about adding your name to mailing lists and newsletters.

10. Do your personal correspondence from your home computer.

of their orders.[35] FedEx, for example, is expected to attempt a major business shift in the near future, to focus on its information systems that track and coordinate the delivery of packages, which is done through a type of extranet.[36]

One of the biggest concerns for intranet users is keeping the network secure, that is, preventing outsiders (or unauthorized insiders) from breaking into the system and accessing sensitive information. One way of doing this is to install a security system known as a *firewall*, which usually includes both hardware and software to block unauthorized users.

▶ Back to the Case

The above material implies that Dunlap as well as other managers at Sunbeam can use computer networking to enhance the success of downsizing and other management decisions. A local area network could be designed to quickly report production data, for example, from various plant locations to a central computer where it would be combined, summarized, and analyzed. Such networking would allow Dunlap to quickly translate information into action focused not only on downsizing to eliminate unproductive company areas and related costs, but to enhance profitability by investing more in productive company areas.

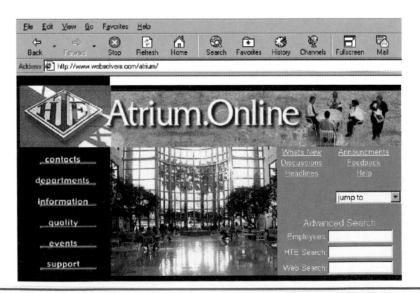

 **Figure 21.12**   *Intranet home page for HTE*

Internet tools like the World Wide Web, e-mail, and an intranet could also be useful to Dunlap in downsizing as well as improving company profitability. The company Web site and its linked pages could be designed to accomplish purposes like promoting Sunbeam's products and helping customers locate retail outlets where the products are available. E-mail could be used to allow speedy communications among Sunbeam stakeholders like Dunlap and the Sunbeam management team, investors, customers, and nonmanagement employees. Finally, an intranet could be designed to allow employees abilities like speedy communication with one another and quick access to company databases to learn more about issues such as jobs available within the company, customer profiles, or manufacturing specifications.

Management Skills Module

This section is specially designed to help you develop management skills. An individual's management skill is based on an understanding of management concepts and the ability to apply those concepts in management situations. As a result, the following activities are designed both to heighten your understanding of management concepts and to help you gain facility in applying those concepts in various management situations.

UNDERSTANDING MANAGEMENT CONCEPTS

▶ Action Summary

Reread the learning objectives below. Each objective is followed by questions. Answering these questions accurately will help you retain the most important concepts discussed in this chapter. After answering each question, check your answer against the answer key at the end of the chapter. (*Hint*: If you have any doubts regarding the correct response, consult the page number that follows the answer.)

Circle:

From studying this chapter, I will attempt to acquire

1. An understanding of the relationship between data and information.

a b c d e   **a.** Data can be: (a) information (b) opinion (c) premises (d) facts (e) gossip.

a b c d e   **b.** Information can be defined as conclusions derived from: (a) data analysis (b) opinion (c) premises (d) gossip (e) none of the above.

2. Insights into the main factors that influence the value of information.

a b c d e   **a.** All of the following are primary factors determining the value of information except: (a) appropriateness (b) expense (c) quality (d) timeliness (e) quantity.

T F   **b.** The appropriateness of the information increases as the volume of the information increases.

3. Knowledge of some potential steps for evaluating information.

a b c d e   **a.** All of the following are main activities in evaluating information except: (a) acquiring information (b) comparing value with cost of information (c) selecting data to be evaluated (d) using information in decision making (e) discounting expected value for deficiencies and inaccuracies.

T F   **b.** The primary concern of management in evaluating information is the dollar value of the benefits gained compared to the cost of generating the information.

4. An understanding of the importance of a management information system (MIS) to an organization.

T F   **a.** A management information system is a network established within an organization to provide managers with information that will assist them in decision making.

a b c d e   **b.** "Determining information needs" is which of the steps necessary to operate an MIS: (a) first (b) second (c) third (d) fourth (e) none of the above.

Circle:

5. A feasible strategy for establishing an MIS.

a b c d e   **a.** All of the following are stages in the process of establishing an MIS except: (a) planning (b) designing (c) improving (d) implementing (e) all of the above are stages.

a b c d e   **b.** Which of the following activities has the potential of improving an MIS: (a) stressing that MIS personnel should strive to accomplish the purpose of an MIS (b) operating an MIS in a "people-conscious" manner (c) encouraging line managers to continually request additional information through the MIS (d) a and b (e) all of the above.

6. Information about what a management decision support system is and how it operates.

T F   **a.** A management decision support system is a set of decision aids aimed at helping managers make nonprogrammed decisions.

T F   **b.** There is basically no difference between a corporate database and a user database.

T F   **c.** Dialogue capability allows the MDSS user to interact with an MIS.

7. An appreciation for the roles of computers and networks like the Internet in handling information.

a b c d e   **a.** All of the following are main computer functions except: (a) input (b) storage (c) control (d) heuristic (e) output.

a b c d e   **b.** All of the following are possible pitfalls in using the computer except: (a) thinking that a computer is independently capable of creative activities (b) failing to realize that a computer is capable only of following precise and detailed instructions (c) training and retraining all computer operating personnel (d) spending too much money on computer assistance (e) overestimating the value of computer output.

T F   **c.** An LAN and the Internet are basically identical.

T F   **d.** A Web site can help managers achieve many different organizational goals.

❚ Action Summary Answer Key

1. a. d, p. 470
    b. a, p. 470
2. a. b, p. 470
    b. F, p. 471
3. a. d, p. 473
    b. T, p. 472

4. a. T, p. 474
    b. a, pp. 474–475
5. a. e, p. 478
    b. d, pp. 480–481

6. a. T, p. 484
    b. F, p. 485
    c. F, p. 486

7. a. d, p. 482
    b. c, pp. 483–484
    c. F, p. 486
    d. T, pp. 488–489

❚ Issues for Review and Discussion

1. What is the difference between data and information?
2. List and define four major factors that influence the value of information.
3. What are operational control decisions and strategic planning decisions? What characterizes information appropriate for making each of these decisions?
4. Discuss the major activities involved in evaluating information.
5. What factors tend to limit the usefulness of information, and how can these factors be overcome?
6. Define *MIS* and discuss its importance to management.
7. What steps must be performed to operate an MIS properly?
8. What major steps are involved in establishing an MIS?
9. Why is planning for an MIS such an important part of establishing an MIS?
10. Why does the designing of an MIS begin with analyzing managerial decision making?
11. How should managers use the symptoms of an inadequate MIS as listed in Table 21.1?
12. How could building cooperation between MIS personnel and line managers improve an MIS?
13. How can management use cost–benefit analysis to improve an MIS?

14. Describe five possible causes of resistance to using an MIS. What can managers do to ensure that these causes do not affect their organization's MIS?
15. Is a computer a flexible management tool? Explain.
16. How do the main functions of a computer relate to one another?
17. Summarize the major pitfalls managers must avoid when using a computer.
18. How does an MDSS differ from an MIS? Define *"what if" analysis* and give an illustration of how a manager might use it.
19. How are local area networks and the Internet different? How are they similar? Explain fully.
20. Define a Web site and explain the relationship between a home page and branch pages.
21. Discuss three different organizational goals that a Web site might help the manager achieve. Be sure to clearly show how a Web site would help.
22. List three challenges to using e-mail and how to meet them.
23. Discuss the value of a firewall to an intranet.

APPLYING MANAGEMENT CONCEPTS

▶ Cases

➤ INTRODUCTORY CASE WRAP-UP

▶ Case Discussion Questions

"Making Changes Without the Right Information at Sunbeam?" (p. 469) and its related Back-to-the Case sections were written to help you better understand the management concepts contained in this chapter. Answer the following discussion questions about this Introductory Case to further enrich your understanding of chapter content:

1. If you were Albert J. Dunlap, what three functions would you use a computer to perform? Be as specific as possible.
2. List three decisions that an MDSS could help Dunlap to make. For each decision, describe the data that must be in the database in order to provide such help.
3. The main steps of the controlling process are measuring performance, comparing performance to standards, and taking corrective action. Discuss a possible role of an MIS at Sunbeam in each of these steps.

▶ Skills Exercise: Applying the VYJ Leadership Model

The Introductory Case emphasized that Albert J. Dunlap, the top manager at Sunbeam Corporation, was fired because he could not achieve an acceptable profit level. Locate the company's Web site on the Internet. What features of the site could help the company be more profitable? Be sure to explain how each feature could help achieve the added profit. What features would you add to the present site to help achieve even greater profitability? Explain why you would add each feature. (*Note*: If you cannot locate the Sunbeam site, answer the same questions for a site of your choice.)

CASE STUDY: *Relax and Let Loudcloud Handle Your Web Site for the New Millenium*

The already famous 29-year-old cofounder of Netscape (now owned by AOL/Time Warner), Marc Andreessen, is determined to build a profitable, secure, long-lasting company. His brainchild, Loudcloud, Inc., not only offers hosting and consulting services, but it allows businesses to outsource the entire creation and management of their net-based communications. Loudcloud builds and manages all aspects of a client's Internet infrastructure from the hardware and software to the network itself. It accomplishes this by using its unique Opsware technology to automate, scale, and monitor Internet functions that used to be done by hand.

Marc Andreessen started Loudcloud in 1999 along with former Netscape/AOL executives Ben Horowitz, Tim Howes, and Sik Rhee; some of the Internet's earliest innovators. Andreessen is now chairman of his second-generation Web company and Ben Horowitz is CEO. According to Andreessen, our economy is undergoing a new wave of technological breakthroughs, but instead of enabling companies to do things faster and better, it is all about saving money and time.

After AOL bought Netscape, Horowitz watched as one company after another succeeded in having its Web site displayed prominently on AOL, become swamped by on-site hits, and then crash. They just didn't know how to handle the traffic on their Web sites! "It was stupid and frustrating," declares CEO Horowitz.

Loudcloud's management team has developed a set of enhanced Smart Cloud Services for customers to choose from. Loudcloud engineers are able to automate the management and construction of large and small corporate Web sites, ultimately saving CEOs and entrepreneurs huge sums of money. They save the expense of hiring a team of highly skilled technicians and they can remain focused on their core business instead of becoming sidetracked by the complexities of evolving Internet technology. Loudcloud takes care of everything for a monthly fee.

In an interview with *Fortune*, Andreessen said, "There's a triangulation between what's possible with the technology, what business needs people have, and what's actually practical." He believes if you can find that "sweet spot," you can make a successful business. Loudcloud is currently managing the Web sites of Nike, Britannica, and Ford Motor, among others.

As a 22-year-old computer engineer, Andreessen cofounded Netscape Communications, the distributor of the first widely available, easy-to-use Web browser, in 1994. During his five years there he learned what it means to build a flexible business strategy that will enable a company to adapt to change and survive. He says that despite the death of many Internet operations in 1999, the opportunities on the Internet have never been greater. Here are just five of the Internet truths he summed up for George Anders of *Fast Company*:

1. Small teams work best. Even within big companies, the best way to take advantage of Internet opportunities may be to put 50 people on a project, instead of 3,500. That's the best way to make sure vital software is developed quickly and with a tight focus.

2. The Net allows you to get closer than ever to your customers. Click-stream analysis allows companies to understand customers' thought patterns as never before. That makes it imperative for companies to put such knowledge to work fast because if they don't their competitors will.

3. Information travels faster than ever. The implications of this are jarring at times—but ultimately they will be beneficial.

4. Open systems become a lot more appealing than they were before. With the Internet, it's possible to have the whole world debugging your software, suggesting new products, or providing customer service. This is now an alternative to the traditional "cathedral of knowledge"—big centrally run companies that do their development in secret and share only finished products. Both models work well. It is hard to say which one will dominate as the Internet becomes a bigger factor in business operations.

5. E-mail remains the Internet's killer application. It's simple but it meets human needs—putting many people in easy reach of one another around the world for business and social contact.

Andreessen goes on to caution companies about what the Internet cannot do. It is still hard to change consumers' preferences. All successful brands like Amazon, AOL, eBay, and Yahoo! were "built by grassroots adoption and word of mouth." Advertising on the Internet only reinforced work that had already been done over time.

Traditional businesses must get used to the instantaneous market feedback received on the Internet. Andreessen stresses that if you retool your software—it will be out on the Web immediately and tested by your real customers so you will know right away if it is working. This can be scary, but it can also be very helpful. Companies need to learn to "turn on a dime"—there is no time to waste in the evolving world of Internet communication.

Andreessen believes that a corporation's successful use of the Internet is based on its ability to adapt to change. This all depends on the management strategy. If the culture is built on the concept of change like it is at Microsoft, Intel, or Cisco, employees will remain loyal and see a rough time through, but if management has not shared the ups and downs of the business with staff, people will leave and the company will flounder. The information available to management via the Internet is only as good as the people who are disseminating it and using it. Great employees are what make a great company.

At Loudcloud and at all start-ups, according to Andreessen, the danger "is not hiring bad people; it's hiring good people instead of great people. Competent managers can usually screen out bad people, but they have a hard time screening out good people." At Loudcloud, CEO Horowitz has a staff of seven full-time Human Resource recruiters—an unusually high number for a company with fewer than 500 employees. It is their job to hire only people at the very top of the talent pool. Horowitz holds weekly one-on-one meetings with his managers and insists that every employee be reviewed and review his manager every 90 days. Horowitz is vigilant about maintaining the highest standards among personnel.

In order to compete in the Internet environment, managers must learn to customize software to their specific needs. For instance, Loudcloud is managing infrastructure services for both Atriax, a Foreign Exchange Portal, and Fox Broadcasting Company. At Fox the goal is to enable the company's Web site to handle unexpected traffic spikes smoothly, especially when Fox has big promotions going. At Atriax, Loudcloud's job is to make sure that Atriax's marketplace is always up and open for the corporate, institutional, and banking foreign exchange professionals around the globe who depend on Atriax to make transactions.

Andreessen and Horowitz and the entire Loudcloud management team are well aware of the risks involved in processing information and plotting out secure business strategies for today's Internet. They believe that the global infrastructure of the Web will ultimately make this a better world. The result of their efforts remains to be seen.

QUESTIONS

1. In a modern, Internet-savvy company like Loudcloud, do appropriateness, quality, timeliness, and quantity still influence the value of information?

2. What information should be on Loudcloud's intranet? Be as specific as possible. Why would you include this information?

3. Explain the role of e-mail at Loudcloud. What advice for using e-mail would you pass on to management?

4. Discuss the major steps necessary to properly operate Loudcloud's MIS. Is any one step more important than any other? Explain.

CONMEDIA SEGMENT 5

Information Technology and the Internet

In this segment you will see what Mia Cipriano's new job as senior vice president for development at Conmedia entails. Her day is long and sometimes frustrating. Small things, like a call from Sam, the publisher, who criticizes her for answering her own phone, reveal just how unaccustomed to corporate life she is. Mia's assistant Kim is having trouble too. You learn that Kim is doing some research using the Conmedia's management information system, which is in need of a major overhaul. As you observe what happens when Kim fails to properly evaluate the data Mia wants, consider whether Kim realizes the importance of her job. Without good market research, Mia will not be able to fulfill her top priority: strategic planning for a new webzine. Big decisions depend on Mia's input, and, at the moment, so does her reputation. As you watch things get worse, bear in mind the factors that influence the value of information. From a management perspective you might want to focus on the need for easy access to data in today's competitive environment. This scenario zeroes in on the world of business you will be entering. Chances are you will play some role in transforming modern management.

As Mia and Sam discuss the management information system, think about what you might do to improve it to suit Mia's needs. Pay attention to what Mia says as she mulls over her next move, which may be to hire a freelancer to do market research. Put yourself in her place. Note the factors that must go into her decision-making process.

On top of everything, Mia has lost touch with her old design team, Jack and Sarah (and possibly her other dot-comer's as well). As you leave Mia, try to assess how she is feeling and why. Remember that it takes time to integrate management information system improvements into the operations of an organization. Nevertheless, it looks like Mia has her work cut out for her. By now your head should be spinning with your own solutions for implementing just the right management information system for Conmedia's needs, including the use of intranets.

QUESTIONS

1. How would you solve Mia's immediate need for accurate, up-to-date data? If she chooses to hire a freelancer to do the market research, explain how she will justify the cost.

2. Using Table 21.1 "Symptoms of an Inadequate MIS," in your text as a guide, list the problems you noted during this video sequence with the MIS at Conmedia.

3. Which of the management decision support system (MDSS) decision aids would be most helpful to Mia—user database, model base, or dialogue capability? Do you think she might want to have more than one? Explain your reasoning by giving thought to what she will need to do in the future as well as to what she needs to do right now.

INFORMATION TECHNOLOGY, THE INTERNET, AND *YOU*

You waited until the last minute to tackle your term project. Your history paper is due tomorrow. The professor requires one illustration (worth 10 points of your grade) and four separate sources. There's no time to go to the library, so you log on to the Internet and find nine Web sites on your topic. You stay up all night and pull together your paper. In the meantime, you've missed this morning's class. No problem. You e-mail your work to the professor at his home e-mail address. Two weeks later he returns your research paper with a failing grade. It turns out your Web site sources were inaccurate. Furthermore, your professor was unable to download your illustration on his computer. As a student you lost points on your grade; as a manager you might have lost your company's money.

1. What could you have done differently, had you not been in such a hurry? What did you learn about the value of information on the World Wide Web? What did you learn about the possible pitfalls of depending on your computer to ensure your success? Do you think this was a useful lesson from a business standpoint?

www.prenhall.com/certo

This book is accompanied by a rich assortment of online activities aimed at developing your management skills. Reviewing news headlines, Internet exercises, an online study guide, and other research and Internet resources can help personalize management skills development for individual students or an entire class.

chapter
chapterchapterchapterchapterchapterchapter

22 Competitiveness: Quality and Innovation

LEGO's Mindstorms Market Research Causes Problem

REMINDER: THE INTRODUCTORY CASE WRAP-UP (PP. 518–519) CONTAINS DISCUSSION QUESTIONS AND A SKILLS EXERCISE TO FURTHER ILLUSTRATE THE APPLICATION OF CHAPTER CONCEPTS TO THIS VIGNETTE.

Well before it reached its target market, MindStorms, the new LEGO toy, benefited from infusions of creative effort and quality control. Courtesy of the LEGO Group.

More than anything on his Christmas list, David Griffin wanted MindStorms, a $200 LEGO robot-construction set designed for kids age 11 and up. So, unable to wait for Christmas Day, he bought a set at a Toys "Я" Us in Leominster, Massachusetts.

In the 11-and-up demographic group, David Griffin is pretty far up: He is a 41-year-old computer engineer, and he is part of a large group of adult MindStorms buyers that *LEGO Group* AG did not anticipate when it put the set on the market. Surveys that LEGO collects with warranty-card returns show that nearly half of the people playing with the set are 25 to 45 years old.

"I really could have gone wild buying add-ons and accessories," Mr. Griffin confesses. "But I was making the purchase under the stern eye of my wife."

Before MindStorms came on the market in mid-September, LEGO expected to sell about 12,000 sets in the United States this year, but since it hit the shelves, demand has been so brisk that the Danish toy giant now expects sales of about 80,000, says John Dion, a LEGO spokesman. Even with ramped-up production, a number of retailers may not get MindStorms in time for Christmas.

"We're still waiting for product," says John Reilly, a spokesman for Consolidated Corporation's K·B toy chain. "I get about a dozen kids coming in every day asking for the new LEGO system," says David Hesel, owner of the Toy Shop in Concord, Massachusetts, who has been told along with other small operators that he won't be getting any MindStorms until next year.

The toy is taking on an unusual life of its own among adult fans. On the Internet, they trade advice about how to break down the system and rebuild it better. Many older users are also swapping handmade programs that supersede the kit's basic software.

The 750-piece MindStorms set includes a palm-size microcomputer called the RCX, light and touch sensors, a bunch of LEGO's trademark interlocking blocks, and an infrared, wireless communications system that lets the RCX receive programming from a personal computer. Owners can build robots that walk, fight with other robots, pick up objects, and sound alarms when doors open.

(continued)

Hobby programmers are trying to teach their MindStorms to do things LEGO never thought of. Mr. Griffin, who works for Compaq Computer Corp., says he wants to program his to run the vacuum cleaner. MindStorms hackers who exchange tips on the World Wide Web say they are trying to use the system to answer the phone and hang up on unwanted callers or to help them operate hidden cameras.

What's Ahead

The Introductory Case focuses on how LEGO has offered the marketplace a new, revolutionary, highly desirable toy called MindStorms but will not achieve high sales of the toy because company market research didn't accurately predict consumer interest in the product. The remainder of this chapter presents useful information for managers like those at LEGO who are interested in maintaining not only the quality of products, but also the quality of important internal company operations like market research. This chapter discusses

1) Fundamentals of quality
2) Quality through strategic planning
3) The quality improvement process
4) Innovation and creativity

FUNDAMENTALS OF QUALITY

Quality is the extent to which a product does what it is supposed to do—how closely and reliably it satisfies the specifications to which it is built.

Quality was defined in Chapter 20 as how well a product does what it is supposed to do—how closely and reliably it satisfies the specifications to which it is built. In that chapter, quality was presented as the degree of excellence on which products or services can be ranked on the basis of selected features. This chapter expands on the topic of product quality.

Defining Total Quality Management

Total quality management (TQM) is the continuous process of involving all organization members in ensuring that every activity related to the production of goods or services has an appropriate role in establishing product quality.

Total quality management (TQM) is the continuous process of involving all organization members in ensuring that every activity related to the production of goods or services has an appropriate role in establishing product quality.[1] In other words, all organization members emphasize the appropriate performance of activities throughout the company in order to maintain the quality of products offered by the company. Under the TQM concept, organization members work both individually and collectively to maintain the quality of products offered to the marketplace.

Although the TQM movement actually began in the United States, its establishment, development, and growth throughout the world are largely credited to the Japanese. The Japanese believe that a TQM program should be companywide and must include the cooperation of all people within a company. Top managers, middle managers, supervisors, and workers throughout the company must strive together to ensure that all phases of company operations appropriately affect product quality. The company operations referred to include areas like market research, research and development, product planning, design, production, purchasing, vendor management, manufacturing, inspection, sales, after-sales customer care, financial control, personnel administration, and company training and education.

"Quality Is Job 1" at Ford

Ford Motor Company has advertised for a number of years that "Quality Is Job 1" at Ford. Symbolic of that commitment is the company's refusal, a few years ago, to release its new Thunderbird model in time for *Motor Trend*'s Car of the Year competition; Ford chose to delay the Thunderbird's release because it had not yet solved certain quality problems. This decision is especially striking because the Thunderbird was the leading contender for the award that year, which would have meant millions of dollars in additional sales and some highly visible publicity for Ford.

Its commitment to quality has made Ford the leader among American automobile manufacturers in meeting the Japanese quality

---

challenge. American automakers have been regaining market share in recent years largely because of the improved quality of their products.

The TQM concept has been adopted by a majority of Japanese firms. In fact, TQM is generally credited with being a major factor in establishing Japan as a major competitor in the world marketplace. Although U.S. firms have been moving toward accepting and implementing the TQM concept, there are still some basic differences between the traditional (U.S.) and Japanese positions on establishing and maintaining total quality.

TQM is a means to the end of product quality. The excellence or quality of all management activities (planning, organizing, influencing, and controlling) in an organization inevitably influences the quality of final goods or services offered by that organization to the marketplace. In general, the more effective its TQM program, the higher the quality of goods and services the organization can offer to the marketplace. The Quality Spotlight feature has been used throughout this text to illustrate how quality is related to planning, organizing, influencing, and controlling issues. ■

The Importance of Quality

Many managers and management theorists warn that U.S. organizations without high-quality products will very soon be unable to compete in the world marketplace. A 1990 book by Armand V. Feigenbaum put the problem succinctly:[2]

> *Quality. Remember it? American manufacturing has slumped a long way from the glory days of the 1950s and '60s when "Made in the U.S.A." proudly stood for the best that industry could turn out. . . . While the Japanese were developing remarkably higher standards for a whole host of products, from consumer electronics to cars and machine tools, many U.S. managers were smugly dozing at the switch. Now, aside from aerospace and agriculture, there are few markets left where the U.S. carries its own weight in international trade. For American industry, the message is simple: Get Better or Get Beat.*

Producing high-quality products is not an end in itself. Rather, successfully offering high-quality goods and services to the marketplace typically results in three important ends for the organization:

1. A positive company image
2. Lower costs and higher market share
3. Decreased product liability costs

Positive Company Image A reputation for high-quality products creates a positive image for an organization, and organizations gain many advantages from having such an image. A positive image helps a firm recruit valuable new employees, accelerate sales of its new products, and obtain needed loans from financial institutions. To summarize, high-quality products generally result in a positive company image, which leads to numerous organizational benefits.[3]

Lower Costs and Higher Market Share Activities that support product quality benefit the organization by yielding lower costs and greater market share. Figure 22.1 illustrates this point. As shown in the top half of this figure, greater market share or gain in product sales is a direct result of customer perception of improved product quality. As shown in the bottom half of the figure, organizational activities that contribute to product quality result in such benefits as increased productivity, lower rework and scrap costs, and lower warranty costs, which, in turn, result in lower manufacturing costs and lower costs of servicing products after they are sold. Figure 22.1 also makes the important point that both greater market share and lower costs attributed to high quality normally result in greater organizational profits.

Decreased Product Liability Costs Product manufacturers are increasingly facing costly legal suits over damages caused by faulty products. More and more frequently, organizations that design and produce faulty products are being held liable in the courts for damages resulting from the use of such products. To take one dramatic example, Pfizer, a company that develops mechanical heart valves, recently settled an estimated 180 lawsuits by heart-implant patients claiming that the valves used in their implants were faulty.[4] Successful TQM efforts typically result in improved products and product performance, and the normal result of improved products and product performance is lower product liability costs.

Established Quality Awards

Recognizing all these benefits of quality, U.S. companies have been placing greater emphasis on manufacturing high-quality products in recent years. Several major awards have been

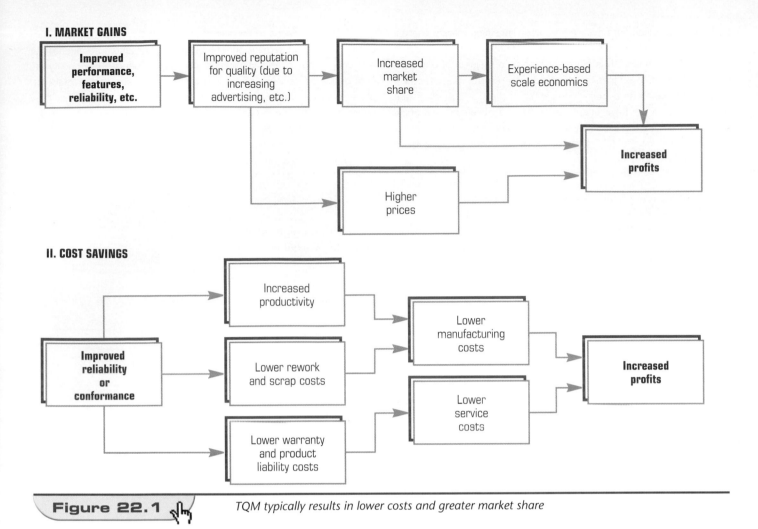

I. MARKET GAINS

Improved performance, features, reliability, etc. → Improved reputation for quality (due to increasing advertising, etc.) → Increased market share → Experience-based scale economics → Increased profits

Higher prices

II. COST SAVINGS

Improved reliability or conformance → Increased productivity → Lower manufacturing costs → Increased profits

Lower rework and scrap costs

Lower warranty and product liability costs → Lower service costs

Figure 22.1 *TQM typically results in lower costs and greater market share*

established in the United States and abroad to recognize those organizations that produce exceptionally high-quality products and services.

The most prestigious international award is the Deming Award, established in Japan in honor of W. Edwards Deming, who introduced Japanese firms to statistical quality control and quality improvement techniques after World War II.

The most widely known award in the United States is the Malcolm Baldrige National Quality Award, awarded by the American Society of Quality and Control. This award was established in 1988.[5]

A few major awards recognize outstanding quality in particular industries. One example is the Shingo Prize for Excellence in American Manufacturing, sponsored by several industry groups, including the Association for Manufacturing Excellence and the National Association of Manufacturers, and administered by Utah State University. Another example, this one from the health care industry, is the Healthcare Forum/Witt Award: Commitment to Quality.

The president of the United States and several states have established a variety of quality awards. NASA, for example, gives awards for outstanding quality to its exceptional subcontractors.

As these examples suggest, quality is an increasingly important element in an organization's ability to compete in today's global marketplace.

▶ Back to the Case

Based on the above information, product quality at LEGO can be defined as the extent to which customer needs are satisfied through the purchased toys. Total quality management

(TQM) would be the process of involving all workers from all organizational levels in providing a high-quality experience to customers.

Clearly, many different organization members at LEGO have significant roles in determining the quality of the entertainment that customers receive through purchased toys. Although the technological marvel of a toy like MindStorms is an obvious dimension of the quality of the experience that is provided customers, issues like customer support and friendliness to customers after the toy is purchased probably help build the perception of product quality in the customers' minds.

All individuals at LEGO, product designers who design toys, market researchers who study customer needs, and line workers who actually manufacture the toys, play a critical role in establishing the level of product quality that LEGO offers its customers.

In today's international marketplace, it is extremely important even for a company like LEGO to maintain a reputation of high product quality. Such a reputation typically results in a positive image for the company as a whole and can make it easier for management to recruit competent employees, reduce operating costs, and increase market share that can enhance company profits and decrease product liability costs.

Achieving Quality

Ensuring that all company operations play a productive role in maintaining product quality may seem like an overwhelming task. The task is indeed formidable, but several sets of valuable guidelines have been formulated to make it more achievable. Guidelines from five internationally acclaimed experts—Philip B. Crosby, W. Edwards Deming, Joseph M. Juran, Shigeo Shingo, and Armand V. Feigenbaum—on how to achieve product quality are summarized in the sections that follow.[6]

Crosby's Guidelines for Achieving Quality

Philip B. Crosby is known throughout the world as an expert in the area of quality and is considered a pioneer of the quality movement in the United States.[7] His work provides managers with valuable insights on how to achieve product quality. According to Crosby, an organization must be "injected" with certain ingredients relating to integrity, systems, communications, operations, and policies before it will be able to achieve significant progress in product quality.

Crosby calls these ingredients the "vaccination serum" that prevents the disease of low companywide quality. The ingredients of Crosby's vaccination serum are presented in Table 22.1.

Deming's Guidelines for Achieving Quality

W. Edwards Deming, who was originally trained as a statistician and began teaching statistical quality control in Japan shortly after World War II, is recognized internationally as a primary contributor to Japanese quality improvement programs. Deming advocated that the way to achieve product quality is to continuously improve the design of a product and the process used to manufacture it.[8] According to Deming, top management has the primary responsibility for achieving product quality.

Deming advised management to follow 14 points to achieve a high level of success in improving and maintaining product quality.[9]

Deming's 14 Points

1. Create and publish to all employees a statement of the aims and purposes of the organization. Management must continually demonstrate its commitment to this statement.
2. Learn the new philosophy—this means top management and everybody else in the organization.
3. Understand the purpose of inspection—for improvement of processes and reduction of cost.
4. End the practice of awarding business on the basis of price tag alone.
5. Improve constantly and forever the system of production and service.
6. Institute training.
7. Teach and institute leadership.
8. Drive out fear. Create trust. Create a climate for innovation.

9. Optimize the efforts of teams, groups, staff areas toward the aims and purposes of the company.
10. Eliminate exhortations to the workforce.
11. (a) Eliminate numerical quotas for production. Instead, learn and institute methods for improvement.

   (b) Eliminate management by objectives. Instead, learn the capabilities of processes and how to improve them.
12. Remove barriers that rob people of pride of workmanship.
13. Encourage education and self-improvement for everyone.
14. Take action to accomplish the transformation.

Juran's Guidelines for Achieving Quality   Like Deming, Joseph M. Juran taught quality concepts to the Japanese and became a significant leader in the quality movement throughout the world. Juran's philosophy emphasizes that management should pursue the mission of quality improvement and maintenance on two levels:

1. The mission of the firm as a whole to achieve and maintain high quality
2. The mission of individual departments within the firm to achieve and maintain high quality

 **Table 22.1**   Crosby's Vaccination Serum for Preventing Poor Total Quality Management

Integrity

A. The chief executive officer is dedicated to having the customer receive what was promised, believes that the company will prosper only when all employees feel the same way, and is determined that neither customers nor employees will be hassled
B. The chief operating officer believes that management performance is a complete function requiring that quality be "first among equals"—schedule and cost
C. The senior executives, who report to those in A and B, take requirements so seriously that they cannot stand deviations
D. The managers, who work for the senior executives, know that the future rests with their abilities to get things done through people—right the first time
E. The professional employees know that the accuracy and completeness of their work determine the effectiveness of the entire workforce
F. The employees as a whole recognize that their individual commitments to the integrity of requirements are what make the company sound

Systems

A. The quality management function is dedicated to measuring conformance to requirements and reporting any differences accurately
B. The quality education system (QES) ensures that all employees of the company have a common language of quality and understand their personal roles in causing quality to be routine
C. The financial method of measuring nonconformance and conformance costs is used to evaluate processes
D. The use of the company's services or products by customers is measured and reported in a manner that causes corrective action to occur
E. The companywide emphasis on defect prevention serves as a base for continual review and planning using current and past experience to keep the past from repeating itself

Communications

A. Information about the progress of quality improvement and achievement actions is continually supplied to all employees
B. Recognition programs applicable to all levels of responsibility are a part of normal operations
C. Each person in the company can, with very little effort, identify error, waste, opportunity, or any concern to top management quickly—and receive an immediate answer
D. Each management status meeting begins with a factual and financial review of quality

Operations

A. Suppliers are educated and supported in order to ensure that they will deliver services and products that are dependable and on time
B. Procedures, products, and systems are qualified and proven prior to implementation and then continually examined and officially modified when the opportunity for improvement is seen
C. Training is a routine activity for all tasks and is particularly integrated into new processes and procedures

Policies

A. The policies on quality are clear and unambiguous
B. The quality function reports on the same level as those functions that are being measured and has complete freedom of activity
C. Advertising and all external communications must be completely in compliance with the requirements that the products and services must meet

Juran insists that quality improvement and maintenance are a clear process requiring managers to become involved in the study of symptoms of quality problems, the identification of quality problems implied by the symptoms, and the application of solutions to these problems. For maximum effect of a quality effort, strategic planning for quality should be similar to the organization's strategic planning for any other organizational issue, such as finance, marketing, and human resources. That is, strategic planning for quality should include setting short- and long-term quality goals, comparing quality results with quality plans, and integrating quality plans with other corporate strategic areas.[10] More discussion on the relationship between quality and strategic planning follows.

Shingo's Guidelines for Achieving Quality   The late Shigeo Shingo served as president of Japan's Institute of Management Improvement and there distinguished himself as one of the world's leading experts on improving the manufacturing process. He and Taiichi Ohno are credited with creating the revolutionary Toyota Production Systems.

Shingo first learned quality production techniques from Americans, who advocated statistical techniques. He later broke with this approach, however, in favor of what he called "mistake-proofing," or in Japanese, *poka yoke*.

The essence of *poka yoke* is that a production system should be made so mistake-proof that it is impossible for it to produce anything except good products. Traditionally, quality efforts were largely confined to inspecting work after it was done— to catch and then fix defects, if possible. Even statistical quality control is dependent on product inspection to diagnose problems with production systems. Recognizing the waste and cost of such inspections, Shingo developed methods to ensure that products are produced correctly the first time, every time.

Figure 22.2 shows an example of a *poka yoke* device designed to prevent errors in a brake wire clamp mounting.[11] Before the improvement, the mounting bridge would accommodate either left or right parts, regardless of which one was needed. This often caused confusion, leading to the installation of the wrong part. A *poka yoke* bridge was devised to set on mounts to ensure that only the correct part could be inserted.

Feigenbaum's Guidelines for Achieving Quality   Armand V. Feigenbaum is credited with originating the term *total quality control*, today more often referred to as *total quality management*, or *TQM*. The basic idea of TQM is that every operation in an organization can benefit from the application of quality improvement principles. Defects are costly and unacceptable throughout the organization, not just on the manufacturing floor.[12]

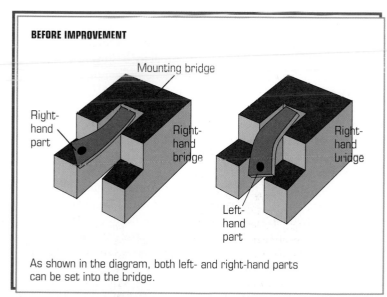

BEFORE IMPROVEMENT

As shown in the diagram, both left- and right-hand parts can be set into the bridge.

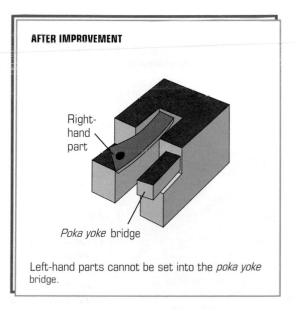

AFTER IMPROVEMENT

Left-hand parts cannot be set into the *poka yoke* bridge.

EFFECTS: Confusion of left and right parts was reduced to zero.

Poka yoke *device*   **Figure 22.2**

The above information gives us insights about how an organization like LEGO can achieve high product quality. Based on the ideas of Philip Crosby, LEGO's management can achieve its high product quality through focusing on complete dedication to quality, its quality-oriented systems, its communications—constantly discussing and monitoring quality—its sound quality-oriented operations decisions regarding issues like which suppliers to use, and its clear policies emphasizing guidelines for achieving a high-quality product.

Based on the ideas of Deming, LEGO can achieve its quality product by continually improving the design of its products and the process used, like market research, to actually provide the experience to its customers. Taking action like focusing on the purpose of improving product quality, promoting cooperation to facilitate the development of product quality, and emphasizing teamwork as a means to product quality are probably all management activities that are instrumental in achieving high product quality at LEGO.

Based on the Ideas of Juran, LEGO can achieve a high-quality product by emphasizing that maintaining product quality is the challenge of the entire organization as well as of individual departments. In addition, LEGO can maintain product quality because all organization members constantly search for symptoms of quality problems and then take action to solve those quality problems.

It would be difficult to conclude that the thoughts of any one of these three theorists completely outline how an organization like LEGO can achieve product quality. Instead, managers should collectively use all of their ideas in formulating a best way to establish product quality within a particular organization.

QUALITY THROUGH STRATEGIC PLANNING

Managers in most organizations spend significant time and effort on strategic planning. Properly designed strategic planning can play an important role in establishing and maintaining product quality.[13] As you recall, strategic planning was defined earlier in this text as long-range planning that focuses on the organization as a whole. The following sections discuss the steps of the strategic management process and suggest how each step can be used to encourage product quality.

Environmental Analysis and Quality

The initial step in the strategic management process is environmental analysis. *Environmental analysis* was defined in Chapter 8 as the study of the organizational environment to pinpoint factors that significantly influence organizational operations. In establishing the role of environmental analysis to enhance product quality, managers should pay special attention to quality-related environmental factors. Consumer expectations about product quality, the quality of products offered by competitors, and special technology under development that will enhance the quality of organizational activities are examples of such factors.

Suppliers are often emphasized during environmental analysis by managers who stress quality. Suppliers are those companies that sell materials used in the final assembly of a product by another company. For example, General Motors has many suppliers who furnish the company with parts that are used in the final assembly of GM automobiles. Managers need to keep in mind that the satisfactory performance of a final product will be only as good as the quality of parts obtained from company suppliers. Defective parts from suppliers can result in delayed delivery schedules, reduced sales, and lower productivity. Making a special study of suppliers during the environmental analysis allows managers to identify those suppliers who will help improve product quality by furnishing high-quality parts.

▶ Part of the strategic planning process for dry cleaning entrepreneurs in general is assessing and limiting the environmental damage caused by the dumping of dry cleaning chemicals.

Establishing Organizational Direction and Quality

In this step of the strategic management process, the results of the environmental analysis are used to determine the path that the organization will take in the future.

This path is then documented and distributed throughout the organization in the form of a mission statement and related objectives. Assuming that environmental analysis results indicate that product quality is important to the organization, a manager can use the organizational mission statement and its related objectives to give general direction to organization members regarding the focus on product quality.

The following is an example of a mission statement used to encourage total quality by Charles Steinmetz, president of All America, Inc., the largest privately owned pest control company in the United States:[14]

> *All America Termite & Pest Control, Inc., operating as Sears Authorized Termite & Pest Control, was founded to provide the residential market a once-a-year pest control service as well as premium termite protection.*
>
> *The purpose of our company is to provide our customers the highest quality of customer service available in our industry while providing unlimited personal and financial potential to our employees.*
>
> *We will commit the time, energy, expertise, and resources needed to provide premier customer service. Furthermore, we realize there are no other choices, options, or alternatives in our pursuit of quality.*
>
> *This requires us to give each customer full value for his or her money and to provide that value the first time and every time we have an opportunity to be of service.*
>
> *We will resolve any customer problems quickly, whether real and apparent or hidden or imaginary. If for any reason we cannot satisfy any customer, we will stand behind our satisfaction or money-back guarantee.*
>
> *Our commitment to our employees is no less important. We will provide all employees with the training necessary for them to become proficient at their job as well as proper equipment, safe materials, and a safe working environment.*
>
> *We will provide ample personal and family benefits to provide reasonable security and offer unlimited compensation, significant opportunity for advancement, and an environment that limits success only by the limits of each employee's hard work, dedication, and capabilities.*

A look at how different companies set the direction of their product quality effort reveals that different companies define product quality in very different ways. For example, some companies define it as a stronger product that will last longer, or as a heavier, more durable product. Other companies define product quality as the degree to which a product conforms to design specifications, or as product excellence at an acceptable cost to the company and an acceptable price to the consumer. In still other companies, quality is defined as the degree to which a product meets consumer requirements.

Whatever definition of product quality management decides on, this definition must be communicated to all organization members so they will work together in a focused and efficient way to achieve predetermined product quality.

Strategy Formulation and Quality

After determining organizational direction, the next step in the strategic management process is strategy formulation—deciding what actions should be taken to best deal with competitors. Incorporating product quality into the SWOT (Strengths, Weaknesses, Opportunities, Threats) analysis will help managers develop quality-based strategies. It may, for example, become apparent as a result of a SWOT analysis that organization members are not adequately trained to deal with certain product quality issues. Obviously, a strategy based on this organizational weakness would be to improve quality-oriented training.[15]

Several management strategies have proved especially successful in improving and maintaining high-quality operations and products. Among them are the following:

➤ *Value adding*—All assets and effort should, as far as possible, directly add value to the product or service. All activities, processes, and costs that do not directly add value to the product should, as far as possible, be eliminated because non–value-adding costs can be very wasteful. This particular strategy is largely responsible for the drastic reductions in staff positions in most large organizations in recent years. For instance, investment analysis does not add value to the product coming off the production line. Therefore, many

▶ Jonathan Ayers is president of the world's largest manufacturer of air conditioners, Carrier Corp., which earns nearly $10 billion a year in revenues and has customers all over the world. Ayers has made Internet technology part of the company's core strategy ever since taking over as president in 1999, and the firm now buys more than 50 percent of its components and services through a Web-based procurement system. Besides cutting costs by an estimated $100 million, use of the Internet has helped Ayers improve quality in many areas, bringing customer satisfaction to new highs.

companies are simplifying their investment strategies and placing greater emphasis on production processes.

➤ *Leadership*—The traditional vision of "The Boss," whip in hand, *driving* lazy, reluctant workers to ever-higher production goals set from on high by management, is disappearing. In quality-focused organizations, "associates" (no longer called "workers" in many quality-focused organizations) are *led*. Management sets the organizational vision and values, and then works with the associates to perfect the production process.

➤ *Empowerment*—Associates are organized into self-directed teams and empowered to do their jobs and even to change work processes if that will improve product quality. They are trained, retrained, and cross-trained in a variety of jobs. "Facilitators" (formerly called "supervisors") work with the associates to provide the resources necessary to meet customer needs.

➤ *Partnering*—The organization establishes "partnerships" with its suppliers and customers—that is, it actively works with them to find ways to improve the quality of its products and services. Management strives to reduce the number of suppliers to only those that can meet two requirements:

1. Suppliers must prove themselves reliable and cost-effective
2. Suppliers must prove the sustained quality of their products

Many quality-focused companies formally certify their suppliers.

➤ *Gathering correct and timely information*—The new global marketplace is exacting and unsympathetic. Managers no longer have time to wait for indirect traditional financial reports of performance to make the decisions required to compete successfully.

Managers no longer have time to wade through mountains of tables, reports, and other documents to find the right information. Consequently, in a quality management environment, information systems provide managers with immediate access to critical nonfinancial and financial information, specifically tailored to the needs of the individual manager.

Computerized information systems are especially useful here. Everyone is trained in computers, from executive management through production staff.

Computer terminals are now as commonplace on factory floors as they are in offices.

➤ *Continuous improvement and innovation*—The clarion themes of the quality movement are continuous improvement and constant innovation. Last year's best performance is not good enough today, and today's best practices will not be good enough perhaps even a month from now.

Tom Peters reported, in *Thriving on Chaos: Handbook for a Management Revolution*, that in 1982, Toyota, the company that established the model for quality in automobile manufacturing, was implementing an average of *5,000* employee suggestions (i.e., improvements) every day. Note that this number does not include improvements initiated by management. Peters advocated, "as a starting point," that U.S. companies target the percentage of revenues stemming from new products and services introduced in the previous 24 months at 50 percent.[16] While these numbers might seem extreme—and they almost certainly are for some companies—they suggest the urgent need to tailor strategic planning to today's rapidly changing and ruthlessly competitive marketplace.

Strategy Implementation and Quality

When the results of environmental analysis indicate that product quality is important to an organization, product quality direction has been established through the organization's mission statement and its related objectives, and a strategy has been developed for achieving or maintaining product quality, management is ready to implement its product quality strategy. Implementation, of course, is putting product quality strategy into action.

This might seem like a straightforward step, but in reality, it is quite complex. To succeed at implementing product quality strategy, managers must rise to some serious challenges. First of all, they must be sensitive to the fears and frustrations of employees who have to implement the new strategy. They must then provide the organizational resources necessary to implement the strategy, monitor implementation progress, and create and effectively use a network of individuals throughout the organization who can help overcome implementation barriers.

Two tools managers commonly employ to implement product quality strategy are policies and organization structure. Each of these tools is discussed in the following sections.

Policies for Quality   A policy was defined in Chapter 9 as a standing plan that furnishes broad, general guidelines for channeling management thinking toward taking action consistent with reaching *organizational* objectives. A quality-oriented policy is a special type of policy. A **quality-oriented policy** is a standing plan that furnishes broad, general guidelines for channeling management thinking toward taking action consistent with reaching *quality* objectives.

Quality-oriented policies can be made in virtually any organizational area. They can focus on such issues as the quality of new employees recruited, the quality of plans developed within the organization, the quality of decision-related information gathered and distributed within the organization, the quality of parts purchased from suppliers to be used in the final assembly of products, and the quality of the training used to prepare employees to work in foreign subsidiaries.

A **quality-oriented policy** is a standing plan that furnishes broad, general guidelines for channeling management thinking toward taking action consistent with reaching quality objectives.

Organizing for Quality Improvement   Juran says that "to create a revolutionary rate of quality improvement requires . . . a special organization structure." He suggests organizing a "quality council," consisting largely of upper managers, to direct and coordinate the company's quality improvement efforts.

The quality council's main job is to establish an appropriate infrastructure, which would include:[17]

1. A process for nominating and selecting improvement projects
2. A process for assigning project improvement teams
3. A process for making improvements
4. A variety of resources, such as time for diagnosis and remedy of problems, facilitators to assist in the improvement process, diagnostic support, and training
5. A process for review of progress
6. A process for dissemination of results and for recognition
7. An appropriate employee merit rating system to reward quality improvement
8. Extension of business planning to include goals for quality improvement

Juran points out that upper management's role in quality improvement is to get actively involved in every element of the infrastructure—even to the point of serving on some improvement project teams.

Notice also that Juran's structure involves employees at all levels. All employees, including managers, serve on quality improvement teams. True, the quality council itself comprises mostly upper management, but it, too, may include other employees.

Strategic Control and Quality

Strategic control emphasizes monitoring the strategic management process to make sure that it is operating properly. In terms of product quality, strategic control focuses on monitoring company activities to ensure that product quality strategies are operating as planned. In achieving strategic control of product quality, management must measure how successful the organization has become in achieving product quality.

Philip Crosby states that in order to control product quality efforts, management needs to monitor several organizational areas. These areas include management's own understanding of and attitude toward quality, how quality efforts appear to others within the organization, how organizational problems are handled, the cost of quality as a percentage of sales, quality improvement actions taken by management, and how management summarizes the organization's quality position.

According to Crosby, organizations go through five successive stages of quality maturity as they approach the maximum level of quality in all phases of organizational activity:

1. *Uncertainty*—There is no comprehension of quality as a management tool. Problems are fought as they occur, with ad hoc methods.
2. *Awakening*—Quality management is recognized as a valuable tool, but the organization is still unwilling to provide adequate resources to attack quality problems.
3. *Enlightenment*—A quality improvement program is established. Top management becomes committed to the concept and implements all the steps necessary for the organization to face problems openly and resolve them in an orderly manner.
4. *Wisdom*—Management now thoroughly understands quality management. Quality problems are identified early, and employees are encouraged to suggest improvements to prevent defects from occurring.
5. *Certainty*—Quality management has become an essential part of the organization's system. Problems are almost always prevented, and quality improvement is a continuous activity.

► Back to the Case

According to the preceding information, strategic planning is a tool that managers in an organization like LEGO can use to achieve product quality. Strategic planning employs strategies and tactics to help management focus on what must be done to maintain product quality in both the long and the short run.

Management can use strategic planning to further product quality by emphasizing quality throughout the strategic management process. During environmental analysis, for example, management can strive to discover information, such as the level of quality that customers expect and technological improvements that might be employed to make the quality of products even greater. MindStorms is an example of such technological improvement to enhance product quality. Given such information, management can decide the direction that product quality should pursue and then use a mission statement and related goals to communicate this direction to all other organization members. Related product quality strategy should then be developed, implemented, and controlled to make sure that it is working.

THE QUALITY IMPROVEMENT PROCESS

Two approaches may be taken to improve quality. The first is the one advocated by most of the quality experts, including Deming, Juran, Crosby, and Feigenbaum. This process can be described as "incremental improvement"—or improve one thing at a time. Actually, many incremental improvements may be undertaken simultaneously throughout an organization; recall Toyota's average of instituting 5,000 improvements per day in 1982.

The second approach, advocated by Michael Hammer, consists of completely reengineering a process.[18] This approach requires starting with a clean slate. Management looks at operations and asks, "If we were to start over today, how would we do this?"

Each approach is discussed in detail in the following sections.

The Incremental Improvement Process

Researches and consultants have advocated a variety of incremental approaches to achieving excellent quality in products and processes. Despite their differences, almost all of these plans bear some remarkable similarities. Although a specific improvement process may not precisely follow the outline in Figure 22.3, most such processes at least approximate it.

> *Step 1: An area of improvement is chosen, which often is called the improvement "theme"*—Either management or an improvement team may choose the theme. Examples are:
> > ➤ Reduction in production cycle time
> > ➤ Increase in the percentage of nondefective units produced
> > ➤ Reduction in the variability of raw material going into production
> > ➤ Increase in on-time deliveries

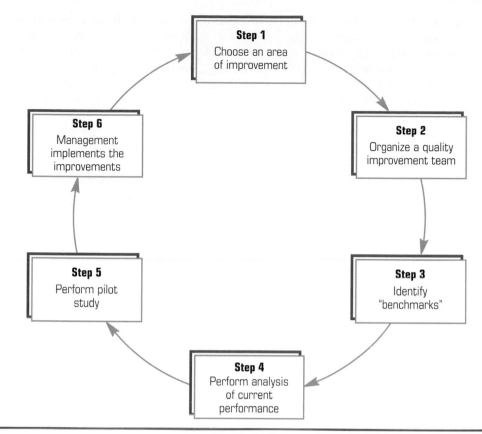

The incremental approach to improving quality

Figure 22.3

➤ Reduction in machine downtime
➤ Reduction in employee absenteeism

Many other examples are possible, of course, but these suffice to make the point that an improvement objective must be chosen.

Consider a pizza company whose delivery business is lagging behind that of its competitors, chiefly because of slow deliveries. The improvement theme in this case may be a reduction in delivery time (i.e., cycle time).

➤ *Step 2: If a quality improvement team has not already been organized, one is organized*—Members of this team might include:

➤ One or more associates directly responsible for the work being done
➤ One or more customers receiving the benefits of the work
➤ One or more suppliers providing input into the work
➤ A member of management
➤ Perhaps one or more experts in areas particularly relevant to solving the problem and making the improvement

For the pizza delivery company, the team might include two pizza builders, a driver, a university student customer, a local resident customer, and a store manager.

➤ *Step 3: The team "benchmarks" the best performers—that is, identifies how much improvement is required in order to match the very best performance*—For example, the pizza company may discover in this step that the benchmark (i.e., the fastest average time between the moment an order is taken until the moment of front-door delivery) established by a competitor is 20 minutes.

Suppose the company's current average delivery performance is 35 minutes. That leaves a minimum possible improvement of 15 minutes on the average.

➤ *Step 4: The team performs an analysis to find out how current performance can be improved to meet, or beat, the benchmark*—Factors to be analyzed here include potential problems related to equipment, materials, work methods, people, and the environment, such as legal constraints, physical conditions, and weather. To return to the pizza delivery company, suppose the team discovered that the pizza-building process could be shortened by 4 minutes. Also suppose they found an average lag of 5 minutes between the time the pizza is ready and the time the delivery van picks it up. Finally, suppose the team discovered that a different oven could shorten cooking time by 7 minutes. Total potential savings in delivery time, then, would be 16 minutes—which would beat the benchmark by 1 minute.

> *Step 5: The team performs a pilot study to test the selected remedies to the problem*—In the pizza case, suppose the team conducted a pilot program for a month, during which the new pizza-building process was implemented, a new driver and van were added, and a new oven was rented. At the end of the month, suppose actual improvement was 17 minutes on average.

The question then becomes, "Is the improvement worth the cost?" In this case, the improved pizza-building process is improving other customer service as well, thereby increasing the company's overall sales capacity. By beating the benchmark, the company can establish a new delivery system standard—a significant marketing advantage. Suppose, then, that a cost–benefit study favors the changes.

> *Step 6: Management implements the improvements*—Making many such incremental improvements can greatly enhance a company's competitiveness. Of course, as more and more companies achieve better and better quality, the market will become more and more demanding. The key, therefore, is to continually improve both product and process.

This section discussed the incremental improvement process in organizations in general terms. The following People Spotlight feature provides insights about how to keep organization members involved in incremental improvement by discussing a very successful incremental improvement process at Bearings, Inc.

Keeping People Involved in Incremental Improvement: Bearings, Inc.

For over three years, operations at Bearings, Inc., have steadily improved as a result of a specially designed incremental improvement program. The program is both simple and effective. Bearings employees are asked to submit ideas for improving company operations, and ideas found to be worthwhile by management are implemented. What began as management's desire to informally solicit unedited ideas from the people who actually do the work has evolved into a program that steadily produces a swell of suggestions—one of which has trimmed $900,000 from the cost of running the program itself.

During the initial phase of the program, employees were simply invited to write down their ideas for improving company operations and to submit them to management. As the program became more formal, ideas were collected and printed in a quarterly report called *Quality Idea Briefs* and sent for review to over 4,000 organization members. Ideas presented in this report have focused on issues ranging from increasing customer satisfaction and sales to decreasing the cost of operations and the time it takes to manufacture bearings.

Submissions to *Quality Idea Briefs* have nearly tripled since the program began—in one recent year, over 8,000 ideas were submitted by workers. Bearings' success in getting workers to participate in the improvement program can probably be credited to the care management takes to inform workers of the exact status of their submitted ideas. Nearly 35 percent of all the ideas that made it into *Quality Idea Briefs* have been transformed into operating policy, and the workers who submitted the other 65 percent have been apprised of the reasons their ideas could not be implemented. Bearings workers feel proud when their ideas are accepted for implementation and respected when management takes the time to explain to them why their ideas are inappropriate. ■

Reengineering Improvements

Hammer argues that significant improvement requires "breaking away from . . . outdated rules and . . . assumptions. . . ." It demands a complete rethinking of operations. He, too, recommends that management organize a team representing the functional units involved in the process to be reengineered, as well as other units that depend on the process.

One important reason for reengineering instead of attempting incremental improvements is the need to integrate computerized production and information systems. This is an expensive change, and one that is very difficult to accomplish piecemeal through an incremental approach.

Hammer outlines seven principles of reengineering:

➤ *Principle 1: Organize around outcomes, not tasks*—Traditionally, work has been organized around different tasks, such as sawing, typing, assembling, and supervising. This first principle of reengineering would, instead, have one person or team performing all the steps in an identified process. The person or team would be responsible for the outcome of the total process.

➤ *Principle 2: Have those who use the output of the process perform the process*—For example, a production department may do its own purchasing, and even its own cost accounting. This principle would require a broader range of expertise from individuals and teams, and a greater integration of activities.

➤ *Principle 3: Subsume information-processing work into the real work that produces the information*—Modern computer technology now makes it possible for a work process to process information simultaneously. For example, scanners at checkout counters in grocery stores both process customer purchases and update accounting and inventory records at the same time.

➤ *Principle 4: Treat geographically dispersed resources as though they were centralized*—Hammer uses Hewlett-Packard as an example of how this principle works. Each of the company's 50 manufacturing units had its own purchasing department, which prevented the company from achieving the benefits of scale discounts. Rather than centralize purchasing, which would have reduced responsiveness to local manufacturing needs, Hewlett-Packard introduced a corporate unit to coordinate local purchases, so that scale discounts could be achieved. That way, local purchasing units retained their decentralized authority and preserved their local responsiveness.

➤ *Principle 5: Link parallel activities instead of integrating their results*—Several processes are often required to produce products and services. Too often, though, companies segregate these processes so that the product comes together only at the final stage. Meanwhile, problems may occur in one or more processes, and those problems may not become apparent until too late, at the final step. It is better, Hammer says, to coordinate the various processes so that such problems are avoided.

➤ *Principle 6: Put the decision point where the work is performed and build control into the process*—Traditional bureaucracies separate decision authority from the work. This principle suggests that the people doing the work are the ones who should make the decisions about that work. The salesperson should have the authority and responsibility to approve credit, for example. This principle saves time and allows the organization to respond more effectively and efficiently to customer needs.

Some managers worry that this principle will reduce control over the process. However, control can be built into the process. In the example cited, criteria for credit approval can be built into a computer program, so the salesperson has guidance for every credit decision.

➤ *Principle 7: Capture information once and at the source*—Computerized online databases help make this principle achievable. It is now easy to collect information when it originates, store it, and send it to those who need it.

Reengineering allows major improvements to be made all at once. While reengineering can be an expensive way to improve quality, today's rapidly changing markets sometimes demand such a drastic response.

▶ Back to the Case

The preceding information gives insights into the quality improvement process that LEGO's management can follow within the company. For example, LEGO's management can emphasize the incremental improvement process. This process emphasizes choosing an area of improvement like market research, organizing a quality team to assess the market research area, having the team establish benchmarks indicating standards that market research activities

(continued)

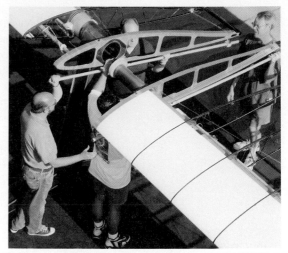

▶ Technicians slip the main span of a Centurion wing section into another during "fit check" operations that ensure quality for the innovative aircraft. The assembly of major framework sections was a milestone in the development of the lightweight remote control aircraft and a creative idea brought to fruition. The project was sponsored by a division of NASA's Dryden Flight Research Center.

should reach in the future, having the team study market research operations to see how current performance can reach or surpass benchmarks, having the team run a pilot study to see how proposed remedies to market research problems would actually work, and having the team implement remedies that are perceived to have value based on the results of the pilot study.

LEGO's management could also use reengineering to improve quality. Using this philosophy, management would not be searching for incremental improvements such as improving market research, but more revolutionary improvements—for instance, totally rethinking and redesigning LEGO's production process. Based on information in the case, incremental improvement would probably be a more appropriate philosophy for LEGO's management to follow than reengineering.

INNOVATION AND CREATIVITY

Innovation is the process of taking useful ideas and turning them into useful products, services, or methods of operation.

Creativity is the ability to combine ideas in a unique way or to make useful associations among ideas.

This chapter has discussed improving quality in organizations by explaining the incremental improvement process and reengineering. The last part of this chapter discusses innovation and creativity, two important keys to quality improvement in organizations. **Innovation** is defined as the process of taking useful ideas and turning them into useful products, services, or methods of operation.[19] These useful ideas are the result of creativity, the prerequisite for innovation. **Creativity** is the ability to combine ideas in a unique way or to make useful associations among ideas.[20] In essence, creativity provides new ideas for quality improvement in organizations and innovation puts the ideas into action. This section focuses primarily on creativity in organizations, making sure that ideas necessary to fuel innovation are plentiful. Discussion focuses on creativity in individuals and encouraging creativity in organization members.[21]

DIGITAL FOCUS

▶ Siemens Uses ShareNet to Encourage Innovation

Siemens, with a rich history of over 150 years, is a world leader in electrical engineering and electronics. Major business areas of the company include:

➤ *Information and Communications*—The company offers communication network solutions and a portfolio of cordless and mobile phones.

➤ *Automation and Control*—Company products include production and logistics automation equipment aimed at increasing productivity.

➤ *Power*—Siemens offers affordable power and heat through its environmentally friendly power plants.

➤ *Transportation*—Siemens offers a number of products and services that integrate transportation systems and improve vehicle safety.

To remain competitive, Siemens has adopted the goal of becoming a global network of innovation. One tool being implemented to meet this goal is an online knowledge-management vehicle called ShareNet. ShareNet, an online database, helps employees to find and share expert advice about solving work problems within Siemens. Actually, ShareNet is an online forum that allows people to post business cases that can be reused by others. Siemens offers incentives like free trips to employees who contribute expertise to ShareNet or who use ShareNet knowledge contributed by others. Through the use of technology, Siemens has the potential to identify and implement the ideas of nearly 460,000 employees in over 190 countries.

Supporters of ShareNet believe that the system will help Siemens to collect a wealth of expertise and apply it to solving company problems. This is one example of how Siemens is implementing innovation by unlocking the profit potential of the knowledge and expertise of its best employees.

Creativity in Individuals

Within each individual, creativity is a function of three components. These components are expertise, creative thinking skills, and motivation. Figure 22.4 illustrates these three components and depicts how, when overlapping, they result in creativity.

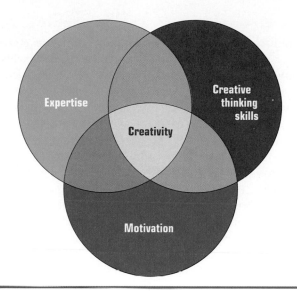

The three components of creativity

Figure 22.4

Expertise, as depicted in Figure 22.4, is everything an individual knows and can do in the broad domain of his or her work. This knowledge pertains to work-related techniques and procedures as well as a thorough understanding of overall work circumstances. Take, for example, a produce worker in a supermarket. Her expertise includes basic abilities in trimming and cleaning fresh fruits and vegetables, building appealing product displays that encourage customers to buy products, and building customer relations. As with all organization members, the abilities of this produce worker can be acquired through formal education, experience, and interaction with peers and other professionals.

Creative thinking is the capacity to put existing ideas together in new combinations. Overall, creative thinking determines how flexibly and imaginatively individuals approach problems. This capacity depends mainly on an individual's personality and work habits. Continuing with the above example, the produce worker will tend to be more creative if she feels comfortable disagreeing with people about how the produce department presently functions. Such disagreement will often result in new thoughts about how to improve the department, such as keeping produce fresher for longer periods. In addition, she will tend to have more creative success if she keeps plodding along to face and solve department problems, such as buying new technology to keep produce cool and not necessarily always looking for quick problem solutions. This enduring attention to problems will afford the produce worker the attention necessary to generate creative solutions to complex organizational problems.

Motivation, as depicted in Figure 22.4, refers to an individual's need or passion to be creative. If an individual feels a need to be creative, that individual is more likely to do so. Expertise and creative thinking are the individual's raw materials for being creative, but motivation determines whether or not an individual will actually be creative. An individual can be driven to be creative either extrinsically through organizational rewards and punishments, or intrinsically through personal interest and passion related to a situation. Normally, people will be most creative when motivated by personal interest, satisfaction, and the challenge of the work. Continuing with our supermarket example, the produce worker could have the expertise and critical thinking necessary to be creative, but unless she is motivated, she probably will not be creative. Generally, the produce worker will be more motivated to be creative if she is personally interested in supermarket problems, tends to be personally satisfied by solving these problems, and sees solving the problems as challenging.

▶ The invention of the 3M "Post-it" note is now a legend. The scraps of paper that 3M scientist Art Fry used to mark the pages in his hymnal were always falling out during choir practice. At about the time he noticed this, Fry was also trying to figure out what to do with a new low-tack adhesive that a coworker named Spencer Silver had invented. Fry's creative application of the invention resulted in a revolutionary product that few office workers today want to be without.

Encouraging Creativity in Organization Members

The previous section discusses components of creativity: expertise, creative thinking skills, and motivation. This next section is based on the premise that managers can influence the existence of these components in individuals and provides sound advice that managers can use to encourage organization members to be creative. To encourage individual creativity in organizations, managers should:

1. *Match individual expertise with work assignments*—Because expertise is an important component of creativity, managers should ensure that organization members are in work areas matched to their levels of expertise. Needless to say, if individuals do not have knowledge of how to adequately function in a job situation, being creative in that job will be virtually impossible. To promote productivity, work situations should be challenging and should require effort and focus. However, work situations significantly beyond an individual's level of expertise will result in frustration and confusion and will eliminate any creative potential that an individual might possess. If an individual's expertise is significantly below the requirements of a particular work situation, management might provide the individual with training necessary to raise the level of expertise or transfer the individual to a more suitable work situation. Once the individual's expertise and the requirements of the work situation are made more equivalent, potential for individual creativity will be restored.

2. *Provide resources necessary for creativity*—In order for organization members to be creative, they need time and money—time in which to be creative and money to invest in assets such as help from consultants. Managers must allocate these resources carefully, knowing what creative challenges organization members face and how much time and money will be needed to meet the challenges. Unfortunately, many managers unknowingly discourage creativity in organizations by creating unrealistic work deadlines. Such deadlines not only discourage creativity, but tend to generate mistrust between managers and organization members and cause worker burnout.

3. *Reward creativity*—Managers can encourage creativity through organizational rewards. In essence, managers should reward workers when they are creative. Rewards should be given extrinsically, such as through annual performance appraisals or by assigning bonuses to be paid over time based on a percentage of the benefit that an individual's idea yields the organization. Managers can also assign rewards that focus on intrinsic motivation by recognizing the high value of creative efforts as well as the skill and perseverance necessary to generate creative solutions to problems. To magnify the impact of such rewards in encouraging personal creativity, managers should be creativity role models. As role models, managers should consistently focus attention on generating creative solutions to complex organizational problems.

▶ When Vance Patterson, CEO of Patterson Fan Co. of South Carolina, saw a couple of employees cooking hamburgers on a grill made of spare parts from the company's industrial fan products, he was intrigued and said so. The employees built him a similar grill for his birthday, with the same flared parts that allowed heat to circulate more evenly. Some months later, in 1998, Patterson patented the grill in the names of the two inventors, James Ballentine and Robert Carter, and himself, and formed a new company to manufacture and sell the Town & Country Grill.

▶ Back to the Case

The above information implies that LEGO's management should use creativity and innovation to enhance organizational quality. New thoughts and ideas would come through creativity, and putting the ideas into action would come through innovation. To encourage creativity at LEGO, management must help organization members to develop expertise in their work area, develop critical thinking skills, and be motivated to be creative.

MindStorms, as a product, is an example of how LEGO's management innovated based on a creative idea to improve the quality of product offerings. Based on the case, LEGO's management obviously afforded appropriately skilled people the time and money necessary to generate the creative idea that spawned MindStorms. Now, management must reward those that spawned the idea and emphasize this new product as a model for how, in the future, creative ideas must grow and flourish at LEGO.

Management Skills Module

This section is specially designed to help you develop management skills. An individual's management skill is based on an understanding of management concepts and the ability to apply those concepts in management situations. As a result, the following activities are designed both to heighten your understanding of management concepts and to help you gain facility in applying those concepts in various management situations.

UNDERSTANDING MANAGEMENT CONCEPTS

▶ Action Summary

Reread the learning objectives below. Each objective is followed by questions. Answering these questions accurately will help you to retain the most important concepts discussed in this chapter. After answering each question, check your answer against the answer key at the end of the chapter. (*Hint:* If you have any doubts regarding the correct response, consult the page number that follows the answer.)

Circle:

From studying this chapter, I will attempt to acquire

1. An understanding of the relationship between quality and total quality management.

T F   **a.** Overall, product quality and total quality management are the same.

a b c d e   **b.** A TQM program is *not* characterized by: (a) a continual process (b) efforts by all organization members (c) a focus on only a few critical work activities (d) a focus on the production process (e) efforts to involve organization members.

2. An appreciation for the importance of quality.

T F   **a.** High product quality can result in reduced costs but generally not increased market share.

T F   **b.** Increasing product quality can reduce product liability costs for an organization.

3. Insights into how to achieve quality.

a b c d e   **a.** According to Crosby, in order to achieve quality, an organization must implement critical ingredients relating to: (a) integrity (b) systems (c) communications (d) operations (e) all of the above.

T F   **b.** According to Deming, a company can improve its product quality by choosing suppliers based on quality rather than on price alone.

T F   **c.** According to Juran, a company can improve its product quality by focusing on the quality of the organization as a whole as well as the quality of individual departments.

a b c d e   **d.** According to Shingo, *poka yoke* means: (a) production (b) mistake-proofing (c) worker commitment (d) quality (e) diversity.

T F   **e.** According to Feigenbaum, defects are unacceptable only on the manufacturing floor.

4. An understanding of how strategic planning can be used to promote quality.

T F   **a.** Establishing an appropriate mission statement is important for achieving quality.

T F   **b.** Establishing and using appropriate policies and organization structure are important steps in quality-oriented strategy formulation.

5. Knowledge about the quality improvement process.

T F   **a.** The incremental improvement approach involves improving one thing at a time.

a b c d e   **b.** The following is a principle of the reengineering approach to improving quality: (a) organize around outcomes (b) link parallel activities (c) put decision points where the work is performed (d) capture information at the source (e) all are principles of reengineering for quality.

T F   **c.** In management, innovation usually precedes creativity.

a b c d e   **d.** To encourage creativity in organizations, managers can: (a) reward creativity (b) provide resources necessary for creativity (c) match individual expertise with work assignments (d) a and b (e) a, b, and c.

1. a. F, p. 500
   b. c, p. 500
2. a. F, p. 501
   b. T, p. 501

3. a. e, p. 503
   b. T, pp. 503–504
   c. T, pp. 504–505
   d. b, p. 505
   e. F, p. 505

4. a. T, pp. 506–507
   b. F, p. 509

5. a. T, p. 510
   b. c, p. 513
   c. F, p. 514
   d. e, p. 516

▶ Issues for Review and Discussion

1. What is the difference between product quality and total quality management (TQM)?
2. Is a successful TQM program important to an organization? Explain.
3. Discuss three benefits resulting from the achievement of high product quality.
4. What guidelines does Crosby offer organizations that want to achieve quality?
5. What guidelines does Deming offer on achieving quality?
6. What guidelines does Juran offer on achieving quality?
7. What guidelines does Shingo offer on achieving quality?
8. Discuss how establishing organizational direction as part of the strategic management process can be used to raise the chances of success of a product quality effort.
9. Can quality be a significant component of a company's strategy? Explain.
10. Discuss the significance of policies and organization structure as components of an effort to maintain product quality.
11. Using Crosby's "five successive stages of quality maturity" as a basis, how would you control TQM efforts in an organization?
12. Discuss how the strategies of partnering and empowerment can improve quality within an organization.
13. When organizing for quality, which structural changes would you anticipate would make the greatest contributions to achieving total quality?
14. Under which circumstances would you use the incremental improvement process to improve quality?
15. Under which circumstances would you use the reengineering approach to improve quality?
16. Discuss Hammer's principles of reengineering for improvement.
17. Would you be concerned with workforce diversity in a program aimed at enhancing product quality? Why or why not? If you would be concerned, what actions would you take?
18. Discuss the relationships among TQM, innovation, and creativity.

APPLYING MANAGEMENT CONCEPTS

▶ Cases

▶ INTRODUCTORY CASE WRAP-UP

▶Case Discussion Questions

"LEGO's MindStorms Market Research Causes Problem" (pp. 499–500) and its related Back-to-the Case sections were written to help you better understand the management concepts contained in this chapter. Answer the following discussion questions about the Introductory Case to further enrich your understanding of chapter content:

1. Can a successful TQM program at LEGO decrease the company's product liability costs? If not, why? If so, how?
2. Explain how Crosby's advice relates to ensuring high-quality company activities at LEGO in the future.
3. What steps can LEGO management take to ensure that creative ideas will continue to enhance the quality of company operations?

▶Skills Exercise: Applying Total Quality Management (TQM)

TQM is a management philosophy that indicates that every operation in an organization can benefit from the application of quality improvement principles. The Introductory Case describes a situation wherein LEGO has missed and will miss sales of its new MindStorms robot construction set because the company did not anticipate significant purchases of the toy by adults. Assume that LEGO's market research department should be improved in order to prevent missed sales of any new toy in the future. Design a plan to improve the quality of LEGO's market research efforts. Be as specific as possible in stipulating and explaining the steps of your plan.

CASE STUDY: *HUMAN INGENUITY GETS A BOOST IN LEAR CORPORATION'S "REALITY ROOM"*

Lear Corporation was founded in Detroit in 1917, as a manufacturer of welded and stamped steel assemblies for the automotive and aircraft industries. By 2000, Lear had gained the capability to make an entire vehicle interior. It had also invested in the latest computer-aided design (CAD) software and Virtual Reality technology. Today, it is the world's largest manufacturer of automotive seating and interiors, with locations in 32 countries. Lear is based in Southfield, Michigan, and now works exclusively for the automobile industry.

At Lear, designers, engineers, and sculptors used to work with 3-D clay renderings of seats and doors. Everyone involved could actually touch the angles and curves. Once Lear had installed its Reality Center, however, it was no longer necessary to build prototypes. When you turn the lights off in the Reality Center and look up at the VR screen (20 feet wide and 8 feet high), you feel as though you are inside a luxurious automobile interior—you watch as lifelike images go by the windshield. All this is made possible through the use of a triple projection screen and three digitized drawing boards. However, the virtual design–engineering team soon realized that they needed to be able to feel the firmness of a seat and the suppleness of the leather upholstery. It wasn't enough to have a projected computerized image; they needed to see and feel the physical version of what they were making. The auto executives who are buying the interiors Lear creates want to be able to touch what they are getting. Therefore, Lear still makes at least one physical prototype of every product.

The team also learned that VR technology makes everything too perfect. "Real life isn't flawless," says Jaron Rothkop, a senior industrial designer at Lear. Now the team builds "mistakes" into its virtual designs. For instance, they might scan in leather interiors with imperfections in them, so when customers see the virtual version of what they are buying, they know it is close to what they will get in reality.

"Technology is a tool: It's not your job," says Rothkop. In order to keep the creative flow of ideas going among team members, Lear built its Reality Center with collaboration in mind. "We wanted it to be a working room, like a design studio," explains Rothkop. "The hot thing in virtual reality is the stereoscopic cave, a space in which people can sit and be completely surrounded by a screen." This arrangement would have simulated being inside a car, but only one or two people at a time can sit in the cave and that is not conducive to team work. The Lear team chose to make its VR room a more open space with a flatter screen. They even have space in front of the screen for a real truck so the designers can work with tactile materials when necessary.

After investing in this expensive technology, Lear executives could have combined the role of designer, sculptor, and animator into a single job, thereby cutting staffing expenses. For instance, the VR and CAD capabilities allow one experienced design engineer to sculpt with the cursor, in theory eliminating the job of the sculptor. However, Lear listened to its creative design team members, who felt that their work was dependent on the specialized skills of each person, especially since they still find it necessary to work with real materials. At Lear, "the Reality Center has no control booth, so everyone can operate the system," says Rothkop. "People get very comfortable here."

In the summer of 1999, the Lear design team heard that GM was thinking of outfitting the shell of a commercial van with deluxe leather seating, flip-down flat panel screens, and other high-tech gadgets. It turned out that the Lear team had a similar idea in the works, so they took that idea to GM's van division executives, who liked it. In order to get the contract, however, Lear had to move quickly. The Lear team used its Reality Center to come up with a makeover and even created a physical prototype of their efforts to show GM within a year. In 2001, the Chevrolet Express LT came off the production line at General Motors. Lear had won the contract to design and manufacture the van's interior by ingenious use of its new technology.

People from GM were impressed. "It would have taken two, maybe three years to make a van like this in the GM system," says Larry Sydowski, GM's program manager for the Express LT. "In that time the demand for such a vehicle might have come and gone—or worse, a rival carmaker might have implemented the idea first."

"We always thought of Lear as a great seating company," says Linda Cook, GM's planning director for commercial trucks and vans. "We didn't realize how much else it could do. Lear really needed that technology to get our attention."

"Technology makes things faster and more cost-effective, but it's not perfect," says John Phillips, Lear's director of advanced product development, who is in charge of the Reality Center. "It requires you to be as flexible as you can be. VR and CAD can streamline the design process but human ingenuity and teamwork are what make a car interior real to the senses."

In order to ensure that the company will remain competitive in years to come, Lear Corporation partners with university campuses that attract high-caliber students. They actively seek "the type of individual who is a self-starter, a person who enjoys creating tomorrow's solutions today in a highly effective and empowered team atmosphere." They even offer "Co-op Programs" that allow serious students to participate in a cooperative assignment.

At Lear, Virtual Reality has become an essential design tool, necessary to survival in an increasingly competitive marketplace, and with the help of technology, the company is thriving. Even with a lean staff and a trim budget, Lear grew its business backlog in 2000 to $3.5 billion.

Lear's Internet home page sports the message "Advance Relentlessly," and that is just what it is doing. Creativity provides the momentum that propels this 84-year-old corporation forward and keeps it at the forefront of the automotive interior industry—where it belongs!

QUESTIONS

1. How has the investment in powerful new technology contributed to both innovation and creativity at Lear? Explain.
2. Describe how management at Lear Corporation encourages creativity in its employees.
3. Without the latest computer-aided design (CAD) software and the Reality Center, do you think Lear would have won the contract for GM's Chevrolet Express LT? Explain.
4. Would you be interested in working at Lear after graduation? Why or why not?

chapter

23 Management's Digital Dimension

objectivesobjectivesobjectives

▶ Objectives

From studying this chapter, I will attempt to acquire

● An understanding of digital dimensioning and the digital dimensioning process

● Insights concerning how digital expertise and digital environment relate to digital success

● An appreciation for digital strategy and digital direction

● Knowledge about how implementation and control relate to digital dimensioning

● An awareness of how strategic management and digital dimensioning relate

● Understanding of how planning, organizing, and digital dimensioning relate to the job of a manager

● Insights into how influencing, controlling, and digital dimensioning relate to the job of a manager

CHAPTER OUTLINE

Introductory Case: *Office Depot Recognized for Digital Excellence*

Defining Digital Dimensioning

Ethics Spotlight ▶ IBM Helps Developing Nations Bridge the Digital Divide

The Digital Dimensioning Process
Enlisting Digital Expertise
Analyzing Digital Environment

Across Industries ▶ Electric Utilities Industry—CMS Energy Corporation Focuses on Digital Environment

Establishing Digital Direction

Quality Spotlight ▶ SMA's Digital Direction Reflects Quality Goal

Formulating Digital Strategy
Implementing Digital Strategy
Controlling Digital Dimensioning

Digital Dimensioning and Strategic Planning

Digital Dimensioning: The Manager's Whole Job?
Digital Dimensioning and Planning
Digital Dimensioning and Organizing
Digital Dimensioning and Influencing
Digital Dimensioning and Controlling

Office Depot Recognized for Digital Excellence

REMINDER: THE INTRODUCTORY CASE WRAP-UP (P. 539) CONTAINS DISCUSSION QUESTIONS AND A SKILLS EXERCISE TO FURTHER ILLUSTRATE THE APPLICATION OF CHAPTER CONCEPTS TO THIS VIGNETTE.

Office Depot, Inc. operates an international chain of over 700 retail stores located throughout 35 states, the District of Columbia, and five Canadian provinces. The stores carry a broad selection of merchandise including office supplies, business machines, computers, computer software, and office furniture. Each store has a multipurpose services center offering business-related services like printing and copying.

Office Depot's Web site makes retail sales more efficient for consumers and for the firm. Customer's find the site's voice interaction feature surprisingly "human."

Office Depot recently gained significant national and international acclaim by appearing on *Informationweek*'s e-business List of 100 Outstanding E-Retailers. The Delray Beach, Florida, company initially designed its Web site, OfficeDepot.com, to cater to consumers and small businesses. At OfficeDepot.com, customers place product orders and pay online as well as check the status of their orders and inventories at Office Depot warehouses and stores around the country. Additionally, the site includes self-service functions like customers making lists of products they are most likely to buy and then placing repeat orders from those lists.

The latest feature of OfficeDepot.com is its new voice interaction capability. This new vehicle has been developed to enrich the online shopping experience of customers. The automated audio response from the OfficeDepot.com Web site to customers seems so real that customers often forget they are dealing with technology. For example, according to Ken Jackowitz, Office Depot's vice president of business systems, when one customer said to the OfficeDepot.com audio system that he needed more time, the automated voice started to hum. Such customers believe the talking robotic system is so effective, you think you are talking to a human being.

By almost any measure, Office Depot's digital presence has been an outstanding success. The company benefits from OfficeDepot.com not only because the site generates new sales, but because the cost of filling Web-based orders is lower than the cost of filling traditional telephone orders. According to some estimates, Office Depot, which sells everything from paper clips to computers, is the second-largest Internet retailer in the world (behind Amazon.com), doing just under $1 billion in Web-based business in 2000. Certainly, part of Office Depot's overall company success is due to its large, traditional catalog operation. Significantly, however, unlike Amazon, Office Depot's e-business is known for making a profit.

According to Bill Seltzer, the vice president and chief information officer in charge of the Web site, plans for site improvement are constantly being developed. Seltzer says that improvement focuses on continually bettering its functionality and speed.

The Introductory Case pointed out that Office Depot has received much acclaim from the success of its digital efforts. The company Web site allows customers to perform basic functions like ordering and paying online but also incorporates recently established features like voice interaction capability. This chapter covers concepts that would be useful to managers like those at Office Depot who are striving to build a successful digital dimension for their organization. The chapter:

1) Defines digital dimensioning
2) Discusses the digital dimensioning process
3) Discusses the relationship between digital dimensioning and strategic planning
4) Discusses digital dimensioning as part of the manager's whole job

DEFINING DIGITAL DIMENSIONING

Digital dimensioning is the process of designing and implementing those digital activities that will best help a specific organization reach its goals.

E-business is any organizational activity that is enhanced by an Internet initiative.

This chapter outlines the simple yet powerful digital steps that managers can take to enhance the success of their digital efforts and, as a result, the probability that their organizations will be successful. Collectively, these steps are called **digital dimensioning,** the process of designing and implementing those digital activities that will best help a specific organization reach its goals. Digital dimensioning is an important management activity that modern managers must understand and practice to be successful in the world of e-business. In the context of this book, **e-business** is any organizational activity that is enhanced by an Internet initiative.[1]

Figure 23.1 embellishes the definition of digital dimensioning by emphasizing that digital dimensioning activities should always be aimed at achieving organizational goals. Managers should not take digital action of any sort unless they have a clear view of organizational goals and how contemplated digital action will help to achieve those goals.

It is worth noting that most reports of digital dimensioning take for granted that organizational stakeholders have Internet access. In reality, however, Internet access is mainly available to people in the United States, Europe, and developed East Asia. Much less Internet access is available to people in developing nations like Africa, the Middle East, and Latin America. The following Ethics Spotlight illustrates how IBM is supporting developing countries to help them take better advantage of the Internet.

SPOTLIGHT ethics — IBM Helps Developing Nations Bridge the Digital Divide

Hindered by poverty and a poor telecommunications infrastructure, only 1 percent to 3 percent of the population in developing countries uses the Internet. In developed countries, however, as much as 25 percent to 50 percent of the population uses the Internet. According to Ashfaq Ishaq, executive director of the International Child Art Foundation, the digital revolution provides an opportunity for the rich to help bridge the existing *digital divide* between the rich and the poor throughout the world. The International Child Art Foundation, based in Washington, is a nonprofit organization that promotes children's artwork and collaborates with selected high-tech companies to help children in developing nations get Internet access and training.

Robin Willner, director of corporate community relations at IBM, feels that simply donating Internet-related hardware and software is not enough. Although IBM does make such donations, the company tries to go much further. IBM's *digital divide* programs have focused on using the Internet and technology to "reinvent" education in underdeveloped communities. The company is funding an effort to provide technology training to 6,000 science teachers in countries like Brazil, Vietnam, and Mexico. IBM sees its *digital divide* program as using technology to turn around many historic inequities in societies throughout the world.

Ishaq is working to make an emphasis on education and technology in developing countries a part of the mission of almost all major corporations. He constantly talks to CEOs about how the Internet can be used to educate everybody. Virtually every major technology company is helping to bridge the *digital divide*, not only to enhance societies throughout the world, but because they know they need to support community and economic development in their market areas. The future of any individual business is inextricably linked to the overall intellectual and financial strength of its community. ∎

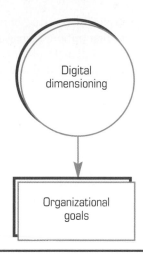

Digital dimensioning

Organizational goals

Digital dimensioning aims at reaching organizational goals

Figure 23.1

THE DIGITAL DIMENSIONING PROCESS

As defined in the previous section, digital dimensioning is a process or series of steps. The major steps in this process, as shown in Figure 23.2, are:

1. Enlisting digital expertise
2. Analyzing digital environment
3. Establishing digital direction
4. Formulating digital strategy
5. Implementing digital strategy
6. Controlling digital dimensioning

The following sections highlight each step of the digital dimensioning process and outline broad relationships among them

Enlisting Digital Expertise

Like any organizational effort, digital dimensioning activities will be successful *only if* individuals with appropriate skills perform them. These skills relate to the digital arena and involve aspects of the technical skill, people skill, and conceptual skill mentioned in Chapter 1. That aspect of *technical skill* that focuses on the digital arena is the ability to use appropriately e-business hardware and software, while that aspect of *people skill* that focuses on the digital arena is the ability to influence people to become focused and involved in carrying out e-business activities. That aspect of *conceptual skill* that focuses on the digital arena is the ability to see the organization as a whole and design e-business activities to suit that view.

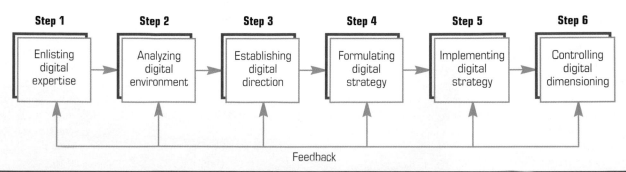

Steps of the digital dimensioning process

Figure 23.2

If managers do not have sufficient digital expertise in their organizations, three primary options are available to enlist it. As the first option, management can train present organization members so that they develop needed digital expertise. Such training must be based on carefully designed programs aimed at enhancing digital expertise deficiencies. Interestingly, IBM recently found that training people internally just was not a quick enough alternative to providing needed digital expertise. To accelerate its process of attaining needed digital expertise, IBM bought Aragon Consulting Group of St. Louis, an e-business marketing strategy and research company. This IBM acquisition typifies several of its other acquisitions aimed at quickly gaining Internet expertise to meet overwhelming internal and client demand for e-business services.

A second option available to a manager to enlist needed digital expertise in an organization is to hire new organization members who already possess the expertise. A carefully focused recruitment effort can yield significant increases in digital expertise within an organization in a relatively short time. Sometimes, however, recruiting employees with valuable digital expertise is not an easy task. As more companies look to integrate both Internet and intranet applications into their organizations, digital expertise can become a core competency that virtually all organizations are attempting to develop. Increased demand for people with e-business expertise can make it more difficult to find such new employees and can heighten related salary costs. This high demand can also make it difficult for an organization to retain its e-business professionals once hired.

As a third option, management can enlist needed digital expertise in an organization by hiring an e-business consultant. Hiring such a consultant can immediately supply a manager with a wealth of needed digital expertise. Management must keep in mind, however, that this is not an automatic solution for e-business problems. Instead, hiring an e-business consultant will generally help to solve problems only if the consultant possesses the needed people, technical, and conceptual skills that are prerequisites for e-business success. Hiring a consultant without these skills can be disastrous and can result in having an e-business partner too preoccupied with incidentals like Web site speed, too prone to cost overruns, and reluctant to ask for needed expertise that exists only outside the consultant's firm. Management will find an appropriate business consultant only by exercising appropriate due diligence.

Overall, this section discusses three primary options managers can use to enlist digital expertise in an organization, a prerequisite for gaining e-business success. Depending on the unique needs of a specific organization, management can implement any one or some combination of these options. Managers must conscientiously monitor the level of digital expertise and maintain a level necessary to carry out desired digital activities. Without involving digital expertise appropriately, the e-business activities of any organization could be destined for failure.

▶ To analyze their environment, trucking companies use computer-aided monitors to track the cost of truckers making unauthorized side trips, getting lost, or taking less-than-optimal routes. Now that most long-haul truck drivers are carefully monitored, savings passed along to the drivers have calmed most of their early misgivings. Here, Warren Hunter plans his route from a truck stop in Texas.

Analyzing Digital Environment

After enlisting appropriate digital expertise, the next step of the digital dimensioning process is analyzing an organization's digital environment. This analysis mainly involves monitoring, assessing, and making conclusions about organizational surroundings that could impact the success of its digital efforts. The purpose of the analysis is to clearly define factors that can impact an organization's digital success not only in the present, but also in the future. The analysis focuses on all critical factors both inside and outside the organization that could influence progress toward building e-business competitive advantage. From organization to organization, these factors may be varied but usually include issues like the types and nature of supplier relationships, the digital skills of present employees, and digital activities of competitors. The following Across Industries feature illustrates how a management team reacted to an analysis of the digital environment of an organization in the Electric Utility Industry.

▶ Electric Utilities Industry—CMS Energy Corporation Focuses on Digital Environment

Industry experts have recently been voicing with more regularity the opinion that although relatively few utility companies are presently allowing residential customers to pay bills online, many such companies will likely offer the option in the near future. These experts have also been stating with more regularity that the Internet is an invaluable medium that utility companies can use to gain significant competitive advantage.

One notable utilities company reacting to this evolution of the digital environment is Consumers Energy, the principal subsidiary of CMS Energy Corporation. Consumers Energy's management team considered this expert opinion along with its personal knowledge that many of its customers owned computers, many were currently online, and many would like the convenience of paying bills online. Further, Consumers Energy management knew of the growing popularity of the Internet within society as a whole and that advances in encryption technology seemed to make online bill-paying technically viable. Management also knew that cutting operational expenses by having customers key in their own billing information seemed to make online bill-paying financially beneficial.

Considering all of this digital environment information, Consumers Energy management initiated a new online service that allowed residential customers to review and pay their natural gas or electric bill through the utility's Web site. Five weeks after the initiation of the program, the company had almost 6,500 out of 2.4 million customers paying bills online, and it expects 100,000 to be paying bills online within 2 years. Overall, the company seems to be on its way to establishing a competitive advantage through digital applications.

One aspect of analyzing the digital environment typically involves monitoring the impact that Internet activity is having on the industry in which an organization exists. According to Michael E. Porter, from the viewpoint of a specific manager, Internet activity can have both positive and negative impacts on the structure of an industry. Such impact can be on the bargaining power of suppliers, the threat of substitute products or services, buyers, barriers to entry, and rivalry among existing competitors within that industry.[2]

One illustration of positive impact on an industry is that by making the overall industry more efficient, the Internet expands the size of the market. An example of negative impact on an industry is that because the Internet can lower operational costs, new competitors can enter an industry more easily. A summary of Porter's thoughts concerning the positive and negative impacts of the Internet on industry structure are shown in Figure 23.3 In this figure, (−) indicates a negative impact on the industry from the viewpoint of a specific manager while (+) indicates a positive impact on the industry from the viewpoint of that manager.

Building on Porter's ideas, one aspect of analyzing digital environment involves monitoring it to determine the positive and negative impact that Internet activity is having. Once this determination has occurred, a manager can use subsequent steps of the digital dimensioning process to outline methods for maximizing the positive impact and minimizing the negative impact.

Threat of substitute products or services

(+) By making the overall industry more efficient, the Internet can expand the size of the market

(−) The proliferation of Internet approaches creates new substitution threats

Bargaining power of suppliers

Rivalry among existing competitors

Buyers
Bargaining power of channels **Bargaining power of end users**

(+/−) Procurement using the Internet tends to raise bargaining power over suppliers, though it can also give suppliers access to more customers

(−) The Internet provides a channel for suppliers to reach end users, reducing the leverage of intervening companies

(−) Internet procurement and digital markets tend to give all companies equal access to suppliers, and gravitate procurement to standarized products that reduce differentiation

(−) Reduced barriers to entry and the proliferation of competitors downstream shifts power to suppliers

(−) Reduces differences among competitors as offerings are difficult to keep proprietary

(−) Migrates competition to price

(−) Widens the geographic market, increasing the number of competitors

(−) Lowers variable cost relative to fixed cost, increasing pressures for price discounting

(+) Eliminates powerful channels or improves bargaining power over traditional channels

(−) Shifts bargaining power to end consumers

(−) Reduces switching costs

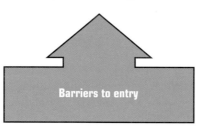

Barriers to entry

(−) Reduces barriers to entry such as the need for a salesforce, access to channels, and physical assets—anything that Internet technology eliminates or makes easier to do reduces barriers to entry

(−) Internet applications are difficult to keep proprietary from new entrants

(−) A flood of new entrants has come into many industries

Figure 23.3 *How the Internet influences industry structure*

Back to the Case

Based on the above information, managers like those at Office Depot need to recognize that digital dimensioning is a process of designing and implementing those digital activities that will best help Office Depot to reach its goals. Such managers must understand that for Office Depot to remain successful in the long run, it must be e-business competitive. Competitors like Staples and Corporate Express are planning to make significant digital dimensioning strides. To keep up with competitors, Office Depot management must focus on digital dimensioning, continually choosing and putting into action those digital activities that will best help Office Depot reach its goals.

To carry out the digital dimensioning process, Office Depot management would likely follow the six steps of the process. In Step 1, it should enlist appropriate digital expertise. Management would carefully evaluate the employees at Office Depot based on the amount of digital expertise possessed. Results of this evaluation would indicate if digital expertise at

Office Depot needed to be improved. If improvement is necessary, management could implement one or a combination of three primary options:

1. Hiring new employees with needed digital expertise
2. Training present employees in deficient digital skills areas
3. Engaging an e-business consultant

In Step 2 of the digital dimensioning process, Office Depot management analyzes its digital environment, and defines in detail its digital surroundings. This analysis should answer diverse questions like:

1. What kind of e-business activities are competitors like Office Max presently performing?
2. What digital services do Office Depot customers need?
3. How does Office Depot's marketing work?
4. Is Office Depot successful in recruiting talented employees?
5. What impact is Internet activity having on Office Depot's industry?

Establishing Digital Direction

In the third step of the digital dimensioning process, managers establish the digital direction that their organizations will take. Step 3 builds on the results of Steps 1 and 2; that is, a manager builds the direction of an organization's digital activities only after he or she has enlisted appropriate digital expertise and thoroughly understands the organization's digital environment. This step can entail making digital direction tangible through a mission statement and related goals. This digitally oriented mission statement and goals can be independent organizational exhibits or be presented as components of the organization's overall mission statement and goals. The following Quality Spotlight illustrates how SMA Health Plan, Inc., is reaching the established goal of improving the quality of medical care through digital applications.

SMA's Digital Direction Reflects Quality Goal

SMA Health Plan, Inc., is a managed health care plan serving approximately 75,000 members in the state of Louisiana. In the managed health care industry, "E-Healthcare" is the buzzword of the day, with discussion focusing on all kinds of revolutionary new, Internet-based methods for increasing organizational efficiency and effectiveness. In reality, however, most health care organizations are still using the Internet primarily for marketing and distributing general health-related information and not as a tool supporting daily clinical operations.

At SMA, however, management has set a goal to raise the quality of patient care and has established the Internet as a primary means for reaching that goal. Overall, SMA is looking to digital technology to improve business processes, decrease administrative expenses, and ultimately increase the quality of care.

Reports regarding initial digital applications at SMA have been positive. By using a new Web-based database, nurses can access a secure site on the Internet to quickly and easily review the appropriateness of action taken in each medical case in their areas of responsibility. Through the site, for example, staff can identify the clinical condition for which the patient was hospitalized, review the severity of illness and intensity of service provided by the attending clinician, and determine an appropriate discharge plan.

In many ways, this digital focus at SMA involves making a transition from a paper-based medical care process to a Web-based process. Staff are able to perform more reviews and manage more cases because they are building case histories via the Web site and not doing all of their documentation by hand. Overall, since the new paperless process allows staff members to be more efficient, they have additional time to perform more tasks as necessary.

Given the initial success of Web-based applications at SMA, new phases of digital applications that are consistent with established digital direction will likely be planned and implemented. Ultimately, physicians and case management staff at SMA will be freer to focus on delivering quality care to patients and not managing paper. ■

One critical factor influencing digital direction in an organization is management's overall philosophy about pursuing digital activities. Consider the reported management philosophy at Ryerson Tull, Inc.[3] The company, headquartered in Chicago, is North America's largest distributor and processor of metals and industrial plastics and has annual sales of approximately $3 billion. In addition, Ryerson Tull has more than 70 facilities in North America; has joint venture relationships in Mexico, India, and China; and has over 5,000 employees worldwide.

At Ryerson Tull, management's philosophy concerning digital activities is that a company should not wait to create, in some think-tank environment, the best digital strategy that will solve all of its industry problems at once. Instead, a company should engage in real digital activities and learn from experience about how to solve problems. This philosophy implies that companies should learn about digital activities through trial and error and probably start with small digital projects to eventually graduate to larger and larger projects. Following this philosophy, Ryerson Tull is pursuing foundation digital activities aimed at offering customers digital solutions to an array of fundamental business problems. Additionally, the company has become an equity partner in an industry-related portal. Given management philosophy about how to pursue digital activities, expect Ryerson Tull to modify, heighten, or even change its array of digital activities, based on what is learned over time from its involvement in the digital arena.

Formulating Digital Strategy

The fourth step of the digital dimensioning process, formulating digital strategy, focuses on how to achieve the organization's digital goals. Overall, this step involves building a plan that outlines steps that the organization will take to reach its digital goals as outlined in Step 3 of the digital dimensioning process. Once a manager has analyzed the digital environment of an organization and has set digital direction, he or she is ready to build a strategy for reaching digital goals.

Recent events at Dow Chemical Company clearly show how goals can give rise to digital strategy. Dow is a global organization that develops and manufactures science- and technology-based products in chemicals, plastics, and agriculture. The company has customers all around the world, with operations in North America, Europe, Latin America, the Pacific, and Africa.

One goal established at Dow is to make the company a sustainable growth company. To focus on achieving this goal, Dow adopted the digital strategy of investing very heavily in e-business activities and is now spending millions of dollars to transform its century-old manufacturing business into a world-class e-business. Dow still makes the same products, but through e-business activities it is becoming a more precise, lower-cost supplier. The company plans to leverage the Internet to sell high-margin engineering and other services that complement its core business. To bring focus and accountability to this new digital thrust, the company has even established a new position, vice president of e-business.[4]

Implementing Digital Strategy

The fifth step of the digital dimensioning process is implementing digital strategy. Since, at this stage, the manager has now completed Steps 1 through 4 of the digital dimensioning process, he or she is now ready to intelligently implement the organization's digital strategy. The manager has analyzed the digital environment, established a direction for digital focus, formulated a strategy for achieving the established direction, and is now ready to implement the strategy.

In order to implement digital strategy successfully, managers must perform activities like allocating resources necessary to build systems required by digital strategy and building organization culture so that digital strategy can grow and flourish. Also, knowing how to change an organization to enhance digital focus is typically very valuable to a manager during digital strategy implementation.

Consider events at Bold Furniture, Inc., of Spring Lake, Michigan, as an illustration of how digital strategy formulation relates to digital strategy implementation.[5] Bold Furniture manufactures a wide array of products including desks, storage shelves, and filing cabinets. Well-known for a broad array of finishes, the company offers products in somewhat traditional finishes like maple and cherry along with more modern finishes like azure, verdant, and wine.

▶ Matthew Live and Chris Jones are betting that their digital strategy will prove as easy for them to implement as it is for customers to use. Their company, Kingsley Management LLC, is a Boston-based car wash operation with 15 outlets in New York, North Carolina, and Florida. Trademarked "Swash," the technology offers a state-of-the-art wash, wax, undercarriage wash, sealant, rinse, and dry, all for under $8 and all performed by software-controlled equipment that even offers a video preview of the service. Entering new markets is relatively easy for the start-up firm because its labor needs are low.

Bold Furniture recently established a digital strategy as a cornerstone of its business plan. This strategy requires a major investment in designing and refining a Web site with e-commerce capability, database management tools, customer service features, and links with dealer partners. Jim Weaver, CEO of Bold Furniture, without disclosing proprietary information, confirmed that his digital strategy includes the construction of a sophisticated Web site costing from $50,000 to $100,000 to build, plus ongoing maintenance costs.

Once a company like Bold Furniture has formulated a digital strategy, implementing that strategy is the next challenge for management. At Bold Furniture, implementation issues such as getting people to develop the digital infrastructure needed to support the planned new Web site, digitally establishing needed relationships with dealer partners, and building e-commerce capability so that customers can actually order products are all critical to the success of the new digital strategy. Regardless of management's perceived value of Bold Furniture's new digital strategy, the strategy will be of no worth to the company if it cannot be implemented successfully.

▶ Back to the Case

Based on the above information, Step 3 of the digital dimensioning process is determining digital direction. In establishing Office Depot's digital direction, after management has enlisted appropriate digital expertise and understands the company's digital environment, management should begin establishing Office Depot's mission and goals for its digital presence. For example, management may discover during environmental analysis that there is a shortage of digitally talented employees in most Office Depot stores. As a result, management could set a goal of establishing digital tools to assist individual Office Depot stores throughout the world in recruiting such employees.

In taking Step 4 of the digital dimensioning process, management formulates Office Depot's digital strategy. This step involves outlining the plan for achieving digital goals. Continuing with the above sample goal, management might establish the plan of designing a "Find a Job" section of the corporate Web site that enables Office Depot Web site visitors to explore positions available in each Office Depot store. Part of the plan could be including e-mail capability on the Web site that visitors can use to express interest in certain job openings, which could be done by e-mailing the managers of those stores where the openings exist directly from the Office Depot corporate Web site.

For Step 5 of the digital dimensioning process, Office Depot management implements its digital strategy, or puts its plan for reaching digitally related goals into action. Continuing the above "Find a Job" example, in this step management would face actually constructing and putting into operation the new portion of the site aimed at recruiting. Management would ensure action like setting up systems to receive notification of job openings from Office Depot stores throughout the world, loading such openings on the corporate site, and establishing the process for taking job openings off the site when filled.

Controlling Digital Dimensioning

Controlling an organization's digital dimensioning activities is a special type of organizational control. This control focuses on monitoring and evaluating the digital dimensioning process to make sure that results materialize as planned. Essentially, controlling digital dimensioning entails monitoring digital activities to ensure that digital goals are achieved. While controlling digital dimensioning, if digital goals are not achieved, management might be required to take action like improving digital strategy, improving how digital strategy is implemented, or reviewing the results of the analysis of the digital environment to see if digital goals were set too high. Management must keep in mind that controlling digital dimensioning might even entail improving the process used to control digital dimensioning.

When controlling digital dimensioning activities, managers must be aware that action taken to improve the effectiveness of digital activities, once implemented, should be monitored very carefully. In some cases, improvements aimed at enhancing the attainment of digital goals will indeed be effective and will result in the goals being achieved, but in other cases such improvements may create *new* issues that actually increase the difficulty of reaching digital goals.

Recent events at Luminate Software Corporation illustrate that activities aimed at making digital improvements can actually result in new issues that management must handle before digital success can be achieved.[6] Luminate provides organizations with comprehensive Internet infrastructure for e-business applications. Through a Web site called Luminate.Net, the company offered its customers an outsourcing service that freed them from certain significant e-business costs in areas related to hardware, software, and installation. Essentially, Luminate positioned itself as the means that customer IT departments could use to keep up with the continuing whirlwind developments in e-business applications and related technology.

Luminate launched a new Web site showcasing a new, improvement-oriented digital service. The improvement entailed the company beginning to deliver its software to customers over the Internet rather than following its old practice of physical, on-site installation. The improvement was built on management's observation that the practice of on-site software installation was losing momentum in the marketplace while the practice of providing software via the Web was gaining momentum.

Negative reaction to Luminate's new, improvement-oriented change was swift and significant. The day after the new Internet service was launched, the company received hundreds of mostly complaining e-mails. Interestingly, the e-mails came primarily from people inside Luminate rather than from customers. Some believe that employees reacted in this fashion because management announced the Internet-based software delivery change to employees at the same time it told customers and did not involve employees in formulating the improvement-oriented plans.

The lesson seems clear. Regardless of the validity of planned digital controlling improvements, the success of those improvements can be negatively influenced by their implementation. At Luminate, management's implementation of planned digital improvements precipitated significant negative employee reaction to the improvements. Only by neutralizing this negative reaction can Luminate management create an environment in which the improvements can bring maximum benefit to the organization.

Overall, the digital dimensioning process is presented as a series of discrete steps. Certainly, this "discrete steps" approach facilitates learning about digital dimensioning. In practice, however, managers may sometimes find that digital dimensioning requires working on two or more steps at the same time, or even working on the steps in a somewhat different order. In reality, managers must not focus on any one step of the digital dimensioning process without considering one or more other steps. For example, managers should not formulate digital strategy without considering how it might be implemented and controlled. Figure 23.4 illustrates that managers may sometimes find themselves considering several or even all digital dimensioning steps together.

DIGITAL DIMENSIONING AND STRATEGIC PLANNING

As you recall from Chapter 8, *strategic planning* is long-range planning that focuses on the organization as a whole.[7] In planning strategically, managers consider the organization as a total unit and ask themselves what must be done in the long term to reach established targets. Long term is usually defined as a period of time extending about three to five years into the future. Major strategic planning tasks include analyzing organizational environment, establishing organizational direction, formulating organizational strategy, and implementing organizational control and strategic control.

On reflection, the digital dimensioning process seems somewhat similar to the strategic planning process. Similarity of strategic planning terms like *analyzing organizational environment* and digital dimensioning terms like *analyzing digital environment* seem to establish the similarity. Overall, management can think of digital dimensioning and strategic planning as somewhat similar processes, but digital dimensioning has a much narrower scope and purpose. Strategic planning aims at developing a logic concerning all organizational functions while digital dimensioning aims at developing a logic concerning primarily digital functions.

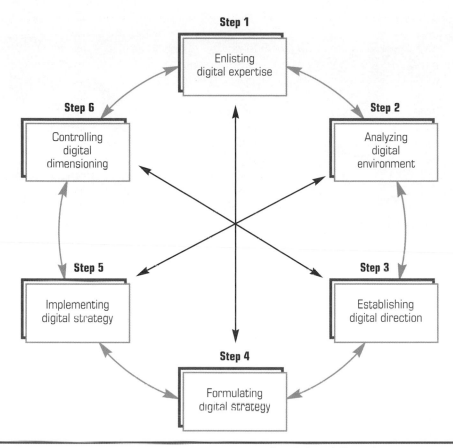

Step 1
Enlisting digital expertise

Step 2
Analyzing digital environment

Step 3
Establishing digital direction

Step 4
Formulating digital strategy

Step 5
Implementing digital strategy

Step 6
Controlling digital dimensioning

Managers may sometimes consider all digital dimensioning steps together

Figure 23.4

Management must establish the unique relationship between strategic planning and digital dimensioning as determined by distinctive organizational needs. In some organizations with established strategic planning processes, perhaps the digital dimensioning process can be thought of primarily as a subset of the strategic management process. In such cases, simply by establishing the digital dimensioning process as a special emphasis or subset of a strategic planning process, management can ensure that digital dimensioning receives necessary attention.

In organizations that do not have an established strategic planning process, perhaps the digital dimensioning process should be established as a special, unique organizational process, making sure that digital thrust receives needed attention. In such organizations, digital dimensioning should not be thought of as a substitute for strategic management. Instead, it should be considered a process that gives strategic focus to an important organizational ingredient, digital activity.

Management must be careful to avoid the belief that issues in the digital environment change so rapidly that digital dimensioning is relatively valueless. Stories abound of organizations going from an idea to a business plan to tangible online activities in a matter of only months. Many such organizations, once established, reportedly maintain a hectic pace of quickly reacting to changes in environmental factors like competitive positioning or technology advances. Management sometimes seems to be constantly uncovering digital environment issues and responding to them quickly and often.

Granted, modern times may require that managers respond to the digital environment changes quickly and often. Such change, however, does not reduce the need for sound digital dimensioning; it increases it. Management should strenuously avoid the dangerous pitfall of foregoing thoughtful digital dimensioning because it seemingly takes too long or requires too much energy. Without thoughtful digital dimensioning, success becomes much more a matter of almost random chance than of management expertise.

▶ Hampton Inn & Suites has incorporated digital technology into many aspects of its strategic plan. Not only does the hotel company's Web site (www.hamptoninn.com) allow travelers to find and locate a hotel near their destination, but it also provides pictures of the hotel, road maps for downloading, and room rates. The rooms themselves include well-lit workspaces, Internet access, and free local phone calls. All these elements of the strategic plan acknowledge that guests rely on the Internet while planning their trip as well as while on the road.

▶ Back to the Case

Controlling Office Depot's digital dimensioning is the last step of the digital dimensioning process. By controlling Office Depot's digital dimensioning, management makes sure that the digital activities are having proper impact. Again continuing with "Find a Job," management might monitor the new site feature to see if it is working technically. Controlling here could also involve checking to see if the new "Find a Job" section is actually helpful in recruiting new, needed talent. If the site is not working technically, management must make sure it is debugged. If needed employees are not being recruited via the site as planned, management must explore changes like modifying its content or enhancing its visual design. In other words, management must take steps to find out why "Find a Job" is not getting expected results and make sure that changes needed to get the results are made.

When management performs the above six digital dimensioning steps at Office Depot, it may sometimes seem that the steps are being performed sequentially. In reality, to ensure the success of Office Depot's digital dimensioning efforts, management should take no single digital dimensioning step without considering all other steps. For example, the "Find a Job" strategy should not be implemented without reflecting on how the strategy can be controlled and the appropriateness of the digital direction that it reflects.

Management at a company like Office Depot should never view digital dimensioning as a substitute for strategic planning. Strategic planning would focus on many issues within the company in addition to digital dimensioning. If a company like Office Depot has an established strategic planning process, digital dimensioning might be established as part of that process. If the company does not have an established strategic planning process, however, management may wish to establish digital dimensioning as a special process that brings needed focus to digital issues within the organization.

DIGITAL DIMENSIONING: THE MANAGER'S WHOLE JOB?

This chapter presents digital dimensioning as a major activity that modern managers must perform to enhance organizational success in the digital era. Digital dimensioning, however, is not and should never be seen as a manager's *entire* job. As emphasized throughout this book, management is the process of working with and through people and other organizational resources to accomplish organizational goals. Wisdom accumulated over the last century by practicing managers as well as management scholars indicates that managers manage by performing four primary activities: planning, organizing, influencing, and controlling.

Given the burgeoning growth and significance of the modern digital business world, many would argue that managers must now ensure that digital dimensioning is a significant part of their job. One method for ensuring this significance is for managers to visualize digital dimensioning as a primary management activity along with planning, organizing, influencing, and controlling. This visualization ensures that digital dimensioning will impact the way a manager plans, organizes, influences, and controls. Conversely, this visualization also ensures that planning, organizing, influencing, and controlling impact the way managers carry out digital dimensioning activities. Figure 23.5 illustrates how managers might visualize this close relationship between digital dimensioning and the more traditionally accepted management functions. The following sections discuss how digital dimensioning can impact each of the more traditional functions, and vice versa, as managers perform their jobs.

Digital Dimensioning and Planning

As you recall from Chapter 6, *planning* is the process of establishing organizational goals, choosing tasks that must be performed in order to reach those goals, outlining how the tasks should be performed, and determining when the tasks should be performed. Assuredly, planning focuses on goal accomplishment; through plans, managers outline what must be done to reach goals.

According to Figure 23.5, planning can impact digital dimensioning and digital dimensioning can impact planning. Planning can impact digital dimensioning, for example, if a manager applies planning knowledge to best structure goals for the organization's digital dimensioning thrust. On the other hand, digital dimensioning can impact planning. As an example, an organization's digital dimension can help a manager to make better planning decisions. Evidence suggests that managers are faced with making planning decisions more often and more quickly than in the past. Since sound planning decisions are generally based, at least in part, on data analysis, this evidence also suggests that managers must analyze planning-related data more often and more quickly than in the past. Digital tools can afford managers online access and analysis of virtually limitless data almost instantaneously. Through digital dimensioning, managers can establish tools to enhance the speed of data gathering and analysis and the probability of making sound planning decisions.[8]

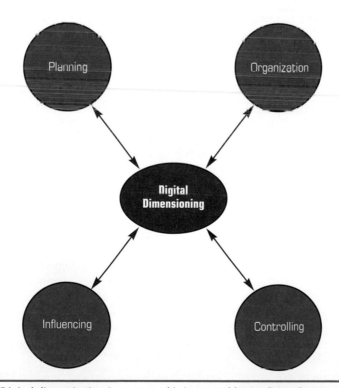

Digital dimensioning impacts and is impacted by traditional management functions

Figure 23.5

Digital Dimensioning and Organizing

As you recall from Chapter 10, *organizing* is the process of establishing orderly uses for all resources within an organization. Resources include the organization's people, raw materials, equipment, and financial assets. In determining orderly uses, managers focus on how to use resources to best carry out plans aimed at reaching organizational goals. Organizing assists managers in making objectives apparent throughout the organization and emphasizing the tasks outlined during planning to specific individuals or groups. Essentially, organizing assigns work to people that, once completed, will result in the organization reaching its targets. Organizing schemes are built on the notion that output of individuals results in success for departments, which in turn results in success for the entire organization.

Certainly, organizing can impact digital dimensioning. For example, managers organize when establishing who should do what jobs in the digital dimensioning effort. The people assigned to carry out digital dimensioning activities will certainly have an impact on the success of digital thrust. The quality of equipment purchased, which is also an organizing issue, will certainly impact the success of digital efforts. While poor-quality equipment can render digital efforts unreliable and of little value, high-quality equipment can enhance the overall perception and success of digital efforts.

Digital dimensioning can also impact organizing. As an example, digital dimensioning can be used to create ways to allow people to work together on specific projects from various locations around the world if necessary. More specifically, by employing person-to-person collaborative tools via the Internet, management can help people to work together as if they were in the same physical office. As the name implies, **person-to-person collaborative tools** are Internet-based applications that enable people to communicate from various locations in cities, states, or countries. As companies become more decentralized, collaborative technologies have tremendous potential for handling organizing issues like facilitating teamwork, improving workflow, and communicating more efficiently and effectively. Person-to-person collaborative tools help management to avoid communication bottlenecks associated with sending documents back and forth via mail delivery or faxes, discussing work issues over the phone, or bringing workers together for face-to-face meetings. Overall, these tools help managers to gain maximum benefit from their greatest asset, the intelligence and expertise of their workers.[9]

Person-to-person collaborative tools are Internet-based applications that enable people to communicate from various locations in cities, states, or countries.

Digital Dimensioning and Influencing

As you recall from Chapter 14, *influencing* is the process of guiding the activities of people in appropriate directions. Appropriate directions, of course, are those that lead to the attainment of organizational goals. Influencing involves focusing on employees as people and dealing with such issues as morale, arbitration of conflict, and the development of positive working relationships. For many managers, success is primarily determined by how well they influence others.

Management must keep in mind that how they influence others can impact the success of digital dimensioning efforts. For example, how a manager chooses to motivate individuals performing digital dimensioning activities can impact the quality of work those individuals produce. If the manager motivates mainly through punitive means, workers may produce high-quality digital dimensioning output in the short run. However, in the long run, such a motivation plan will probably result in a diminishing quality of such output, and this diminishing quality will lessen the success of digital efforts.

Digital dimensioning can also impact the success of management's influencing efforts. For example, as a means of motivating organization members, many managers choose to build and operate special incentive programs. In such programs, as a result of outstanding performance, employees receive special rewards. For some companies, it might make sense to build and operate their own special incentive program. For other organizations, it might make sense to enlist the services of an organization specializing in the design and administration of such programs.

Some such incentive programs, like those at salesdriver.com, are Internet based.[10] Salesdriver.com offers Web-enabled incentive programs specifically tailored to motivate large sales teams. The company Web site allows managers to build and quickly run online sales contests and to reward contest winners with online merchandise and travel options. Contest themes, like "Marketing Warfare" and "Go for the Pin," can be customized to suit the needs of individual organizations and offer managers the ability to view the performance of contest participants at any time during the contest.

Digital Dimensioning and Controlling

As you recall from Chapter 19, *controlling* is the process of making sure that events occur as planned. As implied by this definition, planning and controlling should be thought of as inseparable, the Siamese twins of management. Planning is a manager's map showing how to reach organizational goals. Certainly, without such a map, consistently achieving organizational targets would be highly unlikely. Simply having the plan, however, does not guarantee success in attaining organizational goals. The plan needs to be reviewed periodically to ensure that all the right steps are being taken. Sometimes, a planning review leads to the conclusion that a plan should be changed, perhaps because circumstances have changed or because the plan was improperly conceived.

Controlling can certainly impact the success of digital dimensioning. For example, assume that an organization's digital plan has been designed and implemented, but management lacks a focus on controlling digital efforts. Here, management believes that controlling is important but has been only haphazardly monitoring digital efforts to gauge digital progress. Such a monitoring pattern will not afford management the best opportunity to uncover and neutralize issues that are slowing the progress of digital activities. Through such haphazard controlling, optimization of digital efforts based on controlling will be virtually nonexistent.

Digital dimensioning can also influence controlling. As an example, many companies maintain Web sites that offer a wide array of products to consumers. Such companies include L.L. Bean, Gap, Brooks Brothers, and The Sharper Image. Such Internet based sales outlets are venues that by their very nature can help management gather feedback regarding the effectiveness and efficiency of company efforts. Skilled customer service representatives, for example, can use real-time chat technology to discover customer attitudes regarding issues like product quality, ease of Web site use, and Web site visual appeal. The responses to such issues can be documented, analyzed, and used to make specific improvements to the site, in such areas as e-mail response adequacy, Web site functionality and features, and appropriateness of shipping charges.[11] Undoubtedly, management can use a digital vehicle for gathering control-related feedback aimed at improving company success.

▶ Back to the Case

Managers must remember that in order to succeed at Office Depot or any other organization, digital dimensioning is only one major function that they must perform. Digital dimensioning is only part of a manager's complete job—planning, organizing, influencing, controlling, and digital dimensioning. What a manager knows about planning, organizing, influencing, and controlling can enhance the success of his or her digital dimensioning. Conversely, what a manager knows about digital dimensioning can help to magnify the impact of his or her planning, organizing, influencing, and controlling. Overall, managers collectively carry out these activities to increase the probability of organizational success. Weakness in carrying out any of the activities can significantly decrease the probability of organizational success.

Management Skills Module

This section is specially designed to help you develop management skills. An individual's management skill is based on an understanding of management concepts and the ability to apply those concepts in management situations. As a result, the following activities are designed both to heighten your understanding of management concepts and to help you gain facility in applying those concepts in various management situations.

UNDERSTANDING MANAGEMENT CONCEPTS

▶ Action Summary

Reread the learning objectives below. Each objective is followed by questions. Answering these questions accurately will help you retain the most important concepts discussed in this chapter. After answering each question, check your answer against the answer key at the end of this chapter. (*Hint*: If you have any doubts regarding the correct response, consult the page number that follows the answer.)

Circle:

From studying this chapter, I will attempt to acquire

1. An understanding of digital dimensioning and the digital dimensioning process.

T F   **a.** Digital dimensioning is measuring various aspects of a company Web site.

a b c d e   **b.** Which of the following is *not* a major step of the digital dimensioning process: (a) controlling digital dimensioning (b) establishing digital direction (c) reviving digital efforts (d) implementing digital strategy (e) analyzing digital environment.

2. Insights concerning how digital expertise and digital environment relate to digital success.

T F   **a.** If a manager determines that sufficient digital skill does not exist within an organization, he or she should probably *not* pursue digital activities within that organization.

T F   **b.** The purpose of analyzing an organization's digital environment is to define factors that can impact the organization's digital success both in the present and the future.

3. An appreciation for digital strategy and digital direction.

T F   **a.** Once a manager establishes the digital direction that his or her organization will take, the next step in digital dimensioning is to control that direction.

T F   **b.** Digital strategy is the organization's plan to reach the organization's digital goals.

4. Knowledge about how implementation and control relate to digital dimensioning.

a b c d e   **a.** Put the following steps of the digital dimensioning process in the proper order of performance: (1) enlisting digital expertise (2) implementing digital strategy (3) controlling digital dimensioning (4) analyzing digital environment (5) formulating digital strategy (6) establishing digital direction. a. 1,4,6,5,2,3; b. 4,1,3,2,5,6; c. 1,2,3,4,5,6; d. 6,5,1,4,3,2; e. 5,6,1,2,4,3

T F   **b.** Digital control is a special type of organizational control.

5. An awareness of how strategic management and digital dimensioning relate.

T F   **a.** Management should establish a unique relationship between strategic planning and digital dimensioning as determined by distinctive organizational needs.

T F   **b.** For some industries, an organization's environment changes so rapidly that the worth of digital dimensioning is somewhat limited.

6. Understanding of how planning, organizing, and digital dimensioning relate to the job of a manager.

T F   **a.** Planning can impact digital dimensioning, but digital dimensioning cannot impact planning.

T F   **b.** Through person-to-person collaborative tools, digital dimensioning can impact a manager's organizing efforts.

7. Insights into how influencing, controlling, and digital dimensioning relate to the job of a manager.

T F   **a.** Digital dimensioning can enhance a manager's efforts to communicate with and motivate employees.

T F   **b.** Information gathered from customers via a company Web site can give managers insights into improving the quality of products sold along with the usefulness of the Web site itself.

1. **a.** F, p. 524
   b. c, p. 525
2. **a.** F, p. 526
   b. T, p. 527

3. **a.** F, p. 530
   b. T, p. 530
4. **a.** a, p. 525
   b. T, p. 531

5. **a.** T, pp. 532–533
   b. F, p. 533
6. **a.** F, p. 535
   b. T, p. 536

7. **a.** T, p. 536
   b. T, p. 537

Issues for Review and Discussion

1. What is the relationship between digital dimensioning and organizational goals?
2. Draw the model depicting the digital dimensioning process. Explain how a manager can use this process.
3. Describe three options available to a manager attempting to enlist needed digital expertise in an organization.
4. Explain the importance of analyzing the digital environment in the digital dimensioning process.
5. Can Internet activity change the structure of an industry? Explain.
6. Should a manager normally establish digital direction for an organization before analyzing the organization's digital environment? Explain.
7. Give an example of a digital goal and a related digital strategy that a manager could use to reach that goal. Be as specific as possible.
8. List three factors that managers should consider when implementing strategy. Explain why it is important to consider each factor.
9. Defend the concept that controlling digital dimensioning is a special type of organizational control.

10. What is meant by the phrase "managers may sometimes consider all digital dimensioning steps together"?
11. How are digital dimensioning and strategic management related?
12. Because factors in the digital environment change so rapidly, there is little value in digital dimensioning. Agree or disagree and explain why.
13. Do you think that "digital dimensioning" is as important to managing an organization as planning, organizing, influencing, or controlling? Why?
14. Give three examples of how digital dimensioning can impact planning and how planning can impact digital dimensioning.
15. Give three examples of how digital dimensioning can impact organizing and how organizing can impact digital dimensioning.
16. Give three examples of how digital dimensioning can impact influencing and how influencing can impact digital dimensioning.
17. Give three examples of how digital dimensioning can impact controlling and how controlling can impact digital dimensioning.

APPLYING MANAGEMENT CONCEPTS

Cases

▶ INTRODUCTORY CASE WRAP-UP

Case Discussion Questions

"Office Depot Recognized for Digital Excellence" (p. 523) and its related Back-to-the-Case sections were written to help you better understand the management concepts contained in this chapter. Answer the following questions about this Introductory Case to further enrich your understanding of chapter content:

1. Describe digital dimensioning as it relates to Office Depot. Be as specific as possible.
2. If you were Bill Seltzer, what would you do to make sure that OfficeDepot.com was continually improved?
3. Assuming that you were top management at Office Depot, which step of the digital dimensioning process would you find most challenging? Why?

Skills Exercise: Analyzing Office Depot's Digital Environment

Locate the Web site of one of Office Depot's significant competitors. After studying this site, list four characteristics that you have discovered outlining how this competitor operates. How might these characteristics impact Office Depot's future digital direction?

The small business Hattie Bryant and her husband Bruce Camber founded in 1994 is virtual. Bryant thinks small business owners are America's truest heroes. As a matter of fact, the company's mission is to change the nature of "star worshipping" in our culture and to define "hero" in a different way. Each week on *Small Business School*, the television show they produce, Bryant profiles a small business owner who has had a positive, transforming impact on his or her employees and community. The role small businesses play in our nation's economy is a very important one. Small businesses represent the spirit of America. People who start with nothing but a dream and become successful are heroes, as far as Bryant and Camber are concerned. Their satisfied audience seems to agree.

With phone, fax, and Broadband Internet connectivity, Bryant and Camber work from their fifth-floor apartment in San Diego. Their business administrator works from her home office in New Orleans. Their producer and camera man work from a studio in Dallas. Together, working from three different cities, this group produces and distributes 26 one-half-hour episodes of the show each year.

Hattie Bryant has been working from home for the past 20 years—at first to save money, but now she loves the lifestyle. The couple usually work from 6 A.M. until 4:30 P.M., when they go for a jog through the park or on the beach. "In the morning, I make coffee, turn on the computer, and put on my sweatshirt and jeans," says Bryant. The couple work in their offices, one on either side of the kitchen. Bryant spends hours calling potential participants, while Cambers manages the company's Web site, www.smallbusinessschool.com, and responds to the hundreds of e-mails that arrive each day from viewers, sponsors, and small business owners. Meanwhile, the office assistant answers phones—1,800 miles away in New Orleans.

Small Business School currently uses three business phone lines and one personal line. It also has two U.S. West Venture phones for small businesses, which provide for intercom, conference calls, caller ID, and multiple lines. "We can literally work anywhere in the world today," says Camber.

The staff is dependent on high-speed access to the Internet. Shows are sent across the Net for review. Correspondence between staff and film crew is done by phone and e-mail. Documents are received over an FTP server, which was installed in order to enable Bryant and Camber to access documents and taped Small Business School shows from their office assistant's computer in New Orleans and vice versa.

Bryant and Camber both work on IBM Aptiva computers with flat-screen monitors. In addition, they each have an IBM Think Pad with a DVD drive that is used for giving presentations and when they travel. A good part of the year is spent traveling, as each show is shot on location across the United States, from Tampa to Seattle to Hawaii.

After filming, the nine-member crew spends a week at the Dallas production studio, editing down the footage, crafting the story, and taping voice-overs. Back in San Diego, Bryant and Camber receive the first cut of the program—either over the Internet or via snail mail. Each show is recut for a second airing with a new focus, thus avoiding reruns during the course of a full year of programming. Each completed half-hour broadcast is then fed via satellite to the hosting TV stations. "We go through a Think Pad a year," Camber says.

Bryant and Camber's digital dimensioning strategy will become even more Internet dependent over the next year as they launch the school online. Visitors to the site will be able to log on and access past episodes from archives and take nondegree classes on running a company. A fee of $199 for 10 shows plus study guides and materials will be charged. The couple believe that they will soon have thousands of students from around the world. Camber's latest addition to the digital power base is IBM's Start Now e-commerce Solutions, which he feels "addresses the company's scalability concerns" within his budget. "We've gotten e-mails from government officials in Mongolia and even Pakistan," says Camber. "They all want to know what makes American small businesses so successful."

So much of Small Business School's operation is digital and new that Camber and Bryant are creating their business model as they go. Their management focus is to have the Web site, the TV program, and Bryant's speaking engagements function as separate profit centers. Bryant views the show as "the only how-to about small business." She has even written a book entitled *Beating the Odds*. The series can now be seen in 90 million households in the United States on 225 public television stations. It is broadcast throughout the world by the U.S. government-owned Worldnet Global Satellite. The couple gets e-mail from viewers as far away as Maritius and Mongolia.

The show's sponsors include IBM, the U.S. Postal Service, Qwest, and Verizon. Bryant and Camber raise the $50,000 it costs to produce each show and market the finished product to local PBS member stations. Small Business School has revenues of $2 million a year.

Bryant and Camber keep the show profitable by using digital dimensioning to organize and control almost every aspect of their enterprise. Their business strategy is dependent on it, and so far their timing is right on target.

QUESTIONS

1. Do Camber and Bryant seem to understand the concept of digital dimensioning? Explain.

2. List two ways to improve Small Business School's digital dimension. How would your improvements enhance company success?

3. Do you think it would be easier than, harder than, or about as difficult to analyze the digital environment for Small Business School as it might be to analyze the digital environment for a large corporation? Explain.

4. How does "digital" enhance Small Business School's ability to respond quickly to the marketplace, while remaining focused on its own organizational goals? Explain fully.

QUICKTAKES SEGMENT 6
Topics for Special Emphasis

In this segment, we find Hal, Karen, and John discussing John's feelings about how his first three months on the job have gone. Do you remember the questions John had in his interview with Hal and Karen (part I) about planning and efficiency issues at Quicktakes? In this discussion, we see John expressing concern about these issues again, as well as concerns related to issues of effectiveness.

An interesting aspect of John's comments is the perspective in which he formulates his ideas. John has identified some very specific concerns about how particular jobs or tasks are completed, but he also seems to be interested in a bigger picture. He seems to be interested in something more than how specific employees do their job. The discussion about effectiveness and efficiency quickly turns to a broader discussion of how the company's management looks at the importance of and relationship among certain jobs, and also at issues of motivation.

The meeting takes a turn in a different direction when John brings up an opportunity he sees in going after some markets where Quicktakes does not do much. It is interesting to find out that Quicktakes has previously tried to address this segment, culturally targeted video, with little success. The real interesting thing in this discussion is the subtle change in the way the talk goes. In previous discussions, we saw the management team at Quicktakes just talking about planning issues, with little discussion of solutions. In this segment, we see Hal, Karen, and John talking about what might have limited success in the past and ways that they can try to make a second attempt in this market. The managers at Quicktakes seem to be getting interested in increasing the productivity, efficiency, and quality of what they are doing. Maybe you are not the only one using this textbook—sounds like Quicktakes is using it too!

QUESTIONS

1. John points out some concerns with certain parts of the business and how well certain jobs get done. Hal's reaction is to get the specific people responsible into the meeting. John discourages this and suggests that the problems might not really be related to the individuals involved. What do you think John is really saying? Do you think he is right? If you were hired by Quicktakes as a consultant to help with some of these issues, what might you recommend? How might you use the Internet to address some of the issues?

2. John identifies some issues in motivating people in the company to be more concerned about how efficiently things get done and the quality of what goes out the door. What types of policies or processes do you think are in place at Quicktakes to deal with these types of concerns? Do you think they are adequate? Why or why not?

3. You heard a discussion about issues Quicktakes has had in targeting culturally specific markets. Why do you think things might not have worked so well for them in these markets? What do you think about the ideas they are considering now? What else would you tell them to do?

COMPETITIVENESS: QUALITY AND INNOVATION AND *YOU*

You are from a small town in Minnesota where the population is heavily Caucasian. You love being a freshman on an urban campus. You have invited your Japanese roommate to spend winter break with your family. Eager to learn as much as possible about Japanese traditions, you decide to attend a meeting of the Asian Society. When you get there, everyone is speaking Japanese. Most of the students seem to know one another. You are intimidated and disappointed. You almost walk out, but curiosity gets the better of you. By the end of the evening, you are engaged in an open discussion with the president of the club. He tells you the Asian Society's original purpose was to teach others about Japanese culture. When only Japanese students showed up for meetings, the group got lazy and gave up trying to attract students from different ethnic backgrounds. You suggest they send announcements out via the campus intranet and hold a gala Japanese dinner complete with sushi. The dinner is a success. As a result, the club grows in popularity, hosting more and more cultural events. Now the Asian Society has more members than ever.

1. What has this experience taught you about creativity and innovation? How will this serve as an inspiration to you in your managerial career?

---

www.prenhall.com/certo

This book is accompanied by a rich assortment of online activities aimed at developing your management skills. Reviewing news headlines, Internet exercises, an online study guide, and other research and Internet resources can help personalize management skills development for individual students or an entire class.

Endnotes

Chapter 1

1. For an interesting discussion of how much return a company should be getting on its management resources, see Robert Simons and Antonio Davila, "How High Is Your Return on Management?" *Harvard Business Review* (January/February 1998): 70–80; Peter F. Drucker, "Management's New Role," *Harvard Business Review* (November/December 1969): 54.

2. Frances Cairncross, "Survey: Pay: Who Wants to Be a Billionaire?" *The Economist* 351, no. 8118 (May 8, 1999): s14–s17.

3. Leah Rozen, "The Keys to the Kingdom: How Michael Eisner Lost His Grip," *People Weekly* 53, no. 13 (April 3, 2000): 60.

4. Robert Albanese, *Management* (Cincinnati Southwestern, 1988), 8.

5. Gary Hamel and C. K. Prahalad, "Seeing the Future First," *Fortune*, September 5, 1994, 64–70.

6. For a recent example of tactics taken by Chase Manhattan Corporation to enhance its efficiency see Matt Murray, "Chase Combines International Units in Efficiency Move," *Wall Street Journal*, February 19, 1998, C17.

7. William Wiggenhorn, "Motorola U: When Training Becomes an Education," *Harvard Business Review* (July/August 1990): 71–83.

8. Robert L. Katz, "Skills of an Effective Administrator," *Harvard Business Review* (January/February 1955): 33–41.

9. Ruth Davidhizar, "The Two-Minute Manager," *Health Supervisor* 7 (April 1989): 25–29; for an article that demonstrates how important human skills are for middle managers, see also Philip A. Rudolph and Brian H. Kleiner, "The Art of Motivating Employees," *Journal of Managerial Psychology* 4 (1989): i–iv.

10. Henri Fayol, *General and Industrial Management* (London: Sir Isaac Pitman & Sons, 1949).

11. B. C. Forbes, *Forbes*, March 15, 1976, 128.

12. Don Hellriegel, John W. Slocum, Jr., and Richard W. Woodman, *Organizational Behavior*, 6th ed. (St. Paul: West Publishing Company, 1992), 681.

13. John Ivancevich and Michael T. Matteson, *Organizational Behavior and Management* (Homewood, IL: BPJ/Irwin, 1990), 593–95.

14. Patrick J. Purcell, "Older Workers: Employment and Retirement Trends," *Monthly Labor Review* 123, no. 10 (October 2000): 19–30.

15. John W. Slocum, Jr., William L. Cron, and Linda C. Yows, "Whose Career Is Likely to Plateau?" *Business Horizons* (March/April 1987): 31–38.

16. Joseph E. McKendrick, Jr., "What Are You Doing the Rest of Your Life?" *Management World*, September/October 1987, 2; Carl Anderson, *Management: Skills, Functions, and Organizational Performance*, 2d ed. (Boston: Allyn and Bacon, 1988).

17. Paul H. Thompson, Robin Zenger Baker, and Norman Smallwood, "Improving Personal Development by Applying the Four-Stage Career Model," *Organizational Dynamics* (Autumn 1986): 49–62.

18. Kenneth Labich, "Take Control of Your Career," *Fortune*, November 18, 1991, 87–90; Buck Blessing, "Career Planning: Five Fatal Assumptions," *Training and Development Journal* (September 1986): 49–51.

19. Thomas J. Peters, Jr., "The Best New Managers Will Listen, Motivate, Support," *Working Woman*, September 1990, 142–43, 216–17.

20. For an interesting discussion of conflict of interest and dual-career couples, see Owen Ullmann and Mike McNamee, "Couples, Careers, and Conflicts," *BusinessWeek*, February 21, 1994, 32–34.

21. For additional information see Sue Shellenbarger, "For the Burseks, Best Parent Regimen Is Back-to-Back Shifts," *Wall Street Journal*, February 25, 1998, B1; Jacqueline B. Stanfield, "Couples Coping with Dual Careers: A Description of Flexible and Rigid Coping Styles," *Social Science Journal* 35, no. 1 (1998): 53–64; R. S. Hall and T. D. Hall, "Dual Careers—How Do Couples and Companies Cope with the Problems?" *Organizational Dynamics* 6 (1978): 57–77.

22. This section is based on Samuel C. Certo and Matthew W. Certo, *Digital Dimensioning: Finding the Ebusiness in Your Business* (New York: McGraw-Hill, 2001).

23. Todd Pack, "Will This Be Your Next PC? Cellular Phone Makers Are Betting You'll Say Yes," *Orlando Sentinel*, March 24, 2001, B1.

24. Kenneth J. Rose and James A. Hendricks, "Accountants Overseas," *Management Accounting* 80, no. 7 (January 1999): 34–38.

25. Lori Jacobson, "Shop, Click, Send," *Potentials* 32, no. 11 (November 1999): 6.

26. Shari Weiss, "Drinks Recipes Drive Visitors to Friday's Internet Links," *Nation's Restaurant News* 34, no. 34 (August 21, 2000): 34.

27. James F. Wolf, "The Legacy of Mary Parker Follett," *Bureaucrat* 17 (Winter 1988–89): 53–57.

28. "Hazardous Materials Disaster Management," *Environmental Manager*, October 1994, pp. 7–9.

29. Philip M. Burgess, "Making It in America's New Economy," *Vital Speeches of the Day* 60 (September 15, 1994): 716–19. For a useful discussion of special training issues related to such employees, see Adrienne S. Harris, "And the Prepared Will Inherit the Future," *Black Enterprise*, February 1990, 121–28.

30. Stephen J. Harrison and Ronald Stupak, "Total Quality Management: The Organizational Equivalent of Truth in Public Administration Theory and Practice," *Public Administration Quarterly* 16 (Winter 1993): 416–29

Chapter 2

1. James H. Donnelly, Jr., James L. Gibson, and John M. Ivancevich, *Fundamentals of Management* (Plano, TX: Business Publications, 1987), 6–8; Harold Koontz, Cyril O'Donnell, and Heinz Weihrich, *Management*, 8th ed. (New York: McGraw-Hill, 1984), 52–69; W. Warren Haynes and Joseph L. Massie, *Management*, 2d ed. (Upper Saddle River, NJ: Prentice Hall, 1969), 4–13.

2. David W. Hays, "Quality Improvement and Its Origin in Scientific Management," *Quality Progress*, May 5, 1994, 89–90.

3. Frederick W. Taylor, *The Principles of Scientific Management* (New York: Harper & Bros., 1947), 66–71.

4. For more information on the work of Frederick Taylor, see Edward Rimer, "Organization Theory and Frederick Taylor," *Public Administration Review* 53 (May/June 1993): 270–72; Alan Farnham, "The Man Who Changed Work Forever," *Fortune*, July

21, 1997, 114; Hans Picard, "Quit Following Marx's Advice," *ENR* 246, no. 12 (March 26, 2001): 99.

5. Franz T. Lohrke, "Motion Study for the Blinded: A Review of the Gilbreths' Work with the Visually Handicapped," *International Journal of Public Administration* 16 (1993): 667–68. For information illustrating how the career of Lillian Gilbreth is an inspiration for modern women managers, see Thomas R. Miller and Mary A. Lemons, "Breaking the Glass Ceiling: Lessons from a Management Pioneer," *S.A.M. Advanced Management Journal* 63, no. 1 (Winter 1998): 4–9.

6. Edward A. Michaels, "Work Measurement," *Small Business Reports* 14 (March 1989): 55–63.

7. Henry L. Gantt, *Industrial Leadership* (New Haven, CT: Yale University Press, 1916), 57.

8. For more information on the Gantt chart, see G. William Page, "Using Project Management Software in Planning," *Journal of the American Planning Association* 55 (Autumn 1989): 494–99; Jeff Angus, "Software Speeds Up Project Management," *Informationweek,* September 8, 1997, 85–88.

9. Doug Green and Denise Green, "MacSchedule Has Rich Features at Low Price," *InfoWorld,* July 12, 1993, 88.

10. Gantt, *Industrial Leadership*, 85.

11. Chester I. Barnard, *Organization and Management* (Cambridge, MA: Harvard University Press, 1952). For more current discussion of Barnard's work, see Christopher Vasillopulos, "Heroism, Self Abnegation and the Liberal Organization," *Journal of Business Ethics* 7 (August 1988): 585–91.

12. Alvin Brown, *Organization of Industry* (Upper Saddle River, NJ: Prentice Hall, 1947); Henry S. Dennison, *Organization Engineering* (New York: McGraw-Hill, 1931); Luther Gulick and Lyndall Urwick, eds., *Papers on the Science of Administration* (New York: Institute of Public Administration, 1937); J. D. Mooney and A. C. Reiley, *Onward Industry!* (New York: Harper & Bros., 1931); Oliver Sheldon, *The Philosophy of Management* (London: Sir Isaac Pitman and Sons, 1923).

13. Henri Fayol, *General and Industrial Management* (London: Sir Isaac Pitman and Sons, 1949). See also David Frederick, "Making Sense of Management I," *Credit Management,* December 2000, 34–35.

14. Charles A. Mowll, "Successful Management Based on Key Principles," *Healthcare Financial Management* 43 (June 1989): 122, 124.

15. Fayol, *General and Industrial Management*, 19–42. For an excellent discussion of the role of accountability and organization structure, see Elliott Jaques, "In Praise of Hierarchy," *Harvard Business Review* 68 (January/February 1990): 127–33.

16. For an interesting discussion on how modern training programs are teaching managers to establish productive authority relationships in organizations, see A. Glenn Kiser, Terry Humphries, and Chip Bell, "Breaking Through Rational Leadership," *Training and Development Journal* 44 (January 1990): 42–45. For an interesting discussion on how "chain of command" helps to minimize the negative impact of oil spills, see James Hunt, Bruce Carter, and Frank Kelly, "Clearly Defined Chain-of-Command Helps Mobilize Oil Spill," *Occupational Health & Safety,* June 1993, 40–45. For a discussion of the impact of remuneration on an organization, see Jeffrey Bradt, "Pay for Impact," *Personnel Journal* (January 1992): 76–79. For a discussion of centralization, see Paul T. Mill and Josephine Bonan, "Site-Based Management: Decentralization and Accountability," *Education Digest,* September 1991, 23–25.

17. For detailed summaries of these studies, see *Industrial Worker,* 2 vols. (Cambridge, MA: Harvard University Press, 1938); and F. J. Roethlisberger and W. J. Dickson, *Management and the Worker* (Cambridge, MA: Harvard University Press, 1939). For a more recent discussion of the Hawthorne Studies, see Bev Geber, "The Hawthorne Effect: Orwell or Buscaglia?" *Training* 23 (November 1986): 113–14.

18. Stephen Jones, "Worker Interdependence and Output: The Hawthorne Studies Reevaluated," *American Sociological Review* (April 1990): 176–90.

19. Jennifer Laabs, "Corporate Anthropologists," *Personnel Journal* (January 1992): 81–91; Samuel C. Certo, *Human Relations Today: Concepts and Skills* (Burr Ridge, IL: Irwin, 1995), 4; Scott Highhouse, "Well-Being: The Foundations of Hedonic Psychology," *Personnel Psychology* 54, no. 1 (Spring 2001): 204–6.

20. C. West Churchman, Russell L. Ackoff, and E. Leonard Arnoff, *Introduction to Operations Research* (New York: Wiley, 1957), 18.

21. Hamdy A. Taha, *Operations Research: An Introduction* (New York: Macmillan, 1988), 1–2.

22. James R. Emshoff, *Analysis of Behavioral Systems* (New York: Macmillan, 1971), 10. For an interesting account of how the scientific method can be applied to studying management problems like information system problems, see Allen S. Lee, "A Scientific Methodology for the MIS Case Studies," *MIS Quarterly* 13 (March 1989): 33–50.

23. Catherine L. Morgan, "A Survey of MS/OR Surveys," *Interfaces* 19 (November/December 1989): 95–103; H. J. Zimmermann, "Some Observations on Practicing Successful Operational Research," *The Journal of the Operational Research Society* 49, no. 4 (April 1998): 413–19.

24. The discussion concerning these characteristics is adapted from Donnelly, Gibson, and Ivancevich, *Fundamentals of Management,* 302–3; Efraim Turban and Jack R. Meredith, *Fundamentals of Management Science* (Plano, TX: Business Publications, 1981), 15–23.

25. Harold Koontz, "The Management Theory Jungle Revisited," *Academy of Management Review* 5 (1980): 175–87. For applications of the contingency approach, see David J. Lemak and Wiboon Arunthanes, "Global Business Strategy: A Contingency Approach," *Multinational Business Review* 5, no. 1 (Spring 1997): 26–37. For a practical application of the contingency approach to management, see Henri Barki, Suzanne Rivard, and Jean Talbot, "An Integrative Contingency Model of Software Project Risk Management," *Journal of Management Information Systems* 17, no. 4 (Spring 2001): 37–69.

26. Don Hellriegel, John W. Slocum, and Richard W. Woodman, *Organizational Behavior* (St. Paul, MN: West Publishing, 1986), 22.

27. J. W. Lorsch, "Organization Design: A Situational Perspective," *Organizational Dynamics* 6 (1977): 2–4; Louis W. Fry and Deborah A. Smith, "Congruence, Contingency, and Theory Building," *Academy of Management Review* (January 1987): 117–32.

28. For a more detailed development of von Bertalanffy's ideas, see "General System Theory: A New Approach to Unity of Science," *Human Biology* (December 1951): 302–61.

29. L. Thomas Hopkins, *Integration: Its Meaning and Application* (New York: Appleton-Century-Crofts, 1937), 36–49. For an interesting illustration of how wholeness applies to managed care, see Jill Wechsler, "Managed Care Firms Are Kicking Butts!" *Managed Healthcare* 8, no. 4 (April 1998): 32–36.

30. Joe Schwartz, "Why They Buy," *American Demographics* 11 (March 1989): 40–41.

31. Ken Starkey, "What Can We Learn from the Learning Organization?" *Human Relations* 51, no. 4. (April 1998): 531–46.

32. David A. Garvin, "Building a Learning Organization," *Harvard Business Review* 74, no. 4. (July 1993): 78. For more recent discussion of learning organizations, see Bente Elkjaer, "The Dance of Change: The Challenges of Sustaining Momentum in Learning Organizations," *Management Learning* 32, no. 1 (March 2000): 153–56.

33. Peter Senge, *The Fifth Discipline, The Art & Practice of the Learning Organization* (New York: Doubleday/Currency, 1990). Used by permission of Doubleday, a division of Random House, Inc.

Chapter 3

1. For a good discussion of many factors involved in the modern meanings of social responsibility, see Frederick D. Sturdivant and Heidi Vernon-Wortzel, *Business and Society: A Managerial Approach,* 4th ed. (Homewood, IL: Irwin, 1990), 3–24. The definition of corporate social responsibility is adapted from Keith Davis and Robert L. Blomstrom, *Business and Society: Environment and Responsibility,* 3rd ed. (New York: McGraw-Hill, 1975), 6. For illustrations of how social responsibility makes good economic sense, see David Woodruff, "Herman Miller; How Green Is My Factory," *BusinessWeek,* September 16, 1992, 54–56; Ernest Beck, "Body Shop Founder Roddick Steps Aside as CEO," *Wall Street Journal,* May 13, 1998, B14.

2. Peter L. Berger, "New Attack on the Legitimacy of Business," *Harvard Business Review* (September/October 1981): 82–89.

3. Keith Davis, "Five Propositions for Social Responsibility," *Business Horizons* (June 1975): 9–24. For additional comments supporting social responsibility activities, see Robert Gray, "Responsibility Up the Agenda," *Marketing,* May 3, 2001, 39; Lois A. Mohr, Deborah J. Webb, and Katherine E. Harris, "Do Consumers Expect Companies to Be Socially Responsible? The Impact of Corporate Social Responsibility on Buying Behavior," *Journal of Consumer Affairs* 35, no. 1 (Summer 2001): 45–72.

4. For extended discussion of arguments for and against social responsibility, see William C. Frederick, Keith Davis, and James E. Post, *Business and Society: Corporate Strategy, Public Policy, Ethics,* 6th ed. (New York: McGraw-Hill, 1988), 36–43.

5. For comments on a new way of exploring the relationship between the financial performance of an organization and its social responsibility activities, see Sandra A. Waddock and Samuel B. Graves, "Finding the Link Between Stakeholder Relations and Quality of Management," *Journal of Investing* 6, no. 4 (Winter 1997): 20–24.

6. K. E. Apperle, A. B. Carroll, and J. D. Hatfield, "An Empirical Examination of the Relationship between Corporate Social Responsibility and Profitability," *Academy of Management Journal* (June 1985): 446–63; J. B. McGuire, A. Sundgren, and T. Schneeweis, "Corporate Social Responsibility and Firm Financial Performance," *Academy of Management Journal* (December 1988): 854–72; Vogel, "Ethics and Profits Don't Always Go Hand in Hand," *Los Angeles Times,* December 28, 1988, 7.

7. For Friedman's view, see "Freedom and Philanthropy: An Interview with Milton Friedman," *Business and Society Review* (Fall 1989): 11–18.

8. Milton Friedman, "Does Business Have Social Responsibility?" *Bank Administration* (April 1971): 13–14.

9. Eric J. Savitz, "The Vision Thing: Control Data Abandons It for the Bottom Line," *Barron's,* May 7, 1990, 10–11, 22.

10. For a discussion of radical environmentalism, see Jeffrey Salmon, "We're All 'Corporate Polluters' Now," *Wall Street Journal,* July 2, 1997, A–14.

11. Joan E. Rigdon, "The Wrist Watch: How a Plant Handles Occupational Hazard with Common Sense," *Wall Street Journal,* September 28, 1992, 1.

12. Sandra L. Holmes, "Executive Perceptions of Corporate Social Responsibility," *Business Horizons* (June 1976): 34–40.

13. For insights regarding SC Johnson Wax's position on social responsibility involvement, see Reva A. Holmes, "At SC Johnson Wax Philanthropy Is an Investment," *Management Accounting* (August 1994): 42–45.

14. Bill Richards, "Nike Hires an Executive from Microsoft for New Post Focusing on Labor Policies," *Wall Street Journal,* January 15, 1998, B14.

15. Samuel C. Certo and J. Paul Peter, *The Strategic Management Process,* 3rd ed. (Chicago: Irwin, 1995), 219; Marianne M. Jennings, "Manager's Journal: Trendy Causes Are No Substitute for Ethics," *Wall Street Journal,* December 1, 1997, A22.

16. Carlo Wolff, "Living with the New Amenity," *Lodging Hospitality,* (December 1994): 66–68.

17. Harry A. Lipson, "Do Corporate Executives Plan for Social Responsibility?" *Business and Society Review* (Winter 1974–75): 80–81.

18. S. Prakash Sethi, "Dimensions of Corporate Social Performance: An Analytical Framework," *California Management Review* (Spring 1975): 58–64.

19. For information on the growing trend for business to make contributions to support education, see Joel Keehn, "How Business Helps the Schools," *Fortune,* October 21, 1991, 161–71.

20. Frank H. Cassell, "The Social Cost of Doing Business," *MSU Business Topics* (Autumn 1974): 19–26.

21. Donald W. Garner, "The Cigarette Industry's Escape from Liability," *Business and Society Review* 33 (Spring 1980): 22.

22. Meinolf Dierkes and Ariane Berthoin Antal, "Whither Corporate Social Reporting: Is It Time to Legislate?" *California Management Review* (Spring 1986): 106–21.

23. Condensed from Jerry McAfee, "How Society Can Help Business," *Newsweek,* July 3, 1978, 15. Copyright 1978 by Newsweek, Inc. All rights reserved. Reprinted by permission.

24. "Borden Chemicals Lashes Back at EPA," *Chemical Marketing Reporter,* November 7, 1994, 5, 19.

25. Leonard J. Brooks Jr., "Corporate Codes of Ethics," *Journal of Business Ethics* (February/March 1989): 117–29.

26. For an interesting discussion of the ethical dilemma of fairly allocating an individual's time between work and personal life, see Paul B. Hoffmann, "Balancing Professional and Personal Priorities," *Healthcare Executive* (May/June 1994): 42.

27. Archie B. Carroll, "In Search of the Moral Manager," *Business Horizons* (March/April 1987): 7–15.

28. Sundeep Waslekar, "Good Citizens and Reap Rewards," *Asian Business* (January 1994): 52. See also Genine Babakian, "Who Will Control Russian Advertising?" *Adweek* [Eastern Edit.] August 1, 1994, 16.

29. John F. Akers, "Ethics and Competitiveness—Putting First Things First," *Sloan Management Review* (Winter 1989): 69–71; Natalie M. Green, "Creating an Ethical Workplace," *Employment Relations Today* 24, no. 2 (Summer 1997): 33–44.

30. "Helping Workers Helps Bottom Line," *Employee Benefit Plan Review,* July 1990.

31. Sandy Lutz, "Psych Hospitals Fight for Survival," *Modern Healthcare,* May 8, 1995, 62–65.

32. Patrick E. Murphy, "Creating Ethical Corporate Structures," *Sloan Management Review* (Winter 1989): 81–87; Louis J. D'Amore, "A Code of Ethics and Guidelines for Socially and Environmentally Responsible Tourism," *Journal of Travel Research* (Winter 1993): 64–66.

33. James B. Treece, "Nissan Rattles Japan with Tough Ethics Code," *Automotive News*, May 4, 1998, 1, 49.

34. Richard A. Spinell, "Lessons from the Salomon Scandal," *America*, December 28, 1991, 476–77; Touche Ross, *Ethics in American Business* (New York: Touche Ross & Co., January 1988). For a recent view on developing a code of ethics for the workplace, see O. C. Ferrell, "An Assessment of the Proposed Academy of Marketing Science Code of Ethics for Marketing Educators," *Journal of Business Ethics*, 19, no. 2 (April 1999): 225–28.

35. For additional insights on how and why to create an ethical workplace, see Larry L. Axline, "The Bottom Line on Ethics," *Journal of Accountancy* (December 1990): 87–91; Curt Smith, "The Ethical Workplace," *Association Management* 52, no. 6 (June 2000): 70–73.

36. Alan L. Otten, "Ethics on the Job: Companies Alert Employees to Potential Dilemmas," *Wall Street Journal*, July 14, 1986, 25.

37. Gene R. Laczniak, "Framework for Analyzing Marketing Ethics," *Journal of Macromarketing* (Spring 1983): 7–18. See also Patricia Haddock and Marilyn Manning, "Ethically Speaking," *Sky* (March 1990): 128–31.

38. Saul W. Gellerman, "Managing Ethics from the Top Down," *Sloan Management Review* (Winter 1989): 73–79. For an interesting discussion of what management should do when charged with unethical actions see John A. Byrne, "Here's What to Do Next, Dow Corning," *BusinessWeek*, February 24, 1992, 33.

Chapter 4

1. For a discussion of diversity issues in the United Kingdom, see Ian Dodds, "Differences Can Be Strengths," *People Management* (April 20, 1995): 40–43. See also Raymond Pomerleau, "A Desideratum for Managing the Diverse Workplace," *Review of Public Personnel Administration* 14 (Winter 1994): 85–100. For a list of companies well-known for their positive work in the area of diversity, see Roy S. Johnson, "The 50 Best Companies for Asians, Blacks and Hispanics," *Fortune* 138, no. 3 (August 3, 1998): 94–96.

2. Liz Winfeld and Susan Spielman, "Making Sexual Orientation Part of Diversity," *Training & Development* (April 1995): 50–51.

3. Judith C. Giordan, "Valuing Diversity," *Chemical & Engineering News*, February 20, 1995, 40.

4. Ann M. Morrison, "Leadership Diversity as Strategy," in *The New Leaders: Guidelines on Leadership Diversity in America* (San Francisco: Jossey-Bass, 1992), 11–28.

5. Prem Benimadh, "Adding Value through Diversity," *Canadian Business Review* (Spring 1995): 6–11; Tara Parker-Pope, "Inside P&G, a Pitch to Keep Women Employees," *Wall Street Journal*, September 9, 1998, B1.

6. William B. Johnston and Arnold E. Packer, "Executive Summary," *Workforce 2000: Work and Workers for the Twenty-First Century* (Indianapolis: Hudson Institute, June 1987), xiii–xiv. For discussion of organizational impact of changing demographics, see Constance L. Hays, "McCormick Faces Changing Demographics, Changing Tastes," *New York Times*, February 20, 1998, D1.

7. Roosevelt Thomas, "Affirmative Action or Affirming Diversity," *Harvard Business Review* (1990): 110.

8. Rosabeth Moss Kanter, *Men and Women of the Corporation* (New York: Basic Books, 1977).

9. Rosabeth Moss Kanter, "Numbers: Minorities and Majorities," in *Men and Women of the Corporation* (New York: Basic Books, 1977), 206–44. For a discussion of successful steps Price Waterhouse takes to keep women on the payroll, see Anonymous, "Secrets of Success," *HR Focus* 74, no. 8 (August 1997): 10.

10. Ann M. Morrison, *Breaking the Glass Ceiling: Can Women Reach the Top of America's Largest Corporations?* (Reading, MA: Addison Wesley, 1992).

11. Susan Webb, *Step Forward: Sexual Harassment in the Workplace* (New York: MasterMedia, 1991); Susan B. Garland, "Finally, a Corporate Tip Sheet on Sexual Harassment," *BusinessWeek*, July 13, 1998, 39.

12. Ella Bell, "The Bicultural Life Experience of Career Oriented Black Women," *Journal of Organizational Behavior* 11 (November 1990): 459–78.

13. Catherine Dorton Fyock and Anne Marrs Dorton, "Welcome to the Unretirement Generation," *HR Focus* (February 1995): 22–23. For insights on how to manage older employees, see Carol Hymowitz, "Young Managers Learn How to Bridge the Gap with Older Employees," *Wall Street Journal*, July 21, 1998, B1.

14. Jeffrey Sonnenfeld, "Dealing with the Aging Workforce," *Harvard Business Review* 56 (1978): 81–92.

15. William B. Johnston and Arnold E. Packer, "Executive Summary," *Workforce 2000: Work and Workers for the Twenty-First Century* (Indianapolis: Hudson Institute, June 1987): xii–xiv.

16. Jean Kim, "Issues in Workforce Diversity," Panel Presentation at the First Annual National Diversity Conference (San Francisco, May 1991).

17. *The Holy Bible*, Authorized King James Version (Nashville: Holman Bible Publishers, 1984).

18. J. Stewart Black and Hal B. Gregersen, "Serving Two Masters: Managing the Dual Allegiance of Expatriate Employees," *Sloan Management Review* (Summer 1992): 61–71.

19. Les Donaldson and Edward E. Scannell, *Human Resource Development: The New Trainer's Guide*, 2nd ed. (Reading, MA: Addison-Wesley, 1986), 8–9.

Chapter 5

1. For additional information on this topic, see Samuel C. Certo, *Human Relations Today: Concepts and Skills* (Chicago: Austen Press/Irwin, 1995), 352–75.

2. "Dossier: Telecommunications in Asia, Malaysia, Thailand," *International Business Newsletter*, June 1993, 12.

3. Robert N. Lussier, Robert W. Baeder, and Joel Corman, "Measuring Global Practices: Global Strategic Planning Through Company Situational Analysis," *Business Horizons* 37 (September/October 1994): 56–63; For a detailed look at a successful internationally managed company, Hitachi Maxell, see Ray Moorcroft, "International Management in Action," *British Journal of Administrative Management* (March/April 2001): 12–13.

4. Alyssa A. Lappen, "Worldwide Connections," *Forbes*, June 27, 1988, 78–82.

5. Gale Eisenstodt, " 'We Are Happy,' " *Forbes*, May 8, 1995, 44–45.

6. "Global Investment: The Smart Money Is Flowing South," *Harvard Business Review* 71 (September/October 1993): 13–14.

7. Ben J. Wattenberg, "Their Deepest Concerns," *Business Month* (January 1988): 27–33; American Assembly of Collegiate Schools of Business, *Accreditation Council Policies, Procedures, and Standards* (St. Louis, MO: Assembly Collegiate School of America, 1990–92); Sylvia Nasar, "America's Competitive Revival," *Fortune*, January 4, 1988, 44–52.

8. For additional information regarding various forms of organization based on international involvement, see Arvind Phatak, *International Dimensions of Management* (Boston: Kent, 1993).

9. "Nu Horizons Electronics," *Fortune,* June 13, 1994, 121. For an empirical study assessing the mobility of knowledge within a multinational corporation, see Anil K. Gupta and Vijay Govindarajan, "Knowledge Flows within Multinational Corporations," *Strategic Management Journal* 21, no. 4 (April 2000): 473–96.

10. U.S. Department of Commerce, *The Multinational Corporation: Studies on U.S. Foreign Investment* 1 (Washington, DC: Government Printing Office).

11. Benjamin Gomes-Casseres, "Group versus Group: How Alliance Networks Compete," *Harvard Business Review* 72 (July/August 1994), 62 74.

12. Grover Starling, *The Changing Environment of Business* (Boston: Kent, 1980), 140.

13. This section is based primarily on Richard D. Robinson, *International Management* (New York: Holt, Rinehart & Winston, 1967), 3–5. For focus on complexity related to differing ethical values of various societies, see Paul F. Buller, John J. Kohls, and Kenneth S. Anderson, "When Ethics Collide: Managing Conflicts Across Cultures," *Organizational Dynamics* 28, no. 4 (Spring 2000): 52–65.

14. 1971 Survey of National Foreign Trade Council, cited in Frederick D. Sturdivant, *Business and Society: A Managerial Approach* (Homewood, IL: Richard D. Irwin, 1977), 425. For an interesting discussion of diversification as an advantage to internationalizing, see Jeff Madura and Ann Marie Whyte, "Diversification Benefits of Direct Foreign Investment," *Management International Review* 30 (First Quarter 1990): 73–85.

15. Barrie James, "Reducing the Risks of Globalization," *Long Range Planning* 23 (February 1990): 80–88.

16. "NCR's Standard Contract Clause," *Harvard Business Review* 72 (May/June 1994): 125.

17. Brenda Paik Sunoo, "Loosening Up in Brazil," *Workforce* 3 (May 1998): 8–9.

18. For a review of the possible hazardous effects of repatriation, see Jobert E. Abueva, "Many Repatriations Fail, at Huge Cost to Companies," *New York Times,* May 17, 2000, E1.

19. Roberta Maynard, "Importing Can Help a Firm Expand and Diversify," *Nation's Business* (January 1995): 11.

20. Karen Paul, "Fading Images at Eastman Kodak," *Business and Society Review* 48 (Winter 1984): 56. For a discussion of how Eastman Kodak is attempting to reduce costs associated with its exporting, see Robert J. Bowman, "Cheaper by Air?" *World Trade* 7 (October 1994): 88–91.

21. G. Sam Samdani, "Mobil Develops a Way to Extract Hg from Gas Streams," *Chemical Engineering* 102 (April 1995): 17.

22. Robert Neff, "The Japanese Are Back—But There's a Difference," *BusinessWeek,* Industrial/Technology Edition, October 31, 1994, 58–59.

23. Ken Korane, "Geo Metro: Economy Is Key" *Machine Design* 67 (April 6, 1995): 146–48.

24. Francisco Granell, "The European Union's Enlargement Negotiations with Austria, Finland, Norway, and Sweden," *Journal of Common Market Studies* 33 (March 1995): 117–41; Gwenan Roberts, "Swedish Lawyers Look South," *International Financial Law Review* 14 (May 1995): 12–14; Jim Rollo, "EC Enlargement and the World Trade System," *European Economic Review* 39 (April 1995): 467–73. For a history surrounding the formation of NAFTA, see Richard N. Cooper, "The Making of NAFTA: How the Deal Was Done," *Foreign Affairs* 80, no. 3 (May/June 2001): 136.

25. Jim Mele, "Mexico in '95: From Good to Better," *Fleet Owner,* January 1995, 56–60; William C. Symonds, "Meanwhile, to the North, NAFTA Is a Smash," *BusinessWeek,* February 27, 1995, 66; Robert Selwitz, "NAFTA Expansion Possibilities," *Global Trade & Transportation,* October 1994, 17.

26. N. Carroll Mohn, "Pacific Rim Prices," *Marketing Research: A Magazine of Management & Applications,* Winter 1994, 22–27; Louis Kraar, "The Growing Power of Asia," *Fortune,* October 7, 1991, 118–31.

27. For an interesting account of organizing to go global, see Regina Fazio Maruca, "The Right Way to Go Global: An Interview with Whirlpool CEO David Whitwam," *Harvard Business Review* 72 (March/April 1994): 134–45.

28. Howard V. Perlmutter, "The Tortuous Evolution of the Multinational Corporation," *Columbia Journal of World Business* (January/February 1969): 9–18; Rose Knotts, "Cross-Cultural Management: Transformations and Adaptations," *Business Horizons* (January/February 1989): 29–33.

29. Geert Hotstede, "Motivation, Leadership, and Organization: Do American Theories Apply Abroad?" *Organizational Dynamics* 9 (Summer 1980): 42–63.

30. Walter Sweet, "International Firms Strive for Uniform Nets Abroad," *Network World,* May 28, 1990, 35–36.

31. To gain a feel for the broad range of activities occurring at a transnational company like Nestlé, see Joel Chernoff, "Advancing Corporate Governance in Europe," *Pensions & Investments,* June 12, 1995, 3, 37; E. Guthrie McTigue and Andy Sears, "The Safety 80," *Global Finance,* May 1995, 62–65; Robert W. Lear, "Whatever Happened to the Old-Fashioned Boss?" *Chief Executive,* April 1995, 71; Claudio Loderer and Andreas Jacobs, "The Nestlé Crash," *Journal of Financial Economics* 37 (March 1995): 315–39; Roberto Ceniceros, "Companies Aiding Workers, Starting to Assess Damage," *Business Insurance,* January 30, 1995, 22–23.

32. This section is mainly based on Thomas Donaldson, "Values in Tension: Ethics Away from Home," *Harvard Business Review* 74, no. 5 (September/October 1996): 48–62.

33. Anabelle Perez, "Sports Apparel Goes to Washington: New Sweatshop," *Sporting Goods Business* 30, no. 7 (May 12, 1997): 24.

34. Edward M. Mervosh and John S. McClenahen, "The Care and Feeding of Expats," *Industry Week* 246, no. 22 (December 1, 1977): 68–72.

35. Valerie Frazee, "Research Points to Weaknesses in Expat Policy," *Workforce* 3, no. 1 (January 1998): 9.

Chapter 6

1. Harry Jones, *Preparing Company Plans: A Workbook for Effective Corporate Planning* (New York: Wiley, 1974), 3; Richard G. Meloy, "Business Planning," *The CPA Journal* 63, no. 8 (March 1998): 74–75.

2. Robert G. Reed, "Five Challenges Multiple-Line Companies Face," *Market Facts* (January/February 1990): 5–6; Brian Burrows and Ken G. B. Blakewell, "Management Functions and Librarians," *Library Management* (1989): 2–61. For a recent article on minimizing risk, see Editorial Staff, "Prior Planning Is Key to Averting a Crisis," *Investor Relations Business,* July 23, 2001, 8.

3. C. W. Roney, "The Two Purposes of Business Planning," *Managerial Planning* (November/December 1976): 1–6; Linda C. Simmons, "Plan. Ready. Aim," *Mortgage Banking* 56, no. 5 (February 1996): 95–96. For an interesting account of the planning function in an international setting, see Gabriel Ogunmokun, "Planning: An Exploratory Investigation of Small

Business Organizations in Australia," *International Journal of Management* 15, no. 1 (March 1998): 60–71.

4. Wendy Zellner, "Moving Tofu into the Mainstream," *BusinessWeek* May 25, 1992, 94.

5. Harold Koontz and Cyril O'Donnell, *Management: A Systems and Contingency Analysis of Management Functions* (New York: McGraw-Hill, 1976), 130.

6. For an interesting discussion on how the importance of planning relates to even day-to-day operations, see Teri Lammers, "The Custom-Made Day Planner," *Inc.*, February 1992, 61–62.

7. Kenneth R. Allen, "Creating and Executing a Business Plan," *American Agent & Broker* (July 1994): 20–21.

8. For a discussion of U.S. shortsightedness in planning, see Michael T. Jacobs, "A Cure for America's Corporate Short-termism," *Planning Review* (January/February 1992): 4–9. For a discussion of the close relationship between objectives and planning, see "Mistakes to Avoid: From a Business Owner," *Business Owner* (September/October 1994): 11.

9. For an overview of strategic planning, see Bryan W. Barry, "A Beginner's Guide to Strategic Planning." *The Futurist* 32 no. 3 (April 1998): 33–36.

10. For an example of a subsystem, see Sherry D. Ryan and David A. Harrison, "Considering Social Subsystem Costs and Benefits in Information Technology Investment Decisions: A View from the Field on Anticipated Payoffs," *Journal of Management Information Systems* 16, no. 4 (Spring 2000): 11–40.

11. James F. Lincoln, "Intelligent Selfishness and Manufacturing," *Bulletin 434* (New York: Lincoln Electric Company).

12. John F. Mee, "Management Philosophy for Professional Executives," *Business Horizons* (December 1956): 7.

13. Paul Psarouthakis, "Getting There by Goal Setting," *Supervisory Management* (June 1989): 14–15, David J. Campbell and David M. Furrer, "Goal Setting and Competition as Determinants of Task Performance," *Journal of Organizational Behavior* 16, no. 4 (July 1995): 377–90.

14. Peter F. Drucker, *The Practice of Management* (New York: Harper & Bros., 1954), 62–65, 126–29. For an interesting discussion of objectives set in the customer service area, see John Marshall, "Northwest Chain Store Enhances Customer Service and Lowers Operational Costs by Replacing Outdated POS Terminals," *Chain Store Age Executive*, June 1994, 92. For an interesting discussion on objectives and innovation, see Barton G. Tretheway, "Everything New Is Old Again," *Marketing Management* 7, no. 1 (Spring 1998): 4–13. For a recent tribute to Drucker, see A. J. Vogo, "Drucker, of Course," *Across the Board* 37, no. 10 (November/December 2000): 1.

15. Charles H. Granger, "The Hierarchy of Objectives," *Harvard Business Review* (May/June 1964): 64–74; Richard E. Kopelman, "Managing for Productivity: One-Third of the Job," *National Productivity Review* 17, no. 3 (Summer 1998): 1–2. Reprinted with the permission of American Management Association International. New York, NY. All rights reserved.

16. See also Edwin A. Locke, Dong-Ok Chah, Scott Harrison, and Nancy Lustgarten, "Separating the Effects of Goal Specificity from Goal Level," *Organizational Behavior and Human Decision Processes* (April 1989): 270–87; Mike Deblieux, "The Challenge and Value of Documenting Performance," *HR Focus* (March 1994): 3. To better understand the role of setting objectives in compensation plans, see William J. Liccione, "Effective Goal Setting: A Prerequisite for Compensation Plans with Incentive Value," *Compensation & Benefits Management* 13, no. 1 (Winter 1997): 19–25.

17. Robert L. Mathis and John H. Jackson, *Personnel: Human Resource Management* (St. Paul, MN: West Publishing, 1985), 353–55.

18. Robert Rodgers and John E. Hunter, "Impact of Management by Objectives on Organizational Productivity," *Journal of Applied Psychology* (1991): 322–35; Jerry L. Rostund, "Evaluating Management Objectives with the Quality Loss Function," *Quality Progress* (August 1989): 45–49; William H. Franklin Jr., "Create an Atmosphere of Positive Expectations," *Administrative Management* (April 1980): 32–34; Peter Crutchley, "Management by Objectives," *Credit Management* (May 1994): 36–38; William J. Kretlow and Winford E. Holland, "Implementing Management by Objectives in Research Administration," *Journal of the Society of Research Administrators* (Summer 1988): 135–41.

19. Charles H. Ford, "Manage by Decisions, Not by Objectives," *Business Horizons* (February 1980): 17–18. For an interesting description of how firms in Sweden employ MBO, see Terry Ingham, "Management by Objectives—A Lesson in Commitment and Cooperation," *Managing Service Quality* 5, no. 6 (1995): 35–38.

20. Henry Mintzberg, "A New Look at the Chief Executive's Job," *Organizational Dynamics* (Winter 1973): 20–40. For a recent interview with Mintzberg, see Stephen Bernhut, "In Conversation: Henry Mintzberg," *Ivey Business Journal* 65, no. 1 (September/October 2000): 18–23.

21. For similar questions focusing on strategic planning, see Hans Hinterhuber and Wolfgang Popp, "Are You a Strategist or Just a Manager?" *Harvard Business Review* (January/February 1992): 105–13. For an example of how a CEO plans organizational change, see Peter Spiegel, "Old Dog, New Tricks?" *Forbes*, June 1, 1998, 47.

22. James M. Hardy, *Corporate Planning for Nonprofit Organizations* (New York: Association Press, 1972), 37. For an interesting article that describes how CEOs gain assistance from their boards of directors, see Ben L. Lytle, "Putting Directors to Work Adding Value," *Directors and Boards* 20, no. 3 (Spring 1996): 10–12.

23. Milton Leontiades, "The Dimensions of Planning in Large Industrialized Organizations," *California Management Review* 22 (Summer 1980): 82–86.

24. For a discussion of outside consultants who develop plans for business clients, see Donald F. Kuratko and Arnold Cirtin, "Developing a Business Plan for Your Clients," *National Public Accountant* (January 1990): 24–27.

25. The section "Qualifications of Planners" is adapted from John Argenti, *Systematic Corporate Planning* (New York: Wiley, 1974), 126. For an interesting look at the role of power and politics in the planning process, see Renee Berger, "People, Power, Politics," *Planning* 63, no. 2 (February 1997): 4–9.

26. Michael Muckian and Mary Auestad Arnold, "Manager, Appraise Thyself," *Credit Union Management* (December 1989): 26–28.

27. Edward J. Green, *Workbook for Corporate Planning* (New York: American Management Association, 1970).

28. Z. A. Malik, "Formal Long-Range Planning and Organizational Performance," Ph.D. diss. (Rensselaer Polytechnic Institute, 1974).

Chapter 7

1. For an excellent discussion of various decisions that managers make, see Michael Verespej, "Gutsy Decisions of 1991," *Industry Week* (February 17, 1992): 21–31. For an interesting discussion of decision making in government agencies, see Burton Gummer, "Decision Making under Conditions of Risk, Ambiguity, and

Uncertainty: Recent Perspectives," *Administration in Social Work* 2 (1998): 75–93.

2. Abraham Zaleznik, "What Makes a Leader?" *Success,* June 1989, 42–45; Daphne Main and Joyce C. Lambert, "Improving Your Decision Making," *Business and Economic Review* 44, no. 3 (April/June 1998): 9–12.

3. Mervin Kohn, *Dynamic Managing: Principles, Process, Practice* (Menlo Park, CA: Cummings, 1977), 38–62. For an interesting discussion of how to train managers to become better decision makers by slowing down the decision-making process, see Jack Falvey, "Making Great Managers," *Small Business Reports* (February 1990): 15–18. See also Herbert A. Simon, *The New Science of Management Decision* (New York: Harper & Bros., 1960), 5–8.

4. William H. Miller, "Tough Decisions on the Forgotten Continent," *Industry Week* (June 6, 1994): 40–44.

5. *The D of Research and Development* (Wilmington, DE: DuPont, 1966), 28–29; apparently, DuPont's basic tenets regarding how the scope of decisions influences how decisions should be made have evolved over many years; see, for example, George J. Titus, "Forty-Year Evolution of Engineering Research: A Case Study of DuPont's Engineering Research and Development," *IEEE Transactions on Engineering Management* 41 (November 1994): 350–54.

6. Marcia V. Wilkof, "Organizational Culture and Decision Making: A Case of Consensus Management," *R&D Management* (April 1989): 185–99. For an interesting discussion of various tools used to build consensus, see Richard L. Luebbe and B. Kay Snavely, "Making Effective Team Decisions with Consensus Building Tools," *Industrial Management* 39, no. 5 (September/October 1997): 1–7.

7. Charles Wilson and Marcus Alexis, "Basic Frameworks for Decision," *Academy of Management Journal* 5 (August 1962): 151–64.

8. For a discussion of the importance of understanding decision makers in organizations, see Walter D. Barndt Jr., "Profiling Rival Decision Makers," *Journal of Business Strategy* (January/February 1991): 8–11. See also Ernest Dale, *Management: Theory and Practice* (New York: McGraw-Hill, 1973), 548–49.

9. "New OCC Guidelines for Appraising Management," *Issues in Bank Regulation* (Fall 1989): 20–22. For an interesting discussion of decision-making processes used in the United States versus those used in the United Kingdom, see Mark Andrew Mitchell, Ronald D. Taylor, and Faruk Tanyel, "Product Elimination Decisions: A Comparison of American and British Manufacturing Firms," *International Journal of Commerce & Management* 8, no. 1 (1998): 8–27.

10. For an extended discussion of this model, see William B. Werther Jr., "Productivity Through People: The Decision-Making Process," *Management Decisions* (1988): 37–41.

11. These assumptions are adapted from James G. March and Herbert A. Simon, *Organizations* (New York: Wiley, 1958), 137–38.

12. William C. Symonds, "There's More than Beer in Molson's Mug," *BusinessWeek,* February 10, 1992, 108.

13. Chester I. Barnard, *The Function of the Executive* (Cambridge, MA: Harvard University Press, 1938).

14. For further elaboration on these factors, see Robert Tannenbaum, Irving R. Weschle, and Fred Massarik, *Leadership and Organization: A Behavioral Science Approach* (New York: McGraw-Hill, 1961), 277–78.

15. For more discussion of these factors, see F. A. Shull Jr., A. I. Delbecq, and L. L. Cummings, *Organizational Decision Making* (New York: McGraw-Hill, 1970).

16. For a worthwhile discussion of forecasting and evaluating the outcomes of alternatives, see J. R. C. Wensley, "Effective Decision Aids in Marketing," *European Journal of Marketing* (1989): 70–79.

17. Timothy A. Park and Frances Antonovitz, "Econometric Tests of Firm Decision Making under Uncertainty: Optimal Output and Hedging Decisions," *Southern Economic Journal* (January 1992): 593–609; Mats Danielson, "A Framework for Analyzing Decisions under Risk," *European Journal of Operational Research* 104, no. 3 (February 1, 1998): 474–84.

18. For a discussion of risk and decisions, see Sim B. Sitkin and Amy L. Pablo, "Reconceptualizing the Determinants of Risk Behavior," *Academy of Management Review* (January 1992): 11. See also Michael J. Ryan, "Constrained Gaming Approaches to Decision Making under Uncertainty," *European Journal of Operational Research* (August 25, 1994): 70–81. To see how information can help reduce the risk in decision making, see Helga Drummond, " 'It Looked Marvelous in the Prospectus': TAURUS, Information and Decision Making," *Journal of General Management* 23, no. 3 (Spring 1998): 73–87.

19. Steven C. Harper, "What Separates Executives from Managers," *Business Horizons* (September/October 1988): 13–19; Russ Holloman, "The Light and Dark Sides of Decision Making," *Supervisory Management* (December 1989): 33–34.

20. The scope of this text does not permit elaboration on these three decision-making tools. However, for an excellent discussion on how they are used in decision making, see Richard M. Hodgetts, *Management: Theory, Process and Practice* (Philadelphia: Saunders, 1975), 234–66. For a discussion of the computer as a decision-making tool, see Robert Addleman, "Scientific Decision-Making," *Healthcare Forum* (March/April 1994): 47–50.

21. Richard C. Mosier, "Expected Value: Applying Research to Uncertainty," *Appraisal Journal* (July 1989): 293–96. See also Amartya Sen, "The Formulation of Rational Choice," *American Economic Review* 84 (May 1994): 385–90. For an illustration of how probability theory can be applied to solve personal problems, see Jeff D. Opdyke, " 'Will My Nest Egg Last?'—Probability Theory, an Old Math Technique, Is Providing New—and Better — Answers to That Question," *Wall Street Journal,* June 5, 2000, 7.

22. Peter Boys, "Answers Grow on Decision Trees," *Accountancy* (January 1990): 86–89. For an example of how financial analysts use decision trees to reduce risk, see Joseph J. Mezrich, "When Is a Tree a Hedge?" *Financial Analysts Journal* 50, no. 6 (November/December 1994): 75–81.

23. John F. Magee, "Decision Trees for Decision Making," *Harvard Business Review* (July/August 1964). To see how decision trees can be applied to the problem of stress management, refer to Lin Grensing-Pophal, "If the Answer Is 'No,' Then 'Let It Go': Using the 'Stress Relief Decision Tree,' " *Manage* (July 1994): 18–20.

24. Rakesh Sarin and Peter Wakker, "Folding Back in Decision Tree Analysis," *Management Science* 40 (May 1994): 625–28; Eric H. Sorensen, Keith L. Miller, and Chee K. Ooi, "The Decision Tree Approach to Stock Selection," *Journal of Portfolio Management* 27, no. 1 (Fall 2000): 42–52.

25. This section is based on Samuel C. Certo, *Supervision: Quality and Diversity Through Leadership* (Homewood, IL: Austen Press/Irwin, 1994), 198–202.

26. Clark Wigley, "Working Smart on Tough Business Problems," *Supervisory Management* (February 1992): 1.

27. Joseph Alan Redman, "Nine Creative Brainstorming Techniques," *Quality Digest* (August 1992): 50–51; K. Chung and Carl R. Adams, "A Study on the Characteristics of Group Decision Making Behavior: Cultural Difference Perspective of Korea vs.

U.S.," *Journal of Global Information Management* 5, no. 3 (Summer 1997): 18–29.

28. David M. Armstrong, "Management by Storytelling," *Executive Female* (May/June 1992): 38–41.

29. André Delbecq, Andrew Van de Ven, and D. Gustafson, *Group Techniques for Program Planning* (Glenview, IL: Scott, Foresman, 1975); Philip L. Roth, L. F. Lydia, and Fred S. Switzer, "Nominal Group Technique—An Aid for Implementing TQM," *CPA Journal* (May 1995): 68–69; Karen L. Dowling, "Asynchronous Implementation of the Nominal Group Technique: Is It effective?" *Decision Support Systems* 29, no. 3 (October 2000): 229–48.

30. N. Delkey, *The Delphi Method: An Experimental Study of Group Opinion* (Santa Monica, CA: Rand Corporation, 1969); Delia Neuman, "High School Students' Use of Databases: Results of a National Delphi Study," *Journal of the American Society for Information Science* 46 (1995): 284–98; Gene Rowe and George Wright, "The Delphi Technique as a Forecasting Tool: Issues and Analysis," *International Journal of Forecasting* 15, no. 4 (October 1999).

Chapter 8

1. Tony Grundy and Dave King, "Using Strategic Planning to Drive Strategic Change," *Long-Range Planning* (February 1992): 100–108. For reasons why strategic thinking matters more to managers now than ever before, see Keith H. Hammonds, "Michael Porter's Big Ideas," *Fast Company*, March 2001, 150–56.

2. Charles R. Greer, "Counter-Cyclical Hiring as a Staffing Strategy for Managerial and Professional Personnel: Some Considerations and Issues," *Academy of Management Review* 9 (April 1984): 324–30; Dyan Machan, "The Strategy Thing," *Forbes*, May 23, 1994, 113–14. For an example of a successful business strategy, see Laura Huller, "Target Reiterates Stable Strategy," *Dsn Retailing Today*, June 4, 2001, 6.

3. Richard B. Robinson Jr. and John A. Pearce II, "Research Thrusts in Small Firm Strategic Planning," *Academy of Management Review* 9 (January 1984): 128–37. For a detailed discussion of strategy formulation in small family-owned businesses, see Nancy Drozdow and Vincent P. Carroll, "Tools for Strategy Development in Family Firms," *Sloan Management Review* 39, no. 1 (Fall 1997): 75–88.

4. This section is based on Samuel C. Certo and J. Paul Peter, *Strategic Management: Concepts and Applications* (Chicago: Austin Press/Irwin, 1995), 3–27.

5. Samuel C. Certo and J. Paul Peter, *The Strategic Management Process*, 4th ed. (Chicago: Austen Press/Irwin, 1995), 32; William Drohan, "Principles of Strategic Planning," *Association Management* 49, no. 1 (January 1997): 85–87. For a recent study examining the interaction between organizations and environment, see Max Boisot and John Child, "Organizations as Adaptive Systems in Complex Environments: The Case of China," *Organization Science* 10, no. 3 (May/June 1999): 237–52.

6. This section is based on William F. Glueck and Lawrence R. Jauch, *Business Policy and Strategic Management* (New York: McGraw-Hill, 1984), 99–110.

7. John F. Watkins, "Retirees as a New Growth Industry? Assessing the Demographic and Social Impact," *Review of Business* (Spring 1994): 9–14.

8. Bruce Henderson, "The Origin of Strategy," *Harvard Business Review* (November/December 1989): 139–43. For tips used to analyze competitors more effectively, see Dan Simpson, "Competitive Intelligence Can Be a Bad Investment," *Journal of Business Strategy* 18, no. 6 (November/December 1997): 8–9.

9. Peter Wright, "MNC—Third World Business Unit Performance: Application of Strategic Elements," *Strategic Management Journal* 5 (1984): 231–40; Inga S. Baird, Marjorie A. Lyles, and J. B. Orris, "The Choice of International Strategies by Small Businesses," *Journal of Small Business Management* 32, no. 1 (January 1994): 48–60.

10. M. Klemm, S. Sanderson, and G. Luffman, "Mission Statements: Selling Corporate Values to Employees," *Long-Range Planning* (June 1991): 73–78. For a recent review of effective mission statements, see Shirleen Holt, "Mission Possible," *BusinessWeek*, August 16, 1999, F12.

11. Colin Coulson-Thomas, "Strategic Vision or Strategic Cons: Rhetoric or Reality," *Long-Range Planning* (February 1992): 81–89; Rhymer Rigby, "Mission Statements," *Management Today* (March 1998): 56–58.

12. This section is based primarily on Thomas H. Naylor and Kristin Neva, "Design of a Strategic Planning Process," *Managerial Planning* (January/February 1980): 2–7; Donald W. Mitchell, "Pursuing Strategic Potential," *Managerial Planning* (May/June 1980): 6–10; Benton E. Gup, "Begin Strategic Planning by Asking Three Questions," *Managerial Planning* (November/December 1979): 28–31, 35; Rainer Feurer and Kazem Chaharbaghi, "Dynamic Strategy Formulation and Alignment," *Journal of General Management* 20, no. 3 (Spring 1995): 76–91.

13. For a practical example of SWOT applied in the business world, see Robert H. Woods, "Strategic Planning: A Look at Ruby Tuesday," *Cornell Hotel & Restaurant Administration Quarterly* (June 1994): 41–49.

14. Philip Kotler, *Marketing Management Analysis, Planning and Control*, 7th ed. (Upper Saddle River, NJ: Prentice Hall, 1991), 39–41.

15. Harold W. Fox, "The Frontiers of Strategic Planning: Intuition or Formal Models?" *Management Review* (April 1981): 8–14. See also J. Scott Armstrong and Roderick J. Brodie, "Effects of Portfolio Planning Methods on Decision Making: Experimental Results," *International Journal of Research in Marketing* (January 1994): 73–84; Robin Wensley, "Making Better Decisions: The Challenge of Marketing Strategy Techniques—A Comment on 'Effects of Portfolio Planning Methods on Decision Making: Experimental Results' by Armstrong and Brodie," *International Journal of Research in Marketing* (January 1994): 85–90.

16. This discussion of Porter's model is based on chapters 1 and 2 of Porter's *Competitive Strategy* (New York: The Free Press, 1980), and chapter 1 of Porter's *Competitive Advantage: Creating and Sustaining Superior Performance* (New York: The Free Press, 1985). For an application of Porter's concepts, see William P. Munk and Barry Shane, "Using Competitive Analysis Models to Set Strategy in the Northwest Hardboard Industry," *Forest Products Journal* (July/August 1994): 11–18.

17. Ian C. MacMillan, Donald C. Hambrick, and Diana L. Day, "The Product Portfolio and Profitability—A PIMS-Based Analysis of Industrial-Product Businesses," *Academy of Management Journal* (December 1982): 733–55.

18. Bill Saporito, "Black & Decker's Gamble on Globalization," *Fortune*, May 14, 1984, 40–48; Walecia Konrad and Bruce Einhorn, "Famous Amos Gets a Chinese Accent," *BusinessWeek*, September 28, 1992, 76.

19. Doron P. Levin, "Westinghouse's New Chief Aims to Push New Lines, Revitalize Traditional Ones," *Wall Street Journal*, November 28, 1983, 10.

20. William Sandy, "Avoid the Breakdowns Between Planning and Implementation," *Journal of Business Strategy* (September/October 1991): 30–33.

21. Thomas V. Bonoma, "Making Your Marketing Strategy Work," *Harvard Business Review* (March/April 1984): 69–76. For a recent article illustrating the importance of strategy implementation, see Loizos Heracleous, "The Role of Strategy Implementation in Organization Development," *Organization Development Journal* 18, no. 3 (Fall 2000): 75–86.

22. For a good discussion of the importance of monitoring the progress of the strategic planning process, see William B. Carper and Terry A. Bresnick, "Strategic Planning Conferences," *Business Horizons* (September/October 1989): 34–40. See also Stephen Bungay and Michael Goold, "Creating a Strategic Control System," *Long-Range Planning* (June 1991): 32–39.

23. For a detailed discussion of the characteristics of strategic and tactical planning, see George A. Steiner, *Top Management Planning* (Toronto, Canada: Collier-Macmillan, 1969), 37–39.

24. Russell L. Ackoff, *A Concept of Corporate Planning* (New York: Wiley, 1970), 4.

25. "The New Breed of Strategic Planner," *BusinessWeek,* September 17, 1984, 62–67.

Chapter 9

1. Charles B. Ames, "Straight Talk from the New CEO," *Harvard Business Review* (November/December 1989): 132–38.

2. Fremont E. Kast and James E. Rosenzweig, *Organization and Management: A Systems Approach* (New York: McGraw-Hill, 1970), 443–49. For a classic discussion on expanding this list of characteristics to 13, see P. LeBreton and D. A. Henning, *Planning Theory* (Upper Saddle River, NJ: Prentice Hall, 1961), 320–44. These authors list the dimensions of a plan as (1) complexity, (2) significance, (3) comprehensiveness, (4) time, (5) specificity, (6) completeness, (7) flexibility, (8) frequency, (9) formality, (10) confidential nature, (11) authorization, (12) ease of implementation, and (13) ease of control.

3. Jennifer A. Knight, "Loss Control Solution to Limiting Costs of Workplace Violence," *Corporate Cashflow* (July 1994): 16–17.

4. Kirkland Wilcox and Richard Discenza, "The TQM Advantage," *CA Magazine,* May 1994, 37–41.

5. From "Seize the Future—Make Top Trends Pay Off Now," *Success* (March 1990): 39–45.

6. For an interesting article outlining how currency exchange rates complicate budgets that relate to operations in more than one country, see Paul V. Mannino and Ken Milani, "Budgeting for an International Business," *Management Accounting* (February 1992): 36–41; See also J. Fred Weston and Eugene F. Brigham, *Essentials of Managerial Finance* (New York: Holt, Rinehart & Winston, 1971), 107; Mark M. Klein, "Questions to Ask Before You Sharpen Your Budget Knife," *Bottomline* (March 1990): 32–37; Pierre Filiatrault and Jean-Charles Chebat, "How Service Firms Set Their Marketing Budgets," *Industrial Marketing Management* (February 1990): 63–67.

7. Kjell A. Ringbakk, "Why Planning Fails," *European Business* (July 1970). See also William G. Gang, "Strategic Planning and Competition: A Survival Guide for Electric Utilities," *Fortnightly,* February 1, 1994, 20–23. For a good discussion on involving people in the planning process, see Margaret M. Lucas, "Business Plan Is the Key to Agency Success," *National Underwriter* 94 (March 5, 1990): 15, 17.

8. For information that ranks U.S. cities on the possible site selection criterion of growth, see John Case, "Where the Growth Is," *Inc.,* June 1991, 66–79. See also Walt Yesberg, "Get a Grip on Building Costs," *ABA Banking Journal* 82 (March 1990): 90, 92;

Robert Bowman, "Key Logistics Issues in Site Selection," *Distribution* 88 (December 1989): 56–57.

9. Douglas P. Woodward, "Locational Determinants of Japanese Manufacturing Start-Ups in the United States," *Southern Economic Journal* (January 1992): 690–708.

10. Greg Nakanishi, "Building Business Through Partnerships," *HR Magazine,* June 1991, 108–12. For an interesting description of a company that performs human resource planning for other companies, see Eryn Brown, "PeopleSoft: Tech's Latest Publicly Traded Cult," *Fortune,* May 25, 1998, 155–56. For a recent study assessing the importance of human resource planning, see Senga Briggs and William Keogh, "Integrating Human Resource Strategy and Strategic Planning to Achieve Business Excellence," *Total Quality Management* 10, no. 4/5 (July 1999): S447–53.

11. Charles F. Kettering, "A Glimpse at the Future," *Industry Week* (July 1, 1991): 34.

12. William C. House, "Environmental Analysis: Key to More Effective Dynamic Planning," *Managerial Planning* (January/February 1977): 25–29. The basic components of this forecasting method, as well as of other methods, are discussed in Chaman L. Jain, "How to Determine the Approach to Forecasting," *Journal of Business Forecasting Methods & Systems* (Summer 1995): 2, 28. For information about software applications designed to help companies in their planning and forecasting, see Anonymous, "Planning and Forecasting," *Financial Executive* 17, no. 3 (May 2001): 14–15.

13. Marshall L. Fisher et al., "Making Supply Meet Demand in an Uncertain World," *Harvard Business Review* (May/June 1994): 83–89; Tony Dear, "Fast and Slow Approaches to Sales Forecasting," *Logistics Focus* 6, no. 4 (May 1998): 24–25.

14. Olfa Hemler, "The Uses of Delphi Techniques in Problems of Educational Innovations," no. 8499, RAND Corporation, December 1966. For an interesting article employing the Delphi method to analyze international trends, see Michael R. Czinkota and Ilkka A. Ronkainen, "International Business and Trade in the Next Decade: Report from a Delphi Study," *Journal of International Business Studies* 28, no. 4 (Fourth Quarter 1997): 827–44.

15. James E. Cox Jr., "Approaches for Improving Salespersons' Forecasts," *Industrial Marketing Management* 18 (November 1989): 307–11; Jack Stack, "A Passion for Forecasting," *Inc.,* November 1997, 37–38.

16. N. Carroll Mohn, "Forecasting Sales with Trend Models—Coca-Cola's Experience," *Journal of Business Forecasting* 8 (Fall 1989): 6–8. For an interesting article that describes the use of time series analysis in predicting the alcohol consumption of Europeans, see David E. Smith and Hans S. Solgaard, "Global Trends in European Alcoholic Drinks Consumption." *Marketing and Research Today* 26, no. 2 (May 1998): 80–85. For a historical perspective of time series analysis, see D. S. G. Pollock, "Statistical Visions in Time: A History of Time Series Analysis, 1662–1938," *Economica* 67, no. 267 (August 2000): 459–61.

17. For elaboration on these methods, see George A. Steiner, *Top Management Planning* (London: Collier-Macmillan, 1969), 223–27.

18. Willard Fazar, "The Origin of PERT," *The Controller* (December 1962). See also Harold L. Wattel, *Network Scheduling and Control Systems CAP/PERT* (Hempstead, NY: Hostra University, 1964). For a discussion of software packages that draw preliminary PERT and Gantt charts, see Pat Sweet, "A Planner's Best Friend?" *Accountancy* (February 1994): 56, 58. Also see Curtis F. Franklin Jr., "Project Managers Toolbox," *CIO* 11, no. 2 (October 15, 1997):

64–70. For an extension of the Gnatt chart, see Harvey Maylor, "Beyond the Gantt Chart: Project Management Moving On," *European Management Journal* 19, no. 1 (February 2001): 92–100.

19. R. J. Schonberger, "Custom-Tailored PERT/CPM Systems," *Business Horizons* 15 (1972): 64–66. See also H. M. Soroush, "The Most Critical Path in a PERT Network," *Journal of the Operational Research Society* 45 (March 1994): 287–300.

20. Avraham Shrub, "The Integration of CPM and Material Management in Project Management," *Construction Management and Economics* 6 (Winter 1988): 261–72; Michael A. Hatfield and James Noel, "The Case for Critical Path," *Cost Engineering* 40, no. 3 (March 1998): 17–18.

21. For extended discussion of these steps, see Edward K. Shelmerdine, "Planning for Project Management," *Journal of Systems Management* 40 (January 1989): 16–20.

Chapter 10

1. Douglas S. Sherwin, "Management of Objectives," *Harvard Business Review* (May/June 1976): 149–60. See also Lloyd Sandelands and Robert Drazin, "On the Language of Organization Theory," *Organizational Studies* 10 (1989): 457–77.

2. Henri Fayol, *General and Industrial Management* (London: Sir Isaac Pitman and Sons, 1949), 53–54.

3. For a discussion emphasizing the importance of continually adapting organization structure, see Michael A. Verespej, "When Change Becomes the Norm," *Industry Week* (March 16, 1992): 35–36.

4. Saul W. Gellerman, "In Organizations, as in Architecture, Form Follows Function," *Organizational Dynamics* 18 (Winter 1990): 57–68. For a discussion of how evaluation can contribute to increased worker productivity, see Eugene F. Finklin, "Techniques for Making People More Productive," *Journal of Business Strategy* (March/April 1991): 53–56.

5. Max Weber, *Theory of Social and Economic Organization,* trans. and ed. A. M. Henderson and Talcott Parsons (London: Oxford University Press, 1947); Stanley Vanagunas, "Max Weber's Authority Models and the Theory of X-Inefficiency: The Economic Sociologist's Analysis Adds More Structure to Leibenstein's Critique of Rationality," *American Journal of Economics and Sociology* 48 (October 1989): 393–400; Thomas A. Stewart, "Get with the New Power Game," *Fortune,* January 13, 1997, 58–62.

6. Sandra T. Gray, "Fostering Leadership for the New Millennium," *Association Management* (January 1995): L-78–L-82.

7. Lyndall Urwich, *Notes on the Theory of Organization* (New York: American Management Association, 1952). For a recent look at the implications of organizational structure on misbehavior, see Granville King III, "The Implications of an Organization's Structure on Whistleblowing," *Journal of Business Ethics* 20, no. 4 (July 1999): 315–26.

8. For an interesting discussion of a nontraditional organization structure, see David M. Lehmann, "Integrated Enterprise Management: A Look at the Functions, the Enterprise, and the Environment—Can You See the Difference?" *Hospital Material Management Quarterly* 19, no. 4 (May 1998): 22–26.

9. Sally Helgesen, *The Female Advantage: Women's Ways of Leadership* (New York: Doubleday/Currency, 1990); Tom Peters, "The Best New Managers Will Listen, Motivate, Support," *Working Woman,* September 1990, 142–43, 216–17.

10. David Stamps, "Off the Charts," *Training* 34, no. 10 (October 1997): 77–83.

11. Geary A. Rummler and Alan P. Brache, "Managing the White Space on the Organization Chart," *Supervision* (May 1991): 6–12. For an article arguing in favor of having organizations designed by function, see Jack Cohen, "Managing the Managers," *Supermarket Business* 44 (September 1989): 16, 244.

12. Roderick E. White and Thomas A. Poynter, "Organizing for Worldwide Advantage," *Business Quarterly* 54 (Summer 1989): 84–89.

13. Y. K. Shetty and Howard M. Carlisle, "A Contingency Model of Organization Design," *California Management Review* 15 (1972): 38–45. For additional discussion of factors influencing formal structure, see Paul Dwyer, "Tearing Up Today's Organization Chart," *BusinessWeek* (November 18, 1994): 80–90.

14. For insights on how Ralph Larsen, CEO of Johnson & Johnson, views problems and how his view might influence the formal structure of his organization, see Brian Dumaine, "Is Big Still Good?" *Fortune,* April 30, 1992, 50–60.

15. For a review focusing on division of labor, see Anonymous, "Division of Labor Welcomed," *Business Insurance* 34, no. 10 (March 6, 2000): 8.

16. Carol Ann Dorn, "Einstein: Still No Equal," *Journal of Business Strategy* (November/December 1994): 20–23.

17. C. R. Walker and R. H. Guest, *The Man on the Assembly Line* (Cambridge, MA: Harvard University Press, 1952). For an excellent example of how technology can affect division of labor, see John P. Walsh, "Technological Change and the Division of Labor: The Case of Retail Meatcutters," *Work and Occupations* 16 (May 1989): 165–83.

18. J. Mooney, "The Principles of Organization," in *Ideas and Issues in Public Administration,* ed. D. Waldo (New York: McGraw-Hill, 1953), 86. For a discussion of the importance of cooperation and coordination in division of labor, see Jason Magidson and Andrew E. Polcha, "Creating Market Economies within Organizations," *The Planning Forum* (January/February 1992): 37–40. See also Peter Jackson, "Speed versus Heed," *CA Magazine,* November 1994, 56–57. For an application of the coordination principle, see Gail Karet and Tim Studt, "Managing Biotech Requires Cross-functional Coordination," *Research & Development* 43, no. 3 (March 2001): 12–17.

19. Bruce D. Sanders, "Making Work Groups Work," *Computerworld* 24 (March 5, 1990): 85–89.

20. George D. Greenberg, "The Coordinating Roles of Management," *Midwest Review of Public Administration* 10 (1976): 66–76; Stephen Ackroyd, "How Organizations Act Together: Interorganizational Coordination in Theory and Practice," *Administrative Science Quarterly* 43, no. 1 (March 1998): 217–21.

21. Henry C. Metcalf and Lyndall F. Urwich, eds., *Dynamic Administration: The Collected Papers of Mary Parker Follett* (New York: Harper & Bros., 1942), 297–99; James F. Wolf, "The Legacy of Mary Parker Follett," *Bureaucrat Winter* (1988–89): 53–57. For a recent discussion of the work of Mary Parker Follett, see Vavid M. Boje and Grace Ann Rosile, "Where's the Power in Empowerment? Answers from Follett and Clegg," *Journal of Applied Behavioral Science* 37, no. 1 (March 2001): 90–117.

22. Leon McKenzie, "Supervision: Learning from Experience," *Health Care Supervisor* 8 (January 1990): 1–11. For a recent discussion of span of control, see Anonymous, "Span of Control vs. Span of Support," *Journal for Quality and Participation* 23, no. 4 (Fall 2000): 4.

23. Harold Koontz, "Making Theory Operational: The Span of Management," *Journal of Management Studies* (October 1966): 229–43; see also John S. McClenahen, "Managing More People in the '90s," *Industry Week* 238 (March 1989): 30–38.

24. V. A. Graicunas, "Relationships in Organization," *Bulletin of International Management Institute* (March 1933): 183–87. L. F. Urwick, "V. A. Graicunas and the Span of Control," *Academy of Management Journal* 17 (June 1974): 349–54; Luther Gulick, Lyndall Urwick, James D. Mooney, Henri Fayol, et al. "Papers on the Science of Administration," *International Journal of Public Administration* 21, no. 2–4 (1998): 441–641.

25. For discussion about why managers should increase spans of management see Stephen R. Covey, "The Marketing Revolution," *Executive Excellence* 14, no. 3 (March 1997): 3–4.

26. John R. Brandt, "Middle Management: 'Where the Action Will Be,'" *Industry Week* (May 2, 1994): 30–36.

27. Philip R. Nienstedt, "Effectively Downsizing Management Structures," *Human Resources Planning* 12 (1989): 155–65; Robin Bellis-Jones and Max Hand, "Improving Managerial Spans of Control," *Management Accounting* 67 (October 1989): 20–21.

28. S. R. Maheshwari, "Hierarchy: Key Principle of Organization," *Employment News* 21, no. 49 (March 8–March 14): 1–2.

29. Cass Bettinger, "The Nine Principles of War," *Bank Marketing* 21 (December 1989): 32–34; Donald C. Hambrick, "Corporate Coherence and the Top Management Team," *Strategy & Leadership* 25, no. 5 (September/October 1997): 24–29.

30. Henri Fayol, *General and Industrial Administration* (Belmont, CA: Pitman, 1949).

Chapter 11

1. Andre Nelson, "Have I the Right Stuff to Be a Supervisor?" *Supervision* 51 (January 1990): 10–12. For a recent responsibility-related trend, see Anonymous, "Office Professionals' Responsibilities Set to Soar," *British Journal of Administrative Management* (May/June 2001): 6.

2. J. E. Osborne, "Job Descriptions Do More Than Describe Duties," *Supervisory Management* (February 1992): 8. See also G. F. Scollard, "Dynamic Descriptions: Job Descriptions Should Work for You," *Management World* (May 1985): 34–35; Charlene Marmer Solomon, "Repatriation Planning Checklist," *Personnel Journal* (January 1995): 32; Peggy Anderson and Marcia Pulich, "Making Performance Appraisals Work More Effectively," *The Health Care Supervisor* 16, no. 4 (June 1998): 20–27.

3. Robert J. Theirauf, Robert C. Klekamp, and Daniel W. Geeding, *Management Principles and Practices: A Contingency and Questionnaire Approach* (New York: Wiley, 1977), 334.

4. Deborah S. Kezsbom, "Managing the Chaos: Conflict Among Project Teams," *AACE Transactions* (1989): A.4.1–A.4.8. For an example of how overlapping responsibilities can impact a political organization, see Carolyn Ban and Norma Riccucci, "New York State Civil Service Reform in a Complex Political Environment," *Review of Public Personnel Administration* 14, no. 2 (Spring 1994): 28–40.

5. Chuck Douros, "Clear Division of Responsibility Defeats Inefficiency," *Nation's Restaurant News* (February 21, 1994): 20.

6. Robert D. Melcher, "Roles and Relationships: Clarifying the Manager's Job," *Personnel* 44 (May/June 1967): 34–41.

7. This section is based primarily on John H. Zenger, "Responsible Behavior: Stamp of the Effective Manager," *Supervisory Management* (July 1976): 18–24.

8. Stephen Bushardt, David Duhon, and Aubrey Fowler, "Management Delegation Myths and the Paradox of Task Assignment," *Business Horizons* (March/April 1991): 37–43; Jack J. Phillips, "Authority: It Just Doesn't Come with Your Job," *Management Solutions* 31 (August 1986): 35–37.

9. Max Weber, "The Three Types of Legitimate Rule," trans. Hans Gerth, *Berkeley Journal of Sociology* 4 (1953): 1–11. For a current illustration of this concept, see Gail DeGeorge, "Yo, Ho, Ho, and a Battle for Bacardi," *BusinessWeek,* April 16, 1990, 47–48.

10. John Gardner, "The Anti-Leadership Vaccine," *Carnegie Foundation Annual Report,* 1965.

11. Chester I. Barnard, *The Functions of the Executive* (Cambridge, MA: Harvard University Press, 1938).

12. For an illustration of how line authority issues can impact the operation of the IRS, see Anonymous, "TEI Recommends Changes in IRS Appeals Large Case Program," *Tax Executive* 48, no. 4 (July/August 1996): 265.

13. Patti Wolf, Gerald Grimes, and John Dayani, "Getting the Most Out of Staff Functions," *Small Business Reports* 14 (October 1989): 68–70.

14. Harold Stieglitz, "On Concepts of Corporate Structure," *Conference Board Record* 11 (February 1974): 7–13.

15. Wendell L. French, *The Personnel Management Process: Human Resource Administration and Development* (Boston: Houghton Mifflin, 1987), 66–68.

16. Derek Sheane, "When and How to Intervene in Conflict," *Personnel Management* (November 1979): 32–36; John M. Ivancevich and Michael T. Matteson, "Intergroup Behavior and Conflict," in their *Organizational Behavior and Management* (Plano, TX: Business Publications, 1987), 305–45.

17. Robert Albanese, *Management* (Cincinnati: South-Western Publishing, 1988), 313. For an excellent discussion of the role of accountability and organization structure, see Elliott Jacques, "In Praise of Hierarchy," *Harvard Business Review* 68 (January/February 1990): 127–33; Michael T. McCue and John Gress, "Accountability: A New Commandment," *Managed Healthcare Executive* 11, no. 6 (June 2001): 14.

18. "How Ylvisaker Makes 'Produce or Else' Work," *BusinessWeek,* October 27, 1973, 112. For an interesting discussion of the importance of establishing an environment of accountability in a small women's specialty retail store, see Nan Napier, "Change Is Big Even for a Little Guy," *Business Quarterly* (Winter 1994): 21–27.

19. William H. Newman and E. Kirby Warren, *The Process of Management: Concepts, Behavior, and Practice,* 4th ed. (Upper Saddle River, NJ: Prentice Hall, 1977), 39–40; Dave Wiggins, "Stop Doing It All Yourself! Some Keys to Effective Delegation," *Journal of Environmental Health* 60, no. 9 (May 1998): 29–30. See also Kristin Gilpatrick, "Step Up to Delegation," *Credit Union Management* 24, no. 4 (April 2001): 18.

20. R. S. Drever, "The Ultimate Frustration," *Supervision* (May 1991): 22–23.

21. Ted Pollock, "Secrets of Successful Delegation," *Production* (December 1994): 10–11; Robert B. Nelson, "Mastering Delegation," *Executive Excellence* 7 (January 1990): 13–14; Jimmy Calano and Jeff Salzman, "How Delegation Can Lead Your Team to Victory," *Working Woman,* August 1989, 86–87, 95.

22. Roz Ayres-Williams, "Mastering the Fine Art of Delegation," *Black Enterprise* (April 1992): 91–93.

23. Harold Koontz, Cyril O'Donnell, and Heinz Weihrich, *Essentials of Management,* 8th ed. (New York: McGraw-Hill, 1986), 231–33.

24. For an interesting discussion of whether or not to centralize the marketing function, see Richard Kitaeff, "The Great Debate: Centralized vs. Decentralized Marketing Research Function," *Marketing Research: A Magazine of Management & Applications,* (Winter 1994): 59; Charlotte Sibley, "The Pros and Cons of Centralization and Decentralization," *Medical Marketing and Media* 32, no. 5 (May 1997): 72–76; Christine Tierney and

Katherine Schmidt, "Schrempp, the Survivor? To Tighten His Grip, He Will Centralize Decision-Making," *BusinessWeek*, March 5, 2001, 54.

25. Steve Weinstein, "A Look at Fleming's New Look," *Progressive Grocer* 74 (1995): 47–49.

26. H. Gilman, "J.C. Penney Decentralizes Its Purchasing," *Wall Street Journal*, May 8, 1986, 6.

27. Donald O. Harper, "Project Management as a Conrol and Planning Tool in the Decentralized Company," *Management Accounting* (November 1968): 29–33.

28. Information for this section is mainly from John G. Staiger, "What Cannot Be Decentralized," *Management Record* 25 (January 1963): 19–21. At the time the article was written, Staiger was vice president of administration, North American Operations, Massey-Ferguson, Limited.

Chapter 12

1. For an interesting discussion of human resource department challenges, see Robert Galford, Laurie Broedling, Edward E. Lawler III, Tim Riley et al., "Why Doesn't This HR Department Get Any Respect?" *Harvard Business Review* 76, no. 2 (March/April 1998): 24–40.

2. To see how the performance of these steps can be shared in an organization, see Brenda Paik Sunoo, "Growing without an HR Department" *Workforce* 77, no. 1 (January 1998): 16–17. For a recent review of effective recruitment techniques, see Daniel Bates, "Do You Have Great People?: Roadshow Recruitment," *SBN Pittsburgh* 7, no. 10 (February 1, 2001): 32.

3. Bruce Shawkey, "Job Descriptions," *Credit Union Executive* 29 (Winter 1989/1990): 20–23; Howard D. Feldman, "Why Are Similar Managerial Jobs So Different?" *Review of Business* 11 (Winter 1989): 15–22. For a discussion of the legal importance of job analysis, see James P. Clifford, "Job Analysis. Why Do It, and How Should It Be Done?" *Public Personnel Management* 23 (1994): 321–40.

4. "Job Analysis," *Bureau of Intergovernmental Personnel Programs*, December 1973, 135–52; Gundars E. Kaupins, "Lies, Damn Lies, and Job Evaluations," *Personnel* 66 (November 1989): 62–65; Jim Meade, "Identifying Criteria for Success Helps in Making Effective Hiring Decisions," *HR Magazine* 43, no. 5 (April 1998): 49–50.

5. James H. Martin and Elizabeth B. Franz, "Attracting Applicants from a Changing Labor Market: A Strategic Marketing Framework," *Journal of Managerial Issues* (Spring 1994): 33–53.

6. Fred K. Foulkes, "How Top Nonunion Companies Manage Employees," *Harvard Business Review* (September/October 1981): 90; John Perham, "Management Succession: A Hard Game to Play," *Dun's Review* (April 1981): 54–55, 58.

7. Walter S. Wikstrom, "Developing Managerial Competence: Concepts, Emerging Practices," *Studies in Personnel Policy,* no. 189, National Industrial Conference Board (1964): 95–105.

8. Patricia Panchak, "Resourceful Software Boosts HR Efficiency," *Modern Office Technology* 35 (April 1990): 76–80.

9. Ray H. Hodges, "Developing an Effective Affirmative Action Program," *Journal of Intergroup Relations* 5 (November 1976): 13. For a more philosophical argument supporting affirmative action, see Leo Goarke, "Affirmative Action as a Form of Restitution," *Journal of Business Ethics* 9 (March 1990): 207–13. For a discussion of EEOC operations, see Ellen Rettig, "EEOC Gets Tough with Employers," *Indianapolis Business Journal* 20, no. 46 (January 24, 2000): 1.

10. R. Roosevelt Thomas, Jr., "From Affirmative Action to Affirming Diversity," *Harvard Business Review* 68 (March/April 1990): 107–17. For a recent article supporting the notion of affirmative action, see Albert R. Hunt, "A Persuasive Case for Affirmative Action," *Wall Street Journal*, February 1, 2001: A23.

11. For an article describing the importance of careful employee selection, see Tim Fulton, "Firms shouldn't gamble on employee selection," *Atlanta Business Chronicle*, March 26, 1999, Volume 21, Issue 42, p. B3.

12. For more discussion of the stages of the selection process, see David J. Cherrington, *Personnel Management: The Management of Human Resources* (Dubuque, IA: Wm. C. Brown, 1987), 186–231.

13. This section is based on Andrew F. Sikula, *Personnel Administration and Human Resource Management* (New York: Wiley, 1976), 188–90. For information on various tests available, see O. K. Buros, ed., *The 8th Mental Measurements Yearbook* (Highland Park, NJ: Gryphon Press, 1978).

14. For an example of an aptitude test for accident proneness, see Hiroshi Matsuoka, "Development of a Short Test for Accident Proneness," *Perceptual and Motor Skills* 85, no. 3 (December 1997): 903–6.

15. Daniel P. O'Meara, "Personality Tests Raise Questions of Legality and Effectiveness," *HR Magazine*, January 1994, 97–100.

16. Clive Fletcher, "Testing the Accuracy of Psychometric Measures," *People Management* 3, no. 21 (October 23, 1997): 64–66. For a discussion of EEOC guidelines concerning appropriate pre-employment testing for Americans with disabilities, see Melanie K. St. Clair and David W. Arnold, "Preemployment Screening: No More Test Stress," *Security Management* (February 1995): 73.

17. David Littlefield, "Menu for Change at Novotel," *People Management* (January 26, 1995): 34–36; D. W. Bray and D. L. Grant, "The Assessment Center in the Measurement of Potential for Business Management," *Psychological Monographs* 80 (1966): 1–27; Susan O. Hendricks and Susan E. Ogborn, "Supervisory and Managerial Assessment Centers in Health Care," *Health Care Supervisor* 8 (April 1990): 65–75.

18. Barry M. Cohen, "Assessment Centers," *Supervisory Management* (June 1975): 30. See also Paul Taylor, "Seven Staff Selection Myths," *Management* 45, no. 4 (May 1998): 61–65.

19. Ann Howard, "An Assessment of Assessment Centers," *Academy of Management Journal* 17 (March 1974): 177.

20. William Umiker and Thomas Conlin, "Assessing the Need for Supervisory Training: Use of Performance Appraisals," *Health Care Supervisor* 8 (January 1990): 40–45. For a look at innovative training techniques, see Rob Eure, "E-Commerce (A Special Report): The Classroom—On the Job: Corporate E-Learning Makes Training Available Anytime, Anywhere," *Wall Street Journal*, March 12, 2001, R33.

21. Bass and Vaughn, *Training in Industry*. For discussion on using technology to improve lecture effectiveness, see Anonymous, "Switches Offer Classroom Control," *Computer Dealer News* 14, no. 17 (May 4, 1998): 58.

22. David Sutton, "Further Thoughts on Action Learning," *Journal of European Industrial Training* 13 (1989): 32–35.

23. Anne Fisher, "Don't Blow Your New Job," *Fortune*, June 22, 1998, 159–62.

24. For more information on training techniques, see Cherrington, *Personnel Management*, 304–36.

25. Samuel C. Certo, "The Experiential Exercise Situation: A Comment on Instructional Role and Pedagogy Evaluation," *Academy of Management Review* (July 1976): 113–16. For a worthwhile discussion of the advantages of facilitation over lec-

turing for overcoming trainee resistance to learning, see Margaret Kaeter, "Coping with Resistant Trainees," *Training* 31 (1994): 110–14. For more information on instructional roles in various situations, see Bernard Keys, "The Management of Learning Grid for Management Development," *Academy of Management Review* (April 1977): 289–97.

26. "Training Program's Results Measured in Unique Way," *Supervision* (February 1992): 18–19.

27. William Keenan Jr., "Are You Overspending on Training?" *Sales and Marketing Management* 142 (January 1990): 56–60.

28. For a review of the literature linking performance appraisal and training needs, see Glenn Herbert and Dennis Doverspike, "Performance Appraisal in the Training Needs Analysis Process: A Review and Critique," *Public Personnel Management* (Fall 1990): 253–70. See also Mike Deblieux, "Performance Reviews Support the Quest for Quality," *HR Focus* (November 1991): 3–4.

29. Douglas McGregor, "An Uneasy Look at Performance Appraisal," *Harvard Business Review* (September/October 1972): 133–34; David A. Waldman and David E. Bowen, "The Acceptability of 360 Degree Appraisals: A Customer-Supplier Relationship Perspective," *Human Resource Management* 37, no. 2 (Summer 1998): 117–29.

30. Linda J. Segall, "KISS Appraisal Woes Goodbye," *Supervisory Management* 34 (December 1989): 23–28.

31. Robert M. Gerst, "Assessing Organizational Performance," *Quality Progress* (February 1995): 85–88. See also George A. Rider, "Performance Review: A Mixed Bag," *Harvard Business Review* (July/August 1973): 61–67; Robert Loo, "Quality Performance Appraisals," *Canadian Manager* 14 (December 1989): 24–26.

Chapter 13

1. John H. Zimmerman, "The Principles of Managing Change," *HR Focus* (February 1995): 15–16.

2. Rosabeth Moss Kanter, "The New Managerial Work," *Harvard Business Review* (November/December 1989): 85–92. For a review of planned change models as related to a nursing environment, see Constance Rimmer Tiffany et al., "Planned Change Theory: Survey of Nursing Periodical Literature," *Nursing Management* (July 1994): 54–59.

3. John S. Morgan, *Managing Change: The Strategies of Making Change Work for You* (New York: McGraw-Hill, 1972), 99.

4. Bart Nooteboom, "Paradox, Identity, and Change in Management," *Human Systems Management* 8 (1989): 291–300. For an interesting discussion of how to handle employee stress, see Alan Farnham, "Who Beats Stress Best—And How," *Fortune*, October 7, 1991, 71–86.

5. For a discussion of the value of outside change agents, see John H. Sheridan, "Careers on the Line," *Fortune*, September 16, 1991, 29–30. See also John H. Zimmerman, "The Deming Approach to Construction Safety Management," *Professional Safety* (December 1994): 35–37.

6. Myron Tribus, "Changing the Corporate Culture—A Roadmap for the Change Agent," *Human Systems Management* 8 (1989): 11–22. For a recent review of the effects of structural change within an organization, see Shawn Young, "Structural Changes Pay Off in Profits for Top U.S. Long-Distance Carriers," *Wall Street Journal*, January 19, 1999.

7. For an interesting case illustrating the changing nature of organization structure at Procter & Gamble, see Aelita G. B. Martinsons and Maris G. Martinsons, "In Search of Structural Excellence," *Leadership & Organization Development Journal* 15 (1994): 24–28.

See also Saul W. Gellerman, "In Organizations, as in Architecture, Form Follows Function," *Organizational Dynamics* 18 (Winter 1990): 57–68.

8. C. J. Middleton, "How to Set Up a Project Organization," *Harvard Business Review* (March/April 1967): 73. See also George J. Chambers, "The Individual in a Matrix Organization," *Project Management Journal* 20 (December 1989): 37–42, 50.

9. John F. Mee, "Matrix Organization," *Business Horizons* (Summer 1964).

10. Robert E. Jones, K. Michelle Jones, and Richard F. Deckro, "Strategic Decision Processes in Matrix Organizations," *European Journal of Operational Research* 78 (1994): 192–203. See also Middleton, "How to Set Up a Project Organization," 74; Deborah S. Kezsbom, "Managing the Chaos: Conflict Among Project Teams," *AACE Transactions*, 1989, A.4.1–A.4.8; Harvey F. Kolodny, "Managing in a Matrix," *Business Horizons* (March/April 1981): 17–24.

11. This section is based primarily on R. Blake, J. Mouton, and L. Greiner, "Breakthrough in Organization Development," *Harvard Business Review* (November/December 1964): 133–55. For a discussion of other methods for implementing OD change, see William F. Glueck, *Organization Planning and Development* (New York: American Management Association, 1971).

12. Blake, Mouton, and Greiner, "Breakthrough in Organization Development."

13. W. J. Heisler, "Patterns of OD in Practice," *Business Horizons* (February 1975): 77–84.

14. Martin G. Evans, "Failures in OD Programs—What Went Wrong," *Business Horizons* (April 1974): 18–22.

15. David Coghlan, "OD Interventions in Catholic Religious Orders," *Journal of Managerial Psychology* 4 (1989): 4–6. See also Paul A. Iles and Thomas Johnston, "Searching for Excellence in Second-Hand Clothes?: A Note," *Personnel Review* 18 (1989): 32–35; Ewa Maslyk-Musial, "Organization Development in Poland: Stages of Growth," *Public Administration Quarterly* 13 (Summer 1989): 196–214.

16. For an interesting discussion of resistance to change from inherited staff, see Margaret Russell, "Records Management Program-Directing: Inherited Staff," *ARMA Records Management Quarterly* 24 (January 1990): 18–22.

17. This strategy for minimizing resistance to change is based on "How Companies Overcome Resistance to Change," *Management Review* (November 1972): 17–25. See also Hank Williams, "Learning to Manage Change," *Industrial and Commercial Training* 21 (May/June 1989): 17–20; John P. Kotter and Leonard A. Schlesinger, "Choosing Strategies for Change," *Harvard Business Review* (March/April 1979): 106–13; Arnold S. Judson, *A Manager's Guide to Making Changes* (New York: Wiley, 1966), 118.

18. Newton Margulies and John Wallace, *Organizational Change: Techniques and Applications* (Chicago: Scott, Foresman, 1973), 14.

19. Edgar C. Williams, "Changing Systems and Behavior: People's Perspectives on Prospective Changes," *Business Horizons* (August 1969): 53.

20. Hans Selye, *The Stress of Life* (New York: McGraw-Hill, 1956). See also James C. Quick and Jonathan D. Quick, *Organizational Stress and Preventive Management* (New York: McGraw-Hill, 1984).

21. James D. Bodzinski, Robert F. Scherer, and Karen A. Gover, "Workplace Stress," *Personnel Administrator* 34 (July 1989): 76–80; Richard M. Steers, *Introduction to Organizational Behavior* (Glenview, IL: Scott, Foresman, 1981), 340–41.

22. Corinne M. Smereka, "Outwitting, Controlling Stress for a Healthier Lifestyle," *Healthcare Financial Management* 44 (March 1990): 70–75.

23. J. Clifton Williams, *Human Behavior in Organizations* (Cincinnati: South-Western, 1982), 212–13; Thomas L. Brown, "Are You Living in 'Quiet Desperation'?" *Industry Week* (March 16, 1992): 17.

24. Stewart L. Stokes Jr., "Life after Rightsizing," *Information Systems Management* (Fall 1994): 69–71. For a discussion of other stressors, see "Workplace Stress," *HR Magazine,* Society of Human Resource Management, August 1991, 75–76.

25. For an interesting article addressing how managers can handle their own stress, see Thomas Brown, "Are You Stressed Out?" *Industry Week* (September 16, 1991): 21.

26. Fred Luthans, *Organizational Behavior* (New York: McGraw-Hill, 1985), 146–48. For one successful method of reducing workplace stress, see J. Michael Krivyanski, "Employer-Sponsored Programs Try to Keep Workplace Stress in Check," *Business Times Journal* 20, no. 38 (April 6, 2001): 34.

27. Donald B. Miller, "Career Planning and Management in Organizations," *S.A.M. Advanced Management Journal* 43 (Spring 1978): 33–43.

28. William H. Davidow and Michael S. Malone, *The Virtual Corporation* (New York: HarperCollins, 1992).

29. P. Maria Joseph Christie and Reuven R. Levary, "Virtual Corporations: Recipe for Success," *Industrial Management* (July/August 1998): 7–11.

30. Charles C. Snow, Raymond E. Miles, and Henry J. Coleman Jr., "Managing 21st Century Network Organizations," *Organizational Dynamics* (Winter, 1992): 5–20; Shawn Tully, "The Modular Corporation," *Fortune,* February 8, 1993, 22–26.

31. Judith R. Gordon, *Organizational Behavior: A Diagnostic Approach* (Upper Saddle River, NJ: Prentice Hall, 1999), 385.

32. Christopher Burnatt, "Virtual Organizations in the Small Business Sector: The Case of Cavendish Management Resources," *International Small Business Journal* 15, no. 4 (July/September 1997): 36–47.

33. Anthony M. Townsend, Samuel M. DeMarie, and Anthony R. Hendrickson, "Virtual Teams: Technology and the Workplace of the Future," *Academy of Management Executive* 12, no. 3 (August 1998): 17–29; M. Hammer and J. Champy, *Reengineering the Corporation* (New York: HarperCollins, 1993).

34. For other examples of types of virtuality in organizations, see Daniel E. O'Leary, Daniel Kuokka, and Robert Plant, "Artificial Intelligence and Virtual Organizations, *Communication of the Ach* 40, no. 1 (January 1997): 52–59.

35. This section draws heavily from Thomas H. Davenport and Keri Pearlson, "Two Cheers for the Virtual Office," *Sloan Management Review* (Summer 1998): 51–65. For a further look at the advantages of a virtual office, see Stephen Roth, "Consultants Use a Virtual Office to Make New Services a Reality," *The Business Journal* 19, no. 20, (January 26, 2001): 8.

Chapter 14

1. Derek Torrington and Jane Weightman, "Middle Management Work," *Journal of General Management* 13 (Winter 1987): 74–89. For a useful discussion of how to influence people, see Martin Wilding, "Win Friends and Influence People by Being Sincere," *Marketing,* February 23, 1995, 16; Esther Bogin, "From Staff to Dream Team," *Financial Executive,* January/February 1995, 54–56.

2. Bernard Reilly and Joseph DiAngelo Jr., "Communication: A Cultural System of Meaning and Value," *Human Relations* 43 (February 1990): 29–40. Christine Clements, Richard J. Wagner,

and Christopher Roland, "The Ins and Outs of Experimental Training," *Training & Development* (February 1995): 52–56. For a discussion of communication techniques, see Anonymous, "The Elements of Effective Communication," *Agency Sales* 30, no. 12 (December 2000): 45–46.

3. This section is based on the following classic article on interpersonal communication: Wilbur Schramm, "How Communication Works," *The Process and Effects of Mass Communication,* ed. Wilbur Schramm (Urbana, IL: University of Illinois Press, 1954), 3–10. For tips on how to increase communication skills, see T. J. Saftner, "Talk the Talk: How Well Do You Communicate?" *Career World* 26, no. 4 (January 1998): 24–27.

4. David S. Brown, "Barriers to Successful Communication: Part I, Macrobarriers," *Management Review* (December 1975): 24–29. For a discussion of successful communication, see Jeanelle Barrett, "Successful Communication for Business and Management," *Business Communication Quarterly* 63, no. 4 (December 2000): 102.

5. James K. Weekly and Raj Aggarwal, *International Business: Operating in the Global Economy* (New York: Dryden Press, 1987).

6. Davis S. Brown, "Barriers to Successful Communication: Part II, Microbarriers," *Management Review* (January 1976): 15–21. For study results having implications for e-mail as a communication microbarrier, see Norman Frohlich and Joe Oppenheimer, "Some Consequences of E-mail vs. Face-to-Face Communication in Experiment," *Journal of Economic Behavior & Organization* 35, no. 3 (April 15, 1998): 389–403.

7. Sally Bulkley Pancrazio and James J. Pancrazio, "Better Communication for Managers," *Supervisory Management* (June 1981): 31–37. See also Gene E. Burton, "Barriers to Effective Communication," *Management World* (March 1977): 4–8; John S. Fielden, "Why Can't Managers Communicate?" *Business* 39 (January/February/March 1989): 41–44.

8. Lydia Strong, "Do You Know How to Listen?" *Effective Communications on the Job,* ed. M. Joseph Dooher and Vivienne Marquis (New York: American Management Association, 1956), 28. See also John R. White, "Some Thoughts on Lexicon and Syntax," *Appraisal Journal* 57 (July 1989): 417–21.

9. Robert E. Callahan, C. Patrick Fleenor, and Harry R. Knudson, *Understanding Organizational Behavior: A Managerial Viewpoint* (Columbus, OH: Charles E. Merrill, 1986). For a discussion of the process of generating feedback, see Elizabeth Wolfe Morrison and Robert J. Bies, "Impression Management in the Feedback-Seeking Process: Literature Review and Research Agenda," *Academy of Management Review* (July 1991): 522–41.

10. For more on nonverbal issues, see J. T. Sheppard, "Silent Signals," *Supervisory Management* (March 1986): 31–33.

11. Verne Burnett, "Management's Tower of Babel," *Management Review* (June 1961): 4–11.

12. Reprinted, by permission of the publisher, from "Ten Commandments of Good Communication," by American Management Association AMA-COM et al., from *Management Review* (October 1955). © 1955 American Management Association, Inc. All rights reserved. See also Robb Ware, "Communication Problems," *Journal of Systems Management* (September 1991): 20; "Communicating: Face-to-Face," *Agency Sales Magazine,* January 1994, 22–23.

13. Ted Pollock, "Mind Your Own Business," *Supervision,* May 1994, 24–26; Joseph R. Bainbridge, "Joint Communication: Verbal and Nonverbal," *Army Logistician* 30, no. 4: (July/August) 40–42.

14. Albert Mehrabian, "Communication without Words," *Psychology Today,* September 1968, 53–55. For a practical article emphasizing the role of gestures in communication, see S. D. Gladis, "Notes

Are Not Enough," *Training and Development Journal* (August 1985): 35–38. See also Nicole Steckler and Robert Rosenthal, "Sex Differences in Nonverbal and Verbal Communication with Bosses, Peers, and Subordinates," *Journal of Applied Psychology* (February 1985): 157–63; Andrew J. DuBrin, *Contemporary Applied Management* (Plano, TX: Business Publications, 1982): 127–34; W. Alan Randolph, *Understanding and Managing Organizational Behavior* (Homewood, IL: Richard D. Irwin, 1985), 349–50; Karen O. Down and Jeanne Liedtka, "What Corporations Seek in MBA Hires: A Survey," *Selections*, Winter 1994, 34–39.

15. Gerald M. Goldhaber, *Organizational Communication* (Dubuque, IA: Wm. C. Brown, 1983). For a discussion on the important role of organizational communication within a corporation, see Bauke Visser, "Organizational Communication Structure and Performance," *Journal of Economic Behavior & Organization* 42, no. 2 (June 2000): 231–52.

16. Kenneth R. Van Voorhis, "Organizational Communication: Advances Made During the Period from World War II Through the 1950s," *Journal of Business Communication* 11 (1974): 11–18. See also Phillip J. Lewis, "The Status of 'Organizational Communication,' in Colleges of Business," *Journal of Business Communication* 12 (1975): 25–28.

17. Paul Preston, "The Critical 'Mix' in Managerial Communications," *Industrial Management* (March/April 1976): 5–9. For a discussion of implementing organizational communication reflecting a worldwide structure, see "Iridium Delays Full Start of Global System," *New York Times,* September 10, 1998, C6.

18. For a discussion of how to communicate failures upward in an organization, see Jay T. Knippen, Thad B. Green, and Kurt Sutton, "How to Communicate Failures to Your Boss," *Supervisory Management* (September 1991): 10.

19. "Upward/Downward Communication—Critical Information Channels," *Small Business Report* 10 (October 1985): 85–88; Anne B. Fisher, "CEOs Think That Morale Is Dandy," *Fortune,* November 18, 1991, 70–71. For an article stressing the importance of upward and downward communication for managers, see W. H. Weiss, "Communications: Key to Successful Supervision," *Supervision* 59, no. 9 (September 1998): 12–14.

20. William V. Haney, "Serial Communication of Information in Organizations," in *Concepts and Issues in Administrative Behavior,* ed. Sidney Mailick and Edward H. Van Ness (Englewood Cliffs, NJ: Prentice Hall, 1962), 150. For a discussion involving implications of off-site patterns of communication, see Robert M. Egan, Wendy Miles, John R. Birstler, and Margaret Klayton-Mi, "Can the Rift between Allison and Penny Be Mended?" *Harvard Business Review* 76, no. 4 (July/August 1998): 28–35.

21. Alex Bavelas and Dermot Barrett, "An Experimental Approach to Organizational Communication," *Personnel* 27 (1951): 366–71.

22. Polly LaBarre, "The Other Network," *Industry Week* (September 19, 1994): 33–36.

23. George de Mare, "Communicating: The Key to Establishing Good Working Relationships," *Price Waterhouse Review* 33 (1989): 30–37; Alan Zaremba, "Working with the Organizational Grapevine," *Personnel Journal* 67 (July 1988): 38–42; Stanley J. Modic, "Grapevine Rated Most Believable," *Industry Week* (May 15, 1989): 11, 14.

24. Keith Davis, "Management Communication and the Grapevine," *Harvard Business Review* (January/February 1953): 43–49.

25. Linda McCallister, "The Interpersonal Side of Internal Communications," *Public Relations Journal* (February 1981): 20–23. See also Joseph M. Putti, Samuel Aryee, and Joseph Phua, "Communication Relationship Satisfaction and Organizational Commitment," *Group and Organizational Studies* 15 (March 1990): 44–52. For an article defending the value of grapevines, see W. Kiechel, "In Praise of Office Gossip," *Fortune,* August 19, 1985, 253–54.

Chapter 15

1. Elise Goldman, "The Significance of Leadership Style," *Educational Leadership* 55, no. 7 (April 1998): 20–22. For a worthwhile look at the importance of instilling leadership in all members of a corporation, see Scott Payne, "Corporate Training Trend: Building Leadership," *Grand Rapids Business Journal,* November 13, 2000, B2.

2. David Nadler and Michael L. Tushman, "Beyond the Charismatic Leader: Leadership and Organizational Change," *California Management Review* 32 (Winter 1990): 77–97; Peter R. Scholtes, *The Leader's Handbook: A Guide to Inspiring Your People and Managing the Daily Workflow* (New York: McGraw-Hill, 1998).

3. Abraham Zaleznik, "Executives and Organizations: Real Work," *Harvard Business Review* (January/February 1989): 57–64; Abraham Zaleznik, "Managers and Leaders: Are They Different?" *Harvard Business Review* (May/June 1977): 67–78.

4. Theodore Levitt, "Management and the Post-Industrial Society," *Public Interest* (Summer 1976): 73.

5. Patrick L. Townsend and Joan E. Gebhardt, "We Have Lots of Managers . . . We Need Leaders," *Journal for Quality and Participation* (September 1989): 18–20; Craig Hickman, "The Winning Mix: Mind of a Manager, Soul of a Leader," *Canadian Business* 63 (February 1990): 69–72. For discussion of how successful executives place more importance and emphasis on leadership than management, see Michael E. McGrath, "The Eight Qualities of Success," *Electronic Business* 24, no. 4 (April 1998): 9–10.

6. Ralph M. Stogdill, "Personal Factors Associated with Leadership: A Survey of the Literature," *Journal of Psychology* 25 (January 1948): 35–64.

7. Cecil A. Gibb, "Leadership," in *Handbook of Social Psychology,* ed. Gardner Lindzey (Reading, MA: Addison-Wesley, 1954); Eugene E. Jennings, "The Anatomy of Leadership," *Management of Personnel Quarterly* 1 (Autumn 1961).

8. J. Oliver Crom, "What's New in Leadership?" *Executive Excellence* 7 (January 1990): 15–16.

9. For an interesting discussion of followers in a leadership situation, see Robert E. Kelly, "In Praise of Followers," *Harvard Business Review* (November/December 1988): 142–48. For a discussion of a leader in a military situation, see Sherrill Tapsell, "Managing for Peace," *Management* 45, no. 5 (June 1998): 32–37.

10. Robert Tannenbaum and Warren H. Schmidt, "How to Choose a Leadership Pattern," *Harvard Business Review* (March/April 1957): 95–101.

11. William E. Zierden, "Leading Through the Follower's Point of View," *Organizational Dynamics* (Spring 1980): 27–46. See also Tannenbaum and Schmidt, "How to Choose a Leadership Pattern."

12. Robert Tannenbaum and Warren H. Schmidt, "How to Choose a Leadership Pattern," *Harvard Business Review* (May/June 1973): 162–80.

13. Victor H. Vroom and Philip H. Yetton, *Leadership and Decision-Making* (Pittsburgh: University of Pittsburgh Press, 1973); Victor H. Vroom and Arthur G. Jago, *The New Leadership* (Upper Saddle River, NJ: Prentice Hall, 1988).

14. Gary A. Yukl, *Leadership in Organizations,* 2d ed. (Upper Saddle River, NJ: Prentice Hall, 1989).

15. Vishwanath V. Baba and Merle E. Ace, "Serendipity in Leadership: Initiating Structure and Consideration in the Classroom," *Human Relations* 42 (June 1989): 509–25. For a further discussion of leadership style, see Maria Guzzo, "People to Watch: Mike Parton—Classic Leadership Style," *Pittsburgh Business Times Journal,* June 23, 2000, 14.

16. Rensis Likert, *New Patterns of Management* (New York: McGraw-Hill, 1961).

17. Andrew W. Halpin, *The Leadership Behavior of School Superintendents* (Chicago: University of Chicago Midwest Administration Center, 1959); Harvey A. Hornstein, Madeline E. Heilman, Edward Mone, and Ross Tartell, "Responding to Contingent Leadership Behavior," *Organizational Dynamics* 15 (Spring 1987): 56–65.

18. A. K. Korman, "'Consideration,' 'Initiating Structure,' and Organizational Criteria— A Review," *Personnel Psychology* 19 (Winter 1966): 349–61. See also Rick Roskin, "Management Style and Achievement: A Model Synthesis," *Management Decision* 27 (1989): 17–22.

19. P. Hersey and K. H. Blanchard, "Life Cycle Theory of Leadership," *Training and Development Journal* (May 1969): 26–34.

20. Mary J. Keenan, Joseph B. Hurst, Robert S. Dennis, and Glenna Frey, "Situational Leadership for Collaboration in Health Care Settings," *Health Care Supervisor* 8 (April 1990): 19–25. See also Claude L. Graeff, "The Situational Leadership Theory: A Critical View," *Academy of Management Review* 8 (1983): 285–91; Robert P. Vecchio, "Situational Leadership Theory: An Examination of a Prescriptive Theory," *Journal of Applied Psychology* 72 (August 1987): 444–51; Jane R. Goodson, Gail W. McGee, and James F. Cashman, "Situational Leadership Theory: A Test of Leadership Prescriptions," *Group and Organizational Studies* 14 (December 1989): 446–61.

21. Fred E. Fiedler, "Engineer the Job to Fit the Manager," *Harvard Business Review* (September/October 1965): 115–22. See also Fred E. Fiedler, *A Theory of Leadership Effectiveness* (New York: McGraw-Hill, 1967).

22. From *A Theory of Leadership Effectiveness,* pp. 255–56 by F. E. Fiedler. © 1967 by McGraw-Hill, Inc. Used with permission of McGraw-Hill Company.

23. L. H. Peters, D. D. Harike, and J. T. Pohlmann, "Fiedler's Contingency Theory of Leadership: An Application of the Meta-analysis Procedures of Schmidt and Hunter," *Psychological Bulletin* 97 (1985): 224–85.

24. Robert J. House and Terence R. Mitchell, "Path-Goal Theory of Leadership," *Journal of Contemporary Business* (Autumn 1974): 81–98; Gary A. Yukl, *Leadership in Organizations.*

25. Alan C. Filley, Robert House, and Steven Kerr, *Managerial Process and Organizational Behavior* (Glenview, IL: Scott, Foresman, 1976), 256–60. For a worthwhile review of the path-goal theory of leadership, see Gary A. Yukl, *Leadership in Organizations.*

26. To learn how some managers are reacting to modern challenges, see Jaclyn Fierman, "Winning Ideas from Maverick Managers," *Fortune,* February 6, 1995, 66–80. For a fresh approach to leadership that modern managers are taking, see George Fraser, "The Slight Edge: Valuing and Managing Diversity," *Vital Speeches of the Day* 64, no. 8 (February 1, 1998): 235–40.

27. Andrew J. DuBrin, *Reengineering Survival Guide* (Cincinnati, OH: Thomson Executive Press, 1996), 115–29.

28. Karl W. Kuhnert and Philip Lewis, "Transactional and Transformational Leadership: A Constructive/Developmental Analysis," *Academy of Management Review* (October 1987): 648–57; Shirley M. Ross and Lynn R. Offermann, "Transformational Leaders: Measurement of Personality Attributes," *Personality and Social Psychology Bulletin,* October 1997, 1078–86.

29. For more discussion on specific steps that transformational leaders take, see Robert Miles, "Transformation Challenge," *Executive Excellence* 15, no. 2 (February 1998): 15.

30. Bernard M. Bass, *Leadership and Performance beyond Expectations* (New York: Free Press, 1985); Noel M. Tichy and David M. Ulrich, "The Leadership Challenge: A Call for Transformational Leadership," *Sloan Management Review* (Fall 1984): 59–68.

31. For an in-depth look at the positive effects of coaching on employee productivity, see Bill Blades, "Great Coaching Can Increase Revenue," *Arizona Business Gazette,* January 18, 2001, 5.

32. For more information on empathy and leadership, see William G. Pagonis, "The Work of the Leader," *Harvard Business Review* (November/December 1992): 118–26.

33. Charles C. Manz, "Helping Yourself and Others to Master Self-Leadership," *Supervisory Management* (November 1991): 19–38; Manz and Henry P. Sims Jr., "SuperLeadership: Beyond the Myth of Heroic Leadership," *Organizational Dynamics* (Spring 1991): 28–40.

34. A profile of a successful female entrepreneurial leader in a multicultural situation is contained in Daniel J. McCarthy, Sheila M. Puffer, and Alexander I. Naumov, "Case study—Olga Kirova: A Russian Entrepreneur's Quality Leadership," *International Journal of Organizational Analysis* 5, no. 3 (July 1997): 267–90.

35. S. Kerr and J. M. Jermier, "Substitutes for Leadership: Their Meaning and Measurement," *Organizational Behavior and Human Performance* 22 (1978): 375–403; C. C. Manz and H. P. Sims Jr., "Leading Workers to Lead Themselves: The External Leadership on Self-Managing Work Teams," *Administrative Science Quarterly* (March 1987): 106–29.

36. J. R. Meindl and S. B. Ehrlich, "The Romance of Leadership and the Evaluation of Organizational Performance," *Academy of Management Journal* 30 (1987): 91–109.

37. Data in this section come from the following sources: Ralph M. Stogdill, *Handbook of Leadership* (New York: Free Press, 1974); U.S. Department of Labor, Bureau of Labor Statistics, 1989, *Employment and Earnings* (Washington, DC: Government Printing Office): 29; "Workforce 2000 Is Welcome Today at Digital," *Business Ethics* (July/August 1990): 5–16; Amy Salzman, "Trouble at the Top," *U.S. News and World Report,* June 17, 1991; Susan B. Garland, "Throwing Stones at the Glass Ceiling," *BusinessWeek,* August 19, 1991, 29. For a study summarizing the positive effects that many women have had in the workforce, see Sara Nesbitt, "Women Business Leaders Boost Economy," *The Colorado Springs Business Journal* 11, no. 31 (October 22, 1999): 7.

38. See the following articles: J. B. Rosener, "Ways Women Lead," *Harvard Business Review* (May/June 1990): 103–11; B. M. Bass Leadership. "Good, Better, Best," *Organizational Dynamics* (Winter 1985): 26–40.

Chapter 16

1. Philip A. Rudolph and Brian H. Kleiner, "The Art of Motivating Employees," *Journal of Managerial Psychology* 4 (1989): i–iv; Carole L. Jurkiewicz, Tom K. Massey Jr., and Roger G. Brown, "Motivation in Public and Private Organizations: A Comparative Study," *Public Productivity & Management Review* 21, no. 3 (March 1998): 230–50.

2. Mike DeLuca, "Motivating Your Staff Is Key to Your Success," *Restaurant Hospitality* (February 1995): 20.

3. Craig Miller, "How to Construct Programs for Teams," *Reward & Recognition* (August/September 1991): 4–6; Walter F. Charsley, "Management, Morale, and Motivation," *Management World* 17 (July/August 1988): 27–28.

4. Victor H. Vroom, *Work and Motivation* (New York: Wiley, 1964); Thomas L. Quick, "How to Motivate People," *Working Women* 12 (September 1987): 15, 17.

5. J. Stacy Adams, "Towards an Understanding of Inequity," *Journal of Abnormal and Social Psychology* 67 (1963): 422–36. For a rationale linking expectancy and equity theories, see Joseph W. Harder, "Equity Theory Versus Expectancy Theory: The Case of Major League Baseball Free Agents," *Journal of Applied Psychology* (June 1991): 458–64. For group rewards as an alternative to individual rewards in human motivation, see Donald J. Campbell, Kathleen M. Campbell, and Ho-Beng Chia, "Merit Pay, Performance Appraisal, and Individual Motivation: An Analysis and Alternative," *Human Resource Management* 37, no. 2 (Summer 1998): 131–46.

6. L. W. Porter and E. E. Lawler, *Managerial Attitudes and Performance* (Homewood, IL: Richard D. Irwin, 1968). For more information on intrinsic and extrinsic rewards, see Pat Buhler, "Rewards in the Organization," *Supervision* 50 (January 1989): 5–7.

7. Eric G. Flamholtz and Yvonne Randle, "The Inner Game of Management," *Management Review* 77 (April 1988): 24–30.

8. Abraham Maslow, *Motivation and Personality*, 2d ed. (New York: Harper & Row, 1970). For an up-to-date discussion of the value of Maslow's ideas, see Edward Hoffman, "Abraham Maslow: Father of Enlightened Management," *Training* 25 (September 1988): 79–82. See also Abraham Maslow, *Eupsychian Management* (Homewood, IL: Richard D. Irwin, 1965).

9. For a discussion of an empowerment tool managers can use to help employees satisfy esteem and self-actualization needs, see Chris Argyris, "Empowerment: The Emperor's New Clothes," *Harvard Business Review* 76, no. 3 (May/June 1998): 98–105.

10. For critiques of Maslow, see Jack W. Duncan, *Essentials of Management* (Hinsdale, IL: Dryden Press, 1975), 105; C. P. Alderfer, "An Empirical Test of a New Theory of Human Needs," *Organizational Behavior and Human Performance* 4 (1969): 142–75; D. T. Hall and K. Nougaim, "An Examination of Maslow's Need Hierarchy in an Organizational Setting," *Organizational Behavior and Human Performance* 3 (1968): 12–35; Hoffman, "Abraham Maslow: Father of Enlightened Management;" Dale L. Mort, "Lead Your Team to the Top," *Security Management* 32 (January 1988): 43–45.

11. Clayton Alderfer, *Existence, Relatedness, and Growth* (New York: Free Press, 1972). For a reconstruction of Maslow's hierarchy, see Francis Heylighen, "A Cognitive-Systemic Reconstruction of Maslow's Theory of Self-Actualization," *Behavioral Science* (January 1992): 39–58.

12. Chris Argyris, *Personality and Organization* (New York: Harper & Bros., 1957). See also Charles R. Davis, "The Primacy of Self-Development in Chris Argyris's Writings," *International Journal of Public Administration* 10 (September 1987): 177–207.

13. David C. McClelland and David G. Winter, *Motivating Economic Achievement* (New York: Free Press, 1969); David C. McClelland, "Power Is the Great Motivator," *Harvard Business Review* (March/April 1976): 100–10. See also Burt K. Scanlan, "Creating a Climate for Achievement," *Business Horizons* 24 (March/April 1981): 5–9; Lawrence Holp, "Achievement Motivation and Kaizen," *Training and Development Journal* 43 (October 1989): 53–63; McClelland, *The Achieving Society* (New York: Van Nostrand, 1961); McClelland and David H. Burnham, "Power Is the Great Motivator," *Harvard Business Review* (January/February 1995): 126–39.

14. Michael Sanson, "Fired Up!" *Restaurant Hospitality* (February 1995): 53–64.

15. Douglas McGregor, *The Human Side of Enterprise* (New York: McGraw-Hill, 1960). For a current illustration of how Theory X-Theory Y relates to modern business, see Kenneth B. Slutsky, "Viewpoint: Why Not Theory Z?" *Security Management* 33 (April 1989): 110, 112. See also W. J. Reddin, "The Tri-Dimensional Grid," *Training and Development Journal* (July 1964). For a discussion of Theories X, Y, and Z as they relate to the adoption of new technology in organizations, see Richard T. Due, "Client/Server Feasibility," *Information Systems Management* (Summer 1994): 79–82.

16. For more discussion on the implications of job rotation in organizations, see Alan W. Farrant, "Job Rotation Is Important," *Supervision* (August 1987): 14–16.

17. L. E. Davis and E. S. Valfer, "Intervening Responses to Changes in Supervisor Job Designs," *Occupational Psychology* (July 1965): 171–90; M. D. Kilbridge, "Do Workers Prefer Larger Jobs?" *Personnel* (September/October 1960): 45–48.

18. This section is based on Frederick Herzberg, "One More Time: How Do You Motivate Employees?" *Harvard Business Review* (January/February 1968): 53–62.

19. Scott M. Meyers, "Who Are Your Motivated Workers?" *Harvard Business Review* (January/February 1964): 73–88; John M. Roach, "Why Volvo Abolished the Assembly Line," *Management Review* (September 1977): 50; Matt Oechsli, "Million Dollar Success Habits," *Managers Magazine* 65 (February 1990): 6–14; J. Barton Cunningham and Ted Eberle, "A Guide to Job Enrichment and Redesign," *Personnel* 67 (February 1990): 56–61; Richard J. Hackman, "Is Job Enrichment Just a Fad?" *Harvard Business Review* (September/October 1975): 129–38.

20. Bob Smith and Karen Matthes, "Flexibility Now for the Future," *HR Focus* (January 1992): 5.

21. D. A. Bratton, "Moving Away from Nine to Five," *Canadian Business Review* 13 (Spring 1986): 15–17.

22. Douglas L. Fleuter, "Flextime—A Social Phenomenon," *Personnel Journal* (June 1975): 318–19; Lee A. Graf, "An Analysis of the Effect of Flexible Working Hours on the Management Functions of the First-Line Supervisor," Ph.D. diss. (Mississippi State University, 1976); Jill Kanin-Lovers, "Meeting the Challenge of Workforce, 2000," *Journal of Compensation and Benefits* 5 (January/February 1990): 233–36; William Wong, "Rather Come in Late or Go Home Earlier? More Bosses Say OK," *Wall Street Journal*, July 12, 1973, 1.

23. B. F. Skinner, *Contingencies of Reinforcement* (New York: Appleton-Century-Crofts, 1969). See also E. L. Thorndike, "The Original Nature of Man," *Educational Psychology* 1, 1903; Fred Luthans and Robert Kreitner, *Organizational Behavior Modification and Beyond* (Glenview, IL: Scott, Foresman, 1985).

24. For an interesting discussion of accounting as a means of rewarding employees, see Mahmoud Ezzamel and Hugh Willmott, "Accounting, Remuneration, and Employee Motivation in the New Organization," *Accounting and Business Research* 28, no. 2 (Spring 1998): 97–110.

25. P. M. Padokaff, "Relationships between Leader Reward and Punishment Behavior and Group Process and Productivity," *Journal of Management* 11 (Spring 1985): 55–73. For a practical discussion of punishment, see Bruce R. McAfee and William

Poffenberger, *Productivity Strategies: Enhancing Employee Job Performance* (Upper Saddle River, NJ: Prentice Hall, 1982).

26. "New Tool: Reinforcement for Good Work," *Psychology Today* (April 1972): 68–69.

27. W. Clay Hamner and Ellen P. Hamner, "Behavior Modification on the Bottom Line," *Organizational Dynamics* 4 (Spring 1976): 6–8.

28. James K. Hickel, "Paying Employees to Control Costs," *Human Resources Professional* (January/February 1995): 21–24.

29. Rensis Likert, *New Patterns of Management* (New York: McGraw-Hill, 1961). For an interesting discussion of the worth of Likert's ideas, see Marvin R. Weisbord, "For More Productive Workplaces," *Journal of Management Consulting* 4 (1988): 7–14. The following descriptions are based on the table of organizational and performance characteristics of different management systems in Rensis Likert, *The Human Organization* (New York: McGraw-Hill, 1967), 4–10.

30. For a discussion of a novel monetary incentive program, see Charles A. Cerami, "Special Incentives May Appeal to Valued Employees," *HR Focus* (November 1991): 17; See also Reginald Shareef, "A Midterm Case Study Assessment of Skill-Based Pay in the Virginia Department of Transportation," *Review of Public Personnel Administration* 18, no. 1 (Winter 1998): 5–22.

31. Marilyn Moats Kennedy, "What Makes People Work Hard?" *Across the Board* 35, no. 5 (May 1998): 51–52.

Chapter 17

1. For an article illustrating the importance of managing groups in organizations, see Gregory E. Kaebnick, "Notes from Underground: Walter Corbitt Talks about Monitoring Paperwork for 35,000 Underground Storage Tanks," *Inform* 3 (July/August 1989): 21–22, 48.

2. Edgar H. Schein, *Organizational Psychology* (Upper Saddle River, NJ: Prentice Hall, 1965), 67.

3. Dorwin Cartwright and Ronald Lippitt, "Group Dynamics and the Individual," *International Journal of Group Psychotherapy* 7 (January 1957): 86–102.

4. For insights into how to be more successful in dealing with people in groups, see Anonymous, "Becoming More Persuasive," *Association Management* 50, no. 7 (July 1998): 24–25.

5. Edgar H. Schein, *Organizational Psychology*, 2nd ed. (Upper Saddle River, NJ: Prentice Hall, 1970), 182.

6. For a recent study exploring diversity and task group processes, see Warren E. Watson, Lynn Johnson, and Deanna Meritt, "Team Orientation, Self-Orientation, and Diversity in Task Groups," *Group & Organization Management* 23, no. 2 (June 1998): 161–88.

7. For useful guidelines on how to make committees work, see Arthur R. Pell, "Making Committees Work," *Managers Magazine* 64 (September 1989): 28. To understand further the possible duties of a committee, see Stephanie Balzer, "Committee to Study $500M Civic Plaza Expansion," *The Business Journal* 21, no. 39. (June 22, 2001): 7.

8. Cyril O'Donnell, "Group Rules for Using Committees," *Management Review* 50 (October 1961): 63–67. See also "Making Committees Work," *Infosystems*, October 1985, 38–39. For an example of problems created by committees not doing their jobs, see Joann S. Lublin and Elizabeth MacDonald, "Management: Scandals Signal Laxity of Audit Panels," *Wall Street Journal*, July 17, 1998, B1.

9. These and other guidelines are discussed in "Applying Small-Group Behavior Dynamics to Improve Action-Team Performance," *Employment Relations Today* (Autumn 1991): 343–53. For additional guidelines, see Peggy S. Williams, "Physical Fitness for Committees: Getting on Track," *Association Management* 4 (June 1989): 104–11.

10. See Irving L. Janis, *Groupthink* (Boston: Houghton Mifflin, 1982). For insights on how to avoid groupthink, see Michael J. Woodruff, "Understanding—and Combatting—Groupthink," *Supervisory Management* (October 1991):8. Peter Kay, "Group Think," *Philadelphia Business Journal*, July 2–July 8, 1999, 11.

11. For suggestions on how to build a team, see Edward Glassman, "Silence Is Not Consent," *Supervisory Management* (March 1992): 6–7; Robert B. Reich, "Entrepreneurship Reconsidered: The Team as a Hero," *Harvard Business Review* (May/June 1987): 77–83; Anonymous, "Teamwork Translates into High Performance," *HR Focus* 75, no. 7 (July 1998): 7.

12. Bernard Bass, *Organizational Psychology* (Boston: Allyn and Bacon, 1965), 197–98. For more insights on characteristics of productive groups, see Edward Glassman, "Self-Directed Team Building without a Consultant," *Supervisory Management* (March 1992): 6.

13. Raef T. Hussein, "Informal Groups, Leadership, and Productivity," *Leadership and Organization Development Journal* 10 (1989): 9–16.

14. Keith Davis and John W. Newstrom, *Human Behavior at Work: Organizational Behavior* (New York: McGraw-Hill, 1985), 310–12. See also Muhammad Jamal, "Shift Work Related to Job Attitudes, Social Participation, and Withdrawal Behavior: A Study of Nurses and Industrial Workers," *Personnel Psychology* 34 (Autumn 1981): 535–47.

15. For the importance of determining such information, see Dave Day, "New Supervisors and the Informal Group," *Supervisory Management* 34 (May 1989): 31–33. For a classic study illustrating sociometry and sociometric procedures, see Muzafer Sherif, "A Preliminary Experimental Study of Intergroup Relations," *Social Psychology at the Crossroads*, ed. John H. Rohrer and Muzafer Sherif (New York: Harper & Bros., 1951).

16. Homans, *The Human Group*.

17. William G. Dyer, *Teambuilding: Issues and Alternatives* (Reading, MA: Addison-Wesley, 1987): 4. See also Dawn R. Deeter-Schmelz and Rosemary Ramsey, "A Conceptualization of the Functions and Roles of Formalized Selling and Buying Teams," *Journal of Personal Selling & Sales Management* (Spring 1995): 47–60.

18. J. H. Shonk, *Team-Based Organizations* (Homewood, IL: Irwin, 1922).

19. Jack L. Lederer and Carl R. Weinberg, "Equity-Based Pay: The Compensation Paradigm for the Re-Engineered Corporation," *Chief Executive* (April 1995): 36–39.

20. Kevin R. Zuidema and Brian H. Kleiner, "Self-Directed Work Groups Gain Popularity," *Business Credit* (October 1994): 21–26.

21. Sami M. Abbasi and Kenneth W. Hollman, "Self-Managed Teams: The Productivity Breakthrough of the 1990s," *Journal of Managerial Psychology* 9 (1994): 25–30.

22. For more information on cross-functional teams, see D. Keith Denton, "Multi-Skilled Teams Replace Old Work Systems," *HR Magazine*, September 1992, 48–56; Michael D. Hutt, Beth A. Walker, and Gary L. Frankwick, "Hurdle the Cross-Functional Barriers to Strategic Change," *Sloan Management Review* (Spring 1995): 22–30; John Teresko, "Reinventing the Future," *Industry Week* (April 17, 1995): 32–38; Margaret L. Gagne and Richard Discenza, "Target Costing," *Journal of Business & Industrial Marketing* 10 (1995): 16–22.

23. Bruce W. Tuckman and Mary Ann C. Jensen, "Stages of Small Group Development Revisited," *Group and Organizational Studies* 2 (1977): 419–27; Melissas Masikiewicz, "Are You a Team Player?" *Career World* 26, no. 6 (March 1988): 19–21.

24. Hans J. Thamhain, "Managing Technologically Innovative Team Efforts Toward New Product Success," *Journal of Product Innovation Management* (March 1990): 5–18.

25. For insights about motivation and teams, see Gerben van der Vegt, Ben Emans, and Evert van de Vliert, "Motivating Effects of Task and Outcome Independence in Work," *Group & Organization Management* 23, no. 2 (June 1998): 124–43.

26. Jerre L. Stead, "People Power: The Engine in Reengineering," *Executive Speeches* (April/May 1995): 28–32.

27. Fernando Bartolome, "Nobody Trusts the Boss Completely—Now What?" *Harvard Business Review* (March/April 1989): 114–31.

28. Cass Bettinger, "Use Corporate Culture to Trigger High Performance," *Journal of Business Strategies* (March/April 1989): 38–42. For an article devoted to corporate culture, see J. Lee Howard, "Building a Corporate Culture," *The Business Journal* 14, no. 31. (November 5, 1999): 19.

29. The text discussion of these mechanisms is based on Edgar H. Schein, *Organizational Culture and Leadership* (San Francisco: Jossey-Bass, 1985), 223–43. For an example of using a new building to change corporate culture, see Anonymous, "Business: Places to Linger," *The Economist* 348, no. 8079 (August 1, 1998): 55–56.

Chapter 18

1. Martin Fishbein and Isek Ajyen, *Belief, Attitude, Intention and Behavior: An Introduction to Theory and Research* (Reading, MA: Addison-Wesley, 1975). For an example of a possible employee attitude toward jobs, see Brenda Paik Sunoo, "Optimists Love Their Jobs," *Workforce* 77, no. 5 (May 1998): 17. For a look at the possible impact of attitude on organizations, see Peter Schnitzler, "Friendly, Fearless Attitude Goes a Long Way," *Indianapolis Business Journal* 22, no. 9 (May 14, 2001): 36.

2. Milton Kokeach, *The Nature of Human Values* (New York: Free Press, 1973); William K. Tracey, *The Human Resources Glossary* (New York: AMACOM, 1991), 366. For a discussion of possible ways values can affect business transactions, see Brent Snavely, "A Matter of Values," *Crain's Detroit Business* 17, no. 26, (June 25, 2001): 1.

3. John K. Schermerhorn, James G. Hunt, and Richard N. Osborn, *Managing Organizationul Behavior*, 4th ed. (New York: Wiley, 1991), 115–17; Kevin Barksdale, "Why We Should Update HR," *Journal of Management* 22, no. 4 (August 1998): 526–30.

4. For a look at an attitude survey that was recently conducted, see Penny Singer, "After Merger, a Study of Employee Attitudes," *New York Times,* October 31, 1999, 6.

5. Barry M. Staw and Jerry Ross, "Stability in the Midst of Change: A Dispositional Approach to Job Attitudes," *Journal of Applied Psychology* (August 1985): 469–80.

6. Martin Fishbein and Mark Stasson, "The Role of Desires, Self-Predictions, and Perceived Control in the Prediction of Training Session Attendance," *Journal of Applied Social Psychology* 20 (1990): 173–98; Robert P. Steel and Nestor K. Ovalle II, "A Review and Meta-Analysis of Research on the Relationship between Behavioral Intentions and Employee Turnover," *Journal of Applied Psychology* (November 1984): 873–86.

7. Staw and Ross, 469–80. For an example of how attitudes about race can influence behavior, see Bill Dedman, "For Some Reason,

the Race Does Matter," *The Orlando Sentinel*, September 20, 1998, C3.

8. Angelo J. Kinicki, Kenneth P. Carson, and George W. Bohlander, "Relationships between an Organization's Actual Human Resource Efforts and Employee Attitudes," *Group Organization Management* 17 (June 1992): 135–52.

9. Michael R. Carrell, Norbert Elbert, and Robert Hatfield, *Human Resource Management,* 5th ed. (Upper Saddle River, NJ: Prentice Hall, 1995), 699–702.

10. M. J. Martinko and W. I. Gardner, "The Leader-Member Attribution Process," *Academy of Management Review* 12 (1987): 235–49.

11. Richard M. Steers and J. Stewart Black, *Organizational Behavior* (New York: HarperCollins, 1994), 80–83.

12. For an article that explores way to eliminate stereotypes, see Patty Sullivan, "Breaking Stereotypes," *Alaska Business Monthly*, February 1, 1999, 50.

13. Jerald Greenberg, "Looking Fair vs. Being Fair: Managing Impressions of Organizational Justice," *Research in Organizational Behavior,* ed. B. M. Staw and L. L. Cummings (Greenwich, CT: JAI Press, 1990).

14. L. Alan Witt and Jennifer G. Myers, "Perceived Environmental Uncertainty and Participation in Decision Making in the Prediction of Perceptions of the Fairness of Personnel Decisions," *Review of Public Personnel Administration* (May/August 1993): 48–55.

15. R. Karambayya, J. Brett, and A. Lytle, "Effects of Formal Authority and Experience on Third-Party Roles, Outcomes, and Perceptions of Fairness," *Academy of Management Journal* 35 (1992): 426–38.

16. Carrell, Elbert, and Hatfield, 780–84.

17. For an illustration of operant learning, see Linda S. Morris, "Firms Use High-Impact Rewards to Retain Workers," *Business First* 17, no. 47 (June 22, 2001): 1.

18. Edwin A. Locke and G. P. Latham, *A Theory of Goal Setting and Task Performance* (Upper Saddle River, NJ: Prentice Hall), 1990.

19. Kenneth N. Wexley and Gray P. Latham, *Developing and Training Human Resources in Organizations* (New York: HarperCollins, 1991). For an interesting article discussing reinforcement of groups rather than individuals, see Donald J. Campbell, Kathleen M. Campbell, and Ho-Beng Chia, "Merit Pay, Performance Appraisal, and Individual Motivation: An Analysis and Alternative," *Human Resource Management* 37, no. 2 (Summer 1998): 131–46.

20. Joseph B. Treasfer, "Employer Drug Testing Driving Down Use in Society," *New York Times,* 1993, 21.

Chapter 19

1. For an illustration of the complexity of control in an international context, see Jean-Francois Hennart, "Control in Multinational Firms: The Role of Price and Hierarchy," *Management International Review,* Special Issue 1991, 71–96. See also Anonymous, "Defining Controls," *The Internal Auditor* 55, no. 3 (June 1998): 47.

2. K. A. Merchant, "The Control Function of Management," *Sloan Management Review* 23 (Summer 1982): 43–55. For an example of how a control system can be used with a formal planning model, see A. M. Jaegar and B. R. Baliga, "Control Systems and Strategic Adaptations: Lessons from the Japanese Experience," *Strategic Management Journal* 6 (April/June 1985): 115–34.

3. Robert L. Dewelt, "Control: Key to Making Financial Strategy Work," *Management Review* (March 1977): 18. For discussion relating planning and controlling to leadership, see Sushil K. Sharma and Savita Dakhane, "Effective Leadership: The Key to

Success," *Employment News* 23, no. 10 (June 6–June 12, 1988): 1, 15.

4. For more discussion on Murphy's Law, see Grady W. Harris, "Living with Murphy's Law," *Research-Technology Management* (January/February 1994): 10–13.

5. Robert J. Mockler, ed., *Readings in Management Control* (New York: Appleton-Century-Crofts, 1970), 14.

6. For insights about the process that Delta Air Lines uses to control distribution costs, see Perry Flint, "Delta's 'Shot Heard 'Round the World,'" *Air Transport World* (April 1995): 61–62.

7. Francis V. McCrory and Peter Gerstberger, "The New Math of Performance Measurement," *Journal of Business Strategy* (March/April 1991): 33–38; Anonymous, "Measuring Performance Can Prevent Failure," *Metal Center News* 38, no. 7 (June 1998): 80–82.

8. James M. Bright, "A Clear Picture," *Credit Union Management* (February 1995): 28–29.

9. For a discussion of how standards are set, see James B. Dilworth, *Production and Operations Management: Manufacturing and Nonmanufacturing* (New York: Random House, 1986), 637–50. For more information on various facets of standards and standard setting, see the following: Len Eglo, "Save Dollars on Maintenance Management," *Chemical Engineering* 97 (June 1990): 157–62; Alden M. Hayashi, "GE Says Solid State Is Here to Stay," *Electronic Business* 14 (April 1, 1988): 52–56; Frank Rose, "A New Age for Business?" *Fortune*, October 8, 1990, 156–64; Edward Bassct, "Diamond Is Forever," *New England Business* 12 (October 1990): 40–44; David Sheridan, "Getting the Big Picture," *Training* (September 1990): 12–15; Thomas A. Foster and Joseph V. Barks, "The Right Chemistry for Single Sourcing," *Distribution* 89 (September 1990): 44–52; Joseph Conlin, "The House That G.E. Built," *Successful Meetings* 38 (August 1989): 50–58; Robert W. Mann, "A Building-Blocks Approach to Strategic Change," *Training and Development Journal* 44 (August 1990): 23–25; Joel Chernoff, "Global Standards Due Soon," *Pensions & Investments* 26, no.1 (January 12, 1998): 1, 29.

10. For an example of a company surpassing performance standards, see Peter Nulty, "How to Live by Your Wits," *Fortune*, April 20, 1992, 19–20.

11. To better understand the importance of corrective action, see Zheng Gu, "Predicting Potential Failure, Taking Corrective Action Are Keys to Success," *Nation's Restaurant News* 33, no. 25 (June 21, 1999): 31–32.

12. For a review of other common problems in organizations, see Robert E. Quinn, Regina M. O'Neill, and Lynda St. Clair, "Pressing Problems in Modern Organizations (That Keep Us Up at Night): Transforming Agendas for Research and Practice," (New York: AMACOM): 1999.

13. For an illustration of the problem/symptom relationship, see Elizabeth Dougherty, "Waste Minimization: Reduce Wastes and Reap the Benefits," *R & D* 32 (April 1990): 62–68.

14. Harold Koontz, Cyril O'Donnell, and Heinz Weilhrich, *Essentials of Management* (New York: McGraw-Hill, 1986), 454–59.

15. For an example of concurrent control in the health care industry, see Teri Lammers, "The Troubleshooter's Guide," *Inc.* (January 1992): 65–67.

16. For a discussion of the basic concepts of feedback control, see J. Greg Ziegler and J. Robert Connell, "For Optimum Control: Modify the Process, Not the Controls (Part 1)," *Chemical Engineering* (May 1994): 132–40.

17. Vijay Sathe, *Controller Involvement in Management* (Upper Saddle River, NJ: Prentice Hall, 1982).

18. James D. Wilson, *Controllership: The Work of the Managerial Accountant* (New York: Wiley, 1981). For an example of individu-als in organizations with more specific and limited controlling responsibilities, see the discussion by the director of production control at Nisssan in John Williams, "Total Logistics—The Profit Driver," *Logistics Focus* (August 1994): 20–24. For a discussion of cost control for stadium owners, see Lee Ann Gjertsen, "Stadiums Spawn Risk Management Challenges," *National Underwriter* 102, no. 32 (August 10, 1998): 7, 16.

19. For other ways in which cost-benefit analysis can be used by managers, see G. S. Smith and M. S. Tseng, "Benefit-Cost Analysis as a Performance Indicator," *Management Accounting* (June 1986): 44–49; "The IS (Information System) Payoff," *Infosystems* (April 1987): 18–20. For an illustration of how to apply cost-benefit analysis, see John Sauter, "Justifying Training Needs in the IRS: A Cost-Benefit Analysis," *Public Manager* 29, no. 4 (Winter 2000/2001): 31–33.

20. To explore the relationship between nonverbal behavior and power, see Herman Aguinis, Melissa M. Simonsen, and Charles A. Pierce, "Effects of Nonverbal Behavior on Perceptions of Power Bases," *The Journal of Social Psychology* 138, no. 4 (August 1998): 455–69.

21. See Amitai Etzioni, *A Comparative Analysis of Complex Organizations* (New York: Free Press, 1961), 4–6. For a study discussing the utility of various types of power to managers, see Gary Yukl and Cecilia Falbe, "Importance of Different Power Sources in Downward and Lateral Relations," *Journal of Applied Psychology* (June 1991): 416–23.

22. John P. Kotter, "Power, Dependence, and Effective Management," *Harvard Business Review* (July/August 1977): 128.

23. Kotter, "Power, Dependence, and Effective Management," 135–36. For a discussion on how empowering subordinates can increase the power of a manager, see Linda A. Hill, "Maximizing Your Influence," *Working Woman* (April 1995): 21–22+.

24. Kotter, "Power, Dependence, and Effective Management," 131.

25. For further discussion of how to overcome the potential negative effects of control, see Ramon J. Aldag and Timothy M. Stearns, *Management* (Cincinnati, OH: South Western Publishing, 1987), 653–54. See also Arnold F. Emch, "Control Means Action," *Harvard Business Review* (July/August 1954): 92–98; K. Hall and L. K. Savery, "Tight Rein, More Stress," *Harvard Business Review* (January/February 1986): 160–64.

26. James T. McKenna, "Eastern, Maintenance Heads Indicted by U.S. Grand Jury," *Aviation Week & Space Technology* 133 (July 1990): 84–86.

27. W. Jerome III, *Executive Control: The Catalyst* (New York: Wiley, 1961), 31–34. See also William Bruns Jr. and E. Warren McFarlan, "Information Technology Puts Power in Control Systems," *Harvard Business Review* (September/October 1987): 89–94; C. Jackson Grayson Jr., "Management Science and Business Practice," *Harvard Business Review* (July/August 1973): 41–48.

28. For an article emphasizing the importance of management understanding and being supportive of organizational control efforts, see Richard M. Morris III, "Management Support: An Underlying Premise," *Industrial Management* 31 (March/April 1989): 2–3.

Chapter 20

1. James B. Dilworth, *Production and Operations Management: Manufacturing and Non-Manufacturing* (New York: Random House, 1986), 3.

2. John W. Kendrick, *Understanding Productivity: An Introduction to the Dynamics of Productivity Change* (Baltimore: Johns Hopkins

University Press, 1977), 114. For useful discussion on how to motivate people to do more to enhance productivity, see Geoffrey Colvin, "What Money Makes You Do," *Fortune,* August 17, 1998: 213–14. For a recent article assessing the role of productivity within a company, see Michael H. Moskow, "Productivity: Key to the Economic Future," *Executive Speeches* 15, no. 6 (June/July 2001): 24–28.

3. Lester C. Thurow, "Other Countries Are as Smart as We Are," *New York Times,* April 5, 1981.

4. For an example of virtual offices created to increase worker productivity, see Michael K. Takagawa, "Turn Traditional Work Spaces into Virtual Offices," *Human Resources Professional* (March/April 1995):11–14.

5. W. Edwards Deming, *Out of the Crisis* (Boston: MIT Centre for Advanced Engineering Study, 1986). See also Rafael Aguayo, *Dr. Deming: The American Who Taught the Japanese about Quality* (New York: Carol Publishing Group, 1990), 160–64.

6. John J. Dwyer Jr., "Quality: Can You Prove It?" *Fleet Owner* (April 1995): 36. For coverage of quality assurance, see Anonymous, "Quality Assurance," *Manufacturing Engineering,* August 2000, Volume 125, Issue 2, pp. 270–291.

7. Gerry Davidson, "Quality Circles Didn't Die—They Just Keep Improving,"*CMA Magazine,* February 1995, 6. See also John B. Miner, *Organizational Behavior: Performance and Productivity* (New York: Random House, 1988), 308–16.

8. John Peter Koss, "Plant Robotics and Automation," *Beverage World* (April 1995): 108; Rob Spencer, "A Driving Force: Use of Robotics Remains Strong in Auto Industry," *Robotics World* 19, no. 1 (January/February 2001): 18–21.

9. Robert E. Kemper and Joseph Yehudai, *Experiencing Operations Management: A Walk-Through* (Boston: PWS-Kent Publishing Company, 1991), 48.

10. Richard B. Chase and Nicholas J. Aquilano, *Production and Operations Management: A Life Cycle Approach* (Homewood, IL: Richard D. Irwin, 1981), 4. For a worthwhile discussion of forecasting product demand as a continual operations management activity, see Jim Browne, "Forecasting Demand for Services," *Industrial Engineering* (February 1995): 16–17.

11. Roger W. Schmenner, "Operations Management," *Business Horizons* 41, no. 3 (May/June, 1998): 3–4.

12. For a thorough discussion of product strategy, see Olav Sorenson, "Letting the Market Work for You: An Evolutionary Perspective on Product Strategy," *Strategic Management Journal* 21, no. 5 (May 2000): 577–92.

13. For an example of the kinds of layout issues that concern printers in Europe, see Jill Roth, "Molto Bene," *American Printer* (March 1994): 54–58.

14. For ways to ensure that human resource strategy is progressive, see Kevin Barksdale, "Why We Should Update HR Education," *Journal of Management Education* 22, no. 4 (August 1998): 526–30.

15. For a review of the advantages and disadvantages of JIT, see Brian Milligan, "JIT Works, but Still Has Bugs," *Purchasing* 129, no. 11 (December 22, 2000): 23–34.

16. Lee J. Krajewski and Larry P. Ritzman, *Operations Management: Strategy and Analysis* (Reading, MA: Addison-Wesley, 1987), 573. See also A. Ansari and Modarress Batoul, "Just-in-Time Purchasing: Problems and Solutions," "*Journal of Purchasing and Materials Management* (August 1986): 11–15; Albert F. Celley, William H. Clegg, Arthur W. Smith, and Mark A. Vonderembse, "Implementation of JIT in the United States," *Journal of Purchasing and Materials Management* (Winter 1987): 9–15. For issues to con-

sider when contemplating the use of just-in-time in marketing, see S. Altan Erdem and Cathy Owens Swift, "Items to Consider for Just-In-Time Use in Marketing Channels: Toward Development of a Decision Tool," *Industrial Marketing Management* 27, no. 1 (January 1998): 21–29.

17. John D. Baxter, "Kanban Works Wonders, but Will It Work in U.S. Industry?" *Iron Age* (June 7, 1982): 44–48.

18. For discussion of cost control focusing on corporate jets, see Mel Mandell, "Why Sharing Jets Is Cost Effective," *World Trade* 11, no. 7 (July 1998): 85.

19. George S. Minmier, "Zero-Base Budgeting: A New Budgeting Technique for Discretionary Costs," *Mid-South Quarterly Business Review* 14 (October 1976): 2–8. See also Peter A. Phyrr, "Zero-Base Budgeting," *Harvard Business Review* (November/December 1970): 111–21; E. A. Kurbis, "The Case for Zero-Base Budgeting," *CA Magazine,* April 1986, 104–5; Linda J. Shinn and M. Sue Sturgeon, "Budgeting from Ground Zero," *Association Management* 42 (September 1990): 45–48; Gregory E. Becwar and Jack L. Armitage, "Zero-Base Budgeting: Is It Really Dead?" *Ohio CPA Journal* 48 (Winter 1989): 52–54; Aaron Wildavsky and Arthur Hammann, "Comprehensive versus Incremental Budgeting in the Department of Agriculture," in *Planning Programming Budgeting: A Systems Approach to Management,* ed. Fremont J. Lyden and Ernest G. Miller (Chicago: Markham, 1968), 143–44.

20. Chris Argyris, "Human Problems with Budgets," *Harvard Business Review* (January/February 1953): 108.

21. This section is based primarily on J. Fred Weston and Eugene F. Brigham, *Essentials of Managerial Finance,* 7th ed. (Hinsdale, IL: Dryden Press, 1985). See also F. L. Patrone and Donald duBois, "Financial Ratio Analysis for the Small Business," *Journal of Small Business Management* (January 1981): 35.

22. For an excellent discussion of ratio analysis in a small business, see Patrone and duBois, "Financial Ratio Analysis," 35–40.

23. Lester R. Bittle, *Management by Exception* (New York: McGraw-Hill, 1964); Frederick W. Taylor, *Shop Management* (New York: Harper & Bros., 1911), 126–27.

24. These two rules are adapted from *Boardroom Reports* 5 (May 1976): 4.

25. Robert J. Lambrix and Surenda S. Singhvi, "How to Set Volume-Sensitive ROI Targets," *Harvard Business Review* (March/April 1981): 174.

26. For a listing and discussion of quantitative tools and their appropriate uses, see Kemper and Yehudai, *Experiencing Operations Management,* 341–55. For a clear discussion, illustrations, and examples of linear programming, break-even analysis, work measurement, acceptance sampling, payoff tables, value analysis, computer-aided design (CAD), computer-aided engineering (CAE), computer-aided manufacturing (CAM), manufacturing resource planning, program evaluation and review technique (PERT), capacity requirements planning (CRP), and input/output control, see Jay Heizer and Barry Render, *Production and Operations Management: Strategies and Tactics* (Needham Heights, MA: Allyn and Bacon, 1993).

Chapter 21

1. Garland R. Hadley and Mike C. Patterson, "Are Middle-Paying Jobs Really Declining?" *Oklahoma Business Bulletin* 56 (June 1988): 12–14; A. Essam Radwan and Jerome Fields, "Keeping Tabs on Toxic Spills," *Civil Engineering* 60 (April 1990): 70–72; Dean C. Minderman, "Marketing: Desktop Demographics," *Credit Union Management* 13 (February 1990): 26.

2. Henry Mintzberg, "The Myths of MIS," *California Management Review* (Fall 1972): 92–97; Jay W. Forrester, "Managerial Decision Making," in *Management and the Computer of the Future*, ed. Martin Greenberger (Cambridge, MA, and New York: MIT Press and Wiley, 1962), 37.

3. The following discussion is based largely on Robert H. Gregory and Richard L. Van Horn, "Value and Cost of Information." in *Systems Analysis Techniques*, ed. J. Daniel Conger and Robert W. Knapp (New York; Wiley, 1974), 473–89.

4. John T. Small and William B. Lee, "In Search of MIS," *MSU Business Topics* (Autumn 1975): 47–55.

5. G. Anthony Gorry and Michael S. Scott Morton, "A Framework for Management Information Systems," *Sloan Management Review* 13 (Fall 1971): 55–70.

6. Stephen L. Cohen, "Managing Human-Resource Data Keeping Your Data Clean," *Training & Development Journal* 43 (August 1989): 50–54.

7. Michael A. Verespej, "Communications Technology: Slave or Master?" *Industry Week* (June 19, 1995): 48–55; John C. Scully, "Information Overload?" *Managers Magazine*, May 1995, 2.

8. T. Mukhapadhyay and R. B. Cooper, "Impact of Management Information Systems on Decisions," *Omega* 20 (1992): 37–49.

9. Robert W. Holmes, "Twelve Areas to Investigate for Better MIS," *Financial Executive* (July 1970): 24. A similar definition is presented and illustrated in Jeffrey A. Coopersmith, "Modern Times: Computerized Systems Are Changing the Way Today's Modern Catalog Company Is Structured," *Catalog Age* 7 (June 1990): 77–78. For an interesting example of how a company can decentralize an MIS, see John E. Framel and Leo F. Haas III, "Managing the Dispersed Computing Environment at Mapco, Inc.," *Journal of Systems Management* 43: 6–12.

10. Kenneth C. Laudon and Jane Price Laudon, *Management Information Systems: Organization and Technology* (New York: Macmillan, 1993), 38.

11. For an article dicussing how a well-managed MIS promotes the usefulness of information, see Albert Lederer and Veronica Gardner, "Meeting Tomorrow's Business Demands through Strategic Information Systems Planning," *Information Strategy: The Executive's Journal* (Summer 1992): 20–27.

12. This section is based on Richard A. Johnson, R. Joseph Monsen, Henry P. Knowles, and Borge O. Saxberg, *Management Systems and Society: An Introduction* (Santa Monica, CA: Goodyear, 1976), 113–20; James Emery, "Information Technology in the 21st Century Enterprise," *MIS Quarterly* (December 1991): xxi–xxiii.

13. Robert G. Murdick, "MIS for MBO," *Journal of Systems Management* (March 1977): 34–40.

14. F. Warren McFarlan, "Problems in Planning the Information System," *Harvard Business Review* (March/April 1971): 75.

15. David S. Stoller and Richard L. Van Horn, *Design of a Management Information System* (Santa Monica, CA: RAND Corporation, 1958).

16. Craig Barrow, "Implementing an Executive Information System: Seven Steps for Success," *Journal of Information Systems Management* 7 (Spring 1990): 41–46.

17. Bertram A. Colbert, "The Management Information System," *Management Services* 4 (September/October 1967): 15–24.

18. Adapted from Henry Mintzberg, "The Manager's Job: Folklore and Fact," *Harvard Business Review* (July/August 1975): 58.

19. William R. King and David I. Cleland, "Manager Analysis Teamwork in MIS," *Business Horizons* 14 (April 1971): 59–68; Regina Herzlinger, "Why Data Systems in Nonprofit Organizations Fail," *Harvard Business Review* (January/February 1977): 81–86; John Sculley, "The Human Use of Information," *Journal for Quality and Participation* (January/February 1990): 10–13; Richard Discenza and Donald G. Gardner, "Improving Production by Managing for Retention," *Information Strategy: The Executive's Journal* (Spring 1992): 34–38.

20. David Harvey, "Making Sense of the Data Deluge," *Director* 42 (April 1989): 139–40.

21. Robert Chaiken, "Pitfalls of Computers in a CPA's Office," *Ohio CPA Journal* 46 (Spring 1987): 45–46; John E. Framel, "Managing Information Costs and Technologies as Assets," *Journal of Systems Management* 41 (February 1990): 12–18; Martin D. J. Buss, "Penny-Wise Approach to Data Processing," *Harvard Business Review* (July/August 1981): 111; James A. Yardley and Parez R. Sopanwala, "Break-Even Utilization Analysis," *Journal of Commercial Bank Lending* 72 (March 1990): 49–56.

22. Steven L. Mandell, *Computers and Data Processing: Concepts and Applications with BASIC* (St. Paul, MN: West Publishing, 1982), 370–91.

23. Mark G. Simkin, *Computer Information Systems for Business* (Dubuque, IA: William C. Brown, 1987), 299–301.

24. For additional information on these software packages, see *Lotus 1-2-3 Reference Manual* (Cambridge, MA: Lotus Development Corporation, 1985); Timothy J. O'Leary, *The Student Edition of Lotus 1-2-3* (Reading, MA: Addison-Wesley, 1989); *IFPS User's Manual* (Austin, TX: Execucom Systems Corporation, 1984).

25. Ron Evans, "Systems for Growing Firms," *Black Enterprise* (April 1993). 44–45.

26. Kathleen Kiley, "Spin-Offs Stake Claim in LAN Rush," *Catalog Age* (May 1995): 24; David Reeve, "How Much Is Too Much?" *Computing Canada* (May 11, 1994): 47.

27. Jill Ellsworth and Matthew V. Ellsworth, *Marketing on the Internet: Multimedia Strategies for the World Wide Web* (New York: Wiley, 1995), 3; James Coates, "A Mailbox in Cyberspace Brings the World to Your PC," *Chicago Tribune*, March 26, 1995, sec. 19, 1.

28. David Sachs and Henry Stair, *Hands-on Internet: A Beginning Guide for PC Users* (Upper Saddle River, NJ: Prentice Hall, 1994), 3.

29. Projections in this section are based on: Steven Lewis, "World Web Growth Shocker," *Asian Business*, February 2001, 28.

30. Ellsworth and Ellsworth, *Marketing and the Internet*, xv.

31. Steve Williams, "The Internet—Exploring Its Uses for Economic Development," *Economic Development Review* (Winter 1995): 64–69; Gerry Khermouch, "Holiday Inn Books in the Net; Apollo 13 Launches in Cyberspace," *Brandweek*, June 19, 1995, 16.

32. The following two sections are based on Samuel C. Certo, *Supervision* (New York: Irwin/McGraw-Hill, 2000).

33. Anonymous, "Fast Fact," *Fast Company*, October 1998, 84.

34. Emily Esterson, "Inner Beauties," *Inc. Technology*, no. 4 (1998): 79–109.

35. Wayne Kawamoto, "Click Here for Efficiency," *BusinessWeek Enterprise*, December 7, 1998, 12, 14.

36. Douglas A. Blackmon, "Will FedEx Shift from Moving Boxes to Bytes?" *Wall Street Journal*, November 20, 1998, B1, B8.

Chapter 22

1. "The Push for Quality," *BusinessWeek*, June 8, 1987, 131. For a recent study assessing the importance of total quality management in the workplace, see Thomas J. Douglas and William Q. Judge Jr., "Total Quality Management Implementation and Competitive Advantage: The Role of Structural Control and Exploration," *Academy of Management Journal* 44, no. 1 (February 2001): 158–69.

2. A. V. Feigenbaum, *Total Quality Control* (New York: McGraw-Hill, 1983).

3. For a broadening discussion of a positive image, see Susan Watkins, "A Positive Image Is Not Just the Business of Business," *Public Management* 82, no. 7 (July 2000): 8–10.

4. From Michael Schroeder, "Heart Trouble at Pfizer," *BusinessWeek*, February 26, 1990, 47–48.

5. For a discussion of companies that have recently won the Malcolm Baldrige National Award, see Karen Bemowski, "1994 Baldrige Award Recipients Share Their Expertise," *Quality Progress* (February 1995): 35–40.

6. For more information on these three contributions, see Charles H. Fine and David H. Bridge, "Managing Quality Improvement," *Quest for Qualilty: Managing the Total System*, ed. by M. Sepheri (Norcross, GA: Institute of Industrial Engineers, 1987), 66–74.

7. For some of Crosby's more notable books in this area, see Philip B. Crosby, *Quality Is Free* (New York: McGraw-Hill, 1979); *Quality without Tears* (New York: McGraw-Hill, 1984); *Let's Talk Quality: 96 Questions You Always Wanted to Ask Phil Crosby* (New York: McGraw-Hill, 1989); and *Leading* (New York: McGraw-Hill, 1990).

8. Michael J. O'Connor, "A Way of Corporate Life," *Supermarket Business* (May 1995): 69–75.

9. Deming's 14 Points (January 1990 revision) reprinted by permission from *Out of Crisis* by W. Edwards Deming by permission of MIT and W. Edwards Deming, Published by MIT, Center for Advanced Engineering Study, Cambridge, MA 02139. Copyright 1986 by W. Edwards Deming.

10. Tracy Benson Kirker, "The Teacher's Still a Student," *Industry Week* (May 2, 1994): 37–38. Thomas A. Stewart, "A conversation with Joseph Juran," *Fortune*, January 11, 1999, 168–70.

11. Alan Robinson, *Modern Approaches to Manufacturing Improvements: The Shingo System* (Productivity Press, 1990), 267–68. See also Gary S. Vasilash, "On Training for Mistake-Proofing," *Production* (March 1995): 42–44.

12. Tim Stevens, "Dr. Feigenbaum," *Industry Week* (July 4, 1994): 12–16.

13. Ross Johnson and William O. Winchell, *Strategy and Quality* (Milwaukee, WI: American Society for Quality Control, 1989), 1–2.

14. Company Mission Statement, All America Inc., 1991, used by permission.

15. For a discussion supporting the importance of training to a companywide quality effort, see "Dr. W. Edwards Deming," *EBS Journal* (Spring 1989): 3.

16. Tom Peters, *Thriving on Chaos: Handbook for a Management Revolution* (New York: Harper & Row, 1987), 88, 98, 326.

17. Joseph Juran, *Juran on Quality Leadership: How to Go from Here to There* (Juran Institute, Inc., 1987), 6.

18. Michael Hammer, "Reengineering Work: Don't Automate, Obliterate," *Harvard Business Review* (July/August 1990): 104–12.

19. For an article on the advantages of innovation-minded employees, see John Rendleman, "Innovation: Light Speed Ahead," *Informationweek*, July 9, 2001, 18.

20. For a discussion of why some reengineering attempts fail, see Michael Hammer, "Beating the Risks of Reengineering," *Fortune* (May 15, 1995): 105–14.

21. For an article reviewing ways to instill creativity into employees, see John Bessart, "When Sparks Fly: Igniting Creativity in Groups," *Technovation* 21, no. 6 (June 2001): 396–97.

Chapter 23

1. Amir Hartman and John Sifonis with John Kador, *Net Ready: Strategies for Success in the E-Economy* (New York: McGraw-Hill, 2000), xvii–xviii.

2. Michael E. Porter, "Strategy and the Internet," *Harvard Business Review* (March 2001): 63–78.

3. Myra Pinkham, "Ryerson Tull Tries Dual E-Business Strategy," *Metal Center News* 40, no. 9 (August 2000): 50–54.

4. Robert Preston and Rutrell Yasin, "Transformation Isn't Easy—Dow's New Chemistry," *Internetweek*, July 24, 2001, 1, 54+.

5. Tom Burke, "Bold Plans on the Internet," *FDM* 73, no. 5 (April 2001): 36–38.

6. Cora Daniels, "The Trauma of Rebirth," *Fortune*, September 4, 2000, 367–74.

7. Samuel C. Certo and J. Paul Peter, *The Strategic Management Process* (Chicago: Irwin/Austen Press, 1995).

8. Anonymous, "Decision Making in the Digital Age," *Credit Union Executive Journal* 41, no. 2 (March/April 2001): 26–29.

9. Ed Miller, "Person-to-Person Collaboration," *Computer-Aided Engineering* 20, no. 3 (March 2001): 58.

10. Lynn Miller, "What's New," *HRMagazine* 45, no. 8 (August 2000): 177–80.

11. Shari Weiss, "Drinks Recipes Drive Visitors to Friday's Internet Links," *Nation's Restaurant News* 34, no. 34 (August 21, 2000): 34.

Credits

Chapter 1

Introductory Case: Case based on Moira Cotlier, "Case Study: Lands' End," *Catalog Age* 18, no. 5 (February 2001): 51–52; Jeffrey Marshall, "E-Service" 17, no. 1 (January/February 2001): 17; Janet Purdy Levaux, "Adapting Products and Services for Global E-Commerce," *World Trade* 14, no. 1 (January 2001): 52–54. **Figure 1.5:** Paul Hersey and Kenneth Blanchard, *Management of Organizational Behavior: Utilizing Human Resources,* 5th ed. © 1988, p. 8. Reprinted by permission of Prentice Hall, Inc., Upper Saddle River, NJ. **Figure 1.6:** Douglas T. Hall, *Careers in Organizations.* © 1976. Scott, Foresman and Company. Reprinted by permission. **Table 1.2:** Reprinted, by permission of the publisher, from "Improving Professional Development by Applying the Four-Stage Career Model," by Paul H. Thompson, Robin Zenger Baker, and Norman Smallwood, *Organizational Dynamics* (Autumn 1986): 59. © 1986. American Management Association, New York. All rights reserved. **Case Study:** *State of Small Business,* May 29, 2001, 63; "The Auctioneer," *Wall Street Journal,* November 22, 1999, R68; *Worth,* May 2001, 87; "Capital Wrap Up," *BusinessWeek,* April 24, 2000, 66; "Behind Every Successful Woman There Is a Woman," *Fortune,* October 25, 1999; "The E.Biz 25" <www.businessweek.com/2000>; "TheNew AuctioneerCompany"<www.time.com/time/digital.com/1999>; Biography Resource Center <www.galenet.com>; "Auction Site eBay Beats Forecasts," *Associated Press Online,* April 20, 2001; "Fresh Flowers," *Forbes,* April 10, 1995; "Meg Whitman Is No Jerry Yang"<www.zdnet.com/zdn/stories/comments>, June 21, 2000; "Meg's Blame Game," *Upside,* May 2001; "the e.biz 25," *BusinessWeek,* May 14, 2001, 30, 37, 68, The Standard.com; Meg Whitman, "Q & A with eBay's Meg Whitman," April 19, 2001 <www.businessweek.com/1999>; <www.ebay.com/aboutebay/overview/management.html>, eBay Inc. Capsule, Hoover's Online, May 2001; *Fast Company,* May 2001, 72, 74; *Computerworld,* January 10, 2000, 48.

Chapter 2

Introductory Case: David Leonhardt, "McDonald's: Can It Regain Its Golden Touch?" *BusinessWeek,* March 9, 1998, 70; Shannon Stevens, "McDonald's Realigns Marketing Arm," *Brandweek* 39, no. 11 (March 16, 1998): 4; Ralph Raffio, "Did Somebody Say . . . ," *Restaurant Business* 97, no. 4 (February 15, 1998): 28–46. **Quality Spotlight:** Jeremy Main, "How to Win the Baldrige Award," *Fortune Magazine,* April 23, 1990, 101–16; Christopher W. I. Hart, Christopher Bogan, and Dan O'Brien, "When Winning Isn't Everything," *Harvard Business Review* (January/February 1990): 209. **Digital Focus:** Elena Bowes and Laurel Wentz, "Like a Virgin," *Advertising Age* 71, no. 49 (November 27, 2000): 1, 16. **People Spotlight:** Ben Nagler, "Recasting Employees into Teams," *Workforce* 77, no. 1 (January 1998): 101–16. **Case Study:** "Up the Food Chain," *BusinessWeek,* May 7, 2001, 54; "Food," *BusinessWeek,* January 8, 2001; "A Definite Sell? Gimme 100 Shares," *BusinessWeek,* April 2, 2001; <www1.albertsons.com/corporate/>; "Albertson's Picks an Outsider," *Wall Street Journal,* April 24, 2001, B1; Robert Slater, *Get Better or Get Beaten* (New York: McGraw-Hill, 2001); "Albertson's Names GE Executive to Top Post," *Dallas Morning News,* April 24, 2001, 3D; "Follow-Through," *Forbes,* May 28, 2001, 26; "Check Out the E-Groceries," *BusinessWeek,* May 21, 2001; "Supermarket Chain Ends Net Service in Dallas Area," *Dallas Morning News,* May 5, 2001; "Self Check-Out Gets a Test Run," *Contra Costa Times,* May 2, 2001; "Boise Idaho-Based Grocery Store Chain Names New CEO," *Philadelphia Daily News,* April 25, 2001; "Boise, Idaho-Based Albertson's Steps Up Recycling Efforts," *The Times-News,* April 20, 2001; CNBC Squawk Box, May 2001, transcript available from Burrelle's, 1-800-777-8398.

Chapter 3

Introductory Case: This case is based on contents of IBM's corporate Web site: IBM.com. **Across Industries:** Anonymous, "Candy Wrapper," *Candy Industry* 166, no. 3 (March 2001): 52. **Table 3.2:** Sandra L. Holmes, "Executive Perceptions of Social Responsibility, *Business Horizons* (June 1976). Copyright, 1976, by the Foundation for the School of Business at Indiana University. Reprinted by permission. **Global Spotlight:** Ray Moorcroft, "International management in Action," *British Journal of Administrative Management* (March/April 2001): 12–13. **Figure 3.1:** The Eli Broad College of Business, Michigan State University, **Diversity Spotlight:** Glenn Hasek, "Breaking Barriers: Education Erases False Perceptions of Minority Opportunities," *Hotel & Motel Management* 207 (February 24, 1992): 21–22. **Figure 3.2:** Kenneth E. Newgren, "Social Forecasting: An Overview of Current Business Practices," in Archie B. Carroll, ed., *Managing Corporate Social Responsibility.* Copyright © 1977 by Little, Brown and Company (Inc.). Reprinted by permission of the author. **Figure 3.3:** Reprinted by permission of the *Harvard Business Review,* from "How Companies Respond to Social Demands" by Robert W. Ackerman (July/August 1973): 96. Copyright © 1973 by the President and Fellows of Harvard College; all rights reserved. **Figure 3.4:** John L. Paulszek, "How Three Companies Organize for Social Responsibility." Reprinted by permission from *Business and Society Review* (Summer 1973): 18. Warren, Gorham and Lamont, Inc., 210 South St., Boston, MA. All rights reserved. **Figure 3.5:** Reprinted by permission of Johnson & Johnson. **Figure 3.6:** Reprinted by permission from "Code of Ethics and Standards of Conduct" (Orlando, FL: Martin Marietta, n.d.): 3. **Case Study:** Jeffrey E. Garten, *The Mind of the C.E.O.,* 138–142, 185, 186, 223, 197; "Auto Makers Juggle Substance and Style in New Green Policies," *Wall Street Journal,* May 15, 2001; "Ford, Firestone Face Safety Concerns, Each Other," *Wall Street Journal,* May 24, 2001; "Ford Plans to Recall 47,000 Year-2002 SUV's," *Wall Street Journal,* May 21, 2001; "Auto Sales Were Down Last Month," *New York Times,* May 2, 2001; "A Pre-emptive Strike on Global Warming," *New York Times,* May 15, 2001; "2 Approaches to Aftermath of Tire Recall," *New York Times,* April 4, 2001; "Ford's New Big Rig Is Larger Than Life," *New York Times,* May 6, 2001, L1; "Ford Tries to Burnish Image by Looking to Cut Emissions," *New York Times,* May 4, 2001; "Ford's 70-Year Itch Could Be Relieved," *New York Times,* May 3, 2001; "Ford, Firestone Settle Explorer Rollover Suit," *Wall Street Journal,* January 9, 2001; "Sport Utility Vehicles," *Automotive Industries* 180, no. 24 (October 2000); "A Blowout of Trust," *Automotive Industries* 180, no. 41 (October 2000); "Ford, Firestone Dilemma Will Bring Changes," *Automotive News,* September 18, 2000; "Ford Distances Itself from Recall Report," *New York Times,* May 18, 2001; <www.ford.com/2000annual>; <www.ford.com/servlet/ccmcs/ford/index>.

Chapter 4

Introductory Case: This cased is based on Anonymous, "Denny's Hit with Bias Suit," *The Grand Rapids Press*, August 24, 2001, A4; Jim Adamson, "How Denny's Went from Icon of Racism to Diversity Award Winner," *National Productivity Review* 20 (Winter 2000): 55–68; Anonymous, "Best Companies for Minorities," *Fortune*, July 9, 2001; Advantica's corporate Web site. **Table 4.1:** Ann M. Morrison, *The New Leaders: Leadership Diversity in America*, adapted from pp. 18–27. Copyright 1992 by Ann M. Morrison and Jossey-Bass, Inc., Publishers. Reprinted by permission of Jossey-Bass, Inc., Publishers. **Diversity Spotlight:** Parker R. Goodwin, *Laying the Groundwork for Diversity Training at CAE-LINK: Demographic and Process Issues* (Reprinted by permission) Binghamton University (1993): 31–33. **Figure 4.1:** Based on Howard N. Fullerton Jr., "Labor Force Projections to 2008: Steady Growth and Changing Composition," *Monthly Labor Review* 122 (November 1999): 19–32. **Global Spotlight:** "Connecting the World," *Focus for and about the People of AT&T* (September 1992). **Case Study:** Networks were graded in a range of categories including: minority actors in prime time; writers, producers, and directors in prime time; the development of deals with qualified minorities for programming; employment in the management, corporate, and executive ranks; and commitment to diversity issues. The NAACP did not participate as it plans to release its own assessment. "CBS Taps Thomas Sr. VP, Diversity," *Daily Variety*, April 5, 2000, 4; "TV Shows Adding Minority Characters," *Associated Press Online*, May 25, 2000; "Latinos Lament Dearth of TV Roles," *Associated Press Online*, July 3, 2000; Karissa Wang, "Much Talk, Few Results on Diversity Initiatives," *Electronic Media*, July 24, 2000, 13; Manuel Mendoza, "Networks Try to Balance Picture," *Dallas Morning News*, November 9, 2000; Greg Braxton, "TV's Fall Programming Lineup: Is This Their Final Answer," *Los Angeles Times*, May 20, 2000; "Analysis: Progress of TV Networks to Include People of Color in Front of and Behind the Camera," *All Things Considered* (NPR), May 24, 2001; "Ethnic Groups Condemn American TV Networks Over Lack of Diversity," *AP Worldstream*, May 24, 2001; Greg Braxton, "Company Town," *Los Angeles Times*, May 25, 2001; "Study: White Men Dominate Network TV," *Associated Press Online*, May 1, 2001; Howard Rosenberg, "Howard Rosenberg/Television: CBS Makes Its Fall Picks . . . But Omits One Family," *Los Angeles Times*, May 17, 2000.

Chapter 5

Introductory Case: Anonymous, "The World's Most Admired Companies Go for the Long Term and People Factor," *Management Services* 44, no. 11 (November 2000): 4; Anonymous, "The People Make It All Happen," *Discount Store News* (October 1999): 103, 105+; Mike Troy, "Wal-Mart to Add Japan to Global Lineup," *Retailing Today*, January 22, 2001, 1, 42. **Figure 5.2:** Jon H. Barrett, *Individual Goals and Organizational Objectives: A Study of Integration Mechanisms*, 5. Copyright © 1970 by the Institute for Social Research, The University of Michigan. Reprinted with permission. **Diversity Spotlight:** Margaret Blackburn White, "Women of the World: Diversity Goes Global at IBM," *Diversity Factor* 7, no. 4 (Summer 1999): 13–16. **Figure 5.4:** Joseph L. Massie and John Douglas, *Managing*. © 1985, p. 244. Reprinted by permission of Prentice Hall, Inc., Upper Saddle River, NJ. **Table 5.2:** Howard M. Carlisle, *Management Concepts and Situations*, 598. © 1976. Published by Science Research Associates. Reprinted by permission of the author. **Table 5.3:** Reprinted by permission from A. N. Geller, *Executive Information Needs in Hotel Companies* (New York: Peat Marwick Main, 1984): 17. © Peat Marwick Main & Co., 1984. **Across Industries:** Paul Eisenstein, "A Remarkably un-Japanese Way to Reorganise," *Professional Engineering*, November 3, 1999, 14–15. **Case**

Study: *Marketplace Morning Report,* May 9, 2001, Minnesota Public Radio, transcript available from Burrelle's, 1-800-0777-8398; "McDonald's French Fries under Scrutiny in India." <www.nyc/news/world/article>. (May). "For Hindus and Vegetarians, Surprise in McDonald's French Fries," *New York Times,* May 19, 2001; <www.a2zdekhi.com/a2zdelhi/potpourri/oct-business.htm>. (May 25, 2001). "Sena Takes McDonald's French Fries to Labs," *The Times of India,* May 25, 2001; "Hindu Group Vandalizes McDonald's Shop to Protest Use of Beef in French Fries," *AP Worldstream,* May 25, 2001; "A Misguided Beef with McDonald's," *BusinessWeek,* May 21, 2001; "Ruling Party Demands Closure of McDonald's Store in Western State," *AP Worldstream,* May 8, 2001; "Hindu Group Protests Use of Beef in McDonald's French Fries," *AP Worldstream,* May 5, 2001; "Hindu Group to Protest McDonald's Use of Beef in French Fries," *AP Worldstream,* May 4, 2001; <www.cnn.worldnews.com>. (May 22, 2001). <www.hoovers.com/co/capsule>. (May 25, 2001). <www.media.mcdonalds.com/secured/products/international/maharahamac.html>. (May 25, 2001). <www.financialexpress.com/fe/daily/2001030/fco30071.html>. (May 25, 2001). <http://news.india-today.com/ntoday/nesarchives/100/12/n27.shtml>. (May 25, 2001). <http://det news. com/1996/menu/stories/69311.htm>. (May 25, 2001).

Chapter 6

Introductory Case: Based on Karen Mazurkewich, "Ready for Take-off," *Far Eastern Economic Review* 163, no. 39 (September 28, 2000): 43; John Evan Frook, "From the Top," *Internetweek,* September 14, 1998, 22. **Figure 6.5:** William R. King and David I. Cleland, "A New Method for Strategic Systems Planning," *Business Horizons* (August 1975): 56. Copyright, 1975, by the Foundation for the School of Business Administration at Indiana University. Reprinted by permission. **Ethics Spotlight:** Anonymous, "Community Comes First," *Chain Store Age* 75, no. 13 (December 1999): 69–70. **Case Study:** "Express Delivery," *Inc, Tech 2001, No. 1;* "AccuSHIP.com Introduces Web-based Enterprise Solution for Shipping Logistics Management," *Business Wire,* April 18, 2000; "Delivery Faster Than You Can Say Overnight," *Business Wire,* July 11, 2000; "Accuship: Freight and Freightage," *Export Today's Global Business* (January 2001): 64; "A Neutral Network?" *Global Business* (January 2001): <www.accuship.com/about/business_reporting.html>.

Chapter 7

Introductory Case: This case contributed by S. Trevis Certo, Texas A & M University; Melanie Warner, "Gateway to Wealth," *Fortune,* September 8, 1997, 80; Roger O. Crockett, "Gateway Loses the Folksy Shtick," *BusinessWeek,* July 6, 1998, 80–84. **Table 7.1:** Herbert A. Simon, *The Shape of Automation* (New York: Harper & Row, 1965): 62. Used with permission of the author. **Digital Focus:** Bill Breen, "Changes Is Sweet," *Fast Company*, June 2001, 168–77. **Figure 7.3:** Republished with permission of E. I. du Pont de Nemours & Company. **Global Spotlight:** James M. Hagen, "Educator Insights: Ben & Jerry's—Japan: Strategic Decision by an Emergent Global Marketer," *Journal of International Marketing* 8, no. 2 (2000): 98–110. Company history is based on information from the company Web site. **People Spotlight:** Kevin Kelly, "The New Soul of John Deere," *BusinessWeek,* January 31, 1994, 64–66. **Figure 7.7:** Copyright © 1964 by the President and Fellows of Harvard College; all rights reserved. **Figure 7.8:** Samuel C. Certo, *Supervision: Quality and Diversity Through Leadership* (Chicago: Austen Press/Irwin, 1995): 202. **Case Study:** Flemming Flyvholm, "The Bright Young Thing," *Wireless,* March/April 2001. <www.speednamc.com/lang/global/>. (June 1, 2001).

Chapter 8

Introductory Case: A. David Gianatasio, "Gillette Sharpens Global Effort for Venus Razor," *Adweek*, March 26, 2001, 2; Mark Maremont, "Gillette's New Strategy Is to Sharpen Pitch to Women," *Wall Street Journal*, May 11, 1998, B1; Mark Maremont, "A Cut Above? Gillette Finally Reveals Its Vision of the Future, and It Has 3 Blades—But Firm's Bet that Shavers Will Pay a 30% Premium Is a Double-Edged Sword—Secrecy at 'Plywood Ranch,' " *Wall Street Journal*, April 14, 1998, A1. **Table 8.1:** (a) and (b) based on E. Meadows, "How Three Companies Increased Their Productivity," *Fortune Magazine*, March 10, 1980, 92–101. (c) based on William B. Johnson, "The Transformation of a Railroad," *Long-Range Planning* 9 (December 1976): 18–23. **Figure 8.1:** Samuel C. Certo and J. Paul Peter, *Strategic Management: Concepts and Applications* (New York: McGraw-Hill, Inc., 1991). Reprinted by permission of The McGraw-Hill Companies. **Table 8.2:** Arvind V. Phatak, *International Dimensions of Management*, 2nd ed., 1989, 6. Copyright © 1989 by Wadsworth, Inc. Reprinted by permission of the publisher. **Ethics Spotlight:** Jan Ziegler, "Proving That Ethics Are Efficient," *Business and Health* 18, no. 2 (January 2000): 15–16. Company code of values is based on company Web site information. Victoria Fraza, "Raising the Bar," *Industrial Distribution* 89, no. 4 (April 2000): 72-75. **Figure 8.3:** © 1970 by the Boston Consulting Group, Inc. All rights reserved. Published by permission. **Figure 8.4:** Reprinted by permission from p. 32 of *Strategy Formulation: Analytical Concepts* by Charles W. Hofer and Dan Schendel. Copyright © 1978 by South-Western College Publishing Company, a division of International Thomson Publishing. All rights reserved. **Figure 8.5:** Reprinted with the permission of The Free Press, a Division of Simon & Schuster from *Competitive Advantage: Creating and Sustaining Superior Performance* by Michael E. Porter. Copyright, 1988 by Michael E. Porter. **Across Industries:** Jack Neff, "Johnson Layers Diversity," *Advertising Age* (Midwest region edition), February 19, 2001, S1–S2. **Case Study:** Jennifer Keeney, "Jet Blue Flies High." <www.fsb.com/fortunesb/articles/>. (June 1, 2001). "A Smokeless Herb," *Fortune*, May 28, 2001, 78, 79; "Generation Dot-Com Gets Its Wings." <www.informationweek.com/018/neeleman.htm> (June 1, 2001). Holly Hegeman. "Yeah Baby, JetBlue Is Here." <www.thestreet.com/pf/comment/wingtips/764487.html>. (June 1, 2001). Geoffrey Jones. "JetBlue Airways Enters US Low-Fares Market." <www.flugrevue.rotor.com/>. (June 1, 2001). <ABCNEWS.com>. "How JetBlue's TV System Works." (June 1, 2001). "Jet Blue Skies." <www.forbes.com/2001/01/31/0131jetblue_print.html>. (June 1, 2001). "From Darien to the Skies: JetBlue Has Local Roots," *The Advocate*," April 8, 2001; Margaret Anthony, "JetBlue Lands in New York," *T-Directfolio Magazine*, March 29, 2000. <www.jetblue.com/learnmore/pressDetail.asp?newsld=46>.

Chapter 9

Introductory Case: This case is based on Frank Gibney Jr., "Seeking a Safer SUV," *Time*, January 22, 2001, 57; Cathy Booth Thomas, "A Nasty Turn for Ford?" *Time*, January 15, 2001, 45; Joann Muller, "Putting the Explorer under the Microscope: Ford Is Going All-Out to Ensure the Revamped SUV Is Glitch-Free," *BusinessWeek*, February 12, 2001, 40. **Ethics Spotlight:** Yoshihiko Shimizu, "Toyota Buckles Down to Overtake GM," *Tokyo Business Today* (Japan) 59 (February 1991): 32–34. **Digital Focus:** Stephanie Armour, "Firings Flag Firms' Need for Net Policy," *USA Today*, April 1, 1998, 1B; Jake Lloyd-Smith, "Salomon Gets Tough Over E-Mail Abuse," *South China Morning Post*, April 27, 1998, 1. **Tables 9.1/9.2:** E. S. Groo, "Choosing Foreign Locations: One Company's Experience," *Columbia Journal of World Business* (September/October 1977): 77. Used with permission. **Global**

Spotlight: Anonymous, "Shell Chemicals Profile: A Global Way of Doing Business," *Chemical Week*, May 23, 2001, S10; Anonymous, "Looking at Our Business in a Different Light," *Shell Chemical Brochure*, 2001, 8. **Figure 9.4:** Bruce Colman, "An Integrated System for Manpower Planning," *Business Horizons* (October 1970): 89–95. Copyright 1970, by the Foundation for the School of Business at Indiana University. Reprinted by permission. **Figure 9.6:** Philip Kotler, *Marketing Managing Analysis Planning and Control*. © 1967, p. 291. Adapted by permission of Prentice Hall, Inc., Upper Saddle River, NJ. **Case Study:** <www.whitewave.com/asp/Page 23 – 35k>. (June 3, 2001); Barbara J. Kelly, "White Wave's Soy Milk Gains Foothold in DairyCase," *Natural Foods*, February 25, 2000; <hoovers.com/co/capsule/6/0,2163,61086,00.html>. (June 5, 2001); Bethany Mclean, "Profiles in Persistence," *FSB*, May 2001; Rob Mahoney, "White Wave, Inc.," *Prepared Foods*, October 1999; "Steven Demos," *Beverage Industry*, July 2000, 78; <biz.yahoo.com/prnews/010309/mnf008.html>. (June 5, 2001); Patrick Sweeney, "Riding a Wave of Success in Boulder," *The Denver Business Journal*, October 16, 2000; "Soy Foods Chic: White Wave Celebrates Soyfoods Month by Helping Americans Do What Comes Naturally—Indulge Themselves with Food and Drink."<biz.yahoo.com/prnews/01309/mnf008.html>. (June 5, 2001); "White Wave Reflects on Growth and Dean Foods Investment," *Nutrition Business Journal*, June 2000.

Chapter 10

Introductory Case: Susan O'Keefe, "Lucent: The Next Master of the Universe?" *Telecommunications* 32, no. 4 (April 1998): 28–38; "2 Key Posts Filled and Reorganization Planned," *New York Times*, October 25, 1997, 3; Robert Ristelhueber, "Shaking Up the Old Order," *Electronic Business* 24, no. 1 (January 1998): 66–67 1. **Global Spotlight:** Amy Zuber, "Seeking Its Salad Days, McD Shakes Up Management Team," *Nation's Restaurant News*, May 14, 2001, 1,109. **Quality Spotlight:** Robert F. Huber, "Mercedes Manufacturing Strategy Is to Keep the Company's Market Niche Full," *Production* 103 (October 1991): 60–63. **Across Industries:** Mary M. Fanning, "A Circular Organization Chart Promotes a Hospital-Wide Focus on Teams," *Hospital & Health Services Administration* 42, no. 2 (Summer 1997): 243 254. **Case Study:** Eric Bonabeau and Christopher Meyer, "Swarm Intelligence," *Harvard Business Review* (May 2001). Eric Bonabeau is chief scientist at Icosystem Corporation; Christopher Meyer is the director of Cap Gemini Ernst & Young Center for Business Innovation.

Chapter 11

Introductory Case: Marianne Kolbasuk McGee, "Lessons from a Cultural Revolution," *Informationweek* (October 25, 1999): 46–62; P&G company Web site; Anonymous, 2000; The Year in Review: People," *Advertising Age* (December 18, 2000); Anonymous 71, no. 52 (Midwest edition): 38. **Digital Focus:** Frank Hayes, "Where Have All Coders Gone?" *Computerworld* 32, no. 21 (May 25, 1998): 12; Brian Reed, "IS Departments: Wake Up and Get Online," *Hotel and Motel Management* 211, no. 11 (June 17, 1996): 27. **Table 11.1:** Reprinted, by permission of the American Management Association, from "Roles and Relationships Clarifying the Manager's Job," by Robert D. Melcher, *Management Review* (May/June/1967): 35, 38–39. © 1967 American Management Association, New York. Used with permission of the publisher, American Management Association. All rights reserved. <www.amanet.org>. **Ethics Spotlight:** Joseph Conlin, "The House That GE Built," *Successful Meetings* 38 (August 1989): 50–58. **Figure 11.3:** David B. Starkweather, "The Rationale for Decentralization in Large Hospitals," *Hospital Administration* 15 (Spring 1970): 139. Courtesy of

Dr. P. N. Ghei, Secretary General Indian Hospital Association, New Delhi, India. **People Spotlight:** Laura Stepanek, "Lessons in Discipline," *Security Distributing & Marketing* 31, no. 4 (March 2001): 80–82; Web site. **Case Study:** "Gateway Vows to Win PC Price War," *Los Angeles Times*, May 31, 2001; "Customers to Become Winners of Computer Price War Today," *PR Newswire*, May 30, 2001; Katrina Brooker, "I Built This Company, I Can Save It," *Fortune*, 94; Brad Graves, "Gateway Continues Shakeup with San Diego Move," *Orange County Business Journal*, April 30, 2001, 55; Andrew Simons, "On the Road Again: Gateway Moving More OC Staff," *Orange County Business Journal*, March 26, 2001, 68; Todd Spangler, "The Cow Comes Home," *Inter@ctive Week*, March 19, 2001, 2; Andrew Simons, "Gateway at Crossroads with Management Shift," *Orange County Business Journal*, March 12, 2001, 1; Gary McWilliams, "Gateway Will Match Its Rivals' PC Prices," *Wall Street Journal*, May 30, 2001; Gary McWilliams, "Gateway Co-Founder Starts Comeback Plan with a Restatement," *Wall Street Journal*, March 1, 2001, 1.

Chapter 12

Introductory Case: Susana Schwartz, "NW Mutual Improves Agent Recruitment Process," *Insurance & Technology* 22, no. 7 (July 1997): 14–16; "America's Most Admired Life Insurance Companies," *Fortune*, March 2, 1998. **Figure 12.2:** Reprinted with the permission of Macmillan Publishing Company, from *The Management of People at Work: Readings in Personnel*, 2nd ed. by Dale S. Beach. Copyright © 1985. Adapted by permission of Prentice Hall, Upper Saddle River, NJ. **Figures 12.3, 12.4, 12.5:** Walter S. Wikstrom, "Developing Managerial Competence: Concepts, Emerging Practices," *Studies in Personnel Policy* No. 189, 9, 14. Used with permission. **Figure 12.6:** Reprinted by permission from L. C. Megginson, *Providing Management Talent for Small Business* (Baton Rouge, LA, Division of Research, College of Business Administration, Louisiana State University, 1961): 108. **Table 12.1:** Dale Feuer, "Where the Dollars Go." Reprinted from the October 1985 issue of *Training*, The Magazine of Human Resources Development, 53. Copyright 1985, Lakewood Publications, Inc., Minneapolis, MN 612-333-0471. All rights reserved. **People Spotlight:** Jennifer Koch Laabs, "Optimas 2001—General Excellence: Thinking Outside the Box at The Container Store," *Workforce*, March 2001, 34–38. **Across Industries:** Bernie Knill, "Furniture Making, MES Style," *Material Handling Engineering* 53, no. 5 (May 1998): 42–46. **Diversity Spotlight:** Anonymous, "Coke Ties Pay, Performance," *Orlando Sentinel*, March 11, 2000, C1; Angela G. King, "Coca-Cola Takes the High Road," *Black Enterprise* 31, no. 7 (February 2001): 29. **Table 12.2:** Compiled from Andrew F. Sikula, *Personnel Administration and Human Resource Management* (New York: John Wiley & Sons, 1976): 208–11. **Case Study:** NPR's *Morning Edition*, May 2, 2001, 8:20 A.M. New York City, Elaine Korry interviews new college graduates; Kara Scannell, "The Few. The Proud. The . . . M.B.A.'s," *Wall Street Journal*, June 5, 2001; Jonathan D. Glater, "Would-Be Entrepreneurs Shun Dot-Comsby," *New York Times*, May 2, 2001; Kris Meher, "Business Schools Go All Out to Get Students Jobs," *Wall Street Journal*, June 5, 2001; Kemba J. Dunham, "The Jungle," *Wall Street Journal*, June 5, 2001; Jennifer Merritt, "MBA Programs Are Going Back to School," *BusinessWeek*, May 7, 2001; Suzanne Koudis, "MBA Students Want Old-Economy Bosses," *Fortune*, April 16, 2001; Mica D. Schneider, "Canada: Nirvana for MBAs?" *BusinessWeek*, May 7, 2001; Jonathan D. Glater, "Dear Employee: Welcome and Goodbye," *Wall Street Journal*, May 4, 2001; Matt Richtel, "What, Us Worry?" *New York Times*, May 5, 2001; Mary Lord, "The Need to Be Nimble," "Best Graduate Schools," *U.S. News & World Report*, 2002 Edition; David Wessel, "Intel Cost-Cutting Spares a College Tour," *Wall Street Journal*,

June 14, 2001; Cheryl Dahle, "Is the Internet Second Nature?" *Fast Company*, July 2001; Cheryl Dahle, "Intel Puts Its Chips on the Net," *Fast Company*, 2001.

Chapter 13

Introductory Case: Mahlon Apgar IV, "The Alternative Workplace: Changing Where and How People Work," *Harvard Business Review* (May–June, 1998): 121–136; Stephanie Armour, "Success of Telecommuting Dispels Myth," *USA Today*, April 17, 1998, 2B; Anonymous, "How AT&T Took Telecommuting On-line," *The Management Accounting Magazine*, December 1996/January 1997, 14. **Figure 13.1:** Don Hellriegel and John W. Slocum Jr. "Integrating Systems Concepts and Organizational Strategy," *Business Horizons* 15 (April 1972): 73. Copyright 1972 by the Foundation for the School of Business at Indiana University. Reprinted by permission. **Ethics Spotlight:** Chester Dawson, "Mazda's Dilemma," *Far Eastern Economic Review*, July 27, 2000, 42–44. **Figures 13.4, 13.5:** John F. Mee, "Matrix Organization," *Business Horizons* (Summer 1964): 71. Copyright 1964 by the Foundation for the School of Business at Indiana University. Reprinted by permission. **Diversity Spotlight:** Beverly Geber, "The Disabled: Ready, Willing and Able," *Training* 27 (December 1990): 29–36. **Figure 13.7:** Reprinted by permission of *Harvard Business Review*. From "Breakthrough in Organization Development" by Robert R. Blake, Jane S. Mouton, Louis Barnes, and Larry Greiner (November/December 1964): 136. Copyright © 1964 by the President and Fellows of Harvard College; all rights reserved. **Digital Focus:** Michael J. Blotzer, "Web-based Training," *Occupational Hazards* 62, no. 9 (September 2000): 35–38. **Figure 13.8:** Thomas H. Davenport and Keri Pearlson, "Two Cheers for the Virtual Office," *Sloan Management Review* (Summer 1998): 53. Copyright 1998 by Sloan Management Review Association. All rights reserved. **Table 13.1:** Carolyn Corbin, "Tips to Ensure Good Communication in a Virtual Office," *Workforce* (November 1997; supplement). Used with the permission of ACC. **Case Study:** Daniel Pink, "Not Holding a Job Is New Work System," *New York Times*, May 25, 2001, BU6; Sheryl Nance-Nash, "Conflict Doesn't Kill Companies; It Makes Them Stronger," <http://www.fsb.com/fortunesb/articles/0,2227,322,00.html>. My Virtual Corp. Web site: <http//www.myvirtualcorp.com.>. "Boss of Virtual Assistants," <http//www.usnews.com/usnews/issue/991101/nycu/core18.htm>. Samuel Fromartz, "Extreme Outsourcing," <http://www.fsb.com/fortunesb/o,2227,1711,00.htm>. Reinerman, "Introduction: My Virtual Corp., <www.louisville.edu/-j0monb01/mycorp.htm>.

Chapter 14

Introductory Case: Company Press Release "Eaton Corporation Begins Full Production at Plant in Hastings," Nebraska, October 16, 1998; Company Press Release, "Eaton Automotive Receives Three Top Quality Awards from Ford Motor Company," March 31, 2000. **Table 14.1:** Reprinted by permission from Stephen C. Harper, "Business Education: A View from the Top," *Business Forum* (Summer 1987): 25. Reprinted with permission. **People Spotlight:** Jerry Useem, "A Manager for All Seasons," *Fortune*, April 30, 2001, 66–72. **Figures 14.3, 14.4:** Wilber Schramm, *The Process and Effects of Mass Communication*. © 1954 University of Illinois Press, Champaign, IL. Reprinted by permission. **Across Industries:** David Bell, "How Local Government Managers Should Communicate in Organizations," *Public Management* 79, no. 7 (July 1997): 24–25. Reprinted with permission from the July 1997 issue of *Public Management* published by the International City/County Management Association ICMA, Washington, DC. **Figure 14.5:** Permission of the publisher, from Alex Bavelas and Dermont Barrett, "An Experimental Approach to

Organizational Communication," *Personnel* (March 1951): 370. © 1951 American Management Association, New York. Used with permission of the publisher, American Management Association. All rights reserved. www.amanet.org. **Quality Spotlight:** Alan Salomon, "Bass Gains Base of Confidence," *Hotel & Motel Management* 206 (November 25, 1991): 2, 42. **Figure 14.6:** Reprinted by permission of *Harvard Business Review.* An exhibit from "Management Communication and the Grapevine" by Keith Davis (September/October 1953): 45. Copyright © 1953 by the President and Fellows of Harvard College; all rights reserved. **Table 14.2:** Keith Davis, *Human Behavior at Work*, 396. Copyright © 1972 by McGraw-Hill, Inc. Used with permission of the publisher, American Management Association. All rights reserved. <www.amanet.org>. **Case Study:** Kristina Zimblist, "Fashion's Family Trees," *Harper's Bazaar*, May 2001, 150; "Dr. No," *Forbes*, May 28, 2001, 72; Sara Gay Forden "The House of Gucci"(New York: William Morrow, 2000).

Chapter 15

Introductory Case: *Making It Happen*, H. J. Heinz Company Annual Report 1998, 4–7. **Ethics Spotlight:** Stewart D. Friedman, "Leadership DNA: The Ford Motor Story," *Training & Development* 55, no. 3 (March 2001): 22–29. **Figure 15.2:** Reprinted by permission of *Harvard Business Review.* From "How to Choose a Leadership Pattern" by Robert Tannenbaum and Warren H. Schmidt (May/June 1973). Copyright © 1973 by the President and Fellows of Harvard College; all rights reserved. **Digital Focus:** Patricia A. Galagan, "Mission E-Possible: The Cisco E Learning Story," *Training & Development* 55, no. 2 (February 2001): 46–56. **Figure 15.4:** Reprinted from *Leadership and Decision-Making* by Victor H. Vroom and Philip W. Yetton (Table 2.1, p. 13), by permission of the University of Pittsburgh Press. © 1973 by University of Pittsburgh Press. **Figure 15.5:** Reprinted from *The New Leadership: Managing Participation in Organizations* by Victor H. Vroom and Arthur G. Jago, 1988, Upper Saddle River, NJ: Prentice Hall, Copyright 1987 by V. H. Vroom and A. G. Jago. Used with permission of the authors. **Figure 15.6:** Paul Hersey and Kenneth H. Blanchard, *Management of Organizational Behavior: Utilizing Human Resources*, 3rd ed., 103. © 1977. Reprinted by permission of Prentice Hall, Inc., Upper Saddle River, NJ. **Table 15.1:** F. E. Fiedler, *A Theory of Leadership Effectiveness*, 34. Copyright © 1967 by McGraw-Hill, Inc. Used with permission of McGraw-Hill Book Company. **Figure 15.7:** Reprinted by permission of the *Harvard Business Review.* From "Engineer the Job to Fit the Manager" by Fred Fiedler (September/October 1965). Copyright © 1965 by the President and Fellows of Harvard College; all rights reserved. **Figure 15.8:** G. H. Cpaowksi, "Characteristics of the Emerging Leader Versus Characteristics of the Manager," *Management Review* (March 1994). Used with permission of the publisher, American Management Association. All rights reserved. <www.amanet.org>. **Table 15.2:** Andrew J. DuBrin, *Participant Guide to Module 10: Development of Subordinates* (McGregor, TX: Leadership Systems Corporation, 1985), 11. **Diversity Spotlight:** Kevin D. Thompson, "Blazing New Trails," *Black Enterprise* 21 (January 1991): 54–57. **Case Study:** Cerner Corporation Home Page, <www.cerner.com/>. "Kansas City Software Company CEO's Harsh E-Mail Affects Stock Price," *Kansas City Star*, March 24, 2001; "Kansas City-Based Software Developer Announces Record Earnings," *Kansas City Star*, April 19, 2001; "You Have Mail and You'd Better Respond," *New York Times*, April 6, 2001; "oops," *Fortune*, April 16, 2001, 58; "Success Stories," <www.nasbic.org/success/stories/cerner.cfm>. (April 18, 2001); "The Best 100 Companies to Work For" (cover story), *Fortune*, January 8, 2001; "Daily Camera, Boulder, Colo.," Tech Buzz Column, *Daily Camera*, April 8, 2001; "A Stinging Office Memo Boomerangs," *New York Times*, April 5, 2001; "Lots of Empty Spaces in Cerner Parking Lot Get CEO Riled Up," *Wall Street Journal*, March 30, 2001, B83.

Chapter 16

Introductory Case: Cased based on Bob Violino, "What Slowdown?— E-Biz Spending Still Soaring," *Internetweek*, January 22, 2001, 1; Ted Kemp, "New Prescription: e-Business—Donald Hayden Leads Bristol-Myers Squibb's Search for Web Opportunities," *Internetweek*, October 30, 2000, 185; Ram Charan *Informationweek Online*, November 1, 1999. **Figure 16.3:** Lyman Porter and Edward Lawler III, *Managerial Attitudes and Performance*, 165. Copyright © 1968 Richard D. Irwin Inc. Reprinted by permission. **People Spotlight:** Robert J. Grossman, "HR Woes at Xerox," *HRMagazine*, 46, no. 5, May 2001, 34–45. **Figure 16.5:** Blair Kolasa. **Across Industries:** Liza Cheraskin and Michael A. Campion, "Study Clarifies Job-Rotation Benefits," *Personal Journal* 75, no. 11 (November 1996): 31–38; Tom Russell, "Reinvent Rotation Rule," *Government Executive* 30, no. 7 (July 1998): 62. **Table 16.1:** Reprinted by permission of *Harvard Business Review.* From "One More Time: How Do You Motivate Employees?" by Frederick Herzberg (January/February 1968). Copyright © 1968 by the President and Fellows of Harvard College; all rights reserved. **Figure 16.6:** A. H. Maslow, *Motivation and Personality*, 2nd ed. (Upper Saddle River, NJ: 1970). Reprinted by permission of Prentice Hall, Inc., Upper Saddle River, NJ. **Table 16.2:** Edward G. Thomas, "Workers Who Set Their Own Time Clocks" (Spring 1987): 50. Reprinted by permission from *Business and Society Review.* **Diversity Spotlight:** Catherine L. Carlozzi, "Diversity Is Good for Business," *Journal of Accountancy*, September 1999, 81–86. **Case Study:** For a description refer to www.bluetooth.com/developer/specification/specification.asp Cahners industry forecast. Jan-Eric Ohmann, "The Niche Player," *Wireless*, March/April 2001; Karen J. Marcelo, "How Secure Is Bluetooth?" *Wireless*, March/April 2001; Robert Diamond, "What's Up at Palm," *Wireless*, Premier 2001 <www.axis.com/corporate/ corp/index. htm>.

Chapter 17

Introductory Case: This case is based on Tim Gilbert, "Great Teamwork Pays Off for Xerox," *Journal for Quality and Participation* 22, no. 4 (July/August 1999): 48–51; Michael Sweet, "A Speedy Little Laser," *Smart Computing in Plain English* 12, no. 4 (April 2001): 18; Nikhil Deogun and John Hechinger, "Xerox Nears Sale of Half Its Stake in Fuji Venture," *Wall Street Journal*, March 2, 2001, B6. **Figure 17.2:** Reprinted by permission of *Harvard Business Review.* From "Committees on Trial" (Problems in Review) by Rollie Tillman Jr. (May/June 1960): 163. Copyright © 1960 by the President and Fellows of Harvard College; all rights reserved. **Figure 17.4:** Figure 11.5 from *Social Psychology* by Muzafer Sherif and Carolyn W. Sherif. Copyright © 1969 by Muzafer Sherif and Carolyn W. Sherif. Reprinted by permission of Addison-Wesley Educational Publishers, Inc. **Quality Spotlight:** Roberto Ceniceros, "Insurance Department Takes Team Approach to Quality," *Business Insurance* 35, no. 18 (April 30, 2001): 92. **Across Industries:** Tim Minahan, "Harley-Davidson Revs Up Development Process Purchasing" (May 7, 1998): 18–23; Jay Koblenz, "Revving Up to the Motorcycle Craze," *Black Enterprise* 29, no. 1 (August 1998): 120–121; Tom Weir, "Facing a Wealth of Decisions Spend a Little Time with Ryan Leaf's $11.25 Million Bonus," *USA Today*, August 26, 1998, 3C; Joe Singer and Steve Duvall, "High-Performance Partnering by Self-Managed Teams in Manufacturing," *Engineering Management Journal* 12, no. 4 (December. 2000): 9–15. **Diversity Spotlight:** Kate Fitzgerald, "Diversity Turns Airline Around," *Advertising Age* (February 19, 2001): S6–S7. **Figure 17.7:** Hans J. Thamhain, "Managing Technologically Innovative Team Efforts Toward New Product Success," *Journal of Product Innovation*

Management (March 1990): 5–18. **Case Study:** Carol Lavin Bernick, "When Your Culture Needs a Makeover," *Harvard Business Review*, June 2001, from which the case study is taken.

Chapter 18

Introductory Case: This case is based on Nick Wingfield, "Webvan's Founder, Borders, Ends Ties to the Web Grocer," *Wall Street Journal*, February 15, 2001, B12; Anonymous, *Progressive Grocer*, June 1999, Volume 78, Issue 6, p. 7; Peter Elstrom, Linda Himelstein, and Andy Reinhardt, "Startups That Could Make It into the Majors," *BusinessWeek*, June 21, 1999, 164. **Table 18.1:** Angelo J. Kinicki, Kenneth P. Carson, and George W. Bohlander, "Relationships between an Organization's Actual Human Resource Efforts and Employee Attitudes," *Group & Organization Management*, June 1992, 142. Reprinted by permission of Sage Publishers. **Global Spotlight:** Adapted by Michael R. Carrell and Norbert Elbert, *Human Resource Management* (Upper Saddle River, NJ: Prentice Hall, 1995); adapted from James A. McCaffrey and Craig R. Hafner, "When Two Cultures Collide: Doing Business Overseas," *Training and Development Journal*, October 1985, p. 26. © 1985; *Training and Development Journal*, American Society for Training and Development. Reprinted with permission. All rights reserved. **Case Study:** Rekha Balu, "Act Local, Think Global," *Fast Company*, June 2001; "Unilever's Indian Jewel (int'l edition). <www.businessweek.com>. "Personal Products Make Significant Gains." <www.hll.com/00personal.htm>. "Soap Opera in Bombay, *Forbes*, June 11, 2001, "Indian Products Drive," *Manufacturing Chemist* 170, no. 2 (February 1999): 8; "Unilever Annual Meetings. Shareholders Elect New Directors. All Resolutions Approved," *Business Wire*, May 3, 2000; Jim Rogers, "Trapped in the Past," *Worth*, May 2001.

Chapter 19

Introductory Case: Case based on Steve Konicki, "Fork in E-biz Expressway?" *Informationweek*, August 14, 2000, 22–24; Lee Copeland, "DaimlerChrysler Drives *FastCar* Web Initiative," *Computerworld*, August 14, 2000, 2; Alan Hall, "How the Web Is Retooling Detroit: It Could Bring Cars to Market Sooner and for Less," *BusinessWeek*, November 27, 2000, 194B–194D; John Teresko, "Remaking the Automakers," *Industry Week*, October 4, 1999, 40–44. **Across Industries:** Emily Knight and Gordon M. Amsler, "Checking in under Marriott's First Ten Program," *National Productivity Preview* 17, no. 4 (Autumn 1998): 53–56. Reprinted by permission of John Wiley & Sons, Inc. **People Spotlight:** Ron Ruggless, "Luby's Ongoing Slump Results in 1st Dividend Halt, Resignations," *Nation's Restaurant News*, November 6, 2000, 4, 132. **Diversity Spotlight:** Carlo Wolff, "Adding Dimension to Diversity," *Lodging Hospitality* 55, no. 12 (October 1999): 25–28. **Case Study:** <www.knighttransportation.com>. "The Best CEOs," *Worth*, May 2001; Anne Brady, "Trucker Knight Happily Keeps Foot off Brakes," *Wall Street Journal*, May 14, 2001, B7C; "Truckload Carriers Speculate on the Future," *Fleet Owner* 93, no. 5 (May 1998): 61; Lisa Otteson, "The Truck Stops Here," *Security Management* 44, no. 10 (October 2000): 71; Bruce Upbin, "Happy Drivers, Happy Customers," *Forbes*, November 4, 1996.

Chapter 20

Introductory Case: Carl Quintanilla, "New Airline Fad: Faster Airport Turnarounds," *Wall Street Journal*, August 4, 1994, B1, B2. **UNFigure 20.1:** *USAir Group, Inc., Boeing Co.* "JetBlue Says It's Hip to Be Cheap," *Houston Chronicle*, August 7, 2001, 5; Julie Hyman, "In Air, Smooth

Sailing Versus Turbulence Southwest Will Top Market, Study Says," *Washington Times*, August 24, 2000, B9. **Digital Focus:** Jaikumar Vijayan, "Legacy Access Lets Sallie Mae Go on Web," *Computerworld*, July 27, 1998, 61–62. **Figure 20.1:** Reprinted from *Out of Crisis* by W. Edwards Deming by permission of MIT and W. Edwards Deming. Published by MIT, Center for Advanced Engineering, Cambridge, MA 02139. Copyright 1986 by W. Edwards Deming. **Ethics Spotlight:** Joann Muller with Nicole St. Pierre, "Ford vs. Firestone: A Corporate Whodunit," *BusinessWeek*, June 11, 2001, 46–47; Sara Nathan, "Tire-related Accidents Shatter Lives," *USA Today*, December 26, 2000, 02B; Marc S. Reisch, "Firestone's Tire Problem," *Chemical & Engineering News* 99, no.1 (January 1, 2001): 12–14. **Quality Spotlight:** Stephen Barr, "Adidas on the Rebound," *CFO: The Magazine for Senior Financial Executives* (September 1991): 48–56; Richard A. Melcher, "Now This Should Get Adidas on Its Feet," *BusinessWeek*, July 20, 1992, 42. **Figure 20.3:** Richard B. Chase and Nicholas J. Aquilano, *Production and Operations Management: A Life Cycle Approach*, 4th ed., 5. © 1985 Richard D. Irwin, Inc. Reprinted by permission. **Figure 20.4:** Richard B. Chase and Nicholas J. Aquilano, *Production and Operations Management: A Life Cycle Approach*, 4th ed., 5. © 1985 Richard D. Irwin, Inc. Reprinted by permission. **Case Study:** <www.pirelli.com>. Micheline Maynard, "Tiremaking Technology Is on a Roll," *Fortune*, May 28, 2001, 148B; "Kismet the Robot." <www.npr.org/programs/morning/features/2001/apr/010409.kismet.html>. Thomas Hayden and Peter Hadfield, "The Age of Robots," *U.S. News & World Report*, April 23, 2001, 45; Lisa Eccles, "MIT Scientists Create a More Sociable Robot," *Electronic Design*, April 30, 2001, 30.

Chapter 21

Introductory Case: Martha Brannigan and James R. Hagerty, "Sunbeam, Its Prospects Looking Worse, Fires CEO Dunlap," *Wall Street Journal*, June 15, 1998, A1, A14. **Figure 21.1:** Reprinted by permission from G. Anthony Gorry and Michael S. Scott Morton, "A Framework for Management Information Systems," *Sloan Management Review* 13 (Fall 1971): 59. Reprinted by permission of the publisher. **Figure 21.2:** The Eli Broad College of Business, Michigan State University. **Global Spotlight:** Oles Gadacz, "Steel Giant Pioneers Korean IS," *Datamation* 35 (June 1, 1989): 64g–64h. **Diversity Spotlight:** Jay L. Johnson, "Target's New Dynamics," *Discount Merchandiser* 31 (August 1991): 30–46; Terry E. Hedrick, "New Challenges for Government Managers," *Bureaucrat* 19 (Spring 1990): 17–20. **Figure 21.4:** Adapted from Robert G. Murdick, "MIS for MBO," *Journal of Systems Management* (March 1977): 34–40. Used with permission of *Journal of Systems Management*, 24587 Bagley Road, Cleveland, OH 44138. **Figure 21.5:** Reprinted by permission from R. E. Breen et al., *Management Information Systems: A Subcommittee Report on Definitions* (Schenectady, NY: General Electric Co., 1969): 21. **Figure 21.7:** "Parts of the Personal Computer and What They Do," *Time* (January 3, 1983), 39. Copyright 1982 Time Inc. Magazine Company. Reprinted by permission. **Figure 21.11:** Design Survey, *Internet World*, September 1, 2000, 53. **Across Industries:** Stephen Kreider Yoder, "Technology: The Business Plan," *Wall Street Journal*, November 14, 1994, R16. **Case Study:** <www.loudcloud.com/news/releases/comp-01062.html>. *BW Online*, Table: "Loudcloud's Lessons for Internet Startups." <www.businessweek.com>. (April 16, 2001). George Anders, "Marc Andreessen: Act II," *Fast Company* (February 2001); David Sheff, "Crank It Up," *Wired* (August 2000); Marc Andreessen, "Make the Best of a Bust." <www.upside.com>. "Next Generation," *Fortune*, May 14, 2001.

Chapter 22

Introductory Case: Joseph Pereira, "LEGO's Robot Set for Kids Grabs Crowds of Grown-Ups," *Wall Street Journal*, December 10, 1998, B1. Reprinted by permission. **Quality Spotlight:** Tom Peters, *Thriving on Chaos: Handbook for a Management Revolution* (New York: Harper & Row, 1987), 87. **Figure 22.1:** David A. Gavin, "What Does Product Quality Really Mean?" *Sloan Management Review* 26 (Fall 1984): 37. Reprinted by permission of the publisher. Copyright 1984 by the Sloan Management Review Association. All rights reserved. **Table 22.1:** Philip B. Crosby, *Quality Without Tears* (New York: McGraw-Hill, 1979): 8–9. Copyright 1979. Reprinted with permission of McGraw-Hill, Inc. **Figure 22.2:** From *Zero Quality Control: Source Inspection and the Poka Yoke System* by Shigeo Shingo. English translation. Copyright © 1986 by Productivity Press, Inc., P.O. Box 13390, Portland, OR 97213-0390, (800) 394-6868. Reprinted by permission. **Digital Focus:** Jack Ewing (contributing author: Faith Keenan), "Sharing the Wealth: How Siemens Is Using Knowledge Management to Pool the Expertise of All Its Workers," *BusinessWeek*, March 19, 2001, EB36–EB40; Siemens corporate Web site. **Figure 22.4:** Teresa M. Amabile, "How to Kill Creativity," *Harvard Business Review* (September–October 1998): 78. **Case Study:** <www.lear.com> Home Page; Corporate Pages Including Executive Summary from April 23, 2001; Career Pages and Press Releases; Fara Warner, "Lear Won't Take a Back Seat," *Fast Company*, June 21, 2001.

Chapter 23

This chapter is based on Samuel C. Certo and Matthew W. Certo, *Digitial Dimensioning: Finding the E-Business in Your Business* (New York: McGraw-Hill, 2001). **Introductory Case:** Bob Trott, "Audio Portals Give Web Sites the Gift of Speech," *InfoWorld*, February 12, 2001, 32; David Stires, "Office Depot Finds an E-Business That Works," *Fortune*, February 19, 2001, 232; Bob Violino, "Office Depot Builds Winning Strategy on the Web," *Informationweek*, December 13, 1999, 84–86. **Ethics Spotlight:** Adam Rombel, "The Global Digital Divide," *Global Finance* 14, no. 12 (December 2000): 47. **Across Industries:** Denise Worach, "Online Billing: Savings Oversold?" *Public Utilities Fortnightly* (Spring 2000): 32–40. **Figure 23.3:** From Michael E. Porter, "Strategy and the Internet," *Harvard Business Review* (March 2001): 76. **Quality Spotlight:** Kathleen Danaher and Allan Portelle, "Using the Internet to Improve Daily Operations," *Health Management Technology* 21, no. 2 (February 2000): 40–43. **Case Study:** Jennifer Netherby, "A Big Vision for Small Companies," *House of Business*, May–June 2001; <www.smallbusinesstoday.org>. *SmallBusinessSchool.org.* "New IBM Start Now Solutions Provide Rapid ROI for Small and Medium Businesses," *Business Wire*, June 26, 2001.

Photo Credits

Chapter 1: p. 7, Mark Wilson Photographer; p. 8, Cory Lum; p. 14, Jonathan Saunders; p. 15, John Abbott Photography; **Chapter 2:** p. 25, Ed Carreon/SIPA Press; p. 28, Brown Brothers; p. 28, Douglas Levere/Douglas Levere Photography; p. 29, Brad Trent Photography; p. 32, Tim Parker Photography; **Chapter 3:** p. 49, Paulo Fridman; p. 75, John Abbott Photography; p. 54, R. Crandall/The Image Works; p. 62, Clark Jones Photography; p. 66, Peter Yates/Peter Yates Photography;

Chapter 4: p. 73, Ralf-Finn Hestoft/Corbis/SABA Press Photos, Inc.; p. 77, © 2000 Richard Lee/All Rights Reserved; p. 80, Ruby Washington/New York Times Pictures; p. 88, Wieck/New York Times Pictures; **Chapter 5:** p. 97, Spencer Tirey, AP/Wide World Photos; p. 103, Hugues Vassal/PressCom; p. 105, Alan Levenson; p. 109, Adrian Beadshaw/Getty Images, Inc.; p. 113, Cherry Kim Photography, © 2003 Cherry Kim; **Chapter 6:** p. 123, Ed Andrieski/AP Wide World Photos; p. 129, Reid Horn; p. 136, Action Press/Corbis/SABA Press Photos, Inc.; p. 137, Webb Chappell; **Chapter 7:** p. 145, Photo courtesy of Gateway 2000, Inc., © 1997; p. 150, Alan Levenson; p. 153, Jilly Wendell; p. 154, © Kim KulishCorbis/SABA Press Photos, Inc.; p. 159, Thomas McDonald; **Chapter 8:** p. 167, Montes De Oca and Associates, Inc.; p. 170, Kaku Kurita, Getty Images, Inc.; p. 172, Greg Girard/Contact Press Images, Inc.; p. 175, Paul Sakuma/AP Wide World Photos; p. 182, Eric Risberger/AP Wide World Photos; **Chapter 9:** p. 191, Ford Motor Company; p. 193, Michale L. Abramson/Michael L. Abramson Photography; p. 198, Bob Riha/Getty Images, Inc.; p. 200, Graham Trott; p. 203, Helen H. Davis/The Denver Post; **Chapter 10:** p. 213, The Terry Wild Studio, Inc.; p. 214, Jeremy Woodhouse/New England Stock Photo; p. 219, Ann Grillo/New York Times Pictures; p. 225, © Elizabeth Young; **Chapter 11:** p. 244, Rebecca Cooney/New York Times Pictures; p. 248, Mary Ellen Mark; **Chapter 12:** p. 257, The Northwestern Mutual Life Insurance Company; p. 259, R. Quackenbush Photography, Inc.; p. 266, © Kim Kulish/Corbis/SABA Press Photos, Inc.; p. 270, © Tim Wright/timwrightphoto.com; **Chapter 13:** p. 279, Churchill and Klehr Photography; p. 283, Leslie Flores Photography; p. 286, Robert Holmgren/Robert Holmgren Photography; p. 293, David Perry Photographer; **Chapter 14:** p. 303, Eaton Corporation; p. 308, Evan Kafka; p. 313, Scott Olson/Agence France-Press; p. 316, Louis Psihoyos/Matrix International, Inc.; p. 318, Alan S. Weiner; **Chapter 15:** p. 325, Roy Bottcrell/Getty Images, Inc.; p. 332, United Natural Foods, Inc.; p. 342, Diana Koenigsberg Photography; p. 345, Jimmy Lenner/Orpheus Chamber Ensemble, Inc.; **Chapter 16:** p. 358, AP/Wide World Photos; p. 361, © 2000 Rick Friedman Photography; p. 367, Marc Joseph Photographs; **Chapter 17:** p. 375, Montes De Oca and Associates, Inc.; p. 379, Chris Chapman Photography; p. 381, Mark Hirsch; p. 388, Todd V. Philips/Index Stock Imagery, Inc.; p. 392, Louis Psihoyos/ Matrix International, Inc.; **Chapter 18:** p. 399, Robin Nelson/Black Star; p. 401, Michael Quan/New York Times Pictures; p. 408, Paul Miller; p. 411 (left and right), © Frances M. Roberts/Richard B. Levine/Frances M. Roberts; p. 413, Spencer Grant/Photo Researchers, Inc.; **Chapter 19:** p. 421, Use of copyrighted image courtesy of DaimlerChrysler Corporation; p. 425, Ralf-Finn Hestoft/Corbis/SABA Press Photos, Inc.; p. 431, Wyatt McSpadden Photography; p. 434, Carol Halebian/New York Times Pictures; **Chapter 20:** p. 444, Todd Buchanan; p. 447, Lara Jo Regan/Corbis SABA Press Photos, Inc.; p. 450, Tim Parker Photography; p. 455, Stuart Isett/Getty Images, Inc.; p. 457, USG Corporation; **Chapter 21:** p. 469, The Terry Wild Studio, Inc.; p. 472, Boeing Commercial Airplane Group; p. 476, © 2000 by Marty Katz; p. 487, Rich Frishman Photography and Videograph, Inc.; **Chapter 22:** p. 499, The LEGO Group/Switzer Communications, Inc.; p. 506, Robert Holmgren/Robert Holmgren Photography; p. 508, © 2001 by Dennis Kleiman Photography; p. 513, Dryden Flight Research Center/NASA Headquarters; p. 515, Darrell Eager/Darrell Eager Photography; p. 516, Peter Ross; **Chapter 23:** p. 526, Joe Raedle/Getty Images, Inc.; p. 530, Chuck Eaton; p. 534, Jeff Greenberg/The Image Works.

Glossary

Accountability refers to the management philosophy whereby individuals are held liable, or accountable, for how well they use their authority or live up to their responsibility of performing predetermined activities. *p. 244*

Activities are specified sets of behavior within a project. *p. 204*

Adjourning, the fifth and last stage of the team development process, is the stage in which the team finishes its job and prepares to disband. *p. 389*

Affirmative action programs are organizational programs whose basic purpose is to eliminate barriers against and increase employment opportunities for underutilized or disadvantaged individuals. *p. 264*

Alderfer's ERG theory is an explanation of human needs that divides them into three basic types: existence needs, relatedness needs, and growth needs. *p. 359*

Appropriate human resources are the individuals in the organization who make a valuable contribution to management system goal attainment. *p. 258*

Argyris' maturity-immaturity continuum is a concept that furnishes insights into human needs by focusing on an individual's natural progress from immaturity to maturity. *p. 359*

Assessment center is a program in which participants engage in, and are evaluated on, a number of individual and group exercises constructed to simulate important activities at the organizational levels to which they aspire. *p. 266*

Attitude is a predisposition to react to a situation, person, or concept with a particular response. *p. 400*

Attribution is the process by which people *interpret* the behavior of others by assigning to it motives or causes. *p. 407*

Attribution error is the tendency to overestimate internal causes of behavior and underestimate external ones when judging other people's behavior. *p. 409*

Authority is the right to perform or command. *p. 240*

Behavior modification is a program that focuses on managing human activity by controlling the consequences of performing that activity. *p. 366*

Behavioral approach to management is a management approach that emphasizes increasing organizational success by focusing on human variables within the organization. *p. 31*

Beliefs are accepted facts or truths about an object or person that have been gained from either direct experience or a secondary source. *p. 401*

Bicultural stress is stress resulting from having to cope with membership in two cultures simultaneously. *p. 80*

Brainstorming is a group decision-making process in which negative feedback on any suggested alternative to any group member is forbidden until all group members have presented alternatives that they perceive as valuable. *p. 159*

Break-even analysis is a control tool that summarizes the various levels of profit or loss associated with various levels of production. *p. 460*

Break-even point is that level of production where the total revenue of an organization equals its total costs. *p. 460*

Budget is a control tool that outlines how funds in a given period will be spent, as well as how they will be obtained. *p. 196*

Budget is a control tool that outlines how funds will be obtained and spent in a given period. *p. 455*

Bureaucracy is the term Max Weber used to describe a management system characterized by detailed procedures and rules, a clearly outlined organizational hierarchy, and impersonal relationships among organization members. *p. 217*

Business ethics involves the capacity to reflect on values in the corporate decision-making process, to determine how these values and decisions affect various stakeholder groups, and to establish how managers can use these observations in day-to-day company management. *p. 63*

Business portfolio analysis is the development of business-related strategy based primarily on the market share of businesses and the growth of markets in which businesses exist. *p. 177*

Capacity strategy is an operational plan of action aimed at providing the organization with the right facilities to produce the needed output at the right time. *p. 449*

Career is a sequence of work-related positions occupied by a person over the course of a lifetime. *p. 12*

Career plateauing is a period of little or no apparent progress in the growth of a career. *p. 13*

Centralization refers to the situation in which a minimal number of job activities and a minimal amount of authority are delegated to subordinates. *p. 247*

Change agent is an individual inside or outside the organization who tries to modify an existing organizational situation. *p. 282*

Changing an organization is the process of modifying an existing organization to increase organizational effectiveness. *p. 280*

Classical approach to management is a management approach that emphasizes organizational efficiency to increase organizational success. *p. 26*

Classical organizing theory comprises the cumulative insights of early management writers on how organizational resources can best be used to enhance goal attainment. *p. 217*

Closed system is one that is not influenced by, and does not interact with, its environment. *p. 36*

Coaching is a leadership that instructs followers on how to meet the special organizational challenges they face. *p. 343*

Code of ethics is a formal statement that acts as a guide for making decisions and acting within an organization. *p. 64*

Cognitive learning is an approach theory that focuses on thought processes and assumes that human beings have a high capacity to act in a purposeful manner, and so to choose behaviors that will enable them to achieve long-run goals. *p. 412*

Command group is a formal group that is outlined in the chain of command on an organization chart. Command groups handle routine activities. *p. 377*

Commitment principle is a management guideline that advises managers to commit funds for planning only if they can anticipate, in the foreseeable future, a return on planning expenses as a result of the long-range planning analysis. *p. 168*

Committee is a task group that is charged with performing some type of specific activity. *p. 378*

Communication macrobarriers are factors hindering successful communication that relate primarily to the communication environment and the larger world in which communication takes place. *p. 309*

Communication microbarriers are factors hindering successful communication that relate primarily to such variables as the communication message, the source, and the destination. *p. 309*

Complete certainty condition is the decision-making situation in which the decision maker knows exactly what the results of an implemented alternative will be. *p. 155*

Complete uncertainty condition is the decision-making situation in which the decision maker has absolutely no idea what the results of an implemented alternative will be. *p. 155*

Comprehensive analysis of management involves studying the management function as a whole. *p. 30*

Computer is an electronic tool capable of accepting data, interpreting data, performing ordered operations on data, and reporting on the outcome of these operations. Computers are extremely helpful in generating information from raw data. *p. 482*

Computer network is a system of two or more connected computers that allows computer users to communicate, cooperate, and share resources. *p. 486*

Computer-aided design (CAD) is a computerized technique for designing new products or modifying existing ones. *p. 463*

Computer-aided manufacturing (CAM) is a technique that employs computers to plan and program equipment used in the production and inspection of manufactured items. *p. 463*

Conceptual skills are skills involving the ability to see the organization as a whole. *p. 11*

Concurrent control is control that takes place as some unit of work is being performed. *p. 428*

Consensus is an agreement on a decision by all individuals involved in making that decision. *p. 148*

Consideration behavior is leadership behavior that reflects friendship, mutual trust, respect, and warmth in the relationship between leader and followers. *p. 335*

Content theories of motivation are explanations of motivation that emphasize people's internal characteristics. *p. 354*

Contingency approach to management is a management approach emphasizing that what managers do in practice depends on a given set of circumstances—a situation. *p. 35*

Contingency theory of leadership is a leadership concept that hypothesizes that, in any given leadership situation, success is determined primarily by (1) the degree to which the task being performed by the followers is structured, (2) the degree of position power possessed by the leader, and (3) the type of relationship that exists between the leader and the followers. *p. 338*

Control is making something happen the way it was planned to happen. *p. 422*

Control function—computer activities that dictate the order in which other computer functions are performed. *p. 483*

Control tool is a specific procedure or technique that presents pertinent organizational information in a way that helps managers to develop and implement an appropriate control strategy. *p. 458*

Controller is the staff person whose basic responsibility is to assist line managers with the controlling function by gathering appropriate information and generating necessary reports that reflect this information. *p. 429*

Controlling is the process managers go through to control. It is a systematic effort to compare performance to predetermined standards, plans, or objectives to determine whether performance is in line with those standards or needs to be corrected. *p. 422*

Coordination is the orderly arrangement of group effort to provide unity of action in the pursuit of a common purpose. It involves encouraging the completion of individual portions of a task in an appropriate, synchronized order. *p. 223*

Corporate culture is a set of shared values and beliefs that organization members have regarding the functioning and existence of their organization. *p. 391*

Corporate social responsibility is the managerial obligation to take action that protects and improves both the welfare of society as a whole and the interests of the organization. *p. 48*

Corrective action is managerial activity aimed at bringing organizational performance up to the level of performance standards. *p. 427*

Cost leadership is a strategy that focuses on making an organization more competitive by producing products more cheaply than competitors can. *p. 180*

Cost–benefit analysis is the process of comparing the cost of some activity with the benefit or revenue that results from the activity to determine the activity's total worth to the organization. *p. 431*

Creativity is the ability to combine ideas in a unique way or to make useful associations among ideas. *p. 514*

Critical path is the sequence of events and activities within a program evaluation and review technique (PERT) network that requires the longest period of time to complete. *p. 205*

Critical question analysis is a strategy development tool that consists of answering basic questions about the present purposes and objectives of the organization, its present direction and environment, and actions that can be taken to achieve organizational objectives in the future. *p. 176*

Cross-functional team is an organizational team composed of people from different functional areas of the organization who are all focused on a specified objective. *p. 387*

Culture is the set of characteristics of a given group of people and their environment. *p. 112*

Data are facts or statistics. *p. 470*

Database is a reservoir of corporate facts consistently organized to fit the information needs of a variety of organization members. *p. 485*

Decentralization refers to the situation in which a significant number of job activities and a maximum amount of authority are delegated to subordinates. *p. 247*

Decision is a choice made between two or more available alternatives. *p. 146*

Decision tree is a graphic decision-making tool typically used to evaluate decisions involving a series of steps. *p. 157*

Decision tree analysis is a statistical and graphical multiphased decision-making technique that shows the sequence and interdependence of decisions. *p. 463*

Decision-making process comprises the steps the decision maker takes to make a decision. *p. 152*

Decline stage is the fourth and last stage in career evolution; it occurs near retirement age, when individuals of about 65 years of age show declining productivity. *p. 13*

Decoder/destination is the person or persons in the interpersonal communication situation with whom the source is attempting to share information. *p. 308*

Delegation is the process of assigning job activities and related authority to specific individuals in the organization. *p. 245*

Delphi technique is a group decision-making process that involves circulating questionnaires on a specific problem among group members, sharing the questionnaire results with them, and then continuing to recirculate and refine individual responses until a consensus regarding the problem is reached. *p. 160*

Demographics are statistical characteristics of a population. *p. 77*

Demographics are the statistical characteristics of a population. Organizational strategy should reflect demographics. *p. 172*

Department is a unique group of resources established by management to perform some organizational task. *p. 219*

Departmentalization is the process of establishing departments within the management system. *p. 219*

Dialogue capability is the ability of an MDSS user to interact with an MDSS. *p. 486*

Differentiation is a strategy that focuses on making an organization more competitive by developing a product or products that customers perceive as being different from products offered by competitors. *p. 179*

Digital pertains to components related to the Internet and Internet-supporting technologies like voice recognition or wireless technologies. *p. 15*

Digital dimension is that segment of management that focuses on meeting management challenges through the application of the Internet and Internet-supportive technologies. *p. 15*

Digital dimensioning is the process of designing and implementing those digital activities that will best help a specific organization reach its goals. *p. 524*

Digital dimensioning is the process of determining and using a unique combination of Internet and Internet-supportive tools that best helps management meet organizational challenges and thereby enhance organizational goal attainment. *p. 15*

Direct investing is using the assets of one company to purchase the operating assets of another company. *p. 108*

Discrimination is the act of treating an issue, person, or behavior unjustly or inequitably on the basis of stereotypes or prejudices. *p. 79*

Diversity is the degree of basic human differences among a given population. Major areas of diversity are gender, race, ethnicity, religion, social class, physical ability, sexual orientation, and age. *p. 74*

Diversity training is a learning process designed to raise managers' awareness and develop their competencies to deal with the issues endemic to managing a diverse workforce. *p. 88*

Divestiture is a strategy adopted to eliminate a strategic business unit that is not generating a satisfactory amount of business and has little hope of doing so in the future. *p. 181*

Division of labor is the assignment of various portions of a particular task among a number of organization members. Division of labor calls for specialization. *p. 223*

Domestic organization is a company that essentially operates within a single country. *p. 100*

Downward organizational communication is communication that flows from any point on an organization chart downward to another point on the organization chart. *p. 314*

E-business is any organizational activity that is enhanced by an Internet initiative. *p. 524*

E-mail is a computerized information system that allows individuals the electronic capability to create, edit, and send messages to one another. *p. 490*

Economics is the science that focuses on understanding how people of a particular community or nation produce, distribute, and use various goods and services. *p. 171*

Effectiveness is the degree to which managers attain organizational objectives; it is doing the right things. *p. 449*

Efficiency is the degree to which organizational resources contribute to production; it is doing things right. *p. 449*

Employee-centered behavior is leader behavior that focuses primarily on subordinates as people. *p. 336*

Entrepreneurial leadership is leadership that is based on the attitude that the leader is self-employed. *p. 344*

Environmental analysis is the study of the organizational environment to pinpoint environmental factors that can significantly influence organizational operations. *p. 170*

Equal Employment Opportunity Commission (EEOC) is an agency established to enforce federal laws regulating recruiting and other employment practices. *p. 263*

Equity theory is an explanation of motivation that emphasizes the individual's perceived fairness of an employment situation and how perceived inequities can cause certain behaviors. *p. 356*

Establishment stage is the second stage in career evolution; individuals of about 25 to 45 years of age typically start to become more productive, or higher performers. *p. 13*

Esteem needs are Maslow's fourth set of human needs—including the desires for self-respect and respect from others. *p. 358*

Ethics is our concern for good behavior; our obligation to consider not only our own personal well-being but also that of other human beings. *p. 63*

Ethnocentric attitude reflects the belief that multinational corporations should regard home-country management practices as superior to foreign-country management practices. *p. 110*

Ethnocentrism is the belief that one's own group, culture, country, or customs are superior to others'. *p. 78*

Events are the completions of major project tasks. *p. 204*

Expected value (EV) is the measurement of the anticipated value of some event, determined by multiplying the income an event would produce by its probability of producing that income ($EV = I \times P$). *p. 156*

Exploration stage is the first stage in career evolution; it occurs at the beginning of a career, when the individual is typically 15 to 25 years of age, and it is characterized by self-analysis and the exploration of different types of available jobs. *p. 12*

Exporting is selling goods or services to another country. *p. 108*

Extranet is a program that expands an Intranet to allow organizational outsiders to perform such activities such as placing orders and checking on the status of their orders. *p. 491*

Extrinsic rewards are rewards that are extraneous to the task accomplished. *p. 357*

Feedback is, in the interpersonal communication situation, the destination's reaction to a message. *p. 311*

Feedback control is control that takes place after some unit of work has been performed. *p. 428*

Fixed costs are expenses incurred by the organization regardless of the number of products produced. *p. 460*

Fixed-position layout is a layout plan appropriate for organizations involved in a large number of different tasks that require low volumes, multipurpose equipment, and broad employee skills. *p. 451*

Flat organization chart is an organization chart characterized by few levels and a relatively broad span of management. *p. 226*

Flextime is a program that allows workers to complete their jobs within a workweek of a normal number of hours that they schedule themselves. *p. 365*

Focus is a strategy that emphasizes making an organization more competitive by targeting a particular customer. *p. 180*

Forecasting is a planning tool used to predict future environmental happenings that will influence the operation of the organization. *p. 200*

Formal group is a group that exists within an organization by virtue of management decree to perform tasks that enhance the attainment of organizational objectives. *p. 376*

Formal organizational communication is organizational communication that follows the lines of the organization chart. *p. 314*

Formal structure is defined as the relationships among organizational resources as outlined by management. *p. 218*

Forming is the first stage of the team development process, during which members of the newly formed team become oriented to the team and acquainted with one another as they explore issues related to their new job situation. *p. 389*

Friendship group is an informal group that forms in organizations because of the personal affiliation members have with one another. *p. 382*

Functional authority consists of the right to give orders within a segment of the management system in which the right is normally nonexistent. *p. 244*

Functional similarity method is a method for dividing job activities in the organization. *p. 237*

Gangplank is a communication channel extending from one organizational division to another but not shown in the lines of communication outlined on an organization chart. Use of Fayol's gangplank may be quicker, but could prove costly in the long run. *p. 227*

Gantt chart is a scheduling tool composed of a bar chart with time on the horizontal axis and the resource to be scheduled on the vertical axis. It is used for scheduling resources. *p. 203*

Gender-role stereotypes are perceptions about the sexes based on what society believes are appropriate behaviors for men and women. *p. 79*

General environment is the level of an organization's external environment that contains components normally having broad long-term implications for managing the organization; its components are economic, social, political, legal, and technological. *p. 171*

Geocentric attitude reflects the belief that the overall quality of management recommendations, rather than the location of managers, should determine the acceptability of management practices used to guide multinational corporations. The geocentric attitude is considered most appropriate for long-term organizational success. *p. 110*

Graicunas' formula is a formula that makes the span-of-management point that as the number of a manager's subordinates increases arithmetically, the number of possible relationships between the manager and the subordinates increases geometrically. *p. 225*

Grapevine is the network of informal organizational communication. *p. 317*

Grid organization development (grid OD) is a commonly used organization development technique based on a theoretical model called the *managerial grid*. *p. 287*

Group is any number of people who (1) interact with one another, (2) are psychologically aware of one another, and (3) perceive themselves to be a group. *p. 376*

Groupthink is the mode of thinking that group members engage in when the desire for agreement so dominates the group that it overrides the need to realistically appraise alternative problem solutions. *p. 379*

Growth is a strategy adopted by management to increase the amount of business that a strategic business unit is currently generating. *p. 181*

Halo effect results from allowing one particular aspect of someone's behavior to influence one's evaluation of all other aspects of that person's behavior. *p. 408*

Hierarchy of objectives is the overall organizational objectives and the subobjectives assigned to the various people or units of the organization. *p. 132*

Host country is the country in which an investment is made by a foreign company. *p. 105*

Human relations movement is a people-oriented approach to management in which the interaction of people in organizations is studied to judge its impact on organizational success. *p. 33*

Human relations skill is the ability to work with people in a way that enhances organizational success. *p. 33*

Human resource inventory is an accumulation of information about the characteristics of organization members; this information focuses on members' past performance as well as on how they might be trained and best used in the future. *p. 260*

Human resource planning is input planning that involves obtaining the human resources necessary for the organization to achieve its objectives. *p. 198*

Human resources strategy is an operational plan to use the organization's human resources effectively and efficiently while maintaining or improving the quality of work life. *p. 452*

Human skills are skills involving the ability to build cooperation within the team being led. *p. 11*

Hygiene, or **maintenance, factors** are items that influence the degree of job dissatisfaction. *p. 364*

Importing is buying goods or services from another country. *p. 108*

Influencing is the process of guiding the activities of organization members in appropriate directions. It involves the performance of four management activities: (1) leading, (2) motivating, (3) considering groups, and (4) communicating. *p. 304*

Informal group is a collection of individuals whose common work experiences result in the development of a system of interpersonal relations that extend beyond those established by management. *p. 382*

Informal organizational communication is organizational communication that does not follow the lines of the organization chart. *p. 317*

Informal structure is defined as the patterns of relationships that develop because of the informal activities of organization members. *p. 219*

Information is the set of conclusions derived from data analysis. *p. 470*

Information appropriateness is the degree to which information is relevant to the decision-making situation the manager faces. *p. 471*

Information quality is the degree to which information represents reality. *p. 472*

Information quantity is the amount of decision-related information a manager possesses. *p. 472*

Information technology is technology that focuses on the use of information in the performance of work. *p. 481*

Information timeliness is the extent to which the receipt of information allows decisions to be made and action to be taken so the organization can gain some benefit from possessing the information. *p. 472*

Innovation is the process of taking useful ideas and turning them into useful products, services, or methods of operation. *p. 514*

Input function—computer activities through which the computer enters the data to be analyzed and the instructions to be followed to analyze the data appropriately. *p. 482*

Input planning is the development of proposed action that will furnish sufficient and appropriate organizational resources for reaching established organizational objectives. *p. 196*

Interest group is an informal group that gains and maintains membership primarily because of a common concern members have about a specific issue. *p. 382*

Intermediate-term objectives are targets to be achieved within one to five years. *p. 131*

Internal environment is the level of an organization's environment that exists inside the organization and normally has immediate and specific implications for managing the organization. *p. 173*

International joint venture is a partnership formed by a company in one country with a company in another country for the purpose of pursuing some mutually desirable business undertaking. *p. 108*

International management is the performance of management activities across national borders. *p. 98*

International market agreement is an arrangement among a cluster of countries that facilitates a high level of trade among these countries. *p. 109*

International organization is a company primarily based within a single country but having continuing, meaningful transactions in other countries. *p. 100*

Internet is a large interconnected network of computer networks linking people and computers all over the world via phone lines, satellites, and other telecommunications systems. *p. 486*

Intranet is an internal corporate communication network that uses the structure and standards of the Internet to allow employees of a single firm to communicate and share information with each other electronically. *p. 491*

Intrinsic rewards are rewards that come directly from performing a task. *p. 357*

Job analysis is a technique commonly used to gain an understanding of what a task entails and the type of individual who should be hired to perform that task. *p. 259*

Job-centered behavior is leader behavior that focuses primarily on the work a subordinate is doing. *p. 336*

Job description is a list of specific activities that must be performed to accomplish some task or job. *p. 259*

Job description is a list of specific activities that must be performed to accomplish some task or job. *p. 236*

Job design is an operational plan that determines who will do a specific job and how and where the job will be done. *p. 452*

Job enlargement is the process of increasing the number of operations an individual performs in a job. *p. 364*

Job enrichment is the process of incorporating motivators into a job situation. *p. 364*

Job rotation is the process of moving workers from one job to another rather than requiring them to perform only one simple and specialized job over the long term. *p. 363*

Job specification is a list of the characteristics of the individual who should be hired to perform a specific task or job. *p. 259*

Jury of executive opinion method is a method of predicting future sales levels primarily by asking appropriate managers to give their opinions on what will happen to sales in the future. *p. 200*

Just-in-time (JIT) inventory control is a technique for reducing inventories to a minimum by arranging for production components to be delivered to the production facility "just in time" to be used. *p. 453*

Lateral organizational communication is communication that flows from any point on an organization chart horizontally to another point on the organization chart. *p. 316*

Law of the situation indicates that managers must continually analyze the unique circumstances within their organizations and apply management concepts to fit those circumstances. *p. 17*

Layout is the overall arrangement of equipment, work areas, service areas, and storage areas within a facility that produces goods or provides services. *p. 451*

Layout strategy is an operational plan that determines the location and flow of organizational resources around, into, and within production and service facilities. *p. 451*

Leader flexibility is the ability to change leadership style. *p. 338*

Leadership is the process of directing the behavior of others toward the accomplishment of objectives. *p. 326*

Leadership style is the behavioral pattern a leader establishes while guiding organization members in appropriate directions. *p. 335*

Learning is a more or less permanent change in behavior resulting from practice, experience, education, or training. *p. 411*

Learning organization is an organization that does well in creating, acquiring, and transferring knowledge, and in modifying behavior to reflect new knowledge. *p. 39*

Lecture is primarily a one-way communication situation in which an instructor trains an individual or group by orally presenting information. *p. 269*

Level dimension of a plan is the level of the organization at which the plan is aimed. *p. 193*

License agreement is a right granted by one company to another to use its brand name, technology, product specifications, and so on in the manufacture or sale of goods and services. *p. 108*

Life cycle theory of leadership is a leadership concept that hypothesizes that leadership styles should reflect primarily the maturity level of the followers. *p. 336*

Line authority consists of the right to make decisions and to give orders concerning the production-, sales-, or finance-related behavior of subordinates. *p. 241*

Local area network (LAN) is a computer network characterized by software that manages how information travels through cables to arrive at a number of connected single-user computer workstations. *p. 486*

Location strategy is an operational plan of action that provides the organization with a competitive location for its headquarters, manufacturing, services, and distribution activities. *p. 450*

Long-term objectives are targets to be achieved within five to seven years. *p. 131*

Loss is the amount of the total costs of producing a product that exceeds the total revenue gained from selling the product. *p. 460*

Maintenance stage is the third stage in career evolution; individuals of about 45 to 65 years of age either become more productive, stabilize, or become less productive. *p. 13*

Majority group refers to that group of people in the organization who hold most of the positions that command decision-making power, control of resources and information, and access to system rewards. *p. 74*

Management is the process of reaching organizational goals by working with and through people and other organizational resources. *p. 7*

Management by exception is a control tool that allows only significant deviations between planned and actual performance to be brought to a manger's attention. *p. 459*

Management by objectives (MBO) is a management approach that uses organizational objectives as the primary means of managing organizations. *p. 133*

Management decision support system (MDSS) is an interdependent set of computer-oriented decision aids that help managers make nonprogrammed decisions. The following characteristics are typical of an MDSS. *p. 484*

Management functions are activities that make up the management process. The four basic management activities are planning, organizing, influencing, and controlling. *p. 7*

Management information system (MIS) is a network established within an organization to provide managers with information that will assist them in decision making. An MIS gets information to where it is needed. *p. 474*

Management inventory card is a form used in compiling a human resource inventory. It contains the organizational history of an individual and indicates how that individual might be used in the organization in the future. *p. 261*

Management manpower replacement chart is a form used in compiling a human resource inventory. It is people oriented and presents a composite view of individuals management considers significant to human resource planning. *p. 261*

Management responsibility guide is a tool that is used to clarify the responsibilities of various managers in the organization. *p. 239*

Management science approach is a management approach that emphasizes the use of the scientific method and quantitative techniques to increase organizational success. *p. 34*

Management system is an open system whose major parts are organizational input, organizational process, and organizational output. *p. 37*

Managerial effectiveness refers to management's use of organizational resources in meeting organizational goals. *p. 9*

Managerial efficiency is the degree to which organizational resources contribute to productivity. It is measured by the proportion of total organizational resources used during the production process. *p. 9*

Managerial grid is a theoretical model based on the premise that concern for people and concern for production are the two primary attitudes that influence management style. *p. 287*

Manpower planning is an operational plan that focuses on hiring the right employees for a job and training them to be productive. *p. 452*

Materials control is an operational activity that determines the flow of materials from vendors through an operations system to customers. *p. 457*

Matrix organization is a traditional organizational structure that is modified primarily for the purpose of completing some kind of special project. *p. 285*

McClelland's acquired needs theory is an explanation of human needs that focuses on the desires for achievement, power, and affiliation that people develop as a result of their life experiences. *p. 360*

Message is encoded information that the source intends to share with others. *p. 308*

Message interference refers to stimuli that compete with the communication message for the attention of the destination. *p. 310*

Minority group refers to that group of people in the organization who are smaller in number or who possess fewer granted rights and lower status than the majority groups. *p. 74*

Mission statement is a written document developed by management, normally based on input by managers as well as nonmanagers, that describes and explains the organization's mission. *p. 174*

Model base is a collection of quantitative computer programs that can assist MDSS users in analyzing data within databases. *p. 485*

Motion study finds the best way to accomplish a task by analyzing the movements necessary to perform that task. *p. 28*

Motion-study techniques are operational tools that are used to improve productivity. *p. 453*

Motivating factors, or **motivators,** are items that influence the degree of job satisfaction. *p. 364*

Motivation is the inner state that causes an individual to behave in a way that ensures the accomplishment of some goal. *p. 354*

Motivation strength is an individual's degree of desire to perform a behavior. *p. 355*

Multinational corporation (MNC) is a company that has significant operations in more than one country. *p. 101*

Needs-goal theory is a motivation model that hypothesizes that felt needs cause human behavior. *p. 354*

Negative reinforcement is a reward that consists of the elimination of an undesirable consequence of behavior. *p. 367*

Nominal group technique is a group decision-making process in which every group member is assured of equal participation in making the group decision. After each member writes down individual ideas and presents them orally to the group, the entire group discusses all the ideas and then votes for the best idea in a secret ballot. *p. 160*

Nonprogrammed decisions are typically one-shot decisions that are usually less structured than programmed decisions. *p. 146*

Nonverbal communication is the sharing of information without using words. *p. 313*

Norming, the third stage of the team development process, is characterized by agreement among team members on roles, rules, and acceptable behavior while working on the team. *p. 389*

On-the-job training is a training technique that blends job-related knowledge with experience in using that knowledge on the job. *p. 270*

Open system is one that is influenced by, and is continually interacting with, its environment. *p. 36*

Operant learning is an approach that holds the behavior leading to positive consequences is more likely to be repeated. *p. 411*

Operating environment is the level of the organization's external environment that contains components normally having relatively specific and immediate implications for managing the organization. *p. 173*

Operations control is an operational plan that specifies the operational activities of an organization. *p. 453*

Operations management is performance of managerial activities entailed in selecting, designing, operating, controlling, and updating production systems. *p. 448*

Organization chart is a graphic representation of organizational structure. *p. 218*

Organization development (OD) is the process that emphasizes changing an organization by changing organization members and bases these changes on an overview of structure, technology, and all other organizational ingredients. *p. 287*

Organizational communication is interpersonal communication within organizations. *p. 314*

Organizational mission is the purpose for which, or the reason why, an organization exists. *p. 174*

Organizational objectives are the targets toward which the open management system is directed. They flow from the organization's purpose or mission. *p. 129*

Organizational purpose is what the organization exists to do, given a particular group of customers and customer needs. *p. 129*

Organizational resources are all assets available for activation during normal operations; they include human resources, monetary resources, raw materials resources, and capital resources. *p. 8*

Organizing is the process of establishing orderly uses for all the organization's resources. *p. 214*

Output function—computer activities that take the results of input, storage, processing, and control functions and transmit them outside the computer. *p. 483*

Overlapping responsibility refers to a situation in which more than one individual is responsible for the same activity. *p. 238*

Parent company is the company investing in international operations. *p. 105*

Path–goal theory of leadership is a theory of leadership that suggests that the primary activities of a leader are to make desirable and achievable rewards available to organization members who attain organizational goals and to clarify the kinds of behavior that must be performed to earn those rewards. *p. 340*

People change is a type of organizational change that emphasizes modifying certain aspects of organization members to increase organizational effectiveness. *p. 287*

People factors are attitudes, leadership skills, communication skills, and all other characteristics of the organization's employees. *p. 283*

Perception is the interpretation of a message by an individual. *p. 310*

Perception is the psychological process of selecting stimuli, organizing the data into recognizable patterns, and interpreting the resulting information. *p. 406*

Perceptual process is the series of actions that individuals follow in order to select, organize, and interpret stimuli from the environment. *p. 406*

Performance appraisal is the process of reviewing past productive activity to evaluate the contribution individuals have made toward attaining management system objectives. *p. 271*

Performing, the fourth stage of the team development process, is characterized by a focus on solving organizational problems and meeting assigned challenges. *p. 389*

Person-to-person collaborative tools are Internet-based applications that enable people to communicate from various locations in cities, states, or countries. *p. 536*

Personal power is the power derived from a manager's relationships with others. *p. 432*

Physiological needs are Maslow's first set of human needs—for the normal functioning of the body, including the desires for water, food, rest, sex, and air. *p. 358*

Plan is a specific action proposed to help the organization achieve its objectives. *p. 192*

Planning is the process of determining how the management system will achieve its objectives; it determines how the organization can get where it wants to go. *p. 124*

Planning tools are techniques managers can use to help develop plans. *p. 200*

Plant facilities planning is input planning that involves developing the type of work facility an organization will need to reach its objectives. *p. 196*

Pluralism is an environment in which cultural, group, and individual differences are acknowledged, accepted, and viewed as significant contributors to the entirety. *p. 86*

Policy is a standing plan that furnishes broad guidelines for channeling management toward taking action consistent with reaching organizational objectives. *p. 194*

Polycentric attitude reflects the belief that because foreign managers are closer to foreign organizational units, they probably understand them better, and therefore foreign management practices should generally be viewed as more insightful than home-country management practices. *p. 110*

Porter–Lawler theory is a motivation theory that hypothesizes that felt needs cause human behavior and that motivation strength is determined primarily by the perceived value of the result of performing the behavior and the perceived probability that the behavior performed will cause the result to materialize. *p. 356*

Position power is power derived from the organizational position a manager holds. *p. 432*

Position replacement form is used in compiling a human resource inventory. It summarizes information about organization members who could fill a position should it open up. *p. 261*

Positive reinforcement is a reward that consists of a desirable consequence of behavior. *p. 367*

Power is the extent to which an individual is able to influence others so that they respond to orders. *p. 432*

Precontrol is control that takes place before some unit of work is actually performed. *p. 428*

Prejudice is a preconceived judgment, opinion, or assumption about an issue, behavior, individual, or group of people. *p. 78*

Premises are the assumptions on which an alternative to reaching an organizational objective is based. *p. 126*

Principle of the objective is a management guideline that recommends that before managers initiate any action, they should clearly determine, understand, and state organizational objectives. *p. 132*

Probability theory is a decision-making tool used in risk situations—situations in which the decision maker is not completely sure of the outcome of an implemented alternative. *p. 156*

Problem-solving team is an organizational team set up to help eliminate a specified problem within the organization. *p. 386*

Problems are factors within an organization that are barriers to organizational goal attainment. *p. 427*

Procedural justice is the perceived fairness of the process used for deciding workplace outcomes such as merit increases and promotions. *p. 409*

Procedure is a standing plan that outlines a series of related actions that must be taken to accomplish a particular task. *p. 195*

Process (functional) layout is a layout pattern based primarily on grouping together similar types of equipment. *p. 451*

Process control is a technique that assists in monitoring production processes. *p. 463*

Process strategy is an operational plan of action outlining the means and methods the organization will use to transform resources into goods and services. *p. 451*

Process theories of motivation are explanations of motivation that emphasize how individuals are motivated. *p. 354*

Processing function—computer activities involved with performing the logic and calculation steps necessary to analyze data appropriately. *p. 483*

Product layout is a layout designed to accommodate a limited number of different products that require high volumes, highly specialized equipment, and narrow employee skills. *p. 451*

Product life cycle is the five stages through which most products and services pass: introduction, growth, maturity, saturation, and decline. *p. 202*

Product strategy is an operational plan of action outlining which goods and services an organization will produce and market. *p. 450*

Production is the transformation of organizational resources into products. *p. 442*

Production control ensures that an organization produces goods and services as planned. *p. 442*

Productivity is the relationship between the total amount of goods or services being produced (output) and the organizational resources needed to produce them (input). *p. 442*

Profits are the amount of total revenue that exceeds total costs. *p. 460*

Program is a single-use plan designed to carry out a special project in an organization that, if accomplished, will contribute to the organization's long-term success. *p. 196*

Program evaluation and review technique (PERT) is a scheduling tool that is essentially a network of project activities showing estimates of time necessary to complete each activity and the sequence of activities that must be followed to complete the project. *p. 204*

Programmed decisions are decisions that are routine and repetitive and that typically require specific handling methods. *p. 146*

Programmed learning is a technique for instructing without the presence or intervention of a human instructor. Small pieces of information requiring responses are presented to individual trainees, and the trainees determine from checking their responses against provided answers whether their understanding of the information is accurate. *p. 269*

Projection is the unconscious tendency to assign one's own traits, motives, beliefs, and attitudes to others. *p. 408*

Punishment is the presentation of an undesirable behavior consequence or the removal of a desirable one that decreases the likelihood that the behavior will continue. *p. 367*

Pure-breakdown (repair) policy is a maintenance control policy that decrees that machine adjustments, lubrication, cleaning, parts replacement, painting, and needed repairs and overhaul will be performed only after facilities or machines malfunction. *p. 454*

Pure-preventive maintenance policy is a maintenance control policy that tries to ensure that machine adjustments, lubrication, cleaning, parts replacement, painting, and needed repairs and overhauls will be performed before facilities or machines malfunction. *p. 454*

Quality is the extent to which a product reliably does what it is intended to do. *p. 443*

Quality is the extent to which a product does what it is supposed to do—how closely and reliably it satisfies the specifications to which it is built. *p. 500*

Quality assurance is an operations process involving a broad group of activities that are aimed at achieving the organization's quality objectives. *p. 445*

Quality circles are small groups of workers that meet to discuss quality-related problems on a particular project and communicate their solutions to these problems to management at a formal presentation session. *p. 446*

Quality-oriented policy is a standing plan that furnishes broad, general guidelines for channeling management thinking toward taking action consistent with reaching quality objectives. *p. 509*

Ratio analysis is a control tool that summarizes the financial position of an organization by calculating ratios based on various financial measures. *p. 456*

Recruitment is the initial attraction and screening of the supply of prospective human resources available to fill a position. *p. 259*

Relevant alternatives are alternatives that are considered feasible for solving an existing problem and for implementation. *p. 151*

Repatriation is the process of bringing individuals who have been working abroad back to their home country and reintegrating them into the organization's home-country operations. *p. 106*

Repetitiveness dimension of a plan is the extent to which the plan is to be used over and over again. *p. 192*

Responsibility is the obligation to perform assigned activities. *p. 236*

Responsibility gap exists when certain organizational tasks are not included in the responsibility area of any individual organization member. *p. 238*

Retrenchment is a strategy adopted by management to strengthen or protect the amount of business a strategic business unit is currently generating. *p. 181*

Reverse discrimination is the term used to describe inequities affecting members of the majority group as an outcome of programs designed to help underrepresented groups. *p. 83*

Risk condition is the decision-making situation in which the decision maker has only enough information to estimate how probable the outcome of implemented alternatives will be. *p. 155*

Robotics is the study of the development and use of robots. *p. 447*

Role conflict is the conflict that results when a person has to fill competing roles because of membership in two cultures. *p. 80*

Role overload refers to having too many expectations to comfortably fulfill. *p. 80*

Rule is a standing plan that designates specific required action. *p. 195*

Salesforce estimation method predicts future sales levels primarily by asking appropriate salespeople for their opinions of what will happen to sales in the future. *p. 201*

Scalar relationships refer to the chain-of-command positioning of individuals on an organization chart. *p. 226*

Scheduling is the process of formulating a detailed listing of activities that must be accomplished to attain an objective, allocating the resources necessary to attain the objective, and setting up and following timetables for completing the objective. *p. 203*

Scientific management emphasizes the "one best way" to perform a task. *p. 27*

Scope dimension of a plan is the portion of the total management system at which the plan is aimed. *p. 192*

Scope of the decision is the proportion of the total management system that a particular decision will affect. The broader the scope of a decision, the higher the level of the manager responsible for making that decision. *p. 148*

Security, or safety, needs are Maslow's second set of human needs—reflecting the human desire to keep free from physical harm. *p. 358*

Selection is choosing an individual to hire from all those who have been recruited. *p. 264*

Selective perception is the tendency to collect information that not only supports one's own motives, beliefs, and attitudes, but also minimizes the emotional distress caused by unfamiliar or troublesome stimuli. *p. 409*

Self-actualization needs are Maslow's fifth, and final, set of human needs—reflecting the human desire to maximize personal potential. *p. 359*

Self-managed team is an organizational team established to plan, organize, influence, and control its own work situation with only minimal direction from management. *p. 387*

Self-serving bias is the tendency to overestimate external causes of behavior and underestimate internal ones when judging one's own behavior. *p. 409*

Serial transmission involves the passing of information from one individual to another in a series. *p. 316*

Short-term objectives are targets to be achieved in one year or less. *p. 131*

Signal is a message that has been transmitted from one person to another. *p. 308*

Single-use plans are plans that are used only once—or, at most, several times—because they focus on unique or rare situations within the organization. *p. 194*

Site selection involves determining where a plant facility should be located. It may use a weighting process to compare site differences. *p. 196*

Situational approach to leadership is a relatively modern view of leadership that suggests that successful leadership requires a unique combination of leaders, followers, and leadership situations. *p. 328*

Social audit is the process of measuring the present social responsibility activities of an organization. It monitors, measures, and appraises all aspects of an organization's social responsibility performance. *p. 61*

Social needs are Maslow's third set of human needs—reflecting the human desire to belong, including longings for friendship, companionship, and love. *p. 358*

Social obligation approach is an approach to meeting social obligations that considers business to have primarily economic purposes and confines social responsibility activity largely to conformance to existing legislation. *p. 57*

Social responsibility approach is an approach to meeting social obligations that considers business as having both societal and economic goals. *p. 57*

Social responsiveness is the degree of effectiveness and efficiency an organization displays in pursuing its social responsibilities. *p. 55*

Social responsiveness approach is an approach to meeting social obligations that considers business to have societal and economic goals as well as the obligation to anticipate potential social problems and to work actively toward preventing them from occurring. *p. 57*

Social values are the relative degrees of worth society places on the manner in which it exists and functions. *p. 172*

Sociogram is a sociometric diagram that summarizes the personal feelings of organization members about the people in the organization with whom they would like to spend free time. *p. 383*

Sociometry is an analytical tool that can be used to determine what informal groups exist in an organization and who the members of those groups are. *p. 383*

Source/encoder is the person in the interpersonal communication situation who originates and encodes information to be shared with another person or persons. *p. 308*

Span of management is the number of individuals a manager supervises. *p. 224*

Stability is a strategy adopted by management to maintain or slightly improve the amount of business a strategic business unit is generating. *p. 181*

Staff authority consists of the right to advise or assist those who possess line authority. *p. 242*

Stakeholders are all individuals and groups that are directly or indirectly affected by an organization's decisions. *p. 55*

Standard is the level of activity established to serve as a model for evaluating organizational performance. *p. 425*

Standing plans are plans that are used over and over because they focus on organizational situations that occur repeatedly. *p. 194*

Statistical quality control is the process used to determine how many products should be inspected to calculate a probability that the total number of products will meet organizational quality standards. *p. 445*

Stereotype is a positive or negative assessment of members of a group or their perceived attributes. *p. 78*

Stereotype is a fixed, distorted generalization about members of a group. *p. 408*

Storage function—computer activities involved with retaining the material entered into the computer during the performance of the input function. *p. 483*

Storming, the second stage of the team development process, is characterized by conflict and disagreement as team members try to clarify their individual roles and challenge the way the team functions. *p. 389*

Strategic business unit (SBU) is, in business portfolio analysis, a significant organizational segment that is analyzed to develop organizational strategy aimed at generating future business or revenue. SBUs vary in form, but all are a single business (or collection of businesses), have their own competitors and a manager accountable for operations, and can be independently planned for. *p. 177*

Strategic control, the last step of the strategy management process, consists of monitoring and evaluating the strategy management process as a whole to ensure that it is operating properly. *p. 182*

Strategic planning is long-range planning that focuses on the organization as a whole. *p. 168*

Strategy is a broad and general plan developed to reach long-term organizational objectives; it is the end result of strategic planning. *p. 168*

Strategy formulation is the process of determining appropriate courses of action for achieving organizational objectives and thereby accomplishing organizational purpose. Strategy development tools include critical question analysis, SWOT analysis, business portfolio analysis, and Porter's Model for Industry Analysis. *p. 176*

Strategy implementation, the fourth step of the strategy management process, is putting formulated strategy into action. *p. 182*

Strategy management is the process of ensuring that an organization possesses and benefits from the use of an appropriate organizational strategy. *p. 169*

Stress is the bodily strain that an individual experiences as a result of coping with some environmental factor. *p. 291*

Stressor is an environmental demand that causes people to feel stress. *p. 293*

Structural change is a type of organizational change that emphasizes modifying an existing organizational structure. *p. 284*

Structural factors are organizational controls, such as policies and procedures. *p. 283*

Structure refers to the designated relationships among resources of the management system. *p. 218*

Structure behavior is leadership activity that (1) delineates the relationship between the leader and the leader's followers or (2) establishes well-defined procedures that the followers should adhere to in performing their jobs. *p. 335*

Suboptimization is a condition wherein organizational subobjectives are conflicting or not directly aimed at accomplishing the overall organizational objectives. *p. 132*

Subsystem is a system created as part of the process of the overall management system. A planning subsystem increases the effectiveness of the overall management system. *p. 127*

Successful communication refers to an interpersonal communication situation in which the information the source intends to share with the destination and the meaning the destination derives from the transmitted message are the same. *p. 308*

Superleadership is leadership that inspires organizational success by showing followers how to lead themselves. *p. 343*

Suppliers are individuals or agencies that provide organizations with the resources they need to produce goods and services. *p. 173*

SWOT analysis is a strategy development tool that matches internal organizational strengths and weaknesses with external opportunities and threats. *p. 177*

Symptom is a sign that a problem exists. *p. 427*

System is a number of interdependent parts functioning as a whole for some purpose. *p. 36*

System approach to management is a management approach based on general system theory—the theory that to understand fully the operation of an entity, the entity must be viewed as a system. This requires understanding the interdependence of its parts. *p. 36*

Tactical planning is short-range planning that emphasizes the current operations of various parts of the organization. *p. 183*

Tall organization chart is an organization chart characterized by many levels and a relatively narrow span of management. *p. 226*

Task group is a formal group of organization members who interact with one another to accomplish nonroutine organizational tasks. Members of any one task group can and often do come from various levels and segments of an organization. *p. 377*

Team is a group whose members influence one another toward the accomplishment of (an) organizational objective(s). *p. 386*

Technical skills are skills involving the ability to apply specialized knowledge and expertise to work-related techniques and procedures. *p. 10*

Technological change is a type of organizational change that emphasizes modifying the level of technology in the management system. *p. 284*

Technological factors are any types of equipment or processes that assist organization members in the performance of their jobs. *p. 283*

Technology consists of any type of equipment or process that organization members use in the performance of their work. *p. 481*

Testing is examining human resources for qualities relevant to performing available jobs. *p. 265*

Theory of reasoned action states that when a behavior is a matter of *choice*, the best predictor of the behavior is the person's *intention* to perform it. *p. 403*

Theory X is a set of essentially negative assumptions about human nature. *p. 363*

Theory Y is a set of essentially positive assumptions about human nature. *p. 363*

Theory Z is the effectiveness dimension that implies that managers who use either Theory X or Theory Y assumptions when dealing with people can be successful, depending on their situation. *p. 363*

Time dimension of a plan is the length of time the plan covers. *p. 192*

Time series analysis method is a method of predicting future sales levels by analyzing the historical relationship in an organization between sales and time. *p. 201*

Tokenism refers to being one of very few members of a group in an organization. *p. 79*

Total costs are the sum of fixed costs and variable costs. *p. 460*

Total power is the entire amount of power an individual in an organization possesses. It is made up of position power and personal power. *p. 432*

Total quality management (TQM) is the continuous process of involving all organization members in ensuring that every activity related to the production of goods or services has an appropriate role in establishing product quality. *p. 500*

Total revenue is all sales dollars accumulated from selling the goods or services produced by the organization. *p. 460*

Training is the process of developing qualities in human resources. *p. 89*

Training is the process of developing qualities in human resources that will enable them to be more productive. *p. 267*

Training needs are the information or skill areas of an individual or group that require further development to increase the productivity of that individual or group. *p. 268*

Trait approach to leadership is an outdated view of leadership that sees the personal characteristics of an individual as the main determinants of how successful that individual could be as a leader. *p. 328*

Transformational leadership is leadership that inspires organizational success by profoundly affecting followers' beliefs in what an organization should be, as well as their values, such as justice and integrity. *p. 342*

Transnational organizations also called *global organizations*, take the entire world as their business arena. *p. 113*

Triangular management is a management approach that emphasizes using information from the classical, behavioral, and management science schools of thought to manage the open management system. *p. 38*

Unity of command is the management principle that recommends that an individual have only one boss. *p. 226*

Universality of management means that the principles of management are applicable to all types of organizations and organizational levels. *p. 11*

Unsuccessful communication refers to an interpersonal communication situation in which the information the source intends to share with the destination and the meaning the destination derives from the transmitted message are different. *p. 309*

Upward organizational communication is communication that flows from any point on an organization chart upward to another point on the organization chart. *p. 316*

User database is a database developed by an individual manager or other user. *p. 485*

Value analysis is a cost control and cost reduction technique that examines all the parts, materials, and functions of an operation. *p. 463*

Values are the global beliefs that guide one's actions and judgments across a variety of situations. *p. 401*

Variable budget (also known as a *flexible budget*) is one that outlines the levels of resources to be allocated for each organizational activity according to the level of production within the organization. *p. 456*

Variable costs are expenses that fluctuate with the number of products produced. *p. 460*

Verbal communication is the sharing of information through words, either written or spoken. *p. 313*

Virtual corporation is an organization that goes significantly beyond the boundaries and structure of a traditional organization. *p. 291*

Virtual office is a work arrangement that extends beyond the structure and boundaries of the traditional office arrangement. *p. 295*

Virtual organization is an organization having the essence of a traditional organization, but without some aspect(s) of traditional boundaries and structure. *p. 294*

Virtual teams are groups of employees formed by managers that go beyond the boundaries and structure of traditional teams. *p. 295*

Virtual training is a training process that goes beyond the boundaries and structure of traditional training. *p. 295*

Vroom expectancy theory is a motivation theory that hypothesizes that felt needs cause human behavior and that motivation strength depends on an individual's degree of desire to perform a behavior. *p. 355*

Vroom-Yetton-Jago (VYJ) Model of leadership is a modern view of leadership that suggests that successful leadership requires determining, through a decision tree, what style of leadership will produce decisions that are beneficial to the organization and will be accepted and committed to by subordinates. *p. 332*

"What if" analysis is the simulation of a business situation over and over again, using somewhat different data for selected decision areas. *p. 485*

Work measurement methods are operational tools that are used to establish labor standards. *p. 453*

Work methods analysis is an operational tool used to improve productivity and ensure the safety of workers. *p. 453*

Work team is a task group used in organizations to achieve greater organizational flexibility or to cope with rapid growth. *p. 379*

World Wide Web is a segment of the Internet that allows managers to have an information location called a Web site available continually to Internet users. Each Web site has a beginning page called a home page, and each home page generally has several supporting pages called branch pages that expand on the thoughts and ideas contained in the home page. *p. 488*

Zero-base budgeting requires managers to justify their entire budget request in detail rather than simply referring to budget amounts established in previous years. *p. 156*

Index

Notes

Notes

Notes

Notes

END-USER LICENSE AGREEMENT AND LIMITED WARRANTY

READ THIS LICENSE CAREFULLY BEFORE OPENING THIS PACKAGE. BY OPENING THIS PACKAGE, YOU ARE AGREEING TO THE TERMS AND CONDITIONS OF THIS LICENSE. IF YOU DO NOT AGREE, DO NOT OPEN THE PACKAGE. PROMPTLY RETURN THE UNOPENED PACKAGE AND ALL ACCOMPANYING ITEMS TO THE PLACE YOU OBTAINED THEM FOR A FULL REFUND OF ANY SUMS YOU HAVE PAID FOR THE SOFTWARE. *THESE TERMS APPLY TO ALL LICENSED SOFTWARE ON THE DISK EXCEPT THAT THE TERMS FOR USE OF ANY SHAREWARE OR FREEWARE ON THE DISKETTES ARE AS SET FORTH IN THE ELECTRONIC LICENSE LOCATED ON THE DISK:*

1. GRANT OF LICENSE and OWNERSHIP: The enclosed computer programs ("Software") are licensed, not sold, to you by Prentice Hall, Inc. ("We" or the "Company") and in consideration of your payment of the license fee, which is part of the price you paid, and your agreement to these terms. We reserve any rights not granted to you. You own only the disk(s) but we and/or our licensors own the Software itself. This license allows you to use and display your copy of the Software on a single computer (i.e., with a single CPU) at a single location for <u>academic</u> use only, so long as you comply with the terms of this Agreement. You may make one copy for back up, or transfer your copy to another CPU, provided that the Software is usable on only one computer.

2. RESTRICTIONS: You may <u>not</u> transfer or distribute the Software or documentation to anyone else. Except for backup, you may <u>not</u> copy the documentation or the Software. You may <u>not</u> network the Software or otherwise use it on more than one computer or computer terminal at the same time. You may <u>not</u> reverse engineer, disassemble, decompile, modify, adapt, translate, or create derivative works based on the Software or the Documentation. You may be held legally responsible for any copying or copyright infringement which is caused by your failure to abide by the terms of these restrictions.

3. TERMINATION: This license is effective until terminated. This license will terminate automatically without notice from the Company if you fail to comply with any provisions or limitations of this license. Upon termination, you shall destroy the Documentation and all copies of the Software. All provisions of this Agreement as to limitation and disclaimer of warranties, limitation of liability, remedies or damages, and our ownership rights shall survive termination.

4. LIMITED WARRANTY AND DISCLAIMER OF WARRANTY: Company warrants that for a period of 60 days from the date you purchase this SOFTWARE (or purchase or adopt the accompanying textbook), the Software, when properly installed and used in accordance with the Documentation, will operate in substantial conformity with the description of the Software set forth in the Documentation, and that for a period of 30 days the disk(s) on which the Software is delivered shall be free from defects in materials and workmanship under normal use. The Company does not warrant that the Software will meet your requirements or that the operation of the Software will be uninterrupted or error-free. Your only remedy and the Company's only obligation under these limited warranties is, at the Company's option, return of the disk for a refund of any amounts paid for it by you or replacement of the disk. THIS LIMITED WARRANTY IS THE ONLY WARRANTY PROVIDED BY THE COMPANY AND ITS LICENSORS, AND THE COMPANY AND ITS LICENSORS DISCLAIM ALL OTHER WARRANTIES, EXPRESS OR IMPLIED, INCLUDING WITHOUT LIMITATION, THE IMPLIED WARRANTIES OF MERCHANTABILITY AND FITNESS FOR A PARTICULAR PURPOSE. THE COMPANY DOES NOT WARRANT, GUARANTEE, OR MAKE ANY REPRESENTATION REGARDING THE ACCURACY, RELIABILITY, CURRENTNESS, USE, OR RESULTS OF USE, OF THE SOFTWARE.

5. LIMITATION OF REMEDIES AND DAMAGES: IN NO EVENT, SHALL THE COMPANY OR ITS EMPLOYEES, AGENTS, LICENSORS, OR CONTRACTORS BE LIABLE FOR ANY INCIDENTAL, INDIRECT, SPECIAL, OR CONSEQUENTIAL DAMAGES ARISING OUT OF OR IN CONNECTION WITH THIS LICENSE OR THE SOFTWARE, INCLUDING FOR LOSS OF USE, LOSS OF DATA, LOSS OF INCOME OR PROFIT, OR OTHER LOSSES, SUSTAINED AS A RESULT OF INJURY TO ANY PERSON, OR LOSS OF OR DAMAGE TO PROPERTY, OR CLAIMS OF THIRD PARTIES, EVEN IF THE COMPANY OR AN AUTHORIZED REPRESENTATIVE OF THE COMPANY HAS BEEN ADVISED OF THE POSSIBILITY OF SUCH DAMAGES. IN NO EVENT SHALL THE LIABILITY OF THE COMPANY FOR DAMAGES WITH RESPECT TO THE SOFTWARE EXCEED THE AMOUNTS ACTUALLY PAID BY YOU, IF ANY, FOR THE SOFTWARE OR THE ACCOMPANYING TEXTBOOK. BECAUSE SOME JURISDICTIONS DO NOT ALLOW THE LIMITATION OF LIABILITY IN CERTAIN CIRCUMSTANCES, THE ABOVE LIMITATIONS MAY NOT ALWAYS APPLY TO YOU.

6. GENERAL: THIS AGREEMENT SHALL BE CONSTRUED IN ACCORDANCE WITH THE LAWS OF THE UNITED STATES OF AMERICA AND THE STATE OF NEW YORK, APPLICABLE TO CONTRACTS MADE IN NEW YORK, AND SHALL BENEFIT THE COMPANY, ITS AFFILIATES AND ASSIGNEES. THIS AGREEMENT IS THE COMPLETE AND EXCLUSIVE STATEMENT OF THE AGREEMENT BETWEEN YOU AND THE COMPANY AND SUPERSEDES ALL PROPOSALS OR PRIOR AGREEMENTS, ORAL, OR WRITTEN, AND ANY OTHER COMMUNICATIONS BETWEEN YOU AND THE COMPANY OR ANY REPRESENTATIVE OF THE COMPANY RELATING TO THE SUBJECT MATTER OF THIS AGREEMENT. If you are a U.S. Government user, this Software is licensed with "restricted rights" as set forth in subparagraphs (a)-(d) of the Commercial Computer-Restricted Rights clause at FAR 52.227-19 or in subparagraphs (c)(1)(ii) of the Rights in Technical Data and Computer Software clause at DFARS 252.227-7013, and similar clauses, as applicable.

Should you have any questions concerning this agreement or if you wish to contact the Company for any reason, please contact in writing: Director of New Media, Higher Education Division, Prentice Hall, Inc., 1 Lake Street, Upper Saddle River, NJ 07458.